TB. - 01 - 95

To the Students:

This text was created to provide you with a high-quality educational resource. As a publisher specializing in college textbooks for business and economics, our goal is to provide you with learning materials that will serve you well in your college studies and throughout your career.

The educational process involves learning, retention, and the application of concepts and principles. You can accelerate your learning efforts utilizing the supplements accompanying this text:

- Study Guide for use with Individual Taxation, 1995 Edition;
- Two 1993 Individual Tax Return Practice Problems; and
- Federal Tax Return Preparation with TurboTax (includes ten individual tax return problems).

These learning aids are designed to improve your performance in the course by highlighting key points in the text and providing you with assistance in mastering basic concepts.

Check your local bookstore, or ask the manager to place an order for you today.

We at Irwin sincerely hope this text package will assist you in reaching your goals, both now and in the future.

INDIVIDUAL TAXATION

1995 Edition

INDIVIDUAL TAXATION

1995 Edition

GENERAL EDITORS

James W. Pratt, D.B.A., C.P.A.
William N. Kulsrud, Ph.D., C.P.A.

CONTRIBUTING AUTHORS:

Marguerite R. Hutton, Ph.D., C.P.A.
Western Washington University

Sally M. Jones, Ph.D., C.P.A.
University of Virginia at Charlottesville

William N. Kulsrud, Ph.D., C.P.A.
Indiana University

Michael A. O'Dell, Ph.D., C.P.A.
Arizona State University

Nathan Oestreich, Ph.D., C.P.A.
San Diego State University

James W. Pratt, D.B.A., C.P.A.
University of Houston

Edward J. Schnee, Ph.D., C.P.A.
University of Alabama

Jerrold J. Stern, Ph.D.
Indiana University

Steven C. Thompson, Ph.D., C.P.A.
University of Houston

John C. Tripp, Ph.D., C.P.A.
University of Denver

Michael J. Tucker, J.D., Ph.D., C.P.A.
Quinnipiac College

James L. Wittenbach, D.B.A., C.P.A.
University of Notre Dame

Burr Ridge, Illinois
Boston, Massachusetts

Sponsoring editor: Ron M. Regis
Developmental editor: Elaine Cassidy
Project editor: Mary Conzachi
Production manager: Laurie Kersch
Designer: Jeanne M. Rivera
Compositor: Publication Services, Inc.
Typeface: 10/12 Times Roman
Printer: R.R. Donnelley & Sons Company

ISBN 0-256-12724-7
ISSN 0742-7832

Printed in the United States of America

1 2 3 4 5 6 7 8 9 0 DOC 0 9 8 7 6 5 4 3

PREFACE

This text is designed for use in a first course in Federal taxation for undergraduate or graduate accounting, business, or law students. The numerous examples and computational illustrations used to explain the more complex rules concerning the Federal income taxation of individuals should also make this text suitable for use in a self-study program.

Although the primary emphasis of this text is the income taxation of individuals, the final chapter, "Taxation of Business Forms and Their Owners," provides a comparison of the tax consequences of operating a business as a sole proprietorship, partnership, regular corporation, or "S" corporation. For those students who will not have the opportunity to take another course in Federal taxation, this chapter offers an overview of the tax factors that should be considered in the selection of a particular business form. For others, this chapter provides an introduction to some of the topics generally included in a second course in Federal taxation. This text's companion volume, *Corporate, Partnership, Estate and Gift Taxation*, is designed for use in such a course.

The *1995 Edition* has been revised to reflect the changes introduced by the Revenue Reconciliation Act of 1993 as well as all other significant judicial and administrative developments during the past year. In the event that other significant changes in the tax law occur during the year, we will continue our policy of providing users with timely update supplements.

Former users will also recognize a number of other changes in the 1995 Edition. Most notatable among these are concept review questions and problems contained in a new section following key topics called "Check Your Knowledge." These questions—complete with answers—are designed to reinforce major tax concepts as well as enrich the student's learning experience with real life examples. "Check Your Knowledge" questions, which are contained in most chapters, help students identify the most critical aspects of each topic and enable them to assess their comprehension of the material.

Several other new features of the text can be traced to Chapter 2. In prior editions, this chapter has dealt solely with sources and applications of the tax law, primarily the tools required to do tax research. The 1995 Edition expands this chapter to reflect a new emphasis on tax practice and is fittingly retitled Tax Practice and Research. As revised, this chapter now begins with an introduction to the nature of tax practice and a short section on what a career as a tax professional entails. The chapter has also been rewritten to explain the rules of conduct that must be followed by those who perform tax services. In its new form, it specifically addresses the role of ethics in our tax system, explaining the responsiblities of taxpayers as well as tax practitioners. The emphasis in this discussion concerns key penalties that influence positions taken on tax returns. This new focus on tax practice is reflected throughout the text with questions entitled "You Make the Call" that require students to deal with ethical issues that often confront taxpayers and tax practitioners.

In addition to the standard discussion questions and computational problems contained at the end of every chapter of this text, several chapters contain comprehensive tax return problems and cumulative problems that require an understanding of material presented in earlier chapters and completion of some tax forms. Also, Appendix I contains two comprehensive tax return problems for individual taxpayers. These problems require completion of some of the most common tax forms and are ideal for course projects. Each of these problems requires approximately 6 to 10 hours for completion. These tax return problems are intended to supplement other end-of-chapter problems by requiring students to relate tax rules to actual tax return compliance procedures.

A comprehensive package of instructional aids is available with this text.

- *Solutions Manual:* containing solutions to the discussion questions and computational problems at the end of each chapter. These solutions are referenced to specific pages and examples from the text, and where appropriate, to supporting statutory or administrative authorities. Each and every solution has been carefully checked by external reviewers to ensure that any errors are eliminated.

- *Instructor's Guide:* containing solutions to the tax research problems, tax return problems (including the two comprehensive tax return problems contained in Appendix I), and a test bank containing over 900 objective questions (true-false and multiple choice), with answers referenced back to specific pages and examples in the text.

- *Chapter Lecture Outlines:* containing a summary of the key points of each chapter and *Transparency Masters* for selected illustrations, with a large typeface for easier viewing.

- *CompuTest III:* a microcomputer testing system for use with an IBM-PC or IBM-compatible, along with data disks containing all the questions from the test bank included in the Instructor's Guide. This software package can be used to create quizzes or exams in a minimum amount of time.

- *A Student Study Guide,* written by Professor Nathan Oestreich (San Diego State University). It provides students with chapter highlights and self-review exams and answers.

- *Two 1993 Individual Tax Return Practice Problems,* written by Professor Thomas M. Dalton (University of San Diego). It contains original data source forms (e.g., Forms W-2, 1099-DIV, 1099-INT, real estate closing statements) for the manual preparation of 1993 Form 1040 for two married couples. It also contains blank copies of the tax return forms required to be completed by students.

- *Federal Tax Return Preparation with TurboTax,* prepared by Professor Edmund D. Fenton, Jr. (Gonzaga University). It contains ten Federal tax return problems for individuals, ranging in difficulty from simple to complex, which can be prepared and printed using one of the best tax return preparation programs available.

We are greatly indebted to those who have made many useful suggestions regarding the prior editions of this text. We specifically thank the following professors, who either reviewed all or a part of the text or checked the accuracy of all the end-of-chapter discussion questions and problems:

Thomas M. Dalton, University of San Diego;
James A. Fellows, University of South Florida;
Ramon Fernandez, University of Saint Thomas;
James Gale, Northern Virginia Community College;
Susan Kattlelus, Eastern Michigan University;
Monica Neuman, Western State College/Colorado; and
John Strefeler, University of Nevada/Reno.

These individuals made excellent suggestions for improvement of the text or accompanying solutions manual, and their comments greatly aided our editorial efforts. In this regard, we continue to invite all readers—students and instructors—to call errors and omissions to our attention. As with any work of this magnitude, it is extremely difficult to identify all errors and shortcomings without help, particularly in the dynamic area of Federal taxation. Because this text is revised annually, errors can be *quickly* corrected and constructive criticism will be incorporated on a *continuing* basis.

Finally, we are most appreciative of the professional and technical services received from the staff at Publication Services. This *1995 Edition* would not have been possible without their help.

April, 1994   *James W. Pratt*
                                                                                    William N. Kulsrud

CONTENTS IN BRIEF

PART I

INTRODUCTION TO THE FEDERAL TAX SYSTEM

1 An Overview of Federal Taxation... 1-1
2 Tax Practice and Research.. 2-1
3 Taxable Entities, Tax Formula, Introduction to Property Transactions...................... 3-1
4 Personal and Dependency Exemptions; Filing Status;
   Determination of Tax for an Individual; Filing Requirements............................. 4-1

PART II

GROSS INCOME

5 Gross Income... 5-1
6 Gross Income: Inclusions and Exclusions... 6-1

PART III

DEDUCTIONS AND LOSSES

7 Overview of Deductions and Losses... 7-1
8 Employee Business Expenses.. 8-1
9 Capital Recovery: Depreciation, Amortization, and Depletion................................ 9-1
10 Certain Business Deductions and Losses... 10-1
11 Itemized Deductions.. 11-1
12 Deductions for Certain Investment Expenses and Losses...................................... 12-1

PART IV

ALTERNATIVE MINIMUM TAX AND TAX CREDITS

13 The Alternative Minimum Tax and Tax Credits.. 13-1

PART V

PROPERTY TRANSACTIONS

14 Property Transactions: Basis Determination and Recognition of Gain or Loss............. **14-1**
15 Nontaxable Exchanges... **15-1**
16 Property Transactions: Capital Gains and Losses....................................... **16-1**
17 Property Transactions: Disposition of Trade or Business Property........................ **17-1**

PART VI

EMPLOYEE COMPENSATION AND TAXATION OF BUSINESS FORMS

18 Employee Compensation and Retirement Plans.. **18-1**
19 Taxation of Business Forms
    and Their Owners.. **19-1**

Appendices and Index

Appendix A: **Tax Rate Schedules and Tables**.. **A-1**

Appendix B: **Tax Forms**... **B-1**

Appendix C: **Modified ACRS and Original ACRS Tables**.................................. **C-1**

Appendix D: **Table of Cases Cited**... **D-1**

Appendix E: **Table of Code Sections Cited**... **E-1**

Appendix F: **Table of Regulations Cited**.. **F-1**

Appendix G: **Table of Revenue Procedures and**
    Revenue Rulings Cited.. **G-1**

Appendix H: **Glossary of Tax Terms**.. **H-1**

Appendix I: **Two Individual Comprehensive Tax Return**
    Problems for 1993.. **I-1**

Index... **J-1**

CONTENTS

PART I

INTRODUCTION TO THE FEDERAL TAX SYSTEM

1 AN OVERVIEW OF FEDERAL TAXATION

Introduction	**1-1**
The Nature of a Tax	**1-1**
Development of U.S. Taxation	**1-2**
Excise and Customs Duties	**1-2**
Federal Income Tax	**1-3**
Federal Wealth Transfer Taxes	**1-5**
Federal Taxes as a Source of Revenue	**1-5**
Key Tax Terms	**1-5**
Major Types of Taxes	**1-9**
Income Taxes	**1-9**
Wealth Transfer Taxes	**1-12**
Employment Taxes	**1-19**
Excise Taxes	**1-24**
Additional Types of Taxes	**1-25**
Goals of Taxation	**1-26**
Economic Objectives	**1-27**
Social Objectives	**1-28**
Other Objectives	**1-29**
A Prelude to Tax Planning	**1-31**
Problem Materials	**1-34**

2 TAX PRACTICE AND RESEARCH

Introduction	**2-1**
Tax Practice in General	**2-1**
Taxation as a Professional Career	**2-3**
Rules of Tax Practice: Responsibilities and Ethics	**2-4**
Taxpayer Penalties	**2-5**
Accuracy-Related Penalties	**2-6**
Fraud	**2-10**
Tax Preparer Penalties	**2-12**
Sources and Applications of Tax Laws	**2-19**
Authoritative Sources of Tax Law	**2-20**

Statutory Law.. **2-20**

The Making of a Tax Law.. 2-21
Organization of the Code.. 2-22
Tax Treaties.. 2-24

Administrative Interpretations.. **2-25**

Regulations.. 2-25
Revenue Rulings.. 2-27
Revenue Procedures... 2-27
Letter Rulings... 2-28
Technical Advice Memoranda... 2-29

Judicial Interpretations.. **2-29**

Trial Courts... 2-30
Appellate Courts... 2-32
Case Citation.. 2-35

Secondary Sources... **2-40**

Tax Services... 2-41
Tax Periodicals.. 2-42

Tax Research.. **2-43**

Obtaining the Facts.. 2-43
Diagnosing the Issue... 2-43
Locating the Authorities... 2-44
Evaluating the Authority... 2-45
Deriving the Solution.. 2-46
Communicating the Findings... 2-47

Problem Materials... **2-48**

3 TAXABLE ENTITIES, TAX FORMULA, INTRODUCTION TO PROPERTY TRANSACTIONS

Introduction... 3-1
The Taxable Entity... 3-2

Taxable Entities.. **3-2**

Individual Taxpayers... 3-2
Corporate Taxpayers.. 3-4
Fiduciary Taxpayers.. 3-5
Partnerships... 3-6
Electing Small Business Corporations: "S" Corporations................... 3-8
Limited Liability Companies.. 3-8

Tax Formula.. **3-11**

Analyzing the Tax Formula.. 3-11

Introduction to Property Transactions.................................... **3-27**

Gain or Loss Realized.. 3-28
Gain or Loss Recognized.. 3-30
Character of the Gain or Loss.. 3-31
Trade or Business Property... 3-34

Tax Planning Considerations.. **3-38**

Choice of Business Form.. 3-38
Itemized Deductions vs. Standard Deduction............................... 3-39
Employee Business Expenses... 3-40

Problem Materials.. **3-41**

4

PERSONAL AND DEPENDENCY EXEMPTIONS; FILING STATUS; DETERMINATION OF TAX FOR AN INDIVIDUAL; FILING REQUIREMENTS

Personal and Dependency Exemptions..................................... 4-1

  Personal Exemptions.. 4-2
  Dependency Exemptions.. 4-3

Filing Status... 4-13

  Evolution of Filing Status....................................... 4-13
  Married Individuals.. 4-15
  Head of Household... 4-16

Computation of Tax for Individual Taxpayers............................ 4-21

  Tax Tables.. 4-21
  Tax Rate Schedules.. 4-23
  Special Tax Computation Rules.................................. 4-25
  Determination of Net Tax Due or Refund......................... 4-30

Filing Requirements.. 4-31

  Due Dates for Filing Returns.................................... 4-35
  Estimated Tax Payments.. 4-37
  Statute of Limitations.. 4-40
  Indexation and the Federal Income Tax........................... 4-41

Appendix.. 4-45

  Tax Return Illustrations.. 4-45

Problem Materials... 4-55

PART II

GROSS INCOME

5

GROSS INCOME

  Introduction.. 5-1

Gross Income Defined.. 5-2

  Economic Concept of Income.................................... 5-3
  Accounting Concept of Income.................................. 5-5
  Income for Tax Purposes: The Judicial Concept.................... 5-5

Refinements of the Gross Income Definition............................ 5-9

  Form-of-Benefit Principle....................................... 5-9
  Return of Capital Doctrine...................................... 5-10
  Indirect Economic Benefits...................................... 5-13

Reporting Income: Tax Accounting Methods............................ 5-16

  Accounting Periods.. 5-16
  Accounting Methods... 5-18
  Cash Method of Accounting..................................... 5-21
  Accrual Method of Accounting.................................. 5-25
  Changes in Accounting Methods................................. 5-26

Accounting for Income: Special Considerations................................. **5-29**

    Claim of Right Doctrine... **5-29**
    Prepaid Income... **5-31**
    Interest Income.. **5-35**

Identification of the Taxpayer... **5-40**

    Income from Personal Services.. **5-40**
    Income from Property... **5-41**
    Unearned Income of Children under 14................................... **5-41**
    Interest-Free and Below-Market Loans................................... **5-42**
    Income from Community Property... **5-46**

Tax Planning.. **5-49**

    Timing Income Recognition.. **5-49**
    Income-Splitting Techniques.. **5-49**
    Excluded Economic Income... **5-51**

Problem Materials... **5-52**

6

GROSS INCOME: INCLUSIONS AND EXCLUSIONS

    Introduction... **6-1**

Investments... **6-1**

    Dividends.. **6-2**
    Interest... **6-4**
    Annuities.. **6-9**

Employee Compensation and Other Benefits............................... **6-14**

    Reimbursement of Employee Expenses..................................... **6-15**
    Employer Gifts... **6-15**
    Employer Awards.. **6-16**
    Social Security Benefits... **6-16**
    Unemployment Benefits.. **6-19**
    Employee Insurance... **6-19**
    Death Benefits... **6-24**
    Employer-Provided Meals and Lodging.................................... **6-25**
    Additional Employee Benefits... **6-26**
    Military Personnel... **6-31**

Personal Transfers between Individuals.................................. **6-31**

    Gifts and Inheritances... **6-32**
    Alimony and Separate Maintenance....................................... **6-32**

Transfers by Unrelated Parties... **6-38**

    Prizes and Awards.. **6-38**
    Scholarships and Fellowships... **6-39**
    Government Transfer Payments.. **6-40**

Business Gross Income.. **6-41**

    Agreement Not to Compete and Goodwill.................................. **6-41**
    Business Interruption Insurance Proceeds............................... **6-42**
    Damages Awarded.. **6-42**
    Lease Cancellation Payments.. **6-42**
    Debt Cancellation.. **6-43**
    Leasehold Improvements... **6-44**
    Contributions to Capital... **6-45**

Miscellaneous Items.. 6-45

    Fees Received.. 6-45
    Asset Discovery.. 6-45
    Car Pool Receipts.. 6-45
    Income Tax Refunds.. 6-46
    Temporary Living Costs.. 6-46
    Damages Awarded to Individuals.. 6-46

Tax Planning.. 6-49

    Investments... 6-49
    Employee Benefits... 6-50
    Employee versus Self-Employed... 6-52
    Divorce... 6-53

Problem Materials.. 6-54

PART III

DEDUCTIONS AND LOSSES

7

OVERVIEW OF DEDUCTIONS AND LOSSES

    Deduction Defined... 7-1

Deductions for Expenses: General Requirements........................ 7-2

    General Rules: Code §§ 162 and 212...................................... 7-2
    Related to Carrying on a Business or an Income-Producing Activity....... 7-3
    Ordinary and Necessary Expenses.. 7-7
    Reasonable Expenses.. 7-8
    Paid or Incurred During the Taxable Year............................... 7-9
    Employee Business Expenses... 7-15

Deductions for Losses... 7-15

Classification of Expenses.. 7-16

    Importance of Classification... 7-16
    Deductions for A.G.I... 7-17
    Itemized Deductions.. 7-18
    Self-Employed versus Employee.. 7-19

Limitations on Deductions... 7-22

    Hobby Expenses and Losses.. 7-23
    Personal Living Expenses... 7-26
    Capital Expenditures... 7-27
    Business Investigation Expenses and Start-Up Costs..................... 7-29
    Public Policy Restrictions... 7-31
    Lobbying and Political Contributions................................... 7-33
    Expenses and Interest Relating to Tax-Exempt Income.................... 7-35
    Related Taxpayer Transactions.. 7-36
    Payment of Another Taxpayer's Obligation............................... 7-39
    Substantiation... 7-40

Tax Planning Considerations... 7-41

    Maximizing Deductions.. 7-41
    Timing of Deductions... 7-42
    Expenses Relating to Tax-Exempt Income................................. 7-42
    "Points" on Mortgages.. 7-42
    Hobbies.. 7-43

Problem Materials... 7-44

8 EMPLOYEE BUSINESS EXPENSES

Education Expenses... 8-1

    Requirements for Deduction.. 8-2
    Travel as a Form of Education.. 8-3
    Types and Classification of Education Deductions....................... 8-4

Moving Expenses... 8-5

    Distance Requirement.. 8-5
    Time Test... 8-6
    Deductible Moving Expenses.. 8-7
    Classifying and Reporting the Moving Expense Deduction............... 8-9

Home Office Expenses... 8-10

    Requirements for Deductibility... 8-11
    Amount Deductible.. 8-13
    Daycare and Storage Use... 8-15
    Rental of Residence... 8-15
    Residential Phone Service.. 8-16

Transportation Expenses.. 8-17

    Deductible Transportation versus Nondeductible Commuting............. 8-18
    Computing Car Expenses.. 8-23
    Classification of Transportation and Travel Expenses..................... 8-25

Travel Expenses... 8-26

    Away-from-Home Test... 8-26
    Combined Business and Pleasure Travel................................... 8-28
    Foreign Conventions... 8-31
    Cruise Ships... 8-32

Entertainment Expenses... 8-33

    Deduction Requirements.. 8-34
    Entertainment Facilities... 8-38
    Exceptions to Directly-Related-to and Associated-with Tests.............. 8-38
    Fifty Percent Limitation on Entertainment and Meal Expenses............ 8-39
    Limitations on Deductions for Tickets...................................... 8-41
    Business Gifts... 8-41

Travel and Entertainment Recordkeeping Requirements.................... 8-42

Reporting Business Expenses and Losses.................................... 8-46

    Sole Proprietors and Self-Employed Persons............................. 8-46
    Employees... 8-46

Tax Planning Considerations.. 8-55

    Moving Expenses.. 8-55
    Travel and Entertainment Expenses....................................... 8-55
    Home Office Deduction... 8-56

Problem Materials.. 8-57

9 CAPITAL RECOVERY: DEPRECIATION, AMORTIZATION, AND DEPLETION

Depreciation and Amortization for Tax Purposes........................... 9-2

    General Rules for Depreciation Deductions............................... 9-2
    Historical Perspective... 9-3

Modified Accelerated Cost Recovery System................................ 9-4

An Overview of MACRS... 9-4
Property Subject to MACRS... 9-5
Classes of Property... 9-6
Calculating Depreciation.. 9-7
Straight-Line Methods... 9-18
Dispositions of Assets from General Asset Accounts........................ 9-20
Limited Expensing Election: Code § 179.. 9-22
Limitations for Automobiles.. 9-24
Limitations for Personal Use.. 9-26
Other Considerations... 9-33

Amortization.. 9-34

Goodwill and Covenants Not to Compete.. 9-34
5-Year Elective Amortization.. 9-36
Leasehold Improvements... 9-36

Depletion.. 9-37

Computing the Depletion Deduction.. 9-37

Research and Experimental Expenditures............................... 9-39

Research and Experimental Expenditures Defined............................. 9-40
Alternative Tax Treatments.. 9-40
Other Related Provisions.. 9-42

Expenses of Farmers and Ranchers...................................... 9-42

Expenses Related to Livestock... 9-42
Soil and Water Conservation, Fertilizer, Land Clearing..................... 9-43
Development Expenses.. 9-44

Tax Planning Considerations.. 9-45

Depreciation and After-Tax Cash Flow... 9-45
Accelerating Depreciation with Cost-Segregation............................. 9-46
Goodwill Amortization Rule Benefits Buyers and Sellers.................... 9-46

Problem Materials.. 9-48

10 CERTAIN BUSINESS DEDUCTIONS AND LOSSES

Bad Debts... 10-1

Treatment of Business versus Nonbusiness Bad Debts....................... 10-2
General Requirements... 10-4
Deduction Methods.. 10-5

Casualty and Theft Losses... 10-7

General Rules.. 10-7
Casualty and Theft Defined.. 10-8
Loss Computation.. 10-9
Casualty Gains and Losses.. 10-11
Year Deductible.. 10-13

Net Operating Losses.. 10-16

Carryback and Carryforward Years.. 10-16
Net Operating Loss Computation... 10-17
Recomputing Taxable Income for Year to Which
    Net Operating Loss Is Carried.. 10-20

Inventories... **10-23**

    Costs to Be Inventoried... **10-24**
    Allocating Inventoriable Costs.. **10-26**
    Dollar Value LIFO... **10-29**
    The LIFO Election... **10-32**
    Lower of Cost or Market... **10-33**

Tax Planning Considerations... **10-35**

    Casualty and Theft Losses... **10-35**
    Bad Debts.. **10-36**
    Net Operating Losses.. **10-36**

Problem Materials.. **10-37**

11   ITEMIZED DEDUCTIONS

Medical Expenses.. **11-2**

    In General... **11-2**
    When Deductible.. **11-3**
    Deduction Limitations... **11-5**
    Special Items and Equipment.. **11-6**
    Special Care Facilities.. **11-7**
    Medical Travel and Transportation....................................... **11-8**
    Medical Insurance Costs and Reimbursements............................. **11-9**
    Health Insurance Costs of Self-Employed Taxpayers...................... **11-10**

Personal Casualty and Theft Losses... **11-11**

    Year Deductible... **11-11**
    Reporting Casualty Losses.. **11-11**

Taxes... **11-12**

    General Requirements for Deductibility.................................. **11-12**
    Income Taxes... **11-14**
    Property Taxes... **11-15**
    Reporting Deductions for Taxes... **11-17**

Interest Expense.. **11-18**

    Limitations on Deductions of Interest Expense.......................... **11-18**
    Classification of Interest Expense..................................... **11-27**
    When Deductible.. **11-31**
    Where Reported... **11-32**

Charitable Contributions.. **11-33**

    Deduction Requirements... **11-34**
    Limitations on Deductions.. **11-35**
    Contribution Carryovers.. **11-45**

Miscellaneous Itemized Deductions... **11-46**

Other Itemized Deductions... **11-47**

Three Percent Cutback Rule.. **11-48**

Tax Planning Considerations... **11-51**

    Maximizing Personal Deductions... **11-51**
    Medical Expenses... **11-52**
    Charitable Contributions... **11-52**
    Miscellaneous Deductions... **11-53**

Problem Materials.. **11-54**

12 DEDUCTIONS FOR CERTAIN INVESTMENT EXPENSES AND LOSSES

Passive Activity Limitations **12-1**

General Rule **12-3**
Taxpayers Subject to Limitations **12-7**
Passive Activities **12-8**
Definition of an Activity **12-9**
Rental versus Nonrental Activities **12-12**
Material Participation **12-14**
Recharacterized Passive Income **12-19**

Passive Activity Interest Expense **12-20**

Rental of Residence (Vacation Home Rentals) **12-23**

Basic Rules **12-24**
Allocation of Expenses **12-26**

Problem Materials **12-30**

PART IV

ALTERNATIVE MINIMUM TAX AND TAX CREDITS

13 THE ALTERNATIVE MINIMUM TAX AND TAX CREDITS

Introduction **13-1**

Alternative Minimum Tax **13-2**

Policy Objectives **13-2**
Overview of AMT **13-3**
AMT Rates and Exemptions **13-4**
Adjustments and Tax Preference Items in General **13-6**
AMT Adjustments **13-7**
AMT Adjustments Applicable to All Taxpayers **13-7**
AMT Adjustments Applicable Only to Individuals **13-11**
Adjustment Applicable Only to Corporations **13-14**
Special Tax Shelter Loss Adjustments **13-15**
Tax Preference Items **13-16**
Alternative Minimum Tax Computations **13-19**
Minimum Tax Credit **13-23**

Income Tax Credits **13-29**

Overview of Tax Credits **13-29**
General Business Credit **13-31**
Investment Credit **13-32**
Targeted Jobs Credit **13-37**
Alcohol Fuel Credit **13-38**
Research and Experimental (R&E) Credit **13-39**
Low-Income Housing Credit **13-43**
Disabled Access Credit **13-43**
Empowerment Zone Employment Credit **13-44**
Other Components of the General Business Credit **13-45**
General Business Credit Carryover Rules **13-46**
Foreign Tax Credit **13-46**

Nonbusiness Credits... **13-47**

    Child and Dependent Care Credit.. **13-48**
    Credit for the Elderly and Permanently Disabled......................... **13-53**
    Credit for Interest on Certain Home Mortgages.......................... **13-54**
    Credit for Qualified Electric Vehicles.................................... **13-54**

Refundable Credits.. **13-55**

    Tax Withheld at the Source... **13-55**
    Earned Income Credit.. **13-55**
    Other Refundable Credits.. **13-58**

Problem Materials.. **13-59**

PART V

PROPERTY TRANSACTIONS

14

PROPERTY TRANSACTIONS: BASIS DETERMINATION AND RECOGNITION OF GAIN OR LOSS

Determination of Gain or Loss... **14-1**

    Introduction... **14-1**
    General Rule of Recognition... **14-2**
    Computing Amount Realized... **14-3**

Basis Determination Rules... **14-6**

    Property Acquired by Purchase.. **14-6**
    Property Acquired by Gift... **14-7**
    Property Acquired from a Decedent...................................... **14-9**
    Property Acquired in a Nontaxable Exchange............................. **14-11**
    Property Converted from Personal Use to Business Use................... **14-11**
    Property Converted from Business Use to Personal Use.................. **14-12**
    Adjustments to Basis.. **14-12**

Effect of Liabilities on Amount Realized................................. **14-14**

Concepts Related to Realization and Recognition....................... **14-15**

    Sale or Other Disposition... **14-15**
    Allocations of Purchase Price and Basis................................. **14-19**

Installment Sale Method... **14-21**

    General Rules... **14-21**
    Election out of Installment Reporting.................................... **14-22**
    Gain Reported under the Installment Method............................. **14-23**
    Limitations on Certain Installment Sales................................. **14-26**
    Reporting Gain on Installment Sales..................................... **14-30**

Disallowed Losses... **14-30**

    Wash Sales.. **14-31**
    Sales between Related Parties... **14-31**

Tax Planning Considerations... **14-33**

    Gift versus Bequest... **14-33**
    Charitable Transfers Involving Property Other than Cash................. **14-34**
    Changes in the Use of Property.. **14-34**
    Sales to Related Parties... **14-34**
    Use of Installment Sales... **14-34**

Problem Materials.. **14-36**

15 NONTAXABLE EXCHANGES

Introduction.. 15-1

Types of Nontaxable Exchanges.. 15-2

Sale of a Personal Residence.. 15-3

Section 1034.. 15-4
Replacement Period.. 15-4
Computation of Gain Recognized and Basis of New Residence........... 15-6
Basis of Replacement Residence.. 15-8
Sale of New Residence.. 15-10
Ownership by Husband and Wife.. 15-12
Section 121 Exclusion of Gain... 15-13

Involuntary Conversions... 15-20

Involuntary Conversion Defined.. 15-20
Replacement Property.. 15-22
Replacement Period.. 15-24
Election Required... 15-24
Amount of Gain Recognized.. 15-25

Like-Kind Exchanges.. 15-28

Qualified Property.. 15-29
Like-Kind Property.. 15-29
Receipt of Property Not of a Like-Kind (Boot)............................ 15-32
Basis in Property Received... 15-34
Exchange Requirement.. 15-38
Treatment Mandatory... 15-41
Holding Period.. 15-41

Other Nontaxable Transactions... 15-44

Changes in Form of Doing Business... 15-44
Certain Exchanges of Stock in Same Corporation........................... 15-44
Certain Exchanges of U.S. Obligations.................................... 15-45
Repossession of Real Property.. 15-45
Rollover Gain from Low-Income Housing.................................... 15-45
Certain Exchanges of Insurance Policies.................................. 15-45

Tax Planning Considerations... 15-46

Current Recognition versus Deferral....................................... 15-46
Current Gain Resulting in Future Reductions.............................. 15-46
Section 1034 Considerations.. 15-46
Section 121 Considerations... 15-47
Importance of Capital Budgeting in Decision Making...................... 15-47

Problem Materials.. 15-48

16 PROPERTY TRANSACTIONS: CAPITAL GAINS AND LOSSES

General Requirements for Capital Gain................................. 16-3

Capital Assets.. 16-3

Definition of a Capital Asset... 16-3
Inventory... 16-4
Disposition of a Business.. 16-5

Sale or Exchange Requirement... **16-7**

Worthless and Abandoned Property.................................... **16-7**
Certain Casualties and Thefts... **16-8**
Other Transactions... **16-10**

Holding Period.. **16-10**

Stock Exchange Transactions.. **16-10**
Special Rules and Exceptions.. **16-11**

Capital Gain and Loss Netting Process................................ **16-13**

The Process... **16-13**
The Results.. **16-14**
Treatment of Capital Gains... **16-15**
Treatment of Capital Losses... **16-18**
Reporting Capital Gains and Losses.................................. **16-20**

Capital Gain Treatment Extended to Certain Transactions.............. **16-21**

Patents.. **16-21**
Lease Cancellation Payments... **16-22**

Special Treatment for Certain Investments............................ **16-22**

Losses on Small Business Stock: § 1244 Stock........................ **16-22**
Qualified Small Business Stock... **16-23**
Rollover of Gain on Certain Publicly Traded Securities................ **16-26**
Dealers in Securities.. **16-26**
Subdivided Real Estate.. **16-27**

Other Related Provisions.. **16-28**

Nonbusiness Bad Debts.. **16-28**
Franchise Agreements, Trademarks, and Trade Names................. **16-28**
Short Sales... **16-29**
Options... **16-30**

Corporate Bonds and Other Indebtedness............................. **16-32**

Original Issue Discount.. **16-33**
Market Discount.. **16-36**
Conversion Transactions.. **16-37**
Bond Premium.. **16-38**

Tax Planning Considerations.. **16-39**

Timing of Capital Asset Transactions.................................. **16-39**
Section 1244 Stock... **16-39**

Problem Materials.. **16-41**

17

PROPERTY TRANSACTIONS:
DISPOSITIONS OF TRADE OR BUSINESS PROPERTY

Introduction.. **17-1**

Section 1231.. **17-2**

Historical Perspective.. **17-2**
Section 1231 Property.. **17-3**
Other § 1231 Property.. **17-4**
Section 1231 Netting Process.. **17-7**
Look-Back Rule... **17-10**

Depreciation Recapture... **17-14**

Historical Perspective.. **17-14**
When Applicable... **17-15**
Types of Depreciation Recapture.. **17-15**
Full Recapture—§ 1245.. **17-15**
Partial Recapture—§ 1250.. **17-18**
Additional Recapture—Corporations.. **17-28**
Other Recapture Provisions.. **17-30**
Installment Sales of Trade or Business Property........................... **17-30**

Tax Planning Considerations... **17-34**

Timing of Sales and Other Dispositions................................... **17-34**
Selecting Depreciation Methods... **17-35**
Installment Sales... **17-35**

Problem Materials... **17-36**

PART VI

EMPLOYEE COMPENSATION AND TAXATION OF BUSINESS FORMS

18 EMPLOYEE COMPENSATION AND RETIREMENT PLANS

Introduction.. **18-1**

Taxation of Current Compensation... **18-1**

Statutory Fringe Benefits... **18-2**

Deferred Compensation.. **18-2**

Receipt of Property for Services.. **18-4**

General Rule of § 83.. **18-4**
The § 83(b) Election.. **18-5**

Qualified Retirement Plans for Corporations............................... **18-5**

Tax Benefits of Qualified Plans... **18-6**
Taxability of Qualified Plan Lump Sum Distributions....................... **18-7**
A Comprehensive Example.. **18-9**
Additional Taxes on Premature or Excess Distributions.................... **18-9**
Rollover Contribution... **18-10**
Plan Loans.. **18-10**
Types of Qualified Plans.. **18-10**

Qualification Requirements... **18-12**

Existence of a Qualified Trust.. **18-13**
Anti-Discrimination Rules... **18-13**
Scope of Plan Participation and Coverage................................. **18-14**
Vesting Requirements and Forfeitures..................................... **18-15**
Funding and Contribution Limitations..................................... **18-16**
Top Heavy Plans.. **18-18**
Deductibility of Contributions by Employer............................... **18-18**
Determination Letters... **18-19**

Qualified Plans for Self-Employed Individuals............................ **18-19**

Contribution Limitations.. **18-20**

Qualified Plans for Employees... **18-21**

    Cash or Deferred Arrangements.. 18-21
    Individual Retirement Accounts... 18-23
    Excess Contributions.. 18-25
    Simplified Employee Pensions.. 18-25

Retirement Planning Using Nonqualified Deferred Compensation....... **18-26**

    Constructive Receipt.. 18-26
    Unfunded Deferred Compensation Plans............................... 18-27
    Funded Deferred Compensation Plans................................. 18-27

Stock Options... **18-28**

    Option Exercise.. 18-29

Incentive Stock Options... **18-29**

    Holding Period Requirements.. 18-30
    Qualification Requirements.. 18-31
    Nonqualified Stock Options.. 18-32
    Stock Appreciation Rights... 18-33

Tax Planning Considerations.. **18-34**

    Planning for Retirement Income... 18-34
    Advantages of IRAs... 18-34
    Spousal IRAs... 18-35
    What Is an Active Participant?... 18-36
    Making a Nondeductible Contribution to An IRA......................... 18-36

Problem Materials... **18-38**

19 TAXATION OF BUSINESS FORMS AND THEIR OWNERS

Sole Proprietorships.. **19-1**

Partnerships.. **19-5**

    Taxation of Partnership Operations...................................... 19-5
    Transactions between Partnership and Partners......................... 19-11

S Corporations.. **19-13**

    Election of S Corporation Status... 19-14
    Making the S Election... 19-14
    Taxation of S Corporation Operations.................................... 19-15
    Transactions between an S Corporation and Its Shareholders............. 19-15

C Corporations.. **19-19**

    Taxation of Corporate Operations in General............................ 19-19
    Differences between Corporate and Individual Taxation.................. 19-22

Formation of a Business... **19-30**

    Formation of a Sole Proprietorship...................................... 19-31
    Formation of Partnerships... 19-32
    Formation of Corporations.. 19-33

Problem Materials... **19-47**

Appendices and Index

Appendix A: Tax Rate Schedules and Tables.. **A-1**

Appendix B: Tax Forms.. **B-1**

Appendix C: Modified ACRS and Original ACRS Tables................................. **C-1**

Appendix D: Table of Cases Cited... **D-1**

Appendix E: Table of Code Sections Cited... **E-1**

Appendix F: Table of Regulations Cited... **F-1**

Appendix G: Table of Revenue Procedures and Revenue Rulings Cited.............. **G-1**

Appendix H: Glossary of Tax Terms.. **H-1**

Appendix I: Two Individual Comprehensive Tax Return Problems for 1993.............. **I-1**

Index.. **J-1**

PART I

INTRODUCTION TO THE FEDERAL TAX SYSTEM

CONTENTS

CHAPTER 1 ▪ AN OVERVIEW OF FEDERAL TAXATION

CHAPTER 2 ▪ TAX PRACTICE AND RESEARCH

CHAPTER 3 ▪ TAXABLE ENTITIES, TAX FORMULA, INTRODUCTION TO PROPERTY TRANSACTIONS

CHAPTER 4 ▪ PERSONAL AND DEPENDENCY EXEMPTIONS; FILING STATUS; DETERMINATION OF TAX FOR AN INDIVIDUAL; FILING REQUIREMENTS

LEARNING OBJECTIVES

Upon completion of this chapter you will be able to:

- Trace the historical development of our Federal income tax system

- Explain the key terms used to describe most taxes

- Identify the different types of Federal taxes found in the United States, including

    - Income taxes

    - Wealth transfer taxes

    - Employment taxes

    - Excise taxes

- Understand the relationship between estate and gift taxes

- Explain the differences in the employment taxes levied on employees versus those levied on self-employed individuals

- Identify some of the more common social and economic goals of our Federal tax system

CHAPTER OUTLINE

Introduction	1-1	Wealth Transfer Taxes	1-12
The Nature of a Tax	1-1	Employment Taxes	1-19
Development of U.S. Taxation	1-2	Excise Taxes	1-24
Excise and Customs Duties	1-2	Additional Types of Taxes	1-25
Federal Income Tax	1-3	Goals of Taxation	1-26
Federal Wealth Transfer Taxes	1-5	Economic Objectives	1-27
Federal Taxes as a Source		Social Objectives	1-28
of Revenue	1-5	Other Objectives	1-29
Key Tax Terms	1-5	A Prelude to Tax Planning	1-31
Major Types of Taxes	1-9	Problem Materials	1-34
Income Taxes	1-9		

Chapter 1

AN OVERVIEW OF
FEDERAL TAXATION

INTRODUCTION

The system of Federal taxation that has been developed in the United States is among the most sophisticated and complex national tax programs in the world today. This system of taxation has an impact on almost every business and investment decision as well as many personal decisions. Decisions a business enterprise must make, such as the form it will take (i.e., sole proprietorship, partnership, or corporation), the length and nature of its operations, and the manner in which it will be terminated cannot be made without consideration of the tax consequences. An individual's decisions regarding employment contracts and alternative forms of compensation, as well as place and duration of employment, will be affected by the Federal tax structure. Even such personal choices as housing, family size, marital relationships, and termination of these relationships by divorce or death involve some of the most complex rules of the Federal tax law. This complexity places a *premium* on knowledge of the various types of Federal taxes imposed on those who by chance or choice must operate within the system's boundaries.

The purpose of this book is to introduce the reader to the Federal income taxation of individuals. A corollary objective of the authors is to aid the reader in the development of his or her *tax awareness* (i.e., ability to recognize tax problems, pitfalls, and planning opportunities). Such an awareness is not only an important attribute of accountants and lawyers—it is *essential* for everyone who chooses a career in business.

THE NATURE OF A TAX

The Supreme Court of the United States has defined a *tax* as "an exaction for the support of the Government."[1] Thus, what a tax does is to provide a means through which the government derives a majority of the revenues necessary to keep it in operation. A tax is not merely a source of revenue, however. As discussed in a later section of this chapter, taxes have become a powerful instrument which policymakers use to attain social as well as economic goals.

---

[1] *U.S. v. Butler,* 36-1 USTC ¶9039, 16 AFTR 1289, 297 U.S. 1, 70 (USSC, 1936). An explanation of case citations such as this is presented in Chapter 2.

A tax normally has one or more of the following characteristics:

1. There is no *direct relationship* between the exaction of revenue and any benefit to be received by the taxpayer. Thus, a taxpayer cannot trace his or her tax payment to an Army jeep, an unemployment payment, a weather satellite, or any of the myriad expenditures that the Federal government authorizes.

2. Taxes are levied on the basis of *predetermined criteria*. In other words, taxes can be objectively determined, calculated, and even planned around.

3. Taxes are levied on a *recurring* or *predictable* basis. Most taxes are levied on an annual basis, although some, like the estate tax, are levied only once.

4. Taxes *may be distinguished* from regulations or penalties. A regulation or penalty is a measure specifically designed to control or stop a particular activity. For instance, at one time Congress imposed a charge on the products of child labor. This charge was specifically aimed at stopping the use of children in manufacturing and thus was a regulation rather than a tax, even though it was called a "tax." Also, taxes can be distinguished from licenses and fees, which are payments made for some special privilege granted or services rendered (e.g., marriage license or automobile registration fee).

The major types of taxes imposed by taxing authorities within the United States (e.g., income, employment, and wealth transfer taxes) are discussed later in this chapter. As will be noted, one or more of the above characteristics can be found in each of these various taxes.

DEVELOPMENT OF U.S. TAXATION

The entire history of the United States, from its beginnings as a colony of England to the present day, is entwined with the development of Federal taxation. From its infancy until well into the current century, the United States Federal tax system closely paralleled the tax laws of its mother country, England.[2]

EXCISE AND CUSTOMS DUTIES

Shortly after the colonies won independence and became the United States of America, tariffs became the Federal government's principal revenue-raising source.[3] At the time of its adoption in 1789, the U.S. Constitution gave Congress the power to levy and collect taxes. Promptly exercising this authority, Congress passed as its first act the Tariff Act of 1789, which imposed a system of duties (called excise taxes) on imports.

---

[2] The states in turn have developed their own systems of taxation which often parallel— but sometimes diverge from—the Federal tax system.

[3] A tariff is a duty imposed on an importer. Since it is a cost of the product being imported, it usually is passed on to the consumer as part of the product's price. Thus, the higher the tariff imposed on a product, the higher must be its price if importation is to be profitable.

FEDERAL INCOME TAX

As time passed and the Federal government enlarged the scope of its activities, it became more and more apparent to political leaders that additional sources of revenue would have to be devised to supplement the tariff system. A tax on income was a likely alternative, but Congress was limited by constitutional constraints imposed on its power to levy and collect taxes. Under the original Constitution, any *direct* tax imposed by Congress was required to be *apportioned* among the states on the basis of relative populations. Under such a system it would be possible, and indeed likely, that each state would have a different Federal tax rate for its citizens because the sizes of the states' populations differed. If such a system had been tried, it would have been politically and practically unworkable.

> **Example 1.**   Assume that Congress imposed a $50,000 tax on income. Assume further that the United States was composed of only three states with populations as follows: Vermont—2,000; Texas—3,000; and New York—5,000. Under the original Constitution, if the income tax were a direct tax, it would be allocated among the states according to population, and each state's tax burden would be as follows: Vermont, $10,000 (20% of total population × $50,000 tax); Texas, $15,000 (30% of $50,000); and New York, $25,000 (50% of $50,000).

> **Example 2.**   Assume the sum of the residents' income in each state above was as follows: Vermont—$100,000; Texas—$300,000; and New York—$1,000,000. In such a case, the average rate of tax on income in each state would be as follows: Vermont, 10% ($10,000 tax ÷ $100,000 income); Texas, 5% ($15,000 ÷ $300,000); and New York, 2.5% ($25,000 ÷ $1,000,000). Since incomes are not distributed among the states in the same proportion as residents, the Federal government would be required to assess taxes on citizens of different states at *different rates*—a resident of Vermont might pay taxes at a rate of 10% while a resident of New York paid only 2.5%.

Despite the apportionment requirement, Congress enacted the first Federal income tax in 1861 to finance the vastly increased expenditures brought on by the Civil War. The tax was applied uniformly to all residents—the apportionment requirement being ignored, apparently on the belief that the income tax was not a direct tax. In *Springer v. U.S.*,[4] however, a taxpayer challenged the Civil War income tax, asserting that the tax was unconstitutional because it was direct, and that any direct tax required apportionment.

The distinction between *direct* taxes and indirect taxes has never been completely clarified. According to some, a direct tax is one that cannot be avoided or at least shifted to another with ease. Two taxes generally considered direct taxes are head taxes and property taxes; neither of these can be escaped without difficulty. Customs duties and other excise taxes are normally considered indirect taxes, since they can be avoided by not purchasing the particular good. Beyond these examples, however, the issue is

---

[4]   102 U.S. 586 (USSC, 1880).

unresolved. In *Springer,* the Supreme Court specifically addressed the question of whether an income tax was a direct tax. Upholding the constitutionality of the income tax, the Court indicated that only head taxes and real estate taxes were direct taxes and that all others were indirect. Although this case dealt squarely with the issue, the decision did not end the controversy.

The income tax was allowed to expire shortly after the Civil War, in 1872, but was reenacted in almost identical form in 1894. Upon reinstatement, it again was attacked as a direct tax requiring apportionment. In *Pollock v. Farmers' Loan and Trust Co.,*[5] the Supreme Court focused specifically on the income tax as it applied to income from real estate. The Court believed this case to be different from *Springer* and held that a tax on income from real estate was the equivalent of a tax on the real estate itself. Accordingly, the Court held that the tax was unconstitutional because it was a direct tax imposed without apportionment. After this decision, the constitutionality of an income tax was again suspect.

Undaunted by the *Pollock* decision, proponents of a Federal income tax continued their efforts and in 1909 were successful in bringing about a corporate income tax. This tax was upheld by the Supreme Court in *Flint v. Stone Tracy Co.*[6] when the Court held that it was an excise tax measured by corporate income, rather than a direct tax.

Concurrent with its passage of the 1909 corporate income tax, Congress proposed an amendment to the Constitution that would allow it to levy a tax on *all* incomes *without* apportionment among the states based on population. This effort culminated in the passage of the Sixteenth Amendment on February 25, 1913, which provided that,

> The Congress shall have the power to lay and collect taxes on incomes from whatever source derived, without apportionment among the several States, and without regard to any census or enumeration.

Without hesitation, Congress enacted the Revenue Act of 1913 on October 3, 1913 and made it retroactive to March 1, 1913.

Because of special exemptions and the progressive tax rates of the 1913 income tax law, it too was challenged as a denial of due process of law as guaranteed by the Fifth Amendment to the Constitution. In 1916 the Supreme Court upheld the validity of the new income tax law in *Brushaber v. Union Pacific Railroad Co.*[7] Although many changes have taken place, the United States has not been without a Federal income tax since 1913.

As historical conditions changed and the Federal government's need for additional revenues increased, Congress exercised its income taxing authority by the passage of many separate pieces of legislation that resulted in greater complexity in the Federal income tax law. Each new revenue act was a reenactment of a previous revenue act with added amendments. This process created great confusion for those working with the law, since it could be necessary to research over 100 separate sources to determine exactly what law was currently in effect. In addition, the reenactment of a statute sometimes suggested

---

[5] 3 AFTR 2602, 157 U.S. 429 (USSC, 1895).   [7] 240 U.S. 1 (USSC, 1916).

[6] 3 AFTR 2834, 220 U.S. 107 (USSC, 1911).

that any intervening interpretation of that statute (law) by the courts or the Treasury was approved by Congress, although no such Congressional approval was expressly stated. Congress resolved the confusion in 1939 with its systematic arrangement of all tax laws into the Internal Revenue Code of 1939, a permanent codification that required no reenactment.

The 1939 Code was revised in 1954 and again in 1986. Thus, today's governing Federal tax law is the *Internal Revenue Code of 1986*. The 1986 Code has already been amended by the Revenue Act of 1987, the Technical and Miscellaneous Revenue Act of 1988, the Revenue Reconciliation Act of 1989, the Revenue Reconciliation Act of 1990, the Unemployment Compensation Amendments Act of 1992, the Comprehensive Energy Policy Act of 1992, and the Revenue Reconciliation Act of 1993, and it will continue to be amended to incorporate changes in the tax law as those changes are enacted.

FEDERAL WEALTH TRANSFER TAXES

In 1916, the very same year the Supreme Court upheld the constitutionality of the Federal income tax, Congress enacted the first Federal law to impose a tax on the transfer of property triggered by the death of an individual. The value of the transfer was measured by the fair market value of the various assets included in the decedent's estate, and consequently the tax imposed on the transfer is referred to as the estate tax. The Federal estate tax imposed a progressive tax on the value on the decedent's taxable estate.

Because an individual could avoid the imposition of the Federal estate tax simply by giving away his or her property before death, Congress enacted the first Federal gift tax in 1924[8] to prevent full scale avoidance of the estate tax.

Like the Federal income tax, these Federal wealth transfer taxes have undergone significant changes since first enacted, adding to their complexity. Also, like the Federal income tax, there is little likelihood that Congress will abandon them in the foreseeable future.

FEDERAL TAXES AS A SOURCE OF REVENUE

Among sources of revenue, only the Federal income tax can claim a dominant role in providing the funds with which the U.S. government operates. The chart in Exhibit 1-1 illustrates the role of the Federal income tax in providing funding for the 1993 fiscal year. Note the limited role of excise taxes. Federal transfer taxes are even less significant and are included in the "other" category as a revenue source.

KEY TAX TERMS

Before examining the various types of Federal taxes in more detail, the reader must first become familiar with basic tax terminology. Some of the more common terms are briefly presented below.

---

[8] Although repealed in 1926, the Federal gift
tax was reinstated in 1932.

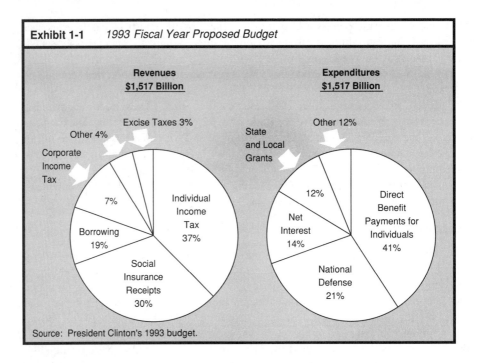

Exhibit 1-1   *1993 Fiscal Year Proposed Budget*

Source: President Clinton's 1993 budget.

Tax Base. A tax base is that amount upon which a tax is levied. For instance, in the case of Federal income taxation, the tax base is *taxable income*. Taxable income is the taxpayer's total income *less* exclusions, deductions, and exemptions that might be available to a particular taxpayer. In the case of the Federal wealth transfer taxes, the tax base is the fair market value of the property transferred by gift or at death *reduced* by certain exclusions, exemptions, or deductions allowed by Congress.

Income. Any *permanent* increment to wealth generally is defined as income. Temporary increments such as loans are not considered to be income. Sometimes income is subject to Federal taxation and other times it is not. The taxability of these increments to wealth generally depends upon whether Congress has *exempted* a particular form of income from taxation. Increments to wealth take many forms. Such increments may take the form of cash, property other than cash, or even services that are rendered to the taxpayer. As a general rule, Congress—and the various Federal courts assigned to interpret its laws—consider *any* increment to wealth to be taxable income *unless* it is *excluded* by definition (e.g., loans that must be repaid), by specific statutory authority in the Internal Revenue Code of 1986, or by the Constitution. Each of these possibilities is examined in detail in Chapters 5 and 6, which deal with gross income.

Deduction. A deduction is a reduction in the gross (total) amount which must be included in the taxable base. For instance, when an individual taxpayer incurs expenses such as medical expenses, interest on a loan or home mortgage, or property taxes, he or she generally will be allowed to deduct these expenses to arrive at taxable income for Federal tax purposes. Similarly, corporations are allowed to deduct most of their costs of doing business to determine corporate taxable income. It is *extremely important* to note, however, that deductions are a matter of legislative grace—unless Congress has specifically authorized a particular deduction, the expense will not be deductible.

> **Example 3.** Individual T purchased his family residence in 1990 for $70,000. T sells his residence in 1994 for $60,000. T may not take a deduction for the $10,000 loss (a permanent reduction in wealth) in determining his taxable income *because* Congress has not authorized a deduction for this particular type of loss.

Most deductions available to individual taxpayers and to other taxable entities (i.e., corporations, estates, and trusts) are discussed in detail in Chapters 7, 8, 9, 10, 11, and 12 of this text.

Exclusions. Certain increments to wealth that are *not included* in a particular Federal tax base are referred to as exclusions. Since the Constitution grants Congress the authority to tax income *from whatever source derived,* exclusions obviously are the creations of Congress. For various social, political, or economic reasons, Congress has chosen to exclude many sources of income and wealth transfers from their usual Federal tax base. The more common Congressional objectives of exclusions are discussed in a later section of this chapter.

> **Example 4.** N receives a $10,000 graduation gift from her aunt. N does not have to include this amount in determining taxable income because Congress has specifically excluded gifts from income. If N had received the $10,000 in exchange for rendering services to her aunt, or if N had received the $10,000 for appearing on a television game show, then in both cases she would have to include (report) the amount in income subject to taxation.

> **Example 5.** Refer to *Example 4* above. If N's aunt transfers $10,000 to N in the current year as a graduation gift, and this is the only gift made by the aunt to N in the current year, this transfer will not be subjected to the Federal gift tax. Congress has provided an annual exclusion from gift taxation of $10,000 per donee per year.

Tax Rates. A tax rate is some percentage applied to the tax base to determine a taxpayer's liability. Tax rates usually are either proportional or progressive. A *proportional* tax rate is one that remains at a constant percentage regardless of the size of the tax base. A *progressive* tax rate structure is one in which an increasing percentage rate is applied to increasing increments of the tax base. A *regressive* tax rate structure is one in which a decreasing percentage rate is applied to increasing increments of the tax base.

> **Example 6.** A has a tax base of $5,000 and pays a tax of $500, or 10%. B's similar tax base is $10,000 and the tax on this amount is $1,000, or 10%. If the same constant rate of 10% is applied to any amount of tax base, the tax is proportional.

> **Example 7.** R has a tax base of $10,000 and pays a tax of $500 on the first $5,000, and a tax of $1,000 on the next $5,000. The total tax of $1,500 was calculated by applying a 10% rate to the first $5,000 increment of the tax base and then applying a 20% rate to the excess tax base over $5,000. Since a higher percentage rate is applied as the tax base increases, this is a progressive rate structure.

Most excise taxes (e.g., sales taxes) employ a proportional tax rate. However, both the Federal income and transfer tax rates, as well as most state income tax rates, are progressive. The 1994 Federal income tax rate schedules for individual taxpayers appear on the inside front cover of this text for ready reference. The tax rates for corporations, estates, and trusts are presented on the inside back cover of the text. The Federal gift and estate tax rates are reproduced in Appendix A at the back of the text. A glance at either of these sources will indicate the progressive nature of the Federal tax system.

Marginal, Average, and Effective Tax Rates. The *marginal* tax rate of any rate structure is that percentage at which the *next* dollar added to the tax base will be taxed. For example, under the 1994 Federal income tax rate structure for individuals, the highest marginal tax rate is 39.6 percent (i.e., no one will be taxed on income at a rate greater than 39.6 percent).

> **Example 8.** H, an unmarried taxpayer, has taxable income of $20,000 for 1994. Referring to tax rate Schedule X on the inside front cover of this text, an unmarried taxpayer with taxable income of $20,000 has a tax of $3,000. H's marginal tax rate is therefore 15%. If H is a married taxpayer filing a separate tax return but reporting the same $20,000 of taxable income, his marginal tax rate would be 28%.

A taxpayer's knowledge of his or her marginal tax rate is essential in any tax-planning effort to minimize taxes. Without it, the tax impact of an additional dollar of the tax base or an additional dollar deduction could not be determined.

> **Example 9.** Refer to *Example 8*. If unmarried taxpayer H is considering depositing $2,000 in an Individual Retirement Account, an amount currently allowed as a deduction for Federal income tax purposes, he could determine his immediate tax savings to be $300 (the 15% marginal tax rate × the $2,000 income not taxed). Similarly, if H had a 31% marginal tax rate and wanted to know the after-tax amount of a proposed $6,000 increase in salary, he would simply multiply 69% (100% − 31%) times the $6,000.

Many individuals, including those who are highly educated, do not understand the marginal tax rate concept. All too often one hears the expression, "I can't afford to earn more because it will throw me into a higher tax bracket and I will keep less than I do now after taxes." This theoretically cannot occur unless the marginal tax rate exceeds 100 percent.

Marginal tax rates are also confused with *average* tax rates (tax divided by tax base) and *effective* tax rates (tax divided by total economic income). In decrying the harshness of the income tax, people often point to their marginal rate and declare that they are paying that percent (e.g., 28%) of their income to the government. Such is clearly not the case.

Example 10.   K, an unmarried taxpayer, has taxable income of $25,000 and pays a tax of $4,212. Although her marginal tax rate is 28%, K's average tax rate is 16.84% ($4,212 ÷ $25,000), a far cry from 28%.

Example 11.   Assume the same facts as in *Example 10* except that K's total economic income is $35,000, the $10,000 difference between total income and taxable income being attributable to exclusions and deductions (e.g., interest on tax-exempt bonds and the personal exemption). In such case, K would pay taxes at an effective rate of 12.03% [$4,212 ÷ ($25,000 + $10,000)].

Tax Credits.   A tax credit is a dollar-for-dollar offset against a tax liability. A credit is quite different from a deduction, since it directly reduces the tax liability itself, whereas a deduction simply reduces the base amount subject to the tax.

Example 12.   T is a single taxpayer with a 31% marginal tax rate. An additional $100 tax deduction would result in a tax reduction to T of $31 (31% × $100). If the $100 qualified as a tax credit, however, T would have a $100 tax reduction—the equivalent of a $323 tax deduction at a marginal tax rate of 31%.

Tax credits are discussed in detail in Chapter 13 of this text.

MAJOR TYPES OF TAXES

Taxing authorities within the United States have a wide array of taxes with which they raise revenues or attempt to effect social, political, or economic change. The average individual will feel the impact of quite a number of taxes during his or her lifetime. Any attempt to accumulate wealth requires diligent tax planning, and to ignore the growing size of the Federal, state, and local taxes will serve no useful purpose toward this end. Although the principal thrust of this text is aimed at the Federal income and wealth transfer taxes, some of the other types of taxes merit a brief introduction.

INCOME TAXES

An income tax is an extraction of some of the taxpayer's economic gain, usually on a periodic basis. In addition to the Federal government, many states and some local governments impose a tax on income. As noted earlier in Exhibit 1-1, the individual income tax is expected to provide 37 percent of the Federal government's revenues in 1993. Of all the sources providing revenues to the Federal government, the individual income tax is the largest. In contrast, the corporate income tax is expected to provide only 7 percent of the Federal government's projected revenues for 1993.[9]

---

[9]   Such heavy reliance on the income tax as a source of government revenues is peculiar to the United States. Most Western European nations have turned to a Value Added Tax (VAT). A VAT is a system of taxing the increment in value of goods as they move through the production and manufacturing process to the market place. The VAT operates very much like a national sales tax and has occasionally been proposed, though unsuccessfully, for the United States.

The Federal government imposes an income tax on individuals, corporations, estates, and trusts. Usually, a final tax reckoning (reporting and paying taxes due) is made at the end of each year. In order to ensure tax collections, however, Congress has created a pay-as-you-go requirement. Basically, this process requires employers to withhold and remit to the Federal government income taxes on wages paid to employees. Individuals with income from sources other than wages, and most other tax entities are required to make estimated tax prepayments during the year.[10]

Application of the Federal income tax to individuals is discussed in Chapters 3 and 4. Computation of a corporation's Federal income tax is explained in Chapter 19. The Federal income taxation of a business operated in either the partnership or corporate form is also examined in Chapter 19. For now, the procedures for determining the Federal income tax liability of corporate and individual taxpayers are reduced to computational formulas presented in Exhibits 1-2 and 1-3 as follows. The components of these formulas are introduced and discussed in greater detail in Chapter 3.

Most states in the United States impose an income tax of some sort.[11] Generally, state income taxes are designed to operate much like the Federal income tax. Almost all the states have a tax-withholding procedure and most use the income determination for Federal income tax purposes as the tax base. Some states allow a deduction for Federal income taxes, while others exclude income that is subject to Federal income taxation.

Exhibit 1-2   *Tax Formula for Corporate Taxpayers*

Income (from whatever source)	$xxx,xxx
Less: Exclusions from gross income	− xx,xxx
Gross income	$xxx,xxx
Less: Deductions	− xx,xxx
Taxable income	$xxx,xxx
Applicable tax rates	xx%
Gross tax	$ xx,xxx
Less: Tax credits and prepayments	− x,xxx
Tax due (or refund)	$ xx,xxx

---

[10]   This procedure was developed by Congress during World War II to accelerate annual tax payments needed to finance the war effort. The process served so well to increase compliance with and facilitate administration of the Federal income tax law that Congress chose not to abandon it at the close of the war.

[11]   States *not* currently imposing an income tax on individuals are Alaska, Florida, Nevada, South Dakota, Texas, Washington, and Wyoming. Tennessee and New Hampshire impose an income tax on an individual's dividend and interest income. Every state imposes either a corporate income tax or a tax on the privilege of conducting business within the state's boundaries. See subsequent discussion of franchise taxes.

Exhibit 1-3 *Tax Formula for Individual Taxpayers*

Income (from whatever source)......................		$xxx,xxx
Less: Exclusions from gross income.................		− xx,xxx
Gross income...		$xxx,xxx
Less: Deductions *for* adjusted gross income........		− xx,xxx
Adjusted gross income...............................		$xxx,xxx
Less: 1. The larger of		
a. Standard deduction...................	$x,xxx	
or	*or*	− x,xxx
b. Total itemized deductions.............	$x,xxx	
2. Personal and dependency		
exemptions × exemption amount.......		− x,xxx
Taxable income.......................................		$xxx,xxx
Applicable tax rates		
(from Tables or Schedules X, Y, or Z)...............		xx%
Gross tax..		$ xx,xxx
Less: Tax credits and prepayments.................		− x,xxx
Tax due (or refund)...................................		$ xx,xxx

Interest income from Federal government obligations is not subject to state income taxation, and interest income from state and local government obligations generally is not subject to either Federal or state income taxation. Most states have developed their own set of rates, exemptions, and credits; however, the filing date for the state income tax return generally coincides with the due date of the taxpayer's Federal income tax return.[12]

One particular problem that has developed in the area of state taxation is the so-called "unitary tax." Several states[13] tax businesses on the basis of their global activities, not just their local operations. This asserted right to tax income that has not been earned within the state's boundaries has been subjected to many challenges in the courts; but, as of this date, the unitary tax has not been struck down as unconstitutional.[14] Foreign corporations object to this worldwide combined reporting for many reasons, the most obvious being that it may result in the imposition of state taxation even when no taxable income has been generated by intrastate operations.

---

[12] For individuals and partnerships, the due date of the Federal income tax return is the fifteenth day of the fourth month following the close of the tax year. For corporate taxpayers, the due date of the Federal return is the fifteenth day of the *third* month following the close of the tax year.

[13] Among those states that tax businesses on the basis of worldwide income are Alaska, California, Colorado, Florida, Idaho, Illinois, Indiana, Massachusetts, Montana, New Hampshire, New York (oil companies only), North Dakota, Oregon, and Utah.

[14] The U.S. Supreme Court upheld California's system of taxing global profits of U.S.-based multinational businesses in *Container Corporation of America v. Franchise Tax Board*, 103 S.Ct. 2933 (USSC, 1983).

WEALTH TRANSFER TAXES

Unlike Federal and state income taxes, wealth transfer taxes are not significant revenue producers. For example, collection of the Federal transfer taxes for 1993 represented less than 2 percent of Federal income.[15] Historically, the primary function of wealth transfer taxes has been to *hinder* the accumulation of wealth by family units. Thus, the goal of wealth redistribution generally underlies the design of estate and gift tax systems.

The Federal Estate Tax. Since 1976, the Federal estate tax and Federal gift tax have been combined into one tax known as the unified transfer tax. The unified transfer tax eliminates the distinction previously required between taxable lifetime transfers and transfers at death. Like the Federal income tax rate structure, the unified transfer tax rates are progressive. Unlike the income tax, however, the Federal transfer tax is *computed cumulatively* on taxable gifts made during a donor's lifetime and taxable transfers made at the donor's death. This is done by adding taxable gifts for the current year to all taxable gifts made in prior years (since 1976), calculating the gross tax on the sum of the gifts, and *subtracting* gift taxes assessed on the prior years' gifts. Under this system, a decedent's taxable estate is treated as the decedent's *final* gift.

The procedure for computing the Federal estate tax liability is reduced to summary form in Exhibit 1-4 as follows.

Exhibit 1-4 *Computation of Federal Estate Tax Liability*

Gross estate....................................		$x,xxx,xxx
Less the sum of:		
Expenses, indebtedness, and taxes.........	$ xx,xxx	
Losses....................................	x,xxx	
Charitable bequests.......................	xx,xxx	
Marital deduction..........................	xxx,xxx	− xxx,xxx
Taxable estate..................................		$ xxx,xxx
Plus: Taxable gifts made after		
December 31, 1976................		+ xx,xxx
Total taxable transfers..........................		$ xxx,xxx
Tentative tax on total transfers.................		$ xxx,xxx
Less the sum of:		
Gift taxes paid on post-1976 taxable gifts...	$ x,xxx	
Unified transfer tax credit..................	xx,xxx	
Other tax credits..........................	x,xxx	− xx,xxx
Estate tax liability.............................		$ xx,xxx

---

[15] Commissioner of Internal Revenue, *1993 Annual Report,* IRS Publication 55.

A decedent's gross estate includes the value of *all* property owned at date of death, wherever located. This includes the proceeds of an insurance policy on the life of the decedent if the decedent's estate is the beneficiary, or if the decedent had any ownership rights[16] in the policy at time of death. Property included in the gross estate generally is valued as of the date of death.[17]

The taxable estate is the gross estate reduced by deductions allowed for funeral and administrative expenses, debts of the decedent, certain taxes and losses, and charitable gifts made from the decedent's estate. It is important to note that there is no limit imposed on the charitable deduction. If an individual is willing to leave his or her entire estate for public, charitable, or religious use, there will be no taxable estate.[18] Finally, an *unlimited* marital deduction is allowed for the value of property passing to a surviving spouse. Thus, if a married taxpayer, no matter how wealthy, is willing to leave all of his or her property to the surviving spouse, no Federal transfer tax will be imposed on the estate. Only upon the subsequent death of the surviving spouse will the couple's wealth be subject to taxation.

Under current Federal estate tax laws, taxable gifts made after 1976 are added to the taxable estate to arrive at total taxable transfers. A tentative transfer tax is then computed on the base amount. All gift taxes paid on post-1976 gifts, as well as certain tax credits, are subtracted from this tentative tax in arriving at the Federal estate tax due, if any. Most estate tax credits have a single underlying purpose—to reduce or eliminate the effect of multiple taxation of a single estate. Estate taxes paid to the various states or foreign countries on property owned by the decedent and located within their boundaries are examples of estate tax credits. However, the major credit available to reduce the Federal estate tax is the *unified credit*.

The unified credit is a lifetime credit available for all taxable transfers, including taxable gifts made after 1976. It must be used when available; a taxpayer may not decide to postpone use of the credit if he or she makes a taxable transfer in the current year. Currently, the unified credit is $192,800. This amount of credit completely offsets the tax on $600,000 of taxable transfers (see Appendix A for the Unified Transfer Tax Rate Schedule currently in effect). Thus, an individual may make substantial transfers of wealth *before* any tax liability is incurred.

> **Example 13.** T had never made any taxable gifts prior to her death in 1994. The tentative tax on T's taxable estate is $250,000, and tax credits *other than* the unified tax credit total $5,000. The Federal estate tax due on T's estate will be $52,200 ($250,000 tentative tax − $192,800 unified tax credit − $5,000 other credits).

---

[16] Ownership rights in a life insurance policy include the power to change the policy's beneficiary, the right to cancel or assign the policy, and the right to borrow against the policy.

[17] For further discussion of the valuation of a decedent's gross estate, see *Corporate, Partnership, Estate and Gift Taxation*, 1995 Edition (Burr Ridge: Richard D. Irwin), Chapter 13.

[18] For federal income tax purposes, an individual's charitable contribution deduction may be subject to several limitations. See Chapter 11 for more details.

Exhibit 1-5   *Computation of Federal Gift Tax Liability*

Fair market value of all gifts made in the current year.............................		$xxx,xxx
Less the sum of:		
Annual exclusions ($10,000 per donee)......	$xx,xxx	
Marital deduction............................	xx,xxx	
Charitable deduction........................	x,xxx	− xx,xxx
Taxable gifts for current year.....................		$xxx,xxx
Plus: Taxable gifts made in prior years.......		+ xx,xxx
Taxable transfers to date..........................		$xxx,xxx
Tentative tax on total transfers to date...........		$ xx,xxx
Less the sum of:		
Gift taxes computed at current rates on prior years' taxable gifts..........	$ x,xxx	
Unified transfer tax credit...................	x,xxx	− x,xxx
Gift tax due on current gifts......................		$ xx,xxx

---

The Federal Gift Tax. As stated earlier, the purpose of the Federal gift tax was to prevent the avoidance of the Federal estate tax by lifetime transfers of property. Until 1977, the Federal gift tax rates were 75 percent of the Federal estate tax rates. This rate differential encouraged taxable lifetime transfers, which in effect accelerated transfer tax payments to the Federal government. The Tax Reform Act of 1976 eliminated this rate difference, and as discussed above, there now is only *one* Federal transfer tax rate structure.

The procedure for computing the Federal gift tax liability is presented as a formula in Exhibit 1-5. To arrive at taxable gifts for the year, the taxpayer's total gifts may be reduced by the annual exclusion and by the deductions allowed for property transferred to a spouse or charity. In computing taxable gifts for the current year, note that a donor is allowed an annual exclusion of $10,000 per donee. The annual exclusion is allowed *each year* even if the donor had made gifts in the prior year to the same donee.

> **Example 14.** T, a widower, wanted his son, daughter-in-law, and their five children to share his wealth. On December 25, 1994 he gave $10,000 to each family member. He repeats these gifts in 1995. Although T has transferred $140,000 [$10,000 × 7 (number of donees) × 2], he has not made taxable gifts in either 1994 or 1995.

The marital and charitable deductions for Federal gift tax purposes are the same as for the Federal estate tax—*unlimited*. Thus, if a taxpayer gives his or her spouse a $2,000,000 anniversary present or transfers $100,000 to his or her church, a taxable gift has not been made.

If taxable gifts have been made for the current year, the cumulative computational procedure of the unified transfer tax must be applied.

Example 15.   In 1989 R made her first taxable gift of $350,000. Tax (before credits) on this amount was $104,800. In 1994 R makes a second taxable gift of $350,000. The tax (before credits) on the second gift is $125,000, computed as follows:

Taxable gift in 1994....................	$350,000
Plus: Taxable gift in 1989..........	+ 350,000
Cumulative taxable gifts...............	$700,000
Tax on $700,000......................	$229,800*
Less: Tax on 1989 gift.............	− 104,800*
Tax on 1994 gift......................	$125,000

* See the unified transfer tax rate schedules contained in Appendix A. Also, note that the current year's tax rate is used to compute the tax reduction for the 1989 gift.

Note that the cumulative system of wealth transfer taxation *and* the progressive rate schedule cause a higher tax on the 1994 gift, even though the gift was the same amount as the 1989 gift.

Computation of the current year's gift tax liability is a two-step process. First, a tentative tax is calculated by applying the unified tax rates in effect for the current year to the cumulative lifetime taxable transfers made by the individual. Next, the tentative tax liability is reduced by (1) the taxes attributable to prior years' taxable gifts, and (2) the unified transfer tax credit. Note that in computing the reduction for prior years' taxable transfers, the unified tax rates in effect in the current year are used—even though the tax reduction so computed may exceed the actual gift taxes paid on the prior transfers. This procedure was developed in 1977 when the gift tax rates were increased to the same level as the estate tax rates. Since the tentative tax liability is calculated by applying the current tax rates to *all* lifetime taxable transfers, any gifts made before 1977 are included at rates substantially higher than those in effect for the year the gifts were made. Without the procedure, the current year's gift tax liability would include some additional tax on prior years' gifts—in effect, a double taxation of pre-1977 gifts.

The only credit available to offset the Federal gift tax liability is the unified transfer tax credit. As illustrated previously (in Examples 13 and 14), a taxpayer's unified transfer tax credit for any given year is the scheduled unified credit available for that particular year.

Example 16. Assume the same facts in *Example 15*. The tax on R's 1989 gift is $104,800, and she must use $104,800 of her available unified credit so that the actual gift tax due is reduced to zero. The tax on R's 1994 gift is $37,000, computed as follows:

Taxable gift for 1994............................		$350,000
Plus: 1989 taxable gift		+ 350,000
Taxable transfers to date.......................		$700,000
Tentative tax on total transfers to date		
(see Exhibit 1-5).............................		$229,800
Less: Gift taxes on 1989 gift................		− 104,800
Tentative tax on 1994 gift.......................		$125,000
Less: Remaining unified transfer tax credit:		
Total credit available............	$192,800	
Less: Unified transfer		
tax credit used in 1989.......	− 104,800	− 88,000
Gift tax due on 1994 gift.......................		$ 37,000

Another unique feature of the Federal gift tax involves the *gift-splitting* election available to a married donor. If a donor makes the election on his or her current gift tax return, one half of all gifts made during the year will be considered to have been made by the donor's spouse. The election is valid *only if* both spouses *consent* to gift-splitting.

Example 17. In 1994 husband H makes two gifts of $100,000 each to his son and daughter. His wife W makes a gift of $5,000 to the daughter only. H and W elect gift-splitting on their 1994 gift tax returns. As a result, H will report a gift to the son of $50,000 and a gift to the daughter of $52,500 [1/2 of ($100,000 + $5,000)], and will claim two $10,000 gift tax exclusions. W will report exactly the same gifts and claim two $10,000 exclusions.

Without gift-splitting, H would still be entitled to $20,000 of exclusions, but W could only claim an exclusion of $5,000 for her gift to the daughter. Thus, by electing to split gifts, a married donor can, in effect, make use of any annual exclusions not needed by his or her spouse. More importantly, if taxable gifts are made under a gift-splitting arrangement, *two* lifetime unified credits (i.e., one for each spouse) will be available to reduce the resulting gift tax liability.

State and Local Transfer Taxes. Many states and some local jurisdictions impose an inheritance tax on the *right to receive* property at death. Unlike an estate tax, which is imposed on the estate according to value of property transferred by the decedent at death, an inheritance tax is imposed on the recipient of property from an estate.[19] The amount of an inheritance tax payable usually is directly affected by the degree of kinship between the recipient and the decedent. The inheritance tax typically provides an exemption from

---

[19] It is not uncommon for the decedent's will to provide that his or her estate pay any inheritance tax imposed on the recipient of property from the estate.

the tax, which increases as the relationship between the recipient (e.g., surviving spouse, children, grandchildren, parents, etc.) and the decedent becomes closer. In addition, as the relationship becomes closer, the transfer tax rates decrease. Thus, the more closely related one is, the smaller the inheritance tax will be. Generally, little if any inheritance tax exemption is available for transfers to unrelated recipients, and the highest rate is imposed.

State estate taxes take one of two forms. One type, similar to the Federal estate tax, permits deductions from the gross estate such as the marital deduction, funeral and administrative expenses, and debts of the decedent. The rates imposed on the resulting taxable estate are considerably lower than those of the Federal unified transfer tax rates. The more common form of a state estate tax, however, is based on whatever amount qualifies for the *maximum* state death tax credit allowed for Federal estate tax purposes. Section 2011 of the Internal Revenue Code contains a schedule of the maximum amount of a credit that may be taken against the Federal estate tax for any estate, inheritance, legacy, or succession taxes actually paid to a state. This schedule is presented in Exhibit 1-6. States imposing an inheritance tax usually will have an estate tax so that they will collect the maximum amount of transfer taxes allowed as a credit under Code § 2011.

> **Example 18.** At his death, T resided in a state that imposes an estate tax based on the maximum amount allowed as a credit for Federal estate tax purposes. If T's Federal adjusted taxable estate is $1,540,000, the state's estate tax will be $70,800.

States that impose *both* an estate and inheritance tax, and which impose their estate tax based on the maximum amount allowed as a credit for Federal estate tax purposes, will reduce the state estate tax by any inheritance tax imposed on the heirs.

> **Example 19.** At her death, F resided in a state that imposed both an estate and inheritance tax. The state's estate tax is based on the maximum allowed credit for Federal estate tax purposes. If the state imposed an inheritance tax of $7,000 on the heirs of F's $440,000 adjusted taxable estate, the state estate tax would be $3,000 ($10,000 minimum state death tax credit − $7,000 inheritance tax).

Nine states impose a state gift tax.[20] Like the Federal gift tax, state gift tax laws usually provide for lifetime exemptions and annual exclusions and very often incorporate by reference the Federal gift tax law. For instance, the New York State statute permitting a state gift tax deduction for charitable contributions reads as follows:

> New York adopts the Federal provisions permitting deductions for charitable, public, and similar gifts less exclusions. The Federal figure is reduced by the gifts, less exclusions, which are not qualified charitable New York gifts (e.g., gifts of out-of-state real property).[21]

---

[20] Delaware, Louisiana, New York, North Carolina, Oregon, Rhode Island, South Carolina, Tennessee, and Wisconsin.

[21] § 1009, Tax Law (CCH New York Tax Reports, No. 88-937). See Chapter 2 for an explanation of citation symbols.

Exhibit 1-6   *Federal Estate Tax Credit for State Death Taxes*

Table for Computation of
Maximum Credit for State Death Taxes

(A) Adjusted* Taxable Estate Equal to or More Than—	(B) Adjusted Taxable Estate Less Than—	(C) Credit on Amount in Column (A)	(D) Rates of Credit on Excess Over Amount in Column (A)
$ 40,000	$ 90,000	$ 0	0.8%
90,000	140,000	400	1.6
140,000	240,000	1,200	2.4
240,000	440,000	3,600	3.2
440,000	640,000	10,000	4.0
640,000	840,000	18,000	4.8
840,000	1,040,000	27,600	5.6
1,040,000	1,540,000	38,800	6.4
1,540,000	2,040,000	70,800	7.2
2,040,000	2,540,000	106,800	8.0
2,540,000	3,040,000	146,800	8.8
3,040,000	3,540,000	190,800	9.6
3,540,000	4,040,000	238,800	10.4
4,040,000	5,040,000	290,800	11.2
5,040,000	6,040,000	402,800	12.0
6,040,000	7,040,000	522,800	12.8
7,040,000	8,040,000	650,800	13.6
8,040,000	9,040,000	786,800	14.4
9,040,000	10,040,000	930,800	15.2
10,040,000	. . . . .	1,082,800	16.0

*The adjusted taxable estate is the Federal taxable estate reduced by $60,000.

State gift tax rates usually follow the pattern of state inheritance taxes. That is, the closer the relationship between donee and donor, the lower the gift tax rate and the larger the gift tax exemption.

EMPLOYMENT TAXES

The Federal government and most states impose some form of employment tax on either self-employed individuals, employees,[22] or employers. The most common form of state employment tax is levied on wages, with the proceeds used to finance the state's unemployment benefits program. State unemployment taxes are imposed on employers who have employees working within the state's boundaries, but only if the employees would be eligible for unemployment benefits from the state. Most states' unemployment taxes are based on the same taxable wage base as that used for the Federal unemployment tax (see discussion below), and employers are allowed to take state unemployment taxes paid as a credit against the Federal unemployment tax liability.

The Federal government imposes two types of taxes on employment—a social security tax and an unemployment tax. The Federal Insurance Contribution Act (FICA) imposes a tax on self-employed individuals, employees, and employers. The FICA tax is paid by both an employee and his or her employer if the employee is eligible for social security and Medicare health insurance benefits. Although subject to a different tax rate, self-employed individuals are required to pay FICA taxes on net earnings from self-employment. The Federal Unemployment Tax Act (FUTA) imposes a tax *only* on the employer. Self-employed individuals are not eligible for unemployment benefits and thus are not subject to the FUTA tax. The tax base and rate structure of both these Federal employment taxes are presented below.

FICA Taxes.   Proceeds from the FICA tax are used by the Federal government to finance its payment of social security benefits [i.e., old age, survivors', and disability insurance (social security) payments and Medicare health insurance (MHI) payments]. The tax base and tax rates have increased annually since 1978. In 1993 Congress removed all limitations on the MHI component so that all wages and self-employed income are now subject to the MHI component of FICA effective in 1994. As was done previously, Congress will continue to raise the social security component's income ceiling every year. Usually this is done a few months before the beginning of the new tax year.

The FICA tax currently imposed on wages and self-employment income has two components: (1) a 1.45 percent tax for Medicare health insurance (MHI), and (2) a 6.2 percent tax for old age, survivors', and disability insurance (social security). Before 1994, each component of the FICA tax had a base amount beyond which no tax was levied. After 1993, the social security component continues to be limited by a statutory

---

[22] The term "employee" is used to identify persons whose work effort, tools, place of work, and work time periods are subject to the supervision and control of another (the employer). A person who provides his or her own tools and who has the *right* to exercise control over when, where, and for whom services are rendered (i.e., an independent contractor) generally is classified as self-employed rather than as an employee. See Chapter 8 for a discussion of the importance this classification has in the deductions allowed to individuals for Federal income tax purposes.

ceiling that changes every year, but the Medicare health insurance tax is levied against all compensation or self-employed income without any ceiling amount. For 1994 the base amount for the social security portion of the FICA tax is limited to $60,600.

Employees and Employers.   FICA taxes are imposed at the combined rate of 7.65 percent (6.2% social security + 1.45% MHI) on each dollar of an employee's wages up to $60,600 plus 1.45 percent on each additional dollar of wages. After 1993 there is no maximum amount on the MHI component of the FICA tax because the 1.45 percent MHI tax is applicable to *all* compensation. The employer is required to pay a matching amount of FICA taxes for each employee (i.e., the same tax rates on each employee's wage base up to the same limits).[23]

> **Example 20.**   During 1994 employee E earns wages of $24,000. As a result, E will pay $1,836 (7.65% × $24,000) FICA taxes, and her employer must pay the same amount as an employment tax.

> **Example 21.**   During 1994 employee F earns wages of $240,000. As a result F will pay $7,237.20 FICA taxes, and her employer must pay the same amount as an employment tax. It is important to note that the 1.45% MHI tax has no ceiling amount. The calculation is as follows:

> | | |
> |---|---|
> | Social security portion = 6.2% × $60,600 limit...... | $3,757.20 |
> | Plus: MHI portion = 1.45% × $240,000............. | + 3,480.00 |
> | Total FICA taxes.................................... | $7,237.20 |

An employer is required to withhold both Federal income taxes and FICA taxes from each employee's wages paid during the year. The employer is then required to pay these withheld amounts plus the employer's matching FICA taxes for each employee to the IRS on a regular basis, usually weekly or monthly.[24] Employers also are required to file Form 941, Employer's Quarterly Federal Tax Return, by the end of the first month following each quarter of the calendar year (e.g., by April 30, 1994 for the quarter ended March 31, 1994), and pay any remaining amount of employment taxes due for the previous quarter.[25]

In some instances, an employee who has had more than one employer during the year may have paid *excess* FICA taxes for the year and will be entitled to a Federal income tax credit or refund for the excess.

---

[23] Employers are allowed a tax deduction for all payroll taxes. See Chapter 7 for a discussion of business deductions.

[24] The frequency of these payments depends on the total amount of Federal income taxes withheld and the FICA taxes due on the employer's periodic payroll. The amount of Federal income and FICA taxes to be withheld from each employee's wages, and the reporting and payment requirements are specified in Circular E, *Employer's Tax Guide,* a free publication of the Internal Revenue Service.

[25] Because of significant penalties for underpayment of these Federal employment taxes, most employers exercise great care to make payments on a timely basis. See Circular E for a discussion of these penalties and due dates.

Example 22.   During 1994 E earned $40,000 from his regular job and $40,000 from a part-time job. Both of E's employers withheld $3,060 ($40,000 × 7.65%) from his wages, and with a matching amount, made payments to the IRS. Since E has paid a total of $6,120 (2 × $3,060) FICA taxes and the maximum amount due for 1994 is $4,917.20 [$3,757.20 social security portion (6.2% × $60,600) + $1,160 MHI portion ($40,000 + $40,000 = $80,000 × 1.45%)], E will be entitled to a tax credit or refund of the $1,202.80 excess ($6,120 − $4,917.20). Note that this simply represents the FICA taxes withheld on E's wages in excess of the $60,600 maximum amount subject to the 6.2% social security rate (i.e., $80,000 − $60,600 = $19,400 × 6.2% = $1,202.80).

Self-Employed Taxpayers.   Like employees, self-employed individuals are required to pay FICA taxes (commonly known as self-employment tax). For 1994 the social security portion of self-employment tax rate is 12.4 percent and the MHI portion is 2.9 percent. These rates are *twice* the FICA tax rates imposed on an employee's wages. Effective for 1994, the ceiling amount for the social security portion of self-employment tax is $60,600, the same as for employees. However, also effective for 1994, there is no ceiling on the MHI portion. Accordingly, all self-employment income, and all compensation, is subject to the MHI portion of the tax.

Apparently in order to provide some relief from this "doubling-up effect," self-employed taxpayers are allowed an income tax deduction for one-half the amount of self-employment taxes actually paid.[26] In addition, a self-employed taxpayer is allowed to *reduce* net earnings from self-employment by an amount equal to one-half the combined 15.3 percent tax rate times net earnings from self-employment (i.e., 7.65% × net earnings from self-employment) in arriving at each of the self-employment tax bases.[27] As illustrated in Example 23, this last so-called deduction may not be of benefit to some self-employed taxpayers.

Each component of the self-employment tax required to be paid is computed as follows:

First: Multiply one-half the self-employment tax rate times net earnings from self-employment.

Second: Subtract the amount determined in step 1 from net earnings from self-employment.[28]

Third: Compare the result in step 2 with the maximum base amount for the social security portion of the self-employment tax ($60,600 for 1994) and select the smaller amount.

---

[26]   § 164(f). See Chapter 2 for an explanation of citations to the Internal Revenue Code of 1986.

[27]   § 1402(a)(12).

[28]   Note that the first and second steps can be combined simply by multiplying the individual's net earnings from self-employment by 100% − one-half the current combined self-employment tax rate (i.e., 100% − 7.65% = 92.35%).

Fourth: Multiply the amounts from steps 2 and 3 by the tax rate for each separate component.

Fifth: Add the amounts of the separate components from step 4. This is the amount of self-employment tax required to be paid.

Example 23. Individuals C and D have net earnings from self-employment for 1994 of $50,000 and $150,000, respectively. Self-employment taxes for C and D are determined as follows:

C	Social Security	MHI
Net earnings from self-employment..............	$ 50,000	$ 50,000
Subtract: 7.65% of net earnings from self-employment.............	(3,825)	(3,825)
	$ 46,175	$ 46,175
Smaller of maximum tax base or amount determined above..................	$ 46,175	$ 46,175
Times: Each component's tax rate.............	× 12.4%	× 2.9%
Tax on each component........................	$5,725.70	$1,339.08
Social security tax...............................	$5,725.70	
Plus: MHI tax..................................	1,339.08	
Equals: C's self-employment tax..............	$7,064.78	

D	Social Security	MHI
Net earnings from self-employment..............	$ 150,000	$ 150,000
Subtract: 7.65% of net earnings from self-employment.............	(11,475)	(11,475)
	$ 138,525	$ 138,525
Smaller of maximum tax base or amount determined above..................	$ 60,600	$ 138,525
Times: Each component's tax rate.............	× 12.4%	× 2.9%
Tax on each component........................	$7,514.40	$4,017.22
Social security tax...............................	$ 7,514.40	
Plus: MHI tax..................................	4,017.22	
Equals: D's self-employment tax..............	$11,531.62	

C will be allowed to deduct $3,532.39 (one-half of $7,064.78 self-employment tax paid) for income tax purposes, and D will be allowed to deduct $5,765.81 (one-half of $11,531.62). Although both will receive a benefit from the income tax deduction, note that only C has received any benefit from the so-called second

deduction in arriving at his self-employment tax base for the social security component. Because D's reduced net earnings for self-employment are still greater than the maximum tax base for the social security component, she is required to pay the maximum amount of this component of the self-employment tax for 1994 (i.e., $60,600 \times 12.4\% = \$7,514.40$).

Self-employed individuals are required to pay quarterly estimated Federal tax payments, including self-employment taxes, if the estimated amount is $500 or more. A self-employed taxpayer also is required to file Schedule SE, Computation of Social Security Self-Employment Tax, with his or her annual Federal income tax return (Form 1040).

In some instances, a self-employed individual may also earn wages subject to FICA withholding while working as a full or part-time employee. In such a case, the maximum earnings base subject to the social security component of the self-employment tax is reduced by the wages earned as an employee.

Example 24. During 1994 T received wages of $30,000 and had self-employment income of $40,000. In computing T's self-employment tax, the maximum taxable base for the social security tax is reduced by the wages paid because T's employer has already withheld the appropriate FICA amount on these wages.

	Social Security
Maximum tax base............................	$ 60,600
Less: Wages subject to FICA tax.............	(30,000)
Reduced maximum tax base...................	$ 30,600
Net earnings from self-employment.............	$ 40,000
Subtract: 7.65% of net earnings from self-employment.............	(3,060)
	$ 36,940
Smaller of reduced maximum tax base or amount determined above..................	$ 30,600
Times: Social security tax rate...............	$\times$ 12.4%
Tax on social security component...............	$3,794.40
Social security tax.............................	$3,794.40
Plus: MHI tax ($36,940 $\times$ 2.9%)..............	1,071.26
Equals: T's self-employment tax...............	$4,865.66

T will also have an income tax deduction of $2,432.83 (one-half of the $4,865.66 self-employment taxes paid).

FUTA Taxes. A Federal unemployment tax is imposed on employers who pay wages of $1,500 or more during any calendar quarter in the calendar year, or who employ at least one individual on each of some 20 days during the calendar year or previous year.[29] Certain exceptions are made for persons employing agricultural or domestic workers.

FUTA tax revenues are used by the Federal government to augment unemployment benefit programs of the various states. The current FUTA tax rate is 6.2 percent of the first $7,000 of wages paid during the year to each covered employee. This translates into a *maximum* FUTA tax of $434 (6.2% × $7,000) *per employee* per year. Since most states also impose an unemployment tax on employers, a credit is allowed against an employer's FUTA tax liability for any similar tax paid to a state. Currently, the maximum FUTA tax credit allowed for this purpose is 5.4 percent of the covered wages (i.e., maximum of $378 per employee). Thus, the maximum FUTA tax paid is normally $56 ($434 − $378, or 0.8% × $7,000) per employee.

All employers subject to FUTA taxes must file Form 940, Employer's Annual Federal Unemployment Tax Return, on or before January 31 of the following year. If the employer's tax liability exceeds certain limits, estimated tax payments must be made during the year.[30] Most states require an employer to file unemployment tax returns and make tax payments quarterly.

EXCISE TAXES

The purpose of an excise tax is to tax certain privileges as well as the manufacture, sale, or consumption of specified commodities. Federal excise taxes are imposed on the sale of specified articles, various transactions, occupations, and the use of certain items. This type of tax is not imposed on the profits of a business or profession, however. The major types of excise taxes are as follows:

1. Occupational taxes;

2. Facilities and services taxes;

3. Manufacturers' taxes;

4. Retail sales of products and commodities taxes; and

5. Luxury taxes.

Occupational Taxes. Some businesses must pay a fee before engaging in their business. These types of businesses include, but are not limited to, liquor dealers, dealers in medicines, and dealers in firearms.

Facilities and Services Taxes. The person who pays for services and facilities must pay the tax on these items. The institution or person who furnishes the facilities or services must collect the tax, file returns, and turn over the taxes to the taxing authorities. A few of the common services subject to the facilities and services excise tax include air travel, hotel or motel lodging, and telephone service.

---

[29] § 3306(a)(1).

[30] See instructions in Circular E, *Supra*, Footnote 24.

Manufacturers' Taxes. As a rule, certain manufactured goods are taxed at the manufacturing level to make collection easier. Most of these items are of a semi-luxurious or specialized nature, such as sporting goods or firearms. This excise tax applies to the sale or use by the manufacturer, producer, or importer of specified articles. The taxes may be determined by quantity of production (e.g., pounds or gallons) or by a percentage of the sales price. When sales price is used as an index, the tax is based on the sales price of the manufacturer, producer, or importer.

Retail Sales of Products and Commodities Taxes. This excise tax applies to the retail sale or use of diesel fuel, special motor fuels, and fuel used in noncommercial aviation. The tax is collected from the person buying the product by the seller, and the seller must file and pay the tax unless the buyer purchased it tax-free.

Luxury Taxes. This type of excise tax is merely an extension of the excise tax imposed by state and local governments on certain retail sales of products. In an obvious attempt to obtain more revenue from those with greater ability to pay, Congress enacted a fairly comprehensive 10 percent luxury tax in 1990, which was applicable to sales of autos, boats, aircraft, jewelry, and furs at prices above certain levels. In 1993 Congress retroactively repealed this luxury tax on all but passenger cars with a sales price greater than $30,000. As an example, the luxury tax on a car with a cost of $35,000 would be $500 ($35,000 − $30,000 = $5,000 × 10%). The tax is collected and remitted to the IRS by the retailer.

State Excise Taxes. Many states and local governments also have excise taxes. They vary in range of coverage and impact, but most parallel the Federal excise taxes. For instance, most states have an excise tax on gasoline, liquor, and cigarettes, as does the Federal government.

ADDITIONAL TYPES OF TAXES

Many other types of taxes are used to augment state, local, and Federal income; employment; excise; and wealth transfer taxes. The three levels of government have never been reluctant to exercise their imagination in creating and developing new ways of supplementing governmental revenues. A few of the other more common types of taxes are briefly explained below.

Franchise Tax. A franchise tax is a tax on the privilege of doing business in a state or local jurisdiction. The measure of the tax generally is the net income of the business or the value of the capital used within the taxing authorities' jurisdictions.

Sales Tax. A sales tax is imposed on the gross receipts from the retail sale of tangible personal property (e.g., clothing, automobiles, and equipment) and certain services. Each state or local government determines the tax rate and the services and articles to be taxed. The seller will collect the tax at the time of the sale, and then periodically remit the taxes to the appropriate taxing authority. It is not uncommon for a state or local government to allow the seller to retain a nominal percentage of the collected taxes to compensate for the additional costs incurred by the seller in complying with the tax requirements.

Use Tax. A use tax is a tax imposed on the use within a state or local jurisdiction of tangible property on which a sales tax was not paid. The tax rate normally equals that of the taxing authority's sales tax.

Doing-Business Penalty. This penalty tax is imposed on a business that has not obtained authorization from the state or local government to operate within its border. Usually, a business must pay a fee for a state charter or some other kind of license as permission to enter business within the state.

Real Property Tax. A real property tax is a tax on the value of realty (land, buildings, homes, etc.) owned by nonexempt individuals or organizations within a jurisdiction. Rates vary with location. This type of tax normally supports local services, such as the public school system or the fire department, and is levied on a recurring annual basis.

Tangible Personal Property Tax. This tax is levied on the value of tangible personalty located within a jurisdiction. Tangible personalty is property not classified as realty and includes such items as office furniture, machinery and equipment, inventories, and supplies. The tax normally must be paid annually, with each local jurisdiction determining its own tax rate and the items to tax.

Intangible Personal Property Tax. This tax is imposed on the value of intangible personalty (i.e., stocks, bonds, and accounts and notes receivable) located within a jurisdiction. The tax generally is paid annually, with each local jurisdiction setting its own tax rate and items to be taxed.

GOALS OF TAXATION

In subsequent chapters, the specific provisions that must be followed to compute the tax will be discussed in detail. Some may view this discussion as a hopeless attempt to explain what seems like an endless barrage of boring rules—rules that, despite their apparent lack of "rhyme or reason," must be considered if the final tax liability is to be determined. The frustration that students of taxation often feel when studying the rules of Federal tax law is not completely unfounded. Indeed, a famous tax scholar, Boris Bittker, once commented on the increasing intricacy of the tax law, saying, "Can one hope to find a way through a statutory thicket so bristling with detail?"[31] As this statement suggests, many provisions of the law are, in fact, obscure and often appear to be without purpose. However, each provision of the tax law originated with some goal, even if no more than to grant a benefit to some Congressman's constituency. A knowledge of the goals

---

[31]   Boris I. Bittker and Lawrence M. Stone, *Federal Income Taxation,* 5th Ed. (Boston: Little, Brown & Co., 1980) liii.

underlying a particular provision is an important first step toward a comprehension of the provision. An understanding of the purpose of the law is an invaluable tool in attacking the "statutory thicket." In studying taxation, it becomes apparent that many provisions have been enacted with similar objectives. The following discussion reviews some of the goals of taxation that often serve as the reasons behind the rule.

ECONOMIC OBJECTIVES

At first glance, it seems clear that the primary goal of taxation is to provide the resources necessary to fund governmental expenditures. At the Federal level, however, this is not entirely true. As many economists have pointed out, any taxing authority that has the power to control the money supply—as does our Federal government—can satisfy its revenue needs by merely creating money. Nevertheless, complete reliance on the Treasury's printing press to provide the needed resources is not a viable alternative. If the government's expenditures were financed predominantly with funds that it created rather than those obtained through taxation, excess demand would result, which in turn would cause prices to rise, or inflation. Thus, taxation in serving a revenue function also operates along with other instruments of policy to attain a stable price level.

Although Congress can create its own resources, revenue objectives often can explain a particular feature of the law. Consider the personal and dependency exemption deductions, the purpose of which is to free from tax the income needed to maintain a minimum standard of living. Although the cost of living has risen substantially over the years, Congress has been reluctant to increase the amount of these exemptions. The exemption deduction was set at $600 from 1948 to 1969 and was only recently increased over $1,000. In effect, the deduction changed very little over the past 38 years, despite significant increases in the price level during this time. The reluctance to alter the exemption amount derives primarily from the potential impact on revenues.[32] A slight increase in the exemption without a corresponding increase in revenues from other sources would result in a tremendous revenue loss because of the number of exemptions taxpayers claim—approximately 227 million in 1980. For similar reasons, Congress has refrained, until recently, from adjusting the tax rate schedules to compensate for inflation, since to do so would significantly reduce its inflow of resources. In 1985, however, both the personal and dependency exemption amount *and* the individual tax rate schedules were adjusted (indexed) for the increase in the Consumer Price Index that occurred during the previous year.

Revenue considerations also can explain why tax accounting methods sometimes differ from those used for financial accounting. Prior to 1954, an accrual basis taxpayer could neither defer taxation of prepaid income nor deduct estimates of certain expenses, such as the expected costs of servicing warranty contracts. In 1954, the treatment of such items was changed to conform with financial accounting principles that permit deferral

---

[32] In order to keep pace with price level changes since 1949, the personal and dependency exemptions would have to be approximately $6,000 each in 1987. The Tax Reform Act of 1986 increased the exemp-tion amount to $1,950 for 1988 and indexed for inflation thereafter. For 1994 the exemption amount is $2,450—still a far cry from $6,000.

of income and accrual of expenses in most situations. The expected revenue loss attributed to this change was $50 million. Within a year after the change, however, the Treasury requested that Congress repeal the new provisions retroactively because estimates of the revenue loss were in excess of several billion dollars. In short, Congress responded and, as a result, the treatment of prepaid income and certain accruals for tax and financial accounting purposes differs—a difference attributable to revenue considerations.

The role of Federal taxation in carrying out economic policy extends beyond the realm of revenue raising and price stability. Taxation is a major tool used by the government to attain satisfactory economic growth with full employment. The title of the 1981 tax bill is illustrative: *The Economic Recovery Tax Act of 1981* (ERTA). As the title suggests, a major purpose of this legislation was directed toward revitalizing the health of the economy. ERTA significantly lowered tax rates to spur the economy out of a recession. Its objective was to place more *after-tax* income in the hands of taxpayers for their disposal. By so doing, it was hoped that taxpayers would consume more and thus increase aggregate demand, resulting in economic growth.

Congress also has used the tax structure to directly attack the problem of unemployment. In 1977 employers were encouraged to increase employment by the introduction of a general jobs tax credit, which effectively reduced the cost of labor. In 1978 Congress eliminated the general jobs credit and substituted a targeted jobs credit. This credit could be obtained only if employers hired certain targeted groups of individuals who were considered disadvantaged or handicapped. This credit was expanded in 1983 to stimulate the hiring of economically disadvantaged youth during the summer. As the credit for jobs suggests, Congress believes that major economic problems can be solved using the tax system.

A subject closely related to economic growth and full employment is investment. To stimulate investment spending, Congress has enacted numerous provisions. For example, accelerated depreciation methods—the accelerated cost recovery system (ACRS)—may be used to compute the deduction for depreciation, thus enabling rapid recovery of the taxpayer's investment.

Congress encourages certain industries by granting them favorable tax treatment. For example, the credit for research and experimental expenditures cited above clearly benefits those engaged in technology businesses. Other tax provisions are particularly advantageous for other groups such as builders, farmers, and producers of natural resources. Special privileges also are available for exporters. As will become clear in later chapters, the income tax law is replete with rules designed to encourage, stimulate, and assist various enterprises as Congress has deemed necessary over the years.

SOCIAL OBJECTIVES

The tax system is used to achieve not only economic goals but social objectives as well. Some examples are listed below:

1.   The deduction for charitable contributions helps to finance the cost of important activities that otherwise would be funded by the government.

2.   The deduction for interest on home mortgages subsidizes the cost of a home and thus encourages home ownership.

3. The targeted jobs credit noted above exists to fight unemployment problems of certain disadvantaged groups of citizens.

4. Larger standard deductions are granted to taxpayers who are 65 or over, or are blind, to relieve their tax burden.

5. Deductions for contributions to retirement savings accounts encourage individuals to provide for their future needs.

These examples are representative of the many provisions where social considerations provide the underlying rationale.

The above discussion is but a brief glimpse of how social and economic considerations have shaped our tax law. Interestingly, most of the provisions mentioned have been enacted in the past 20 years. During this time, Congress has relied increasingly on the tax system as a means to strike at the nation's ills. Whether the tax law can be used successfully in this manner is unclear. Many believe that attacking such problems should be done directly through government expenditure programs—not through so-called *tax expenditures*. A tax expenditure is the estimated amount of revenue lost for failing to tax a particular item (e.g., scholarships), for granting a certain deduction (e.g., charitable contributions), or for allowing a credit (e.g., targeted jobs credits). The concept of tax expenditures was developed by noted tax authority Stanley S. Surrey. While Assistant Secretary of the Treasury for Tax Policy during 1961–1969, Surrey and his supporters urged that certain activities should not be encouraged by subsidizing them through reduced tax liabilities. They argued that paying for government-financed activities in such a roundabout fashion makes their costs difficult if not impossible to determine. In addition, they asserted that such expenditures are concealed from the public eye as well as from the standard budgetary review process. Others, however, argued that the tax system could be used effectively for this purpose. Whether either view is correct, Congress currently shows no apparent signs of discontinuing use of the tax system to influence taxpayers' behavior.

OTHER OBJECTIVES

Although social and economic goals provide the rationale for much of our tax law, many provisions can be explained in terms of certain well-established principles of taxation. These principles are simply the characteristics that "good" taxes exhibit. Most tax experts agree that a tax is good if it satisfies the following conditions:[33]

1. The tax is *equitable* or fair;

2. The tax is *economically efficient* (i.e., it advances a goal where appropriate and otherwise is as neutral as possible);

3. The tax is *certain* and not arbitrary;

---

[33] These qualities were first identified by Adam Smith. See *The Wealth of Nations*, Book V, Chapter II, Part II (New York: Dutton, 1910).

4. The tax can be administered by the government and complied with by the taxpayer at a *low cost* (i.e., it is *economical* to operate); and

5. The tax is *convenient* (i.e., administration and compliance can be carried out with the utmost simplicity).

These five qualities represent important principles of taxation that must be conformed with in pursuing social and economic goals. As discussed below, these criteria have greatly influenced our tax law.

Equity. A tax system is considered equitable if it treats all persons who are in the same economic situation in the same fashion. This aspect of equity is referred to as *horizontal equity.* In contrast, *vertical equity* implies that taxpayers who are not in the same situation will be treated differently—the difference in treatment being fair and just. There are two major obstacles in implementing the equity concept as explained. First, there must be some method to determine when taxpayers are in the same economic situation. Second, there must be agreement on reasonable distinctions between those who are in different situations. The manner in which these obstacles are addressed explains two significant features of our tax system.

As indicated above, the first major difficulty in implementing the equity concept is identification of some technique to determine when taxpayers are similarly situated. For tax purposes, it is well settled that similarity is measured in terms of a taxpayer's *ability to pay.* Hence, taxpayers with equal abilities to pay should pay equal taxes. To the dismay of some tax policymakers, however, there is no simple, unambiguous index of an individual's ability. A taxpayer's ability to pay is the composite of numerous factors including his or her wealth, income, family situation, health, and attitude. Clearly, no one measure captures all of these factors. This being so, tax specialists generally have agreed that the best objective measure of ability to pay is income. This agreement, that income is a reasonable surrogate for ability to pay and thus serves the equity principle, explains in part why the primary tax used by the Federal government is an *income* tax.

The second obstacle in implementing the equity concept concerns the treatment of taxpayers who are differently situated. In terms of income, the problem may best be explained by reference to two taxpayers, A and B. If A's income (e.g., $100,000) exceeds B's (e.g., $20,000), it is assumed that A has more ability to pay and thus should pay more tax. The dilemma posed is not whether A and B should pay differing amounts of tax, but rather, what additional amount may be fairly charged to A. If a proportional tax of five percent is levied against A and B, A pays $5,000 (5% of $100,000) and B pays $1,000 (5% of $20,000). While application of this tax rate structure results in A paying $4,000 more than B absolutely, A pays the same amount in relative terms; that is, they both pay the *same* 5 percent. Those charged with the responsibility of developing Federal tax policy have concluded that paying more tax in absolute terms does not adequately serve the equity goal. For this reason, a progressive tax rate structure is used, requiring relatively more tax to be paid by those having more income. With respect to A and B above, this structure would require that A pay a greater percentage of his income than B.

The equity principle explains (at least partially) not only the basic structure of our predominant tax device—an income tax and its progressive tax rate structure—but also explains many other provisions in our law. In fact, some of the factors mentioned earlier

that affect a taxpayer's ability to pay are recognized explicitly by separate provisions in the Code. For example, a taxpayer may deduct medical expenses and casualty losses—items over which the taxpayer has little or no power—if such items exceed a certain level. Similarly, a taxpayer's family situation is considered by allowing exemption deductions for dependents whose support is the taxpayer's responsibility.

There are many other specific situations where the equity principle controls the tax consequences. For example, fairness dictates that taxes should not be paid when the taxpayer does not have the *wherewithal to pay* (i.e., the money to pay the tax). This is true even though the transaction results in income to the taxpayer.

> **Example 25.** Upon the theft of valuable machinery, LJM Corporation received a $20,000 insurance reimbursement. Assuming the machinery had a cost (adjusted for depreciation) of $5,000, LJM has realized a $15,000 gain ($20,000 − $5,000). Although the corporation has realized a gain, it also has lost the productive capacity of the machinery. If LJM reinvests the entire $20,000 proceeds in similar assets within two years of the theft, the gain is not taxed. This rule derives from Congressional belief that equity would not be served if taxes were levied when the taxpayer did not have the wherewithal to pay. In addition, the taxpayer's total economic situation has not been so materially altered as to require recognition of the gain.

Administrative Concerns. The final three qualities of a good tax—certainty, economy, and simplicity—might be aptly characterized as administrative in nature. Numerous provisions exist to meet administrative goals. Some of these are so obvious as to be easily overlooked. For example, the certainty requirement underlies the provision that a tax return generally is due each April 15, while economy of collection is the purpose, at least in part, for withholding. Similarly, provisions requiring the taxpayer to compute the tax using tables provided by the IRS are motivated by concerns for simplicity.

Perhaps the most important aspect of the administrative principles is that they often conflict with other principles of taxation. Consequently, one principle must often be adhered to at the expense of another. For example, our tax system could no doubt be more equitable if each individual's ability to pay was personally assessed, much like welfare agents assess the needs of their clients. However, this improvement could be obtained only at a substantial administrative cost. The administrative principle is first in importance in this case, as well as in many others.

A PRELUDE TO TAX PLANNING

Although taxes affect numerous aspects of our lives, their impact is not uncontrollable. Given an understanding of the rules, taxes can be managed with considerable success. Successful management, however, is predicated on good tax planning.

Tax planning is simply the process of arranging one's actions in light of their potential tax consequences. It should be emphasized that the tax consequences sometimes turn on how a particular transaction is structured—that is, *form* often controls taxation.

Example 26.   Z is obligated to make monthly payments of interest and principal on a note secured by his home. During the year, he was short of cash so his mother, B, who lives with Z, made the payments for him. Since B made the payments directly, she may not deduct the interest expense because interest is deductible only if it relates to a debt for which the taxpayer is personally liable. Moreover, her son cannot deduct the expense since he did not make payment. Note that the deduction could have been obtained had the payment been structured properly. If Z had received a gift of cash from his mother and then made payment, he could have claimed the interest deduction. Alternatively, if B had been jointly liable on the note, she could have deducted the interest payments she made.

In the example above, note that regardless of how the transaction is structured, the result is the same *except for* the tax ramifications. By merely planning and changing the form of the transaction, tax benefits are obtained. Before jumping to the conclusion that form always governs taxation, a caveat is warranted. Courts often are obliged to disregard form and let substance prevail. Notwithstanding the form versus substance difficulty, the point to be gained is that the pattern of a transaction often determines the tax outcome.

The obvious goal of most tax planning is the minimization of the amount that a person or other entity must transfer to the government. The legal minimization of taxes is usually referred to as *tax avoidance*. Although the phrase "tax avoidance" may have a criminal connotation, there is no injustice in legally reducing one's taxes. The most profound statement regarding the propriety of tax avoidance is found in a dissenting opinion authored by Justice Learned Hand in the case of *Commissioner v. Newman*. Justice Hand wrote:[34]

> Over and over again courts have said that there is nothing sinister in so arranging one's affairs so as to keep taxes as low as possible. Everybody does so, rich or poor, and all do right, for nobody owes any public duty to pay more than the law demands: taxes are enforced exactions, not voluntary contributions. To demand more in the name of morals is pure cant.

This statement is routinely cited as authority for taking those steps necessary to reduce one's taxes. It should be emphasized that tax planning and tax avoidance involve only those actions that are legal. *Tax evasion* is the label given to illegal activities that are designed to reduce the tax liability.

The planning effort for Federal income taxation (the principal area covered in this text) requires an understanding of the answer to *four* basic questions regarding the flow of cash and cash equivalents into and out of various tax entities. These questions regard the amount, character, and timing of income, deductions and credits, and recognition (reporting) of these items. The answers depend upon the tax entity that receives or transfers the cash or cash equivalents, its tax accounting period and methods, and whether

---

[34]   159 F.2d 848 (CA-2, 1947).

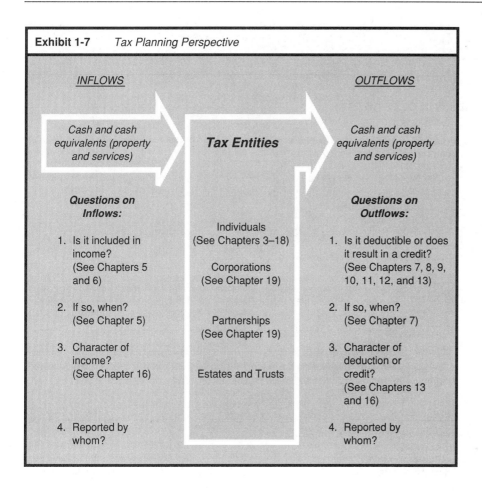

Exhibit 1-7   *Tax Planning Perspective*

INFLOWS

OUTFLOWS

Cash and cash equivalents (property and services)

Tax Entities

Cash and cash equivalents (property and services)

Questions on Inflows:

1. Is it included in income? (See Chapters 5 and 6)

2. If so, when? (See Chapter 5)

3. Character of income? (See Chapter 16)

4. Reported by whom?

Individuals (See Chapters 3–18)

Corporations (See Chapter 19)

Partnerships (See Chapter 19)

Estates and Trusts

Questions on Outflows:

1. Is it deductible or does it result in a credit? (See Chapters 7, 8, 9, 10, 11, 12, and 13)

2. If so, when? (See Chapter 7)

3. Character of deduction or credit? (See Chapters 13 and 16)

4. Reported by whom?

the entity is considered a taxpayer separate from its owners or simply a conduit through which items of income, gain, loss, deduction, or credit flow to its owners. The tax entities recognized for Federal tax purposes, and the tax planning questions, are presented in Exhibit 1-7.

Tax planning efforts often involve deferring the recognition of income or shifting the incidence of its tax to a lower tax bracket entity (e.g., from parents to children), or accelerating, deferring, or shifting deductions and credits to tax periods or among tax entities with higher or lower tax rates. Keeping this overall scheme of tax minimization in mind, many of the subsequent chapters of this text conclude with a discussion of tax planning considerations.

PROBLEM MATERIALS

DISCUSSION QUESTIONS

1-1 *Tax Bases*. Describe the tax bases for the Federal income tax and for each of the Federal wealth transfer taxes.

1-2 *Tax Rates*. Distinguish between a proportional tax rate structure and a progressive tax rate structure. What is the significance of the marginal tax rate under either a proportional or a progressive rate structure?

1-3 *Progressive, Proportional, and Regressive Taxes*. The media often refer to sales taxes as regressive. Similar comments are made when discussing social security taxes (FICA). Are the media correct? Include in your comments an explanation of the different types of tax rate structures.

1-4 *Deduction vs. Credit*. Distinguish between a deduction and a credit. If a credit is allowed for 20 percent of an expenditure in lieu of a deduction for the total expenditure, under what circumstances should you prefer the credit? The deduction?

1-5 *Individual vs. Corporate Taxable Income*. Based on the tax formulas contained in Exhibits 1-2 and 1-3, what are the significant differences in computing a corporation's taxable income as opposed to computing an individual's taxable income?

1-6 *Withholding Taxes at Source*. What do you believe is the principal reason that Congress continues the pay-as-you-go requirements of employers withholding Federal income taxes from the wages paid their employees?

1-7 *Marital Deduction*. Describe the marital deduction allowed for Federal estate and gift taxes. How might an individual use this deduction to avoid all Federal wealth transfer taxes?

1-8 *Unified Credit*. How is the unified transfer tax credit applied in determining taxable wealth transfers?

1-9 *Annual Gift Tax Exclusion*. What is the amount of the annual Federal gift tax exclusion? If a widow were interested in making gifts to her daughter and seven grandchildren, how much could she transfer to them in any given year before incurring a taxable gift?

1-10 *Gift-Splitting Election*. What is the gift-splitting election allowed for Federal gift tax purposes? How might the marital deduction be used to explain why Congress allows this election?

1-11 *Estate vs. Inheritance Taxes*. Distinguish between an estate and an inheritance transfer tax. How are these two taxes often integrated by a state in its wealth transfer tax system?

1-12 *Federal Employment Taxes*. Distinguish between FICA and FUTA taxes. Between an employee and his or her employer, who bears the greater burden of these taxes?

1-13 *Unemployment Taxes.* For 1994 what is the maximum FUTA tax an employer can expect to pay if he or she has three employees during the year and the minimum salary paid is $10,000? If the employer also is subject to state unemployment taxes, what is the maximum amount of credit he or she will be allowed against the FUTA tax liability?

1-14 *Sales vs. Use Tax.* Distinguish between a sales and a use tax. Assume you live in state A but near the border of state B and that state A imposes a much higher sales tax than does state B. If you were planning to purchase a new automobile, what might you be tempted to do? How might state A discourage your plan?

1-15 *Tax Expenditures.* It is often suggested that many of our social problems can be cured through use of tax incentives.

   a.   Discuss the concept of tax expenditures.
   b.   Expand on the text's discussion of the pros and cons of tax expenditures vis-à-vis direct governmental expenditures.

1-16 *Goals of Taxation.* In a recent discussion concerning what a fair tax is, the following comments were made: (1) the fairest tax is one that someone else has to pay; (2) people should be taxed in accordance with the benefits they obtain (i.e., taxes are the price paid for the benefit); (3) a head tax would be the fairest; and (4) why tax at all, just use the printing press. Discuss the first three of these comments in terms of equity and explain whether the fourth represents a viable alternative.

PROBLEMS

1-17 *Marginal Tax Rates.* T, a single taxpayer, has taxable income of $40,000 for 1994. If T anticipates a marginal tax rate of 15 percent for 1995, what income tax savings could she expect by accelerating $1,000 of deductible expenditures planned for 1995 into the 1994 tax year?

1-18 *Tax Rate Schedules and Rate Concepts.* An examination of the tax rate schedules for single taxpayers (see the inside cover of the text) indicates that the tax is a "given dollar amount" plus a percentage of taxable income exceeding a particular level.

   a.   Explain how the "given dollar amounts" are determined?
   b.   Assuming the taxpayer has a taxable income of $50,000 and is single, what is his tax liability for 1993?
   c.   Same facts as (b). What is the taxpayer's marginal tax rate?
   d.   Same facts as (b). What is the taxpayer's average tax rate?
   e.   Assuming the taxpayer has tax-exempt interest income from municipal bonds of $30,000, what is the taxpayer's effective tax rate?

1-19 *Tax Equity.* Taxpayer R has a taxable income of $20,000. Similarly, S has a taxable income of $20,000. Each taxpayer pays a tax of $1,000 on his income.

   a.   Discuss whether the tax imposed is equitable. Include in your discussion comments concerning horizontal and vertical equity.
   b.   Assume S has a taxable income of $40,000 and pays a tax of $2,000 on his income. Discuss whether the tax imposed is equitable in light of this new information.

1-20 *Taxable Gifts.*   M made the following cash gifts during 1994:

To her son............................	$50,000
To her daughter........................	50,000
To her niece..........................	10,000

a.   If M is unmarried, what is the amount of taxable gifts she has made in 1994?

b.   If M is married and her husband agrees to split gifts with her, what is the total amount of taxable gifts made by M and her husband for 1994?

1-21 *Taxable Estate.*   R dies in 1994. R made taxable gifts during his lifetime in 1982, 1983, 1985, 1988, and 1991 but paid no Federal transfer taxes due to the unified transfer tax credit. What effect will these taxable gifts have on determining the following:

a.   R's Federal taxable estate?

b.   The rates imposed on the Federal taxable estate?

1-22 *Estate Tax Computation.*   T died in a car accident on January 4, 1994. He owned the following property on his date of death:

Cash..................................	$ 75,000
Stocks and bonds......................	400,000
Residence.............................	230,000
Interest in partnership..................	450,000
Miscellaneous personal property........	25,000

Upon T's death, he owed $80,000 on the mortgage on his residence. T also owned a life insurance policy. The policy was term life insurance which paid $100,000 to his mother upon his death. Its value immediately before his death was $0. T had all of the incidents of ownership with regard to the policy.

During his life, T had made only one gift. He gave a diamond ring worth $30,000 (it was an old family heirloom) to his daughter in 1988. No gift taxes were paid on the gift due to the annual exclusion (gift-splitting was elected) and the unified transfer tax credit. The ring was worth $50,000 on his date of death.

T's will contained the following provisions:

a.   To my wife I leave all of the stocks and bonds.

b.   To my alma mater, State University, I leave $50,000 to establish a chair for a tax professor in the Department of Accounting in the School of Business.

c.   The residue of my estate is to go to my daughter.

Compute T's estate tax. Assume that his state imposes a state death tax equal to the maximum credit allowable for state death taxes. No other credits are available.

1-23 *State Estate Taxes.*   At the time of her death, T resided in a state that imposes an estate tax based on the maximum amount allowed as a credit for Federal estate tax purposes.

a.   If T's Federal taxable estate is $500,000, how much estate taxes will be imposed by the state?

b.   If the state also imposes $3,000 of inheritance taxes on the heirs of T's estate, what will its estate tax levy be?

1-24 *Excess FICA Taxes.* During 1994 E earned $48,000 of wages from employer X and $20,000 of wages from employer Y. Both employers withheld and paid the appropriate amount of FICA taxes on E's wages.

    a. What is the amount of excess taxes paid by E for 1994?

    b. Would it make any difference in the amount of E's refund or credit of the excess of FICA taxes if he was a full-time employee of each employer for different periods of the year, as opposed to a full-time employee of X and a part-time employee of Y for the entire year?

1-25 *Self-Employment Tax.* During 1994 H had earnings from self-employment of $40,000 and wages of $48,000 from employer X. Employer X withheld and paid the appropriate amount of FICA taxes on H's wages. Compute H's self-employment tax liability for 1994. What is the amount of H's income tax deduction for the self-employment taxes paid?

1-26 *Tax Awareness.* Assume that you are currently employed by Corporation X in state A. Without your solicitation, Corporation Y offers you a 20 percent higher salary if you will relocate to state B and become its employee. What tax factors should you consider in making a decision as to the offer?

LEARNING OBJECTIVES

Upon completion of this chapter you will be able to:

- Describe the basic features of tax practice: compliance, planning, litigation, and research.
- Identify typical career paths in taxation.
- Understand the rules of conduct that must be followed by those who perform tax services.
- Appreciate the role of ethics in tax practice and the responsibilities of tax practitioners.
- Explain the key penalties that influence positions taken on tax returns.
- Describe the process in which Federal tax law is enacted and subsequently modified or evaluated by the judiciary
- Interpret citations to various statutory, administrative, and judicial sources of the tax law
- Identify the source of various administrative and judicial tax authorities
- Locate most statutory, administrative, and judicial authorities
- Evaluate the relative strength of various tax authorities
- Understand the importance of communicating the results of tax research

CHAPTER OUTLINE

Introduction	2-1	Revenue Procedures	2-27
Tax Practice in General	2-1	Letter Rulings	2-28
Taxation as a Professional Career	2-3	Technical Advice Memoranda	2-29
Rules of Tax Practice: Responsibilities		Judicial Interpretations	2-29
and Ethics	2-4	Trial Courts	2-30
Taxpayer Penalties	2-5	Appellate Courts	2-32
Accuracy-Related Penalties	2-6	Case Citation	2-35
Fraud	2-10	Secondary Sources	2-40
Tax Preparer Penalties	2-12	Tax Services	2-41
Sources and Applications of Tax Laws	2-19	Tax Periodicals	2-42
Authoritative Sources of Tax Law	2-20	Tax Research	2-43
Statutory Law	2-20	Obtaining the Facts	2-43
The Making of a Tax Law	2-21	Diagnosing the Issue	2-43
Organization of the Code	2-22	Locating the Authorities	2-44
Tax Treaties	2-24	Evaluating the Authority	2-45
Administrative Interpretations	2-25	Deriving the Solution	2-46
Regulations	2-25	Communicating the Findings	2-47
Revenue Rulings	2-27	Problem Materials	2-48

Chapter 2

TAX PRACTICE AND RESEARCH

INTRODUCTION

Before jumping into the rules and regulations that must be applied to determine the taxpayer's final tax liability, one should have at least an appreciation of the basic nature of tax practice and how to go about finding answers to tax questions. This chapter lays the necessary foundation by first exploring exactly what it is that tax professionals do and the rules of conduct that they must observe while doing it. The chapter concludes by identifying the various sources of tax law and how they may be accessed and used to solve a particular tax question.

TAX PRACTICE IN GENERAL

There are essentially four aspects of tax practice: compliance, planning, litigation, and research. Although these may be thought of as discrete areas, as a practical matter, tax professionals are normally involved in all four.

Tax Compliance. The area of tax compliance generally encompasses all of the activities necessary to meet the statutory requirements of the tax law. This largely involves the preparation of the millions of tax returns that must be filed by individuals and other organizations each year. Interestingly, the reliance of individuals on professional return preparation is rather a recent phenomenon. There was a time when most individuals prepared their own returns and H & R Block was unheard of. However, the ever-increasing complexity of the tax law has made professional assistance almost a necessity and in fact created a tax preparation industry. It is currently estimated that 4 out of every 10 taxpayers seek the services of a professional tax preparer every year. Tax preparation services are typically performed by Certified Public Accountants (CPAs), attorneys, enrolled agents (individuals who have passed a two-day examination given by the IRS), and commercial tax return preparation services. But there are no special requirements that must be met to become a tax return preparer. Consequently, anyone willing to try his or her hand at mastering the tax law—as well as any shysters who think there is a buck to be made—can hang out a shingle. In fact, the advent of personal computers and sophisticated yet user-friendly software have made tax preparation easier for everyone, including those who want to get into the tax preparation business. Note, however, that only CPAs, attorneys, and enrolled agents are authorized to practice before the IRS and therefore able to represent taxpayers beyond the initial audit (e.g., at the Appellate level).

As might be imagined, the day-to-day tasks of those working in the tax compliance area typically surround preparation of a tax return. They collect the appropriate information from the taxpayer then analyze and evaluate such data for use in preparing the required tax return or other tax filing. But tax compliance goes far beyond merely placing numbers in boxes. In many cases, completion of the return requires tax research to determine the appropriate treatment of a particular item. Preparation of a return may also uncover tax planning opportunities that can be shared with the client to obtain future savings. In addition, tax compliance involves representation of the taxpayer before the IRS during audits and appeals.

Tax Planning. Perhaps the most rewarding part of tax practice is tax planning and the sense of satisfaction one gets from helping clients minimize their tax liability. As explained in the previous chapter, tax planning is simply the process of arranging one's financial affairs in light of their potential tax consequences. Unlike the weather, taxpayers often have some degree of control over their tax liability, and it is the job of the tax adviser to help the taxpayer whenever possible. A great deal of tax planning is simply an outgrowth of the tax compliance process. Well-trained tax professionals often recognize a situation where a little planning could bring a more favorable result. In these so-called *closed fact* situations, it is typically too late to do anything until the opportunity once again presents itself, typically the next year. On the other hand, taxpayers about to embark on a transaction—an *open fact* situation—may engage a tax adviser to determine the tax consequences and how to structure the transaction to obtain the most beneficial outcome.

Tax Litigation. As might be expected, taxpayers and the IRS do not always agree on the tax treatment of a particular item. Many disputes and controversies are settled during an appeals process within the IRS itself. Others, however, are ultimately resolved in a court of law. Tax litigation is a very specialized but often lucrative area of tax practice. In most cases, tax litigation can be pursued only by licensed attorneys. However, accountants and others, including the taxpayer himself, can represent the taxpayer in certain situations. In addition, accountants often assist legal counsel and provide litigation support.

Tax Research. Tax research may be the most interesting part of tax practice. Tax research is simply the process of obtaining information and synthesizing it to answer a particular tax question. Regardless of the area of tax practice—compliance, planning, or litigation—tax research plays an important part.

Tax research generally involves identifying tax issues, finding relevant information on the issue, and assessing the pertinent authority to arrive at a conclusion. Unfortunately, the law is not so straightforward that the answer to any tax question is readily available. Consequently, being able to do the research is an important skill for anyone involved in tax. For example, a decorator that works out of her home may want to know whether the cost of maintaining a home office can be deducted in computing taxable income. It may seem that a common problem like this could be easily resolved, but it is often much more difficult than might be imagined. To answer this question, the tax adviser may be required to sift through mounds of information—rules, regulations, IRS pronouncements, and court cases—in order to determine the proper treatment. Even if an answer seems apparent, the dynamic nature of the tax law often requires the practitioner to constantly update his or her research to ensure that it is current and has not been changed by some recent development.

TAXATION AS A PROFESSIONAL CAREER

The need for tax advisory services has grown almost exponentially in recent years. The growth is not surprising given the growth in the tax law. Over the last 25 years, from the Tax Reform Act of 1969 to the Revenue Reconciliation Act of 1993, there have been tax law changes of some import virtually every year. During this time Congress has turned to the tax system again and again to attack not only the country's economic ills but its social problems as well. In addition, growing budget deficits at the Federal level have meant less Federal money for state governments. This in turn has caused state and local governments to increase their taxes, thus making state and local taxes more important than ever before. The end result is a tax law, both Federal and state, that is forever changing and quite complex. Consequently, individuals and organizations have increasingly needed to call upon tax specialists to help them cope with the law. These demands on the tax profession have created tremendous opportunities for those interested in careers in taxation.

The tax specialists of today wear a number of hats. They act as tax consultants as well as business advisers. They help individuals and business owners with tax compliance, keep them informed of changes in the tax law, and assist them in personal financial planning. Tax advisers not only consult on Federal and state income tax matters; they also prepare sales, payroll, and franchise tax returns. Industry and government also employ tax specialists who are involved in planning and compliance. Here are some examples of activities in which the tax specialist might be involved:

- A husband and wife want to transfer their business to their children. Should they sell the business to the kids or would they be better off just giving it to them? A tax specialist can compare the income tax consequences of a sale to that of a gift or bequest and help design the best plan in light of the couple's wishes.

- A taxpayer wants to sell her corporation. Should she sell the stock or cause the corporation to sell its assets? A tax specialist can explain the tax and nontax factors affecting the decision.

- An individual and his son are forming a new business. Should it be operated as a corporation, an S corporation, a partnership, or a limited liability company? A tax specialist can help with the analysis.

- A corporation is planning on opening operations in a foreign country. A tax specialist can help reorganize the company to help minimize U.S. and foreign taxes.

- A corporation is considering the establishment of a retirement plan. A tax adviser who specializes in employee benefits can provide information regarding the tax considerations.

- A taxpayer is seeking a divorce. A tax specialist can explain the tax consequences.

- A corporation and its subsidiaries are thinking about filing a consolidated tax return. The tax specialist can assist the taxpayer in filing such a return, preparing estimated tax payments, or reviewing a corporation's tax returns.

- The IRS wants to deny the taxpayer a deduction for meals and entertainment. The tax specialist might represent an individual during the IRS examination or present oral and written arguments before an IRS appeals conference and (if qualified) before the U.S. Tax Court.

In these and similar matters, the tax specialist is often an important member of the client's professional advisory team and works with high-caliber individuals. For example, if a business owner is seeking estate planning advice, the team typically includes the individual's attorney, accountant, life insurance agent, and tax adviser.

Thousands of men and women enjoy successful careers in taxation. They are highly respected as professionals and are well compensated for their work. Those in tax rarely find their jobs boring or dull. Tax work, particularly once one has paid one's dues and built a firm foundation, is interesting and challenging. Moreover, working in a tax department along with other professionals with like interests can be a vastly rewarding personal experience. Tax professionals also serve the public good by raising the standard of tax practice and administration and by working with other groups to improve the tax system.

RULES OF TAX PRACTICE: RESPONSIBILITIES AND ETHICS

Over the last several years there has been a great deal of attention focused on ethics in business. This attention has not escaped the world of taxation. Unethical behavior of taxpayers and tax preparers has always been a serious concern of the tax system, primarily because of its reliance on voluntary compliance.

Anyone who has ever filed an income tax return recognizes the potential for bilking the system. It is as easy as underreporting income or overstating deductions. What is perhaps more important is that it can be done with so little risk. The audit rate is so low—only 0.96 percent for 1993 (1,187,000 returns audited, 123,882,000 filed)—that dishonest taxpayers can exploit the system with little chance that they will ever get caught. That the tax system is such an easy mark was underscored recently in testimony given before the House Ways and Means Oversight Subcommittee by two practitioners convicted of tax fraud for illegal refund schemes. In his testimony, Barry Becht, a 36-year-old former tax return preparer, explained that, before he was convicted and sent to Federal prison, he had "helped" his clients reduce their tax liabilities by over $750,000 simply by overstating their deductions. Surprisingly, Becht did not share in his client's windfalls. Allegedly his only purpose was to build up his practice! The other convicted felon, Frazier Todd, reported that he had gained more than $500,000 in only two years using electronic filing schemes. Shortly after college and with the help of a few courses on computers, accounting, and business, Todd had set up a tax-preparation service near public housing in Atlanta. There he was able to strike deals with low-income taxpayers who allowed him to use their names and social security numbers to falsify wage statements (W-2 forms). He then proceeded to file returns electronically, which enabled him to obtain a refund before the IRS discovered that the returns were phony. Unfortunately, the stories of Becht and Todd are just two illustrations of how easy it is to abuse the system. Near the close of 1993, the IRS estimated that the "tax gap," the amount of unpaid taxes (income, payroll, and excise) due to cheating and fraud, was over $150 million annually.

The problems of tax fraud do not go unnoticed, however. To safeguard the system, encourage compliance, and promote ethical behavior, the government has adopted a number of mechanisms. Among these is an intricate set of penalties that can be applied to both taxpayers and tax return preparers. These penalties cover a variety of violations, such as failure to file and pay taxes on a timely basis, negligence in preparing the tax return, and outright fraud. While the penalties are usually monetary in nature, criminal penalties—such as the jail sentences given to Mr. Becht and Mr. Todd—may result if the taxpayer goes beyond these civil offenses and purposefully attempts to evade tax. The failure-to-file and failure-to-pay penalties—penalties that typically result not because taxpayers are trying to deceive the government but simply because they are late in filing and paying their taxes—are discussed in Chapter 4. The focus in this chapter is on the responsibilities of taxpayers and tax return preparers in filing returns and the major penalties that may be imposed with respect to positions taken on returns.

TAXPAYER PENALTIES

In a 1985 IRS survey, one out of every five people reported that they cheated on their tax return. In the same survey, 41 percent said they believed that their fellow taxpayers also cheated. Similarly, Professor Peggy Hite found in a 1993 survey of Indiana residents that 40 percent of the 688 individuals asked indicated that they definitely would not voluntarily report prize income, such as money won in a lottery or similar contests and sweepstakes.[1] Another 30 percent were somewhat wishy-washy in their answers, suggesting that, depending on the circumstances, they also would not report the income. But anyone thinking about cheating should recognize that it can be quite expensive. The IRS has over 140 penalties in its arsenal that it could apply. In their simplest form, these penalties provide that as long as taxpayers do not cheat and make a good faith effort to determine their tax liability, they have no reason to worry. But in reality the ethical problems created by the tax system for taxpayers and tax preparers can be difficult to resolve. Unfortunately, the law rarely provides clear-cut answers, leaving taxpayers wondering what they should do.

As an illustration, consider two taxpayers, both with bad backs, who bought $5,000 hot tubs on the hope that they might have some therapeutic value. Can the taxpayers deduct their costs as a medical expense? Even if they researched the question every day of the week for a month, the answer may not be clear. Should the fact that the answer is not clear preclude them from deducting their expenses? Some taxpayers might be inclined to simply abandon the issue, pay the tax and never worry about it again. But others might believe that there is some support for their position and want to take the deduction. So assume in this case taxpayer A deducts the expense and taxpayer B deducts not only the cost of the tub but, banking on the audit lottery, also deducts the entire cost of the house on the grounds that it serves as a rehabilitation facility. What happens if both returns are audited and the agent rejects the deductions of both taxpayers? Obviously the system of punishment should fit the crime. And this is what Congress has attempted to do by creating a penalty system that fairly treats taxpayers who in good faith believe that their

---

[1] "Nearly 1 in 3 Would Cheat on Taxes," *The Indianapolis Star,* April 7, 1994, B1.

position has validity but at the same time discourages taxpayers from taking frivolous positions, hoping that the audit lottery will never pick their number.

As the penalty discussion below will reveal, the tax law has its own way of dealing with taxpayers who stray too far from the correct position. While the system is complex, it is somewhat analogous to the way a mother treats her teenage son who is apt to stay out beyond his 12 o'clock curfew. If the son is a few minutes late, there will probably be no penalty if he has a reasonable explanation. On the other hand, if he gets home two hours late, the penalty will probably be severe unless he called to say he would be late. But if he never called, punishment is a virtual certainty unless his story is truly believable and backed by witnesses. And, of course, if her son lies, he will be grounded forever. Although the rules for breaking curfew are not completely analogous to those for taxpayers that take erroneous positions on returns, the comparison may be useful. If a taxpayer takes an incorrect position with respect to a *small* amount, there will be no penalty as long as there is a *reasonable basis* for the position. On the other hand, if the tax dollars involved are *substantial,* a penalty is normally imposed unless the taxpayer has *substantial authority* for the position or, alternatively, has disclosed the position and has a reasonable basis for it. Of course, if the taxpayer commits blatant fraud, the penalties could be quite harsh. These ethical standards for taxpayers are embedded in two types of penalties: accuracy-related penalties and penalties for fraud.

ACCURACY-RELATED PENALTIES

What happens if a waiter simply fails to report all of his tips? What if a 70-year-old grandmother fails to file her return believing that senior citizens do not have to pay tax? And what if the taxpayer deducts the cost of his daughter's wedding as business entertainment? As might be expected, the IRS does not treat such transgressions lightly. If the taxpayer's behavior can be characterized as negligent, a penalty in addition to the regular tax may be imposed. In 1989 Congress consolidated several existing penalties relating to negligence into a so-called accuracy-related penalty. The accuracy-related penalty is generally 20 percent of the portion of the tax underpayment. The principal accuracy-related penalties include[2]

- Negligence or disregard of rules and regulations
- Substantial understatement of income tax
- Substantial valuation misstatement.

Note that these penalties do not stack on top of each other. The IRS must pick which one it wants to assess.

Negligence Penalty (Insubstantial).   The negligence penalty, as an accuracy-related penalty, is 20 percent of the portion of the tax underpayment that is attributable to negligence or disregard of the rules and regulations.[3] For example, assume a taxpayer forgets to report $1,000 that he received for consulting during the year. If the taxpayer is in the

---

[2]   § 6662.   [3]   § 6662(c).

31 percent tax bracket, the underpayment is $310 and the penalty would be $63 (20% × $310). Note that when the day of reckoning comes, the taxpayer will be required to pay the underpayment, interest on the underpayment from the original due date, and the penalty, if any. The taxpayer may also owe interest on the penalty. Interest on the penalty generally starts to run when the taxpayer has been notified of the penalty, usually sometime after the audit. Under § 6601(e)(2)(B) interest must be paid on the failure-to-file penalty, accuracy-related penalties, and the fraud penalty. The interest begins on the due date of the return.

Negligence is generally defined as any failure to do what a reasonable and ordinarily prudent person would do under the circumstances. To avoid the negligence penalty, the taxpayer must make a reasonable attempt to comply with the law. The negligence penalty is usually imposed when the taxpayer fails to report income or claims large amounts of unsubstantiated expenses. For example, a waitress who fails to report her cash tips would probably get hit with the penalty, as would the businessperson who claims thousands of dollars of business entertainment expenses with little or no substantiation—a specific requirement for travel and entertainment expenses. A taxpayer is automatically considered negligent and liable for the 20 percent penalty if he or she fails to report any type of income for which there is an information return filed by the party paying the income (e.g., Form 1099). In other situations, determination of whether the penalty should be imposed is in the hands of the auditor. It is important to note, however, that taxpayers who intentionally attempt to deceive the government are normally not subject to the negligence penalty but rather the more severe fraud penalty discussed below.

For most taxpayers, the most important aspect of the negligence penalty concerns its relationship to positions taken on returns.

> **Example 1.**   This year D graduated with a marketing degree from the University of Arkansas and immediately took a job with a publishing company as a sales representative. The company did not provide her with an office, so she worked out of her home. After talking with her boss at work, she found out that he deducted his home office expenses as business expenses on his return. Knowing little about tax, she followed her boss's lead and deducted $3,000 of expenses related to her home office. Two years later D's return was audited and the agent informed her that he planned to deny her deduction for the home office expenses. Assuming the agent is correct, another issue is raised: should the negligence penalty apply since D has taken an incorrect position on the return?

In answer to the question posed by the example above, the law has recently changed. Prior to 1994 the taxpayer could avoid the negligence penalty as long as the position was not frivolous and it was disclosed on the return. But that approach apparently inspired taxpayers to play the audit lottery. For example, aggressive taxpayers might take a questionable deduction, disclose it, then hope that they would never be audited. Even if they got caught, there was little risk since disclosure protected them against a negligence penalty in every situation except where the position was frivolous or patently improper. In other words, as long as the position was nonfrivolous—that is, the taxpayer had some basis on which to argue the disclosed position (e.g., a merely arguable or

merely colorable claim)—the negligence penalty could be avoided.[4] Believing that the ethical standard set by this rule was far too low, the Revenue Reconciliation Act of 1993 changed the rules. Under the new approach, taxpayers are forced to be far more cautious about the positions they take on their returns.

Beginning in 1994, a negligence penalty can be assessed unless the taxpayer has a *reasonable basis* for the position taken on the return regardless of whether it is disclosed on the return.[5] What the new approach means to taxpayers is that in situations where the potential tax understatement is insubstantial they can ethically take a position that is contrary to the rules and regulations without fear of the negligence penalty as long as the position has a reasonable basis. Of course, the critical issue here is what constitutes a reasonable basis.

Although any definition of a "reasonable basis" would be subject to debate, the regulations do provide some guidance. According to the regulations, the reasonable basis standard is met if the return position is "arguable, but fairly unlikely to prevail in court."[6] Practitioners generally interpret this to mean that a position has a reasonable basis if it has at least a 20 percent chance of succeeding (without regard to the possibility that it might not be discovered at all). Apparently, this represents a slight increase in the level of support required by the nonfrivolous standard for disclosed positions under prior law. In the final analysis, however, the standard leaves a great deal to be desired. The regulations do provide one additional insight that may be useful: the "too good to be true" rule. This rule indicates that the reasonable basis standard is not met if the taxpayer fails to make a reasonable attempt to determine the correctness of a position that seems too good to be true.

Substantial Understatement Penalty. The substantial understatement penalty, like its sibling, the negligence penalty, is an accuracy-related penalty that is 20 percent of the portion of the underpayment of tax due to any substantial understatement of income tax.[7] The understatement is considered substantial if it exceeds the larger of (1) 10 percent of the correct tax or (2) $5,000.

The major difference between the substantial understatement penalty and the negligence penalty concerns the level of authority required to avoid penalty for an erroneous *undisclosed* position. In effect, Congress is telling taxpayers that if the risky position they are taking involves a substantial amount of tax and they are *unwilling to disclose* the position, the degree of support they must have is greater than simply a reasonable basis. The substantial understatement penalty applies to undisclosed positions unless the taxpayer has *substantial authority* for the position. It is unclear what the substantial authority requirement calls for, but it seems clear that it is somewhat more stringent

---

[4] Reg. §§ 1.6662-3(b)(3) and 1.6694-2(c)(2).

[5] See Predmore, "New Reasonable Basis Standard for Return Disclosure Likely to Be Troublesome," *Journal of Taxation* (January, 1994), p. 25, which indicates that, until the regulations are modified, "disclosure of a not frivolous position should suffice to avoid the

negligence penalty." Discussions with other practitioners suggest that nonfrivolous positions probably can no longer be protected through disclosure.

[6] Reg. § 1.6662-4(d).

[7] § 6662(d).

than the 1 in 3 test of the realistic possibility success standard discussed below but less demanding than the more-likely-than-not requirement, a more than 50 percent chance, related to certain positions taken with respect to certain tax shelter investments. For purposes of the substantial authority analysis, only materials published by Congress, the IRS, and the courts are relevant. Conclusions suggested by tax professionals in treatises, legal periodicals (which provide the basis of many arguments), or the like are not to be considered.[8]

The degree of support necessary to avoid the substantial understatement penalty drops down a notch if the taxpayer is willing to disclose the position. The substantial understatement penalty can be avoided if the taxpayer makes *adequate disclosure* and has a *reasonable basis* for his position. What constitutes adequate disclosure is many times clearer than what constitutes a reasonable basis. Disclosure is considered adequate if the position is explained on a special form intended just for this purpose, Form 8275 or 8275-R, or on the return in accordance with rules issued by the IRS each year.[9] In effect, when the tax dollars involved are material, taxpayers must meet a much higher standard—substantial authority—than is normally applied unless they are willing to disclose the position.

Substantial Valuation Misstatement. The tax law often requires taxpayers and tax return preparers to provide valuations for certain items. For example, taxpayers are generally entitled to a deduction for the fair market value of property given to qualified charitable organizations. What happens if a taxpayer in the 31 percent bracket gives a work of art that he says is worth $6,000 when its value is really closer to $2,000? The answer is that he has saved $1,240 ($4,000 $\times$ 31%) if he wins the audit lottery. But if the IRS does catch him, the taxpayer may face an accuracy-related penalty for substantial valuation misstatement. A 20 percent penalty is imposed on the underpayment of tax attributable to the misstatement.[10] The taxpayer avoids the penalty, however, if the misstatement does not exceed 200 percent of the correct value or if the amount of tax underpayment attributable to the misstatement is less than $5,000 ($10,000 for corporations). Thus the taxpayer above, who overstated the correct value by 300 percent, would still escape the valuation penalty since the amount of tax attributable to the misstatement, $1,240, is less than the $5,000 threshold. However, the taxpayer could still be subject to the negligence or the substantial understatement penalties.

Summary of Penalties for Inaccurate Returns. There is little doubt that there is a great deal of confusion over penalties concerning erroneous positions on tax returns and what one can do to avoid them. Nevertheless, Exhibit 2–1 attempts to summarize the three accuracy-related penalties discussed above and what defenses are available to the taxpayer. After a great deal of studying, it may become clear that the likelihood of a penalty depends on three factors: the amount of the potential understatement, whether the taxpayer has disclosed the position adequately, and the level of support that there is for the position. As a rule, if the tax dollars are not significant, a reasonable basis protects the taxpayer from penalty. On the other hand, if the tax dollars are substantial, the taxpayer is protected only if there is substantial authority or if there is disclosure

---

[8] Reg. § 1.6692-4(d)(3)(iii).

[9] Reg. § 1.6694-2(c)(3).

[10] § 6662(e).

Exhibit 2-1   *The 20 Percent Penalty for Inaccurate Returns and Defenses: § 6662*

1. Negligence (insubstantial)

   • Defined: Reasonable attempt to comply with the tax laws
   • Defenses:
     — Reasonable basis (disclosure is unnecessary)
     — Exercise of reasonable care in preparing tax return
     — Reasonable cause and good faith

2. Substantial understatement

   • Defined: Understatement greater than 10% of tax or $5,000, whichever is larger
   • Defenses:
     — Understatement does not exceed threshold
     — Disclosure with reasonable basis
     — No disclosure with substantial authority
     — Reasonable cause and good faith

3. Substantial valuation misstatement

   • Defined: Misstatement more than 200% of correct valuation
   • Defenses:
     — Misstatement does not exceed threshold
     — Amount of underpayment of tax is less than $5,000
     — Reasonable cause and good faith

---

with reasonable basis. Exhibit 2–2 summarizes the various standards of compliance and ranks them according to their level of certainty. Note that in all cases the taxpayer can avoid the penalties by showing that there was *reasonable cause* for the position taken or that he or she acted in *good faith*. Obviously, these are both purely subjective determinations based on the individual facts and circumstances.

FRAUD

When the taxpayer attempts to defraud the government, the tax law imposes a minimum penalty equal to 75 percent of the amount of underpayment attributable to the fraud.[11] *In addition,* the taxpayer may also be subject to the criminal penalties for fraud. Criminal penalties can be as high as $100,000 ($500,000 for corporate taxpayers) and imprisonment for up to five years. Despite these penalties, taxpayers by the thousands are willing to play the audit lottery, including some rich and famous tax felons:[12]

• Leona Helmsley, New York hotel magnate, who will forever be remembered for her offhand comment to her housekeeper, "we don't pay taxes; only the little people pay taxes." Helmsley, convicted in 1992 for deducting millions of dollars

---

[11]   § 6663.

[12]   See in part "Famous Faces from IRS Hall of

Shame," *Sacramento Bee,* March 29, 1994, Metro Final Scene, D3.

Exhibit 2-2 *Standards of Compliance Required to Avoid Penalties*

1. Frivolous position

   • Defined: Patently improper
     — No protection for frivolous positions

2. Not frivolous position

   • Defined: Not patently improper, merely arguable
     — Pre-1994: Protection against negligence with disclosure
     — Post-1993: Apparently no protection

3. Reasonable basis

   • Defined: Arguable but fairly unlikely to prevail in court
     — Protects against insubstantial negligence
     — Protects against substantial understatement if position disclosed

4. Realistic possibility of success

   • Defined: More than one in three chances for success
     — Protects against insubstantial negligence without disclosure
     — Protects against substantial negligence with disclosure

5. Substantial authority

   • Defined: Supporting authorities are substantial (Congress, IRS, or court cases)
     — Protects against insubstantial and substantial negligence without disclosure (except tax shelter item)

6. More-likely-than-not

   • Defined: Greater than 50 percent chance of succeeding
     — Protects against insubstantial and substantial negligence without disclosure including tax shelter items

7. Reasonable cause and good faith

   • Defined: Facts and circumstances determination
     — Protects normally against all penalties

---

of personal expenses, including renovations to her personal residence, was fined over $7 million and sentenced to four years in prison (served 18 months).

• Pete Rose, baseball player and all-time leader in hits (4,256). Rose failed to report income from memorabilia shows and gambling and served five months in prison.

• Spiro Agnew, vice-president during the Nixon era. Agnew, who failed to report income from bribes, was fined $10,000 and had a three-year suspended sentence.

• Chuck Berry, famous rock and roll star of Johnny B. Goode fame. Berry under-reported his income by $110,000 in 1979 and served four months in prison.

• Aldo Gucci, famous designer. Gucci pleaded guilty to $7 million of tax fraud in 1989 and was sentenced to one year in jail and fined $30,000.

- Al Capone, racketeer and mobster. Capone, convicted of tax evasion in 1931, was fined $50,000 and served eight years of a ten-year sentence, then retired to his Miami estate.

- Willie Nelson, country and western singing star. Nelson ran up his tax bill to over $32 million. He served no time in prison, but part of the bill was paid from part of his ranch, which was seized by the IRS.

Civil fraud has not been clearly defined, but it requires more than simply negligent acts or omissions by the taxpayer. There is a fine line between fraud and negligence (to which a lesser penalty applies, as explained above). Fraud does not occur by accident. It is a willful and deliberate attempt to evade tax. For example, consider a taxpayer who is entitled to a deduction of $19,000. What penalty applies if he transposed the digits and claimed a deduction of $91,000? Fraud occurs only if it can be shown that the taxpayer knew that the amounts reported on the return were false. In this regard, the IRS must prove this to be true by a "preponderance of evidence." Thus for the transposition error above, the fraud penalty can be upheld if the IRS can carry its burden of proof and show that the taxpayer intentionally transposed the numbers. Lacking this, the negligence or substantial understatement penalty would probably be assessed. Note that before the *criminal* fraud penalty can be imposed, the IRS must show that the taxpayer intentionally tried to evade tax "beyond a shadow of any reasonable doubt." All of those in the "hall of shame" above found that this is not an impossible task. As a practical matter, the penalty imposed—negligence, civil, or criminal fraud—depends on the severity of the offense and the ability of the IRS to carry the burden of proof.

> **Example 2.**   Dr. Bradford Calloway paid his children, all of whom were under 12 years of age, $11,000 for performing various tasks relating to his business. The kids did such chores as mail sorting, trash collecting, and answering the telephone. Although expenses incurred in carrying on a business such as these are normally deductible, the IRS did not believe that children that age could perform work worth that much money for any business. The Tax Court agreed with the IRS, and the judge added a fraud penalty, explaining that "We find it inherently incredible that Calloway, an intelligent and educated professional man, would pay a total of $11,138.56 for such services, performed by small children on a part-time basis, or that he could seriously believe that such payments represented reasonable and deductible compensation for services rendered in his medical practice . . . particularly in the face of his accountant's contrary advice."[13]

TAX PREPARER PENALTIES

Understanding the penalty structure becomes doubly hard when a tax preparer is involved. What are the responsibilities of tax preparers when the client in unscrupulous or simply wants to take an aggressive position? As a practical matter, it is not the totally dishonest taxpayer that presents difficulties for tax return preparers. Most practitioners can

---

[13] A. J. Cook, *A. J.'s Tax Court* (St. Luke's Press, 1987), p. 96.

easily walk away from such engagements. The more perplexing and more common problems concern situations where the client wants the preparer to take an aggressive position on issues for which the answer is unclear. Similarly, taxpayers may want to pursue a particular position because they view the law as arbitrary or capricious or they are not receptive to the preparer's response. These situations often present an ethical dilemma for the preparer. What side should the practitioner take? Should the preparer sign the return if he or she disagrees with the taxpayer? First, it needs to be emphasized that the tax practitioner is being paid to be an advocate for the client, not an independent third party hired to provide an unbiased or neutral opinion. It is the job of the tax expert to explain the relevant considerations and possible consequences, including positions that may be contrary to the law but which may be defensible. That done, it is not the right of the practitioner to impose his or her own set of moral values on the client. The final decision is to be made by the client after reviewing the alternatives provided. If the practitioner believes that the client's actions violate his or her personal code of ethics, the practitioner should withdraw from the engagement.

Beyond the basic preparer-client relationship, there are a number of other forces at work that affect whether the preparer signs the return containing a risky position. First, even if an answer to a particular question does exist, the costs of uncovering it probably cannot be recovered from the client. Second, given the small percentage of tax returns that are audited, there is only a slight chance that either the taxpayer or preparer will ever come face to face with the IRS. Third, preparers, like most people, want to please their customers and find it hard to just say no. When these dynamics are present, they make it relatively easy for practitioners to resolve an issue in favor of the client, notwithstanding the lack of reasonable support for the position. This is particularly true when the practitioner knows that the unprincipled competitor down the street will do whatever the client wants and at a cheaper price. On the other hand, the practitioner's sense of public duty, concern about his or her personal and professional reputation, and possible legal liability may cause him or her to be something less than an advocate for the client. As might be expected, the practitioner's proper role in these situations is not clearly defined. There are, however, in addition to the preparer's own personal code of ethics, some guidelines that a preparer generally must follow in carrying on a tax practice.

Individuals who prepare tax returns are subject to a variety of rules regulating their professional conduct. The rules governing tax practice are contained in Treasury Circular Number 230 and various provisions of the Internal Revenue Code. In addition, CPAs and attorneys engaged in tax practice must also follow the rules of conduct imposed by their professional organizations: the American Institute of Certified Public Accountants (AICPA) and the American Bar Association (ABA). The general rules of conduct prescribed by the AICPA for all CPAs concern a variety of matters such as independence, integrity, objectivity, advertising, contingent fees, and responsibilities of the accountant when undertaking an engagement—but none of these are directly related to tax practice. Acknowledging that individuals engaged in tax practice have ethical concerns beyond those covered in the general rules of conduct, the AICPA began issuing Statements on Responsibilities in Tax Practice (SRTP) in 1964. These statements, currently eight in number, provide additional guidelines for professional conduct of CPAs in tax practice. Similarly, the ABA Standing Committee on Ethics and Professional Responsibility has also issued certain opinions regarding an attorney's conduct when practicing before the IRS.

Tax Return Positions. As might be imagined, the rules and applicable penalties concerning practitioner conduct as set forth by Circular 230, the Internal Revenue Code, the AICPA, and the ABA deserve a chapter devoted solely to these topics. In essence, however, the most important penalty for those preparing returns is that contained in § 6694(a) of the Internal Revenue Code. Section 6694(a) provides that a $250 penalty is imposed on the preparer of a tax return if any part of an understatement of the liability on a return is due to an *undisclosed* position for which there was not a *realistic possibility* of success. This standard is met "if a reasonable and well informed analysis by a person knowledgeable in the tax law would lead such a person to conclude that the position has approximately a one in three, or greater, likelihood of being sustained on its merits."[14] The AICPA's Statements on Responsibilities in Tax Practice also adopt this standard in *SRTP No. 1,* which states that a CPA should not recommend to a client a position (or prepare or sign a return that contains a position) with respect to the tax treatment of any item on a return unless the CPA has a good faith belief that the position has a realistic possibility of success. The ABA and a recently proposed change in Circular 230 also embrace the realistic possibility standard. A violation of this standard under Circular 230 can result in disbarment from practice before the IRS, but only if the violation is willful, reckless, or the result of gross incompetence.

At first glance, it would appear that the size of penalty imposed by the IRS, $250, is so small that it would do little to dissuade preparers from taking whatever position a client wishes. The ramifications of a violation under Circular 230 also seem more academic than real since disbarment occurs only if the violation was willful or reckless. What may not be apparent, however, is the significance of this standard *and* its violation should a disgruntled client end up suing the preparer for malpractice. In a civil action against a preparer, the courts, both judges and juries, typically rely on expert testimony to assess whether the preparer should be held liable. In such case, it is not too hard to imagine a judge or jury believing that the preparer was negligent once an expert has explained that the preparer has already been penalized under § 6694(a). Even if the preparer is ultimately exonerated, the costs to defend such action could be substantial. Moreover, failing to observe such a standard could ultimately cost the practitioner the loss of his or her professional license to practice as a CPA or attorney. In short, it is not the size of the penalty that the practitioner fears but the other consequences that the penalty may trigger.

> **Example 3.** T, a CPA, has prepared the tax return for D&G Home Products for the past 15 years. It is normally a week-long job and worth well over $10,000 to T's practice. He also does the monthly preparation of financial statements worth another $20,000 per year. This year D&G spent over $100,000 on a Super Bowl excursion for its customers. In preparing the return, D&G insists that it should be able to deduct all of the expenses, but T has some reservations. T understands there have been some recent changes in the law in this area but does not have time to adequately research the issue, and, even if he did, he doubts whether he could charge for the time spent. He also knows that this is a lucrative engagement

---

[14] Reg. § 1.6694-2(b).

and he wants to continue the relationship with the client. Finally, T recognizes that it is highly unlikely that the return will ever be audited. Consequently, T decides to sign the return and worry about it only if a problem arises. But what happens if the return is audited, the position is overturned, and a preparer penalty is assessed on the grounds that the return contained an undisclosed position that did not have a realistic possibility of success? While the penalty would be monetarily small, the real concern is the effect of the reversal on the client. D&G may have a short memory once it is forced to pay the tax, interest, and perhaps a substantial understatement penalty and interest on the penalty. It may not remember conversations with T and his admonitions. In the end, the corporation may feel that it was misled and sue T for malpractice and hundreds of thousands of dollars. In such a proceeding, D&G may have the upper hand since it has been determined by a court of law that the position was unrealistic under that standards of § 6694(a) and T has therefore failed to meet his ethical responsibilities as established for tax practitioners in the AICPA's Statements on Responsibilities in Tax Practice.

The decision that all practitioners ultimately face with every return they prepare is whether they can in good faith sign the tax return as preparer. The key factor in making this decision is whether the position advanced on the return has a realistic possibility of success. In fact, a proposed change to Circular 230 states specifically that a practitioner *may not sign a return unless the realistic possibility standard is met or adequate disclosure exists*.

It should be emphasized that a preparer can breathe much more easily if the client is willing to adequately disclose the position. *SRTP No. 1* sets the ethical standard, allowing the preparer to prepare and sign the return provided the position is not frivolous and it is disclosed. Similarly, the preparer penalty of § 6694(a) does not apply to disclosed positions. In many cases, however, the client does not want to disclose the position, therefore returning the preparer to the original dilemma—determining whether there is a realistic possibility that the position will be upheld. Note that, even if there is a disclosure, the *taxpayer* can still be liable for negligence penalties unless there is a *reasonable basis* for the taxpayer's treatment of the disclosed item. Thus, even though preparers can absolve themselves from liability as long as the position is nonfrivolous and there is disclosure, the taxpayer is subject to a higher standard.

Example 4. This year P&P, a large public accounting firm, prepared the return for T Corporation, a valued *Fortune* 500 client. The return contained a somewhat risky position involving a material amount of tax. Assuming the position has a realistic possibility of being upheld, P&P can sign the return without fear of penalty regardless of whether the position is disclosed. However, if the position is rejected, the taxpayer could very well be subject to the substantial understatement penalty unless there is substantial authority for the position or the taxpayer discloses and has a reasonable basis for the position. Thus, if there is no disclosure, if the return is audited, and if it is determined that the realistic possibility standard is satisfied but the substantial authority test is not, P&P is off the hook but T must pay a 20 percent penalty. These differing results place the preparer and taxpayer in a conflict that can be avoided only if the preparer carefully communicates the distinction. Even then the client might be miffed and find another preparer.

In addition to the $250 penalty for preparing a return that contains an undisclosed position for which there is not a realistic possibility of success, the tax law provides a number of other penalties to encourage ethical conduct by preparers. For example, a penalty of $1,000 per return is imposed where the prepaper willfully attempts to understate the liability of the taxpayer or where the preparer understates the taxpayer's liability by reckless or intentional disregard of the rules or regulations.[15] The law also contains a number of criminal penalties for preparers with fines of up to $10,000 and imprisonment for up to three years.[16]

Other Guidelines for CPAs.   As suggested above, the Statements on Responsibilities in Tax Practice provide a number of other guidelines for CPAs who are tax practitioners. There are currently eight statements. *STRP No. 1,* regarding tax positions, was covered at length above. The remaining statements generally fall into one of two categories: (1) return preparation issues (STRP Numbers 2, 3, and 4) and (2) issues that arise after a return is filed (STRP Numbers 5, 6, and 7). Some of these statements are described below.

- *STRP No. 2: Answers to Questions on the Return.* A CPA should make a reasonable effort to obtain from the client, and provide, appropriate answers to all questions on a tax return before signing as preparer. As a general rule, questions simply cannot be ignored.

- *STRP No. 3: Certain Procedural Aspects of Preparing Returns.* A CPA ordinarily may rely on information provided by the client or a third party in preparing a return and is not required to examine or review documents or other evidence supporting client information in order to sign the return. The CPA cannot ignore, however, the implications of information furnished or information known by the CPA, and is required to make reasonable inquiries where information as presented appears to be incomplete or incorrect. In effect, the CPA cannot put on blinders and ignore information relevant to the return.

- *STRP No. 4: Use of Estimates.* A CPA may prepare returns involving the use of the taxpayer's estimates if it is impractical to obtain exact data and the estimated amounts are reasonable under the facts and circumstances known to the CPA.

- *STRP No. 6: Knowledge of Error (Return Preparation).* A CPA should advise the client promptly upon learning of an error in a previously filed return, or upon learning of a client's failure to file a required return. The advice of the CPA may be oral and should include a recommendation of the measures to be taken. The CPA is not obliged to inform the IRS and may not do so without the permission of the client, except where required by law. If the error in a prior year might cause a material understatement of tax liability, the CPA may not be able to prepare the current year return and must therefore withdraw from the engagement.

---

[15]   § 6694(b).   [16]   See §§ 7206, 7207, and 7216.

- *STRP No. 7: Knowledge of Error (Administrative Proceeding).* When the CPA represents a client in an administrative proceeding regarding a return with an error known to the CPA that has resulted or may result in more than an insignificant effect on the client's tax liability, the CPA should request permission from the client to disclose the error to the IRS. Absent such permission, the CPA should consider withdrawing from the engagement.

The above discussion is just a brief introduction to the penalties and rules of practice that serve to define the proper conduct for taxpayers and preparers. In reality, there are a number of other penalties and rules that may apply in certain situations.[17] Nevertheless, this introduction may provide a sense of what are the most common ethical problems facing tax practitioners. Moreover, it underscores the importance of being able to find authoritative answers for questions, the subject of the next section.

✔ CHECK YOUR TAX KNOWLEDGE

Review Question 1.   The system of penalties provides an escape for taxpayers if the positions taken on their returns meet certain standards. In effect, meeting a certain standard enables the taxpayer to avoid a penalty. Practitioners generally associate a probability of success rate for each standard. What probabilities would you assign?

Frivolous	_____
Substantial authority	_____
Nonfrivolous	_____
More-likely-than-not	_____
Reasonable basis	_____
Realistic possibility of success	_____

None of these probabilities other than *realistic possibility of success* have been quantified by the law. However, practitioners would typically rank the standards in the following order with the associated probabilities of success. Although the probabilities might vary from firm to firm and practitioner to practitioner, the order would remain the same.

1. More-likely-than-not	$>50\%$
2. Substantial authority	≥ 40
3. Realistic possibility of success	≥ 33
4. Reasonable basis	≥ 20
5. Nonfrivolous	≥ 5
6. Frivolous	< 5

---

[17] For a more complete discussion, see the related text, *Corporate Partnership, Estate and Gift Taxation* (Richard D. Irwin, 1995), Chapter 17.

Review Question 2.   Pete Hartman operates an accounting practice in northern Virginia just outside of Washington. One of his long-time clients is Jim Anderson. Last year the IRS audited Jim's 1992 tax return, and he ultimately had to pay additional taxes as well as interest on that amount. Jim now wants to deduct a portion of this interest as a business expense. He reasons that because business expenses are deductible and the interest was directly attributable to back taxes on business income the deduction should be allowed. There has also been another development this year. Jim's daughter has been diagnosed to have dyslexia. The problem is not severe but it was enough to cause Jim to enroll his daughter in a private school that is better equipped to provide the additional help she needs. The tuition for the school is $20,000, and Jim wants to deduct the cost as a medical expense. After some research, Pete believes that both positions are somewhat risky. Jim has asked Pete about the downside risk of taking this position on his return. Pete estimates that taking the deduction for the interest will reduce Jim's tax liability of $30,000 about $1,000. If he were to claim only the medical expense deduction by itself, it would reduce his tax liability by about $6,000. Try the following questions.

a.   What is the maximum penalty that Jim might pay if he deducts only the interest and it is considered erroneous but not fraudulent?

Jim would be subject to an accuracy-related penalty (negligence), which is 20 percent of the amount of the underpayment due to the overstatement of deductions. In this case, the penalty would be $200 (20% × $1,000). In addition, Jim would owe the additional $1,000 in tax plus interest on the underpayment *and* interest on the penalty.

b.   True-False. Jim will not be subject to penalty with respect to the interest deduction as long as his position has a reasonable basis even if he does not specifically disclose the position on the return.

True. Based on recent changes, the negligence penalty will not be assessed as long as the taxpayer has a reasonable basis for the position regardless of whether the position is disclosed on the tax return.

c.   True-False. Jim will not be subject to penalty with respect to the tuition deduction as long as his position has a reasonable basis even if he does not specifically disclose the position on the return.

False. In this situation, Jim's $6,000 understatement would be considered substantial since it exceeds the larger of $5,000 or 10 percent of the correct tax, $3,000 (10% × $30,000). When the understatement in question is substantial, the substantial understatement penalty applies. This penalty can be avoided only if the taxpayer has substantial authority for his position *or* he discloses the position and such position has reasonable basis. Here Jim will not have disclosed the position, so a reasonable basis for the position will not suffice.

d. Jim has indicated that he does not want to flag either position. Pete would not be subject to a preparer penalty with respect to the tuition deduction if the position is *not* disclosed as long as the position

      (1)   has a reasonable basis
      (2)   is nonfrivolous
      (3)   has a realistic possibility of success
      (4)   more than one of the above
      (5)   all of the above

(3). To avoid the $250 preparer penalty of § 6694(a), an undisclosed position must have a reasonable possibility of success, a higher standard than reasonable basis. However, if the position is disclosed, the preparer penalty will not apply as long as it is not a frivolous position.

e. True-False. By signing the tax return, Pete would not be violating the AICPA Statement on Responsibilities of Tax Practice assuming both positions have a reasonable basis.

False. The AICPA has also adopted the realistic possibility of success standard, suggesting that tax practitioners should not sign returns containing undisclosed positions that do not meet this standard.

f. Pete understands that the SRTP indicate that he is not supposed to sign the return where there is an undisclosed position unless the position has a realistic possibility of success. However, he has no real idea whether the chances are 20 percent, 30 percent, 40 percent, or whatever based on what he has found. Can Pete sign a return containing a position for which there is no reasonable basis without violating the AICPA statements if he discloses the position?

Yes. The SRTP provide that a practitioner can sign any return as long as the position is disclosed and it is not frivolous.

SOURCES AND APPLICATIONS OF TAX LAW

As stated at the outset of this chapter, before delving into the rules and regulations of taxation, it is important at a minimum to have an appreciation of not only the nature of tax practice but also the sources of the tax law and how they can be used for solving questions. The second half of this chapter identifies the various components of the tax law, explains how they can be accessed, and reviews the basic methods of tax research.

AUTHORITATIVE SOURCES OF TAX LAW

Sources of tax law can be classified into two broad categories: (1) the law, and (2) official interpretations of the law. The law consists primarily of the Constitution, the Acts of Congress, and tax treaties. In general, these sources are referred to as the *statutory* law. Most statutory law is written in general terms for a typical situation. Since general rules, no matter how carefully drafted, cannot be written to cover variations on the normal scheme, interpretation is usually required. The task of interpreting the statute is one of the principal duties of the Internal Revenue Service (IRS) as representative of the Secretary of the Treasury. The IRS annually produces thousands of releases that explain and clarify the law. To no one's surprise, however, taxpayers and the government do not always agree on how a particular law should be interpreted. In situations where the taxpayer or the government decides to litigate the question, the courts, as final arbiters, are given the opportunity to interpret the law. These judicial interpretations, administrative interpretations, and the statutory law are considered in detail below.

STATUTORY LAW

The Constitution of the United States provides the Federal government with the power to tax. Disputes concerning the constitutionality of an income tax levied on taxpayers without apportionment among the states were resolved in 1913 with passage of the Sixteenth Amendment. Between 1913 and 1939, Congress enacted revenue acts that amounted to a complete rewrite of all tax law to date, including the desired changes. In 1939, due primarily to the increasing complexity of the earlier process, Congress codified all Federal tax laws into Title 26 of the *United States Code,* which was then called the *Internal Revenue Code of 1939.* Significant changes in the Federal tax laws were made during World War II and the post-war period of the late 1940s. Each change resulted in amendments to the 1939 Code. By 1954, the codification process had to be repeated in order to organize all additions to the law and to eliminate obsolete provisions. The product of this effort was the *Internal Revenue Code of 1954.* After 1954, Congress took great care to ensure that each new amendment to the 1954 Code was incorporated within its organizational structure with appropriate cross-references to any prior provisions affected by a new law. Among the changes incorporated into the 1954 Code in this manner were the Economic Recovery Tax Act (ERTA) of 1981, the Tax Equity and Fiscal Responsibility Act (TEFRA) of 1982, and the Deficit Reduction Act (DRA) of 1984. In 1986, Congress again made substantial revision in the tax law. Consistent with this massive redesign of the 1954 Code, Congress changed the title to the *Internal Revenue Code of 1986.* Like the 1954 Code, the 1986 Code is subject to revisions introduced by a new law. Recent changes incorporated into the 1986 Code were the Revenue Reconciliation Act of 1989, the Revenue Reconciliation Act of 1990, and the Revenue Reconciliation Act of 1993.

The legislative provisions contained in the Code are by far the most important component of tax law. Although procedure necessary to enact a law is generally well known, it is necessary to review this process with a special emphasis on taxation. From a tax perspective, the *intention* of Congress in producing the legislation is extremely important since the primary purpose of tax research is to interpret the legislative intent of Congress.

THE MAKING OF A TAX LAW

Article I, Section 7, Clause 1 of the Constitution provides that the House of Representatives of the U.S. Congress has the basic responsibility for initiating revenue bills.[18] The Ways and Means Committee of the House of Representatives must consider any tax bill before it is presented for vote by the full House of Representatives. On bills of major public interest, the Ways and Means Committee holds public hearings where interested organizations may send representatives to express their views about the bill. The first witness at such hearings is usually the Secretary of the Treasury, representing the President of the United States. In many cases, proposals for new tax legislation or changes in existing legislation come from the President as a part of his political or economic programs.

After the public hearings have been held, the Ways and Means Committee usually goes into closed session, where the Committee prepares the tax bill for consideration by the entire House. The members of the Committee receive invaluable assistance from their highly skilled staff, which includes economists, accountants, and lawyers. The product of this session is a proposed bill that is submitted to the entire House for debate and vote.

After a bill has been approved by the entire House, it is sent to the Senate and assigned to the Senate Finance Committee. The Senate Finance Committee may also hold hearings on the bill before its consideration by the full Senate. The Senate's bill generally differs from the House's bill. In these situations, both versions are sent to the Joint Conference Committee on Taxation, which is composed of members selected from the House Ways and Means Committee and from the Senate Finance Committee. The objective of this Joint Committee is to produce a compromise bill acceptable to both sides. On occasion, when compromise cannot be achieved by the Joint Committee or the compromise bill is unacceptable to the House or the Senate, the bill "dies." If, however, compromise is reached and the Senate and House approve the compromise bill, it is then referred to the President for his approval or veto. If the President vetoes the bill, the legislation is "killed" unless two-thirds of both the House and the Senate vote to override the veto. If the veto is overridden, the legislation becomes law.

It should be noted that at each stage of the process, information is produced that may be useful in assessing the intent of Congress. One of the better sources of Congressional intent is a report issued by the House Ways and Means Committee. This report contains the bill as well as a general explanation. This explanation usually provides the historical background of the proposed legislation along with the reasons for enactment. The Senate Finance Committee also issues a report similar to that of the House. Because the Senate often makes changes in the House version of the bill, the Senate's report is also an important source. Additionally, the Joint Conference Committee on Taxation issues its own report, which is sometimes helpful. Two other sources of intent are the records of the debates on the bill and publications of the initial hearings.

---

[18] Tax bills do not originate in the Senate, except when they are attached to other bills.

Committee reports and debates appear in several publications. Committee reports are officially published in pamphlet form by the U.S. Government Printing Office as the bill proceeds through Congress. The enacted bill is published in the *Internal Revenue Bulletin* and the *Internal Revenue Cumulative Bulletin*. The debates are published in the *Congressional Record*. In addition to these official government publications, several commercial publishers make this information available to subscribers.

The diagram on the following page illustrates the normal flow of a bill through the legislative process and the documents that are generated in this process.

ORGANIZATION OF THE CODE

Once a tax bill becomes tax law, it is incorporated into the existing structure of the *Internal Revenue Code*.[19] The ability to use the Internal Revenue Code is essential for all individuals who have any involvement with the tax laws. It is normally the starting point for research. The following format is the basic organization of the Code.

Title 26 of the United States Code (referred to as the Internal Revenue Code)

    Subtitle A—Income Taxes

        Chapter 1—Normal Taxes and Surtaxes

            Subchapter A—Determination of Tax Liability

                Part I—Tax on Individuals

                    Sections 1 through 5

When working with the tax law, it is often necessary to make reference to or *cite* a particular source with respect to the Code. The *section* of the Code is the source normally cited. A complete citation for a section of the Code would be too cumbersome. For instance, a formal citation for Section 1 of the Code would be "Subtitle A, Chapter 1, Subchapter A, Part I, Section 1." In most cases, citation of the section alone is sufficient. Sections are numbered consecutively throughout the Code so that each section number is used only once. Currently the numbers run from Section 1 through Section 9602. Not all section numbers are used, so that additional ones may be added by Congress in the future without the need for renumbering.[20]

---

[19] All future use of the term Code or Internal Revenue Code refers to the *Internal Revenue Code of 1986*.

[20] It is interesting to note that when it adopted the 1954 Code, Congress deliberately left section numbers unassigned to provide room for future additions. Recently, however, Congress has been forced to distinguish new sections by alphabetical letters following a particular section number. See, for example, Sections 280, 280A, 280B, and 280C of the 1986 Code.

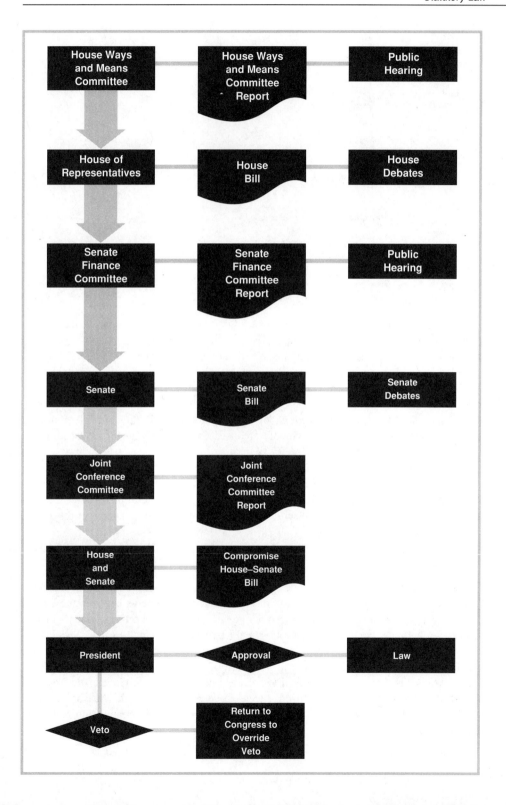

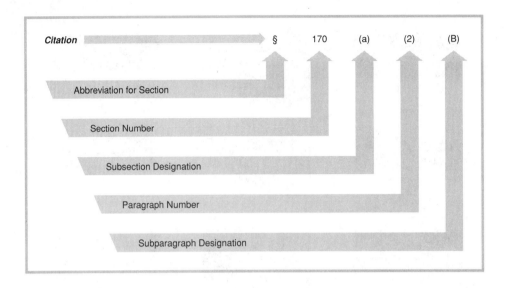

Citation of a particular Code section in tax literature ordinarily does not require the prefix "Internal Revenue Code" because it is generally understood that, unless otherwise stated, references to section numbers concern the Internal Revenue Code of 1986 as amended. However, since most Code sections are divided into subparts, reference to a specific subpart requires more than just its section number. Section 170(a)(2)(B) serves as an example.

All footnote references used throughout this text are made in the form given above. In most cases, the "§" or "§§" symbols are used in place of the terms "section" or "sections," respectively.

Single-volume or double-volume editions of the Internal Revenue Code are published after every major change in the law. Commerce Clearing House, Inc. (CCH) and the Research Institute of America (RIA) publish these editions. Additionally, the Code is included in each of the major tax services that are discussed in a later section of this chapter.

TAX TREATIES

The laws contained in tax treaties represent the third and final component of the statutory law. Tax treaties (also referred to as tax conventions) are agreements between the United States and other countries that provide rules governing the taxation of residents of one country by another. For example, the tax treaty between the United States and France indicates how the French government taxes U.S. citizens residing in France and vice versa. Tax treaties, as law, have the same authority as those laws contained in the Code. Treaty provisions may override provisions of the Internal Revenue Code if the treaty is signed after the enactment of the Code. (See Code § 7872.) For this reason, persons involved with an international tax question must be aware of tax treaties and recognize that the Code may be superseded by a tax treaty.

ADMINISTRATIVE INTERPRETATIONS

After Congress has enacted a tax law, the Executive branch of the Federal government has the responsibility for enforcing it. In the process of enforcing the law, the Treasury interprets, clarifies, defines, and analyzes the Code in order to apply Congressional intention of the law to the specific facts of a taxpayer's situation. This process results in numerous administrative releases including the following:

1. Regulations

2. Revenue rulings and letter rulings

3. Revenue procedures

4. Technical advice memoranda

REGULATIONS

Congress has authorized the Secretary of the Treasury to prescribe and issue all rules and regulations needed for enforcement of the Code.[21] The Secretary, however, usually delegates the power to write the regulations to the Commissioner of the Internal Revenue Service. Normally, regulations are first published in proposed form—*proposed regulations*—in the Federal Register. Upon publication, interested parties have 30 days for comment. At the end of 30 days, the Treasury responds in light of the comments in any of three ways: it may (1) withdraw the proposed regulation; (2) amend it; or (3) leave it unchanged. In the latter two cases, the Treasury normally issues the regulation in its final form as a *Treasury decision* (often referred to as TDs) and it is published in the Federal Register. Thereafter, the new regulation is included in Title 26 of the *Code of Federal Regulations*.

The primary purpose of the regulations is to explain and interpret particular Code sections. Although regulations have not been issued for all Code sections, they have been issued for the great majority. In those cases where regulations exist, they are an important authoritative source on which one can usually rely. Regulations can be classified into three groups: (1) legislative; (2) interpretive; and (3) procedural.

Legislative Regulations. Occasionally, Congress will give specific authorization to the Secretary of the Treasury to issue regulations on a particular Code section. For example, under § 1502, the Secretary is charged with prescribing the regulations for the filing of a consolidated return by an affiliated group of corporations. There are virtually no Code sections governing consolidated returns, and the regulations in effect serve in lieu of the Code. In this case and others where it occurs, the regulation has the force and effect of a law, with the result that a court reviewing the regulation usually will not substitute its judgment for that of the Treasury Department unless the Treasury has clearly abused its discretion.[22]

---

[21] § 7805(a).

[22] *Anderson, Clayton & Co. v. U.S.*, 77-2 USTC ¶9727, 40 AFTR2d 77-6102, 562 F.2d 972 (CA-5, 1977), *Cert. den.* at 436 U.S. 944 (USSC, 1978).

Interpretative Regulations.   Interpretative regulations explain the meaning of a Code section and commit the Treasury and the Internal Revenue Service to a particular position relative to the Code section in question. This type of regulation is binding on the IRS but not on the courts, although it is "a body of experience and informed judgment to which courts and litigants may properly resort for guidance."[23] Interpretive regulations have considerable authority and normally are invalidated only if they are inconsistent with the Code or are unreasonable.

Procedural Regulations.   Procedural regulations cover such areas as the information a taxpayer must supply to the IRS and the internal management and conduct of the IRS in certain matters. Those regulations affecting vital interests of the taxpayers are generally binding on the IRS, and those regulations stating the taxpayer's obligation to file particular forms or other types of information are given the effect of law.

Citation for Regulations.   Regulations are arranged in the same sequence as the Code sections they interpret. Thus, a regulation begins with a number that designates the type of tax or administrative, definitional, or procedural matter and is followed by the applicable Code section number. For example, Treasury Regulation Section 1.614-3(f)(5) serves as an illustration of how regulations are cited throughout this text.

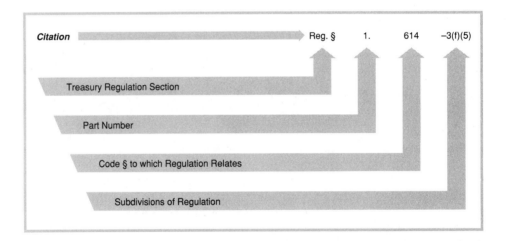

The part number of a Treasury regulation is used to identify the general area covered by the regulation as follows.

Part Number	Law Subject
1	Income Tax
20	Estate Tax
25	Gift Tax
31	Employment Tax
48–49	Excise Tax

---

[23] *Skidmore v. Swift and Co.,* 323 U.S. 134 (USSC, 1944).

The various subdivisions of a regulation are not necessarily related to a specific subdivision of the Code.

Sometimes the Treasury issues temporary regulations when it is necessary to meet a compelling need. For example, temporary regulations are often issued shortly after enactment of a major change in the tax law. These temporary regulations have the same binding effect as final regulations until they are withdrawn or replaced. Such regulations are cited as Temp. Reg. §.

Temporary regulations should not be confused with proposed regulations. The latter have no force or effect.[24] Nevertheless, proposed regulations provide insight into how the IRS currently interprets a particular Code section. For this reason, they should not be ignored.

REVENUE RULINGS

Revenue rulings also are official interpretations of the Federal tax laws and are issued by the National Office of the IRS. Revenue rulings do not have quite the authority of regulations, however. Regulations are a direct extension of the law-making powers of Congress, whereas revenue rulings are an application of the administrative powers of the Internal Revenue Service. In contrast to rulings, regulations are usually issued only after public hearings and must be approved by the Secretary of the Treasury.

Unlike regulations, revenue rulings are limited to a given set of facts. Taxpayers may rely on revenue rulings in determining the tax consequences of their transactions; however, taxpayers must determine for themselves if the facts of their cases are substantially the same as those set forth in the revenue ruling.

Revenue rulings are published in the weekly issues of the *Internal Revenue Bulletin*. The information contained in the *Internal Revenue Bulletins* (including, among other things, revenue rulings) is accumulated and usually published semiannually in the *Cumulative Bulletin*. The *Cumulative Bulletin* reorganizes the material according to Code section. Citations for the *Internal Revenue Bulletin* and the *Cumulative Bulletin* are illustrated on the following page.

REVENUE PROCEDURES

Revenue procedures are statements reflecting the internal management practices of the IRS that affect the rights and duties of taxpayers. Occasionally they are also used to announce procedures to guide individuals in dealing with the IRS or to make public something the IRS believes should be brought to the attention of taxpayers. Revenue procedures are published in the weekly *Internal Revenue Bulletins* and bound in the *Cumulative Bulletin* along with revenue rulings issued in the same year. The citation system for revenue procedures is the same as for revenue rulings except that the prefix "Rev. Proc." is substituted for "Rev. Rul."

---

[24] Federal law (i.e., the Administrative Procedure Act) requires any federal agency, including the Internal Revenue Service, that wishes to adopt a substantive rule to publish the rule in proposed form in order to give interested persons an opportunity to comment. Proposed regulations are issued in compliance with this directive.

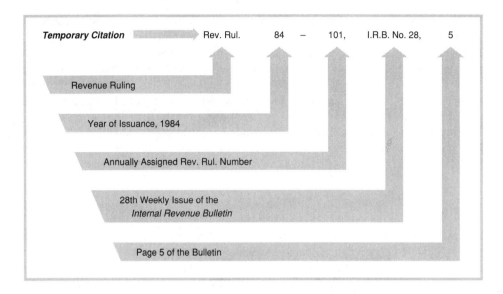

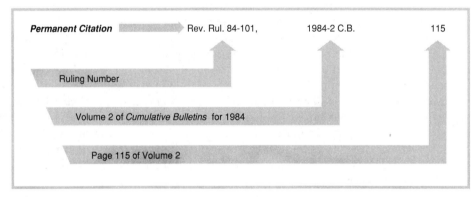

LETTER RULINGS

Taxpayers who are in doubt about the tax consequences of a contemplated transaction may ask the National Office of the IRS for a ruling on the tax question involved. Generally, the IRS has discretion about whether to rule or not and has issued guidelines describing circumstances under which it will issue a ruling on a question posed by a taxpayer.[25] Unlike revenue rulings, letter rulings (or private rulings) apply *only* to the particular taxpayers asking for the ruling and are not applicable to all taxpayers. For those requesting a ruling, the response might provide insurance against

---

[25] See Rev. Proc. 82-22, 1982-1 C.B. 469 for a description of the areas in which the IRS has refused to issue advanced rulings. Note, also, that the IRS is required to charge taxpayers a fee for letter rulings, opinion letters, determination letters, and similar requests. The fees range from $50 to $1,000. See § 6591.

surprises because, as a practical matter, a favorable ruling should preclude any controversies with the IRS on a subsequent audit. During the process of obtaining a ruling, the IRS may recommend changes in a proposed transaction to assist the taxpayers in achieving the result they wish. Since 1976, the IRS has made individual rulings publicly available after deleting information that tends to identify the taxpayer. Such rulings appear in digests by the leading tax commentators and by publishers such as CCH and RIA.

TECHNICAL ADVICE MEMORANDA

Either a taxpayer or an IRS district's Appeals Division may request advice from the National Office of the IRS about the Code, Regulations, and statutes and their impact on a specific set of facts. Generally, such requests take place during an audit or during the appeals process of the audit, and give both the taxpayer and the revenue agent an opportunity to resolve a dispute over a technical question. If the National Office renders advice favorable to the taxpayer, normally it must be applied. However, if the advice is against the taxpayer, the taxpayer does not lose his or her right to further pursue the issue in question with the IRS.

Citations for letter rulings and technical advice follow a multi-digit file number system. IRS Letter Ruling 9042002 serves as an example.

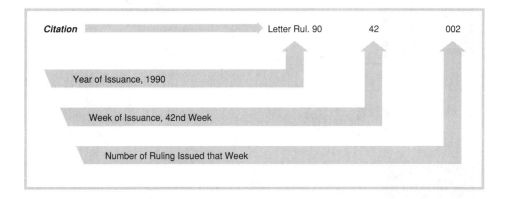

JUDICIAL INTERPRETATIONS

The Congress passes the tax law and the Executive branch of the Federal government enforces and interprets it, but under the American system of checks and balances, it is the Judiciary branch that ultimately determines whether the Executive branch's interpretation is correct. This provides yet another source of tax law—court decisions. It is therefore absolutely essential for the student of tax as well as the tax practitioner to have a grasp of the judicial system of the United States and how tax cases move through this system.

Before litigating a case in court, the taxpayer must have exhausted the administrative remedies available to him or her within the Internal Revenue Service. If the taxpayer has not exhausted his or her administrative remedies, a court will deny a hearing because the claim filed in the court is premature.

All litigation begins in what are referred to as *courts of original jurisdiction,* or *trial courts,* which "try" the case. There are three trial courts: (1) the Tax Court; (2) the U.S. District Court; and (3) the U.S. Claims Court. Note that the taxpayer may select any one (and only one) of these three courts to hear the case. If the taxpayer or government disagrees with the decision by the trial court, it has the right to appeal to either the U.S. Court of Appeals or the U.S. Court of Appeals for the Federal Circuit, whichever is appropriate in the particular case. If a litigating party is dissatisfied with the decision by the appellate court, it may ask for review by the Supreme Court, but this is rarely granted. The judicial system is illustrated and discussed below.

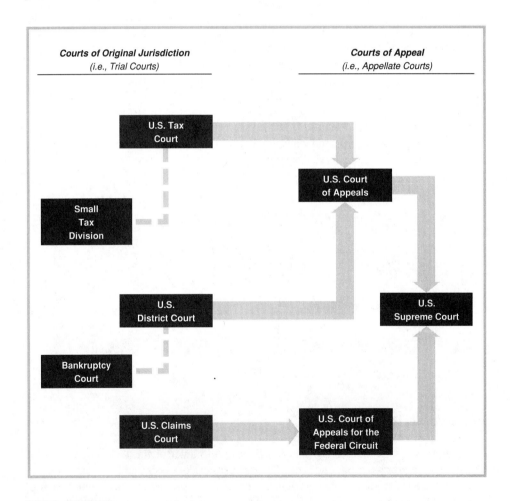

TRIAL COURTS

U.S. Tax Court. The Tax Court, as its name suggests, specializes in tax matters and hears no other types of cases. The judges on the court are especially skilled in taxation. Usually, prior to being selected as a judge by the President, the individual was a practitioner or IRS official who was noted for his or her expertise. This Court is

composed of 19 judges who "ride circuit" throughout the United States (i.e., they travel and hear cases in various parts of the country). Occasionally, the full Tax Court hears a case, but most cases are heard by a single judge who submits his or her opinion to the chief judge, who then decides whether the full court should review the decision.

Besides its expertise in tax matters, two other characteristics of the Tax Court should be noted. Perhaps the most important feature of the Tax Court is that the taxpayer does not pay the alleged tax deficiency before bringing his or her action before the court. The second facet of the Tax Court that bears mentioning is that a trial by jury is not available.

U.S. District Courts. For purposes of the Federal judicial system, the United States is divided into 11 geographic areas called circuits which are subdivided into districts. For example, the second circuit, which is composed of Vermont, Connecticut, and New York, contains the District Court for the Southern District of New York, which covers parts of New York City. Other districts may include very large areas, such as the District Court for the State of Arizona, which covers the entire state. A taxpayer may take a case into the District Court for the district in which he or she resides, but only after the disputed tax deficiency has been paid. The taxpayer then sues the IRS for a refund of the disputed amount. The District Court is a court of general jurisdiction and hears many types of cases in addition to tax cases. This is the only court in which the taxpayer may obtain a jury trial. The jury decides matters of fact but not matters of law. However, even in issues of fact, the judge may, and occasionally does, disregard the jury's decision.

U.S. Claims Court. The United States Claims Court was established on October 1, 1982. Prior to that time it was called the "U.S. Court of Claims." The U.S. Claims Court hears cases involving certain claims against the Federal government, including tax refunds. This Court is made up of 16 judges and usually meets in Washington, D.C. A taxpayer must pay the disputed tax deficiency before bringing an action in this court, and may not obtain a jury trial. Appeals from the U.S. Claims Court are taken to the U.S. Court of Appeals for the Federal Circuit, an appellate court created at the same time as the U.S. Claims Court.

The chart on the following page illustrates the position of the taxpayer in bringing an action in these courts.

Small Claims Cases. When the amount of a tax assessment is relatively small, the taxpayer may elect to submit the case to the division of the Tax Court hearing small claims cases called the Small Tax Division of the Tax Court. If the amount of tax at issue is $10,000 per year or less, the taxpayer can obtain a decision with a minimum of formality, delay, and expense; but the taxpayer loses the right to appeal the decision. The Small Tax Division is administered by the chief judge of the Tax Court, who is authorized to assign small claims cases to special trial judges. These cases receive priority on the trial calendars, and relatively informal rules are followed whenever possible. The special trial judges' opinions are not published on these cases, and the decisions are not reviewed by any other court or treated as precedents in any other case.

Bankruptcy Court. Under limited circumstances, it is possible for the bankruptcy court to have jurisdiction over tax matters. The filing of a bankruptcy petition prevents creditors, including the IRS, from taking action against a taxpayer, including the filing of a proceeding before the Tax Court if a notice of deficiency is sent after the filing of a petition in bankruptcy. In such cases, a tax claim may be determined by the bankruptcy court.

	U.S. Tax Court	U.S. District Court	U.S. Claims Court
Jurisdiction	Nationwide	Specific district in which court is sitting	Nationwide
Subject Matter	Tax cases only	Many different types of cases, both criminal and civil	Claims against the Federal government, including tax refunds
Payment of Contested Amount	Taxpayer does not pay deficiency, but files suit against IRS Commissioner to stop collection of tax	Taxpayer pays alleged deficiency and then files suit against the U.S. government for refund	Taxpayer pays alleged deficiency and then files suit against the U.S. government for refund
Availability of Jury Trial	No	Yes	No
Appeal Taken to	U.S. Court of Appeals	U.S. Court of Appeals	U.S. Court of Appeals for the Federal Circuit
Number of Courts	1	95	1
Number of Judges per Court	19	1	16

APPELLATE COURTS

U.S. Courts of Appeals. The appropriate appellate court depends on which trial court hears the case. Taxpayer or government appeals from the District Courts and the Tax Court are taken to the U.S. Court of Appeals that has jurisdiction over the court in which the taxpayer lives. Appeals from the U.S. Claims Court are taken to the U.S. Court of Appeals for the Federal Circuit, which has the same powers and jurisdictions as any of the other Courts of Appeals except that it only hears specialized appeals. Courts of Appeals are national courts of appellate jurisdiction. With the exceptions of the Court of Appeals for the Federal Circuit and the Court of Appeals for the District of Columbia, these appellate courts are assigned various geographic areas of jurisdiction as follows:

**Court of
Appeals for
the Federal
Circuit (CA-FC)**

U.S. Claims
Court

**District of
Columbia
Circuit (CA-DC)**

District of
Columbia

**First
Circuit (CA-1)**

Maine
Massachusetts
New Hampshire
Puerto Rico
Rhode Island

**Second
Circuit (CA-2)**

Connecticut
New York
Vermont

**Third
Circuit (CA-3)**

Delaware
New Jersey
Pennsylvania
Virgin Islands

**Fourth
Circuit (CA-4)**

Maryland
N. Carolina
S. Carolina
Virginia
W. Virginia

**Fifth
Circuit (CA-5)**

Canal Zone
Louisiana
Mississippi
Texas

**Sixth
Circuit (CA-6)**

Kentucky
Michigan
Ohio
Tennessee

**Seventh
Circuit (CA-7)**

Illinois
Indiana
Wisconsin

**Eighth
Circuit (CA-8)**

Arkansas
Iowa
Minnesota
Missouri
Nebraska
N. Dakota
S. Dakota

**Ninth
Circuit (CA-9)**

Alaska
Arizona
California
Guam
Hawaii
Idaho
Montana
Nevada
Oregon
Washington

**Tenth
Circuit (CA-10)**

Colorado
New Mexico
Kansas
Oklahoma
Utah
Wyoming

**Eleventh
Circuit (CA-11)**

Alabama
Florida
Georgia

Taxpayers may appeal to the Courts of Appeal as a matter of right, and the Courts must hear their cases. Very often, however, the expense of such an appeal deters many from proceeding with an appeal. Appellate courts review the record of the trial court to determine whether the lower court completed its responsibility of fact finding and applied the proper law in arriving at its decision.

District Courts must follow the decision of the Appeals Court for the circuit in which they are located. For instance, the District Court in the Eastern District of Missouri must follow the decision of the Eighth Circuit Court of Appeals because Missouri is in the Eighth Circuit. If the Eighth Circuit has not rendered a decision on the particular issue involved, then the District Court may make its own decision or follow the decision in another Circuit.

The Tax Court is a national court with jurisdiction throughout the entire country. Prior to 1970, the Tax Court considered itself independent and indicated that it would not be bound by the decisions of the Circuit Court to which its decision would be appealed. In *Golsen,*[26] however, the Tax Court reversed its position. Under the *Golsen rule,* the Tax Court now follows the decisions of the Circuit Court to which a particular case would be appealed. Even if the Tax Court disagrees with a Circuit Court's view, it will decide based upon the Circuit Court's view. On the other hand, if a similar case arises in the jurisdiction of another Circuit Court that has not yet ruled on the same issue, the Tax Court will follow its own view, despite its earlier decision following a contrary Circuit Court decision.

U.S. Courts of Appeals generally sit in panels of three judges, although the entire court may sit in particularly important cases. They may reach a decision that affirms the lower court or that reverses the lower court. Additionally, the Appellate Court could send the case back to the lower court (remand the case) for another trial or for rehearing on another point not previously covered. It is possible for the Appellate Court to affirm the decision of the lower court on one particular issue and reverse it on another.

Generally, only one judge writes a decision for the Appeals Court, although in some cases no decision is written and an order is simply made. Such an order might hold that the lower court is sustained, or that the lower court's decision is reversed as being inconsistent with one of the Appellate Court's decisions. Sometimes other judges (besides the one assigned to write the opinion) will write additional opinions agreeing with (concurring opinion) or disagreeing with (dissenting opinion) the majority opinion. These opinions often contain valuable insights into the law controlling the case, and often set the ground for a change in the court's opinion at a later date.

U.S. Supreme Court. The Supreme Court of the United States is the highest court of the land. No one has a *right* to be heard by this Court. It only accepts cases it wishes to hear, and generally those involve issues that the Court feels are of national importance. The Supreme Court generally hears very few tax cases. Consequently, taxpayers desiring a review of their trial court decision find it solely at the Court of Appeals. Technically, cases are submitted to the Supreme Court through a request process known as the "Writ of Certiorari." If the Supreme Court decides to hear the case, it grants the Writ of Certiorari; if it decides not to hear the case, it denies the Writ of Certiorari. It is important to note that there is another path to review by the U.S. Supreme Court—*by appeal*—as opposed to by Writ of Certiorari. This "review by appeal" may be available when a U.S. Court of Appeals has held that a state statute is in conflict with the laws or treaties of the United States. The "review by appeal" may also be available when the highest court in a state

---

[26] *Jack E. Golsen,* 54 T.C. 742 (1970).

has decided a case on grounds that a Federal statute or treaty is invalid, or when the state court has held a state statute valid despite the claim of the losing party that the statute is in conflict with the U.S. Constitution or a Federal law. Review by the U.S. Supreme Court is still discretionary, but a Writ of Certiorari is not involved.

The Supreme Court, like the Courts of Appeals, does not conduct another trial. Its responsibility is to review the record and determine whether or not the trial court correctly applied the law in deciding the case. The Supreme Court also reviews the decision of the Court of Appeals to determine if the court used the correct reasoning.

In general, the Supreme Court only hears cases when one or more of the following conditions apply:

1. When the Court of Appeals has not used accepted or usual methods of judicial procedure or has sanctioned an unusual method by the trial court;

2. When a Court of Appeals has settled an important question of Federal law and the Supreme Court feels such an important question should have one more review by the most prestigious court of the nation;

3. When a decision of a Court of Appeals is in apparent conflict with a decision of the Supreme Court;

4. When two or more Courts of Appeals are in conflict on an issue; or

5. When the Supreme Court has already decided an issue but feels that the issue should be looked at again, possibly to reverse its previous decision.

CASE CITATION

Tax Court Decisions.   Prior to 1943, the Tax Court was called the Board of Tax Appeals. The decisions of the Board of Tax Appeals were published as the *United States Board of Tax Appeals Reports* (BTA). Board of Tax Appeals cases are cited as follows:

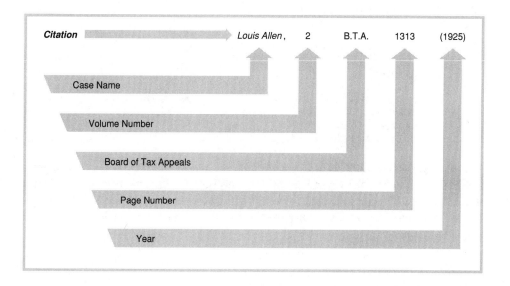

The Tax Court renders two different types of decisions with two different citation systems: regular decisions and memorandum decisions.

Tax Court *regular* decisions deal with new issues that the court has not yet resolved. In contrast, decisions that deal only with the application of already established principles of law are called *memorandum* decisions. The United States government publishes regular decisions in *United States Tax Court Reports* (T.C.). Tax Court regular decisions are cited as follows:

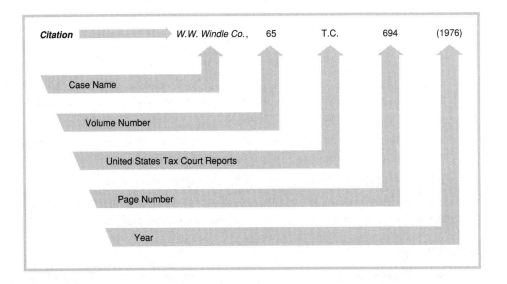

Like revenue rulings and the *Cumulative Bulletins*, there is a time lag between the date a Tax Court regular decision is issued and the date it is bound in a *U.S. Tax Court Report* volume. In this case, the citation appears as follows:

Temporary Citation:

        W.W. Windle Co., 65 T.C. _____, No. 79 (1976).

Here the page is left out, but the citation tells the reader that this is the 79th regular decision issued by the Tax Court since Volume 64 ended. When the new volume (65th) of the Tax Court Report is issued, then the permanent citation may be substituted for the old one. Both CCH and RIA have tax services that allow the researcher to find these temporary citations.

The IRS has adopted the practice of announcing its acquiescence or nonacquiescence to the regular decisions of the Tax Court that are adverse to the position taken by the government.[27] That is, the Service announces whether it agrees with the Tax Court or not. The IRS does not follow this practice for the decisions of the other courts, or even for memorandum decisions of the Tax Court, although it occasionally announces that it will or will not follow a decision of another Federal court with a similar set of facts. The IRS may withdraw its acquiescence or nonacquiescence at any time and may do so even retroactively. Acquiescences and nonacquiescences are published in the weekly *Internal Revenue Bulletins* and the *Cumulative Bulletins*.

Although the U.S. government publishes the Tax Court's regular decisions, it does not publish memorandum decisions. However, both CCH and RIA publish them. CCH publishes the memorandum decisions under the title *Tax Court Memorandum Decisions* (TCM), while RIA publishes these decisions as *Tax Court Reporter and Memorandum Decisions* (T.C. Memo). In citing Tax Court memorandum decisions, some authors prefer to use both the RIA and the CCH citations for their cases.

In an effort to provide the reader the greatest latitude of research sources, this dual citation policy has been adopted for this text. The case of *Alan K. Minor* serves as an example of the dual citation of Tax Court memorandum decisions.

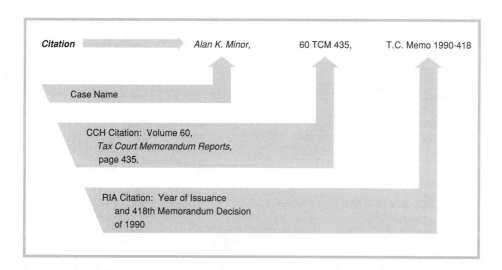

Citation → *Alan K. Minor,* 60 TCM 435, T.C. Memo 1990-418

Case Name

CCH Citation: Volume 60,
  Tax Court Memorandum Reports,
  page 435.

RIA Citation: Year of Issuance
  and 418th Memorandum Decision
  of 1990

Citations for U.S. District Court, Court of Appeals, and Claims Court. Commerce Clearing House, Research Institute of America, and West Publishing Company all publish decisions of the District Courts, Courts of Appeals, and the Claims Court. When available, all three citations of a case are provided in this text.[28] CCH publishes the decisions of these courts in its *U.S. Tax Cases* (USTC—not to be confused with the U.S.

---

[27] The IRS' acquiescence is symbolized by "A" or "Acq." and its nonacquiescence by "NA" or "Nonacq."

[28] When all three publishers have not printed the case, only the citations to the cases published are provided.

Tax Court Reports) volumes, and RIA offers these decisions in its *American Federal Tax Reports* (AFTR) series.[29] West Publishing Company reports these decisions in either its *Federal Supplement Series* (F. Supp.—District Court decisions), or its *Federal Second Series* (F.2d—Claims Court and Courts of Appeals decisions).

The citation of the U.S. District Court decision of *Cam F. Dowell, Jr. v. U.S.* is illustrated for each of the three publishing companies as follows:

CCH Citation:

Cam F. Dowell, Jr. v. U.S., 74-1 USTC ¶9243, (D.Ct. Tx., 1974).

Interpretation: This case is reported in the first volume of the *U.S. Tax Cases,* published by CCH for calendar year 1974 (74-1), located at paragraph (¶) 9243, and is a decision rendered in 1974 by a U.S. District Court located in Texas (Tx.).

RIA Citation:

Cam. F. Dowell, Jr. v. U.S., 33 AFTR2d 74-739, (D.Ct Tx., 1974).

Interpretation: Reported in the 33rd volume of the second series of the *American Federal Tax Reports* (AFTR2d), published by RIA for 1974, and located at page 739.

West Citation:

Cam F. Dowell, Jr. v. U.S., 370 F.Supp. 69 (D.Ct. Tx., 1974).

Interpretation: Located in the 370th volume of the *Federal Supplement Series* (F.Supp), published by West Publishing Company, and located at page 69.

The multiple citation of the U.S. District Court case illustrated above appears as follows:

Cam F. Dowell, Jr. v. U.S., 74-1 USTC ¶9243, 33 AFTR2d 74-739, 370 F.Supp. 69 (D.Ct. Tx., 1974).

---

[29]   Until the acquisition of Prentice Hall by RIA, Prentice Hall published cases under its own name. Accordingly, researchers need-ing cases from before 1993 will often encounter Prentice Hall as publisher of these reporters now carried under RIA's name.

Decisions of the Claims Court (Ct. Cls.), the Courts of Appeals (e.g., CA-1, CA-2, etc.), and the Supreme Court (USSC) are published by CCH and RIA in the same reporting source as District Court decisions (i.e., USTCs and AFTRs). Claims Court and Court of Appeals decisions are reported by West Publishing Company in its *Federal Second Series* (F.2d). Supreme Court decisions are published by West Publishing Company in its *Supreme Court Reports* (S.Ct.), and the U.S. Government Printing Office publishes Supreme Court decisions in its *Supreme Court Reports* (U.S.).

An example of the multiple citation of a Court of Appeals decision follows:

Citation:

Millar v. Comm., 78-2 USTC ¶9514, 42 AFTR2d 78-5246, 577 F.2d 212 (CA-3, 1978).

A multiple citation of a Supreme Court decision would appear as follows:

Citation:

Fausner v. Comm., 73-2 USTC ¶9515, 32 AFTR2d 73-5202, 413 U.S. 838 (USSC, 1973).

Note that in each of the citations above, the designation "Commissioner of the Internal Revenue Service" is simply abbreviated to "Comm." In some instances, the IRS or U.S. is substituted for Comm., and older cases used the Commissioner's name. For example, in *Gregory v. Helvering,* 293 U.S. 465 (USSC, 1935), Mr. Helvering was the Commissioner of the Internal Revenue Service at the time the case was brought to the Court. Also note that the citation contains a reference to the Appellate Court rendering the decision (i.e., CA-3, or USSC) and the year of issuance.

Exhibits 2–3 and 2–4 summarize the sources of case citations from various reporter services.

Exhibit 2-3 *Reporters of Tax Court Decisions*

Reporter	Abbr.	Type	Publisher
Tax Court Reports	TC	Regular	Government Printing Office
Tax Court Memorandum Decisions	TCM	Memorandum	Commerce Clearing House
Tax Court Memorandum Decisions	TC Memo	Memorandum	Research Institute of America

---

Exhibit 2-4 *Reporters of Decisions Other Than Tax Court*

Reporter	Abbr.	Courts Reported	Publisher
Supreme Court Reports	U.S.	Supreme Court	Government Printing Office
Supreme Court Reporter	S. Ct.	Supreme Court	West Publishing
Federal Supplement	F.Supp.	District Courts	West Publishing
Federal Reporter	F. F.2d	Cts. of Appeal and Claims Ct.	West Publishing
American Federal Tax Reports	AFTR AFTR2d	District Courts Claims Court, Cts. of Appeal, and Supreme Ct.	Research Institute of America
United States Tax Cases	USTC	Same as AFTR and AFTR2d	Commerce Clearing House

SECONDARY SOURCES

The importance of understanding the sources discussed thus far stems from their role in the taxation process. As mentioned earlier, the statutory law and its official interpretations constitute the legal authorities that set forth the tax consequences for a particular set of facts. These legal authorities, sometimes referred to as *primary authorities,* must be distinguished from so-called *secondary sources* or *secondary authorities*. The secondary sources of tax information consist mainly of books, periodicals, articles, newsletters, and editorial judgments in tax services. When working with the tax law, it must be recognized that secondary sources are unofficial interpretations—mere opinions—that have no legal authority.

Although secondary sources should not be used as the supporting authority for a particular tax treatment (except as a supplement to primary authority or in cases where primary authority is absent), they are an indispensable aid when seeking an understanding of the tax law. Several of these secondary materials are discussed briefly below.

TAX SERVICES

"Tax service" is the name given to a set of books that contains a vast quantity of tax-related information. In general, a tax service is a compilation of the following: the Code, regulations, court decisions, IRS releases, and explanations of these primary authorities by the editors. As the listing of contents suggests, a tax service is invaluable since it contains, all in one place, a wealth of tax information, including both primary and secondary sources. Most tax services are available on CD-ROM. Moreover, these materials are updated constantly to reflect current developments—an extremely important feature given the dynamic nature of tax law. The major tax services are

Publisher	Name of Publication
Commerce Clearing House	*Standard Federal Tax Reporter—Income Taxes*
Research Institute of America	*United States Tax Reporter and Federal Tax Coordinator—2nd Series*
The Bureau of National Affairs, Inc.	*Tax Management Portfolios—U.S. Income*
Mertens	*Law of Federal Income Taxation*

The widespread use of computers has found other applications in tax research. For example, *LEXIS* is a computerized data base that a user can access through his or her personal computer. The *LEXIS* data base contains almost all information available in an extensive tax library. Suppliers of tax services are currently making their own computer-based system available to their customers, or are in the process of perfecting such a system. Undoubtedly computers will be basic to tax research in the future, particularly within the large law and accounting firms that have enough work to make the use of such a system economical.

Commerce Clearing House, Research Institute of America, and other publishers issue weekly summaries of important cases and other tax developments that many practitioners and scholars find helpful in keeping current with developments in the tax field. The Bureau of National Affairs publishes the *Daily Tax Bulletin,* a comprehensive daily journal of late-breaking tax news that often reprints entire cases or regulations of particular importance. *Tax Notes,* published by Tax Analysts, is a weekly publication addressing legislative and judicial developments in the tax field. *Tax Notes* is particularly helpful in following the progress of tax legislation through the legislative process.

TAX PERIODICALS

In addition to these services, there are a number of quality publications (usually published monthly) that contain articles on a variety of important tax topics. These publications are very helpful when new tax acts are passed, because they often contain clear, concise summaries of the new law in a readable format. In addition, they serve to convey new planning opportunities and relay the latest IRS and judicial developments in many important sub-specialities of the tax profession. Some of the leading periodicals include the following:

Estate Planning	Taxation for Lawyers
Journal of Corporate Taxation	Taxes—The Tax Magazine
Journal of Partnership Taxation	The International Tax Journal
Journal of Real Estate Taxation	The Review of Taxation of Individuals
Journal of Taxation	The Tax Adviser
Tax Law Journal	The Tax Executive
Tax Law Review	The Tax Lawyer
Taxation for Accountants	Trusts and Estates

In addition to these publications, many law journals contain excellent articles on tax subjects.

Several indexes exist that may be used to locate a journal article. Through the use of a subject index, author index, and in some instances a Code section index, articles dealing with a particular topic may be found. Three of these indexes are

Title	Publisher
Index to Federal Tax Articles	Warren, Gorham and Lamont
Federal Tax Articles	Commerce Clearing House
The Accountant's Index	American Institute of Certified Public Accountants

In addition, the *United States Tax Reporter,* published by RIA, contains a section entitled "Index to Tax Articles."

TAX RESEARCH

Having introduced the sources of tax law, the remainder of this chapter is devoted to working with the law—or more specifically, the art of tax research. Tax research may be defined as the process used to ascertain the optimal answer to a question with tax implications. Although there is no perfect technique for researching a question, the following approach normally is used:

1. Obtain all of the facts

2. Diagnose the problem from the facts

3. Locate the authorities

4. Evaluate the authorities

5. Derive the solution and possible alternative solutions

6. Communicate the answer

Each of these steps is discussed below.

OBTAINING THE FACTS

Before discussing the importance of obtaining all the facts, the distinction between closed-fact research and open- or controlled-fact research should be noted. If the research relates to a problem with transactions that are complete, it is referred to as closed-fact research and normally falls within the realm of tax practice known as tax compliance. On the other hand, if the research relates to contemplated transactions, it is called controlled- or open-fact research and is an integral part of tax planning.

In researching a closed-fact problem, the first step is gathering all of the facts. Unfortunately, it is difficult to obtain all relevant facts upon first inquiry. This is true because it is essentially impossible to understand the law so thoroughly that all of the proper questions can be asked before the research task begins. After the general area of the problem is identified and research has begun, it usually becomes apparent that more facts must be obtained before an answer can be derived. Consequently, additional inquiries must be made until all facts necessary for a solution are acquired.

DIAGNOSING THE ISSUE

Once the initial set of facts is gathered, the tax issue or question must be identified. Most tax problems involve very basic questions such as these:

1. Does the taxpayer have gross income that must be recognized?

2. Is the taxpayer entitled to a deduction?

3. Is the taxpayer entitled to a credit?

4. In what period is the gross income, deduction, or credit reported?

5. What amount of gross income, deduction, or credit must be reported?

As research progresses, however, such fundamental questions can be answered only after more specific issues have been resolved.

> **Example 5.**   R's employer owns a home in which R lives. The basic question that must be asked is whether the home constitutes income to R. After consulting the various tax sources, it can be determined that § 61 requires virtually all benefits to be included in income unless another provision specifically grants an exclusion. In this case, § 119 allows a taxpayer to exclude the value of employer-provided housing if the housing is on the employer's premises, the lodging is furnished for the convenience of the employer, and the employee is required by the employer to accept the housing. Due to the additional research, three more specific questions must be asked:
>
> 1.   Is the home on the employer's premises?
>
> 2.   Is the home provided for the employer's convenience?
>
> 3.   Is R required to live in the home?

As the above example suggests, diagnosing the problem requires a continuing refinement of the questions until the critical issue is identified. The refinement that occurs results from the awareness that is gained through reading and rereading the primary and secondary authorities.

> **Example 6.**   Assume the same facts in *Example 5*. After determining that one of the issues concerns whether R's home is on the business premises, a second inquiry is made of R concerning the location of his residence. (Note that as the research progresses, additional facts must be gathered.) According to R, the house is located in a suburb, 25 miles from his employer's downtown office. However, the house is owned by the employer, and hence R suggests that he lives on the employer's premises. He also explains that he often brings work home and frequently entertains clients in his home. Having uncovered this information, the primary authorities are reexamined. Upon review, it is determined that in *Charles N. Anderson,*[30] the court indicated that an employee would be considered on the business premises if the employee performed a significant portion of his duties at the place of lodging. Again the question must be refined to ask: Do R's work and entertainment activities in the home constitute a significant portion of his duties?

LOCATING THE AUTHORITIES

Identification of the critical issue presented by any tax question begins by first locating, then reading and studying the appropriate authority. Locating the authority is ordinarily done using a tax service. With the issue stated in general terms, the subject is found in the

---

[30]   67-1 USTC ¶9136, 19 AFTR2d 318, 371
F.2d 59 (CA-6, 1966).

index volume and the location is determined. At this point, the appropriate Code sections, regulations, and editorial commentary may be perused to determine their applicability to the question.

> **Example 7.**   In the case of R above, the problem stated in general terms concerns income. Using an index, the key word, *income,* could be located and a reference to information concerning the income aspects of lodging would be given.

Once information relating to the issue is identified, the authoritative materials must be read. That is, the appropriate Code sections, regulations, rulings, and cases must be examined and studied to determine how they relate to the question. As suggested above, this process normally results in refinement of the question, which in turn may require acquisition of additional facts.

EVALUATING THE AUTHORITY

After the various authorities have been identified and it has been *verified* that they are applicable, their value must be appraised. This evaluation process, as will become clear below, primarily involves appraisal of court decisions and revenue rulings.

The Code.   The Internal Revenue Code is the final authority on most tax issues since it is the Federal tax law as passed by Congress. Only the courts can offset this authority by declaring part of the law unconstitutional, and this happens rarely. Most of the time, however, the Code itself is only of partial help. It is written in a style that is not always easy to understand, and it contains no examples of its application. Accordingly, to the extent the Code can be understood as clearly applicable, no stronger authority exists, except possibly a treaty. But in most cases, the Code cannot be used without further support.

Treasury Regulations.   As previously discussed, the regulations are used to expand and explain the Code. Because Congress has given its authority to make laws to the Executive branch's administrative agency—the Treasury—the regulations that are produced are a very strong source of authority, although not as strong as the Code itself. Normally, the major concern with regulations is whether they are consistent with the Code. If the regulations are inconsistent, the Court will not hesitate to invalidate them.

Judicial Authority.   The value of a court decision depends on numerous factors. On appraising a decision, the most crucial determination concerns whether the outcome is consistent with other decisions on the same issue. In other words, consideration must be given to how other decisions have evaluated the one in question. An invaluable tool in determining the validity of a case is a *citator*. A tax citator is a volume containing an alphabetical listing of virtually all tax cases. After the name of each case, there is a record of other decisions that have cited (in the text of their facts and opinions) the first case.

Example 8.   Assume the same facts as in *Example 6*. Examination of the *Anderson* case in a citator reveals that it has been cited by courts in other decisions numerous times. For example, two cases in which the *Anderson* decision was discussed are *U.S. Jr. Chamber of Commerce*[31] and *Jan J. Wexler*.[32]

It is important to note that tax citators often use abbreviations for subsequent case history. For example, the abbreviations *aff'g* and *aff'd* mean "affirming" and "affirmed" and indicate that an appeals court has upheld the decision in question. Similarly, *rev'g* and *rev'd* mean "reversing" and "reversed" and indicate that a trial court's decision was overturned. Finally, *rem'g* and *rem'd* mean "remanding" and "remanded" and indicate that the case has been sent back to a lower court for reconsideration.

The validity of a particular decision may be assessed by examining how the subsequent cases viewed the cited decision. For example, subsequent cases may have agreed or disagreed with the decision in question, or distinguished the facts of the cited case from those examined in a later case.

Another important factor that must be considered in evaluating a court decision is the level of the court that issued it. Decisions issued by trial courts have less value than those issued by appellate courts. And, of course, decisions of the Supreme Court are the ultimate authority.

A court decision's value rises appreciably if the IRS agrees with its result. As discussed earlier, the IRS usually indicates whether it acquiesces or does not acquiesce to regular Tax Court decisions. The position of the Service may also be published in a revenue ruling.

Rulings.   The significance of revenue rulings lies in the fact that they reflect current IRS policy. Since agents of the IRS are usually reluctant to vary from that policy, revenue rulings carry considerable weight.

Revenue rulings are often evaluated in court decisions. Thus, a tax service should be used to determine whether relevant rulings have been considered in any decisions. By examining the Court's view of the ruling, possible flaws may be discovered.

Private letter rulings issued to the taxpayer must be followed for that taxpayer by the IRS as long as the transaction is carried out in the manner initially approved. Variation from the facts on which the ruling was based permits the Service to revise its position. As mentioned earlier, a private letter ruling applies only to the particular taxpayer to whom it was issued. However, such a ruling should prove helpful to any other taxpayer faced with a substantially identical fact pattern.

DERIVING THE SOLUTION

Once all the relevant authorities have been evaluated, a conclusion must be drawn. Before deriving the final answer or answers, however, an important caveat is warranted: the researcher must ensure that the research reflects all current developments. The new matters section of a tax service can aid in this regard. The new matters section updates

---

[31]   64-2 USTC ¶9637, 14 AFTR2d 5223, 334 F.2d 660 (Ct. Cls., 1964).

[32]   75-1 USTC ¶9235, 35 AFTR2d 75-550, 507 F.2d 842 (CA-6, 1975).

the textual discussion with any late-breaking developments. For instance, the section will contain any new cases, regulations, or pronouncements of the Internal Revenue Service that may bear on the discussion of the topic covered in the main text.

COMMUNICATING THE FINDINGS

The final product of the research effort is a memorandum recording the research and a letter to the interested parties. Although many formats are suitable for the memorandum, one technique typically used is structured as follows:

1. Description of the facts

2. Statement of the issues or questions researched

3. Report of the conclusions (brief answers to the research questions)

4. Discussion of the rationale and authorities that support the conclusions

5. Summary of the authorities consulted in the research

A good tax memorandum is essential. If the research findings are not communicated intelligently and effectively, the entire research effort is wasted.

PROBLEM MATERIALS

DISCUSSION QUESTIONS

2-1 *Taxpayer Penalties.* In reviewing his last year's return, T noticed that he had inadvertently deducted the entire cost of a new air-conditioning system. Such cost should have been capitalized and depreciated.

    a.   T wants to know what penalties, if any, might be assessed if his return is audited and the IRS uncovers his mistake.

    b.   What should T do?

2-2 *Tax Positions.* R operates a small accounting practice in Columbus. While preparing the return for his long-time client C, he found out that C wants to deduct the cost of lawn care for her home. C is a landscape architect who recently started using a room at her home as an office. She feels that this is clearly a business expense. During the interview she seemed to have a point. "What if my clients came to my house and the yard was less than picture perfect? It would kill my business," she explained. R has reviewed the proposed regulations on the home office deduction, and they specifically state that lawn care is not deductible. Nevertheless, he understands C's point. R just cannot say no, and he is thinking about preparing the return and deducting a portion of lawn care allocable to C's home office.

    a.   Assume the position is erroneous and is not disclosed. Will C be subject to any penalty? Explain.

    b.   Assume the position is erroneous and is disclosed. Will C be subject to any penalty? Explain.

2-3 *Avoiding Preparer Penalties.* H recently quit a national public accounting firm and purchased the practice of a local accountant. Her first busy season with this new set of clients has been eye-opening. Some of the taxpayers have been taking very questionable positions on certain recurring items. Somewhat paranoid, H is now quite concerned about incurring penalties. What can she do to guard against possible preparer penalties?

2-4 *Knowledge of Error.* Last March, P put the finishing touches on the tax return of one of his most prized clients, Great Buy Corporation. When preparing the monthly financial statement for June, P noticed that $30,000 of sales somehow got left off of the return. What should P do?

2-5 *Knowledge of Error.* This year P got a new client from the firm down the street, Dewey, Cheatham and Howe. After reviewing the client's prior year return, he found, as he had expected, an error in the way Dewey had computed depreciation. What should P do?

2-6 *Making a New Tax Law.* Describe the Congressional process of making a tax bill into final law.

2-7 *Legislative vs. Interpretative Regulations.* Explain the difference between a legislative Treasury Regulation and an interpretative Regulation.

2-8 *Proposed vs. Final Regulations.* Distinguish between proposed and final Regulations. How would either type of Regulation involving Code § 704 be cited?

2-9 *Revenue Rulings and Revenue Procedures.* Distinguish between a Revenue Ruling and a Revenue Procedure. Where can either be found in printed form?

2-10 *Private vs. Published Rulings.* Distinguish between a private letter ruling and a Revenue Ruling. Under what circumstances would a taxpayer prefer to rely on either of these sources?

2-11 *Technical Advice Memoranda.* What are Technical Advice Memoranda? Under what circumstances are they issued?

2-12 *Trial Courts.* Describe the trial courts that hear tax cases. What are the advantages or disadvantages of litigating a tax issue in each of these courts?

2-13 *The Appeals Process.* A taxpayer living in Indiana has exhausted her appeals within the IRS. If she chooses to litigate her case, trace the appeals process assuming she begins her effort in each of the following trial courts:

    a. The U.S. Claims Court
    b. The U.S. District Court
    c. The U.S. Tax Court
    d. The Small Tax Division of the U.S. Tax Court

2-14 *Tax Court Decisions.* Distinguish between a Regular Tax Court decision and a Memorandum decision.

2-15 *Authority of Tax Law Sources.* Assuming that you have discovered favorable support for your position taken in a controversy with an IRS agent in each of the sources listed below, indicate how you would use these authoritative sources in your discussion with the agent.

    a. A decision of the U.S. District Court having jurisdiction over your case if litigated
    b. Treasury Regulation
    c. The Internal Revenue Code
    d. A decision of the Supreme Court
    e. A decision of the Small Claims Court
    f. A decision of the U.S. Tax Court
    g. A private letter ruling issued to another taxpayer
    h. A Revenue Ruling
    i. A tax article in a leading periodical

2-16 *Tax Services.* What materials are generally found in leading tax services? Which does your library have?

YOU MAKE THE CALL

2-17 T is the owner of a small CPA firm that has developed a very good auditing and tax practice over the years. Recently, while visiting the home of S, his best client (revenues of about $15,000 annually for audit and tax services), T learned some very disturbing information about S's business practices. During a tour of her home, S accidentally revealed that some very expensive personal entertainment equipment acquired in 1993 had been charged to her corporation (cost of approximately $30,000). S stated that everyone she knew charged personal assets to their business accounts and that it appeared to be generally accepted practice. She said she hoped T would not mind.

When T returned to his office, he immediately checked S's 1993 corporate income tax return and found that depreciation had been taken on the $30,000 cost of assets listed simply as "Equipment." Of course, T never suspected the assets were for personal use in S's home.

What should T do? This client is too good to lose, but T is worried about the consequences of allowing this type of behavior to continue.

PROBLEMS

2-18 *Interpreting Citations.* Interpret each of the following citations:

    a. Reg. § 1.721-1(a).
    b. Rev. Rul. 60-314, 1960-2 C.B. 48.
    c. Rev. Proc. 86-46, 1986-2 C.B. 739.
    d. Rev. Rul. 92-35, I.R.B. No. 35, 21.
    e. § 351.

2-19 *Citation Abbreviations.* Explain each of the abbreviations below.

    a. B.T.A.
    b. Acq.
    c. D. Ct.
    d. CA-9
    e. F. Supp.
    f. NA.
    g. Ct. Cls.
    h. USTC
    i. AFTR
    j. *Cert. Den.*
    k. *aff'g* and *aff'd*
    l. *rev'g* and *rev'd*
    m. *rem'g* and *rem'd*

2-20 *Interpreting Citations.* Identify the publisher and interpret each of the following citations:

    a. 41 TCM 289.
    b. 93 S. Ct. 2820 (USSC, 1973).
    c. 71-1 USTC ¶9241 (CA-2, 1971).
    d. 236 F. Supp. 761 (D. Ct. Va., 1974).
    e. T.C. Memo 1977-20.
    f. 48 T.C. 430 (1967).
    g. 6 AFTR2d 5095 (CA-2, 1960).
    h. 589 F.2d 446 (CA-9, 1979).
    i. 277 U.S. 508 (USSC, 1928).

2-21 *Citation Form.* Record the following information in its proper citation form.

    a. Part 7, subdivision (a)(2) of the income tax Regulation under Code § 165
    b. The 34th Revenue Ruling issued March 2, 1987, and printed on pages 101 and 102 of the appropriate document
    c. The 113th letter ruling issued the last week of 1986

2-22 *Citation Form.*   Record the following information in its proper citation form.

  a. A 1982 U.S. Tax Court case in which Roger A. Schubel sued the IRS Commissioner for a refund, published in volume 77 on pages 701 through 715 as a regular decision

  b. A 1974 U.S. Tax Court case in which H. N. Schilling, Jr. sued the IRS Commissioner for a refund, published by (1) Commerce Clearing House in volume 33 on pages 1097 through 1110 and (2) Prentice Hall as its 246th decision that year

  c. A 1966 Court of Appeals case in which Boris Nodiak sued the IRS Commissioner in the second Circuit for a refund, published by (1) Commerce Clearing House in volume 1 of that year at paragraph 9262, (2) Prentice Hall in volume 17 on pages 396 through 402, and (3) West Publishing Company in volume 356 on pages 911 through 919.

RESEARCH PROBLEMS

2-23 *Using a Citator.*   Use either the Commerce Clearing House or Research Institute of America Citator in your library and locate *Richard L. Kroll, Exec. v. U.S.*

  a. Which Court of Appeals Circuit heard this case?

  b. Was this case heard by the Supreme Court?

  c. James B. and Doris F. Wallach are included in the listing below the citation for Kroll. In what court was the Wallach case heard?

2-24 *Using a Citator.* Using any available citator, locate the case of *Corn Products v. Comm.*, 350 U.S. 46. What effect did the decision in *Arkansas Best v. Comm.* (58 AFTR2d 86-5748, 800 F.2d 219) have on the precedential value of the *Corn Products* case?

2-25 *Locating Court Cases.* Locate the case of *Robert Autrey, Jr. v. United States*, 89-2 USTC ¶9659, and answer the following questions.

  a. What court decided the case on appeal?

  b. What court originally tried the case?

  c. Was the trial court's decision upheld or reversed?

2-26 *Locating Court Cases.* Locate the case of *Estate of James C. Freeman*, 67 T.C. 202, and answer the following questions.

  a. What court tried the case?

  b. Identify the various types of precedential authority the judge used in framing his opinion.

2-27 *Locating Court Cases.*   Locate the cited court cases and answer the questions below.

  a. *Stanley A. and Lorriee M. Golantly,* 72 T.C. 411 (1979). Did the taxpayers win their case?

  b. *Hamilton D. Hill,* 41 TCM 700, T.C. Memo ¶71,127 (1971). Who was the presiding judge?

  c. *Patterson (Jefferson) v. Comm.,* 72-1 USTC ¶9420, 29 AFTR2d 1181 (Ct. Cls., 1972). What was the issue being questioned in this case?

2-28   *Completing Citations.*   To the extent the materials are available to you, complete the following citations:

    a.   Rev. Rul. 85-153, _____ C.B. _____.

    b.   *Lawrence W. McCoy,* _____ T.C. _____ (1962).

    c.   *Reginald Turner* _____ TCM _____, T.C. Memo 1954-38.

    d.   *RCA Corp. v. U.S.,* _____ USTC _____ (CA-2, 1981).

    e.   *RCA Corp. v. U.S.,* _____ AFTR2d _____ (CA-2, 1981).

    f.   *RCA Corp. v. U.S.,* _____ F.2d _____ (CA-2, 1981).

    g.   *Comm. v. Wilcox,* _____ S. Ct. _____ (USSC, 1946).

    h.   _____, 79-1 USTC ¶9139 (USSC, 1979).

    i.   _____, 34 T.C. 842 (1960).

    j.   *Brian E. Knutson,* 60 TCM 540, T.C. Memo _____.

    k.   *Samuel B. Levin v. Comm.,* 43 AFTR2d 79-1057 (_____).

2-29   *Examination of Tax Sources.*   For each of the tax sources listed below, identify at least one of the tax issues involved. In addition, if the source has a temporary citation, provide its permanent citation (if available).

    a.   *Battelstein Investment Co. v. U.S.,* 71-1 USTC ¶9227, 27 AFTR2d 71-713, 442 F.2d 87 (CA-5, 1971).

    b.   *Joel Kerns,* 47 TCM, _____ T.C. Memo 1984-22.

    c.   *Patterson v. U.S.,* 84-1 USTC ¶9315 (CA-6, 1984).

    d.   *Webster Lair,* 95 T.C. 484 (1990).

    e.   *Thompson Engineering Co., Inc.,* 80 T.C. 672 (1983).

    f.   *Towne Square, Inc.,* 45 TCM 478, T.C. Memo 1983-10.

    g.   Rev. Rul. 85-13, I.R.B. No. 7, 28.

    h.   Rev. Proc. 85-49, I.R.B. No. 40, 26.

    i.   *William F. Sutton, et al. v. Comm.,* 84 T.C. _____ No. 17.

    j.   Rev. Rul. 86-103, I.R.B. No. 36, 13.

    k.   *Hughes Properties, Inc.,* 86-1 USTC ¶9440, 58 AFTR2d 86-5062, _____ U.S. _____ (USSC, 1986).

    l.   Rev. Rul. 93-60, I.R.B. No. 20, 5.

2-30   *Office in the Home.*   T comes to you for advice regarding the deductibility of expenses for maintaining an office in his home. T is currently employed as an Executive Vice President for Zandy Corporation. He has found it impossible to complete his job responsibilities during the normal forty-hour weekly period. Although the office building in which he works is open nights and weekends, the heating and air conditioning systems are shut down at night (from 6 p.m.) and during the entire weekend. As a result, T has begun taking work home with him on a regular basis. The work is generally done in the den of T's home. Although T's employer does not require him to work at home, T is convinced that he would be fired if his work assignments were not completed on a timely basis. Given these facts, what would you advise T about taking a home-office deduction?

    Partial list of research aids:

        § 280A
        Reg. § 1.280A
        M.G. Hill, 43 TCM 832, T.C. Memo 1982-143

2-31 *Journal Articles.* Refer to Problem 2-30 above. Consult an index to periodicals (e.g., AICPA's *Accountants Index*; Warren, Gorham, and Lamont's *Index to Federal Tax Articles*; or CCH's *Federal Tax Articles*) and locate a journal article on the topic of tax deductions for an office in the home. Copy the article. Record the citation for the article (i.e., author's name, article title, journal name, publication date, and first and last pages of the article) at the top of your paper. Prepare a two-page summary of the article, including all relevant issues, research sources, and conclusions. Staple your two-page summary to the article. The grade for this exercise will be based on the relevance of your article to the topic, the accuracy and quality of your summary, and the quality of your written communication skills.

2-32 *Deductible Medical Expenses.* B suffers from a severe form of degenerative arthritis. Her doctor strongly recommended that she swim for at least one hour per day in order to stretch and exercise her leg and arm muscles. There are no swimming pools nearby, so B spent $15,000 to have a swimming pool installed in her back yard. This expenditure increased the fair market value of her house by $5,000. B consults you about whether she can deduct the cost of the swimming pool on her individual tax return. What do you recommend?

> **Hint:** You should approach this problem by using the tax service volumes of either Commerce Clearing House or Research Institute of America. Both tax services are organized according to Code Sections, so you should start with Code § 213. You will find the Code Sections on the back binding of the volumes. Research Institute of America has a very extensive index, so look under the term "medical expenses."

2-33 *Deductible Educational Expenses.* T is a CPA with a large accounting firm in Houston, Texas. He has been assigned to the international taxation group of his firm's tax department. As a result of this assignment, T enrolls in an international tax law course at the University of Houston Law School. The authorities of the University require T to enroll as a regular law student; and, theoretically, if he continues to attend courses, T will graduate with a law degree. Will T be able to deduct his tuition for the international tax law course as a business expense?

> **Hint:** Go to either the RIA or CCH tax service and use it to find the analysis of Code § 162. When you have found the discussion of § 162, find that part of the subsection dealing with educational deductions. Read the appropriate Regulations and then note the authorities listed after the Regulations. Read over the summaries provided and then choose those you think have the most relevance to the question asked above. Read these cases and other listed authorities, and formulate a written response to the question asked in light of these cases and other authorities. Finally, for the authorities you choose, go to the RIA or CCH Citator and use it to ensure that your authorities are current.

LEARNING OBJECTIVES

Upon completion of this chapter you will be able to:

- Identify the entities that are subject to the Federal income tax

- Explain the basic tax treatment of individuals, corporations, partnerships, S corporations, and fiduciary taxpayers (trusts and estates)

- Understand the basic tax formulas to be followed in computing the tax liability for individuals and corporations

- Define many of the basic terms used in the tax formula such as gross income, adjusted gross income, taxable income, exclusion, deduction, and credit

- Calculate the gain or loss on the disposition of property and explain the tax consequences, including the special treatment of capital gains and losses

CHAPTER OUTLINE

Introduction	3-1	Introduction to Property Transactions	3-27
The Taxable Entity	3-2	Gain or Loss Realized	3-28
Taxable Entities	3-2	Gain or Loss Recognized	3-30
Individual Taxpayers	3-2	Character of the Gain or Loss	3-31
Corporate Taxpayers	3-4	Trade or Business Property	3-34
Fiduciary Taxpayers	3-5	Tax Planning Considerations	3-38
Partnerships	3-6	Choice of Business Form	3-38
Electing Small Business		Itemized Deductions vs. Standard	
Corporations: "S" Corporations	3-8	Deduction	3-39
Limited Liability Companies	3-8	Employee Business Expenses	3-40
Tax Formula	3-11	Problem Materials	3-41
Analyzing the Tax Formula	3-11		

Chapter **3**

TAXABLE ENTITIES, TAX FORMULA, INTRODUCTION TO PROPERTY TRANSACTIONS

INTRODUCTION

The amount of income tax ultimately paid by any taxpayer is determined by applying the many rules comprising our income tax system. This chapter examines some of the fundamental features of this system. They are

- *Taxable Entities*—those entities that are subject to taxation and those that are merely *conduits*

- *Tax Formulas*—the mathematical relationships used to compute the tax for the various taxable entities

- *Property Transactions*—the tax treatment of sales, exchanges, and other dispositions of property

As will become clear, this chapter, in covering the essentials, provides a bird's-eye view of the entire income tax system. For many, this may be sufficient. This one chapter may contain enough tax law and have more than enough detail for some. Nevertheless, it is just part of the picture. Many of the details as well as the conceptual basis for some of these provisions are skipped and left to later chapters. This can be frustrating to those who want more or know that more exists, but the major purpose of this chapter is to establish the basic framework in which the implications of any particular transaction on taxable income can be assessed. To this end, the chapter gives not only a brief description of what is taxable and what is deductible but also a glimpse of such esoteric topics as the passive loss rules and the alternative minimum tax. Remember, the goal is not necessarily to provide a detailed discussion of all the rules but to provide a foundation so that problems, pitfalls, and opportunities can be recognized.

THE TAXABLE ENTITY

The income tax must be imposed on the income of some type of entity. Unfortunately, there is no uniform agreement on what is the theoretically correct unit of taxation. There are a variety of legal, economic, social, and natural entities that Congress could select: individuals (natural persons), family units, households (those living together), sole proprietorships, partnerships, corporations, trusts, estates, governments, religious groups, nonprofit organizations, and other voluntary or cooperative associations. Despite the disagreement over which of these or other entities are the proper choices, Congress has provided that only certain entities are responsible for actually paying the tax. According to the Code, individuals, most corporations, and fiduciaries (estates and trusts) are taxable entities. Other entities, such as sole proprietorships, partnerships, and so-called "S" corporations, are not required to pay tax on any taxable income they might have. Instead, the taxable income of these entities is allocated to their owners, who bear the responsibility for paying any tax that may be due.

> **Example 1.**   R and S are equal partners in a partnership that had taxable income of $50,000 in the current year. The partnership does not pay tax on the $50,000. Rather, the income is allocated equally between R and S. Thus, both R and S will report $25,000 of partnership income on their individual returns and pay the required tax.

In the following sections, the general tax treatment of the taxable entities—individuals, corporations, and fiduciaries—is explained along with the treatment of partnerships and "S" corporations. The specific tax treatment of entities other than individuals is discussed separately in Chapter 19. However, it should be emphasized that many of the tax rules applying to one entity also apply to other entities. These similarities will be pointed out as the various rules are discussed.

TAXABLE ENTITIES

INDIVIDUAL TAXPAYERS

Citizens and Residents of the United States.   Section 1 of the Internal Revenue Code indicates that a tax is imposed on the taxable income of all individuals. As might be expected, the term *individual* generally applies to U.S. citizens. However, it also includes persons who are *not* U.S citizens but who are considered residents, so-called *resident aliens*. Thus, if Princess Di decides to move to New York to escape the tabloids of London, she could be subject to U.S. taxes even though she is not a U.S. citizen. The same could be said for a Japanese citizen working for Honda in Marysville, Ohio or a Canadian citizen who lives and works in Detroit. Whether these people are residents requires application of a complicated test.[1] The key point to remember is that foreign citizens who are not merely

---

[1]   See § 7701(b) for a definition of the "substantial presence test" that is used to determine if an individual is a resident alien and subject to U.S. tax.

visiting but stay for an extended period must worry about the need for filing.[2] As discussed below, the tax would be levied on both their U.S. income and any foreign income.

Foreign Taxpayers. Individuals who are not U.S. citizens and who do not qualify as residents may be subject to U.S. tax. These persons, referred to as *nonresident aliens*, are taxed on certain types of income that are received from U.S. sources.[3] If the income is derived from a trade or business carried on in the United States, that income is taxed in the same way as it is for a citizen or resident. Most other income earned in the United States is taxed at a flat rate of 30 percent. However, the United States generally does not tax interest income earned by nonresident aliens.

Age. It should be noted that the age of an individual is not a factor in determining if he or she is a taxpaying entity. Whether the individual is eight years old or eighty years old, he or she is still subject to tax on any taxable income he or she might receive. Contrary to the belief of some people, a child's income is taxed to the child and not the parent. As explained later, age may have an impact on *both* the method of computing the tax and the amount of tax owed; it does not, however, affect the individual's status as a taxpayer.

Sole Proprietorship. Another aspect of individual taxation requiring consideration is the taxation of sole proprietorships. For financial accounting purposes, the business activities of the proprietor are treated as distinct from other activities. The sole proprietorship is considered a separate accounting entity for which separate records and reports are maintained. For tax purposes, however, the sole proprietorship is not a separate entity subject to tax. The sole proprietorship does not file its own tax return. Rather, the income and deductions of the proprietorship are reported on the individual's personal income tax return along with any other tax items. In essence, the sole proprietorship serves as a conduit; that is, any income it has flows through to the individual.

> **Example 2.** K is employed as an accounting professor at State University, where she earns a salary of $42,000. K also operates a consulting practice as a sole proprietorship, which earned $10,000 during the year. The sole proprietorship does not file a separate return and pay tax. Instead, K reports the sole proprietorship's income along with her salary on her individual return (Form 1040) and pays the tax required. The operations of the sole proprietorship are reported on a special form, Schedule C, which accompanies Form 1040.

Worldwide Income. The Federal income tax on individuals applies not only to domestic (U.S.) source income, but also to income from foreign sources. It is therefore possible to have foreign source income taxed by more than one country (e.g., the foreign country and the United States). Several provisions exist to prevent or minimize double taxation, however. For example, U.S. citizens and residents living abroad may take either a direct reduction in U.S. tax (foreign tax credit)[4] or deduct such taxes.[5] In lieu of taking a credit or deduction for foreign taxes, any U.S. citizen who works abroad may exclude

---

[2] Reg. § 1.871-2(b).

[3] § 871.

[4] § 901.

[5] § 164(a).

from his or her U.S. income certain amounts of income earned abroad.[6] This exclusion is limited to $70,000 for any 12-month period. To qualify, the taxpayer (referred to as an *expatriate*) must either be a bona fide resident of a foreign country (or countries) or be physically present in a foreign country for 330 days in any 12 consecutive months.

> **Example 3.** Z, a U.S. citizen, is an aircraft mechanic who was temporarily assigned to a lucrative job in Seoul, South Korea. Z lived in Seoul all of 1994 except for two weeks when he came back to the United States to visit relatives. From his Korean job, he earned $90,000 in 1994. Because Z was present in the foreign country for 330 days during 12 consecutive months, he meets the physical presence test and may exclude $70,000 of his $90,000 salary. The remaining $20,000 plus any other income, such as dividends and interest, are subject to tax.

In addition to the relief measures mentioned above, tax treaties often exist that deal with the problem of double taxation by the United States and foreign countries.

CORPORATE TAXPAYERS

Section 11 of the Code imposes a tax on all corporations. The tax applies to both domestic corporations and foreign corporations with trades or businesses operated in the United States.[7] Although § 11 requires all corporations to pay tax, other provisions in the law specifically exempt certain types of corporations from taxation. For example, a corporation organized not for profit, but for religious, charitable, scientific, literary, educational, or certain other purposes generally is not taxable.[8] However, if a nonprofit organization conducts a business unrelated to the purpose for which its exemption was granted, any taxable income resulting from that business would be subject to tax.[9] In addition to the special provisions governing taxation of nonprofit corporations, the rules applying to S corporations vary from those applying to C or "regular" corporations as explained below.

The overall income tax treatment of corporations is quite similar to that of individuals. In fact, all of the basic rules governing income, exclusions, deductions, and credits apply to individuals as well as C corporations and, for that matter, fiduciaries. For example, the general rule concerning what is deductible, found in Code § 162, allows *all* taxpayers a deduction for trade or business expenses. Similarly, § 103 provides that *all* taxpayers are allowed to exclude interest income from state and local bonds. Although many of the general rules are the same for both individuals and corporations, there are several key differences.

The most obvious difference can be seen by comparing the corporate and individual formulas for determining taxable income as found in Exhibits 3-1 and 3-2. The concepts of adjusted gross income and itemized deductions common to the individual tax formula are conspicuously absent from the corporate formula. Other major differences in determining taxable income involve the treatment of particular items, such as dividend income and charitable contributions. These and other differences are discussed in detail

---

[6] § 911(a).

[7] § 882(a). See Chapter 19 for more details.

[8] § 501(a).

[9] § 501(b).

in Chapter 19. It should be emphasized once again, however, that most of the basic rules apply whether the taxpayer is a corporation or an individual.

One difference in the taxation of individuals and corporations that is not apparent from the basic formula, but which should be noted, concerns the tax rates that each uses in computing the tax liability (see the inside back cover of the text). A comparison of the individual and corporate tax rates shows a somewhat similar progression: 15 to 39.6 percent for individuals and 15 to 39 percent for corporations. But note that the rates apply at quite different levels of income.

Perhaps the most critical aspect of corporate taxation that is generally not shared with any other taxable entity concerns the potential for double taxation. When a corporation receives income and subsequently distributes that income as a dividend to its shareholders, the effect is to tax the income twice: once at the corporate level and again at the shareholder level. Double taxation can occur because the corporation is not allowed to deduct any dividend payments to its shareholders. As one might suspect, many have questioned the equity of this treatment, arguing that it penalizes those who elect to do business in the corporate form. Note, however, that this treatment is consistent with the fact that the corporation is considered a separate taxable entity. Moreover, it is often argued that the corporation and its owners in reality do not bear the burden of the corporate tax. According to the argument, corporations are able to shift the tax burden either to consumers by charging higher prices or to employees by paying lower wages. In addition, those who reject the double tax theory often note that closely held corporations, whose owners are also employees of the business, are able to avoid double taxation to the extent they can characterize any corporate distributions as deductible salary payments rather than nondeductible dividends. Whether in fact double taxation does or does not occur, it appears that this feature, which has been part of the U.S. tax system since its inception, is unlikely to change in the immediate future.

Special rules apply to the formation of a corporation, corporate dividend distributions, and distributions made to shareholders in exchange for their stock. Penalty taxes also may be assessed against corporations that try to shelter income from high personal tax rates by accumulating it in the corporation. These topics and others related to the income taxation of corporations and their owners are discussed in Chapter 19.

FIDUCIARY TAXPAYERS

A *fiduciary* is a person who is entrusted with property for the benefit of another, the *beneficiary*. The individual or entity that acts as a fiduciary is responsible for managing and administering the entrusted property, at all times faithfully performing the required duties with the utmost care and prudence.

Two types of fiduciary relationships are the trust and the estate. The trust is a legal entity created when the title of property is transferred by a person (the *grantor*) to the fiduciary (the *trustee*). The trustee is required to implement the instructions of the grantor as specified in the trust agreement. Typically, the property is held in trust for a minor or some other person until he or she reaches a certain age or until some specified event occurs.

An estate is also recognized as a legal entity, established by law when a person dies. Upon the person's death, his or her property generally passes to the estate, where it is administered by the fiduciary until it is distributed to the beneficiaries. Both trusts and estates are treated as taxpaying entities.

The Code specifically provides for a tax on the taxable income of estates and trusts.[10] Determining the tax for such entities is very similar to determining the tax for individuals, with one major exception.[11] When distributions are made to beneficiaries, the distributed income is generally taxed to the beneficiary rather than to the estate or trust.[12] In essence, the trust or estate is permitted to reduce its taxable income by the amount of the distribution—acting as a *conduit*, since the distributed income flows through to the beneficiaries.

> **Example 4.** T is the trustee of a trust established for the benefit of A and B. The trust generated $4,000 of income subject to tax for 1994 and no distributions were made to either A or B during the year. The trustee files an annual fiduciary tax return for 1994 and pays the tax based on the $4,000 taxable amount.

> **Example 5.** Assume that for 1995 the trust in *Example 4* had $10,000 of income subject to tax and that distributions of $2,000 each were made to A and B. The trustee files an annual trust return for 1995 and pays a tax based on $6,000 ($10,000 taxable income − $4,000 distribution). A and B each include $2,000 in their income tax returns for 1995.

Distributions made by a trust or estate from its corpus (also called the trust property or principal), including undistributed profits from prior years, generally are not taxable to the beneficiary.[13] This is because these distributions are part of a gift or inheritance or have been taxed previously. Similarly, the trust or estate is not entitled to deductions for these non-taxable distributions.[14]

PARTNERSHIPS

The partnership is a conduit for Federal income tax purposes. This means that the partnership itself is not subject to Federal income tax and that all items of partnership income, expense, gain, loss, or credit pass through to the partners and are given their tax effect at the partner level.[15] The partnership is required to file an information return reporting the results of the partnership's transactions and how those results are divided among the partners. Using this information, the partners each report their respective shares of the various items on their own tax returns.[16] Because a partner pays taxes on his or her share

---

[10] §§ 1(e) and 641(a).

[11] § 641(b).

[12] §§ 651 and 661.

[13] § 662.

[14] § 661. For further information on the income taxation of fiduciaries, see *Corporate,*

Partnership, Estate and Gift Taxation, 1995 Edition (Homewood: Richard D. Irwin, Inc.), Chapter 14.

[15] § 701.

[16] § 702(a).

of the partnership income, distributions made by the partnership to the partner generally are not taxable to the partner.[17]

> **Example 6.** For its calendar year 1994, EG Partnership had taxable income of $18,000. During the year, each of its two equal partners received cash distributions of $4,000. The partnership is not subject to tax, and each partner must include $9,000 in his annual income tax return, despite the fact that each partner actually received less than this amount in cash. The partnership must file an annual income tax return reporting the results of its operations and the effect of these operations on each partner.

A characteristic of a partnership (as well as an S corporation) that deserves special emphasis is the treatment of losses. If a business is typical, it will take several years of operation before it can be declared a profitable venture. Until that time, expenses normally exceed revenues and the result is a net loss. In the case of a conduit entity such as a partnership, that net loss flows through to the owners, who are generally allowed to offset it against any other income they may have. In contrast, if a regular C corporation sustains a loss, referred to as a net operating loss, or NOL, the shareholders do not benefit from that loss directly. A C corporation is allowed, like individuals, to use the loss to offset taxable income of prior or subsequent years. Generally, losses are carried back 3 years and forward 15 years. For example, the taxpayer would first carry back the loss to the third prior year and offset it against any taxable income. In such case, the taxpayer would file a claim for a tax refund. Any remaining loss is carried to the second prior year and then to the first prior year. Any remaining loss is carried forward for 15 years. The key point to remember is that the losses of a partnership flow through and thus may provide immediate benefit, whereas those of a C corporation do not flow through and can be used only if the corporation has income in other tax years.

In some respects, the partnership is treated as a separate entity for tax purposes. For example, many tax elections are made by the partnership,[18] and a partnership interest generally is treated as a single asset when sold.[19] In transactions between the partners and the partnership, the partners generally are treated like nonpartners.[20] However, an individual partner who performs services in his or her role as a partner is not an employee for tax purposes. As a result, the partner does not qualify for the favorable tax treatment of employee fringe benefits (see Chapter 6), and his or her share of any trade or business income is generally subject to self-employment taxes. These and other controlling provisions related to the Federal income tax treatment of partnerships are introduced in Chapter 19.

---

[17] § 731(a).

[18] § 703(b).

[19] § 741 states that the sale or exchange of an interest in a partnership shall generally be treated as the sale of a capital asset.

[20] § 707(a).

ELECTING SMALL BUSINESS CORPORATIONS: "S" CORPORATIONS

The Internal Revenue Code allows certain closely held corporations to elect to be treated as conduits (like partnerships) for Federal income tax purposes. The election is made pursuant to the rules contained in Subchapter S of the Code.[21] For this reason, such corporations are referred to as *S corporations*. Not all corporations are eligible to select S status. The only corporations that qualify are those that have 35 or fewer shareholders and meet certain other tests.

If a corporation elects S corporation status, it is taxed in virtually the same fashion as a partnership. Like a partnership, the S corporation's items of income, expense, gain, or loss pass through to the shareholders to be given their tax effect at the shareholder level. Salaries and wages of shareholders and other employees are reported on a Form W-2 and are subject to withholding of income taxes and FICA (that is matched by the employer-corporation). Although employees generally qualify for favorable treatment of fringe benefits, shareholder-employees owning 2 percent or more of the corporation's stock do not. As a result, the value of any fringe benefits, such as medical insurance coverage, is taxable to the employee-shareholder.

The S corporation files an information return similar to that of a partnership, reporting the results of the corporation's transactions and how those results are allocated among the shareholders. The individual shareholders report their respective shares of the various items on their own tax returns. Chapter 19 contains an introductory discussion of the taxation of S corporations and their shareholders.

LIMITED LIABILITY COMPANIES

As of this writing, 36 states have passed legislation creating a relatively new form of business entity: the limited liability company (LLC). What is this new creature and how is it taxed? Perhaps the best characterization of an LLC is that it is a cross between a partnership and a corporation. From a nontax perspective, an LLC is like a corporation in that *all* of the owners (or members, as they are usually called) enjoy limited liability. The tax law, however, does not specifically recognize an LLC. Instead, it looks at its characteristics to determine whether it more closely resembles a corporation or a partnership. Consequently, if the LLC is properly formed and does not take on too many corporate characteristics it will be taxed as a partnership. Alternatively, if an LLC does in fact look too much like a corporation, it will be taxed as a regular C corporation.

✔ CHECK YOUR KNOWLEDGE

Review Question 1.   Section 1 of the Internal Revenue Code imposes a tax on all individuals. If taken literally, this would mean that the United States taxes not only Bill Clinton but also Saddam Hussein and Boris Yeltsin. Are these foreign citizens subject to U.S. tax? Explain and also comment on how the North American Free Trade Agreement (NAFTA) might make the definition of "individual" more important.

---

[21]   §§ 1361 through 1379.

The U.S. income tax applies only to U.S. citizens and resident aliens. As a result, it would not apply to Hussein and Yeltsin since they are not citizens and do not live in the United States. But note that citizenship is generally irrelevant. The key question is whether the individual could be considered a resident. The passage of NAFTA may mean that more Canadian and Mexican citizens could be living and working in the United States. Under the general rules, they could be considered residents subject to U.S. tax unless a treaty provision provides special treatment.

Review Question 2. Macaulay Culkin of *Home Alone* fame has made millions of dollars from his movie appearances.

a. Must Macaulay file his own return and report the income, or do his parents simply include it on their return?

Although there are some special rules that can apply, parents normally do not report the income of their children on their return. A child is treated as a taxable entity, separate and distinct from his or her parents. Consequently, if a child's income exceeds the filing requirement threshold, he or she must usually file a return.

b. Do you think there could be any advantage derived from the fact that a child is a separate taxpayer?

Besides all of the other things that children are—both good and bad—they can also be mini tax shelters. Since they are separate taxpayers, they have their own set of tax rates and other tax characteristics. Therefore, to the extent that parents are able to shift income from the parents' high bracket to the child's low bracket (and still control the use of the income), taxes can be saved. These opportunities and some limitations that restrict such schemes are discussed more fully in Chapters 4 and 5.

Review Question 3. After all these years, Dick and Jane have decided to start their own business: the Sumo Bar and Grill. They have everything lined up but still have to decide what form the business should take. Originally, the couple did not even think about it. They planned to simply operate the business as a sole proprietorship.

a. If they do pursue this course, will they need to file a separate return for the business?

A sole proprietorship is not considered a separate taxable entity. Instead, all of the information related to the proprietorship is included on the individual's personal tax return. The results of operation are summarized on Schedule C. The net profit or loss is transferred from Schedule C to page 1 of Form 1040. In addition, since such income is also subject to self-employment tax, the net profit is also transferred to Schedule SE, where the special computation is made.

b. After Dick and Jane talked to their attorney, it was clear that they did not want to be a partnership or a sole proprietorship. Why?

Typically, individuals want to protect themselves from liability. While insurance may provide some protection, most individuals want the added safety of limited liability that only the corporate or LLC form offers.

c. At first Dick and Jane thought they would be a corporation. But according to their accountant, this new thing called an LLC allows business owners to achieve what he believes is tax nirvana. What is all the fuss about LLCs? Can you not get the same thing with S corporations? What do you think? How are LLCs taxed? What form of business organization seems best for Dick and Jane's business?

The beauty of an LLC is that the owners have limited liability yet the entity is taxed like a partnership. As a result, all of the income, as well as any loss, flows through to the partners. The significance of this treatment is twofold. First, if any loss occurs, it can be used to offset any other income Dick and Jane may have. If a C corporation is chosen, early losses do not provide any benefit until the business starts to make money. The NOL carryback feature for corporations is useless, because the business is brand new. Moreover, if it is like most businesses, Dick and Jane's will experience losses—at least until the clientele develop a love for Sumo wrestling. The second attraction of an LLC is the fact that its income avoids the double tax that can occur with C corporations. But why opt for an LLC? Is not this same treatment available with an S corporation? In this regard, the LLC is virtually identical to an S corporation, but there are many differences that some argue make the LLC more attractive. The only difference that can be gleaned from the discussion above is that an S corporation is limited to 35 shareholders while a partnership or LLC can have an unlimited number of partners. This may be irrelevant for Dick and Jane but could be extremely important for some businesses (e.g., a large public accounting firm). Another difference concerns the type of owner allowed. For example, an S corporation can generally have only individuals (and no nonresident aliens) as shareholders, but there are no restrictions on the type of partner or member that a partnership or an LLC can have. This too may be unimportant for Dick and Jane but there are still other considerations too technical to touch on here.

As a practical matter, prior to the advent of the LLC, most advisors would have suggested that Dick and Jane choose to be an S corporation. Since 1986 S corporations have generally been the most popular form of conducting business—at least when there were no more than 35 shareholders—because they were the only form of business that offered limited liability to all of its owners and a single level of tax. But the advent of the LLC changes all of this. In the next few years, it will be interesting to see if LLCs become more popular than S corporations. In any event, they provide yet one more option for the business owner to select.

TAX FORMULA

Computing an income tax liability is normally uncomplicated, requiring only a few simple mathematical calculations.[22] These steps, referred to as the tax formula, are shown in Exhibits 3-1 and 3-2. The tax formula is presented here in two forms: the simpler general formula that establishes the basic concepts as applicable to corporate taxpayers (Exhibit 3-1) and the more complex formula for individual taxpayers (Exhibit 3-2). The formulas in Exhibits 3-1 and 3-2 will be useful references while studying the various aspects of Federal income tax law in the subsequent chapters. To make such reference easier, both formulas are reproduced on the inside back cover of the text.

The tax formula for each type of entity is incorporated into the Federal income tax forms. Exhibit 3-1 may be compared with Form 1120 (the annual income tax return for corporations) and Exhibit 3-2 with Form 1040 (the return for individuals). These forms are included in Appendix B at the back of the text.

Examination of the two formulas reveals the importance of tax terms such as *gross income*, *deductions*, and *exemptions*. Each of these terms and countless others used in the tax law have very specific meanings. Indeed, as later chapters will show, taxpayers often have been involved in litigation solely to determine the definition of a particular term. For this reason, close attention must be given to the terminology used in taxation.

ANALYZING THE TAX FORMULA

Income. The tax computation begins with a determination of the taxpayer's total income, both taxable and nontaxable. As the formula in Exhibit 3-2 suggests, income is defined very broadly to include income from any source.[23] The list of typical income items in Exhibit 3-3 illustrates its comprehensive nature. A specific definition of income is developed in Chapter 5.

Exclusions. Although the starting point in calculating the tax is determining total income, not all of the income identified is taxable. Over the years, Congress has specifically exempted certain types of income from taxation, often in an attempt to accomplish some specific goal.[24] In tax terminology, income exempt from taxation and thus not included in a taxpayer's gross income is referred to as an "exclusion." Exhibit 3-4 shows a sample of the numerous items that can be excluded when determining gross income. Exclusions are discussed in detail in Chapter 6.

Gross Income. The amount of income remaining after the excludable items have been removed is termed *gross income*. When completing a tax return, gross income is usually the only income disclosed, because excluded income normally is not reported.

---

[22] §§ 1 and 63.

[23] § 61(a).

[24] See Chapter 6 for a discussion of the social and economic reasons for excluding certain items of income from taxation.

Exhibit 3-1   *Tax Formula for Corporate Taxpayers*

Income (from whatever source)...............................	$xxx,xxx
Less: Exclusions from gross income..........................	− xx,xxx
Gross Income...	$xxx,xxx
Less: Deductions.......................................	− xx,xxx
Taxable Income...	$xxx,xxx
Applicable tax rates......................................	xx%
Gross tax...	$ xx,xxx
Less: Tax credits and prepayments..........................	− x,xxx
Tax due (or refund).......................................	$ xx,xxx

Exhibit 3-2   *Tax Formula for Individual Taxpayers*

Total income (from whatever source)............		$xxx,xxx
Less: Exclusions from gross income...........		− xx,xxx
Gross Income....................................		$xxx,xxx
Less: Deductions *for* adjusted		
gross income.........................		− xx,xxx
Adjusted gross income.........................		$xxx,xxx
Less: 1. The larger of		
a. Standard deduction................	$x,xxx	
or	*or*	− x,xxx
b. Total itemized deductions..........	$x,xxx	
2. Number of personal and		
dependency exemptions ×		
exemption amount....................		− x,xxx
Taxable income..................................		$xxx,xxx
Applicable tax rates		
(from Tables or Schedules X, Y, or Z).........		xx%
Gross income tax...............................		$ xx,xxx
Plus: Additional taxes (e.g., self-employment		
taxes and recapture of tax credits)......		+ x,xxx
Less: Tax credits and prepayments............		− x,xxx
Tax due (or refund).............................		$ xx,xxx

Exhibit 3-3 *Partial List of Items Included in Gross Income*

Alimony and separate maintenance payments
Annuities
Awards
Bonuses
Commissions
Debts forgiven to debtor by a creditor
Dividends from corporations
Employee expense reimbursements
Fees and other compensation for personal services
Gains from illegal transactions
Gains from transactions in property
Gross profit from sales
Hobby income
Income from an interest in an estate or trust

Income from rental operations
Income in respect of a decedent
Interest
Pensions and other retirement benefits
Prizes and gambling or lottery winnings
Pro rata share of income of a partnership
Pro rata share of income of an S corporation
Punitive damages
Rewards
Royalties
Salaries and wages
Tips and gratuities
Trade or business income
Unemployment compensation

Exhibit 3-4 *Partial List of Exclusions from Gross Income*

Amounts received from employer-financed health and accident insurance to the extent of expenses
Amounts received from health, accident, and disability insurance financed by the taxpayer
Amounts received under qualified educational assistance plans
Certain death benefits from employers
Certain specified employee fringe benefits
Child support payments received
Contributions by employer to employer-financed accident and health insurance coverage
Dependent care assistance provided by employer
Gifts and inheritances
Group prepaid legal service plan benefits

Improvements by lessee to lessor's property
Interest on most state and local government debt
Meals and lodging furnished for the convenience of one's employer
Personal damage awards
Premiums paid by employer on group-term life insurance (for coverage up to $50,000)
Proceeds of life insurance paid on death
Proceeds of borrowing
Qualified transportation plan benefits
Scholarship and fellowship grants (but only for tuition, fees, books, and supplies)
Social security benefits (within limits)
Veteran's benefits
Welfare payments

Example 7.   E is divorced and has custody of her only child. E's income for the current year is from the following sources:

Salary...	$34,000
Alimony from former spouse.....................	12,000
Child support for child...........................	6,000
Interest from First Savings & Loan...............	1,200
Interest on U.S. Government Treasury Bonds.....	1,600
Interest on State of Texas Bonds.................	2,000
Total...	$56,800

Even though E's total income is $56,800, her gross income for tax purposes is only $48,800 because the child support and the interest income from the State of Texas are excluded. All the other items are included in gross income. Note that the interest from the Federal government is taxable, even though interest from state and local governments is generally excluded from gross income.

Deductions.   *Deductions* are those items that are subtracted from gross income to arrive at taxable income. The deductions normally allowed may be classified into two major groups:

1. *Business and Production-of-Income Expenses*—deductions for expenses related to carrying on a trade or business or some other income-producing activity, such as an investment[25]

2. *Personal Expenses*—deductions for certain expenses of an individual taxpayer which are primarily personal in nature such as charitable contributions and medical expenses[26]

Observe that the Code allows a deduction only for business or investment expenses. Personal expenses—other than a handful of special items—are not deductible. As someone once said, the Code's treatment of deductions is relatively simple: the costs of earning a living are deductible but the costs of living are not. The problem is determining into which category the expense falls.

A trade or business is an activity that is entered into for profit and involves significant taxpayer participation, either personally or through agents. It typically involves providing goods or services to customers, clients, or patients. If the activity qualifies as a trade or business, all the costs normally associated with operating a business are generally deductible. In most cases, it is easy to determine whether a taxpayer is engaged in a trade or business, but not always. For example, consider a taxpayer who travels around the world looking for antiques and incurs $10,000 of travel expenses but ultimately sells one item for $100. In this situation, the taxpayer might argue that he has a $9,900 loss from the activity that he should be able to offset against other income. On the other hand, it could easily be argued that the taxpayer was not really trying to make a profit. In such case, the IRS may deny the taxpayer's deduction. In these and similar situations,

---

[25]   §§ 162 and 212.   [26]   §§ 170 and 213.

the determination of whether the taxpayer is truly in a trade or business must be based on all the facts and circumstances.

Interestingly, the Code also takes the view that an individual who is employed is in the business of being an employee. This is an extremely important assumption since it enables employees to deduct their business expenses (e.g., professional dues, subscriptions, and similar costs). However, a number of special rules must be observed. For example, the Code allows an employee to deduct only 50 percent of the unreimbursed costs of meals and entertainment. Similarly, there are restrictions on the deduction of expenses for education, travel, transportation, moving, and home offices. Most of these special rules are discussed in detail in Chapter 8.

The rental of real estate is generally not considered to be a trade or business, unless the tenants are transient (i.e., stay for short periods of time, as in a hotel or motel) or there are extraordinary services provided to tenants. Nevertheless, the expenses are normally deductible as expenses related to an income-producing activity and are classified as deductions for adjusted gross income.

As one might suspect at this point, Congress is quite cautious in granting deductions. There are rules, rules, and more rules that try to ensure that only true business expenses are deductible. The tax law is particularly concerned about deduction of losses (i.e., the excess of deduction over revenues) from activities in which the taxpayer may have an interest. The problem became particularly acute in the 1970s and 1980s, when certain activities were designed primarily to generate tax losses (tax shelter limited partnerships and rental real estate were the biggest culprits). In an attempt to eliminate widespread abuse, Congress enacted the so-called *passive loss* rules in 1986. These highly complex rules generally limit the deduction of losses from activities, including rental real estate, in which the taxpayer is a mere investor and does not materially participate. The passive loss rules are covered in detail in Chapter 12.

Classifying Deductions.   A comparison of the general tax formulas used by corporations and by individuals reveals some differences in the treatment of deductions. For a corporate taxpayer, all deductions are subtracted directly from gross income to arrive at taxable income. In contrast, the individual formula divides deductions into two groups:[27] one group of deductions is allowed to reduce gross income, resulting in what is referred to as *adjusted gross income* (A.G.I.), while a second group is subtracted from A.G.I. As explained more fully below, the first group of deductions is generally composed of certain business expenses and other special items. The deductions in this group are referred to as deductions *for* adjusted gross income. The second group of expenses consists of two categories of allowable deductions: (1) deductions *from* adjusted gross income, and (2) deductions for personal and dependency exemptions. Deductions from adjusted gross income, normally referred to as *itemized deductions*, may be deducted only if they exceed a stipulated amount known as the *standard deduction* (e.g., $3,800 for single taxpayers in 1994). The deduction for any personal and dependency exemptions claimed (e.g., $2,450 per exemption in 1994) is deductible regardless of the amount of other deductions.

[27]   § 62.

Dividing deductions into two groups is done primarily for administrative convenience. Congress substantially reduced the number of individuals who claim itemized deductions because such deductions need to be reported only if they exceed the taxpayer's standard deduction. This reduction in the number of tax returns with itemized deductions significantly reduced the IRS audit procedures involving individual taxpayers. Since corporate taxpayers have only business deductions, no special grouping was needed and thus the term *adjusted gross income* does not exist in the corporate formula.

Adjusted Gross Income. The amount of an individual taxpayer's adjusted gross income (A.G.I.) serves two primary purposes. First, it is simply a point of reference used for classifying deductions: deductions are classified as either for or from A.G.I. Second, the calculation of the amount of several itemized deductions is made with reference to A.G.I. For example, medical expenses are deductible only if they exceed 7.5 percent of A.G.I., while personal casualty losses may be deducted only if they exceed 10 percent of A.G.I. In addition, recent changes in the tax law make A.G.I. even more important for some taxpayers. As explained below, most itemized deductions and the deduction for exemptions are reduced if adjusted gross income exceeds certain levels.

> **Example 8.** This year proved to be very difficult for T; his divorce became final, and shortly thereafter he became very sick. For the year, he earned $45,000 and paid $5,000 in alimony to his ex-wife and $10,000 for medical expenses that were not reimbursed by insurance. T's A.G.I. is $40,000 ($45,000 − $5,000) because alimony is a deduction for A.G.I. As computed below, T's medical expense deduction is limited to $7,000 because he is allowed to deduct only the amount that exceeds 7.5% of his A.G.I.

Medical expenses (unreimbursed)....		$10,000
Adjusted gross income..............	$40,000	
Times:.............................	× 7.5%	
Threshold..........................	$ 3,000	(3,000)
Deductible medical expenses........		$ 7,000

Deductions for Adjusted Gross Income. Code § 62 specifically lists the deductions allowable in arriving at A.G.I. This listing is a potpourri of items, as illustrated in Exhibit 3-5. They have been given various names besides deductions for A.G.I. For example, practitioners often refer to this category of deductions as being "above the line"—the line being A.G.I. Some commentators and authors label these as deductions from gross income. This text will use the "deduction for" terminology. Classification of a deduction as one for A.G.I. is significant for numerous reasons, as explained fully in Chapter 7. The most important of these reasons, however, is that unlike itemized deductions, deductions for A.G.I. need not exceed a minimum level before they are subtracted when computing taxable income.

Exhibit 3-5 *List of Deductions for Adjusted Gross Income*

Alimony and separate maintenance payments paid
Certain deductions of life tenants and income beneficiaries of property
Certain portion of lump-sum distributions from pension plans subject to the
    special averaging convention
Certain required repayments of supplemental unemployment compensation
    benefits
Contributions to pension, profit sharing, and other qualified retirement plans
    on behalf of a self-employed individual
Contributions to the retirement plan of an electing Subchapter S corporation
    on behalf of an employee/shareholder
Deductions attributable to property held for the production of rents and
    royalties
Individual retirement account contributions (within limits)
Losses from the sale or exchange of property
Moving expenses
One-half of any self-employment tax
Penalties for premature withdrawal of deposits from time savings accounts
Reforestation expenses
Reimbursed trade or business expenses of employees
Trade or business deductions of self-employed individuals (including
    unreimbursed expenses of qualified performing artists)

Itemized Deductions and the Standard Deduction.   Itemized deductions are all deductions other than the deductions for A.G.I. and the deduction for personal and dependency exemptions.[28] While deductions for A.G.I. are deductible without limitation, itemized deductions are deducted only if their total exceeds the taxpayer's *standard deduction*. For example, if T has total itemized deductions of $3,000 and his standard deduction amount is $3,800, he normally would claim the standard deduction in lieu of itemizing deductions. In contrast, if T's itemized deductions were $5,000, he would no doubt elect to itemize in order to maximize his deductions.

The standard deduction was introduced along with the concept of adjusted gross income and deductions *for* and *from* A.G.I. as part of the overall plan to eliminate the need for every taxpayer to list or itemize certain deductions on his or her return. As suggested above, by allowing the taxpayer to claim some standard amount of deductions in lieu of itemizing each one, the administrative problem of verifying the millions of deductions that otherwise would have been claimed has been eliminated. The standard deduction also simplifies return preparation in that most individuals no longer have to determine the amount of deductions to which they are entitled. For this reason, the amount of the standard deduction is theoretically set at a level that equals or exceeds the average person's expenditures for those items qualifying as deductions from A.G.I. Consequently, the great majority of taxpayers claim the standard deduction in lieu of itemizing deductions.

---

[28] § 63.

The amount of each taxpayer's standard deduction differs depending on his or her filing status.[29] The amounts for each filing status are adjusted annually for inflation. For 1993 and 1994, the amounts are as follows:

	Standard Deduction Amount	
Filing Status	1993	1994
Single...	$3,700	$3,800
Unmarried head of household....................	5,450	5,600
Married persons filing a joint return		
(and surviving spouse).........................	6,200	6,350
Married persons filing a separate return..........	3,100	3,175

Exhibit 3-6 contains a partial list of itemized deductions. The most common itemized deductions are those granted for a few personal expenses: medical expenses, state and local property and income taxes, casualty and theft losses, and interest expense related to a home mortgage and investments.

Miscellaneous Itemized Deductions. Itemized deductions are also allowed for a group of other expenses referred to as *miscellaneous itemized deductions*. Miscellaneous itemized deductions include the deductions for unreimbursed employee business expenses (e.g., dues to professional organizations, subscriptions to professional journals, travel), tax return preparation fees and related costs, and certain investment expenses (e.g., safety deposit box fees, investment advice). The classification of an expense as a miscellaneous itemized deduction is extremely important because a limitation is imposed on their deduction. Only the portion of miscellaneous itemized deductions exceeding 2 percent of adjusted gross income is deductible. Congress imposed this limitation in hopes of simplifying the law. The floor is intended to relieve taxpayers from the burden of recordkeeping (unless they expect to incur substantial expenditures) and relieve the IRS of the burden of auditing these expenditures.

---

[29] § 63(c) contains the standard deduction amounts for 1988. The amounts for subsequent years are adjusted for inflation and announced by the IRS annually. Filing status is discussed in Chapter 4.

Exhibit 3-6 *Partial List of Itemized Deductions*

Not Subject to 3 Percent Cutback Rule

Medical expenses (amount in excess of 7.5 percent of A.G.I.):
  Prescription drugs and insulin
  Medical insurance premiums
  Fees of doctors, dentists, nurses, hospitals, etc.
  Medical transportation
  Hearing aids, dentures, eyeglasses, etc.
Investment interest (to extent of investment income)
Casualty and theft losses (amount in excess of 10 percent of A.G.I.)
Wagering losses (to the extent of wagering income)

Subject to Cutback Rule

Certain state, local, and foreign taxes:
  State, local, and foreign income taxes
  State, local, and foreign real property taxes
  State and local personal property taxes
Mortgage interest on personal residences (limited)
Charitable contributions (not to exceed 50 percent of A.G.I.)
Miscellaneous itemized deductions (amount in excess of 2 percent of A.G.I.):
  Costs of preparation of tax returns
  Fees and expenses related to tax planning and advice
  Investment counseling and investment expenses
  Certain unreimbursed employee business expenses (including
    travel and transportation, professional dues, subscriptions,
    continuing education, union dues, and special work clothing)

Example 9. R, single, is employed as an architect for the firm of J&B Associates, where he earned $25,000. His itemized deductions for the year were interest on his home mortgage, $3,000; charitable contributions, $900; tax return preparation fee, $200; and professional dues, $400. R's total itemized deductions are computed as follows:

Miscellaneous itemized deductions:		
Tax return preparation fee........................	$200	
Professional dues................................	400	
Total miscellaneous itemized deductions...........	$600	
A.G.I. limitation (2% $\times$ $25,000)...................	(500)	
Total deductible miscellaneous itemized deductions..		$ 100
Other itemized deductions:		
Interest on home mortgage........................		3,000
Charitable contributions...........................		900
Total itemized deductions............................		$4,000

Because R's itemized deductions of $4,000 exceed the standard deduction for single persons, $3,800 (1994), he will deduct the entire $4,000. Note that only $100 of R's miscellaneous itemized deductions are deductible, whereas all his other itemized deductions are deductible.

Three Percent Cutback Rule. In search of more revenue, Congress imposed a new limitation on the amount of itemized deductions that high-income taxpayers may deduct in tax years after 1990. Today, taxpayers must reduce total itemized deductions otherwise allowable (*other than* medical expenses, casualty and theft losses, and investment interest) by 3 percent of their A.G.I. in excess of $111,800 ($55,900 for married individuals filing separately). However, this reduction cannot exceed 80 percent of the deductions. This 80 percent limit ensures that taxpayers subject to the cutback rule can deduct at least 20 percent of their so-called "3 percent" deductions. As a result, a taxpayer's itemized deductions are never completely phased out.

The 3 percent cutback rule is discussed in detail in Chapter 11.

Additional Standard Deduction for Elderly or Blind Taxpayers. Congress has traditionally extended some type of tax relief to the elderly and blind, presumably to take into account their special situations. Currently, an unmarried taxpayer who is either blind or age 65 at the close of the taxable year is allowed to increase his or her standard deduction by an additional $950 (for 1994). If an unmarried taxpayer is *both* blind and 65 or older, he or she is allowed to increase the standard deduction by $1,900. A married couple is allowed $750 (for 1994) for each status for a maximum increase on a joint return of $3,000.

> **Example 10.** In 1994, S celebrated her sixty-fifth birthday. Instead of using the $3,800 standard deduction amount allowed for single taxpayers for 1994, S will be allowed a standard deduction of $4,750 ($3,800 basic standard deduction + $950 additional standard deduction) for 1994.
>
> If S were married filing a joint return for 1994, the standard deduction amount allowed would be $7,100 ($6,350 + $750). If both S and her husband were 65 or older, the standard deduction would be $7,850 [$6,350 standard deduction + (2 × $750 additional standard deduction)].

Both age and blindness are determined at the close of the taxable year. Guidelines are provided for determining whether an individual is legally blind, and specific filing requirements must be met.[30] An individual is considered to have attained age 65 on the day *preceding* his or her sixty-fifth birthday.[31] Thus, if a taxpayer's sixty-fifth birthday is January 1, 1995, he or she is considered to be 65 on December 31, 1994.

---

[30] §§ 151(d) and 151(d)(3). A taxpayer is legally blind if he or she cannot see better than 20/200 in the better eye with corrective lenses, or the taxpayer's field of vision is not more than 20 degrees. A statement must be attached to the tax return for the year. The statement must be prepared by a physician or optometrist when a taxpayer is less than totally blind. Reg. § 1.151-1(d)(2).

[31] Reg. § 1.151-1(c)(2).

Limitations on Use of Standard Deductions. Not all individuals are entitled to the full benefit of the standard deduction. No standard deduction is allowed for the following individuals:

1. A married person filing a separate return if his or her spouse itemizes deductions;[32]

2. A nonresident alien;[33] and

3. An individual filing a return for a period of less than 12 months because of a change of accounting period.[34]

In addition, the standard deduction is limited for an individual who is claimed as a dependent on another taxpayer's return. This limitation is discussed in Chapter 4.

Exemptions. Congress has always recognized the need to insulate from tax a certain amount of income required by the taxpayer to support himself and others. For this reason, every individual taxpayer is entitled to a basic deduction for himself and his dependents. This deduction is called an exemption. For 1994, an individual taxpayer is entitled to a deduction of $2,450 for each *personal* and *dependency* exemption.[35] *Personal exemptions* are those allowed for the taxpayer. Generally, every taxpayer is entitled to claim a personal exemption for himself or herself. However, taxpayers *cannot* claim a personal exemption on their own return if they can be claimed as a dependent on another taxpayer's return.[36] If husband and wife file a joint return, they are treated as two taxpayers and are therefore entitled to claim two personal exemptions. *Dependency exemptions* may be claimed for qualifying individuals who are supported by the taxpayer.[37] In addition to the 3 percent cutback in itemized deductions, high-income taxpayers are required to reduce the amount of their total deduction for personal and dependency exemptions. All the special rules governing the deduction for exemptions are discussed in detail in Chapter 4.

Taxable Income and Tax Rates. After all deductions have been identified, they are subtracted from gross income to arrive at taxable income. Taxable income is the tax base to which the tax rates are applied to determine the taxpayer's gross tax liability (i.e., the tax liability before any credits or prepayments).

The tax rate schedule to be used in computing the tax varies, depending on the nature of the taxable entity. For example, one set of tax rates applies to all regular corporations (see inside back cover of text). In contrast, individuals use one of four tax rate schedules (see inside front cover) depending on their filing status, of which there are four. These are

1. Unmarried individuals (i.e., single) who are not surviving spouses or heads of households

2. Heads of household

---

[32] If one spouse elects to itemize deductions on a separate return, the other spouse *must* also itemize deductions. § 63(c)(6)(A).

[33] § 63(c)(6)(B).

[34] § 63(c)(6)(C).

[35] § 151(d)(1). For 1989, the exemption was $2,000. For years *after* 1989, the amount has been indexed for inflation.

[36] § 151(d)(2).

[37] § 152.

3.   Married individuals filing jointly and surviving spouses

4.   Married individuals filing separately

These tax rate structures are all graduated with the rates of 15, 28, 31, 36, and 39.6 percent. Although the rates in each schedule are identical, the degree of progressivity differs. For example, in 1994 the 31 percent marginal rate applies to single taxpayers when income exceeds $55,100, but this rate does not apply to married individuals filing jointly until income exceeds $91,850. The various filing statuses and rate schedules are discussed in Chapter 4.

Credits.   Unlike a deduction, which reduces income in arriving at taxable income, a credit is a direct reduction in tax liability. Normally, when the credit exceeds a person's total tax, the excess is not refunded—hence, these credits are referred to as *nonrefundable* credits. In some instances, however, the taxpayer is entitled to receive a payment for any excess credit. This type of credit is known as a *refundable* credit.

Credits have frequently been preferred by Congress and theoreticians because they affect all taxpayers equally. In contrast, the value of a deduction varies with the taxpayer's marginal tax rate. However, credits often have complicated rules and limitations. A partial list of tax credits is included in Exhibit 3-7, and most of these are discussed in detail in Chapter 13.

Prepayments.   Attempting to accelerate the collection of revenues for the war effort in 1943, Congress installed a "pay-as-you-go" system for certain taxes. Under this system, income taxes are paid in installments as the income is earned.

Prepayment, or advance payment, of the tax liability can be made in several ways. For individual taxpayers, the two most common forms of prepayment are Federal income taxes withheld from an employee's salaries and wages and quarterly estimated tax payments made by the taxpayer. Certain corporate taxpayers must make quarterly estimated tax payments as well. Quarterly estimated tax payments are required for taxpayers who have not prepaid a specified level of their anticipated Federal income tax in any other way, and there are penalties for failure to make adequate estimated prepayments.

Exhibit 3-7   *Partial List of Tax Credits*

Foreign tax credit
Earned income credit
Child and dependent care credit
Credit for the elderly
Credit for producing fuel from a nonconventional source
Credit for increasing research activities
Credit for employment of certain new employees
Low income housing credit
Credit for rehabilitating certain buildings

These prepayments serve two valuable purposes. As suggested above, prepayments allow the government to have earlier use of the tax proceeds. Secondly, prepayments reduce the uncertainty of collecting taxes since the government, by collecting at the source, gets the money before the taxpayer has a chance to put it to a different use. In effect, the government collects the tax while the taxpayer has the wherewithal (ability) to pay the tax.

Other Taxes. There are several types of other taxes that must be reported and paid with the regular Federal income tax. A partial list of these taxes is included in Exhibit 3-8. Two deserve special mention.

Self-employment Tax. As explained in Chapter 1, self-employed individuals as well as general partners in partnerships are, like employees, required to pay FICA taxes (commonly known as self-employment taxes). Since the tax is paid on income from sole proprietorship and partnership businesses carried on by individual partners, it is convenient for the IRS to collect this tax along with the income tax on Form 1040. The individual calculates the tax on Schedule SE and claims the income tax deduction for one-half of the self-employment tax paid on page 1 of Form 1040.

Alternative Minimum Tax. In 1969 there was an outcry by the media and others that the rich did not pay their fair share of taxes. Indeed, the House Ways and Means Committee Report indicated that in 1964 over 1,100 returns with adjusted gross incomes over $200,000 paid an average tax of 22 percent. Moreover, it reported that there were a significant number of cases where taxpayers with economic income of $1 million or more paid an effective tax amounting to less than 5 percent of their income. As might be expected, faced with such facts Congress decided to take action. However, instead of risking the wrath of their constituents by simply repealing the various loopholes that enabled these taxpayers to avoid taxes, Congress elected to take a politically cautious approach: a direct tax on the loopholes. In effect, the taxpayer simply added up all of the loopholes and paid a flat tax on them. As a result, the minimum tax was born. The whole thrust of this new tax was to ensure that all individuals paid a minimum tax on their income. It currently applies to all taxpayers, individuals, corporations, and fiduciaries.

Over the years, the minimum tax evolved into a monster and was adorned with its current name, the alternative minimum tax (AMT). Despite the changes and increased

---

Exhibit 3-8 *Partial List of Other Taxes*

Alternative minimum tax on corporations
Alternative minimum tax on individuals and fiduciaries
Self-employment tax
Social security tax on tip income not reported to employer
Tax on premature withdrawal from an Individual Retirement Account
Tax from recapture of investment credit
Uncollected employee F.I.C.A. and R.R.T.A. tax on tips

complexity, it remains basically the same. The mathematical steps for computing the AMT are relatively simple:

> Regular taxable income
> ± Adjustments and preferences
>
> Alternative minimum taxable income
> − Exemption
>
> Tax base
> × Rate
>
> Tentative alternative minimum tax
> − Regular tax
>
> Alternative minimum tax

As the formula above illustrates, the taxpayer starts with taxable income and then adds back certain income that is excluded for regular tax purposes and subtracts certain deductions that are normally allowed. These modifications to regular taxable income are referred to as *preference items* and *adjustments*. In this regard, it is important to recognize that the AMT effectively functions as an entirely separate system with its own rules. For example, while most interest from state and local bonds is not taxable, such interest is taxable for AMT purposes if the bonds are used to fund some private activity such as a downtown mall. Similarly, deductions that are usually allowed for regular tax purposes, such as exemptions, miscellaneous itemized deductions, and state and local taxes, are not allowed in computing the AMT. In effect, there are two rules for some items: one rule for regular tax purposes and another for AMT purposes. After taking into account all of the special adjustments required under this alternative system, the new result is called alternative minimum taxable income. This amount is then reduced by an allowable exemption ($45,000 for married taxpayers filing jointly; $30,000 for single and head of household taxpayers) to arrive at the the tax base. A two-tier rate structure is then applied (26% on the first $175,000 and 28% on the excess). The product is referred to as the tentative AMT. This amount is then compared to the regular tax, and the taxpayer pays the higher. Technically, the excess of the tentative AMT over the regular tax is the AMT, but the bottom line is that the taxpayer pays the higher.

Example 11. H and W are married with four children. This year they filed a joint return and reported regular taxable income of $100,000. Various adjustments required under the AMT were $55,000. The couple must pay an AMT of $5,296, computed as follows:

Regular taxable income.........................	$100,000
± Adjustments....................................	55,000
Alternative minimum taxable income.............	$155,000
− Exemption......................................	(45,000)
Tax base..	$110,000
× Rate...	× 26%
Tentative alternative minimum tax................	$ 28,600
− Regular tax....................................	(23,304)
Alternative minimum tax........................	$ 5,296

Note that the AMT is only $5,296, but the taxpayer must pay a total of $28,600 (regular tax of $23,304 + AMT of $5,296).

There is no good rule of thumb as to when the AMT is triggered. For the vast majority of taxpayers it is simply not an issue. These individuals are not subject to the tax since they have low to moderate taxable incomes with few adjustments, causing them to fall below the $30,000 or $45,000 exemption. It is typically high-income taxpayers who have substantial adjustments that fall prey to the tax. Obviously the key lies in the nature of the adjustments. For now it is sufficient to say that beyond the few mentioned above there are several more such as those relating to depreciation, depletion, and stock options. Full coverage is deferred until Chapter 13. Nevertheless, even at this early juncture it is important to recognize that the AMT exists and often alters what appears to be very favorable tax treatment. In effect, the AMT makes some tax benefits more apparent than real. As these items come up throughout the text, the implications for the AMT are duly noted.

✔ CHECK YOUR KNOWLEDGE

Review Question 1. It's time for "Tax Jeopardy." Here are the answers; supply the questions.

a.   The type of expenses taxpayers can deduct.

What are business expenses? Around tax time, there is a single question that can be heard reverberating across the land: What can I deduct? The answer is business expenses. All taxpayers are allowed to deduct the ordinary and necessary expenses incurred in carrying on a trade or business. The vast majority of all deductions fall into this category. Note also that this rule allows the deduction of employee business expenses. In addition, taxpayers are entitled to deduct expenses related to investment activities (e.g., investment advice or repairs and maintenance on rental property).

b. The type of expenses taxpayers cannot deduct.

What are personal expenses? Although business expenses are deductible, personal expenses normally are not deductible. For example, the costs of food, shelter, clothing, and personal hygiene cannot be deducted.

c. Five notable exceptions to the rule that personal expenses are not deductible. (Hint: they are all reported on Schedule A of Form 1040, found in Appendix B of this book.)

What are the following?

1. Medical expenses (but only if they exceed 7.5% of A.G.I.)
2. Taxes
    - State and local income taxes (but not federal)
    - Real estate taxes
    - Personal property taxes
3. Interest
    - Home mortgage interest
    - Investment interest (but only to the extent of investment income)
4. Charitable contributions
5. Casualty and theft losses

d. The name given by the IRS to deductions for A.G.I. (Hint: see page 1 of Form 1040 in Appendix B of this book.)

What are "adjustments to income"?

e. The only type of tax-exempt income reported on the return. (Hint: see page 1 of Form 1040.)

What is tax-exempt interest income (reported on line 8b of page 1 of Form 1040)?

f. Something the individual tax formula has that the corporate tax formula does not have.

What is adjusted gross income? What is the standard deduction? What are exemptions?

g. A benefit received by the elderly and blind.

What is the increased standard deduction for taxpayers who are age 65 or over or who are blind?

h. Deductions that are deductible regardless of their amount.

What are deductions for A.G.I.? If a taxpayer's itemized deductions do not exceed the standard deduction, the taxpayer receives no benefit from the itemized deductions.

i. A deduction that may be claimed by virtually all taxpayers.

What is the exemption deduction, or the standard deduction? As explained above, however, certain persons are not entitled to a standard deduction. For

example, married persons filing a separate return must itemize. In addition, as fully explained in Chapter 4, taxpayers cannot claim a personal exemption on their own return if they can be claimed as a dependent on another taxpayer's return.

j.   A loss from this activity may not be deductible.

What are losses from rental real estate and any other activity in which the taxpayer does not materially participate? Before losses from an activity can be deducted (e.g., a loss that passes through from a partnership or a loss from renting a duplex), they must run through the gauntlet of tests prescribed by the passive loss rules covered in Chapter 12.

k.   A tax on loopholes.

What is the alternative minimum tax?

Review Question 2.   Are deductions of a sole proprietor deductible *for* or *from* adjusted gross income? (Hint: see Adjustments to Income on Page 1 of Form 1040 and Schedule C in Appendix B of this book.)

The trade or business expenses of a sole proprietor or someone who is self-employed are deductible for A.G.I. Note that these are not shown as one of the adjustments to income on Page 1 of Form 1040. Instead, they are netted against the sole proprietor's income on Schedule C, and this net profit is included in the taxpayer's total income reported on Page 1 of Form 1040.

INTRODUCTION TO PROPERTY TRANSACTIONS

The tax provisions governing property transactions play a very important part in our tax system. Obviously, their major purpose is to provide for the tax treatment of transactions involving a sale, exchange, or other disposition of property. However, the basic rules covering property transactions can also impact the tax liability in other indirect ways. For example, the amount of the deduction granted for a charitable contribution of property may depend on what the tax result would have been had the property been sold rather than donated. As this example suggests, a basic knowledge of the tax treatment of property transactions is helpful in understanding other facets of taxation. For this reason, an overview of property transactions is presented here. Chapters 14, 15, 16, and 17 examine this subject in detail.

The tax consequences of any property transaction may be determined by answering the following three questions:

1.   What is the amount of gain or loss *realized*?

2.   How much of this gain or loss is *recognized*?

3.   What is the *character* of the gain or loss recognized?

Each of these questions is considered in the following sections.

Exhibit 3-9   *Computation of Amount Realized*

> Amount of money received (net of money paid)
> **Add:**   Fair market value of any other property received
> Liabilities discharged in the transaction (net of
> liabilities assumed)
> **Less:**   Selling costs
> Equals: **Amount realized**

GAIN OR LOSS REALIZED

A realized gain or loss results when a taxpayer sells, exchanges, or otherwise disposes of property. In the simple case where property is purchased for cash and later sold for cash, the gain or loss realized is the difference between the purchase price and the sale price, adjusted for transaction costs. The determination of the realized gain or loss is more complicated when property other than cash is received, when liabilities are involved, or when the property was not acquired by purchase. As a result, a more formal method for computing the gain or loss realized is used. The formulas for computing the gain or loss realized are shown in Exhibits 3-9, 3-10, and 3-11. As these exhibits illustrate, the gain or loss realized in a sale or other disposition is the difference between the *amount realized* and the *adjusted basis* in the property given up.

Amount Realized.   The amount realized is a measure of the economic value received for the property given up. It generally includes the amount of any money plus the fair market value of any other property received, reduced by any selling costs.[38] In determining the amount realized, consideration must also be given to any liabilities from which the taxpayer is relieved or which the taxpayer incurs. From an economic standpoint, when a taxpayer is relieved of debt, it is the same as if cash were received and used to pay off the debt. In contrast, when a taxpayer assumes a debt (or receives property that is subject to a debt), it is the same as if the taxpayer gave up cash. Consequently, when a sale or exchange involves the transfer of liabilities, the amount realized is increased for the net amount of any liabilities discharged or decreased for the net amount of any liabilities incurred.

Adjusted Basis.   The adjusted basis of property is similar to the concept of "book value" used for accounting purposes. It is the taxpayer's basis at the time of acquisition— usually cost—increased or decreased by certain required modifications.[39] The taxpayer's basis at the time of acquisition, or original basis, depends on how the property was acquired. For purchased property, the taxpayer's original basis is the property's cost. When property is acquired by gift, inheritance, or some form of tax-deferred exchange, special rules are applied in determining the original basis. Once the original basis is ascertained, it must be increased for any capital improvements and reduced by depreciation and other capital recoveries. The adjusted basis represents the amount of investment that can be recovered free of tax.

---

[38]   § 1001(b).   [39]   §§ 1011 through 1016.

Exhibit 3-10 *Determination of Adjusted Basis*

Basis at time of acquisition:
 For purchased property, use cost
 Special rules apply for the following methods of acquisition:
  Gift
  Bequest or inheritance
  Nontaxable transactions
Add: Capital improvements, additions
Less: Depreciation and other capital recoveries
Equals: **Adjusted basis in property**

Example 12. This year, L sold 100 shares of M Corporation stock for $41 per share for a total of $4,100. He received a settlement check of $4,000, net of the broker's sales commission of $100. L had purchased the shares several years ago for $12 per share for a total of $1,200. In addition, he paid a sales commission of $30. L's realized gain is $2,770, computed as follows:

Amount realized ($4,100 − $100).........	$4,000
Less: Adjusted basis ($1,200 + $30)......	− 1,230
Gain realized.............................	$2,770

Example 13. During the year, T sold his office building. As part of the sales agreement, T received $20,000 cash, and the buyer assumed the mortgage on the building of $180,000. T also paid a real estate brokerage commission of $7,000. T originally acquired the building for $300,000 in 1980, but since that time had deducted depreciation of $230,000 and had made permanent improvements of $10,000. T's gain realized is computed as follows:

Amount realized:		
Cash received......................	$ 20,000	
Liability assumed by buyer...........	+180, 000	
Selling expenses....................	−7, 000	
		$193,000
Less: Adjusted basis		
Original cost........................	$300,000	
Depreciation claimed................	−230, 000	
Capital improvements...............	+10, 000	
		−80, 000
Gain realized...........................		$113,000

Exhibit 3-11 *Computation of Gain or Loss Realized*

Amount realized from sale or other disposition
Less: Adjusted basis in property (other than money) given up
Equals: **Gain or loss realized**

GAIN OR LOSS RECOGNIZED

The gain or loss *realized* is a measure of the economic gain or loss that results from the ownership and sale or disposition of property. However, due to special provisions in the tax law, the gain or loss reported for tax purposes may be different from the realized gain or loss. The amount of gain or loss that affects the tax liability is called the *recognized* gain or loss.

Normally, all realized gains are recognized and included as part of the taxpayer's total income. In some instances, however, the gain recognition may be deferred or postponed until a subsequent transaction occurs.

> **Example 14.**   M exchanged some land in Oregon costing $10,000 for land in Florida valued at $50,000. Although M has realized gain of $40,000 ($50,000 − $10,000), assuming certain requirements are satisfied, this gain will not be recognized, but rather postponed. This rule was adopted because the taxpayer's economic position after the transaction is essentially unchanged. Moreover, the taxpayer has not received any cash or wherewithal with which she could pay any tax that might result.

Chapter 15 contains a discussion of the more common types of property transactions in which the recognition of an individual taxpayer's realized gains are postponed.

Any loss realized must be specifically allowed as a deduction before it is recognized. Individuals generally are allowed to deduct *three* types of losses. These are

1. Losses incurred in a trade or business (e.g., an uncollectible receivable)

2. Losses incurred in an activity engaged in for profit (e.g., sale of investment property such as stock at a loss)

3. Casualty and theft losses

Losses in the first two categories generally are deductions for adjusted gross income. Casualty and theft losses from property used in an individual's trade, business, or income-producing activity also are allowed as deductions for adjusted gross income. However, casualty and theft losses from personal use property are classified as itemized deductions and are deductible only to the extent they exceed $100 per casualty or theft and other specific limitations. Other than casualty and theft losses, all other losses from dispositions of personal use assets are *not* deductible. The rules governing the deductibility of losses in the first three categories are covered in Chapter 10. The special rules governing the deduction of "capital" losses are introduced below and covered in greater detail in Chapter 16.

CHARACTER OF THE GAIN OR LOSS

From 1913 through 1921, all includible income was taxed in the same manner. Since 1921, however, Congress has provided special tax treatment for "capital" gains or losses. As a result, in determining the tax consequences of a property transaction, consideration must be given to the character or nature of the gain or loss—that is, whether the gain or loss should be classified as a *capital* gain or loss or an *ordinary* gain or loss. Any *recognized* gain or loss must be characterized as either an ordinary or a capital gain or loss.

Capital Gains and Losses. Although capital gains and losses arise in numerous ways, they normally result from the sale or exchange of a *capital asset*. Any gain or loss due to the sale or exchange of a capital asset is considered a capital gain or loss.

Capital assets are defined in § 1221 of the Code as being anything *other* than the following:

1. Inventory, or other property held primarily for sale to customers in the ordinary course of a trade or business

2. Depreciable property or real property used in a trade or business of the taxpayer

3. Trade accounts or notes receivable

4. Certain copyrights, literary, musical, or artistic compositions, and letters or memoranda held by the person whose personal efforts created them, and certain specified other holders of these types of property

5. U.S. Government publications acquired other than by purchase at the price at which they are sold to the general public

The term *capital assets*, therefore, includes most passive investments (e.g., stocks and bonds) and most personal use assets of a taxpayer. However, property used in a trade or business is not a capital asset and is subject to special tax treatment, as discussed later in this chapter.

Holding Period. The exact treatment of the results of sales and exchanges of capital assets depends on how long the assets were held by the taxpayer. A long-term gain or loss is one resulting from the sale or disposition of an asset held for *more than one year*.[40] A short-term gain or loss occurs when an asset is held for *one year or less*.[41] The length of time that a property is held is called the *holding period*.[42] The distinction between long-term and short-term capital gains and losses is required as part of the netting process described below.

Combining Capital Gains and Losses: Netting Process. Generalization about the treatment of capital gains and losses is difficult because the actual treatment can be determined only after the various capital gains and losses for a taxable year are combined, or netted, to determine the net gain or loss during the year.

---

[40] § 1222(3) and (4).

[41] § 1222(1) and (3).

[42] § 1223.

The first step in the netting process is to classify the gains and losses as either short-term capital gains or losses (STCG or STCL) or long-term capital gains or losses (LTCG or LTCL). Short-term capital gains and losses are combined to arrive at a *net* short-term capital gain or loss (NSTCG or NSTCL). Similarly, long-term capital gains and losses are combined to arrive at a *net* long-term capital gain or loss (NLTCG or NLTCL). The final step in the netting process concerns the netting of NSTCG or NSTCL with NLTCL or NLTCG. There are six possible combinations of a taxpayer's capital gains and losses. These combinations and the results are summarized in Exhibit 3-12.

Exhibit 3-12   *Taxation of Individual Taxpayer's Capital Gains and Losses*

Netting Process	General Tax Treatment
Case 1. NSTCG[1] and NLTCG[2] cannot be combined	NSTCG is treated as ordinary income; NLTCG is taxed at a maximum of 28%
Case 2. NSTCG > NLTCL = Overall NSTCG[1]	Treated as ordinary income
Case 3. NLTCG > NSTCL = Overall NLTCG[2]	Taxed at a maximum of 28%
Case 4. NSTCL > NLTCG = Overall NSTCL	Deduct up to $3,000 from ordinary income; unused NSTCL carried forward until exhausted and treated as if incurred in year to which carried; the loss retains its character as NSTCL
Case 5. NLTCL > NSTCG = Overall NLTCL	Deduct up to $3,000 from ordinary income; unused NLTCL carried forward until exhausted and treated as if incurred in year to which carried; the loss retains its character as NLTCL
Case 6. NSTCL and NLTCL cannot be combined	Deduct NSTCL from ordinary income first, up to $3,000; if full $3,000 has not been offset by NSTCL, offset ($3,000 − NSTCL) by NLTCL; unused NSTCL and NLTCL carried forward until exhausted and treated as if incurred in year to which it is carried; NSTCL and NLTCL retain their character when carried forward

[1] The term *capital gain net income* is used by the Code to describe a NSTCG with no further netting allowed as well as the excess of a NSTCG over a NSTCL.
[2] The term *net capital gain* is used by the Code to describe a NLTCG with no further netting allowed as well as the excess of a NLTCG over a NSTCL.

Tax Treatment of Capital Gains. A special tax calculation ensures that an *individual* taxpayer's long-term capital gains are taxed at a maximum marginal tax rate of 28 percent instead of a higher rate that could otherwise apply. This calculation is covered in detail in Chapter 16. Note, however, that this special tax treatment is reserved solely for the taxpayer's long-term capital gains, or more precisely, the taxpayer's *net capital gain* [i.e., the excess of NLTCG over NSTCL (if any)]. In contrast, no special treatment is extended to a taxpayer's short-term capital gains [i.e., *capital gain net income*, the excess of NSTCG over NLTCL (if any)]. Net short-term capital gains receive the same treatment as ordinary income.

Example 15. Assuming taxpayers A and B realized the following capital gains and losses, netting would be performed as follows:

	Taxpayer A		Taxpayer B	
	Short-term	Long-term	Short-term	Long-term
STCG	$8,000		$14,000	
STCL	(3,000)		(9,000)	
LTCG		$1,000		$1,000
LTCG		5,000		
LTCL				(3,000)
NSTCG	$5,000		$ 5,000	
NSTCL				
NLTCG		$6,000		
NLTCL				($2,000)

Taxpayer A has both a NSTCG and a NLTCG, and no further netting of these transactions occurs. This is *Case 1* in Exhibit 3-12. A will combine her NSTCG with other income and receive no special treatment. A's NLTCG will be taxed at a maximum rate of 28%. In contrast, taxpayer B has a NSTCG of $5,000 and a NLTCL of $2,000, which are combined to yield an overall NSTCG of $3,000 (technically referred to as capital gain net income). This overall NSTCG receives no special treatment.

Tax Treatment of Capital Losses. When the result of an individual's capital asset transactions is a net capital loss (i.e., *Cases 4, 5,* and *6* in Exhibit 3-12), the loss is deductible up to an *annual limit* of $3,000.[43] The deductible capital loss is a deduction *for* adjusted gross income. Any losses in excess of the annual limit are carried forward for an indefinite period.

Example 16. In 1994 T has a net short-term capital loss of $2,000, a net long-term capital loss of $5,000, other includible income of $40,000, and no other deductions for adjusted gross income. In arriving at his $37,000 A.G.I., T is allowed to deduct only $3,000 of the $7,000 net capital loss. The remaining $4,000 net capital loss must be carried forward to future years.

---

[43] § 1211(b).

When an individual has both a net short-term and net long-term capital loss, the net short-term capital loss must be used first toward the $3,000 capital loss deduction limit.

> **Example 17.** Assume the same facts in *Example 16*. In arriving at his $3,000 capital loss deduction, R must use all $2,000 of the net short-term capital loss and only $1,000 of the net long-term capital loss. The remaining $4,000 net long-term capital loss may be carried forward to future years.

Details of capital gain and loss treatment and the capital loss carryover rules are discussed in Chapter 16.

Corporate Taxpayers. Although corporations net their capital gains and losses in the same manner as individuals, there are important differences in the tax treatment of the overall results. Corporate taxpayers receive no special treatment for long-term capital gains. Long-term capital gains of corporations are taxed in the same manner as other income. Corporations are also not allowed to deduct capital losses against ordinary income. A corporate taxpayer's capital losses can be used *only to offset* its capital gains.[44] Any excess losses are first *carried back* to the three preceding years and offset against any capital gains. Absent any capital gains in the three prior years, or if the loss carried back exceeds any capital gains, the excess may be *carried forward* for five years.[45] The rules related to the treatment of a corporate taxpayer's capital gains and losses are illustrated and further discussed in Chapter 19.

TRADE OR BUSINESS PROPERTY

Depreciable property and real property used in a trade or business are not capital assets, but are subject to several special provisions. Any depreciation of properties sold or exchanged may be subject to the depreciation recapture provisions if the property transaction results in a gain. Any other gains and any losses are netted under a separate netting process, and the net result generally is subject to favorable treatment.

Depreciation Recapture. Depreciation expense is generally allowable as a business or income-producing deduction that directly reduces taxable income and also reduces the basis in the property being depreciated. If the property is subsequently sold, a gain is increased or a loss is decreased because of this basis adjustment. If a gain were given preferential capital gain treatment, the taxpayer would benefit. In essence, he or she would have converted the ordinary deduction into long-term capital gain.

To prevent any such unintended benefit, all or part of depreciation related to real property and all depreciation related to other property used in a trade or business are subject to the depreciation recapture provisions. In effect, any gain on the sale of depreciable properties is ordinary income to the extent of all or a part of the depreciation deductions claimed on the property. This amount is referred to as the "depreciation recapture potential."[46] Any gain in excess of the depreciation recapture amount is generally subject to a special netting process under § 1231.

---

[44] § 1211(a).   [46] §§ 1245 and 1250.

[45] § 1212(a).

Section 1231 Gains and Losses. Section 1231 provides for an elaborate netting process of the results of certain casualties and thefts with the gains and losses from sales or exchanges of *§ 1231 assets*. Section 1231 assets generally include depreciable property and land used in a trade or business and held for more than one year. The results of such sales or exchanges are included in the netting process *only* after the application of the above recapture provisions.

If after the netting process is complete, a gain results, the *overall gain* generally is treated as a long-term capital gain. That gain is combined with other capital gains and losses for the year. In the case of an *overall loss*, the net loss is treated as an ordinary loss rather than a capital loss.

The special rules related to depreciation recapture and § 1231 gains and losses are examined in detail in Chapter 17.

✔ CHECK YOUR KNOWLEDGE

Try the following true-false questions.

Review Question 1. An individual always receives special treatment for his or her capital gains.

False for two reasons. An individual can receive special treatment only for long-term capital gains. Short-term capital gains are treated just like ordinary income. Second, if the taxpayer's tax bracket does not exceed 28 percent, there is no benefit since the favorable treatment for long-term capital gains simply limits the applicable tax rate to 28 percent. If income including the long-term capital gains puts the taxpayer in the 15 percent tax bracket, then the capital gain is taxed at a rate of 15 percent.

Review Question 2. J is interested in the stock market. This year she realized a $1,000 short-term capital gain and an $8,000 long-term capital loss. She will report a $1,000 short-term capital gain and carry over the $8,000 long-term capital loss.

False. She first nets the short-term gain of $1,000 against her $8,000 long-term loss, resulting in an overall long-term capital loss of $7,000. She may deduct $3,000 of this loss as a deduction for A.G.I. The remaining loss is carried over to the following year, where it will be treated as if she had realized a $4,000 long-term capital loss.

Review Question 3. K makes $300,000 a year and plays the stock market. So far this year she has realized a $3,000 long-term capital gain. It is now December 31. K should sell stock and recognize a $3,000 long-term capital loss.

Who knows! If she recognizes a $3,000 loss, the loss is offset against the gain and therefore reduces income that would have been taxed at a 28 percent rate. This would produce a tax benefit from the loss of only $840 ($3,000 × 28%). If she waits and uses the loss against ordinary income, it will produce a tax benefit of $1,188

(39.6% × $3,000), or $348 ($1,188 − $840) more. However, if she postpones the loss until some subsequent year hoping to use it to offset income taxed at a higher rate, she will lose the time value of the $840.

Review Question 4.   A corporation receives no special treatment for its long-term capital gains.

True. The capital gains of a corporation are treated in the same manner as ordinary income.

Review Question 5.   Since a corporation receives no special treatment for its capital gains, there is no need to distinguish them from ordinary income.

False. There are several reasons for making the distinction, but probably the most important concerns their relationship to capital losses. If a corporation suffers a capital loss, it can deduct such loss only to the extent of capital gains. Note that a corporation, unlike an individual, is not permitted to offset its capital losses against ordinary income. If there are insufficient capital gains to absorb the loss in the year the loss is realized, the loss is carried back three years and then forward five years. If no capital gains are found during this carryover period, the loss is lost.

Review Question 6.   John Doe is the typical American taxpayer. He is married, has a dog and two kids. He also owns two cars: a brand new Ford and a 1987 Chevrolet. He bought the Ford for $17,000 and the Chevy for $10,000. Both of the cars were used for personal purposes. This year John and his family moved to New York and decided they did not need the cars, so he sold them. He sold the Chevy for only $3,000. The story on the Ford was different. The Ford happened to be a Mustang convertible, and because Mustangs were in demand and were on back order, a car nut was willing to give him $19,000, a $2,000 premium for not having to wait. How will these sales affect John's taxable income? Explain whether the taxpayer has a gain or loss, its character, and in the case of a loss whether it is deductible for or from A.G.I.

John reports a capital gain of $2,000. The first step is to determine John's gain or loss *realized*. In this case, the determination is simple. On the sale of the Chevy, John realized a loss of $7,000 ($3,000 − $10,000), and on the sale of the Mustang he realized a gain of $2,000 ($19,000 − $17,000). The second step is to determine whether he *recognizes* the gain and loss realized. John must recognize the gain. As a general rule, all income is taxable unless the taxpayer can point to a specific provision that specifically exempts the income from tax. In this case, there is no exclusion. On the other hand, the $7,000 loss is not deductible. Although all income is normally taxable, only those items specifically authorized are deductible. Only three types of losses are deductible: (1) losses incurred in carrying on a trade or business; (2) losses incurred in an activity engaged in for profit (e.g., investment losses); and (3) casualty and theft losses. In this case, the loss on the sale of the Chevy is purely personal, and therefore no deduction is allowed. Thus John is not allowed to net the loss against the gain but must report only the gain of $2,000. While

this may seem like a surprising result, understand that tax is a one-way street: as a general rule, all income is taxable and only those expenses and losses specifically allowed are deductible. The final step is determining the character of the gain, that is, whether the gain is capital gain or ordinary income. In order for a taxpayer to have a capital gain, there must be a sale or exchange of a capital asset. The Code defines a capital asset as essentially everything but inventory and real or depreciable property used in a trade or business. In this case, the car is not used in business and it does not represent inventory, so it is a capital asset. As a result, John reports a capital gain of $2,000.

Review Question 7. Indicate whether the following assets are capital assets.

   a.   2,000 boxes of Frosted Flakes held by a grocery store

   b.   A crane used in the taxpayer's bungee-jumping business

   c.   A warehouse owned by Wal-Mart

   d.   IBM stock held for investment

   e.   The personal residence of Jane Doe

The Code generally defines a capital asset as essentially everything but inventory and real or depreciable property used in a trade or business. Based on this definition, the Frosted Flakes are not a capital asset since they are held as inventory by the grocery; the crane is not a capital asset since it is depreciable property used in a business; and the warehouse is not a capital asset since it is real property used in a business. The personal residence and IBM stock are both capital assets since they are neither inventory nor property used in a trade or business.

TAX PLANNING CONSIDERATIONS

CHOICE OF BUSINESS FORM

One of the major decisions confronting a business from a tax perspective concerns selecting the form in which it conducts its operations. A taxpayer could choose to operate a business as a sole proprietorship, a partnership, a limited liability company, an S corporation, or a regular C corporation. Each of these entities has its own tax characteristics that make it more or less suitable for a particular situation. The following discussion highlights a number of the basic factors that should be considered.

Perhaps the most important consideration in choosing a business form is the outlook for the business. A business that expects losses will typically opt for a business form different from the one that expects profits. A key advantage of a conduit entity (i.e., partnership or S corporation) applies in years in which a business suffers losses. Like income, losses flow through to the owners of the entity and generally can be used to offset other income at the individual level. In contrast, losses suffered by a regular C corporation are bottled up inside the corporate entity and can benefit only the corporation. Losses of a regular corporation generally are carried back 3 years and carried forward 15 years to offset income that the corporation has in prior or subsequent years.

A profitable business may also benefit from choosing the proper form of organization. To illustrate, consider a business that is generating taxable income of $1 million per year. If the taxpayer conducts the business as a sole proprietorship or through one of the conduit entities, the top tax rate applied to the income is 39.6 percent. In contrast, if a C corporation is used to operate the business, the top rate is 34 percent. Tax savings may also be generated at lower levels of income. This possibility can be seen in the tax rate schedules for corporations and individuals. A quick comparison reveals that the first $50,000 of income of a corporate taxpayer is taxed at a 15 percent rate, whereas married taxpayers receive the benefits of a 15 percent rate on a maximum of $38,000. Obviously, the tax-wise individual might try to structure the activities so that the best of both worlds could be obtained. Consider a business that produces income of $88,000. If a corporation is used, the company could pay a deductible salary of $38,000 to the owner, leaving $50,000 of taxable income in the corporation. By so doing, the maximum tax rate paid on the income would be 15 percent. Had the business been operated as a sole proprietorship or an S corporation, $50,000, the income in excess of $38,000, would have been taxed at a 28 percent rate, or 13 percentage points higher. This may seem appealing, but it is a very simplistic analysis and leaves vital elements out of the equation. For example, this scheme completely ignores the problem of double taxation; it assumes that the taxpayer will be able to withdraw the $50,000 left in the corporation at a later time in a deductible fashion so as to avoid the second tax. Unfortunately, doing so is not as easy as it may appear, and this plan as well as any other requires careful analysis. Suffice it to say here, however, that careful planning at the outset of a new business can save the taxpayer substantial taxes in the future.

A major disadvantage of partnerships and S corporations concerns the treatment of certain fringe benefits. As explained in Chapter 6, the Code contains a host of fringe benefits that generally are deductible by the employer and nontaxable to the employee. For example, a corporation is entitled to deduct the costs of group-term life insurance provided to an employee, and the benefit (i.e., the payment of the premiums) is not treated as taxable compensation to the employee but is tax-free. Note that if the employee purchases the insurance directly, it is purchased with compensation that has been previously taxed. As a result, the employee acquires the benefit with after-tax dollars. The favorable tax treatment of fringe benefits is generally available only to employees of a business. Unfortunately, partners and shareholders in S corporations who work in the business are not considered employees for this purpose and consequently cannot obtain many of the tax-favored fringe benefits. In contrast, shareholders in regular C corporations who work in the business are treated as employees and are therefore able to take advantage of the various benefits.

ITEMIZED DEDUCTIONS VS. STANDARD DEDUCTION

A typical complaint of many taxpayers is that they have insufficient deductions to itemize and therefore cannot benefit from any deductions they have in a particular year. Nevertheless, with a little planning, not all of those deductions will be wasted. Taxpayers in this situation should attempt to bunch all their itemized deductions into one year. By so doing, they may itemize one year and claim the standard deduction the next. By alternating each year, total deductions over the two-year period are increased. This could be accomplished simply by postponing or accelerating the payment of expenses. Cash basis taxpayers have this flexibility because they are entitled to deduct expenses when paid.

> **Example 18.**   Last year, X, a widow age 61, made the final payment on her home mortgage. As a result, she no longer has the interest deductions that in the past enabled her to itemize. In fact, the only deductible expenses she anticipates are property taxes on the house and charitable contributions to her church. However, these expenses together do not exceed the standard deduction as her estimates below show.
>
> | | 1994 | 1995 |
> |---|---|---|
> | Property taxes............... | $1,200 | $1,200 |
> | Charitable contributions...... | 2,000 | 2,000 |
> | Total........................ | $3,200 | $3,200 |

If the pattern above continues, X will not benefit from any of the itemized deductions since they do not exceed the standard deduction for single taxpayers, $3,800. In short, she would obtain a total of $7,600 ($3,800 × 2) of deductions over the two-year period. Note, however, what would happen if X simply shifted the payment of the charitable contributions from one year to the other by paying it either earlier or later. In such case, total itemized deductions in one year would be $5,200 and she could itemize, while in the other year she could claim the standard

deduction. As a result, she would obtain total deductions over the two-year period of $9,000 ($5,200 + $3,800), or $1,400 more than if she merely claimed the standard deduction.

EMPLOYEE BUSINESS EXPENSES

Most employee business expenses are typically paid by the employer, either through direct payment or reimbursement. As such, the expenses are deductible by the employer. In the case of reimbursements, the employee has equal amounts of income and deduction if the reimbursement equals the expense. The net effect on adjusted gross income is zero.

If an employer requires employees to incur some business expenses, the employee can claim them only to the extent he or she itemizes and has miscellaneous itemized deductions in excess of 2 percent of A.G.I. As a result, the employee may receive little or no tax benefit from the expenses.

In reviewing the employee's compensation package, employers might consider changing their reimbursement policies. If an employer adopts more generous reimbursement policies in lieu of compensation increases, the employees may benefit.

Example 19.   E is an employee with gross income of $20,000. She typically has annual employee business expenses of $750 that are not reimbursed. Since E does not itemize, she derives no tax benefit from the expenses.

If, instead of the above arrangement, E received a salary of $19,250 and the $750 were reimbursed, she would be in the same position before tax. However, she would pay $113 ($750 × 15 percent marginal tax on her salary) less in Federal income taxes.

PROBLEM MATERIALS

DISCUSSION QUESTIONS

3-1 *Taxable Entities.* List the classes of taxable entities under the Federal income tax. Identify at least one type of entity that is not subject to the tax.

3-2 *Double Taxation.* It has been stated that corporate earnings are subject to double taxation by the Federal government. Elaborate.

3-3 *Fiduciary.* In some regards, the fiduciary is a conduit for Federal income tax purposes. Explain.

3-4 *Partnership and S Corporation Returns.* The partnership and S corporation tax returns are often referred to as information returns only. Explain.

3-5 *Income from Partnerships.* Y is a general partner in the XYZ Partnership. For the current calendar year, Y's share of profits include his guaranteed compensation of $50,000 and his share of remaining profits, which is $22,000. What is the proper income tax and payroll tax (F.I.C.A. or self-employment tax) treatment of each of the following to Y for the current calendar year?

    a. The guaranteed compensation of $50,000
    b. The remaining income share of $22,000

3-6 *Income from S Corporations.* K is the president and chief executive officer of KL, Inc., an S corporation that is owned equally by individuals K and L. K receives a salary of $80,000, and her share of the net income, after deducting executive salaries, is $50,000. What is the proper income tax and payroll tax (F.I.C.A. or self-employment tax) treatment of each of the following to K for the current calendar year?

    a. The salary, assuming it is reasonable in amount
    b. The net income of $50,000 that passes through to K
    c. The $3,600 that the company paid for group employee medical insurance for K and her family

3-7 *Tax Formula.* Reproduce the tax formula for individual taxpayers in good form and briefly describe each of the components of the formula. Discuss the differences between the tax formula for individuals and that for corporations.

3-8 *Gross Income.* How is gross income defined in the Internal Revenue Code?

3-9 *Deductions.* Distinguish between deductions *for* and deductions *from* adjusted gross income.

3-10 *Standard Deduction.* What is the standard deduction? Explain its relationship to itemized deductions. Which taxpayers are entitled to additional standard deductions?

3-11 *Itemized Deductions.* List seven major categories of itemized deductions. How and when are these reduced? Is the standard deduction reduced? If so, under what circumstances?

3-12 *Employee Business Expenses.*   Expenses incurred that are directly related to one's activities as an employee are trade or business expenses. True or False?

3-13 *Additional Standard Deduction.*   H and W are married and are 74 and 76 years of age, respectively. Assuming they have gross income of $14,500 for 1994, determine their standard deduction and their personal exemption deductions.

3-14 *Exemptions.*   Differentiate between personal exemptions and dependency exemptions. Which taxpayers are denied a personal exemption?

3-15 *Credits.*   There are numerous credits that are allowed to reduce a taxpayer's Federal income tax liability. List at least four such credits.

3-16 *Credits.*   Credits of equal amount affect persons in different tax brackets equally, whereas deductions of equal amount are more beneficial to taxpayers in higher tax brackets. Explain.

3-17 *Prepayments.*   What is meant by the concept of "wherewithal to pay" for tax purposes? How do prepayments of an individual's income taxes in the form of withholding and quarterly estimates represent the application of this concept?

3-18 *Alternative Minimum Tax.*   What is the alternative minimum tax? Explain what is meant by *alternative* and *minimum* in this context.

3-19 *Amount Realized.*   What is meant by "the amount realized in a sale or other disposition?" How is the amount realized calculated?

3-20 *Adjusted Basis.*   Describe the concept of adjusted basis. How is the basis in purchased property determined?

3-21 *Gain or Loss Realized.*   Reproduce the formula for determining the gain or loss realized in a sale or other disposition of property.

3-22 *Gain or Loss Recognized.*   Differentiate between the terms "gain or loss realized" and "gain or loss recognized."

3-23 *Losses.*   Which losses are deductible by individual taxpayers?

3-24 *Capital Assets.*   Define the term "capital asset."

3-25 *Holding Period.*   The determination of the holding period is important in determining the treatment of capital gains and losses. What is the difference between a long-term holding period and a short-term holding period?

3-26 *Capital Gains.*   Describe the capital gain and loss netting process and identify the two results with *overall* capital gains. How are these gains treated?

3-27 *Capital Losses of Individuals.*   There are "limitations" on the capital loss deduction for individuals. Identify these limitations.

3-28 *Capital Losses of Corporations.*   What is the limitation on the deduction for excess capital losses of a corporate taxpayer?

3-29 *Carryover of Excess Capital Losses.*   Excess capital losses of individuals may be offset against gains for other years. Specify the carryover and/or carryback period for such excess losses. How do the carryover/back provisions differ for corporate taxpayers?

3-30 *Depreciation Recapture.*   What combination of events causes *depreciation recapture?* Why does the tax law require that part or all of depreciation recapture be treated as ordinary income?

3-31 *Section 1231 Assets.*   Generally, what assets are included in the classification "Section 1231 assets?"

3-32 *Section 1231 Netting Process.*   Give an overall description of the netting process for § 1231 gains and losses and describe the treatment of the net result.

YOU MAKE THE CALL

3-33 Shortly after Murray began working in the tax department of the public accounting firm of Dewey, Cheatham and Howe, he was preparing a tax return and discovered an error in last year's work papers. In computing the gain on the sale of the taxpayer's duplex, the preparer had failed to increase the amount realized by the $50,000 mortgage assumed by the buyer. Apparently, the mistake was overlooked during the review process. Upon discovering the mistake, Murray went to his immediate supervisor, Norm (who actually prepared last year's return), and pointed out the error. Norm, knowing that the client would probably flip if he found out he had to pay more tax, told Murray "let's just wait and see if the IRS catches it. Forget it for now." What should Murray do?

PROBLEMS

3-34 *To Whom Is Income Taxed?*   In each of the following separate cases, determine how much income is to be taxed to each of the taxpayers involved:

   a. Alpha Partnership is owned 60 percent by William and 40 percent by Patricia, who agree to share profits according to their ownership ratios. For the current year, Alpha earned $12,000 in ordinary income and made no cash distributions.

   b. Beta Trust is managed by Susan for the benefit of Gregory. The trust is required to distribute all income currently. For the current year, Beta Trust had net ordinary income of $5,500 and made cash distributions to Gregory of $7,000.

   c. Gamma Corporation earned net ordinary income of $24,000 during the current calendar year. The corporation is a regular U.S. corporation. Heather and Kristie each own 50 percent of the stock and received dividend distributions of $1,350 each during the year.

3-35 *Selecting a Form of Doing Business.*   Which form of business—sole proprietorship, partnership, S corporation, limited liability company, or regular corporation—is each of the following taxpayers likely to choose? An answer may include more than one business form.

   a. Edmund and Gloria are starting a new business that they expect to operate at a net loss for about five years. Both Edmund and Gloria expect to have substantial incomes during those years from other sources.

   b. Robin would like to incorporate her growing retail business for non-tax reasons. Because she needs all of the net profits to meet personal obligations, Robin would like to avoid the corporate "double tax" on dividends.

3-36 *Income from C Corporations.* M is the president and chief executive officer of MN, Inc., a corporation that is owned solely by M. During the current calendar year, MN, Inc. paid M a salary of $80,000, a bonus of $22,000, and dividends of $30,000. The corporation's gross income is $350,000, and its expenses excluding payments to M are $225,000.

   a. Compute the corporation's taxable income and determine its gross income tax.

   b. Assuming M's only other income is interest income of $12,500, determine M's adjusted gross income.

   c. Does this situation represent double taxation of corporate profits? Explain.

3-37 *Income from Partnerships.* J is a one-fourth partner in JKLM Partnership. The partnership had gross sales of $880,000, cost of sales of $540,000, and operating expenses excluding payments to partners of $145,000 for the current calendar year. Partners' compensation for services of $90,000 ($45,000 to J) were paid, and distributions of $120,000 ($30,000 to J) were made for the year.

   a. Determine the partnership's net income for tax reporting purposes.

   b. Determine the amount of income J must report from the partnership for the year.

   c. Determine how much of the income in (b) is self-employment income.

3-38 *Income from Fiduciaries.* G created a trust for the benefit of B to be managed by T. For the current year, the trust had gross income of $45,000, income-producing deductions of $1,900, and cash distributions to B of $12,500.

   a. Determine the taxable income of the trust.

   b. Assuming B's only other income is interest of $22,300, determine B's adjusted gross income.

3-39 *Tax Treatment of Various Entities.* Office Supplies Unlimited is a small office supply outlet. The results of its operations for the most recent year are summarized as follows:

Gross profit on sales............................	$95,000
Cash operating expenses.......................	43,000
Depreciation expense...........................	16,500
Compensation to owner(s)......................	20,000
Distribution of profit to owner(s)................	5,000

In each of the following situations, determine how much income is to be taxed to each of the taxpayers involved.

   a. The business is a sole proprietorship owned by T.

   b. The business is a partnership owned by R and S with an agreement to share all items equally. S is guaranteed a salary of $20,000 (see above).

   c. The business is a corporation owned equally by U and K. K is employed by the business and receives a salary of $20,000 (see above).

3-40 *Gross Income.*   The following represent some of the more important items of income for Federal tax purposes. For each, indicate whether it is fully includible in gross income, fully excludable from gross income, or partially includible and partially excludable.

a. Alimony received from a former spouse
b. Interest from State and local governments
c. Money and other property inherited from a relative
d. Social security benefits
e. Tips and gratuities
f. Proceeds of life insurance received upon the death of one's spouse

3-41 *Classifying Deductions.*   The following represent some of the more important deductions for Federal tax purposes. For each, indicate whether it is deductible for A.G.I. or as an itemized deduction.

a. Alimony paid to one's former spouse *A.G.I (Adjusted Gross Income)*
b. Charitable contributions *ITEMIZED*
c. Trade or business expenses of a self-employed person *A.G.I schedule C*
d. Expenses of providing an apartment to a tenant for rent *A.G.I*
e. Interest incurred to finance one's principal residence *ITEMIZED · Schedual A*
f. Reimbursed trade or business expenses of an employee *A.G.I*
g. Unreimbursed trade or business expenses of an employee *ITEMIZED*

3-42 *Determining Adjusted Gross Income and Taxable Income.*   Fred and Susan are married and file a joint income tax return. Neither is blind or age 65. They have two children whom they support, and the following income and deductions for 1994:

Gross income.................................	$40,000
Deductions for A.G.I...........................	1,200
Total itemized deductions......................	5,900
Credits and prepayments.......................	1,350

Determine Fred and Susan's adjusted gross income and taxable income for the calendar year 1994.

3-43 *Tax Formula.*   The following information is from the 1994 joint income tax return of Gregory and Stacy Jones, both of good sight and under 65 years of age.

Gross income.................................	$64,000
Adjusted gross income........................	55,350
Taxable income...............................	31,050
Number of personal exemptions................	2
Number of dependency exemptions.............	2

Determine the amount of the Jones' deductions for A.G.I. and the amount of their itemized deductions.

3-44   *Tax Formula.*   Complete the following table of independent cases for a single person with good eyesight and under age 65 in 1994:

	A	B	C
Gross income...................	$50,000	$65,000	$_____
Deductions for A.G.I............	_____	8,000	7,000
Adjusted gross income (A.G.I.)..	42,000	_____	68,000
Itemized deductions.............	7,500	3,000	_____
Standard deduction..............	_____	_____	_____
Exemptions......................	2	1	1
Taxable income..................	_____	_____	59,000

3-45   *Worldwide Income Subject to Tax.*   T, a U.S. citizen, has income that was earned outside the United States. The income was $20,000, and a tax of $2,000 was paid to the foreign government. Determine the general treatment of this income and the tax paid under the following circumstances:

a.   The tax paid was on income earned on foreign investments, and the U.S. tax attributable to this income is $2,800.

b.   Same as (a), except the U.S. tax attributable to this income is $1,800.

c.   Same as (a), except the income is from services rendered while absent from the United States for 13 successive months.

3-46   *Alternative Minimum Tax.*   L is single, has no dependents, and uses the cash method and the calendar year for tax purposes. The following information was derived from L's records for 1994:

Taxable income (regular income tax).............$22,000
AMT adjustments and preferences............... 21,000

Although L does have substantial gross income and deductions, she does not itemize. Calculate L's regular income tax and alternative minimum tax, if any.

3-47   *Asset Classification.*   For each of the assets in the list below, designate the appropriate category using the symbols given:

C – Capital asset
T – Trade or business asset (§ 1231)
O – Other (neither capital nor § 1231 asset)

a.   Personal residence
b.   Stock in Xerox Corporation
c.   Motor home used for vacations
d.   Groceries held for sale to customers
e.   Land held for investment
f.   Land and building held for use in auto repair business
g.   Trade accounts receivable of physician's office
h.   Silver coins held primarily for speculation

3-48 *Gain or Loss Realized.* During the current year, W disposed of a vacant lot which he had held for investment. W received cash of $12,000 for his equity in the lot. The lot was subject to a $32,000 mortgage that was assumed by the buyer. Assuming W's basis in the lot was $23,000, how much is his realized gain or loss?

3-49 *Adjusted Basis.* M owns a rental residence that she is considering selling, but she is interested in knowing her exact tax basis in the property. She originally paid $39,000 for the property. M has spent $8,000 on a new garage, $2,500 for a new outdoor patio deck, and $4,500 on repairs and maintenance. M has been allowed depreciation on the unit in the amount of $7,500. Based on this information, calculate M's basis in the rental residence.

3-50 *Gain or Loss Realized, Adjusted Basis.* S sold a rental house for $72,000. She received cash of $6,000 and a vacant lot worth $30,000. The buyer assumed the $36,000 mortgage loan outstanding against S's property. S had purchased the house for $52,000 four years earlier and had deducted depreciation of $12,000. How much are S's amount realized, her adjusted basis in the house sold, and her gain or loss realized in this transaction?

3-51 *Capital Gain and Loss Netting Process.* Individual D executed the following transactions during 1994:

Transaction	Sales Price	Adjusted Basis	Holding Period
Sale of 100 shares of XYZ..............	$2,000	$1,000	Long-term
Sale of land held for investment.........	9,000	3,000	Long-term
Sale of silver held for speculation........	5,000	7,000	Short-term
Sale of personal jewelry................	4,000	6,000	Long-term

Based on these transactions, calculate D's net capital gain or net capital loss for 1994.

3-52 *Excess Capital Loss.* T, an individual taxpayer, had a short-term capital gain of $4,000 and a long-term capital loss of $9,000 during 1994. How much is T's allowable capital loss deduction for 1994? What is the treatment of the short-term gain?

3-53 *Excess Capital Loss.* Individual R completed the following transactions during 1994:

Transaction	Sales Price	Adjusted Basis	Holding Period
Sale of 150 shares of LMK..............	$1,800	$2,400	Long-term
Sale of land held for investment.........	8,000	6,800	Long-term
Sale of gold held for speculation........	4,000	7,000	Short-term

Based on these transactions, calculate R's capital loss deduction, if any, for 1994.

3-54 *Individual's Tax Computation.* Richard Hartman, age 29, single with no dependents, received a salary of $24,000 in 1994. During the year, he received $700 interest income from a savings account and a $1,500 gift from his grandmother. At the advice of his father, Richard sold stock he had held as an investment for five years, for a $3,000 gain. He also sustained a loss of $1,000 from the sale of land held as an investment and owned for four months. Richard had itemized deductions of $1,300. For 1994 compute the following for Richard:

a. Gross income
b. Adjusted gross income
c. Taxable income
d. Income tax before credits and prepayments (use the appropriate 1994 tax rate schedule located on the inside front cover of this text)
e. Income tax savings that would result if Richard made a deductible $2,000 contribution to a qualified Individual Retirement Account

3-55 *Tax Treatment of Income From Entities.* The G family—Mr. G, Mrs. G, and G Jr.—owns interests in the following successful entities:

1. X Corporation is a calendar year regular corporation owned 60 percent by Mr. G and 15 percent by G Jr. During the year, it paid salaries to Mr. G of $80,000 to be its president and to G Jr. of $24,000 to be a plant supervisor. The company earned a net taxable income of $75,000, and paid dividends to Mr. G and G Jr. in the amounts of $42,000 and $10,500, respectively.
2. Mrs. G owned a 60 percent capital interest in a retail outlet, P Partnership. The partnership earned a net taxable income of $60,000 and made distributions during the year of $72,000. The profit and the distributions were allocated according to relative capital interests.
3. Mr. G and G Jr. each own 25 percent interest in H Corporation, an electing S Corporation. The corporation is a start-up venture and generated a net tax loss of $28,000 for the calendar year. No dividend distributions were made by H. Both Mr. G and G Jr. have bases in their H Corporation stock of $30,000.
4. G Jr. is the sole beneficiary of G Trust created by Mrs. G's father. The trust earned a net taxable income of $16,000 and made distributions of $4,500 to G Jr.

Determine the amount of income or loss from each entity that is to be reported by the following:

a. Mr. and Mrs. G on their joint calendar year tax return
b. G Jr. on his calendar year individual return
c. X Corporation
d. P Partnership
e. H Corporation
f. G Trust

3-56 *Comprehensive Taxable Income Computation.* Indy Smith, single, is an anthropology professor at State University. His tax records that he brought to you for preparation of his return revealed the following items.

Income

Salary from State University	$58,000
Part-time consulting	5,000
Dividend income	500
Reimbursement of travel to Denver by State University	200

Expenses

Interest on personal residence	$ 7,000
Travel expenses related to consulting	1,000
Tax return preparation fee	500
Safe deposit box to hold bonds	50
Travel and lodging to present academic paper in Denver related to his teaching position	450

In addition, Indy claims a dependency exemption for his father. Compute Indy's taxable income for calendar year 1994.

3-57 *Comprehensive Taxable Income Computation.* Eli and Lilly have been happily married for 30 years. Eli, 67, is a research chemist at Pharmaceuticals Inc. Lilly, 64, recently retired but stays busy managing the couple's investments, including a duplex. The majority of the couple's income is derived from Eli's employment, from which he received a salary of $90,000 this year. Other income includes dividends from stocks of $5,000 and interest on State of Illinois bonds of $1,000. In addition, rents collected from the duplex were $10,000 while rental expenses (e.g., maintenance, utilities, depreciation) were $6,000. Eli made a tax-deductible contribution of $2,000 to his individual retirement account. The couple also paid the following expenses: unreimbursed medical expenses, $7,000; interest on the home mortgage, $10,000; property taxes on the home, $3,000; charitable contributions, $4,000; and rental of safe deposit box, $100. Determine the couple's taxable income for 1994.

RESEARCH PROBLEM

3-58 *Using the Internal Revenue Code.* Locate a copy of the *Internal Revenue Code of 1986.* Read §§ 61 through 65, 67, 151, and 152. Read the titles of §§ 71 through 135, 161, and 162.

a. Describe how Congress defined "gross income."

b. Why is the "exemption deduction" properly called a deduction from adjusted gross income?

c. A taxpayer is self-employed and incurs an ordinary and necessary expense in his business endeavor. What is the authority for deducting the expense? Why is it considered a deduction *for* adjusted gross income?

d. A taxpayer pays alimony to her former husband. Within limits, it is deductible *for* adjusted gross income. Why?

Upon completion of this chapter you will be able to:

- Identify the various requirements that a taxpayer must meet in order to claim a personal or dependency exemption

- Explain the phase-out of the deduction for personal and dependency exemptions

- Apply the rules to determine the taxpayer's filing status

- Compute the tax liability of an individual taxpayer using the tax rate schedules and the tax tables

- Explain the special approach used in computing the tax liability of certain children

- Describe the filing requirements for individual taxpayers and the role of the statute of limitations as it applies to the filing of tax returns

- Explain when taxes must be paid and the penalties that apply for failure to pay on a timely basis

■ CHAPTER OUTLINE ■

Personal and Dependency Exemptions 4-1
  Personal Exemptions 4-2
  Dependency Exemptions 4-3
Filing Status 4-13
  Evolution of Filing Status 4-13
  Married Individuals 4-15
  Head of Household 4-16
Computation of Tax for Individual
  Taxpayers 4-21
  Tax Tables 4-21
  Tax Rate Schedules 4-23
  Special Tax Computation Rules 4-25

Determination of Net Tax Due
  or Refund 4-30
Filing Requirements 4-31
  Due Dates for Filing Returns 4-35
  Estimated Tax Payments 4-37
  Statute of Limitations 4-40
  Indexation and the Federal Income
    Tax 4-41
Appendix 4-45
  Tax Return Illustrations 4-45
  Problem Materials 4-55

Chapter **4**

PERSONAL AND DEPENDENCY EXEMPTIONS; FILING STATUS; DETERMINATION OF TAX FOR AN INDIVIDUAL; FILING REQUIREMENTS

As seen in Chapter 3, numerous factors must be considered in the determination of an individual's net tax liability. Beginning in this chapter and continuing through Chapter 18, a detailed examination of these factors is conducted. This chapter is devoted to four particular concerns of individual taxpayers:

1. Personal and dependency exemptions;

2. Filing status;

3. Calculation of the tax liability using the tax rate schedules and tax tables; and

4. Filing requirements.

PERSONAL AND DEPENDENCY EXEMPTIONS

Since the inception of the income tax, policymakers have recognized the need to protect from tax some minimum amount of income that could be used for the support of the taxpayer and those who depend on him. The device used to accomplish this objective is the deduction allowed for exemptions. There are two types of exemptions for which deductions are allowed: personal exemptions and dependency exemptions.[1] Taxpayers

---

[1] §§ 151(a), 151(b), and 151(c). For 1993, the deduction allowed for each personal and dependency exemption was $2,350.

may deduct the *exemption amount* for each of their exemptions. The exemption amount for 1994 is $2,450.[2] Each type of exemption is discussed below.

PERSONAL EXEMPTIONS

There are *two* types of personal exemptions:

1. Exemption for the taxpayer
2. Exemption for the taxpayer's spouse

Each individual taxpayer normally is entitled to one personal exemption. When a *joint return* is filed by a married couple, *two* personal exemptions may be claimed. This occurs not because one spouse is the dependent of the other, but because the husband and wife are each entitled to his or her own personal exemption. If a married individual files a *separate return*, however, a personal exemption may be claimed for his or her spouse only if the spouse has no gross income and is not claimed as a dependent of another taxpayer.[3]

Disallowance of Personal Exemption. A taxpayer is denied a personal exemption if he or she qualifies as a dependent of another taxpayer (see discussion below).[4] This rule prevents two taxpayers (e.g., a child and his or her parent) from benefiting from two exemptions for the same person.

> **Example 1.** J is 21 years of age and a full-time college student. J receives a partial scholarship and works part-time, but the majority of his support is received from his parents. Assuming J is eligible to be claimed as a dependent on his parents' return, he is not entitled to a personal exemption deduction on his own return. This rule applies *regardless* of whether J's parents actually claim an exemption for him.

---

[2] Since 1988 the exemption amount has been increased to reflect price level changes based on changes in the consumer price index. The exact amount is announced by the IRS in the fall of the preceding year. For instance, the exemption amount for 1995 will be announced by December 15, 1994. §§ 1(f) and 151(d)(3). If the exemption amount had been adjusted for inflation and real growth in income since 1948, when it was $600, it would be about $8,650 in 1993. See Steurle, "Decline in the Value of the Dependent Exemption," 62 *Tax Notes* 109 (October 4, 1993).

[3] § 151(b).

[4] § 151(d)(2).

DEPENDENCY EXEMPTIONS

As indicated above, an individual taxpayer also is entitled to an exemption for each person who is considered a *dependent*—generally one who depends on the taxpayer for his or her support. Technically, an individual qualifies as a dependent only if *all* five of the following requirements are satisfied.

1. *Support Test.* The taxpayer must provide more than 50 percent of the dependent's total support.

2. *Gross Income Test.* The dependent's gross income must be less than the exemption amount. An exception is provided for a child of the taxpayer who is under age 19 or a child of the taxpayer who is a full-time student *and* is under age 24.

3. *Relationship or Member of the Household Test.* The dependent must be a relative of the taxpayer or a member of the taxpayer's household.

4. *Joint Return Test.* The dependent must not have filed a joint return with his or her spouse.

5. *Citizenship or Residency Test.* The dependent must be a U.S. citizen, resident, or national, or a resident of Canada or Mexico.

In reporting dependency exemptions, the taxpayer must provide the Social Security number of every dependent who has reached the age of one as of the close of the taxable year. Failure to do so results in the imposition of a small penalty.[5]

Support Test. To satisfy the support requirement, the taxpayer must provide over half of the amount spent for the dependent's total support.[6] Total support includes not only amounts expended by others on behalf of the dependent but also any amounts spent by the dependent. Note that only the amount *actually spent* for support is relevant. Income and other funds available to the dependent for spending are ignored unless they are spent.

> **Example 2.** During the year, C paid $10,000 to maintain her father, F, in a nursing home that provides all of his needs. No other amounts were spent for his support. C made these payments, even though her father could afford them since he has cash in the bank and tax-exempt bonds valued at $200,000. Although F has funds available for providing his own support, they are not considered in applying the support test because the funds were not spent. Consequently, the support test is satisfied.

---

[5] Although some parents may be skeptical, the year that this requirement became effective the number of exemptions dropped 7 million below what had been expected, resulting in about $2.8 billion in additional tax revenue. Interestingly, over 48 percent of the drop was attributable to single taxpayers. See IRS Pub. 1500 (August 1991).

[6] § 152(a).

Exhibit 4-1   *Partial List of Support Items*

Automobile	Lodging
Care for a dependent's pet	Medical care
Charitable contributions by	Medical insurance premiums
or on behalf of dependent	Singing lessons
Child care	Telephone
Clothing	Television
Dental care	Toys
Education	Transportation
Entertainment	Utilities
Food	Vacations
Gifts	

Support is generally measured by the cost of the item to the individual providing it. However, when support is provided in a noncash form, such as the use of property or lodging, the amount of support is the fair market value or fair rental value.

What constitutes an item of support is not always clear. If, for example, a child receives a stereo or car, are these items considered support, or do only necessities qualify? The Regulations provide some guidance as to the nature of support, indicating that it includes food, shelter, clothing, medical and dental care, education, recreation, and transportation.[7] Support is not limited to these items, however. Examination of the numerous cases and rulings reveals a hodgepodge of qualifying expenditures as well as some that are not. For example, the costs for boats, life insurance, and lawn mowers are not considered support. Additionally, the value of any services performed for the dependent by the taxpayer is ignored.[8] Exhibit 4-1 presents a sampling of those items that constitute support.

The determination of support also is complicated by several items accorded special treatment. For example, scholarships and fellowships received by the taxpayer's child or step-child are not considered support items. Accordingly, such amounts are not treated as being provided by either the taxpayer or the dependent.[9]

---

[7] Reg. § 1.152-1(a)(2)(i).

[8] *Markarian v. Comm.*, 65-2 USTC ¶9699, 16 AFTR2d 5785, 352 F.2d 870 (CA-7, 1965).

[9] Reg. § 1.152-1(c). Note that G.I. Bill benefits are not treated as scholarships and therefore are included as support items provided by the recipient.

Example 3. J was the recipient of an athletic scholarship that covered 100% of her tuition, books, supplies, room, and board. In addition, J was paid a small cash allowance. J's parents also provided her with $2,000 cash to be used for clothing, entertainment, and miscellaneous expenses.

The scholarship package, which was related to J's continued scholastic activity, was valued at $5,500 per year. Nevertheless, assuming the other four tests are met, J's parents are entitled to a dependency exemption, since the scholarship is not included in her support.[10]

Although social security benefits generally are not taxable income to the recipient, they are considered as provided by the person covered by social security. Thus, social security benefits are included in determining support to the extent they are spent for support items.[11] State welfare payments are considered provided by the state, and therefore are not treated as provided by the parent or any other taxpayer. This is true even though the parent is entrusted to oversee the prudent expenditure of the funds.[12]

Example 4. F received support during the current year from various sources, including amounts contributed by his son, S. The amounts spent toward F's support were provided as follows:

F's social security benefits.................	$5,500
Taxable interest income....................	400
Amount provided by S.....................	2,100
Total.................	$8,000

S is not entitled to a dependency exemption for F because he did not provide more than 50% of F's total support ($2,100 is not greater than 50% of $8,000).

Example 5. This year M received social security benefits of $6,000, $3,500 of which was immediately deposited in a savings account. The amounts spent toward M's support were provided as follows:

M's social security benefits spent..........	$2,500
Taxable interest income....................	600
Amount provided by M's brother, B.........	4,000
Total.....	$7,100

Assuming the other tests are met, B is entitled to a dependency exemption for M since he provided more than one-half of her support expenditures ($4,000 is > 50% of $7,100).

---

[10] Any part of a scholarship providing benefits other than tuition, fees, and supplies, is *includible* in the recipient's gross income to the extent of those benefits. See Chapter 6 for a discussion of taxable scholarships.

[11] Reg. § 1.152-1(a)(2)(ii).

[12] See Rev. Rul. 71-468, 1971-2 C.B. 115 and *Helen Lutter*, 61 T.C. 685, *aff'd*. at 75-1 USTC ¶9439, 35 AFTR2d 75-1414, 514 F.2d 1095 (CA-7, 1975), *cert. den.*

In many instances, an individual who is not self-supporting is supported by more than one taxpayer. Generally, no dependency exemption is allowed for such persons; however, two exceptions exist. Exemptions may be allowed under multiple support agreements or to divorced or separated parents with respect to their children.

Multiple Support Agreements. A dependency exemption may be assigned to a taxpayer under a multiple support agreement if *all* of the following tests are met:[13]

1. No one person contributed over half the support of the individual.

2. Over half the support was provided by a group, all of whose members must be qualifying relatives of the individual.

3. The citizenship, joint return, and gross income requirements are met by the individual.

4. The dependency exemption is assigned by agreement to a group member *who contributed more* than 10 percent of the total support.

The assignment is effective only if each of the members contributing more than 10 percent signs a declaration to the effect that he or she will not claim the exemption. This declaration is made on Form 2120 (see Appendix B), which is then filed with the return of the taxpayer claiming the exemption.

> **Example 6.** M is single and received her support of $12,000 for 1994 from the following sources:
>
> | | Amount | Percentage |
> | --- | --- | --- |
> | Social security benefits | $ 4,000 | 33.33% |
> | Taxable interest income | 800 | 6.67 |
> | From D, M's daughter | 4,700 | 39.17 |
> | From S, M's son | 1,500 | 12.50 |
> | From G, M's grandchild | 1,000 | 8.33 |
> | | $12,000 | 100.00% |
>
> Together, D, S, and G contribute more than 50% of M's support for 1994 ($7,200 > 50% of $12,000). If a multiple support agreement is executed, either D or S may be allowed the exemption deduction. G is not eligible since he did not contribute more than 10% of the total support. Also, note that S may claim M as a dependent even though D provided more of M's support.

Children of Divorced or Separated Parents. Special rules apply to children of parents who are divorced or legally separated under a decree of divorce or separate maintenance, or are separated under a written separation agreement, or lived apart at all times during the last six months of the calendar year. If over half of a child's support is provided by one parent or collectively by both parents (including amounts contributed by the new spouse of a parent), and the child is in custody of one or both parents for more than

---

[13] § 152(c).

half of the year, the dependency exemption generally is allowed to the parent with custody for the greater portion of the year.[14] Thus, the custodial parent ordinarily receives the exemption regardless of the amount paid by either parent. Under certain conditions, however, the *noncustodial parent* may claim the exemption.

The noncustodial parent is entitled to the dependency exemption if the custodial parent signs a written declaration that he or she will not claim the exemption for the child, *and* the declaration is attached to the tax return of the noncustodial parent.[15]

> **Example 7.** R and S were divorced in early 1994. S has custody of their only child. R paid child support of $3,700 in 1994. Since S is the custodial parent, she is entitled to the dependency exemption. However, if S signs a statement granting the dependency exemption to R and he attaches the statement to his 1994 tax return, R is entitled to the dependency exemption for the child.

Gross Income Test. The second test that must be satisfied before an individual may be claimed as a dependent concerns his or her gross income. A dependency exemption generally is not allowed for a person whose gross income equals or exceeds the exemption amount ($2,450 for 1994).[16] In applying this test, the technical definition of "gross income" must be heeded.[17] It does not include items that are excluded from income. Accordingly, a person whose only sources of income are excluded from gross income (e.g., social security and municipal bond interest) may qualify as a dependent.

It also should be noted that gross income is not always synonymous with includible gross receipts. Regulation § 1.61-3 indicates that gross income for a merchandising business generally means the total sales less the cost of goods sold *plus* any income from investments or other sources. The importance of this distinction between gross receipts and gross income is demonstrated in the following example.

> **Example 8.** T provides 60% of the support for his single brothers, F and R, for the 1994 calendar year. F's sole source of income is from the sale of fireworks. During the year, he sold fireworks costing $4,000 for $5,500. R's sole source of income is derived from rental property. During the year, he collected rents of $3,200 while incurring expenses of $1,700 for repairs, maintenance, and interest. Although F and R each earned $1,500 (F: $5,500 − $4,000 = $1,500; R: $3,200 − $1,700 = $1,500), F's *gross income* was $1,500, whereas R's was $3,200. As a result, T can only claim an exemption for F, since F's gross income was less than the $2,450 exemption amount for 1994.

---

[14] §§ 152(e)(1) and 152(e)(5).

[15] § 152(e)(2). A special rule applies to agreements executed before 1985. See § 152(e)(4). Also, if the exemption was assigned under a multiple support agreement, *that* agreement controls. § 152(e)(3).

[16] § 151(c)(1)(A).

[17] See Chapters 5 and 6 for detailed discussion of "gross income."

Absent a special rule, the gross income limitation might cause a taxpayer to discourage his or her children from working, since even a modest income would cause the loss of the dependency exemption for the parent. Accordingly, Congress provided that the gross income limitation *does not apply* to a child of the taxpayer who has not attained age 19 during the year or a child of the taxpayer who is a full-time student *and* has not reached age 24.[18] *Child* means a natural or adopted child of the taxpayer. Foster children and children placed in the taxpayer's home by an authorized agency pending adoption by the taxpayer are also included.[19] *Student* means that the child was enrolled *full-time* during at least five calendar months of the year in a qualifying educational institution. A student satisfies the full-time condition if he or she is enrolled for the number of hours or courses that the school requires for a student to be considered in full-time attendance. School attendance only at night does not qualify. However, attendance at night as a part of a full-time program is acceptable.[20]

Relationship or Member of the Household Test. The third of the five hurdles that must be cleared before an individual can be claimed as a dependent concerns the individual's relationship to the taxpayer. Regardless of the amount of support that the taxpayer provides for another person, no exemption is allowed unless the prospective dependent is properly related to the taxpayer.[21] Apparently the authors of the dependency rules believed that the tax law should not grant an exemption unless there is some obligation on the part of the taxpayer to support an individual. Such an obligation normally exists between relatives or others who are members of the taxpayer's household. Therefore, to qualify as a dependent, an individual must satisfy one of nine qualifying relationship tests. All of these are *familial* (i.e., related by blood, marriage, or adoption) except one. These are:

1. A son or daughter (including an adopted child, a foster child who lives with the taxpayer the entire taxable year, or a child placed with the taxpayer by an authorized agency pending legal adoption by the taxpayer), or a descendant of either

2. A stepson or stepdaughter

3. A brother, sister, stepbrother, or stepsister

4. The father or mother, or an ancestor of either

5. A stepfather or stepmother

---

[18] § 151(c)(1)(B).

[19] Reg. § 1.151-3(a).

[20] Reg. § 1.151-3(b).

[21] § 152(a). Note: Recall that there is no dependency exemption for a spouse. The exemption for a spouse is the *personal* exemption.

6. A niece or nephew[22]

7. An aunt or uncle[23]

8. A son-in-law, daughter-in-law, father-in-law, mother-in-law, brother-in-law, or sister-in-law

9. Any person who lives in the taxpayer's home and is a member of the taxpayer's household for the entire *taxable* year. Even though such a person is not legally related to the taxpayer (i.e., a familial relative), he or she is treated the same as one who satisfies one of the legal relationships as long as he or she lives with the taxpayer the entire taxable year; for this purpose, temporary absences due to illness, school, vacation, business, or military service are ignored; in addition, a person cannot be claimed as a dependent if the relationship with the taxpayer violated local law (e.g., cohabitation).[24]

A relationship created by marriage does not cease upon divorce or the death of the spouse. Thus, for tax purposes, a divorce would not terminate an individual's relationship with his or her mother-in-law.[25] Additionally, if a dependent dies before the close of the tax year, the taxpayer may still claim a dependency exemption.

Example 9. This year F provided all the support for several individuals, none of whom had more than $2,450 of income. Each person and his or her status as a relative is shown below:

1. S, F's son, living in Los Angeles and attending UCLA. S is a relative; a son is a familial relative and such persons need not live in the home.

2. B, F's 29-year-old brother who moved in with F on November 1 after leaving the military. B is a relative; a brother is a familial relative and such persons need not live in the home.

3. C, F's 27-year-old cousin who moved in with F on October 1 after being unemployed for 10 months. C is not a relative; a cousin is not considered a familial relative and, therefore, qualifies only if he lives with the taxpayer the entire taxable year.

---

[22] A niece or nephew must be a daughter or son of a brother or sister of the taxpayer. § 152(a)(6).

[23] An aunt or uncle must be a sister or brother of the father or mother of the taxpayer. § 152(a)(7). For example, the person married to your mother's sister would be her brother-in-law, but he would not qualify as your uncle for purposes of this definition.

Technically, such a person would be your "uncle-in-law," a relationship not defined in Code § 152.

[24] § 152(b)(5).

[25] Reg. § 1.152-2(d).

4. BL, the brother of F's former wife. BL is a relative; BL is F's brother-in-law, a familial relative; such a relationship continues to exist whether F is divorced or his wife dies.

5. Z, a friend who has been living with F since December 1 of the prior year. Z is a "relative"; a person who lives with the taxpayer the *entire* taxable year qualifies as a relative even though such person is not related by blood or marriage.

Joint Return Test. The fourth of the five dependency tests looks to see if the prospective dependent is married. A taxpayer normally cannot claim an exemption for a married individual if such person files a joint return.[26] This rule appears to reflect a presumption that married taxpayers normally rely on themselves for support rather than others. Note, however, that if a joint return is filed solely for a refund (i.e., the tax is zero and all withholding is refunded), the return is ignored and the individual may be claimed as a dependent (assuming the other tests are met).[27] Also observe that the test is met as long as a joint return is *not* filed. If the married individual files a separate return, he or she may still be claimed as a dependent. In certain situations, parents of newlyweds and others may find it beneficial for their child to file a married, separate return.

> **Example 10.** B and C were married on December 21, 1994. B, a budding 25-year-old attorney, earned $38,000 for the year. C, age 23, is a full-time graduate student. Because C was fully supported by her parents, she was eligible to be claimed as a dependent on her parents' return. However, C's parents may not claim C as a dependent if B and C elect to file a joint return. The family must determine whether or not they are better off if: (1) B and C file a joint return and C claims her exemption on their joint return; or (2) B and C each file married filing separately and they relinquish C's exemption to her parents. A partial analysis would suggest the first alternative is far superior. If a joint return is filed, all of B's income would be taxed at 15% (see inside front cover of text for rates). Alternatively, the filing of separate returns would cause a substantial portion of B's taxable income to be taxed at 28%. In this case, it would appear that the additional tax caused by filing separate returns would more than offset any savings to be derived from shifting the exemption to C's parents.

> **Example 11.** D and E were married on December 28, 1994. During 1994 D, age 22, attended State University full-time. In addition, she worked part-time, earning $5,000 for the year. E, age 21, was also a full-time student, fully supported by his parents. In this case, E's parents are entitled to claim an exemption for E even if D and E elect to file a joint return. The joint return requirement would not be violated because the couple owes no tax (the couple's standard deduction eliminates their taxable income). Consequently, under the IRS view, they would be filing merely to obtain a refund of any withholding and not filing an actual return.

---

[26] § 151(c)(2).   [27] Rev. Rul. 54-567, 1954-2 C.B. 108.

Citizenship or Residency Test. A dependent must be a citizen or national (e.g., an American Samoan) of the United States or a resident of the United States, Canada, or Mexico. An adopted child of a citizen qualifies, even though not a resident, if he or she was a member of the taxpayer's household for the entire taxable year.[28]

Return Filed by a Dependent. The fact that a person files his or her own tax return does not bar another taxpayer (who otherwise meets all the necessary tests) from claiming him or her as a dependent. This is true as long as the dependent does not file a joint return for any reason other than to claim a refund of the entire amount of taxes withheld. Otherwise, the joint return test would not be met and the dependency exemption would be denied.

Phase-out of Personal and Dependency Exemptions. Since 1989 Congress has reduced the benefits that high-income taxpayers receive from their personal and dependency exemptions. Under § 151(d), taxpayers must reduce their deduction for personal and dependency exemptions by 2 percent for each $2,500 or fraction thereof ($1,250 for married persons filing separate returns) by which a taxpayer's A.G.I. exceeds the applicable threshold. These thresholds depend on the taxpayer's filing status, and the amounts are adjusted for inflation annually.

Filing Status	Threshold A.G.I.	
	1993	1994
Single individuals (not surviving spouse or head of household).........................	$108,450	$111,800
Married filing jointly or surviving spouse..........	162,700	167,700
Head of household...............................	135,600	139,750
Married filing separately.........................	81,350	83,850

The reduction in the exemption deduction may be computed as follows:

$$\frac{\text{A.G.I.} - \text{Threshold}}{\$2,500 \text{ (or } \$1,250)} = \frac{\text{Factor}}{\text{(round-up)}} \times \frac{2}{\text{percentage points}} = \frac{\text{Percentage}}{\text{reduction}}$$

Example 12. H and W are married with four children. They are entitled to claim six exemptions. In 1994 their A.G.I. is $208,700. The reduction in the couple's exemption deduction is computed as follows:

A.G.I.........................	$208,700
Threshold....................	− 167,700
Excess......................	$ 41,000

$$\frac{\$41,000}{\$2,500} = 16.4, \text{ rounded to } 17 \times 2 = 34\%$$

H and W are required to reduce their exemption deduction by 34%. Assuming the total exemption deduction is $14,700 ($2,450 × 6), the deduction is reduced by $4,998 (34% × $14,700) to $9,702 ($14,700 − $4,998). In effect, the couple receives only 66% of their normal exemption deduction.

---

[28] § 152(b)(3).

Note that the exemption deduction is completely eliminated if A.G.I. exceeds the threshold by more than $122,500. For example, if a married couple's A.G.I. exceeds $290,200, their total deduction for exemptions would be eliminated [($290,201 − $167,700 = $122,501) ÷ $2,500 = 49.004, rounded up to 50 × 2 = 100% reduction].

✔ CHECK YOUR KNOWLEDGE

Try these 10 true-false questions concerning exemptions. If the statement is false, explain why.

Review Question 1.   All individuals are entitled to claim a personal exemption.

False. An individual who may be claimed as a dependent on another taxpayer's return cannot claim a personal exemption. This prohibits taxpayers from claiming two exemptions for the same person.

Review Question 2.   Certain people that are normally considered relatives (e.g., cousins) do not qualify as relatives for purposes of the exemption tests.

True. A cousin is not a familial relative.

Review Question 3.   An individual, such as a cousin, can qualify as a "relative" even though he or she is not a familial relative.

True. An individual who lives in the taxpayer's home the entire taxable year is treated as a relative even though such person and the taxpayer would not be "related" under the statutory definition.

Review Question 4.   T takes care of his mom. He satisfies the support test if he provides more than 10 percent of her total support.

False. A taxpayer must generally provide more than 50 percent of an individual's support in order to claim the individual as a dependent. However, an individual who provides more than 10 percent of a person's support may be able to claim a dependency exemption under a multiple support agreement.

Review Question 5.   In determining whether T provides more than 50 percent of his mom's support, her savings of over $100,000 are not counted except to the extent they are actually spent.

True. Funds available for an individual's support are ignored in applying the support test. Only amounts spent (or the value of support items provided, such as lodging) are considered.

Review Question 6.   T received a scholarship to attend Harvard worth over $15,000. Such amount is ignored in determining whether her parents provided more than one-half of her support.

True.

Review Question 7.   T's mom has no income other than social security benefits of $5,000 and interest from City of Duluth bonds of $6,000. T may claim an exemption for her mom.

True. A dependency exemption normally cannot be claimed for an individual if such person's gross income exceeds the exemption amount. For this purpose, gross income includes only income that is subject to tax. In this case, T's mom's income from social security is excluded as is the interest from the municipal bonds.

Review Question 8.   T's 14-year-old son earned $5,000 from his paper route this year. T may not claim an exemption for his son.

False. As a general rule, an individual cannot be claimed as a dependent if he or she has gross income for the year that exceeds the personal exemption amount, $2,450 for 1994. However, the gross income test does not apply to a child of the taxpayer who has not reached the age of 19 or who is a full-time student and has not reached the age of 24.

Review Question 9.   In the case of a divorced couple with children, the custodial parent normally receives the exemption for the children even if the noncustodial parent provides all of the child support.

True. The custodial parent is entitled to the exemption unless he or she assigns it to the noncustodial parent.

Review Question 10.   T and his wife's only income for the year was from T's salary of $200,000. A contribution to an individual retirement account will reduce the amount that he may deduct for personal and dependent exemptions.

False. Because of their high income, T and his wife must reduce their exemption deduction based on the amount that their A.G.I exceeds the applicable threshold, $167,700 in 1994 for a married taxpayer filing a joint return. Since the contribution is deducted for adjusted gross income and therefore reduces his A.G.I., the exemption phase-out is also reduced.

FILING STATUS

EVOLUTION OF FILING STATUS

The tax rates that are applied to determine the taxpayer's tax liability depend on the taxpayer's filing status. From 1913 to 1948, there was only one set of tax rates that applied to individual taxpayers. During this period, each taxpayer filed a separate return, even if he or she were married. For example, if both a husband and wife had income, each would file a separate return, reporting their respective incomes. This system, however, proved inequitable due to the differing state laws governing the ownership of income (or property).

In the United States, the rights that married individuals hold in property are determined using either the common law or community property system. There are nine community property states: Arizona, California, Idaho, Louisiana, Nevada, New Mexico, Texas, Washington, and Wisconsin. In a community property state, income generated through the personal efforts of either spouse is generally owned *equally* by the community (i.e., the husband and wife). In common law states, income belongs to the spouse that earns the income. The differing treatments of income by community property and common law states produced the need for a special rate schedule for married taxpayers.

Married Status.   The category of married couples filing jointly and its unique rate schedule were added to the law because of an inequity that existed between married couples in community property states and non–community property jurisdictions (separate or common law property states). As noted above, earnings derived from personal services performed by married persons in community property states generally are owned jointly by the two spouses. Accordingly, both husband and wife in a community property state would file returns showing one-half of their earned income, even though only one may have been employed. Note that the total income of the couple would be split equally between the husband and wife regardless of who earned the income. If a couple in a non–community property state relied on one spouse's earnings, the employed spouse filed a return showing the entire amount of those earnings.

Since the tax rates are progressive, a married couple in a non–community property state would bear a larger tax burden than one in a community property state if only one spouse was employed outside the home or one spouse earned substantially more than the other. To eliminate this inequity, Congress elected to grant the benefits of income splitting to all married couples. This was accomplished by authorizing a new tax schedule for married persons filing jointly. A joint return results in the same amount of tax as would be paid on two "married, filing separate" returns showing half the total income of a married couple.

> **Example 13.**   L and M are married and reside in California with their two children. L is an executive with a major corporation and M works in the home. Under state law, L's salary of $70,000 is owned equally by L and M. Each may file a separate return and report $35,000 of the salary.

> **Example 14.**   S and T are married and reside in Virginia with their two children. S is an executive with a major corporation and T works in the home. If S were to file a separate return, she would report the entire $70,000 salary on that return. Since the tax rate schedules for individuals are progressive, S would pay a higher tax than the total paid by L and M in *Example 13*. Consequently, the total tax burden on S and T would be greater than that on L and M. By filing a joint return, S and T are placed in a position equivalent to that of L and M.

Head-of-Household Status.   Introduction of the joint return in 1948 was not viewed by the public as merely a solution to a problem caused by differing state laws. Many saw it as a tax break for those who had family obligations. As a result, single parents and other unmarried taxpayers with dependents tried to persuade Congress that they should be entitled to some tax relief due to their family responsibilities. Their arguments were based on the fact that they suffered a greater tax burden than single-earner married

couples. In 1957, a tax reduction was allowed in the form of a new tax rate schedule for taxpayers who qualify as a *head of household*. The rates were designed to be lower than the original rates, which applied to all taxpayers, but *higher* than the rates for married persons filing jointly.

Single Status. The most recent change in the overall tax rate structure was the addition of a separate tax rate schedule for single persons. This change was made because a single person was paying a higher rate of tax on the same income than married persons filing jointly and heads of households. The reduced rates for single taxpayers still are higher than those for a head of household, but lower than those in the original rate structure. As a result of this final change, the original tax rate structure that once applied to all taxpayers now applies only to married persons filing separately.

Summary. The Federal income tax on individuals is based on four tax rate schedules. Taxpayers must file under one of the following classifications, listed in order from lowest to highest in tax rates:

1. Married filing jointly (including surviving spouses)

2. Head of household

3. Single

4. Married filing separately

The 1994 tax rate schedules for these classifications are reproduced on the inside front cover of this text.[29]

MARRIED INDIVIDUALS

Marital status is determined on the last day of an individual's taxable year. A person is married for tax purposes if he or she is married under state law, regardless of whether he or she is separated or in the process of seeking a divorce.[30]

Joint Return. A husband and wife generally may file a return using the rates for married persons filing jointly.[31] If a joint return is filed, husband and wife are jointly and severally (individually) liable for any tax, including any later assessments of tax, related to *that* joint return. As a result, one spouse may be held liable for paying the entire tax, even though the other spouse earned all the income. For this reason, a spouse should be cautious in signing a joint return. However, under the *innocent spouse rule*, a spouse will not be held liable for tax and penalties attributable to misstatements by the other spouse if the assessment is large relative to his or her financial situation, he or she did not know of the misstatements in the return, and he or she did not have reason to know of it.[32]

---

[29] The 1994 tax tables had not been issued by the IRS at the date of publication of this text. However, the 1993 tax tables are reproduced in Appendix A.

[30] Special rules apply to a taxpayer whose spouse dies during the year. See §§ 7703(a)(1) and 6013(a)(2).

[31] § 6013(a). However, a special rule applies if the spouse is a nonresident alien. See § 6013(g). Also, both spouses must have the *same* taxable year.

[32] § 6013(e). Generally, the understatement of tax must exceed $500 and certain other tests must be met.

Surviving Spouse.   Certain widows and widowers may use the tax rates for married persons filing jointly. In order to use these lower rates, the person must qualify as a *surviving spouse*. There are two requirements. First, the spouse must have died within the two taxable years preceding the current taxable year. Second, the taxpayer must provide over half the cost of maintaining a home in which he or she and a *dependent* son, stepson, daughter, or stepdaughter live.[33] Remarriage terminates surviving spouse status. Of course, a joint return can be filed with the new spouse.

> **Example 15.**   H and W were married in 1984 and had two children, S and D. H died in 1994. After H's death, W continued to provide a home and all the support of S and D. As a result, W is entitled to claim S and D as dependents. For 1994 H may file a joint return with W. W may file as a surviving spouse in 1995 and 1996, using the same rates as married persons filing jointly. In subsequent years, W may file as a head of household.

Separate Returns.   Normally, it will be advantageous for married persons to file a joint return because it is simpler to file one return than it is to file two, and the tax will be as low or lower than the tax based on the rules for married persons filing separately. In some situations, a taxpayer may prefer to file a separate return. For example, a person may wish to avoid liability for the tax on the income—especially any unreported income—of his or her spouse. Similarly, a husband and wife who are separated and are contemplating divorce may wish to file separate returns.

Separate returns may be to the taxpayers' advantage in certain circumstances. Although rare, use of the separate rate schedules may result in a lower total tax than by using the rates applicable to a joint return. Filing of separate returns may also prove beneficial when the filing of a joint return would prevent another taxpayer (e.g., a parent) from claiming a dependency exemption deduction for either the husband or the wife (see *Example 10* above).

HEAD OF HOUSEHOLD

Head-of-household rates may be used if the taxpayer satisfies two conditions. First, the taxpayer must be unmarried or considered unmarried (i.e., an abandoned spouse) on the last day of the tax year. The second condition generally requires that the taxpayer provide over one-half of the cost of maintaining the home in which a *dependent familial relative* lives for more than half the taxable year.[34] As might be expected, the same individuals that are considered "relatives" for exemption purposes generally qualify as relatives when applying the head-of-household rules (e.g., children, grandchildren, parents, grandparents). However, there is an exception. Even though a person who is not truly

---

[33]   § 2(a).   [34]   § 2(b)(1).

Exhibit 4-2 *Relatives for Dependency and Head-of-Household Tests*

Relative *Familial relatives*	For Dependent Exemption	For Head-of-Household Test
Child, stepchild, adopted child, or descendant	Yes	Yes
Grandchild	Yes	Yes
Parent, stepparent, or ancestor	Yes	Yes
Grandparent	Yes	Yes
Brother, stepbrother	Yes	Yes
Sister, stepsister	Yes	Yes
Mother-in-law	Yes	Yes
Father-in-law	Yes	Yes
Brother-in-law	Yes	Yes
Sister-in-law	Yes	Yes
Son-in-law	Yes	Yes
Daugther-in-law	Yes	Yes
If related by blood		
Aunt	Yes	Yes
Uncle	Yes	Yes
Nephew	Yes	Yes
Niece	Yes	Yes
Other individuals		
Person lives in taxpayer's home entire taxable year	Yes	No

related to the taxpayer but who lives in the taxpayer's home for the entire taxable year is treated as a relative for purposes of the dependency exemption, such is not the case here. In order for the taxpayer to qualify for head-of-household status, the individual living in the home must be a familial relative.[35] Exhibit 4-2 gives a listing of those who are normally considered relatives for purposes of meeting both the head-of-household and dependency rules. Note they are all the same except for the nonfamilial relative.

An individual is normally a qualifying relative *only* if he or she is the taxpayer's dependent *and* lives in the taxpayer's household. Three exceptions exist to this general rule.

1. A parent need not live in the taxpayer's home; however, the taxpayer still must pay more than half of the cost of keeping up a home for his or her mother or father. For example, the taxpayer qualifies if he or she paid more than half the cost of the parent's living in a rest home or home for the elderly.

---

[35] §§ 2(b)(3), 152(a)(9), and 152(c).

Example 16.　D, an unmarried individual, lives in San Francisco and pays more than half of the cost of maintaining a home in Reno for her dependent parents. Although her parents do not live with her in San Francisco, D qualifies for the head-of-household rates.

2.　An *unmarried* child, grandchild, stepchild, or adopted child of the taxpayer need not be a dependent. This exception permits a divorced parent to qualify as head-of-household even though the former spouse claims the exemption for the child.

Example 17.　M is divorced and maintains a household for herself and her 10-year-old daughter. Although M is the custodial parent, she allows her former husband to claim the exemption for the child. M still qualifies for the head-of-household rates.

3.　A *married* child, grandchild, stepchild, or adopted child of the taxpayer who *could* be claimed as a dependent except that the taxpayer has signed a written declaration allowing the noncustodial parent to claim the dependent.

It should be noted that a person for whom a dependency exemption is claimed solely under a multiple support agreement (e.g., the taxpayer did not provide over half the cost of maintaining the home) is not considered a qualifying relative and *cannot* qualify the taxpayer as a head of household. In addition, a nonresident alien cannot be a head of household.[36]

Costs of Maintaining a Home.　In determining whether a taxpayer qualifies for head-of-household status, it is necessary to determine whether he or she pays over half of the cost of maintaining a home for the taxable year. This determination must also be made for surviving spouse filing status. The costs of maintaining the home include the costs for the mutual benefit of the occupants and include such expenses as property taxes, mortgage interest, rent, utilities, insurance, repairs, upkeep, and food consumed on the premises. The cost of maintaining a home does not include clothing, educational expenses, medical expenses, or transportation.[37]

Abandoned Spouse Provision.　Without a special provision, an individual whose spouse has simply abandoned him or her might be forced to file using the high rates for married individuals filing separately. Aware of this problem, Congress has provided that a married individual who files a separate return may file as head of household if he or she qualifies as an *abandoned spouse*. To qualify, the individual must provide over half the cost of maintaining a home that houses him or her and a child for whom a dependency exemption deduction is *either* claimed or could be claimed by the taxpayer except for the fact that the exemption was assigned to the noncustodial parent.[38] The child must live in the home with the taxpayer for more than half the taxable year and the taxpayer's spouse must not live in the home at any time during the last six months of the year. If each of these requirements is met, an abandoned spouse qualifies as a head of household.

---

[36]　Supra, footnote 35.

[37]　Reg. § 1.2-2(d).

[38]　§ 2(c) and § 7703(b). An adopted child of the taxpayer is considered a son or daughter for this test.

Exhibit 4-3   *Determination of Filing Status*

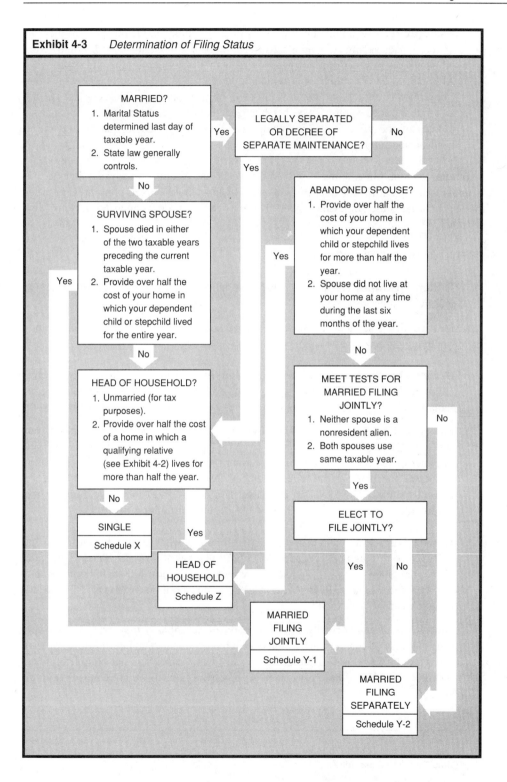

Example 18.   M and N are married with six children. In October, M stormed out of the house, saying he would never return. N was hopeful that M would return and consequently had not taken action to obtain a divorce by the end of the year. Although M and N are eligible to file a joint return, M indicated that he would not. Consequently, N's filing status is married filing separately. She does not qualify as an abandoned spouse since her husband lived in the home during the last six months of the year. In the following year, however, N could qualify and file as head of household.

Single.   Single filing status is defined by exception. A single taxpayer is anyone who is unmarried and does not qualify as a head of household or surviving spouse. Even though these rates are somewhat lower, they may not be used by married persons filing separately.[39]

✔ CHECK YOUR KNOWLEDGE

Review Question 1.   List the available rate schedules in the order of their progressivity (most to least).

Married filing separately, single, head of household, and married filing jointly (including surviving spouses).

Review Question 2.   H died in 1992, survived by his wife, W, and two young children, S and D. What rate schedule may W use in 1994 assuming she has not remarried?

She should be able to file as a surviving spouse and use the joint return rate schedule. A taxpayer qualifies as a surviving spouse if his or her spouse has died in either of the two taxable years preceding the current year (i.e., 1992 or 1993 in this case) and he or she provides over half the cost of a home in which he or she and a dependent child live. In this case, H died in 1992, so it would appear that W provides a home in which she and her dependent children live.

Review Question 3.   Q, divorced, is alive and well in Los Angeles. She has a 19-year-old daughter who attends school full-time at Arizona State. Q provides all her daughter's support, including payment of her dorm bill each month. Can Q file as a head of household? What additional questions must be asked before this question can be answered?

An individual can normally file as a head of household if they provide over *one-half* the cost of maintaining a home in which a dependent familial relative lives for more than *one-half* of the taxable year. In this case, it is not completely clear whether the half-and-half test is met. As a general rule, the relative must live in the

---

[39] Single filing status is referred to in Code § 1(c) as "Unmarried individuals (Other Than   Surviving Spouses and Heads of Households)."

home of the taxpayer one-half of the year. Here Q's daughter may only live in Q's home during the summer months, and it would therefore appear that Q could not qualify. However, temporary absences due to special circumstances such as those due to education, business, vacation, and military service are ignored. Since the daughter's absence is temporary, the test is satisfied. Note that Q's daughter need not be a dependent since this requirement is relaxed in the case of an unmarried child of the taxpayer.

COMPUTATION OF TAX FOR INDIVIDUAL TAXPAYERS

Once filing status and taxable income have been determined, the tax computation for most individuals is fairly straightforward. The gross tax is computed using the tax tables or the tax rate schedules. This amount is then reduced by any tax credits available to the taxpayer and any tax prepayments in arriving at the tax due or the refund. Children under age 14 with unearned income and all persons claimed as dependents are subject to special rules in the computation of their income tax.

TAX TABLES

The vast majority of individuals must determine their tax using *tax tables*, provided by the IRS along with the instructions for preparing individual income tax returns. The tables are derived directly from the rate schedules to simplify compliance and reduce taxpayer errors. The tax for any particular range of taxable income is determined by using the midpoint of the range and the appropriate rate schedule. For example, the tax in the 1993 tables for a single taxpayer with taxable income of $19,010 is $2,854, which is the tax computed on $19,025 (see Exhibit 4-4 for an excerpt and Appendix A for the complete 1993 Tax Tables).

The tables cover taxpayers in each filing status with taxable incomes less than $100,000. A taxpayer who qualifies generally is required to use the tax tables.[40]

Example 19. William W. Bristol was single for 1993 and had no dependents. Bill's only income was wages of $24,910 and taxable interest of $150. Since his itemized deductions totaled only $1,650, Bill claims the $3,700 standard deduction allowed for 1993. Federal income tax of $3,020 was withheld from Bill's salary. Bill's taxable income and tax for 1993 are calculated as follows:

---

[40] § 3.

Exhibit 4-4 *Excerpts From Tax Tables for 1993*

If line 37 (taxable income) is—		And you are—				If line 37 (taxable income) is—		And you are—			
At least	But less than	Single	Married filing jointly *	Married filing sepa-rately	Head of a house-hold	At least	But less than	Single	Married filing jointly *	Married filing sepa-rately	Head of a house-hold
		Your tax is—						Your tax is—			
19,000						**31,000**					
19,000	19,050	2,854	2,854	3,117	2,854	31,000	31,050	6,042	4,654	6,477	5,138
19,050	19,100	2,861	2,861	3,131	2,861	31,050	31,100	6,056	4,661	6,491	5,152
19,100	19,150	2,869	2,869	3,145	2,869	31,100	31,150	6,070	4,669	6,505	5,166
19,150	19,200	2,876	2,876	3,159	2,876	31,150	31,200	6,084	4,676	6,519	5,180
19,200	19,250	2,884	2,884	3,173	2,884	31,200	31,250	6,098	4,684	6,533	5,194
19,250	19,300	2,891	2,891	3,187	2,891	31,250	31,300	6,112	4,691	6,547	5,208
19,300	19,350	2,899	2,899	3,201	2,899	31,300	31,350	6,126	4,699	6,561	5,222
19,350	19,400	2,906	2,906	3,215	2,906	31,350	31,400	6,140	4,706	6,575	5,236
19,400	19,450	2,914	2,914	3,229	2,914	31,400	31,450	6,154	4,714	6,589	5,250
19,450	19,500	2,921	2,921	3,243	2,921	31,450	31,500	6,168	4,721	6,603	5,264
19,500	19,550	2,929	2,929	3,257	2,929	31,500	31,550	6,182	4,729	6,617	5,278
19,550	19,600	2,936	2,936	3,271	2,936	31,550	31,600	6,196	4,736	6,631	5,292
19,600	19,650	2,944	2,944	3,285	2,944	31,600	31,650	6,210	4,744	6,645	5,306
19,650	19,700	2,951	2,951	3,299	2,951	31,650	31,700	6,224	4,751	6,659	5,320
19,700	19,750	2,959	2,959	3,313	2,959	31,700	31,750	6,238	4,759	6,673	5,334
19,750	19,800	2,966	2,966	3,327	2,966	31,750	31,800	6,252	4,766	6,687	5,348
19,800	19,850	2,974	2,974	3,341	2,974	31,800	31,850	6,266	4,774	6,701	5,362
19,850	19,900	2,981	2,981	3,355	2,981	31,850	31,900	6,280	4,781	6,715	5,376
19,900	19,950	2,989	2,989	3,369	2,989	31,900	31,950	6,294	4,789	6,729	5,390
19,950	20,000	2,996	2,996	3,383	2,996	31,950	32,000	6,308	4,796	6,743	5,404

Salary...		$24,910
Taxable interest..................................		+ 150
Equals: Adjusted gross income...................		$25,060
Less: Standard deduction for 1993..............	$3,700	
Personal exemption for 1993..............	2,350	− 6,050
Equals: Taxable income..........................		$19,010
Tax on $19,010 for 1993 (See Exhibit 4-4)........		$ 2,854
Less: Income tax withheld.......................		− 3,020
Equals: Tax due or (refund)......................		($ 166)

A completed Form 1040EZ for William W. Bristol, based on the information in this example, is shown in the Appendix at the end of the chapter.

Example 20. Clyde F. and Delia C. Cooper were married during all of 1993 and had income from the following sources:

Salary, Clyde....................................		$31,795
Federal income tax withheld...................	$2,970	
Part-time salary, Delia...........................		17,750
Federal income tax withheld...................	1,280	
Interest from City Savings.......................		950
Interest from U.S. Government...................		150

Clyde and Delia are the sole support for their two children, ages 2 and 7. During 1993, they paid job-related child care expenses of $3,500 and made deductible contributions of $4,000 to their Individual Retirement Accounts ($2,000 each). Their itemized deductions for the year do not exceed their standard deduction of $6,200. The Coopers' taxable income and tax for 1993 are calculated as follows:

Salary ($31,795 + $17,750).....................		$ 49,545
Plus: Taxable interest ($950 + $150)............		+ 1,100
Less: Contributions to IRAs......................		− 4,000
Equals: Adjusted gross income...................		$ 46,645
Less: Standard deduction for 1993..............	$6,200	
Exemptions for 1993.....................	9,400	− 15,600
Equals: Taxable income.........................		$ 31,045
Tax on $31,045 for 1993 (See Exhibit 4-4)........		$ 4,654
Less: Child care credit (.20 × $3,500)...........		− 700
Equals: Net tax..................................		$ 3,954
Less: Income tax withheld ($2,970 + $1,280)....		− 4,250
Equals: Tax due or (refund).....................		($ 296)

A completed Form 1040A based on this information is included in the Appendix at the end of the chapter.

TAX RATE SCHEDULES

A taxpayer who is unable to use the tax tables uses the tax rate schedules in computing his or her tax. These schedules contain the rates as stated in § 1 of the Internal Revenue Code. The 1993 tax rate schedules are included, along with the 1993 tax tables, in Appendix A. The 1994 tax rate schedules are summarized in Exhibit 4-5. For future reference, the tax rate schedules for 1994 are also reproduced on the inside front cover of this text.

Exhibit 4-5 *Individual Tax Rate Schedules for 1994*

SINGLE

If taxable income is		Tax liability		Of the amount over
Over	But not over			
$ 0	$ 22,750		15%	$ 0
22,750	55,100	$ 3,412.50 +	28%	22,750
55,100	115,000	12,470.50 +	31%	55,100
115,000	250,000	31,039.50 +	36%	115,000
250,000	—	79,639.50 +	39.6%	250,000

MARRIED FILING JOINTLY AND QUALIFYING WIDOWS AND WIDOWERS

If taxable income is		Tax liability		Of the amount over
Over	But not over			
$ 0	$ 38,000		15%	$ 0
38,000	91,850	$ 5,700 +	28%	38,000
91,850	140,000	20,778 +	31%	91,850
140,000	250,000	35,704.50 +	36%	140,000
250,000	—	75,304.50 +	39.6%	250,000

HEADS OF HOUSEHOLDS

If taxable income is		Tax liability		Of the amount over
Over	But not over			
$ 0	$ 30,500		15%	$ 0
30,500	78,700	$ 4,575 +	28%	30,500
78,700	127,500	18,071 +	31%	78,700
127,500	250,000	33,199 +	36%	127,500
250,000	—	77,299 +	39.6%	250,000

MARRIED FILING SEPARATELY

If taxable income is		Tax liability		Of the amount over
Over	But not over			
$ 0	$ 19,000		15%	$ 0
19,000	45,925	$ 2,850 +	28%	19,000
45,925	70,000	10,389 +	31%	45,925
70,000	125,000	17,852.25 +	36%	70,000
125,000	—	37,652.25 +	39.6%	125,000

A typical example illustrating the use of the tax rate schedules is given below.

Example 21. R, single, has taxable income of $60,000 for 1994. R's gross tax liability is $13,989.50, computed as follows:

Tax on $55,100................................	$12,470.50
Plus: Tax on income above $55,100	
[($60,000 − $55,100) × 31%]..............	1,519.00
Tax liability.....................................	$13,989.50

SPECIAL TAX COMPUTATION RULES

Unfortunately, the computation of the tax is not always as straightforward as shown in *Example 21* above. For certain individuals, special rules must be followed.

Persons Claimed as Dependents. As one might deduce from the brief introduction to tax rates, one of the most fundamental principles of tax planning concerns minimizing the marginal tax rate that applies to the taxpayer's income. The significance of this principle is easily understood when it is recognized that Federal marginal tax rates have at times exceeded 90 percent. Even with the reduction of marginal rates to their current levels, minimizing the tax rate can provide benefits.

Historically, one of the most popular techniques to minimize the tax rate has been to shift income to a lower bracket taxpayer such as a child. As discussed in Chapter 5, this could be accomplished most easily by giving the child income-producing property. For example, a parent might establish a savings account for a child. In this way, the income would be taxed to the child at his or her low rate rather than the parents' high rate. In addition, this strategy—absent any special rules—takes advantage of the personal exemption and standard deduction available to a child.

Congress has long recognized the tax-saving potential inherent in such plans. For this reason, it is not surprising that it has taken steps to limit the opportunities. These are:

1. **Personal exemption.** A taxpayer who can be claimed as a dependent on another taxpayer's return is not entitled to a personal exemption. This rule effectively prohibits all children from claiming a personal exemption. Observe that *without this rule*, a child could currently receive up to $2,450 income tax free.

2. **Standard deduction.** The standard deduction available to a taxpayer who can be claimed as a dependent on another taxpayer's return is limited to the *greater* of $600 (also $600 for 1993) or his or her earned income—but not to exceed $3,800. Without this rule, a child could receive unearned income such as interest of up to $3,800 (i.e., the normal standard deduction in 1994) tax free.

3. **Kiddie tax.** The *unearned income* of a child under age 14 is generally taxed as if the parent received it to the extent it exceeds $1,200 (2 × $600 standard deduction).[41] Absent this provision, affectionately known as the *kiddie tax*, a parent could shift up to $22,750 in income to the child in 1994, who would pay taxes at a 15 percent rate rather than at the parents' rate.

---

[41] § 1(i).

The effect of these provisions is to severely limit the success of any schemes designed to shift income.

Example 22.   V, age 15, lives at home and may be claimed as a dependent on her parents' return. Several years ago, V's grandfather died, leaving her with a tidy sum to help send her to college. For 1994 V received interest income of $2,975. Her taxable income is computed as follows:

Adjusted gross income..........		$2,975
Less: Standard deduction........	$600	
Personal exemption....... +	0	− 600
Taxable income.................		$2,375

Note that, in computing V's taxable income, her standard deduction is limited to $600 (the larger of earned income, $0, or $600). The limitation is imposed because she is eligible to be claimed as a dependent on another taxpayer's return. For the same reason, she is not allowed to claim her own personal exemption deduction. Although the benefits of the normal standard deduction and personal exemption are denied, she avoids the kiddie tax because she is over 13 years of age. Consequently, her tax is $356 (15% × $2,375). By escaping the kiddie tax, some tax savings are probably achieved since the income is taxed at her 15% rate rather than a higher rate had her parents actually received the income.

Example 23.   Assume the same facts in *Example 22*, except that V also earns $2,000 from a part-time job. V's taxable income is determined as follows:

Adjusted gross income:		
Earned income...............	$2,000	
Interest income...............	+ 2,975	$4,975
Less: Standard deduction........	$2,000	
Personal exemption....... +	0	− 2,000
Taxable income.................		$2,975

As in *Example 22*, because V is a dependent, she is not allowed to claim her personal exemption deduction, nor may she claim the full standard deduction of $3,800. Note, however, that her standard deduction has increased because of her earned income. Her standard deduction is now $2,000 (the *larger* of earned income, $2,000, or $600). In effect, V is able to shelter income from tax with the standard deduction to the extent it is earned from personal services.

Kiddie Tax.   The kiddie tax provisions apply only to children who have not attained the age of 14 before the close of the taxable year and who have at least one living parent (or foster parent). If the child becomes 14 before the close of the year, he or she is treated as being 14 for the entire taxable year and the rules do not apply. Moreover, the kiddie tax rules are triggered only when the designated child has *net unearned income*. For this purpose, unearned income generally includes dividends, interest, rents, and royalties.

Net unearned income is unearned income in excess of $1,200 (also $1,200 for 1993).[42] In short, when a child under 14 has unearned income exceeding $1,200, the special tax computation must be made. The effect of this calculation is that the first $600 of unearned income is offset by the standard deduction and the second $600 of unearned income is taxed at the child's rates (currently 15%). Any unearned income exceeding $1,200 is taxed at the parents' top rates.

Example 24. J is 12 years old. Each year he receives interest income from a savings account and earned income from his paper route. The table below shows several sample calculations of J's taxable income assuming various amounts of earned and unearned income. In addition, the amount taxed at his rates and his parents' rates is computed.

	A	B	C	D
Unearned income...................	$1,400	$ 400	$1,400	$2,800
Earned income.....................	350	700	700	5,000
Total...............................	$1,750	$1,100	$2,100	$7,800
Standard deduction:				
Greater of $600 or earned income not to exceed $3,800 standard deduction.............	− 600	− 700	− 700	− 3,800
Personal exemption.................	−	−	−	−
Taxable income (a).................	$1,150	$ 400	$1,400	$4,000
Taxed at parents' rates				
Unearned income > $1,200 (b)...	$ 200	$ 0	$ 200	$1,600
Taxed at child's rates [(a) − (b)].....	$ 950	$ 400	$1,200	$2,400

In case B, there is no net unearned income because J's unearned income was less than $1,200. J has net unearned income in cases A, C, and D. In each case, the amount taxed at the parents' rate is the amount by which the child's unearned income exceeded $1,200. Any other income is taxed at the regular rates for the child.

When the child has net unearned income, the tax must be computed as if such income had been the parents' income. The child is required to pay the tax computed using his or her parents' rates except in rare cases where the tax computed in the normal manner is greater (in which case the higher tax must be paid).

Although the thrust of the kiddie tax is to tax income that would be taxed at a 15 percent rate at a higher rate, determination of the child's actual tax is somewhat complicated. The tax is computed on Form 8615 (see Appendix A) using the following approach:

---

[42] § 1(i)(4). If greater than $1,200, the sum of $600 and the allowable itemized deduc- tions specifically allocable to production of the unearned income is used.

Taxable income from parents' return...............................	$xxx
Add: Net unearned income of child (children)......................	+ xxx
Equals: Total income taxed at parents' rate.......................	$xxx
Tax on total income taxed at parents' rate.......................	$xxx
Minus: Tax on parents' income....................................	− xxx
Equals: Parental tax on child's net unearned income..............	$xxx
Add: Tax on child's remaining taxable income at 15 percent........	+ xxx
Equals: Total tax on child's taxable income......................	$xxx

The first step in this process requires the calculation of the parental tax. This is accomplished by combining the income of the parents with the net unearned income of the child and then calculating the total tax on this combined income as if the parents had reported all the income. Then, by subtracting the tax on the parents' income (from the parents' return), the amount of tax that the parents would have paid on the child's net unearned income is determined. This *parental tax* is, therefore, the tax that the parents would have paid on the net unearned income had they reported it directly.

The final part of the calculation involves determining the tax on the child's remaining taxable income at the child's tax rate of 15 percent. This tax is added to the parental tax to arrive at the child's total tax.

In those situations where the parents are divorced, the parental tax is computed using the taxable income of the custodial parent (or joint income if he or she has remarried). Where the parents file separate returns, the tax is computed using the greater of the parents' two taxable incomes.

In computing the tax on the parent *including* the child's net unearned income, such income is not considered when computing any of the parents' deductions or credits (e.g., the deduction for miscellaneous itemized deductions, which is limited to the amount that exceeds 2% of adjusted gross income).

Where there is more than one child under 14 with net unearned income, the parental tax must be computed using the net unearned income of all children. As shown below, the tax so computed is then allocated pro rata based on each child's relative contribution to total net unearned income.

$$\frac{\text{Child's net unearned income}}{\text{All children's net unearned income}} \times \frac{\text{Parental}}{\text{tax}} = \frac{\text{Child's share}}{\text{of parental tax}}$$

Example 25. During 1994 T, age 11, received $4,600 in dividends from stock given to him in 1990 by his now-deceased grandfather. Similarly, his sister, V, age 6, had $1,800 of dividend income. Since T and V are under 14 and have net unearned income of $3,400 ($4,600 − $1,200) and $600 ($1,800 − $1,200), respectively, their tax must be computed in the special manner. The children's parents had income of $80,000. In addition, due to special medical problems of the father, they incurred $11,000 of medical expenses. The couple also has other itemized deductions of $10,000. T's tax is computed as follows:

1. Tax on parents computed in the normal manner:

   Adjusted gross income... $80,000

   Deductions:

       Medical expenses [$11,000 − (7.5% × $80,000)]............. − 5,000

       Other itemized deductions................................... − 10,000

       Exemptions (4 × $2,450)..................................... − 9,800

   Taxable income computed in the normal manner.................. $55,200

   Tax [$5,700 + 28% ($55,200 − $38,000)]....................... $10,516

2. Tax on parents including net unearned income of all children:

   Parents' taxable income computed in the normal manner........ $55,200

   Net unearned income of children:

       ($3,400 + $600).. + 4,000

   Taxable income including net unearned income................. $59,200

   Tax [$5,700 + 28% ($59,200 − $38,000)]....................... $11,636

3. Parental tax:

   Tax on parents including net unearned income................. $11,636

   − Tax on parents computed in the normal manner............... − 10,516

   = Parental Tax... $ 1,120

4. T's share of parental tax [$1,120 × ($3,400 ÷ $4,000)] = $ 952

5. Tax on T excluding net unearned income:

   Dividend income... $ 4,600

   − Net unearned income....................................... − 3,400

   − Standard deduction (as limited for dependents)............. − 600

   − Exemption deduction (none for dependents)................. − 0

   Taxable income.. $ 600

   Tax (15% × $600).. $ 90

6. Total tax on T:

   Tax on T excluding net unearned income...................... $ 90

   + Parental Tax.. + 952

   = T's total tax... $ 1,042

Note that in this case the total parental tax of $1,120 is simply the product of the net unearned income of $4,000 and the parents' marginal tax rate of 28%. Also note that the parents' deduction for medical expenses is computed without including the net unearned income of the children (i.e., the percentage limitation is based on $80,000 rather than $84,000).

Election to Report Child's Income on Parents' Return. In order to simplify the return filing process, parents may elect to include on their own return the unearned income of a child if certain conditions are satisfied.[43] Note that this is contrary to the normal procedure where the child files his or her own return and pays the tax computed with respect to the parents' rates. This election eliminates the hassle of filing separate returns for each child. However, the election can only be made where the child is under age 14, his or her income is between $600 and $5,000, and consists solely of interest or dividends. The election is not available if estimated taxes have been paid or taxes have been withheld on dividend or interest income (i.e., the child is subject to back-up withholding).

DETERMINATION OF NET TAX DUE OR REFUND

Once the tax is determined using the tax tables, tax rate schedules, or the special tax computation procedures described above, it is reduced by the amount of any credits or prepayments. The primary prepayments are the Federal income tax withheld from the taxpayer's salary or wages by an employer, quarterly estimated tax payments, and the estimated tax paid when an extension of time to file a return is requested. Estimated tax payments and extensions of time to file are discussed later in this chapter.

Numerous credits are allowed in computing the Federal income tax. The credit most frequently encountered on an uncomplicated income tax return is the child care credit. This and other credits are discussed in detail in Chapter 13.

✔ CHECK YOUR KNOWLEDGE

Review Question 1. What are the top and bottom tax rates for individuals?

In 1993 the Clinton administration and Congress raised the top rate from 31 percent to 39.6 percent. The top rate applies if a taxpayer (regardless of filing status) has more than $250,000 in taxable income. The bottom rate is 15 percent (note that this is less than the self-employment tax rate).

Review Question 2. Several years ago Grandma gave her grandchild K, now 13, $20,000 to be used for her college education. All of the money was invested in stock. This year K's dad, acting on her behalf, sold some of the stock for a $4,000 short-term capital gain. K's parents are in the 36 percent tax bracket.

a. Compute K's taxable income and K's tax.

Income (unearned).................	$4,000
Standard deduction:	
Greater of $600 or earned income –	600
Exemption.........................	0
Taxable income....................	$3,400

---

[43] § 1(i)(7).

K's personal exemption and standard deduction are limited since she can be claimed as a dependent on her parent's return. Consequently, she is not entitled to an exemption, and her standard deduction is $600 since she has no earned income. In computing K's tax, the amount of unearned income in excess of $1,200 is $2,800 ($4,000 − $1,200), which must be taxed at her parents' rates while the remainder is taxed at her rates. Thus her tax is $1,098 [(36% × $2,800) + ($600 × 15%)].

b. What suggestion might you give to K and her dad?

K should wait to sell the stock until next year, when she turns 14 and the kiddie tax does not apply. If she does so, the gain would be taxed at 15 percent rather than 36 percent, and the family would save $588 [(36% − 15% = 21%) × $2,800].

c. Assume there were no kiddie tax. How much income could be shifted to a child and taxed at the child's 15 percent rate rather than the parents' rate?

The 15 percent bracket for 1994 extends from taxable income of $0 to $22,750.

FILING REQUIREMENTS

Individual taxpayers with extremely low levels of income are not required to file a Federal income tax return. In general, a taxpayer is not required to file an income tax return for the year if his or her gross income is less than the *total* of his or her standard deduction (including the additional amount for the elderly but not the blind) *plus* personal exemptions (but not dependency exemptions).[44] These taxpayers generally are not liable for any Federal income tax. The filing requirement is based on gross income, so taxpayers who have gross incomes exceeding specified thresholds *must* file even if they owe no Federal income tax. A partial list of filing requirements for 1994 and how they are computed is illustrated in Exhibit 4-6.

In addition to the general requirement for filing (gross income is at least as much as the taxpayer's standard deduction + personal exemptions), certain individuals *must* file returns. These include

1. Any taxpayer who has self-employment income of $400 or more

2. An individual who is claimed as a dependent on another taxpayer's return *and* who has unearned income at least equal to his or her minimum standard deduction (i.e., generally $600, but increased by the additional amount for elderly or blind taxpayers)[45]

3. Any person who receives any advance payments of earned income credit

---

[44] § 6012(a)(1).

[45] § 6012(a)(1)(C)(i). As stated earlier, certain children under the age of 14 are not required to file a tax return *if* their parents *elect* to include the child's income on their return and pay the appropriate additional tax.

Exhibit 4-6   *Gross Income Filing Requirements for 1994*

	Personal Exemption +	Standard Deduction +	Elderly Standard Deduction =	1994 Gross Income
Single person < 65 years old	$2,450	$3,800	–	$ 6,250
Single person ≥ 65 years old	2,450	3,800	$ 950	7,200
Head of household < 65	2,450	5,600	–	8,050
Head of household ≥ 65	2,450	5,600	950	9,000
Married filing jointly, both < 65	4,900	6,350	–	11,250
Married filing jointly, both ≥ 65	4,900	6,350	1,500	12,750
Married filing separately	2,450			2,450
Surviving spouse < 65	2,450	6,350	–	8,800
Surviving spouse ≥ 65	2,450	6,350	750	9,550
Dependents				Special Rules

Form 1040.   The individual taxpayer is required to file Form 1040, along with related forms and schedules. A complicated return involves many forms and schedules in addition to the Form 1040, whereas a simpler return may require only a few or no attached schedules.

Two simplified forms are provided for taxpayers with uncomplicated tax calculations. The Form 1040EZ is available for taxpayers who are single or married filing jointly and have no dependents. To qualify, the taxpayer's income must consist only of salaries and wages plus interest income of $400 or less. The only allowable deductions on this form are the personal exemption amount and the standard deduction.

The Form 1040A is available for a large number of taxpayers who do not itemize their deductions and have no income other than salaries and wages, dividends, interest, and unemployment compensation. This form provides for deductions for individual retirement account (IRA) contributions, personal and dependency exemptions, and the earned income credit.

Example 26.   Jeremy S. Allen, a registered nurse, and Shelly R. Allen, an air traffic controller, are married and file a joint income tax return for 1993. They are the sole support of their three children: William, Susan, and Gregory. The following information is from their records for 1993:

Salaries and wages, Jeremy.......................		$30,975
Federal income tax withheld....................	$4,400	
Salaries and wages, Shelly.......................		43,000
Federal income tax withheld....................	5,100	
Interest income—Mercantile National Bank........		1,800
Interest income—U.S. Government Bonds..........		600
Interest income—Ben Franklin Savings.............		400
Dividends—GRE, Inc. (A Kansas corporation)......		200
Itemized deductions are as follows:		
Hospitalization insurance.......................		700
Unreimbursed fees of doctors, hospitals, etc.....		2,100
Unreimbursed prescription drugs................		200
Real estate taxes on residence..................		1,200
State income taxes paid.........................		3,500
Interest paid on original home mortgage........		8,500
Investment interest.............................		400
Charitable contribution—First Church............		1,300
Charitable contribution—		
Home State University........................		200
Preparation of prior year's tax return.............		225

The Allens' adjusted gross income is $76,975 ($30,975 + $43,000 + $2,800 interest income + $200 dividend income) since there were no deductions for A.G.I. The deductible amount of their itemized deductions is $15,100, summarized as follows:

Medical expenses exceeding $5,773	
(i.e., 7.5% × $76,975 A.G.I.).........................	$ 0
Deductible taxes ($1,200 + $3,500)....................	4,700
Qualifying home mortgage interest.....................	8,500
Investment interest....................................	400
Charitable contributions...............................	1,500
Miscellaneous itemized deductions	
exceeding $1,540 (i.e., 2% × $76,975 A.G.I.).........	0
Total itemized deductions..............................	$15,100

The Allens' taxable income, gross tax, and tax refund for 1993 are determined as follows:

Adjusted gross income....................................		$76,975
Less: Itemized deductions................................	$15,100	
Personal and dependency		
exemptions ($2,350 × 5)............................	+ 11,750	− 26,850
Equals: Taxable income...................................		$50,125
Gross Tax (from 1993 Tax Schedule):		
Tax on $36,900...	$5,535	
Tax on excess ($50,125 − $36,900) × 28%...............	+ 3,703	$ 9,238
Less: Prepayments ($4,400 + $5,100)....................		− 9,500
Equals: Tax due or (refund)..............................		($ 262)

Exhibit 4-7   *List of Common Forms and Schedules Used by Individual Taxpayers*

Form 1040   **U.S. Individual Income Tax Return**

Accompanying Schedules:

Schedule A	Itemized deductions
Schedule B	Interest and dividend income
Schedule C	Profit (or loss) from business or profession
Schedule D	Capital gains and losses
Schedule E	Supplemental income schedule (rents, royalties, etc.)
Schedule F	Farm income and expenses
Schedule R	Credit for the elderly
Schedule SE	Computation of social security self-employment tax

Accompanying Forms:

Form 2106	Employee business expenses
Form 2119	Sale or exchange of principal residence
Form 2210	Underpayment of estimated tax by individuals
Form 2441	Credit for child and dependent care expenses
Form 3800	General business credit
Form 3903	Moving expense adjustment
Form 4562	Depreciation
Form 4684	Casualties and thefts
Form 4797	Supplemental schedule of gains and losses
Form 6251	Alternative minimum tax computation
Form 6252	Computation of installment sale income
Form 8582	Passive activity losses
Form 8615	Computation of tax for children under age 14 who have investment income of more than $1,000
Form 8814	Parents' election to report child's interest and dividends

Other Common Forms:

Form 1040A	U.S. Individual Income Tax Return
Form 1040EZ	Income tax return for single filers with no dependents
Form 4868	Application for automatic extension of time to file
Form 2688	Application for extension of time to file

The Allens' completed 1993 tax return is shown in the Appendix at the end of the chapter. It consists of a Form 1040 plus Schedules A and B.

The more common tax forms and schedules used by individual taxpayers are listed in Exhibit 4-7. Copies of these forms are contained in Appendix B at the end of the text.

DUE DATES FOR FILING RETURNS

The day on which a Federal return must be filed with the IRS depends upon what type of return is involved. Generally the tax returns must be filed on or before the due dates, which are as follows:[46]

Type of Return	Due Date
Annual Individual Income Tax Returns	Fifteenth day of the fourth month following the close of the tax year (April 15 for calendar year individuals)
Annual C Corporation and S Corporation Income Tax Returns	Fifteenth day of third month following the close of the tax year (March 15 for calendar year corporations)
Annual Partnership, Estate, and Trust Income Tax Returns	Fifteenth day of the fourth month following the close of the tax year (April 15 for calendar year entities)
Estate Tax Returns	Nine months after the date of the decedent's death
Gift Tax Returns	April 15 (All gift tax returns are for a Calendar year)

Any return that is mailed via the U.S. Postal Service is deemed to be delivered when mailed, so any return postmarked on or before the above due dates is timely filed. If any of these due dates fall on Saturday, Sunday, or a legal holiday, the return must be filed on the succeeding day that is not a Saturday, Sunday, or legal holiday.

Extension of Time to File. The Internal Revenue Code provides extensions of time for filing returns. The extension must be requested on or before the due date of the return. Currently, there is an *automatic* four-month extension for filing the individual income tax return (Form 1040). Thus the extended due date for calendar year individuals is August 15. If the taxpayer desires to use the four-month extension, he or she simply fills out Form 4868 and mails it to the IRS by the original due date along with a check covering the estimated balance due. It should be noted that an extension of time to file is not an extension of time to pay. There is *no extension* of time to pay estimated tax due.[47]

If the taxpayer needs additional time to prepare the return after the automatic four-month extension, he or she must file Form 2688 or write a letter explaining the circumstances. This extension is discretionary with the IRS and probably will not be granted unless unusual circumstances indicate that the taxpayer is laboring under "undue hardship" in compiling the necessary records.

---

[46] § 6072(a).   [47] Reg. § 1.6081-4(a).

Example 27. As a result of a severe flood in early April, T lost all records necessary for the filing of his Federal income tax return for the prior year. T should file Form 4868 and pay any income tax he estimates to be due by April 15. If T requires more than four months to gather duplicate copies of his records (e.g., bank statements, canceled checks, and prior years' Federal income tax returns), he should file Form 2688 or write a letter to the District Director of the IRS requesting an additional extension of time. Under these circumstances, there is no doubt that T will be granted his request.

Interest and Penalties. Whenever a taxpayer fails to pay the amount of tax owed by the due date of the return, interest is charged at a rate 3 percent higher than the Federal short term rate. For the first quarter of 1994, the annual interest rate charge on such a deficiency is 7 percent (4% + 3%), compounded daily on the unpaid balance.[48] An interest charge normally results when the taxpayer files for an extension and pays the estimated tax due that ultimately turns out to be less than that due when the return is actually filed. In addition, if the balance due is more than 10 percent of the tax shown on the taxpayer's return or the amount due is not paid by August 15, the IRS charges a late-payment penalty. This *failure-to-pay* penalty is one-half of 1 percent (0.5%) per month (or any fraction of a month), up to a maximum of 25 percent of the amount due.[49] However, no penalty for failure to pay is assessed when there is reasonable cause or an extension of time to file is properly obtained and the tax due is less than 10 percent of the total tax shown on the return.

Example 28. W was simply too busy to file his Federal tax return for the most recent calendar year. Thus on April 15 he requested an automatic extension of time to file until August 15. W had prepaid taxes of $5,800 in the form of withholding, and he estimated that his total tax would be $6,200. Therefore, he paid $400 when he filed the request for an extension. When he finally did file on June 15, W's return showed a total tax of $6,850 and a tax due of $650. W is not required to pay the penalty for failure to pay since his tax due is less than 10 percent of the total tax [$650 < 10%× $6,850]. However, assuming the current rate of interest on underpayments is 7%, W must pay interest of $8 ($650 at 7% annually, compounded daily for 61 days).

In the event a tax return is not filed by the due date (including extensions), the IRS will impose a *failure-to-file* penalty of 5 percent per month—up to a maximum of 25 percent—on the amount of tax due on the return.[50] Like the failure-to-pay penalty, any fraction of a month is counted as a full month. A minimum penalty of $100 (limited to the total tax on the return) applies if the return is not filed within 60 days of the due date.

---

[48] § 6601(a). The 7 percent rate is scheduled to remain in effect until April 1994, at which time it will be increased, reduced, or allowed to remain unchanged, based on a predetermined formula.

[49] § 6651(a)(2).

[50] § 6651(a)(1). If the failure to file is fraudulent, the penalty is 15 percent per month up to a maximum of 75 percent. § 6551(f).

When both of the preceding penalties apply, the penalty for failure to file is reduced by the amount of the penalty for failure to pay. Since both penalties are technically an addition to the tax, interest must be paid on the penalty as well as the unpaid tax.

Example 29. K forgot to file her Federal tax return for the most recent calendar year. K had prepaid taxes of $4,600 in the form of withholding. When she finally filed the return on June 15, K's return showed a total tax of $5,200 and a tax due of $600. Assuming the current rate of interest on underpayments is 10 percent, K must pay the tax due of $600, a penalty of $60, and interest of $8, for a total of $668, computed as follows:

Tax due...		$600
Penalty for failure to pay ($600 × .005 × 2).............		− 6
Penalty for failure to file ($600 × .05 × 2)...............	$60	
Net of penalty for failure to pay.......................	− 6	+ 54
Interest [($600 + $54 + $6) at 7 percent annually, compounded daily for 61 days, rounded]..............		+ 8
Total due..		$668

Note that the minimum penalty rule is not triggered because the return was filed within 60 days of the due date. If the minimum penalty provision had applied, the penalty would have been $100 (the lesser of the total tax on the return, $5,200, or $100).

As mentioned in Chapter 2, many other penalties exist to ensure proper compliance with the tax laws. For example, the Code provides for an *accuracy-related* penalty of 20 percent of the amount of understatement due to negligence or intentional disregard of the rules (e.g., failing to report income), or substantial valuation infractions.[51] In addition, severe penalties, both civil and criminal, exist for fraud.[52] Still another important penalty to be considered is that for failure to pay estimated taxes during the year. This penalty is discussed below.

Amended Return. After the original return has been filed, an individual taxpayer generally has until the later of three years from the date of filing the original return, or two years from the time the tax was paid, to amend his or her return.[53] This is done by filing Form 1040X (see Appendix B).

ESTIMATED TAX PAYMENTS

Under the "pay-as-you-go" system for collection of taxes, taxpayers are required to prepay Federal income taxes in the form of withholding from certain types of income and estimated tax payments. Withholding is normally adequate for taxpayers receiving only salaries and wages. However, those taxpayers with other income *must* estimate the

---

[51] § 6653(a)(1).

[52] § 6653(b).

[53] § 6511(a).

tax that will be due (including the self-employment tax, the alternative minimum tax, and certain other taxes) and make periodic payments of the estimated tax. Corporations are also required to make estimated tax payments.

A penalty is imposed for taxpayers who fail to make adequate estimates. This penalty is separate from the penalty for failure to pay the tax and the interest which is charged.[54] The failure-to-pay penalty applies to underpayments of tax due as of the due date (e.g., April 15) of the return. The estimated tax penalty is charged from the date the estimated tax installment was due (e.g., June 15th) until the tax was paid (or, if the tax is paid late, the due date of the return). The penalty is assessed at the same rate as the interest which is charged on tax deficiencies; however, it is not assessed where the net tax due after withholding is less than $500.

The estimates are due on April 15, June 15, September 15, and January 15 for a calendar year taxpayer. To avoid penalty, the total prepayments must *generally* equal or exceed the lesser of the following:

1. Ninety percent of the tax shown on the return, or

2. One hundred percent of the tax shown on the return for the individual for the preceding year (110% if adjusted gross income in the prior year exceeded $150,000).[55]

Example 30.   For 1994 T, a single individual, reported an adjusted gross income of $165,000, a taxable income of $140,000, and a tax liability (after credits) of $40,000. In 1995 his tax liability is $60,000. Under the general rules T must have paid the lesser of 90% of the current year's tax, $54,000, or 100% of last year's tax, $40,000, in order to avoid underpayment penalty. However, because T's adjusted gross income exceeded $150,000 in the prior year, 1994, he is subject to the special 110 percent rule regarding his estimated tax payments for the current year, 1995. As a result, he can avoid underpayment penalties with respect to 1995 only if he pays the lesser of the following:

1. 90% of the current year's tax of $60,000................ $54,000
2. 110% of last year's tax of $40,000...................... 44,000

Thus, if T pays at least $44,000 on a timely basis during 1995, he will not be subject to any penalty for failing to pay estimated taxes.

Whether the payments are adequate or not is determined at the end of each quarter. For this purpose, withholding is treated as if it occurred proportionately throughout the year. At the end of each quarter, the payments to date are compared to the appropriate portion of the amount required to be paid.

---

[54] § 6654(a).   [55] § 6654(d).

Example 31. For 1993 and 1994 G's gross tax was $12,000 and $16,000, respectively. G's withholding for 1994 was $6,500 and his estimated tax payments were $1,500 on April 15 and June 15 and $500 on September 15 and January 15. G's underpayment is determined as follows:

| | Payment Due Date | | | |
	4/15	6/15	9/15	1/15
Percentage due................................	25%	50%	75%	100%
Ninety percent of current year's tax				
($16,000 × .90 × percentage due)..........	$3,600	$7,200	$10,800	$14,400
One hundred percent of prior year's tax				
($12,000 × percentage due)................	$3,000	$6,000	$ 9,000	$12,000
Payments to date:				
Withholding................................	$1,625	$3,250	$ 4,875	$ 6,500
Estimated tax payments....................	+ 1,500	+ 3,000	+ 3,500	+ 4,000
Total..	$3,125	$6,250	$ 8,375	$10,500

G's payments are adequate for the first quarter and the second quarter, since the payments up to each date exceed the lesser of the two required amounts (the prior year's tax in both cases). As of the third payment date, G is underpaid by $625 ($9,000 − $8,375); and as of the last payment date, he is underpaid by $1,500 ($12,000 − $10,500). The penalty is computed based on these amounts from the due date until the day they are paid (or April 15, if earlier).

Assuming the current rate of penalty is 7 percent and G does not pay his tax early, G's penalty would be $41, which is the penalty on $625 from September 15 through January 15 [$625 × (.07 × 122 days/365 days) = $15] *plus* that on $1,500 from January 15 through April 15 [$1,500 × (.07 × 90 days/365 days) = $26].

The penalty for failure to make adequate estimated tax payments is calculated on Form 2210 (see Appendix B for a sample form). Unless a taxpayer can reduce the penalty by applying the annualized income installment or otherwise, he or she may simply let the IRS calculate this penalty and assess a deficiency for it. In addition, the IRS may waive the underpayment penalty in the event of a casualty or unusual circumstances where it might be inequitable to impose the additional tax. The IRS may also waive the penalty for retired taxpayers who are age 62 or disabled where the underpayment was due to reasonable cause rather than willful neglect.

Annualized Income Installment. If the income for a year is earned disproportionately during the year, the taxpayer may be able to avoid penalty for one or more of the first three payments under the *annualized income installment* method.[56] Under this method, no penalty is imposed when the payment to date exceeds the tax which would be due on the income for the months preceding the payment date determined on an annualized basis.

---

[56] § 6654(d).

Example 32. F, a calendar year individual, is engaged in a seasonal business which earns most of its income during the fourth quarter. F is able to demonstrate that the income was earned as follows:

	Payment Due Date			
	4/15	*6/15*	*9/15*	*1/15*
Months preceding payment......	3	5	8	12
Net income earned for the months preceding the payment.....................	$10,000	$18,000	$25,000	$50,000
Annualized amount [Net income × (12 ÷ No. of months to date)]........	$40,000	$43,500	$37,500	$50,000

To apply this exception, the tax on the annualized income is determined. There is an underpayment only if the estimated tax payments are less than the appropriate portion of the tax on the annualized income.

The required payment for April 15 is the fraction 3 months ÷ 12 months times the tax on $40,000. If the tax on $40,000 is $8,000, F has no underpayment for the first payment so long as she paid $2,000 ($8,000 × 3/12) or more. If she had paid less, the underpayment would be the amount by which $2,000 exceeded the payments. A similar process would be followed for each quarter.

To apply the annualized income installment calculations, a taxpayer completes a worksheet that accompanies the Form 2210. If this method is used to the benefit of the taxpayer for one payment, it must be used for *all* four payments.

STATUTE OF LIMITATIONS

Even in the administration of the Federal tax laws, all things must finally come to an end. As the U.S. Supreme Court has stated,

> Congress has regarded it as ill advised to have an income tax system under which there would never come a day of final settlement and which required both a taxpayer and the Government to stand ready forever and a day to produce vouchers, prove events, and recall details of all that goes into an income tax contest.[57]

Accordingly, there are certain time periods within which the IRS must take action *against* a taxpayer. If the Service does not take action within the prescribed time period, it is *barred* from pursuing the matter further. Technically the period in which an action must be commenced is called the Statute of Limitations. If the Statute of Limitations runs (expires) without any action on the part of the IRS, then the government is prohibited from assessing additional taxes for the expired periods.

---

[57] *Rothensies v. Electric Storage Battery Co.,*   296, 301 (USSC, 1946).
47-1 USTC ¶9106, 35 AFTR 297, 329 U.S.

Under the general rule, the IRS has three years from the date a return is filed to assess an additional tax liability against the taxpayer. If the tax return is filed before its due date, the three-year period for assessment begins *on* the due date.

> **Example 33.** R, a calendar year taxpayer, files a 1994 income tax return (due April 15) on March 8, 1995. The IRS will be prevented from assessing R additional taxes for 1994 any time after April 15, 1998.

> **Example 34.** Refer to *Example 33*. If R files a 1994 income tax return on October 15, 1995, the IRS may assess additional taxes for 1994 at any time through October 15, 1998.

There are several important exceptions to the three-year time period for assessing additional taxes. First, if the taxpayer has filed a false or a fraudulent return with the intention to *evade* the tax, then the tax may be assessed (or a proceeding may be initiated in court without assessment) at *any time* in the future. Similarly, if the taxpayer fails to file a return, the Statute of Limitations will not begin to run. Interestingly, a willful failure to file, a negligent failure to file, or an innocent failure to file are all treated the same. Thus, under any of these circumstances there is no limit to the time in which the IRS may make an assessment or begin a court proceeding against the taxpayer.

In the case of a *substantial omission of income* from a tax return, the Statute of Limitations is extended to six years. A substantial omission is defined as an omission of income in excess of 25 percent of the gross income *reported* on the return.[58] If the omission of gross income was committed with the intent of evading the tax, however, the assessment period would be unlimited.

> **Example 35.** T, a calendar year taxpayer, unintentionally failed to include $8,000 of dividends in his 1994 tax return filed on April 15, 1995. If the $8,000 omitted is more than 25 percent of the gross income reported on T's 1994 return, the IRS may assess an additional income tax liability against him at any time until after April 15, 2001.

The periods within which assessments must be made are summarized in Exhibit 4-8, which follows.

INDEXATION AND THE FEDERAL INCOME TAX

Inflation has significant effects on a progressive tax rate structure stated in terms of a *constant* dollar. Taxpayers whose *real* incomes remain constant will have increasing levels of income, stated in terms of *nominal* dollars. Accordingly, their incomes will *creep up* into higher tax brackets. As an illustration, assume a taxpayer who earned $100,000 in 1993 is entitled to an annual raise at least equal to any increase in the Consumer Price Index (2.7 percent increase in 1993). Although his 1994 salary will creep up to

---

[58] § 6501(e).

Exhibit 4-8 *Periods within Which Assessments Must Be Made*

Circumstances of Return	Period of Assessment
Normal return has been filed	Three years from date of filing or due date, whichever is later
Return filed with substantial omission of gross income	Six years from date of filing or due date, whichever is later
No return is filed	No time limit
False or fraudulent return	No time limit

$102,700, his before-tax income in terms of 1993 prices remains at $100,000. At first glance, the taxpayer is as well off in 1994 as he was in 1993. Note, however, that the salary increase could push him into a higher tax bracket, in which case he would have less after-tax income in real terms in 1994 than he had in 1993. Over time, this *bracket creep*, as it has been labeled, results in a larger portion of the taxpayer's earnings being paid to the Federal government. In effect, unlegislated tax increases occur.

For many years, Congress simply ignored the bracket creep phenomenon, choosing instead to allow the hidden tax increases to occur. As might be expected, this was a very palatable approach to politicians, particularly considering the alternative. The concerns of the few who objected were mollified in part by tax reduction packages enacted in 1981 and 1986. Both the Economic Recovery Tax Act of 1981 and the Tax Reform Act of 1986 directly reduced tax rates. These specific tax rate adjustments have since been followed by a permanent remedy for bracket creep: indexation.

Congress began adding the concept of indexation to the tax law in 1985. In 1986 it specified the amounts of the standard deduction, exemption amounts, and tax brackets for 1987 and 1988 (and the exemption amount for 1989). Thereafter, each of these amounts and many others have been annually adjusted for price level changes as measured by the Consumer Price Index.[59]

✔ CHECK YOUR KNOWLEDGE

Review Question 1.   Z, age 16, earned $2,000 from umpiring baseball games and refereeing soccer matches during the year. Z—rather Z's parents—wants to know whether he is required to file a tax return since this was his only income.

A taxpayer is not normally required to file a return if his or her income is less than the sum of the personal exemption amount and the standard deduction. However, this general rule does not apply to an individual who can be claimed as a dependent

---

[59]   See §§ 1(f),1(g)(4),639(c)(4), and 151(d)(3).

on another return since he or she is not entitled to claim a personal exemption and the standard deduction may be limited. In this case, all of Z's income is earned income and is therefore offset by his standard deduction of $2,000 (the greater of $600 or earned income). Consequently, it seems that there is no need for him to file a return. However, even though he is not subject to the income tax, he still must consider self-employment taxes (assuming the income is self-employment income). A return is required if a taxpayer has self-employment income of at least $400. As a result, Z must file a return.

Review Question 2.   After spending three years on the auditing staff of a large accounting firm, Norm took a job as controller of a small construction company. On the first day of the job, Norm looked around his new office and noticed a bunch of tax forms on the corner of his desk. One looked like the 1040 for his boss, and the others were corporate and partnership returns related to the company. At first he panicked. But then he realized that it was only the end of February and he had until April 15 to figure out what needed to be done. Should Norm relax?

Doubtful. Although returns for calendar year individuals and partnerships are normally due on April 15, the return for a C corporation or an S corporation is due on March 15.

Review Question 3.   As always, April 15 arrived and T had not even begun to prepare his tax return. Not to worry, he thought. He could simply file for an extension.

   a. Assume T does not file for an extension and simply files his return late. Are there any penalties?

Maybe. A failure-to-file as well as a failure-to-pay penalty may be imposed. Both penalties apply only if there is a tax due. If T is entitled to a refund, there is no penalty. The failure-to-file penalty is 5 percent per month on the balance due, not to exceed 25 percent.

   b. How long is the extension?

An automatic extension of four months until August 15 is available.

   c. Is an extension for time to file the return also an extension of time to pay the tax?

No. If T does not pay a sufficient amount of his tax by April 15, he faces penalties and interest imposed on the balance due.

   d. Assuming T's gross tax liability before withholding is $10,000, how much must he pay by April 15 in order to avoid penalty?

T must pay 90 percent of the gross tax, or $9,000, by April 15. After that date, a penalty of ½ of 1 percent per month is imposed up to a maximum of 25 percent.

   e. If T fails to pay his tax and he is subject to penalties, how does interest work? Must he pay interest on just the tax due or on both the tax and the penalties?

He pays interest not only on the tax due but also the penalties since the penalties are considered an additional tax.

Review Question 4.   Penalties for failing to file a return and failing to pay at least 90 percent of the tax due by the due date must be distinguished from penalties for failure to adequately make estimated tax payments during the year (underpayment penalties). Try the following true-false questions concerning estimated tax payments.

a. T finally filed her 1993 tax return and is now worrying about 1994. As a general rule, an individual taxpayer must pay 22.5 percent of her 1994 tax (even though she has no idea what it will be) 15 days after the end of each quarter (i.e., April 15, July 15, October 15, and January 15).

False. Although it is true that the taxpayer must normally pay 90 percent of the current tax due during the year (or 22.5 percent per installment), the installments are due on April 15, June 15, September 15, and January 15. Notwithstanding the fact that these payments are not truly paid on a quarterly basis, most people refer to them as "quarterly" estimated tax payments.

b. In lieu of paying 90 percent of their tax liability, individual taxpayers may avoid the underpayment penalty by paying 90 percent of last year's tax liability.

False. Penalty can be avoided if the taxpayer pays 90 percent of the current year's tax or 100 percent of last year's tax. Moreover, the 100 percent rule is increased to 110 percent if the taxpayer's adjusted gross income in the prior year exceeded $150,000.

c. T earns a salary but also does some tinkering in the stock market. In October she realized that she should have paid estimated taxes throughout the year given what her income was going to be. Asking her employer to withhold an extra $36,500 in taxes during October, November, and December will help solve T's estimated tax problems for April, June, and September.

True. Withholding is treated as being paid ratably throughout the year. Therefore the additional $36,500 is not simply applied to the later due dates. Instead, T is treated as having paid $100 per day each day of the year. For example, she is treated as having an additional $10,500 (105 × $100) on April 15.

Review Question 5.   T filed her 1994 tax return on March 15, 1995. The IRS is barred from assessing a deficiency on

a. March 15, 1996
b. March 15, 1997
c. March 15, 1998
d. April 15, 1997
e. April 15, 1998

The statue of limitations runs out on April 15, 1998, three years from the later of the due date or the date of filing.

APPENDIX

TAX RETURN ILLUSTRATIONS

The following pages provide realistic examples of uncomplicated tax returns for individual taxpayers. The information from *Examples 19*, *20*, and *26* of this chapter is used.

Form 1040EZ Return for William W. Bristol (Example 19)

Department of the Treasury—Internal Revenue Service

Form 1040EZ

Income Tax Return for Single and Joint Filers With No Dependents (T) **1993**

OMB No. 1545-0675

Use the IRS label
(See page 10.)
Otherwise, please print.

Print your name (first, initial, last)

WILLIAM W. BRISTOL

If a joint return, print spouse's name (first, initial, last)

Home address (number and street). If you have a P.O. box, see page 11. Apt. no.

651 SOUTH HAMPTON

City, town or post office, state and ZIP code. If you have a foreign address, see page 11.

LITTLE CITY, KS 62228

See instructions on back and in Form 1040EZ booklet.

Your social security number 187 52 9034

Spouse's social security number

Presidential Election Campaign
(See page 11.)

Note: Checking "Yes" will not change your tax or reduce your refund.
Do you want $3 to go to this fund? ▶
If a joint return, does your spouse want $3 to go to this fund? ▶

Yes ☒ No ☐
☐ ☐

Filing status

1 ☒ Single   ☐ Married filing joint return (even if only one had income)

Report your income

Attach Copy B of Form(s) W-2 here.
Attach any tax payment on top of Form(s) W-2.

Note: You **must check** Yes or No.

Dollars   Cents

2 Total wages, salaries, and tips. This should be shown in box 1 of your W-2 form(s). Attach your W-2 form(s). 2 | 24,910.00

3 Taxable interest income of $400 or less. If the total is over $400, you cannot use Form 1040EZ. 3 | 150.00

4 Add lines 2 and 3. This is your **adjusted gross income.** 4 | 25,060.00

5 Can your parents (or someone else) claim you on their return?
☐ Yes. Do worksheet on back; enter amount from line G here.
☒ No. If **single**, enter 6,050.00. If **married**, enter 10,900.00. For an explanation of these amounts, see back of form. 5 | 6,050.00

6 Subtract line 5 from line 4. If line 5 is larger than line 4, enter 0. This is your **taxable income.** 6 | 19,010.00

Figure your tax

7 Enter your Federal income tax withheld from box 2 of your W-2 form(s). 7 | 3,020.00

8 **Tax.** Look at line 6 above. Use the amount on **line 6** to find your tax in the tax table on pages 24–28 of the booklet. Then, enter the tax from the table on this line. 8 | 2,854.00

Refund or amount you owe

9 If line 7 is larger than line 8, subtract line 8 from line 7. This is your **refund.** 9 | 166.00

10 If line 8 is larger than line 7, subtract line 7 from line 8. This is the **amount you owe.** For details on how to pay, including what to write on your payment, see page 16. 10 |

Sign your return

Keep a copy of this form for your records.

I have read this return. Under penalties of perjury, I declare that to the best of my knowledge and belief, the return is true, correct, and accurately lists all amounts and sources of income I received during the tax year.

Your signature *William W. Bristol*
Date 3-7-94 Your occupation RESTAURANT MGR

Spouse's signature if joint return
Date   Spouse's occupation

For IRS Use Only — Please do not write in boxes below.

☐ ☐ ☐ ☐
☐ ☐ ☐ ☐

For Privacy Act and Paperwork Reduction Act Notice, see page 4.   Cat. No. 11329W   Form 1040EZ (1993)

Form 1040A Return for Clyde F. and Delia C. Cooper (Example 20)

Form	Department of the Treasury—Internal Revenue Service		
1040A	**U.S. Individual Income Tax Return** (T) **1993**	IRS Use Only—Do not write or staple in this space.	

OMB No. 1545-0085

Label
(See page 15.)

L
A
B
E
L

H
E
R
E

Use the IRS label. Otherwise, please print or type.

Your first name and initial: CLYDE F.   Last name: COOPER

Your social security number: 234 56 7890

If a joint return, spouse's first name and initial: DELIA C.   Last name: COOPER

Spouse's social security number: 345 67 8901

Home address (number and street). If you have a P.O. box, see page 16.
1234 FINE STREET   Apt. no.

City, town or post office, state, and ZIP code. If you have a foreign address, see page 16.
DESIRABLE, OK 66666

For Privacy Act and Paperwork Reduction Act Notice, see page 4.

Presidential Election Campaign Fund (See page 16.)

	Yes	No
Do you want $3 to go to this fund?		X
If a joint return, does your spouse want $3 to go to this fund?		X

Note: Checking "Yes" will not change your tax or reduce your refund.

Check the box for your filing status
(See page 16.)
Check only one box.

1 ☐ Single
2 ☒ Married filing joint return (even if only one had income)
3 ☐ Married filing separate return. Enter spouse's social security number above and full name here. ▶ _____
4 ☐ Head of household (with qualifying person). (See page 17.) If the qualifying person is a child but not your dependent, enter this child's name here. ▶ _____
5 ☐ Qualifying widow(er) with dependent child (year spouse died ▶ 19___). (See page 18.)

Figure your exemptions
(See page 19.)

If more than seven dependents, see page 22.

6a ☒ **Yourself.** If your parent (or someone else) can claim you as a dependent on his or her tax return, **do not** check box 6a. But be sure to check the box on line 18b on page 2.

b ☒ **Spouse**

No. of boxes checked on 6a and 6b: **2**

c **Dependents:**

(1) Name (first, initial, and last name)	(2) Check if under age 1	(3) If age 1 or older, dependent's social security number	(4) Dependent's relationship to you	(5) No. of months lived in your home in 1993
GARY R. COOPER		777 99 6541	SON	12
DEBORAH D. COOPER		456 99 8765	DAUGHTER	12

No. of your children on 6c who:
• lived with you **2**
• didn't live with you due to divorce or separation (see page 22)

d If your child didn't live with you but is claimed as your dependent under a pre-1985 agreement, check here . . . . ▶ ☐

Dependents on 6c not entered above ___

e Total number of exemptions claimed.

Add numbers entered on lines above **4**

Figure your total income

Attach Copy B of your Forms W-2 and 1099-R here.

If you didn't get a W-2, see page 24.

If you are attaching a check or money order, put it on top of any Forms W-2 or 1099-R.

7 Wages, salaries, tips, etc. This should be shown in box 1 of your W-2 form(s). Attach Form(s) W-2. | 7 | 49,545 | 00

8a **Taxable** interest income (see page 25.) If over $400, also complete and attach Schedule 1, Part I. | 8a | 1,100 | 00

b **Tax-exempt** interest. DO NOT include on line 8a.   8b ___

9 Dividends. If over $400, also complete and attach Schedule 1, Part II.   9 ___

10a Total IRA distributions.   10a ___   10b Taxable amount (see page 26.)   10b ___

11a Total pensions and annuities.   11a ___   11b Taxable amount (see page 26.)   11b ___

12 Unemployment compensation (see page 30).   12 ___

13a Social security benefits.   13a ___   13b Taxable amount (see page 30.)   13b ___

14 Add lines 7 through 13b (far right column). This is your **total income.** ▶ | 14 | 50,645 | 00

Figure your adjusted gross income

15a Your IRA deduction (see page 32).   15a | 2,000 | 00

b Spouse's IRA deduction (see page 32).   15b | 2,000 | 00

c Add lines 15a and 15b. These are your **total adjustments.** | 15c | 4,000 | 00

16 Subtract line 15c from line 14. This is your **adjusted gross income.** If less than $23,050 and a child lived with you, see page 63 to find out if you can claim the "Earned income credit" on line 28c. ▶ | 16 | 46,645 | 00

Cat. No. 11327A   **1993 Form 1040A page 1**

Return for Clyde F. and Delia C. Cooper *continued*

1993 Form 1040A page 2

Name(s) shown on page 1	CLYDE F. AND DELIA C. COOPER	Your social security number 234 56 7890

Figure your standard deduction, exemption amount, and taxable income

17	Enter the amount from line 16.	17	46,645	00

18a Check ☐ **You** were 65 or older   ☐ Blind } **Enter number of**
   if: ☐ **Spouse** was 65 or older ☐ Blind } **boxes checked ▶ 18a**

b If your parent (or someone else) can claim you as a dependent, check here . . . . ▶ 18b ☐

c If you are married filing separately and your spouse files Form 1040 and itemizes deductions, see page 36 and check here ▶ 18c ☐

19 Enter the **standard deduction** shown below for your filing status. **But if you checked any box on line 18a or b,** go to page 36 to find your standard deduction. **If you checked box 18c,** enter -0-.
- Single—$3,700   • Head of household—$5,450
- Married filing jointly or Qualifying widow(er)—$6,200
- Married filing separately—$3,100

19	6,200	00

20	Subtract line 19 from line 17. If line 19 is more than line 17, enter -0-.	20	40,445	00
21	Multiply $2,350 by the total number of exemptions claimed on line 6e.	21	9,400	00
22	Subtract line 21 from line 20. If line 21 is more than line 20, enter -0-. This is your **taxable income.**	▶ 22	31,045	00

Figure your tax, credits, and payments

If you want the IRS to figure your tax, see the instructions for line 22 on page 37.

23	Find the tax on the amount on line 22. Check if from: ☒ Tax Table (pages 50–55) or ☐ Form 8615 (see page 38).	23	4,654	00

24a Credit for child and dependent care expenses. Complete and attach Schedule 2. 24a 700 00

b Credit for the elderly or the disabled. Complete and attach Schedule 3. 24b

c	Add lines 24a and 24b. These are your **total credits.**	24c	700	00
25	Subtract line 24c from line 23. If line 24c is more than line 23, enter -0-.	25	3,954	00
26	Advance earned income credit payments from Form W-2.	26		
27	Add lines 25 and 26. This is your **total tax.**	▶ 27	3,954	00

28a Total Federal income tax withheld. If any tax is from Form(s) 1099, check here. ▶ ☐ 28a 4,250 00

b 1993 estimated tax payments and amount applied from 1992 return. 28b

c **Earned income credit.** Complete and attach Schedule EIC. 28c

d	Add lines 28a, 28b, and 28c. These are your **total payments.**	▶ 28d	4,250	00

Figure your refund or amount you owe

29	If line 28d is more than line 27, subtract line 27 from line 28d. This is the amount you **overpaid.**	29	296	00
30	Amount of line 29 you want **refunded to you.**	30	296	00
31	Amount of line 29 you want **applied to your 1994 estimated tax.**	31		
32	If line 27 is more than line 28d, subtract line 28d from line 27. This is the **amount you owe.** For details on how to pay, including what to write on your payment, see page 42.	32		
33	Estimated tax penalty (see page 43). Also, include on line 32.	33		

Sign your return

Keep a copy of this return for your records.

Under penalties of perjury, I declare that I have examined this return and accompanying schedules and statements, and to the best of my knowledge and belief, they are true, correct, and accurately list all amounts and sources of income I received during the tax year. Declaration of preparer (other than the taxpayer) is based on all information of which the preparer has any knowledge.

Your signature *Clyde F. Cooper*	Date 4-2-94	Your occupation PROFESSIONAL MODEL
Spouse's signature. If joint return, BOTH must sign. *Delia C. Cooper*	Date 4-2-94	Spouse's occupation COMPUTER PROGRAMMER

Paid preparer's use only

Preparer's signature ▶	Date	Check if self-employed ☐	Preparer's social security no.
Firm's name (or yours if self-employed) and address ▶		E.I. No.	
		ZIP code	

1993 Form 1040A page 2

Return for Clyde F. and Delia C. Cooper *continued*

Schedule 1
(Form 1040A)

Department of the Treasury—Internal Revenue Service

Interest and Dividend Income
for Form 1040A Filers (T)

1993

OMB No. 1545-0085

Name(s) shown on Form 1040A
CLYDE F. AND DELIA C. COOPER

Your social security number
234 :56: 7890

Part I

Interest income

(See pages 25 and 56.)

Note: *If you received a Form 1099–INT, Form 1099–OID, or substitute statement from a brokerage firm, enter the firm's name and the total interest shown on that form.*

1 List name of payer. If any interest is from a seller-financed mortgage and the buyer used the property as a personal residence, see page 56 and list this interest first. Also, show that buyer's social security number and address.

		Amount	
CITY SAVINGS	1	950	00
U.S. GOVERNMENT		150	00

2 Add the amounts on line 1.	2	1,100	00
3 Excludable interest on series EE U.S. savings bonds issued after 1989 from Form 8815, line 14. You MUST attach Form 8815 to Form 1040A.	3		
4 Subtract line 3 from line 2. Enter the result here and on Form 1040A, line 8a.	4	1,100	00

Part II

Dividend income

(See pages 25 and 57.)

Note: *If you received a Form 1099–DIV or substitute statement from a brokerage firm, enter the firm's name and the total dividends shown on that form.*

5 List name of payer		Amount	
	5		

6 Add the amounts on line 5. Enter the total here and on Form 1040A, line 9.	6		

For Paperwork Reduction Act Notice, see Form 1040A instructions.   Cat. No. 12075R   **1993 Schedule 1 (Form 1040A) page 1**

Return for Clyde F. and Delia C. Cooper continued

Schedule 2
(Form 1040A)

Department of the Treasury—Internal Revenue Service

Child and Dependent Care Expenses for Form 1040A Filers (T) **1993**

OMB No. 1545-0085

Name(s) shown on Form 1040A CLYDE F. AND DELIA C. COOPER

Your social security number 234 56 7890

You need to understand the following terms to complete this schedule: **Dependent care benefits, Earned income, Qualified expenses,** and **Qualifying person(s).** See **Important terms** on page 58. Also, if you had a child born in 1993 and line 17 of Form 1040A is less than $23,050, see **A change to note** on page 59.

Part I

Persons or organizations who provided the care

You MUST complete this part.

1	(a) Care provider's name	(b) Address (number, street, apt. no., city, state, and ZIP code)	(c) Identifying number (SSN or EIN)	(d) Amount paid (see page 61)	
	HAPPY TRAILS PRESCHOOL	2391 BRONCO ST. DESIRABLE, OK 66789	74-3966431	3,500	00

(If you need more space, use the bottom of page 2.)

2 Add the amounts in column (d) of line 1.	2	3,500	00

3 Enter the number of **qualifying persons** cared for in 1993 . . . ▶ | 2 |

Did you receive dependent care benefits?	**NO** ──────▶ Complete only Part II below.
	YES ──────▶ Complete Part III on the back now.

Part II

Credit for child and dependent care expenses

4 Enter the amount of **qualified expenses** you incurred and paid in 1993. DO NOT enter more than $2,400 for one qualifying person or $4,800 for two or more persons. If you completed Part III, enter the amount from line 25. | 4 | 3,500 | 00 |

5 Enter YOUR **earned income.** | 5 | 31,795 | 00 |

6 If married filing a joint return, enter YOUR SPOUSE'S earned income (if student or disabled, see page 61); **all others,** enter the amount from line 5. | 6 | 17,756 | 00 |

7 Enter the **smallest** of line 4, 5, or 6. | 7 | 3,500 | 00 |

8 Enter the amount from Form 1040A, line 17. | 8 | 46,645 | 00 |

9 Enter on line 9 the decimal amount shown below that applies to the amount on line 8.

If line 8 is—		Decimal amount is	If line 8 is—		Decimal amount is
Over	But not over		Over	But not over	
$0—10,000		.30	$20,000—22,000		.24
10,000—12,000		.29	22,000—24,000		.23
12,000—14,000		.28	24,000—26,000		.22
14,000—16,000		.27	26,000—28,000		.21
16,000—18,000		.26	28,000—No limit		.20
18,000—20,000		.25			

9	× .20

10 Multiply **line 7** by the decimal amount on line 9. Enter the result. Then, see page 61 for the amount of credit to enter on Form 1040A, line 24a. | 10 = | 700 | 00 |

Caution: *If you paid $50 or more in a calendar quarter to a person who worked in your home, you must file an employment tax return. Get* **Form 942** *for details.*

For Paperwork Reduction Act Notice, see Form 1040A instructions.   Cat. No. 10749I   **1993 Schedule 2 (Form 1040A) page 1**

Form 1040, with Schedules A and B Return for Jeremy S. and Shelly R. Allen
(Example 26)

Form **1040** Department of the Treasury—Internal Revenue Service
U.S. Individual Income Tax Return (T) **1993**

IRS Use Only—Do not write or staple in this space.

For the year Jan. 1–Dec. 31, 1993, or other tax year beginning , 1993, ending , 19   OMB No. 1545-0074

Label
(See instructions on page 12.)

Your first name and initial   Last name
JEREMY S. ALLEN

If a joint return, spouse's first name and initial   Last name
SHELLY R. ALLEN

Home address (number and street). If you have a P.O. box, see page 12.   Apt. no.
8473 SMITHSON PLA

City, town or post office, state, and ZIP code. If you have a foreign address, see page 12.
BORING, OR 97832

Use the IRS label. Otherwise, please print or type.

Your social security number
123 45 9875

Spouse's social security number
456 85 2147

For Privacy Act and Paperwork Reduction Act Notice, see page 4.

Presidential Election Campaign
(See page 12.)
Do you want $3 to go to this fund? . . . .   Yes [X] No
If a joint return, does your spouse want $3 to go to this fund? . . . .   [X]

Note: Checking "Yes" will not change your tax or reduce your refund.

Filing Status
(See page 12.)
Check only one box.

1   Single
2 [X] Married filing joint return (even if only one had income)
3   Married filing separate return. Enter spouse's social security no. above and full name here. ▶
4   Head of household (with qualifying person). (See page 13.) If the qualifying person is a child but not your dependent, enter this child's name here. ▶
5   Qualifying widow(er) with dependent child (year spouse died ▶ 19   ). (See page 13.)

Exemptions
(See page 13.)

6a [X] Yourself. If your parent (or someone else) can claim you as a dependent on his or her tax return, **do not** check box 6a. But be sure to check the box on line 33b on page 2 .
b [X] Spouse . . . .

c **Dependents:**

(1) Name (first, initial, and last name)	(2) Check if under age 1	(3) If age 1 or older, dependent's social security number	(4) Dependent's relationship to you	(5) No. of months lived in your home in 1993
WILLIAM A.		789 65 4321	SON	12
SUSAN B.		456 65 9874	DAUGHTER	12
GREGORY C.		321 65 9873	SON	12

If more than six dependents, see page 14.

No. of boxes checked on 6a and 6b   **2**
No. of your children on 6c who:
• lived with you   **3**
• didn't live with you due to divorce or separation (see page 15)
Dependents on 6c not entered above

d   If your child didn't live with you but is claimed as your dependent under a pre-1985 agreement, check here ▶ ☐
e   Total number of exemptions claimed

Add numbers entered on lines above ▶ **5**

Income

Attach Copy B of your Forms W-2, W-2G, and 1099-R here.

If you did not get a W-2, see page 10.

If you are attaching a check or money order, put it on top of any Forms W-2, W-2G, or 1099-R.

7   Wages, salaries, tips, etc. Attach Form(s) W-2   7   73,975 00
8a   **Taxable** interest income (see page 16). Attach Schedule B if over $400 . . . . .   8a   2,800 00
b   Tax-exempt interest (see page 17). DON'T include on line 8a   8b
9   Dividend income. Attach Schedule B if over $400   9   200 00
10   Taxable refunds, credits, or offsets of state and local income taxes (see page 17) . .   10
11   Alimony received   11
12   Business income or (loss). Attach Schedule C or C-EZ   12
13   Capital gain or (loss). Attach Schedule D   13
14   Capital gain distributions not reported on line 13 (see page 17)   14
15   Other gains or (losses). Attach Form 4797   15
16a   Total IRA distributions . 16a   b Taxable amount (see page 18)   16b
17a   Total pensions and annuities 17a   b Taxable amount (see page 18)   17b
18   Rental real estate, royalties, partnerships, S corporations, trusts, etc. Attach Schedule E   18
19   Farm income or (loss). Attach Schedule F   19
20   Unemployment compensation (see page 19)   20
21a   Social security benefits 21a   b Taxable amount (see page 19)   21b
22   Other income. List type and amount—see page 20   22
23   Add the amounts in the far right column for lines 7 through 22. This is your **total income** ▶   23   76,975 00

Adjustments to Income
(See page 20.)

24a   Your IRA deduction (see page 20) 24a
b   Spouse's IRA deduction (see page 20) 24b
25   One-half of self-employment tax (see page 21) . . . 25
26   Self-employed health insurance deduction (see page 22) 26
27   Keogh retirement plan and self-employed SEP deduction 27
28   Penalty on early withdrawal of savings 28
29   Alimony paid. Recipient's SSN ▶ 29
30   Add lines 24a through 29. These are your **total adjustments** . . . . ▶   30

Adjusted Gross Income

31   Subtract line 30 from line 23. This is your **adjusted gross income.** If this amount is less than $23,050 and a child lived with you, see page EIC-1 to find out if you can claim the "Earned Income Credit" on line 56 . . . . ▶   31   76,975 00

Cat. No. 11320B   Form **1040** (1993)

Return for Jeremy S. and Shelly R. Allen *continued*

Form 1040 (1993)   Page **2**

Tax Compu- tation (See page 23.)	32	Amount from line 31 (adjusted gross income)	32	76,975 00
	33a	Check if: ☐ **You** were 65 or older, ☐ Blind; ☐ **Spouse** was 65 or older, ☐ Blind. Add the number of boxes checked above and enter the total here . . . . ▶ **33a**		
	b	If your parent (or someone else) can claim you as a dependent, check here . ▶ **33b** ☐		
	c	If you are married filing separately and your spouse itemizes deductions or you are a dual-status alien, see page 24 and check here. . . . . ▶ **33c** ☐		
	34	Enter the larger of your: { **Itemized deductions** from Schedule A, line 26, **OR** **Standard deduction** shown below for your filing status. **But if you checked any box on line 33a or b,** go to page 24 to find your standard deduction. If you checked **box 33c,** your standard deduction is zero. • Single—$3,700 • Head of household—$5,450 • Married filing jointly or Qualifying widow(er)—$6,200 • Married filing separately—$3,100 }	34	15,100 00
If you want the IRS to figure your tax, see page 24.	35	Subtract line 34 from line 32	35	61,875 00
	36	If line 32 is $81,350 or less, multiply $2,350 by the total number of exemptions claimed on line 6e. If line 32 is over $81,350, see the worksheet on page 25 for the amount to enter .	36	11,750 00
	37	**Taxable income.** Subtract line 36 from line 35. If line 36 is more than line 35, enter -0-	37	50,125 00
	38	Tax. Check if from **a** ☒ Tax Table, **b** ☐ Tax Rate Schedules, **c** ☐ Schedule D Tax Worksheet, or **d** ☐ Form 8615 (see page 25). Amount from Form(s) 8814 ▶ **e** ___	38	9,238 00
	39	Additional taxes (see page 25). Check if from **a** ☐ Form 4970 **b** ☐ Form 4972 . . .	39	
	40	Add lines 38 and 39. . . . . ▶	40	9,238 00
Credits (See page 25.)	41	Credit for child and dependent care expenses. Attach Form 2441	41	
	42	Credit for the elderly or the disabled. Attach Schedule R . .	42	
	43	Foreign tax credit. Attach Form 1116	43	
	44	Other credits (see page 26). Check if from **a** ☐ Form 3800 **b** ☐ Form 8396 **c** ☐ Form 8801 **d** ☐ Form (specify) ___	44	
	45	Add lines 41 through 44	45	
	46	Subtract line 45 from line 40. If line 45 is more than line 40, enter -0- . . . . . ▶	46	9,238 00
Other Taxes	47	Self-employment tax. Attach Schedule SE. Also, see line 25.	47	
	48	Alternative minimum tax. Attach Form 6251	48	
	49	Recapture taxes (see page 26). Check if from **a** ☐ Form 4255 **b** ☐ Form 8611 **c** ☐ Form 8828	49	
	50	Social security and Medicare tax on tip income not reported to employer. Attach Form 4137 .	50	
	51	Tax on qualified retirement plans, including IRAs. If required, attach Form 5329	51	
	52	Advance earned income credit payments from Form W-2	52	
	53	Add lines 46 through 52. This is your **total tax** . . . . ▶	53	9,238 00
Payments Attach Forms W-2, W-2G, and 1099-R on the front.	54	Federal income tax withheld. If any is from Form(s) 1099, check ▶ ☐	54	9,500 00		
	55	1993 estimated tax payments and amount applied from 1992 return .	55			
	56	**Earned income credit.** Attach Schedule EIC	56			
	57	Amount paid with Form 4868 (extension request)	57			
	58a	Excess social security, Medicare, and RRTA tax withheld (see page 28) .	58a			
	b	Deferral of additional 1993 taxes. Attach Form 8841	58b			
	59	Other payments (see page 28). Check if from **a** ☐ Form 2439 **b** ☐ Form 4136	59			
	60	Add lines 54 through 59. These are your **total payments** . . . . ▶	60	9,500 00
Refund or Amount You Owe	61	If line 60 is more than line 53, subtract line 53 from line 60. This is the amount you **OVERPAID** . ▶	61	262 00
	62	Amount of line 61 you want **REFUNDED TO YOU**. . . . . ▶	62	262 00
	63	Amount of line 61 you want **APPLIED TO YOUR 1994 ESTIMATED TAX** ▶	63			
	64	If line 53 is more than line 60, subtract line 60 from line 53. This is the **AMOUNT YOU OWE.** For details on how to pay, including what to write on your payment, see page 29 . ▶	64	
	65	Estimated tax penalty (see page 29). Also include on line 64	65			

Sign Here Keep a copy of this return for your records.	Under penalties of perjury, I declare that I have examined this return and accompanying schedules and statements, and to the best of my knowledge and belief, they are true, correct, and complete. Declaration of preparer (other than taxpayer) is based on all information of which preparer has any knowledge.

Your signature	Date	Your occupation
Jeremy S. Allen	4/15/94	REGISTERED NURSE
Spouse's signature. If a joint return, BOTH must sign.	Date	Spouse's occupation
Shelly R. Allen	4/15/94	AIR TRAFFIC CONTROLLER

Paid Preparer's Use Only	Preparer's signature ▶		Date	Check if self-employed ☐	Preparer's social security no.
	Firm's name (or yours if self-employed) and address ▶			E.I. No.	
				ZIP code	

Return for Jeremy S. and Shelly R. Allen   *continued*

SCHEDULES A&B	**Schedule A—Itemized Deductions**	OMB No. 1545-0074
(Form 1040)	(Schedule B is on back)	1993
Department of the Treasury Internal Revenue Service (T)	▶ Attach to Form 1040. ▶ See Instructions for Schedules A and B (Form 1040).	Attachment Sequence No. 07

Name(s) shown on Form 1040
JEREMY S. AND SHELLY R. ALLEN

Your social security number

Medical and Dental Expenses		**Caution:** *Do not include expenses reimbursed or paid by others.*			
	1	Medical and dental expenses (see page A-1)	1	3,000 00	
	2	Enter amount from Form 1040, line 32.	2	76,975 00	
	3	Multiply line 2 above by 7.5% (.075)	3	5,773 00	
	4	Subtract line 3 from line 1. If zero or less, enter -0-. ▶	4	– 0 –	
Taxes You Paid (See page A-1.)	5	State and local income taxes	5	3,500 00	
	6	Real estate taxes (see page A-2)	6	1,200 00	
	7	Other taxes. List—include personal property taxes ▶	7		
	8	Add lines 5 through 7 ▶	8	4,700 00	
Interest You Paid (See page A-2.)	9a	Home mortgage interest and points reported to you on Form 1098	9a	8,500 00	
	b	Home mortgage interest not reported to you on Form 1098. If paid to the person from whom you bought the home, see page A-3 and show that person's name, identifying no., and address ▶	9b		
Note: Personal interest is not deductible.	10	Points not reported to you on Form 1098. See page A-3 for special rules	10		
	11	Investment interest. If required, attach Form 4952. (See page A-3.)	11	400 00	
	12	Add lines 9a through 11 ▶	12	8,900 00	
Gifts to Charity (See page A-3.)		**Caution:** *If you made a charitable contribution and received a benefit in return, see page A-3.*			
	13	Contributions by cash or check	13	1,500 00	
	14	Other than by cash or check. If over $500, you **MUST** attach Form 8283	14		
	15	Carryover from prior year	15		
	16	Add lines 13 through 15 ▶	16	1,500 00	
Casualty and Theft Losses	17	Casualty or theft loss(es). Attach Form 4684. (See page A-4.) ▶	17		
Moving Expenses	18	Moving expenses. Attach Form 3903 or 3903-F. (See page A-4.) ▶	18		
Job Expenses and Most Other Miscellaneous Deductions (See page A-5 for expenses to deduct here.)	19	Unreimbursed employee expenses—job travel, union dues, job education, etc. If required, you **MUST** attach Form 2106. (See page A-4.) ▶	19		
	20	Other expenses—investment, tax preparation, safe deposit box, etc. List type and amount ▶ $225 TAX RETURN PREPARATION	20	225 00	
	21	Add lines 19 and 20	21	225 00	
	22	Enter amount from Form 1040, line 32.	22	76,975 00	
	23	Multiply line 22 above by 2% (.02)	23	1,540 00	
	24	Subtract line 23 from line 21. If zero or less, enter -0- ▶	24	– 0 –	
Other Miscellaneous Deductions	25	Other—from list on page A-5. List type and amount ▶	25		
Total Itemized Deductions	26	Is the amount on Form 1040, line 32, more than $108,450 (more than $54,225 if married filing separately)? • **NO.** Your deduction is not limited. Add lines 4, 8, 12, 16, 17, 18, 24, and 25 and enter the total here. Also enter on Form 1040, line 34, the **larger** of this amount or your standard deduction. • **YES.** Your deduction may be limited. See page A-5 for the amount to enter. ▶	26	15,100 00	

For Paperwork Reduction Act Notice, see Form 1040 instructions.	Cat. No. 11330X	Schedule A (Form 1040) 1993

Return for Jeremy S. and Shelly R. Allen *continued*

Schedules A&B (Form 1040) 1993	OMB No. 1545-0074	Page **2**

Name(s) shown on Form 1040. Do not enter name and social security number if shown on other side.

JEREMY S. AND SHELLY R. ALLEN

Your social security number 123 45 9875

Schedule B—Interest and Dividend Income

Attachment Sequence No. **08**

Part I
Interest Income

(See pages 16 and B-1.)

Note: If you received a Form 1099-INT, Form 1099-OID, or substitute statement from a brokerage firm, list the firm's name as the payer and enter the total interest shown on that form.

Note: If you had over $400 in taxable interest income, you must also complete Part III.

Interest Income		Amount	
1 List name of payer. If any interest is from a seller-financed mortgage and the buyer used the property as a personal residence, see page B-1 and list this interest first. Also show that buyer's social security number and address ►			
MERCANTILE NATIONAL BANK		1,800	00
U.S. GOVERNMENT BONDS		600	00
BEN FRANKLIN SAVINGS	1	400	00
2 Add the amounts on line 1	2	2,800	00
3 Excludable interest on series EE U.S. savings bonds issued after 1989 from Form 8815, line 14. You MUST attach Form 8815 to Form 1040	3		
4 Subtract line 3 from line 2. Enter the result here and on Form 1040, line 8a ►	4	2,800	00

Part II
Dividend Income

(See pages 17 and B-1.)

Note: If you received a Form 1099-DIV or substitute statement from a brokerage firm, list the firm's name as the payer and enter the total dividends shown on that form.

Note: If you had over $400 in gross dividends and/or other distributions on stock, you must also complete Part III.

Dividend Income		Amount	
5 List name of payer. Include gross dividends and/or other distributions on stock here. Any capital gain distributions and nontaxable distributions will be deducted on lines 7 and 8 ►			
GRE, INC.	5	200	00
6 Add the amounts on line 5	6	200	00
7 Capital gain distributions. Enter here and on Schedule D* .	7		
8 Nontaxable distributions. (See the inst. for Form 1040, line 9.)	8		
9 Add lines 7 and 8	9		
10 Subtract line 9 from line 6. Enter the result here and on Form 1040, line 9 . ►	10	200	00

*If you received capital gain distributions but do not need Schedule D to report any other gains or losses, see the instructions for Form 1040, lines 13 and 14.

Part III
Foreign Accounts and Trusts

(See page B-2.)

If you had over $400 of interest or dividends OR had a foreign account or were a grantor of, or a transferor to, a foreign trust, you must complete this part.	Yes	No
11a At any time during 1993, did you have an interest in or a signature or other authority over a financial account in a foreign country, such as a bank account, securities account, or other financial account? See page B-2 for exceptions and filing requirements for Form TD F 90-22.1		X
b If "Yes," enter the name of the foreign country ►		
12 Were you the grantor of, or transferor to, a foreign trust that existed during 1993, whether or not you have any beneficial interest in it? If "Yes," you may have to file Form 3520, 3520-A, or 926 .		X

For Paperwork Reduction Act Notice, see Form 1040 instructions.

Schedule B (Form 1040) 1993

PROBLEM MATERIALS

DISCUSSION QUESTIONS

4-1 *Personal and Dependency Exemptions.* Distinguish between personal and dependency exemptions.

4-2 *Tests for Dependency Exemptions.* List and briefly describe the five tests that must be met before a taxpayer is entitled to a dependency exemption for another individual. Must all five tests be met?

4-3 *Support.* Briefly describe the concept of support. As part of your definition, include examples of support items.

4-4 *Support—Special Items.* With respect to the support test, discuss survivor's treatment of each of the following items: athletic scholarships, social security survivors' benefits paid to an orphan, and aid to dependent children paid by the state government.

4-5 *Gross Income Test.* Describe the gross income test that is applied to the dependency exemption. Must all dependents for whom a dependency exemption is claimed meet this test?

4-6 *Gross Income Test—Dependency Exemption.* M provides more than half of the support for her father, F, who is single for tax purposes. F's other support is in the form of interest income of $5,000 and social security benefits of $9,000.

    a. May M claim a dependency exemption for supporting F in 1994?
    b. Would your answer differ if F's interest income were only $1,500.

4-7 *Relationship Test—Dependency Exemption.* Assuming Q provides over 50 percent of their support and the dependent meets the gross income, relationship, and citizenship tests, which of the following relatives may be claimed as a dependent?

    a. Widow of Q's deceased son
    b. Q's husband's brother
    c. Daughter of Q's husband's brother
    d. Q's mother's brother
    e. Q's grandmother's brother
    f. Q's great grandson

4-8 *Joint Return Test—Dependency Exemption.* K and L were married in 1994 and elected to file a joint return. K had interest income of $5,000 and a salary of $30,000 for the year. L had interest income of $2,250 and received the remainder of her support from her mother and K.

    a. If L's mother provided more than 50 percent of L's support, can she claim a dependency exemption for L?
    b. If not, under what circumstances could the exemption be claimed?

4-9 *Community Property Law.* How does the treatment of earned income differ between a community property state and a noncommunity property (i.e., separate property) state for Federal income tax purposes? Why?

4-10   *Filing Status, Tax Schedules.*   List the four sets of rate schedules that apply to individual taxpayers. Refer to them by filing status and schedule designation (e.g., Schedule Z). Which taxpayers must use the rate schedules rather than the tax rate tables?

4-11   *Determination of Marital Status.*   Married taxpayers are subject to a separate set(s) of tax rates. When is marital status determined? What authority (state or federal) controls marital status?

4-12   *Exceptions—Marital Status.*   In certain instances, a person who is married may use the rates for unmarried persons. In another instance, a single person may use the rates for married persons filing jointly. Elaborate.

4-13   *Head of Household—Requirements.*   What are the specific requirements for head-of-household status? List at least ten relatives who may qualify the taxpayer for head-of-household filing status.

4-14   *Head of Household—Divorced Parents.*   May a divorced parent with custody of a child qualify as a head of household even though his or her former spouse is entitled to the dependency exemption for the child? Explain.

4-15   *Head of Household—Taxpayer's Home.*   Must the person who qualifies a taxpayer as a head of household (i.e., the taxpayer's child or other dependent) live in the taxpayer's home? Are there any exceptions to this rule?

4-16   *Costs of Maintaining Home.*   Which of the following expenses are included in determining the cost of a home when determining whether a taxpayer qualifies as a head of household?

    a.   Food consumed on the premises
    b.   Transportation for a dependent to and from school
    c.   Clothing for a dependent
    d.   Property taxes on residence
    e.   Rent paid on residence

4-17   *Abandoned Spouse.*   M is married and lives with her dependent son, S. M receives child support sufficient to provide 65 percent of S's support from S's father, who lived in a nearby city for the entire year. M provides over one-half of the cost of providing the home in which she and S live.

    a.   What is M's filing status and what is the number of exemption deductions that she may claim?
    b.   How would your answers differ if M agreed to let S's father claim the dependency exemption for S?

4-18   *Tax Tables.*   Are taxpayers required to use the tax tables? Which taxpayers are ineligible to use the tables?

4-19   *Limited Standard Deduction.*   W is 16 years old, single, and claimed as a dependent by his parents. His 1994 gross income is $4,000.

    a.   If W's taxable income is $3,400, what is the character of his income, earned or unearned?
    b.   If W's taxable income is $2,500, what is the character of his income, earned or unearned?
    c.   If W's taxable income is $200, what is the character of his income, earned or unearned?

4-20 *Kiddie Tax.* G is 13 years old and claimed as a dependent by her parents. G's top marginal tax rate is 15 percent and her parents' is 28 percent. Calculate G's taxable income and the rate at which it will be taxed in the following instances:

a. Interest of $950
b. Interest of $1,600
c. Interest of $600 and wages of $2,400
d. Interest of $3,400 and wages of $500

4-21 *Filing Requirements.* Which individuals are exempted from filing a Form 1040 (or equivalent Form 1040A or Form 1040EZ)?

4-22 *Due Date.* P is a calendar year individual taxpayer with taxable income of $45,000 and a tax due of $350 for the current year.

a. When is P's tax return due?
b. Assuming P uses the fiscal year ending June 30, when is her annual income tax return due?

4-23 *Extensions.* Q is a calendar year individual taxpayer with taxable income of $25,000 and a tax refund of $150 for the current year.

a. If Q is unable to file on time, she may request an automatic extension of time to file her tax return. How long is the maximum extension period?
b. If Q is unable to complete her return by the extended due date and she has an appropriate reason, how long of an additional extension can she request?

4-24 *Due Dates for Estimated Tax Payments.* R is a calendar year taxpayer whose estimated tax liability for 1994 is $4,000. What are the amounts and the due dates of R's estimated tax payments?

4-25 *Amount of Estimated Tax Payments.* H is a calendar year taxpayer who estimates his Federal income tax to be $5,500 and his self-employment tax to be $4,500 for 1994. For 1993, H's Federal income tax was $4,950, and his self-employment tax was $3,975. What is the amount of estimated tax that H must pay on each due date to avoid a penalty for failure to make adequate estimated tax payments?

4-26 *Penalties and Interest.* J is a calendar year individual whose gross tax for 1994 is $10,000. J had taxes of $5,750 withheld and made estimated tax payments of $500 each due date. She submitted $1,350 along with her request for an automatic extension on April 15. The remaining $900 was paid when J's tax return was filed on July 9. J's 1993 tax totaled $9,950.

a. Does J owe a penalty for failure to file for 1994?
b. Does J owe a penalty for failure to pay for 1994? If so, for what period?
c. Does J owe a penalty for failure to make adequate estimated tax payments for 1994? If so, over what period?
d. Does J owe interest on any of the amounts paid? If so, for what period?

4-27 *Statute of Limitations.* What is the importance of the Federal Statute of Limitations to the taxpayer? To the IRS? Generally, how long is the statute of limitations on tax matters?

4-28 *Six-Year Statute of Limitations.* Under what circumstances will the regular three-year statutory period for assessments be extended to six years?

4-29 *Indexation and the Individual Income Tax.* Congress has provided for indexation of certain deductions. What items are subject to indexation? What index is to be used as an estimate of price-level changes?

PROBLEMS

4-30 *Exemptions.* In each of the following situations determine the proper number of personal and dependency exemptions available to the taxpayer. Unless otherwise implied, assume that all tests are satisfied.

    a. R's mother, age 85, lives in his home. R figures that including the value of the lodging, he provides support of about $6,000. The remainder of her support is paid for with her social security benefits of $4,000.

    b. This year D sent his father, F, monthly checks of $200, or $2,400 for the year. F used these checks along with $2,300 of rental income ($4,400 of rents less $2,100 of expenses) to pay all of his support.

    c. H and W are married with one daughter, D, age 7. D models children's clothing and earned $4,000 of wages this year. D also has a trust fund of $50,000 established by her grandparents. All of D's wages were saved and none were used to pay for her support. Similarly none of the funds of the trust were used to pay for D's support.

    d. Professor and Mrs. Smith participated in the foreign exchange student program at their son's high school. In December of 1993, a student, Hans, arrived from Germany, spent the spring of 1994 with the Smiths, then returned to Germany.

    e. B and C are happily married with one son, S. S, age 20, is a full-time student at the University of Cincinnati. S worked as a painter during the summer to help put himself through school. He earned wages of $4,000, $2,500 of which was used to pay for his room and board at school and $1,500 for miscellaneous living expenses (e.g., gas for his car, dates, laundry, etc.). He lived with his parents during the summer. The value of their support including meals and lodging was $5,000. He also received a National Merit Scholarship which paid for his tuition of $5,000.

4-31 *Personal and Dependency Exemptions.* In each of the following situations determine the proper number of personal and dependency exemption deductions available to the taxpayer.

    a. A is single and 44 years of age. He provides full support for his mother, who is 67 and lives in a small retirement community in A's hometown.

    b. D and K are married and file a joint return for the year. D is 67 years of age and K is 62. They have no dependents.

    c. E and O are married and file a joint return for the year. They provide all the support for their two younger children for the entire year. E and O also provided all the support for their oldest child (age 19) for the eight months she was a full-time student. After graduating from high school, she accepted a job that paid $3,000 in salaries. Nevertheless, her parents contributed over one-half of her support for the entire year.

4-32 *Exemption Phase-out.* H and W are married with two children, ages 3 and 5. Compute the couple's deduction for exemptions assuming they file a joint return and have adjusted gross income as follows:

   a. $100,000

   b. $176,000

   c. $300,000

4-33 *Married Dependents.* In November of this year, Jim Jenkins married his college sweetheart, Kate Brown. Jim was 24 and Kate was 22. Jim had graduated two years ago. Kate still had one more year of school. The majority of Kate's support this year was provided by her parents. Jim earned $15,000 during the year while Kate received $900 of interest from her savings account. Assume Kate's parents are in the 28 percent tax bracket and would give the couple any tax savings to be derived from claiming Kate as a dependent.

   a. May Kate's parents claim an exemption for Kate assuming the couple files a joint return?

   b. Would the couple be better off filing separate returns (and thus receiving any taxes saved by Kate's parents) or filing a joint return? Show all computations you must make to determine your answer.

4-34 *Itemized Deductions and Exemptions.* G and H are married and file a joint return for 1994. They have A.G.I. of $200,400 for the year and the following itemized deductions and personal and dependency exemptions:

State and local taxes............................	$ 5,300
Residence interest..............................	14,500
Investment interest.............................	500
Charitable contributions.........................	6,200
Personal and dependency exemptions............	4

   a. Calculate G and H's taxable income for 1994.

   b. Calculate G and H's taxable income for 1994 assuming their A.G.I. was $210,400, a $10,000 increase over (a).

   c. By what amount did taxable income increase due to this $10,000 increase in adjusted gross income? Why wasn't it $10,000?

4-35 *Multiple Support Agreements.* G's support is provided as follows:

Social security benefits.................................	$3,600
Taxable interest income.................................	800
Support from:	
A, G's oldest son—Cash..............................	1,600
B, G's daughter—Fair value of lodging and cash........	2,300
C, G's youngest son—Cash...........................	700

   a. Who is entitled to a dependency exemption for G in absence of any agreement as to who gets the deduction?

   b. Who may claim a dependency exemption for G under a multiple support agreement?

   c. How would your answer to (b) differ if A contributed $650 instead of $1,600?

4-36 *Children of Divorced Parents.* For each of the following, determine whether M or F is entitled to the dependency exemption in 1994 for their only child, S. M and F were divorced in 1991 and M has custody, except when F has visitation privileges. Together, M and F provide 100 percent of S's support.

   a. M was granted the dependency exemption under the divorce decree. F pays child support for the year totaling $1,500. Total support expenditures for S are $3,600.

   b. No mention of the dependency exemption was made in the divorce decree. F pays child support for S of $2,400, and the total support for S is $4,500.

   c. F was granted the dependency exemption in the divorce decree and he paid child support of $1,800 for the year. The total support for S for the year was $3,500.

4-37 *Filing Status and Standard Deduction.* Determine the most beneficial filing status and the standard deduction for each of the following taxpayers for 1994:

   a. M is a 54-year-old unmarried widow whose spouse died in 1989. During all of 1994 M's son, for whom she claims a dependency exemption, lives with her.

   b. S is a 67-year-old bachelor who lives in New York City. S pays over half the cost of maintaining a home in Tampa, Florida for his 89-year-old mother. He is entitled to a dependency exemption under a multiple support agreement executed by his brother, his sister, and himself.

   c. R is a widower whose wife died in 1993. R maintained a household for his three dependent children during 1994 and provided 100 percent of the cost of the household.

   d. J is divorced and has custody of his 9-year-old child. J provides over half the cost of the home in which he lives with his child, but his ex-wife is entitled to the dependency exemption for the child for 1994.

4-38 *Head of Household.* Indicate whether the taxpayer would be entitled to file using the head of household rate schedule.

   a. Y is divorced from her husband. She maintains a home in which she and her 10-year-old son live. Her ex-husband pays child support to her that she uses to provide all of the support for the child. In addition, Y has relinquished her right to claim her son as a dependent to her former spouse.

   b. C is divorced from his wife. He provides 75 percent of the support for his mother who lives in a nursing home. His mother receives $5,000 of interest income annually.

   c. J's grandson, L, had a falling-out with his parents and moved in with him this year. J did not mind because he had grown lonely since his wife died three years ago. L is 17 years old and earned $5,000 this year as a part-time grocery clerk.

   d. B's wife died four years ago and he has not remarried. Last year his daughter, D, graduated from Arizona State University and moved to Hawaii. Unfortunately, D was unable to earn enough money to make ends meet and had to rely on checks from dad. B paid for D's own apartment and provided the majority of her support.

   e. M's wife died last year. This year he maintains a home for his 25-year-old daughter, E, who is attending graduate school. E earned $8,000 as a teaching assistant. Nevertheless, M provided the majority of E's support.

   f. Same as (e) except E is the taxpayer's sister.

   g. F's husband died this year. She continues to provide a home for her two children, ages 6 and 8.

4-39 *Dependent's Personal Exemption and Standard Deduction.* K is 16 years old and is claimed as a dependent on her parents' income tax return. She earned wages of $2,800 and collected interest of $1,200 for the year. What is the amount of K's taxable income for the year?

4-40 *Dependent's Personal Exemption and Standard Deduction.* B is 20 years old and is claimed as a dependent on his sister's tax return. B earned $1,600 from a part-time job during the year. What is B's taxable income?

4-41 *Computation of Tax.* R and S are married and have two dependents. Compute their 1994 tax liability, assuming they file a joint return and their taxable income is

    a. $75,000
    b. $175,000
    c. $260,000

4-42 *High-Income Taxpayer.* H and W are married and file a joint return for 1994. They have no dependents and both are under age 40. H earned a salary of $120,000. W is self-employed and earned a net profit from business of $89,000. H and W have personal itemized deductions totaling $14,800 (all subject to the 3% cutback problem).

    a. What are the amounts of their adjusted gross income and taxable income on their joint income tax return?
    b. Calculate the 1994 tax liability, including W's self-employment tax. Assume that the 1994 self-employment tax is 15.3 percent on income up to $60,600 (2.9% MHI with no limit).

4-43 *Tax Tables.* S earned a salary during 1993 of $54,600. She is single and had no dependents for the year. Her only other income was taxable interest income of $560. Determine S's taxable income and her Federal income tax. (**Note:** This tax table computation is for 1993 because the 1994 tax tables will not be available until late 1994. See Appendix A for the 1993 tax tables.)

4-44 *Tax Rate Schedules.* W and T were married and filed a joint return for 1994. Their adjusted gross income for the year was $102,000. Their total itemized deductions were $9,700 and they were entitled to three personal and dependency exemptions. Neither W nor T is 65 years old and both have good sight. Determine W and T's taxable income and their Federal income tax liability before prepayments and credits for 1994.

4-45 *Application of the Kiddie Tax.* For each of the following situations, determine the child's taxable income and the amounts that would be taxed at the child's and parents' rates for the 1994 tax year.

    a. When J's rich uncle died, he left her 1,000 shares of stock. This year the stock paid J $1,400 in dividends, her only income. J is seven years old and her parents claim an exemption for her.
    b. L, age 13, works in his father's record shop on weekends. During the year, he earned $1,100 from this job. In addition, L had $700 of interest income attributable to a gift from his grandfather. L's father claims an exemption for him.
    c. Same as (b) except L's earned income was $2,100 and interest income was $1,700.

4-46 *Computation of the Kiddie Tax.* G's great aunt gave her a certificate of deposit which matures in ten years when she is 21. The certificate pays interest of $2,000 annually. G's parents file a joint return. Their 1994 taxable income is $75,000. Compute G's tax.

4-47 *Failure-to-File Penalty.* T, overwhelmed by other pressing concerns, simply forgot to file his tax return for 1993 until July 20, 1994. When filed, T's 1993 return showed a tax due before withholding and estimated taxes of $10,000.

    a. Will T be penalized for failure to file his return if the total income taxes withheld by his employer were $11,000?

    b. Assuming T's employer withheld $9,000, what is the amount of the failure-to-file penalty, if any?

4-48 *Failure-to-Pay Penalty.* On April 13, 1995 R, a calendar year taxpayer, sat down to prepare his 1994 tax return. Realizing that he simply did not have time to accumulate all of his records, R decided to file for an extension. R's tax liability for the previous year, 1993, was $8,000. During 1994 R's employer withheld $2,500 and R paid estimated taxes of $500. R estimates that his final tax liability for 1994 will be $12,000.

    a. Assuming R obtains an extension to file his 1994 return, when will his return normally be due?

    b. Based on the facts above, what amount must R pay by April 15 to avoid a failure-to-pay penalty?

    c. R completed and filed his return on July 20, 1995. Unfortunately, his initial estimate of his tax was low and his final tax (before withholding and estimated tax payments) was $15,000. Assuming R paid the amount determined in part (b) above, what is the amount of the failure-to-pay penalty, if any?

4-49 *Estimated Taxes and Underpayment Penalty.* K works as a salesman for the National Hospital Supply Corporation, selling surgical and other hospital supplies. He receives a salary plus a percentage commission on sales over a certain threshold. In 1994 K's tax liability before prepayments was $20,000. His 1993 tax liability was $12,000. In each year his A.G.I. was less than $150,000.

    a. What is the lowest required tax installment (including withholding) that K can make and avoid the penalty for underpaying his taxes during the year? (Ignore the annualized income installment.)

    b. Assume that K paid estimated taxes of $1,000 on each due date. In addition, K's employer withheld a total of $3,000 during the year. K filed and paid the balance of his liability on April 15, 1995. Assume the applicable interest rate charged on underpayments for each period in 1994 is 10 percent. Compute K's penalty, if any, for failure to pay estimated taxes. Compute the penalty for the first installment only.

    c. Assume that K works solely for commissions and that he had no income through March 31, 1994 because he decided to take a winter vacation. Income for the remainder of the year was sufficient to generate a tax liability before prepayments of $20,000. What implications do these facts have on the calculation of the underpayment penalty for 1994?

4-50 *Penalties for Inadequate Estimated Tax Payments.* Z is a calendar year individual whose gross tax for 1994 is $40,000. Z had taxes of $8,000 withheld and did not make estimated tax payments. Z's tax due was paid with his timely filed return on April 15, 1995. His 1993 tax was $30,000.

    a. Calculate Z's penalty for failure to make adequate estimated tax payments, if any.

    b. Does Z owe interest on any of the amounts paid? If so, for what period?

    c. Same as (a) above, except Z's adjusted gross income for 1993 was $160,000.

4-51 *Penalties and Interest.* Y filed her tax return for 1993 on April 15, 1994. Upon discovering an inadvertent error, Y filed an amended return and submitted additional tax of $1,250.

    a. Does Y owe a penalty for failure to pay? If so, how much?

    b. Does Y owe interest on the $1,250 paid with the amended return? If so, how much?

4-52 *Statute of Limitations.* T, a calendar year taxpayer, filed her 1993 Federal income tax return on January 29, 1994 and received a tax refund check for overpaid 1993 taxes on May 17, 1994.

    a. Assuming that T did not file a false return or have a substantial omission of income, what is the last date on which the IRS may assess an additional income tax liability against her for the 1993 tax year?

    b. If T unintentionally had a substantial omission of income from her 1993 return, what is the last day on which the IRS may assess her an additional 1993 income tax liability?

    c. If T had never bothered to file her 1993 tax return, what is the last day on which the IRS may assess her an additional 1993 income tax liability?

TAX RETURN PROBLEMS

4-53 *Form 1040EZ.* Samuel B. White was single for 1994 and had no dependents. Sam's only income was wages of $19,500 and taxable interest of $65. Federal income tax of $2,430 was withheld from Sam's salary.

    Calculate Sam's Federal income tax and his tax due or refund for 1994. A Form 1040EZ may be completed based on this information. Supply fictitious occupation, social security number, and address. (**Note:** If the 1994 tax forms are not available, use 1993 forms.)

4-54 *Form 1040A.* Charles D. and Alice A. Davis were married during all of 1993 and had income from the following sources:

Salary, Charles....................................		$22,000
Federal income tax withheld....................	$2,660	
Part-time salary, Alice............................		11,400
Federal income tax withheld....................	1,280	
Interest from Home Savings......................		320
Interest from U.S. Government Bonds............		430

Charles and Alice provide the sole support of their two children. During 1994 they paid job-related child care expenses of $2,200. Their itemized deductions for the year are insufficient for them to itemize, but a deductible $2,000 was deposited in each of their individual retirement accounts.

    Calculate the Federal income tax and the tax due (or refund) for Mr. and Mrs. Davis, assuming they file a joint return. If the 1994 tax tables are not available, use the tax rate schedules on the inside front cover of the text. A Form 1040A may also be completed. Supply fictitious information for the address, occupations, social security numbers, and children's names. (**Note:** If the 1994 tax forms are not available, use 1993 forms.)

4-55   *Form 1040.*   William A. Gregg, a high school educator, and Mary W. Gregg, a microbiologist, are married and file a joint income tax return for 1994. Neither William nor Mary is over 50 years old, and both have excellent sight. They provide the sole support of their three children: Barry, Kimberly, and Rachel. The following information is from their records for 1994:

Salaries and wages, William......................		$32,000
Federal income tax withheld.....................	$3,420	
Salaries and wages, Mary........................		44,000
Federal income tax withheld.....................	4,730	
Interest income—Home Savings and Loan.........		410
Interest income—City Bank.......................		220
Tax-exempt interest income......................		1,400
Dividends—Alto, Inc. (a Florida company).........		180
Itemized deductions as follows:		
Hospitalization insurance......................		320
Unreimbursed fees of doctors, hospitals, etc.....		740
Unreimbursed prescription drugs................		310
Real estate taxes on residence.................		1,350
State income taxes paid........................		1,440
State sales taxes paid..........................		720
Interest paid on original home mortgage.........		8,430
Charitable contribution—Faith Church............		1,720
Charitable contribution—State University.........		200
Quarterly estimated taxes paid....................		3,500

Calculate the 1994 Federal income tax and the tax due (or refund) for the Greggs assuming they file a joint return. Form 1040, along with Schedules A and B, may be completed. Supply fictitious information for the address and social security numbers. (**Note:** If the 1994 tax forms are not available, use 1993 forms.)

RESEARCH PROBLEMS

4-56   *Support by Noncustodial Parent.*   G incurred several expenses while exercising visitation rights with his children from a dissolved marriage. Determine which, if any, of the following expenses are treated as provided by G toward the support of his children: travel by G to visit the children, transportation and entertainment for children, lodging in G's residence, and gifts of toys and clothing.

Research aids:

> *Brandes v. Comm.*, 29 TCM 1436, T.C. Memo 1970-313.
> *Gilliam v. Comm.*, 28 TCM 956, T.C. Memo 1969-188.
> *Hout v. Comm.*, 25 TCM 1468, T.C. Memo 1966-281.
> *Hastings v. Comm.*, 16 TCM 928, T.C. Memo 1957-202.

4-57   *Nonresident Alien Spouse.*   C is a citizen of the United States who resides indefinitely in Europe. C is married to N, a citizen of Greece. C has $32,000 of gross income subject to United States tax and would like to file jointly with N. Can C accomplish this goal? If so, what steps are necessary? How is the income of N treated?

Research aids:

> Code § 6013(g) and Reg. § 1.6013-6.

PART II

GROSS INCOME

CONTENTS

CHAPTER 5 ▪ GROSS INCOME

CHAPTER 6 ▪ GROSS INCOME: Inclusions and Exclusions

LEARNING OBJECTIVES

Upon completion of this chapter you will be able to:

- Define income for tax purposes and explain how it differs from the definitions given to it in accounting or economics

- Explain the concept of the taxable year and identify who is eligible to use fiscal years

- Apply the cash and accrual methods of accounting to determine the tax year in which items are reported

- Determine the effect of a change in accounting method

- Describe some of the special rules governing the treatment of prepaid income, interest income, interest-free loans, and income from long-term contracts

- Identify which taxpayer is responsible for reporting income and paying the taxes on such income

CHAPTER OUTLINE

Introduction	5-1	Accounting for Income:	
Gross Income Defined	5-2	Special Considerations	5-29
Economic Concept of Income	5-3	Claim of Right Doctrine	5-29
Accounting Concept of Income	5-5	Prepaid Income	5-31
Income for Tax Purposes:		Interest Income	5-35
The Judicial Concept	5-5	Identification of the Taxpayer	5-40
Refinements of the Gross Income		Income from Personal Services	5-40
Definition	5-9	Income from Property	5-41
Form-of-Benefit Principle	5-9	Unearned Income of Children	
Return of Capital Doctrine	5-10	under 14	5-41
Indirect Economic Benefits	5-13	Interest-Free and Below-Market	
Reporting Income: Tax Accounting		Loans	5-42
Methods	5-16	Income from Community Property	5-46
Accounting Periods	5-16	Tax Planning	5-49
Accounting Methods	5-18	Timing Income Recognition	5-49
Cash Method of Accounting	5-21	Income-Splitting Techniques	5-49
Accrual Method of Accounting	5-25	Excluded Economic Income	5-51
Changes in Accounting Methods	5-26	Problem Materials	5-52

Chapter 5

GROSS INCOME

INTRODUCTION

Determination of the final income tax liability begins with the identification of a taxpayer's gross income. Before that can be done, however, one obviously must understand what constitutes *income* for tax purposes. The primary purpose of this chapter is to examine the income concept and thus provide some general guidelines regarding what is and what is not subject to taxation. As a practical matter, income is normally easy to spot. Salary, interest, dividends, rents, gains from the sales of property, and most other items that one customarily thinks of as income are in fact income for tax purposes. In fact, these represent the bulk of all income that is reported to Uncle Sam. But what if a taxpayer is lucky enough to receive an inheritance, a gift, or a scholarship? Are these taxable? What about court-awarded damages? And if a taxpayer borrows $1,000, is there income? What happens if Publishers Clearing House gives you $10 million? Is the IRS as happy as you are? And how do those Mississippi flood victims treat their government aid? Is their relief taxable? The list of possible income items goes on and on. Fortunately, these items are more the exception than the rule. In any event, newcomers to tax should understand that there are no hard and fast rules that can be applied to every conceivable situation. The Supreme Court clearly stated the problem in a case concerning the income status of embezzled funds:

> In fact, no single conclusive criterion has yet been found to determine in all situations what is sufficient gain to support the imposition of an income tax. No more can be said in general than that all relevant facts and circumstances must be considered.[1]

---

[1] *Comm. v. Wilcox*, 46-1 USTC ¶9188, 34 AFTR 811, 327 U.S. 404 (USSC, 1946).

Notwithstanding the Court's observations, three important generalizations developed in this chapter are

1. "Income" is broadly construed for tax purposes to include virtually any type of gain, benefit, or profit that has been realized.

2. Although the scope of the income concept is broad, certain types of income are exempted from taxation by statute, administrative ruling, or judicial decree.

3. Taxpayers who realize income may not be required to recognize and report it immediately but may be able to postpone recognition until some time in the future.

To sum up, there are three basic questions to address concerning income:

1. Did the taxpayer have income?

2. If the taxpayer had income, was it realized?

3. If the taxpayer has realized income, must it be recognized now or is it permanently excluded or perhaps temporarily deferred and reported at some future date?

The first part of this chapter examines the concept of income. Once one is sensitive to the concept of income, consideration must be given to *if and when* the income must be reported as well as *who* must report it. The latter part of the chapter focuses on the timing of income recognition and the identification of the reporting entity.

GROSS INCOME DEFINED

The definition of income found in the Internal Revenue Code reflects the language of the constitutional amendment empowering Congress to impose taxes on income.[2] Section 61(a) of the Code defines *gross income* as follows:

> Except as otherwise provided in this subtitle, gross income means all income from whatever source derived, including (but not limited to) the following items:
>
> 1. Compensation for services, including fees, commissions, fringe benefits, and similar items;
> 2. Gross income derived from business;
> 3. Gains derived from dealings in property;
> 4. Interest;
> 5. Rents;
> 6. Royalties;
> 7. Dividends;

---

[2] See Chapter 1.

8. Alimony and separate maintenance payments;

9. Annuities;

10. Income from life insurance and endowment contracts;

11. Pensions;

12. Income from discharge of indebtedness;

13. Distributive share of partnership gross income;

14. Income in respect of a decedent; and

15. Income from an interest in an estate or trust.

Despite the statute's detailed enumeration of income items, the list is not comprehensive. The items specified are only a sample of the more common types of income. Taxable income includes many other economic benefits not identified above.

As a practical matter, Code § 61 furnishes little guidance for determining whether a particular benefit should be treated as income. The statute provides no criteria or factors that could be used for assessment. For example, the general definition does not provide any clue as to whether a gift or an inheritance constitutes taxable income. Similarly, the statute is not helpful in determining whether income arises upon the discovery of buried treasure. These and similar issues, as will be seen, are often answered by reference to other, more specific, sections of the Code. On the other hand, many questions cannot be resolved by reference to the statute or the regulations. In situations where clear statutory guidance is absent, the difficult task of ascertaining how far the definitional boundary of income extends falls to the courts. To this end, the courts have utilized the meanings given income in both economics and accounting to mold a workable definition of income for tax purposes.

ECONOMIC CONCEPT OF INCOME

Economists define income as the amount that an individual could have spent for consumption during a period while remaining as well off at the end of the period as at the beginning of the period. This concept of income may be expressed mathematically as the sum of an individual's consumption during the period plus the change in the individual's net worth between the beginning and end of the period.[3]

---

[3] The economic definition of income given here is often referred to as the Haig-Simons definition as derived from the following works: Robert M. Haig, "The Concepts of Income—Economic and Legal Aspects," *The* *Federal Income Tax* (New York: Columbia University Press, 1921); Henry C. Simons, *Personal Income Taxation* (Chicago: University of Chicago Press, 1921).

Example 1. K's records revealed the following assets and liabilities as of December 31, 1994 and 1995:

	12-31-94	12-31-95
Assets (fair market value)......	$100,000	$140,000
Liabilities......................	(20,000)	(30,000)
Net worth.....................	$ 80,000	$110,000

During the year, K spent $25,000 on rent, food, clothing, entertainment, and other items. From an economic perspective, K's income for 1995 is $55,000 determined as follows:

Consumption...	$25,000
Change in net worth ($110,000 − $80,000)...............	30,000
Economic income..	$55,000

There are two key aspects of an economist's definition. The first is the emphasis on a change in net worth. According to the economist, a taxpayer has income under any circumstances that cause his or her net worth to increase. Note that this view is extremely broad. Taxpayers who receive an inheritance, are the beneficiaries of a life insurance policy, discover buried treasure, or have their debts canceled have all had an increase in net worth and would therefore have income using this definition. Some may object to this comprehensive approach. It is nevertheless consistent with § 61, which states that income includes *all* income regardless of its source.

The second and perhaps more critical aspect of the economist's definition from a tax perspective is the notion that consumption and the change in net worth must be computed using market values on an accrual basis rather than on a realization basis. For example, economists include in income any increase in the value of an individual's shares of stock during the period, even though the shares are not sold and the individual does not *realize* the increase in value. In addition, economists would include in income the rental value of one's car or home, as well as the value of food grown for personal use, since such items constitute consumption. Gifts and inheritances would also be considered income by an economist since these items would affect an individual's net worth. Although the economist's approach to income is theoretically sound, it has significant drawbacks from a practical view.

For practical application, the meaning given to income must be objective to minimize controversies. The economist's reliance on market values to measure net worth and consumption violates this premise. Few assets have readily determinable and accurate values. Valuation of most assets would be a subjective determination. For example, an individual may be able to value shares of stock by referring to an active publicized market, but how is the value of a favorite chair to be computed? The difficulty in making such valuations would no doubt lead to countless disputes and administrative hassles. These practical problems of implementing the economic concept of income have caused the courts to adopt a different interpretation.

It should be pointed out, however, that the economist's approach to measuring income—the so-called "net worth method"—is sometimes used when the IRS decides that the taxpayer's records do not adequately reflect income.[4] Application usually occurs where the taxpayer has not maintained records, or has falsified or destroyed any records that were kept. In these situations, the IRS reconstructs income by determining the change in net worth during the year and adding estimated living expenses.

ACCOUNTING CONCEPT OF INCOME

The principle of realization distinguishes the accountant's concept of income from that of the economist. Under this principle, accountants recognize income when it is *realized*. Income is generally considered realized when (1) the earnings process is complete, and (2) an exchange or transaction has taken place.[5] Normally, some type of *conversion* occurs that substantially changes the taxpayer's relationship to the asset. To illustrate, consider a taxpayer who discovers oil on his property. He may have "income" in the economic sense (at least to the extent that the value of his property and his net worth have increased). But he has not realized that increase in net worth and does not have income in the accounting sense until he converts his discovery into another asset (e.g., he sells the property or the oil). Observe that these two criteria provide the objective determination of value traditionally believed necessary for the work that accountants perform. As a result, accounting income usually does not recognize changes in market values of assets during a period (as would economic income) unless such changes have been realized.

INCOME FOR TAX PURPOSES: THE JUDICIAL CONCEPT

The landmark decision of the Supreme Court in *Eisner v. Macomber* in 1918 provided the first glimpse of how the concept of income would be interpreted for tax purposes.[6] In this case, the court embraced the realization principle of accounting, indicating that income must be *realized* before it can be taxed. As later decisions suggested, the primary virtue of the realization principle is not that it somehow yields a better or more theoretically precise income figure. Rather, it provides an objective basis for measuring income, eliminating the problems that would arise if income were determined using subjective valuations. In short, the realization principle is a well-entrenched part of the tax law because it makes the law so much easier to administer.

---

[4] *Holland v. U.S.,* 54-2 USTC ¶9714, 46 AFTR 943, 348 U.S. 121 (USSC, 1954). Net worth, however, is to be determined using the tax basis in assets and not their fluctuating market values [*S. Bedeian,* 54 T.C. 295 (1970)].

[5] "Basic Concepts and Accounting Principles Underlying Financial Statements of Busi-

ness Enterprises," *Accounting Principles Board Statements No. 4* (New York: American Institute of Certified Public Accountants, 1970), ¶134.

[6] 1 USTC ¶32, 3 AFTR 3020, 252 U.S. 189 (USSC, 1920).

A second issue addressed by the *Eisner* decision concerned the scope of the income concept. How far did it reach? Did income include gifts, scholarships, court-awarded damages, a personal secretary, and other types of benefits? In essence, the Court again followed the accounting approach, stating that income was restricted to gains realized from property or personal services.

Hence, finding a $10 bill, receiving a prize or award, or profiting from a canceled debt would not have been taxable under *Eisner,* since the benefits were obtained without any effort by the taxpayer. Later decisions, however, expanded the concept of income by rejecting the notion that only gains derived from capital or labor are recognized. The courts have taken what is often referred to as an "all-inclusive" approach; that is, *all* gains are presumed to be taxable except those specifically exempted. The Supreme Court's opinion in *Glenshaw Glass Co.* provides the definition of income that is perhaps most commonly accepted today.[7] This case involved the treatment of punitive damages awarded to Glenshaw Glass for fraud and antitrust violations of another company. In holding that such awards were income, the Court stated:[8]

> Here we have instances of undeniable accessions to wealth, clearly realized, and over which the taxpayer has complete dominion. The mere fact that the payments were extracted from wrongdoers as punishment for unlawful conduct cannot detract from their character as taxable income to the recipients.

Thus, income for tax purposes is construed to include any type of gain, benefit, profit, or other increase in wealth that has been realized and is not exempted by statute. Note that the courts have adopted key elements of both the economic and accounting definition of income: income is any increase in the taxpayer's *net worth* (i.e., wealth) that has been *realized.* Also note that, even though it all sounds very technical and precise, the rule, like so many rules in taxation, may be difficult to apply in a given situation. For example, if a tenant paints the walls of her apartment or plants some gladiolus in the garden, has the landlord realized income? Arriving at a solution for this and any particular set of facts can be quite frustrating, but one can generally take heart that these are rare and, moreover, a common sense approach generally works: if it smells like income, it probably is income.

It should be emphasized that even though a taxpayer may have "income" that has in fact been realized, this by itself does not guarantee that it will be taxed. In tax parlance, the question still remains as to whether the taxpayer must "recognize" the income (i.e., report the income for tax purposes). There are *three* relatively common exceptions to the general rule that all income must be recognized immediately:

1. *Excluded income.* Income that has been realized need not be recognized if it is specifically exempted from taxation by virtue of some provision in the Code. For example, as discussed in Chapter 6, interest income from state and local bonds is specifically excluded under § 103 while gifts and inheritances (which obviously increase net worth) are excluded under § 102. In these cases, the income permanently escapes tax and normally creates a difference between taxable income and

---

[7]   55-1 USTC ¶9308, 47 AFTR 162, 348 U.S.   [8]   *Ibid.*
426 (USSC, 1955).

financial accounting income. It should be noted that, notwithstanding the Code's all-inclusive concept of income, the tax base is far from comprehensive because of the numerous exclusions and exemptions that have crept into the law over the years.[9]

2. *Accounting methods.* A taxpayer may be able to defer recognition of income to a subsequent year by following some particular method of accounting (e.g., the installment sales method or the completed contract method).

3. *Nontaxable exchanges.* Income realized on a sale or exchange may be deferred under a special nonrecognition rule. For example, a taxpayer who sells his home and realizes a gain is not required to recognize the income if he reinvests the sales proceeds in another home within a certain period of time. Similarly, a taxpayer who swaps one parcel of land costing $10,000 for another parcel worth $50,000 is not required to recognize the $40,000 gain under the like-kind exchange rules. The theory underlying nonrecognition in these situations is that the taxpayer has not liquidated his investment to cash but has continued it, albeit in another form. In effect, the law is willing to defer the tax until such time when the taxpayer does in fact convert the asset to cash and has the wherewithal to pay the tax. It is important to note, however, that in these and similar cases, the gain is only deferred; it does not escape tax permanently as is the case with excluded income.

In summary, income for tax purposes can generally be defined as any increase in wealth (net worth) or consumption that has been realized. Moreover, such income normally must be recognized unless it is specifically excluded or postponed due to an accounting rule or deferral provision.

✔ CHECK YOUR KNOWLEDGE

On December 30, 1993, at one of the most lavish affairs in the history of New York, Donald Trump tied the knot with Marla Maples. According to a brief article in the *New York Times,* Maples was adorned with a diamond tiara containing 325 diamonds and weighing 105 carats, estimated to be worth about $2 million. Interestingly, it later came out that Donald had not purchased a special present for the new Mrs. Trump. Instead, Marla had borrowed the tiara from a jeweler without charge to wear for the occasion. In addition, an eight-carat ring that Trump had given has fiancée earlier was also borrowed. Is there a tax question here?[10] Before answering, consider carefully the economic and accounting definitions of income.

---

[9] For an excellent discussion of the concept of income and the notion of a comprehensive tax base see Boris Bittker, "A Comprehensive Tax Base as a Goal of Income Tax Reform," 80 *Harvard Law Review* 925 (1967).

[10] For a complete discussion and the genesis of this question, see Sheppard, "Something Borrowed: The Tax Treatment of Marla's Tiara," 61 *Tax Notes* 1541.

If the proverbial smell test is applied, most people would probably find it difficult to detect the scent of income in this situation. Indeed, it is doubtful whether the IRS would sniff this one out or even care. Only narrow-minded taxaholic professors trying to illustrate the key aspects of the income definition could find a tax issue in this picture. The question posed by this unusual but illustrative scenario is whether Maples has realized any income and, if so, must it be recognized? Applying the economist's definition requires a check of her net worth. It would appear that she is no better off before the wedding than after since she had to return the precious stones to the jeweler. But has there been any consumption? Arguably so. She was allowed to wear the gems all during the wedding without paying a nickel. The rental value of the jewelry plus any unreimbursed cost of providing security no doubt meets the economist's concept of income. (In fact, as discussed later in this chapter, if a taxpayer loans money interest-free to another, the taxpayer is generally required to impute interest at the going rate and report the imputed interest income just as if he or she had actually received it.) Nevertheless, even if Maples has income under the all-inclusive rule of § 61, the question remains as to whether the income is exempt by some other provision of the Code. In this case, Maples may be able to argue that the value of one night's use of the jewelry (no doubt nominal in amount) is simply a gift from Donald's friendly jeweler. If the use is truly a gift, then it is not taxable since gifts are specifically excluded from income. But is the transfer a gift? Probably not, if the rationale of *Duberstein* is followed.[11] In this landmark case, Duberstein received a Cadillac from a business associate who was showing his gratitude for customer referrals that had led to sales. The transferor of the Cadillac had deducted the car as a business expense, but Duberstein did not report his newly acquired status symbol on his tax return. Although the Tax Court agreed with Duberstein, the Supreme Court did not. The Court indicated that, in order for the taxpayer to exclude a transfer, the transferor must have a "detached and disintegrated generosity." According to the Court, the transferor was not so motivated, and it consequently required Duberstein to report the value of the car in income. This same rationale could be applied in this situation. Apparently it is common practice for jewelers (e.g., Hollywood jewelers) to loan their merchandise to celebrities as a marketing ploy, not from some other, charitable impulse. Based on this theory, it could be concluded that Mrs. Trump has taxable income. Only time will tell whether the IRS believes the issue is worth pursuing. In any event, the story nicely explains the essence of the income concept: an increase in net worth or consumption that has been realized and is not exempted by statute.

---

[11] *Comm. v. Duberstein,* 60-2 USTC ¶9515, 5 AFTR2d 1626, 363 U.S. 278 (USSC, 1960).

REFINEMENTS OF THE GROSS INCOME DEFINITION

As one might imagine, in the early years of the tax law, when there were few specific rules, people found it easy to take the position that Congress never intended to tax their particular type of "income." To support such contentions, taxpayers, never lacking for imagination, often concocted ingenious arguments explaining why they should escape tax. In one memorable case, a taxpayer who received a gift (gifts are specifically excluded from income) argued that the income from the gifted property was also exempt since the income was merely an extension of the gift. Unfortunately, the court did not accept this gift-that-keeps-on-giving theory and taxed the income. But this was typical of the development of the tax law. As the courts dealt with this and other income issues, their decisions set a number of precedents that shaped and refined the concept of income. Because of their significance, some of the principles established by early court decisions were given statutory effect; that is, the rule evolving from the decision was subsequently enacted as part of the law, or codified. For example, § 102(b) now provides that income from gifted property is not part of the gift and is fully taxable.

Other court rulings have been incorporated into the Regulations either directly or by way of reference. Several of these rulings, however, have not found their way into the Code or Regulations. Nevertheless, they provide authoritative guidance for the determination of taxable income. This section examines three major principles that are relevant to the income concept. These concern:

1. *Form of Benefit.*   Must income be realized in a particular form, such as cash, before it becomes taxable?

2. *Return of Capital.*   Does gross income mean gross receipts or net gain after allowance for a tax-free recovery of the taxpayer's capital investment?

3. *Indirect Economic Benefits.*   Are benefits provided by an employer (such as a company car) taxable where they are not intended as compensation?

FORM-OF-BENEFIT PRINCIPLE

Many taxpayers erroneously believe that income need be reported only when cash is received. The Regulations clearly state, however, that gross income includes income realized in any form.[12] Thus, income is not limited to receipts of cash but also extends to receipts of property, services, and *any other economic benefits*. For example, taxpayers may realize income when their debts are canceled or they purchase property at a price less than its fair market value—a so-called *bargain purchase*. In situations where income is received in a form other than cash, a cash-equivalent approach is adopted.[13] Under this method, the measure of income is its fair market value at the time of receipt.

---

[12]   Reg. § 1.61-1(a).   [13]   Reg. § 1.446-1(a)(3).

Example 2.   Several years ago on the televsion show *60 Minutes,* a segment was devoted to what the commentators implied was a tax travesty. In truth, it was a sad tale. According to the story, a generous employer who wanted to reward his employees for their long years of service gave them stock in the company. At that time, the stock had a value of about $100 per share. The employees, as one might guess, were extremely pleased. Unfortunately, a sudden turn of events caused the value of the shares to plummet. By the close of the year, the stock was practically worthless. Some employees still holding the stock were upset but accepted their misfortune graciously. On April 15, however, those still holding the stock found themselves in tax shock. What was the problem? As may be apparent from the discussion of the form-of-benefit principle, the employees were required to report compensation income equal to the value of stock at the time of receipt, $100 per share. This meant that many employees had to report thousands of dollars of income even though the stock was currently worthless. They had income without any way to pay the tax. Although the employees might be able to claim a deduction for worthless stock, it might not provide total relief since such loss would be a capital loss, the deduction of which is limited.

Example 3.   Borrower B owed Lender L $10,000, evidenced by a note payable due in six months. If L allows B to cancel the note for a payment of $9,000, B must normally recognize gross income of $1,000.

RETURN OF CAPITAL DOCTRINE

The return of capital doctrine is best illustrated by a simple loan transaction. When a taxpayer lends money and it is later repaid, no income is recognized since the repayment represents merely a *return of capital* to the taxpayer. Although there is no statutory provision to this effect, it is a well-recognized rule. Moreover, the taxpayer's net worth has not increased (one asset, a receivable, has simply been replaced by another, cash). However, any interest on the loan that is paid to the taxpayer would be income.

Sale or Disposition.   The application of the return of capital doctrine is not limited to loans. One of the first refinements made to the income concept concerned the use of the return of capital principle to determine the income from a sale of property. In 1916 the Supreme Court held that the total proceeds received on a sale were not to be treated as income.[14] Rather, the portion of the proceeds representing the taxpayer's capital (i.e., adjusted basis) could be recovered tax free. Thus, it is the return of capital doctrine that allows the taxpayer to determine the income upon a sale or disposition of property by reducing the amount realized (cash + the fair market value of other receipts such as property) by the adjusted basis of the property. Using this approach—now contained in § 1001(a)—the taxpayer's income on dispositions of property is limited to the *gain* realized.

---

[14]   *Doyle v. Mitchell Bros.,* 1 USTC ¶17, 3 AFTR 2979, 247 U.S. 179 (USSC, 1918). See also, *Southern Pacific Company v.* *Lowe,* 1 USTC ¶19, 247, 3 AFTR 2989, 247 U.S. 330 (USSC, 1918).

Example 4. R sold XYZ stock for $10,000. He purchased the stock for $6,000. R's realized gain is $4,000 ($10,000 amount realized − $6,000 adjusted basis) rather than the gross amount of the sales price, $10,000, since the return of capital doctrine permits him to recover his $6,000 investment tax free.

The return of capital doctrine also stands for the important proposition that gross income is not the same as gross receipts. This is reflected in Regulations, which provide that in the manufacturing, merchandising, or mining business, *gross income* means total sales less costs of goods sold.[15]

Damages. The return of capital doctrine may also apply to amounts awarded for injury inflicted upon the taxpayer. Section 104, discussed in the following chapter, specifically excludes from income the amount of any damages awarded for personal injury or sickness on the grounds that the amount received represents a return of the personal capital destroyed. For this same reason, early rulings and decisions held that compensatory damages awarded for such personal wrongs as breach of contract to marry, slander and libel, and alienation of affection are nontaxable.[16] In many cases, amounts are also awarded to penalize the party responsible for the wrongdoing. These so-called punitive damages are taxable unless related to a physical injury or sickness.[17] Similarly, where the damages awarded represent reimbursement for lost profits, the amounts are considered taxable since they are merely substitutions for income.[18]

Example 5. After ten consecutive losing seasons as head football coach at Trample University and a swing at his offensive line coach, Coach F was fired. Shortly thereafter, F developed an ulcer, which forced him to have surgery. It was subsequently determined that the operation had been improperly performed. F sued the university for lost wages and the court awarded him $25,000. The $25,000 is fully taxable since it represents a substitution of income. F also sued the surgeon for $200,000 for malpractice and won. The $200,000 is not taxable since it represents a return of capital.

---

[15] Reg. § 1.61-3(a).

[16] For example, see *C.A. Hawkins,* 6 B.T.A. 1023 (1927); *L. McDonald,* 9 B.T.A. 1340 (1930); and Rev. Rul. 74-77, 1974-1 C.B. 33.

[17] § 104(a).

[18] *Phoenix Coal Co. v. Comm.,* 56-1 USTC ¶9366, 49 AFTR 445, 231 F.2d 420 (CA-2, 1956).

Example 6. G, an aging Hollywood starlet, sued a national gossip publication for malicious and defamatory remarks concerning how she made her way to the top. The suit demanded $800,000 for compensatory damages and $200,000 for punitive damages. The court only awarded her $500,000. In absence of any court allocation, the amount representing punitive damages, $100,000, is taxable, whereas the amount representing compensatory damages, $400,000, is nontaxable. These amounts were determined as follows:

$$\frac{\$200,000}{\$200,000 + \$800,000} \times \$500,000 = \$100,000 \text{ taxable}$$

$$\frac{\$800,000}{\$200,000 + \$800,000} \times \$500,000 = \$400,000 \text{ nontaxable}$$

Damages awarded to businesses are generally subject to the same tests applied to individuals. Awards or settlements for antitrust violations or patent infringements are examples of substitutions for income and thus are taxable. This is true for both actual and punitive damages. Compensation for damages to property are taxable to the extent that amounts received exceed the adjusted basis of the assets. Where the award is for damages to the goodwill of the business, the entire amount is usually taxable since the taxpayer normally does not have any recoverable basis in the goodwill.[19]

Example 7. M left her car running and ran inside the bank to make a deposit. When she came back, she stopped in shock as she watched her car plunge through the front of a furniture store. The furniture store ultimately received $50,000 in damages for property for which it had a basis of $35,000. The store realized a gain of $15,000. This gain must be recognized unless certain special rules concerning involuntary conversions discussed in Chapter 15 are followed.

Other Considerations. The scope of the return of capital doctrine extends beyond situations involving damages and simple sales transactions. Numerous Code sections are grounded on this principle, and often contain detailed rules for ascertaining how a receipt should be apportioned between capital and income. For example, amounts received under a life insurance policy are not taxable on the theory that the proceeds—at least in part—represent a return of the taxpayer's premium payments.[20] Similarly, where the taxpayer purchases an annuity (i.e., an investment which makes a series of payments to the investor in the future), the return of capital doctrine provides that each payment is in part a tax-free return of capital.[21] In addition, somewhat intricate provisions exist to determine whether a corporate distribution represents a distribution of earnings (i.e., a dividend) or a tax-free return of the taxpayer's investment.[22] The special rules governing life insurance, annuities, and dividends are covered in detail in Chapter 6.

---

[19] *Raytheon Production Corp. v. Comm.*, 44-2 USTC ¶9424, 32 AFTR 1155, 144 F.2d 100 (CA-1, 1944).

[20] § 101.

[21] § 72.

[22] §§ 301 and 316.

INDIRECT ECONOMIC BENEFITS

Another refinement to the otherwise all-inclusive definition of gross income concerns certain benefits provided by employers for employees. Early rulings and decisions exempted benefits conferred to employees that did not represent compensation and were provided for the convenience of the employer. For example, in 1919, the IRS ruled that lodging furnished seamen aboard ship was not taxable.[23] Similarly, in 1925, the Court of Claims held that the value of quarters provided an Army officer was not includible in income.[24] Explanations offered for exempting the lodging from income emphasized that the employee was granted the benefit solely because the employer's business could not function properly unless an employee was furnished that benefit on the employer's premises. The Court also observed that the benefits were not designed as a form of compensation for the employee, but rather were an outgrowth of business necessity. These early holdings established the view that certain benefits an employee receives indirectly from his or her employer are nontaxable. Current law grants an exclusion only if the employee can demonstrate that the benefit served a business purpose of the employer other than to compensate the employee.[25]

> **Example 8.** In the following situations an employee is permitted to exclude the benefit received under the rationale discussed above.
>
> 1. An employer provides the employee with a place to work and supplies tools and machinery with which to do the work. Similarly, an employee is not taxed when his or her secretary types a letter.
>
> 2. An employer provides tuition-free, American-style schools for its overseas employees.
>
> 3. An employer provides an executive with protection in response to threats made by terrorists.
>
> 4. An employer requires its employees to attend a convention held in a resort in Florida and pays the travel costs to the employees.

It is often difficult to determine whether a particular benefit represents compensation or, alternatively, serves the business needs of the employer. For example, free parking places and similar fringe benefits provided by an employer could arguably fall into either category, depending upon the circumstances. After many years of controversy concerning the taxation of fringe benefits, Congress addressed the problem in 1984. To emphasize that fringe benefits are taxable, Congress modified the listing of typical

---

[23] O.D. 265, 1 C.B. 71 (1919).

[24] *Jones v. U.S.*, 1 USTC ¶129, 5 AFTR 5297, 60 Ct.Cls. 552 (1925). Section 119, discussed in Chapter 6, currently provides specific rules that must be satisfied before meals and lodging may be excluded.

[25] *George D. Patterson v. Thomas*, 61-1 USTC ¶9310, 7 AFTR2d 862, 289 F.2d 108 (CA-2, 1960).

income items found in § 61 to specifically include "fringe benefits and similar items." However, several exceptions exempting certain benefits still exist. These exceptions are discussed in Chapter 6 concerning exclusions.

✔ CHECK YOUR KNOWLEDGE

Review Question 1. After exploring the cavernous pits of his patient's mouth, Dr. Will Floss, a dentist, concluded that the gentleman had to have a root canal. Floss explained to the patient the nature of the work and that it could very well be the first in a series of expensive steps required to put his teeth back in working order. He estimated the total cost at $5,000. At that moment, the patient, a wily floor-covering dealer, immediately recalled Floss's need for new carpeting. As a result, he suggested that he would be happy to make a deal: carpeting, pad, and installation in exchange for the dental work. The two agreed, the teeth were repaired, and the carpeting was installed. Any tax problem here?

The issue is whether either party must report income. Many individuals think that barter transactions, exchanges of property for services or property other than cash, are not taxable. However, taxpayers who believe bartering escapes the eye of the tax collector are in for a rude awakening by the IRS. Barter transactions are fully taxable under the form-of-benefit principle. It makes no difference whether the taxpayer's net worth is increased by cash or property. In either case, the taxpayer is better off and must recognize income. Here the dentist recognizes income equal to the value of the services rendered, $5,000, and the carpet salesman has revenue equal to the value of services received.

Review Question 2. Intel Corporation, a leading manufacturer of computer chips in the United States, recently sued another chip manufacturer, American Micro, for using its patented technology. The courts awarded Intel millions of dollars for the infringement. In a similar situation several years ago, Brian Bosworth, an All-American linebacker from Oklahoma University and a first-round draft pick of the Seattle Seahawks, retired from football after playing 24 of 44 games during his only three seasons. The cause of his short career can be traced to a debilitating shoulder injury. It was rumored that despite the end of his career, he could still receive $7.3 million of the $9.8 million remaining on his 10-year contract. In a comparable story, Theresa Burke and more than 8,000 other women employees of the Tennessee Valley Authority claimed unlawful discrimination in the payment of salaries on the basis of sex. The TVA had increased the salaries in certain male-dominated pay schedules, but not in certain female-dominated pay schedules. Moreover, TVA lowered salaries in the latter. The female employees asked for and were awarded back pay, costs, and attorney's fees. Burke and the other women each received amounts in settlement according to a formula based on their length of service and rates of pay. What tax treatment might be proposed for these taxpayers?

The basic question in all of these situations is the same: does Intel, Bosworth, or Burke have taxable income? The key is recognizing that the amounts received may be taxable or nontaxable depending on the application of the return of capital doctrine and perhaps other provisions of the Code. The problem that Intel faces is

demonstrating that the award for the patent infringement is not merely a replacement of lost income. It would appear that the corporation would have a difficult time overcoming a long string of cases that indicates that patent infringement awards are taxable. Nevertheless, there is no certainty in these matters without knowledge of all of the facts and a great deal of research. On the other hand, Bosworth probably had an easier time excluding his insurance benefits since they represent a return of his personal capital. And what about Ms. Burke? It would seem that knife could cut either way. On the one hand, the amounts received reimbursed her for back pay and arguably should be taxable as a substitution of income. On the other hand, the amounts could be viewed as a nontaxable reimbursement for a personal injury, sexual discrimination. If this seems difficult, it was and continues to be. The courts struggled with the issue. The Sixth Circuit Court of Appeals held that the amounts were not taxable, but that decision was reversed by the Supreme Court.

Review Question 3.   When Lee Iacocca ran Chrysler and Roger Smith was the CEO of GM, they probably received the use of a company car. The same can probably be said for their successors and the owners of every car dealership in the country as well as their salesmen. (If only accountants could receive such a deal!) Assume that each individual can drive the car for only 3,000 miles, after which he or she must evaluate the experience then exchange the old car for a new one and do it all over again. This is a nice arrangement: use a Jeep Grand Cherokee one month and a Viper the next. Great benefits, but what are the tax consequences?

Once again the question concerns income. Is the value of the use of the company car taxable? Can the taxpayers argue that their use (including all personal trips) is not compensation but simply an incidental benefit that they must endure in order to evaluate the car? Does the indirect benefit rule apply? Is there a special provision that exempts fringe benefits of this nature? In a long line of cases, it has been established that the value of a car provided by an employer is compensation to the extent of the employee's personal use. The twist on the basic fact pattern— the required evaluation—may, however, suggest a different conclusion. The fringe benefit rules enacted in 1984 and discussed more fully in Chapter 6 do allow an exclusion for certain full-time automobile salesmen who use demonstration vehicles in the sales area in which the automobile dealer's sales office is located. Note that this rule applies only to salesmen. Thus an owner or executive would not qualify for an exclusion under this exception unless he or she also is considered a salesman. There may be another escape hatch for executives and other management personnel, however, buried in the Regulations concerning product testing.[26] These Regulations allow the employee to exclude the benefit if the employee receives goods for testing and evaluation if a laundry list of requirements is met. The key point to remember here is not necessarily knowing the specific answer to this question but recognizing that an important theory exists—the indirect benefit doctrine—that is a valuable weapon on which the taxpayer can sometimes rely to avoid taxation of what at first glance has all the characteristics of taxable income.

---

[26] Regulation § 1.132-5(n).

REPORTING INCOME: TAX ACCOUNTING METHODS

Once the taxpayer has realized an item of taxable income, he or she must determine *when* the income should be reported. This determination, however, requires an understanding of the nature of accounting periods and accounting methods that may be used for tax purposes. This section examines some of the fundamental rules of tax accounting and how they govern the timing of income recognition.

ACCOUNTING PERIODS

Taxable income is usually computed on the basis of an annual accounting period commonly known as the taxable year.[27] There are two types of taxable years: a calendar year and a fiscal year. A calendar year is a 12-month period ending on December 31, whereas a fiscal year generally is any period of 12 months ending on the last day of any month other than December.[28] Any taxpayer may use a calendar year. Fiscal years may be used only by taxpayers who maintain adequate books and records. A taxpayer filing his or her *first* return may adopt either a calendar year or a fiscal year without IRS consent simply by filing a return. After adoption, however, any change does require IRS consent.[29]

Income from Partnerships, S Corporations, Fiduciaries.   Reporting income derived from an interest in a partnership, an S corporation, or an estate or trust presents a special problem. As explained in Chapter 3, income realized by a partnership or an S corporation is not taxable to either of these because they are not treated as separate taxable entities. Rather, the partnership or S corporation merely serves as a conduit through which the income flows. Consequently, partners or S shareholders report their distributive shares of the entity's income in their taxable year within which (or with which) the partnership or S corporation tax year ends. Partners or S shareholders must report their share of the income regardless of the amounts distributed to them.

> **Example 9.**   DEF Company, a fiscal year taxpayer, is a partnership owned equally by D, E, and F. For the taxable year ending September 30, 1994, the company had net income of $90,000. During the 12-month period ending on September 30, 1994, D withdrew $20,000 from his capital account. For his year ending December 31, 1994, D must report his share of partnership income, $30,000 ($\frac{1}{3}$ of $90,000), even though he only received a distribution of $20,000. Note that any income earned by the partnership from October 1994 through December 1994 is not reported until D files his 1995 tax return, which is normally due on April 15, 1996.

---

[27]   § 441(a) and (b).

[28]   Reg. § 1.441-1(d) and (e). The taxpayer may elect to end the tax year on a particular day of the week rather than a date, resulting in a tax year that varies in length between 52 and 53 weeks. See Reg. § 1.441-2.

[29]   A request for a change is made on Form 1128. The initial selection of, or a change in, tax year may result in a short tax year, in which case the tax may have to be computed on an annualized basis. See §§ 442 and 443.

Income realized by a trust or an estate is generally taxed to the beneficiaries to the extent it is actually distributed or required to be distributed. Income that is not taxed to the beneficiaries is taxed to the estate or trust.

Limitation on Fiscal Years. One effect of allowing fiscal years for reporting is to enable certain taxpayers to *defer* the taxation of income. For instance, in *Example 9* above, the election by the partnership to use a fiscal year creates an opportunity for D. Note that D's share of the partnership's income for October 1994 through December 1994 is not reported until D files his 1995 tax return, which is normally filed on April 15, 1996. A small corporation that primarily provides personal services could obtain a similar deferral.

> **Example 10.** G&H Inc., a law firm, is a regular C corporation owned by two attorneys, G and H. The corporation reports using a fiscal year ending on January 31. During 1994 the corporation paid G and H small salaries. Just before the close of its taxable year ending January 31, 1995, the corporation paid a bonus to G and H equal to its taxable income. By deducting the bonus, the corporation reports no income for its taxable year ending January 31, 1995, and G and H defer reporting the bonus until they file their 1995 tax return on April 15, 1996.

In 1986, Congress felt that the use of fiscal years to create deferral of income as shown above was improper. As a result, provisions were enacted that restrict the use of fiscal years by partnerships, S corporations, and so-called personal service corporations (i.e., corporations where the principal activity is the performance of services, substantially all of which are performed by employees who are also the owners of the business). Although certain exceptions enable these entities to use a fiscal year on a limited basis, as a general rule, these taxpayers normally must use the calendar year.[30]

Annual Accounting and Progressive Rates. The use of an annual accounting period in combination with other features of the taxation process causes numerous difficulties. For example, consider the effect of the tax system's use of both an annual accounting period and a progressive tax rate structure. Each year the taxpayer computes his or her taxable income for that period and applies a progressive rate structure to the income of that year. If income varies from one year to the next, taxes paid on the *total* income of those two years are likely to exceed the total taxes that would have resulted had the taxpayer earned the income equally each year.

---

[30] §§ 441(i), 444, 706(b), and 1378.

Example 11.   Taxpayer R is a salesman whose income is derived solely from commissions. Taxpayer S earns a salary. Both taxpayers are single. In 19X1 and 19X2 R's taxable income was $83,200 and $16,800, respectively, while S had taxable income of $50,000 each year. The tax effect on R and S (rounded to the nearest dollar and using 1994 tax rates) is as follows:

	R		S	
	Taxable Income	Tax	Taxable Income	Tax
19X1.....................	$ 83,200	$21,314	$ 50,000	$11,127
19X2.....................	16,800	2,520	50,000	11,127
Total...................	$100,000	$23,834	$100,000	$22,254

Note that although R and S have the same total income of $100,000 for the two year period, R's total tax bill of $23,834 exceeds S's bill of $22,254 by $1,580.

As the above example demonstrates, the use of an annual accounting period may create inequities. In this particular case, R could reduce his tax bite if he could defer some of his income from one year to the next so as to split his income between years as equally as possible. In other cases, Congress has responded by enacting special provisions. For example, where a taxpayer has a loss during the year, the net operating loss rules allow the taxpayer to utilize the loss by permitting it to be carried back or forward to profitable years.[31] Without these carryback and carryover provisions, the taxpayer would receive no benefit from any losses realized.

ACCOUNTING METHODS

Once a tax year is identified, the taxpayer must determine in which period a transaction is to be reported. The year in which a particular item becomes part of the tax calculation is not a trivial matter. The time of recognition can make a substantial difference in the taxpayer's total tax liability not only because of the time value of money but also because other changes may occur from year to year. For instance, tax rates may go up or down from one year to the next. Such change does not necessarily take an act of Congress. A taxpayer may simply marry, divorce, incorporate, or change from a taxable to tax-exempt entity. In such case, deferral of income to the low-rate year and acceleration of deductions to the high-rate year could produce significant savings. Similarly, Congress may completely revise the treatment of an item. For example, in 1993 Congress raised the top tax rate from 31 to 39.6 percent, eliminated the deduction for business club dues, dropped the amount of the deduction for business meals and entertainment from 80 to 50 percent, eliminated the deduction for certain moving expenses, increased the

---

[31]   § 172. See Chapter 10 for a discussion of the net operating loss rules.

Medicare tax, increased the amount of social security benefits that are subject to tax, and raised the amount of business equipment that may be expensed from $10,000 to $17,500. Changes like these have become an annual rite in the tax area, consequently making timing critical.

The rules that determine when a particular item is reported are generally referred to as accounting methods. The Code identifies four permissible methods of accounting:[32]

1. The cash receipts and disbursements method

2. The accrual method

3. Any other method permitted by the Code (e.g., a method for a specific situation such as the completed contract method or the use of LIFO to value inventories)[33]

4. Any combination of the three methods above permitted by the Regulations

The term "accounting method" is not limited to the overall method of accounting used by the taxpayer (e.g., the cash or accrual method). It generally includes the treatment of *any particular item* if such treatment affects *when* the item will be reported. For example, the use of LIFO to value inventories would be considered an accounting method since the use of this method determines when the cost of a product will become part of cost of goods sold.

It should be emphasized that the taxpayer is not required to adopt one overall method of accounting. For example, a taxpayer with inventories *must* use the accrual method to account for inventories and related sales. However, the same taxpayer could use the cash method to report interest income or other items. This approach (referred to as the *hybrid method*) is completely acceptable as long as the taxpayer applies the same methods consistently.

Taxpayers are generally allowed to select the methods of accounting they wish to use. In all cases, however, the IRS has the right to determine if the method used *clearly reflects income*, and, if not, to make the necessary adjustments.[34] For example, assume that each year a taxpayer changes the way it computes the amount of overhead that it capitalizes as part of inventory (e.g., on the basis of direct labor hours one year, machine hours the next). In such case, the IRS might require the taxpayer to use one method consistently so that income would not be distorted from year to year but would be clearly reflected.

---

[32] § 446(c).

[33] Reg. § 1.446-1(c)(1)(iii).

[34] § 446(b).

Tax Methods vs. Financial Accounting Methods. At first glance, many people—particularly accountants—would no doubt conclude that a method of accounting that conforms with generally accepted accounting principles (GAAP) would be regarded as clearly reflecting income.[35] Although this is ordinarily true, it is not always the case.[36] Conflicts sometimes exist because the objectives of the income tax system differ from that of financial accounting. The primary goal of financial accounting is to provide useful information to management, shareholders, creditors, and other interested parties. In contrast, the goal of the income tax system is to ensure that revenues are fairly collected. Due to these different goals, the tax law may disregard fundamental accounting principles. Perhaps the most obvious example can be found in the tax law's allowance of the cash method of accounting. Despite its failure to properly match revenues and expenses, the cash method is normally tolerated because from an administrative view it is simple and objective. Such administrative concerns often dictate a different approach for tax purposes. For example, an accrual basis taxpayer is often required to report prepaid income when received rather than when earned. Although this practice violates the matching principle, it ensures that the tax is imposed when the taxpayer has the cash to pay it.

The operation of differing objectives can also be seen in the use of estimates. One of the major responsibilities of financial accountants is to ensure that financial statement users are not misled. This demand normally encourages accountants to be conservative, which in turn may cause them to understate rather than overstate income. Although the government does not want taxpayers to overstate income, it certainly does not want to endorse principles that would tend toward understatement. Thus, the tax law generally does not allow taxpayers to estimate future expenses such as bad debts or warranty costs and deduct them currently, as is the case with financial accounting. Instead, the deduction is allowed only when there is objective evidence that a cost has been incurred. The government frowns on estimates of expenses, presumably because taxpayers would tend to overstate them.

Reporting of prepaid income and the treatment of estimated expenses are just two examples of where financial accounting principles deviate from tax accounting. The key point to recognize is that a particular item may be treated one way for financial accounting purposes and another way for tax purposes. As a practical matter, this may mean that two sets of books are maintained, or what is perhaps more likely, one set based on financial accounting principles to which adjustments must be made to arrive at taxable income.

---

[35] Reg. § 1.446-1(a)(2).

[36] For an excellent example, see *Thor Power Tool Co.*, 79-1 USTC ¶9139, 43 AFTR2d 79-362, 439 U.S. 522 (USSC, 1979).

CASH METHOD OF ACCOUNTING

General Rule. Virtually all individuals—as well as many corporations, partnerships, trusts, and estates—use the cash method of accounting. Its prevalence is no doubt attributable to the fact that it is easy to use. Under the cash method, taxpayers simply report items of income and deduction in the year in which they are received or paid.[37] In effect, the cash method allows taxpayers merely to refer to their checkbooks to determine taxable income.

In using the cash method, items of income need not be in the form of cash but need only be capable of valuation in terms of money. Under this rule, sometimes termed the *cash equivalent doctrine,* the taxpayer reports income when the equivalent of cash is received.[38] Thus, where property or services are received, the fair market value of these items serves as the measure of income.

Due to the cash equivalent doctrine, reporting of income arising from notes and accounts receivable differs. Notes received by a cash basis taxpayer are usually considered property and hence constitute income equal to the value of the note.[39] Where a promise to pay is *not* evidenced by a note (e.g., credit sales resulting in accounts receivable), no income is recognized by a cash basis taxpayer until payment is received.[40] This treatment results because unsupported promises to pay normally are not considered as having a fair market value.

Constructive Receipt Doctrine. Taxpayers using the cash method of accounting have substantial control over income recognition since they may control the timing of the actual receipt of cash. If the requirement calling for *actual* receipt were strictly adhered to, the cash basis taxpayer could easily frustrate the purpose of progressive taxation. For example, taxpayers could select the year with the lowest tax rate and simply cash their salary or dividend checks or redeem their interest coupons in that year. To curtail this practice, the doctrine of constructive receipt was developed. Under this principle, a taxpayer is *deemed* to have received income even though such income has not actually been received. It should be noted that there is no corresponding doctrine for deductions (i.e., there is no constructive payment doctrine).

The constructive receipt doctrine is currently expressed in Regulation § 1.451-2(a) as follows:

> Income, although not actually reduced to the taxpayer's possession, is constructively received by him in the taxable year in which it is credited to his account, set apart for him or otherwise made available so that he could have drawn upon it during the taxable year if notice of intention to withdraw had been given. However, income is not constructively received if the taxpayer's control of its receipt is subject to substantial limitations or restrictions.

---

[37] Reg. § 1.446-1(c)(1)(i).

[38] Reg. § 1.446-1(a)(3).

[39] *A.W. Wolfson,* 1 B.T.A. 538 (1925).

[40] *Bedell v. Comm.,* 1 USTC ¶359, 7 AFTR 8469, 30 F.2d 622 (CA-2, 1929).

As the Regulation suggests, the taxpayer is treated as having received income where three conditions are satisfied:

1. The taxpayer has control over the amount without substantial limitations and restrictions

2. The amount has been set aside or credited to the taxpayer's account

3. The funds are available for payment by the payer (i.e., the payer's ability to make payment must be considered)

Some of the common situations to which the rule is applied are illustrated in the following examples.

> **Example 12.** B refereed a football game on Saturday night, December 31, 1994 and did not receive the check for his services until after the banks had closed. He cashed the check on January 3, 1995. B must report the income in 1994. In the case of a check, a taxpayer is deemed to have received payment in the year the check is received rather than when it is cashed.[41]

> **Example 13.** T mailed a check on December 29, 1994 to S, which S received in January 1995. S is not in constructive receipt of the check since it was not available to him for his immediate use and enjoyment. However, if S requested that T mail him the check so that he receive it in 1995, or if S could have received the check by merely appearing in person and claiming it, S would be deemed to have received the payment in 1994.

> **Example 14.** When G made a deposit on January 15, 1995, the bank updated her passbook on December 31, 1994 to show that $200 of interest was credited to her account for the last quarter of 1994. G withdrew the interest on January 31. G must report the interest in 1994. Interest credited to the taxpayer's account is taxable when credited, regardless of whether it is in the taxpayer's possession, assuming that it may be withdrawn.[42]

> **Example 15.** B Corporation mailed dividend checks dated December 20 on December 28, 1994. R, a shareholder in B, received her check on January 4, 1995. R reports the dividend income in 1995 as long as the payer customarily pays dividends by mail so that the shareholder receives it after the end of the year.[43]

> **Example 16.** R's secretary received several checks for services that R had performed. Payments received by a taxpayer's agent are considered constructively received by the taxpayer.[44]

---

[41] *C. F. Kahler,* 18 T.C. 31 (1952).

[42] Reg. § 1.451-2(b).

[43] *Ibid.; S.L. Avery,* 4 USTC ¶1277, 13 AFTR 1168, 292 U.S. 210 (USSC, 1934). See also

H.B. McEuen v. Comm., 52-1 USTC ¶9281, 41 AFTR 1169, 196 F.2d 127 (CA-5, 1952).

[44] *T. Watson,* 2 TCM 863 (1943).

Example 17. A taxpayer who agrees not to cash a check until authorized by the payer has not constructively received income if the payer does not have sufficient funds in the bank to cover the check.[45]

The tax treatment of many deferred compensation arrangements between employers and employees is tied to the constructive receipt doctrine. The Service has ruled that where the taxpayer has entered into a deferral agreement *before* the services are performed, such income is not considered received.[46] This is true even though the taxpayer has control over whether the payments are to be made currently or are to be deferred. The Service's conclusion rests on the principle that once the employee has made the agreement, he or she does not have the right to receive currently the deferred amounts. This presumes, however, that the taxpayer has not received cash equivalents such as notes and that the payments are not secured in any fashion. Similarly, the taxpayer cannot be protected through some type of escrow or trust account to which funds are transferred since such amounts may be treated as having been set aside for withdrawal by the taxpayer.

Example 18. F Corporation employs R as a major league baseball player. They enter into a contractual arrangement whereby F promises to pay R $500,000 this year and $100,000 annually for five years after he retires. R will not be treated as having constructively received the deferred payments when the employment contract is signed because he has no legally enforceable right to demand payment currently. In addition, R has not received a negotiable note but merely an unsecured promise to pay.

Limitations on the Use of the Cash Method. As a method of accounting, the cash method's principal advantage lies in its simplicity. On other counts, the cash method scores poorly, ranking a distant second to the accrual method. From an accounting perspective, the cash method is entirely inappropriate since income and expense are recognized without regard to the taxable year in which the economic events responsible for the income or expense actually occur. Similarly, when some parties to a transaction use different methods of accounting, there may be a mismatching of income and deductions. For example, an accrual basis corporation could accrue expenses payable to a cash basis individual. In such case, the corporation could obtain deductions without ever having to make a disbursement and, moreover, without the individual taxpayer recognizing any offsetting income.

While the above are clearly shortcomings, the major flaw found in the cash method is that it is easily abused. Taxpayers have often secured benefits by merely timing their transactions appropriately: recognizing income in one year, deductions in the next, or what is more likely, deductions in years in which the taxpayer is in a high tax bracket and income in years in which the taxpayer is in a low tax bracket.

---

[45] *A.V. Johnston,* 23 TCM 2003, T.C. Memo 1964-323.

[46] Rev. Rul. 60-31, 1960-1 C.B. 174. For further discussion, see Chapter 18.

To attack these problems, Congress has limited the use of the cash method of accounting. The following entities are normally prohibited from using the cash method:[47]

1. Regular C corporations;

2. Partnerships that have regular C corporations as partners (other than certain personal service corporations described below); and

3. *Tax shelters,* generally defined as any enterprise (other than a regular C corporation) in which interests have been offered for sale in any offering required to be registered under Federal or State security agencies.

Despite these general restrictions, Congress believed that the simplicity of the cash method justified its continued use in certain instances. For example, Congress felt that it would be costly for small businesses to switch to the accrual method. Similarly, it recognized that the accrual method would create undue complexity for farming businesses if such a method were required to account for growing crops and livestock. In addition, Congress believed that personal service corporations, which have traditionally used the cash method, should be allowed to continue their use. Accordingly, the following entities are allowed to use the cash method.[48]

1. Any corporation or partnership whose annual *gross receipts* for *all* preceding years do not exceed $5 million. This test is satisfied for any prior year only if the average annual gross receipts[49] for the three-year period ending with such year does not exceed $5 million. Once this average *exceeds* $5 million, the corporation cannot use the cash method for the following year.

2. Certain farming businesses.

3. Qualified personal service corporations. A regular C corporation is qualified if substantially all of the activities consist of performing services in the fields of health, law, engineering, architecture, accounting, actuarial science, performing arts, or consulting, *and* at least 95 percent of its stock is held by the employees who are providing the services. The latter test is considered satisfied if the stock is owned by a retired employee or by the estate or heirs of a deceased employee.

---

[47] § 448(a).

[48] § 448(b).

[49] Gross receipts include total sales (net of returns and allowances but not reduced by costs of goods sold) and amounts received for services, interest, rents, royalties, and annuities. For sales of capital assets and real or depreciable property used in trade or business, gross receipts are reduced by the taxpayer's adjusted basis in such property. See Temp. Reg. § 1.448-1T(f)(2)(iv).

Example 19. G's Grocery, a regular C corporation, started business in 19X1. Since that time it has had annual gross receipts as follows:

Year	Gross Receipts	Average Annual Gross Receipts[*]
19X1	$ 4,000,000	$4,000,000
19X2	2,000,000	3,000,000
19X3	6,000,000	4,000,000
19X4	10,000,000	6,000,000

$$* \ \frac{\text{Current} + \text{Prior two years}}{3 \text{ (or if less, years in existence)}}$$

It initially adopted the cash method in 19X1. It was able to use the cash method through 19X4 because the average annual gross receipts for all prior years did not exceed $5 million. Note that although its gross receipts were $6,000,000 in 19X3, its *average annual* gross receipts for that year were only $4,000,000 [($4,000,000 + $2,000,000 + $6,000,000) ÷ 3]. Consequently, the cash method could be used for 19X4. It will be denied use of the cash method for 19X5 since the average annual gross receipts for 19X4 exceed $5 million [($2,000,000 + $6,000,000 + $10,000,000) ÷ 3 = $6,000,000].

It should be noted that the above exceptions do not apply to tax shelters. Any enterprise considered a tax shelter must use the accrual method.

ACCRUAL METHOD OF ACCOUNTING

Taxpayers using the accrual method of accounting report income in the year in which it is considered earned under the so-called *all events test*. Under this test, income is earned when all the events have occurred that fix the right to receive such income and the amount of income can be determined with reasonable accuracy.[50] As the all events test indicates, income generally accrues only if the taxpayer has an unconditional right to receive the income. This right normally arises when the title to the property passes to the buyer.[51] With sales of inventory, however, taxpayers may accrue income when the goods are shipped, when the product is delivered or accepted, or when title passes, as long as the method is consistently used.[52] Note that the accrual method *must* be used in accounting for sales, purchases, and inventories if inventories are an income-producing factor. However, the taxpayer who must use the accrual method in this instance may still account for other items of income and expense using the cash method. The accrual method, as noted earlier, must be used by regular C corporations and partnerships with C corporations as partners unless one of several exceptions is satisfied.

---

[50] Reg. § 1.451-1(a).

[51] *Lucas v. North Texas Lumber Co.,* 2 USTC ¶484, 8 AFTR 10276, 281 U.S. 11 (USSC, 1929).

[52] Reg. § 1.446-1(c)(1)(ii).

There are several special rules relating to the accrual method of accounting that cause variations in the normal scheme. For example, dividends would normally accrue under the all events test on the date of record. An exception exists, however, so that dividends are reported when received.[53] In addition to this exception, others exist that are discussed later in this chapter.

CHANGES IN ACCOUNTING METHODS

Taxpayers are initially given great freedom in the methods of accounting they may use. However, once a particular method has been adopted (e.g., when it is first used to account for an item), it may not be changed unless consent is granted by the IRS.[54] Taxpayers seeking a change must apply for permission by filing Form 3115, Application for Change in Accounting Method, within 180 days of the beginning of the tax year when the change is to become effective. The IRS does not rubber-stamp these requests. Permission is granted only if the taxpayer is willing to make any adjustments required by the IRS. Under Code § 481, the IRS is authorized to require adjustments if a change in method would result in the omission of income or the duplication of deductions.

> **Example 20.**   T, Inc. operates a computer consulting company. It has always used the cash method to account for its income from services. In 1994, it decided that it should switch to the accrual method. At the end of 1993, T's outstanding receivables were $10,000. If T were allowed to switch to the accrual method and no adjustment were required, the $10,000 would escape taxation. The $10,000 would not be taxed in 1993 since T was on the cash basis in that year and no collections were made. Similarly, the $10,000 would not be taxed in 1994 because T is on the accrual method in that year and the income did not accrue in 1994 but rather 1993. Thus, without an adjustment, the $10,000 of income would be omitted from both the 1993 and 1994 returns, never to be taxed.

Example 20 illustrates why the law requires taxpayers who wish to change to agree to an adjustment. Prior to 1954, however, taxpayers were normally not required to make an adjustment for duplications or omissions. For this reason, if the *IRS* requires the taxpayer to change accounting methods, any portion of the adjustment attributable to years prior to 1954 is disregarded. In contrast, if the *taxpayer* voluntarily changes an accounting method, any portion attributable to years before 1954 must be taken into account.[55]

---

[53] Reg. § 1.451-2(b), *Tar Products Corp. v. Comm.*, 42-2 USTC ¶9662, 29 AFTR 1190, 130 F.2d 866 (CA-3, 1942).

[54] § 446(f) authorizes the IRS to impose penalties if consent is not secured.

[55] § 481(a).

Accounting for the Adjustment. Taxpayers are normally required to report any adjustment attributable to the change in the year of the change and pay any additional tax due (or receive a refund).[56] In certain situations, this may create a severe hardship for the taxpayer (e.g., the required inclusion of several years' income in a single year). However, § 481(c) allows the IRS to alter this approach. The IRS has used this authority to develop a system that encourages taxpayers to switch from an erroneous method they may be using to a correct method.[57] For this purpose, an erroneous method—a so-called *Category A method*—is a method not permitted by the Code, Regulations, or Supreme Court decision. For example, if the taxpayer failed to use the accrual method to account for inventories or did not use the uniform capitalization rules to account for indirect costs, the methods that were used would be considered erroneous. The system devised by the IRS to govern changes also contains rules for changes from one permissible method of accounting—a *Category B method*—to another permissible method.

Under the procedures prescribed by the IRS, the treatment of the adjustment depends on who initiates the adjustment (a voluntary change by the taxpayer or an involuntary change required by the IRS) and the type of adjustment (Category A, erroneous, or Category B, permissible). Taxpayers who voluntarily change from a Category A method are treated far more favorably than those who are forced to change by the IRS as part of an audit proceeding. If the IRS requires the taxpayer to change from a Category A method, the entire adjustment is taken into account in the year of the change. In contrast, if the taxpayer voluntarily changes from a Category A method to a correct method of accounting, a positive adjustment is normally spread over three years (the year of the change and the following two years) and a negative adjustment is brought into income entirely in the year of change. When the change involves a Category B method, the taxpayer may be able to spread the adjustment over six years, the year of the change and the following five years. Special rules may apply, however.

> **Example 21.** J has operated a small hardware store as a sole proprietorship since 1972. This year the IRS audited J's 1991 tax return and determined that J had failed to use the accrual method of accounting for inventories. Instead, J had expensed all of his inventory as it was acquired. Consequently, the IRS required J to change his method of accounting. Based on a physical count and valuation of his inventory, the IRS determined that J had understated his income in prior years by $300,000. Because the change was initiated by the IRS and involved a Category A method (a method not permitted by the Code), J must pay all of the tax attributable to the $300,000 adjustment this year.[58] Had J voluntarily changed to the proper method, he would have been entitled to a forward spread of three years, reporting $100,000 in each of 1991, 1992, and 1993. By so doing, he would have deferred the tax to 1991, 1992, and 1993.

---

[56] *Ibid.*

[57] Rev. Proc. 92-20, 1992-1 C.B. 685.

[58] In computing the tax that must be paid, § 482(b) provides special rules.

Example 22.   During 1993, R asked for and obtained permission to change from the cash method to the accrual method. This change resulted in a positive income adjustment of $60,000. Because this is a Category B method and was initiated by the taxpayer, R could spread the $60,000 of income over six years, $10,000 in 1993 and $10,000 in each of the following five years.

Changes in accounting method are not to be confused with correction of errors. Errors such as mathematical mistakes or the improper calculation of a deduction or credit can be corrected by the taxpayer without permission of the IRS by simply filing an amended return. Alternatively, the IRS may discover the mistake and require the taxpayer to make a correction. However, if the statute of limitations has run on a return containing an error, no correction can be made. In these cases, the taxpayer's income is forever over- or understated, as the case may be.

✔ CHECK YOUR KNOWLEDGE

Review Question 1.   On Sunday, December 31, 1961 in Green Bay, Wisconsin, Paul Hornung, All-American quarterback from Notre Dame, star of the Green Bay Packers, and later a sports analyst, won a Corvette for being the most valuable player in the NFL championship game.[59] After the game, the editor of *Sport* magazine, the sponsor of the award, gave nothing to Hornung to evidence his ownership of the car, which was being held at a dealership in New York. Hornung picked up the car on January 3, 1962 in New York. What are the tax concerns here?

There is little question that Hornung must report income (although that was uncertain in 1961). The important issue to be resolved is when. Was Hornung in constructive receipt of the car when the editor gave him the keys that snowy afternoon in December 1961? Although Hornung, wanting to report the income in 1961, argued that he had received the car, the court disagreed. In a decision that should be mandatory reading for its witty analysis, the court explained that the basis of constructive receipt is unfettered control over the date of actual receipt. In this case, the facts indicated that Hornung did not have such control. He did not receive the car or even the keys or title to the car in 1961. Moreover, the car was in a dealership that was not only 1,000 miles away but was also closed. In addition, the car had not been set aside for Hornung's use and delivery was not solely up to him. Accordingly, the doctrine of constructive receipt was inapplicable.

Review Question 2.   Mr. Mike, an accountant, is the proud owner of Maggie, a West Highland terrier. Shortly after Mike acquired Maggie, he discovered the need to take her to get the appropriate shots. It did not take long for Mike to pick a vet. He elected to use one of his long-time clients for whom he prepares tax returns, Nonhuman Companion Inc., which operates a chain of veterinary clinics throughout Arizona and California. Mike's visit to the vet was the first time he had actually been to his client's office.

---

[59] *Paul V. Hornung*, 47 T.C. 428 (1967).

While there he noticed that the clinic not only provided veterinarian and kennel services but also a great variety of food, toys, and pet paraphernalia for sale. To his best recollection, the corporation used the cash method of accounting. Is this the correct method?

There are two rules concerning accounting methods that come into play here. First, a corporation is normally required to use the accrual method of accounting. However, several exceptions may apply. The accrual requirement is waived if the corporation is an S corporation or its average annual gross receipts are less than $5 million for all preceding tax years. If neither of these exceptions applies, the corporation could possibly use the accrual method if it is considered a personal service corporation, since it provides services in the health field. Interestingly, the IRS has addressed this question and ruled that veterinarian services do qualify. Nevertheless, there could be a concern that "substantially all the activities" do not consist of performing "health" services. The second rule that operates in this situation concerns accounting for inventory. A corporation must use the accrual method to account for inventory even if it otherwise qualifies to use the cash method. The IRS recently held that a partnership that provided veterinary services was required to switch from the cash method to the accrual method when over 50 percent of the partnership's receipts were from merchandise (pet food, supplies, and drugs).[60]

ACCOUNTING FOR INCOME: SPECIAL CONSIDERATIONS

CLAIM OF RIGHT DOCTRINE

Occasionally income may be received before the taxpayer's rights to such income have been clearly established. The tax difficulty posed in these instances concerns whether the taxpayer should report the income currently or wait until the proper claims to the income have been identified. For these situations, the courts have established a rule of law termed the *claim of right doctrine*. Under this rule, if a taxpayer actually or constructively *receives* income under a claim of right (i.e., he claims the income is rightfully his) and such income is not restricted in use, it must be included in gross income.[61] In other words, earnings received must be included in income if the taxpayer has an *unrestricted claim,* notwithstanding the possibility that the income may be subsequently relinquished if the taxpayer's claim is later denied.

---

[60] Technical Advice Memorandum 9218008.

[61] *North American Oil Consolidated v. Burnet,*
3 USTC ¶943, 11 AFTR 16, 286 U.S. 417
(USSC, 1932).

Example 23.   Television station WXYZ received $100,000 from KLM Company to air the firm's commercials during a local talk show in the month of December. During this month, the ratings dropped sharply when the star of the show quit. Shortly thereafter, KLM contacted the station, indicating that it wanted to discontinue its sponsorship and requesting return of $75,000 of the payment. In view of their interpretation of the agreement, the station continued to air the firm's commercials and retained the $100,000. KLM brought suit to recover the $75,000. Under the claim of right doctrine, WXYZ must include the entire $100,000 in income even though it may have to repay the amount or a portion thereof to KLM. The amount is included because WXYZ received the money and could use the amount without restriction.

The claim of right doctrine applies to both cash and accrual basis taxpayers. As previously discussed, income is usually reported by an accrual basis taxpayer only when all the events have occurred that fix the taxpayer's right to receive such income. However, in the case of contested income, the taxpayer's rights to such amounts have not been fixed, and under the all events test he or she would not report it. The all events test notwithstanding, the claim of right doctrine carves out an exception to this rule for contested income the taxpayer has *received*. An accrual basis taxpayer who *receives* contested income under a claim of right without restrictions on its use must report the amount in income even though his or her rights to the income have not been fixed.[62] Alternatively, if the accrual basis taxpayer has *not received* the contested income, it will not be included because his or her rights thereto have not been fixed.[63] Thus, an *accrual basis* taxpayer's reporting of contested income depends on whether or not the taxpayer has received it.

Example 24.   RST, Inc., an accrual basis taxpayer, shipped parts to MNO Corporation and sent a bill for $25,000. MNO used the parts and reported that they did not perform according to specifications. If MNO had paid the $25,000 and subsequently sued to recover the purchase price, RST would be required to include the $25,000 in income since the amount was received and the claim of right doctrine applies (i.e., RST has an unrestricted claim to the income). On the other hand, if MNO had not paid the $25,000, RST would not be required to accrue the income because the amount was *not* received and the all events test has not been satisfied (RST's rights to the income have not been fixed).

---

[62]   *Ibid.*   [63]   Reg. § 1.446-1(c)(1)(ii).

The claim of right doctrine has been used in many differing instances to cause the inclusion of income in the year received. Some examples where the rule has been applied to make the income taxable are

1.   Contingent legal fees that must be returned upon a reversal by an appellate court;[64]

2.   Illegal income and gains (e.g., embezzled amounts);[65] and

3.   Bonuses and commissions that were improperly computed and had to be subsequently repaid.[66]

The claim of right doctrine does not apply where the taxpayer receives the income but recognizes an obligation to repay.[67] For example, a landlord would not be required to report the receipt of a tenant's security deposit as income because the deposit must be repaid upon the tenant's departure if the apartment unit is undamaged.

In those situations where the taxpayer repays an amount that previously had been included in income, a deduction is allowed. Section 1341 provides a special rule for computing the deduction, which ensures that the tax benefit of the deduction is the equivalent to the tax paid on the income in the prior year.

PREPAID INCOME

Over the years, a web of exceptions and special rules have developed regarding the reporting of prepaid income by an *accrual basis* taxpayer. Absent these rules, the accrual basis taxpayer (in accordance with the all events test) would defer recognition of prepaid income until it becomes earned, as is the case in financial accounting. For tax purposes, however, accrual basis taxpayers often report prepaid income in the year received. This treatment normally results from application of the claim of right doctrine, which requires income recognition when the taxpayer receives earnings under an unrestricted claim. For example, prepaid rental income must be reported when received since the taxpayer accepts the money under a claim of right without restrictions on its use. Unfortunately, no general rule is completely reliable to determine when prepaid income must be reported. Rather, the reporting procedure depends on the type of income received. As discussed below, special rules exist for prepaid income from rents, interest, services, warranties, goods, dues, subscriptions, and similar items. Note, however, these rules apply to *accrual basis* taxpayers only. A *cash basis* taxpayer reports all of these prepaid items of income in the year the cash is received.

---

[64]   *Michael Phillips v. Comm.*, USTC ¶10,067, 50 AFTR 718, 238 F.2d 473 (CA-7, 1956).

[65]   *James v. U.S.*, 61-1 USTC ¶9449, 7 AFTR2d 1361, 366 U.S. 213 (USSC, 1961).

[66]   *U.S. v. Lewis*, 51-1 USTC ¶9211, 40 AFTR 258, 340 U.S. 590 (USSC, 1951).

[67]   *Comm. v. Turney*, 36-1 USTC ¶9168, 17 AFTR 679, 82 F.2d 661 (CA-5, 1936).

Prepaid Interest, Rents, and Royalties. Several types of advance payments are included in income when received without question. For example, prepaid interest is income when received.[68] Prepaid rent and lump-sum payments, such as bonuses or advanced royalties received upon execution of a lease or other agreement, are also income when received.[69] As subsequently explained, however, the term *rent* does not include payments for the use or occupancy of rooms or space where *significant services* are also rendered to the occupant (e.g., hotels, motels, and convalescent homes are not considered as having received rents).[70] Because of the significant service element, these prepayments are reported using the rules applying to prepaid service income. Prepaid rents must be distinguished not only from services but also from lease or security deposits. Amounts received from a lessee that are refundable provided the lessee complies with the terms of the lease are not income since the lessor recognizes an obligation to repay.[71] The deposits become income only when the lessor becomes entitled to their unrestricted use upon the lessee's violation of the agreement.

Prepaid Service Income. For many years, the IRS argued that the claim of right doctrine required accrual basis taxpayers to report prepayments for services in the year received. After much litigation, however, the Service relented and created special rules. Revenue Procedure 71-21 explains that the procedures used for reporting advance payments for services vary, depending on when the services will be performed.[72] The income is reported as it is *earned* where under an agreement all of the services are required to be performed by the end of the next tax year (i.e., the tax year following the year of receipt). If services *may* be performed after the next tax year, all income is reported when received.

Example 25. AAA Inc. is an accrual basis, calendar year taxpayer that sells riding lawn mowers. The company sells one-, two-, and three-year service contracts. In a late September sale in 1993, the company sold the following contracts, the income from which would be reported as follows:

		Income Recognition	
Contract Terms	Proceeds	1994	1995
One-year	$ 2,400	$ 600	$1,800
Two-year	8,000	8,000	0
Three-year	10,000	10,000	0

For the one-year contracts the taxpayer reports $600 ($3/_{12}$ of $2,400) of income, representing that amount earned for the last three months of the year. Deferral is

---

[68] *Franklin Life Insurance v. U.S.*, 68-2 USTC ¶9459, 22 AFTR2d 5180, 399 F.2d 757 (CA-7, 1968).

[69] *South Dade Farms, Inc. v. Comm.*, 43-2 USTC ¶9634, 31 AFTR 842, 138 F.2d 818 (CA-5, 1943); *W.M. Scott*, 27 B.T.A. 951.

[70] Rev. Proc. 71-21, 1971-2 C.B. 549.

[71] *Clinton Hotel Realty Corp. v. Comm.*, 42-2 USTC ¶9559, 29 AFTR 758, 128 F.2d 968 (CA-5, 1942).

[72] *Supra*, Footnote 70.

permitted since all of the services are required to be performed by the end of the succeeding year, 1995. Deferral is not permitted in the case of two- and three-year contracts because the services may be performed after the close of the next year.

As previously noted, the treatment accorded service income also applies to *rents* where significant services are also rendered for the occupant. This treatment permits hotels, motels, and the like to enjoy the deferral provision as outlined above for services. For example, a calendar year, accrual basis ski lodge need not report prepayments received in November for rooms to be used in February but may defer income recognition until the rooms are actually used.

Advanced Payments for Goods. Normally, an accrual basis taxpayer reports advanced payments for sales of merchandise when they are earned (e.g., when the goods are shipped). This treatment enables the taxpayer to defer recognition of the prepayments. However, this approach is allowed only if the taxpayer follows the same method of reporting for financial accounting purposes.[73]

> **Example 26.** C Corporation, a calendar year taxpayer, manufactures kitchen appliances. In late December 1994, it received $50,000 for kitchen appliances that it will produce and ship in May 1995. The corporation may postpone recognition of the income until 1995, assuming that such income is also reported on the financial accounting income statement in 1995.

Long-Term Contracts. Section 460 contains special rules for the reporting of income from long-term contracts. A long-term contract is defined as any contract for the manufacture, building, installation, or construction of property that is not completed within the same taxable year in which it was entered into. However, a *manufacturing* contract is still not considered long-term unless it also involves either (1) the manufacture of a unique item not normally carried in finished goods inventory (e.g., a special piece of machinery), or (2) items that normally require more than 12 months to complete. If a manufacturing contract does not qualify as a long-term contract, deferral may still be available under the rules regarding advance payments for goods discussed above. Note that contracts for services normally do not qualify for treatment as long-term contracts.

The tax law has long allowed taxpayers who enter into a long-term contract to use the percentage of completion method or the completed contract method (subject to certain limitations) to account for advance payments.[74] The percentage of completion method requires the taxpayer to recognize a portion of the gross profit on the contract based on the estimated percentage of the contract completed. In contrast, the completed contract method allows the taxpayer to defer income recognition until the contract is complete and acceptance has occurred. When available, taxpayers usually opted to use the completed contract method in order to postpone recognition of income. In some extreme cases, taxpayers have been able to postpone income for many years on the claim that the contract was not complete.

---

[73] Reg. § 1.451-5(b). See Reg. § 1.451-4(c)(1) for certain situations where the prepayments must be reported earlier.

[74] Reg. § 1.451-3.

Over the years, Congress became concerned about the opportunities for deferral as well as the potential for abuse. Consequently, it took various steps, slowly but surely limiting the use of the completed contract method. These actions culminated with the virtual repeal of the method in 1989. As a result, long-term contracts currently entered into normally must be accounted for using the percentage of completion method.[75] However, there are two situations where the completed contract method can still be used. These include[76]

1. *Home construction contracts.* Contracts in which 80 percent of the costs are related to buildings containing four or fewer dwelling units. Special rules apply to contracts if the buildings contain more than four units (i.e., so-called residential construction contracts).[77]

2. *Contracts of small businesses.* Construction contracts that are completed within two years of commencement and are performed by a contractor whose average annual gross receipts for the three preceding tax years do not exceed $10 million.

When using the percentage of completion method, the portion of the total contract price reported during the year and matched against current costs is computed as follows

$$\text{Total contract price} \times \frac{\text{Direct and allocable indirect costs incurred this period}}{\text{Total estimated costs of contract}}$$

Note that if less than 10 percent of the contract's costs have been incurred, the taxpayer may elect to defer reporting until the year in which the 10 percent threshold is reached.[78]

Example 27.   In October 1994, W Corporation entered into a contract to build a hotel to be completed by May 1996. The contract price was $1 million. The company's estimated total costs of construction were $800,000. W's average annual gross receipts exceed $10 million, and it is therefore required to use the percentage of completion method. Total costs incurred during 1994 were $600,000. In 1995, the contract was completed at a total cost of $840,000. The income reported in 1994 and 1995 is computed below:

	1994	1995
Revenue recognized...	$750,000*	$250,000
Current costs..........	(600,000)	(240,000)
Total...............	$150,000	$ 10,000

$$*\frac{\$600,000}{\$800,000} = 75\% \times \$1,000,000$$

---

[75] § 460(a).

[76] § 460(e).

[77] A 70% percentage of completion method may be used for certain residential construction contracts.

[78] § 460(b)(5).

Any contract for which the percentage of completion method is used is subject to the special *look-back* provisions.[79] Under these rules, once the contract is complete, annual income is recomputed based on final costs rather than estimated costs. Interest is then paid to the taxpayer if there was an overstatement of income. Conversely, the taxpayer must pay interest if income was understated.

Example 28.   Same facts as in *Example 27* above. Based on total actual costs of $840,000, W's 1994 income should have been $114,000, computed as follows:

	1994
Revenue recognized...	$714,000*
Current costs.........	(600,000)
Total...............	$114,000

$$\frac{^*\$600,000}{\$840,000} = 71.4\% \times \$1,000,000$$

Because the contract was in reality only 71.4% complete and not 75% complete, W overstated income in 1994 by $36,000 ($150,000 − $114,000). Consequently, the IRS is required to pay the taxpayer interest on the overpayment of the related tax.

Prepaid Dues and Subscriptions.   Amidst much controversy concerning the reporting of prepaid income, Congress provided specific rules for the reporting of prepaid dues and subscriptions. Section 455 permits the taxpayer to elect to recognize prepaid subscription income (amounts received from a newspaper, magazine, or periodical) ratably over the subscription period. Section 456 provides that taxpayers may elect to report prepaid dues ratably over the membership period.

INTEREST INCOME

The period in which a taxpayer recognizes interest income usually follows the basic tax accounting rules for cash and accrual basis taxpayers. In some cases, however, these taxpayers must observe special provisions that may cause reporting to vary from the normal pattern.

General Rules.   As a general rule, cash basis taxpayers recognize interest income when received, while accrual basis taxpayers recognize the income when it is earned. As previously noted, both accrual and cash basis taxpayers that receive interest before it is earned (prepaid interest) must report the income when it is received.

---

[79]   § 460(b)(2).

Example 29.   T operates a small business that manufactures pottery dishes. When one of her customers was unable to pay her bill, T accepted a $10,000 note, dated October 1, 1994, payable with 6% interest on October 1, 1995. Assuming T is a cash basis taxpayer, she will report $600 of interest income ($10,000 × 6%) in 1995. If T uses the accrual method, she would include $150 ($10,000 × $3/12$ × 6%) in her gross income for 1994 and $450 ($10,000 × $9/12$ × 6%) in 1995. Had the customer paid all of the interest, $600, in 1994 as a showing of good faith, T would report the entire $600 in 1994 regardless of whether she is a cash or accrual basis taxpayer.

In many instances, a taxpayer will purchase an interest-bearing instrument between payment dates. When this occurs, it is assumed that the purchase price includes the interest accrued to the date of the purchase. Thus, when the buyer later receives the interest payment, the portion accrued to the date of purchase is considered a nontaxable return of capital that reduces the taxpayer's basis in the instrument. On the other hand, the seller must include as interest income the amount accrued to the date of the purchase, regardless of the seller's method of accounting.

Example 30.   S owned a $1,000, 12% AT&T bond that paid interest semiannually on November 1 and May 1. He purchased the bond at par several years ago. On September 1, 1994, S sold the bond for $1,540 including $40 of the accrued interest ($1,000 × 12% × $4/12$). S must report $40 of interest income accrued to the date of sale. In addition, S will report a capital gain of $500 ($1,540 − $40 interest − $1,000 basis). The result is the same if S is a cash or accrual basis taxpayer.

Example 31.   Assume B purchased for $1,540 the bond that S sold in the example above. On November 1, B receives an interest payment of $60 ($1,000 × 12% × $6/12$). B treats the interest accrued to the date of purchase, $40, as a nontaxable return of basis. Thus, B's basis is reduced to $1,500 ($1,540 − $40). The remaining $20 of interest is included in B's gross income.

As a practical matter, the broker's statement normally reflects the interest accrued to the date of the sale or purchase.

Discount.   When accounting for interest income, any discount relating to the debt instrument—the excess of the face value of the obligation over the purchase price—must be considered. Discount typically results when the rate at which the instrument pays interest is less than the market rate. In such case, the discount essentially functions as a substitute for interest. Consistent with this view, the tax law attempts to ensure that the discount is treated as interest income and is normally reported currently. Special provisions have been introduced over the years to clarify the reporting of the discount income as well as to prohibit taxpayers from converting the discount income into capital gain.

Example 32. During 1992, T purchased a $10,000, 8% corporate bond for $8,000, or a $2,000 discount. In 1994 the bond matured and the taxpayer redeemed the bond for its par value of $10,000. The redemption is treated as an exchange, and the taxpayer recognizes a long-term capital gain of $2,000 ($10,000 redemption price − $8,000 basis). In this case, the taxpayer has converted the discount of $2,000, which from an economic view is ordinary interest income, to capital gain. Moreover, the taxpayer has deferred the reporting of such income from the time it accrues to the time the bond is sold. Although this opportunity still exists for certain older bonds, some of the provisions discussed below (and in greater detail in Chapter 16) eliminate this possibility for bonds issued in the future.

The tax treatment of discount depends in part on when it arises. The discount often occurs at the time the instrument is issued. For example, certain instruments such as U.S. savings bonds, Treasury bills, and so-called zero coupon bonds do not bear interest and are usually *issued* at discounts. Other debt obligations that do bear interest (such as corporate bonds) also may be issued at a discount, usually if the coupon rate is set lower than the current rate. Discount could also result after the instrument is issued. For example, where interest-bearing instruments are issued at par, discount may arise upon a subsequent purchase. The specific treatment of discount is examined below.

Non–Interest-Bearing Obligations Issued at a Discount. The Code provides special rules for non–interest-bearing obligations that are issued at a discount and redeemable for a fixed amount that increases over time. The instruments to which these rules would normally apply are Series E and EE U.S. savings bonds. Series E bonds were issued between 1941 and 1980, having maturities up to 40 years. Beginning in 1980, these bonds were replaced by Series EE bonds. These bonds are issued at a discount and are generally redeemable at any time up until the final maturity date at a price that increases with the passage of time. No interest payments are made while the bond is held. The holder's interest income is represented by the difference between the redemption price and purchase price. For reporting purposes, taxpayers may elect to include in income the annual increase in the redemption price of the bond.[80] In essence, this election allows a cash basis taxpayer to use the accrual method with respect to these bonds. If income is not reported on an annual basis, the taxpayer reports the entire difference between the redemption and issue prices as income when the bond is redeemed.

Example 33. S purchased Series EE bonds with a face value of $10,000 at a cost of $8,000. The redemption price of the bonds increases during the year by $100. If S elects to report the income annually, she will include $100 in her gross income. Alternatively, S could wait until she redeems the bond to report the income. For example, if S later redeemed the bonds for $9,500, she would report $1,500 income (the difference between the redemption price of $9,500 and her cost of $8,000).

---

[80] § 454(a)

The taxpayer may make the election to report the interest annually at any time. When the election is made, all interest previously deferred on all Series E and EE bonds must be reported. This procedure effectively allows the taxpayer to choose the year in which the interest income is to be reported. However, once the election is made, it applies to *all* Series E and EE bonds subsequently acquired. Should the taxpayer desire to change to reporting the income at redemption, consent from the IRS is required.

Series E and EE bonds may be exchanged within one year of their maturity date for Series HH bonds that *pay* interest semiannually. By exchanging the Series E or EE bonds for Series HH bonds, the taxpayer is able to postpone the recognition of any unreported income attributed to the Series E or EE bonds to the year in which the Series HH bonds are redeemable.[81]

> **Example 34.**   In June 1960, B purchased Series E bonds at a cost of $6,000. He did not report the income annually. When the bonds mature in 1994, B will receive $40,000 and will have to report a gain of $34,000 ($40,000 − $6,000). B could effectively shift the $34,000 of income to a year of his choice by exchanging the Series E bonds for Series HH and redeeming the Series HH bonds at a later date. By so doing, B may be able to create a significant tax savings by recognizing the income in a year in which a lower tax rate would apply (e.g., his retirement years).

As discussed in Chapter 6, certain taxpayers who cash in Series EE bonds and use the proceeds for educational expenses may be able to exclude the interest.

Government Obligations.   Special rules also govern the treatment of the discount arising upon the purchase of short-term government obligations such as Treasury bills. Typically, a taxpayer purchases a short-term Treasury bill at a discount and redeems it for par value shortly thereafter. In this instance, Code § 454(b) applies to cash basis taxpayers to ensure that the gain on the redemption—in effect, the discount—is treated as ordinary interest income. Specifically, any gain realized by cash basis taxpayers from the sale or redemption of non–interest-bearing obligations issued by governmental units that have a fixed maturity date that is one year or less from the date of issue is always ordinary income. This ordinary income is reported *in the year* of sale or redemption. In contrast, accrual basis taxpayers are required to amortize the discount (i.e., include it in income) on a *daily* basis under Code § 1281(a).

> **Example 35.**   On December 1, 1994, B, a cash basis calendar year taxpayer, purchased a $10,000 non–interest-bearing Treasury bill. She purchased the bill at 97 ($9,700) and redeemed the bill on March 1, 1995 at par. B recognizes a $300 gain ($10,000 − $9,700) on the redemption, and the entire gain is treated as ordinary income in 1995. The same result would occur if B had *sold* the Treasury bill for $10,000 on January 15, 1995. Note that if B were an accrual basis taxpayer, the $300 discount would have been included in income on a daily basis. Consequently, a portion of the income would be reported in 1994 and the remainder in 1995.

---

[81]   § 454(c); Reg. § 1.454-1(a); § 1037.

Original Issue Discount. When interest-bearing obligations such as corporate bonds are *issued* at a discount, a complex set of provisions operates to prevent taxpayers from not only deferring the discount income but also converting it to capital gain as depicted in *Example 32*. These rules apply only to discount that arises when the bonds are originally issued. This discount is technically referred to as *original issue discount* (OID) and is determined as follows:

Redemption price......................................	$x,xxx
− Issue price...	− xxx
= Original issue discount................................	$x,xxx

The thrust of the provisions is to require the holder of the bond to amortize the discount into income during the period the bond is held. A complete discussion of the treatment of OID is provided in Chapter 16.

✔ CHECK YOUR KNOWLEDGE

Review Question 1. For financial accounting purposes, prepaid income is generally reported as it is earned. Does the same treatment apply for tax purposes? Explain the treatment of prepaid interest, rents, royalties, services, and advance payments for goods.

As a general rule, prepaid income must be reported when received. This is obviously true for cash basis taxpayers and surprisingly true for accrual basis taxpayers. The unusual treatment for accrual basis taxpayers stems from the claim of right doctrine, which requires recognition of income whenever the amount has been received and the taxpayer does not recognize an obligation to repay. This treatment applies to prepaid interest, rents, and royalties. It does not apply to prepaid service income (including prepaid rents if significant services are provided) if the service contract is completed by the year following the year of receipt. It also does not apply to advance payments for goods, which are normally reported in the same manner as they are for financial accounting purposes (the normal accrual method).

Review Question 2. After the changes made during the 1980s, some commentators pronounced the use of the completed contract method dead. Is this true? Are there any circumstances under which the completed contract method can be used?

The completed contract may be dead for large construction companies that build mammoth projects such as airplanes, stadiums, dams, office towers, and the like. But it is alive and well for the majority of construction companies. The completed contract method may be used by any home builder (regardless of size) and small construction companies (those with average annual gross receipts of less than $10 million).

Review Question 3.   During the autumn of 1986, it became clear that the Reagan administration and Congress planned to cut tax rates from a top rate of 50 percent to something around 28 percent. As a result, the papers and financial press were filled with planning ideas. Some advisers suggested that people who had cash sitting in money market accounts should buy Treasury bills. Why?

An investment in Treasury bills allows the taxpayer to defer the interest until the bonds are redeemed. Consequently, many advisers suggested purchasing Treasury bills at a discount during the fall of 1986 with the idea of redeeming them when income tax rates dropped in 1987.

IDENTIFICATION OF THE TAXPAYER

A final consideration in the taxation of income concerns identification of the taxpayer to whom the income is taxed. Generally, this is not a mind-boggling task. The person who receives the income usually must pay the tax. As discussed below, however, receipt or nonreceipt of income does not always govern who must report it.

INCOME FROM PERSONAL SERVICES

In the famous case of *Lucas v. Earl,* the Supreme Court was required to determine whether a husband was taxable on earnings from personal services despite a legally enforceable agreement made with his wife that the earnings would be shared equally.[82] At the time of this decision, such agreements effectively split income between a husband and wife; this resulted in a reduced tax liability since each individual was treated as a separate taxable entity and a progressive income tax rate structure existed. The Court eliminated the usefulness of this technique, however, by holding that the income is taxable to the taxpayer who earns it. Thus, anticipatory assignments of income that one has a *right* to receive are an ineffective device to escape taxation. In explaining what has become the assignment of income doctrine, the Court gave birth to the well-known *fruit of the tree* metaphor. According to Justice Holmes, the fruit (income) must be attributed to the tree from which it grew (Mr. Earl's services).

Section 73 directly addresses the treatment of a child's earnings. This provision indicates that amounts received for the services of a child are included in the *child's* gross income. Thus, a parent or a guardian who collects income earned by a child would not report the income; rather the income would be reported by the child since he or she earned it. As discussed in Chapter 4, however, the *unearned* income of a child under age 14 may be reported on his or her parents' tax return and taxed at the parents' rates.

---

[82]   2 USTC ¶496, 8 AFTR 10287, 281 U.S. 111 (USSC, 1930).

INCOME FROM PROPERTY

The assignment of income doctrine also applies when income from property is received. Under this rule, income from property is included in the gross income of the taxpayer who owns the property. This principle was derived from another famous case, *Helvering v. Horst.*[83] In this case, Mr. Horst clipped the interest coupons from bonds he owned and gave them to his son, who later collected them. The Supreme Court held Mr. Horst taxable since he owned and controlled the source of income (i.e., the bonds). Accordingly, income from property can be effectively assigned only if the taxpayer relinquishes ownership of the property.

UNEARNED INCOME OF CHILDREN UNDER 14

Perhaps the most fundamental principle in tax planning concerns minimizing the marginal tax rate that applies to the taxpayer's income. The significance of this principle is easily understood when one realizes that Federal marginal tax rates have at times exceeded 90 percent. Although the current disparity between the top and bottom rates, 24.6 percent (39.6%−15%), is not as great as in some years, the potential for significant tax savings still exists.

Minimizing the tax rate is normally accomplished by shifting income to a lower bracket taxpayer. As discussed above, the assignment of income doctrine makes it virtually impossible for taxpayers to shift income arising from services. Opportunities do exist, however, for shifting income through transfers of property. The most popular technique in this regard has traditionally involved transferring income-producing property to a child. In this manner, not only is the tax rate applying to the income reduced, but the income also stays within the family unit, normally to be used as the parent directs.

As part of the tax overhaul in 1986, Congress took steps to reduce tax avoidance opportunities available through income shifting to a child. This was accomplished by enacting a special provision affectionately referred to as the "kiddie" tax.[84] The thrust of this rule—as explained in Chapter 4—is to tax the *unearned* income of a child under the age of 14 as if it were the parents' income and thus at the parents' rates. By limiting the tax to unearned rather than earned income, Congress was taking direct aim at parents and others who shifted income by making gifts of property. Accordingly, shifting techniques based on gifts of property such as stocks, bonds, and rental property that produce unearned income (e.g., dividends, interest, and rents) are now severely limited.

---

[83] 40-2 USTC ¶9787, 24 AFTR 1058, 311 U.S. 112 (USSC, 1940).   [84] § 1(i).

INTEREST-FREE AND BELOW-MARKET LOANS

To be successful in shifting income to another, the assignment of income doctrine generally requires that the taxpayer transfer the income-producing property itself, not merely the income from the property. Consequently, shifting income normally requires a completed gift of the property. Taxpayers, however, are understandably reluctant to forever relinquish ownership and control of the property. For this reason, taxpayers have attempted to design techniques that enable them to retain ownership of the property yet shift income.

Prior to 1984, one popular method for shifting income from one family member to another, or from a corporation to its shareholders (or employees), utilized interest-free loans. Under the typical arrangement, a father who was in the 50 percent tax bracket would make a loan to his son who was in a tax bracket far lower than his father's (or who perhaps paid no taxes at all). Upon receipt of the loan, the son (or his representative if he was a minor) would invest the funds. As a result, any income earned on the investment would be taxed to the son at a lower rate than would have been paid had the father received the income directly. This arrangement could secure substantial tax savings, particularly where there was a great disparity between the tax rates of the two family members.

The success of the tax-saving technique described above was attributable to the terms of the loan agreement. These terms required the son to repay the loan on demand *without interest*. Had the father charged interest, he would still have income attributable to the amount loaned, and no income shifting would have occurred. By not charging interest, however, the interest income that the father would have earned was successfully shifted to the son and tax savings resulted. In addition, the interest that was not charged, a valuable benefit for the son, was not considered a taxable gift. Moreover, this arrangement was extremely appealing because it did not require the father to part with the property forever. Since he had only loaned the funds to his son, he could demand repayment of the funds at any time.

The IRS did not view interest-free loans as a valid means to shift income, but rather a tax avoidance device designed to circumvent the assignment of income rules. After much unsuccessful litigation, the Service finally struck a severe blow in 1984, when the Supreme Court decided in *Dickman* that the interest-free use of the loan amount (i.e., the forgone interest) did constitute a taxable gift by the lender.[85] Despite this victory, the decision did not preclude income shifting. Instead, it merely imposed a cost on using the tax-saving technique equal to the gift tax—which could be zero if the gift of the forgone interest was less than the amount of the annual exclusion of $10,000. As a result, the use of interest-free loans to shift income still appeared viable. However, Congress eliminated this opportunity in 1984 by enacting Code § 7872, which imputes interest income to the lender where the actual interest is considered inadequate.

---

[85]   84-1 USTC ¶13,560, 53 AFTR2d 84-1608,
       104 S.Ct. 1932 (USSC, 1984).

Treatment of Below-Market Loans. In general, § 7872 applies to loans when the interest charged is below the current market rate of interest. As pictured below, when such a loan is made, the treatment is determined *assuming* that the borrower pays the interest to the lender at the market rate, which the lender is then deemed to transfer back to the borrower:

This hypothetical scenario results in the following tax consequences:

1. The borrower may be allowed a deduction for the interest hypothetically paid to the lender, while the lender reports the fictitious payment as *interest income*.

2. The lender treats the hypothetical payment to the borrower as either compensation, dividend, or gift depending on the nature of the loan. Similarly, the borrower treats the payment as either compensation, dividend, or gift as the case may be. In determining the character of the lender's hypothetical payment, the Code classifies loans into three types according to the relationship between the lender and the borrower.

    > *Gift loans*—those where the forgone interest is in the nature of a gift;
    > *Compensation-related loans*—those made by an employer to an employee or an independent contractor; and
    > *Corporation-shareholder loans*—those made by a corporation to a shareholder.[86]

The thrust of these rules is to treat the borrower as having paid the proper amount of interest, which is funded by the lender through compensation, dividends, or gift.

---

[86] In this regard, Proposed Reg. § 1.7872-4(d)(2) indicates that a payment to a shareholder-employee is presumed to be a dividend if the corporation is (1) closely held and such person owns more than 5 percent of its stock, or (2) publicly held and such person owns $1/2$ of one percent of the stock.

Example 36.   Lender L loaned $100,000 to borrower B payable on demand without interest. Assume the statutory rate of interest required to be charged is 10 percent compounded semiannually. Thus, the interest hypothetically paid by B and which must be imputed to L is $10,250. The following table shows the effect on L and B, assuming the loan is

1.   A gift loan.

2.   A compensation-related loan.

3.   A corporation-shareholder loan.

	Lender L				Borrower B			
	Interest Income	Gift Made	Comp. Expense	Dividend Paid	Interest Expense	Gift Received	Comp. Income	Dividend Received
(1)	$10,250	$10,250			$(10,250)	$10,250		
(2)	10,250		$(10,250)		(10,250)		$10,250	
(3)	10,250			$10,250	(10,250)			$10,250

The first situation reveals the effects where the interest forgone by the lender is considered a gift (e.g., loans between family members). In this case, income shifting is prohibited since L does not avoid taxation on the income from the loan. Rather, he or she is deemed to receive an interest payment from B on the amount loaned. In addition, L is treated as having made a taxable gift to B of $250 ($10,250 gift − $10,000 annual exclusion). On the other hand, B is entitled to exclude the $10,250 gift from income. B's hypothetical interest payment may or may not be deductible, depending on whether it is treated as investment interest, business interest, or personal interest (see Chapter 11 for a discussion of interest).

The second situation assumes that the loan is made by an employer to an employee, and, thus, the hypothetical payment by the lender is considered compensation. In this case, the lender is treated as having received interest income that is offset by a deduction for compensation expense to B. Note, however, that if B is an employee, L would be responsible for employment taxes and withholding. The effect on the borrower, B, depends on whether the hypothetical interest payment is deductible. If so, there generally will be no effect since such deduction offsets B's compensation income.

The third situation demonstrates the undesirable consequences that a corporation encounters when its deemed payment is considered a dividend rather than compensation. This problem would normally arise where the loan is made to an individual who is both a shareholder and an employee of the corporation. In this situation, like the second situation above, L (a corporation) has income from the deemed payment. In contrast to the second situation, however, L receives no offsetting deduction since dividend payments are not deductible. The effect on B again depends on whether the hypothetical interest payment is deductible.

These provisions govern not only the treatment of gift, compensation-related, and corporate-shareholder loans, but also any other type of below-market loan designed to achieve tax avoidance or affect the tax liability of the lender or the borrower.

> **Example 37.** During the year, J joined a country club. The club requires each member to lend the club $10,000 without interest. Assuming interest rates are currently 8 percent, the club is effectively receiving annual dues of $800 from each member. More importantly from the member's standpoint, the dues are paid with tax-free dollars.
>
> Had J received the $800 directly, she would be required to pay taxes. By making the loan to the club, she has effectively converted taxable income to tax-exempt income. Under Code § 7872, however, this arrangement would not be effective since J would be treated as having received the $800 income and would have no offsetting deduction for the payment to the club.

Exempted Loans. To restrict the application of § 7872 to predominantly abusive situations, Congress carved out several exceptions to the rules described above. Under the first exception, § 7872 does not apply to *gift* loans as long as the loans outstanding during the year do not exceed $10,000 *and* the borrower does not use the loan proceeds to purchase or carry income-producing assets. Without this latter requirement, income of small amounts could still be shifted. The effect of this provision is to exempt small loans where income shifting is absent.

Congress also granted compensation-related and corporation-shareholder loans an exemption from the onerous rules of § 7872 if they do not exceed $10,000. The exemption does not apply to these loans, however, if tax avoidance is one of the principal purposes of the loan.

Interest Income Cap. Another special rule imposes a limit on the amount of imputed interest income for loans between individuals. Generally, if the amount of outstanding loans does not exceed $100,000 and their principal purpose is not tax avoidance, the deemed payment by the borrower to the lender is limited to the borrower's investment income. This rule follows from the theory that the amount of income shifted by the lender is limited to that which the borrower actually earns. In addition, to enable loans where tax avoidance is obviously not a motive, the lender is treated as having no imputed interest income if the borrower's investment income does not exceed $1,000. However, the lender is still deemed to have made a gift of the forgone interest.

> **Example 38.** R has a son, T, who earns a salary and has $800 investment income. During the year, R loaned T $90,000 without interest to purchase a home. Interest imputed at the IRS rate is $12,000. R has no interest income since the loan is less than $100,000 and investment income is less than $1,000. However, R is charged with a taxable gift of $2,000 ($12,000 − $10,000 exclusion). Note that if T had $7,000 of investment income, R also would have been charged with interest income of $7,000.

INCOME FROM COMMUNITY PROPERTY

In the United States, the rights that married individuals hold in property are determined using either the common law or community property system. The community property system developed in continental Europe and was adopted in several states having a French or Spanish origin. The nine states currently recognizing the community property system are Arizona, California, Idaho, Louisiana, Nevada, New Mexico, Texas, Washington, and Wisconsin. The remaining 41 states use the common law system, which originated in England.

The community property system categorizes property into two types: separate property, which is considered belonging separately to one of the spouses, and community property, which is considered owned equally by each spouse. In general, separate property consists only of those assets owned before marriage or acquired by gift or inheritance while married. All property acquired during a marriage except by gift or inheritance is community property.

Income from separate property may be community property or separate property depending on the state of jurisdiction. In Texas, Louisiana, and Idaho, income from separate property is community property. Accordingly, for Federal tax purposes each spouse is responsible for one-half of the income. In the other six states, income from separate property is separate property and must be reported by the person owning the property. Income from personal services is generally treated as belonging to the community. The following example illustrates how these differing rules must be taken into account.

> **Example 39.** A husband and wife elect to file separate returns. The husband received a $30,000 salary and $1,000 dividends on stock he had purchased prior to the couple's marriage. The husband also receives $500 of taxable interest from a certificate of deposit that he had purchased in his own name while married. The wife's income would vary depending on the state in which she lived:
>
> | | Texas | Arizona | Common Law States |
> |---|---|---|---|
> | Salary.................. | $15,000 | $15,000 | $0 |
> | Dividends.............. | 500 | 0 | 0 |
> | Interest................ | 250 | 250 | 0 |
> | Wife's income.......... | $15,750 | $15,250 | $0 |

Community Income Where Spouses Live Apart. The treatment of community income can create financial problems, particularly where spouses live apart during the year and are later divorced before the end of the taxable year. For example, consider R and S, who were married but lived apart during the first half of the year before their divorce became final. Under these circumstances, the property settlement should consider the accrued tax liability that arises due to any community income. Accounting for the liability may be difficult or impossible, however, if one of the spouses has abandoned the other. In such cases, the abandoned spouse becomes liable for the tax on income earned by a spouse who cannot be located to share the financial responsibility. To eliminate these difficulties, special provisions were enacted.

Section 66 provides that a spouse will be taxed only on the earnings attributed to his or her personal services if during the year the following requirements are satisfied:

1. The two married individuals live apart at all times.

2. The couple does not file a joint return with each other.

3. No portion of the earned income is transferred between the spouses.

This rule only applies to income from personal services and not income from property.

> **Example 40.** M and N, residents of Texas, decided in November 1991 to obtain a divorce, which became final on March 31, 1993. N earns $2,000 each month and M is unemployed. N has a savings account that yielded $200 of taxable interest during the first three months of 1993. Assuming the two live apart during all of 1993 and none of the earned income is transferred between them, N will report all of the $6,000 ($2,000 × 3) attributable to her personal services and $100 of the interest. M will report his $100 share of the taxable interest.

✔ CHECK YOUR KNOWLEDGE

> **Review Question 1.** In 1960 18-year-old Randy Hundley signed a contract to play baseball for the Chicago Cubs.[87] The contract provided for a bonus of $110,000 (a grand sum in those days) to be paid over a five-year period at a rate of $22,000 per year: $11,000 to Randy and $11,000 to his father, Cecil. The payment to Randy's father was pursuant to an oral agreement the two had made when Randy was 16. According to the agreement, Cecil, a former semiprofessional baseball player and coach, acted as Randy's coach and business manager in exchange for 50 percent of any bonus that Randy might receive if he should obtain a baseball contract.
>
> At about the same time that the Cubs were striking a deal with Hundley, the Philadelphia Phillies reached an agreement with Richie Allen, another future star.[88] According to this arrangement, Allen was to receive a $70,000 bonus: $30,000 paid to him over five years and $40,000 paid to his mother. How should the bonuses be treated? Should they both be treated the same?

---

[87] *Cecil Randolph Hundley, Jr.*, 48 T.C. 339 (1967).

[88] *Richard A. Allen*, 50 T.C. 466 (1968).

The question in both cases is whether the child has effectively split the income between himself and his parent or merely made an anticipatory assignment of income. If the latter is true, all of the income would be taxed to the child and none to the parent. In both cases, the IRS argued that the payment to Randy's father and Richie's mother should be treated as being first made to the child and then followed by a nondeductible gift. Despite the similarity of the cases, the Court believed that the services provided by Hundley's father were instrumental in his son's success, whereas Allen's mother made no tangible contribution. As a result, Hundley was allowed to deduct the payment to his father as a business expense and, therefore, split the income between them. In contrast, no deduction was allowed to Allen and he was required to pay taxes on the entire bonus.

Review Question 2.   M wants to shift income to her 14-year-old daughter so that it will be taxed at the daughter's 15 percent rate rather than at M's 36 percent rate. M plans on loaning her daughter $10,000 interest-free for this purpose. Will her plan to shift income to the daughter work?

As a general rule, interest-free loans can no longer be used successfully to shift income, since interest income must be imputed to the lender. In this case, M would be treated as having received an interest payment from her daughter, thus defeating the entire plan. At first blush, some might believe that because the loan is less than $10,000, the de minimus rule operates and M is not required to impute interest; this is a typical misconception. It is true that imputation is not required if the loan is less than $10,000, but only if the borrower does not invest the loan amount in income-producing property. Of course, if the borrower does not invest in income-producing property there is no income and nothing is shifted. Therefore, the $10,000 de minimis rule does not create any opportunity. In this particular case, the $100,000 rule also would come into play. This exception provides that the maximum amount of interest to be imputed to the lender is equal to the net investment income of the borrower (zero, if net investment income is less than $1,000). This provision does provide a small opportunity. If the daughter invests the $10,000 to produce $900 of interest income, no income would be imputed to M and $900 would be successfully shifted. M would be treated as having made a gift of $900 to her daughter, but there would be no gift tax because of the annual exclusion of $10,000.

TAX PLANNING

TIMING INCOME RECOGNITION

The proper timing of income recognition can reap great benefits for the taxpayer. As a general rule, postponement of income recognition is wise since the tax on such income is deferred. The major advantage of tax deferral is that the taxpayer has continued use of the funds that otherwise would have been used to pay taxes. Deferral of the tax is in essence an interest-free loan from the government.

When considering deferral, attention must be given to the marginal tax rates that may apply to the income. For example, taxpayers often postpone income until their retirement years, when they are usually in a lower tax bracket. Although deferral may be wise in this situation, it may be unwise where tax rates rise by operation of law or because of the taxpayer's increase in earnings. Ideally, the taxpayer should attempt to level out taxable income from one year to the next and equalize the tax rate that applies annually (to avoid the situation of R in *Example 11* and duplicate that of S).

The opportunities for most individuals to postpone income are limited, particularly in light of the constructive receipt doctrine. Several techniques do exist, however, as outlined below:

1. Taxpayers who own securities may postpone the sale of investments at a profit. Methods exist for locking in the gain in the current year without having to realize it (selling short against the box or "put" options).

2. Installment sales of property enable the taxpayer not only to avoid the bunching of income in a single year but also to defer the tax.

3. Income on Series E and EE bonds, Treasury bills, and certain certificates of deposit may be deferred until they are redeemed.

4. Investments in Individual Retirement Accounts (IRAs), Keogh plans, and qualified retirement plans are all made with before-tax dollars (since these contributions are deductible), and earnings on these investments are not taxed until they are withdrawn.

5. Deferred compensation arrangements may be suitable, as in the case of a professional athlete, celebrity, or executive (see Chapter 18).

INCOME-SPLITTING TECHNIQUES

As stressed earlier, the most fundamental rule in tax planning concerns minimizing the marginal tax rate that applies to the taxpayer's income. Minimizing the applicable rate is usually accomplished through use of some type of income splitting or shifting technique.

Example 41.   Mr. and Mrs. J pay taxes at a rate of 36%. The couple helps support Mr. J's 67-year-old retired mother, M, by giving her $5,000 annually. Such gifts do not entitle the couple to claim M as a dependent. Consequently, in 1994, M may claim an exemption deduction of $2,450 and a standard deduction of $4,600 ($3,800 regular + $950 additional for unmarried and over 65 years of age), for total deductions of $7,200. In providing M's support through gifts, the couple is using after-tax dollars. That is, the couple would have to earn $7,812 to provide M with $5,000 in support [$7,812 − (36% of $7,812) = $5,000]. Instead, the couple could transfer income-producing property to M to provide the needed support. By so doing, the income would not be subject to tax (assuming M's only other income is tax-exempt such as social security benefits), and the cost of support would be far less expensive. Although this arrangement requires the couple to give up the property permanently (since any type of reversionary interest would cause the income to be taxed back to the couple), in many family situations, M would probably give the property back when she no longer needs it or when she dies. In addition, other techniques are available that can circumvent the problem of permanently departing with the property.

The above example demonstrates how income can be shifted successfully. Where income is to be shifted to children, however, the taxpayer must contend with the "kiddie" tax.

The "kiddie" tax clearly limits opportunities for shifting unearned income to children. However, it does not eliminate them. It should be emphasized that the "kiddie" tax does not apply to children 14 and over. Thus, tax savings similar to those illustrated in *Example 41* can be obtained with little difficulty where the children have reached 14. Moreover, the "kiddie" tax does not apply until unearned income exceeds $1,200 (in 1994). Consequently, for a child under 14, the first $600 of unearned income bears no tax because of the standard deduction, and the next $600 is taxed at the child's rates. Although the "kiddie" tax severely curtails the amount of tax that could otherwise be saved through shifting income to children, taxpayers attempting to shift modest amounts of income are not affected.

Example 42.   In 1994, Father, who earns $90,000 and is in the 31% tax bracket decided to start a college fund for his seven-year-old, Son. To this end, he opened a savings account for Son and deposited $1,000 in the account annually. Assuming the account pays 10% interest annually, interest income for the next several years would be determined as follows:

Son's Age	Balance	Interest	Son's Tax	Son's After-Tax Income
7	$ 1,000	$ 100	$ 0	$ 100
8	2,100	210	0	210
9	3,310	331	0	331
10	4,641	464	0	464
11	6,105	610	2	608
12	7,713	771	26	745
13	9,458	945	52	893
14	11,351	1,135	80	1,055

As the table shows, Son pays no taxes at all for the first four years due to the $600 standard deduction. Moreover, for the next several years Son pays taxes at his low 15% rate because his unearned income does not exceed $1,200 and consequently is not subject to the "kiddie" tax. Note that in this case the "kiddie" tax never applies since Son's unearned income begins to exceed $1,200 only after he turns 14. In contrast, if Father had embarked on a similar program for himself, all income would have been taxed at a rate of 31%.

For taxpayers wanting to shift more unearned income to their children, other techniques are available. One way of coping with the "kiddie" tax is by making investments with income that is deferred until the child becomes 14 or older. For example, the taxpayer could give a child Series EE savings bonds. The income from these bonds can be deferred by not electing to report the accumulated interest until after the child turns 14. Interest thereafter would be reported annually. Similarly, discount bonds—those *without* original issue discount—could be purchased. In this case, the interest is not reported until the bond is sold.

The "kiddie" tax applies to unearned income and not earned income. As a result, earned income can be successfully shifted by paying the child for performing some task. Of course, shifting does not occur unless the payment is deductible by the parent. Such payments, when made by a parent directly to a child under 18, have the added benefit of not being subject to social security taxes.

EXCLUDED ECONOMIC INCOME

In arranging one's affairs, it should be observed that certain "economic" income does not fall within the definition of income for tax purposes and thus can be obtained tax free.

> **Example 43.** Taxpayer R received a gift from her rich uncle of $100,000, which she is considering investing in either a condominium or corporate stocks. The condominium in which she is interested is the one in which she currently lives and rents for $8,000 annually. In lieu of purchasing the condominium, she could continue to rent and invest the $100,000 in preferred stocks paying dividends of 10% annually, or $10,000 of income per year. Assume that R pays taxes at a marginal rate of 30%. The return after taxes on the preferred stock will be 7%, or $7,000. The return from the investment in the condominium is represented by the rent that she does not pay of $8,000, which is nontaxable. In essence, the condominium pays a dividend-in-kind (i.e., shelter), which is tax-exempt. Consequently, R would obtain a higher yield on her investment by purchasing the condominium. Note that income for tax purposes does not include the value of the condominium which would be considered income in the economic sense because the use of the condominium's shelter represents consumption. This same type of analysis applies to all types of investments in consumer goods that provide long-term benefits, such as washers and refrigerators.

PROBLEM MATERIALS

DISCUSSION QUESTIONS

5-1 *Economic versus Tax Concept of Income.* It has been said that the income tax discriminates against the person who lives in a rented home as compared with the person who owns his or her own residence. Comment on the truth of this assertion and why such discrimination may or may not be justified.

5-2 *Net Worth Method.* Explain the circumstances in which the economist's approach to measuring income might be used for tax purposes and what specific steps might be taken to implement such an approach.

5-3 *What Is Income?* Listed below are several items that may or may not constitute income for purposes of economics and income taxes. Indicate whether each item would be considered income for each of these purposes, including comments on why differences, if any, might exist.

    a. Beef raised and consumed by a cattle rancher.
    b. Interest received on state or local bonds.
    c. Air transportation provided by an airline to one of its flight attendants.
    d. Appreciation of XRY stock from $1,000 to $6,000 during the year.
    e. Proceeds collected from an insurance company for a casualty loss and reinvested in similar property.
    f. A loan obtained from a friend.
    g. $105 received from sale of stock purchased one year ago for $100; inflation during the past year averaged 5 percent.
    h. A gift received as a Christmas present.

5-4 *Cash Equivalent Doctrine.* A financial newsletter recently reported the many advantages that may be obtained from belonging to a barter club or organization. Would tax benefits be included among these advantages (e.g., no taxable income realized on the exchange of services)?

5-5 *Return of Capital Doctrine—General.* Explain the return of capital doctrine and discuss three situations in which the doctrine operates.

5-6 *Indirect Benefits.* A, an assistant manager for a department store, often is required to work overtime to help mark down merchandise for special sales. On these occasions, her employer pays the cost of her evening meal. Does the meal constitute income? Explain.

5-7 *Annual Accounting Period-Planning.* Briefly explain the notion of "income bunching" and why it is a problem.

5-8   *Relationship between Tax and Financial Accounting Methods.*   Does conformity with generally accepted accounting principles satisfy the requirement of § 446(c) that income must be clearly reflected? Explain, including some illustrations where income for tax purposes will differ from that for financial accounting purposes.

5-9   *Cash Basis Taxpayer's Receipt of Notes.*   Does a cash basis taxpayer recognize income when a note is received or when collections are made?

5-10   *Constructive Receipt Doctrine.*   Discuss the planning opportunities related to the cash method of accounting and how these are affected by the constructive receipt doctrine.

5-11   *Accrual Method of Accounting.*   Address the following questions:

a.   When does a taxpayer using the accrual method of accounting normally report income?

b.   Under what circumstances is an accrual basis taxpayer treated like a cash basis taxpayer for purposes of reporting income?

5-12   *Category A vs. Category B Methods.*   T Corporation is considering altering the way in which it accounts for a particular item. Its accountant has stated that the ultimate disposition of the item and the effect of the change on income depend on whether the method is considered a Category A or Category B method of accounting as well as who initiates that change. Explain.

5-13   *Change in Accounting Method—Pre-1954 Balances.*   J has operated a furniture store in Littleville, Ohio since 1947. This year, he hired an accountant who immediately discovered that J was not using the accrual method to account for his inventory costs. According to the accountant, a change to this method will result in additional income of $200,000, a portion of which is attributable to the years 1947 through 1953. What would you advise J to do?

5-14   *Changing Accounting Methods: Procedures.*   F files the tax returns for his three-year-old son, S. Up until this year, F had always reported the interest on S's Series EE savings bonds annually. F now wishes to report the interest income when the bonds are redeemed (e.g., when the child reaches age 14). Can F change the way he reports the interest? If so, how?

5-15   *What Is an Accounting Method?*   This year, T hired a new accountant, A. As part of A's routine review procedures, A determined that T's previous accountant had improperly computed the gross profit percentage to be used in recognizing income on an installment sale. Based on the previous accountant's calculation, 40 percent of each year's receipts were to be included in income, whereas according to A's calculation the proper percentage was 50 percent. Explain what A should do upon finding the discrepancy.

5-16   *Claim of Right.*   Consider the questions below.

a.   Is the application of the claim of right doctrine limited to situations that involve only contested income? Explain.

b.   Explain the difference between the claim of right and constructive receipt doctrines.

5-17   *Prepaid Rent.*   In light of the tax treatment, should landlords of apartment complexes characterize an initial $500 deposit from their tenants as a security deposit or as a payment of the last month's rent in advance? Explain.

5-18   *Prepaid Services.*   Identify several types of services where the accrual basis provider will not be permitted to defer any prepayments of income related to such services. Explain.

5-19   *Long-Term Contracts.*   Indicate which method of accounting for long-term contracts—completed contract or percentage of completion—the taxpayer may use in the following situations. Assume each contract is considered a long-term contract unless otherwise implied.

  a.   A contract to build an office building. The taxpayer's annual gross receipts for the last five years have exceeded $11 million.
  b.   A contract to build a home to be finished next year. The taxpayer's annual gross receipts for the last five years have exceeded $11 million.
  c.   A contract to build a high-rise apartment complex containing 120 units. The contractor's average gross receipts are $11 million.
  d.   A contract to manufacture 15,000 seats for a football stadium. The taxpayer has several contracts for this type of seat. Average gross receipts are $12 million.
  e.   A contract to manufacture a special part for the Space Shuttle. Average annual gross receipts were $12 million.

5-20   *Taxpayer Identification—Family Trusts.*   In recent years, many taxpayers have fallen victim to vendors of the so-called "family trust" tax shelter. Under this arrangement the taxpayer signs a contractual agreement entitling the trust to all of the taxpayer's income which is subsequently distributed to the beneficiaries of the trust. Explain how this arrangement is supposed to save taxes and why it fails.

5-21   *Income Reporting by Partnerships and S Corporations.*   Explain how partners and shareholders in S corporations may defer the reporting of income by having their respective entities select fiscal years for reporting rather than calendar years.

5-22   *Income from Community Property.*   Under what circumstances will knowledge of the community property system be relevant? Is it necessary for persons residing in common law states to understand the community property system?

5-23   *Planning—Timing Income Recognition.*   Although it is generally desirable to defer income recognition and the related taxes, when would acceleration of income be preferred?

5-24   *Planning—Income Splitting.*   How might R, who operates a shoe store as a sole proprietorship, reduce the taxes that are imposed on his family using income-splitting techniques?

5-25   *"Kiddie" Tax.*   R has been advised that due to recent changes in the tax law he can no longer save taxes by shifting income to his children.

  a.   Explain the origin of such advice.
  b.   Refer to *Example 42* in this chapter. Determine how much more Father is able to accumulate for Son's education by using the savings account over the period shown in the example.

YOU MAKE THE CALL

5-26 In the last episode in the adventures of Dr. Will Floss, the tax-evading dentist identified earlier in this chapter, he was found exploring the cavities of his patient's mouth. As may be remembered, Dr. Floss had just made a deal with a patient whereby he exchanged a root canal for some carpet complete with pad and installation. Floss's accountant, Al, was faced with a dilemma. After dumping his records on Al's desk, Floss had proudly proclaimed that it was another great year. Al could remember his exact words: "Made over $200,000 but reported only $50,000. Not bad," said Floss. "Am I glad I talked to Dr. Moller!" Unfortunately, Al had to lower the boom on Floss's plan, explaining to him that he was required to report his barter income. However, Floss has stated flatly that he will not report the income. "If Moller doesn't report his, I'm not reporting mine," insists Floss. What should Al the accountant do about his client Floss and his friend Moller? If Floss goes to another accountant, does Al have any responsibilities?

PROBLEMS

5-27 *What Is Income?* In each of the following situations indicate whether taxable income should be recognized.

    a. Q purchased an older home for $20,000. Shortly after its purchase, the area in which it was located was designated a historical neighborhood, causing its value to rise to $50,000.

    b. R, a long-time employee of XYZ Inc., purchased one of the company's cars worth $7,000 for $3,000.

    c. I borrowed $10,000 secured by property that had an adjusted basis of $3,000 and a fair market value of $15,000.

    d. S, a 60 percent shareholder in STV Corporation, uses a company car 70 percent of the time for business and 30 percent for personal purposes. The rental value of the car is $200 per month.

5-28 *What Is Income?* In each of the following situations indicate whether taxable income should be recognized.

    a. R discovered oil on his farm, causing the value of his land to increase by $100 million.

    b. While jogging, L found a portable stereo radio valued at $200.

    c. E agreed to rent his lake cottage to F for $1,000 during the summer. After living there for two weeks, E and F agreed that E would only charge $700 if F made certain improvements.

    d. D borrowed $100,000, $20,000 each from S, T, U, V, and W. He gave them each a one-year note bearing interest at a rate of 25 percent. At the end of the year, D borrowed $200,000 from X, promising to pay him back in one year plus 30 percent interest. D used part of the $200,000 from X to pay the interest due to S, T, U, V, and W. D also convinced them to extend the original notes for another year. D has no intention of ever repaying the principal of the notes.

5-29 *What Is Income?*   In each of the following situations indicate whether taxable income should be recognized.

    a. L sued her former employer for sex discrimination evidenced in his compensation policy. She was awarded $100,000, $39,000 of which represented reimbursement for mental anguish.

    b. M, a sales clerk for a department store, purchased a microwave oven from the store's appliance department. The store has a policy allowing employees a 10 percent discount. This discount results in $45 savings to M.

    c. R received a bottle of perfume and a case of grapefruit from her boss at the annual Christmas party. The items were valued at $25.

5-30 *Constructive Receipt.*   When would a cash basis taxpayer recognize income in the following situations? Assume the taxpayer reports on a calendar year.

    a. R, a traveling salesman, was out of town on payday, December 31. He picked up his check when he arrived back on January 3.

    b. C owns a bond with interest coupons due and payable on December 31. C clipped the coupons and redeemed them on January 7.

    c. R is an officer and controlling shareholder in XYZ Corporation. In December the corporation authorized bonuses for all officers. The bonus was paid in February of the following year.

5-31 *Constructive Receipt.*   For each of the following situations, indicate whether the taxpayer has constructively received the income.

    a. R received a bonus as top salesman of the year. He received the check for $20,000 at 10 P.M. on December 31 at a New Year's Eve party. All the banks were closed.

    b. On January 3, D received the check for January's rent of her duplex. The envelope was postmarked December 31.

    c. On December 25, C Corporation rewarded its top executive, E, with 100 shares of stock for a job well done. E was unable to find a buyer until March 15 of the following year.

    d. Immediately after receiving her check on December 31, Z went to her employer's bank to cash it. The bank would not cash it since the employer's account was overdrawn.

5-32 *Constructive Receipt.*   For each of the following situations, indicate whether the taxpayer has constructively received the income.

    a. X Corporation declared a dividend on December 15 and mailed dividend checks on December 28. R received her check for $200 on January 4.

    b. F owns a small apartment complex. His son, S, lives in one of the units and manages the complex. Several tenants left their January rent checks with S during the last week of December. S delivered the checks to his father in January.

    c. This year, the cash surrender value of L's life insurance policy increased by $500. In order to obtain the value, L must cancel the policy.

5-33 *Changes in Accounting Method.* JB and his sons have operated a small "general store" in Backwoods, Idaho, since 1947. This year, JB hired a new accountant, who immediately told him he should be using the accrual method to account for his inventories and related sales. According to the accountant's best guess, as of January 1, 1954 the store's balances in accounts receivable and inventory were $40,000 and $50,000, respectively. On that same date, JB owed $10,000 in accounts payable related to his inventory. The receivables were primarily attributable to sales of seed to farmers as well as appliances. JB has always used the cash method of accounting, reporting all of his income when he receives it and deducting all costs when paid. According to the accountant, as of the close of the current year, JB had $70,000 in receivables outstanding (none of which had been reported in income), inventory of $130,000 (all expensed), and outstanding accounts payable for recent purchases of inventory of $20,000.

    a. If JB is audited, what method of accounting will the IRS claim that he should be using? Is the method he is currently using a Category A or Category B method?

    b. If the IRS audits JB and requires him to change his method of accounting, what is the adjustment amount and when will JB report it?

    c. Same as (b) except JB voluntarily changes his method of accounting.

    d. If JB changes to the accrual method of accounting to account for inventories and sales, may he continue to report other items of income (e.g., interest income) and expense (e.g., supplies) using the cash method?

5-34 *Advanced Payments for Goods.* HIJ Furniture, an accrual basis company for both tax and financial accounting purposes, normally does not sell the items displayed in its showrooms, nor does it keep those items in stock. Instead, it obtains partial payment from the customer and orders the items directly from the manufacturer. During 1994, HIJ collected $60,000 with respect to furniture sales still on order at the close of the year. (The partial payments collected by HIJ do not exceed their cost for the items ordered.) Must HIJ report any of the $60,000 as income in 1994?

5-35 *Percentage of Completion.* THZ Corporation is a large construction company. This year it contracted with the city of Old York to build a new performing arts center for a price of $5,000,000. Estimated total costs of the project were $4,000,000. Annual costs incurred were as follows:

1995..........................	$2,000,000
1996..........................	500,000
1997..........................	1,000,000
Total..........................	$3,500,000

    a. What method(s) of accounting may the corporation use to report income from the project?

    b. How much income would be reported each year under the percentage of completion method?

    c. Would any interest be due to (or from) the IRS as a result of this contract? If so, compute for the first year only, assuming the taxpayer is in the 34 percent tax bracket and the interest rate is 10 percent.

    d. Assume that the costs incurred in 1995 were $100,000. How much income is the taxpayer required to report in 1995?

5-36 *U.S. Savings Bonds.* During 1994, S purchased U.S. Government Series EE Bonds for $700. The redemption value of the bonds at the end of the year was $756.

    a. What options are available to S with respect to reporting the income from the bonds?

    b. What advantage might be obtained by exchanging the Series EE Bonds for Series HH Bonds?

5-37 *Contested Income.* In 1994, GLX Company, an accrual basis taxpayer, received $10,000 for supplying running shoes to T for sale in his sporting goods store. During 1994, T claimed the shoes had defective soles and requested GLX to refund the $10,000 payment.

    a. Must GLX report any of the $10,000 as income in 1994?

    b. Had GLX not received payment in 1994, would your answer in (a) change?

    c. Assume GLX and T resolved their dispute in 1995 and GLX refunded $2,000 to T. What would be the effect, if any, on GLX?

5-38 *Deposits and Prepaid Rents.* Q owns several duplexes. From each new tenant she requires a $150 security deposit and $300 for the last month's rent. The deposit is refundable assuming the tenant complies with all the terms of the lease. During the year, Q collected $1,000 in deposits and $2,400 of prepaid rents for the last month of occupancy. In addition, she refunded $400 to previous tenants but withheld $300 due to damages. How much must Q include in income assuming she is an accrual basis taxpayer?

5-39 *Prepaid Service Income: Accrual Method.*

    a. LL Corporation, a calendar year and accrual basis taxpayer, is engaged in the lawn care business, providing fertilizer treatments four times a year. It sells one- and two-year service contracts. On September 1, 1994, it sold a contract for $100 and provided one treatment for the customer in 1994. What amount must be included in income in 1994 and 1995 if the contract is a one-year contract?

    b. Same as (a) except that the contract is for two years.

    c. A professional basketball team that reports on the calendar year and uses the accrual method collected $700,000 in pre-season ticket sales in August and September of 1994. Of its 41-game home season, 15 games were played prior to the end of the year. What amount must be included in income in 1994?

    d. A posh resort hotel in Florida reports on the calendar year and uses the accrual method. During 1994, it collected $10,000 in advance payments for rooms to be rented during January and February 1995. What amount of income must be included in 1994 and 1995?

5-40 *Income from Transferred Property.* E's grandmother owns several vending machines on campus. To help him through college, she allows E to collect and keep all the receipts from the machines. During the year, E spent approximately two hours a month to collect $5,000. Who must report the income and what is the amount to be included?

5-41 *Partnership Income.* QRS, a partnership, had taxable income of $120,000 for the fiscal year ended September 30, 1994. For the first quarter ending December 31, 1994, taxable income was $30,000. During 1994, Q, a partner with a 30 percent interest in profits and losses, withdrew $1,000 per month for a total of $12,000. What is Q's taxable income from QRS for 1994?

5-42   *Reporting Interest Income.*   On November 1, 1993, G received a substantial inheritance and promptly made several investments. Indicate in each of the following cases the amount of interest income that he must report and the period in which the income is properly reported, assuming that G uses (1) the cash method of accounting, or (2) the accrual method of accounting. G reports using the calendar year.

    a.   G purchased a $10,000, 90-day U.S. Treasury bill at 99. The bill matured on January 30, 1994, when G redeemed it at par.

    b.   G purchased $100,000 of AFN Inc. 10 percent bonds for $95,000. The bonds were issued at par in 1985. The bonds pay interest semiannually on March 1 and September 1. On March 1, 1994, G received an interest payment of $5,000.

5-43   *Interest-Free Loans.*   This year Dr. W, an orthopedic surgeon, and her husband, H, an attorney, established a trust for their five-year-old daughter, D. In conjunction with setting up the trust, the couple loaned the trust $200,000 payable on demand without interest. Assuming the interest that should have been charged under the applicable rate was $23,000, explain the effect of the loan on all of the parties.

5-44   *Shareholder Advances.*   In 1963, J started ACC Corporation, a construction company. J owns all of the stock of the corporation and is also its president. Like many owners of closely-held corporations, J pretty much treats the corporation's checkbook as his own. He often asks the bookkeeper to make out checks to him that he ostensibly uses for business purposes. Over time, J does repay the amounts used for personal purposes, or turns in receipts for amounts used for business. In the meantime, the bookkeeper charges these checks to a special account titled "J Suspense." Upon the accountant's review this year, he noted that the account showed a balance of $15,000 (indicating an amount due from J). Explain the tax consequences.

5-45   *Interest-Free Loans.*   F is chief executive officer of CVC Corporation and has taxable income in excess of $200,000 annually. During the year, he loaned his 20-year-old son, S, $30,000, payable on demand without interest. S promptly invested the $30,000 and earned $1,200, which was his only income during the year.

    a.   Assuming the interest that should have been charged under applicable rate is $3,000, compute the effect of the loan on the taxable income of both F and S.

    b.   Would F be able to shift income to his son if he had made a loan of only $9,000?

5-46   *Code § 7872: Exceptions.*   For each of the following independent cases, indicate the income and gift tax consequences for both the lender and the borrower.

    a.   J loaned his 19-year-old son, K, $8,000 interest-free which K used to purchase a car. K had $400 investment income from a savings account for the year.

    b.   Same as (a) except K decided to invest the money in a certificate of deposit yielding $800 of interest income producing a total net investment income of $1,200 for the year.

    c.   G loaned her 29-year-old daughter, D, $50,000 interest-free to help her acquire a franchise for a fast-food restaurant. All of D's funds were invested in the business and consequently she had no investment income for the year.

    d.   P Corporation loaned its sole shareholder, Q, $150,000 interest-free.

    e.   Same as (d) except Q owns no stock in P but is simply a key employee.

5-47 *Cash Method Eligibility.* Given the facts below, indicate whether the taxpayer may use the cash method for 1994 in the following situations.

a. Sweatshirt Corporation, a publicly traded corporation: annual gross receipts for 1990 and previous years were $1 million annually; gross receipts for 1992 were $3 million; and for 1993, $8 million.

b. Dewey, Cheatham, and Howe, a national public accounting firm, operated as a partnership. Annual gross receipts for the last five years have exceeded $50 million.

c. McSwane, McMillan, and McClain, Inc., an architectural firm, operated as a regular C corporation. Annual gross receipts for the last two years have exceeded $7 million. McSwane, McMillan, and McClain own all of the stock and perform services for the firm.

d. Buttons and Bows, Inc., an S corporation.

e. A trust established for John Doe.

f. Plantation Office Park, a publicly traded limited partnership: annual gross receipts have never exceeded $2 million. The partnership is a tax shelter.

5-48 *Shifting Income to Children.* Mr. and Mrs. D wish to shift income to their seven-year-old son, C, to be used for his college education. Explain whether the following would serve their goals or, alternatively, how they effect any technique designed to shift income.

a. Paying C an allowance for making his bed and picking up his clothes.

b. Paying C for helping to wash cars at his dad's car wash.

c. Buying C Series EE savings bonds.

d. Arranging to have Mrs. D's employer pay C part of her salary.

e. The social security rules.

f. The rules governing personal exemptions.

CUMULATIVE PROBLEM

5-49 David K. Gibbs, age 37, and his wife Barbara, age 33, have two children, Chris and Ellen, ages 2 and 12. David is employed as an engineer for an oil company, and his wife recently completed a degree in accounting and will begin working for a public accounting firm next year. David has compiled the following information for your use in preparing his tax return for 1994.

1. For the current year, David received a salary of $50,000. His employer withheld Federal income taxes of $9,000 and the appropriate amount of FICA taxes.

2. At the annual Christmas party, he received a card indicating that he would receive a bonus of $3,000 for his good work during the year. The bonus check was placed in his mailbox at work on December 30. Since David was out of town for the holidays, he did not pick up the bonus check until January 2.

3. A bond issued by AM&T Inc. was sold on May 30, 1994 for $9,700, $700 of which represented interest accrued to the date of the sale. The Gibbs had purchased the bond (issued at par value of $10,000 on March 1, 1980) in 1991 for $10,000.

4. Because of some financial difficulties the couple had encountered, Barbara was able to obtain a salary advance from her new employer of $1,500. Her first paycheck in January 1995 was to be reduced by this amount.

5. The couple has a $500 U.S. savings bond, which they purchased for $300 and gave to their daughter several years ago. The proper election to report the income from the bond annually was made. The bond's redemption value increased $30 this year.

6. David was an instant winner in the state lottery and won $50.

7. The couple's only itemized deductions were interest on their home mortgage, $6,500; and property taxes on their home of $900.

Compute Mr. and Mrs. Gibbs' Federal income tax liability (or refund) for 1994. If a tax return is required by your instructor, prepare Form 1040, including Schedules A and B.

RESEARCH PROBLEMS

5-50 During the year, J, a college accounting professor, received complimentary copies of various textbooks from numerous publishers. J gives some of these books to students and the school library. J also keeps some of the books for his personal use and reference. A few times during the year J sold an unwanted text to a wholesale book dealer who periodically checked with him and other professors for texts. Must J report any income related to receipt of these books?

5-51 R recently became a member of a religious order. As a member, she was subject to the organization's complete control. The organization often required its members to terminate their employment in order to work in other jobs consistent with the organization's philosophy. For example, the organization supplied personnel to missions, hospitals, and schools. The organization also requires all members to take an oath of poverty and pay over all their earnings to it. Members' living expenses are paid for by the organization out of its own funds. Is R taxed on her earnings?

5-52 In each of the following cases, indicate who is responsible for reporting the income.

    a. Dr. A instructed the hospital for which he worked to pay his salary to his daughter C.

    b. R, a famous entertainer, agreed to perform at a concert gratuitously (without fee) for the benefit of a charitable organization.

    c. In a contest for the best essay on why education is important, T, age 25, won the right to designate a person under 17 to receive $1,000.

5-53 M owed her good friend, F, $20,000. In addition, M planned on making a charitable contribution to her church of $10,000. Instead of using cash to pay her friend and to make the contribution, M is considering transferring stock to each in the appropriate amount. The stock is currently worth $100 per share. M had purchased the 300 shares of stock several years ago for $6,000 ($20 per share). Will M realize any income if she transfers the stock rather than paying cash?

5-54 Sam Sellit is a salesman for Panoramic Pools of St. Louis, a construction company that builds and sells prefabricated swimming pools. Over the past several years, Sam has progressed to become the top salesman for the St. Louis franchise. Sam has done so well that he is considering purchasing his own franchise and starting a company in San Antonio. This year he contacted the home office in Pittsburgh about the possibility of opening up his own shop. The vice president in charge of expansion, Greg Grow, suggested that the two of them meet at the company's annual meeting of franchisees in Orlando. Greg knew that Sam, although not a franchisee, would be attending because he was the top salesman in the St. Louis office, and the company invites the top salesman from each office as well as his or her spouse to attend the meeting.

    While at the four-day meeting (Tuesday through Friday) in Orlando, Sam and his wife, Sue, met with Greg and discussed the potential venture. In addition, Greg allowed Sam and Sue to attend the parts of the meeting that were only for franchisees so that they could get a glimpse of how the company operated. Of course, while they were in Orlando, Sam and his wife visited all of the tourist attractions. On Tuesday, there were no meetings scheduled and everyone spent the day at Disney World and Epcot Center. On Thursday afternoon, no meetings were scheduled and the couple went with Greg and his wife to Sea World. Sam attended meetings for several hours on Friday while his wife played golf. The couple stayed over through Sunday and continued their sightseeing activities.

    The company picked up the tab for the couple's trip, reimbursing Sam $3,500 which included the costs of air fare, meals, lodging, and entertainment. What are the tax consequences to Sam?

5-55 Large Corporation manufactures computers. Its total sales of computers last year were well over $100 million. With each computer it offers a three-year warranty, covering parts and labor. The company estimates the future costs of warranty work related to current-year sales and defers the recognition of income until such time that it expects the warranty work will be done. Currently, the corporation reports 60 percent of the warranty income in the year of sale because the majority of warranty work occurs shortly after the computer has been sold. Thirty percent of the warranty income is reported in the second year of the warranty, and the remaining 10 percent is reported in the last year of the warranty. The company's estimates were based on sophisticated statistical techniques. Such techniques have produced estimates that appear extremely accurate based on the last 10 years of data. No insurance is purchased to cover the warranty risk. Upon audit this year, the IRS agent indicated that the company cannot defer the warranty income and assessed a large tax deficiency. Advise the taxpayer as to whether it should pay the additional tax or pursue the matter in court.

LEARNING OBJECTIVES

Upon completion of this chapter you will be able to:

- Identify which items an individual taxpayer must include in the computation of gross income

- Determine which items an individual taxpayer can exclude from the computation of gross income

- Understand generally what goals Congress had in mind in passing the applicable rules and exceptions for inclusions and exclusions

- Recognize tax planning opportunities related to the more common types of income inclusions and exclusions available to individual taxpayers

CHAPTER OUTLINE

Introduction	6-1	Government Transfer Payments	6-40
Investments	6-1	Business Gross Income	6-41
Dividends	6-2	Agreement Not to Compete and	
Interest	6-4	Goodwill	6-41
Annuities	6-9	Business Interruption Insurance	
Employee Compensation and Other		Proceeds	6-42
Benefits	6-14	Damages Awarded	6-42
Reimbursement of Employee		Lease Cancellation Payments	6-42
Expenses	6-15	Debt Cancellation	6-43
Employer Gifts	6-15	Leasehold Improvements	6-44
Employer Awards	6-16	Contributions to Capital	6-45
Social Security Benefits	6-16	Miscellaneous Items	6-45
Unemployment Benefits	6-19	Fees Received	6-45
Employee Insurance	6-19	Asset Discovery	6-45
Death Benefits	6-24	Car Pool Receipts	6-45
Employer-Provided Meals and		Income Tax Refunds	6-46
Lodging	6-25	Temporary Living Costs	6-46
Additional Employee Benefits	6-26	Damages Awarded to Individuals	6-46
Military Personnel	6-31	Tax Planning	6-49
Personal Transfers between Individuals	6-31	Investments	6-49
Gifts and Inheritances	6-32	Employee Benefits	6-50
Alimony and Separate Maintenance	6-32	Employee versus Self-Employed	6-52
Transfers by Unrelated Parties	6-38	Divorce	6-53
Prizes and Awards	6-38	Problem Materials	6-54
Scholarships and Fellowships	6-39		

Chapter **6**

GROSS INCOME
Inclusions and Exclusions

INTRODUCTION

Gross income includes *all* income unless specifically exempted by the U.S. *Constitution*, by *statute*, or by the evolving but authoritative *definition* of income (outlined in Chapter 5). Both the Sixteenth Amendment and Code § 61(a) grant this broad approach to Federal income taxation. Consequently, it is the taxpayer's responsibility to (1) prove that a particular type of income is excluded, and (2) provide the specific authority that permits the exclusion.

Income can be (1) taxable (includible) in total, (2) taxable in part and nontaxable (excludable) in part, or (3) nontaxable in total. In most instances, income that is non-taxable in total is completely omitted from the tax return. For example, it is not possible to determine who received certain nontaxable employee benefits by looking at the tax returns. In contrast, some income that is partially taxable and partially nontaxable is reported in full on the tax return and the nontaxable portion is subtracted in arriving at gross income. For instance, income included on certain brokerage statements is reported in full on the tax return, the nontaxable portion is subtracted, and the taxable portion remains a part of gross income.

This chapter contains a discussion of the more frequently encountered sources of income. To provide some order and logic to the discussion, these sources are classified in the following pages as (1) investments, (2) employee compensation and other benefits, (3) personal transfers between individuals, (4) transfers by unrelated parties, (5) business gross income, and (6) miscellaneous items.

INVESTMENTS

Gross income from investments includes the taxpayer's share of gross income from a partnership and an S corporation (see Chapter 19). Although only the net income or loss is actually recorded on the tax return, the taxpayer is deemed to have reported each

item individually, including the business's gross income.[1] This distinction, for example, can be important in determining whether an individual qualifies as a dependent. Gross income also includes the total amount of rents and royalties before any expenses are deducted.[2] In contrast, only the gain on investments in stocks, bonds, and annuities is treated as gross income. Depending on the source, all the interest may be nontaxable.

DIVIDENDS

Corporate distributions may be of several types. Those commonly received are

1. Cash or property dividends

2. Return of capital

3. Stock dividends

Cash and Property Dividends. A *dividend* is a distribution of cash or other assets to a shareholder with respect to the individual's stock. Dividends are taxable to the extent the distribution comes from the corporation's current or accumulated earnings and profits (E&P). [Basically, current E&P is a corporation's taxable income for the current year after certain specified adjustments are made. Accumulated E&P is a corporation's undistributed E&P from previous years. (In general, see Chapter 19.)] In the case of noncash assets distributed to a shareholder, the value of the dividend received is the property's fair market value on the date of the distribution.[3] The taxable amount becomes the asset's basis. To avoid double taxation at the corporate level, corporate shareholders are allowed a special dividend-received deduction (discussed in Chapter 19).[4]

In contrast to a regular corporation, a mutual fund is usually treated as a conduit in that dividends distributed to its shareholders are deductible in computing the mutual fund's taxable income. As a result, a mutual fund is taxed only on its undistributed income. *Ordinary dividends* received by shareholders of a mutual fund are included in gross income in the years of receipt.[5] *Capital gain dividends* are treated as long-term capital gains irrespective of how long the shareholder has owned the stock in the mutual fund.[6] Furthermore, undistributed capital gain dividends that have been allocated to shareholders by the mutual fund are taxable.[7] Corporate shareholders of a mutual fund are entitled to the dividend-received deduction with respect to ordinary dividends only. A mutual fund is required to provide each shareholder with Form 1099-DIV detailing the types of dividends paid or allocated during the year.

---

[1] § 702(b) and (c). Business gross income is revenues or net sales less cost of goods sold.

[2] § 61(a)(5) and (6) and Reg. § 1.61-8.

[3] § 301(b).

[4] §§ 243 through 246. Generally, the deduction is a percentage of the dividends received from a domestic corporation deter-mined as follows: (1) 70% when the stock ownership percentage (SOP) is less than 20%, (2) 80% when the SOP is 20% or more but less than 80%, and (3) 100% when the SOP is 80% or more.

[5] Reg. § 1.852-4(a).

[6] Reg. § 1.852-4(b).

[7] § 852(b)(3)(D).

Return of Capital. Distributions of cash and other assets to shareholders by corporations in *excess* of their current and accumulated E&P do not qualify as dividends.[8] Instead, they are a return of capital, and are therefore nontaxable to the extent of the shareholder's basis in the stock.[9] After the shareholder's basis in the stock is reduced to zero, additional distributions in excess of E&P are capital gains.[10]

> **Example 1.** C, Inc. distributes $100,000 to shareholders when its current E&P is $60,000 and it has no accumulated E&P. T, a 10% shareholder, has a basis in C, Inc. stock of $3,000. T receives $10,000, of which $6,000 (10% × $60,000) is from C's current E&P. Thus, T has a $6,000 taxable dividend; the $3,000 equal to his basis in the stock is a nontaxable return of investment, and the remaining $1,000 is capital gain.

There are a number of other types of distributions that do not qualify as dividends. Some of these are listed below.

1. In some instances, earnings on deposits with banks, credit unions, investment companies, and savings and loan associations are referred to as dividends when they actually possess all the characteristics of interest. These dividends are reported as interest.[11]

2. Mutual insurance companies distribute amounts referred to as dividends to owners of unmatured life insurance policies. These dividends are treated as a nontaxable return of a portion of the insurance premium paid.[12]

3. Cooperatives distribute patronage dividends to cooperative members. These dividends are treated as a return of part of the original price paid for items purchased by members.[13]

4. As noted above, dividends from regulated investment companies (mutual funds) that represent gains on sales of investments from the fund are treated as long-term capital gains.[14]

Stock Dividends. In some instances, corporations wish to pay dividends but have insufficient cash or other assets to distribute. One approach is to issue stock dividends to shareholders without giving them an opportunity to receive cash, other assets, or other stock. If the stock dividend is common stock distributed to common shareholders, it is nontaxable.[15] Shareholders simply increase the number of common shares held. The basis in their original holdings is divided equally among all shares of common.[16] The holding period for the new common stock is the same as the holding period of the original common stock.

---

[8] § 316(a).

[9] § 301(c)(2).

[10] § 301(c)(3).

[11] Reg. § 1.61-7(a).

[12] § 316(b)(1).

[13] § 1385(b).

[14] § 1382(b).

[15] § 305(a).

[16] § 307(a).

Example 2. V owns 100 shares of Z common with a basis of $2,200 ($22 per share). He receives 10 shares of Z common as a stock dividend. If V did not have the right to receive cash or other assets in lieu of the stock, he has no taxable income and his $2,200 basis is allocated among the 110 shares of common for a $20 per share basis ($2,200 ÷ 110).

When nonconvertible preferred stock is distributed to common shareholders as a stock dividend, it too is nontaxable.[17] After the distribution, shareholders own both common and preferred stock. The basis in their original holdings of common stock is allocated between the common and the preferred stock based on their relative fair market values. The holding period for the preferred stock is the same as the holding period of the common stock.[18]

Example 3. Q owns 100 shares of S common with a basis of $2,200. She receives 10 shares of S preferred as a stock dividend. The market value is $4,000 ($40 per share) for common and $1,000 ($100 per share) for preferred. If Q did not have the right to receive cash or other assets in lieu of the stock, she has no taxable income. Her basis for the preferred stock is $440 [$1,000 ÷ ($4,000 + $1,000 = $5,000 total value) = 20% × $2,200] and her basis for the common stock is $1,760 [either ($2,200 − $440) or ($4,000 ÷ $5,000) × $2,200].

Reinvested Dividends. Shareholders who have the right to choose between receiving their dividends in cash *or* in additional shares of stock do not qualify for the stock dividend exclusion. Regardless of whether these shareholders elect to receive cash or stock, they have taxable dividend income (to the extent of E&P, as discussed above).[19] This same treatment applies to all situations in which a dividend can change a common shareholder's proportionate ownership interest in the common stock.[20]

INTEREST

Generally, interest is taxable income regardless of (1) its source (a bank, business, friend, or relative), (2) the form of the interest-bearing instrument (savings account, bond, or note), or (3) how the funds were used. Two exceptions are (1) the exclusion for interest on certain state and local government obligations, and (2) the exclusion for interest on educational savings bonds.

---

[17] § 305(a) and (b)(5). However, § 306 may require a taxpayer to recognize ordinary income for all or a portion of the gain when the preferred stock is sold.

[18] § 1223(5).

[19] § 305(b)(1).

[20] § 305(b)(2).

Interest on State and Local Government Obligations. From the inception of the Federal income tax law, interest on obligations of a state, a territory, a U.S. possession, or any of their political subdivisions has been *nontaxable*.[21] This treatment stems from an uncertainty about whether taxing this interest would be unconstitutional and also from political pressure exerted by the affected governments.[22] The exclusion is exceedingly beneficial to these governments because it means they can pay a lower interest rate and still attract investors, especially those investors who are subject to taxes at the highest marginal rates.

Example 4. K, Inc. invests $10,000 in corporate bonds that pay 13% annually and $10,000 in state bonds that pay 9% annually. If K, Inc.'s marginal tax rate is 34%, its after-tax earnings on the corporate bonds are less than its earnings on the state bonds.

	Corporate Bonds	State Bonds
Annual interest income............	$1,300	$900
Federal income tax (34%).........	442	0
After-tax income..................	$ 858	$900

If K's marginal tax rate is 15%, however, its after-tax earnings for the corporate bonds increase to $1,105 ($1,300 − $195).

A break-even point between taxable and nontaxable rates of return may be calculated with the following formula:

Taxable interest rate × (1 − Marginal tax rate) = Tax-free rate

Applying the numbers in the example above when K, Inc.'s tax rate is 34 percent, the break-even point for the taxable bond is

13% × (1 − 0.34 = 0.66) = 8.58%

Thus, at the 34 percent marginal tax rate, a 13 percent taxable return is equal to an 8.58 percent tax-exempt return.

---

[21] § 103(a); § 103(c).

[22] In *National Life Insurance Co.*, 1 USTC ¶314, 6 AFTR 7801, 277 U.S. 508 (USSC, 1928), the Supreme Court indicated that Federal taxation of *interest* paid by state and local governments was unconstitutional. However, in *Willcuts v. Bunn*, 2 USTC ¶640, 9 AFTR 584, 282 U.S. 216 (USSC, 1931), the Supreme Court reversed a Court of Appeals decision and held that Federal taxation of *gain* (not representing interest) from a sale of state and local securities was constitutional.

Exhibit 6-1 *Comparison of Taxable vs. Tax-Free Investments*

	If your tax-free investment is yielding:					
	4.50%	5.00%	5.50%	6.00%	6.50%	7.00%
Tax Bracket	*Your taxable equivalent yield is:*					
15%	5.29%	5.88%	6.47%	7.06%	7.65%	8.24%
28%	6.25%	6.94%	7.64%	8.33%	9.03%	9.72%
31%	6.52%	7.25%	7.97%	8.70%	9.42%	10.14%
36%	7.03%	7.81%	8.59%	9.38%	10.16%	10.94%
39.6%	7.45%	8.28%	9.11%	9.93%	10.76%	11.59%

The formula can be converted to compute the break-even point for the tax-exempt bond as follows:

$$\text{Tax-free rate} \div (1 - \text{Marginal tax rate})$$

or

$$9\% \div (1 - 0.34 = 0.66) = 13.6\%$$

Thus, at the 34 percent marginal tax rate, a 9 percent tax-exempt return is equal to a 13.6 percent taxable return.

A comparison of the effective yield on tax-free versus taxable investments is provided in Exhibit 6-1 using the five marginal tax brackets for individuals. Given current market conditions, the effective yield on tax-exempt securities will be difficult to match with taxable investments.

In recent years, Congress has reacted to the criticism that this exclusion subsidizes the wealthy (i.e., those subject to the highest tax rates) and has also reacted to the increasing number and complexity of financial offerings developed by state and local governments. Originally, these governments sold securities to fund public projects. In recent years, however, bonds have been issued to fund business construction and other industrial development projects. When this occurs, a governmental unit retains ownership of the facilities and leases them to a business. Because the interest rate on these bonds is lower than it would be on bonds issued by the corporation, the negotiated lease payments can be lower. Congress has curtailed the tax-exempt status of industrial development bonds. With certain specified exceptions, interest on industrial development bonds issued after April 1968 is taxable income.[23]

There are numerous restrictions intended to curb the use of state and local bonds to finance business activities. For example, tax-exempt bonds can no longer be issued to finance airplanes, gambling facilities, liquor stores, health clubs, sky boxes, or other luxury boxes. Nor can the bonds be issued to finance the acquisition of farmland or existing facilities, with certain exceptions.

---

[23] §103 (b).

It should be noted that any exclusion on state and local obligations is for *interest* income received by the bondholder. Thus, *gain* on the sale of tax-exempt securities that does not represent interest is taxable income.[24] In addition, interest received for late payments of tax refunds, trade accounts receivable, or condemnation awards is taxable income.[25]

Educational Savings Bonds. In 1988 Congress took steps to help taxpayers finance the rising costs of higher education by offering a special tax break for those who save to meet such expenses. Code § 135 generally provides that accrued interest on Series EE savings bonds issued after 1989 is exempt from tax when the accrued interest and principal amount of such bonds are used to pay for *qualified educational expenses* of the taxpayer or the taxpayer's spouse or dependents (but only if these relationships are satisfied in the year of the redemption). For this purpose, qualified education expenses include those for tuition or fees to attend college or certain schools offering vocational education. Costs that otherwise qualify must be reduced by any scholarships or fellowships that may be received, as well as any employer-provided assistance.

The interest exclusion is allowed only to the extent that the taxpayer uses the proceeds of the bond redemption to pay qualified educational expenses during the year that he or she redeems a bond. If the redemption proceeds received during the year exceed the amount of education expenses paid during the same year, the amount of the interest exclusion must be reduced proportionately. The amount of the exclusion may be computed as follows:

$$\frac{\text{Qualified educational expenses paid during the year}}{\text{Total redemption proceeds of qualified bonds during the year}} \times \text{Accrued interest} = \text{Exclusion}$$

Example 5. Mr. and Mrs. T purchased Series EE savings bonds in 1994 for $4,000. On June 2, 2007 they cashed in the bonds and received $10,000, $6,000 representing accrued interest and $4,000 representing their original investment. Three months later on September 2, they paid the college expenses for their daughter, D. The expenses included tuition of $9,000 and dorm fees of $5,000. In November, D received a scholarship of $1,000 for being an outstanding accounting major. Only $8,000 ($9,000 tuition − $1,000 scholarship) of D's expenses are considered qualified educational expenses. Since this amount represents only 80% ($8,000/$10,000) of the total redemption proceeds, Mr. and Mrs. T may exclude only 80% of the $6,000 accrued interest, or $4,800.

---

[24] *Willcuts v. Bunn*, 2 USTC ¶640, 9 AFTR 584, 282 U.S. 216 (USSC, 1931). (See footnote 22.)

[25] *U.S. Trust Co. of N.Y. v. Anderson*, 3 USTC ¶1125, 12 AFTR 836, 65 F.2d 575 (CA-2 1933) and *American Viscose Corp. v. Comm.*, 3 USTC ¶881, 10 AFTR 1478, 56 F.2d 1033 (CA-3, 1932).

Note that to qualify for the exclusion, the savings bonds need not be transferred directly to the educational institution. The exclusion applies to interest on *any* post-1989 Series EE savings bond that is realized during the taxable year as long as the taxpayer pays sufficient qualified educational expenses during the same taxable year.

The special exclusion is designed to benefit only those who have moderate incomes. To achieve this objective, the exclusion is gradually reduced once the taxpayer's A.G.I. (as determined in the taxable year when the bonds are redeemed) reaches a certain level. The 1994 income level at which the phase-out begins depends on the taxpayer's filing status as shown below.

Filing Status	Phase-out Range Modified A.G.I.*
Single (including heads of household)............	$41,200–$56,200
Married filing jointly..............................	$61,850–$91,850

*Adjusted annually for inflation

The reduction of the exclusion otherwise allowed is computed as follows:

$$\frac{\text{Excess A.G.I.}}{\substack{\$15,000 \\ (\$30,000 \text{ for joint returns})}} \times \text{Otherwise excludable interest} = \text{Reduction}$$

Married taxpayers filing separately are not eligible for the exclusion. Taxpayers who are married must file a joint return to secure the exclusion.

> **Example 6.**   Mr. and Mrs. B have an A.G.I., after proper modifications, of $71,850, before the exclusion. As a result, the amount of any interest that would otherwise be nontaxable must be reduced by one-third:
>
> $$\frac{(\$71,850 \text{ A.G.I.} - \$61,850 \text{ threshold} = \$10,000)}{(\$91,850 - \$61,850 = \$30,000 \text{ phase-out range})}$$
>
> Assume the couple redeemed qualified bonds this year with accrued interest of $10,000. Only 90% of the proceeds of the bonds (i.e., interest and principal) were spent on qualifying education expenses. They could exclude $6,000 of the interest, computed as follows:
>
> | | |
> |---|---:|
> | Excludable interest (90% × $10,000)........................ | $9,000 |
> | Exclusion phase-out | |
> | (1/3 × $9,000).. | − 3,000 |
> | Amount of interest excluded................................. | $6,000 |

Note that the exclusion would not be available to the couple if their A.G.I. in the year they redeemed the bonds exceeded the phase-out range (e.g., $91,850 for 1994).

Without any special provision, taxpayers with high incomes might try to circumvent the income limitation to obtain the exclusion. For example, a father earning an income of $100,000 might give $10,000 to his 10-year-old daughter who would then be instructed to buy the bonds. When the daughter started college, she would redeem the bonds to pay for her tuition. Absent any restrictions, the daughter could secure 100 percent of the available exclusion since she would have little or no income. To prevent such schemes, the exclusion is available only for bonds that are issued to individuals who are at least 24 years old. In addition, the exclusion is available only to the original purchaser of the bond or his or her spouse. This rule prohibits gifts of qualified bonds.

Example 7. Mr. and Mrs. C have an A.G.I. of $100,000. Assume they currently hold qualified Series EE bonds with $10,000 of accrued interest. To avoid the income limitation, the bonds are given to Mr. C's father, GF, who has little income. This year, GF cashes the bonds in and pays for his grandson's tuition. The payment is sufficient to qualify the grandson as GF's dependent. Even though the redemption proceeds are used to pay for education expenses of the taxpayer's dependent, no exclusion is available for the interest since GF was not the original purchaser of the bond. Had GF originally purchased the bonds for his grandson, the exclusion would be allowed (assuming his grandson is his dependent).

ANNUITIES

An annuity is an investment contract that requires a fixed amount of money to be paid to the owner at specific intervals for either a certain period of time or for life. Annuities may be purchased either by an individual or for an employee by the employer. In addition, a beneficiary may elect to receive life insurance proceeds under an annuity arrangement. When the annuity is purchased by an individual, the interest earned on the investment is tax-deferred. This means the interest is taxable income but not during the current year when it is earned. Instead, the interest is included in gross income at some future date when the annuitant receives cash payments. Until then, the interest is automatically reinvested in full, without payment of Federal income taxes, to earn tax-deferred interest.

Example 8. H invests $20,000 in a single-premium deferred annuity. The interest earned in the first year totals $2,000. Since this is tax-deferred, H has no taxable income, and the $2,000 is added to the $20,000 to continue to earn interest.

When earnings are reinvested, as they are for an annuity, the value of the asset grows at an increasing rate. A formula may be used to determine the *approximate* time period required to double the original investment in these circumstances:

$$72 \div \text{Compound interest rate}$$

If the compound interest rate used is an annual one, the solution provides the number of years required. Or, if the compound interest rate is a monthly one, the solution is in number of months.

Example 9.   An annuity's annual compound interest rate is 12%. At this rate, the original investment will be doubled in approximately six years (72 ÷ 12).

Since the formula provides an *approximate* period, it should be used as a quick "rule of thumb" only. Greater accuracy is obtained by using annuity tables or by making the detailed computations.

Investors are discouraged from withdrawing funds before annuity benefits are scheduled to be received on contracts issued after August 13, 1982. Not only are early withdrawals treated as being distributions of the interest earned on the contract, a 10 percent penalty is assessed on the deferred income. The penalty is waived if the taxpayer satisfies certain requirements provided in the Code.[26]

Annuity payments are commonly scheduled to begin on retirement when the recipients' marginal tax rates are lower. Because of the lower rates, these individuals actually pay less total taxes in addition to receiving the benefits from tax deferral. Annuitants, similar to beneficiaries of life insurance contracts, may elect to receive the principal plus accumulated interest in installments for a stipulated number of years or for the annuitant's lifetime. The important point to remember is that the individual has taxable income equal to the amount of interest received. As discussed in Chapter 5, the portion that is a return of capital is nontaxable.[27] The formula for determining the portion that is a *nontaxable return of capital* for the current period is

$$\frac{\text{Investment in the contract}}{\text{Expected return from the contract}} \times \text{Amount received currently}$$

The taxable portion is the amount received currently less the portion that is a return of capital. When the annuity will be received over a stipulated number of years, the expected return from the contract is the amount to be received each year (or month) multiplied by the number of years (or months) payments are to be received.

Example 10.   W invests $20,000 in a single-premium deferred annuity. At the end of 15 years, W elects to receive the $20,000 principal plus interest over the next ten years. She receives $7,000 in the current year and will receive $7,000 each of the following nine years. W's nontaxable return of capital each year is

$$\frac{\$20,000}{\$7,000 \times 10 \text{ years} = \$70,000} \times \$7,000 = \$2,000$$

W's taxable income each year is $5,000 ($7,000 − $2,000).

Example 11.   Refer to *Example 10*. If W receives only three payments in the first year totaling $1,750 ($7,000 × 3/12), the computation remains the same except the amount received currently is $1,750 (instead of $7,000). Consequently, her nontaxable return of capital in the first year is $500 [($20,000 ÷ $70,000) × $1,750] and her taxable income is $1,250 ($1,750 − $500).

---

[26] See § 72(q)(2).   [27] § 72(b)(1).

Exhibit 6-2 *Ordinary Life Annuities—One Life—Expected Return Multiples*

Age	Multiple	Age	Multiple	Age	Multiple
21	60.9	58	25.9	95	3.7
22	59.9	59	25.0	96	3.4
23	59.0	60	24.2	97	3.2
24	58.0	61	23.3	98	3.0
25	57.0	62	22.5	99	2.8
26	56.0	63	21.6	100	2.7
27	55.1	64	20.8	101	2.5
28	54.1	65	20.0	102	2.3
29	53.1	66	19.2	103	2.1
30	52.2	67	18.4	104	1.9

Note that the solution to *Example 10* is the same if W had simply divided the $20,000 principal by the 10 years (and to *Example 11* if W adjusted the annual amount to months). This is not true, however, when an individual elects to receive the annuity payments over his or her lifetime. For these situations, the Regulations contain several tables based on contract payment terms and the annuitant's age.[28] Because of the Supreme Court decision in *Arizona Governing Committee v. Norris*,[29] tables V through VIII were added to the Regulations; these tables ignore a taxpayer's gender in calculating the expected return. In general, these tables became effective July 1, 1986, and must be used by those taxpayers making post–June 1986 contributions to the annuity contract. A portion of table V, which contains the new multiples, is reproduced in Exhibit 6-2.

When the payments will be received over the life of the annuitant, the expected return from the contract is the amount to be received each year multiplied by the multiple that corresponds to the annuitant's age in the Table.[30] It also is important to note that the portion of any annuity payment to be excluded from gross income cannot *exceed* the unrecovered investment in the contract immediately before the receipt of the payment.[31] In addition, if the annuitant dies before the entire investment is recovered, the amount of the *unrecovered investment* is allowed as a *deduction* on his or her final tax return.[32]

[28] Reg. § 1.72-9.

[29] *Arizona Governing Committee v. Norris*, 82-52 Slip Op. (USSC, 1983). The case specifically dealt with whether monthly retirement benefits received under an employer's deferred compensation plan could be lower for a woman than for a man when the contributions to the plan were equal. In 1978, the Supreme Court held that an employer could not require women to make larger contributions than men in order to obtain the same monthly benefits. *Los Angeles Dept. of Water & Power v. Manhart*, 435 U.S. 702 (USSC, 1978).

[30] § 72(c)(3). Two common types of life annuities are the *single-premium deferred life annuity* and the *single-premium immediate life annuity*. The former provides for annuity income after a specified future date (i.e., when the annuitant retires), whereas the latter provides the annuitant with income for life beginning at once.

[31] § 72(b)(2).

[32] § 72(b)(3).

Example 12.   T, 65 years old, purchased a single-premium immediate life annuity on January 1, 1994 for $11,400. It will pay $100 a month for the rest of her life (i.e., annual payment of $1,200). From Exhibit 6-2, her multiple is 20.0. T's nontaxable return of capital each year is

$$\frac{\$11,400}{\$1,200 \times 20 \ = \ \$24,000} \times \$1,200 \ = \ \$570$$

T's taxable income is $630 ($1,200 − $570). The $570 is considered a return of capital until T recovers her $11,400 investment. Note that if she lives 21 years, the total amount she excludes is limited to $11,400 ($570 × 20 years = $11,400). Thus, T's taxable income for year 21 is the entire $1,200 received. In contrast, if she lives just 15 years, the total amount she excludes is $8,550 ($570 × 15 years), and the unrecovered amount of $2,850 ($11,400 − $8,550) is allowed as a deduction on T's final tax return.

Some employers with qualified pension or profit-sharing plans (see Chapter 18) purchase annuity contracts for their employees' retirement. The taxable income to the employee is dependent on the employee's total *after-tax* investment in the annuity. After-tax funds generally exclude contributions, for example, to certain Individual Retirement Accounts (when individuals are allowed a deduction for the contribution) and to qualified employer retirement plans (since these contributions are made from amounts that are excluded from gross income in the current year). Investments that are not from after-tax funds are ignored in determining the individual's capital investment in the annuity. In some situations, employees may not have invested any after-tax funds in the employer's plan. Consequently, their basis in the annuity contract is zero and all amounts are included in gross income when received by them. In all other instances, calculations for return of capital and taxable income are identical to the procedure outlined in the above paragraphs.

Safe Harbor for Some Annuities.   The Internal Revenue Service has provided taxpayers with a simplified safe harbor method for computing the nontaxable portion of annuity distributions from qualified plans.[33] In addition, the safe harbor method should enable distributees (i.e., recipients) to exclude a larger portion of each annuity payment. The simplified method may be elected if the annuity payments

1.   Start after July 1, 1986;

2.   Depend on the life of the distributee or the joint lives of the distributee and his or her beneficiary;

3.   Are made from a qualified employee plan [under § 401(a)], an employee annuity [under § 403(a)], or an annuity contract [under § 403(b)]; and

4.   Start when the distributee is under age 75 or, if older, there are less than five years of guaranteed payments remaining.

---

[33]   Notice 88-118, 1988-2 C.B. 450.

Exhibit 6-3   *Monthly Payments Table*

Age of Distributee	Number of Payments
55 and under	300
56–60	260
61–65	240
66–70	170
71 and over	120

A taxpayer electing to use the safe harbor method will find the computations less onerous than those previously described for computing the exclusion ratio under § 72. Under this method, the total number of monthly annuity payments expected to be received is based on the distributee's age at the annuity starting date. Consequently, the life expectancy tables (such as Exhibit 6-2) can be ignored. Instead, Exhibit 6-3 is used, and is applicable whether the annuity is single life or joint and survivor type.[34]

The portion of each monthly annuity payment that is nontaxable is determined using the following formula:

$$\frac{\text{Investment in the contract}}{\text{Number of monthly payments}} = \text{Nontaxable return of capital}$$

Example 13.   H, an employee, retired on January 1, 1994 at the age of 65. He started receiving retirement benefits in the form of a joint and 50% survivor annuity to be paid for the joint lives of H and W (his spouse), who is 60. H contributed $48,000 (after-tax contributions) to the plan and will receive a retirement benefit of $2,000 a month. Upon H's death, W will receive a survivor retirement benefit of $1,000 each month. The nontaxable portion of each monthly annuity payment to H is calculated as follows:

$$\frac{\$48,000 \text{ investment}}{240 \text{ payments (see Exhibit 6-3)}} = \$200 \text{ nontaxable return of capital}$$

Should H die prior to receiving his entire investment of $48,000, W will likewise exclude $200 from her $1,000 monthly payment. As explained earlier, after 240 annuity payments have been made, any additional payments will be fully taxable. Should both H and W die prior to receiving 240 payments, a deduction is allowed in the amount of the unrecovered investment in the last income tax return.

---

[34] A single life annuity pays a fixed amount at regular intervals for the remainder of one person's life. A joint and survivor annuity pays a fixed amount at regular intervals to one individual for life, and on his or her death, the payments continue over the life of a designated person such as a spouse or child.

The safe harbor method should help reduce the number of requests the IRS receives each year from retirees and beneficiaries asking the Service to make the necessary computations.

EMPLOYEE COMPENSATION AND OTHER BENEFITS

Employee compensation is included in gross income whether it is in the form of cash or other assets and whether it is salary, commissions, bonuses, tips, vacation pay, or severance pay.[35] In addition, employers incur a number of other expenses for the benefit of their employees. These may be classified as (A) generally includible in, or (B) generally excludable from, the employees' gross income when the expenses are incurred by the employer.

A. *Generally Includible in Gross Income*

    Reimbursement for
        Business transportation and travel
        Business entertainment
        Moving expenses
        Educational expenses
    Employer gifts
    Employer awards

B. *Generally Excludable from Gross Income*

    Employee taxes paid by employer
        Social security (FICA) taxes
        State and Federal unemployment taxes
    Premiums paid on
        Group-term life insurance (up to $50,000 coverage)
        Health insurance
        Accident insurance
        Disability insurance
    Death benefits (first $5,000)
    Meals and lodging (on the premises at the employer's convenience)
    Supper money
    Educational-assistance plans
    Child or dependent care facilities
    Benefits that would qualify as deductible expenses by the employee
    Parking
    Use of company facilities or services
    Purchase discounts
    De minimis benefits
    On-premises athletic facilities
    Tuition reduction by educational institutions

---

[35] § 61(a)(1) and Reg. § 1.61-2(a).

Most employee fringe benefit plans must meet rigid rules to enable the employer to deduct contributions to the plans and for employees to exclude these amounts. Basically, the plans must (1) not discriminate in favor of highly compensated employees, (2) be in writing, (3) be for the exclusive benefit of the employees, (4) be legally enforceable, (5) provide employees with information concerning available plan benefits, and (6) be established with the intent that they will be maintained indefinitely. In addition, several eligibility and benefit tests provide detailed rules that must be met to ensure that employer costs are nontaxable income for employees. Additional employment benefits involving stock option, profit-sharing, and pension plans are discussed in Chapter 18.

REIMBURSEMENT OF EMPLOYEE EXPENSES

Amounts received from employers as reimbursement of expenses are included in an employee's gross income regardless of whether the employee has an offsetting business deduction (see Chapter 8 for an exception when the employees have accounted to their employers). The most commonly reimbursed items are business-related expenses such as transportation, out-of-town travel, entertainment, and moving expenses for a new or transferred employee. In addition, some employers reimburse employees for all or part of their educational expenses. This is likewise included in income (unless it is made under an educational-assistance plan—discussed later in this chapter). Generally, when reimbursement of these items equals the employee's deductible expense, the net effect on adjusted gross income (A.G.I.) is zero. An excess of reimbursement over deductible expenses increases A.G.I. Under-reimbursement also has a zero effect on A.G.I. but may reduce taxable income if the amounts qualify as itemized deductions (see Chapters 8 and 11).

EMPLOYER GIFTS

The inclusion or exclusion of *employer gifts* depends on several factors: (1) whether a legal obligation exists, (2) whether the employer intends to make a gift, (3) whether the employer deducts the cost for tax purposes, and (4) whether the amount is nominal. The existence of a legal obligation generally means the transfer is taxable compensation, not a gift. In contrast, the absence of a legal obligation to make the transfer is favorable, but not conclusive, evidence that the transfer is a gift. The employer's intent also is important. For the transfer to be a gift, it must be made with detached or disinterested generosity and not be a reward for past services or made in expectation of future services.[36] Intent also is evidenced by how the employer handles the gift on the business's tax return. Compensation is deductible whereas a gift is not. An exception is made when the value of the gift is nominal.[37] For example, a holiday gift of a turkey, ham, umbrella, or inexpensive pen may be deducted by the employer but is nontaxable by the employee.

This same reasoning applies to all business-related gifts whether made to employees, clients, or other business contacts.[38] Although the word *nominal* (or *de minimis*) is not defined for employee gifts, it is defined for gifts to nonemployees as being $25 or less.

---

[36] *Comm. v. Duberstein*, 60-2 USTC ¶9515, 5 AFTR2d 1626, 363 U.S. 278 (USSC, 1960).

[37] Rev. Rul. 59-58, 1959-1 C.B. 17.

[38] § 274(b).

Thus, the $25 limitation is presumed to be applicable to all types of gifts. This does not mean that a larger amount cannot qualify as a gift if other factors are favorable. It does mean, however, that both parties benefit when the gift is nominal; the employer deducts the cost as a business expense and the employee excludes the income. This two-sided benefit does not exist for amounts above $25.

EMPLOYER AWARDS

Employer awards to employees, other than de minimis fringe benefits (discussed later in this chapter), are generally treated as compensation with two exceptions: if they are provided (1) for length-of-service or safety achievements, or (2) under a nondiscriminatory qualified award plan. To be nontaxable, the awards must be made with tangible personal property. No exclusion is available for cash payments or the equivalent. The award must be given as part of a meaningful presentation and under conditions and circumstances that do not create a significant likelihood of the payment of disguised compensation. Also, no exclusion for the length-of-service award is available if it or a similar award is made within the individual's first five years of employment with the employer. To be nontaxable, safety awards cannot have been made to more than 10 percent of a company's eligible employees. All employees are considered to be eligible except those in managerial, professional, and clerical positions.[39]

Qualifying awards are deductible by the employer and nontaxable by the employee if the amount does not exceed the statutory limits. Under these limitations, the cost of property cannot exceed $400 per employee annually for length-of-service and safety achievements or $1,600 annually for all qualified plan awards, including length-of-service and safety achievements. For example, an employee achievement award (other than a qualified plan award) that costs the employer $390 and has a fair market value of $440 would be fully excluded from the employee's gross income. Excess costs are taxable income to the extent of the *greater* of (1) the nondeductible cost to the employer due to the limitations, or (2) the property's market value in excess of the limitations. This taxable income must be reported on the employee's Form W-2.

> **Example 14.** R, Inc. pays $525 ($640 market value) for a brooch that it awards to L in recognition of her 15 years of service to the company. No other awards are given to L during the year. R's deduction is limited to $400, and L has taxable income of $240 (the greater of $525 − $400 = $125 and $640 − $400 = $240). The $240 will appear on L's Form W-2 as taxable income.

SOCIAL SECURITY BENEFITS

When taxpayers (employees, self-employed, and others) collect social security benefits, these receipts generally are excludable from gross income.[40] For high-income bracket recipients, however, a portion of the social security benefits received must be included

---

[39]   See §§ 74(c) and 274(j).   [40]   Rev. Rul. 70-217, 1970-1 C.B. 12.

as taxable income. Thus, in effect, these amounts are taxed to some individuals twice; first when included as gross wages and second when included as social security benefits received. Beginning in 1994, retired individuals with high incomes may find that more of their social security benefits are taxable. Under prior law, a maximum of 50 percent of the taxpayer's social security benefits could be taxable. Under the new rules, however, up to 85 percent of the taxpayer's benefits may be subject to tax.[41] The thrust of the new rule is quite simple: as the taxpayer's income increases, the amount of social security subject to tax increases. Unfortunately, the actual calculation of the amount included in gross income is quite cumbersome.

The effect of the revised provisions is to establish two income thresholds:

	Married Filing Jointly	Married Filing Separately	Unmarried Taxpayers
Combined income threshold #1	$32,000	$0	$25,000
Combined income threshold #2	44,000	0	34,000

For most taxpayers, the term *combined income* includes adjusted gross income plus interest on tax-exempt bonds plus one-half of social security benefits received. As before, taxpayers who fall below the first threshold ($32,000 for married filing jointly) are not taxed on their social security benefits. Similarly, the treatment of taxpayers whose income falls below the second threshold (e.g., $44,000 for married filing jointly) is the *same* as it was under prior law. These taxpayers (those with combined income of less than the second threshold amounts—$44,000, $0, and $34,000, respectively) must include the lesser of one-half of their social security benefits or one-half of the excess of their combined income over the specified threshold. For those taxpayers whose combined income *exceeds* the first threshold (e.g., $32,000 for married filing jointly), the calculation can be made using the following schedules:

Married filing jointly

If combined income is		
Over	But not over	Amount taxed:
$32,000	$44,000	Step 1: Lesser of (1) 50% of benefits, or (2) 50% × (Combined income − $32,000)
$44,000		Step 2: Lesser of (1) Step 1 amount, not to exceed $6,000, + 85% × (Combined income − $44,000), or (2) 85% of benefits

---

[41] § 86.

Unmarried taxpayers

If combined income is		
Over	But not over	Amount taxed:
$25,000	$34,000	**Step 1:** Lesser of (1) 50% of benefits, or (2) 50% × (Combined income − $25,000)
$34,000		**Step 2:** Lesser of (1) Step 1 amount, not to exceed $4,500, + 85% × (Combined income − $34,000), or (2) 85% of benefits

Note that the effect of applying these rules is to impose the same tax as under prior law if the taxpayer's combined income does not exceed the second threshold amount ($44,000 or $34,000). Once combined income exceeds this second threshold amount, the 85 percent rate is triggered and a greater amount of social security becomes taxable.

Example 15. George and Mildred, happily married for 45 years, received the following income:

Dividend income......	$50,000
Social security benefits	16,000

In this case, the couple's combined income is $58,000[$50,000 + (50% × $16,000 = $8,000)]. Because the couple's $58,000 combined income exceeds the second threshold of $44,000, the 85% rule is triggered. Their taxable social security is $13,600, computed as follows:

Step 1 amount
Lesser of

50% × social security of $16,000	$ 8,000
or	
50% × ($58,000 − $32,000 = $26,000)	$13,000
Step 1 amount	$ 8,000

Step 2 amount
Lesser of

Step 1 amount ($8,000), not to exceed $6,000,	$ 6,000
+ 85% × ($58,000 − $44,000 = $14,000)	11,900
	$17,900
or	
85% × benefits of $16,000	$13,600
Step 2 amount and taxable social security benefits	$13,600

Example 16. Assume the same facts as in *Example 15* above except that dividend income amounts to $30,000. Because the couple's $38,000 combined income [$30,000 + (50% × $16,000)] falls below the second threshold ($44,000), their taxable social security is $3,000, computed as follows:

Lesser of

50% × social security of $16,000	$8,000
or	
50% × ($38,000 − $32,000 = $6,000)	$3,000
Step 1 amount and taxable social security benefits	$3,000

As indicated above, the base or threshold amount is zero for married filing separately. Consequently, married taxpayers who elect to file separately automatically expose social security benefits to taxation. Deductions are allowed for legal fees incurred in perfecting social security claims, and adjustments are allowed for catch-up and repayment situations. Congress has earmarked all income tax generated by the new law for the Medicare Hospital Insurance (HI) Trust Fund.

Taxpayers whose social security benefits are subject to taxation should give consideration to shifting money out of municipal bonds and into other investment vehicles such as growth stocks that do not pay dividends or into Series EE U.S. savings bonds, which generally do not produce taxable income until they are redeemed.

UNEMPLOYMENT BENEFITS

Employers only, not employees, are subject to Federal and State unemployment taxes. These *taxes* are deductible business expenses for the employer and are not gross income for the employee. However, unemployment benefits *received* under a government program are included in gross income.[42]

EMPLOYEE INSURANCE

It is common for employers to have group insurance coverage for employees. Premiums may be paid by the employer only, by the employee only, or by both the employer and employee under some shared cost arrangement. Generally, employer-paid premiums for health, accident, and disability insurance are deductible business expenses and are excluded from the employee's gross income. On the other hand, life insurance premiums paid by the employer generally are included by the employee and deductible by the employer. As may be expected, however, there are exceptions.

---

[42] § 85(a).

Life Insurance Premiums and Proceeds. Employer-paid life insurance premiums are nontaxable by an employee but *only* for the first *$50,000* of *group-term life insurance* protection.[43] Premiums paid by an employer for any other type of life insurance are fully included in each employee's gross income. In order to qualify as group insurance, the employer must provide coverage for all employees with a few permitted exceptions based on their age, marital status, or factors related to employment. Examples of employment-related factors are union membership, duties performed, compensation received, and length of service.[44] Acceptable discrimination, however, is limited by the Regulations. Thus, employers may establish eligibility requirements that exclude certain types of employees, such as those who work part-time, who are under age 21, or who have not been employed at least six months. But omitting older employees or those with longer service records generally is not permitted.

When group-term insurance protection exceeds $50,000, the employee's taxable income is an amount set forth in the Regulations rather than actual premiums paid. The taxable amount for each $1,000 of insurance in excess of $50,000 is based on the employee's age as of the last day of his or her tax year. For group-term life insurance provided after 1988, the Technical and Miscellaneous Revenue Act of 1988 required the IRS to prescribe higher monthly rates for taxpayers over age 64. Under prior law, taxpayers over age 64 received a favorable tax break, in that the premium cost was computed as if they fell in the 60 to 64 age bracket. Accordingly, the IRS has provided a new table (see Exhibit 6-4) for determining the cost of group-term life insurance provided employees after December 31, 1988.[45]

Example 17. BC, Inc. provides all full-time employees with group-term insurance. Records for three of the employees show the following information. All three were employed by BC for the full year.

Employee	Age	Insurance Coverage	Coverage in Excess of $50,000
D	56	$80,000	$30,000
E	38	62,000	12,000
F	35	40,000	0

D's taxable income is $270 ($9.00 × $30,000 ÷ $1,000). E's taxable income is $15.84 ($1.32 × $12,000 ÷ $1,000). F has no taxable income from group-term life insurance, since the coverage does not exceed $50,000.

---

[43] § 79(a)(1). The $50,000 limit is eliminated for retired employees who are disabled.

[44] Reg. §§ 1.79-0 and 1.79-1(a)(4).

[45] Reg. § 1.79–3. Beginning in 1988, the cost of group-term life insurance that an employee must include in his or her gross income must also be treated as wages for social security withholding purposes.

Exhibit 6-4 *Imputed Costs of Excess Group-Term Life Insurance*

| | Includible Income per $1,000 | |
Employee's Age	Monthly	Annually
Under 30	$0.08	$ 0.96
30 to 34	0.09	1.08
35 to 39	0.11	1.32
40 to 44	0.17	2.04
45 to 49	0.29	3.48
50 to 54	0.48	5.76
55 to 59	0.75	9.00
60 to 64	1.17	14.04
65 to 69	2.10	25.20
70 and over	3.76	45.12

Source: Reg. § 1.79-3.

Regardless of whether life insurance is provided by the employer or not, proceeds received by a beneficiary on the death of the insured ordinarily are excludable from gross income.[46] There are some exceptions, however. For example, insurance proceeds are taxable if the proceeds are a *substitute for taxable income* or if the policy was transferred in exchange for *valuable consideration*.[47] Each of these exceptions is discussed below.

Substitute for Taxable Income. In some instances, life insurance is used to protect a creditor against a bad debt loss on the death of the insured. However, the fact that the debt is offset by life insurance proceeds on the death of the insured does not cause otherwise taxable income to be nontaxable. For example, amounts equal to unreported interest due on the debt are taxable interest income.[48] Similarly, proceeds offsetting debt that was previously written off as uncollectable, or proceeds representing gain not previously reported, are included in gross income.[49]

[46] § 101(a)(1).

[47] Insurance proceeds are also taxable if the policy is an investment contract with little or no *insurance risk* or the owner of the policy does not have an *insurable interest* in the insured. In addition to the insured, a spouse, dependents, business partners, and in some instances, creditors and employers are considered to possess the requisite insurable interest.

[48] *Landfield Finance Co. v. Comm.*, 69-2

USTC ¶9680, 24 AFTR2d 69-5744, 418 F.2d 172 (CA-7, 1969), *aff'g.* 69-1 USTC ¶9175, 23 AFTR2d 69-601, 296 F. Supp. 1118 (DC, 1969).

[49] *St. Louis Refrigerating & Cold Storage Co. v. Comm.*, 47-2 USTC ¶9298, 35 AFTR 1477, 162 F.2d 394 (CA-8, 1947), *aff'g.* 46-2 USTC ¶9320, 34 AFTR 1574, 66 F. Supp. 62 (DC, 1946) and Rev. Rul. 70-254, 1970-1 C.B. 31.

Transfer for Valuable Consideration. If a policy is transferred to another party in exchange for valuable consideration, any *gain* from the proceeds on the insured's death is taxable income.[50] Gain is defined as the insurance proceeds less the owner's basis. Basis is the total purchase price plus all premiums paid by the subsequent owner after the transfer.

> **Example 18.**   XY Corporation purchased a $15,000 life insurance policy from S, the insured, for $7,300. The corporation made five annual premium payments of $600 each on the policy. S died at the end of the fifth year and XY collected $15,000 insurance. Since XY's basis in the policy is $10,300 [($600 × 5 payments) + $7,300], its taxable income is $4,700 ($15,000 − $10,300).

There are four exceptions to *Example 18*. All gain is nontaxable if the purchaser is (1) a partner of the insured, (2) a partnership in which the insured is a partner, (3) a corporation in which the insured is a shareholder or officer, or (4) the insured.[51]

Health Insurance Benefits.   With few exceptions, all medical insurance benefits are excluded from income regardless of who pays the premiums.[52] Any reimbursement of medical costs simply reduces the amount of medical expenses that can be itemized (as deductions from A.G.I.—discussed in Chapter 11).[53] However, in some instances the expenses are paid in one year but reimbursement is not received until a later year. Taxpayers have a choice when this occurs. One, they may anticipate the reimbursement and not deduct any of the reimbursable expenses. This decision means the reimbursement is nontaxable when received. Alternatively, these taxpayers may choose to itemize all medical costs in the year paid even though reimbursement is expected. This decision means the reimbursement is included in gross income when received to the extent a *tax benefit* was obtained for the prior year's deduction.[54] Since only the amount of medical expenditures that exceed 7.5 percent of A.G.I. provides a tax benefit (i.e., reduces an individual's taxable income), it is possible that part of the reimbursement is nontaxable.

> **Example 19.**   J pays $4,000 medical expenses in 1994 and receives reimbursement of $1,100 in 1994 and $2,900 in 1995 from the insurance company. J's 1994 A.G.I. is $20,000, and her other itemized deductions exceed the standard deduction for the year. If J chooses to deduct all unreimbursed medical expenses in 1994, her itemized deduction is $2,900 ($4,000 − $1,100 reimbursed in 1994) and her *tax benefit* is $1,400 [$2,900 − (7.5% × $20,000 A.G.I. = $1,500)]. Thus, only $1,400 of the $2,900 reimbursement received in 1995 is included in gross income. Alternatively, if J decides to forgo the deduction in 1994, she has no taxable income in 1995. In this example, the important factors in J's decision are (1) her marginal tax rates for both years, and (2) the present value to her of the tax deferral for one year.

---

[50]   § 101(a)(2).

[51]   § 101(a)(2)(B).

[52]   § 106.

[53]   §§ 105(b) and 213.

[54]   § 111(a).

In contrast to the above, reimbursement received in one year for a medical expense not paid until a future year is nontaxable.

> **Example 20.** L pays medical expenses of $1,100 in 1994 and $2,900 in 1995. However, he is reimbursed in 1994 by the insurance company for the entire $4,000. L may not deduct the medical expenses, but he also does not have taxable income for the reimbursement.

If medical coverage is financed by the employer, any reimbursement in excess of medical expenses incurred by an employee for himself or herself, a spouse, and dependents is included in gross income.[55] These excess amounts, however, are not included if the premiums were paid by the individual.

Corporations that finance their own medical benefit plans from company funds (instead of through insurance) are required to establish plans that do not discriminate in favor of certain officers, shareholders, or highly paid employees. If the plan is discriminatory, individuals in these three categories must report taxable income equal to any medical reimbursement they received that is not available to other employees.[56] Thus, the purpose is to encourage corporations to extend medical coverage to all of their employees.

Accident and Disability Insurance Benefits. As a general rule, all amounts received under an *employer-financed* accident or disability plan are taxable with few exceptions. When payments are for permanent loss or use of a function or member of the body or for permanent disfigurement, however, they are nontaxable.[57]

> **Example 21.** G lost two fingers while making repairs to her automobile. She received $2,500 from her employer-provided accident insurance policy. The $2,500 is nontaxable income and is not considered to be a reimbursement of any medical expense.

In contrast with employer-financed disability plans, all disability income is *nontaxable* if the taxpayer paid for the disability coverage.[58] Consequently, those employees with long-term disabilities may incur substantial tax costs if their disability income is received from employer-financed plans.

> **Example 22.** After graduation from high school, R was employed by WW Manufacturing Company. The company's employee benefits included disability insurance. R's disability insurance premiums averaged $250 annually. After 15 years with WW, R became seriously ill. The illness left him permanently disabled. After a three-month wait, required by the insurance company, R began receiving $800 monthly disability income. Whether the $800 is taxable income depends on who paid the $250 annual premium on the disability policy. If WW paid the premium, the $800 monthly disability income is taxable income. If R paid the premium,

---

[55] § 105(b).

[56] § 105(h).

[57] §§ 105(a) and (c).

[58] § 104(a)(3) and Reg. § 1.104-1(d).

the $800 is nontaxable. If R paid a portion of the premium, for example 40%, then that portion, $320 (40% × $800), is nontaxable, and the remaining $480 is attributable to the employer's contribution and is, therefore, taxable income.

DEATH BENEFITS

When an employee dies, payments to the deceased's beneficiaries by an employer may qualify as either death benefits, compensation, or gifts. The first $5,000 of payments that qualify as death benefits is deductible by the employer but is excluded from income for the beneficiaries. (Amounts in excess of $5,000 are either compensation or gifts, based on the employer's intent, as discussed earlier in this chapter.) To qualify for this exclusion, the payment must be made *solely* because of an employee's death.[59] It does not matter, however, whether the payment is a legal obligation or a voluntary act of the employer. Any amounts earned by the employee, or amounts that represent other nonforfeitable rights vested in the employee prior to death, would have been paid regardless of death, and consequently do not qualify for the exclusion. Examples of amounts earned by the employee before death are accrued salaries, bonuses, commissions, and vacation pay. All of these are taxable compensation. An exception occurs, however, when lump-sum distributions are made from qualified pension, profit-sharing, or stock bonus plans. These distributions qualify for the exclusion even if the benefits are nonforfeitable.

In most instances, death benefits in excess of $5,000 are deducted by the employer, and are therefore taxable to the beneficiary. The $5,000 limit is per employee and is unaffected by the number of employers or beneficiaries. The exclusion also covers beneficiaries of self-employed individuals but only if lump-sum distributions are made.[60] When more than one beneficiary is involved, the $5,000 exclusion is allocated among all of them, regardless of their relationships to the deceased, based on each one's percentage of the total death benefit paid.

> **Example 23.**   A corporation distributes $8,000 in death benefits to a deceased employee's beneficiaries as follows: $4,000 to the spouse, $2,000 to a son, and $2,000 to a daughter. The exclusion for the spouse is $2,500 ($4,000 ÷ $8,000 = 50% × $5,000) and for each child is $1,250 ($2,000 ÷ $8,000 = 25% × $5,000). Thus, taxable income for the spouse is $1,500 ($4,000 − $2,500) and for each child is $750 ($2,000 − $1,250). The entire $8,000 is a deductible business expense for the corporation.

In some instances, employer distributions in excess of $5,000 qualify as business gifts. This means the employer can deduct only $5,000 as a death benefit and the remainder is subject to the $25 business gift limitation discussed previously in this chapter.[61] Since both the $5,000 death benefit and the gifts are nontaxable, beneficiaries have no gross income.

---

[59]   § 101(b) and Reg. § 101-2(a).   [61]   § 274(b).

[60]   § 101(b)(3).

EMPLOYER-PROVIDED MEALS AND LODGING

The value of meals and lodging provided by an employer to an employee and the employee's spouse and dependents is excluded from income if

1. Provided for the *employer's convenience*;

2. Provided *on* the employer's *business premises*; and

3. In the case of lodging, the employee *is required* to occupy the quarters in order to perform employment duties.[62]

Generally, meals and housing furnished to employees without charge are considered to be for the employer's convenience if a substantial noncompensatory business purpose exists.[63] For example, there may be substantial business reasons to provide meals and lodging to the manager of a motel who is on 24-hour call.[64] But, if the employee has the option to receive other compensation instead, the value of the meals and lodging is included in income.[65]

If all requirements for exclusion are met, the value of meals and lodging is nontaxable for all *employees*, even those who are major shareholders.[66] This provision, however, does not apply to owners who do not qualify as employees. Since it has been held that owners of proprietorships and partnerships cannot be employees of their businesses, the exclusion is not available to them. Consequently, the costs of meals and lodging furnished a proprietor or partner generally are nondeductible business expenses.[67]

Some employees who are required to accept employer-provided meals or housing must pay for them. If the fee is a fixed assessment, employees have nontaxable income equal to the charges.[68] Otherwise, these payments are personal expenses. Special rules apply to qualified campus lodging, primarily covering lodging on or near an educational institution provided for its employees.

> **Example 24.** Employees of the Q Recreational Spa are required to accept housing on the grounds as a condition of employment. Employee N's monthly salary is $1,000. In addition, she pays monthly rent of $200 for housing on the grounds; the housing has a rental value of $450. N's monthly taxable compensation is $800 ($1,000 − $200). If N were *not* required to live on the grounds to perform her duties, her monthly taxable compensation would be $1,250 ($450 − $200 = $250 + $1,000).

---

[62] § 119(a)(2) and Reg. § 1.119-1(b).

[63] Reg. §§ 1.119-1(a)(2) and (b).

[64] *J.B. Lindeman*, 60 T.C. 609 (1973), *acq.*

[65] Reg. § 1.119-1(c)(2).

[66] See *Comm. v. Wilhelm, et al.*, 66-2 USTC ¶9637, 18 AFTR2d 5563, 257 F. Supp. 16 (DC, 1966); but see *Atlanta Biltmore Hotel Corp., et al. v. Comm.*, 65-2 USTC ¶9573, 16 AFTR2d 5285, 349 F.2d 677 (CA-5, 1965).

[67] Rev. Rul. 53-80, 1953-1 C.B. 62 and *Wilson v. Comm.*, 67-1 USTC ¶9378, 19 AFTR2d 1225, 376 F.2d 280 (Ct. Cls., 1967); but see *George A. Papineau*, 16 T.C. 130 (1951), *nonacq.*

[68] Reg. §§ 1.119-1(a)(2), (a)(3), and (b) and Rev. Rul. 59-307, 1959-2 C.B. 48.

Nontaxable meals and lodging must be furnished on the employer's premises. The term *business premises* has been interpreted to be either the primary place of business (e.g., the hotel, restaurant, or construction site) or elsewhere as long as it is near the place of business and where a significant portion of the business is conducted.[69] However, employer-owned housing located two blocks from the primary place of business, a motel, was disallowed because it was not considered to be on the employer's premises.[70] This contrasts with employer-owned housing located across the street from the primary place of business, a hotel, that was held to be on the premises.[71] Apparently, taxpayer success in this second case was based on the amount of business conducted in the home rather than its location.

Definitions of what constitutes meals and lodging are broadly interpreted. For example, lodging includes operating costs such as utilities, as well as the rental value of housing.[72] In addition to restaurant meals, purchases of unprepared food and nonfood items such as napkins and paper towels from grocery stores have been allowed by the courts.[73] However, a 1977 Supreme Court decision seems to end disagreement over whether employer cash reimbursement of meals and groceries qualifies for the exclusion. In *Kowalski*, the Supreme Court ruled that the exclusion applies only to meals (and presumably lodging) furnished *in kind*, and not to cash reimbursements.[74] The full effect this decision will have on the issue of employer-provided meals and lodging is yet to be known. For example, it has long been held that cash allowances or "supper monies" infrequently paid to employees working overtime are nontaxable.[75] A footnote in *Kowalski* specifically states this issue was not considered in the decision. In addition, exclusions for cash allowances paid to military personnel also could be in question as a result of *Kowalski*.

ADDITIONAL EMPLOYEE BENEFITS

The types of fringe benefits a firm provides its employees can be a very important factor in attracting and retaining key people. Fortunately, the Internal Revenue Code contains a number of provisions granting employers and employees favorable tax treatment. For example, to encourage employers to underwrite the cost of child care, the Code allows an employer a deduction and an employee an exclusion for child and dependent care assistance provided through an employer plan.[76] The employee's exclusion, however, is limited to $5,000 annually (and $2,500 for married filing separate returns). Many of the requirements relating to this exclusion parallel those found in the child and dependent care tax credit provisions (discussed in Chapter 13).[77]

---

[69] Rev. Rul. 71-411, 1971-2 C.B. 103.

[70] *Comm. v. Anderson*, 67-1 USTC ¶9136, 19 AFTR2d 318, 371 F.2d 59 (CA-6, 1966), *cert. denied.*

[71] *J.B. Lindeman*, 60 T.C. 609 (1973), *acq.*

[72] See *Comm. v. Dole, et al.*, 65-2 USTC ¶9688, 16 AFTR2d 5756, 351 F.2d 308 (CA-1, 1965), *aff'g.* 43 T.C. 697 (1965), *acq.*, and Rev. Rul. 68-579, 1968-2 C.B. 61.

[73] See *Jacob v. Comm.*, 74-1 USTC ¶9316, 33 AFTR2d 74-972, 493 F.2d 1294 (CA-3, 1974).

[74] *Kowalski v. Comm.*, 77-2 USTC ¶9748, 40 AFTR2d 6128, 434 U.S. 77 (USSC, 1977).

[75] O.D. 514, 2 C.B. 90 (1920).

[76] § 129(a)(1).

[77] § 21.

The Revenue Reconciliation Act of 1990 extended the § 127 exclusion for employer-provided educational assistance benefits of $5,250 per year per employee to December 31, 1991. Furthermore, for taxable years beginning after December 31, 1990, the term "educational assistance" is extended to graduate level courses. Prior law (i.e., tax years beginning after 1987 and before 1991) did not apply to courses leading to advanced academic or professional degrees. To the extent that the educational assistance is not excludable because it exceeds the maximum dollar limitation, it may be excludable as a working condition fringe benefit (discussed below) under Code § 132(d), assuming the education is job related. On December 11, 1991, President Bush signed the Tax Extension Act of 1991 extending Code § 127 for six months only, to June 30, 1992. On August 10, 1993 President Clinton signed the Revenue Reconciliation Act of 1993, which extended § 127 retroactively from June 30, 1992 through December 31, 1994.

In 1984, Congress enacted legislation that, in general, codified many of the fringe benefits allowed in the past but not specified in the Code or Regulations.[78] An overview of this legislation is provided in Exhibit 6-5. Beginning with 1985, only the following additional employee benefits are excluded from income by employees:

1. Working condition fringe benefits

2. No-additional-cost services

3. Qualified employee discounts

4. De minimis fringe benefits

5. On-premises athletic facilities

6. Qualified tuition reduction by educational institutions

Working Condition Fringe Benefits. This exclusion provides that fringe benefits are nontaxable to the extent that employees could deduct the costs if they reimbursed their employer or otherwise paid the costs.[79] For example, many businesses furnish some of their employees with company-owned automobiles. Expenses related to the business usage of the cars are deductible by employers and are excluded from income by the employees. In contrast, personal use of the cars, which includes commuting between the employees' home and work, is taxable compensation (unless it is nontaxable under the de minimis rule discussed later in this section).[80] This income is reported as other compensation, and thus not subject to withholding taxes.[81] If, however, employees reimburse their employers for all personal use of the automobiles, there is no auto-related taxable compensation. Other items qualifying for this exclusion are professional dues and subscriptions. These benefits need not be provided to all employees (i.e., they may be reserved for officers, owners, and highly paid employees).

---

[78] § 132(a)(1) through (4).

[79] Such costs would have been deductible as business expenses under § 162 or as depreciation under § 167. § 132(d); Reg. § 1.132-5.

[80] § 61(a)(1) and Reg. § 1.61-2(d)(1).

[81] Reg. § 1.6041-2 and Ltr. Rul. 8122017. Although not subject to withholding taxes, this income is subject to social security taxes.

Exhibit 6-5 *Nontaxable Fringe Benefits under § 132*

Type of Benefit	Conditions	Examples
No additional cost service—§ 132(b)	Company incurs no substantial additional cost Services sold in normal course of business Same-line-of-business limitations Reciprocal agreements allowed Must be nondiscriminatory	Airplane tickets Hotel rooms Telephone services
Qualified employee discount—§ 132(c)	Offered for sale in normal course of business Same-line-of-business limitation Merchandise discounts limited to employer's gross profit Service discounts limited to 20% of normal price Must be nondiscriminatory Not applicable to investment property or real esate	Retail items
Working condition fringe—§ 132(d)	Nontaxable to extent employee would have deducted the cost had he or she paid for the property or service	Company car Parking Club memberships Professional dues and subscriptions Seminar expenses
De minimis fringe—§ 132(e)	Benefits are so small that accounting for them is unreasonable or administratively impractical	Employee picnics Cocktail parties Holiday gifts Occasional use of: Copying machine Typing services Meals Coffee and donuts
Athletic facilities—§ 132(h)(5)	Located on employer's premises Operated by employer Substantially all use is by employees, spouses, and children	Tennis court Golf course Gym Pool

Several other types of benefits that result in deductible costs for employers and non-taxable income for employees have been available for many years. For example, some employees enjoy free or low-cost parking. Although this expense is not deductible when paid by an employee, the exclusion was extended to cover this fringe benefit when paid by the employer. Thus, the value of parking provided on or near the business premises is nontaxable as a working condition fringe benefit.[82]

No-Additional-Cost Services. Some employers allow employees to use company facilities or services without charge or for a minimal maintenance fee. Unlike the situation with most other benefits, in this case employees have nontaxable income only if the company incurs no substantial additional cost as a result of the employees' usage and the benefit does not discriminate in favor of officers, owners, or highly paid employees.[83] These benefits range from use of company meeting rooms to free tickets in the entertainment industry for seats that would otherwise be empty. The exclusion is limited to services sold in the normal course of business in which the employee works. For example, the value of a hotel room is nontaxable if used by an employee (and/or a spouse or dependent children) who works in the employer's hotel business. It is taxable, however, if the employee works for another line of business of an employer with diversified interests such as hotels and auto rentals.[84] Those employees identified with more than one line of business may exclude the benefits received from all of them. The exclusion is extended to benefits provided under a written reciprocal agreement by another employer that is in the same line of business.[85] Thus, the hotel employee has nontaxable income for free use of a hotel room provided by another company that has a qualified reciprocal agreement with the employer. In accordance with the Regulations under § 132, no-additional-cost services do not include non–excess-capacity services such as the facilitation by a stock brokerage firm of the purchase of stock.

The line of business limitation is relaxed for companies that, on January 1, 1984, were providing substantially all employees with these benefits regardless of the employees' line of business. Such companies may elect to continue the practice, but they must pay a nondeductible 30 percent excise tax. The tax is levied each year on the amount that the total value of the exclusion for these services plus employee discounts (discussed below) exceed 1 percent of total compensation. The election can be revoked by the company at any time.

Qualified Employee Discounts. It is common practice for companies to allow employees to purchase inventory items at a discount. For example, a department store may allow its employees to purchase merchandise at the selling price less a stipulated discount. Such discounts seldom result in taxable income unless they discriminate in favor of highly compensated employees.[86] The exclusion, however, is not available for discounts on investment property or on residential or commercial real estate.

---

[82] § 132(h)(4).

[83] § 132(b).

[84] TAMRA of 1988 clarified that airline employees who are involved in cargo transportation (e.g., baggage and handling) are treated as being in the same line of business as those in passenger transportation. Therefore, an employee working in the cargo area can receive nontaxable air travel. § 132(h).

[85] § 132(g)(1).

[86] § 132(c).

The rules governing nondiscrimination, the requirement that items must be offered for sale in the normal course of business and line of business, and the rules governing coverage of spouses and dependent children discussed above for nontaxable services also pertain to nontaxable discounts. In contrast with services, however, discounts under reciprocal agreements are taxable income. The merchandise discount exclusion is limited to the employer's normal profit (i.e., the discount may not exceed the employer's gross profit). In the case of employer services, the discount may not exceed 20 percent of the price charged to customers. Any discount beyond that amount is taxable income to the employee.

Example 25.   V, an employee of an auto mechanic business, has her automobile repaired by the company. Accounting records show the following information for the parts and service necessary to repair V's car:

	Normal Selling Price	Firm's Cost	V's Cost
Parts.....................................	$200	$120	$112
Service..................................	90	81	70

V's taxable income for the parts is $8 ($120 − $112) and for the service is $2 [($90 − $70 = $20) − ($90 × 20% = $18)].

De Minimis Fringe Benefits.   Exclusion of employee benefits also extends to items of minimal value such as the occasional use of a company's photocopy machines, other equipment, or typing services; annual employee picnics, cocktail parties, or occasional lunches; and inexpensive holiday gifts such as a turkey at Thanksgiving. No dollar amount is specified in determining what qualifies as de minimis. The general guideline is that the value of these benefits is so small that accounting for them is unreasonable or administratively impractical.[87] The exclusion also covers discounts on food served in an eating facility provided by an employer *if* (1) the facility is located on or near the employer's business premises, (2) its revenue equals or exceeds its direct operating costs, and (3) the nondiscriminatory rules discussed above are met.

On-Premises Athletic Facilities.   The Code contains an exclusion for the use of athletic facilities provided on the employer's premises primarily for current or retired employees, their spouses, and their dependent children. Facilities that qualify for the exclusion include gyms, golf courses, swimming pools, tennis courts, and running and bicycle paths. Resorts are not qualifying facilities. Although the athletic facility must be located on premises owned or leased by the employer, it need not be located on the employer's business premises. Because the nondiscrimination rules are not applicable to on-premises athletic facilities, they may be made available to executives only.[88]

---

[87]   § 132(e).

[88]   § 132(h)(5)(B) and Reg. § 1.132-1(e)(1),(2), and (5).

Qualified Tuition Reduction by Educational Institutions. Employees of educational institutions have nontaxable income for reduction in tuition costs provided by their employer or other educational institution *below* the graduate level. This exclusion is available to the employee, a spouse, and dependent children and is extended to these individuals even if the employee is retired, disabled, or deceased.

Under § 117(d), *graduate* students who are engaged in teaching or research activities (e.g., graduate assistants) for an educational institution are allowed to exclude tuition costs provided by the institution for graduate level work as well as undergraduate work. In effect, this new rule extends favorable nontaxable treatment to tuition reduction arrangements for graduate students who teach or serve as a research assistant.[89]

MILITARY PERSONNEL

Military personnel are employees subject to most of the same provisions as nonmilitary employees. However, the character and tax treatment of some military benefits differ from those of nonmilitary employee benefits. All compensation is taxable unless specifically excluded. Examples of taxable compensation are active duty and reservist pay, reenlistment bonuses, lump-sum severance and readjustment pay, and retirement pay. Examples of nontaxable benefits are allowances for subsistence, uniforms, and quarters; extra allowances for housing and living costs while on permanent duty outside the United States, and family separation allowances caused by overseas duty; moving and storage expenses; compensation received by *enlisted* service members (up to $500 per month for commissioned officers) for active duty in an area designated by the President as a combat zone (e.g., Operation Desert Storm); and all pay while a prisoner of war or missing in action.[90] Benefits provided to military veterans by the Veterans Administration also are nontaxable. Examples of these are allowances for education, training, and subsistence; disability income; pensions paid to veterans or family members; and grants for specially equipped vehicles and homes for disabled veterans. In addition, bonuses paid from general welfare funds by state governments to veterans are nontaxable.

PERSONAL TRANSFERS BETWEEN INDIVIDUALS

Assets are transferred from one individual to another as a result of *personal relationships* under many different circumstances. Commonly, cash and other assets are received as gifts, inheritances, child support, and alimony. With the exception of alimony, these asset transfers are nontaxable for Federal income tax purposes. That is, the transferor has no deduction and the transferee has no taxable income.

---

[89] § 117(d) is subject to the compensation limitation in § 117(c).

[90] The TRA of 1986 consolidated existing military benefits and provided the Treasury with the authority to expand the list.

GIFTS AND INHERITANCES

Section 102 excludes the value of property received as a gift, bequest, devise, or inheritance from gross income.[91] However, this exclusion does not extend to income earned on the property.[92] For example, the value of bonds inherited or received as a gift is nontaxable, but any interest income earned on the bonds by the new owner is taxable unless specifically exempted by the Code (e.g., interest on tax-exempt bonds issued by a municipality).

Ordinarily, the source of assets inherited or received as a gift is not relevant. For example, it does not matter if cash received is paid from the donor's *principal* or *income*.[93] There are two exceptions, however. One, this exclusion does not apply to a gift or assignment of income. Thus, a qualifying gift of interest earned on corporate bonds placed in a nonreversionary trust (i.e., the assets will not revert to the grantor) is taxable to the party *receiving* the interest. Two, a gift or bequest of a specific sum of money that is paid from a trust or estate in more than three installments is included in income to the extent it is paid from income.

> **Example 26.**   P inherits $30,000 from his grandmother's estate. The estate consists primarily of stocks in a family-owned business. To avoid forcing the sale of these stocks, P agrees to receive the $30,000 in installments as cash is accumulated in the estate. Eventually, P receives $10,000 from estate principal and $20,000 from estate earnings. If the $30,000 is received in three or fewer installments, the entire amount is excluded from P's income. However, if the $30,000 is received in four or more installments, it is included in P's income to the extent of the $20,000 paid from earnings.

As discussed previously in this chapter, the nontaxability of gifts is determined by the intent of the donor. A nontaxable gift or inheritance must be a voluntary transfer of property and not an exchange for adequate consideration such as services or other property. Thus, a donor is expected to be motivated solely by affection, admiration, sympathy, or similar emotion.

ALIMONY AND SEPARATE MAINTENANCE

Alimony and separate maintenance agreements provide for the transfer of funds between two people. The substance of these transfers is reflected in the Code. That is, amounts that qualify as alimony or separate maintenance are deductible by the payor (hereinafter referred to as the husband) in arriving at A.G.I. and are taxable income to the payee (hereinafter referred to as the wife).[94] As long as all requirements are

---

[91]   § 102(a).

[92]   Reg. § 1.102-1(a).

[93]   § 663(a)(1).

[94]   § 215(a) and 71(a)(1). Identifying the husband as the payor spouse is for illustration purposes only. In reality, the wife may be the payor spouse, in which case the same rules apply.

met, this tax treatment occurs even in states that do not specifically recognize alimony payments.[95] On the other hand, amounts that qualify as property settlements are not deductible by the husband or taxable to the wife. A property settlement is a transfer of property to a spouse in exchange for the release of her marital claims (i.e., claims to property accumulated during marriage). No deduction is allowed for property transfers because, unlike alimony payments, they are not made by the ex-husband in discharge of his "general obligation to support" his ex-wife.

Provisions governing payments and property transfers incident to divorce were changed substantially in 1984. The rules discussed in this section reflect these changes and often are not applicable to agreements made prior to their effective date.[96]

Payments qualify as alimony or separate maintenance only if[97]

1. They are made in *cash*;

2. They are made as a result of a divorce or separation under a *written decree* of separate maintenance or support;

3. They are *required* under a decree or a written instrument incident to a divorce or separation;

4. The spouses or court do *not* elect that they be designated as not qualifying as alimony;

5. The husband and wife do not live together nor do they file a joint return together; and

6. Payments cease with the death of the *recipient*.

Payments meeting these requirements, however, are not treated as alimony if the divorce or separation agreement clearly states they are not alimony for Federal income tax purposes.

As indicated above, the payments from the ex-husband to the ex-wife must be in cash, not property. The following types of payments qualify as alimony or separate maintenance payments:

1. Payments made in cash, checks, and money orders payable on demand.[98]

2. Payments of cash by the ex-husband to the ex-wife's creditors in accordance with the terms of the divorce or separation instrument such as payments of the ex-wife's mortgage (i.e., on house ex-wife owns), taxes, rent, medical and dental bills, utilities, tuition, and other similar expenses.[99]

---

[95] *Douglas G. Benedict*, 82 T.C. 573 (1984).

[96] These changes apply to a pre-1985 divorce decree *only* if both parties expressly agree. Ltr. Rul. 8634040.

[97] § 71(a) and (b) and Reg. § 1.71-1.

[98] Temp. Reg. § 1.71-1T(b), Question 5.

[99] Temp. Reg. § 1.71-1T(b), Question 6.

3. Premiums paid by the ex-husband for term or whole life insurance on the ex-husband's life made pursuant to the terms of the divorce or separation instrument, provided the ex-wife is the owner of the policy.[100]

4. Payments of cash to a third party on behalf of the ex-wife, if they are made at the written request of the ex-wife, such as a contribution to a charitable organization.[101]

5. Payments required to be made to ex-wife's parents or other relatives in discharge of ex-wife's obligation to provide support.[102]

However, the following *do not* qualify as alimony or separate maintenance payments:

1. Assets transferred as a part of the property settlement, such as a home, car, stocks and bonds, life insurance policies, annuity contracts, and so forth.

2. Any payments to maintain property owned by the ex-husband and used by the ex-wife, including mortgage payments, real estate taxes, insurance premiums, and improvements.[103] Such payments increase the ex-husband's equity in the property.

3. Fair rental value of residence owned by ex-husband but used exclusively by ex-wife.[104]

4. Repayment by the ex-husband of a loan previously made to him by his ex-wife as part of the general settlement.[105]

5. Transfers of services (i.e., professional or otherwise).[106]

6. Voluntary payments not required by the divorce or separation agreement.

7. Payments made prior to a divorce or separation.

Example 27. D and G are divorced. The divorce decree requires D to transfer personal assets valued at $30,000 to G, to pay G $2,400 per year until G remarries or dies, and to pay G $50,000 over a period of 12 years. During the year, D pays G the following amounts:

1. $1,000 separate maintenance, voluntarily made prior to their separation or divorce

2. $2,400 separate maintenance, made in accordance with the divorce agreement

---

[100] *Ibid*. See also *Lemuel A. Carmichael*, 14 T.C. 1356(1950) and Rev. Rul. 70-218, 1970-1 C.B. 19.

[101] Temp. Reg. § 1.71-1T(b), Question 7.

[102] *Christiansen*, 60 T.C. 456(1973), *acq*.

[103] Temp. Reg. § 1.71-1T(b), Question 6.

[104] Temp. Reg. § 1.71-1T(b), Question 5.

[105] Reg. § 1.71-1(b)(4).

[106] Temp. Reg. § 1.71-1T(b), Question 5.

3. $30,000 of personal assets, transferred in accordance with the divorce agreement

4. $6,000 of the $50,000 to be paid over 12 years

G's alimony is $8,400 ($2,400 + $6,000). The $1,000 separate maintenance is not alimony because it was paid voluntarily and before any divorce or separate maintenance agreement was made. The $30,000 transfer of personal assets is not alimony since it is a property settlement. Since G has taxable alimony of $8,400, D has a deduction for A.G.I. of $8,400.

Limitations on Front Loading. To discourage "excessive" amounts from being treated as alimony in the early years, Congress redesigned § 71 to preclude the early deduction of large payments that may, in reality, represent property settlements.[107] Moreover, the provision prevents the payor spouse from taking advantage of tax savings that are worth more when larger payments are deducted early as opposed to deferring the deductions to later years. These rules are effective for all instruments executed after 1986 and for pre-1987 instruments that are modified after 1986.

Alimony paid in the first and second years must be *recaptured* in the third year if, during this three years, alimony payments decreased by more than $15,000. Amounts recaptured are included in gross income by the payor and deductible by the payee in arriving at A.G.I. To compute the recapture, the years must be considered in reverse order. Thus, the recapture formula for the second post-separation year is (1) total payments made in the second year less (2) payments made in the third year less (3) $15,000. The recapture formula for the first year is similar with one exception. In the second step, an *average* is computed of the second-year payments (less excess payments for that year, determined in the preceding computation above) plus the third-year payments.

Example 28. Alimony payments by W to H for the first three years after divorce are $25,000, $20,000, and $15,000. Since payments did not decrease by more than $15,000, no recapture is required. Both W's deductions for A.G.I. and H's taxable income are $25,000 the first year, $20,000 the second year, and $15,000 the third year.

Example 29. Alimony payments by M to F for the first three years after divorce are $50,000, $20,000, and $0. Since payments decrease by more than $15,000, recapture is required in the third year. The recapture from the second year is $5,000 ($20,000 paid in the second year − $0 paid in the third year − $15,000). The recapture from the first year is $27,500 [$50,000 paid in the first year − ($20,000 paid in the second year − $5,000 excess from the first calculation = $15,000 + $0 paid in the third year = $15,000 ÷ 2 = $7,500 average for the two years) − $15,000]. M's deduction for A.G.I. and F's taxable income are $50,000 the first year and $20,000 the second year. In the third year, the recaptures exceed payments; thus, M's taxable income and F's deduction for A.G.I. is $32,500 ($5,000 + $27,500).

---

[107] § 71(f).

Different rules apply to divorce instruments executed during 1985 and 1986. There are no front-loading provisions for years prior to 1985.

Recapture rules do not apply for post-1984 divorce instruments if payments

1. Cease because of the death of either spouse during the three-year period;

2. Cease because the payee remarries during the three-year period;

3. Are made under a support agreement, and thus do not qualify as alimony; or

4. Are a fixed portion of income to be paid for at least three years and based on revenues from a business, from property, or from employee or self-employment compensation.

In all situations, the tax effect of payments between divorced or separated individuals must be offsetting. That is, (1) payments that do not qualify as alimony are neither taxable income to the ex-wife nor deductible by the ex-husband, and (2) payments that qualify as alimony are taxable income to her and deductible by him. There is one type of exception to this approach but the outcome remains the same. An alimony obligation may be satisfied by transferring income-producing property to the ex-wife. When this occurs, the income is taxable to her, but instead of a deduction, he excludes the income.[108] Regardless of the method, her A.G.I. is increased by the same amount as his A.G.I. is reduced.

Transfers of property between spouses or former spouses incident to a divorce are nontaxable regardless of the type of property, if liabilities are involved, or if it is an equal exchange or unequal transfer. Consequently, neither party recognizes any gain or loss and the former owner's basis and holding period transfers with the property.[109]

> **Example 30.**   H and W are divorced. The divorce decree transfers investments owned by H to W. The investments have a market value of $24,000 and a basis for H of $16,000. Neither H nor W has taxable income, and W's basis in the investments is $16,000.

Prior to 1985, transfers between former spouses often resulted in gain being recognized by the former owner; the recipient's basis in the property was its market value.

Child Support.   If there are children, it is reasonable to assume that a portion of the husband's payments will be for their care and support. Amounts that qualify as child support are nondeductible personal expenses for the husband and nontaxable income to the wife.[110] Funds qualify as child support *only* if

---

[108] §§ 71(d) and 215.

[109] § 1041(b)(2).

[110] Reg. § 1.71-1(e).

1. A specific amount is fixed or is contingent on the child's status (e.g., reaching a certain age);

2. Paid solely for the support of minor children; and

3. Payable by decree, instrument, or agreement.

If all three requirements are not met, the payments are treated as alimony with no part considered to be child support.[111] All other factors are irrelevant to the issue. For example, the intent of the parties involved, the actual use of the funds, and state or local support laws have no bearing on whether payments qualify as child support. Also, even though state law may be to the contrary, a minor child is anyone under age 21.[112]

> **Example 31.** A divorce decree states that B is to pay $300 per month as alimony and support of two minor children. The agreement also states that the payments will decrease by one-third (1) if the former spouse dies or remarries, and (2) as each child reaches 21 years of age. This type of agreement meets the contingency rule for child support. Consequently, $100 per month qualifies as alimony and $200 per month qualifies as child support.

If child support is not properly established in the original agreement, the parties involved may amend the agreement retroactively.[113] This retroactive amendment is allowed, however, only if taxpayers produce convincing evidence that the amendment corrects a mistake, inadvertence, or clerical error. If such evidence does not exist, it is unlikely that any retroactive adjustment will be accepted.[114] Once child support is established, no payments are considered to be alimony until all past and current child support payments are made.[115]

> **Example 32.** A divorce decree states that H is to pay $100 per month as alimony and $200 per month as support of two minor children. The first payment was due October 1. H paid $150 in October, $300 in November, and $350 in December. These payments are allocated between child support and alimony as follows:

---

[111] See § 71(c)(2) and Temp. Reg. § 1.71-1T, Questions 16 and 17. Also, see *Arnold A. Abramo*, 78 T.C. 154 (1983) *acq.* and *Comm. v. Lester*, 61-1 USTC ¶9463, 7 AFTR2d 1445, 366 U.S. 299 (USSC, 1961).

[112] *W.E. Borbonus*, 42 T.C. 983 (1964).

[113] Rev. Rul. 71-416, 1971-2 C.B. 83 and *Margaret R. Sklar*, 21 T.C. 349 (1953), *acq.*

[114] Rev. Rul. 58-52, 1958-1 C.B. 29 and *A.Z. Gordon*, 70 T.C. 525 (1978).

[115] Reg. § 1.71-1(e).

	Payment	Child Support	Alimony
October......................................	$150	$150	$ 0
November..................................	300	250	50
December..................................	350	200	150
Total......................................	$800	$600	$200

The above allocation is made even if H or state law stipulates that payments are to cover alimony first.

TRANSFERS BY UNRELATED PARTIES

Taxpayers also receive cash and other assets from unrelated parties. That is, neither a family nor business relationship exists between the transferor and transferee. Such transfers include assets received as prizes, awards, scholarships, fellowships, and government transfer payments.

PRIZES AND AWARDS

Prizes and awards generally are taxable income. Thus, winners of sweepstakes, lotteries, employer service awards, contests, door prizes, and raffles held by charitable organizations have taxable income to the extent the fair market value of the winnings exceeds the cost of entering the contests.[116] Fair market value of property won is not necessarily the list price or even the cost to the purchaser. For example, the Tax Court held that the taxable amount for an automobile won was less than its purchase price but more than the amount allowed as a trade-in ten days later, after the car was driven several hundred miles.[117] When property won has no resale market or is nontransferable, the Tax Court has estimated the value that the particular winner could and would pay for similar goods.[118] An exception is provided in the Code for prizes and awards that are made in recognition of religious, charitable, scientific, educational, artistic, literary, or civic achievements, but only if

1. The recipient was selected without any direct action on his or her part to enter the contest or proceeding;

2. The recipient is not required to perform substantial future services as a condition of receiving the prize or award; and

3. The prize or award is given by the payor to a governmental unit or tax-exempt organization.[119]

---

[116] Reg. § 1.74-1(a)(2).

[117] *Lawrence W. McCoy*, 38 T.C. 841 (1962), acq.

[118] *Reginald Turner*, 13 TCM 462, T.C. Memo. 1954-38.

[119] § 74(b).

When these rules are met, the award has no impact on the winner's tax liability; it is neither taxable income nor a deductible charitable contribution.

SCHOLARSHIPS AND FELLOWSHIPS

Although scholarships and fellowships are considered to be prizes and awards, they are specifically exempted from the above provisions.[120] Instead, § 117 excludes all qualifying scholarships and fellowships that are required to be used and, in fact, are used for (1) tuition and fees necessary for enrollment or attendance at an educational institution; and (2) fees, books, supplies, and equipment required for the course of study. Any amounts not used for these purposes are taxable income unless returned to the grantor. However, recall from the earlier discussion in this chapter for employee benefits that certain tuition reductions for employees of educational institutions (including graduate students engaged in teaching or research activities) are nontaxable.[121]

> **Example 33.** J, a junior majoring in engineering at Private University, was awarded a $10,000 scholarship during the current year. She used the funds to pay the following school-related expenses: tuition $6,000, books $850, fees $50, supplies $100, equipment $1,100, and room and board $1,900. Only the amount spent on room and board, $1,900, is included in J's taxable income.

When recipients are degree candidates, the educational activities may take place away from the school. Nevertheless, they must be pursued for the purpose of meeting requirements at a degree-granting institution. Ordinarily, the educational institution must have a faculty, a curriculum, and an organized student body participating in the educational function.[122] Degree candidates also are not subject to dollar limitations.

Regardless of whether the recipient is a degree candidate or not, educational benefits from an employer generally are taxable income to the employee.[123] Even though a current employment relationship may not exist, scholarships granted with the expectation of future services generally are taxable to the recipient. For example, a beauty contest winner of a scholarship was considered to have taxable income since she participated in the televised pageant and was expected to perform promotional services in the future.[124]

Finally, the exclusion does not apply to scholarships provided by individuals who are motivated by family or philanthropic reasons.[125] In any event, taxpayers with taxable scholarship or fellowship income may be allowed a deduction for educational expenses (see Chapters 8 and 11).

---

[120] Rev. Rul. 59-80, 1959-1 C.B. 39.

[121] § 117(d).

[122] Reg. § 1.117-3(b) and § 151(e)(4).

[123] Rev. Rul. 76-71, 1976-1 C.B. 308 and Reg. § 1.117-4(c).

[124] Rev. Rul. 68-20, 1968-1 C.B. 55.

[125] Reg. § 1.117-3(a).

GOVERNMENT TRANSFER PAYMENTS

Many government transfer payments are excluded from income. For example, earlier discussion in this chapter revealed that all or a portion of Social Security benefits are excluded from income. Since medicare benefits are considered to be Social Security, they also are nontaxable. Supplementary medicare payments received as reimbursement of medical expenses deducted in a prior year are taxable, however, to the extent the taxpayer received a *tax benefit* in that year.[126]

Worker's compensation received as a result of a work-related injury is excluded from income.[127] Similar to the typical accident insurance policy discussed earlier in this chapter, worker's compensation provides the injured employee with a fixed amount for the permanent loss of use of a function or member of the body. For example, an individual who loses a hand, fingers, or hearing in a work-related accident receives a nontaxable amount, according to a schedule of payments. This exclusion is extended to compensation received by the survivors of a deceased worker. Other worker's compensation benefits are taxable unless the requirements for accident or health plans, previously discussed, are met.

Both state and Federal government transfer payments that are classified as public assistance (e.g., food stamps) or paid from a general welfare fund (e.g., welfare payments) are nontaxable.[128] Among others, these include payments to foster and adoptive parents, to individuals who are blind, to victims of crimes, for disaster relief, to reduce energy costs for low-income groups, and for urban renewal relocation payments.[129]

Benefits to participants in government programs designated to train or retrain specified groups are frequently nontaxable. Whether these benefits are nontaxable or not is dependent upon the primary purpose of the programs. Thus, if the objective of the program is to provide unemployed or under-employed individuals with job skills that enhance their employment opportunities, amounts received are nontaxable.[130] But, if the primary purpose is to provide compensation for services, participants are government employees with taxable wages.[131]

Most government transfer payments to farmers are included in income.[132] For example, gross income from farming includes government funds received for trees, shrubs, seed, and certain conservation expenditures, and for reducing farm production.[133] If materials are received instead of cash, their fair market value is taxable income. In addition, taxpayers receiving government funds under qualifying conservation cost-sharing plans may elect to exclude the reimbursement of capital improvements. However, the capitalized cost of the projects must be reduced by the excluded amount.[134]

---

[126] Rev. Rul. 70-341, 1970-2 C.B. 31.

[127] § 104(a)(1).

[128] Rev. Rul. 71-425, 1971-2 C.B. 76.

[129] Rev. Ruls. 78-80, 1978-1 C.B. 22; 74-153, 1974-1 C.B. 20; 77-323, 1977-2 C.B. 18; 74-74, 1974-1 C.B. 18; 76-144, 1976-1 C.B. 17; 78-180, 1978-1 C.B. 136; and 76-373, 1976-2 C.B. 16.

[130] Rev. Ruls. 63-136, 1963-2 C.B. 19; 68-38, 1968-1 C.B. 446; 71-425, 1971-2 C.B. 76; and 72-340, 1972-2 C.B. 31.

[131] Rev. Rul. 74-413, 1974-2 C.B. 333.

[132] Reg. § 1.61-4(a)(4).

[133] *R.L. Harding*, 29 TCM 789, T.C. Memo. 1970-179 and Rev. Rul. 60-32, 1960-1 C.B. 23.

[134] See §126 and Temp. Reg. § 16A.126-1.

BUSINESS GROSS INCOME

The amount to be included in gross income for proprietorships, partnerships, and corporations is total revenues plus net sales less cost of goods sold. This same concept is applicable even if the business conducted is illegal or if the activities do not qualify as a trade or business but constitute a hobby. Many of the other includible and excludable business gross income items are discussed earlier in this chapter. Additional income items peculiar to business that deserve discussion are classified as (A) generally includible in, or (B) generally excludable from, gross income.

A. **Generally Includible in Gross Income**

Agreement not to compete
Goodwill
Business interruption insurance proceeds
Damages awarded
Debt cancellation
Lease cancellation payments

B. **Generally Excludable from Gross Income**

Leasehold improvements (unless made in lieu of rent)
Contributions to capital

AGREEMENT NOT TO COMPETE AND GOODWILL

The sale of a business often contains an agreement that the seller will not compete with the buyer in the same or similar business within a particular area or distance. The amount assigned to the agreement is included in ordinary income. The purchaser may amortize (deduct) this amount over 15 years on a straight-line basis.

When the net selling price of the business exceeds the fair market value of all identifiable net assets, the business generally is considered to possess *goodwill*. That is, its potential value exceeds its net assets because of the business name, location, reputation, or other intangible factor. Goodwill is taxable as a capital gain. As provided in the Revenue Reconciliation Act of 1993, acquired goodwill can now be amortized ratably over a period of 15 years. If the contract includes a single amount for both goodwill *and* a noncompetition agreement, the entire amount is treated as goodwill. Under prior law, the seller of a business was generally indifferent as to whether part of the sales price was for goodwill or a covenant not to compete because there was no special treatment for capital gains. The resurrection of favorable capital gain treatment changes the seller's perspective. In negotiating the sale, the seller should now consider the trade-off. Note also that under revised Code § 1060, buyers and sellers are now generally required to report consistent purchase price allocations. In addition, an individual who owns at least 10 percent of an entity and the purchaser of that interest are required to furnish information to the IRS regarding the transaction if the individual or a related person enters into an employment contract, covenant not to compete, or some other type of agreement with the purchaser.

BUSINESS INTERRUPTION INSURANCE PROCEEDS

Some businesses carry insurance policies that provide for the loss of the use of property and of net profits sustained when the business property cannot be used because of an unexpected event such as fire or flood. The Regulations state that the insurance proceeds are included in gross income regardless of whether they are a reimbursement for the loss of the use of property or of net profits.[135] Similarly, insurance proceeds that are to reimburse the business for overhead expenses during the period of interruption are taxable.[136]

DAMAGES AWARDED

Cash may be awarded by the courts or by insurance companies for damages suffered by businesses because of patent infringement, cancellation of a franchise, injury to a business's reputation (see later discussion concerning professional reputation), breach of contract, antitrust action, or unfair competition. Punitive damages are included in gross income.[137] However, compensatory awards may be used *first* to offset any litigation expenses or other expenditures in obtaining the award.[138] *Second*, funds that represent a recovery of capital when damages are awarded because of a loss in value to a business's goodwill or other assets are used to offset or write down the capitalized asset costs.[139] Remaining damages generally are considered to be a reimbursement for a loss of profits and are included in gross income.[140] An exception to the latter classification occurs when compensatory damages are awarded in an antitrust suit. While the punitive damages in these cases are taxable, the compensatory damages are taxable only to the extent that losses sustained by the business resulted in a tax benefit.[141]

LEASE CANCELLATION PAYMENTS

Early termination of lease agreements may result in a lease cancellation payment. Either a lessor or a lessee may receive these payments, depending on which party canceled the lease. In *Hort*, the Supreme Court held that lease cancellation funds received by a lessor are a substitute for rent.[142] Consequently, these receipts are taxable income. Amounts received by a lessee on cancellation of a lease are considered proceeds from the sale of the lease.[143] Thus, the gain is included in gross income. Whether the gain is ordinary or capital depends on the use of the property (see discussion in Chapter 16).

---

[135] Reg. § 1.1033(a)-2(c)(8).

[136] Rev. Rul. 55-264, 1955-1 C.B. 11.

[137] *Comm. v. Glenshaw Glass Co.*, 55-1 USTC ¶9308, 47 AFTR 162, 348 U.S. 426 (USSC, 1955).

[138] *State Fish Corp.*, 49 T.C. 13 (1967), *mod'g.* 48 T.C. 465 (1967).

[139] *Farmers' and Merchants Bank of Cattletsburg, Ky. v. Comm.*, 3 USTC ¶972, 11 AFTR 619, 59 F.2d 912 (CA-6, 1932) and

Thomson v. Comm., 69-1 USTC ¶9199, 23 AFTR2d 69-529, 406 F.2d 1006 (CA-9, 1969).

[140] *Durkee v. Comm.*, 1950-1 USTC ¶9283, 35 AFTR 1438, 162 F.2d 184 (CA-6, 1947), *rem'g.* 6 T.C. 773 (1946).

[141] § 186 and Reg. § 1.186-1.

[142] *Hort v. Comm.*, 41-1 USTC ¶9354, 25 AFTR 1207, 313 U.S. 28 (USSC, 1941).

[143] § 1241.

DEBT CANCELLATION

A business's tax consequences when creditors cancel all or part of its debt are determined by whether the business is in bankruptcy proceedings or is insolvent.[144] When debt is canceled under bankruptcy proceedings, there is no taxable income currently. The taxpayer has a choice in how the reduction is recorded. First, the decrease in debt may be offset by seven tax attributes: (1) net operating losses (NOLs) and NOL carryovers, (2) the general business credit, (3) the minimum tax credit, (4) capital loss carryovers, (5) the basis of the taxpayer's property, (6) passive activity loss and credit carryovers, and (7) foreign tax credit carryovers.[145] All of these attributes are discussed in later chapters. Any debt reduction exceeding these seven tax attributes is ignored. Alternatively, the decrease in debt may be offset by a reduction in the debtor's depreciable assets or real estate held as inventory.[146] These lower asset bases are used for future depreciation and gain or loss calculations (see discussion in Chapters 9 and 16). Thus, the asset reduction represents a tax deferral rather than an exclusion.

Although not in bankruptcy proceedings, a business may be insolvent (i.e., liabilities exceed the value of its assets). If the business continues to be insolvent after debt cancellation, the decrease in debt is offset by the seven tax attributes listed above.[147] If, however, the business is insolvent before but solvent after the cancellation, the cancellation to the extent of solvency is subject to the rules governing solvent businesses.[148] In contrast, when debt of a solvent business not in bankruptcy is cancelled, the taxpayer must report the reduction as taxable income.[149]

> **Example 34.** XYZ Inc. has assets of $375,000 and liabilities of $500,000. If creditors forgive $90,000 of debt, none of the forgiveness will generate taxable income because, as shown below, XYZ is insolvent both before and after the debt cancellation.

	Before	After
Total assets........	$ 375,000	$ 375,000
Total liabilities......	(500,000)	(410,000)
Insolvent..........	$(125,000)	$ (35,000)

If, on the other hand, the creditors forgive $140,000 of debt, XYZ will be solvent after the cancellation (i.e., $375,000 − $360,000 = $15,000). Consequently, the firm would report $15,000 of the forgiveness as taxable income in such case.

---

[144] § 108(a).

[145] § 108(b).

[146] § 108(b)(5).

[147] §§ 108(b), (d)(3), and (e)(1).

[148] § 108(a)(3).

[149] § 61(a)(12).

As explained above, if a business's debt is canceled, the taxpayer must recognize income unless the business is bankrupt or insolvent. To provide relief to those engaged in the real estate business (other than corporations), Congress created a special exception. Under newly amended Code § 108, a taxpayer may elect to exclude the income resulting from the cancellation of indebtedness incurred or assumed in connection with real property used in a trade or business (*qualified real property business indebtedness*). This is true even though the taxpayer is neither bankrupt nor insolvent. The cancellation of debt income does not escape tax, however. The taxpayer must reduce the basis of the depreciable property for any income that is excluded. As a result, the taxpayer forgoes future deductions. The maximum amount of exclusion may not exceed the excess of the outstanding principal amount of the debt over the fair market value of the property.

> **Example 35.** During 1985 T acquired an office building in Houston for $800,000. He borrowed $700,000 of the purchase price by giving First Bank of Houston a note payable with interest at a rate of 14%. The note was secured by the building. By 1994 the value of the building had dropped to $400,000. At that time, the balance on the note was $600,000. Instead of foreclosing and taking the property, the bank agreed it would be better to leave the real estate in the hands of T and renegotiate the terms of the note so that T could handle the payments. As a result, the bank reduced the principal of the note from $600,000 to $400,000. T may elect to exclude the cancellation of debt income of $200,000, but he must reduce the basis of the property by $200,000.

LEASEHOLD IMPROVEMENTS

A lessee often makes improvements to leased real estate. These may range from minor improvements up to the construction of a building on the leased land. If these improvements are made in lieu of rent payments, they are included in the lessor's gross income.[150] Otherwise, the lessor has no taxable income either at the time the improvements are made or at the time the lease is terminated, even if the improvements substantially increase the property's value.[151] The lessor's only taxable income from these improvements will occur indirectly on the sale of the property to the extent the improvements result in a higher net selling price.

> **Example 36.** For the past 10 years W had leased land to X. During the current year the lease expired and W became the owner of a three-stall garage (FMV $19,000) that X had constructed on the property seven years previously. Assuming the improvements were not made in lieu of rent, the FMV of the garage is not currently included in W's gross income.

---

[150] Reg. § 1.109-1.   [151] § 109.

CONTRIBUTIONS TO CAPITAL

Cash or other property received by a business in exchange for an ownership interest are nontaxable transactions for the business. These assets are treated as contributions to capital and not income.[152] Contributions to capital that are not in exchange for an ownership interest also are nontaxable.

MISCELLANEOUS ITEMS

As stated in the first paragraph of this chapter, gross income includes *all* income unless specifically exempted. Although this chapter is not intended to discuss every income item, some additional items are classified for discussion purposes as miscellaneous.

FEES RECEIVED

Ordinarily, fees received for services performed are included in gross income. Thus, fees paid to corporate directors, jurors, and executors are reported as miscellaneous gross income. However, if executor fees are paid regardless of whether the taxpayer performs any services, they may qualify as nontaxable gifts.[153]

ASSET DISCOVERY

Cash or other assets found by a taxpayer are taxable income even if found accidentally, with no effort expended in discovering them.[154] For example, taxpayers were held to have taxable income equal to cash found in a used piano they had purchased.[155]

CAR POOL RECEIPTS

One type of earned income is nontaxable. Vehicle owners operating car pools for fellow commuters may exclude all the revenues received.[156] Car pool expenses are *personal* commuting expenses, and therefore are not deductible. If, however, the car pool activities are sufficient to qualify a taxpayer as being in a trade or business, all revenues are taxable. How much activity constitutes a trade or business is a question of fact not easily answered but, in this type of situation, the definition of trade certainly requires considerably more activity than a single automobile or small van making one round trip daily.

---

[152] §§ 118 and 721.

[153] Rev. Rul. 57-398, 1957-2 C.B. 93.

[154] Rev. Rul. 53-61, 1953-1 C.B. 17.

[155] *Cesarini v. Comm.*, 70-2 USTC ¶9509, 26 AFTR2d 70-5107, 428 F.2d 812 (CA-6, 1970).

[156] Rev. Rul. 55-555, 1955-2 C.B. 20.

INCOME TAX REFUNDS

All income tax refunds are nontaxable except to the extent the taxpayer received a tax benefit in a prior year.[157] A corporation receives a tax benefit for all business expenses, including state and local income taxes but not Federal income taxes, unless the corporation incurs a net operating loss for the year of deduction. State and local income taxes paid by individuals, however, provide a tax benefit only if the taxpayer itemized these deductions in the year paid. There is no tax benefit for the expense if the standard deduction was used instead of itemized deductions.

TEMPORARY LIVING COSTS

If an individual receives insurance to cover temporary living costs incurred because the principal residence was destroyed or damaged by fire, flood, or other casualty, the funds are nontaxable to the extent they are offset by *extra* living costs.[158] These funds also may be excluded if the government prevented the individual from using an undamaged residence because of the existence or threat of a casualty. Extra living costs are limited to those additional costs actually incurred for temporarily housing, feeding, and transporting the taxpayer and members of the household. Typical qualifying costs are hotel or apartment rent and utilities, extra costs for restaurant meals, and additional transportation necessitated by having to live outside the immediate area of the residence.

DAMAGES AWARDED TO INDIVIDUALS

Cash may be awarded by the courts or by insurance companies as damages to individuals because of job discrimination or personal injuries suffered due to alienation of affection, breach of promise to marry, and slander or libel. Job discrimination damages, according to the IRS and two circuit courts of appeal, are considered to be for back pay that was lost because of discrimination, and they are therefore included in gross income.[159] However, the Sixth Circuit Court of Appeals held in *Burke*[160] that settlements received from age and sex discrimination suits asserted under Title VII of the U.S. Civil Rights Act of 1964 represent damages for personal injuries and are therefore fully excluded from gross income under § 104(a)(2). The conflict among the Circuits was recently resolved when the Supreme Court,[161] in reversing *Burke,* concluded that back pay awards pursuant to Title VII of

---

[157]   § 111(a).

[158]   § 123.

[159]   Rev. Rul. 72-341, 1972-2 C.B. 32; *Thompson v. Comm.*, 89-1 USTC ¶9164, 63 AFTR 2d 89-677, 866 F.2d. 709 (CA-4, 1989) and *Sparrow v. Comm.*, 91-2 USTC ¶50, 567, 69 AFTR2d 92-325, 949 F.2d. 434, (CA-DC, 1991).

[160]   *Pistillo v. Comm.*, 90-2 USTC ¶50,469, 66 AFTR2d 90-5448, 912 F.2d 155 (CA-

6, 1990) and *Burke et al. v. U.S.*, 91-1 USTC ¶50,175, 67 AFTR2d 91-749, 929 F.2d 1119 (CA-6, 1991).

[161]   *Burke v. U.S.*, 92-1 USTC ¶50, 254, 69 AFTR2d 92-1293, 112 S. Ct. 1867 (USSC, 1992), *rev'g*, 91-1 USTC ¶50, 175, 67 AFTR2d 91-749, 929 F.2d. 119 (CA-6, 1991).

the Civil Rights Act of 1964 are not excludable from gross income under § 104(a)(2).[162] However, the Tax Court ruled in *Downey*[163] that damages awarded under the Age Discrimination in Employment Act (ADEA) to an airline pilot who was forced to retire at age 60 were tax-free as damages for personal injury under § 104(a)(2). To further complicate matters, a Florida district court recently disagreed with the Tax Court when it held in *Maleszewski*[164] that ADEA damages are not excludable from gross income.

Awards received for personal injuries due to alienation of affection, breach of promise to marry, and slander or libel represent nontaxable income.[165] When damage amounts for these personal injuries are specified as reimbursement for medical expenses, they reduce any itemized medical deduction. If any of these medical expenses were deducted in a prior year, they are included in gross income to the extent the taxpayer received a *tax benefit* for them.[166]

In a recent decision, the Sixth Circuit Court in *Threlkeld*[167] lined up with the Ninth Circuit Court in *Roemer*[168] in holding that damages received for injury to an individual's professional reputation were excludable from income as personal injury damages under § 104(a)(2). In both cases, the courts concluded that the harm to the individual's reputation was a personal injury even though it affected the professional relationships of the victim. The Tax Court changed its original position and now agrees with the Ninth Circuit. However, the Internal Revenue Service has announced that it will not follow the Ninth Circuit's decision in *Roemer*.[169] In the opinion of the IRS, a taxpayer cannot sustain a personal injury within the meaning of § 104(a)(2) when the primary harm suffered is a loss of business income. Therefore, the IRS will continue to tax amounts received for damages to professional reputation.

The Revenue Reconciliation Act of 1989 amended §104(a) with respect to punitive damages received on account of personal injuries. Such amounts, if received after July 10, 1989, are excluded from gross income only if a physical injury or sickness is involved. Consequently, determining the nature of the damage (i.e., compensatory or punitive) has important tax implications.

---

[162] It should be noted that the 1991 Civil Rights Act expanded Title VII's remedial scope to include compensatory and punitive damages. Although this signals a marked change in Title VII (the 1964 Act limits available remedies to back pay), the Supreme Court does not comment on whether back pay awarded under the 1991 Act would be nontaxable.

[163] *Burns P. Downey*, 100 T.C. , No. 40 (1993).

[164] *Chester J. Maleszewski v. U.S.*, 93-1 USTC ¶50,358,72 AFTR2d 93-5172 (D. Ct. Fl., 1993).

[165] Rev. Rul. 74-77, 1974-1 C.B. 33.

[166] Rev. Rul. 75-230, 1975-1 C.B. 93.

[167] *James E. Threlkeld v. Comm.*, 88-1 USTC ¶9370, 61 AFTR2d 1285, 848 F.2d 81 (CA-6, 1988), *aff'g*. 87 T.C. 1294 (1986).

[168] *Roemer, Jr. v. Comm.*, 83-2 USTC ¶9600, 52 AFTR2d 5954, 716 F.2d 693 (CA-9, 1983), *rev'g*. 79 T.C. 398 (1982).

[169] Rev. Rul. 85-143, 1985-2 C.B. 55.

Example 37.   Z's neighbor wrote a letter that was published in the "Voice of the People" section of the local newspaper claiming that Z was incompetent and an incorrigible liar. Z sued his neighbor for libel (i.e., loss of personal reputation), and the court awarded him $50,000. Z also received $6,000 in punitive damages.

The $50,000 represents compensation for personal injury and is nontaxable. However, the $6,000 received for punitive damages is taxable because Z did not suffer any physical injury.

TAX PLANNING

In *Gregory v. Helvering*, Judge Learned Hand stated: "Any one may so arrange his affairs that his taxes shall be as low as possible; he is not bound to choose that pattern which will best pay the Treasury; there is not even a patriotic duty to increase one's taxes."[170] Individuals and businesses have many opportunities to arrange their affairs in ways that decrease their annual Federal income tax liability. Tax advisers must be both knowledgeable and imaginative in order to provide their clients with good tax-planning information. But then, it is the taxpayers' responsibility to use this information wisely to meet their own needs and desires.

INVESTMENTS

Tax-planning strategy must be viewed in terms of each taxpayer's own financial position. When considering investments, both the after-tax return and the risk involved must be evaluated. Before-tax income frequently is lower for tax-exempt and tax-deferred investments than it is for taxable investments with the same degree of risk. Consequently, tax-exempt investments should be most attractive to those in the higher tax bracket. They may not be beneficial to those in the lower bracket. Tax-deferred investments should be most attractive to those expecting a lower tax bracket when the deferral period ends. In addition, investors must consider whether any gains will be taxed as ordinary income or capital gains (see Chapter 15), and whether capital gains will be needed to offset capital losses.

Taxpayers have a variety of investment opportunities available to them. In order to arrive at informed investment decisions, comparative evaluations are necessary. However, such evaluations must be viewed with caution. The very nature of this type of analysis means that tentative assumptions must be made about the future. For example, when comparing a possible stock purchase with an annuity purchase, assumptions must be made about (1) future cash flows for the two investments, (2) future marginal tax rates, and (3) the discount rate to be used in determining the present value of the expected cash flows. A decision should never be based on a simple nonmathematical tax comparison of the total of annual dividend exclusions plus capital gains for the stock, as opposed to the total deferred ordinary income for the annuity. A tax adviser should always remember that while taxation is a very important factor, it is just one of several that must be considered.

On the death of an insured person, life insurance companies ordinarily allow beneficiaries to receive the proceeds in one lump sum, or in installments for a stipulated period or over the beneficiary's life. Tax concerns aside, some beneficiaries may elect to leave the proceeds with the insurance company simply because they like the security of receiving a periodic payment from an established financial institution. Each installment contains a ratable portion of the proceeds plus interest. This interest is taxable income. Thus, life insurance proceeds received in installments are treated the same as annuities.

---

[170] 35-1 USTC ¶9043, 14 AFTR 1191, 55 U.S. 266 (USSC, 1935).

Example 38.   M is the sole beneficiary of her husband's $60,000 life insurance policy. She elects to receive the proceeds in monthly installments for 10 years. Her monthly installment is $500 plus interest on the unpaid principal. In the current year, she receives $6,000 plus $3,700 interest. Her taxable interest income is $3,700.

One feature of life insurance that has enticed many investors over the years is its tax-free cash build-up. Taxpayers have taken advantage of this by borrowing against the policy—in effect receiving use of the income without having to pay tax on it. To discourage the purchase of life insurance as a tax-sheltered investment vehicle, special rules have been established. As a result, taxpayers must closely scrutinize the type of insurance they purchase with respect to its tax treatment. Under the revised rules, a taxpayer who receives amounts before age 59½, including loans, from certain single premium and other investment-oriented life insurance contracts (modified endowment contracts) is treated as receiving income first and then a recovery of basis. In addition, the recipient is subject to an additional 10 percent income tax on the amounts received that are includible in gross income. This provision affects only "modified endowment contracts" entered into on or after June 21, 1988.

An investor who desires nontaxable income may choose to purchase assets such as

1. Qualifying state and local government bonds to obtain the full interest income exclusion

2. Stocks in companies with net income for accounting purposes, but no earnings and profits for tax purposes, to obtain the full exclusion for distributions that are treated as a return of capital

Investors who wish to defer income may choose to purchase

1. Annuities (or to elect that life insurance proceeds be received as annuities) to obtain the deferral of all interest income until received

2. Assets that are expected to appreciate, such as stocks, real estate, and collectables, to obtain the deferral of all appreciation until it is realized

If the taxpayer does not dispose of the assets, the deferral becomes permanent. That is, no one recognizes the income and the assets are inherited at their market values, including the deferred income.

EMPLOYEE BENEFITS

Company fringe benefits can provide employees with tax consequences that range from excellent savings to actual disadvantages. From a tax viewpoint, the best fringe benefits are those that are deductible by the employer and convert otherwise taxable income to nontaxable income for the recipient. For example, payments made to beneficiaries on behalf of a deceased employee are nontaxable up to $5,000 if they qualify as death benefits but are taxable compensation otherwise. In addition, most employee benefits that are provided in lieu of additional salary convert taxable compensation to nontaxable benefits.

Example 39. W is a new employee of Z Corporation. Her compensation package is $20,000. However, she may choose to receive (a) $20,000 salary and no benefits, or (b) $19,000 salary and Z will pay premiums of $600 for medical insurance and $400 for group-term life insurance. If W chooses the first option, she has $20,000 taxable income, but if she selects the second option, she has $19,000 taxable income.

Another very valuable type of fringe benefit is one that is nontaxable income if provided by the employer but is a nondeductible expenditure if paid by the employee. Most fringe benefits are of this type. These include premiums paid for group-term life insurance up to $50,000, qualifying meals and lodging on the premises, supper money, company parking, use of company facilities, and employee discounts. All of these benefits are deductible costs by the employer but nontaxable income to the employee when the necessary requirements discussed in this chapter are met. If, however, the employees pay these costs instead of the employer, there is no tax deduction for them.

A third type of fringe benefit includes expenditures that are deductible expenses, when paid by individuals, but are subject to restrictions. For example, health insurance premiums are deductible for employees who itemize their deductions but *only* to the extent that all qualifying medical expenditures exceed 7.5 percent of A.G.I. (see Chapter 11). Thus, employer-paid health insurance represents different tax savings to different employees.

Example 40. L's compensation includes a salary of $30,000 plus employer-paid health insurance premiums of $600. L's taxable income is $30,000 since the $600 is nontaxable. If the company policy is changed so that L pays the $600 health insurance premiums and the company increases his salary to $30,600, the tax effect on L depends on his individual tax situation.

1. If L does not itemize medical expenses, he has taxable income of $30,600 salary and no deduction for the $600.

2. If L itemizes deductions and his medical expenditures before the health insurance premiums exceed 7.5% of A.G.I., he still has taxable income of $30,600 salary but now has a deduction of $600.

Assume L has a 28% marginal tax rate. In situation 1 above, his tax benefit from employer-paid health insurance premiums is $168 ($600 × 28%). In the second situation, L appears to receive no tax benefit when his company pays the health insurance premiums. However, his A.G.I. is $600 higher when L pays the premium. Since medical expenses equal to 7.5% of A.G.I. are not deductible, this increases the nondeductible portion by $45 ($600 × 7.5%). Thus, at the 28% tax rate, his tax increases by $12.60 ($45 × 28%).

Some employer-provided benefits can be a disadvantage to employees. Recall, for example, that disability income is taxable if the premiums were paid by the employer but nontaxable if they were paid by the individual. The best tax-planning advice when employers pay disability insurance premiums is for employees to convince employers to provide another benefit and let employees pay their own disability premiums.

Considerable leeway in tax planning is available to those employees who are allowed to select their own fringe benefits. Simply looking at the cost of each benefit to the company, however, is inadequate. Each employee should carefully evaluate personal needs and the tax effect of each desirable benefit before selection is made.

EMPLOYEE VERSUS SELF-EMPLOYED

The numerous favorable tax results received with fringe benefits are available only if an employer/employee relationship exists. When all necessary requirements are met, it does not matter if the employees are major shareholders of the employer. This situation creates an incentive to operate some businesses as corporations rather than as proprietorships or partnerships.

One of these fringe benefits, employer-furnished meals and lodging, has been of increasing interest to closely held businesses in recent years. Farming represents a particularly good example of a business that requires someone to be available on the property 24 hours a day. When the working owner lives on the farm, a business deduction plus an employee exclusion for the cost of meals and lodging provided to the farmer can be significant.

Example 41.   A farm owned by M has the following information for the current year:

Gross income.....................................	$130,000
Cost of food consumed by M......................	2,000
Cost of lodging used by M........................	4,200
Salary to M......................................	20,000
Other farm expenses.............................	85,000

If the farm is a proprietorship, net farming income is $25,000 ($130,000 − $20,000 − $85,000) and M has an A.G.I. of $45,000 ($25,000 + $20,000).[171] Similar results occur if the farm is a partnership, except M will report only his share of the $25,000. In contrast, if the farm is a corporation, net income is $18,800 ($130,000 − $2,000 − $4,200 − $20,000 − $85,000) and M has an A.G.I. of $20,000. Thus, M, the proprietor, has $45,000 A.G.I. compared with a combined income of $38,800 ($18,800 + $20,000) for the M Corporation and M, the employee.

---

[171] Technically, a proprietor's salary is not a farming expense but is shown in the example for comparison purposes. Thus, net income is $45,000 ($130,000 - $85,000) and M's A.G.I. is $45,000.

Although the above example seems to result in a tax advantage for the corporate farm, such a conclusion is over-simplified. Other tax factors are important. For example, corporate net income is taxed to the corporation currently and again as dividend income to shareholders when distributed to them (see Chapter 19). Another important factor is that individuals and corporations are subject to different tax rates. Also, if farming losses occur, the results may be very unfavorable with a corporate entity. The important point to remember is that the tax advantage achieved with the corporation for meals and lodging (and other employee benefits) is just one of the necessary ingredients when evaluating whether a business should be incorporated.

DIVORCE

Insufficient attention usually is given to tax planning during separation and divorce. Of course, favorable tax results are easier to accomplish when the individuals are parting amicably, but good results still can occur amid animosity. The more disparate the husband's and wife's tax brackets, the greater the benefits to be achieved. This is because payments classified as alimony or separate maintenance are deductible by the payor and are taxable income to the recipient. In contrast, all other asset transfers are neither deductible expenses nor taxable income.

Example 42.   H and W are divorced. H's marginal tax rate is 36% while W's is 15%. Every $10 of alimony costs H $6.40 after taxes [$10 paid − $3.60 tax savings ($10 × 36%)] and is worth $8.50 to W after taxes [$10 received − $1.50 tax due ($10 × 15%)]. Thus, H pays $6.40 for W to receive $8.50. If W requires $425 after taxes each month, she must receive $500 if the payments qualify as alimony [$500 − ($500 × 15% = $75)] or $425 if they do not. On the surface, it seems that H would rather pay $425 a month than $500 but $500 in alimony results in an after-tax cost of $320 [$500 − ($500 × 36% = $180)] for a monthly savings of $105 ($425 − $320). Naturally, the closer the two marginal rates, the less there is in tax savings.

PROBLEM MATERIALS

DISCUSSION QUESTIONS

6-1   *Basic Concepts.*   Determine whether each of the following statements is true or false. If false, rewrite the statement so that it is true. Be prepared to explain each statement.

    a.   Receipts are included in gross income only if specifically listed in the Code.

    b.   Tax returns show (1) gross receipts from all sources, less (2) excludable income, which equals (3) taxable income.

    c.   Interest earned on tax-exempt municipal bonds is nontaxable income regardless of whether it is received by an individual or by a corporation.

6-2   *Investments—Stocks versus Bonds.*   C has $10,000 to invest but is uncertain whether to purchase H, Inc. stocks or tax-exempt bonds issued by the State of Illinois. List the relevant types of information that C must obtain or estimate in order to make a mathematical calculation of her after-tax return on the two investments she is considering.

6-3   *Investments—Bonds.*   D, Inc. bonds are selling for $1,000 each with an interest rate of 11 percent. Tax-exempt bonds issued by the State of Kentucky are selling for $1,000 each with an interest rate of 8 percent. Which bond provides a taxpayer with the higher after-tax return when the marginal tax rate is

    a.   36 percent?

    b.   15 percent?

6-4   *Investments—Dividend Income.*   Corporate distributions may qualify as dividends, return of capital, or stock dividends. Explain the tax treatment of each of these three distributions. What determines whether a distribution is a dividend, a return of capital, or a stock dividend?

6-5   *Employee Benefits.*   Z, Inc. owns and operates several businesses, including six hotels and two real estate agencies. R, an employee of Z, spends three nights free of charge in one of Z's hotels in Indiana. Is the value of the lodging nontaxable to R, assuming the information below? Explain.

    a.   R works for one of the real estate agencies.

    b.   R tends bar in one of the hotels in Maine.

    c.   R is a tax accountant in Z's corporate headquarters where the tax records of all of Z's businesses are maintained.

6-6   *Employee Benefits—Comparison.*   Compare the tax treatment for each of the items listed below assuming they are paid by (1) the employer, or (2) the employee.

    a.   Parking in the company lot during working hours

    b.   Health insurance premiums

    c.   Disability insurance premiums

    d.   Meals eaten in the company cafeteria when the employee must remain on the premises for job reasons

6-7 *Employee Benefits—Meals and Lodging.*   Employer-provided meals and lodging that qualify as nontaxable income can be an exceedingly valuable employee benefit.

    a. When do employer-provided meals and lodging qualify as nontaxable income?

    b. List at least 10 types of occupations in which employer-provided lodging and/or meals could qualify for the exclusion. Explain why these occupations are appropriate for the exclusion.

6-8 *Employee Benefits.*   Over the years, the list of employee benefits that qualify as deductible expenses by the employer and nontaxable income for the employee has expanded. Assume Congress is interested in further expanding the list of benefits available for this special tax treatment. Prepare a list for Congress of at least three items not discussed in this chapter that would provide many employees with valuable benefits. Explain why these three would be logical additions.

6-9 *Gifts.*   How can gifts to family members reduce the family's income tax liability?

6-10 *Alimony and Child Support.*   A husband and wife who are obtaining a divorce disagree whether certain periodic payments should be classified as alimony or child support.

    a. What difference does it make how the payments are classified?

    b. What if the agreement states the payments are for both alimony and child support without making a specific distinction in dollar allocation between the two?

    c. List three types of compromise offers that could be made by the husband to reach an allocation that might satisfy both the husband and wife. Explain the tax consequences of each of the three possible solutions.

6-11 *Alimony.*   A husband (H) and wife (W) are obtaining a divorce. He agrees to pay alimony of $25,000 in each of the two years after the divorce to enable her to attend graduate school. No alimony will be paid after the second year.

    a. What are his deductible and her taxable amount of alimony for each of the two years, and what are the tax effects in year three?

    b. How could the payment schedule be restructured to maximize his deductions?

    c. How could the payment schedule be restructured to minimize her taxable income?

6-12 *Prizes and Awards.*   Contest winners must report the value of prizes won as taxable income.

    a. What arguments could the taxpayer use to convince the IRS and the courts that the values of the prizes are less than their retail selling prices?

    b. Are any prizes or awards ever nontaxable? Explain.

6-13 *Scholarships and Fellowships.*   CPA firms are interested in encouraging practical research that explores accounting issues with an objective of developing better accounting methods for the profession. Assume the XY firm decides to establish a fund that will support individual research efforts. Recipients of these grants will be selected based on the quality of their past work and on a written proposal of a specific research project to be completed with funds from the XY firm. Do recipients of these grants have taxable or nontaxable income? Explain.

6-14 *Goodwill versus Agreement Not to Compete.* A preliminary agreement covering the sale/purchase of a dental practice includes an allocation of $40,000 to goodwill and the agreement that the seller will not practice dentistry within a five-mile radius for five years.

    a. What are the tax consequences of this $40,000 allocation?

    b. What advice should a tax adviser give the seller?

    c. What advice should a tax adviser give the buyer?

6-15 *Damages Awarded.* As the result of a newspaper article, V claims his character was damaged beyond repair, he lost his job, and he incurred medical expenses for psychiatric care. His lawsuit requested that the court award him the following amounts: $500,000 for personal injury due to slander; $30,000 in lost wages; and $5,000 for psychiatric care.

    a. What are the tax consequences to V if he is awarded the $535,000?

    b. V decides to accept an out-of-court settlement of $150,000. The newspaper and its insurer are willing to allocate the $150,000 in any manner that V requests. How should V have the amount allocated?

PROBLEMS

6-16 *Basic Concepts.* Calculate the amount to be included in gross income for the following taxpayers.

    a. T is self-employed as a beautician. Her records show

Receipts	
Services	$21,000
Product sales	3,000

Expenditures	
Cost of products sold	1,800
Cost of supplies used	2,600
Utilities	2,400
Shop and equipment rent	3,600
Other expenses	1,000

    b. R owns rental property. His records show

Gross rents	$6,000
Depreciation expense	4,200
Repair expense	2,100
Miscellaneous expense	300

    c. S is an employee with the following tax information:

Gross salary	$15,000
Social security (FICA) taxes withheld (rounded for simplicity)	1,000
Federal income tax withheld	2,200
Health insurance premiums withheld	500
Net salary received in cash	11,300
Employer's share of social security taxes	1,000

6-17 *Investments—Cash Dividends.*   Three years ago, Z purchased 50 shares of L common stock for $6,000. Although Z is married, the stocks are recorded in his name alone. The current market value of these shares totals $7,200. He and Mrs. Z file a joint return and neither of them owns any other stock. Mr. Z wants to know what effect each of the following totally separate situations has upon (1) his taxable income and (2) his basis in each share of stock.

   a. L distributes a cash dividend and Z receives $330.

   b. L distributes cash as a return of capital and Z receives $330.

6-18 *Investments—Stock Dividends.*   A, who is single, purchased 100 shares of N Corporation common stock four years ago for $12,000. The stock has a current fair market value of $14,400. A asks how each of the following separate situations affects her (1) taxable income and (2) her basis in each share of stock.

   a. N distributes common stock as a dividend and A receives 10 shares.

   b. N distributes nonconvertible preferred stock as a dividend and A receives 10 shares. The preferred stock has a current fair market value of $100 per share.

6-19 *Investments—Cash Dividends.*   D, Inc. had accumulated earnings and profits at January 1 of the current year of $20,000. During the taxable year, it had current earnings and profits of $10,000. On December 31 of the current year, D, Inc. made a cash distribution of $40,000 to its sole shareholder, G. G paid $25,000 for his stock three years ago.

   a. How will G treat the $40,000 he received on December 31?

   b. Assume G sold all of his stock for $36,000 on January 1 of the following year. Compute his capital gain.

6-20 *Investments—Interest.*   Mr. K died at the beginning of the year. Mrs. K received interest during the year from the following sources:

Corporate bonds..................................	$1,100
Bank savings account............................	200
Personal loan to a friend.........................	500
City of Maryville bonds (issued to build a new high school).....................	600

In addition to the above, Mrs. K was the beneficiary of her husband's $50,000 life insurance policy. She elected to receive the $50,000 proceeds plus interest over the next 10 years. She receives $7,500 in the current year and will receive a like amount each of the following nine years. Calculate the taxable portion of the interest income received by Mrs. K during the year.

6-21 *Educational Savings Bonds Requirements.*   H and W have twin sons, S and T, and two daughters, D and E. The couple purchased Series EE savings bonds, hoping to take advantage of the interest exclusion for their children's education. This year, they cashed in some of the bonds, receiving $5,000. Of this amount, $2,000 represented interest. For each of the following independent situations, indicate how much, if any, of the exclusion is allowed this year.

   a. D enrolled at Michigan State University and paid tuition of $4,000 and fees for room and board of $3,000. To help defray some of these expenses, she used an academic scholarship of $1,000.

   b. While on her way to the first day of class, D fell and broke her leg. She withdrew from classes and received all of her money back.

    c. S˙ is 25 and entered the Ph.D. program at the University of Texas this year. As a teaching assistant, he receives a salary of $7,000 during the year. His parents paid $1,000 of his tuition.

    d. H and W paid for all of T's tuition to attend Arizona State University. The couple's A.G.I. for this year was $100,000. When the couple purchased the particular bonds used to pay for T's tuition, their A.G.I. was $55,000.

    e. E, 22, redeemed bonds this year, receiving $5,000. E used all of the proceeds to pay for her tuition. She received the bonds as a gift from her parents last year. E's A.G.I. for this year is $3,000.

6-22 *Investments—Annuities.* P is single, 65 years old, and retired. On August 1, 1988, he purchased a single-premium deferred life annuity for $40,000 using after-tax funds. This year, P received $5,000 in annuity benefits. He will receive a like amount each year for the rest of his life. (Note: In answering the following questions, use the information in Exhibit 6-2 of this chapter.)

    a. Calculate P's taxable income from the annuity for the current year.

    b. Calculate P's taxable income from the annuity for year 5.

    c. Calculate P's taxable income from the annuity for year 22.

    d. Assume P lives just 15 more years. Calculate the deduction that would be allowed on P's final tax return.

    e. Assume the annuity was purchased by P and his employer jointly. P contributed $12,000 in after-tax funds, and the employer contributed $28,000. Calculate P's taxable income from the annuity for the current year.

6-23 *Annuities.* A, age 66, retired after 30 years of service as an employee of the XYZ Corporation. He started receiving retirement benefits in the form of a single life annuity on January 1 of the current year. A's total after-tax contributions to the plan amounted to $34,000, and his retirement benefit is $1,500 per month.

    a. Determine A's nontaxable portion of each monthly payment, assuming he elects the simplified safe-harbor method.

    b. Assume A lives another 20 years. Will there be a time period in which A will be required to fully include the monthly payments in gross income? If so, when?

6-24 *Investments—Life Insurance.* L is 65 years old and retired. Her husband died early in the year. L was the beneficiary of his $20,000 life insurance policy. L elected to receive $5,200 annually for five years rather than receive a single payment of $20,000 immediately. Calculate L's taxable income from the first payment.

6-25 *Social Security Benefits.* X, who is single and retired, has the following income for the current year:

Taxable interest	$20,000
Dividend income	10,000
Tax-exempt bond interest	8,000
Social security benefits	7,200

    a. Compute the taxable portion of X's social security benefits.

    b. Assume the above information remains the same, except X's taxable interest amounted to $10,000. Compute the taxable portion of his social security benefits.

6-26 *Employee Benefits.* Determine the (1) deductible employer amount, and (2) taxable employee amount for each of the following employer-provided benefits.

   a. Reimbursement of expenses paid by an employee to entertain a client of the business, $200.

   b. Bonus paid an employee when a sales quota was met, $300.

   c. Watches given employees at Christmas, $38 each.

   d. Free parking provided on company property, $500 market value and $220 cost per employee.

   e. Supper money of $15 paid to an employee for each of 10 nights that she worked past 6 P.M., $150.

6-27 *Employee Benefits.* Determine the (1) deductible employer amount, and (2) taxable employee (or beneficiary) amount for each of the following employer-provided benefits.

   a. A death benefit of $6,000 paid to the wife and $4,000 to the son of a deceased employee.

   b. Premiums of $700 paid on $70,000 of group-term life insurance for a 52-year-old woman employee.

   c. Ten percent employee discounts are allowed on the retail price of all merchandise purchased from the employer. During the year, sales to employees totaled $18,000 ($20,000 retail price − $2,000 discount) for merchandise that cost the employer $14,000. The employer reported the $18,000 as sales and the $14,000 as cost of goods sold.

6-28 *Employee Benefits—Medical Insurance.* F's $400 annual health insurance premium is paid by his employer. During the year, F received $870 reimbursement of medical expenses; $650 for this year's expenses and $220 for last year's expenses. Determine F's taxable income from the reimbursement in the current year if

   a. F never itemizes any medical expenses.

   b. F deducted medical expenses from his A.G.I. this year of $900 and last year of $450.

6-29 *Tax Benefit Rule.* During 1993 K had adjusted gross income of $30,000. A list of itemized deductions available to K in preparing her 1993 return is shown below:

State income taxes paid	$2,000
Property taxes on residence	600
Charitable contributions	400
Medical expenses	2,500
Interest paid on residence	1,200

K is single, and her son M, who is 8 years old, lives with her. She qualifies as a head of household. In 1994 K received $2,500 from an insurance company for reimbursement of her 1993 medical expenses. Is K required to include any of the $2,500 reimbursement in her gross income in 1994?

6-30   *Fringe Benefits versus Compensation.*   P is a 46-year-old professor at Z University, a private school in the Midwest. P is married and has triplets who are freshmen at Z University. Among others, P is provided with the following fringe benefits during the current year:

> Group-term life insurance coverage of $75,000. Premium cost to Z University is $300. Tuition reduction of $30,000 for the triplets.

   a.   How much does the group-term life insurance cost Professor P? Assume his marginal tax bracket is 31 percent.
   b.   Would P be equally well off if the university simply paid him an additional $300 in compensation to cover the term insurance?
   c.   Is the tuition reduction for the triplets taxable?
   d.   Assuming tuition remains constant, how much will Professor P save in tuition payments by remaining on the faculty at Z University until the triplets graduate?
   e.   What would be the result for the current year if the university increased Professor P's salary by $30,000 a year to pay for the triplets' tuition?

6-31   *Unemployment Compensation and Disability Income.*   Mr. and Mrs. B are married filing jointly. Mrs. B was permanently disabled the entire year and Mr. B was unemployed part of the year. Both are 55 years old. Their receipts for 1994 were

Disability income—Mrs. B................................	$ 6,200
Social security income—Mrs. B..........................	1,000
Salary—Mr. B...	16,500
Unemployment compensation—Mr. B.....................	4,500

Calculate their taxable income for 1994, assuming the disability insurance premiums were paid

   a.   Entirely by Mrs. B.
   b.   Entirely by Mrs. B's employer.

6-32   *Damages Awarded and Disability Income.*   D works for the XYZ Tool and Die Shop. On March 1, 1994 a stamping press that D was operating malfunctioned, resulting in the loss of the index finger on his right hand. D, claiming the machine was not properly maintained, sued XYZ for the following damages:

Medical expenses during D's one-week stay	
in the hospital..	$ 8,000
Loss of D's finger..	50,000
Punitive damages..	5,000
Total...	$63,000

On April 1, 1995 the court awarded D $63,000.

   a.   Assuming D did not deduct the $8,000 of medical expenses he incurred in 1994, what portion of the $63,000 settlement is included in D's gross income in 1995?
   b.   D did not return to work for three months. During this time period, he received $3,000 in disability income payments. Assuming D paid the annual premium on the disability insurance, how much of the $3,000 is taxable income to D?

6-33   *Meals and Lodging.*   Mr. and Mrs. G own and operate a small motel near Big Mountain resort area. Their only employees are two maids and one cook. The rest of the work is done by Mr. and Mrs. G. In order to be on 24-hour call, they live in a home next to the motel. The home is owned by the business. Both Mr. and Mrs. G eat most of their meals in the motel restaurant. Answer the questions below assuming the business is (1) a corporation, or (2) a partnership.

   a.   Are any of the costs for the meals and lodging deductible by either the business or Mr. and Mrs. G?

   b.   Is the value of the meals and lodging included in Mr. and Mrs. G's gross income?

   c.   Answer the questions in (a) and (b) again, but assume Mr. and Mrs. G paid the business for all their meals in the restaurant and for rent of the home.

6-34   *Military Compensation.*   After graduating from high school last year, K, who is single, joined the U.S. Air Force. Her military compensation for 1994 is

	Cash	Market Value
Salary..	$10,000	
Military housing...............................		$2,500
Computer training on the job....................		1,800
Uniforms......................................		800
Meals on the base.............................		3,600
Reimbursement of moving expenses............	500	

Calculate K's taxable income for the year.

6-35   *Inheritances.*   In each of the following independent situations, determine how much, if any, the taxpayer must include in gross income.

   a.   At the beginning of this year, a taxpayer inherited rental property valued at $87,000 from his grandmother. Rental income from the property after the transfer of title totaled $6,000, and rental expenses were $5,200.

   b.   A taxpayer inherited $50,000 from her employer. She was his housekeeper for ten years and was promised she would be provided for in his will if she continued employment with him until his death.

   c.   A taxpayer lent $15,000 to a friend. To protect the loan, the taxpayer had his friend make him beneficiary on her $20,000 life insurance policy. Six months later the friend died and the taxpayer received $20,000 from the insurance company.

6-36   *Gifts.*   In each of the following independent situations, determine how much, if any, the taxpayer must include in gross income.

   a.   A taxpayer often visits her uncle in a nursing home. In addition, she manages his investment portfolio for him. To show his gratitude, he has given her stock valued at $5,000. He has also implied that if she continues these activities, he will transfer other shares of stock to her.

   b.   A taxpayer saved a child's life during a fire. The child's parents gave him land valued at $5,000 to show their gratitude. They paid $2,200 for the land several years ago.

   c.   Taxpayer's employer gave him $1,200 in recognition of his 20 years of service to the company. The employer deducted the $1,200 as a business expense.

6-37 *Awards.* In each of the following independent situations, determine how much, if any, the taxpayer must include in gross income.

a. The taxpayer, a professional basketball player, was voted as the outstanding player of the year. In addition to the honor, he received an automobile with a sticker price of $16,000. He drove the car for six months and sold it for $12,000. The taxpayer's employer also gave him a gold watch worth $1,200. He wears the watch. Both donors deducted their respective costs for the automobile and the watch as business expenses. The costs of the automobile and watch were $13,500 and $800, respectively.

b. The taxpayer was selected by the senior class as the most outstanding classroom teacher. The high school presented her with a $1,000 check in recognition of her significant accomplishments. She used the money to take a well-earned vacation to Cancun.

c. M, Inc. gave T a watch in recognition of her 20 years of service to the company. The watch cost the employer $400.

6-38 *Child Support and Alimony.* Determine the effect on A.G.I. for the husband (H) and wife (W) in each of the following *continuous* situations. H and W are divorced and do not live in a community property state. They have three children.

a. H pays W $400 per month as alimony and support of the three children.

b. W discovers her attorney did not word the agreement correctly. H and W sign a statement that the *original* agreement is retroactively amended to hold that H pays $100 per month as alimony to W and $300 per month as support of the three children. All other language remains unchanged. What is the effect of this change on future and past payments?

c. Assume the original agreement contained the wording in (b) above. In the first year, H makes only 10 of the 12 payments for a total of $4,000. In the second year, H pays the $800 balance due for the prior year and makes all 12 payments of $400 each on time.

d. On their divorce, W was awarded an automobile. H is required to pay the loan outstanding on the car, $94 per month for 20 months. During the year, H pays $94 for 12 months. This includes $130 interest and $998 loan principal.

e. H owns the home in which W and the children live free of charge. H's mortgage payments are $360 per month for the next 20 years. During the year, his expenses on the home are $2,900 interest, $800 property taxes, $340 insurance, $280 loan principal, and $218 repairs. The rental value of the home is $425 per month.

f. In addition to the monthly alimony and support payments above, H is to pay W $30,000 over a period of 11 years. H pays $2,500 of this amount the first year and $3,600 the second year.

g. H inherits considerable property. As a result, he voluntarily increases the alimony to $150 and child support to $450 per month. He makes 12 payments of $600 each during the year.

6-39 *Alimony.* Determine the effect on A.G.I. for the husband (H) and wife (W) in each of the three years. W is to pay H alimony of $100,000 as follows:

Year	Amount
1	$56,000
2	26,000
3	18,000

6-40 *Divorce—Property Settlement.* Husband (H) and wife (W) are divorced this month. The divorce agreement states that all jointly owned property will be transferred as follows:

	Cost	Market Value	Transferred to
Home.............	$35,000	$65,000	W
Investments.......	3,000	5,000	W
Cash............	7,000	7,000	H and W equally

W will occupy the home and H will rent an apartment. Determine the recognized gain or loss and the basis of the assets to H and W after the transfer. Explain.

6-41 *Divorce—Property Settlement.* H and W, who live in Michigan (a common law state), decided to end their troubled 30-year marriage. Pursuant to the divorce decree, the following assets are transferred from H to W on March 1, 1994:

	Basis to H	Market Value
Stocks (purchased by H on April 10, 1988)....	$300,000	$400,000
Land (purchased by H on June 2, 1984)......	200,000	500,000

In addition to the above, H transferred a life insurance policy on his life with a face value of $200,000 to W, who assumed responsibility for the annual premium.

W sold the stocks for $500,000 on November 1, 1994 and the land for $550,000 on December 1, 1994. H died on December 20, 1994.

a. Determine W's gain on the sale of the stocks and land in 1994.
b. Are any of the life insurance proceeds taxable to W? Explain.

6-42 *Employee Fringe Benefits.* For each of the following independent situations, indicate whether the fringe benefit the employee receives is taxable or nontaxable. Explain your answer.

a. C is a ticket agent for North Central Airways. The airline has a nondiscriminatory policy that allows its employees to fly without charge on a standby basis only. The last week in July, C took a vacation and flew from Kansas City to San Francisco. The value of the round-trip ticket was $400.

b. Assume that C [in part (a) above] also stayed, without charge, for the entire week at a hotel in San Francisco that North Central Airways owns. The value of a week's stay in the hotel was $2,000.

c. Assume in part (a) above that C was unable to obtain an empty seat on North Central the last week in July. Consequently, utilizing the qualified reciprocal arrangement that North Central has with South Shore Airlines, C flew free to San Francisco on South Shore. The value of the round-trip ticket was $400.

d. M is a sales clerk for J-mart Department store. The store has a nondiscriminatory policy whereby its employees may purchase inventory items at a discount. In June, M purchased a microwave oven for $250 that J-mart sells to its customers for $300. J-mart's gross profit rate is 20 percent.

e. F is a CPA and works for a public accounting firm. On F's behalf, the firm paid $375 in subscription fees for three professional accounting journals.

f. Officers of the XYZ Corporation are provided free parking space in a public parking garage located across the street from the firm's office building. The annual cost of the parking space to XYZ is $300 for each officer.

6-43 *Unrelated Party Transfers.* In each of the following independent situations, determine how much, if any, the taxpayer must include in gross income.

a. Taxpayer has been very active as a volunteer hospital worker for many years. In the current year, the city named her as the Outstanding Volunteer of the Year. She later discovered that she was nominated for the award by two nurses at the hospital. The honor included a silver tray valued at $400. In addition, the two nurses collected $700 from hospital personnel and gave her a prepaid one-week vacation for two people.

b. Taxpayer, an undergraduate degree candidate, was selected as one of five outstanding sophomore students in accounting by the Institute of Management Accountants. Selection was based on an application submitted by eligible students. The winner received $15,000. Although there was no stipulation of how the money was to be used, the award was given with the expectation that the money would be used for tuition, books, and fees in the student's junior and senior years.

c. Taxpayer won the bowling league award for the highest total score over a five-week period. Taxpayer received a trophy valued at $65 and $100 cash.

d. Taxpayer purchased church raffle tickets in her eight-year-old son's name and gave the tickets to him. One of the tickets was drawn. The prize was a $600 color television.

e. Taxpayer receives a $20,000 grant from the National Association of Chiefs of Police to conduct a research study on crowd control. The grant stipulates that the research period is for eight months and that $8,000 of it is for travel and temporary living costs.

f. An accounting student accepted an internship with a CPA firm and is paid $3,000. The stated purpose of the internship is to provide students with a basic understanding of how accounting education is applied. It is believed this understanding will help students in remaining course work and later job selection. Although the faculty believes internships would benefit all students, only 40 percent of the accounting majors participate in the program.

6-44 *Businesses.* In each of the following independent situations, determine how much, if any, the taxpayer must include in gross income.

a. A taxpayer sold a beauty shop operated as a proprietorship for $60,000. The assets were valued as follows: tangible assets, $45,000; agreement not to compete, $10,000; and goodwill, $5,000. The seller's basis for the tangible assets is $45,000 but there is no basis for the other two assets.

b. The building in which a drug store is located is damaged by fire. The store had to be closed for two weeks while repairs were made. As a result, the insurance company paid the store $50,000 for lost profits during the period and $15,000 to cover overhead expenses.

c. E, Inc. leases land to V, Inc. The agreement states that the lease period is for five years and the annual lease payment is $1,000 per month. Under the terms of the lease, V immediately constructs a storage building on the land for $40,000. E receives $12,000 from V each year for three years. At the end of the third year, V cancels the lease and pays a cancellation penalty of $6,000. At this time, the building's market value is $30,000. Thus, in the third year, E received $18,000 cash and a building worth an additional $30,000. Determine E's taxable income from the lease for each of the three years.

d. A corporation accepted $100,000 from an insurance company as an out-of-court settlement of a lawsuit for patent infringement.

6-45 *Debt Cancellation.* DEF, Inc. is in the van conversion business. Due to stiff competition and a declining economy in the region served by DEF, the company has incurred significant operating losses during the past year. As of December 31 of the current year, DEF's financial statements reflect the following pertinent information:

Total assets..	$ 750,000
Total liabilities...	1,000,000
Tax attributes	
Adjusted basis of depreciable assets.....................	300,000
NOL carryover..	100,000
Capital loss carryover....................................	25,000

In an attempt to rescue the company from going out of business, DEF's suppliers have agreed to forgive $180,000 of indebtedness.

a. Assuming DEF is not in bankruptcy proceedings, what are the tax consequences to the corporation resulting from the cancellation of the debt?

b. Would your answer to part (a) change if DEF makes an election under Code § 108(b)(5)?

c. Would your answer to part (a) change if the $180,000 of debt is cancelled under bankruptcy proceedings?

d. Assume that the facts in the problem remain the same, except that DEF has total assets of $1 million and total liabilities of $750,000. What impact does the cancellation of $180,000 in debt now have on DEF?

6-46 *Miscellaneous Items.* In each of the following independent situations, determine how much, if any, the taxpayer must include in gross income.

a. A taxpayer's round trip mileage to and from work is 50 miles. Five fellow employees live near him and pay to ride with him. The taxpayer's records for the current year show $3,900 receipts and $3,120 automobile expenses.

b. While walking across campus, a taxpayer found a diamond ring. She notified the authorities on campus and paid $10 for an ad in the lost-and-found section of the newspaper. When six weeks went by with no response, she had the ring appraised. It was valued at $1,200. After six more weeks with no response, she sold the ring for $850.

c. A taxpayer was injured on the job and was out of work for most of the year. He received the following government benefits during the year: $800 in food stamps; $1,500 worker's compensation for the injury; and $1,800 in welfare payments.

d. A taxpayer sued her neighbor for malicious slander. The court awarded her $30,000 for personal injury due to indignities suffered as a result of the slander; $3,500 in lost income; and $200 reimbursement for medical expenses incurred. The taxpayer does not itemize deductions.

CUMULATIVE PROBLEMS

6-47   H, age 40, and W, age 38, are married with two dependent children: M, age 15, and N, age 16. H, who is president of a local bank, is paid a salary of $150,000. He also is the sole proprietor of a jewelry store that had a net profit for 1994 of $75,000. W, a registered nurse at a large hospital, is paid a salary of $50,000. In addition to the above income, H and W received the following during 1994:

a. $6,000 cash dividend on ABC, Inc. stock, which they own jointly. They paid $25,000 for the stock three years ago and it has a current market value of $40,000. ABC, Inc. has $300,000 of current and accumulated E&P.

b. $750 in interest on State of Michigan bonds that H owns.

c. $7,000 in interest on corporate bonds that H and W purchased two years ago at face value for $100,000.

d.   W received a check for $400 from her employer in recognition of her outstanding service to the hospital during the past 10 years.

e.   The bank provides H with $90,000 of group term life insurance protection. The bank provides all full-time employees with group term insurance.

f.   1,000 shares of XYZ common as a stock dividend. Prior to the distribution, H and W owned 9,000 shares of common with a basis of $15,000. H and W did not have the right to receive cash or other assets in lieu of the stock.

g.   Because W must be available should an emergency arise, she is required to eat her lunches in the hospital cafeteria. The value of the free meals provided by her employer during 1994 was $1,100.

h.   H's grandfather passed away in February 1994, leaving H a 400-acre farm in southern Illinois valued at $500,000. H rented the land to F, a neighboring farmer, for $13,000.

i.   In order to drain off the excess surface water from 10 acres, F (see h above) installed drainage pipe at a cost of $1,500.

j.   W sold 50 shares of DEF stock for $100 per share. She bought the stock four years ago for $1,800.

k.   H received a dividend check for $280 from the MNO Mutual Life Insurance Company. H purchased the policy in 1981, and W is the primary beneficiary.

l.   H and W's only itemized deductions were interest on their home mortgage, $18,000; property taxes on their home, $4,000; and charitable contributions, $6,000.

m.   The hospital withheld $11,000 of Federal income taxes on W's salary and the appropriate amount of FICA taxes. The bank withheld $30,000 in Federal income taxes from H's salary and the appropriate amount of FICA taxes. Furthermore, H's quarterly estimated tax payments for 1994 total $25,000.

Part I: Computation of Federal Income Tax.   Calculate H and W's 1994 Federal income tax liability (or refund) assuming they file a joint return.

Part II: Tax Planning Ideas.   H and W are very concerned about the amount of Federal income tax they now pay. Because they want to send M and N to private universities, they have come up with the following strategies, which they hope will reduce their family's total tax liability.

1.   In 1995 M and N will begin working at the jewelry store two nights a week and on Saturdays throughout the school year and 20 hours a week during the summer months. Each child will be paid $4,500 for services during the year.

2.   On January 1, 1995 H and W will sell their corporate bonds for $100,000 and invest the cash proceeds in Series EE savings bonds. H and W will use the bonds to pay for M and N's qualified educational expenses.

3. On January 1, 1995 H and W will gift their stock in ABC, Inc. to M and N equally.

4. Beginning in 1995 H will instruct the farmer who is leasing his Illinois farm to pay the $13,000 in rent directly to M and N (i.e., $6,500 each).

H and W have asked for your opinion concerning the above strategies. For each idea, explain why it will or will not reduce the family's total tax liability. Assuming H and W implement only the strategies that will reduce taxes, how much will the family save in taxes in 1995 compared to 1994? (Note: Calculate the 1995 tax using the tax law and rates applicable to 1994 and assume all other data from Part I above is the same.)

6-48 A and B are married with two children, ages 15 and 16. A, who is 45 years old, is president of Greenville Savings & Loan (a large financial institution located in Greenville, Michigan). During 1994 his salary amounted to $400,000. Additional information pertaining to A and B's financial affairs for 1994 is summarized below:

a. A and B purchased 1,000 shares of GHI, Inc. common stock on January 1, 1994 for $22,000. On May 1, 1994 A and B received 100 shares of GHI, Inc. common as a stock dividend. They did not have the right to receive cash or other assets in lieu of the stock.

b. On November 15, 1993 A and B purchased a small farm (50 acres) five miles from Greenville for $50,000. Although A and B originally planned to move to the farm when A retires, they ended up selling it on October 20, 1994 to a large real estate developer for $200,000.

c. On August 1, 1994 A and B redeemed Series EE bonds that had matured for $30,000. They originally purchased the bonds for $14,000. During the period they held the bonds, A and B never elected to include in income the annual increase in the redemption price.

d. B's father passed away on September 1, 1994. She inherited $100,000, which they deposited in a savings account at the Greenville Savings & Loan. The interest on the deposit amounted to $2,000 for the year.

e. Greenville Savings & Loan provided A with the following benefit package:

Fringe Benefit	Annual Cost to Greenville S & L
Health insurance premium..................	$2,400
Accident and disability premium............	600
Parking space.............................	200
Group-term life insurance of $150,000......	800

f. A and B's only itemized deductions were mortgage interest on their personal residence, $40,000; state and local taxes, $30,000; and charitable contributions, $8,000.

g. The Greenville Savings & Loan withheld $100,000 of Federal income taxes on A's salary and the appropriate amount of payroll taxes.

Part I: Calculation of Taxable Income and Tax Due. Compute A and B's taxable income and Federal income tax liability for 1994 assuming they file a joint return.

Part II: Tax Planning Suggestions. Assume that A and B come to you on July 1, 1994 seeking your advice on ways in which they can reduce their 1994 Federal income tax liability. They provide you with the following additional information:

1. The real estate developer, who is interested in acquiring A and B's 50 acres, is willing to defer the purchase date to November 16, 1994. What would you recommend A and B do? Explain your answer.

2. A and B would like to get the best return possible on the money they will receive from the sale of their farm. Two options they are considering are (1) invest the proceeds in corporate bonds paying 7% annually and (2) purchase State of Michigan bonds paying $5\frac{1}{2}$% annually. What would you recommend A and B do? Explain your answer.

3. A and B have been informed that the Series EE bonds that mature on August 1, 1994 can be exchanged for Series HH bonds that pay interest semiannually. What would you recommend A and B do? Explain your answer.

RESEARCH PROBLEMS

6-49   *Divorce.*   J and M are obtaining a divorce after ten years of marriage. They have two children. A draft of the divorce agreement and property settlement between them states that they will have joint custody of the children. They plan to live in the same general area and each child will live half of each year with each parent. Since J's A.G.I. is $40,000 and M's $15,000, he will pay her $100 per month for each child ($2,400 per year) and $500 per month for her support. The $500 ceases on his or her death, her remarriage, or when her A.G.I. equals his. In addition, J agrees to continue to pay premiums of $50 per month on his life insurance policy payable to her. All jointly owned property will be distributed as follows:

	Basis	Market Value	Transfer to
Home.............	$50,000	$80,000	M
Furnishings........	20,000	15,000	M
Investments.......	10,000	30,000	J

Each will keep his or her individually owned personal items and an automobile. This is an amicable divorce and they both request your advice. Their objective is to maximize total tax benefits without making too many changes to the agreement. Use tax-planning techniques when possible in responding to the following questions.

a. Who will be able to claim the children as dependents?

b. What is each one's filing status for the current year if neither one remarries?

c. Does the $500 per month qualify as alimony? Does the $50 per month qualify as alimony?

d. J expects to make the $500 and $50 payments for three months while legally separated before the divorce. What are the tax effects during this period?

e. What is the tax effect of the distribution of jointly owned property to J and to M?

f. What tax planning advice could you give to J and M that would decrease their combined tax liability?

6-50   *Meals and Lodging.*   H and W are married with three children. The children are 8, 10, and 15 years old. H and W are purchasing a 500-acre farm, which they will manage and operate themselves. In addition, they will employ one full-time farmer year round and several part-time people at peak times. H will be responsible primarily for management of the operations, the crops, and the dairy herd and other farm animals. W will be responsible primarily for the garden, the chickens, providing meals for the family and farm hands, and maintaining the family home. The children are assigned farm chores to help their parents after school and on weekends.

The taxpayers prefer to operate the farm as a partnership but, after all factors are considered, are willing to incorporate the farm if it seems to provide greater benefits. Presently, they ask for detailed information about the residence on the farm and the groceries that will be purchased to feed them and their employees on the farm. Some of their specific questions are listed below.

a. What are the benefits and requirements covering meals and lodging provided by the business?

b. Is it possible to meet the requirements and obtain all or at least some of the benefits if the farm is operated as a proprietorship or partnership, or must it be operated as a corporation?

c. If full benefits are obtained, are any adjustments required for the children, for personal entertainment and meals shared with friends and relatives in the farm home, or any other personal use? If any adjustments are required, which ones, and are they made at cost or market value?

d. If full benefits are obtained, exactly what qualifies? For example, do all groceries qualify, including supplies that are not eaten, such as freezer bags to store frozen foods from the garden, soap, and bathroom supplies? Do all expenses for the home qualify, such as utilities, insurance, and repairs?

e. Should the business or should H and W own the home?

f. Is it acceptable for H and W to purchase the food and be reimbursed by the business?

Some suggested research materials:

Code § 119 and accompanying Regulations.
Kowalski v. Comm., 77-2 USTC ¶9748, 40 AFTR2d 6128, 434 U.S. 77 (USSC, 1977).
Armstrong v. Phinney, 68-1 USTC ¶9355, 21 AFTR2d 1260, 394 F.2d 661.
Rev. Rul. 53-80, 1953-1 C.B. 62.

6-51 *Discharge of Indebtedness.* T, who is single, purchased a new home in 1976 from the XYZ Construction Co. for $55,000. She received a 7.25 percent mortgage from the Federal Savings and Loan Association (FS&L). Currently, the home's fair market value is approximately double its original purchase price. Since interest rates have risen significantly in recent months, FS&L wants to rid itself of the low 7.25 percent mortgage. Lending to others at a much higher interest rate would clearly enhance FS&L's profits. Consequently, during the current year FS&L sent a letter to T offering to cancel the mortgage (which had a remaining principal balance of $35,000) in return for a payment of $29,000. T took advantage of the prepayment opportunity, thus receiving a discount equal to the difference between the remaining principal balance of $35,000 and the amount paid by T of $29,000, or $6,000.

a. Although T is pleased she no longer has a monthly mortgage payment, she is concerned about the possible tax consequences resulting from the discharge of indebtedness. T has come to you for your advice.

b. Assume that the fair market value of T's residence has declined to $25,000 due to the construction of a nearby land fill operation. Does this fact change your answer?

Some suggested research materials:

Code §§ 61(a)(12), 108(a)(1), and 108(e)(5).
Sutphin v. U.S., 88-1 USTC ¶9269, 1 AFTR2d 88-990, 14 F.2d 545 (Ct. Cls., 1988).
Hirsch v. Comm., 40-2 USTC ¶9791, 25 AFTR 1038, 115 F.2d 656 (CA-7, 1940).

6-52 *Compensatory Damages.*   T. J. Taxpayer, CLU, has owned an insurance agency in Santa Rosa, California since 1960. As an independent agent, he represented five companies selling auto, home, commercial, and life insurance. Because of his excellent reputation in the community, T. J. has built a very successful agency. Last year, T. J. applied for an agency license from the American Life Insurance Co. in order to broaden his life insurance business. In reviewing his application, American requested a credit report from Federal Credit. Federal Credit provided copies to American Life as well as other insurance companies.

   The credit report contained numerous false accusations. In addition to questioning Taxpayer's integrity, the report stated that T. J. seldom returned phone calls from clients and lacked understanding of basic insurance practices and concepts. As a result, American Life denied T. J. a license to sell its life insurance. Because the report adversely affected his ability to work with existing clients and to attract new business, T. J.'s profits declined considerably.

   T. J. sued Federal Credit for libel, claiming that the credit report was issued with intent to damage his business or professional reputation. The jury found that Federal Credit had committed libel and awarded him $100,000 in compensatory damages. T. J. has heard conflicting comments from various sources about whether the $100,000 is taxable and comes to you for help. When researching this issue, you come across a number of cases and rulings.

   a.   Two Circuit Courts of Appeal have expressed their opinion concerning the taxability of damages received for injury to an individual's business or professional reputation. What was their conclusion? Give a summary of the analysis each court used in arriving at its decision.
   b.   What is the Tax Court's position concerning compensatory damages? Is the Tax Court's current position a reversal of its previously held position? If so, explain why the Tax Court changed its mind.
   c.   What is the Internal Revenue Service's position with respect to compensatory damages?
   d.   What advice would you give T. J. Taxpayer concerning the taxability of the $100,000?

6-53 *Sex Discrimination.*   Alice Johnson has worked for the LSMFT Corporation for ten years. In March 1992, after talking with various company employees, Alice came to the realization that there was a significant pay differential between men and women. In fact, she discovered that the corporation had modified its compensation package in 1986 whereby the salaries of employees in certain male-dominated pay schedules were increased but those in certain female-dominated pay schedules were either unchanged or reduced.

   As a result, Alice Johnson brought suit (under Title VII of the Civil Rights Act of 1964) in District Court against the LSMFT Corporation alleging unlawful discrimination in the payment of wages based upon gender. Alice sought back pay from the company in the amount of $10,000 to eliminate the discrimination. Rather than incur substantial costs in litigating the issue, LSMFT reached an out-of-court settlement with Alice on January 15, 1994. The settlement requires LSMFT to pay Alice back pay of $8,000 and to develop gender-neutral pay schedules.

   Is the $8,000 subject to tax as wages under § 61(a) or excludable from income under § 104(a)(2) as damages received on account of personal injuries?

PART III

DEDUCTIONS AND LOSSES

CONTENTS

CHAPTER 7 ▪ OVERVIEW OF DEDUCTIONS AND LOSSES

CHAPTER 8 ▪ EMPLOYEE BUSINESS EXPENSES

CHAPTER 9 ▪ CAPITAL RECOVERY: Depreciation, Amortization, and Depletion

CHAPTER 10 ▪ CERTAIN BUSINESS DEDUCTIONS AND LOSSES

CHAPTER 11 ▪ ITEMIZED DEDUCTIONS

CHAPTER 12 ▪ DEDUCTIONS FOR CERTAIN INVESTMENT EXPENSES AND LOSSES

LEARNING OBJECTIVES

Upon completion of this chapter you will be able to:

- Recognize the general requirements for deducting expenses and losses
- Define the terms *ordinary*, *necessary*, and *reasonable* as they apply to business deductions
- Recognize tax accounting principles with respect to deductions and losses
- Explain the proper treatment of employee business expenses
- Describe the importance of properly classifying expenses as deductions *for* or *from* adjusted gross income
- Classify expenses as deductions *for* or *from* adjusted gross income
- Recognize statutory, administrative, and judicial limitations on deductions and losses
- Explain tax planning considerations for optimizing deductions

CHAPTER OUTLINE

Deduction Defined	7-1
Deductions for Expenses: General Requirements	7-2
General Rules: Code §§ 162 and 212	7-2
Related to Carrying on a Business or an Income-Producing Activity	7-3
Ordinary and Necessary Expenses	7-7
Reasonable Expenses	7-8
Paid or Incurred During the Taxable Year	7-9
Employee Business Expenses	7-15
Deductions for Losses	7-15
Classification of Expenses	7-16
Importance of Classification	7-16
Deductions for A.G.I.	7-17
Itemized Deductions	7-18
Self-Employed versus Employee	7-19
Limitations on Deductions	7-22
Hobby Expenses and Losses	7-23
Personal Living Expenses	7-26
Capital Expenditures	7-27
Business Investigation Expenses and Start-Up Costs	7-29
Public Policy Restrictions	7-31
Lobbying and Political Contributions	7-33
Expenses and Interest Relating to Tax-Exempt Income	7-35
Related Taxpayer Transactions	7-36
Payment of Another Taxpayer's Obligation	7-39
Substantiation	7-40
Tax Planning Considerations	7-41
Maximizing Deductions	7-41
Timing of Deductions	7-42
Expenses Relating to Tax-Exempt Income	7-42
"Points" on Mortgages	7-42
Hobbies	7-43
Problem Materials	7-44

Chapter 7

OVERVIEW OF DEDUCTIONS
AND LOSSES

As explained in Chapter 3, the income tax is imposed on taxable income, a quantity defined as the difference between gross income and allowable deductions.[1] The concept of gross income was explored in Chapters 5 and 6. This chapter and the following four chapters examine the subject of deductions.

There is little doubt that when it comes to taxation, the questions asked most frequently concern deductions. What is deductible? Can this expense be deducted? How much can I deduct? This is a familiar refrain around taxpaying time, and rightfully so, since any item which might be deductible reduces the tax that otherwise must be paid. Many of the questions concerning deductions are easily answered by merely referring to the basic criteria. On the other hand, many items representing potential deductions are subject to special rules. The purpose of this chapter is to introduce the general rules which are in fact used for determining the answer to that age-old question: Is it deductible?

DEDUCTION DEFINED

In the preceding chapters, the definition given for income was described as being "all-inclusive" (i.e., gross income includes *all* items of income except those specifically excluded by law). Given this concept of income, it might be assumed that a similarly broad meaning is given to the term deduction. Deductions, however, are defined narrowly. Deductions are only those *particular* expenses, losses, and other items for which a deduction is authorized.[2] The significance of this apparently meaningless definition is found in the last word—"authorized." *Nothing is deductible unless it is allowed by the Code.* It is a well-established principle that before a deduction may be claimed the taxpayer must find some statutory provision permitting the deduction. The courts consistently have affirmed this principle, stating that a taxpayer has no constitutional right to a deduction. Rather, a taxpayer's right to a deduction depends solely on "legislative grace" (i.e., Congress has enacted a statute allowing the deduction).[3]

---

[1] § 63.

[2] § 161.

[3] *New Colonial Ice Co. v. Helvering*, 4 USTC ¶1292, 13 AFTR 1180, 292 U.S. 435 (USSC, 1934).

Although a taxpayer's deductions require statutory authorization, this does not mean that a particular deduction must be specifically mentioned in the Code. While several provisions are designed to grant the deduction for a specific item, such as § 163 for interest expense and § 164 for taxes, most deductions are allowed because they satisfy the conditions of some broadly defined category of deductions. For example, no specific deduction is allowed for the advertising expense of a restaurant owner, but the expense may be deductible if it meets the criteria required for deduction of *business expenses*.

The remainder of this chapter examines those provisions authorizing several broad categories of deductions: § 162 on trade or business expenses, § 212 on expenses of producing income, and § 165 on losses. In addition to these deduction-granting sections, several provisions that expressly deny or limit deductions for certain items are considered. The rules provided by these various provisions establish the basic framework for determining whether a deduction is allowed. Once the deductibility of an item is determined, an additional problem exists for individual taxpayers—the deduction must be classified as either a deduction *for* adjusted gross income or a deduction *from* adjusted gross income (itemized deduction). The classification process is also explained in this chapter.

DEDUCTIONS FOR EXPENSES: GENERAL REQUIREMENTS

Given that the taxpayer can deduct only those items that are authorized, what deductions does Congress in fact allow? The central theme found in the rules governing deductions is relatively straightforward: those expenses and losses incurred in business and profit-seeking activities are deductible while those incurred in purely personal activities are not. The allowance for business and profit-seeking expenses stems in part from the traditional notion that income is a *net* concept. From a conceptual perspective, income does not result until revenues exceed expenses. It generally follows from this principle that it would be unfair to tax the revenue from an activity but not allow deductions for the expenses that produced it.

In light of the Code's approach to deductions, many commentators have aptly stated that the costs of *earning* a living are deductible while the costs of living are not. Although this is a good rule of thumb, it is also an over-generalization. As will become clear, the Code allows deductions not only for the costs of producing income, but also for numerous personal expenses such as interest on home mortgages, property taxes, medical expenses, and charitable contributions. To complicate matters further, the line between personal and business expenses is often difficult to draw. For this reason, the various rules governing deductions must be examined closely.

GENERAL RULES: CODE §§ 162 AND 212

Two provisions in the Code provide the authority for the deduction of most expenses: § 162 concerning trade or business expenses and § 212 relating to expenses for the production of income. Numerous other provisions of the Code pertain to deductions. These other provisions, however, normally build on the basic rules contained in §§ 162 and 212. For this reason, the importance of these two provisions cannot be overstated.

Section 162(a) on trade or business expenses reads, in part, as follows:

> In General.—There shall be allowed as a deduction all the ordinary and necessary expenses paid or incurred during the taxable year in carrying on any trade or business, including—
>
> (1) a reasonable allowance for salaries or other compensation for personal services actually rendered;
> (2) traveling expenses (including amounts expended for meals and lodging other than amounts which are lavish or extravagant under the circumstances) while away from home in the pursuit of a trade or business;
> (3) rentals or other payments required to be made as a condition to the continued use or possession, for purposes of the trade or business, of property to which the taxpayer has not taken or is not taking title or in which he has no equity.

Although § 162(a) specifically enumerates three items that are deductible, the provision's primary importance lies in its general rule: ordinary and necessary expenses of carrying on a trade or business are deductible.

Section 212 contains a general rule very similar to that found in § 162. Section 212, in part, reads as follows:

> In the case of an individual, there shall be allowed as a deduction all the ordinary and necessary expenses paid or incurred during the taxable year—
>
> (1) for the production or collection of income;
> (2) for the management, conservation, or maintenance of property held for the production of income. . . .

Production of income expenses are normally those related to investments, such as investment advisory fees and safe deposit box rentals.

An examination of the language of §§ 162 and 212 indicates that a deduction is allowed under either section if it meets *four* critical requirements. The expense must have all of the following properties:

1. It must be related to carrying on a trade or business or an income-producing activity.

2. It must be ordinary and necessary.

3. It must be reasonable.

4. It must be paid or incurred during the taxable year.

It should be emphasized, however, that satisfaction of these criteria does not ensure deductibility. Other provisions in the Code often operate to prohibit or limit a deduction otherwise granted by §§ 162 and 212. For example, an expense may be ordinary, necessary, and related to carrying on a business, but if it is also related to producing tax-exempt income, § 265 prohibits a deduction. This system of allowing, yet disallowing, deductions is a basic feature in the statutory scheme for determining deductibility.

RELATED TO CARRYING ON A BUSINESS OR AN INCOME-PRODUCING ACTIVITY

The Activity. Whether an expense is deductible depends in part on the type of activity in which it was incurred. A deduction is authorized by § 162 only if it is paid or incurred in an activity which constitutes a trade or business. Similarly, § 212 permits a deduction

only if it is paid or incurred in an activity for the production or collection of income. The purpose of each of these requirements is to deny deductions for expenses incurred in an activity which is *primarily personal* in nature. For example, the costs incurred in pursuing what is merely a hobby, such as collecting antiques or racing automobiles, normally would be considered nondeductible personal expenditures. Of course, this assumes that such activities do not constitute a trade or business.

The Code does not provide any clues as to when an activity will be considered a trade or business or an income-producing activity rather than a personal activity. Over the years, however, one criterion has emerged from the many court cases involving the issue. To constitute a trade or business or an income-producing activity, the activity must be *entered into for profit.*[4] In other words, for the taxpayer's expenses to be deductible, they must be motivated by his or her hope for a profit. For this reason, taxpayers who collect antiques or race automobiles can deduct all of the related expenses if they are able to demonstrate that they did so with the hope of producing income. In such case, they would be considered to be in a trade or business. If the required profit motive is lacking, however, expenses of the activity generally are not deductible except to the extent the activity has income.

As may be apparent, the critical question in this area is what inspired the taxpayer's activities. The factors to be used in evaluating the taxpayer's motivation, along with the special provisions governing activities which are not engaged in for profit—the so-called hobby loss rules—are considered in detail later in this chapter.

A profit motive is the only requirement necessary to establish existence of an *income-producing* activity. However, the courts have imposed an additional requirement before an activity qualifies as a *trade or business*. Business status requires both a profit motive and a sufficient degree of taxpayer involvement in the activity to distinguish the activity from a passive investment. No clear guidelines have emerged indicating when a taxpayer's activities rise to the level of carrying on a business. The courts, however, generally have permitted business treatment where the taxpayer has devoted a major portion of time to the activities or the activities have been regular or continuous.[5]

> **Example 1.**   C owns six rental units, including several condominiums and town-houses. He manages his rental properties entirely by himself. His managing activities include seeking new tenants, supplying furnishings, cleaning and preparing the units for occupancy, advertising, and bookkeeping. In this case, C's involvement with the rental activities is sufficiently continuous and systematic to constitute a business.[6] If the rental activities were of a more limited nature, they might not qualify as a trade or business. The determination ultimately depends on the facts of the particular situation.[7]

---

[4] *Doggett v. Burrett*, 3 USTC ¶1090, 12 AFTR 505, 65 F.2d 192 (CA-D.C., 1933).

[5] *Grier v. U.S.*, 55-1 USTC ¶9184, 46 AFTR 1536, 218 F.2d 603 (CA-2, 1955).

[6] *Edwin R. Curphey*, 73 T.C. 766 (1980).

[7] *Ibid.*

Example 2. H owns various stocks and bonds. Her managerial activities related to these securities consist primarily of maintaining records and collecting dividends and interest. She rarely trades in the market. These activities are those normally associated with a passive investor, and accordingly would not constitute a trade or business under § 162 (they would be considered an income-producing activity under § 212).[8] On the other hand, if H had a substantial volume of transactions, made personal investigations of the corporations in which she was interested in purchasing, and devoted virtually every day to such work, her activities could constitute a trade or business.[9] Again, however, the answer depends on the facts.

Distinguishing between §§ 162 and 212. Prior to enactment of § 212, many investment-related expenses were not deductible because the activities did not constitute a business. The enactment of § 212 in 1942 allowing for the deduction of expenses related to production or collection of income enabled the deduction of investment-oriented expenses. This expansion of the deduction concept to include so-called "nonbusiness" or investment-related expenses eliminates the need for an activity to constitute a business before a deduction is allowed. As a result, the issue of deductibility (*assuming* the other requirements are met) is effectively reduced to a single important question: Is the expense related to an activity engaged in for profit?

It may appear that the addition of § 212 completely removed the need for determining whether the activity resulting in the expense constitutes a business or is merely for the production of income. However, the distinction between business and production of income expenses remains important. For example, the classification of the expense as a deduction for or from adjusted gross income may turn on whether the expense is a trade or business expense or a production of income expense. Production of income expenses (other than those related to rents or royalties) are usually miscellaneous itemized deductions that can be deducted only to the extent they *exceed* 2 percent of adjusted gross income. In contrast, most business expenses are deductions for adjusted gross income and are deductible in full.

Example 3. Refer to *Example 2*. In the first situation, where H is considered a passive investor, her investment-related expenses (e.g., subscriptions to stock advisory services and investment newsletters) would be miscellaneous itemized deductions and deductible only to the extent they exceed 2% of adjusted gross income. In the second situation, however, the same type of expenses would be deductions for adjusted gross income since H's trading activities qualify as a trade or business.

---

[8] *Higgins v. Comm.*, 41-1 USTC ¶9233, 25 AFTR 1160, 312 U.S. 212 (USSC, 1941).

[9] *Samuel B. Levin v. U.S.*, 79-1 USTC ¶9331, 43 AFTR2d 79-1057, 597 F.2d 760 (Ct. Cls., 1979). But see *Joseph Moller v. U.S.* 83-2 USTC ¶9698, 52 AFTR2d 83-6333 (CA-FC, 1983) where, for purposes of the home office deduction, the court held that the taxpayer's management of his substantial investment portfolio could not be a trade or business regardless of how continuous, regular, and extensive the activities were.

Another reason for ascertaining whether the activity constitutes a business relates to the use of the phrase "trade or business" in other Code Sections. The phrase "trade or business" appears in at least 60 different Code Sections, and the interpretation given to this phrase often controls the tax treatment. For example, whether an activity is an active business or a passive investment affects the tax consequences related to losses (deductible or limited), bad debts (short-term capital loss vs. ordinary loss), property sales (capital gain or loss vs. ordinary gain or loss), expenses for offices in the home (deductible vs. nondeductible), and limited expensing of depreciable property (allowed vs. disallowed).[10]

The Relationship. Before an expense is deductible under §§ 162 or 212, it must have a certain relationship to the trade or business or income-producing activity. The Regulations require that business expenses must be directly connected with or must pertain to the taxpayer's trade or business.[11] Similarly, production of income expenses must bear a reasonable and proximate relationship to the income-producing activity.[12] Whether an expenditure is directly related to the taxpayer's trade or business or income-producing activity usually depends on the facts. For example, the required relationship for business expenses normally exists where the expense is primarily motivated by business concerns or arises as a result of business, rather than personal, needs.[13]

> **Example 4.** While driving from one business to another, T struck a pedestrian with his automobile. He paid and deducted legal fees and damages in connection with the accident that were disallowed by the IRS. The Court found that the expenses were not directly related to, nor did they proximately result from, the taxpayer's business. The accident was merely incidental to the transportation and was related only remotely to the business.[14]

Whether a particular item is deductible often hinges on whether the expense was incurred for business or personal purposes. Consider the case of a law enforcement officer who is required to keep in top shape to retain his employment. Is the cost of a health club membership incurred for business or personal purposes? Similarly, can a disc jockey who obtains dentures to improve his speech deduct the cost as a business expense? Unfortunately, many expenses—like these—straddle the business-personal fence and the final determination is difficult. In both the cases above, the Court denied the taxpayers' deductions on the theory that such expenses were inherently personal.

---

[10] See §§ 165, 166, 1221, 280A, and 179.

[11] Reg. § 1.162-1(a).

[12] Reg. § 1.212-1(d).

[13] *U.S. v. Gilmore*, 63-1 USTC ¶9285, 11 AFTR2d 758, 372 U.S. 39 (USSC, 1963).

[14] *Julian D. Freedman v. Comm.*, 62-1 USTC ¶9400, 9 AFTR2d 1235, 301 F.2d 359 (CA-5, 1962); but see *Harold Dancer*, 73 T.C. 1103 (1980), where the Tax Court allowed the deduction when the taxpayer was traveling between two locations of the *same* business. Note how the subtle change in facts substantially alters the result!

Another common question concerns expenses paid or incurred prior to the time that income is earned. In the case of § 212 expenses, it is not essential that the activity produce income currently. For example, expenses may be deductible under § 212 even though there is little likelihood that the property will be sold at a profit or will ever produce income.[15] Deductions are allowed as long as the transaction was entered into for profit.

> **Example 5.** B purchased a vacant lot three years ago as an investment. During the current year she paid $200 to have it mowed. Although the property is not currently producing income, the expense is deductible since it is for the conservation or maintenance of property held for the production of income.

ORDINARY AND NECESSARY EXPENSES

The second test for deductibility is whether the expense is ordinary and necessary. An expense is *ordinary* if it is normally incurred in the type of business in which the taxpayer is involved.[16] This is not to say that the expense is habitual or recurring.[17] In fact, the expense may be incurred only once in the taxpayer's lifetime and be considered ordinary. The test is whether other taxpayers in similar businesses or income-producing activities would customarily incur the same expense.

> **Example 6.** P has been in the newspaper business for 35 years. Until this year, his paper had never been sued for libel. To protect the reputation of the newspaper, P incurred substantial legal costs related to the libel suit. Although the taxpayer has never incurred legal expenses of this nature before, the expenses are ordinary since it is common in the newspaper business to incur legal expenses to defend against such attacks.[18]

It is interesting to note that the "ordinary" criterion normally becomes an issue in circumstances which are, in fact, unusual. For example, in *Goedel*,[19] a stock dealer paid premiums for insurance on the life of the President of the United States, fearing that his death would disrupt the stock market and his business. The Court denied the deduction on the grounds that the payment was not ordinary but unusual or extraordinary.

---

[15] Reg. § 1.212-1(b).

[16] *Deputy v. DuPont*, 40-1 USTC ¶9161, 23 AFTR 808, 308 U.S. 488 (USSC, 1940).

[17] *Dunn and McCarthy, Inc. v. Comm.*, 43-2 USTC ¶9688, 31 AFTR 1043, 139 F.2d 242 (CA-2, 1943).

[18] *Welch v. Helvering*, 3 USTC ¶1164, 12 AFTR 1456, 290 U.S. 111 (USSC, 1933).

[19] 39 B.T.A. 1 (1939).

A deductible expense not only must be ordinary, but also necessary. An expense is *necessary* if it is appropriate, helpful, or capable of making a contribution to the taxpayer's profit-seeking activities.[20] The necessary criterion, however, is rarely applied to deny a deduction. The courts have refrained from such a practice since to do so would require overriding the judgment of the taxpayer.[21] The courts apparently feel that it would be unfair to judge *currently* whether a previous expenditure was necessary at the time it was incurred.

It should be emphasized that not all necessary expenses are ordinary expenses. Some expenses may be appropriate and helpful to the taxpayer's business but may not be normally incurred in that particular business. In such case, no deduction is allowed.

> **Example 7.** W was an officer in his father's corporation. The corporation, unable to pay its debts, was adjudged bankrupt. After the corporation was discharged from its debts, W decided to resume his father's business on a fresh basis. To reestablish relations with old customers and to solidify his credit standing, W paid as much of the old debts as he could. The Supreme Court held that the expenses were necessary in the sense they were appropriate and helpful in the development of W's business. However, the Court ruled that the payments were not ordinary since men do not usually pay the debts of another.[22]

REASONABLE EXPENSES

The third requirement for a deduction is that the expense be reasonable in amount. An examination of § 162(a) reveals that the term "reasonable" is used only in conjunction with compensation paid for services (e.g., a reasonable allowance for salaries). The courts have held, however, that reasonableness is implied in the phrase "ordinary and necessary."[23] In practice, the reasonableness standard is most often applied in situations involving salary payments made by a closely held corporation to a shareholder who also is an employee. In these situations, if the compensation paid exceeds that ordinarily paid for similar services—that which is reasonable—the excessive payment may represent a nondeductible dividend distribution.[24] Dividend treatment of the excess occurs if the amount of the excessive payment received by each employee closely relates to the number of shares of stock owned.[25] The distinction between reasonable compensation and dividend is critical because characterization of the payment as a dividend results in double taxation (i.e., it is taxable to the shareholder-employee and not deductible by the corporation).

---

[20] *Supra*, Footnote 18. See also *Comm. v. Heininger*, 44-1 USTC ¶9109, 31 AFTR 783, 320 U.S. 467 (USSC, 1943).

[21] *Supra*, Footnote 18.

[22] *Supra*, Footnote 18.

[23] *Comm. v. Lincoln Electric Co.*, 49-2 USTC ¶9388, 38 AFTR 411, 176 F.2d 815 (CA-6, 1949).

[24] Reg. § 1.162-7(b)(1).

[25] Reg. § 1.162-8.

Example 8.　B and C own 70 and 30% of X Corporation, respectively. Employees in positions similar to that of B earn $60,000 annually while those in positions similar to C's earn $20,000. During the year, the corporation pays B a salary of $130,000 and C a salary of $50,000. The excessive payment of $100,000 [($130,000 + $50,000) − ($60,000 + $20,000)] is received by B and C in direct proportion to their percentage ownership of stock (i.e., B's salary increased by $70,000 or 70% of the excessive payment). Because the payments are in excess of that normally paid to employees in similar positions and the excessive payment received by each is closely related to his stockholdings, the excessive payment may be treated as a nondeductible dividend.

Some of the factors used by the IRS when considering the reasonableness of compensation are [26]

1.　Duties performed (i.e., amount and character of responsibility)

2.　Volume and complexity of business handled (i.e., time required)

3.　Individual's ability and expertise

4.　Number of available persons capable of performing the duties of the position

5.　Corporation's dividend policies and history

PAID OR INCURRED DURING THE TAXABLE YEAR

Sections 162 and 212 both indicate that an expense is allowable as a deduction only if it is "paid or incurred during the taxable year." This phrase is used throughout the Code in sections concerning deductions. Use of both terms, "paid" and "incurred," is necessary because the year in which deductions are allowable depends on the method of accounting used by the taxpayer.[27] The term *paid* refers to taxpayers using the cash basis method of accounting while the term *incurred* refers to taxpayers using the accrual basis method of accounting. Accordingly, the year in which a deduction is allowed usually depends on whether the cash or accrual basis method of accounting is used.

Cash Basis Taxpayers.　For those taxpayers eligible to use the cash method (as discussed in Chapter 5), expenses are deductible in the taxable year when the expenses are actually paid.[28] However, there are numerous exceptions to this rule that are designed to restrict the flexibility a cash basis taxpayer would otherwise have in reporting deductions. Without these restrictions, a cash basis taxpayer could choose the year of deductibility simply by appropriately timing the cash payment. Before examining these restrictions, it is important to understand when the taxpayer is considered to have paid the expense.

---

[26]　Internal Revenue Manual 4233, § 232.　　[28]　Reg. § 1.446-1(a)(1).

[27]　§ 461(a).

Time of Payment. For the most part, determining when a cash basis taxpayer has paid an expense is not difficult. A cash basis taxpayer "pays" the expense when cash, check, property, or service is transferred. Neither a promise to pay nor a note evidencing such promise is considered payment. Consequently, when a cash basis taxpayer buys on credit, no deduction is allowed until the debts are paid. However, if the taxpayer borrows cash and then pays the expense, the expense is deductible when paid. For this reason, a taxpayer who charges expenses to a credit card is deemed to have borrowed cash and made payment when the charge is made. Thus, the deduction is claimed when the charge is actually made and not when the bank makes payment or when the taxpayer pays the bill.[29] If the taxpayer uses a "pay-by-phone" account, the expense is deductible in the year the financial institution paid the amount as reported on a monthly statement sent to the taxpayer.[30] When the taxpayer pays by mail, payment is usually considered made when the mailing occurs (i.e., dropping it in the post-office box).[31]

Restrictions on Use of Cash Method. Under the general rule, a cash basis taxpayer deducts expenses when paid. Without restrictions, however, aggressive taxpayers could liberally interpret this provision to authorize not only deductions for routine items, but also deductions for capital expenditures and other expenses that benefit future periods (e.g., supplies, prepaid insurance, prepaid rent, and prepaid interest). To preclude such an approach, numerous limitations have been imposed.

One of the more fundamental restrictions applying to cash basis taxpayers concerns inventories. For example, if no limitation existed, a cash basis owner of a department store could easily reduce or eliminate taxable income by increasing purchases of inventory near year-end and deducting their cost. To prevent this possibility, the Regulations require taxpayers to use the accrual method for computing sales and costs of goods sold if inventories are an income producing factor.[32] In such cases, inventory costs must be capitalized, and accounts receivable and accounts payable (with respect to cost of goods sold) must be created. The taxpayer could continue to use the cash method for other transactions, however.

Provisions of both the Code and the Regulations limit the potential for deducting capital expenditures, prepaid expenses, and the like. As discussed later in this chapter, Code § 263 specifically denies the deduction for a capital expenditure; such costs as those for equipment, vehicles, and buildings normally are recovered through depreciation, as discussed in Chapter 9.

The Regulations—at least broadly—deal with other expenditures that are not capital expenditures per se, but which do benefit future periods. According to the Regulations, any expenditure resulting "in the creation of an asset having a useful life which extends *substantially beyond the close of the taxable year* may not be deductible when made, or may be deductible only in part."[33] In this regard, the courts agree that "substantially beyond" means a useful life of more than one year.[34] Perhaps the simplest example of

---

[29] Rev. Rul. 78-39, 1978-1 C.B. 73.

[30] Rev. Rul. 80-335, 1980-2 C.B. 170.

[31] See Rev. Rul. 73-99, 1973-1 C.B. 412 for clarification of this general rule.

[32] Reg. § 1.446-1(c)(2).

[33] Reg. § 1.446-1(a)(1).

[34] *Martin J. Zaninovich*, 69 T.C. 605, *rev'd* in 80-1 USTC ¶9342, 45 AFTR2d 80-1442, 616 F.2d 429 (CA-9, 1980).

this rule as so interpreted concerns payments for supplies. Assuming the supplies would be exhausted before the close of the following tax year, a deduction should be allowable when payment is made. In regard to other prepayments, however, the application of this principle has spawned a hodgepodge of special rules.

Prepaid Rent. An Appeals Court decision suggests that prepayments of rents and prepayments for services may be deducted in the year paid when two conditions are present: (1) the period for which the payment is made does not exceed one year, and (2) the taxpayer is contractually obligated to prepay an amount for a period extending beyond the close of the year.[35] Other advanced payments of rentals can be deducted only during the period to which they relate.

> **Example 9.** R, a farmer, pays taxes based on the calendar year. In 1994 he leases farm land for the twenty-year period December 1, 1994 to November 30, 2014. The lease agreement provides that annual rent for the period December 1 to November 30 is payable on December 20 each year. The yearly rent is $24,000. On December 20, 1994 R pays the $24,000 rental for the next year. The prepayment is deductible because it is for a period not exceeding a year and R is obligated to pay for the entire year in advance on December 20. However, if the lease agreement required only monthly rentals of $2,000 each (instead of an annual payment of $24,000), only $2,000 would be deductible (representing the rent allocable to the month of December) because the remainder of the payment was voluntary.[36]

Prepaid Insurance. Prepayments of insurance premiums normally are not deductible when paid. Instead, the IRS holds that this expense must be prorated over the period that the insurance covers.[37] However, the "one year" exception noted above with respect to prepaid rent may also apply here.

> **Example 10.** On December 15, 1994 T purchased an insurance policy covering theft of his inventory. The policy cost $3,000 and covered 1995–1997. T may not deduct any of the cost in 1994. In each of the following three years, he will deduct $1,000.

Other Prepayments. Perhaps the Service's current view of the proper treatment of most prepayments is best captured in a ruling concerning prepaid feed. In this ruling, the taxpayer purchased a substantial amount of feed prior to the year in which it would be used.[38] The purchase was made in advance because the price was low due to a depressed market. The IRS granted a deduction for the prepayment because there was a business purpose for the advanced payment, the payment was not merely a deposit, and it did not

---

[35] *Supra*, Footnote 34.

[36] *Bonaire Development Co.*, 83-2 USTC ¶9428, 679 F.2d 159 (CA-9, 1983), *aff'g*, 76 T.C. 789 (1981).

[37] Rev. Rul. 70-413, 1970-2 C.B. 103.

[38] Rev. Rul. 79-229, 1979-2 C.B. 210. See also, *Kenneth Van Raden*, 71 T.C. 1083 (1979), *aff'd* in 81-2 USTC ¶9547, 48 AFTR2d 81-5607, 650 F.2d 1046 (CA-9, 1981).

materially distort income. Based on this ruling and related cases, prepayments normally should be deductible if the asset will be consumed by the close of the following year, there is a business purpose for the expenditure, and there is no material distortion of income.

Prepaid Interest. The Code expressly denies the deduction of prepaid interest. Prepaid interest must be capitalized and deducted ratably over the period of the loan.[39] The same is true for any costs associated with obtaining the loan. The sole exception is for "points" paid for a debt incurred by the taxpayer to purchase his or her principal residence. In this regard, the IRS has ruled that points incurred to refinance a home must be amortized over the term of the loan.[40] However, a recent Appeals Court case allowed a taxpayer to deduct the amount of points paid on refinancing a home. The proceeds were used to pay off a three-year, temporary loan that was made to allow the borrower time to secure permanent financing for the home.[41] The court stated that, since the temporary loan was merely an integrated step in securing permanent financing for the taxpayer's residence, the points were deductible currently.

> **Example 11.** K desires to obtain financing for the purchase of a new house costing $100,000. The bank agrees to make her a loan of 80% of the purchase price, or $80,000 (80% of $100,000) for thirty years at a cost of two points (two percentage "points" of the loan obtained). Thus, she must pay $1,600 (2% of $80,000) to obtain the loan. Assuming it is established business practice in her area to charge points in consideration of the loan, the $1,600 in points (prepaid interest) is deductible. However, if the house is not the principal residence of the taxpayer, then the prepaid interest must be deducted ratably over the 30-year loan period.

Accrual Basis Taxpayers. An accrual basis taxpayer deducts expenses when they are incurred. For this purpose, an expense is considered incurred when the *all events test* is satisfied and *economic performance* has occurred.[42] Two requirements must be met under the all events test: (1) all events establishing the existence of a liability must have occurred (i.e., the liability is fixed); and (2) the amount of the liability can be determined with reasonable accuracy. Therefore, before the liability may be accrued and deducted, it must be fixed and determinable.

> **Example 12.** In *Hughes Properties, Inc.*, an accrual basis corporation owned a gambling casino in Reno, Nevada that operated progressive slot machines that paid a large jackpot about every four months.[43] The increasing amount of the jackpot was maintained and shown by a meter. Under state gaming regulations, the jackpot

---

[39] § 461(g).

[40] Rev. Rul. 87-22, 1987-1 C.B.146.

[41] *James R. Huntsman*, 90-2 USTC ¶50,340, 66 AFTR2d 90-5020, 905 F2d 1182 (CA-8,1990). In an *Action on Decision* issued on February 11,1991, the IRS ruled that, although it will not appeal the *Huntsman* decision, it will not follow this decision outside the Eighth Circuit.

[42] § 461(h).

[43] *Hughes Properties, Inc.*, 86-1 USTC ¶9440, 58 AFTR2d 86-5015, 106 S. Ct. 2092 (USSC, 1986).

amount could not be turned back until the amount had been paid to a winner. In addition, the corporation had to maintain a cash reserve sufficient to pay all the guaranteed amounts. At the end of each taxable year, the corporation accrued and deducted the liability for the jackpot as accrued at year-end. The IRS challenged the accrual, alleging that the all events test had not been met, and that the amount should be deducted only when paid. It argued that payment of the jackpot was not fixed but contingent, since it was possible that the winning combination may never be pulled. Moreover, the Service pointed out the potential for tax avoidance: the corporation was accruing deductions for payments that may be paid far in the future, and thus—given the time value of money—overstated the amount of the deduction. The Supreme Court rejected these arguments, stating that the probability of payment was not a remote and speculative possibility. The Court noted that not only was the liability fixed under state law, but it also was not in the interest of the taxpayer to set unreasonably high odds, since customers would refuse to play and gamble elsewhere.

The all events test often operates to deny deductions for certain estimated expenditures properly accruable for financial accounting purposes. For example, the estimated cost of product guarantees, warranties, and contingent liabilities normally may not be deducted— presumably because the liability for such items has not been fixed or no reasonable estimate of the amount can be made.[44] However, the courts have authorized deductions for estimates where the obligation was certain and there was a reasonable basis (e.g., industry experience) for determining the amount of the liability.

The condition requiring *economic performance* was introduced in 1984 due to Congressional fear that the all events test did not prohibit so-called premature accruals. Prior to 1984, the courts—with increasing frequency—had permitted taxpayers to accrue and deduct the cost of estimated expenditures required to perform certain activities *prior* to the period when the activities were actually performed. For example, in one case, a strip-mining operator deducted the estimated cost of backfilling land which he had mined for coal.[45] The court allowed the deduction for the estimated expenses in the current year even though the backfilling was not started and completed until the following year. According to the court, the liability satisfied the all events test since the taxpayer was required by law to backfill the land and a reasonable estimate of the cost of the work could be made. A similar decision involved a taxpayer that was a self-insurer of its liabilities arising from claims under state and Federal worker's compensation laws.[46] Under these laws, the taxpayer was obligated to pay a claimant's medical bills, disability payments, and death benefits. In this situation, the taxpayer was allowed to accrue and deduct the estimated expenses for its obligations even though actual payments would extend over many years. In Congress' view, allowing the deduction in these and similar cases prior to the time when the taxpayer actually performed the services, provided

---

[44] *Bell Electric Co.*, 45 T.C. 158 (1965).

[45] *Paul Harrold v. Comm.*, 52-1 USTC ¶9107, 41 AFTR 442, 192 F.2d 1002 (CA-4, 1951).

[46] *Crescent Wharf & Warehouse Co. v. Comm.*, 75-2 USTC ¶9571, 36 AFTR2d 75-5246, 518 F.2d 772 (CA-5, 1975).

the goods, or paid the expenses, overstated the true cost of the expense, because the time value of money was ignored. Perhaps more importantly, Congress recognized that allowing deductions for accruals in this manner had become the foundation for many tax shelter arrangements. Accordingly, the economic performance test was designed to defer the taxpayer's deduction until the activities giving rise to the liability are performed.

The time at which economic performance is deemed to occur—and hence the period in which the deduction may be claimed—depends on the nature of the item producing the liability. A taxpayer's liabilities commonly arise in three ways, as summarized below.

1. *Liability of taxpayer to provide property and services.* When the taxpayer's liability results from an obligation to provide goods or services to a third party (e.g., perform repairs), economic performance occurs when the taxpayer provides the goods or services to the third party.

2. *Liability for property or services provided to the taxpayer.* When the taxpayer's liability arises from an obligation to pay for services, goods, or the use of property provided to (or to be provided to) the taxpayer (e.g., consulting, supplies, and rent), economic performance occurs when the taxpayer receives the services or goods or uses the property. Note that in this case, economic performance occurs when the taxpayer *receives* the consideration bargained for, while in the situation above it occurs when the taxpayer *provides* the consideration.

3. *Liability for payment arising under worker's compensation laws or any tort.* If the liability arises from an obligation to pay another person under any worker's compensation law or due to the taxpayer's tort, economic performance occurs as the payments are made.

Example 13. In 1994 C, an accrual basis corporation, contracted with P, a partnership, to drill 50 gas wells over a five-year period for $500,000. Absent the economic performance test, C could accrue and deduct the $500,000 fee in 1994 because the obligation is fixed and determinable. However, because economic performance has not occurred (i.e., the services have not been received by C), no deduction is permitted in 1994. Rather, C may deduct the expense when the wells are drilled.

Example 14. Same facts as above. Although P is obligated to perform services for C over the five-year period, P cannot prematurely accrue the cost of providing these services because economic performance has not occurred. Deduction is permitted only as the wells are drilled.

To prohibit the disruption of normal business and accounting practices, certain recurring expenses are exempted from the economic performance rules. The expense may be accrued and deducted if all of the following conditions are met.[47]

---

[47]   § 461(h)(3).

1. The all events test is satisfied.

2. Economic performance does in fact occur within a reasonable period after the close of the taxable year not to exceed eight and one-half months.

3. The item is recurring in nature, and the taxpayer consistently treats such items as incurred in the taxable year.

4. The item is either immaterial, or accrual in the earlier year results in a better match against income than accruing the item when economic performance occurs.

> **Example 15.**   Z, who uses the accrual basis and reports using the calendar year, operates a small construction business. He has contracted with a CPA firm to prepare monthly financial statements for the business for $300 a month. The financial statements for December normally are prepared by the end of January of the following year. Under the exception for recurring expenses, Z may accrue the charge for December even though the services are not performed until the next accounting period. In this case, the all events test is met, economic performance occurs shortly after year-end, and the item is recurring and probably immaterial.

EMPLOYEE BUSINESS EXPENSES

The definition of *trade or business* also includes the performance of services as an employee. In other words, an employee is considered to be in the business of being an employee. As a result, the ordinary and necessary expenses incurred by an employee in connection with his or her employment are deductible under § 162 as business expenses. Examples of deductible expenses typically incurred by employees include union dues, dues to trade and professional societies, subscriptions to professional journals, small tools and supplies, medical exams required by the employer, and work clothes and uniforms as well as their maintenance (where required as a condition of employment and not suitable for everyday use).[48] Expenses such as travel, entertainment, and education may also be deducted as employee business expenses under certain conditions explained in Chapter 8. As explained later in this chapter, employee business expenses—other than those which are reimbursed—are considered miscellaneous itemized deductions and thus deductible only to the extent they exceed 2 percent of A.G.I.

DEDUCTIONS FOR LOSSES

The general rules concerning deduction of losses are contained in § 165. This provision permits a deduction for any loss sustained which is not compensated for by insurance. The deductions for losses of an individual taxpayer, however, are limited to

1. Losses incurred in a trade or business

2. Losses incurred in a transaction entered into for profit

---

[48]   Rev. Rul. 70-474, 1970 C.B. 35.

3. Losses of property not connected with a trade or business if such losses arise by fire, storm, shipwreck, theft, or some other type of casualty

Note that personal losses—other than those attributable to a casualty—are not deductible. For example, the sale of a personal residence at a loss is not deductible.

Before a loss can be deducted, it must be evidenced by a closed and completed transaction. Mere decline in values or unrealized losses cannot be deducted. Normally, for the loss to qualify as a deduction, the property must be sold, abandoned, scrapped, or become completely worthless. The amount of deductible loss for all taxpayers cannot exceed the taxpayer's basis in the property. Special rules related to various types of losses are discussed in Chapter 10.

CLASSIFICATION OF EXPENSES

Once the deductibility of an item is established, the tax formula for individuals requires that the deduction be classified as either a deduction *for* adjusted gross income or a deduction *from* adjusted gross income (itemized deduction).[49] In short, the deduction process requires that two questions be asked. First, is the expense deductible? Second, is the deduction for or from adjusted gross income (A.G.I.)? Additional aspects of the first question are considered later in this chapter. At this point, however, it is appropriate to consider the problem of classification.

The classification process arose with the introduction of the standard deduction in 1944. The standard deduction was introduced to simplify the return form for the majority of individuals by eliminating the necessity of itemizing primarily personal deductions such as medical expenses and charitable contributions. In addition, the administrative burden of checking such deductions was eliminated. Although these objectives were satisfied by providing a blanket deduction in lieu of itemizing actual expenses, a new problem arose. The standard deduction created the need to classify deductions as either deductions that would be deductible in any event (deductions for A.G.I.), or deductions that would be deductible only if they exceeded the prescribed amount of the standard deduction (deductions from A.G.I.).

IMPORTANCE OF CLASSIFICATION

The classification problem is significant for several reasons. First, itemized deductions may be deducted only to the extent they exceed the standard deduction. For this reason, a taxpayer whose itemized deductions do not exceed the standard deduction would lose a deduction if a deduction for A.G.I. is improperly classified as a deduction from A.G.I. This would occur since deductions for A.G.I. are deductible without limitation.

A second reason for properly classifying deductions concerns the treatment of miscellaneous itemized deductions. As part of the tax overhaul in 1986, Congress limited the deduction of miscellaneous itemized deductions—defined below—to that amount which

---

[49] § 62.

exceeds 2 percent of A.G.I. This new limitation is extremely important. Under prior law, taxpayers who itemized deductions could misclassify a deduction for A.G.I. as an itemized deduction with little or no effect, since the expense would be deductible either one place or the other. Under the current scheme, however, misclassification of a deduction for A.G.I. as a miscellaneous itemized deduction would subject the expense to the 2 percent floor, possibly making it wholly or partially nondeductible.

A third reason for properly classifying deductions concerns A.G.I. itself. Limitations on deductions such as medical expenses and charitable contributions are expressed in terms of the taxpayer's A.G.I. For example, miscellaneous itemized deductions are deductible only to the extent they exceed 2 percent of A.G.I., medical expenses are deductible only to the extent they exceed 7.5 percent of A.G.I., and charitable contributions are deductible only to the extent of various limitations (50, 30, or 20 percent) based on A.G.I.

As discussed in Chapter 3, Congress has created two relatively new limitations that are based on A.G.I. First, the amount of itemized deductions (other than for medical expenses, casualty and theft losses, and investment interest) must be reduced by 3 percent of a taxpayer's A.G.I. in excess of $111,800. In addition, the deduction for personal exemptions is phased out as the taxpayer's A.G.I. exceeds a threshold amount (e.g., $167,700 for joint returns and $111,800 for a single taxpayer). Thus, the misclassification of a deduction for A.G.I. as an itemized deduction would result in a higher A.G.I. and could result in a lower deduction for itemized deductions and personal exemptions.

Adjusted gross income for Federal income tax purposes also serves as the tax base or the starting point for computing taxable income for many state income taxes. Several states do not allow the taxpayer to itemize deductions. Consequently, misclassification could result in an incorrect state tax liability.

Still another reason for properly classifying expenses concerns the self-employment tax. Under the social security and Medicare programs, self-employed individuals are required to make an annual contribution based on their net earnings from self-employment. Net earnings from self-employment include gross income from the taxpayer's trade or business less allowable trade or business deductions attributable to the income. Failure to properly classify a deduction as a deduction for A.G.I. attributable to self-employment income results in a higher self-employment tax.

DEDUCTIONS FOR A.G.I.

The deductions for A.G.I. are specifically identified in Code § 62. It should be emphasized, however, that § 62 merely classifies expenses; it does *not* authorize any deductions. Deductions *for* A.G.I. are

1. Trade or business deductions except those expenses incurred in the business of being an employee (e.g., expenses of a sole proprietorship or self-employment normally reported on Schedule C of Form 1040)

2. Two categories of employee business deductions:

   a. expenses that are reimbursed by an employee's employer (and included in the employee's income); and

   b. expenses incurred by a qualified performing artist (see below)

3. Losses from sale or exchange of property

4. Deductions attributable to rents or royalties

5. Deductions for contributions to Individual Retirement Accounts or Keogh retirement plans

6. Alimony deductions

7. Deductions for penalties imposed for premature withdrawal of funds from a savings arrangement

8. Deduction for 25 percent of premiums for family medical care insurance paid by qualified self-employed persons. Although this provision was repealed after December 31, 1993, Congress may revive and extend this deduction in 1994.

9. Deduction for 50 percent of self-employment tax paid by self-employed persons

10. Moving expenses

11. Certain other deductions

All of the above are deductible for A.G.I., while all other deductions are from A.G.I. (i.e., itemized deductions).

ITEMIZED DEDUCTIONS

As seen above, only relatively few expenses are deductible for A.G.I. The predominant expenses in this category are the deductions incurred by taxpayers who are self-employed (i.e., those carrying on as a sole proprietor). All other expenses are deductible from A.G.I. as itemized deductions.

Itemized deductions fall into two basic categories: those that are *miscellaneous itemized deductions* and those that are not. The distinction is significant because miscellaneous itemized deductions are deductible only to the extent they exceed 2% of A.G.I. Miscellaneous itemized deductions are all itemized deductions *other than* the following:

1. Interest

2. Taxes

3. Casualty and theft losses

4. Medical expenses

5. Charitable contributions

6. Gambling losses to the extent of gambling gains

7. Deduction where annuity payments cease before investment is recovered

8. Amortizable bond premium

9. Certain other deductions

The miscellaneous itemized deductions category is comprised primarily of *unreimbursed* employee business expenses, investment expenses, and deductions related to taxes such as tax preparation fees. Examples of these (assuming they are not reimbursed by the employer) include:

1. Employee travel away from home (including meals and lodging)

2. Employee transportation expenses

3. Outside salesperson's expenses [except that "statutory employees" (e.g., full-time life insurance salespersons, certain agent or commission drivers, and traveling salespersons) are allowed to report their income and expenses on a separate Schedule C and avoid the 2% of A.G.I. limitation]

4. Employee entertainment expenses

5. Employee home office expenses

6. Union dues

7. Professional dues and memberships

8. Subscriptions to business journals

9. Job-seeking expenses (in the same business)

10. Education expenses

11. Investment expenses, including expenses for an investment newsletter, investment advice, and rentals of safety deposit boxes

12. Tax preparation fees or other tax-related advice including that received from accountants or attorneys, tax seminars, and books about taxes

With respect to item 12 above, expenses related to tax preparation and resolving tax controversies normally are reported as miscellaneous itemized deductions. However, the IRS allows taxpayers who own a business, farm, or rental real estate or have royalty income to allocate the total cost of preparing their tax return to the cost of preparing Schedule C (trade or business income), Schedule E (rental and royalty income), or Schedule F (farm income) and deduct these costs "for" A.G.I. The same holds true for expenses incurred in resolving tax controversies, including expenses relating to IRS audits or business or rental activities.

SELF-EMPLOYED VERSUS EMPLOYEE

Under the current scheme of deductions for and from A.G.I., an important—and perhaps inequitable—distinction is made based on whether an individual is an employee or self-employed. As seen above, employees generally deduct all unreimbursed business expenses as itemized deductions. In contrast, self-employed taxpayers (i.e., sole proprietors or partners) deduct business expenses for A.G.I. At first glance, the difference appears trivial, particularly for those taxpayers who itemize their deductions. Recall, however, that an employee's business expenses are treated as miscellaneous itemized deductions

and thus deductible only to the extent that these and all other miscellaneous itemized deductions collectively exceed 2 percent of the taxpayer's A.G.I. Due to this distinction, deductibility often depends on the employment status of the taxpayer.

Example 16. T is an accountant. During the year she earns $30,000 and pays dues of $100 to be a member of the local CPA society. These were her only items of income and expense. If T practices as a self-employed sole proprietor (e.g., she has a small firm or partnership), the dues are fully deductible for A.G.I. However, if T is an employee, none of the expense is deductible since it does not exceed the 2% floor of $600 (2% × $30,000). If T's employer had reimbursed her for the expense and included the reimbursement in her income, the expense would have been completely deductible, totally offsetting the amount that T must include in income. If T is employed, but at the same time does some accounting work on her own, part-time, the treatment is unclear.

The logic for the distinction based on employment status is fragile at best. According to the committee reports, Congress believed that it was generally appropriate to disallow deductions for employee business expenses because employers reimburse employees for those expenses that are most necessary for employment. In addition, Congress felt that the treatment would simplify the system by relieving taxpayers of the burden of recordkeeping and at the same time relieving the burden of the IRS of auditing such deductions.

Reimbursed Expenses. As emphasized above, an employee's business expenses are generally deductible as itemized deductions unless a reimbursement is received. Where the employee is fully reimbursed and the reimbursement is included in income, the deduction is fully deductible for A.G.I. If only a portion of the expense is reimbursed and included in income, that portion is deductible for A.G.I. and the remainder is a miscellaneous itemized deduction.

Example 17. Professor K is employed by State University in the finance department. The department has a policy of reimbursing up to $50 for his costs of subscribing to finance journals. During the year, K spent $75 on subscriptions and received a $50 reimbursement. K's tentative A.G.I. is $40,000 (including the $50 reimbursement). He may deduct $50 for A.G.I. The remaining $25 is a miscellaneous itemized deduction which may or may not be deductible depending on whether this amount *plus* all other miscellaneous itemized deductions exceeds the 2% floor of $799 ($39,950 × 2%).

The discussion to this point assumes that all employee reimbursements are included by the employer in the employee's income. This is usually not the case, however. As discussed in Chapter 8, the employee may omit both the reimbursement and the expense from the return if, as is generally true, the reimbursement equals such expense and an adequate accounting is made to the employer. In fact, the IRS does not require the employer to file an information return under such circumstances.[50] As a result, an

---

[50]   Reg. § 1.6041-3(i).

employee expense reimbursement generally is not included in income, and the related expense is not deductible either as a deduction for A.G.I. or as an itemized deduction.

Whether a reimbursement is or is not included in the income of the employee, the effect on A.G.I. is the same. That is, there is no effect on A.G.I. The transaction is a "wash" economically for the employee and is, therefore, a "wash" on the employee's tax return. This concept is demonstrated below.

Example 18. Dr. R is employed by General Hospital. The hospital reimburses employees for the cost of subscribing to medical journals. During the year, Dr. R spent $100 on subscriptions and, after an adequate accounting, received a $100 reimbursement. If the reimbursement is included in Dr. R's income, she is allowed an offsetting deduction for A.G.I. If the reimbursement is not included in her income, she does not take any deduction with respect to the subscription cost.

	Reimbursement Included in Income	Reimbursement not Included in Income
Gross income	$100	$-0-
Deduction for A.G.I.	(100)	(-0-)
A.G.I.	$ -0-	$-0-

Expenses of Performing Artists. Most employee business expenses were relegated to second-class status in 1986 as they became subject to the 2 percent limitation. However, one group of employees, the struggling performing artists, escaped this restriction. These actors, actresses, musicians, dancers, and the like are technically employees but exhibit many attributes of the self-employed. They often work for several employers for little income yet incur relatively large unreimbursed expenses as they seek their fortunes. For these reasons, "qualified performing artists" are permitted to deduct their business expenses *for* A.G.I. To qualify, the individual must perform services in the performing arts as an employee for at least two employers during the taxable year, earning at least $200 from each. In addition, the individual's A.G.I. before business deductions cannot exceed $16,000. Lastly, the artist's business deductions must exceed 10 percent of his or her gross service income, otherwise they too are considered miscellaneous itemized deductions.

Example 19. Z is an actress. This year she worked in two Broadway productions for two different employers earning $7,000 from each for a total of $14,000. Her expenses, including the fee to her agent, were $2,000. She may deduct all of her expenses for A.G.I.

Self-Employed or Employee? The above discussion illustrates the importance of determining whether an individual is self-employed or is treated as an employee. However, whether an individual is self-employed or is an employee is often difficult to determine. An employee is a person who performs services for another individual subject

to that individual's direction and control.[51] In the employer-employee relationship, the right to control extends not only to the result to be accomplished but also to the methods of accomplishment. Accordingly, an employee is subject to the will and control of the employer as to both what will be done and how it will be done. In the case of the self-employed person, the individual is subject to the control of another only as to the end result, and not as to the means of accomplishment. Generally, physicians, lawyers, dentists, veterinarians, contractors, and subcontractors are not employees. An insurance agent or salesperson may be an employee or self-employed, depending on the facts. The courts have developed numerous tests for differentiating between employees and self-employed persons. Each of the following situations would suggest that an employer-employee relationship exists.[52]

1. Complying with written or oral instructions (an independent contractor need not be trained or attend training sessions)

2. Regular written or oral reports on the work's status

3. Continuous relationship—more than sporadic services over a lengthy period

4. Lack of control over the place of work

5. No risk of profit or loss; no income fluctuations

6. Regular payment—hourly, weekly, etc. (an independent contractor might work on a job basis)

7. Specified number of hours required to work (an independent contractor is master of his or her own time)

8. Unable to delegate work—hiring assistants not permitted

9. Not independent—does not work for numerous firms or make services available to general public

LIMITATIONS ON DEDUCTIONS

Some provisions of the Code specifically prohibit or limit the deduction of certain expenses and losses despite their apparent relationship to the taxpayer's business or profit-seeking activities. These provisions operate to disallow or limit the deduction for various expenses unless such expenses are specifically authorized by the Code. As a practical matter, these provisions have been enacted to prohibit abuses identified in specific areas. Several of the more fundamental limitations are considered in this chapter.

---

[51]   Reg. § 31.3401(c)-1(a).

[52]   Rev. Rul. 87-41, 1987-1 C.B. 296. This Revenue Ruling actually contains 20 questions.

HOBBY EXPENSES AND LOSSES

As previously discussed, a taxpayer must establish that he or she pursues an activity with the objective of making a profit before the expense is deductible as a business or production of income expense. When the profit motive is absent, the deduction is governed by § 183 on activities not engaged in for profit (i.e., hobbies). Section 183 generally provides that hobby expenses of an individual taxpayer or S corporation are deductible only to the extent of the gross income from the hobby. Thus, the tax treatment of hobby expenses substantially differs from profit-seeking expenses if the expenses of the activity exceed the income resulting in a net loss. If the loss is treated as arising from a profit-motivated activity, then the taxpayer ordinarily may use it to reduce income from other sources.[53] Conversely, if the activity is considered a hobby, no loss is deductible. Note, however, that hobby expenses may be deducted to offset any hobby income.

Profit Motive. The problem of determining the existence of a profit motive usually arises in situations where the activity has elements of both a personal and profit-seeking nature (e.g., auto racing, antique hunting, coin collecting, horse breeding, weekend farming). In some instances, these activities may represent a profitable business venture. Where losses are consistently reported, however, the business motivation is suspect. In these cases all the facts and circumstances must be examined to determine the presence of the profit motive. The courts have held that the taxpayer simply is required to pursue the activity with a bona fide intent of making a profit.[54] The taxpayer, however, need not show a profit. Moreover, the taxpayer's expectation of profit need not be considered reasonable.[55] The Regulations set out nine factors to be used in ascertaining the existence of a profit motive.[56] Some of the questions posed by these factors are

1. Was the activity carried on in a businesslike manner? Were books and records kept? Did the taxpayer change his or her methods or adopt new techniques with the intent to earn a profit?

2. Did the taxpayer attempt to acquire knowledge about the business or consult experts?

3. Did the taxpayer or family members devote much time or effort to the activity? Did they leave another occupation to have more time for the activity?

4. Have there been years of income as well as years of loss? Did the losses occur only in the start-up years?

5. Does the taxpayer have only incidental income from other sources? Is the taxpayer's wealth insufficient to maintain him or her if future profits are not derived?

6. Does the taxpayer derive little personal or recreational pleasure from the activity?

An affirmative answer to several of these questions suggests a profit motive exists.

---

[53] The limitations imposed on losses from passive activities should not be applicable in this situation since the taxpayer materially participates in the activity. See discussion in Chapter 12 and § 469.

[54] Reg. § 1.183-2(a).

[55] *Ibid.*

[56] Reg. § 1.183-2(b).

Presumptive Rule. The burden of proof in the courts is normally borne by the taxpayer. Section 183, however, shifts the burden of proof to the IRS in hobby cases where the taxpayer shows profits in any three of five consecutive years (two of seven years for activities related to horses).[57] The rule creates a presumption that the taxpayer has a profit motive unless the IRS can show otherwise. An election is available to the taxpayer to postpone IRS challenges until five (or seven) years have elapsed from the date the activity commenced. Making the election allows the taxpayer sufficient time to have three profitable years and thus shift the burden of proof to the IRS. This election must be filed within three years of the due date of the return for the taxable year in which the taxpayer first engages in the activity, but not later than 60 days after the taxpayer has received notice that the IRS proposes to disallow the deduction of expenses related to the hobby. The election automatically extends the statute of limitations for each of these years, thus enabling a later challenge by the IRS. It should be emphasized that this presumptive rule only shifts the burden of proof. Profits in three of the five (or two of seven) years do not absolve the taxpayer from attack.

> **Example 20.** T enjoys raising, breeding, and showing dogs. In the past, she occasionally sold a dog or puppy. In 1994 T decided to pursue these activities seriously. During the year, she incurred a loss of $4,000. T also had a loss of $2,000 in 1995. If T made no election for any of these years (i.e., within three years of the start of the activity), the IRS may assert that T's activities constitute a hobby. In this case, the burden of proof is on T to show a profit motive, since she has not shown a profit in at least three years. If T made an election, then the IRS is barred from assessing a deficiency until five years have elapsed. Five years need to elapse to determine whether T will have profits in three of the five years and, if so, shift the burden of proof to the IRS in any litigation which may occur. If an election is made, however, the period for assessing deficiencies for all years is extended until two years after the due date of the return for the last taxable year in the five-year period.[58] In T's case, an election would enable the IRS to assess a deficiency for 1994 and subsequent years up until April 15, 2001, assuming T is a calendar year taxpayer. If an election were not made, the statute of limitations would normally bar assessments three years after the return is due (e.g., assessments for 1994 would be barred after April 15, 1998).

Deduction Limitation. If the activity is considered a hobby, the related expenses are deductible to the extent of the activity's gross income as reduced by *otherwise allowable deductions*.[59] Otherwise allowable deductions are those expenses relating to the hobby that are deductible under other sections of the Code regardless of the activity in which they are incurred. For example, property taxes are deductible under § 164 without regard to whether the activity in which they are incurred is a hobby or a business. Similarly,

---

[57] § 183(d).

[58] § 183(d)(4).

[59] § 183(b). On classification of the deductions, see Rev. Rul. 75-14, 1975-1 C.B. 90

and Senate Finance Committee Report on H.R. 3838, S. Rep. No. 99-313 (5/29/86), p. 80, 99th Cong., 2nd. Sess.

interest on debt secured by the taxpayer's principal or secondary residence is deductible regardless of the character of the activity. Consequently, any expense otherwise allowable is deducted *first* in determining the gross income limitation. Any other expenses are deductible to the extent of any remaining gross income (i.e., other operating expenses are taken next, with any depreciation deductions taken last). Otherwise allowable deductions are fully deductible as itemized deductions, while other deductible expenses are considered miscellaneous itemized deductions and are deductible only to the extent they exceed 2 percent of A.G.I. (including the hobby income).

Example 21. R, an actor, enjoys raising, breeding, and racing horses as a hobby. His A.G.I. excluding the hobby activities is $68,000. He has a small farm on which he raises the horses. During the current year, R won one race and received income of $2,000. He paid $2,300 in expenses as follows: $800 property taxes related to the farm and $1,500 feed for horses. Additionally, R calculated depreciation with respect to the farm assets at $6,500. Assuming the activity is considered a hobby and R itemizes deductions, he would compute his deductions as follows:

Gross income..............................		$2,000
Otherwise allowable deductions:		
Taxes.................................	(800)	$ 800
Gross income limitation....................	$1,200	
Feed expense:		
$1,500 limited to remaining		
gross income		1,200
Total.................................		$2,000

Note that because depreciation is taken last, there is no deduction for this item.

R would include $2,000 in gross income, increasing his A.G.I. to $70,000. Of the $2,000 in deductible expenses, the property taxes of $800 are deductible in full as an itemized deduction. The remaining $1,200 is considered a miscellaneous itemized deduction. In this case, none of the $1,200 is deductible since this amount does not exceed the 2% floor of $1,400 (2% of $70,000). No deduction is allowed for the remaining feed expense of $300 ($1,500 − $1,200) due to the gross income limitation.

Example 22. Assume the same facts as in *Example 21* except that R's expense for property taxes is $2,400 instead of $800. In this case, because the entire $2,400 is deductible as an otherwise allowable deduction and exceeds the gross income from the hobby, none of the feed expense is deductible. Thus, R would include $2,000 in gross income and the $2,400 of property taxes would be fully deductible from A.G.I.

PERSONAL LIVING EXPENSES

Just as the Code specifically authorizes deductions for the costs of pursuing income—business and income-producing expenses—it also denies deductions for personal expenses. Section 262 prohibits the deduction of any personal, living, or family expenses. Only those personal expenditures expressly allowed by some other provision in the Code are deductible. Some of the personal expenditures permitted by other provisions are medical expenses, contributions, qualified residence interest, and taxes. Normally, these expenses are classified as itemized deductions. These deductions and their underlying rationale are discussed in Chapter 11.

The disallowance of personal expenditures by § 262 complements the general criteria allowing a deduction. Recall that the general rules of §§ 162 and 212 permit deductions for ordinary and necessary expenses *only where a profit motive exists*. As previously seen in the discussion of hobbies, however, determining whether an expense arose from a personal or profit motive can be difficult. Some of the items specifically disallowed by § 262 are:

1. Expenses of maintaining a household (e.g., rent, utilities)

2. Losses on sales of property held for personal purposes

3. Amounts paid as damages for breach of promise to marry, attorney's fees, and other costs of suits to recover such damages

4. Premiums paid for life insurance by the insured

5. Costs of insuring a personal residence

Legal expenses related to divorce actions and the division of income-producing properties are often a source of conflict. Prior to clarification by the Supreme Court, several decisions held that divorce expenses incurred primarily to protect the taxpayer's income-producing property or his or her business were deductible.[60] The Supreme Court, however, has ruled that deductibility depends on whether the expense arises in connection with the taxpayer's profit-seeking activities. That is, the *origin* of the expense determines deductibility.[61] Under this rule, if the spouse's claim arises from the marital relationship—a personal matter—then no deduction is allowed. Division of income-producing property would only be incidental to or a consequence of the marital relationship.

> **Example 23.**   R pays legal fees to defend an action by his wife to prevent distributions of income from a trust to him. Because the wife's action arose from the marital relationship, the legal expenses are nondeductible personal expenditures.[62]

---

[60] *F.C. Bowers v. Comm.*, 57-1 USTC ¶9605, 51 AFTR 207, 243 F.2d 904 (CA-6, 1957).

[61] *Supra,* Footnote 13. Also, compare *Comm. v. Tellier*, 66-1 USTC ¶9319, 17 AFTR2d 633, 383 U.S. 687 (USSC, 1966) with *Boris*

Nodiak v. Comm., 66-1 USTC ¶9262, 17 AFTR2d 396, 356 F.2d 911 (CA-2, 1966).

[62] *H.N. Shilling, Jr.*, 33 TCM 1097, T.C. Memo 1974-246.

Legal expenses related to a divorce action may be deductible where the expense is for advice concerning the tax consequences of the divorce.[63] The portion of the legal expense allocable to counsel on the tax consequences of a property settlement, the right to claim children as dependents, and the creation of a trust for payment of alimony are deductible.

CAPITAL EXPENDITURES

A capital expenditure is ordinarily defined as an expenditure providing benefits which extend beyond the close of the taxable year. It is a well-established rule in case law that a business expense, though ordinary and necessary, is not deductible in the year paid or incurred if it can be considered a capital expenditure.[64] Normally, however, a capital expenditure may be deducted ratably over the period for which it provides benefits. For example, the Code authorizes deductions for depreciation or cost recovery, amortization, and depletion where the asset has a determinable useful life.[65] Capital expenditures creating assets that do not have a determinable life, however, generally cannot be deducted. For example, land is considered as having an indeterminable life and thus cannot be depreciated or amortized. The same is true for stocks and bonds. Expenditures for these types of assets are recovered (i.e., deducted) only when there is a disposition of the asset through sale (e.g., cost offset against sales price), exchange, abandonment, or other disposition.

As a general rule, assets with a useful life of one year or less need not be capitalized. For example, the taxpayer can write off short lived assets with small costs such as supplies (e.g., stationery, pens, pencils, calculators), books (e.g., the Internal Revenue Code), and small tools (e.g., screwdrivers, rakes, and shovels).

Goodwill. Like land, goodwill is an example of an asset that does not have a determinable useful life. Because of this indeterminate life, acquired goodwill historically has been treated as a capitalized asset that could not be depreciated. The only way a taxpayer could receive a current tax benefit from acquired goodwill was to identify components separate and apart from goodwill that had an ascertainable value and limited useful life (e.g., client files and subscription lists). If a taxpayer was successful in establishing the requisite valuation and limited life for a goodwill component, the taxpayer could depreciate the cost of the intangible asset over its useful life using the straight-line method (known as amortization). However, in practice, taxpayers often faced challenges by the IRS, and many attempts to depreciate goodwill components were unsuccessful.

Congress recently enacted Code § 197 to reduce the uncertainty surrounding the depreciation of goodwill and its identifiable components. Effective August 10, 1993 the cost of acquiring intangible assets (including acquired goodwill) may, at the election of the taxpayer, be amortized over a 15-year period. If the election is not made, the cost of acquiring goodwill and related intangibles must be capitalized and no amortization will be allowed.

---

[63] Rev. Rul. 72-545, 1972-2 C.B. 179.

[64] *Supra*, Footnote 18.

[65] §§ 167, 168, 169, 178, 184, 188, and 611 are examples.

Example 24.   B has decided to purchase a newspaper business in a small town for $100,000. It can be determined that $80,000 of the purchase price is allocable to the assets of the business and $20,000 is attributable to goodwill (subscription lists and other intangibles). B may be able to recover all $100,000 of the cost through deductions for depreciation and amortization.

Capital Expenditures vs. Repairs.   The general rule of case law disallowing deductions for capital expenditures has been codified for expenditures relating to property. Code § 263 provides that deductions are not allowed for any expenditures for new buildings or for permanent improvements or betterments made to increase the value of property.[66] Additionally, expenditures substantially prolonging the property's useful life, adapting the property to a new or different use, or materially adding to the value of the property are not deductible.[67] Conversely, the cost of incidental repairs that do not materially increase the value of the property nor appreciably prolong its life, but maintain it in a normal operating state, may be deducted in the current year.[68] For example, costs of painting, inside and outside, and papering are usually considered repairs.[69] However, if the painting is done in conjunction with a general reconditioning or overhaul of the property, it is treated as a capital expenditure.[70]

Example 25.   L operates his own limousine business. Expenses for a tune-up such as the costs of spark plugs, points, and labor would be deductible as routine repairs and maintenance since such costs do not significantly prolong the car's life. In contrast, if L had the transmission replaced at a cost of $600, allowing him to drive it for another few years, the expense must be capitalized.

Acquisition Costs.   As a general rule, costs related to the acquisition of property must be capitalized. For example, freight paid to acquire new equipment or commissions paid to acquire land must be capitalized. In addition, Code § 164 requires that state and local general sales taxes related to the purchase of property be capitalized. The costs of demolition or removal of an old building prior to using the land in another fashion must be capitalized as part of the cost of the land.[71] Costs of defending or perfecting the title to property, such as legal fees, are normally capitalized.[72] Similarly, legal fees incurred for the recovery of property must be capitalized unless the recovered property is investment property or money that must be included in income if received.[73]

Advertising.   Under a strict interpretation of the capitalization rules, the cost of advertising could be considered a capital expenditure because such costs may benefit future periods. Despite the theoretical merits of this argument, this approach generally has been rejected due to the difficulty in determining the amount that each future period benefits. For this reason, advertising costs are ordinarily deductible in the year paid or incurred.

---

[66] § 263(a).

[67] Reg. § 1.263(a)-1(b).

[68] Reg. § 1.162-4.

[69] *Louis Allen*, 2 BTA 1313 (1925).

[70] *Joseph M. Jones*, 57-1 USTC ¶9517, 50 AFTR 2040, 242 F.2d 616 (CA-5, 1957).

[71] § 280B.

[72] Reg. § 1.263(a)-2.

[73] Reg. § 1.212-1(k).

Elections to Capitalize or Deduct.   Various provisions of the Code permit a taxpayer to treat capital expenditures as deductible expenses, as deferred expenses, or as capital expenditures.[74] For example, at the election of the taxpayer, expenses for research and experimentation may be deducted currently, treated as deferred expenses and amortized over at least 60 months, or capitalized and included in the basis of the resulting property.[75]

BUSINESS INVESTIGATION EXPENSES AND START-UP COSTS

Another group of expenses which arguably may be considered capital expenditures are those incurred when seeking and establishing a new business, such as costs of investigation and start-up. Business investigation expenses are those costs of seeking and reviewing prospective businesses prior to reaching a decision to acquire or enter any business. Such expenses include the costs of analysis of potential markets, products, labor supply, and transportation facilities. Start-up or pre-opening expenses are costs that are incurred after a decision to acquire a particular business and prior to its actual operations. Examples of these expenses are advertising, employee training, lining up distributors, suppliers, or potential customers, and the costs of professional services such as attorney and accounting fees.

Historically, the deductibility of expenses of business investigation and start-up has turned on whether the taxpayer was "carrying on" a business at the time the expenditures were incurred. Notwithstanding recent changes, the basic rule still remains: when the taxpayer is in the same or similar business as the one which he or she is starting or investigating, the costs of investigation and start-up are wholly deductible in the year paid or incurred.[76] The deduction is allowed regardless of whether the taxpayer undertakes the business.[77] However, this rule often forces taxpayers to litigate to determine whether a business exists at the time the expenses are incurred. Prior to recent changes, if the taxpayer could not establish existence of a business, the expenditures normally were treated as capital expenditures with indeterminable lives.[78] As a result, the taxpayer could only recover the expenditure if and when he or she disposed of or abandoned the business.

In 1980 Congress realized that the basic rule was not only a source of controversy but also discouraged formation of new businesses. For this reason, provisions permitting amortization of these expenses under certain conditions were enacted.[79] Before examining these provisions, it should be emphasized that the traditional rule still continues to be valid. Thus, if a taxpayer can establish that the investigation and start-up costs are related to a similar existing business of the taxpayer, a deduction is allowed.

---

[74] §§ 174, 175, and 180 are examples.

[75] § 174.

[76] *The Colorado Springs National Bank v. U.S.*, 74-2 USTC ¶9809, 34 AFTR2d 74-6166, 505 F.2d 1185 (CA-10, 1974).

[77] *York v. Comm.*, 58-2 USTC ¶9952, 2 AFTR2d 6178, 261 F.2d 421 (CA-4, 1958).

[78] *Morton Frank*, 20 T.C. 511 (1953).

[79] § 195(a).

Example 26.   S owns and operates an ice cream shop on the north side of the city. A new shopping mall is opening on the south side of the city, and the developers have approached her about locating a second ice cream shop in their mall. During 1994 S pays a consulting firm $1,000 for a survey of the potential market on the south side. Because S is in the ice cream business when the expense is incurred, the entire $1,000 is deductible regardless of whether she undertakes the new business.

Amortization Provision.   Section 195 sets out the treatment for the start-up and investigation expenses of taxpayers who are *not* considered in a similar business when the expenses are incurred *and* who actually enter the new business. Eligible taxpayers may elect to treat qualified expenditures as deferred expenses and amortize them over a period not less than 60 months. Amortization starts in the month the taxpayer begins or acquires the business. Expenses for research and development, interest payments, and taxes are not considered start-up expenditures.[80] Consequently, these costs are not subject to § 195 and may be deducted under normal rules.

Example 27.   J, a calendar year, cash basis taxpayer, recently graduated and received $10,000 from his wealthy uncle as a graduation gift. J paid an accountant $1,200 in September to review the financial situation of a small restaurant he desired to purchase. In December, J purchased the restaurant and began actively participating in its management. J may deduct $20 ($1/60$ of $1,200) for the current year.

Example 28.   S, a famous bodybuilder, has decided to build his first health spa. While the facility is being constructed, a temporary office is set up in a trailer next to the site. The office is nicely decorated and contains a small replica of the facility. S hired a staff who will manage the facility but at this time are calling prospective customers. Elaborate brochures have been printed. All of these costs, including the salaries paid to the staff, the printing of the brochures, and the costs of operating the trailer such as depreciation and utilities, are start-up costs and must be amortized over a period not less than 60 months.

As suggested above, the taxpayer must enter the business to qualify for amortization. Whether the individual is considered as having entered the business normally depends on the facts in each case.

If the taxpayer (who is not in a similar, existing business) does not enter into the new business, the investigation and start-up expenses generally are not deductible. The Tax Court, however, has held that a taxpayer may deduct costs as a loss suffered from a transaction entered into for profit if the activities are sufficient to be considered a "transaction."[81] The IRS has interpreted this rule to mean that those expenditures related to a *general search* for a particular business or investment are not deductible.[82] Expenses are considered general when they are related to whether to enter the transaction and which

---

[80]   § 195(c)(1).

[81]   *Harris W. Seed*, 52 T.C. 880 (1969).

[82]   Rev. Rul. 77-254, 1977-2 C.B. 63.

transaction to enter. Once the taxpayer has focused on the acquisition of a *specific* business or investment, expenses related to an unsuccessful acquisition attempt are deductible as a loss on a transaction entered into for profit.

> **Example 29.**   L, a retired army officer, is interested in going into the radio business. He places advertisements in the major trade journals soliciting information about businesses that may be acquired. Upon reviewing the responses to his ads, L selects two radio stations for possible acquisition. He hires an accountant to audit the books of each station and advise him on the feasibility of purchase. He travels to the cities where each station is located and discusses the possible acquisition with the owners. Finally, L decides to purchase station FMAM. To this end, he hires an attorney to draft the purchase agreement. Due to a price dispute, however, the acquisition attempt collapses. The expenses for advertising, auditing, and travel are not deductible since they are related to the taxpayer's general search. The legal expenses are deductible as a loss, however, since they occurred in the taxpayer's attempt to acquire a specific business.

Job-Seeking Expenses.   The tax treatment of job-seeking expenses of an employee is similar to that for expenses for business investigation. If the taxpayer is seeking a job in the same business in which he or she is presently employed, the related expenses are deductible as miscellaneous itemized deductions subject to the 2 percent floor.[83] The deduction is allowed even if a new job is not obtained. No deduction or amortization is permitted, however, if the job sought is considered a new trade or business or the taxpayer's first job.

> **Example 30.**   B, currently employed as a biology teacher, incurs travel expenses and employment agency fees to obtain a new job as a computer operator. The expenses are not deductible because they are not incurred in seeking a job in the profession in which she was currently engaged. Moreover, the expenses are not deductible even though B obtained the new job. However, the expenses would be deductible if she had obtained a new job in her present occupation.

PUBLIC POLICY RESTRICTIONS

Although an expense may be entirely appropriate and helpful, and may contribute to the taxpayer's profit-seeking activities, it is not considered necessary if the allowance of a deduction would frustrate sharply defined public policy. The courts established this longstanding rule on the theory that to allow a deduction for expenses such as fines and penalties would encourage violations by diluting the penalty.[84] Historically, however, the IRS and the courts were free to restrict deductions of any type of expense where, in their view, it appeared that the expenses were contrary to public policy—even if the policy had not been clearly enunciated by some governmental body. As a result, taxpayers were often forced to go to court to determine if their expense violated public policy.

---

[83]   Rev. Rul. 75-120, 1975-1 C.B. 55, as clarified by Rev. Rul. 77-16, 1977-1 C.B. 37.

[84]   *Hoover Motor Express Co., Inc. v. U.S.*, 58-1 USTC ¶9367, 1 AFTR2d 1157, 356 U.S. 38 (USSC, 1958).

Recognizing the difficulties in applying the public policy doctrine, Congress enacted provisions specifically designed to limit its use.[85] The rules identified and disallowed certain types of expenditures that would be considered contrary to public policy. Under these provisions no deduction is allowed for fines, penalties, and illegal payments.

Fines and Penalties.   A deduction is not allowed for any fine or similar penalty paid to a government for the violation of any law.[86]

> **Example 31.**   S is a salesman for an office supply company. While calling on customers this year, he received parking tickets of $100. None of the cost is deductible because the violations were against the law.

> **Example 32.**   Upon audit of T's tax return, it was determined that he failed to report $10,000 of tip income from his job as a maitre d', resulting in additional tax of $3,000. T was also required to pay the negligence penalty for intentional disregard of the rules. The penalty—20% of the tax due—is not deductible.

Fines include those amounts paid in settlement of the taxpayer's actual or potential liability.[87] In addition, no deduction is allowed for two-thirds of treble damage payments made due to a violation of antitrust laws.[88] Thus, one-third of this antitrust "fine" is deductible.

Illegal Kickbacks, Bribes, and Other Payments.   The Code also disallows the deduction for four categories of illegal payments:[89]

1.   Kickbacks or bribes to U.S. government officials and employees if illegal

2.   Payments to governmental officials or employees of *foreign* countries if such payments would be considered illegal under the U.S. Foreign Corrupt Practices Act

> **Example 33.**   R travels all over the world, looking for unique items for his gift shop. Occasionally when going through customs in foreign countries, he is forced to "bribe" the customs official to do the necessary paperwork and get him through customs as quickly as possible. These so-called grease payments to employees of foreign countries are deductible unless they violate the Foreign Corrupt Practices Act. In general, such payments are not considered to be illegal.

---

[85]   S. Rep. No. 91-552, 91st Cong., 1st Sess. 273-75 (1969). Note, however, that the Tax Court continues to utilize the doctrine despite Congress' attempt to restrict its use—see *R. Mazzei*, 61 T.C. 497 (1974).

[86]   § 162(f).

[87]   § 162(g).

[88]   Reg. § 1.162-21(b).

[89]   § 162(c).

3. Kickbacks, bribes, or other illegal payments to any other person if illegal under generally enforced U.S. or state laws that provide a criminal penalty or loss of license or privilege to engage in business

4. Kickbacks, rebates, and bribes, although legal, made by any provider of items or services under Medicare and Medicaid programs

Those kickbacks and bribes not specified above would still be deductible if they were ordinary and necessary. The payment, however, may not be necessary and thus disallowed if it controverts public policy.

Kickbacks generally include payments for referral of clients, patients, and customers. However, under certain circumstances, trade discounts or rebates may be considered kickbacks.

Example 34. M, a life insurance salesman, paid rebates or discounts to purchasers of policies. Since such practice is normally illegal under state law, the rebate is not deductible.[90]

Expenses of Illegal Business. The expenses related to an illegal business are deductible.[91] Similar to the principle governing taxation of income from whatever source (including income illegally obtained), the tax law is not concerned with the lawfulness of the activity in which the deductions arise. No deduction is allowed, however, if the expense itself constitutes an illegal payment as discussed above. In addition, Code § 280E prohibits the deduction of any expenses related to the trafficking in controlled substances (i.e., drugs).

LOBBYING AND POLITICAL CONTRIBUTIONS

Although expenses for lobbying and political contributions may be closely related to the taxpayer's business, Congress has traditionally limited their deduction. These restrictions usually are supported on the grounds that it is not in the public's best interest for government to subsidize efforts to influence legislative matters.

Lobbying. Prior to 1962, no deduction was permitted for any type of lobbying expense. In 1962, however, Congress altered its position slightly with the addition of § 162(e), which carved out a narrow exception for certain lobbying expenses. This provision allowed a deduction for the expenses of appearing before or providing information to governmental units on legislative matters of *direct interest* to the taxpayer's business. Similarly, a deduction was permitted for expenses of providing information to a trade organization of which the taxpayer was a member where the legislative matter was of direct interest to the taxpayer and the organization. The portion of dues paid to such an organization attributable to the organization's allowable lobbying activities was also deductible. Beginning in 1994, however, these rules for deducting lobbying expenses are

---

[90] *James Alex*, 70 T.C. 322 (1978).

[91] See *Max Cohen v. Comm.*, 49-2 USTC ¶9358, 176 F.2d 394 (CA-10, 1949) and

Neil Sullivan v. Comm., 58-1 USTC ¶9368, AFTR2d 1158, 356 U.S. 27 (USSC, 1958).

even more restrictive. Lobbying expenditures are now deductible only if incurred for the purpose of influencing legislation at the *local* level. Therefore, the expense of influencing national and state legislation (including the costs of hiring lobbyists to represent the taxpayer in these matters) is not deductible. This prohibition is extended to the costs of any direct communication with executive branch officials in an attempt to influence official actions or positions of such official.

The taxpayer must have a direct interest in the local legislation before lobbying expenses may be deducted. Although the definitional boundaries of the term "direct" are vague, a taxpayer is considered as having satisfied the test if it is reasonable to expect that the local legislative matter affects or will affect the taxpayer's business. However, a taxpayer does not have a direct interest in the nomination, appointment, or operation of any local legislative body.[92]

The deduction for lobbying *does not* extend to expenses incurred to influence the general public on legislative matters, elections, or referendums.[93] Expenses related to the following types of lobbying are not deductible:

1. Advertising in magazines and newspapers concerning legislation of direct interest to the taxpayer.[94] However, expenses for "goodwill" advertising presenting views on economic, financial, social, or similar subjects of a general nature, or encouraging behavior such as contributing to the Red Cross, are deductible.[95]

2. Preparing and distributing to a corporation's shareholders pamphlets focusing on certain legislation affecting the corporation and urging the shareholders to contact their representatives in Congress.[96]

Example 35.   T owns a restaurant in Austin, Texas. Legislation has been introduced by the City Council to impose a sales tax on food and drink sold in Austin to be used for funding a dome stadium. T places an ad in the local newspaper stating reasons why the legislation should not be passed. He goes to the City Council and testifies on the proposed legislation before several committees. He pays dues to the Austin Association of Restaurant Owners organization, which estimates that 60% of its activities are devoted to lobbying for local legislation related to restaurant owners. T may deduct the cost of travel and 60% of his dues since the local legislation is of direct interest to him. He may not deduct the ad since it is intended to influence the general public.

---

[92]   Reg. § 1.162-20(b).

[93]   § 162(e)(2).

[94]   Rev. Rul. 78-112, 1978-1 C.B. 42.

[95]   Reg. § 1.162-20(a)(2).

[96]   Rev. Rul. 74-407, 1974-2 C.B. 45, as amplified by Rev. Rul. 78-111, 1978-1 C.B. 41.

Political Contributions. No deduction is permitted for any contributions, gifts, or any other amounts paid to a political party, action committee, or group or candidate related to a candidate's campaign.[97] This rule also applies to indirect payments, such as the payments for advertising in a convention program and admission to a dinner, hall, or similar affair where any of the proceeds benefit a political party or candidate.[98]

EXPENSES AND INTEREST RELATING TO TAX-EXEMPT INCOME

Section 265 sets forth several rules generally disallowing deductions for expenses relating to tax-exempt income. The best known rule prohibits the deduction for any *interest* expense or nonbusiness (§ 212) expense related to tax-exempt *interest* income.[99] Without this rule, taxpayers in high tax brackets could borrow at a higher rate of interest than could be earned and still have a profit on the transaction.

> **Example 36.** D, an investor in the 28% tax bracket with substantial investment income, borrows funds at 9% and invests them in tax-exempt bonds yielding 7%. If the interest expense were deductible, the after-tax cost of borrowing would be 6.48% [(100% − 28% = 72%) × 9%]. Since the interest income is nontaxable, the after-tax yield on the bond remains 7%, or .52 percentage points higher than the effective cost of borrowing. Section 265, however, denies the deduction for the interest expense, thus eliminating the feasibility of this arrangement. It should be noted, however, that business (§ 162) expenses (other than interest) related to tax-exempt interest income may be deductible.

If the income that is exempt is *not* interest, none of the related expenses are deductible.[100]

> **Example 37.** A company operating a baseball team paid premiums on a disability insurance policy providing that the company would receive proceeds under the policy if a player were injured. Because the proceeds would not be taxable, the premiums are not deductible even though the expenditure would apparently qualify as a business expense.[101]

As a practical matter, it would appear difficult to determine whether borrowed funds (and the interest expense) are related to carrying taxable or tax-exempt securities. For example, an individual holding tax-exempt bonds may take out a mortgage to buy a residence instead of selling the bonds to finance the purchase price. In such case, it could be inferred that the borrowed funds were used to finance the bond purchase. Generally, the IRS will allow the deduction in this and similar cases unless the facts indicate that the primary purpose of the borrowing is to carry the tax-exempt obligations.[102] The facts must establish a *sufficiently direct relationship* between the borrowing and the investment producing tax-exempt income before a deduction is denied.

[97] § 162(e).

[98] § 276.

[99] § 265(2).

[100] § 265(1).

[101] Rev. Rul. 66-262, 1966-2 C. B. 105.

[102] Rev. Proc. 72-18, 1972-1 C.B. 740 as clarified by Rev. Proc. 74-8, 1974-1 C.B. 419, and amplified by Rev. Rul. 80-55, 1980-2 C.B. 849.

Example 38.   K owns common stock with a basis of $70,000 and tax-exempt bonds of $30,000. She borrows $100,000 to finance an investment in an oil and gas limited partnership. The IRS will disallow a deduction for a portion of the interest on the $100,000 debt because it is presumed that the $100,000 is incurred to finance all of K's portfolio including the tax-exempt securities.[103]

Example 39.   R has a margin account with her broker. This account is devoted solely to the purchase of taxable investments and tax-exempt bonds. During the year, she buys several taxable and tax-exempt securities on margin. A portion of the interest expense on this margin account is disallowed because the borrowings are considered partially related to financing of the investment in tax-exempt securities.[104]

Business Life Insurance.   Absent a special rule, premiums paid on insurance policies covering officers and employees of the business might be deductible as ordinary and necessary business expenses. However, to ensure that the taxpayer is not allowed to deduct expenses related to tax-exempt income (i.e., life insurance proceeds) a special provision exists. Under § 264, the taxpayer is not allowed any deduction for life insurance premiums paid on policies covering the life of any officer, employee, or any other person that may have a financial interest in the taxpayer's trade or business, if the taxpayer is the *beneficiary* of the policy. Thus premiums paid by a business on a key-person life insurance policy where the company is beneficiary are not deductible. In contrast, payments made by a business on group-term life insurance policies where the employees are beneficiaries are deductible.

RELATED TAXPAYER TRANSACTIONS

Without restrictions, related taxpayers (such as husbands and wives, shareholders and their corporations) could enter into arrangements creating deductions for expenses and losses, and not affect their economic position. For example, a husband and wife could create a deduction simply by having one spouse sell property to the other at a loss. In this case, the loss is artificial because the property remains within the family and their financial situation is unaffected. Although the form of ownership has been altered, there is no substance to the transaction. To guard against the potential abuses inherent in transactions between related taxpayers, Congress designed specific safeguards contained in § 267.

---

[103]   *Ibid.*

[104]   *B.P. McDonough v. Comm.*, 78-2 USTC
¶9490, 42 AFTR2d 78-5172, 577 F.2d 234
(CA-4, 1978).

Related Taxpayers. The transactions that are subject to restriction are only those between persons who are considered "related" as defined in the Code. Related taxpayers are[105]

1. Certain family members: Brothers and sisters (including half-blood), spouse, ancestors (i.e., parents and grandparents), and lineal descendants (i.e., children and grandchildren)

2. Taxpayer and his or her corporation: An individual and a corporation if the individual owns either directly or *indirectly* more than 50 percent of the corporation's stock[106]

3. Personal service corporation and an employee-owner: A corporation whose principal activity is the performance of personal services which are performed by the employee-owners (i.e., an employee who owns either directly or indirectly *any* stock of the corporation)

4. Certain other relationships involving regular corporations, S corporations, partnerships, trusts, and individuals

In determining whether a taxpayer and a corporation are related, the taxpayer's direct and indirect ownership must be taken into account for the 50 percent test. A taxpayer's indirect stock ownership is any stock that is considered as owned, or "constructively" owned by the taxpayer but not actually owned. Section 267 provides a set of constructive ownership rules, also referred to as *attribution rules*, indicating the circumstances when the taxpayer is considered as owning the stock of another. Under the constructive ownership rules, a taxpayer is considered owning indirectly[107]

1. Stock owned directly or indirectly by his or her family as defined above

2. His or her proportionate share of any stock owned by a corporation, partnership, estate, or trust in which he or she has ownership (or of which he or she is a beneficiary in the case of an estate or trust)

3. Stock owned indirectly or directly by his or her partner in a partnership

In using these rules, the following limitations apply: (1) stock attributed from one family member to another *cannot* be reattributed to members of his or her family, and (2) stock attributed from a partner to the taxpayer *cannot* be reattributed to a member of his or her family or to another partner.[108]

---

[105] § 267(b).

[106] A partner and a partnership in which the partner owns more than a 50 percent interest are treated in the same manner. See § 707(b).

[107] § 267(c).

[108] § 267(c)(5).

Example 40.   H and W are husband and wife. HB is H's brother. H, W, and HB own 30, 45, and 25% of X Corporation, respectively. H is considered as owning 100% of X Corporation, 30% directly and 70% indirectly (25% through HB and 45% through W, both by application of attribution rule 1 above). W is considered as owning 75% of X Corporation, 45% directly and 30% indirectly through H by application of attribution rule 1 (note that HB's stock cannot be attributed to H and reattributed to W). HB is considered as owning 55% of X Corporation, 25% directly and 30% indirectly through H by application of attribution rule 1 and the reattribution limitation.

Losses.   The taxpayer is not allowed to deduct the loss from a sale or exchange of property directly or indirectly to a related taxpayer (as defined above).[109] However, any loss disallowed on the sale may be used to offset any gain on a subsequent sale of the property by a related taxpayer.[110]

Example 41.   A father owns land that he purchased as an investment for $20,000. He sells the land to his daughter for $15,000 producing a $5,000 loss. The $5,000 loss may not be deducted because the transaction is between related taxpayers. If the daughter subsequently sells the property for $22,000, she will then realize a $7,000 gain ($22,000 sales price − $15,000 basis). However, the gain may be reduced by the $5,000 loss previously disallowed, resulting in a recognized gain of $2,000 ($7,000 realized gain − $5,000 previously disallowed loss). If the daughter had sold the property for only $19,000, the realized gain of $4,000 ($19,000 − $15,000) would have been eliminated by the previous loss of $5,000. The $5,000 loss previously disallowed is utilized only to the extent of the $4,000 gain. The remaining portion of the disallowed loss ($1,000) cannot be used. Had the father originally sold the property for $19,000 to an outsider as his daughter subsequently did, the father would have recognized a $1,000 loss ($19,000 sales price − $20,000 basis). Note that the effect of the disallowance rule does *not* increase the basis of the property to the related taxpayer by the amount of loss disallowed.

Example 42.   S owns 100% of V Corporation. She sells stock with a basis of $100 to her good friend T for $75, creating a $25 loss for S. T, in turn, sells the stock to V Corporation for $75, thus recouping the amount he paid S with no gain or loss. The $25 loss suffered by S, however, is not deductible because the sale was made *indirectly* through T to her wholly owned corporation.

Unpaid Expenses and Interest.   Prior to enactment of § 267, another tax avoidance device used by related taxpayers involved the use of different accounting methods by each taxpayer. In the typical scheme, a taxpayer's corporation would adopt the accrual basis method of accounting while the taxpayer reported on a cash basis. The taxpayer could lend money, lease property, provide services, etc., to the corporation and charge the

---

[109]   § 267(a)(1).   [110]   § 267(d).

corporation for whatever was provided. As an accrual basis taxpayer, the corporation would accrue the expense and create a deduction. The cash basis individual, however, would report no income until the corporation's payment of the expense was actually received. As a result, the corporation could accrue large deductions without ever having to make a disbursement and, moreover, without the taxpayer recognizing any offsetting income. The Code now prohibits this practice between "related taxpayers" as defined above. Code § 267 provides that an accrual basis taxpayer can deduct an accrued expense payable to a related cash basis taxpayer *only* in the period in which the payment is included in the recipient's income.[111] This rule effectively places all accrual basis taxpayers on the cash method of accounting for purposes of deducting such expenses.

Example 43. B, an individual, owns 100% of X Corporation which manufactures electric razors. B uses the cash method of accounting while the corporation uses the accrual basis. Both are calendar year taxpayers. On December 27, 1994 the corporation accrues a $10,000 bonus for B. However, due to insufficient cash flow, X Corporation was not able to pay the bonus until January 10, 1995. The corporation may not deduct the accrued bonus in 1994. Rather, it must deduct the bonus in 1995, the year in which B includes the payment in his income.

Example 44. Assume the same facts as above, except that B owns only a 20% interest in X. In addition, X is a large law firm in which B is employed. The results are the same as above because B and X are still related parties: a personal service corporation and an employee-owner.

PAYMENT OF ANOTHER TAXPAYER'S OBLIGATION

As a general rule, a taxpayer is not permitted to deduct the payment of a deductible expense of another taxpayer. A deduction is allowed only for those expenditures satisfying the taxpayer's obligation or arising from such an obligation.

Example 45. As part of Q's rental contract for his personal apartment, he pays 1% of his landlord's property taxes. No deduction is allowed because the property taxes are the obligation of the landlord.

Example 46. P is majority stockholder of R Corporation. During the year, the corporation had financial difficulty and was unable to make an interest payment on an outstanding debt. To protect the goodwill of the corporation, P paid the interest. The payment is not deductible, and P will be treated as having made a contribution to the capital of the corporation for interest paid.

An exception to the general rule is provided with respect to payment of medical expenses of a dependent. To qualify as a dependent for this purpose, the person needs only to meet the relationship, support, and citizen tests.[112] If the taxpayer pays the medical expenses of a person who qualifies as a dependent under the modified tests, the expenses are treated as if they were the taxpayer's expenses and are deductible subject to limitations applicable to the taxpayer.

---

[111] § 267(a)(2).   [112] § 213(a)(1).

SUBSTANTIATION

The Code requires that taxpayers maintain records sufficient to establish the amount of gross income, deductions, credits, or other matters required to be shown on the tax return.[113] As a practical matter, recordkeeping requirements depend on the nature of the item. With respect to most deductions, taxpayers may rely on the "*Cohan* rule."[114] In *Cohan*, George M. Cohan, the famous playwright, spent substantial sums for travel and entertainment. The Board of Tax Appeals (predecessor to the Tax Court) denied any deduction for the expenses because the taxpayer had no records supporting the items. On appeal, however, the Second Circuit Court of Appeals reversed this decision indicating that "absolute certainty in such matters is usually impossible and is not necessary."[115] Thus, the Appeals Court remanded the case to make some allowance for the expenditures. From this decision, the "*Cohan* rule" developed, providing that a reasonable estimation of the deduction is sufficient where the actual amount is not substantiated. In 1962, however, Congress eliminated the use of the *Cohan* rule for travel and entertainment expenses and established rigorous substantiation requirements for these types of deductions. Substantiation for other expenses, however, is still governed by the *Cohan* rule. Despite the existence of the *Cohan* rule, records should be kept documenting deductible expenditures since estimates of the expenditures may be substantially less than actually paid or incurred.

---

[113] Reg. § 1.6001-1(a).

[114] *Cohan v. Comm.*, 2 USTC ¶489, 8 AFTR 10552, 39 F.2d 540 (CA-2, 1930).

[115] *Ibid.*

TAX PLANNING CONSIDERATIONS

MAXIMIZING DEDUCTIONS

Perhaps the most important step in minimizing the tax liability is maximizing deductions. Maximizing deductions obviously requires the taxpayer to identify and claim all the deductions to which he or she is entitled. Many taxpayers, however, often overlook deductions that they are allowed because they fail to grasp and apply the fundamental rules discussed in this chapter. To secure a deduction, the taxpayer needs only to show that the expense paid or incurred during the year is ordinary, necessary, and related to a profit-seeking activity. Notwithstanding the special rules of limitation that apply to certain deductions, most deductions are allowed because the *taxpayer* is able to recognize and establish the link between the expenditure and the profit-seeking activity. The taxpayer is in the best position to recognize that an expenditure relates to his or her trade or business, not the tax practitioner. Practitioners typically lack sufficient insight into the taxpayer's activities to identify potential deductions. Thus, it is up to the taxpayer to recognize and establish the relationship between an expenditure and the profit-seeking activity. Failure to do so results in the taxpayer's paying a tax liability higher than what he or she is required to pay.

The taxpayer should not only maximize the absolute dollar amount of deductions, but also the value of the deduction. A deduction's value is equal to the product of the amount of the deduction and the taxpayer's marginal tax rate. Because the taxpayer's marginal rate fluctuates over time, the value of a deduction varies depending on the period in which the deduction is claimed. When feasible, deductions should normally be accelerated or deferred to years when the taxpayer is in a higher tax bracket. In timing deductions, however, the time value of money also must be considered. For example, in periods of inflation, the deferral of a deduction to a high bracket year may not always be advantageous, since a deduction in the future is not worth as much as one currently.

An individual taxpayer's timing of itemized deductions is particularly important in light of the standard deduction and the floor on miscellaneous itemized deductions. Many taxpayers lose deductions because their deductions do not exceed the standard deduction in any one year. These deductions need not be lost, however, if the taxpayer alternates the years in which he or she itemizes or uses the standard deduction. For example, in those years where the taxpayer itemizes, all tax deductible expenditures from the prior year should be deferred while expenditures of the following year should be accelerated. By so doing, the taxpayer bunches itemized deductions in the current year to exceed the standard deduction. In the following year, the taxpayer would use the standard deduction. Itemized deductions are considered in detail in Chapter 11.

Maximizing deductions also requires shifting of deductions to the taxpayer who would derive the greatest benefit. For example, if two sisters are co-obligees on a note, good tax planning dictates that the sister in the higher tax bracket pay the deductible interest expense. In this case, either sister may pay and claim a deduction.

TIMING OF DEDUCTIONS

In the previous section, the importance of maximizing the absolute amount of deductions was emphasized. However, because of the time value of money it is equally important to consider the timing of deductions.

> **Example 47.** R, who pays Federal, state, and local taxes equal to 50% of his income, makes a cash expenditure of $10,000. If the $10,000 is deductible immediately, R will realize a tax benefit of $5,000 ($10,000 × 50%). Moreover, because the tax savings were realized immediately, the present value of the benefit is not diminished. On the other hand, if R is not able to deduct the $10,000 for another five years, the benefit of the deduction is substantially reduced. Specifically, assuming the annual interest rate is 10%, the present value of the $5,000 tax savings decreases to $3,105 ($5,000 × [1 ÷ (1 + 0.10)^5]), a decrease of almost 38%.

As the above example illustrates, accelerating a deduction from the future to the present can substantially increase its value. Awareness of the provisions permitting acceleration of deductions allows taxpayers to arrange their affairs so as to reap the greatest rewards. For example, a taxpayer may choose an investment that the tax law allows him or her to deduct immediately rather than an investment that must be capitalized and deducted through depreciation over the asset's life.

EXPENSES RELATING TO TAX-EXEMPT INCOME

Although expenses related to tax-exempt income are not deductible, expenses related to tax-deferred income are deductible.[116] For example, income earned on contributions to Individual Retirement Accounts are not taxable until the earnings are distributed (usually at retirement). If the taxpayer borrows amounts to contribute to his or her Individual Retirement Account, interest paid on the borrowed amounts may be deductible (if the general rules for deductibility are met) because the income to which it relates is only tax-deferred, not tax-exempt.

"POINTS" ON MORTGAGES

"Points" paid to secure a mortgage on a principal residence normally are deductible in the year paid or incurred. In many cases, however, the points are not paid out of independent funds of the taxpayer but are withheld from the mortgage proceeds. For example, where a lender is charging two points on a $50,000 loan, or $1,000 (2% of $50,000), the $1,000 is withheld by the lender as payment while the remaining $49,000 ($50,000 − $1,000) is advanced to the borrower. The Tax Court has ruled that in these situations, the taxpayer

---

[116] *Hawaiian Trust Co., Ltd. v. U.S.*, 61-1 USTC ¶9481, 7 AFTR2d 1553, 291 F.2d 761 (CA-9, 1961). See also, Letter Rul. 8527082 (April 2, 1985).

has not prepaid the interest (as represented by the points) and thus must amortize the points over the term of the loan.[117] To avoid this result and obtain a current deduction, the taxpayer should pay the points out of separate funds rather than having them withheld by the lender. This requirement will be met if the cash paid by the borrower up to and at the closing (including down payments, escrow deposits, earnest money, and amounts paid at closing) is at least equal to the amount deducted for points.[118]

HOBBIES

Several studies suggest that the factor on which the hobby/business issue often turns is the manner in which the taxpayer carries on the activity.[119] For business treatment, it is imperative that the taxpayer have complete and detailed financial and nonfinancial records. Moreover, such records should be used in decision making and in constructing a profit plan. The activity should resemble a business in every respect. For example, the taxpayer should maintain a separate checking account for the activity, advertise where appropriate, obtain written advice from experts and follow it, and acquire some expertise about the operation.

Although the taxpayer is not required to actually show profits, profits in *three* of *five* consecutive years create a substantial advantage for the taxpayer. Where the profit requirement is satisfied, it is presumed that the activity is not a hobby and the IRS has the burden of proving otherwise. For this reason, the cash basis taxpayer might take steps that could convert a loss year into a profitable year. For example, in some situations it may be possible to accelerate receipts and defer payment of expenses. However, the taxpayer should be cautioned that arranging transactions so nominal profits occur has been viewed negatively by the courts.

---

[117] *Roger A. Schubel*, 77 T.C. 701 (1982).

[118] Rev. Proc. 92-12, 1992-3, I.R.B. 27.

[119] See, for example, Burns and Groomer, "Effects of Section 183 on the Business Hobby Controversy," *Taxes* (March, 1980) pp. 195–206.

PROBLEM MATERIALS

DISCUSSION QUESTIONS

7-1 *General Requirements for Deductions.* Explain the general requirements that must be satisfied before a taxpayer may claim a deduction for an expense or a loss.

7-2 *Deduction Defined.* Consider the following:

    a. It is often said that income can be meaningfully defined while deductions can be defined only procedurally. Explain.

    b. The courts are fond of referring to deductions as matters of "legislative grace." Explain.

    c. Although deductions may only be defined procedurally, construct a definition for a deduction similar to the "all inclusive" definition for income.

    d. Will satisfaction of the requirements of your definition ensure deductibility? Explain.

7-3 *Business versus Personal Expenditures.* Consider the following:

    a. If the taxpayer derives personal pleasure from an otherwise deductible expense, will the expense be denied? Explain.

    b. Name some of the purely personal expenses that are deductible, and indicate whether they are deductions *for* or *from* A.G.I.

7-4 *Business versus Investment Expenses.* Two Code sections govern the deductibility of ordinary and necessary expenses related to profit-motivated activities. Explain why two provisions exist and the distinction between them.

7-5 *An Employee's Business.* Is an employee considered as being in trade or business? Explain the significance of your answer.

7-6 *Year Allowable.* The year in which a deduction is allowed depends on whether the taxpayer is a cash basis or accrual basis taxpayer. Discuss.

7-7 *Classification of Expenses.* F is a self-employed registered nurse and works occasionally for a nursing home. G is a registered nurse employed by a nursing home. Their income, exemptions, credits, etc. are identical. Explain why a deductible expense, although paid in the same amount by both, may cause F and G to have differing tax liabilities.

7-8 *Above and Below-the-Line Deductions.* At a tax seminar, F was reminded to ensure that he properly classified his deductions as either above- or below-the-line. After the seminar, F came home and scrutinized his Form 1040 to determine what the instructor meant and why it was important. Despite his careful examination of the form, F could not figure out what the instructor was talking about or why it was important. Help F out by explaining the meaning of this classification scheme.

7-9 *Performing Artists.* V hopes to become a movie star someday. Currently, she accepts bit parts in various movies waiting for her break. What special tax treatment may be available for V?

7-10 *Classification of Deductions.* J and K are both single, and each earns $30,000 of income and has $2,000 of deductible expenses for the current year. J's deductions are for A.G.I. while K's deductions are itemized deductions.

    a. Given these facts, and assuming that the situation of J and K is identical in every other respect, will their tax liabilities differ? Explain.

    b. Same as (a) except their deductions are $5,000.

7-11 *Constructive Distributions.* D owns all of the stock of DX Inc., which manufactured record jackets. Over the years, the corporation was very successful. This year, D placed his 16- and 14-year-old sons on the payroll, paying them each $10,000 annually. The boys worked on the assembly line a couple of hours each week. Explain D's strategy and the risks it involves.

7-12 *Disguised Distributions.* E owns all of the stock of EZ Inc., which operated a nursery. During the past several years, the company had operated at a deficit and E finally sold all of his stock to C. C drew a very low salary before he could turn things around. Now the business is highly profitable, and C is paying himself handsomely. As C's tax adviser, what counsel if any should be given to C?

7-13 *Income and Expenses of Illegal Business.* B is a bookie in a state where gambling is illegal. During the year, he earned $70,000 accepting bets. His expenses included those for rent, phone, and utilities. In addition, he paid off a state legislator who was a customer and who obviously knew of his activity.

    a. Discuss the tax treatment of B's income and expenses.

    b. Same as (a) except B was a drug dealer.

7-14 *Permanent and Timing Differences.* Financial accounting and tax accounting often differ in the manner in which certain expenses are treated. Identify several expenditures which, because of their treatment, produce permanent or timing differences.

7-15 *Capital Expenditures.* Can a cash basis taxpayer successfully reduce taxable income by purchasing supplies near year-end and deducting their cost?

7-16 *Independent Contractor versus Employee.* Briefly discuss the difference between an independent contractor (self-employed person) and an employee and why the distinction is important.

7-17 *Hobby Expenses.* Discuss the factors used in determining whether an activity is a hobby and the tax consequences resulting from its being deemed a hobby.

7-18 *Public Policy Doctrine.* A taxpayer operates a restaurant and failed to remit the sales tax for August to the city as of the required date. As a result, he must pay an additional assessment of 0.25 percent of the amount due. Comment on the deductibility of this payment.

7-19 *Constructive Ownership Rules.* Explain the concept of constructive ownership and the reason for its existence.

7-20 *Expenses Relating to Tax-Exempt Income.* Discuss what types of expenses relating to tax-exempt income *may* be deductible.

7-21 *Substantiation.* Explain the *Cohan* rule.

PROBLEMS

7-22 *General Requirements for Deduction.* For each of the following expenses identify and discuss the general requirement(s) (ordinary, necessary, related to business, etc.) upon which deductibility depends.

a. A police officer who is required to carry a gun at all times lives in New York. The most convenient and direct route to work is through New Jersey. The laws of New Jersey, however, prohibit the carrying of a gun in the car. As a result, he must take an indirect route to the police station to avoid New Jersey. The indirect route causes him to drive ten miles more than he would otherwise. The cost of the additional mileage is $500. (Note: commuting expense from one's home to the first job site is a nondeductible personal expense.)

b. The current president of a nationwide union spends $10,000 for costs related to re-election.

c. The taxpayer operates a lumber business. He is extremely religious and consequently is deeply concerned over the business community's social and moral responsibility to society. For this reason, he hires a minister to give him and his employees moral and spiritual advice. The minister had no business background although he does offer solutions to business problems.

d. The taxpayer operates a laundry in New York City. He was recently visited by two "insurance agents" who wished to sell him a special bomb policy (i.e., if the taxpayer paid the insurance "premiums," his business would not be bombed). The taxpayer paid the premiums of $500 each month.

7-23 *Accrual Basis Deductions.* In each of the following situations assume the taxpayer uses the accrual method of accounting and indicate the amount of the deduction allowed.

a. R sells and services gas furnaces. As part of his sales package, he agrees to turn on and cut off the buyer's furnace for five years. He normally charges $35 for such service, which costs him about $20 in labor and materials. Based on 1994 sales, R sets up a reserve for the costs of the services to be performed, which he estimates will be $4,500 over the next five years.

b. At the end of 1994, XYZ, a regular corporation, agreed to rent office space from ABC Leasing Corp. Pursuant to the contract, XYZ paid $10,000 on December 1, 1994 for rent for all of 1995.

c. RST Villas, a condominium project in a Vermont ski resort, reached an agreement with MPP Pop-Ins providing that MPP would provide maid services for 1995 for $20,000. RST transferred its note payable for $20,000 at the end of 1995 to MPP on December 1, 1994.

7-24 *Accrual vs. Cash Method of Accounting.* D operates a hardware store. For 1994, D's first year of operation, D reported the following items of revenue and expense:

Cash receipts.............................	$140,000
Purchase of goods on credit.................	90,000
Payments on payables.....................	82,000

By year-end, D had unsold goods on hand with a value of $25,000.

a. Using the cash method of accounting, compute D's taxable income for the year.

b. Using the accrual method of accounting, compute D's taxable income for the year.

c. Which method of accounting is required for tax purposes? Why?

7-25 *Prepaid Interest.*   In each of the following cases, indicate the amount of the deduction for the current year. In each case, assume the taxpayer is a calendar year, cash basis taxpayer.

a.   On December 31, P, wishing to reduce his current year's tax liability, prepaid $3,000 of interest on his home mortgage for the first three months of the following taxable year.

b.   On December 1 of this year, T obtained a $100,000 loan to purchase her residence. The loan was secured by the residence. She paid two points to obtain the loan bearing a 6 percent interest rate.

c.   Same as (b) except the loan was used to purchase a duplex, which she will rent to others. The loan was secured by the duplex.

7-26 *Prepaid Rent.*   This year F, a cash basis taxpayer, secured a ten-year lease on a warehouse to be used in his business. Under the lease agreement he pays $12,000 on September 1 of each year for the following twelve months' rental.

a.   Assuming F pays $12,000 on September 1 for the next 12 months' rental, how much, if any, may he deduct? How would your answer change if F were an accrual basis taxpayer?

b.   In order to secure the lease, F also was required to pay an additional $12,000 as a security deposit. How much, if any, may he deduct?

7-27 *Prepaid Expenses.*   D, a cash basis taxpayer, operates a successful travel agency. One of her more significant costs is a special computer form on which airline tickets are printed as well as stationery on which itineraries are printed. Typically, D buys about a three-month supply of these forms for $2,000. Knowing that she will be in a lower tax bracket next year, D would like to accelerate her deductions to the current year.

a.   Assuming that D pays $12,000 on December 15 for forms which she expects to exhaust before the close of next year, how much can she deduct?

b.   Same as above except D purchases the larger volume of forms because D's supplier began offering special discounts for purchases in excess of $3,000.

7-28 *Expenses Producing Future Benefits.*   B took over as chief executive officer of Pentar Inc., which specialized in the manufacture of cameras. As part of his strategy to increase the corporation's share of the market, he ran a special advertising blitz just prior to Christmas that cost over $1,000,000. The marketing staff estimated that these expenditures very well could increase the company's share of the market by 10 percent over the next three years. Speculate on the treatment of the promotion expenses.

7-29 *Capital Expenditure or Repair.*   This year, Dandy Development Corporation purchased an apartment complex with 100 units. At the time of purchase, it had a 40 percent vacancy rate. As part of a major renovation, Dandy replaced all of the carpeting and painted all of the vacant units. Discuss the treatment of the expenditures.

7-30   *Identifying Capital Expenditures.*   K, a sole proprietor, made the following payments during the year. Indicate whether each is a capital expenditure.

     a.   Sales tax on the purchase of a new automobile
     b.   Mechanical pencil for K
     c.   Mops and buckets for maintenance of building
     d.   Freight paid on delivery of new machinery
     e.   Painting of K's office
     f.   Paving of dirt parking lot with concrete
     g.   Commissions to leasing agent to find new office space
     h.   Rewiring of building to accommodate new equipment

7-31   *Hobby Expenses—Effect on A.G.I.*   C is a successful attorney and stock car racing enthusiast. This year she decided to quit watching the races and start participating. She purchased a car and entered several local races. During the year, she had the following receipts and disbursements related to the racing activities:

Race winnings..............................	$3,000
Property taxes..............................	2,800
Fuel, supplies, maintenance.................	1,000

Her A.G.I. exclusive of any items related to the racing activities is $100,000.

     a.   Indicate the tax consequences assuming the activity is not considered to be a hobby.
     b.   Assuming the activity is treated as a hobby, what are the tax consequences?
     c.   Assuming the activity is deemed a hobby and property taxes are $4,000, what are the tax consequences?
     d.   What is the critical factor in determining whether an activity is a hobby or a business?
     e.   What circumstances suggest the activity is a business rather than a hobby?

7-32   *Hobby—Presumptive Rule.*   In 1992 R, a major league baseball player, purchased a small farm in North Carolina. He grows several crops and maintains a small herd of cattle on the farm. During 1992 his farming activities resulted in a $2,000 loss, which he claimed on his 1992 tax return, filed April 15, 1993. In 1994 his 1992 return was audited, and the IRS proposed an adjustment disallowing the loss from the farming activity, asserting that the activity was merely a hobby.

     a.   Assuming R litigates, who has the burden of proof as to the character of the activity?
     b.   Can R shift the burden of proof at this point in time?
     c.   Assume R filed the appropriate election for 1992 and reported losses of $3,000 in 1993 and profits of $14,000 in 1994, $5,000 in 1995, and $6,000 in 1996. What effect do the reported profits have?
     d.   When does the statute of limitations bar assessment of deficiencies with respect to the 1992 tax return?

7-33 *Investigation Expenses.* H currently operates several optical shops in Portland. During the year he traveled to Seattle and San Francisco to discuss with several doctors the possibility of locating optical shops adjacent to their practices. He incurred travel costs to Seattle of $175 and to San Francisco of $200. The physicians in Seattle agreed to an arrangement and H incurred $500 in legal fees drawing up the agreement. The physicians in San Francisco, however, would not agree, and H did not pursue the matter further.

In the following year, H decided to enter the ice cream business. He sent letters of inquiry to two major franchisers of ice cream stores and subsequently traveled to the headquarters of each. He paid $400 for travel to Phoenix for discussions with X Corporation and $500 for travel to Los Angeles for discussions with Y Corporation. He also paid an accountant $1,200 to evaluate the financial aspects of each franchise ($600 for each evaluation). H decided to acquire a franchise from Y Corporation. He paid an attorney $800 to review the franchising agreement.

   a. Discuss the tax treatment of H's expenses associated with the attempt to expand his optical shop business.

   b. Discuss the tax treatment of the expenses incurred in connection with the ice cream business assuming H acquires the Y franchise and begins business.

   c. Same as (b). Discuss the tax treatment of these expenses assuming H is forced to abandon the transaction after being informed that there is no franchise available in his city.

7-34 *Investigation Expenses.* P incurred significant expenses to investigate the possibility of opening a Dowell's Hamburgers franchise in Tokyo, Japan. Her expenditures included hiring a local firm to perform a feasibility study, travel, and accounting and legal expenses. Her 1994 expenditures total $25,000. With respect to this amount:

   a. Assuming this was P's first attempt at opening a business of her own, how much may she deduct in 1994 if she decides *not* to acquire the franchise?

   b. Assuming this was P's first attempt at opening a business of her own, how much may she deduct in 1994 if she decides to acquire the franchise?

   c. Assuming P was already in the fast food business (she owns a Dowell's franchise in Toledo, Ohio), how much may she deduct in 1994 to acquire the franchise?

7-35 *Capital Expenditures.* Consider the following:

   a. A corporate taxpayer reimbursed employees for amounts they had loaned to the corporation's former president, who was losing money at the racetrack. Comment on the deductibility of these payments as well as those expenditures discussed in *Example 7* of this chapter (relating to payments of debts previously discharged by bankruptcy) in light of the rules concerning capital expenditures.

   b. How are the costs of expenditures such as land and investment securities recovered?

   c. How are the costs of expenditures for goodwill recovered?

   d. Distinguish between a capital expenditure and a repair.

7-36 *Classification of Deductions.* M works as the captain of a boat. His income for the year is $20,000. During the year, he purchased a special uniform for $100. Indicate the amount of the deduction and whether it is for or from A.G.I. for the following situations:

a. M's boat is a 50-foot yacht, and he operates his business as a sole proprietorship (i.e., he is self-employed).

b. M is an employee for Yachts of Fun Inc.

c. M is an employee for Yachts, which reimbursed him $70 of the cost (included in his income on Form W-2).

7-37 *Computing Employee's Deductions.* T, who is single, is currently a supervisor in the tax department of a public accounting firm in Milwaukee. T's total income for the year consisted of compensation of $32,000 and dividend income of $2,100. During the year, she incurred the following expenses:

AICPA dues...	$ 200
State Society of Accountants dues.................	100
Subscriptions to tax journals.......................	300
Tax return preparation.............................	200
Pen and pencil set.................................	50
Cleaning of suits...................................	189
Safe deposit box (holds investment documents)....	30
Annual fee on brokerage account..................	20
Qualified residence interest.......................	4,000

T's employer reimbursed her $50 for the AICPA dues (included in her income).

a. Compute T's taxable income.

b. Assuming T expects her expenses to be about the same for the next several years, what advice can you offer?

7-38 *Computing Employee's Deductions.* Z, a single taxpayer, is employed as a nurse at a local hospital. Z's records reflect the following items of revenue and expense for 1994:

Gross wages......................................	$20,000
Expenses:	
Employee travel expenses, not reimbursed.......	1,100
Cost of commuting to and from work,	
reimbursed (included in gross wages)..........	520
Charitable contributions...........................	700
Interest and taxes on personal residence...........	3,900
Nurse's uniform, reimbursed (included in	
gross wages).................................	250

a. What is Z's A.G.I.?

b. What is Z's total of itemized deductions?

7-39 *Interest.* Mr. E operates a replacement window business as a sole proprietorship. He uses the cash method of accounting. On November 1, 1994 he secured a loan in order to purchase a new warehouse to be used in his business. Information regarding the loan and purchase of the warehouse is shown below. All of the costs indicated were paid during the year.

Term......................................	20 years
Loan origination fee.......................	$ 2,000
Points.....................................	6,000
One year's interest paid in advance........	20,000
Legal fees for recording mortgage lien......	500

What amount may E deduct in 1994?

7-40 *Insurance.* Hawk Harris owns and operates the Waterfield Mudhens, a franchise in an indoor soccer league. Both Hawk and the corporation are cash basis, calendar year taxpayers. During 1994 the corporation purchased the following policies:

Policy Description	Cost	Date Paid
Two-year fire and theft effective 12/1/94.........................	$2,400	12/15/94
One-year life insurance policy on Jose Greatfoot, star forward; the corporation is beneficiary; effective 11/1/94..............	1,000	11/1/94
One-year group-term life insurance policy covering entire team and staff; effective 1/1/94...........................	9,000	1/15/94
One-year policy for payments of overhead costs should the team strike and attendance fall; effective 11/1/94.....................	3,600	9/1/94

In addition to the policies purchased above, the corporation is unable to get insurance on certain business risks. Therefore the corporation has set up a reserve—a separate account—to which it contributes $5,000 on February 1 of each year.
How much may the corporation deduct for 1994?

7-41 *Life Insurance.* The Great Cookie Corporation is owned equally by F and G. Under the articles of incorporation, the corporation is required to purchase the stock of each shareholder upon his or her death to ensure that it does not pass to some undesirable third party. To finance the purchase, the corporation purchased a life insurance policy on both F and G, naming the corporation as beneficiary. The annual premium is $5,000. Can the corporation deduct the premiums?

7-42 *Business Life Insurance.* L, 56, has operated her sole proprietorship successfully since its inception three years ago. This year she has decided to expand. To this end, she borrowed $100,000 from the bank, which would be used for financing expansion of the business. The bank required L to take out a life insurance policy on her own life that would serve as security for the business loan. Are the premiums deductible?

7-43 *Public Policy—Fines, Lobbying, etc.* M is engaged in the construction business in Tucson. Indicate whether the following expenses are deductible.

    a. The Occupational Safety and Health Act (OSHA) requires contractors to fence around certain construction sites. M determined that the fences would cost $1,000 and the fine for not fencing would be only $650. As a result, he did not construct the fences and paid a fine of $650.

    b. M often uses Mexican quarry tile on the floors of homes that he builds. To obtain the tiles, he drives his truck across the border to a small entrepreneur's house and purchases the materials. On the return trip he often pays a Mexican customs official to "expedite" his going through customs. Without the payment, the inspection process would often be tedious and consume several hours. This year he paid the customs officials $200.

    c. M paid $100 for an advertisement supporting the administration's economic policies, which he felt would reduce interest rates and thus make homes more affordable. In addition, he paid $700 for travel to Washington, D.C. to testify before a Congressional Committee on the effects of high interest rates on the housing industry. While there, he paid $100 to a political action committee to attend a dinner, the proceeds from which went to Senator Q.

7-44 *Limitations on Business Deductions.* This is an extension of Problem 7-22(d). In that problem, you are asked to determine if the case contains expenditures that are ordinary, necessary, and reasonable under the provisions of Code § 162. Assume the positive criteria of § 162 are met (i.e., the expenditures are ordinary, necessary, and reasonable). Are there any additional provisions in § 162 that will cause the expenditures to be disallowed?

7-45 *Related Taxpayers—Sale.* E sold stock to her son for $8,000. She purchased the stock several years ago for $11,000.

    a. What amount of loss will E report on the sale?

    b. What amount of gain or loss will the son report if he sells the stock for $12,000 to an unrelated party?

    c. If the son sells for $10,000?

    d. If the son sells for $4,000?

7-46 *Related Taxpayers—Different Accounting Methods.* G, a cash basis, calendar year taxpayer, owns 100 percent of XYZ Corporation. XYZ is a calendar year, accrual basis taxpayer engaged in the advertising business. G leases a building to the Corporation for $1,000 per month. In December, XYZ accrues the $1,000 rental due. Indicate the tax treatment to XYZ and G assuming the payment is

    a. Made on December 30 of the current year; or

    b. Made on April 1 of the following year.

    c. Would your answers above change if G owned 30 percent of XYZ?

7-47 *Constructive Ownership Rules.* How much of RST Corporation's stock is B considered as owning?

Owner	Shares Directly Owned
B...	20
C, B's brother.............................	30
D, B's partner.............................	40
E, B's 60-percent-owned corporation........	100
Other unrelated parties.....................	10

7-48 *Expenses of Another Taxpayer.* B is the only child of P and will inherit the family fortune. P, who is in the 28 percent tax bracket, is willing to give B and his wife $500 a month. Comment on the advisability of P paying the following directly in lieu of making a gift.

  a. Medical expenses of B who makes $20,000 during the year; P (the father) provides 55 percent of B's support.

  b. Interest and principal payments on B's home mortgage on which B and his wife are the sole obligees.

  c. Same as (b) except that P is also an obligee on the note.

7-49 *Losses.* This year was simply a financial disaster for Z. Indicate the effects of the following transactions on Z's taxable income. Ignore any limitations that may exist.

  a. After the stock market crash, Z sold her stock and realized a loss of $1,000.

  b. Z sold her husband's truck for $3,000 (basis $2,000) and her own car for $5,000 (basis $9,000). Both vehicles were used for personal purposes.

  c. Z's $500 camera was stolen.

  d. The land next to Z's house was rezoned to light industrial, driving down the value of her home by $10,000.

7-50 *Planning Deductions.* X, 67, is a widow, her husband having died several years ago. Each year, X receives about $30,000 of interest and dividends. Because the mortgage on her home is virtually paid off, her only potential itemized deductions are her contributions to her church and real estate taxes. Her anticipated deductions are:

Year	Contribution
1995	$2,000
1996	3,000
1997	1,000

What tax advice can you offer X?

7-51 *Timing Deductions.* T currently figures that Federal, state, and local taxes consume about 30 percent of his income at the margin. Next year, however, due to a tax law change his taxes should increase to about 40 percent and remain at that level for at least five or six years. Assuming T buys a computer for $4,000 and he has the option of deducting all of the cost this year or deducting it ratably through depreciation over the next five years, what advice can you offer?

7-52 *Classification and Deductibility.* In each of the following independent situations, indicate for the current taxable year the amounts deductible *for* A.G.I., *from* A.G.I., or *not deductible* at all. Unless otherwise stated, assume all taxpayers use the cash basis method of accounting and report using the calendar year.

a. M spent $1,000 on a life insurance policy covering her own life.

b. G is an author of novels. His wife attempted to have him declared insane and have him committed. Fearing the effect that his wife's charges may have on him and his book sales, G paid $11,000 in legal fees resulting in a successful defense.

c. Taxpayer, a plumber employed by XYZ Corporation, paid union dues of $100.

d. Q Corporation paid T, its president and majority shareholder, a salary of $100,000. Employees in comparable positions earn salaries of $70,000.

e. L operates a furniture business as a sole proprietorship. She rents a warehouse (on a month-to-month basis) used for storing items sold in her store. In late December, L paid $2,000 for rental of the warehouse for the month of January.

f. M is a self-employed security officer. He paid $100 for uniforms and $25 for having them cleaned.

g. N is a security officer employed by the owner of a large apartment complex. He pays $150 for uniforms. In addition, he paid $15 for having them cleaned. His employer reimbursed him $60 of the cost of the uniforms (included in his income on Form W-2).

h. K owns a duplex as an investment. During the year, she paid $75 for advertisements seeking tenants. She was unable to rent the duplex, and thus no income was earned this year.

i. P paid $200 for subscriptions to technical journals to be used in his employment activities. Although P was fully reimbursed by his employer, his employer did not report the reimbursement in P's income.

7-53 *Classification and Deductibility.* In each of the following independent situations, indicate for the current taxable year the amounts deductible *for* A.G.I., *from* A.G.I., or *not deductible* at all. Unless otherwise stated, assume all taxpayers use the cash basis method of accounting and report using the calendar year.

a. O paid the interest and taxes of $1,000 on his ex-wife's home mortgage. The divorce agreement provided that he could claim deductions for the payments.

b. P paid an attorney $1,500 in legal fees related to her divorce. Of these fees, $600 is for advice concerning the tax consequences of transferring some of P's stock to her husband as part of the property settlement.

c. R paid $10,000 for a small warehouse on an acre of land. He used the building for several months before tearing it down and erecting a hamburger stand.

d. H and his wife moved into the city and no longer needed their personal automobiles. They sold their Chevrolet for a $1,000 loss and their Buick for a $400 gain.

e. C is employed as a legal secretary. This year he paid an employment agency $300 for finding him a new, higher-paying job as a legal secretary.

f. X operates his own truck service. He paid $80 in fines for driving trucks that were overweight according to state law.

g. T, an employee, paid $175 to an accountant for preparing her personal income tax returns.

7-54 *Classification and Deductibility.*   In each of the following independent situations, indicate for the current taxable year the amounts deductible *for* A.G.I., *from* A.G.I., or *not deductible* at all. Unless otherwise stated, assume all taxpayers use the cash basis method of accounting and report using the calendar year.

   a. B sold stock to his mother for a $700 loss. B's mother subsequently sold the stock for $400 less than she had paid to B.

   b. Same as (a) but assume the mother sold the stock for $500 more than she had paid to B.

   c. D operates three pizza restaurants as a sole proprietorship in Indianapolis. In July he paid $1,000 in air fares to travel to Chicago and Detroit to determine the feasibility of opening additional restaurants. Because of economic conditions, D decided not to open any additional restaurants.

   d. T owns and operates several gun stores as a sole proprietorship. In light of gun control legislation, he traveled to the state capitol at a cost of $80 to testify before a committee. In addition, he traveled around the state speaking at various Rotary and Kiwanis Club functions on the pending legislation at a cost of $475. T also placed an advertisement in the local newspaper concerning the merit of the legislation at a cost of $50. He pays dues to the National Rifle Association of $100.

   e. D is employed as a ship captain for a leisure cruise company. He paid $1,000 for rent on a warehouse where he stores smuggled narcotics, which he sells illegally.

   f. M, a plumber and an accrual basis taxpayer, warrants his work. This year he estimates that expenses attributable to the warranty work are about 3 percent of sales, or $3,000.

   g. G, a computer operator, pays $75 for a subscription to an investment newsletter devoted to investment opportunities in state and municipal bonds.

7-55 *Employee Business Expenses: Planning.*   J is employed as a salesman by Bigtime Business Forms Inc. He is considering the purchase of a new automobile that he would use primarily for business. Are there any tax factors that J might consider before purchasing the new car?

CUMULATIVE PROBLEMS

7-56 Tony Johnson (I.D. No. 456-23-7657), age 45, is single. He lives at 5220 Grand Avenue, Brooklyn, NY 46289. Tony is employed by RTI Corporation, which operates a chain of restaurants in and around New York City. He has supervisory responsibilities over the managers of four restaurants. An examination of his records for 1994 revealed the following information.

   1. During the year, Tony earned $33,000. His employer withheld $3,200 in Federal income taxes and the proper amount of FICA taxes. Tony obtained his current job through an employment agency to which he paid a $150 fee. He previously was employed as a manager of another restaurant. Due to the new job, it was necessary to improve his wardrobe. Accordingly, Tony purchased several new suits at a cost of $600.

   2. On the days that Tony works, he normally eats his meals at the restaurants for purposes of quality control. There is no charge for the meals, which are worth $2,000.

   3. He provides 60 percent of the support for his father, age 70, who lived with Tony all year and who has no income other than social security benefits of $7,000 during the year. Tony provided over one-half of the cost of maintaining the home.

4. Dividend income from General Motors Corporation stock that he owned was $350. Interest income on savings was $200.

5. Tony and other employees of the corporation park in a nearby parking garage. The parking garage bills RTI Corporation for the parking. Tony figures that his free parking is worth $1,000 annually.

6. Tony subscribes to several trade publications for restaurants at a cost of $70.

7. During the year, he paid $200 to a bank for a personal financial plan. Based on this plan, Tony made several investments, including a $2,000 contribution to an individual retirement account, and also rented for $30 a safety deposit box in which he stores certain investment-related documents.

8. Tony purchased a new home, paying three points on a loan of $70,000. He also paid $6,000 of interest on his home mortgage during the year. In addition, he paid $650 of real property taxes on the home. He has receipts for sales taxes of $534.

9. While hurrying to deliver an important package for his employer, Tony received a $78 ticket for violating the speed limit. Because his employer had asked that he deliver the package as quickly as possible, Tony was reimbursed $78 for the ticket, which he paid.

Compute Tony's taxable income for the year. If forms are used for the computations, complete Form 1040 and Schedule A. (Use 1993 tax forms if the 1994 forms are not available.)

7-57   Wendy White (I.D. No. 526-30-9001), age 29, is single. She lives at 1402 Pacific Beach Ave., San Diego, CA 92230. Wendy is employed by KXXR television station as the evening news anchor. An examination of her records for 1994 revealed the following information.

1. Wendy earned $110,000 in salary. Her employer withheld $22,000 in Federal income taxes and the proper amount of FICA taxes.

2. Wendy also received $10,000 in self-employment income from personal appearances during the year. Her unreimbursed expenses related to this income were: transportation and lodging, $523; meals, $120; and office supplies, $58.

3. Wendy reports the following additional deductions: home mortgage interest, $6,250; charitable contributions, $1,300; state and local income taxes, $3,100; and employment-related expenses, $920.

Compute Wendy's taxable income for the year and her tax due (including any self-employment tax). If forms are used for the computations, complete Form 1040, Schedule A, Schedule C, and Schedule SE.

Reminder: FICA and self-employment taxes are composed of two elements: social security (old age, survivor, and disability insurance) and Medicare health insurance (MHI). In 1994, social security is paid at a rate of 6.2 percent (12.4 percent for self-employed individuals) on the first $60,600 of earned income; MHI is paid at a rate of 1.45 percent (2.9 percent for self-employed individuals) on all earned income.

RESEARCH PROBLEMS

7-58   T and two associates are equal owners in LST Corporation. The three formed the corporation several years ago with the idea of capitalizing on the fitness movement. After a modest beginning and meager returns, the corporation did extremely well this year. As a result, the corporation plans on paying the three individuals' salaries that T believes the IRS may deem unreasonable. T wonders whether he can avoid the tax consequences associated with an unreasonable compensation determination by paying back whatever amount is ultimately deemed a dividend.

   a.   What would be the effect on T's taxable income should he repay the portion of a salary deemed a dividend?

   b.   Would there be any adverse effects of adopting a payback arrangement?

   Partial list of research aids:

   Vincent E. Oswald, 49 T.C. 645.
   Rev. Rul. 69-115, 1969-1 C.B. 50.

7-59   C, a professor of film studies at State University, often meets with her doctoral students at her home. In her home, C has a room that she uses solely to conduct business related to the classes she teaches at the university. In the room she and her students often review the movies the students have made to satisfy requirements in their doctoral program. Can C deduct expenses related to her home office?

7-60   R moved to St. Louis in 1993 and purchased a home. After living there for a year, his family had grown and required a much larger home. On August 1, 1994 they purchased their dream house, which cost far more than their first home. Shortly before he closed on the new residence, he put his first house on the market to sell. After two months had passed, however, he had received no offers. Fearing that he would be unable to pay the debt on both homes, R decided to rent his old home while trying to sell it. Surprisingly, he was able to rent the house immediately. However, in order to secure the party's agreement to rent monthly, he was required to perform a few repairs costing $500. Seven months after he had rented the home, R sold it. During the rental period, R paid the utilities and various other expenses. R has come to you for your advice on how these events in 1994 would affect his tax return.

7-61   In November 1994 B, employed as a life insurance salesman for PQR Insurance Company in Newark, New Jersey, purchased a personal computer for use in his work. B has come to you for help in deciding how to handle this purchase on his 1994 tax return. He, of course, wants to expense the full price of the computer under Code § 179.

   B relates the following salient information to you with respect to this purchase:

   1.   B files a joint return with his wife, L. They have a combined A.G.I. of $65,000 before considering this item. They have sufficient qualified expenditures to itemize deductions on Schedule A, but they have no miscellaneous itemized deductions.

   2.   B paid $3,000 for the laptop computer, which will be used 100% for business use.

3. B bought the computer to analyze client data. He figures this will help him increase his sales because he can analyze the results of various insurance options at the client's home or office (all personalized, of course).

4. PQR does not provide B with company-owned computing equipment. In fact, they refused to pay for B's computer because the expense of providing computers for all of PQR's agents would be too great.

How should B treat this purchase on his 1994 tax return?

7-62 On January 28, 1994 S comes to you for tax preparation advice. She has always prepared her own return, but it has become somewhat complicated and she needs professional advice.

During your initial interview, you discover that S is a teacher at a high school in Chicago, Illinois. She is also the coach of the golf team. In 1991 S decided she wanted to be a professional golfer. So, when she was 32 years old, she began a part-time apprenticeship program with the Professional Golfers' Association of America (PGA), where she was an unpaid assistant to the pro at a local country club. Then, in 1992 she became a member of the PGA and began her professional career.

S has not made much money as a professional golfer. In fact, her expenses exceeded her income in both 1992 and 1993 ($4,000 loss in 1992; $3,500 loss in 1993). Believing she was actively engaged in a trade or business (she kept separate records for her golf activities, practiced about 10 hours each week, and worked with a pro whenever she could), S deducted her golf-related expenses on Schedule C and reported her losses from this activity on her prior returns.

The IRS has challenged S's 1992 and 1993 loss deductions, calling them nondeductible "hobby" losses. Is the IRS correct in this matter? Would she win if the matter is taken to court? What planning steps can S take to ensure that any future losses are deductible trade or business losses?

LEARNING OBJECTIVES

Upon completion of this chapter you will be able to:

- Discuss the rules governing the deduction of several common expenses incurred by employees and self-employed persons
- Recognize when educational expenses are deductible
- Explain the rules concerning the deduction of moving expenses
- Describe when expenses of maintaining a home office are deductible
- Distinguish between deductible transportation expenses and nondeductible commuting costs
- Understand the differences between deductible travel expenses and deductible transportation costs
- Determine when entertainment expenses can be deducted
- Describe the 50 percent limitation on the deduction of meals and entertainment
- Explain the special record-keeping requirements for travel and entertainment expenses
- Discuss the two types of reimbursement arrangements: accountable and nonaccountable plans

CHAPTER OUTLINE

Education Expenses	8-1	Foreign Conventions	8-31
Requirements for Deduction	8-2	Cruise Ships	8-32
Travel as a Form of Education	8-3	Entertainment Expenses	8-33
Types and Classification of Education		Deduction Requirements	8-34
Deductions	8-4	Entertainment Facilities	8-38
Moving Expenses	8-5	Exceptions to Directly-Related-to	
Distance Requirement	8-5	and Associated-with Tests	8-38
Time Test	8-6	Fifty Percent Limitation	
Deductible Moving Expenses	8-7	on Entertainment and Meal	
Classifying and Reporting the Moving		Expenses	8-39
Expense Deduction	8-9	Limitations on Deductions	
Home Office Expenses	8-10	for Tickets	8-41
Requirements for Deductibility	8-11	Business Gifts	8-41
Amount Deductible	8-13	Travel and Entertainment	
Daycare and Storage Use	8-15	Recordkeeping Requirements	8-42
Rental of Residence	8-15	Reporting Business Expenses and	
Residential Phone Service	8-16	Losses	8-46
Transportation Expenses	8-17	Sole Proprietors and Self-Employed	
Deductible Transportation versus		Persons	8-46
Nondeductible Commuting	8-18	Employees	8-46
Computing Car Expenses	8-23	Tax Planning Considerations	8-55
Classification of Transportation		Moving Expenses	8-55
and Travel Expenses	8-25	Travel and Entertainment	
Travel Expenses	8-26	Expenses	8-55
Away-from-Home Test	8-26	Home Office Deduction	8-56
Combined Business and Pleasure		Problem Materials	8-57
Travel	8-28		

Chapter **8**

EMPLOYEE BUSINESS EXPENSES

Over the years, many rules have been developed to govern the deductibility of specific business expenses. These rules normally augment the general requirements of § 162 (identified in Chapter 7) by establishing additional criteria that must be satisfied before a deduction may be claimed. As a practical matter, the primary purpose of many of these rules is to prohibit taxpayers from deducting what are in reality personal expenditures. For example, consider a taxpayer who uses a room at home to work or a taxpayer who takes a customer to lunch. In both cases, the expenses incurred very well may be genuine business expenses and deductible under the general criteria. On the other hand, such expenses could simply be *disguised* personal expenditures. As these examples suggest, some of the expenses that are likely to be manipulated are those often incurred by employees in connection with their employment duties. Such common employee expenses as those for travel and entertainment, education, moving, and home offices have long been the source of controversy. Of course, such costs are incurred by a self-employed person as well as by employees and raise similar problems. This chapter examines the special provisions applicable to these items.

EDUCATION EXPENSES

Historically, the tax law has taken the view that most education expenses are not deductible. For example, an art appreciation course for the taxpayer's cultural enrichment is purely personal in nature. Consequently, its cost is not deductible. Similarly, no deduction is granted for expenses of a college education on the theory that they are costs of preparing the taxpayer to enter a new business—not the costs of carrying on a business. Therefore, such general education expenses are nondeductible capital expenditures for which no amortization is allowed. Other education expenses, however, such as those incurred by an accountant to attend a seminar on a new tax law, are considered essential costs of pursuing income and are deductible like other ordinary and necessary business expenses. To ensure that deductions are permitted only for education expenses that serve current business objectives and are not personal or capital in nature, special tests must be met.

The Regulations allow a deduction if the education expenses satisfy *either* of the following conditions *and* are not considered personal or capital in nature, as discussed below.[1]

1. The education maintains or improves skills required of the taxpayer in his or her employment or other trade or business.

2. The education meets the express requirements imposed by either the individual's employer or applicable law, and the taxpayer must meet such requirements to retain his or her job, position, or rate of compensation.

Education expenses that meet either of these conditions are still not deductible if they are considered personal or capital expenditures under either of the following two tests:[2]

1. The education is necessary to meet the minimum educational requirements of the taxpayer's trade or business.

2. The education qualifies the taxpayer for a new trade or business.

REQUIREMENTS FOR DEDUCTION

Maintain Skills. For the expense to qualify under the first criterion, the education must be related to the taxpayer's present trade or business and maintain or improve the skills used in such business. The taxpayer must be able to establish the necessary connection between the studies pursued and the taxpayer's current employment. For example, a personnel manager seeking an M.B.A. degree was allowed to deduct all of her education expenses when she ingeniously related each course taken to her job (e.g., a computer course enabled her to be more effective in acquiring information from and communicating with computer personnel).[3] In contrast, the Tax Court denied the deductions of a research chemist's cost of an M.B.A., indicating that courses such as advanced business finance, corporate strategy, and business law were only remotely related to the skills needed for his job.[4]

Refresher and continuing education courses ordinarily meet the skills maintenance test.

> **Example 1.** T repairs appliances. To maintain his proficiency, he often attends training schools. The costs of attending such schools are deductible because the education is necessary to maintain and improve the skills required in his job.

Required by Employer or Law. Once the minimum education requirements are met to obtain a job, additional education may be required by the employer or by law to retain the taxpayer's salary or position. Costs for such education are deductible as long as they do not qualify the taxpayer for a new trade or business.

---

[1] Reg. § 1.162-5(a).

[2] Reg. §§ 1.162-5(b)(2) and (3).

[3] *Frank S. Blair, III,* 41 TCM 289, T.C. Memo 1980-488.

[4] *Ronald T. Smith,* 41 TCM 1186, T.C. Memo 1981-149.

Example 2. This year, R took a new job as a high school instructor in science. State law requires that teachers obtain their masters degree within five years of becoming employed. Expenses for college courses for this purpose are deductible even though they lead to a degree since such education is mandatory under state law.

New Trade or Business. If education prepares the taxpayer to enter a new trade or business, no deduction is permitted. In this regard, a mere change of duties usually is not considered a new business.[5] For example, a science teacher may deduct the cost of courses enabling him or her to teach art since the switch is a mere change in duties. The taxpayer becomes qualified for a new occupation if the education enables the taxpayer to perform substantially different tasks, regardless of whether the taxpayer actually uses the skills acquired.

Example 3. R was hired as a trust officer in a bank several years ago. His employer now requires that all trust officers must have a law degree. R may not deduct the cost of obtaining a law degree because the degree qualifies him for a new trade or business.[6] No deduction is allowed even though it is required by his employer and R does not actually engage in the practice of law.

Minimum Education. Expenses of education undertaken to gain entry into a business or to meet the minimum standards required in a business are not deductible. These standards are determined in light of the typical conditions imposed by the particular job. This rule operates to prohibit the deduction of such expenses as those for a review course for the bar or C.P.A. exam and fees to take such professional exams.[7] Similarly, education expenses related to a pay increase or promotion may not be deductible under this rule if the increase or promotion was the primary objective of the education.

TRAVEL AS A FORM OF EDUCATION

Prior to 1986, travel in and of itself was considered a deductible form of education when it was related to a taxpayer's trade or business. For example, an instructor of Spanish could travel around Spain during the summer to learn more about the Spanish culture and improve her conversational Spanish. In such case, the travel cost would have been deductible since it was related to the taxpayer's trade or business. In 1986, Congress became concerned that many taxpayers were using this rule to deduct what were essentially the costs of a personal vacation. Moreover, Congress believed that any business purpose served by traveling for general education purposes was insignificant. To eliminate possible abuse, no deduction is allowed simply because the travel itself is educational.[8] Deductions are allowed for travel only when the education activity otherwise qualifies and the travel expense is necessary to pursue such activity. For example, a deduction for travel would be allowed where a Professor of French literature travels to France to take courses that are offered only at the Sorbonne.

---

[5] Reg. § 1.162-5(b)(3).

[6] Reg. § 1.162-5(b)(3)(ii), Ex. 1.

[7] Rev. Rul. 69-292, 1969-1 C.B. 84.

[8] § 274(m)(2).

TYPES AND CLASSIFICATION OF EDUCATION DEDUCTIONS

Education expenses normally deductible include costs of tuition, books, supplies, typing, transportation, and travel (including meals, lodging, and similar expenses). Typical education expenses are for college or vocational courses, continuing professional education programs, professional development courses, and similar courses or seminars.

The costs of transportation between the taxpayer's place of work and school are deductible. If the taxpayer goes home before going to school, however, the expense of going from home to school is deductible, but only to the extent that it does not exceed the costs of going directly from work. The cost of transportation from home to school on a nonworking day represents nondeductible commuting.

Unreimbursed educational expenditures of an employee are treated as miscellaneous itemized deductions subject to the 2 percent floor. In contrast, if an employer reimburses an employee for such expenses under an *accountable plan* (discussed later in this chapter), the reimbursement is excludable from gross income. Any reimbursement not made under an accountable plan must be included in the employee's gross income, and qualifying deductions must be treated as miscellaneous itemized deductions. Finally, education expenses incurred by a self-employed person are deductible *for* A.G.I.

✔ CHECK YOUR KNOWLEDGE

For each of the following situations, indicate whether the expenditures are deductible as education expenses.

Review Question 1.   Last June, D graduated magna cum laude from the University of Virginia. This fall he entered Johns Hopkins Medical School, paying tuition of thousands of dollars.

The costs of medical school are not deductible for two reasons. First, the education is necessary to meet the minimum educational requirements to become a doctor. Second, the education qualifies the taxpayer to carry on a new trade or business.

Review Question 2.   H, a practicing tax accountant, is taking a series of correspondence courses to become a certified financial planner.

As may be clear by now, very little is black or white in the tax law; here is yet another case. The IRS would probably take the position that the expenses are not deductible because the education qualifies the taxpayer to carry on a new trade or business. From the accountant's perspective, however, the coursework simply improves or maintains the skills that he is already using in his business. It would appear that the education does not necessarily enable the taxpayer to do anything that he could not do before except to hold himself out as a certified financial planner. The accountant would deduct the expense.

Review Question 3.   Ms. McClain, an elementary school teacher, took a sabbatical to Ireland, where she studied the art of storytelling.

Whether her expenses are deductible ultimately depends on the facts and circumstances. As noted above, changes made in 1986 aimed to eliminate deductions for travel that was primarily personal in nature. In this case, the taxpayer appears to be pursuing that which might not be available at home. Assuming she spent a reasonable amount of time studying and researching, the expense would be deductible. In contrast, consider an architect who travels all over Europe simply taking pictures of classic architectural styles that he may incorporate in his work. Without more, a court would probably view his trip as merely a disguised vacation and deny a deduction for his travel expenses.

MOVING EXPENSES

For many years, moving expenses were viewed as nondeductible personal expenses. In 1964, however, Congress revised its position, believing that moving expenses necessitated by the taxpayer's employment should be regarded as a deductible cost of earning income. To this end, Code § 217 was enacted, expressly authorizing a deduction for moving expenses. Section 217 allows self-employed individuals and employees to deduct moving expenses incurred in connection with beginning employment or changing job locations. To ensure that the deduction is allowed only for moves required by the taxpayer's employment, the taxpayer must satisfy *both* a distance test and a time test before the deduction may be claimed.

DISTANCE REQUIREMENT

The thrust of § 217 is to allow a taxpayer to deduct moving expenses only if there is a change in job location *and* the new location is sufficiently far away that it essentially requires the taxpayer to uproot and move his or her residence. This idea is captured in a somewhat misleading 50-mile distance test.[9] The taxpayer does not satisfy the requirement simply by moving 50 miles to a new residence in connection with a new job location. If this were the case, the taxpayer could meet the requirement by simply moving his office down the hall and at the same time moving his residence 50 miles. Instead, the distance test is constructed to determine if the taxpayer's commute to the new job site *without the move* would have increased by more than 50 miles. Technically, the condition is satisfied if the distance between the old residence and the new job site is at least 50 miles greater than the distance between the old residence and the old job site. Note that both distances are measured from the taxpayer's *former residence*. Thus, if the taxpayer's old commute was four miles, the new commute (absent a move) would have to be at least 54 miles ($54 - 4 = 50$) before the test is satisfied.

---

[9] The Revenue Reconciliation Act of 1993 increased the distance requirement from 35 miles to 50 miles beginning in 1994.

Example 4. During the year, R was promoted to district sales manager, requiring her to move from Tucson to Phoenix. To determine whether the 50-mile test is met, the distances shown below must be compared.

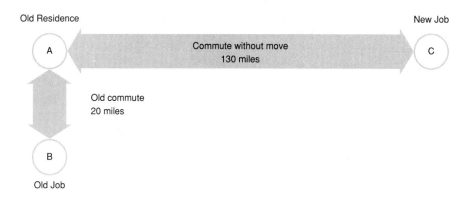

Since the distance between R's old residence and new job (AC = 130 miles) exceeds the distance between R's old residence and old job (AB = 20 miles) by more than 50 miles (130 − 20 = 110), the distance requirement is satisfied. In this case, it is quite clear that if the taxpayer had not moved, her commute would have increased significantly (110 miles). Consequently, § 217 grants her a deduction for the costs of moving her residence to a place where the commute is more reasonable. In applying the test, note that the location of the new residence is irrelevant.

If the taxpayer has no old job site, the distance test is satisfied if the new job site is 50 miles from the old residence.[10]

TIME TEST

If taxpayers were not required to maintain employment at the new job site for a minimum amount of time, they could move from place to place, taking temporary jobs in each location to justify the deduction of what in effect are personal travel expenses. To prohibit this possibility, the second test generally requires the taxpayer to work for a *sustained period* of time upon arrival at the new job location. This condition is met if the taxpayer is a *full-time* employee in the area of the new job location for at least 39 weeks during the 12-month period immediately following arrival.[11] Alternatively, the taxpayer may satisfy the test by being an employee or self-employed on a *full-time* basis for at least 78 weeks during the 24-month period after arrival. Note, however, that—like the first test—39 of these 78 weeks must be during the first 12-month period. In either case, the taxpayer need not work for the same employer or for 39 weeks in a row. The time

---

[10] § 217(c)(1).

[11] § 217(c)(2).

requirement is waived if the taxpayer dies, becomes disabled, is involuntarily dismissed, or is transferred by the new employer.[12]

> **Example 5.** N, an accountant, left his job in Boston to take a new job with a firm in Orlando. After working for the firm for eight months, he became dissatisfied and quit to open his own practice as a sole proprietor. Due to the poor economy, N closed the business after six months and moved to Denver. N may not deduct his expenses of moving to Orlando. Since he was employed for only 32 weeks (eight months) during the 12-month period after arrival in Orlando, he does not meet the 39-week test for employees. Similarly, he does not meet the alternative 78-week test since he was employed or self-employed only 56 weeks (14 months) of the 24-month period in Orlando after his arrival. Whether the costs of moving to Denver are deductible depends on whether either of the tests can be satisfied.

In many instances, taxpayers do not know by the end of the tax year whether they will be able to satisfy the time test. Accordingly, the law permits the taxpayer to claim the deduction on the assumption that the test will be satisfied. If the test is subsequently failed, the taxpayer must increase income in the year of failure by the amount of the previous deduction. In lieu of claiming the deduction prior to satisfaction of the test, the taxpayer may wait until the test is satisfied and file an amended return for the year of the moving expense.

DEDUCTIBLE MOVING EXPENSES

For many years, taxpayers were allowed to deduct a variety of moving expenses. These included not only direct expenses such as the cost of moving the taxpayer's personal belongings and the cost of traveling to the new location but also a limited amount of indirect expenses (up to $3,000). For example, a taxpayer could deduct expenses for house-hunting trips, temporary living at the new location, and expenses related to disposing of the taxpayer's former residence. In 1993, however, Congress eliminated the deduction for all indirect moving expenses. Beginning in 1994, only direct moving expenses are deductible. They are:[13]

1. Costs of moving household goods and personal belongings; and

2. Costs of traveling from the old location to the new location.

Costs of Moving Household Goods and Personal Belongings. This category of direct moving expenses includes the following:[14]

- Packing, crating, and transporting the taxpayer's personal possessions (e.g., the cost of hiring a moving company or renting a truck)

---

[12] § 217(d).

[13] §§ 217(b)(1)(A) and (B).

[14] Reg. § 1.217-2(b)(3).

- Storage and insurance of goods and personal effects while "in-transit" (i.e., any consecutive 30-day period after the day the items are moved from the former home and before they are delivered to the new home)

- Connecting and disconnecting utilities required by the moving of the taxpayer's appliances

- Moving a pet

- Shipping a car

Losses sustained on dispositions of memberships in clubs, expenses of refitting rugs and drapes, mortgage prepayment penalties (although these are usually deductible as interest), and similar expenses are not deductible.

Costs of Traveling. Once the taxpayer's furniture and other items are out the door, the taxpayer's household must follow. Only the costs of moving a taxpayer's family members (including pets) are deductible. Those for such nonfamily members as servants, chauffeurs, governesses, or nurses do not qualify. The following travel expenses are deductible:

- Transportation costs. The taxpayer may use actual expenses (i.e., the costs of oil, gasoline, tolls, and parking—but not those for general repairs or maintenance) or 9 cents per mile.

- Lodging expenses. The taxpayer may deduct the costs of lodging incurred in traveling to the new location. Beginning in 1994, no deduction is allowed for any meal expenses related to the move.[15]

Example 6. J, who was employed by the San Francisco 49ers, was traded to the Kansas City Chiefs during the year. Although he had lived in San Francisco for years, J decided he would move permanently to Kansas City. Prior to the move, J and his wife made several trips to Kansas City looking for a new home. After finding just the right one, they hired a moving company to pack and move all their belongings. During the summer, the entire family made the long trek to Kansas City. Upon arrival, however, complications arose and they were not able to move in immediately. They ended up staying at a hotel for three weeks before they were able to take possession. J incurred the following expenses in making the move:

Costs of traveling to Kansas City to look for a house..............	$ 900
Costs of moving van (including costs of $500 for packing and crating)	15,000
Costs of storage in Kansas City....................................	1,000
Transportation costs (2,000 miles @ 9 cents per mile).............	1,800
Three-week hotel stay (meals and lodging)........................	3,000
Real estate commission on sale of former residence..............	30,000

---

[15] § 217(b)(1)(B).

J is allowed to deduct only the direct expenses related to the move: the van, storage, and transportation, for a total of $17,800. The indirect expenses, house-hunting, temporary living, and selling expenses are not deductible. However, J may treat the costs of selling his home as a reduction in the amount realized on the sale of the home, decreasing any gain realized or increasing any loss realized. Note that if J's new employer reimburses J for any of the expenses, he must include the reimbursement in income.

CLASSIFYING AND REPORTING THE MOVING EXPENSE DEDUCTION

Moving expenses of an employee or a self-employed person are deductible for A.G.I.[16] All moving expenses are reported on Form 3903.

As noted above, any reimbursements received for moving expenses must be included in gross income as compensation. Such reimbursements and other amounts paid on the employee's behalf normally are included in the employee's total income reported on Form W-2.

✔ CHECK YOUR KNOWLEDGE

Review Question 1. After 15 years with the firm, J was finally promoted to partner. The substantial raise that came along with the promotion enabled him to build the house of his dreams. The new home is nestled in the woods near Lake Lemon, 60 miles from his old condo in the city. His new commute is 58 miles. Will J be able to deduct his moving expenses?

No. The distance requirement focuses on what would have happened to the taxpayer's commute had he not moved. As a general rule, J's commute absent the move must have increased by more than 50 miles. In other words, the distance between the old home and the *new job site* must exceed the distance between the old home and the *old job site* by more than 50 miles. Note that in order to satisfy this requirement there normally must be a change in job location. In this case, his commute without the move does not increase since the job location did not change. Therefore, his moving expenses are not deductible.

Review Question 2. Mitch's three grueling years in law school finally paid off. This year he graduated from Harvard and took a job with a firm in Memphis for $80,000 a year. He does not itemize his deductions. Can he deduct any of his moving expenses?

Yes. Deduction of moving expenses normally requires the taxpayer to change job sites. However, if the taxpayer is not currently employed and has no former job site, the distance test is met if the new job site is more than 50 miles from the taxpayer's old residence. Also note that because moving expenses are deductible for A.G.I., Mitch can claim the deduction even though he does not itemize.

---

[16] From 1987 through 1993, moving expenses were itemized deductions.

Review Question 3.   Grandma and Grandpa retired this year and moved from Detroit to Florida at a cost of $15,000. Both took part-time jobs at a local fast-food restaurant. Can they deduct their moving expenses?

No. In order to meet the time test, the taxpayer must be employed on a full-time basis for 39 weeks of the 12-month period immediately following arrival at the new location.

Review Question 4.   Indicate whether the following moving expenses are deductible.

    a.   Rental of moving truck

    b.   Boxes to pack household items

    c.   Brake job for car while in route to new location

    d.   28 cents per mile for each mile driven to the new job location

    e.   Meals on the three-day, 900-mile trip to the new location

    f.   Trip to look for a new house after the new job was secured but before the move

Only a and b are deductible. Unusual costs incurred in traveling to the new location such as repairs are not deductible. In lieu of deducting actual transportation expenses, nine cents per mile is allowed. Meals and house-hunting trips are not deductible.

HOME OFFICE EXPENSES

It is currently estimated that over 39 million Americans—39 percent of the labor force—work at home either full or part time. However, simply working at home does not automatically enable a taxpayer to write off the costs of owning or renting. Very narrow standards must be met before a deduction is permitted.

For many years, expenses relating to use of a portion of the taxpayer's home for business purposes were deductible without limitation when they were merely appropriate and helpful in the taxpayer's business. In 1976, however, Congress felt that the appropriate and helpful test was insufficient to prevent the deduction of what were really personal expenses. For example, under the helpful test, a university professor who was provided an office by his employer could convert personal living expenses into deductions by using a den or some other room in his residence for grading papers. In such a situation, it was unlikely that any additional expense was incurred due to the business use. To prevent the deduction of disguised personal expenses, Congress enacted § 280A, severely limiting the deduction of expenses related to the home. Section 280A generally disallows deduction of any expenses related to the taxpayer's home except those otherwise allowable, such as qualified residence interest and taxes, and those for certain business and rental use (the exception for rental use is discussed in Chapter 12).

REQUIREMENTS FOR DEDUCTIBILITY

Under the business use exception, a deduction is allowed for a home office if a portion of the home is "exclusively" used on a "regular" basis for any of three types of business use:[17]

1. As the principal place of business for *any* business of the taxpayer;

2. As a place of business used regularly by patients, clients, or customers in meeting or dealing with the taxpayer in the normal course of his or her trade or business; or

3. In connection with the taxpayer's trade or business when the office is located in a separate structure.

Beyond these basic requirements applicable to all taxpayers, there is one additional test that must be met if the taxpayer is an employee. Employees are entitled to claim a home office deduction only if the home office is for the *convenience of the employer*. Each of these prerequisites is considered below.

Exclusive Use. Under prior law, a taxpayer might write off his whole kitchen just because he opened his briefcase there. The exclusive use requirement was intended to put an end to such shenanigans. A deduction is allowed only when the space in the home is devoted solely to business use. The authors of §280A apparently did not believe a deduction should be allowed where the space was used for both personal and business purposes. The exclusive use requirement does not mean that the home office must be physically separated from the remainder of the home. It is not necessary that the portion of the room be marked off by a permanent partition. It is sufficient if the home office activities are confined to a particular space in a room that is used only for business purposes.[18] To what extent, if any, the IRS will permit personal activities to be carried on in the home office (e.g., making personal phone calls, reading for pleasure, taking care of investments as well as business) is not clear. In any event, the taxpayer should be reminded that the key word is *exclusive*. Two exceptions to the exclusive use test, inventory storage and daycare use, are discussed below.

Regular Use. Section 280A also requires the home office to be used on a regular basis. Fortunately, the Code and Regulations have not adopted precise rules that require the taxpayer to punch a time clock every time he or she steps into the home office. Currently, there is no requirement to keep track of the hours spent in the office. The little guidance that does exist on the issue can be found in IRS publications. The Service does not specifically define *regular* but does explain that occasional or incidental use does not meet the regular use test even if that part of the home is used for no other purpose.[19]

Convenience of the Employer. As noted above, if the taxpayer is an employee, he or she must jump one additional hurdle before claiming the home office deduction. An employee must work at home for the *convenience of the employer*. To

---

[17] § 280A(c).

[18] *George Weightman,* 42 TCM 104, T.C. Memo 1981-301.

[19] § 280A(c)(1). see "Business Use of Your Home," IRS Publication 587(1993), p. 2.

meet this condition, the home office must be more than appropriate and helpful. The Tax Court has suggested that satisfaction of this test requires the taxpayer to show that he or she was unable to do the work performed at home at the employer's office.[20] For example, the Second Circuit has held in *Weissman* that this standard is met if the employer does not provide the employee with space to properly perform his or her employment duties.[21] In this case, a college professor who shared an office and did extensive research at home satisfied the test because in the Court's view the home office was necessitated by lack of suitable working space on campus.

Principal Place of Any Business. A taxpayer satisfies the first business use test if the home office is the principal place of business for *any* business of the taxpayer. Most taxpayers, as employees, fail this test since their only business is that of being an employee and the principal location of that business is at the employer's office. This rule is not foolproof, however. In one decision, the court held that the principal place of business of a taxpayer employed as a concert musician was his home practice room rather than where he gave performances.[22] In contrast, employees who have a *second* business (e.g., selling cosmetics or vitamins) or self-employed persons who operate these activities out of their home normally satisfy the first business use test as long as they can show that the home is in fact the principal place of business.

For years, taxpayers and the IRS have squabbled over when a home office constitutes a taxpayer's principal place of business.[23] The most recent chapter on this controversy is the Supreme Court's 1993 decision in *Nader E. Soliman*.[24] Soliman was an anesthesiologist who worked for three hospitals. However, none of the hospitals provided him an office so he spent 10 to 15 hours a week at his home office doing his billing and scheduling. To Soliman's chagrin, the IRS denied his deductions for his home office expenses. Upon review, the Tax Court was more sympathetic, allowing the deductions on the grounds that the home office was essential to Soliman's business, he had spent substantial time there, and there was no other location available to perform the office function of the business. Although the Fourth Circuit agreed with the Tax Court, the Supreme Court did not. The high court stated that it is not sufficient that the work done in the home office is essential to the business. The court explained that to satisfy the principal place of business test, the home office must be the most important place of business as compared to all the other locations where the taxpayer carries on business. In determining whether the home office is the *most important place of business,* the court identified two factors that should be considered: (1) the relative importance of the functions performed at each of the business locations, and (2) the amount of time spent at each location. In this case, the court believed that the hospital, where Soliman performed his services and treated patients, was his most important place of business.

---

[20] *Robert Chauls,* 41 TCM 234, T.C. Memo 1980-471.

[21] *David J. Weissman v. Comm.,* 85-1 USTC ¶9106, 55 AFTR2d 85-539, 751 F.2d (CA-2, 1984).

[22] *Drucker v. Comm.,* 83-2 USTC ¶9550, AFTR2d 83-5804 (CA-2, 1983).

[23] For example, see *Rudolph Baie,* 74 T.C. 105 (1980).

[24] *Comm. v. Soliman*, 93-1 USTC ¶50,014 (USSC, 1993), *rev'g Nader E. Soliman,* 94 T.C. 20 (1990).

Example 7. T is a manufacturer's representative. He promotes the products of several companies, selling to both wholesalers and retailers all over the state of Ohio. None of the companies he represents provides him an office, so he maintains an office at home. While T works some of the time at his home office, he spends the majority of his working hours at his customer's businesses. Based on the *Soliman* decision, it would appear that T would not be allowed to deduct the costs of maintaining a home office since his clients' premises may be his most important place of business.[25]

As the example above illustrates, the *Soliman* decision may have significant impact on those taxpayers who run a business out of their home office but actually perform services elsewhere. It is estimated that over one-half of the 1.6 million taxpayers who deducted home office expenses in 1991 totaling about $2.4 billion will lose their deductions. Taxpayers such as salespersons, doctors, consultants, repair persons, personal trainers, caterers, and many more may find that they no longer can claim the deduction since their services are not performed in the home office. These taxpayers could still qualify, however, if, as discussed below, they regularly meet with clients in their home office.

Trade or Business. No deduction is permitted for home office expenses if the activities to which they relate do not constitute a business.[26]

Example 8. B, an engineer, regularly uses a room in his home exclusively for evaluating his investments. No deduction is permitted since the activity does not constitute a business.

Meeting Place. The second exception for business use is less restrictive than the first. Under this exception, the home office qualifies if clients regularly meet with the taxpayer there. Interestingly, in *John W. Green,* the taxpayer ingeniously argued that this exception should be satisfied where he regularly received phone calls in his home office. Although a majority of the Tax Court agreed with the taxpayer, the decision was reversed on appeal. The Appellate Court believed that the statute required that the taxpayer *physically* meet with clients in the home office.[27]

Separate Structure. The third exception for business use is the least restrictive of the three. If a separate structure is the site of the home office, it need be used only in connection with the taxpayer's work (e.g., a converted detached garage or barn).

AMOUNT DEDUCTIBLE

If the taxpayer qualifies for the home office deduction, an allocable portion of expenses related to the home may be deducted. The allocation of expenses generally must be based on square footage. Typical expenses include utilities, depreciation, insurance, security systems, repairs (e.g., furnace repair), interest, taxes, and rent. It should be emphasized that the home office deduction is limited to the gross income from the home business as

---

[25] *Supra*, Footnote 19.

[26] S. Rep. No. 94-938, 94th Cong., 2d Sess. 147-49 (1976).

[27] 78 T.C. 428 (1982).

reduced by allowable deductions. This computation is very similar to that for determining deductible hobby expenses. The taxpayer may deduct expenses equal to the extent of gross income reduced by (1) expenses allowable without regard to the use of the dwelling unit (e.g., interest—assuming it is a primary or secondary residence—and taxes), and (2) business or rental expenses incurred in carrying on the activity other than those of the home office (e.g., supplies and secretarial expenses).[28] Any home office expenses that are not deductible due to this limitation may be carried over and used to offset income from the business which led to the deduction, even if the taxpayer does not use the unit in the business in subsequent years.

When the taxpayer is self-employed (i.e., a sole proprietor), all of the taxpayer's expenses, including those attributable to the home office, are deductible for A.G.I. In contrast, if the taxpayer is an employee, the *otherwise allowable* expenses (e.g., interest and taxes) are deductible in full as itemized deductions. The other business expenses, including the home office expenses, are considered miscellaneous itemized deductions and are subject, along with other miscellaneous itemized deductions, to the 2 percent floor. All expenses for business use of a home office must be reported on Form 8829 (see Appendix B for a sample form).

Example 9.   K maintains a qualifying home office. During this year, she earned only $2,000 from the home office activities. Her expenses included the following: interest and taxes allocable to the home office, $600; secretarial services, miscellaneous supplies and postage, $900; and expenses directly related to the home office including insurance, utilities, and depreciation, $1,700. K's potential deduction is $2,000 computed as follows:

Gross income		$2,000
Otherwise allowable deductions:		
Interest and taxes	(600)	$ 600
Other business expenses	(900)	900
Gross income limitation	$ 500	
Home office expenses:		
$1,700 limited to remaining gross income		500
Total potential deduction		$2,000

Whether the $2,000 of deductible expenses are deductible for or from A.G.I. depends on whether K is self-employed or an employee. If K is self-employed, the entire $2,000 is deductible for A.G.I. If the taxpayer is an employee, the $600 of interest and taxes allocable to the home office are deductible as itemized deductions and would be subject to the 3% cutback provision. The remaining $1,400 is considered a miscellaneous itemized deduction subject (along with other miscellaneous itemized deductions) to the 2% floor. Of course, any miscellaneous itemized deductions exceeding the 2% floor are still subject to the 3% cutback provision. The

---

[28]   See § 280A(c)(5).

home office expenses that are not deductible this year, $1,200 [($600 + $900 + $1,700 = $3,200) − $2,000], may be carried over to the following years to be offset against future home office income.

DAYCARE AND STORAGE USE

The home office rules for taxpayers who use their home as a daycare center or as a place to store inventory of a home-based business receive special attention from the Code. In both cases, the normal rules apply except that the exclusive use test is relaxed.

Daycare Use. If a portion of the taxpayer's home doubles as both a living space and a daycare center it would appear that no deduction would be allowed since the exclusive use test would not be satisfied. When the home is used as a daycare center, however, the exclusive use test does not apply.[29] Instead, the expenses attributable to the room are prorated between personal and daycare use based on the number of hours of use per day. Thus, if the taxpayer uses a family room for daycare 40 percent of the time, 40 percent of the expenses allocable to that room would be deductible. A portion of the home qualifies for this special treatment if the taxpayer uses the home to provide daycare services for children, individuals over age 65, or those who are physically or mentally incapable of taking care of themselves.

Storage Use. If the taxpayer regularly uses part of the home to store goods sold at retail or wholesale and the home is the sole fixed location of that business, expenses related to the storage space are deductible.[30] More importantly, the space need not be used exclusively for this purpose. However, the space should be a specific area (e.g., a particular part of a basement or closet).

RENTAL OF RESIDENCE

The *business use* requirements explained above do not apply when the taxpayer simply rents a part of his or her home to a third party. In such case, the taxpayer reports the income from the rental and deducts the expenses without limitation.

In *Feldman,* the taxpayer used the rental exception to avoid the home office rules.[31] Mr. Feldman operated an accounting practice as a separate corporation. Pursuant to an agreement between him and the corporation, Feldman leased a room in his home to the corporation which then provided it for Feldman's use. By so doing, Feldman was able to deduct all expenses allocable to the "rental property." Because the deductions offset the rental payment, no tax was paid on the amount received. In effect, Feldman was able to receive part of his corporation's earnings tax free. Note that had Feldman simply used the home office related to his employment, no deduction would have been allowed since it would not have satisfied the principal place of business or convenience of the employer tests. To eliminate this avoidance possibility, Congress amended the home office provisions. Under the amendment, no home office deduction is allowable where an employee leases a portion of the home to the employer. For this purpose, an independent contractor is treated as an employee for the party for whom the work is performed.[32]

---

[29] § 280A(c)(4).

[30] § 280A(c)(2).

[31] 84 T.C. 1 (1985).

[32] § 280A(c)(6).

RESIDENTIAL PHONE SERVICE

For many years, taxpayers who used their home phone for business or income-producing purposes deducted a portion of the basic charge for local service on the grounds that it was business-related. In 1988, however, Congress saw the issue differently. Apparently it believed that in this day and age the cost of basic phone service to a taxpayer's residence would have been incurred in any event—without regard to any business that the taxpayer might otherwise conduct. As a result, a taxpayer may no longer deduct any charge (including taxes) for local phone service for the *first* phone line provided to any residence. The taxpayer may still deduct the costs of long-distance phone calls or optional phone services such as call waiting or call forwarding, when such costs are related to business. In addition, taxpayers may deduct the costs of additional phone lines into the home that are used for business (e.g., a separate line for a fax machine or modem).

✔ CHECK YOUR KNOWLEDGE

Review Question 1.   Indicate whether the following taxpayers would be allowed to deduct expenses attributable to a home office.

a.   T is on the tax staff of a public accounting firm. From time to time, he brings home returns and does a little work in his home office. In addition, he does most of his technical reading in the home office.

T would not be allowed a deduction since he does not meet the principal place of business or convenience of the employer tests. He fails the first of these tests since his principal place of business is his employer's office. He fails the convenience of the employer test since the employer provides him an office and he could do at the office what he does at home. His work at home appears to be for his own convenience.

b.   R is a decorator. She works out of an office in her home. She spends about 10 hours per week visiting her client's homes and another 10 visiting businesses that carry furniture and home accessories. The remainder of her 40-hour week is spent at her home office doing sketches, ordering, keeping books, and the like.

Although R's home office is essential to her work, the *Soliman* decision requires more. The home must be the most important place of business. The primary considerations in this determination are the relative significance of the functions performed in the home office and the time spent there relative to other locations. As can be seen in this case, applying the wisdom of *Soliman* is difficult. If the past is any indication, the IRS would probably take the position that visiting customers is the most important aspect of her business and deny the deduction notwithstanding the fact that visiting customers takes only 25 percent of her average work week.

c. J operates a floral shop in town. He grows the plants for his shop in a greenhouse behind his home.

Even though the principal place of J's business is arguably at J's shop, J would still qualify for the deduction under the separate structure exception.

Review Question 2. With the kids starting college, income from their regular jobs was not enough, so this year N and her husband started a small blind and drapery operation. They run it out of an office in their home. N orders the fabric and sews the drapes while her husband installs. In their first year of business, the couple had gross income of $2,000. Interest and taxes allocable to the home office were $600. Various supplies and equipment, including a file cabinet, table, Rolodex, sewing machine, and scissors, cost $1,000. Depreciation, utilities, insurance, and similar expenses allocable to the home office were $900. According to their friend Norm, they should be able to deduct all $1,900 since they are all ordinary and necessary business expenses. Is Norm correct? How much can they deduct?

Norm is only partially right. Section 280A limits the deduction of home office expenses. Home office expenses are essentially deductible to the extent of net income from the business before taking into account the home office expenses (other than the interest and taxes). The home office expenses cannot create a loss from the activity. As a result, the couple can deduct $400 ($2,000 − $1,000 − $600). As a result, the couple's net income from the business after the home office deductions is zero. Note that § 280A limitations do not apply to the $1,000 of expenses for items directly used in the business. These costs relate directly to the business (rather than the home) and, therefore, are fully deductible (or depreciable, as explained in Chapter 9).

TRANSPORTATION EXPENSES

Before examining the deduction for transportation expenses, the distinction between transportation expenses and travel expenses should be explained. In tax jargon, transportation and travel are not synonymous. Travel expenses are broadly defined to include not only the costs of transportation but also related expenses such as meals, lodging, and other incidentals when the taxpayer is in a travel status. As discussed below, the taxpayer is in travel status when he or she is *away from home overnight* on business.[33] In contrast, transportation expenses are defined narrowly to include only the actual costs of transportation—expenses of getting from one place to another while in the course of business when the taxpayer is *not* away from home overnight.[34] Transportation expenses normally occur when the taxpayer goes and returns on the same day. The most common transportation expense is the cost of driving and maintaining a car, but the term also includes the cost of traveling by other forms of transportation such as bus, taxi, subway, or train.[35]

---

[33] § 162(a)(2).

[34] Reg. § 1.62-1(g).

[35] *Ibid.*

Example 10.   M is an architect in Cincinnati. At various times during the year, he drove to Cleveland to inspect one of his projects. He often ate lunch and dinner in Cleveland before returning home. M is allowed to deduct only the costs of transportation. The costs of the meals are not deductible since he was not away from home overnight. Had he spent the night in Cleveland and returned the next day, the costs of meals and lodging as well as transportation would be deductible.

The deduction for transportation is allowed under the general provisions of §§ 162 and 212. Therefore, to qualify for deduction, the transportation expense must be ordinary, necessary, and related to the taxpayer's trade or business or income-producing activity. Personal transportation, of course, does not qualify for deduction. Like many other expenses, however, the boundary between business and personal transportation is often difficult to identify. Some of the common problem areas are discussed below.

DEDUCTIBLE TRANSPORTATION VERSUS NONDEDUCTIBLE COMMUTING

The cost of transportation or commuting between the taxpayer's home and his or her place of employment may appear to be a necessary business expense. It is settled, however, that commuting expenses generally are nondeductible personal expenses. This rule derives from the presumption that the commuting expense arises from the taxpayer's *personal preference* to live away from the place of business or employment. This presumption persists even though there often is no place to live within walking distance of employment, much less one that is suitable or within the taxpayer's means. The fact that the taxpayer is forced to live far away from the place of employment is irrelevant and does not alter the personal nature of the expenses.

Example 11.   In *Sanders v. Comm.*, the taxpayers were civilian employees working on an air force base.[36] Despite the fact that they were not allowed to live on the base next to their employment and could only live elsewhere and commute, the transportation costs were not deductible. The Court found it impossible to distinguish between these expenses and those of a suburban commuter, both being personal in origin.

Example 12.   In *Tauferner v. Comm.*, the taxpayer worked at a chemical plant that was located 20 miles from any community due to the dangers involved.[37] The taxpayer was denied deductions for his commuting even though he lived in the nearest habitable spot. Arguably, the nature of his job—not personal convenience— produced additional transportation costs. Nevertheless, the Court did not believe that such hardship changed the personal character of the expenses.

While the costs of commuting normally are not deductible, there are several exceptions. These exceptions are discussed below.

---

[36]   71-1 USTC ¶9260, 27 AFTR2d 71-832, 439 F.2d 296 (CA-9, 1971).

[37]   69-1 USTC ¶9241, 23 AFTR2d 69-1025, 407 F.2d 243 (CA-10, 1969).

Commuting with Tools and Similar Items.   The fact that the taxpayer hauls tools, instruments, or other equipment necessary in pursuing business normally does not cause commuting expenses to be deductible. The Supreme Court has ruled that only the *additional* expenses attributable to carrying the tools are deductible.[38] The IRS determines the taxpayer's "additional expenses" by applying the so-called "same mode" test.[39] Under this test, a deduction is allowed for the extra cost of commuting by one mode with the tools over the cost of commuting by the same mode without the tools. Thus, a carpenter who drives a truck would not be allowed a transportation deduction simply by loading it with tools since carrying the tools created no additional expense. The fact that tools may have caused the carpenter to drive a truck, which is more expensive than some other type of transportation, is irrelevant under the IRS view. The courts, however, have rejected this test in certain cases.[40]

> **Example 13.**   M plays second trumpet in the Dallas orchestra. During the year, his employer indicated they no longer needed a second trumpet and M would have to switch to the tuba to retain his job. If, in order to transport the tuba, M had to change from driving to work in a small car costing $3 per day to driving to work in a van costing $5 per day, the IRS would not allow a deduction for the additional cost. Under the same mode test, the cost of driving the van with the tuba is the same as without the tuba. The courts, however, may allow a deduction for the $2 increase in cost. On the other hand, if M had rented a trailer to carry the tuba at a cost of $2 per day, the IRS would allow the deduction because the cost of driving the van with the tuba is now $2 more than without the tuba.

The IRS view on the treatment of local transporation is summarized in Exhibit 8-1.

Commuting between Two Jobs.   The transportation cost of going from one job to a second job is deductible.[41] The deduction is limited to the cost of going *directly* from one job to the other.

---

[38] *Fausner v. Comm.*, 73-2 USTC ¶95-15, 32 AFTR2d 73-5202, 413 U.S. 838 (USSC, 1973).

[39] Rev. Rul. 75-380, 1975-2 C.B. 59.

[40] *J.F. Grayson*, 36 TCM 1201, T.C. Memo 1977-304. See also *H.A. Pool*, 36 TCM 93, T.C. Memo 1977-20.

[41] *Supra*, Footnote 39.

Exhibit 8-1   *When Are Local Transportation Expenses Deductible?*

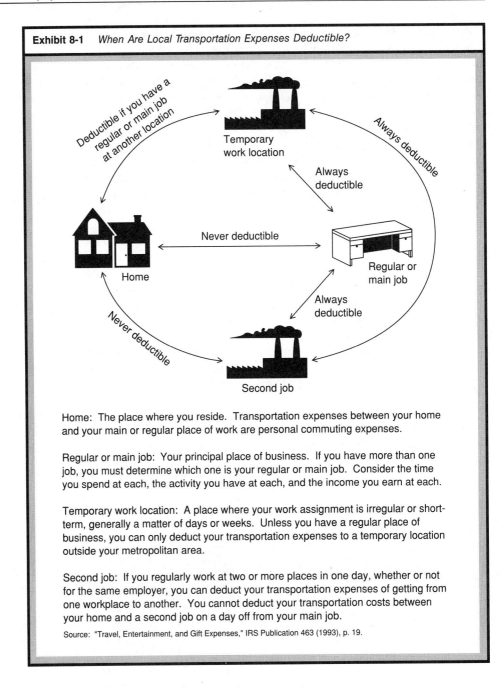

Home: The place where you reside. Transportation expenses between your home and your main or regular place of work are personal commuting expenses.

Regular or main job: Your principal place of business. If you have more than one job, you must determine which one is your regular or main job. Consider the time you spend at each, the activity you have at each, and the income you earn at each.

Temporary work location: A place where your work assignment is irregular or short-term, generally a matter of days or weeks. Unless you have a regular place of business, you can only deduct your transportation expenses to a temporary location outside your metropolitan area.

Second job: If you regularly work at two or more places in one day, whether or not for the same employer, you can deduct your transportation expenses of getting from one workplace to another. You cannot deduct your transportation costs between your home and a second job on a day off from your main job.

Source: "Travel, Entertainment, and Gift Expenses," IRS Publication 463 (1993), p. 19.

Example 14. R works for X Corporation on the morning shift and for Y Corporation on its afternoon shift. The distances he drives are diagrammed below.

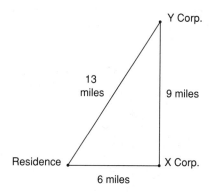

If R leaves X and goes home to eat lunch before going to Y, he actually drives 19 miles to get to Y, or 10 more miles than if he had driven directly $(19 - 9)$. However, only the cost of driving directly, 9 miles, is deductible.

Commuting to a Temporary Assignment. Individuals are often assigned to work at a location other than where they regularly work. When a taxpayer commutes to a *temporary work location,* the commuting expenses are deductible transportation costs if either of the following tests are satisfied:

1. The temporary assignment is *within* the general area of the taxpayer's employment *and* he or she otherwise has a *regular* place of business (e.g., an office);[42] or

2. The temporary assignment is *outside* the general area of the taxpayer's employment (i.e., his or her tax home).[43]

Example 15. C is an auditor for a public accounting firm that has its office in downtown Chicago. C works about 30% of the time in her employer's office, and the remaining 70% is spent at various clients' offices around the city. C may deduct the costs of commuting between her residence and a client's office because the client's office is a temporary work location and C otherwise has a regular place of business (i.e., her employer's office).

Example 16. M is a carpenter. He works for a construction company that builds houses in subdivisions in various areas of Houston. Most of his assignments are located within about 25 miles of downtown Houston. During the year, M worked at two different locations, one on the north side of Houston and the other on the west side. Although M is assigned to temporary work locations, he is not allowed to deduct any of his commuting expenses because he does not otherwise have a regular place of business.

---

[42] Rev. Rul. 90-23, 1990-1 C.B. 28.   [43] Rev. Rul. 190, 1953-2 C.B. 303.

Example 17. Assume the same facts as above except that M was temporarily assigned to a job in Galveston, 60 miles from Houston. He drove to Galveston daily and returned home in the evenings. Under these circumstances, M may deduct the cost of driving the entire 120-mile round trip from his home to Galveston. The following diagram illustrates this approach.

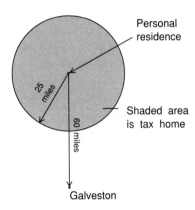

The IRS draws an important distinction between temporary and regular work locations. A work location is temporary if the taxpayer performs services on an irregular or short-term basis (e.g., a matter of days or weeks).[44] In contrast, a work location is considered a *regular* place of business if—as one might expect—the taxpayer performs services there on a regular basis. According to the IRS, a taxpayer may have more than one regular place of business even though he or she does not perform services at that location every week or on a set schedule. When the taxpayer commutes to these different locations on a "regular" basis, the costs of commuting would not be deductible because such locations are not temporary.

Example 18. Dr. T, a podiatrist, has an office on both the north side and south side of Indianapolis. In addition, she performs services at a clinic and a hospital with which she is associated. T may not deduct the costs of transportation between her residence and these various locations because each is considered a regular place of business and not a temporary work location. As discussed below, however, the costs of going between two business locations (e.g., a clinic and a hospital) are deductible.

---

[44] An assignment beyond the taxpayer's tax home is not considered to be temporary if it is expected to last for a year or more. § 162(a).

Transportation between Job Sites. While the transportation costs between a taxpayer's home and the first and last job sites generally are considered nondeductible commuting expenses, transportation costs between two job sites are deductible.[45] Accordingly, once the taxpayer arrives at the first job site any business travel thereafter usually is deductible.

Example 19. R is employed as a tax accountant and works primarily in his employer's office downtown. R drives 34 miles round-trip from his home to the office. After arriving at work one day, R drove 6 miles to a client's office and returned to his employer's office. In this case, R may deduct the cost of driving 12 miles.

Example 20. Assume R drives 17 miles to work in the morning. In the afternoon, he drives 15 miles to a client's office where he conducts some business. From the client's office he drives 9 miles home. In this situation, R may deduct the cost of driving 15 miles because transportation between two job sites is deductible. In addition, it appears that he may deduct the cost of driving 9 miles since transportation between the taxpayer's residence and a temporary work location (i.e., the client's office) is deductible.

Although transportation expenses between the taxpayer's home and work normally are not deductible, the rule concerning travel between job sites creates a favorable exception for taxpayers who maintain a separate trade or business at home. For these taxpayers, the transportation from the first job site—the home—and the second job site would be deductible.

Example 21. V is a landscape engineer and works out of his home. Transportation costs from his home to a client's place of business are deductible since the expenses are incurred in traveling from his principal place of business to a job site.[46]

COMPUTING CAR EXPENSES

Deductions relating to driving and maintaining a car may be computed using actual expenses or a standard mileage rate (automatic mileage method). Under either method, if the car is used for both business and personal purposes, only the car expenses attributable to business or income production are deductible.

Actual Expenses. Actual car expenses normally deducted include the costs for gas, oil, repairs, insurance, depreciation, interest on loans to purchase the car (other than that of an employee), taxes, licenses, garage rent, parking fees, and tolls. Calculating actual expenses usually requires determining the portion of the nondeductible expenses attributable to personal use. Under the actual expense method, the total actual expense is allocated based on mileage.

---

[45] Rev. Rul. 55-109, 1955-1 C.B. 261.

[46] See *Raymond Garner,* 42 TCM 1181, T.C. Memo 1981-542, and *Joe J. Adams,* 43 TCM 1203, T.C. Memo 1982-223.

Example 22.   R, self-employed, drove 20,000 miles during the year: 16,000 on business and 4,000 for personal purposes. Total actual expenses were as follows:

General expenses:	
Gas...	$ 800
Maintenance (oil, repairs).........................	200
Insurance......................................	400
Interest expense.................................	600
Depreciation....................................	2,000
Total..	$4,000

Other business expenses:	
Tolls incurred on business trips...................	$ 10
Parking fees when calling on clients..............	90
Total..	$ 100

Since R used the car 80% (16,000 ÷ 20,000) for business, he may deduct 80% of the general expenses, $3,200 (80% × $4,000). In addition, he may deduct the entire $100 cost for the parking and tolls since they were incurred solely for business purposes, for a total deduction of $3,300. Note that the nonbusiness portion of the interest expense would not be deductible, assuming it is not attributable to a loan secured by his first or second home. If R were an employee, none of the interest would be deductible because business interest of an *employee* is not deductible.

Standard Mileage Rate.   The automatic mileage method generally allows a deduction of 28 cents per mile for *all* business miles driven during the year.[47] The business portion of expenses for interest (if self-employed), state and local property taxes, parking, and tolls also may be added to the amount computed using the mileage rate. Other expenses such as depreciation, insurance, and maintenance are built into the mileage rate and cannot be added.

Example 23.   Same facts as in *Example 22*. R's deduction using the standard mileage rate would be $5,060, as computed below.

Business mileage (16,000 × $0.28).................	$4,480
Interest ($600 × 80%).............................	480
Parking and tolls.....................................	100
Total...	$5,060

Note that in arriving at the deduction, gas, maintenance, insurance, and depreciation are not added to the amount computed using the standard rate since they are built into the rate. Conversely, interest (if self-employed), parking, and tolls are added since they are not included in the rate.

---

[47]   Rev. Proc. 91-67, I.R.B. No. 52, 11. Rural letter carriers are permitted to use 150% of this rate, 42 cents per mile.

The standard mileage rate may be used *only* if it is adopted in the first year the car is placed in service. In addition, the following conditions must be satisfied:[48]

1. The car must be owned by the taxpayer, not leased.

2. The car must not be one of two or more cars being used simultaneously in a business, such as in a fleet operation. When a taxpayer alternates in using different cars on different occasions, the cars are treated as one and the mileage is combined.

3. The car must not be for hire, such as a taxi.

4. Additional first year depreciation or depreciation using an accelerated method must not have been claimed in a prior year.

If these conditions are satisfied, the taxpayer may switch methods from year to year. However, use of the standard mileage method precludes the taxpayer from using the Modified Accelerated Cost Recovery System (MACRS) for computing depreciation in a subsequent year, and depreciation must be computed under one of the alternative methods.[49] Note that selecting the actual method in the first year generally *prohibits* the taxpayer from ever using the standard mileage rate for that automobile.

Taxpayers who use the standard mileage rate are required to reduce the adjusted basis of their automobiles just as if they had claimed depreciation. For example, for 1990 and 1991, the basis is reduced by 11 cents per mile, and for 1992, by 11.5 cents for each mile driven.[50]

CLASSIFICATION OF TRANSPORTATION AND TRAVEL EXPENSES

The *unreimbursed* transportation and travel expenses of an employee are treated as miscellaneous itemized deductions subject to the 2 percent floor. In contrast, if an employee is reimbursed for such expenses under a qualified arrangement known as an *accountable plan* (discussed later in this chapter), the reimbursement is excludable from gross income. Any reimbursement not made under such a plan must be included in the employee's gross income, and any qualifying deductions must be treated as miscellaneous itemized deductions. If the expenses are incurred by a self-employed person, the expenses are deductible for A.G.I. An employee reports the expenses on Form 2106, a copy of which is reproduced in the last section of this chapter.

Travel and transportation expenses related to property held for the production of income are also considered miscellaneous itemized deductions unless the income is rents or royalties, in which case the deductions would be for A.G.I. In addition, the deduction for meals may be limited to 50 percent of their cost. This limitation is discussed in detail with entertainment expenses later in this chapter.

---

[48] *Ibid.*

[49] *Supra,* Footnote 47.

[50] *Supra,* Footnote 47.

TRAVEL EXPENSES

Section 162 of the Code provides for the deduction of travel expenses while "away from home" in the pursuit of a trade or business.[51] A similar deduction is allowed for travel expenses connected with income-producing activities not constituting a business.[52] The definition of travel expenses is not as narrow as that of transportation expenses. Travel expenses include not only the costs of transportation but also the costs of meals (but limited to 50 percent of actual costs, as discussed later), lodging, cleaning and laundry, telephone, and other similar expenses related to travel.[53] Whether these additional expenses such as meals and lodging are deductible depends on whether the taxpayer is considered "away from home."

AWAY-FROM-HOME TEST

The taxpayer must be *away from home* before travel expenses are deductible. The "away-from-home" test poses two questions: For what period does the taxpayer need to be away from home, and where is the taxpayer's home for tax purposes? With respect to the first question, the Supreme Court has ruled that the away-from-home test generally requires the taxpayer to be away from home *overnight*.[54] Later interpretations of this decision have indicated that the taxpayer will be considered to be "overnight" when it is reasonable for the taxpayer to stop for needed sleep or rest. A trip where the taxpayer leaves and returns the same day is not travel and, consequently, only the transportation cost would be deductible. Meals eaten during the trip, lodging, etc., would not be deductible.

The second and more critical aspect of the away-from-home test concerns the determination of the taxpayer's *tax home*. The IRS and the Tax Court have defined the term *tax home* to mean the business location of the taxpayer or the general vicinity of the taxpayer's employment, regardless of the location of the taxpayer's personal residence.[55] The Court of Appeals in several circuits, however, has held that "home" should be interpreted in the normal fashion (i.e., as the place where the taxpayer normally maintains his or her residence;[56] see *Example 25*). The interpretation problems usually arise when taxpayers live in one location but also conduct substantial business at another location where they often stay because it is impractical to return to the residence. To illustrate, consider a construction worker who lives with his family in Milwaukee but obtains a job to work on the construction of a nuclear power plant near Chicago. During the week, he stays in a motel in Chicago and eats his meals. The issue here is the location of the taxpayer's tax home. If the taxpayer normally works in Chicago, the IRS would take the position that the taxpayer's tax home is in Chicago and deny the deductions for meals and lodging. On the other hand, if the taxpayer normally works in Milwaukee and takes a job in Chicago, he may be able to secure a deduction for his Chicago expenses if he could demonstrate that the Chicago job is only a *temporary* assignment. The IRS permits

---

[51] *Supra,* Footnote 34.

[52] §§ 212(1) and (2).

[53] Reg. § 1.162-2(a).

[54] *U.S. v. Correll,* 68-1 USTC ¶9101, 20 AFTR2d 5845, 389 U.S. 299 (USSC, 1967).

[55] G.C.M. 23672, 1943 C.B. 66, superseded by Rev. Rul. 74-291, 1974-1 C.B. 42.

[56] For example, see *Rosenspan v. U.S.,* 71-1 USTC ¶9241, 27 AFTR2d 71-707, 438 F.2d 905 (CA-2, 1971).

taxpayers to deduct travel expenses incurred away from the principal place of business if an assignment away from home is temporary and not indefinite. Under recently revised § 162(a), assignments in a single location lasting a year or more are not temporary but indefinite.[57] Consequently, if a taxpayer anticipates an assignment to last more than a year or it actually exceeds one year, none of the taxpayer's travel expenses are deductible (not even those for the first 12 months). According to the IRS, the nature of assignments lasting less than a year depends on the facts and circumstances of each case. In most cases, however, the IRS treats assignments lasting less than a year as temporary.

> **Example 24.** D is employed as an engineer, living and working in Kansas City. Her employer assigned D to a job in El Paso where she lived and worked for five months before returning to Kansas City and resuming her regular employment. The IRS would permit D to deduct her travel expenses since the assignment is temporary. If D's assignment in El Paso was extended beyond the original period to exceed a year, none of D's expenses would be deductible.

If the taxpayer has no principal place of employment, the tax home is normally his regular place of abode.[58] However, if the taxpayer has no permanent place of residence, the courts have consistently denied the taxpayer's deductions for meals and lodging since there is no "home" to be away from. This rule has been applied to itinerant construction workers and salespeople whom the courts view as being *at home* wherever their work may take them.[59]

The purpose of the away-from-home provision is to reduce the burden of the taxpayer who, because of business needs, must maintain two places of abode and consequently incurs additional and duplicate living expenses. The rule is based on the principle that a taxpayer normally lives and works in the same general vicinity. Thus, when taxpayers choose to live in an area other than where they work, the resulting expenses normally are considered personal. This rule often is difficult to apply in particular situations. For this reason, the deduction of travel expenses ultimately depends on the facts.

> **Example 25.** C works at a testing laboratory in a remote mountain area of New Mexico, 70 miles from his home. His residence, however, is the closest place to the laboratory to live. C normally commutes to work but sometimes stays at the testing facilities' quarters overnight when he works overtime. In this situation, the IRS would not allow a deduction for travel expenses since C's tax home is at the testing laboratory, and when staying there he is not away from home. Some Appellate Courts, however, may permit the deduction for meals and lodging since he is away from his residence.[60]

---

[57] *Supra,* Footnote 44.

[58] Criteria exist for determining whether a taxpayer has a regular place of abode. See Rev. Rul. 73-529, 1973-2 C.B. 37.

[59] *George H. James v. U.S.,* 62-2 USTC ¶9735, 10 AFTR2d 5627, 308 F.2d 204 (CA-9, 1962).

[60] For example, see *Lee E. Coombs,* 79-2 USTC ¶9719, 45 AFTR2d 80-444, 608 F.2d 1269 (CA-9, 1979).

COMBINED BUSINESS AND PLEASURE TRAVEL

As discussed above, travel costs are deductible only while away from home in pursuit of business or income-producing activities. When traveling away from home, however, taxpayers often combine business with pleasure with the hope that they can deduct what is really a personal vacation. With an eye to this possibility, the Regulations provide special guidance as to how much can be deducted in this situation. The rules governing combined business and pleasure travel differ depending on whether the taxpayer is traveling inside or outside of the United States.

Domestic Travel. The taxpayer who travels within the United States (all 50 states and the District of Columbia) may deduct *all* of the costs of travel to and from the destination if the trip is primarily for business.[61] If the trip is primarily for business, the taxpayer will not lose all or even a part of the deduction merely because he or she takes a personal side-trip or extends the trip for a short vacation. However, the costs of any personal side-trips are not allowed. Travel which is primarily for personal purposes is not deductible even though some business is conducted. Note that the taxpayer either deducts *all* of the *to-and-from* travel expenses or deducts *none* of them—there is no allocation. Of course, any travel expenses (e.g., meals and lodging) directly related to business upon arriving at the destination qualify.

> **Example 26.**   F, a CPA, flew from Dallas to Denver for the annual convention of the Texas Society of Certified Public Accountants. The air fare was $500. Meals and lodging for the three days she attended were $150 and $230, respectively. Upon conclusion of the convention, F drove to the mountains and skied for two days before returning home. The travel to the mountains, including meals and lodging, cost $350. F may deduct all of the air fare, $500, because costs of transportation are fully deductible without allocation when the trip is primarily for business. In addition, F may deduct 50% of the meal costs, $75 (50% × $150), and $230 for lodging because these travel expenses are directly related to business. The expenses of $350 for the ski trip are nondeductible personal expenses.

> **Example 27.**   Assume the same facts as in *Example 26,* except that F skied for five days. In this case, the trip may be treated as primarily personal thus preventing any deduction of the $500 air fare from Dallas to Denver. Fifty percent of the expenses for meals and all of the lodging costs while at the convention on business are still deductible.

Obviously the most troublesome question concerning domestic travel is whether the nature of the trip is primarily business or pleasure. In this regard, the Regulations, Rulings, and reported decisions offer little guidance—saying only that the answer depends on the facts and circumstances in each case. Among the factors normally considered, the amount of time devoted to business as compared to personal activities is often decisive. Another factor emphasized is the type of location where the business occurs (e.g., a resort hotel or a more businesslike setting). The increasing number of professional

---

[61]   Reg. § 1.162-2(b)(1).

organizations that schedule their conventions and seminars in resort areas has caused the IRS to closely scrutinize deductions for alleged business trips which are merely disguised vacations. Congress took action regarding expenses related to nonbusiness conventions (e.g., investment and tax seminars), completely disallowing their deduction after 1986.[62] For a business meeting, however, if it can be clearly shown that the expenses were incurred for business purposes, the deduction is not disallowed merely because the meeting occurs at a resort.

> **Example 28.** This year, Dr. H, a surgeon, attended a week-long course on arthroscopic surgery in Palm Beach. His wife accompanied him and attended a seminar on personal financial planning. H may deduct his costs of transportation as well as the travel expenses incurred after arriving in Palm Beach because the expenses are related to business. None of his wife's expenses are deductible because they relate not to her trade or business but to investments and taxes.

Travel Expense of Spouse and Dependents. The IRS has always taken a dim view of taxpayers who combine business travel with pleasure and in the process deduct the cost of taking their families with them. For years, the Service attacked this abuse with a longstanding regulation that denied the deduction of a family member's travel expenses unless the taxpayer could demonstrate that the family member's presence served a bona fide business purpose.[63] Apparently this ammunition was incapable of adequately policing the problem. Consequently, Congress provided the IRS more help with new legislation in 1993.[64] Currently, no deduction is allowed for any travel expenses paid or incurred with respect to a spouse, dependent, or other individual accompanying the taxpayer (or an officer or employee of the taxpayer) on business unless (1) the individual is an employee of the person paying or reimbursing the expenses, (2) the travel of such individual has a bona fide business purpose, and (3) such expenses are otherwise deductible. The rule does not apply to deductible moving expenses.

> **Example 29.** T is the owner and president of TDI Corporation, which owns seven car dealerships in and around Des Moines. This year General Motors held a meeting for all of its dealers in Maui, and T took his wife and 18-year-old daughter. TDI reimbursed T for all of his traveling expenses including those of his wife and daughter. TDI is not allowed to claim a deduction for the travel expenses of T's wife and daughter unless they are both employees of the company and it can establish that their presence had a bona fide business purpose. Note that T and TDI may be able to overcome the first requirement by employing both his wife and daughter. Satisfying the second test is more difficult. In this regard, the regulations provide that performance of incidental services does not cause a family member's

---

[62] § 274(h)(7).

[63] Reg. § 1.162-2(c); Rev. Rul. 55-57, 1955-1 C.B. 315.

[64] § 274(m).

expenses to qualify. The courts, however, have allowed a deduction for a spouse's expenses when the facts have shown that the spouse's presence enhanced the image of the taxpayer or the spouse acted as a business assistant.[65]

Foreign Travel.   When the taxpayer travels outside the United States, the travel expenses must satisfy more stringent requirements for deduction. Generally, the costs of transportation to and from the foreign destination and other travel expenses must be allocated between business (or income-producing activities) and personal activities. If the travel is *primarily* business, the costs of transportation are fully deductible without allocation if one of the following conditions is satisfied:[66]

1. *Travel outside the United States does not exceed one week* (seven consecutive days). In counting the days out of the United States, the day of departure from the United States is excluded while the day of return to the United States is included. (For example, leaving on Sunday and returning on the following Sunday is exactly seven days.)

2. *More than 75 percent of the days on the trip were devoted to business.* A day is treated as a business day if during any part of the day the taxpayer's presence is required at a particular place for a business purpose. Moreover, the day is considered a business day even though the taxpayer spends more time during normal working hours on nonbusiness activity than on business activity. Weekends, holidays, or other "stand-by" days that fall between the taxpayer's business days are also considered business days. However, such days are not business days if they fall at the end of the taxpayer's business activities and the taxpayer merely elects to stay for personal purposes. The day of departure and the day of return are both treated as business days.

3. Taxpayer has no substantial control over arranging the business trip.

4. Personal vacation is not a major consideration in making the trip.

If the travel is not primarily for business or fails to satisfy one of the above conditions, an *allocation* of the to-and-from travel expenses must be made. In such cases, the deductible travel expenses are determined by the following allocation formula:

$$\frac{\text{Business days on trip}}{\text{Total days on trip}} \times \begin{array}{c}\text{Total} \\ \text{to-and-from} \\ \text{Travel Expenses}\end{array} = \begin{array}{c}\text{Deductible} \\ \text{to-and-from} \\ \text{Travel Expenses}\end{array}$$

---

[65] See *Fraser Wilkins*, 72-2 USTC ¶9707, 30 AFTR2d 72-5639, 348 F. Supp. 1282 (D.Ct. Neb., 1972); *Pierre C. Warwick*, 64-2 USTC ¶9864, 14 AFTR2d 5817, 236 F. Supp. 761 (D.Ct. Va., 1974).

[66] § 274(c); Reg. § 1.274-4.

A deduction for the to-and-from travel expenses is not allowed if the trip is primarily personal. However, travel costs (e.g., meals and lodging) directly related to business upon arriving at the destination are deductible.

> **Example 30.** B, an executive, arranged a trip to Japan primarily for business. He left Chicago for Tokyo on July 1 and returned on July 20. During his trip, he spent 15 days on business (including the two travel days) and five days sight-seeing. His air fare was $1,000 and his lodging plus 50% of the meal costs totaled $100 per day. Unless B can show that a personal vacation was not a major consideration for the trip, he must allocate his expenses because none of the other conditions are satisfied. In such case, B may deduct $2,250 [(15 business days ÷ 20 total days = 75%) × $3,000 total expenses]. If B had returned July 8 or spent one less day sight-seeing, no allocation would be required since he would have been out of the United States less than a week or would have spent more than 75% of his time on business activities.

Luxury Water Travel. When lawmakers lowered the boom on entertainment and meal expenses in 1986, they also took a swipe at unhurried businesspersons who travel by cruise ships, ocean liners, and other luxury water transportation. As a general rule, deductions for transportation by water are limited to *twice* the highest per diem amount allowed to Federal employees while away from home but serving in the 48 contiguous states.[67]

> **Example 31.** To conduct a business meeting in London, T traveled by ocean liner, taking five days at a total cost of $3,000. Assuming the top per diem rate for Federal employees serving in the United States is $200 per day, T's deduction is limited to $2,000 ($200 × 2 × 5).

FOREIGN CONVENTIONS

Notwithstanding the restrictions imposed on deductions related to foreign travel, substantial abuse existed until 1976. Most of this abuse involved travel to foreign conventions, seminars, cruises, and the like, which if properly scheduled amounted to government-subsidized vacations. To eliminate this possibility, specific safeguards were enacted in 1976 and revised in 1978. Currently, no deduction is allowed for travel expenses to attend a convention, seminar, or similar meeting outside of North America *unless* the taxpayer establishes the following:[68] (1) the meeting is directly related to the active conduct of his or her trade or business, and (2) it is as reasonable to hold the meeting outside North America as within North America. North America includes the United States, its possessions, Canada, Mexico, the Trust Territory of the Pacific Islands, and qualifying Caribbean Countries and Bermuda.

---

[67] § 274(m)(1).

[68] See § 274(h)(1), (3), and (6).

Example 32.   B, a professor of international business, traveled to Spain to present a paper on tax incentives for exports at the International Accounting Convention. Since it is as reasonable to hold an international meeting in Spain as in North America, and presentation of the paper is directly related to B's business, she may deduct her travel expenses subject to the normal rules for travel outside the United States.

CRUISE SHIPS

No deduction is allowed for the cost of attending a meeting conducted on a cruise ship unless the following requirements are met:[69] (1) the ship is a vessel registered in the United States and it sails *only* between ports in the United States or its possessions; (2) the meeting is directly related to the taxpayer's business; and (3) certain detailed information regarding the cruise is submitted with the return. For qualifying cruises, the maximum deduction is $2,000 per calendar year for each taxpayer. An employer, however, may deduct the cost of sending an individual to a foreign convention or on any type of cruise if the amount is included in the employee's income.

✔ CHECK YOUR KNOWLEDGE

Try the following true-false questions.

1. F is director of sales for QVS in Los Angeles but chooses to live 90 miles away in Santa Barbara. Each day he drives to and from work. Once in a while he will leave the office to call on a customer and then return. F may not deduct his cost to commute but can deduct the cost of driving to make calls.

   True. As a general rule, commuting is not deductible regardless of the distance traveled. However, the cost of going from one job site to another site is deductible.

2. A taxpayer must have a regular work location in order to deduct the costs of commuting to a temporary work assignment outside his tax home.

   False. In order to deduct the cost of commuting to a work location *within* the taxpayer's tax home, the taxpayer must have a regular place of business. The same requirement does not apply to commuting outside the taxpayer's tax home.

3. The costs of depreciation and insurance for an automobile vary significantly depending on the type of car and driver. Consequently, these items are not reflected in the standard mileage rate; however, the taxpayer can add the appropriate amount of depreciation and insurance expense to the amount computed using the standard rate in computing deductible automobile expenses.

   False. Depreciation and insurance are included in the rate.

---

[69] § 274(h)(2).

4. T is the district manager for Mississippi Catfish, a fast-food chain with over 100 stores. He lives in New Orleans. On Monday he traveled to Baton Rouge and returned the same day. On Tuesday he traveled to Houston, spent the night, and returned on Wednesday. T may deduct the costs of lunch both in Baton Rouge and in Houston.

    False. In order to deduct the costs of meals and lodging, the taxpayer must be in a travel status (i.e, away from home overnight). Thus T cannot deduct the cost of lunch on his day trip to Baton Rouge. He is allowed to deduct the cost of his lunch while in Houston since he was there overnight.

5. This year, Dr. F, an ophthalmologist, attended a four-day meeting of his professional organization in Cancun. He remained another three days to lay on the beach and fish. Dr. F may deduct $\frac{4}{7}$ of his airfare.

    False. If the trip is primarily for business, the taxpayer is allowed to deduct all of the transportation costs to and from the destination.

ENTERTAINMENT EXPENSES

Perhaps no single deduction has created as much controversy as that for entertainment expenses. The difficulty lies in the fact that there is no simple way to distinguish entertainment expenses incurred out of business necessity from those incurred for personal purposes. The problem is the dual personality of entertainment. Entertainment can be purely for fun and amusement. Or it can be used to break the ice with a potential customer, to relax, or to create an engaging atmosphere for closing the sale or getting the contract. Over the years, Congress and various administrations have continually struggled to devise the proper test that would prohibit taxpayers from deducting what might be a personal expenditure. In this respect, the past year was no different as Congress made several major changes affecting entertainment expenses.

The Kennedy administration was the first to have some success in limiting the entertainment deduction. In 1961, President Kennedy recommended abolishing the deduction for entertaining customers at parties, night clubs, and the like, as well as disallowing the deduction for country club dues. Although Kennedy's suggestions were not enacted, Congress did move to make it more difficult to deduct entertainment expenses with the enactment of Code § 274. This provision—discussed below—still stands as the major hurdle that must be overcome before entertainment expenses may be deducted. Under § 274, entertainment expenses must not only satisfy the normal criteria for business and income-producing expenses but also several additional requirements, including certain recordkeeping standards. Despite these additional conditions, the so-called *Kennedy rules* still were viewed by many to be inadequate.

President Carter's administration ventured into the battle over entertainment deductions in 1977, blasting the taxpayer's right to deduct the cost of what is now the infamous "three martini lunch." The Carter attacks were generally unsuccessful, however. It was not until President Reagan's term that the entertainment deduction was drastically curtailed. Present law now presumes that virtually every entertainment and meal expense contains a personal element that is not deductible. As discussed below, only 50 percent of the cost of allowable meals and entertainment is currently deductible.

DEDUCTION REQUIREMENTS

To be deductible, an entertainment expense must first survive the gauntlet of tests applied to all potential deductions by § 162. That is, the expense must be reasonable, ordinary, and necessary, and incurred in carrying on a trade or business.

> **Example 33.** D is a sales representative of M Corporation, a manufacturer of cookware. Twice a month, she takes buyers from the leading retail department stores to lunch where they discuss the corporation's new products. Business meals are customary, appropriate, and helpful in commissioned sales and thus are deductible.

As a practical matter, most entertainment expenses satisfy the ordinary and necessary tests with little difficulty. It is the additional requirements of § 274 that provide the greatest obstacles.

The restrictions contained in § 274 apply to any expense related to an activity customarily considered to provide entertainment, amusement, or recreation.[70] The provision applies to expenses for entertaining guests such as those for the following: food, liquor, sporting events, movie and theater productions, social, athletic and country clubs, yachts, hunting and fishing trips, and company-provided vacations. Business gifts also are governed by this provision.[71] It should be emphasized that expenses ostensibly for other purposes also are subject to the requirements of § 274 if they are of an entertaining nature.

> **Example 34.** A national magazine desiring publicity often sends the company president flying in a hot air balloon emblazoned with the corporation's logo. Although the expense is for advertising, § 274 applies since the activity constitutes entertainment.

As might be expected, when the IRS questions the taxpayer about his or her deductions for entertainment, the auditor does not ask whether the taxpayer had a good time. Unfortunately, the agent is concerned with whether the taxpayer has satisfied either of two principal tests. Under § 274, no deduction is allowed unless the taxpayer can adequately substantiate that the entertainment expense is *either* "directly related to" or "associated with" the taxpayer's business or falls within one of ten exceptions.

---

[70] § 274(a)(1).   [71] § 274(d).

Directly-Related-To Expenses. The Regulations set forth what the taxpayer must establish for an entertainment expenditure to be considered *directly related to* the taxpayer's business or income-producing activity. Expenses are treated as directly related under the so-called *general test* if the taxpayer shows all of the following:[72]

1. More than a general expectation of deriving some income or other specific benefit (other than goodwill) existed as a result of making the expenditure; no resulting benefit must be shown, however.

2. Business was actually discussed or engaged in during the entertainment.

3. The combined business and entertainment was principally characterized by business.

Business Benefit. Prior to the enactment of § 274, entertainment deductions were liberally granted where they were shown to promote the customer's goodwill. Section 274 rejects this prior standard. Under current law, the taxpayer must have more than just a general expectation of deriving some income or some specific business benefit. Although this standard is hardly the epitome of clarity, it is clear that the likelihood of a benefit must be greater than a remote possibility.

> **Example 35.** T, an insurance salesman, sees his old college chum, C, in a bar. T buys his buddy a few drinks then takes him to a ballgame, using an extra ticket T has. Before the night is over, T mentions that if C ever needs insurance he should give T a call. In this case, T's prospect of a business benefit is slight, too distant, and thus not directly related. It simply creates goodwill, which is insufficient to obtain a deduction. However, T may be able to benefit from hindsight. If C later calls him about insurance, T could rightfully claim the deduction.

Actively Engage in Business. Under the general test, the taxpayer must actually discuss or engage in business. This means that at some point during the entertainment—at half-time, during the intermission, between innings—the taxpayer must forsake the merriment of the moment and get down to business, negotiating, dealing, bargaining with respect to a bona fide business transaction. Since this is obviously difficult to police, the Regulations have given the IRS two helpful presumptions.[73] First, it is presumed that no business can take place if the taxpayer is not present. If the taxpayer is at home mowing the lawn while the client is enjoying the game using tickets given to him by the taxpayer, the implication is that no business can take place. (In such case, the taxpayer may be able to deduct the cost of the tickets as a business gift as discussed below.) Second, it is presumed that no business can take place where there are substantial distractions. The Regulations insist that such distractions are present at night clubs, sporting events, social gatherings, cocktail lounges, theaters, and wherever the taxpayer meets with a group including not only business associates but others. Despite these presumptions, a

---

[72] Reg. § 1.274-2(c)(3).   [73] Reg. § 1.274-2(c)(7).

deduction is still allowed if the taxpayer can establish to the contrary that he or she actively engaged in the discussion of business. As a practical matter, most taxpayers take advantage of this latitude, claiming the deduction and hoping that they will never be called upon to justify it.

Principal Character Is Business.   During the entertainment, business must predominate. This does not mean that the taxpayer must spend more time on business than enjoying the activity. It does mean that the business aspects must be more than incidental. As above, the Regulations rest on the rebuttable presumption that the primary character of certain activities—those on a hunting or fishing trip, a yacht or pleasure boat—is not business.

The Regulations also specify several other situations where the entertainment expense will be considered directly related. For example, entertainment is directly related if it is provided in a clear business setting—a setting where the guest recognizes the taxpayer's business motive (e.g., a hospitality room provided by a book publisher at a convention of accounting professors).[74] Expenditures for entertainment provided for those who render services for the taxpayer also are regarded as directly related. For example, a vacation trip awarded by a manufacturer to the retailer selling a number of its products qualifies.[75]

Associated-With Expenses.   It is often difficult to qualify the entertainment under the directly related test, generally due to the presumption regarding distractions or simply because the taxpayer could not squeeze in any business during the show or game. However, the entertainment may still qualify for deduction if it satisfies the *associated-with test*. Entertainment expenses are considered *associated with* the taxpayer's business if the entertainment is immediately before or after a substantial business discussion.[76] The key distinction between associated-with and directly-related-to expenses concerns when the business activity occurs. The associated-with test allows the business to occur immediately preceding or following the entertainment while the directly-related-to standard requires business during the entertainment. Note that to satisfy the "immediately preceding or following" requirement it is sufficient that the entertainment merely takes place on the same day as business. In some cases, the entertainment may be on the day before or after the business activity.

> **Example 36.**   B operates a chain of sporting goods stores in Dallas. Before school begins each fall, he invites area coaches to one of his stores, where he presents his new lines of equipment. Immediately afterwards, he takes them to a Cowboy football game. B may deduct the costs of tickets to the game since there was substantial business activity immediately before the entertainment. Note that due to the distractions presented by the game no deduction would be permitted if B merely took the coaches to the game and discussed business there.

---

[74] Reg. § 1.274-2(d)(4).

[75] Reg. § 1.274-2(d)(5).

[76] *Supra*, Footnote 70; Reg. § 1.274-2(d).

Business Meals. For many years, taxpayers were allowed to deduct the cost of meals with business associates regardless of whether they satisfied the directly-related-to or associated-with requirements. More importantly, the costs could be deducted even if business was not discussed. The effect of these rules was to allow a deduction for entertaining that created goodwill. In 1986, Congress believed that this favorable treatment was no longer justified and therefore tightened the rules.

Currently, expenses for meals, like other entertainment expenses, are not deductible unless they satisfy the directly-related-to or associated-with tests.[77] Under these criteria, the business meal is not deductible unless there is a substantial and bona fide business discussion either before, after, or during the meal.[78] In addition, the taxpayer or an employee of the taxpayer normally must be present at the meal.[79] For example, if the taxpayer merely reserves a table for dinner at a restaurant for a customer, but neither the taxpayer nor one of his or her employees attends the dinner, no deduction is allowed. For purposes of this rule, an independent contractor who performs significant services for the taxpayer such as an attorney or accountant is considered an employee.

A common question regarding the deduction for business meals concerns the costs of the taxpayer's own meals. From a purely theoretical view, the cost would presumably be a nondeductible personal expense since the taxpayer has to eat in any event. In *Richard A. Sutter,* the Tax Court took just such a view in disallowing a taxpayer's deduction for his own meals at business lunches.[80] The Court said:

> We think the presumptive nondeductibility of personal expenses (the taxpayer's meals) may be overcome only by clear and detailed evidence as to each instance that the expenditure in question was *different from* or *in excess* of that which would have been made for the taxpayer's personal purposes (emphasis supplied).

Despite the Court's holding, the IRS has been quite gracious. The Service permits the taxpayer to deduct the *entire cost* of his or her own meal except in abusive situations where it is evident that a substantial amount of personal expenditures are being deducted.[81] Where abuse is apparent, the IRS would invoke the *Sutter* rule and allow a deduction only to the extent it exceeds the amount the taxpayer would normally spend.

Another common question concerns the costs of entertaining those who are not directly involved in the business activities to which the entertainment relates. The portion of any entertainment expense attributable to the customer's and the taxpayer's spouses is deductible where the purpose is business rather than personal or social.[82] For example, when the taxpayer entertains a business client and it is impractical to entertain the client without the spouse, the expenses of both the taxpayer's spouse and the client's spouse are deductible. Any expenses of other persons not closely connected with those who attended the business discussion are not deductible.

---

[77] An individual who is *away from home* on business and eats alone need not satisfy these tests.

[78] §§ 274(a) and (b).

[79] § 274(k)(1)(B).

[80] 21 T.C. 170 (1953).

[81] Rev. Rul. 63-144, 1963-2 C.B. 129.

[82] Reg. § 1.274-2(d)(4).

ENTERTAINMENT FACILITIES

For many years, the costs of owning and maintaining such status symbols as airplanes, luxury skyboxes, yachts, and hunting and fishing lodges could be subsidized by deducting them as entertainment expenses. Typically, taxpayers would deduct expenses like depreciation, utilities, maintenance, insurance, and salaries (e.g., that of the yacht's captain) that were allocable to business usage of the property. In 1978, however, Congress imposed severe restrictions. Currently, costs such as those listed above that are related to any entertainment facility are not deductible.[83] Additional special rules apply to expenses incurred in using a luxury skybox.[84]

These rules governing entertainment facilities do not prohibit the deduction of out-of-pocket expenses incurred while at the entertainment facility. Expenses for such items as food or beverage would be deductible, assuming they meet the directly-related-to or associated-with tests. In addition, the various exceptions of § 274 discussed below may enable an employer to deduct expenses connected with entertainment facilities. For example, an employer may deduct the costs of vacation condominiums, swimming pools, tennis courts, and similar facilities if such entertainment facilities are provided primarily for employees.[85]

Club Dues. For years, the tax law contained an exception to the facility rule that allowed taxpayers to deduct their dues or fees paid for a membership in country clubs and the like if the club was primarily used for business. In the never-ending attack on entertainment expenses, Congress eliminated the deduction for club dues in 1993. Beginning in 1994, no deduction is allowed for the cost of membership in any club organized for business, pleasure, recreation, or any other social purpose.[86] The new rule extends not only to country club dues but to all types of clubs, including luncheon, social, athletic, airline, and hotel clubs. Note that specific expenses incurred at a club such as a business meal continue to be deductible to the extent that they satisfy any other applicable requirements.

EXCEPTIONS TO DIRECTLY-RELATED-TO AND ASSOCIATED-WITH TESTS

In certain innocent situations, entertainment and meal expenses need not meet either the directly-related-to or associated-with requirements. These include expenses for the following:[87]

1. Food and drink furnished on the business premises primarily for employees (e.g., costs of a holiday office party)

2. Recreational or social activities, including facilities primarily for employees (e.g., a summer golf outing, a company health club, an annual picnic)

---

[83] § 274(a)(1)(B); Reg. § 1.274-2(e)(2).

[84] § 274(l)(2).

[85] § 274(e)(5).

[86] § 274(a)(3).

[87] § 274(e)(1)-(9).

3. Entertainment and meal expenses for an employee if the employee reports their value as taxable compensation (e.g., a company-provided vacation for the top salesperson)

4. Entertainment and meal expenses at business meetings of employees, stockholders, and directors (e.g., refreshments at a directors' meeting)

5. Costs of items made available to the general public (e.g., soft drinks at a grand opening, free ham to the first 50 customers)

6. Costs of entertainment and meals sold to customers (e.g., costs of food sold at an event)

FIFTY PERCENT LIMITATION
ON ENTERTAINMENT AND MEAL EXPENSES

Opponents of the deduction for entertainment and meal expenses have long argued that, despite their business relationship, such expenses are inherently personal and should not be deductible. These same critics typically declare that businesspersons should not be able to live high-on-the-hog at the expense of the government. In 1986 the critics got their way, cutting the deduction to 80 percent of the actual cost. In 1993, they did it again, slashing the deduction even further.

Currently, § 274(n) generally limits the amount that can be deducted for meals and entertainment to 50 percent of their actual cost. In effect, 50 percent of the cost is disallowed. For employees whose entertainment expenses are *not reimbursed,* the 50 percent limitation is applied before the 2 percent floor for itemized deductions.

Example 37. B, an employee, pays $3,000 for business entertainment for which he is not reimbursed. B's A.G.I. is $50,000 for the year and he has no other miscellaneous itemized deductions. B's deduction is $500, computed as follows:

Total unreimbursed entertainment expenses..........	$3,000
Less 50% reduction (50% × $3,000)..............	(1,500)
Miscellaneous itemized deductions...................	$1,500
Less 2% of A.G.I. (2% × $50,000)................	(1,000)
Itemized deduction.................................	$ 500

Expenses subject to the 50 percent limitation include the costs of taxes, tips, and parking related to a meal or an entertainment activity. In contrast, the costs of transportation to and from the activity are not subject to limitation.

Example 38.   B is the agent of C, who recently signed a lucrative contract with the Golden State Warriors. After successfully negotiating C's contract, B and C took a cab to a local restaurant where they toasted their success. After dinner, they walked to a nearby nightclub. For the night, B spent $207 for the following:

	Limited Expenses	Other
Meal	$120	
Tax	12	
Tips	30	
Cover charge	38	
Cab		$7
Total	$200	$7

The cost of the cab ride, $7, is not subject to limitation and thus can be deducted in full. Of the remaining $200, only $100 is deductible (50% of $200).

It should be emphasized that the percentage reduction rule applies to meals while away from home overnight on business as well as the traditional quiet business meal. The 50 percent limitation does not apply in several situations, thus allowing the taxpayer to deduct the meal or entertainment in full. These exceptions are discussed below.

Reimbursed Expenses.   When the taxpayer is reimbursed for the meal or entertainment, the limitation is imposed on the party making reimbursement, not the taxpayer.[88]

Example 39.   N, a sales representative for Big Corporation, took a customer to lunch after he secured a large order. He paid $30, for which he was totally reimbursed. N includes the $30 in income and may deduct the entire $30. The corporation can deduct only $15 (50% of $30).

If an employee has a reimbursement or expense allowance arrangement with the employer, but under the arrangement the full amount of business expenses is not reimbursed, special problems arise. These problems are considered along with recordkeeping requirements later in this chapter.

Excludable Fringe Benefit.   The 50 percent limitation does not apply where the food or beverage provided is excludable as a de minimis employee fringe benefit (e.g., holiday turkeys, hams, fruitcakes, and the like given to employees or to subsidized cafeterias).[89]

Code § 274(e) Exceptions.   The percentage reduction rule generally is not imposed on entertainment and meal costs which are exempted from the directly-related-to and associated-with tests noted above.[90] For example, there is no reduction required for the deductible costs of an annual employee Christmas party, summer golf outings, or company-provided vacations treated as compensation. Similarly, the costs of promotional

---

[88] §§ 274(n)(2) and 274(e)(3).

[89] § 274(n)(2)(B).

[90] § 274(n)(2).

items made available to the general public (e.g., 100 baseball tickets given by a radio to the first 100 callers) or the salaries of comedians paid by a nightclub are not subject to the 80 percent limitation.

Charitable Sporting Event. The costs of tickets to a sporting event are not subject to the reduction rule if the event is related to charitable fund-raising.[91] Specifically, the event must be organized for the primary purpose of benefiting a tax-exempt charitable organization, must contribute 100 percent of the proceeds to the charity, and must use volunteers for substantially all work performed in putting on the event. For example, the cost of tickets to attend a golf or tennis celebrity tournament sponsored by the local chapter of the United Way would normally satisfy these requirements and would be fully deductible. Tickets for high school, college, or other scholastic events (e.g., a football game or theater tickets) do not qualify for this exception on the grounds that volunteers do not do all the work (e.g., coaches, their assistants, and other paid individuals provide substantial work such as coaching and recruiting).

LIMITATIONS ON DEDUCTIONS FOR TICKETS

In the entertainment fracas of 1986, lawmakers also struck a blow at the deductible costs of tickets. This deduction is limited to the face value of the ticket.[92] This rule is aimed at amounts paid to a ticket scalper in excess of the regular price of the ticket. Such excess is not deductible. The rule also makes nondeductible any fee paid to a ticket agency for arranging tickets. Note, however, that this rule does not apply to tickets to qualified charitable fundraisers.

BUSINESS GIFTS

In hopes that their generosity will someday be rewarded, taxpayers often make gifts to customers, clients, and others with whom they have a business relationship. Such business-connected gifts are deductible under the general rules of § 162. Under prior law, taxpayers wanting to create goodwill could shower their business associates with gifts and deduct these instruments of goodwill. Moreover, the recipient of such bounty could arguably exclude the presents. Currently, § 274(b) curbs such practice by limiting the deduction for business gifts to $25 per donee per year.[93] For this purpose, the following items *are not* considered gifts:

1. An item costing $4 or less imprinted with the taxpayer's name (e.g., pens)

2. Signs, display racks, or other promotional materials to be used on the business premises of the recipient

Incidental costs such as engraving, mailing, and wrapping are not considered part of the cost of an item for purposes of the $25 limit. However, husband and wife are treated as *one* recipient for purposes of the $25 limitation.

---

[91] § 274(n)(2)(C).

[92] § 274(l)(1).

[93] § 274(b). It is unclear whether the 50 percent limitation applies to gifts. See § 274(n)(1) and Reg. § 1.274-2(b)(1)(iii).

Example 40.   J, a saleswoman of hospital supplies, computes her deduction for business gifts during the year in the following manner.

Description of Gift	Amount	Deduction
H, head of purchasing at St. Jude hospital:		
Perfume....................................	$10	
Solar calculator............................	30	
Total..	$40	$25
Dr. Z:		
Box of golf balls...........................	$18	
Gift wrap...................................	2	
Total..	$20	20
Total business gift deduction...................		$45

Assuming J is an employee, she may deduct the $45 as a miscellaneous itemized deduction.

Employee Achievement Awards.   When a business expresses its gratitude for an employee's performance with a gift, special rules allow amounts greater than $25 to be transferred. The effect of these rules is to allow an employer to make and deduct gifts of up to $1,600 to an employee who is allowed to *exclude* the amount of the gift. The Code generally allows an employer to deduct up to $400 per employee for an *employee achievement award*.[94] An employee achievement award is defined as an item of tangible personal property (e.g., a television or watch, not cash or a gift certificate) transferred to the employee for length of service or for safety achievement. To help ensure that such awards are not merely disguised compensation, the award must be transferred as part of a meaningful presentation. When the employer has a qualified plan in effect—a nondiscriminatory written plan where the average annual award to all employees does not exceed $400—a deduction of up to $1,600 for a particular award is allowed.

TRAVEL AND ENTERTAINMENT RECORDKEEPING REQUIREMENTS

Travel and entertainment expenses (including business gifts) are not deductible unless the taxpayer properly substantiates the expenses.[95] The *Cohan* rule permitting a deduction for an unsupported but reasonable estimation of an expense does not apply in regard to travel and entertainment.[96]

---

[94] § 274(j).

[95] § 274(d).

[96] Reg. § 1.274-5T(a)(4).

Section 274(d) specifically requires the taxpayer to substantiate each of the following five elements of an expenditure:

1. Amount

2. Time

3. Place

4. Business purpose

5. Business relationship (for entertainment only)

In most cases, each item must be supported by adequate records such as a diary, account book, or similar record, *and* documentary evidence including receipts or paid bills. Where adequate records have not been maintained, the taxpayer's personal statement will suffice—but only if there is other corroborating evidence, such as the testimony of the individual who was entertained.[97] Congress has indicated that oral evidence would have the least probative value of any evidence and has also authorized the IRS to ask certain additional questions concerning substantiation on the return (see Part II, lines 19–21 of Form 2106, discussed below). In addition, the legislative history makes it clear that the IRS and the courts will invoke the negligence and fraud penalties in those cases where the taxpayer claims tax benefits far in excess of what can be justified.

A receipt is necessary only for lodging expenses and any other expenses of $25 or more. Canceled checks, without other evidence, may not be sufficient. In the well-known blizzard case of 1975, the importance of properly substantiating each element of the expense was made clear.[98] In this case, the taxpayer did not keep a diary or other record of his substantial travel and entertainment expenses, but he presented the District Court with over 1,700 bills, chits, and memos, as well as 20 witnesses. The District Court allowed the deduction holding that the virtual "blizzard" of bills, etc., met the required tests. The Appellate Court, however, disagreed, indicating that the District Court did not determine whether the elements of each expense were substantiated. Lacking sufficient information on the specific purpose of each expenditure, deductions were denied. A written statement of the purpose is unnecessary, however, where the business purpose or business relationship is obvious from other surrounding facts.

In lieu of substantiating the *amount* of meals and lodging expenses while away from home on business, taxpayers may elect to compute the deduction using a standard daily allowance rate. For example, the standard meal rate is usually $26 per day (up to $38 for high-cost areas) and is reduced by the 50 percent limit on meals.[99]

---

[97] Reg. § 1.274-5(c)(3).

[98] *Cam F. Dowell, Jr. v. U.S.*, 75-2 USTC ¶9819, 36 AFTR2d 75-6314, 522 F.2d 708 (CA-5, 1975), *vac'g.* and *rem'g.* 74-1 USTC ¶9243, 33 AFTR2d 74-739, 370 F. Supp. 69 (D.Ct. Tex., 1974).

[99] "Travel, Entertainment and Gift Expenses," IRS Publication 463 (1993), pp. 5 and 6.

✔ **CHECK YOUR KNOWLEDGE**

Review Question 1.   P, the public defense attorney of South City, occasionally takes all of his staff to lunch. Q, an attorney in private practice, occasionally takes all of her staff to lunch. Can P and Q deduct the costs of the meals?

Too bad, P. This question illustrates the relatively rare situation when the taxpayer's entertainment expenses may fail the ordinary and necessary criterion or perhaps be considered lavish or extravagant. Q, the attorney in private practice, would have no trouble deducting her expenses. However, the IRS denied (with the Tax Court's support) a public defender's deduction since public defenders do not commonly take their staffs to lunch!

Review Question 2.   To illustrate the problems with entertainment expenses, consider the case of Danville Plywood Corporation, a custom manufacturer of plywood. In 1981, Danville sponsored a four-day excursion for 116 people to the Super Bowl in New Orleans. The so-called Super Bowl Sales Seminar cost $103,444 including tickets, airfare, food, and lodging. On its 1981 tax return, the corporation claimed a deduction for the entire amount, euphemistically calling it "advertising expense." The list of attendees included 55 customers, 37 of their spouses, and 2 of their children. The remainder consisted of a few employees of the corporation and their spouses, as well as the owner, a few of his friends, and 2 of his children. According to the corporation, the goal of the seminar was to have discussions with the customers over a period of days in order to ascertain how Danville could do a better job as well as cut down on the travel expenses its salesmen incurred on customer visits. In the past, customers had rarely participated in plant visits so the corporation thought some type of sales meeting held in conjunction with a sporting event might boost attendance. In preparation for the trip, the company instructed its employees regarding some new products and provided other information that they were to share with the customers during the Super Bowl or a side trip to the French Quarter. The company also arranged a display showing some of its products in an area adjacent to the lobby of the hotel where everyone stayed. However, when Danville invited its guests, the letter made no reference to business meetings of any kind, nor did the company reserve rooms where business could be conducted. The corporation did hold a dinner in the hotel for all of its guests, but other individuals were also present. Danville had sponsored a similar trip to the 1980 Super Bowl and had deducted about $98,000. Was Danville able to deduct the expenses of all of the attendees?

Unfortunately, Danville got sacked on this play and none of the costs were deductible. In denying the deduction, the court emphasized that the expenses not only had to meet the tests of § 162 (i.e., ordinary and necessary business expenses) but also had to pass the rigorous requirements of § 274. The court found little difficulty in concluding that these tests were not met. It found incredulous the corporation's attempt to deduct not only the expenses of the president's children but also those of the customers, explaining that their presence did not serve a bona fide business purpose. The court felt similarly about the president's friends as well as the spouses of both the customers and the employees. With respect to the

customers and employees, it noted that there was little if any business discussed—a few idle conversations at most. Moreover, the letters to the customers never mentioned the possibility of business discussions or meetings. Nor were meeting rooms reserved for such purpose. In addition, the court believed that such trips were not commonplace in the industry. Based on these observations, the court concluded that the central focus of the trip was entertainment, not business. Unfortunately, it appears that Danville could have won this game if it had had a better game plan. For example, the deduction may have been secured if only the company's correspondence had properly explained the business nature of the weekend and it had actually conducted a business meeting in a separate room devoted to such purpose. No doubt, it also did not sit well with the IRS that the corporation was so aggressive that it deducted the expenses of the children and the friends. Simply bypassing these deductions may have saved the day.

Review Question 3.   Although there appears to be one test after another that taxpayers must meet before they deduct entertainment expenditures, there are some basic requirements. Describe them.

The entertainment must be either directly related or associated with business. This means that a taxpayer must discuss business either before, after, or during the entertainment activity.

Review Question 4.   D, an attorney in Indianapolis, is an avid Hoosier fan. Somehow he managed to obtain season tickets to the IU basketball games. From time to time, he is unable to attend a game, so he calls a client and surprises him or her with a pair of tickets. Can D deduct the cost of the tickets for his clients?

D can continue to make his friends happy. As a general rule, no deduction is allowed unless the taxpayer or his representative (e.g., an employee) is present, since business cannot take place. However, D could deduct up to $25 as a business gift.

Review Question 5.   E runs an advertising firm and is constantly taking people to lunch. Just yesterday he took the ad director at Channel 12 to dinner at his favorite gourmet restaurant. They both had drinks, salad, prime rib, dessert, and coffee: a total of $30 each. When E eats alone, he typically eats a value meal at the local fast-food place. Can E deduct the cost of his client's meal? Can he deduct the entire cost of his own meal or only the amount in excess of what he normally spends?

E can eat, drink, and be merry. As long as E and his friend discussed business in between bites or the meal followed or preceded a business meeting, he can deduct the entire $60 subject to the 50 percent limitation.

Review Question 6. This year F was admitted to the partnership of her accounting firm. Not only was F required to contribute $50,000 to the partnership but she was also required to join a country club. She joined the plush Meridian Lakes Country Club at a cost of $25,000. In addition, she must pay monthly dues of $300. Assuming F uses the club exclusively for business, can she deduct the membership and dues?

Sorry, F, but it is the price of being a partner. The Code has always denied a deduction for the cost of the membership and beginning in 1994 it specifically prohibits the deduction for the club dues.

Review Question 7. True or False: Taxpayers are generally allowed to deduct only 50 percent of their unreimbursed travel and entertainment expenses.

False. Do not be fooled. A typical mistake is to lump travel and entertainment together. Only meals and entertainment expenses are subject to the 50 percent rule. Travel (other than meals) is not subject to the limitation.

Review Question 8. G&H, a public accounting firm, provides continuing education for its tax staff at a resort in Florida. During the week, the employees spend hour upon hour in seminars devoted to the tax law. The firm pays for the meals and lodging of the participants. Is G&H entitled to deduct the entire costs of the meals or only 50 percent?

The 50 percent limitation normally applies to the costs of all meals and entertainment. However, the limitation does not apply if any of the various exceptions contained in § 274(e) apply. One of these concerns business meetings of employees. Consequently, the firm is allowed to deduct 100 percent of the meal costs.

REPORTING BUSINESS EXPENSES AND LOSSES

SOLE PROPRIETORS AND SELF-EMPLOYED PERSONS

Sole proprietors and self-employed persons are not treated as separate taxable entities. Rather, their income and expenses are compiled and reported simply as a part of their individual return. This information is reported on Schedule C or C-EZ of Form 1040. Page 1 of Schedule C appears on the following page. An examination of Schedule C reveals that it is relatively straightforward and self-explanatory. The net income or loss as reported on line 31 of Schedule C is transferred to Page 1 of Form 1040 and is added to the taxpayer's income. The net income or loss on Schedule C also is used in the computation of self-employment tax. Accordingly, the net amount on Schedule C must also be transferred to Schedule SE.

EMPLOYEES

Both the treatment and reporting of an employee's business expenses vary significantly depending on whether the expenses are reimbursed. As explained in Chapter 7, employee business expenses that are *not* reimbursed are treated as miscellaneous itemized deduc-

tions, and are therefore deductible only to the extent that total miscellaneous itemized deductions exceed 2 percent of A.G.I. In addition, such deductions would be subject to the 3 percent cutback. On the other hand, expenses reimbursed under an accountable plan (discussed below) are *not deductible* by the employee, *but* the reimbursement is excludable from his or her gross income. In such case, there is no effect on the taxpayer's return. This latter treatment normally applies to most employee expense accounts, including those arrangements where the employer reimburses an employee for a particular expense as well as those where the employer gives the employee a fixed allowance (e.g., a per diem amount such as $15 per day for meals and $25 per day for lodging). It should be emphasized, however, that even though an expense may appear to be reimbursed in the normal sense, it may not be treated as reimbursed for determining whether the expense is deductible from A.G.I. or the reimbursement is excludable from gross income.

Accountable and Nonaccountable Plans. Beginning in 1989, an employee's business expenses are treated as reimbursed only if his or her employer has a reimbursement or allowance arrangement that qualifies as an *accountable plan*. An arrangement generally qualifies as an accountable plan if the employee properly substantiates the expenses to the employer, and, in the case of advances or allowances, is required to return to the employer any amount in excess of that which is substantiated.[100] If the arrangement does not meet the accountable plan requirements, it is considered a *nonaccountable plan*. As might be expected, the tax treatment of payments under the two different plans differs drastically.

Reimbursements or advances made under an accountable plan are treated far more favorably than those under a nonaccountable plan. Amounts paid under an accountable plan are normally excluded from gross income, not reported on the employee's Form W-2, and are exempt from employment taxes (i.e., social security and unemployment). In contrast, reimbursements and advances made under a nonaccountable plan must be reported in the employee's gross income, included on Form W-2, and are subject to employment taxes. More importantly, the expenses for which the employee is reimbursed under a nonaccountable plan must be claimed as miscellaneous itemized deductions subject to the 2 percent floor. Under either plan, the employee normally summarizes employee business expenses on Form 2106 (shown on pp. 8-51 and 8-52). When this form is properly completed, expenses not considered reimbursed flow to Schedule A and are deducted as miscellaneous itemized deductions. The reporting of employee business expenses is summarized in Exhibit 8-2 (shown on pp. 8-49 and 8-50).

Under an accountable plan, an employee who substantiates his or her expenses and returns any excess reimbursement reports neither the reimbursements nor the expenses because there is a complete wash. (See Exhibit 8-2, Item 1). *However,* if the employee fails to return any excess reimbursement, a different accounting is required. In this case, the excess reimbursement is treated *as if* paid under a nonaccountable plan. Therefore, the employer must report the *excess* in the employee's Form W-2 as well as pay the related employment taxes. On the other side, the employee must include the excess in gross income. (See Exhibit 8-2, Item 3.)

---

[100] Temp. Reg. § 1.62-2T.

SCHEDULE C (Form 1040)

Department of the Treasury
Internal Revenue Service (O)

Profit or Loss From Business
(Sole Proprietorship)

▶ Partnerships, joint ventures, etc., must file Form 1065.

▶ Attach to Form 1040 or Form 1041.　▶ See Instructions for Schedule C (Form 1040).

OMB No. 1545-0074

1993

Attachment Sequence No. **09**

Name of proprietor

Social security number (SSN)

A Principal business or profession, including product or service (see page C-1)

B Enter principal business code
(see page C-6) ▶

C Business name. If no separate business name, leave blank.

D Employer ID number (EIN), if any

E Business address (including suite or room no.) ▶ ....
City, town or post office, state, and ZIP code

F Accounting method:　**(1)** ☐ Cash　**(2)** ☐ Accrual　**(3)** ☐ Other (specify) ▶ ....

G Method(s) used to value closing inventory:　**(1)** ☐ Cost　**(2)** ☐ Lower of cost or market　**(3)** ☐ Other (attach explanation)　**(4)** ☐ Does not apply (if checked, skip line H)　　Yes　No

H Was there any change in determining quantities, costs, or valuations between opening and closing inventory? If "Yes," attach explanation

I Did you "materially participate" in the operation of this business during 1993? If "No," see page C-2 for limit on losses.

J If you started or acquired this business during 1993, check here . . . . ▶ ☐

Part I　Income

1	Gross receipts or sales. **Caution:** *If this income was reported to you on Form W-2 and the "Statutory employee" box on that form was checked, see page C-2 and check here* . . . . ▶ ☐	1
2	Returns and allowances	2
3	Subtract line 2 from line 1	3
4	Cost of goods sold (from line 40 on page 2)	4
5	**Gross profit.** Subtract line 4 from line 3	5
6	Other income, including Federal and state gasoline or fuel tax credit or refund (see page C-2) . .	6
7	**Gross income.** Add lines 5 and 6 . . . . ▶	7

Part II　Expenses. Caution: *Do not enter expenses for business use of your home on lines 8–27. Instead, see line 30.*

8	Advertising	**8**	19	Pension and profit-sharing plans	**19**
9	Bad debts from sales or services (see page C-3) . .	**9**	20	Rent or lease (see page C-4):	
			a	Vehicles, machinery, and equipment .	**20a**
10	Car and truck expenses (see page C-3)	**10**	**b**	Other business property . .	**20b**
11	Commissions and fees . .	**11**	21	Repairs and maintenance . .	**21**
12	Depletion	**12**	22	Supplies (not included in Part III) .	**22**
13	Depreciation and section 179 expense deduction (not included in Part III) (see page C-3)	**13**	23	Taxes and licenses	**23**
			24	Travel, meals, and entertainment:	
			a	Travel	**24a**
14	Employee benefit programs (other than on line 19) . . .	**14**	**b**	Meals and entertainment .	
15	Insurance (other than health) .	**15**	**c**	Enter 20% of line 24b subject to limitations (see page C-4) .	
16	Interest:				
a	Mortgage (paid to banks, etc.) .	**16a**	**d**	Subtract line 24c from line 24b	**24d**
b	Other	**16b**	25	Utilities	**25**
17	Legal and professional services	**17**	26	Wages (less jobs credit) . .	**26**
18	Office expense	**18**	27	Other expenses (from line 46 on page 2)	**27**

28	**Total expenses** before expenses for business use of home. Add lines 8 through 27 in columns. . . ▶	**28**
29	Tentative profit (loss). Subtract line 28 from line 7	**29**
30	Expenses for business use of your home. Attach **Form 8829**	**30**
31	**Net profit or (loss).** Subtract line 30 from line 29.	
	● If a profit, enter on **Form 1040, line 12,** and ALSO on **Schedule SE, line 2** (statutory employees, see page C-5). Fiduciaries, enter on Form 1041, line 3.	**31**
	● If a loss, you MUST go on to line 32.	
32	If you have a loss, check the box that describes your investment in this activity (see page C-5).	
	● If you checked 32a, enter the loss on **Form 1040, line 12,** and ALSO on **Schedule SE, line 2** (statutory employees, see page C-5). Fiduciaries, enter on Form 1041, line 3.	**32a** ☐ All investment is at risk.
	● If you checked 32b, you MUST attach **Form 6198.**	**32b** ☐ Some investment is not at risk.

For Paperwork Reduction Act Notice, see Form 1040 instructions.　　　　Cat. No. 11334P　　　　**Schedule C (Form 1040) 1993**

Exhibit 8-2 *Reporting Travel, Transportation, Meal, and Entertainment Expenses and Reimbursements*

Type *of Reimbursement or Other Expense Allowance Arrangement*	**Employer** *Reports on Form W-2*
1. **Accountable** *Adequate accounting and excess returned*	*Not reported*
2. *Per diem or mileage allowance (up to government rate)* *Adequate accounting and excess returned*	*Not reported*
3. *Per diem or mileage allowance (exceeds government rate)* *Adequate accounting up to the government rate only and excess not returned*	*Excess reported as wages in Box 1.[3] Amount up to the government rate is reported only in Box 13—it is not reported in Box 1*
4. **Nonaccountable** *Adequate accounting or return of excess either not required or required but not met*	*Entire amount is reported as wages in Box 1.[3]*
5. *No reimbursement*	*Normal reporting of wages, etc.*

Notes: [1]Any allowable expense is carried to line 20 of Schedule A and deducted as a miscellaneous itemized deduction.

[2]These amounts are subject to the applicable limits including the 50% limit on meals and entertainment expenses and the 2% of adjusted gross income limit on the total miscellaneous itemized deductions.

[3]These amounts are subject to income tax withholding and to all employment taxes such as FICA and FUTA.

Source: "Travel, Entertainment, and Gift Expenses," IRS Publication 463 (1993), p. 24.

Example 41. R is a sales representative for C Corporation and has an expense account arrangement. Under this arrangement, R fills out an expense report every two weeks, documenting all of his expenses, and submits it for reimbursement. This year R submitted travel expenses of $5,000, all of which were reimbursed. Assuming this is an accountable plan and R has properly substantiated expenses of $5,000, there is nothing included on his Form W-2 and none of the expenses are reported on his return. In effect, there is no effect on R because the reimbursement and expenses wash. (See Exhibit 8-2, Item 1.)

Exhibit 8-2   *Continued*

Employee *Shows on Form 2106*	**Employee** *Claims on Schedule A*
Not shown	*Not claimed*
All expenses and reim- bursements only *if excess expenses are claimed.*[1] *Otherwise, form is not filed*	*Expenses the employee can prove and which ex- ceed the reimbursements received* [2]
All expenses, and reim- bursements equal to the government rate, only if *expenses in excess of the government rate are claimed.*[1] *Otherwise, form is not filed*	*Expenses the employee can prove and which ex- ceed the government rate* [2]
All expenses[1]	*Expenses the employee can prove* [2]
All expenses[1]	*Expenses the employee can prove* [2]

Example 42.   Assume the plan in *Example 41* was not properly structured and did not require R either to substantiate his expenses or to return any excess reimbursement. In this case, the arrangement would be a nonaccountable plan. Consequently, the $5,000 reimbursement would be included as income in R's Form W-2 and he could deduct the $5,000 as a miscellaneous itemized deduction. In this case, the income and deduction do not necessarily wash (e.g., if R does not itemize), and R ends up with taxable income that economically he does not have. (See Exhibit 8-2, Item 4. The Form 2106 shown on pp. 8-51 and 8-52 reveals how this information would be reported.)

As the above examples illustrate, most employers should opt to establish reimbursement arrangements that meet the accountable plan requirements so that employees are not unduly penalized. Nevertheless, as noted above, even if the employer has an accountable plan, the employee must still substantiate any expenses and return any reimbursements in excess of the expenses substantiated to avoid unfavorable treatment.

Form **2106**	**Employee Business Expenses**	OMB No. 1545-0139
Department of the Treasury Internal Revenue Service (T)	▶ See separate instructions. ▶ Attach to Form 1040.	**1993** Attachment Sequence No. **54**

Your name	Social security number	Occupation in which expenses were incurred
R		

Part I Employee Business Expenses and Reimbursements

STEP 1 Enter Your Expenses		Column A Other Than Meals and Entertainment		Column B Meals and Entertainment	
1	Vehicle expense from line 22 or line 29	1			
2	Parking fees, tolls, and transportation, including train, bus, etc., that **did not** involve overnight travel	2			
3	Travel expense while away from home overnight, including lodging, airplane, car rental, etc. **Do not** include meals and entertainment	3	5,000		
4	Business expenses not included on lines 1 through 3. **Do not** include meals and entertainment	4			
5	Meals and entertainment expenses (see instructions)	5			
6	**Total expenses.** In Column A, add lines 1 through 4 and enter the result. In Column B, enter the amount from line 5	6	5,000		

Note: *If you were not reimbursed for any expenses in Step 1, skip line 7 and enter the amount from line 6 on line 8.*

STEP 2 Enter Amounts Your Employer Gave You for Expenses Listed in STEP 1

7	Enter amounts your employer gave you that were **not** reported to you in box 1 of Form W-2. Include any amount reported under code "L" in box 13 of your Form W-2 (see instructions) . . .	7	-0-		

STEP 3 Figure Expenses To Deduct on Schedule A (Form 1040)

8	Subtract line 7 from line 6	8	5,000		

Note: *If **both columns** of line 8 are zero, **stop here.** If Column A is less than zero, report the amount as income on Form 1040, line 7, and enter -0- on line 10, Column A.*

9	Enter 20% (.20) of line 8, Column B	9			
10	In Column A, enter the amount from line 8. In Column B, subtract line 9 from line 8	10	5,000		
11	Add the amounts on line 10 of both columns and enter the total here. **Also, enter the total on Schedule A (Form 1040), line 19.** (Qualified performing artists and individuals with disabilities, see the instructions for special rules on where to enter the total.) . . . . ▶	11	5,000		

For Paperwork Reduction Act Notice, see instructions.   Cat. No. 11700N   Form **2106** (1993)

Substantiation. A plan generally satisfies the substantiation requirement if the employee meets the normal rules for substantiation of expenses. For example, travel and entertainment expenses must be substantiated under the special rules of § 274(d) discussed earlier in this chapter. Note that an employee whose reimbursement is based on some type of fixed allowance (e.g., a per diem for meals and lodging or a mileage allowance) is *deemed* to have substantiated the amount of his or her expenses up to the amount set by the IRS for per diem, mileage, or other expense allowances.[101] Generally,

---

[101] See Regs. §§ 1.62-2T(e)(2) and 1.274-5T(g).

Form 2106 (1993)

Part II	Vehicle Expenses (See instructions to find out which sections to complete.)			
Section A.—General Information			**(a)** Vehicle 1	**(b)** Vehicle 2

			(a) Vehicle 1	(b) Vehicle 2
12	Enter the date vehicle was placed in service	12	/ /	/ /
13	Total miles vehicle was driven during 1993	13	miles	miles
14	Business miles included on line 13	14	miles	miles
15	Percent of business use. Divide line 14 by line 13	15	%	%
16	Average daily round trip commuting distance	16	miles	miles
17	Commuting miles included on line 13	17	miles	miles
18	Other personal miles. Add lines 14 and 17 and subtract the total from line 13.	18	miles	miles

19   Do you (or your spouse) have another vehicle available for personal purposes? . . . . ☐ Yes ☐ No

20   If your employer provided you with a vehicle, is personal use during off duty hours permitted? ☐ Yes ☐ No ☐ Not applicable

21a   Do you have evidence to support your deduction? . . . . ☐ Yes ☐ No

21b   If "Yes," is the evidence written?   . . . . ☐ Yes ☐ No

Section B.—Standard Mileage Rate (Use this section only if you own the vehicle.)

22	Multiply line 14 by 28¢ (.28). Enter the result here and on line 1. (Rural mail carriers, see instructions.)	22	

Section C.—Actual Expenses		(a) Vehicle 1		(b) Vehicle 2	
23	Gasoline, oil, repairs, vehicle insurance, etc.	23			
24a	Vehicle rentals	24a			
b	Inclusion amount (see instructions)	24b			
c	Subtract line 24b from line 24a	24c			
25	Value of employer-provided vehicle (applies only if 100% of annual lease value was included on Form W-2—see instructions)	25			
26	Add lines 23, 24c, and 25 . .	26			
27	Multiply line 26 by the percentage on line 15 . . .	27			
28	Depreciation. Enter amount from line 38 below	28			
29	Add lines 27 and 28. Enter total here and on line 1.	29			

Section D.—Depreciation of Vehicles (Use this section only if you own the vehicle.)

			(a) Vehicle 1		(b) Vehicle 2	
30	Enter cost or other basis (see instructions)	30				
31	Enter amount of section 179 deduction (see instructions) .	31				
32	Multiply line 30 by line 15 (see instructions if you elected the section 179 deduction) . . .	32				
33	Enter depreciation method and percentage (see instructions) .	33				
34	Multiply line 32 by the percentage on line 33 (see instructions) . .	34				
35	Add lines 31 and 34	35				
36	Enter the limitation amount from the table in the line 36 instructions	36				
37	Multiply line 36 by the percentage on line 15 . . .	37				
38	Enter the **smaller** of line 35 or line 37. Also, enter this amount on line 28 above	38				

the only expense substantiation for such plans is the number of business miles traveled and the number of days away from home spent on business. Due to this rule, employees who receive allowances within the IRS guidelines will have no reimbursements in excess of their substantiated expenses and, therefore, will not have any excess to return.

> **Example 43.**   K works as an accountant for a public accounting firm in Tampa. This year she attended a continuing education course in Jacksonville. The firm gives its employees a meal allowance of $12 per diem, which is within the IRS guidelines. K attended the course for five days. When she returned from the trip, she submitted her expense report requesting reimbursement for meals of $60 (5 × $12). In reality, K, wanting to save as much as she could, spent only $40 on meals. Although K has actually received $20 more than she spent ($60 − $40), she does not have to return the excess because she is deemed to have substantiated expenses of $60.

If the employee has expenses that the employer did not reimburse, the employee should file Form 2106 to claim a deduction for the unreimbursed expenses. Proper completion of this form results in the unreimbursed expenses being claimed as miscellaneous itemized deductions on Schedule A. (See Exhibit 8-2, Item 2.)

> **Example 44.**   Under an accountable plan, T is reimbursed 28 cents per mile for all business miles driven. For the year, he received $1,000. After consulting his records, T determined that his actual expenses exceed 28 cents per mile for a total of $1,200. None of the reimbursement is included on T's Form W-2 because this is an accountable plan and the allowance does not exceed the government rate. T should report the $1,200 of expenses on lines 1–6 of Form 2106. The $1,000 reimbursement is entered on line 7 and subtracted from the $1,200 expense amount to leave $200. The $200 (the amount for which T did not receive a reimbursement) flows through to Schedule A and is treated as a miscellaneous itemized deduction. (See line 11 of Form 2106 and Exhibit 8-2, Item 2.)

> **Example 45.**   J's employer pays her a flat $100 per month to cover her car expenses. The employer does not have an accountable plan. Thus the employer must include the $100 as income in J's Form W-2, and J may deduct her car expenses as miscellaneous itemized deductions. (See Exhibit 8-2, Item 4.)

In certain instances, the employer may give the employee a per diem allowance that exceeds the Federal government allowable rate (e.g., 30 cents per mile instead of the allowable 28 cents per mile). In such cases, special reporting rules apply.[102]

---

[102]   *Supra,* Footnote 99, p. 11.

Partial Reimbursements. Occasionally, the reimbursement received by an employee does not cover all of his or her deductible business expenses. This often occurs when the taxpayer is on a per diem allowance. Because of the 50 percent limitation imposed on meal and entertainment expenses, when there is only a partial reimbursement the employee must determine the particular expenses that were reimbursed. As noted above, the employee is generally able to directly offset 100 percent of any reimbursed meal or entertainment expense against the reimbursement itself. Thus, the employee simply excludes the reimbursement from gross income and does not deduct any of the expenses. In contrast, either of these which is not reimbursed must be reduced by 50 percent and then may be deducted along with other miscellaneous itemized deductions subject to the 2 percent floor. The portion of the meals and entertainment expenses deemed reimbursed is determined in a manner similar to that under prior law, as follows:[103]

$$\frac{\text{Entertainment and meal expenses}}{\text{(before 50\% limit)}} \times \text{Reimbursement}$$

For this purpose, total reimbursable expenses represent those expenses which the reimbursement was intended to cover.

Example 46.   H, a salesman for XYZ corporation, paid the following expenses for which he was reimbursed $700:

Meals...	$ 600
Lodging...	400
Total expenses....................................	$1,000

After allocating the reimbursement, R offsets $420 [$700 × ($600 ÷ $1,000)] of the meals and $280 [$700 × ($400 ÷ $1,000)] of the lodging against the $700 reimbursement. Of the remaining $180 ($600 − $420) of meal expenses, $90 is not deductible under the 50% disallowance rule for meal expenses, and $90 is a miscellaneous itemized deduction subject to the 2% floor. The remaining $120 ($400 − $280) of lodging expenses is also a miscellaneous itemized deduction.

---

[103]   Reg. § 1.62-1(f).

TAX PLANNING CONSIDERATIONS

MOVING EXPENSES

Upon retirement, many individuals move to another location. Normally, the moving expenses would not be deductible. If the taxpayer can obtain a full-time job at the new location, however, the costs of moving become deductible. In this regard, the taxpayer must be sure to satisfy the 39- or 78-week test.

TRAVEL AND ENTERTAINMENT EXPENSES

The rules governing deductions for combined business and pleasure travel permit some vacationing on business trips without jeopardizing the deduction. As long as the trip is primarily for business, the entire cost of traveling to the business/vacation destination is deductible. Although the expenses of personal side-trips are not allowed, these expenses may be incidental to the major costs of getting to the desired location. For example, a taxpayer living in New York can deduct a major portion of the cost of a vacation in Florida—the cost of getting there—by properly scheduling business in Miami. In those situations where vacation time exceeds time spent on business, the taxpayer must be prepared to establish that the trip would not have been taken *but for* the business need.

When traveling, the taxpayer may also be able to deduct the expenses of a spouse if a business purpose for the spouse's presence can be established. Even where a spouse's travel expenses are clearly not deductible, only the *incremental* expense attributable to the spouse's presence is not allowed. When an automobile is used for transportation, there is no incremental expense. In the case of lodging, the single room rate would be fully deductible and only the few extra dollars added for a double room rate would not be deductible.

The importance of adequate records for travel and entertainment expenses cannot be over-emphasized. However, the *actual cost* of travel expenses need not be proved when a per diem or a fixed mileage allowance arrangement exists between the employee and the employer. In these situations, the other elements of the expense—time, place, and business purpose—must still be substantiated by the employer and employee. Moreover, the taxpayer must substantiate the cost of travel where the employee is "related" to the employer (an employee is considered related when he or she either owns more than 10 percent of a corporate employer's stock or is the employer's spouse, brother, sister, ancestor, or lineal descendant). Notwithstanding the relaxation of the substantiation requirements for travel costs, it is advisable to maintain receipts and other records to substantiate the other elements of the expenditure.

The taxpayer should get in the habit of contemporaneously recording the required elements for each expenditure. Although a bothersome task, this must be done to secure deductions for travel and entertainment expenses. *Each* element of each expenditure must be established.

With respect to vehicle expenses, the taxpayer cannot simply deduct the expenses and hope that he or she will never be asked to produce evidence supporting the deduction. Form 2106 (Part II, line 21) specifically asks whether the taxpayer has proper written evidence. Thus, failure to maintain such documentation would mean that the taxpayer could not answer this question in the affirmative, increasing the probability of audit. Of course, indicating that such evidence exists when it in fact does not could subject the taxpayer to negligence or fraud penalties.

HOME OFFICE DEDUCTION

Generally, reporting any gain realized on the sale of a residence may be postponed if the taxpayer purchases another residence with a sales price equivalent to that of the residence sold (see Chapter 15 for details). Claiming the home office deduction in the year of sale, however, results in loss of the deferral privilege for any gain on the sale of the residence attributable to the home office. Thus, before claiming the deduction, the trade-off between a current deduction and subsequent gain recognition must be considered.

PROBLEM MATERIALS

DISCUSSION QUESTIONS

8-1 *Requirements for Education Expenses.* J has been told that, as a practical matter, most education expenses are considered nondeductible personal expenses. Under what conditions, if any, may J deduct expenses for education?

8-2 *Education: Degrees, Promotion, and Employer Assistance.* Y is currently employed as the manager of a fast-food restaurant, earning $29,000. In order to improve her upward mobility in the company, Y decides that she should go to college and earn her degree.

a. Can Y deduct any of the cost of obtaining her bachelor's degree in business?

b. Same as above, except Y already has her bachelor's degree and now decides to take courses which could lead to her receiving an M.B.A.

c. What is the effect on Y if her employer pays for her education costs this year of $6,000? Answer for both a bachelor's degree and an M.B.A.

8-3 *Expenses of Education.* F, vice president of sales for a large corporation, is in the executive M.B.A. program at the University of Michigan. F lives in Chicago and travels to Ann Arbor and Detroit to take certain courses.

a. F's employer reimburses F for the tuition, which is $8,000 per year. Explain how F will treat the reimbursement and the expense. What if F was not reimbursed?

Indicate whether the following expenses incurred by F would be deductible:

b. Meals and lodging when he stays overnight
c. Transportation costs from Chicago and back
d. Books
e. Secretarial fees for typing term projects
f. Copying expenses
g. Value of vacation time used to take classes
h. Tutor

8-4 *Qualifying Educational Expenses.* Indicate whether education expenses would be deductible in the following situations:

a. J is currently an elementary school teacher. State law requires beginning teachers to have a bachelor's degree and to complete a master's degree within five years after first being hired. This year he took two courses toward the master's degree.

b. R is a full-time engineering student and has a part-time job as an engineer with a firm that will employ him as an engineer when he graduates.

c. C is an airline pilot and is presently taking lessons to become a helicopter pilot.

d. H retired from the finance department of the Army and now is getting his M.B.A. He plans to get a job with a financial institution.

8-5 *Moving Expenses.*   Address the following:

   a. What two tests must be satisfied before moving expenses may be deducted?

   b. What moving expenses are deductible?

   c. Are moving expenses deductible *for* or *from* adjusted gross income?

8-6 *Moving Expenses: Real Estate Commissions.*   B's employer transferred him during the year. As a result, B sold his home in North Dakota and moved to New York, where he lives in an apartment. He does not plan to move into a new home. B's real estate commissions were $6,000. B has asked how he should treat the real estate commissions.

8-7 *Home Office Expenses.*   The enactment of the restrictive rules related to home office deductions caused many commentators to conclude that the home office deduction had been essentially eliminated and that the tax advantages of vacation homes had been severely curtailed. Which particular requirement(s) of § 280A prompted such a conclusion?

8-8 *Computing Car Expenses.*   Briefly answer the following:

   a. With respect to a business car, can the taxpayer claim depreciation in addition to the expense determined using the standard mileage rate?

   b. Can a taxpayer switch to the automatic mileage method after using MACRS to compute depreciation? If so, when does the car become fully depreciated?

8-9 *Transportation vs. Travel.*   Explain the distinction between transportation expenses and travel expenses.

8-10 *U.S. Travel vs. Foreign Travel.*   Compare and contrast the rules governing travel in the United States to those rules governing travel outside of the United States.

8-11 *Limitations on Entertainment and Meals.*   T is employed by KL Publishing Corporation. He is a sales representative with responsibility for college textbook sales in Georgia, Florida, and Alabama. T lives in Atlanta. For each of the following situations, indicate whether T's or the corporation's deduction for entertainment or meals would be limited, and if so, how?

   a. T flew to Birmingham on a Tuesday night. After checking in at the hotel, he caught a cab to his favorite restaurant where he ate by himself. The cost of the meal was $20, including a $1 tax and a $3 tip. The cost of the cab ride was $10. The next day he called on a customer.

   b. Same as (a), except that T's employer reimbursed him under an accountable plan for all of his costs.

   c. Same as (a), but further assume that T's A.G.I. for the year was $30,000 and that he has other miscellaneous itemized deductions of $700.

   d. At the year-end Christmas party for employees, the corporation gave T a 10-pound, honey-baked ham, costing $40. The cost of the party (excluding the ham), which was held at a local restaurant, was $300.

   e. During the annual convention of college marketing professors in New Orleans, the corporation rented a room in the convention hotel for one night and provided hors d'oeuvres. The room cost $200 while the food and drink cost $1,000.

8-12 *Reimbursed Expenses.*   Explain the reporting requirements relating to expenses that are reimbursed.

8-13   *Entertainment Expenses.*   Distinguish between entertainment expenses that are considered "directly related to" the taxpayer's business and those that are "associated with" the taxpayer's business.

8-14   *Business Meals.*   Can the taxpayer deduct the cost of his or her own meal when he or she pays for the lunch of a customer and no business is discussed?

8-15   *Entertainment Facilities.*   Under what circumstances are expenses related to an entertainment facility deductible?

8-16   *Substantiation of Travel and Entertainment Expenses.*   What information must the taxpayer be prepared to present upon the audit of his or her travel and entertainment expenditures? Does the taxpayer need to maintain records if he or she has a per diem arrangement with the employer?

8-17   *Foreign Convention.*   Dr. B recently learned that a world famous plastic surgeon will be making a presentation concerning her area of expertise at a convention of physicians in Switzerland. If B attends, can she deduct the costs of airfare, meals, lodging, and registration? Explain.

8-18   *Cruise Ship Seminars.*   The American Organization of Dental Specialists is offering a seven-day seminar on gum disease aboard a cruise ship. Dr. D, a dentist, would like to attend. If D attends, can he deduct his expenses?

8-19   *Reporting Reimbursements.*   R is regional sales manager for a large steel manufacturing corporation. His job requires him to travel extensively to call on customers and salespeople. As a result, he incurs substantial expenses for airfare, hotel, meals, and entertainment, for which he is reimbursed. Under what conditions may R simply ignore reporting the reimbursements and the expenses for tax purposes?

8-20   *Reporting Employee Business Expenses.*   T is a salesperson for Classy Cosmetics Inc. During the year, she incurred various business expenses for which she was reimbursed under an accountable plan. Indicate how T must report the reimbursements and expenses in the following situations, assuming an adequate accounting was made.

   a.   T was on a per diem of $25 per day for lodging and $15 per day for meals. She received $2,000 under the per diem arrangement for expenses totaling $2,200.
   b.   T was reimbursed $3,800 for expenses totaling $3,000.

8-21   *Per Diem Arrangement.*   Al was recently hired by a public accounting firm as a staff accountant. When Al is out of town on business (e.g., staff training or an audit at a client's place of business), the firm gives him $12 a day for dinner. Al normally spends $5 and banks the rest. What are the tax consequences?

8-22   *Substantiation Requirements.*   Indicate whether the following is required in order to properly substantiate a deduction:

   a.   Purpose of an entertainment expenditure
   b.   Date of entertainment expenditure
   c.   Receipt for business meal with client, which cost $15
   d.   Receipt for lodging at Motel Cheap, which cost $12
   e.   Description of what the taxpayer wore on the day he lunched with client
   f.   Diary detailing information normally required for substantiation of entertainment expenses
   g.   Canceled check for $12 for tickets to baseball game that was attended with customer
   h.   Social security number of client entertained

YOU MAKE THE CALL

8-23   The unfortunate experience of Danville Plywood Corporation and its deduction for the Super Bowl described earlier in this chapter raises another issue. The corporation booked what clearly seemed to be entertainment expenses as advertising expenses, perhaps with the hope that the expense would be forever buried. Assume that you were the accountant on the job, noted this, and proposed a reclassification entry to the client who objected. What action should you take?

PROBLEMS

8-24   *Education Expenses.*   Indicate the amount, if any, of deductible education expenses in each of the following cases. Comment briefly on your answer and state whether the deduction is deductible *for* or *from* adjusted gross income:

    a.   C is employed as a plumber, but is training to become a computer programmer. During the year, he paid $500 for tuition and books related to a college course in programming.

    b.   E is a licensed nurse. During the year, she spent $300 on courses to become a registered nurse.

    c.   R paid a $75 fee to take the C.P.A. exam and $800 for a C.P.A. review course. R currently is employed by a public accounting firm.

    d.   R is an IRS agent. This year, he began taking courses toward a law degree emphasizing tax. Tuition and books cost $1,000.

    e.   H is a high school instructor teaching European history. On a one-year sabbatical leave from school, he traveled to Europe, taking slides which he planned on using in his classes. The trip cost $7,000, including $1,000 for meals.

8-25   *Moving Expenses.*   In May of the current year, M found a new job, forcing him to move from Tulsa to Seattle. On June 1, the moving company picked up all of M's possessions. M and his family stayed in a hotel on June 1, left the morning of June 2, and arrived in Seattle on June 4. They incurred the following expenses.

    1.   Air fare and meals for him and his wife while traveling to Seattle to look for a new house, $260 and $50 respectively. They failed to find a home. Consequently, they moved into an apartment, from which they continued their search.

    2.   Lodging in Tulsa on the day they moved out of their house, $70.

    3.   Expenses on the way to Seattle included meals, $80; and lodging, $100.

    4.   Mileage to Seattle, 2,000 miles.

    5.   Car repair on trip to Seattle, $175.

    6.   Moving van, $4,000.

    7.   Storage charges for furniture that would not fit in the apartment: $3 per day for the period June 5–July 31.

    8.   Temporary living expenses for period June 5–July 31: apartment, $10 per day; meals, $20 per day; and cleaning and laundry, $25.

    9.   Realtor's commission on sale of old home, $1,000.

Compute M's moving expense deduction (Form 3903 may be helpful).

8-26 *Home Office.* In each of the following independent situations, indicate whether the taxpayer is entitled to deduct expenses related to the home office:

a. C, a dermatologist employed by a hospital, also owns several rental properties. He regularly uses a bedroom in his home solely as an office for bookkeeping and other activities related to management of the rental properties.

b. R, an attorney employed by a large law firm, frequently brings work home from the office. She uses a study in her home for doing this work as well as paying bills, sorting coupons and conducting other personal activities.

c. M is a research associate employed by the Cancer Research Institute. His duties include designing and carrying out experiments, reviewing data, and writing articles and grant proposals. His employer furnishes M a laboratory but due to insufficient space cannot provide an office for him. Thus, for about three hours each day, M uses a portion of his bedroom (where he and his wife sleep) to do the writing, reviewing, and other related activities.

d. T is a self-employed tax consultant. He has an office downtown and a home office. He occasionally meets with his clients in the home office since it is often more convenient for the clients to meet there.

e. S, an artist, converted a detached garage to a studio for painting. She sells her paintings at her own gallery located in town.

f. D has four toddlers. Since her home is virtually a nursery already, she decided to turn her family room into a day care center.

8-27 *Home Office.* R is considering purchasing a home priced somewhat over her budget. Her brother has suggested that converting a room to a home office would enable her to deduct a substantial part of the costs related to the home, thus making the purchase feasible. R is a sales manager for X Corporation, which transfers its middle management employees frequently. Comment on the following advice given to R by her brother:

a. Establishing a home office is an effective method for reducing the costs of home ownership by the amount of the tax benefits received.

b. There are no disincentives for claiming the home office deduction.

8-28 *Home Office Computations.* T is employed as a law professor at State University. Outside of her university work she teaches continuing education courses for attorneys and occasionally provides legal services. T does all her work for these outside pursuits in her home office. Income and expenses relating to these were

Income:	
Fees for services................................	$2,000
Expenses:	
Depreciation on home office furniture and	
computer.......................................	400
Miscellaneous supplies, books, etc................	500
Expenses attributable to home office:	
Depreciation....................................	500
Insurance and utilities...........................	700
Taxes...	300
Interest...	700

Determine the tax consequences resulting from T's part-time activities.

8-29 *Deductible Moving Expenses.*   Indicate whether the following expenses qualify as deductible moving expenses:

a. Costs of meals and lodging while en route to new location.

b. Insurance on household and personal effects being transported—an option provided by the moving company.

c. Costs of driving the family car to new location.

d. Costs of storing items that would not fit in apartment at the new location; the apartment served as a temporary residence until a home was purchased.

e. Costs of new carpeting and wallpaper to prepare old home to be sold.

f. Real estate commission on sale of former residence.

g. Loss on sale of residence.

h. Payment of six months' rent to settle lease obligation at old location; the lease had six more months to run.

i. Cost of appraisal of new home required as part of loan application.

8-30 *Moving Expenses: Time Test.*   On September 1, 1994, L left her former employment in Indianapolis to seek her fortune in Cincinnati. Indicate whether L could deduct the cost of her moving expenses to Cincinnati under the following conditions.

a. L found a teaching job for the public school system for which she worked ten months, September through June. After school was out, L took a three-month vacation. She then decided to leave Cincinnati and move to Atlanta.

b. Same as (a) except L found a job as a substitute teacher and was considered self-employed.

c. L moved to take a new position as product manager with P&G Corporation. After working three months, she and her new employer had a falling out over what she considered unethical advertising. She quit her job and moved to New York.

8-31 *Moving Expenses: Distance Test.*   P is an accountant for L Corporation. This year, his employer moved from its downtown Manhattan location to a new office in New Jersey. As a result, P decided to move to be closer to the office.

a. Assuming P did not change jobs, is he allowed to deduct any moving expenses?

b. Regardless of your answer to (a), indicate whether P satisfies the distance test in light of the following information:

    —Old office building to new building: 60 miles
    —Old home to new home: 65 miles
    —New home to old office: 51 miles
    —Old home to old office: 30 miles
    —New home to new office: 15 miles
    —Old home to new office: 58 miles

8-32 *Standard Mileage Rate.* R, self-employed, elects to compute her deduction for car expenses using the standard mileage rate. Indicate whether the following expenses may be deducted in addition to expenses computed using the standard rate:

  a. Depreciation
  b. Interest on car loan
  c. Insurance
  d. Parking while calling on customers
  e. Parking tickets incurred while on business
  f. Major overhaul
  g. Personal property taxes on car
  h. Tolls

8-33 *Transportation Expenses.* Indicate the amount, if any, deductible by the taxpayer in each of the following cases. (Ignore the floor on miscellaneous itemized deductions.)

  a. R works in downtown Denver, but chooses to live in the mountains 90 miles away. During the year, he spent $2,700 for transportation expenses to and from work.
  b. Q, a high school basketball coach, liked to scout his opposition. On one Friday afternoon, he left school and drove 40 miles to attend the game of the team he played next. On the way, he stopped for a meal ($5). He watched the game and returned home.
  c. R, a carpenter, commutes to work in a truck. He drives the truck in order to carry the tools of his trade. During the year, R's total transportation costs were $5,000. R estimates that his costs of transportation without the tools would have been $4,000, since he otherwise would have taken public transportation.
  d. G, an attorney, works downtown. She is on retainer, however, with a client who has offices two miles from her home. G often stops at the client's office before going to work. The distance between these locations is as follows: home to office, 20 miles; home to client, 2 miles; and client to office, 22 miles. During the year, G drove directly to work 180 days and via the client's office 50 days.

8-34 *Transportation to Temporary Assignments.* For each of the following cases, indicate the number of business miles driven by the taxpayer. (Ignore the floor on miscellaneous itemized deductions.)

  a. K is employed as a salesperson for Midwest Surgical Supply Company. The company's offices are in downtown Chicago. K's sales territory is the northwest side of Chicago and the adjacent suburbs. During Monday through Thursday, K drives directly from her residence to call on various customers. She sees each customer about once a month. On Friday of each week, she goes directly from her home to her office downtown to turn in orders, attend the weekly sales meeting, and do any other miscellaneous work. A portion of K's trip diary appears below.

		Odometer Reading		
Date	Destination	Begin	End	Mileage
3-17	Springmill Clinic	470	482	12
	Dr. J	482	485	3
	Home	485	500	15
3-18	Office	500	530	30
	Home	530	560	30

b. F, an electrician, works for EZ Electrical. He lives and works in the Los Angeles area. For 200 days of this year, he was assigned to do the wiring on a 30-story office building in downtown Los Angeles. His mileage from his home to the building was 20 miles. For 50 days during the year, he was assigned to a job in San Diego. Most of F's assignments are 20 miles closer than San Diego. F commuted 70 miles from his home to San Diego.

8-35 *Travel Expenses.*   Indicate the amount, if any, deductible by the taxpayer in each of the following situations. (Ignore the floor on miscellaneous itemized deductions.)

a. P, a steelworker, obtained a job with XYZ Corporation to work on a nuclear reactor 200 miles from his residence. P drove to the site early on Monday mornings and returned home late Friday nights. While at the job site he stayed in a boarding house. P anticipates that the job will last for eight months. During the year, he traveled 4,000 miles in going to and from the job. Other expenses while away from home included the following: meals, $1,000; lodging, $900; and laundry, $75.

b. Same as (a), except P anticipates the job to last for more than a year.

c. W plays professional football for the Minnesota Vikings. He has an apartment in St. Paul but he and his wife's permanent personal residence is in Tucson. During the season, W usually stays in St. Paul. In the off-season he returns to Tucson. Expenses for the year include travel between St. Paul and Tucson, $2,000; apartment in St. Paul, $1,800; meals while in St. Paul, $900.

d. R takes a trip to New York primarily for business. R's husband accompanied her. She spent two weeks on business and one week sightseeing in the city. Her train fare was $400 and meals and lodging cost $30 and $50 per day, respectively. R's husband incurred similar expenses.

e. L flew from Cincinnati to Chicago for $300 round-trip. She spent one day on business and four days shopping and sight-seeing. Her meals and lodging cost $30 and $50 per day, respectively.

8-36 *Car Expense Computation.*   E, a salesperson for T Corporation, incurred the following expenses for transportation during the year:

Gas and oil	$ 900
Repairs	200
Insurance	300
Interest on car loan	400
Depreciation	2,000
License	100

In addition, he spent $70 on parking while calling on customers. E drove the car 20,000 miles during the year, 18,000 for business.

a. Compute E's deduction, assuming the standard mileage rate is elected.

b. Compute E's deduction, assuming he claims actual expenses.

8-37 *Travel Outside of the U.S.*   S, an executive for an automotive company, traveled to Paris this year for business meetings with a European subsidiary. Prior to the trip, she thought that the meetings presented an ideal opportunity for her to vacation in Paris as well as to conduct business. For this reason, she scheduled the trip. S's air fare to Paris was $1,000 and her daily meals and lodging were $30 and $50 respectively. Given the additional facts below, indicate the amount, if any, of the deduction that S may claim.

   a. S's trip was primarily business. She spent two days on business (including travel days) and four days sight-seeing.

   b. Her itinerary revealed the following:

Thursday, May 1:	Depart New York, arrive Paris
Friday, May 2:	Business 9-11 a.m.; remainder of day sight-seeing in Paris
Saturday and Sunday, May 3-4:	Tour French countryside
Monday and Tuesday, May 5-6:	Business 9-5
Wednesday-Sunday, May 7-11:	Tour Germany
Monday, May 12:	Business 9-5
Tuesday, May 13:	Depart Paris, arrive New York

   c. Same as (a) except the travel was to Paris for the International Car Exposition, a foreign convention.

   d. Same as (a) except the business meetings took place on a luxury liner cruising the Caribbean.

   e. Same as (a) except S had no control over arranging the trip.

   f. Same as (a) except the trip was primarily personal.

8-38 *Entertainment Expenses.*   R is president of X Corporation, a company that manufactures and distributes office supplies. During the year, he and the company incurred various expenses relating to entertainment. In each of the following situations, indicate the amount of the deduction for entertainment expenses. Briefly explain your answer and classify the deduction as either *for* or *from* adjusted gross income. (Assume all the substantiation requirements are satisfied.)

   a. R and his wife took a potential customer and his wife to a night club to hear a popular singer. Tickets for the event cost $10 each. R was unable to discuss any business during the evening.

   b. After agreeing in the afternoon to supply S's company with typing paper, R took S to a baseball game that evening. Tickets were $8 each. X Corporation reimbursed R $16 for the tickets under an accountable plan.

   c. R and S, a client, went to lunch at an expensive restaurant. R paid the bill for both his meal, $30, and S's meal, $40. No business was discussed during lunch.

   d. X Corporation purchased a vacation condominium for use primarily by its employees. Expenses relating to the condominium, including depreciation, maintenance, utilities, interest, and taxes, were $7,000.

   e. R joined an exclusive country club this year. The membership fee, which is not refundable, was $1,000. In addition, R paid annual dues of $3,600. During the year, R used the club 100 days, 70 days for entertainment directly related to business and 30 days for personal use.

   f. R gave one of the company's best customers a $100 bottle of wine.

   g. X Corporation gave one of its retailers 1,000 golf balls ($1 each) to distribute for promotional purposes. X Corporation's name was imprinted on the balls.

8-39 *Convention and Seminar Expenses.* Dr. F, a pediatrician, is employed at a hospital located in Chicago. He also operates his own practice. During the year, he attended the following seminars and conventions. In each case, he incurred expenses for registration, travel, meals, and lodging. Indicate whether such expenses would be deductible assuming he attended.

a. "The Care and Feeding of Newborns," a seminar in Honolulu sponsored by the American Family Medical Association.

b. While Dr. F was attending the meeting above, his wife attended a concurrent seminar entitled "Tax Planning for Physicians and their Spouses."

c. "The Economics of a Private Practice: Make Your Investment Count," sponsored by the American Management Corporation in Chicago.

d. "Investing and Inside Information," sponsored by the National Association of Investment Specialists in Orlando.

CUMULATIVE PROBLEM

8-40 George (445-42-5432) and Christina Campbell (993-43-9878) are married with two children, Victoria, 7, and Brad, 2. Victoria and Brad's social security numbers are 446-75-4389 and 449-63-4172, respectively. They live at 10137 Briar Creek Lane, Tulsa, OK 74105. George is the district sales representative for Red Duck, a manufacturer of sportswear. His principal job is to solicit orders of the company's products from department stores in his territory, which includes Oklahoma and Arkansas. The company provides no office for him. Christina is a maker of fine quilts which she sells in selected shops in the surrounding area. The couple uses the cash method of accounting and reports on the calendar year. Their records for the year reveal the following information:

1. George received a salary of $35,000 and a bonus of $5,000. His employer withheld Federal income taxes of $6,000 and the proper amount of F.I.C.A. taxes.
2. Christina's income and expenses of her quilting business, Crazy Quilts, include

Quilt sales...	$7,000
Costs of goods sold...............................	600
Telephone (long distance calls).....................	100

Christina makes all of the quilts at home in a separate room that is used exclusively for her work. This room represents 10 percent of the total square footage of their home. Expenses related to operating the entire home include utilities, $2,000; and insurance, $500. Depreciation attributable solely to the home office is $800.

Christina computes her deduction relating to use of her car using actual expenses, which included gas and oil, $900; insurance, $300; and repairs, $100. The car is fully depreciated. Her daily diary revealed that, for the year, she had driven the car a total of 20,000 miles, including the following trips:

Trip Description	Miles
Home to sales outlets and return....................	10,000
Between sales outlets...............................	2,000
Miscellaneous personal trips........................	8,000

3. George incurs substantial expenses for travel and entertainment, including meals and lodging. He is not reimbursed for these expenses. This is the second year that George has used the standard mileage rate for computing his automobile expenses. During the year he drove 50,000 miles; 40,000 of these were directly related to business. Expenses for parking and tolls directly related to business were $90. Total meal and lodging costs for days that he was out of town overnight were $600 and $1,200, respectively. Entertainment expenses were $400.

4. This is George's second marriage. He has one child, Ted (age 11), from his first marriage to Hazel, who has custody of the child. He provides more than 50 percent of the child's support. The 1983 divorce agreement between George and Hazel provides that George is entitled to the exemption for Ted. George paid Hazel $4,800 during the year, $1,600 as alimony and the remainder as child support. Ted's social security number is 122-23-3221.

5. The couple's other income and expenses included the following:

Dividends (IBM stock owned separately by George)....	$ 400
Interest on redeemed Treasury bills...................	700
Interest on City of Reno bonds.......................	566
Interest paid on home mortgage......................	8,000
Real property taxes on home........................	900
Safety deposit box fee...............................	50

6. Both taxpayers elect to give to the Presidential campaign fund.

Compute the couple's tax liability for the year. If forms are used, complete Form 1040 for the year, including Schedules A, B, C, SE, and Form 2106.

RESEARCH PROBLEMS

8-41 *Travel Away from Home.*   M is a traveling salesperson who lives with his family in Cincinnati. His sales territory consists of Indiana, Illinois, and Kentucky. Most of his business, however, is in the Louisville area. For this reason, he normally travels to Louisville weekly and spends three or four days there living in a hotel. He also spends considerable time traveling throughout his territory. M completes the paperwork and other tasks incidental to his work at his home in Cincinnati. M's wife has a good job in Cincinnati and consequently M has never considered moving to Louisville. May M deduct the costs of traveling between his residence in Cincinnati and Louisville (including the costs of meals and lodging while in Louisville)?

8-42 *Business Gifts.*   R is product manager for a large pharmaceutical company. At the annual Christmas party, he handed out $50 gifts (checks from his personal account) to each of the 10 employees that work in his division under his supervision. R's group had been highly successful during the year and he felt that each person contributed to the division's profitability. He also gave his secretary $100. What amount, if any, may R deduct?

LEARNING OBJECTIVES

Upon completion of this chapter, you will be able to:

- Identify the various depreciation methods and accounting conventions available under the Modified Accelerated Cost Recovery System (MACRS)

- Make recommendations concerning the selection of an appropriate depreciation method and accounting convention

- Compute a taxpayer's depreciation deduction under each of the various depreciation methods and accounting conventions

- Explain the depreciation rules for listed property

- Identify property eligible for the election to currently expense rather than depreciate its cost

- Determine the current depletion deduction for various assets

- Explain the options available in selecting the appropriate tax treatment of research and experimentation expenditures

- Recognize tax planning opportunities related to depreciation, amortization, and depletion deductions

CHAPTER OUTLINE

Depreciation and Amortization for Tax
    Purposes   9-2
  General Rules for Depreciation
    Deductions   9-2
  Historical Perspective   9-3
Modified Accelerated Cost Recovery
    System   9-4
  An Overview of MACRS   9-4
  Property Subject to MACRS   9-5
  Classes of Property   9-6
  Calculating Depreciation   9-7
  Straight-Line Methods   9-18
  Dispositions of Assets from General
    Asset Accounts   9-20
  Limited Expensing Election:
    Code § 179   9-22
  Limitations for Automobiles   9-24
  Limitations for Personal Use   9-26
  Other Considerations   9-33
Amortization   9-34
  Goodwill and Covenants Not to
    Compete   9-34
  5-Year Elective Amortization   9-36

  Leasehold Improvements   9-36
Depletion   9-37
  Computing the Depletion Deduction   9-37
Research and Experimental
    Expenditures   9-39
  Research and Experimental
    Expenditures Defined   9-40
  Alternative Tax Treatments   9-40
  Other Related Provisions   9-42
  Expenses of Farmers and Ranchers   9-42
  Expenses Related to Livestock   9-42
  Soil and Water Conservation,
    Fertilizer, Land Clearing   9-43
  Development Expenses   9-44
Tax Planning Considerations   9-45
  Depreciation and After-Tax Cash
    Flow   9-45
  Accelerating Depreciation with
    Cost-Segregation   9-46
  Goodwill Amortization Rule Benefits
    Buyers and Sellers   9-46
Problem Materials   9-48

Chapter 9

CAPITAL RECOVERY
Depreciation, Amortization, and Depletion

The concept of capital recovery originated with the basic premise that income does not result until revenues exceed the capital expended to produce such revenues. For example, consider the situation where a taxpayer purchases an asset at a cost of $1,000 and subsequently sells it. Generally, the sale produces no income unless the asset is sold for a price exceeding $1,000. This result derives from the principle that the taxpayer first must *recover* his or her $1,000 of capital invested (basis) before he or she can be considered as having income. Here, the recovery occurs as the taxpayer offsets the basis of the asset against the amount realized on the sale. This same principle operates where an asset, instead of being sold and providing a readily identifiable benefit, provides benefits indirectly (e.g., a machine used for many years as part of a process to manufacture a product). In this case, the cost of the asset or the capital invested is *recovered* by offsetting (deducting) the asset's cost against the revenues the asset helps to produce. Thus, in the absence of a sale or other disposition of an asset, capital recovery usually occurs when the taxpayer is permitted to deduct the expenditure. Certain capital expenditures such as research and experimental costs are recovered in the year of the expenditure since the tax law allows immediate deduction. For other types of capital expenditures, the taxpayer is allowed to deduct or recover the cost over the years for which the asset provides benefits.

This chapter examines the various cost allocation methods allowed by the Code. These are depreciation, amortization, and depletion. Although each of these methods relates to a process of allocating the cost of an asset over time, different terms for the same process are used because each method relates to a different type of property. Depreciation concerns *tangible property*, amortization concerns *intangible property*, and depletion concerns *natural resources*. Tangible property means any property having physical existence (i.e., property capable of being touched such as plant, property, and equipment). Conversely, intangible property has no physical existence but exists only in connection with something else, such as the goodwill of a business, stock, patents, and copyrights. There

are two types of tangible property: real property and personal property. Real property (or *realty*) is land and anything attached to the land such as buildings, curbs, streets, fences, and other improvements. Personal property is property that is not realty and is usually movable. The concept of personal property or *personalty* should be distinguished from property that a person owns and uses for his or her benefit—usually referred to as *personal-use* property.

. In addition to the cost recovery methods mentioned above, this chapter discusses the tax treatment of other capital expenditures such as those for research and experimentation, and certain expenses of farmers.

DEPRECIATION AND AMORTIZATION FOR TAX PURPOSES

GENERAL RULES FOR DEPRECIATION DEDUCTIONS

The Code allows as a depreciation deduction a reasonable allowance for the exhaustion, wear and tear, and obsolescence of property that is either used in a trade or business or held for the production of income.[1] This rule makes it clear that not all capital expenditures for property are automatically eligible for depreciation. Rather, like all other expenditures, only those that satisfy the initial hurdles can be deducted.

Exhaustion, Wear and Tear, and Obsolescence. Only property that wears out or becomes obsolete can be depreciated. As normally construed, this requirement means that depreciation is allowed only for property that has a *determinable life*.[2] Property such as land which does not wear out and which has no determinable life cannot be depreciated. Similarly, goodwill and works of art cannot be amortized or depreciated since both have an indefinite life. In contrast, intangible assets with definite lives such as covenants not to compete, patents, copyrights, and licenses that cover a fixed term can be amortized.

Business or Income-Producing Property. Like other expenses, no deduction is allowed for depreciation unless the property is used in a trade or business or an income-producing activity. Property used for personal purposes cannot be depreciated. In many instances, however, a single asset may be used for *both* personal purposes and for profit-seeking activities. In these cases, the taxpayer is permitted to deduct depreciation on the portion of the asset used for business or production of income.

> **Example 1.** N is a salesman who uses his car for both business and personal purposes. He purchased the car this year for $18,000. During the year, N drove the car 50,000 miles, 40,000 miles for business and 10,000 miles for personal purposes. Under these circumstances, 80% (40,000 ÷ 50,000) of the cost of the car is subject to depreciation in the current year. Note that the business-use percentage may vary from year to year. If so, the depreciation allowed each year will vary accordingly.

---

[1]　§ 167(a).

[2]　Reg. §§ 1.167(a)-2 and 1.167(a)-3.

Property held for the production of income, even though not currently producing income, may still be depreciated. For example, a duplex held out for rental which is temporarily vacant may still be depreciated for the period during which it is not rented. Similarly, if the taxpayer's trade or business is suspended temporarily, rather than indefinitely, depreciation can be continued despite the suspension of activity.

Depreciable Basis.　The basis for depreciation is the adjusted basis of the property as used for computing gain or loss on a sale or other disposition.[3] This is usually the property's cost. Where property used for personal purposes *is converted* to use in business or the production of income, the basis for depreciation purposes is the lesser of the fair market value or the adjusted basis at the time of conversion.[4] This ensures that no deduction is claimed for declines in value while the property was held for personal purposes.

> **Example 2.**　R purchased a home computer for $1,000 while attending college. He used it solely for personal purposes. After graduation, R went into the consulting business and began using the computer for business purposes. At the time he converted the computer to business use, its value was $400. R may compute depreciation using a basis of $400 (the lesser of the adjusted basis, $1,000, or its value, $400, at the time of conversion).

The basis for depreciation must be reduced by depreciation allowed or allowable.[5] Thus, where a taxpayer fails or forgets to claim a depreciation deduction to which he or she was entitled in prior years, future depreciation charges may not be increased to correct for the error. However, this failure does not prohibit the taxpayer from claiming the proper amount of depreciation in the current year.

> **Example 3.**　In 19X1, D purchased a typewriter to use in her business for $1,000. The typewriter has an estimated useful life of 10 years and no salvage value. D did not claim depreciation to which she was entitled in 19X1 because she was temporarily in a low tax bracket. In 19X2, D elects to use the double declining-balance method of depreciation. D's depreciation deduction for 19X2 is $160 [20% of $800 ($1,000 cost − $200 allowable depreciation)]. Note that in 19X2 D must reduce the depreciable basis of $1,000 by the $200 of depreciation she did not claim in 19X1, since she was entitled to it. However, D can file an amended return for 19X1 to claim the depreciation not taken in that year. This is available as long as the three-year statute of limitations has not run out for 19X1.

HISTORICAL PERSPECTIVE

Prior to 1981, taxpayers could compute depreciation using either of two approaches: (1) the facts-and-circumstances method or (2) the Class Life System. Depreciation methods such as straight-line, declining balance, and sum-of-the-years'-digits were available for most assets under each system. The facts-and-circumstances method enabled

---

[3]　§ 167(g).

[4]　Reg. § 1.167(g)-1.

[5]　Reg. § 1.167(a)-10.

taxpayers to choose useful life and salvage value estimates for depreciable assets based on their experience and judgment of all surrounding facts and circumstances. There were no predetermined or prescribed guidelines. Conflicts often arose between taxpayers and the IRS over useful life selections because taxpayers were motivated to employ short useful lives in order to maximize the present value of tax savings from depreciation deductions.

As an alternative to the facts-and-circumstances system, the Class Life System became part of the law in 1971. It was developed primarily to minimize IRS-taxpayer conflicts over useful life estimates. The system prescribed depreciable life ranges for numerous categories of assets. For example, office furniture and fixtures could be depreciated using lives from 8 years to 12 years under the Class Life System.[6] Taxpayers electing this system were not challenged by the IRS. However, IRS-taxpayer conflicts were not eliminated because many taxpayers continued to employ the facts-and-circumstances system, seeking depreciable lives that were shorter than those available with the Class Life System.

In 1981, the facts-and-circumstances system and Class Life System were all but eliminated for assets placed in service after 1980. In the Economic Recovery Tax Act of 1981 (ERTA), Congress substantially revised the method for computing depreciation by enacting Code § 168 and the Accelerated Cost Recovery System (ACRS). Altered several times since 1981, the current version of this system is known as the Modified Accelerated Cost Recovery System (MACRS). An alternative to MACRS, called the Alternative Depreciation System (ADS), is also available.

A major benefit of MACRS and ADS is the elimination of previous areas of dispute between taxpayers and the IRS. Under these systems, the taxpayer is required to choose from a small set of predetermined options regarding depreciable life and depreciation method. Salvage value is ignored in all cases. Thus, depreciation calculations are more uniform for all taxpayers.

It should be emphasized, however, that some assets may not be depreciated using either of these systems. For this reason, the facts-and-circumstances approach and the Class Life System have continuing validity in certain instances.

MODIFIED ACCELERATED COST RECOVERY SYSTEM

AN OVERVIEW OF MACRS

Once it is determined that property is eligible for depreciation, the amount of the depreciation deduction must be computed. Under current law, taxpayers are required to calculate depreciation for most property using the Modified Accelerated Cost Recovery System (MACRS). As suggested earlier, MACRS is a radical departure from traditional approaches to depreciation. Under MACRS, useful lives for assets are termed *recovery periods* and are prescribed by statute. These recovery periods are for the most part arbitrary, determined without regard to how long the asset may actually last. Regardless

---

[6] Rev. Proc. 77-10, 1977-1 C.B. 548.

of the effects of nature and outside forces, each asset is deemed to have a particular useful life of 3, 5, 7, 10, 15, 20, 27.5, or 39 years. In addition, salvage value is ignored under MACRS. With these rules, possibilities for abuse using unrealistic values for useful life and salvage value are essentially eliminated.

The basic machinery of MACRS that is used to compute depreciation can be summarized as follows:

1. The system establishes eight classes or categories of property (e.g., 3-year property).

2. For each class of property, a specific useful life and depreciation method are prescribed (e.g., for 3-year property the useful life is three years and either the 200 percent declining-balance or straight-line method must be used).

To actually compute depreciation, taxpayers must first determine whether the property is subject to MACRS, then—based on the property's classification—determine the applicable method, recovery period, and accounting convention. These elements of the depreciation calculation are discussed below.

PROPERTY SUBJECT TO MACRS

Taxpayers generally must use MACRS to compute depreciation for all *tangible* property, both real and personal, new or used, if the property was acquired after 1986.[7] MACRS is not used to amortize *intangible* assets such as patents or copyrights, which are amortized using the straight-line method. In addition, MACRS may not be used with respect to the following property: [8]

1. Property depreciated using a method that is not based on years (e.g., the units-of-production or income forecast methods)

2. Automobiles if the taxpayer has elected to use the standard mileage rate (such an election precludes a depreciation deduction)

3. Property for which special amortization is provided and elected by the taxpayer in lieu of depreciation (e.g., amortization of pollution control facilities)

4. Certain motion picture films, video tapes, sound recordings, and public utility property

5. Generally, any property that the taxpayer—or a party related to the taxpayer—owned or used (e.g., leased) prior to 1987

As a practical matter, MACRS is mandatory for all tangible property. But, as will be seen, the taxpayer is allowed to elect out of MACRS and use the Alternative Depreciation System (ADS). In addition, in lieu of depreciation, the taxpayer may be allowed to expense up to $17,500 annually of the aggregate costs of certain assets placed in

---

[7] § 168(a).   [8] § 168(f).

Exhibit 9-1 *Depreciation Methods and Accounting Conventions under MACRS and ADS*

8 MACRS Property Classes	Modified Accelerated Cost Recovery System (MACRS): Use MACRS Property Class Life	Alternative Depreciation System (ADS): Use ADS Life	Accounting Convention[1]
3-year, 5-year, 7-year, 10-year[2]	Choices: 200% DB or SL[3]	Choices: 150% DB or SL	Half-year or mid-quarter
15-year, 20-year	Choices: 150% DB or SL	Choices: 150% DB or SL	Half-year or mid-quarter
Residential rental real estate	27.5 years SL	40 years SL	Mid-month
Nonresidential real estate	39 years SL	40 years SL	Mid-month

Notes:
(1) Taxpayers do *not* have the option of choosing either the half-year or mid-quarter convention. As explained later in this chapter, either the half-year or mid-quarter convention is *required* depending on the timing of asset purchases during the year.
(2) Under certain conditions, $17,500 immediate expensing under Code § 179 is available for most 3-, 5-, 7-, and 10-year assets (i.e., depreciable tangible personal property).
(3) Abbreviations:
  DB = declining balance
  SL = straight-line

---

service during the year. It should be emphasized, however, that there are no elections available enabling the taxpayer to use the facts-and-circumstances method typically used for financial accounting purposes. Exhibit 9-1 identifies the depreciation methods and accounting conventions available under the MACRS and ADS systems.

CLASSES OF PROPERTY

As indicated in Exhibit 9-1, all property subject to MACRS is assigned to one of eight classes.[9] Classification is important because the recovery periods, methods, and accounting conventions to be used in calculating depreciation can vary among the different classes of property. Property is assigned to a particular class based on its *class life* as prescribed in Revenue Procedure 87-56.[10] This Revenue Procedure, an excerpt of which is provided in Exhibit 9-2, specifies not only the class lives of various assets but also the recovery periods to be used for both MACRS and ADS. Note that the "General Depreciation System" column of Exhibit 9-2 pertains to MACRS. Exhibit 9-3 provides examples of property in each of the eight MACRS property classes.

---

[9] § 168(e).

[10] 1987-2 C.B. 674, as modified by Rev. Proc. 88-22, I.R.B. No. 18, 38.

CALCULATING DEPRECIATION

Under MACRS, depreciation is a function of *three* factors: the recovery period, the method, and the accounting convention.

Recovery Periods.   As seen in Exhibit 9-1, recovery periods run various lengths of time depending on the class of property.[11] Although the current recovery periods more closely resemble assets' actual useful lives than did recovery periods of prior years, the relationship is still more arbitrary than real.

In examining the different classes, several features should be observed. First, certain property is assigned to a class without regard to its class life. The most notable example of this is cars, which are assigned to the five-year class (see asset class 00.22 in Exhibit 9-2). Note also that the current structure provides different recovery periods for real property, depending on whether it is residential or nonresidential real estate. As a result, when a building is used for both residential and nonresidential purposes (e.g., a multilevel apartment building with commercial space on the bottom two floors) it must be classified as one or the other. For this purpose, realty qualifies as residential real estate if 80 percent of the gross rents are for the dwelling units.[12]

Depreciation Method.   The depreciation method to be used—like the recovery period—varies depending on the class of the property. A closer look at Exhibit 9-1, however, reveals that the variation is actually between real and personal property. Real property is depreciated using the straight-line method, while personal property is depreciated using either straight-line or a declining-balance method. If a declining balance depreciation method is elected, a switch to straight-line is made in the first year in which a larger depreciation would result. Example 4 illustrates this procedure, and the IRS depreciation tables presented later in this chapter incorporate the switch to straight-line.

Accounting Conventions.   The final factor to be considered in computing depreciation is the accounting convention. The Code establishes three conventions to handle the computation of depreciation when property is placed in service or sold (or otherwise disposed of) during the year.[13] These are the half-year, mid-month, and mid-quarter conventions.

Half-Year Convention.   The half-year convention applies to all property *other than* nonresidential real property and residential rental property. From a practical perspective, the half-year convention applies to *all depreciable tangible personal property*. Under the half-year convention, one-half year of depreciation is allowed regardless of when the asset is placed in service or sold during the year (e.g., ½ × the annual depreciation as normally computed).[14] Since only one-half year's depreciation is allowed in the first year, the recovery period is effectively extended one year so that the remaining one-half may be claimed.

---

[11]   § 168(c).

[12]   § 168(e)(2).

[13]   § 168(d).

[14]   § 168(d)(4).

Exhibit 9-2 *Excerpt from Revenue Procedure 87-56*

Asset Class	Description of Assets Included	Class Life (in years)	Recovery Periods (in years) General Depreciation System	Recovery Periods (in years) Alternative Depreciation System
SPECIFIC DEPRECIABLE ASSETS USED IN ALL BUSINESS ACTIVITIES, EXCEPT AS NOTED:				
00.11	**Office Furniture, Fixtures, and Equipment:** Includes furniture and fixtures that are not structural components of a building. Includes such assets as desks, files, safes, and communications equipment. Does not include communications equipment that is included in other classes...........................	10	7	10
00.13	**Data Handling Equipment, except Computers:** Includes only typewriters, calculators, adding and accounting machines, copiers, and duplicating equipment...	6	5	6
00.21	**Airplanes (airframes and engines), except those used in commercial or contract carrying of passengers or freight, and all helicopters (airframes and engines).....................................**	6	5	6
00.22	**Automobiles, Taxis.............................**	3	5	5
00.23	**Buses...**	9	5	9
00.241	**Light General Purpose Trucks:** Includes trucks for use over the road (actual unloaded weight less than 13,000 pounds)..........	4	5	5
00.242	**Heavy General Purpose Trucks:** Includes heavy general purpose trucks, concrete ready-mix truckers, and ore trucks, for use over the road (actual unloaded weight 13,000 pounds or more)...	6	5	6

Exhibit 9-2 *continued*

Asset Class	Description of Assets Included	Class Life (in years)	Recovery Periods (in years) General Depreciation System	Recovery Periods (in years) Alternative Depreciation System
DEPRECIABLE ASSETS USED IN THE FOLLOWING ACTIVITIES:				
01.1	**Agriculture:** Includes machinery and equipment, grain bins, and fences but no other land improvements, that are used in the production of crops or plants, vines, and trees; livestock; the operation of farm dairies, nurseries, greenhouses, sod farms, mushroom cellars, cranberry bogs, apiaries, and fur farms; the performance of agriculture, animal husbandry, and horticultural services.............................	10	7	10
01.11	**Cotton Ginning Assets.........................**	12	7	12
01.21	**Cattle, Breeding or Dairy........................**	7	5	7
01.22	**Horses, Breeding or Work......................**	10	7	10
01.221	**Any horse that is not a race horse and is more than 12 years old at the time it is placed in service**	10	7	10
01.223	**Any race horse that is more than 2 years old at the time it is placed in service.................**	*	3	12
01.23	**Hogs, Breeding...............................**	3	3	3
01.24	**Sheep and Goats, Breeding...................**	5	5	5
01.3	**Farm buildings except structures included in Class 01.4.......................................**	25	20	25
01.4	**Single-purpose agricultural or horticultural structures..**	15	10	15

Exhibit 9-3 *Examples of MACRS Property*

MACRS Property Class	Examples
3 years	Special tools, race horses, tractors, and property with a class life of 4 years or less
5 years	Automobiles, trucks, computers, and peripheral equipment (such as printers, external disk drives, and modems), typewriters, copiers, R&E equipment, and property with a class life of more than 4 years and less than 10 years
7 years	Office furniture, fixtures, office equipment, most machinery, property with a class life of 10 years or more but less than 16 years, and property with no assigned class life
10 years	Single-purpose agricultural and horticultural structures, assets used in petroleum refining and manufacturing of tobacco and certain food products, and property with a class life of 16 years or more but less than 20 years
15 years	Land improvements (such as sidewalks, roads, parking lots, irrigation systems, sewers, fences, and landscaping), service stations, billboards, telephone distribution plants, and property with a class life of 20 years or more but less than 25 years
20 years	Municipal sewers and property with a class life of 25 years or more
27.5 years	Residential rental real estate, including apartment complexes, duplexes, and vacation rental homes
39 years	Nonresidential real estate, including office buildings, warehouses, factories, and farm buildings

---

Example 4.   On March 1, 1994 T purchased a car to be used solely for business for $10,000. It was his only acquisition during the year. The car had an estimated useful life of four years and an estimated salvage value of $2,000. Although these estimates might be used for financial accounting purposes, under MACRS, salvage value is ignored and T is required to use the recovery period, depreciation method, and accounting convention prescribed for 5-year property, the class to which cars are assigned. T elects to compute his depreciation using the 200% declining-balance method (switching to straight-line where appropriate), a 5-year recovery period, and the half-year convention. The 200% declining-balance rate would be 40% (200% × straight-line rate, $1/5$ or 20%). The declining-balance method would be used until 1998, when a switch to straight-line maximizes the depreciation deduction. Due to the half-year convention, the cost is actually recovered over six years rather than the 5-year recovery period. Depreciation would be computed as follows:

Year	Depreciation Method	Basis for Depreciation Computation	Rate	Depreciation
1994	200% D.B.	$10,000	20%*	$ 2,000
1995	200% D.B.	8,000	40%	3,200
1996	200% D.B.	4,800	40%	1,920
1997	200% D.B.	2,880	40%	1,152**
1998	S.L.	1,730	$^{1.0}/_{1.5}$	1,152***
1999	S.L.	1,730	$^{0.5}/_{1.5}$	576
				$10,000

* Half-year allowance (40% × $^{1}/_{2}$ = 20%).

** Note that straight-line depreciation is the same ($2,880 × $^{1}/_{2.5}$).

*** Declining-balance depreciation would have been $692 ($1,730 × 40%); since straight-line depreciation over the remaining $1^{1}/_{2}$ years is $1,152 and greater than $692, the switch to straight-line is made.

Example 5. Same facts as above except the property was sold on December 20, 1996. In computing depreciation for personal property in the year of sale or disposition, the half-year convention must also be used. Thus, depreciation for 1996 would be $960 ($4,800 × 40% × $^{1}/_{2}$).

To simplify the computation of depreciation, the IRS provides optional tables as shown in Exhibits 9-4 to 9-7.[15] The percentages (or rates) shown in the tables are the result of combining the three factors used in determining depreciation—method, rate, and convention—into a single, composite percentage to be used for each class of property.[16]

Example 6. The depreciation rate for the year that 5-year property is placed in service and for the following year is determined as follows:

Year 1

Straight-line rate (1/5).........................	20%
× Declining-balance rate........................	× 200%
200 percent declining-balance rate............	40%
× Half-year allowance...........................	× 1/2
Depreciation rate per table....................	20%

Year 2

Basis of asset remaining (100% − 20%)......	80%
× 200 percent declining-balance rate............	× 40%
Depreciation rate per table....................	32%

---

[15] Rev. Proc. 87-57, 1987-2 C.B. 687.

[16] Depreciation percentages in the tables are rounded to one-hundredth of a percent for recovery property with a recovery period of less than 20 years, and one-thousandth of a percent for all other property. See Rev. Proc. 87-57 *supra*.

Exhibit 9-4 *MACRS Accelerated Depreciation Percentages Using the Half-Year Convention for 3-, 5-, and 7-Year Property*

Recovery Year	Property Class		
	3-Year	5-Year	7-Year
1	33.33%	20.00%	14.29%
2	44.45	32.00	24.49
3	14.81	19.20	17.49
4	7.41	11.52	12.49
5		11.52	8.93
6		5.76	8.92
7			8.93
8			4.46

Source: Rev. Proc. 87-57, Table 1.
Appendix C has additional depreciation tables.

Example 7.   Same facts as in *Example 4*. Depreciation computed using the table in Exhibit 9-4 would be the same as above, computed as follows:

Year	Unadjusted Basis	×	Accelerated Recovery Percentage	Annual Depreciation
1994	$10,000		20.00%	$ 2,000
1995	10,000		32.00	3,200
1996	10,000		19.20	1,920
1997	10,000		11.52	1,152
1998	10,000		11.52	1,152
1999	10,000		5.76	576
			100.00%	$10,000

Example 7 illustrates the basic steps necessary to compute annual depreciation. These steps are as follows:

1. Identify the *depreciable basis* of the asset (generally its cost): $10,000 in *Example 7*.

2. Determine the MACRS *property class*: 5-year property in *Example 7*.

3. Identify the *depreciation convention* (either half-year or mid-quarter for personal property; mid-month for real estate): half-year convention in *Example 7*.

4. Determine the *recovery period* and *method*. See Exhibit 9-1 for a summary of the available choices: 5-year 200 percent declining balance in *Example 7*.

5. Locate the *appropriate table* based on the depreciation convention, recovery period, and method: Exhibit 9-4 for *Example 7*. (Note the depreciation convention is already reflected in the table percentages for the year of acquisition, but *not* for the year of disposition.)

6. Choose the *table percentages* relating to the recovery period of the asset: 5-year property percentages for *Example 7* (i.e., 20 percent, 32 percent, etc.).

7. Multiply the table percentages by the depreciable (cost) basis of the asset to *compute annual depreciation* amounts: $10,000 multiplied by 20 percent provides $2,000 of depreciation for 1994 in *Example 7*.

When using the depreciation tables, a special adjustment must be made if there is a disposition of the property before its cost is fully recovered. As noted above, under the half-year convention the taxpayer is entitled only to a half-year of depreciation in the year of disposition. Therefore, where the half-year convention applies and the property is used for only a portion of the disposition year, only one-half of the amount of depreciation determined using the table is allowed.

Example 8. Same facts as *Example 7* except the taxpayer sold the property on December 1, 1996. Since the taxpayer did not hold the property the entire taxable year and the half-year convention is in effect, only one-half of the amount of depreciation using the table is allowed. Therefore, depreciation for 1996 would have been $960 ($10,000 $\times$ 19.2% $\times$ ½). Note that this is the same result as obtained in *Example 5* above.

Mid-Month Convention. This convention applies only to real property (i.e., nonresidential real property and residential rental property).[17] Under the mid-month convention, one-half month of depreciation is allowed for the month the asset is placed in service or sold and a full month of depreciation is allowed for each additional month of the year that the asset is in service.[18] For example, if a calendar year taxpayer places a building in service on April 3, the fraction of the annual depreciation allowed is $^{8.5}/_{12}$ (half-month's depreciation for April and eight months' depreciation for May through December).

Example 9. The first-year depreciation rate for residential rental realty that is placed in service in April is determined as follows:

$$\begin{array}{lr}
\text{Straight-line rate } (^1/_{27.5})\dots\dots\dots\dots\dots & 3.636\% \\
\times\ \text{Mid-month convention}\dots\dots\dots\dots\dots & \times\ \ ^{8.5}/_{12} \\
\hline
\text{Depreciation rate per table}\dots\dots\dots\dots & 2.576\% \\
\end{array}$$

---

[17] § 168(d)(2).   [18] § 168(d)(4)(B).

Exhibit 9-5   *MACRS Depreciation Percentages for Residential Rental Property*

Month Placed in Service	1	2	3	...	27	28	29
1	3.485%	3.636%	3.636%		3.636%	1.970%	0.000%
2	3.182	3.636	3.636		3.636	2.273	0.000
3	2.879	3.636	3.636		3.636	2.576	0.000
4	2.576	3.636	3.636		3.636	2.879	0.000
5	2.273	3.636	3.636		3.636	3.182	0.000
6	1.970	3.636	3.636		3.636	3.485	0.000
7	1.667	3.636	3.636		3.637	3.636	0.152
8	1.364	3.636	3.636		3.637	3.636	0.455
9	1.061	3.636	3.636		3.637	3.636	0.758
10	0.758	3.636	3.636		3.637	3.636	1.061
11	0.455	3.636	3.636		3.637	3.636	1.364
12	0.152	3.636	3.636		3.637	3.636	1.667

Source: Rev. Proc. 87-57, Table 6.
Appendix C has additional depreciation tables.

Due to the mid-month convention, the recovery period must be extended one month to claim the one-half month of depreciation that was not claimed in the first month. For example, the entire cost of residential rental property is recovered over 331 months (27½ years is 330 months + 1 additional month to claim the half-month of depreciation not claimed in the first month). As a result, depreciation deductions are actually claimed over either 28 or 29 years depending on the month in which the property was placed in service. This can be seen by examining the composite depreciation percentages for real property reflecting the mid-month convention given in Exhibits 9-5 and 9-6.

Example 10.   S purchased a duplex as an investment for $110,000 on July 17, 1994. Of the $110,000 cost, $10,000 is allocated to the land. The estimated useful life of the duplex is 30 years—the same period as her mortgage—and the estimated salvage value is $15,000. Despite these estimates, under MACRS salvage value is ignored and S is required to use the recovery period, depreciation method, and convention prescribed for residential rental property, the class to which the duplex is assigned. Therefore, S uses a 27.5-year life, the straight-line method, and the mid-month convention. Using the table in Exhibit 9-5, depreciation for the first year would be $1,667 ($100,000 × 1.667%).

When using the depreciation tables, an adjustment must be made if there is a disposition of the real property before its cost is fully recovered. This adjustment is similar to that required where the half-year convention applies, but not identical. In the year of disposition, the taxpayer may deduct depreciation only for those months the property is used by the taxpayer. In addition, under the mid-month convention, the taxpayer is entitled to only a half-month of depreciation for the month of disposition.

Exhibit 9-6 *MACRS Depreciation Percentages for Nonresidential Real Property*

Month Placed in Service	Recovery Year					
	1	2	3 · · ·	31	32	33
1	3.042%	3.175%	3.175%	3.174%	1.720%	0.000%
2	2.778	3.175	3.175	3.175	1.984	0.000
3	2.513	3.175	3.175	3.174	2.249	0.000
4	2.249	3.175	3.175	3.175	2.513	0.000
5	1.984	3.175	3.175	3.174	2.778	0.000
6	1.720	3.175	3.175	3.175	3.042	0.000
7	1.455	3.175	3.175	3.174	3.175	0.132
8	1.190	3.175	3.175	3.175	3.174	0.397
9	0.926	3.175	3.175	3.174	3.175	0.661
10	0.661	3.175	3.175	3.175	3.174	0.926
11	0.397	3.175	3.175	3.174	3.175	1.190
12	0.132	3.175	3.175	3.175	3.174	1.455

Source: Rev. Proc. 87-57, Table 7.
Appendix C has additional depreciation tables.

Example 11. Same facts as *Example 10* except the taxpayer sold the property on May 22, 1996. Depreciation for 1996 would be $1,363 ($100,000 $\times$ 3.636% $\times$ $^{4.5}/_{12}$).

Mid-Quarter Convention. The mid-quarter convention applies only to *personal property*. However, it applies only if more than 40 percent of the aggregate bases of all personal property placed in service during the taxable year is placed in service during the last three months of the year.[19] Property placed in service and disposed of during the same taxable year is not taken into account. Also not taken into account is any amount immediately expensed under § 179 (discussed below) or property used for personal purposes. If the 40 percent test is satisfied, the mid-quarter convention applies to *all* personal property placed in service during the year (regardless of the quarter in which it was actually placed in service).

Example 12. During the year, K Company, a calendar year taxpayer, acquired and placed in service the following assets:

Assets	Acquisition Date	Cost
Office furniture	March 28	$20,000
Machinery	October 9	80,000
Warehouse	February 1	90,000

[19]   § 168(d)(3).

Of the total *personal* property placed in service during the year, more than 40% [$80,000 ÷ ($20,000 + $80,000)] occurred in the last quarter (i.e., October through December). As a result, K must use the mid-quarter convention for computing the depreciation of both the furniture and the machinery.

When applicable, the mid-quarter convention treats all personal property as being placed in service in the middle of the quarter of the taxable year in which it was actually placed in service.[20] Therefore, one-half of a quarter's depreciation—in effect one-eighth ($1/2 \times 1/4$) or 12.5 percent of the annual depreciation—is allowed for the quarter that the asset is placed in service or sold. In addition, a full quarter's depreciation is allowed for each additional quarter that the asset is in service. For example, personal property placed in service on March 3 would be treated as having been placed in service in the middle of the first quarter and the taxpayer would be able to claim $3 1/2$ quarters—$3.5/4$ or 87.5 percent—of the annual amount of depreciation. The percentages of the annual depreciation allowed under the mid-quarter convention for a year in which an asset is placed in service are

	Quarter Placed in Service			
	First January–March	*Second* April–June	*Third* July–September	*Fourth* October–December
Percentage of annual depreciation allowed..............	87.5%	62.5%	37.5%	12.5%

The above chart illustrates that where an asset is placed in service in the first quarter and the mid-quarter convention applies, the taxpayer is allowed to deduct 87.5 percent of the annual depreciation. In contrast, for personal property placed in service during the fourth quarter only 12.5 percent of the annual depreciation may be deducted. Note that the recovery period must be extended by one year so that the balance of the depreciation not claimed in the first year may be deducted. Composite depreciation percentages to be used for 3-year and 5-year property where the mid-quarter convention applies are provided in Exhibit 9-7. Appendix C has depreciation tables for all categories of personal property under the mid-quarter convention.

Example 13.   In 1994 T, a calendar year taxpayer, purchased four automobiles to use in his business at a cost of $10,000 each. These purchases were his only acquisitions of personal property during the year. Three of the cars were purchased in December while the other car was purchased in January. Since more than 40% of the property placed in service during the year was placed in service in the last quarter ($30,000 ÷ $40,000 = 75%), the mid-quarter convention applies in computing depreciation. Thus, the depreciation allowed on the auto purchased in January would be limited to 87.5% of a full year's depreciation, and the depreciation allowed on the three cars purchased in December would be limited to 12.5%

---

[20]   § 168(d)(3).

Exhibit 9-7 *MACRS Accelerated Depreciation Percentages Using the Mid-Quarter Convention for 3- and 5-Year Property*

3-Year Property:

Recovery Year	Quarter Placed in Service			
	1	2	3	4
1	58.33%	41.67%	25.00%	8.33%
2	27.78	38.89	50.00	61.11
3	12.35	14.14	16.67	20.37
4	1.54	5.30	8.33	10.19

5-Year Property:

Recovery Year	1	2	3	4
1	35.00	25.00	15.00	5.00
2	26.00	30.00	34.00	38.00
3	15.60	18.00	20.40	22.80
4	11.01	11.37	12.24	13.68
5	11.01	11.37	11.30	10.94
6	1.38	4.26	7.06	9.58

Source: Rev. Proc. 87-57. Appendix C has additional depreciation tables.

of a full year's depreciation. Since a full year's depreciation would be 40% of cost (straight-line rate of 20% per year × 200% declining-balance = 40%), the depreciation for the January purchase would be limited to 35% of cost (40% × 87.5%), or $3,500 (35% × $10,000). Similarly, the depreciation for the December purchases would be limited to 5% of cost (40% × 12.5%), or $1,500 (5% × $30,000). Total depreciation under the mid-quarter convention is limited to $5,000 ($3,500 + $1,500). These amounts are easily computed using the tables in Exhibit 9-7.

Note that had the mid-quarter convention *not* applied, the depreciation percentage would have been 20%—reflecting the half-year allowance for 5-year property (40% × $\frac{1}{2}$ = 20%), or $8,000 ($40,000 × 20%). Due to the timing of the acquisitions, T's depreciation for the year is reduced by $3,000 ($8,000 − $5,000).

When using the depreciation tables, a special adjustment must be made if there is a disposition of the property before its cost is fully recovered. This adjustment is similar to that for the half-year and mid-month conventions. As noted above, under the mid-quarter convention, the taxpayer is entitled to only one-half of a quarter's depreciation—in effect one-eighth ($\frac{1}{2}$ × $\frac{1}{4}$) or 12.5 percent of the annual depreciation—for the quarter that the asset is sold. In addition, a full quarter of depreciation is allowed for each quarter

that the asset is in service. For example, if property was sold on August 2, the taxpayer could claim $2\frac{1}{2}$ quarters—$^{2.5}/_4$ or 62.5 percent—of the annual amount of depreciation. The percentages of annual depreciation allowed under the mid-quarter convention for the year an asset is sold are

	Quarter Property Sold			
	First January–March	Second April–June	Third July–September	Fourth October–December
Percentage of annual depreciation allowed..............	12.5%	37.5%	62.5%	87.5%

Example 14.   Same facts as in *Example 13* above, except the car acquired in January 1994 was sold on August 9, 1996. Since T did not hold the property the entire taxable year and the mid-quarter convention is in effect, only 62.5% of the amount of depreciation using the table is allowed. Therefore, using the table in Exhibit 9-7, T's depreciation for this car would have been $975 ($10,000 × 15.6% × 62.5%).

STRAIGHT-LINE METHODS

The accelerated depreciation methods prescribed by MACRS are normally desirable since they allow taxpayers to recover their costs more rapidly than the straight-line method. However, there may be circumstances where the slower-paced straight-line method may be more rewarding. For example, if the taxpayer is currently in the 15 percent tax bracket, he or she may want to defer depreciation deductions to years when he or she is in the 28 percent or higher tax bracket. By doing this, the taxpayer may be able to maximize the present value of the tax savings from depreciation deductions (depending upon the taxpayer's discount rate).

Taxpayers can elect to use the straight-line method in lieu of the accelerated method. Two different approaches are available: straight-line under MACRS, or straight-line under ADS.

MACRS Straight-Line.   Although it may seem inconsistent, the *Modified Accelerated Cost Recovery System* offers taxpayers a straight-line method of depreciation.[21] If the taxpayer so elects, the straight-line method is used in conjunction with all of the other rules that normally apply under MACRS; that is, the taxpayer simply uses the straight-line method (in lieu of the accelerated method) along with the applicable recovery period and accounting convention. The depreciation percentages to be used where the taxpayer elects the straight-line method are contained in Exhibit 9-8 (half-year convention property) for 3-, 5-, and 7-year property. Appendix C has straight-line depreciation tables for all categories of personal property under the half-year convention. The depreciation percentages for the straight-line method when the mid-quarter convention applies can be found in Revenue Procedure 87-57.[22]

---

[21] § 168(b)(3)(C).   [22] 1987-2 C.B. 687.

Exhibit 9-8 *MACRS and ADS Straight-Line Depreciation Percentages Using the Half-Year Convention for 3-, 5-, and 7-Year Property*

Recovery Year	Property Class		
	3-Year	5-Year	7-Year
1	16.67%	10.00%	7.14%
2	33.33	20.00	14.29
3	33.33	20.00	14.29
4	16.67	20.00	14.28
5		20.00	14.29
6		10.00	14.28
7			14.29
8			7.14

Source: Rev. Proc. 87-57.
Appendix C has additional depreciation tables.

Example 15.   On June 1, 1994 L purchased 5-year property (to which the half-year convention applies) for $50,000. Using the table in Exhibit 9-8, depreciation for the year would be $5,000 ($50,000 × 10%). Depreciation for 1995 would be $10,000 (20% × $50,000). If L sold the property on January 22, 1996, depreciation would be $5,000 ($50,000 × 20% × ½).

The election to use the straight-line method is made annually by class (of course, the straight-line method must be used for realty). For example, if in 1994 the taxpayer makes the election for 7-year property, *all* 7-year property placed in service during the year must be depreciated using the straight-line method. The election does not obligate the taxpayer to use the straight-line method for any other class. Similarly, the taxpayer need not use the straight-line method for such class of assets placed in service in the following year.

Alternative Depreciation System.   The Alternative Depreciation System (ADS) is an option for taxpayers.[23] This system is similar to MACRS in two ways: salvage value is ignored, and the same averaging conventions must be followed. The major differences between MACRS and ADS consist of longer recovery periods for most assets and, in some cases, slower rates of depreciation. The recovery period to be used for ADS is normally the property's class life. The class life—which is usually longer than the MACRS life—is used unless no class life has been prescribed for the property or a specific class life has been designated in Code § 168. For example, as shown in Exhibit 9-2, the ADS class life for typewriters (asset class 00.13) is six years while the MACRS life is five years. Thus, depreciation under ADS would be computed using a 6-year life while depreciation for MACRS would be computed using a 5-year life. The recovery periods to be used for ADS are summarized in Exhibit 9-9.

---

[23] § 168(g).

Taxpayers electing ADS for real property are restricted to straight-line deprecia-tion. Thus, an office building (nonresidential real property) would be depreciated using straight-line and a 40-year recovery period under ADS. The ADS depreciation percent-ages for real property are found in Exhibit 9-10.

In contrast, either straight-line or 150 percent declining balance depreciation may be chosen for depreciable tangible personal property. The ADS straight-line depreciation percentages for such property, which in fact have class lives of 3, 5, and 7 years, are the same as those for MACRS straight-line and can be found in Exhibit 9-8.

For depreciable tangible personal property, a taxpayer may have as many as four different depreciation options. For example, the ADS options for a typewriter consist of straight-line over six years or 150 percent declining balance over six years. The MACRS alternatives for a typewriter are straight-line over *five* years or *200* percent declining balance over five years. Which of these four choices would be best for depreciating the typewriter? In general, the taxpayer should select the depreciation method that maximizes the present value of tax savings from depreciation deductions. For taxpayers who expect their future marginal tax rate to either remain constant or decline, the fastest depreciation method over the shortest time period will maximize the present value of tax savings from depreciation.

The mechanics of the election to use ADS—except for real property—are identical to those of MACRS discussed above. Except for real property, the taxpayer may elect to use ADS on a class-by-class, year-by-year basis.[24] For realty, the election is made on a property-by-property basis. In addition, the taxpayer *must* use ADS straight-line for depreciating certain property. Such property includes certain "listed property" (discussed later in this chapter), foreign use property (i.e., property used outside the U.S. more than half of a taxable year), property leased to a tax-exempt entity (and foreign persons unless more than 50 percent of the income is subject to U.S. tax), and property that is financed either directly or indirectly by the issuance of tax-exempt bonds (i.e., tax-exempt bond-financed property).[25] ADS is also used for computing depreciation for purposes of the alternative minimum tax (discussed in Chapter 13) and a corporation's earnings and profits (discussed in Chapter 19).

DISPOSITIONS OF ASSETS FROM GENERAL ASSET ACCOUNTS

Quite often, it is impractical for a taxpayer to account for so-called mass assets. The term *mass assets* is defined as a group of individual items of property not necessarily homogeneous but so numerous in quantity that separate identification is impractical. In addition, each asset's value is minor relative to the total value of the group. Examples of mass assets include returnable containers, railroad ties, portable tools, and minor items of office furniture. Despite their relatively minor value, each asset represents a capital expenditure recoverable through depreciation. To simplify accounting for these items, the Code allows the taxpayer to establish *general asset accounts*.[26] Under this accounting

---

[24]   § 168(g)(7).   [26]   § 168(i)(4).

[25]   § 168(g)(1).

Exhibit 9-9 *Alternative Depreciation System Recovery Periods*

General Rule: Recovery period is the property's class life unless

1. There is no class life (see below), or
2. A special class life has been designated (see below).

Type of Property	Recovery Period
Personal property with no class life............................	12 years
Nonresidential real property with no class life..................	40 years
Residential rental property with no class life....................	40 years
Cars, light general purpose trucks, certain technological equipment, and semiconductor manufacturing equipment.................................	5 years
Computer-based telephone central office switching equipment..	9.5 years
Railroad track..	10 years
Single purpose agricultural or horticultural structures...........	15 years
Municipal waste water treatment plants, telephone distribution plants..	24 years
Low-income housing financed by tax-exempt bonds............	27.5 years
Municipal sewers...	50 years

Exhibit 9-10 *ADS Straight-Line Depreciation Percentages Real Property Using the Mid-Month Convention*

Month Placed in Service	Recovery Year		
	1	2–40	41
1	2.396%	2.500%	0.104%
2	2.188	2.500	0.312
3	1.979	2.500	0.521
4	1.771	2.500	0.729
5	1.563	2.500	0.937
6	1.354	2.500	1.146
7	1.146	2.500	1.354
8	0.938	2.500	1.562
9	0.729	2.500	1.771
10	0.521	2.500	1.979
11	0.313	2.500	2.187
12	0.104	2.500	2.396

Source: Rev. Proc. 87-57, Table 13.

procedure, depreciation is computed in the normal manner. However, upon disposition of the asset the entire amount of the proceeds realized (undiminished by the basis of the asset disposed of) is recognized as income. For this reason, the unadjusted basis of the asset disposed of is left in the general asset account to be fully recovered through depreciation in future years.

> **Example 16.**   P Corporation, a nationwide painting company, purchased 1,000 portable paint sprayers at a cost of $300 each (total cost of $300,000). P uses a general asset account to account for the sprayers. The sprayers were shipped to branches of the company in over 50 cities including Miami. During the year, P closed its Miami branch and sold all of the sprayers to local companies for $9,000. P will report the entire $9,000 in income and continue to depreciate whatever sprayers were sold until they are fully depreciated.

LIMITED-EXPENSING ELECTION: CODE § 179

When Congress introduced MACRS, it also enacted a provision allowing taxpayers (other than estates or trusts) to *elect* to treat the cost of qualifying property as a currently deductible expense rather than a capital expenditure subject to depreciation.[27] This measure was intended primarily to stimulate investment; however, its corollary effect was to eliminate the need for maintaining depreciation records where the taxpayer's annual acquisitions were not substantial. The limitation on the amount that can be expensed annually by a taxpayer is normally $17,500. However, two limitations may restrict the amount that the taxpayer may otherwise expense.

1. *Acquisitions of Eligible Property Exceeding $200,000.* Where the aggregate cost of *qualifying* property placed in service during the year exceeds $200,000, the $17,500 amount must be reduced $1 for each $1 of cost in excess of $200,000. For example, taxpayers purchasing $204,000 of property could expense up to $13,500 of the cost while taxpayers purchasing in excess of $217,500 could not benefit from § 179 at all.

2. *Taxable Income Limitation.* The deduction under § 179 cannot exceed the amount of taxable income (prior to consideration of this deduction) derived from all of the taxpayer's trades or businesses (including wage income). Any amount that cannot be deducted can be carried over indefinitely to following years to be used against future income. The $17,500 maximum amount that can be expensed in subsequent years is not increased by the carryover amount, however. Rather than carry over the amount that could not be expensed because of the taxable income limitation, the taxpayer has the option of not reducing the property's basis by the carryover amount so it can be depreciated along with the rest of the property's cost.

The taxpayer may elect to expense all or a portion of an asset so long as the total amount expensed does not exceed the dollar limitation. If only a portion of an asset is expensed, the remaining portion is subject to depreciation.

---

[27]   § 179.

Example 17. T purchased 5-year property for $25,000 and 7-year property for $20,500 during the current year. Both assets are eligible to be expensed subject to the limitations of § 179. Assume T expects her future marginal tax rate to remain constant. To maximize the present value of the tax savings from limited expensing and depreciation deductions, T should expense $17,500 of the 7-year property rather than the 5-year property since the cost of the 5-year property could be recovered more quickly, thus resulting in higher depreciation deductions in the current year. Assuming T elects to expense $17,500 of the 7-year property, her deduction for such property would be $17,929 computed as follows:

	Original cost.............................	$20,500	
−	Expensed portion.........................	− 17,500	$17,500
	Remaining depreciable basis..............	$ 3,000	
×	Depreciation percentage..................	× 14.29%	
	Depreciation deduction...................	$ 429	429
	Total deduction..........................		$17,929

In addition, the taxpayer could claim a deduction for *depreciation* of the 5-year property.

Assume these two assets were the only depreciable assets T purchased during the year. Further assume that the 5-year property was purchased in August (the third quarter of the year) and the 7-year property was purchased in November (the fourth quarter of the year). If immediate expensing had *not* been elected, T would be required to use the mid-quarter convention for both assets since more than 40% of the cost was placed in service during the fourth quarter [$20,500 is 45% of $45,500 ($20,500 + $25,000)]. Because T expenses $17,500 of the $20,500 asset, the cost of the asset placed in service in the fourth quarter is deemed to be $3,000, not $20,500. Thus, the mid-quarter convention is avoided and the taxpayer can maximize depreciation for the year using the half-year convention.

Eligible Property. Only property that satisfies certain requirements is eligible for expensing. To qualify, the property may be new or used and must be[28]

1. Recovery property;

2. Property that would have qualified for the investment credit (e.g., most property other than buildings and their components);

3. Property used in a trade or business, as distinguished from property held for the production of income; and

4. Property acquired by purchase from someone who is generally not a "related party" under § 267 (e.g., gifted or inherited property usually does not qualify nor would property acquired from a spouse or parent).

---

[28] §§ 179(d)(1) and (2).

The Americans with Disabilities Act established a relief measure for businesses that make improvements to facilities that provide accessibility to the disabled. As a general rule, businesses may elect either to expense up to $15,000 or to claim a $5,000 credit.

Recapture.   Without any special rule, taxpayers could use an asset in business for a short period (e.g., one day), expense it for tax purposes, then convert it to nonbusiness use. To prohibit this possible abuse, a special rule applies. If the property is converted to nonbusiness use *at any time*, the taxpayer must *recapture* the benefit derived from expensing.[29] Recapture requires the taxpayer to *include* in income the difference between the amount expensed and the MACRS deductions that would have been allowed for the actual period of business use.

> **Example 18.**   On January 1, 1994 F purchased a computer for $5,000. He used it for business for one year, then gave it to his teenage son as a graduation present and bought himself another computer. F may expense the entire $5,000 cost of the computer. However, in 1995 he must recapture and include in income the difference between the expensed amount and the deduction computed under MACRS, $4,000 [$5,000 expensed − MACRS deduction of $1,000 ($5,000 × 20%)]. Note that the net effect in this case is to allow F a deduction equal to what he otherwise could have claimed under MACRS, $1,000.

LIMITATIONS FOR AUTOMOBILES

Over the years, Congress has become more and more concerned about taxpayers who effectively use the benefits of the tax law to reduce the cost of what are essentially personal expenses. For example, a taxpayer may justify the purchase of a luxury rather than standard automobile on the grounds that the government is helping to defray the additional cost through tax deductions and credits allowed for the purchase. In 1984 Congress enacted Code § 280F to reduce the benefits of depreciation and limited expensing for certain automobiles and other properties that are often used partially for personal purposes. In addition, the recordkeeping requirements for travel and entertainment were tightened and extended to certain property used for personal purposes.

Section 280F carves out a special set of limitations for *passenger automobiles*. A passenger automobile is defined as any four-wheeled vehicle manufactured primarily for use on public streets, roads, and highways that weighs 6,000 pounds or less unloaded.[30] (Normally, a standard sedan weighs approximately 4,500 pounds while vans typically weigh about 5,000 pounds.) For purposes of § 280F, the term *passenger automobiles* does not include vehicles for hire, such as taxi cabs, rental trucks, and rental cars.[31] Ambulances and hearses directly used in a trade or business are also unaffected by the § 280F limitations. In addition, the IRS has prescribed Regulations exempting certain trucks and vans.

---

[29]   § 179(d)(10).

[30]   § 280F(d)(5).

[31]   § 280F(d)(5)(B).

Exhibit 9-11 *Section 280F Depreciation Limits for Autos*

	Limits for Autos Based on Year Placed in Service				
	1989	1990	1991	1992	1993
First year of service	$2,660	$2,660	$2,660	$2,760	$2,860
Second year of service	4,200	4,200	4,300	4,400	4,600
Third year of service	2,550	2,550	2,550	2,650	2,750
Thereafter	1,475	1,475	1,575	1,575	1,675

For passenger automobiles, § 280F generally imposes a ceiling on the amount of annual depreciation and first-year expensing deductions. The *maximum* depreciation and/or § 179 expense for autos is shown in Exhibit 9-11. The limits for a particular auto are determined by the year the auto is placed in service by the taxpayer. Thus, annual limits for autos placed in service in 1993 are determined by the 1993 column in Exhibit 9-11. Maximum depreciation and/or § 179 expensing for an auto placed in service in 1993 is $2,860. Maximum depreciation for this auto is $4,600 for 1994, $2,750 for 1995, and $1,675 thereafter. (*Note:* The limits for autos placed in service in 1994 were not available on the publication date of this text. Consequently, subsequent examples will be based on the 1993 limits.)

The 1993 limitations under § 280F restrict the annual depreciation amounts for autos costing $14,300 or more (assuming 200 percent declining-balance depreciation was selected). The $14,300 amount reflects the $2,860 first-year restriction ($14,300 × 20% allowed for five-year property). Moreover, note that if the taxpayer selects (or is required to use) straight-line depreciation, depreciation on an auto costing more than $8,375 would be restricted by the $1,675 limitation for years following the third year of ownership (i.e., $8,375 × 20 percent = $1,675).

Where the car is used less than 100 percent of the time for business—including the portion of time the car is used for production of income purposes—the maximum amounts given above must be reduced proportionately.

Example 19.   T purchased a car for $20,000 in 1993. She used it 60% of the time for business purposes and 20% of the time traveling to her rental properties. Depreciation and limited expensing may not exceed $2,288 (80% × $2,860) for the first year, $3,680 (80% × $4,600) for the second year, and so on.

If the property's basis has not been fully deducted by the close of the normal recovery period (i.e., apparently the extended recovery period of six years), a deduction for the *unrecovered basis* is allowed in subsequent years. Deductions for the property's unrecovered basis are limited to $1,675 annually until the entire basis is recovered.

Example 20.   On October 1, 1993 R purchased a new automobile for $20,000 which he uses solely for business. As a result of depreciation deduction limits, his recovery period is extended an additional five years to 2002.

	1993	1994	1995	1996	1997	1998	Annually 1999–01	2002
Unadjusted basis.........	$20,000	$20,000	$20,000	$20,000	$20,000	$20,000		
Depreciation percentage...	20%	32%	19.2%	11.52%	11.52%	5.76%		
MACRS depreciation..	$ 4,000	$ 6,400	$ 3,840	$ 2,304	$ 2,304	$ 1,152		
Limit............	$ 2,860	$ 4,600	$ 2,750	$ 1,675	$ 1,675	$ 1,675	$1,675	$1,675
Deduction......	$ 2,860	$ 4,600	$ 2,750	$ 1,675	$ 1,675	$ 1,152	$1,675	$263

In examining the above schedule, notice that in the sixth year, 1998, the depreciation actually calculated, $1,152, is less than the $1,675 limitation. The taxpayer can only deduct $1,152 despite the fact that there is additional basis remaining to be recovered.

Leasing.   Without any special rule, the taxpayer could lease a car and circumvent the limitations on depreciation since the restrictions would appear to apply only to the deduction for depreciation and not lease payments. For instance, in *Example 20* above, the taxpayer might lease the car for $400 per month and claim a deduction of $4,800 for the year—far in excess of the amount allowed for depreciation. To prohibit this possibility, lessees may deduct the amount of the lease payment (applicable to business or income-producing use)—but must *include* certain amounts in income to bring their deductions for use of the car in line for owners. Note that the above limitations do not apply to cars leased 30 days or less, or lessors who are regularly engaged in the auto leasing business.[32]

LIMITATIONS FOR PERSONAL USE

Section 280F also restricts the amount of depreciation that may be claimed for so-called "listed property" that is not used predominantly—more than 50 percent—for business. If the property is not used more than 50 percent *for business* in the year it is placed in service, the following restrictions are imposed:[33]

1.   Limited expensing under § 179 is not allowed.

2.   MACRS may not be used in computing depreciation. Property not qualifying must be depreciated using ADS. As explained above, ADS depreciation is computed using the straight-line method and the asset's class life (except in the case of certain property such as automobiles and computers, where the life to be used is specifically prescribed as five years).

Note that these restrictions are imposed if the property is not used primarily for business in the *first* year. Subsequent usage in excess of 50 percent does not permit the taxpayer to amend the earlier return or later use accelerated depreciation or limited expensing. On the other hand, if qualified usage initially exceeds 50 percent but subsequently drops to 50 percent or below, benefits previously secured must be relinquished. The recapture of these benefits is discussed below. Exhibit 9-12 identifies the depreciation methods available for listed property.

These restrictions apply only to *listed property*. Listed property includes the following:[34]

1. Passenger automobiles (as defined above)

2. Any other property used as a means for transportation (e.g., motorcycles and trucks)

3. Any property generally used for purposes of entertainment, recreation, or amusement (e.g., yacht, photography equipment, video recorders, and stereo equipment) *unless* used exclusively at a regular business establishment (e.g., at the office or at a home office)

4. Any computer or peripheral equipment *unless* used exclusively at a regular business establishment

5. Any cellular telephones and similar communications equipment

Example 21. K purchased a car for $20,000 in 1993. She uses her car 40% of the time for business and the remaining time for personal purposes. Since the property is a car, the limitations on depreciation are first reduced in light of the personal usage. In the first year, depreciation would initially be limited to $1,144 ($2,860 maximum allowed × 40% business use). In addition, since the car is listed property and is not used more than 50% for business, K must use ADS to compute depreciation. Therefore, depreciation in the first year is $800 ($20,000 cost × 40% business use = $8,000 × 10% ADS rate).

Qualified Business Use. In determining whether the property is used more than 50 percent for business, only *qualified business use* is considered.[35] Generally, qualified business use means any use in a trade or business of the taxpayer.[36] Thus, for this test *only*, use in an activity that does not constitute a trade or business is ignored (e.g., use of a computer to monitor the taxpayer's investments does not count toward the 50 percent threshold since the activity is not a business).[37] Additionally, an employee's use of his or her own property in connection with employment is not considered business use unless

---

[34] § 280F(d)(4).

[35] § 280F(b)(1) and (2).

[36] § 280F(d)(6).

[37] Temp. Reg. § 1.280F-6T(d)(2).

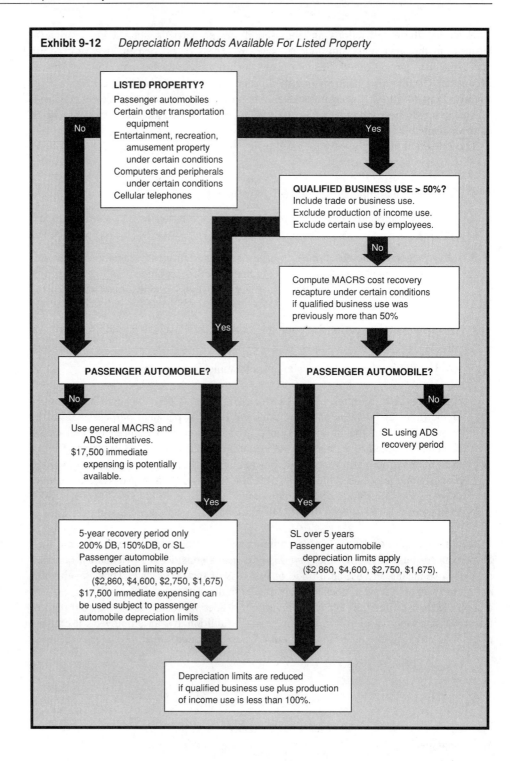

Exhibit 9-12   *Depreciation Methods Available For Listed Property*

it is for the *convenience of the employer* and is *required as a condition of employment*.[38] According to the Regulations, these two requirements generally have the same meaning for § 280F as they have for § 119 relating to the exclusion for meals or lodging.[39] Given this interpretation, a mere statement by the employer expressly requiring the employee to use the property is insufficient. Ordinarily, the property is considered required only if it enables the employee to properly perform the duties of his or her employment.

> **Example 22.** T is employed by X, a newspaper company, to deliver papers in a rural area where the homes are widely scattered. The company does not provide T with a car and does not require T to own a car for employment. Since the car enables T to properly perform his duties and is for the convenience of X, T's use should qualify for purposes of the 50% test even though he is not explicitly required to own a car.

> **Example 23.** J is a budget analyst in the accounting department of a large construction firm. She owns a personal computer that is identical to the one she uses at work. Instead of staying late at the office, J occasionally brings home work for which she uses her computer. J's use of her computer for her work does not qualify.

Recent rulings indicate that the IRS takes a very narrow view regarding what satisfies the convenience-of-the-employer and condition-of-employment tests. In one instance, the Service held that a professor's use of her home computer for writing related to her research—which was required for continued employment—did not satisfy the tests.[40] Although the Service agreed that the use of the computer was related to her work, it found no evidence that employees who did not use home computers were professionally disadvantaged. The Service also felt that her employer did not explicitly require use of the home computer before she was hired. Apparently, the Service will require taxpayers to demonstrate that the work could not properly be performed without the computer or at least that they will be professionally disadvantaged if they do not use the computer. In addition, under the IRS view, taxpayers will be obliged to show that use of the computer was mandatory and not optional.

The reach of this and other rulings goes farther than it first appears. As brought out by the Service, a literal interpretation of the statute indicates that if an employee does not satisfy the convenience-of-the-employer and condition-of-employment tests, *none* of the employee's use is treated as business use. This view does *not* mean that the employee is merely relegated to using ADS for depreciation. Rather, with no business use, the employee is prohibited from claiming any deductions relating to the listed property. Only time will tell whether this interpretation is consistent with Congressional intent.

---

[38] § 280F(d)(3).

[39] Temp. Reg. § 1.280F-6T(a)(2).

[40] Letter Ruling 8615024.

In those cases where qualified business use exceeds 50 percent, any usage for the production of income or other business purposes is included in determining the percentage of the asset that may be depreciated using MACRS. Similarly, if business use is 50 percent or less, the usage for production of income or other nonqualified business purposes is still included in determining the percentage of the asset that may be depreciated using ADS. Note that depreciation is still allowed where the 50 percent test is not met, assuming there is business or investment usage.

> **Example 24.**   V, a financial consultant, purchased a car for $20,000. She uses the car 25% of the time for business and 55% for production of income activities that do not qualify as a business. V must use ADS since business usage is only 25%. Although the time spent for the production of income cannot be counted toward the 50% test, it may be considered in the depreciation computation. Thus, V's depreciation would be $1,600 [$20,000 × (55% + 25%) × 10%]. It should be noted that where the listed property is an automobile, the limitations on depreciation also apply. Here the depreciation limitation is $2,288 [(55% + 25%) × $2,860; note that the production of income usage is considered in making the proper reduction]; thus it does not restrict the amount of the depreciation deduction. Had the usage percentages been reversed, the depreciation deduction would still have been limited to $2,288 ($20,000 × 80% business and investment usage = $16,000 × 20% depreciation percentage = $3,200 but limited to $2,288).

Employer-Provided Cars.   The qualified business use rules directly address the problems of the company-owned car and other company-owned property used by employees. In the case of automobiles, employers typically provide company-owned cars to their employees principally for use in the employer's business. Normally, however, the employee also uses the car for personal purposes if only to commute to work. Under prior law, the employer claimed deductions and credits for the car without limitation (i.e., 100 percent of the car's basis was taken into account) while employees were required to treat the personal use as compensation. In most cases, the compensation income was avoided as long as the employee reimbursed the company for the value of the personal use, which the company in turn reported as income. Section 280F now prescribes specific rules governing depreciation where listed property is used by someone *other than* the owner—such as an employer-provided automobile. The following discussion examines these rules as they apply to employer-provided automobiles; however, such rules extend to other listed property as well.

Where an employee uses an automobile, an *employer* is able to secure 100 percent qualified business use—and thus depreciate the entire cost of the automobile—in one of four ways.[41]

1. The employee's actual business usage is disregarded and the *entire value* of using the vehicle is included in the employee's income.

2. The employee's actual business usage is combined with inclusion of the value of any personal use by the employee as income.

---

[41] Temp. Reg. § 1.280F-6T(d)(4)(iv).

3. The employee's actual business usage is combined with a reimbursement arrangement where the employee reimburses the employer for any personal use (i.e., a fair rent is paid).

4. The use falls under one of four exceptions.

Conditions 2 and 3 cannot be applied to qualify the use of a person owning greater than a 5 percent interest in the business (e.g., the company president, who is also a 30 percent shareholder). In this case, the employer can depreciate the car based only on the employee's actual business usage.

Before looking at several examples of these rules, it should be noted that each requires a valuation of the vehicle's use to the employee. The value can be determined using a facts-and-circumstances approach (e.g., considering such variables as geographic location, make and model, etc.) or one of several safe harbors provided by Temporary Regulations.[42] For example, the Regulations provide a table (i.e., a lease value table) based on the car's total value which provides values for personal use. Another alternative that can be used to value personal use under certain circumstances is the standard mileage allowance.

> **Example 25.**   During the year, X Corporation provided T, an employee, with a new car costing $10,000. T drove the company car 15,000 miles, 9,000 miles or 60% for business purposes, and 6,000 miles or 40% for personal purposes. X Corporation may use any of the first three alternatives to account for the car.
>
> *Alternative No. 1.*   Under this full inclusion method, the employee's actual use is disregarded and the employee must include 100% of the value of the car's use in income, $4,350 (15,000 × 29 cents—the standard mileage rate for 1994)[43] just as if it were salary (i.e., X Corporation includes it on T's Form W-2 and withholds income and FICA taxes). Therefore, all of T's use qualifies and X may depreciate 100% of the car using MACRS. T may then deduct any substantiated business use as a miscellaneous itemized deduction subject to the 2% floor. One advantage of this method for the employer is that it shifts all of the substantiation burden to the employee.
>
> *Alternative No. 2.*   Under this partial inclusion method, only T's personal use is treated as income, or $1,740 (6,000 × 29 cents). X could depreciate the car in the same manner as above. T may be better off under this method since the amount of compensation is reduced. This may have an effect on the amount of deductions or credits T may otherwise claim (e.g., the 2% floor on miscellaneous itemized deductions would be smaller due to the lower amount of income). In this case, X must be able to substantiate the employee's actual business use.

---

[42] Temp. Reg. § 1.61-2T(d)(2)(iii).   [43] Rev. Proc. 93-51, I.R.B. No. 42, 30.

Alternative No. 3. Under the rental reimbursement method, T would pay X Corporation for his personal use, $1,740. X could depreciate the car in the same manner as above. T would be worse off in this situation. Each dollar of reimbursement costs T one dollar, while inclusion of the value of the personal use costs the employee only the tax on the value. Again, X must be able to substantiate the employee's actual business use.

Five Percent Owner. If T owns 5% or more of the business (i.e., X Corporation), the only alternative is to compute depreciation using T's actual business mileage. In this case, X could depreciate 60% of the car using MACRS. Had T's business usage been 50% or less, X would be required to use ADS to compute depreciation.

Additional rules for determining qualified business usage exist for other situations. For example, leasing the property to a 5 percent owner of the business or a related person is not considered qualified business use. Similarly, special rules are provided for aircraft.

Recapture Provisions. If the 50 percent test is satisfied in the year property is placed in service but failed prior to the time when the cost of the asset would be completely recovered using the listed property recovery rules, the taxpayer is required to relinquish the benefits of MACRS. Technically, the taxpayer must recompute the depreciation in the prior years using ADS and include in income the excess of the depreciation actually claimed over the ADS amounts. Depreciation in future years is computed using the straight-line method.

Example 26. In 1994 G purchased a car for $10,000 and used it entirely for business. Depreciation for 1994 was $2,000 ($10,000 × 20%). In 1995 G's business usage dropped to 40%. Since G's business usage is no longer greater than 50%, he must recapture the benefits of accelerated depreciation. Depreciation using the straight-line method in 1994 would have been $1,000 ($10,000 × 10%). Thus, G must include $1,000 ($2,000 original depreciation − $1,000 straight-line depreciation) in income in 1995. Depreciation for 1995 and all subsequent years must be computed using the straight-line method.

Recordkeeping Requirements. Not only has Congress severely restricted tax benefits for listed property, it also has imposed strict recordkeeping requirements for such property. The substantiation rules contained in Code § 274(d), which were formerly reserved solely for travel and entertainment expenses, now extend to expenses related to "listed property." For listed property, the taxpayer is required to substantiate the following: [44]

1. The amount of each expenditure related to the property, including the cost of acquisition, maintenance, and repairs

2. The date of the use of the property

---

[44] Temp. Reg. § 1.274-5T(b)(6).

3. The amount of each business or investment use as well as total use [the number of miles—in the case of a car or other means of transportation—or the amount of time that the property was used for other listed property (e.g., a computer)]

4. The purpose of the use of the property

In those cases where the overall use of the property for a taxable year can be definitely determined without entries, nonbusiness use need not be recorded. For example, in the case of a car, total miles can be determined by comparing the odometer readings at the beginning and the end of the taxable year. Consequently, the taxpayer needs to make entries only for business and investment use.

OTHER CONSIDERATIONS

Anti-Churning Rules. In some cases, a taxpayer's depreciation deductions under MACRS would be higher than those that the taxpayer may currently have. For this reason, Congress believed that some taxpayers would engage in transactions that might enable them to secure the advantages of MACRS.

> **Example 27.** In 1980 H acquired an apartment building as an investment that she chose to depreciate using the straight-line method over 35 years. H made this decision because the use of accelerated depreciation caused a portion of any gain from the subsequent sale of such property to be treated as ordinary income rather than favorable capital gain. With the elimination of favorable capital gain treatment in 1986, there no longer was any disincentive to use the accelerated method. Therefore, H created a plan to benefit from the change. She sold the property to her son who immediately leased it back to her. The rental payments to be paid by H were structured in light of the higher depreciation deductions (27.5-year life instead of 35 years) that her son would be able to take as the new owner of the property.

Sales, exchanges, and other dispositions of assets such as that illustrated above are referred to as "churning" transactions—exchanges of used property solely to obtain the benefits of MACRS.

The thrust of the anti-churning rules is to preclude the use of MACRS for property placed in service prior to the enactment of either version of MACRS, unless the property is transferred in a transaction where not only the owner changes but also the user.[45] In *Example 27* the anti-churning rules prohibit H's son from using MACRS since ownership did not truly change.

---

[45] § 168(e)(4).

There are three sets of rules designed to police churning. For practical purposes these provisions should be given close review whenever the taxpayer is involved in a leasing or nontaxable transaction. For example, a taxpayer would typically be subject to the anti-churning rules in the following situations:

1. Sale followed by immediate leaseback

2. Like-kind exchange

3. Formation and liquidation of a corporation or partnership, including transfers of property to and distributions from these entities

Property Leased to Tax-Exempt Entities.   Prior to 1984, property leased to a tax-exempt entity such as a school, hospital, or government organization normally qualified for depreciation using ACRS (the predecessor of MACRS). Because depreciation provided no tax benefits for tax-exempt entities, these entities often structured arrangements to lease the properties they needed from taxable entities that could utilize the depreciation deductions. By so doing, the tax-exempt entity's effective cost of leasing the property was lower than the cost of purchasing the property outright. In 1984, however, Congress addressed the depreciation issue. As a general rule, depreciation of "tax-exempt use property"—most property leased to a "tax-exempt entity"—must be depreciated using ADS with special rules to determine the applicable recovery period.[46] However, the restrictions described above do not apply to a variety of situations. For example, the rules are inapplicable to "short-term leases."

AMORTIZATION

As previously discussed, MACRS does not apply to intangible property. Therefore, intangibles are subject to the rules existing prior to enactment of ACRS and MACRS. Generally, intangibles are amortized using the straight-line method over their estimated useful life. Special amortization and depreciation rules apply to certain expenditures, however.

GOODWILL AND COVENANTS NOT TO COMPETE

As mentioned in Chapter 6, buyers of a going concern often pay an amount in excess of the fair market value of the concern's tangible assets. This excess purchase price normally is attributable to intangible assets such as goodwill and/or a covenant not to compete. The tax treatment for such intangible assets was changed dramatically by the

---

[46] § 168(g)(1)(C).

Revenue Reconciliation Act of 1993 for acquisitions occurring after August 10, 1993. Acquisitions taking place on or before August 10, 1993 continue to be treated under prior law, which held that goodwill could not be amortized because it was considered as having an unlimited life. Thus, recovery of a taxpayer's basis in goodwill could occur only when the business was subsequently sold or abandoned. In contrast, a covenant not to compete usually has an ascertainable life because the seller typically agrees to refrain from conducting similar business or some other activity for a certain number of years. As a result, prior law held that any cost attributable to the covenant may be amortized over the appropriate period using the straight-line method.

Under prior law, taxpayers attempted to allocate the purchase price to assets other than goodwill since goodwill could not be amortized. In this regard, accountants have been quite creative, assigning the purchase price to a variety of intangibles such as covenants not to compete, favorable contracts, customer lists, accounting control systems, and a long list of other items. As long as the taxpayer was able to establish that the intangible was separate and distinct from goodwill and had a determinable useful life, the taxpayer was entitled to amortize the cost. For example, a taxpayer might allocate a substantial portion of the purchase price of a business to a covenant not to compete and amortize the cost over three years, producing a significant benefit where otherwise there would be no benefit at all if the cost were allocated to goodwill.

Post–August 10, 1993 Acquisitions.   As might be expected, the IRS did not sit idly by and allow taxpayers to do as they pleased. In case after case, the IRS challenged the taxpayer's allocation, and there was a great deal of controversy and litigation. To put an end to the disputes and clear up the uncertainty, Congress enacted § 197. Effective for acquisitions after August 10, 1993 all "Section 197 intangibles" must be amortized over 15 years. (A taxpayer may elect to have the rules of § 197 apply to intangibles acquired after July 15, 1991.) Much like MACRS, § 197 forces the taxpayer to use the 15-year period even if the useful life is actually more or less than 15 years. Section 197 intangibles include a number of items such as goodwill, going-concern value, covenants not to compete, information bases such as customer or subscription lists, know-how, customer-based intangibles, governmental licenses and permits (e.g., liquor licenses, taxicab medallions, landing or takeoff rights, regulated airline routes, television or radio licenses), franchises, trademarks, and trade names.

To further prohibit the deduction of an intangible obtained as part of an acquisition, special rules govern disposition. No loss is allowed on the disposition of an intangible if the business retains other intangible assets acquired in the same or a series of related transactions. Instead, any remaining basis is reallocated among the bases of other § 197 intangibles. Although losses are not recognized, the same treatment does not apply to gains. If the intangible assets are sold at a gain, such gain must be recognized.

Example 28.   Buyer allocates $150,000 to intangible assets in a purchase. Under § 197 Buyer would claim $10,000 per year for 15 years as an amortization deduction. The deduction would not be affected by breaking the $150,000 into separate portions for goodwill, a covenant not to compete, or any other specifically identified intangibles.

Assume that the purchase occurred on January 1, 1994. Buyer will claim a $10,000 deduction every year for 15 years through 2008. Assume that Buyer allocates $105,000 to goodwill and the remaining $45,000 to a covenant not to compete that would expire on January 1, 1997. From 1994 through 1996, Buyer claims an annual amortization deduction of $3,000 ($45,000/15) on the covenant and $7,000 ($105,000/15) on the goodwill. On January 1, 1997, Buyer will have an unrecovered basis of $36,000 on the covenant, which has expired [$45,000 − $9,000 amortization ($3,000 amortization per year for three years)]. However, Buyer can add the $36,000 unrecovered basis to the basis of goodwill and continue to deduct $10,000 per year as amortization of the goodwill.

A number of anti-churning rules exist to prohibit taxpayers from creating and amortizing goodwill and going-concern value. Other intangibles are not covered by these rules.

5-YEAR ELECTIVE AMORTIZATION

To accomplish certain economic and social objectives, Congress has enacted various optional 5-year (60-month) amortization procedures from time to time over the last 40 years. During certain periods, a 5-year amortization election (in lieu of regular depreciation) has been available for expenditures made in connection with child care facilities (§ 188), pollution control facilities (still an option under § 169), railroad rolling stock (§ 184), and rehabilitation of low-income housing [§ 167(k)]. A 60-month amortization election is currently available for qualifying expenditures associated with starting up a business (see Chapter 7).

LEASEHOLD IMPROVEMENTS

Taxpayers often lease property and improve the property while leasing it. In this situation, the lessee is entitled to recover the investment in the improvement.[47] After 1986, the cost of any leasehold improvement made by a lessee is depreciated in the normal manner without regard to the term of the lease. Any unrecovered cost at the end of the lease term would increase the taxpayer's basis for determining gain or loss. The recovery of the costs of acquiring a lease is determined under special rules in Code § 178.

---

[47]   § 168(i)(8); also see § 178(a) when the lease permits renewals.

DEPLETION

A taxpayer who invests in natural resources that are exhausted over time is entitled to recover his or her capital investment. Depletion is the method of recovering this cost and is similar to depreciation.[48] Depletion usually is claimed for investments in oil, gas, coal, copper, and other minerals. Land is not subject to depletion.

To qualify for depletion, the taxpayer must have an economic interest in the mineral deposits.[49] Typically, both the owner of the land who leases the property and the operator to whom the land is leased have the requisite interest since they both receive income from the severance or extraction of the minerals.

COMPUTING THE DEPLETION DEDUCTION

Taxpayers generally are permitted to compute their depletion deduction using either the cost or percentage (statutory) depletion method. The taxpayer computes both cost and percentage depletion and is required to claim the higher amount.[50]

Cost Depletion.   Using cost depletion, the taxpayer recovers the actual investment (adjusted basis in the natural resource) as the mineral is produced. The following formula is used:[51]

$$\text{Annual cost depletion} = \frac{\text{Unrecovered adjusted basis}}{\text{Estimated recoverable units}} \times \frac{\text{Number of units } sold}{\text{during the year}}$$

This formula generally matches the cost of the investment against the revenues produced.

> **Example 29.**   On June 3, 19X1, D, a coal producer, paid $150,000 to acquire the mineral rights in a property which contains coal. He estimates that 90,000 tons of coal are recoverable from the property. During the year, 58,000 tons of coal were produced and 30,000 were sold. D's cost depletion would be $50,000 computed as follows:
>
> $$\frac{\$150,000 \text{ basis}}{90,000 \text{ units}} \times \frac{30,000}{\text{units sold}} = \frac{\$50,000}{\text{depletion}}$$

Similar to depreciation, total *cost* depletion can never exceed the taxpayer's adjusted basis in the property.

Percentage Depletion.   For large oil and gas producers, cost depletion is the only depletion method allowed. However, both cost depletion and percentage depletion are available to small "independent" oil and gas producers as well as royalty owners.[52] Both cost depletion and percentage depletion are also allowed for *all* producers of certain types of minerals (e.g., gold, silver, gravel).

---

[48] § 611.

[49] Reg. § 1.611-1(b).

[50] § 613(a); Reg. § 1.611-1(a).

[51] Reg. § 1.611-2(a).

[52] § 613A(c).

Exhibit 9-13 *Summary of Various Percentage Depletion Rates*

Natural Resource	Percentage Rate
1. Gravel, sand, and other items.............................	5
2. Shale and clay used for sewer pipes; or brick and clay, shale, and slate used for lightweight aggregates................................	7.5
3. Asbestos, coal, sodium, chloride, etc........................	10
4. Gold, silver, oil and gas, oil shale, copper, and iron ore from deposits in the United States...........	15
5. Sulfur and uranium and a series of minerals from deposits in the United States........................	22
6. Metals, other than those subject to 22% or 15% rate...	14

Under the percentage depletion method, the taxpayer's depletion deduction is computed without reference to the taxpayer's cost of the investment. Rather, percentage depletion is based on the amount of income derived from the property.[53] For this reason, the taxpayer may deduct percentage depletion in excess of the adjusted basis of the investment. Thus, the taxpayer is entitled to a deduction for percentage depletion as long as the property continues to generate income.

To compute percentage depletion, a percentage specified in the Code (see Exhibit 9-13) is applied to the *gross* income from the property. The resulting product is the amount of percentage depletion unless limited. For oil and gas properties, percentage depletion is generally limited to the taxpayer's *taxable* income before depletion. Percentage depletion is limited to 50 percent of the taxpayer's taxable income from mineral properties. Gross income is the value of the natural resource when severed from the property before any processing. Taxable income from the property is the difference between income and operating expenses including overhead.

> **Example 30.**   Assume the same facts in *Example 29* and that the 30,000 tons sold were sold for $10 per ton (gross income of $300,000). Further, operating expenses attributable to the coal operation were $260,000. Percentage depletion is computed as follows:

Gross income....................................	$300,000
Statutory percentage for coal....................	× _10%_
Percentage depletion before limitation............	$ 30,000

---

[53] § 613.

Taxable income limitation:

Gross income..................................	$300,000
Less: Operating expenses......................	− 260,000
Taxable income before depletion...............	$ 40,000
Limitation percentage.........................	× 50%
Percentage depletion limit.....................	$ 20,000
Percentage depletion allowable..................	$ 20,000

In this situation, D would use cost depletion of $50,000 as computed in *Example 29* because it exceeds allowable percentage depletion.

Example 31. Assume the same facts in *Example 30* except that barrels of oil are being produced, rather than tons of coal. Cost depletion computations are the same as in *Example 29*. Percentage depletion is computed as follows:

Gross income.................................	$300,000
Statutory percentage for oil..................	× 15%
Percentage depletion before limitation.........	$ 45,000
Gross income.................................	$300,000
Less: Operating expenses.....................	− 260,000
Taxable income before depletion..............	$ 40,000
Percentage depletion limit.....................	$ 40,000
Percentage depletion allowable...............	$ 40,000

D would use cost depletion of $50,000 (computed in *Example 29*) rather than percentage depletion of $40,000 because cost depletion is larger.

Whether percentage or cost depletion is used, the taxpayer must reduce the property's basis (but not below zero) by the amount of depletion claimed. Note that once the basis of the property is reduced to zero, only percentage depletion may be claimed (when the taxpayer is permitted to take percentage depletion), and *no* adjustment is made to create a negative basis.

RESEARCH AND EXPERIMENTAL EXPENDITURES

At first glance, it may appear that the proper tax treatment for research and development expenses requires their capitalization as part of a project's cost. This approach seems appropriate since these costs normally yield benefits only in future periods. Under this theory, the capitalized costs could be recovered over the period during which the project provides benefits or when the project is disposed of or abandoned. Upon closer examination, however, it becomes apparent that this approach is fraught with problems. Since it is difficult to establish any direct relationship between costs of research and develop-

ment and the actual period benefited, it may be impossible to determine the appropriate period for recovery. For example, establishing a useful life for a scientific discovery that has numerous applications and which continually contributes to later research would be guesswork at best. A similar problem exists for unsuccessful efforts. Although a particular effort may not prove fruitful, it may at least indicate what does not work and thus lead to other, perhaps successful, research. In such case, it is not clear whether the costs should be written off or capitalized as part of the subsequent project.

Due to the administrative difficulties inherent in these determinations, the IRS historically granted research and experimental costs favorable treatment by generally allowing the taxpayer to deduct the expenses as incurred or to capitalize the expenses and amortize them over whatever period the taxpayer desires. Although this approach encountered difficulties in the courts, Congress eliminated the problems with enactment of special provisions in 1954.

RESEARCH AND EXPERIMENTAL EXPENDITURES DEFINED

The Code provides separate rules for research and experimental costs.[54] It should be emphasized that the provisions apply to research and *experimental* costs, not to research and *development* costs. The term *experimental* was used instead of *development* to limit the special treatment to laboratory costs.[55] Qualified costs generally include those incident to the development or improvement of a product, a formula, an invention, a plant process, an experimental or pilot model, or similar property. Research and experimental costs do *not* include expenditures for ordinary testing or inspection of materials or products for quality control, efficiency surveys, management studies, consumer surveys, advertising, or promotion. Costs of obtaining a patent, such as legal fees, qualify. However, the costs of acquiring an existing patent, model, or process are not considered research and experimental costs. Expenditures for depreciable property do not qualify but the depreciation allowable on the property is eligible for special treatment.

ALTERNATIVE TAX TREATMENTS

Three alternative methods may be used to account for research and experimental expenditures. The expenses may be deducted as they are paid or incurred, deferred and amortized, or capitalized. Immediate deduction usually is the preferred method since the present value of the tax benefit is greater using this method. Deferral may be preferable in two instances, however. If the taxpayer's income is low in the current year, the tax benefit of the deduction might be increased by deferring the deduction to high-income years when the taxpayer is in a higher marginal tax bracket. Deferral also may be better if an immediate deduction creates or adds to a net operating loss since such losses may be carried over and used only for a limited period of time. The general rule for selecting the best alternative is to choose the one that maximizes the present value of the tax savings from the research and experimental expenditures.

---

[54] § 174.   [55] Reg. § 1.174-2(a).

Expense Election. The taxpayer can elect to deduct all research and experimental expenditures currently.[56] Note, however, that expenditures for depreciable property cannot be expensed currently.[57] If the taxpayer adopts this method in the first tax year in which research and experimental expenses are incurred, the method must be used for all such expenditures in all subsequent years, unless permission is secured to change methods of part or all of the expenditures.[58] The IRS does not need to approve the method the taxpayer adopts initially. Consent is required, however, if the taxpayer wishes to change methods.

Deferral Option. Research and experimental expenditures may be deferred and amortized at the election of the taxpayer.[59] The expenses must be amortized ratably over a period not less than 60 months beginning in the period in which benefits from the expenditures are first realized. It should be emphasized that costs of depreciable property are not deferred expenses; rather, the depreciation expense must be capitalized and amortized over 60 months. Also, if the taxpayer elects to defer the expenditures and a patent is subsequently obtained, the cost must be amortized over the life of the patent, 17 years. If the deferral method is initially elected, the taxpayer must use this method for all future expenses in subsequent tax years unless permission to change methods is obtained.[60]

Election to Capitalize. A taxpayer who does not elect either to amortize research and experimental expenditures over 60 months or to deduct them currently must capitalize them. Capitalizing the expenditure increases the basis of the property to which the expense relates. No deduction is permitted for the capital expenditure until the research project is considered worthless or abandoned. A disposition of the research project such as a sale or an exchange enables the taxpayer to offset the capitalized expenditures—the basis of the project—against any amount realized.

> **Example 32.** L Corporation, a drug manufacturer, is an accrual basis, calendar year taxpayer. During 1994 the corporation performed research to improve various cold and flu medications. On December 1, 1994 a new cold and flu product line was successfully introduced on the market. In connection with this project, L incurred the following costs:
>
> | | |
> |---|---:|
> | Lab equipment (5-year property)................. | $50,000 |
> | Salaries....................................... | 90,000 |
> | Laboratory materials........................... | 5,000 |

---

[56] § 174(a).   [59] § 174(b).

[57] § 174(c).   [60] § 174(b)(2).

[58] § 174(a)(2).

If L Corporation elects to expense the research and experimental costs, it may deduct $105,000 in 1994 as follows:

MACRS depreciation on lab equipment
   (20% of $50,000)................................. $ 10,000
Salaries... 90,000
Laboratory materials................................ 5,000

      Total deductions.................................. $105,000

Note that only the depreciation on the lab equipment may be deducted as a research and experimental cost, *not* the entire cost of the equipment. If L Corporation elects to defer the expense, its monthly amortization beginning December 1, 1994 would be

$$\frac{\$105,000}{60} = \$1,750$$

Alternatively, L could capitalize all the expenses as an asset (including the $10,000 of depreciation) and receive no deduction until a later disposition or abandonment.

OTHER RELATED PROVISIONS

Several other provisions exist relating to the treatment of research and experimental expenditures. In 1981 Congress created a tax credit for research and experimentation. Generally, the credit is 20 percent of the current year's expenditures after adjustments (see Chapter 13).[61] Taxpayers electing the credit are generally required to reduce their research and experimentation expenses by 50 percent of the credit for purposes of computing the amount to either be expensed, deferred, or capitalized.[62] Special rules also exist for contributions of research property by corporations (see Chapter 11).[63]

EXPENSES OF FARMERS AND RANCHERS

Special provisions exist for certain types of expenditures incurred by those engaged in farming and ranching. The rules examined below generally differ from the treatment of expenses that normally would be considered capital expenditures subject to depreciation.

EXPENSES RELATED TO LIVESTOCK

Costs of acquiring animals used for breeding, dairy, work, or sport are treated as capital expenditures and are depreciable under MACRS unless such animals are primarily held for sale and would be appropriately included in inventory. If a farmer raises his or her own livestock, however, expenses incurred such as feed normally can be deducted as

---

[61] § 41.

[62] § 280C(c).

[63] § 170.

paid, assuming the taxpayer uses the cash basis method of accounting.[64] This rule is in sharp contrast to that applying to other self-production costs. Costs incurred by farmers and others in constructing their own equipment and buildings must be capitalized and depreciated.

SOIL AND WATER CONSERVATION, FERTILIZER, LAND CLEARING

Farmers often incur expenses for soil and water conservation. Examples of these expenses are the costs of leveling or terracing the soil to control the flow of water, irrigation and drainage ditches, ponds, dams, eradication of brush, and planting windbreaks. Although normal tax rules would require these expenses to be capitalized, Code § 175 permits a deduction when such expenses are paid or incurred as long as such expenses are consistent with a conservation plan approved by the Soil Conservation Service of the Department of Agriculture. To encourage these practices and still restrict the availability of this benefit, the Code requires that the taxpayer be engaged in the business of farming. In addition, the annual deduction for these expenses is limited to 25 percent of the taxpayer's gross income from farming. This limitation prohibits a taxpayer from using the deductions to reduce nonfarm income. Expenditures exceeding this limitation may be carried over to subsequent years.

Like soil and water conservation expenditures, Code § 180 provides that the cost of fertilizer, lime, and other materials used to enrich farmland can be deducted in the year paid or incurred by those engaged in the business for farming. There is no limitation imposed on the amount of the deduction.

Taxpayers engaged in the farming business must capitalize expenses of clearing land in preparation for farming. These expenses include any cost of making the land suitable for farming such as those for removing and eradicating brush or tree stumps and the treating or moving of earth. Routine brush clearing and other ordinary maintenance related to the land may be expensed, however.

---

[64] Reg. § 1.162-12.

DEVELOPMENT EXPENSES

Expenses incurred in the development of farms and ranches prior to the time when production begins may be capitalized or expensed at the election of the taxpayer.[65] Examples of these expenses are costs of cultivation, spraying, pruning, irrigation, and management fees.

The expensing of development and other farm-related costs prior to the period in which the farm begins to produce income provides an attractive device for high-bracket taxpayers—who have no interest in farming—to shelter their income from other nonfarm sources. These and other tax advantages offered by farming in the sixties brought such an influx of "urban cowboys" to the farming industry that several farm groups protested and demanded protection. Congress first responded to these groups in 1969. Currently, this provision prohibits the immediate expensing of any amount attributable to the planting, cultivation, maintenance, or development of any citrus or almond grove. Any of these development costs that are incurred in the first four years of the grove's life must be capitalized.

Congress adopted additional safeguards in 1976. Section 447 generally requires that corporations (and partnerships having a corporate partner) engaged in the business of farming must use the accrual method of accounting. Since this provision was intended to protect small farmers and family-owned farms, the following are not treated as corporations: (1) S corporations; (2) family-owned corporations (at least 50% of the stock is owned by family members); and (3) any corporation that did not have gross receipts exceeding $1 million in any prior year. In addition, farming syndicates may deduct the costs of feed, seed, fertilizer, and similar farm supplies only as they are actually used.[66] A farming syndicate generally is defined to include partnerships and S corporations where the sale of their interests are specifically regulated by state or local securities laws, or more than 35 percent of their losses during any period are allocated to limited partners or persons who do not actively participate in the management of the business.

In 1986 the prohibition against the deduction of prepaid farming expenses was extended to all farmers that prepay more than 50 percent of their expenses such as feed, seed, and fertilizer.[67] Farmers cannot deduct such expenses until the items are consumed or used. Several exceptions exist, however.

---

[65] *Ibid.*

[66] § 464.

[67] § 464(f).

TAX PLANNING CONSIDERATIONS

DEPRECIATION AND AFTER-TAX CASH FLOW

Many taxpayers, when analyzing an investment, fail to consider the tax aspects. For example, a taxpayer who looks solely to the cash flow projections of investing in a rental property might overlook the effect of depreciation. The depreciation deduction does not require an outlay of cash, but does produce a tax benefit.

Example 33. In January of the current year, L purchased a duplex for $80,000 which she rented to others. Of the $80,000 purchase price, $70,000 was allocable to the building and $10,000 was allocable to the land. L financed the purchase with a $5,000 downpayment and a mortgage calling for monthly payments of interest and principal of $400. During the year, L rented the property for $7,000. Expenses for the year were as follows:

Mortgage interest.................................	$4,000
Taxes...	1,200
Insurance..	500
Maintenance and utilities.........................	300
Depreciation (MACRS: $70,000 × 3.485%).........	2,440
Total expenses...................................	$8,440

The net taxable loss from the real property would be

Rental income.....................................	$ 7,000
Less: Rental expenses............................	− 8,440
Net taxable loss..................................	$ 1,440

Note that the taxable loss contains depreciation expense of $2,440, a noncash expenditure. Assuming L is in the 28 percent tax bracket, the net cash flow from the project would be computed as follows:

Cash inflow:			
Rental income...............................			$7,000
Tax saving from loss			
($1,440 × 28%)...........................			403
Total cash inflow............................			$7,403
Cash outflow:			
Total expenses...........:.................		$8,440	
Less: Depreciation.......................		− 2,440	
		$6,000	
Debt service			
Mortgage payments ($400 × 12).............	$4,800		
Less: Interest (included in			
expenses above).................	− 4,000	+ 800	
Total cash outflow...........................			(6,800)
After-tax cash flow.............................			$ 603

Therefore, L has a positive cash flow of $603 on the project notwithstanding the taxable loss that she suffered of $1,440.

Under certain circumstances, limitations are imposed on the deduction of losses from rental property. These limitations are discussed in Chapter 12.

ACCELERATING DEPRECIATION WITH COST-SEGREGATION

Prior to 1981, some taxpayers used a technique called "component depreciation" to accelerate real estate depreciation deductions. These taxpayers separated the costs of their depreciable buildings into various components with useful lives shorter than the rest of the building. For example, structural components such as wiring, plumbing, and roofing were depreciated over periods of 10 or 15 years rather than the much longer periods typically associated with the useful life of the building shell.

Although MACRS rules do not allow component depreciation for structural components of buildings, taxpayers may still be able to accelerate depreciation on some costs that might otherwise be depreciated over 27.5 or 39 years with the rest of the building's cost. Examples of assets that taxpayers should segregate from the cost of the building and depreciate over five or seven years include movable partitions, computers, separate fire protection systems, manufacturing equipment, and built-in desks and cabinets. Separate humidity-control and air conditioning systems installed specifically for special equipment can also be depreciated over seven years. A rule of thumb for identifying these separate depreciable assets is to assess whether the items would be removed if the business were to relocate. If so, the removable assets can have their own depreciation schedules.

Land improvements represent another set of costs that should be separated since they can be depreciated over 15 years. These include parking lots, landscaping, sewers, and irrigation systems.

To segregate costs successfully, taxpayers or their advisors should work closely with building contractors to document the costs of fast-depreciating assets. Early involvement with the contractor or architect could even lead to building designs that maximize the number of separate depreciable assets while not reducing the productive use of the building.

GOODWILL AMORTIZATION RULE BENEFITS BUYERS AND SELLERS

Prior to August 10, 1993 the goowill portion of the cost of acquiring a business provided no tax benefit to the buyer until the buyer later sold the business because the basis assigned to goodwill could not be amortized. Now that goodwill can be amortized over 15 years, its value is greater because the present value of a series of tax deductions received throughout a 15-year period is higher than the present value of a single deduction received many years in the future (assuming constant or declining marginal tax rates over time). Buyers and sellers will share this increase in value as they negotiate purchase/sale prices of their businesses.

Typically, buyers and sellers have some flexibility regarding the allocation of purchase price between goodwill (a capital asset that produces capital gain for the seller) and other intangibles. Two factors encourage increased allocations to goodwill. First, the seller will recognize capital gain income instead of ordinary income (assuming the allocation choice is between goodwill and a covenant not to compete). Second, for buyers concerned about earnings per share, goodwill is preferable to payments for a covenant not to compete since goodwill must be amortized over 40 years for financial accounting purposes under generally accepted accounting principles (GAAP). In contrast, the covenant may be amortized over its economic life (typically less than 40 years). Buyers not concerned about GAAP should be indifferent between allocations to goodwill versus a covenant not to compete because *all* intangibles are amortizable over 15 years for tax purposes. Thus, at best, increased allocations to goodwill could benefit both buyers and sellers of businesses. At worst, increased goodwill allocations will neither help nor harm buyers or sellers.

PROBLEM MATERIALS

DISCUSSION QUESTIONS

9-1 *Requirements for Depreciation.* Indicate the basic requirements that must be satisfied before property may be depreciated.

9-2 *Depreciation and Amortization: Eligible Property.* Indicate whether a taxpayer could claim deductions for depreciation or amortization of the following property:

    a. Land used in the taxpayer's farming business.

    b. A duplex—the taxpayer lives in one half while he rents the other half out.

    c. The portion of the taxpayer's residence that she uses as a home office.

    d. The taxpayer's former residence, which he listed for rental temporarily until he is able to sell it. The residence was listed in late November and was not rented as of the end of the taxable year.

    e. A mobile home that the taxpayer initially purchased and used while he was in college and this year began renting to several students.

    f. The costs attributable to goodwill and a covenant not to compete.

    g. An automobile used for business. The taxpayer accounts for his deductible car expenses using the standard mileage rate.

9-3 *Definitions: Cost Allocation Methods and Types of Property.* Explain the terms depreciation, amortization, and depletion. Include in your discussion an explanation of tangible and intangible property as well as personal and real property.

9-4 *Depreciation Systems.* Briefly describe the depreciation systems (e.g., MACRS) for computing tax depreciation that one may encounter in practice.

9-5 *Ineligible Property.* What types of property are not depreciated using MACRS? How can the taxpayer avoid MACRS?

9-6 *Depreciation Methods and MACRS Statutory Percentages.*

    a. Indicate the first-year depreciation percentage applicable to office furniture and show how it is determined.

    b. Same as (a) except the property is an apartment building.

9-7 *MACRS and Straight-Line Depreciation.* Assuming a taxpayer desires to use the straight-line method of depreciation, what alternatives, if any, are available?

9-8 *Alternative Depreciation System.* Typically, all depreciation is computed using MACRS. However, Code § 168 also establishes an alternative depreciation system (ADS). As a practical matter, when will use of ADS be most likely?

9-9   *Depreciating Recovery Property.*   During the year, X purchased land and a building for a total of $500,000 and furniture for the building for $100,000. He intends to lease the building. Indicate whether the following factors are taken into account in computing the depreciation of these assets.

   a.   Each asset's useful life as estimated by the taxpayer in light of industry standards.
   b.   Salvage value.
   c.   The month in which the property was placed in service.
   d.   The use of the building by the lessee.
   e.   The taxpayer is a corporation.
   f.   The property is used for investment rather than business use.
   g.   The acquisition cost of the building including the land.
   h.   The lessee.

9-10   *Half-Year Convention.*   Indicate whether the following statements are true or false regarding the half-year convention.

   a.   Depreciation can be claimed for the *entire* year if the asset has been in service for more than six months.
   b.   The half-year convention applies to *all* property placed in service during the year.
   c.   The half-year convention applies *both* in the year of acquisition and the year of disposition of the asset.
   d.   The convention must be considered when expensing an asset under Code § 179.

9-11   *Acquiring a Business.*   L has worked as a salesman in the outdoor advertising business for ten years. This year he decided to go into business for himself. To this end he purchased all of the assets of Billboards Unlimited Corporation for $2 million. The value of the tangible assets such as the office building, furniture, and equipment was $1.4 million. Explain how L will recover the cost of his investment.

9-12   *Luxury Cars.*   Indicate whether the following statements are true or false. If false, explain why.

   a.   W purchased a car used solely for business for $12,000. The limitations imposed by Code § 280F on deductions related to automobiles do not alter what W could claim in the year of acquisition.
   b.   P Corporation is a distributor of hospital supplies. During the year, it purchased a $20,000 car for its best salesperson. Section 280F does not alter the total amount of depreciation deducted while P owns the car. Section 280F alters only the timing of the depreciation deductions.

9-13 *Listed Property.* Indicate whether the following statements are true or false. If false, explain why.

    a. J is a part-time photographer. This year she purchased a camera that cost $1,000 for her video cassette recorder. Thirty percent of her usage was for business while the remainder was personal. J may use the accelerated depreciation recovery percentages of MACRS.

    b. P, a proprietor of a lighting store, purchased computer equipment for $10,000 which he uses 50 percent of the time for business. Under Code § 280F, the maximum deduction for depreciation and limited expensing in the first year is $500, while without § 280F the deduction would be $5,000.

    c. C purchased computer equipment that he uses 60 percent for managing his investments and 35 percent of the time in connection with a mail-order business he operates out of his home. C may claim straight-line depreciation deductions based on 95 percent of the cost of the asset.

    d. G is employed as a research consultant for RND Corporation, a research institute. G uses the company's computer at the office but often takes home work, which she does on her home computer. G's use of her home computer for work done for her employer is considered qualified business use.

    e. T is a college professor who uses a computer, for which he properly claims deductions, to write textbooks in his home office. It is unnecessary for T to maintain records on business usage of the computer.

    f. WS Corporation, a large clothing manufacturer, provides a car for each of its salespeople. It charges each of its salespeople 29 cents for each mile of personal use. WS may disregard any personal use of the cars by its salespeople in computing depreciation.

    g. WS Corporation also provides a car for its chief executive officer, C, who owns 10 percent of the company's stock. All of C's use is for business except for commuting to work, which represents 60 percent of the car's use. C reimburses the company for the personal use. WS may claim accelerated depreciation for the car based on 40 percent of the car's cost.

9-14 *Amortization.* How are the costs of patents, copyrights, and goodwill recovered?

9-15 *Leasing Restrictions.* Address the following:

    a. Construct a numerical example illustrating why a tax-exempt entity would rather lease than buy.

    b. R acquired a ten-year ground lease on three acres on which it constructed a small office building. Explain how R will recover its cost of the building.

9-16 *Depreciation—Allowed or Allowable.* R inherited her mother's personal residence in 1958 and converted it to rental property. Her basis for depreciation was $30,000. The residence had an estimated useful life of 30 years. This year, R sold the residence for $40,000. During the time R held the property, she never claimed a deduction for depreciation on the residence. What amount of gain will R report upon the sale?

9-17 *Salvage Value.* How is salvage value used in computing the depreciation deduction using MACRS?

9-18 *Depreciable Basis and Limited Expensing.* Explain how the taxpayer's depreciable basis may be affected by the amount expensed under the limited expensing election of § 179.

9-19 *Anti-Churning Rules.* Explain the purpose of the anti-churning rules and when they normally will apply.

9-20 *Component vs. Composite Depreciation.* Answer the following:

    a. Distinguish component depreciation from composite depreciation.

    b. May the taxpayer use either method? Explain.

9-21 *Mid-Quarter Convention.* T company, a calendar year taxpayer, purchased $100,000 of equipment on December 3 of this year.

    a. Under what circumstances will the mid-quarter convention apply in computing depreciation of the equipment?

    b. Assume that T can purchase the equipment at any time during the year. How will T time the acquisitions if it wants to maximize the firm's depreciation deductions for the year?

9-22 *Depletion.* Address the following:

    a. Briefly describe how cost and percentage depletion are computed and determine which is used in a particular year.

    b. Assuming the taxpayer has completely recovered her depletable cost basis (e.g., her basis is zero), is she entitled to further depletion deductions?

9-23 *Farming Expenses.* N plans on stepping down from his position as president of a large energy company in five years. At that time, he and his wife would like to move to the country where they would retire and perhaps operate a small dairy farm. N has spotted some land through which a sparkling creek runs. His accountant has suggested that he purchase the land now and begin to operate it despite initial losses. Explain the rationale behind the accountant's advice.

PROBLEMS

9-24 *Depreciation of Converted Personal-Use Property.* F purchased a mobile home to live in while at college. The home cost $12,000. When he graduated, he left the home in the trailer park and rented it. At the time he converted the home to rental property, it had a fair market value of $10,000.

    a. What is F's basis for depreciation?

    b. F now lives 75 miles away from his alma mater. Can he deduct the cost of traveling back to check on his rental property (including those trips on which he also attended a football game)?

9-25 *MACRS Accelerated Depreciation.* In 1994 T, a calendar year taxpayer, decided to move her insurance business into another office building. She purchased a used building for $70,000 on March 15. T also purchased new office furniture for the building. The furniture was acquired for $20,000 on May 1. The first-year expensing option is not elected, yet T wants to depreciate her assets as rapidly as possible. MACRS depreciation tables are located in Appendix C.

    a. Compute T's depreciation deduction for 1994.

    b. Compute T's depreciation deduction for 1995.

    c. Assuming that T sold the office building and the furniture on July 20, 1996, compute T's depreciation for 1996.

    d. Answer (a), (b), and (c) above assuming that the furniture was purchased on October 20.

9-26 *Mid-Quarter Convention.* Q Corporation anticipates purchasing $300,000 of office furniture and fixtures (7-year property) next year. This will be Q's only personal property acquisition for the year. Q Corporation management is willing to purchase and place the property in service any time during the year to accelerate its depreciation deductions. In addition, management wants to depreciate the property as rapidly as possible. MACRS depreciation tables are located in Appendix C.

a. Compute depreciation for the first two years of ownership assuming *all* of the property is purchased and placed in service on February 2.

b. Compute depreciation for the first two years of ownership assuming *all* of the property is purchased and placed in service on December 6.

c. Compute depreciation for the first two years of ownership assuming $177,000 (59%) of the property is purchased and placed in service on February 2 and $123,000 (41%) is purchased and placed in service on December 6.

d. Based on the results of (a) through (c) above, what course of action do you recommend for Q Corporation?

9-27 *MACRS Straight-Line Depreciation.* G Corporation operates a chain of fast-food restaurants. On February 7, 1994 the company purchased a new building for $100,000. In addition, on May 5, 1994 G purchased a used stove for $5,000 and refrigeration equipment for $30,000 (both 7-year property). G does not elect to use the limited expensing provision. The company does elect to compute depreciation using the straight-line method under MACRS. MACRS depreciation tables are located in Appendix C.

a. Why might G elect to use the straight-line method?

b. Assuming G elects to use the straight-line method and a 7-year recovery period for depreciating the stove applies, can it use MACRS accelerated recovery percentages for the refrigeration equipment? For the building?

c. Compute G's depreciation for the stove and building in 1994 assuming it elects the straight-line method for the 7-year property.

d. Compute the depreciation for the stove and building in 1995.

e. If G does not dispose of either the stove or building, what is the final (i.e., last year's) depreciation deduction for the stove and the building?

f. Assuming G disposes of both the stove and the building on October 18, 1995, what is the depreciation for each of these assets in 1995?

9-28 *ADS Depreciation.* P retired several years ago to live on a small farm. To supplement his income, he cuts wood and sells it in the nearby community. This year he purchased a new light duty truck to haul and deliver the wood. He used the truck 20 percent of the time for business. Assuming the truck cost $9,000, compute P's depreciation for the year.

9-29 *Section 179 Election.* Although K is currently a systems analyst for 3L Corporation, her secret desire is to write a best-selling novel. To this end, she purchased a computer for $3,000 this year. She used the computer only for writing her novel. Can she deduct the entire cost of her computer this year even though she has not yet received any income from the novel? Next year?

9-30 *Limitations on § 179 Expensing.* In each of the following situations, indicate whether T may elect to use the limited-expensing provisions of § 179. Assume the acquisition qualifies unless otherwise indicated.

   a. T is a corporate taxpayer.

   b. This year, T purchased a $300,000 building and $50,000 of equipment.

   c. T suffered a net operating loss of $40,000 this year before consideration of the § 179 deduction.

   d. T purchased the asset on the last day of the taxable year.

9-31 *Limited-Expensing Election: Eligible Property.* For each of the following assets, indicate whether the taxpayer may elect to expense a portion or all of the asset's cost.

   a. A $10,000 car used 75 percent for business purposes and 25 percent for personal purposes.

   b. A home computer used by the taxpayer to maintain records and perform financial analyses with respect to her investments.

   c. An apartment building owned by a large property company.

   d. A roll-top desk purchased by the taxpayer's father, who gave it to the taxpayer to use in her business.

9-32 *Limited-Expensing Election Calculations.* N, a single taxpayer, purchased duplicating equipment to use in his business. He purchased the equipment on June 3 of the current year for $20,000. N elects to expense the maximum amount allowable with respect to the equipment.

   a. What portion of the cost of the equipment may N expense for this year?

   b. Compute N's depreciation deduction for the current year.

9-33 *Section 280F Calculations.* In the current year, H purchased a new automobile for $15,000. The first-year expensing election is not made. Use the 1993 limits from Exhibit 9-11 in responding to the questions below.

   a. Assuming the car is used solely for business, prepare a depreciation schedule illustrating the amount of annual depreciation to which H is entitled assuming he holds the car until the entire cost is recovered.

   b. Assume the same facts as (a) except the car is used 80 percent of the time for business and 20 percent of the time for personal purposes. Compute the current year's depreciation deduction.

   c. Same as (b) except the car is used 70 percent of the time for business, 10 percent of the time for production of income activities, and 20 percent of the time for personal purposes.

   d. Same as (a) except the car is used 40 percent of the time for business and 60 percent of the time for personal purposes.

9-34 *Section 280F Calculations.* M purchased a new automobile for $30,000 in 1993. The first-year expensing election is not made. The car is used solely for business. M is in the 28 percent tax bracket. The present value factors for a 10 percent discount rate are as follows: year 1, .91; 2, .83; 3, .75; 4, .68; 5, .62; 6, .56; 7, .51; 8, .47; 9, .42; 10, .39; 11, .35; 12, .32; 13, .29; 14, .26; 15, .24; 16, .22; 17, .20.

   a. Prepare a depreciation schedule.

   b. Compute the total tax savings M will receive throughout the recovery period from depreciation deductions.

   c. Using an after-tax discount rate of 10 percent, compute the present value of tax savings from depreciation deductions under § 280F.

   d. Using an after-tax discount rate of 10 percent, compute the present value of tax savings from depreciation deductions under MACRS *as if* § 280F were repealed.

   e. Compare the results of (b) and (c) above. What impact does discounting have in assessing the tax benefits of depreciation?

   f. Compare the results of (c) and (d) above. What is the discounted after-tax cost of the § 280F limitations for this taxpayer?

9-35 *Research and Experimental Expenditures.* ABC Corporation is developing a new process to develop film. During the year, the company had the following expenditures related to research and development:

Salaries...	$60,000
Laboratory equipment (5-year property)...........	30,000
Materials and supplies...........................	10,000

Compute ABC's deduction for research and experimental expenditures under each of the alternative methods.

9-36 *Depletion.* DEF Company produces iron ore. It purchased a property for $100,000 during the year. Engineers estimate that 50,000 tons of iron ore are recoverable from the property. Given the following information, compute DEF's depletion deduction and undepleted cost basis for each year.

Year	Units Sold (tons)	Gross Income	Taxable Income before Depletion
1	15,000	$300,000	$124,000
2	20,000	400,000	50,000
3	10,000	250,000	90,000

9-37 *Depletion.* Assume the same facts in Problem 9-36 except that barrels of oil are being produced rather than tons of iron ore. Compute DEF's depletion deduction and undepleted cost basis for each year.

CUMULATIVE PROBLEMS

9-38   David and Lauren Hammack are married with one child, Jim, age 12. The couple lives at 2003 Rolling Drive, Indianapolis, Indiana 46222. David is a product manager for G&P corporation, a food company. Lauren operates a clothing store as a sole proprietorship (employer identification number 35-123444). The couple uses the cash method of accounting except where the accrual method is required. They report on the calendar year.

David earned a salary of $60,000 during the year. G&P also provides health insurance for David and his family. Of the total insurance premium, the company paid $750. Income taxes withheld from David's salary were $7,000. The couple paid $9,500 in estimated taxes during the year.

Lauren's father died on June 20. As a result, Lauren received $40,000 as beneficiary of a life insurance policy on her father. In addition, her father's will provided that she receive all of his shares of IBM stock. The stock was distributed to her in October when it was worth $30,000.

On August 1 of this year, the couple purchased a six-month Treasury Bill for $9,700. They redeemed it on February 1 of the following year for its face value, $10,000. In addition, the couple purchased a previously issued AT&T bond with the face value of $1,000 for $890 on June 1. The bond pays interest at 6 percent per year on January 1 and July 1. On July 1 they received an interest payment of $30, which was also reported on Form 1099-INT, sent to them shortly after year-end. The couple plans on reporting any accrued market discount in taxable income when they sell or redeem the bond, in some future year.

Several years ago, the couple invested in Nedco Corporation, acquiring 100 shares of stock for $10,000. They were two of the original 10 investors that helped start the corporation. Unfortunately, the corporation was never successful and the stock became worthless this year. Only $500,000 of stock was ever issued. All of Nedco's stock is considered small business stock under Code § 1244.

Each year, Lauren travels to Paris to attend the annual fashion shows for buyers. When scheduling her trip for this year, Lauren decided to combine business with pleasure. On Thursday, March 6, Lauren departed for Paris, arriving on Friday morning. Friday afternoon was devoted to business discussions with several suppliers. Since the shows began on Monday, she spent the weekend touring Paris. After attending the shows Monday through Wednesday, she returned to Indianapolis on Thursday, arriving late that night. The cost of her round-trip air fare to Paris was $500. Meals were $30 per day and lodging was $100 per day for Friday through the following Wednesday.

In addition to running her own shop, Lauren teaches an M.B.A. course in retailing at the local university. She received a $6,000 salary for her efforts this year. The university withheld $429 in FICA taxes, but did not make additional tax withholdings related to the salary. The school is ten miles from her office. Normally, she goes home from her office to get dinner before she goes to the school to teach (16 miles from her home). According to her log, she made 80 trips from home to school. In addition, the log showed that she had driven 20,000 miles related to her clothing business. She uses the standard mileage rate to compute her automobile expenses.

Lauren's records, which she maintains for her business using the cash method of accounting, reveal the following additional information:

Sales......................................	$120,000
Cost of goods sold..........................	(50,000)
Gross profit.................................	$ 70,000
Advertising..................................	6,000
Insurance...................................	1,400
Rent..	9,000
Wages......................................	15,000
Employment taxes...........................	2,000

The insurance included (1) a $200 premium paid in September for coverage of her car from October through March of the following year; and (2) a $1,200 payment for fire insurance for June 1 through May 31 of the following year. Similarly, rent expense includes a $4,500 payment made on November 1 for rent from November through April. She has a five-year lease requiring semiannual rental payments of $4,500 on November 1 and May 1.

Lauren allows several of her customers to buy things on credit. This year, she sold $2,000 of merchandise to X and allowed him to charge it to his account. To Lauren's dismay, X declared bankruptcy during the year and the debt is now worthless.

During the year, David purchased a new automobile for $15,000 which he uses 60 percent of the time for business (i.e., "qualified business usage" is 60 percent). His actual operating expenses, excluding depreciation, were $3,000.

In addition to the information provided earlier in this problem, the couple paid the following amounts during the year:

State income taxes....................	$5,500
County income taxes..................	500
Real estate taxes......................	2,400
Mortgage interest on their home........	3,600
Charitable contributions................	2,000

David and Lauren's social security numbers are 445-54-5565 and 333-44-5789, respectively. Their son Jim's social security number is 464-57-4681.

Compute David and Lauren's tax liability for the year. Make all computations (including any special elections required) to minimize the Hammacks' tax liability based on *current* tax law. If a tax return is to be prepared for this problem, complete the following forms: 1040 (including Schedules A, C, and SE), and 2106. There is no alternative minimum tax liability. (*Note:* if the § 280F limitations apply to any auto depreciation, you must use the 1993 numbers from Exhibit 9-11 because the 1994 amounts were not available at the publication date of this text.)

9-39   Michelle Kay purchased a small building on February 1 of the current year for $650,000. In addition, she paid $15,000 for land. Ms. Kay obtained a $640,000 mortgage for the acquisition. She and five of her employees use the property solely to store and sell a variety of gift items under the business name of "Michelle's Gifts." The following information pertains to the business:

Sales....................................	$950,000
Cost of goods sold.......................	625,000
Wages for employees ($20,000 each)......	100,000
Payroll taxes for five employees...........	?
Depreciation.............................	?
Advertising..............................	25,000
Mortgage interest........................	60,000
Legal services...........................	20,000
Real estate taxes........................	4,000
Fire insurance...........................	3,000
Meals and entertainment..................	2,500

During the year, Ms. Kay purchased the following assets for the business. She wants to depreciate all business assets as rapidly as the law allows.

	Cost	Month/Day of Acquisition
Personal computer..............	$14,000	March 31
Printer for computer.............	2,000	April 2
Office furniture and fixtures......	20,000	April 29
Machinery (7-year property).....	30,000	May 12

Michelle Kay was divorced from Benjamin Kay two years ago. The divorce decree stipulates that Benjamin Kay would receive the dependency exemption for their son, Eric (now 12 years old), even though Eric lives full-time with Ms. Kay in a home she maintains. During the year, Ms. Kay provided 25 percent of Eric's support and Mr. Kay provided 75 percent. Ms. Kay received $15,000 of alimony and $10,000 of child support from Mr. Kay during the year. Ms. Kay's social security number is 333-46-2974. Her address is 567 North Hollow Drive, Grimview, Illinois, 48124. For business purposes, her employer ID number is 66-2869969. She uses the cash method of accounting for all purposes.

Unrelated to her business, Ms. Kay paid the following amounts during the year:

Estimated federal income taxes............	$22,000
State income taxes.......................	3,500
County income taxes.....................	1,500
Real estate taxes........................	2,000
Mortgage interest on her home...........	5,600
Charitable contributions...................	2,900
Deductible contribution to individual retirement account (Note: This is a deduction *for* A.G.I. It is one of the "adjustments to income" on page 1 of Form 1040.)............................	2,000
Health insurance for Ms. Kay.............	1,000

Compute Ms. Kay's tax liability for the year based on *current* tax law. (Hint: Ms. Kay's adjusted gross income is less than $100,000.) If a tax return is to be prepared for this problem, complete the following forms: 1040 (including Schedules A, C, and SE) and 4562. There is no alternative minimum tax liability. For grading purposes, attach a sheet to Schedule C showing supporting calculations for payroll taxes.

RESEARCH PROBLEMS

9-40 *Depreciation.*   S is a land developer. During the year, he finished construction of a complex containing a new shopping mall and office building. To enhance the environment of the complex, substantial landscaping was done including the planting of many trees, shrubs, and gardens. In addition, S acquired a massive sculpture that served as the focal point of the complex. S also purchased numerous pictures, which were hung in the shopping center and office building. Can S claim depreciation deductions for any of the items noted above?

9-41 *Amortization.*   During the year, the metropolis of Burnsberg accepted bids from various cable television companies for the right to provide service within its city limits. The accepted bid was submitted by Cabletech Inc. in the amount of $500,000. For this amount, the city granted the company a license to operate for 10 years. The terms of the agreement further provided that the company's license would be renewed if the city was satisfied with the services provided. May Cabletech amortize the cost of the license?

Upon completion of this chapter you will be able to:

- Determine when a deduction is allowed for a bad debt
- Understand the different tax treatment for business and nonbusiness bad debts
- Explain what constitutes a deductible casualty or theft loss
- Compute the amount of the deduction for casualty and theft losses
- Determine the net operating loss deduction and explain how it is treated
- Explain the basic tax accounting requirements for inventories
- Identify the costs that must be capitalized as part of inventory and the role of the uniform capitalization rules in making this determination
- Explain how inventory costs are assigned to costs of goods sold using the FIFO and LIFO assumptions
- Compute ending inventory using double-extension dollar-value LIFO
- Apply the lower of cost or market rule in valuing ending inventory

CHAPTER OUTLINE

Bad Debts 10-1
  Treatment of Business versus
    Nonbusiness Bad Debts 10-2
  General Requirements 10-4
  Deduction Methods 10-5
Casualty and Theft Losses 10-7
  General Rules 10-7
  Casualty and Theft Defined 10-8
  Loss Computation 10-9
  Casualty Gains and Losses 10-11
  Year Deductible 10-13
Net Operating Losses 10-16
  Carryback and Carryforward Years 10-16
  Net Operating Loss Computation 10-17

Recomputing Taxable Income for
  Year to Which Net Operating Loss
  Is Carried 10-20
Inventories 10-23
  Costs to Be Inventoried 10-24
  Allocating Inventoriable Costs 10-26
  Dollar Value LIFO 10-29
  The LIFO Election 10-32
  Lower of Cost or Market 10-33
Tax Planning Considerations 10-35
  Casualty and Theft Losses 10-35
  Bad Debts 10-36
  Net Operating Losses 10-36
Problem Materials 10-37

Chapter **10**

CERTAIN BUSINESS DEDUCTIONS AND LOSSES

The rules governing the treatment of expenses and losses discussed in Chapter 7 set forth the general requirements that must be met if the taxpayer wishes to claim a deduction. As already seen, the basic test—whether the item was incurred in carrying on business or profit-seeking activities—is often just the initial hurdle in obtaining a deduction. Other provisions in the Code may impose additional conditions or limitations that must be considered. This chapter examines some of the special rules that relate to certain business losses and expenses of the taxpayer, including the provisions for bad debts, casualty losses, the net operating loss deduction, and inventories.

BAD DEBTS

Loans are made for a variety of reasons. Some are made in connection with the taxpayer's trade or business while others are made for purely personal purposes. People also make loans hoping to make a profit. Regardless of the motive, with the extension of credit comes the possibility—as every lender knows—that the loan will never be repaid. When the borrower, in fact, cannot repay the loan, the taxpayer has what is termed a *bad debt* and may be entitled to a deduction. For tax purposes, a bad debt is considered a special form of loss subject to the specific rules of Code § 166. This provision governs the treatment of all types of bad debts: those that arise from the sale of goods or services such as accounts receivable, as well as those resulting from a direct loan of money. Moreover, § 166 applies regardless of the form of the debt (e.g., a secured or unsecured note receivable or a mere oral promise to repay).[1]

---

[1] Notes issued by a corporation (with interest coupons or in registered form) that are considered capital assets in the hands of the taxpayer are treated as worthless securities, as discussed in Chapter 12.

TREATMENT OF BUSINESS VERSUS NONBUSINESS BAD DEBTS

The tax treatment of a bad debt vastly differs depending on whether it is a *business* or *nonbusiness* bad debt. Business bad debts may be deducted without limitation. In contrast, nonbusiness bad debts are deductible only as short-term capital losses and are therefore subject to the limitation on deductions of capital losses (i.e., to the extent of capital gains plus $3,000).[2] Congress provided this distinctive treatment for nonbusiness bad debts in part to ensure that investments cast in the form of loans are handled in virtually the same manner as other investments that become worthless. As a general rule, an investment in a company's stock or bonds that becomes worthless also receives capital loss treatment.

Another difference between business and nonbusiness bad debts concerns the method allowed to claim a deduction. For some debts, it may be apparent that a portion of the loan will become uncollectible but determination of the exact amount must await final settlement. In the case of a nonbusiness bad debt, there is no deduction for partial worthlessness.[3] A deduction is postponed until the ultimate status of the debt is determined.

> **Example 1.**　R loaned his neighbor $5,000 in 1993. During 1994 his neighbor declared bankruptcy, and it is estimated that R will recover no more than 20 cents on the dollar or a maximum of $1,000 from the debt. Although R can establish that he has a bad debt of at least $4,000 ($5,000 − $1,000), no deduction is permitted in 1994 since the debt is nonbusiness, and it is partially worthless. If in 1995 R settles for $500, without any capital gains or other capital losses, he may deduct $3,000 of this loss as a *short-term* capital loss and carry over the remaining $1,500 ($5,000 − $3,000 − $500) to the following year. On the other hand, if the debt had arisen from R's business, R could deduct $4,000 in 1994 based on his estimate of the uncollectible amount, and the $500 remainder of the loss, in 1995, all against ordinary income.

Because of their significantly different treatments, the determination of whether a particular debt is a business or nonbusiness bad debt has produced substantial controversy.

Business Bad Debts.　Business bad debts are defined as those that arise in connection with the taxpayer's trade or business.[4] To qualify, the loan must be closely related to the taxpayer's business activity. Simply making a loan to a business associate does not make the loan business related; it must support the business activity. Common business bad debts include the following:

1. Uncollectible accounts receivable (for accrual basis taxpayers only)

2. Loans to suppliers to ensure a reliable source of materials

3. Loans to customers, clients, and others to preserve business relationships or nurture goodwill

---

[2] § 166(d)(1)(B). See Chapter 16 for a detailed discussion of capital gains and losses.

[3] Reg. § 1.166-5(a)(2).

[4] § 166(d)(2).

4. Loans to protect business reputation

5. Loans or advances to employees

6. Loans by employees to protect their employment

7. Loans made by taxpayers in the business of making loans

It is important to note that corporate taxpayers are not subject to the nonbusiness bad debt rules.[5] All loans made by a corporation are deemed to be related to its trade or business. Thus, any bad debt of a corporation is considered to be a *business* bad debt.

Nonbusiness Bad Debts. A nonbusiness bad debt is defined as any debt other than one acquired in connection with the taxpayer's trade or business.[6] From a practical perspective, nonbusiness bad debts are simply those that do not qualify as business bad debts.

The most common nonbusiness bad debts are losses on personal loans, such as those made to friends or relatives. As suggested above, however, nonbusiness bad debt treatment also extends to loans that are made to make a profit and that essentially function as investments. For example, a loan to an acquaintance to start a new business is in effect an investment and thus a nonbusiness debt. Similarly, a loan to a business to protect an investment in such enterprise would be considered a nonbusiness debt. For example, an investor may loan funds to a struggling corporation in which he owns stock, hoping that the infusion of cash might sustain it and save the original investment.

Although the dividing line between business and nonbusiness bad debts usually is clear, controversy typically arises in several common situations. One troublesome area involves taxpayers who frequently make loans to make a profit but who do not make such loans their full-time occupation. In such cases, the Service takes the view that the taxpayers are not in the business of making loans and thus any bad debts are not business bad debts. These situations can become even more difficult when the taxpayer devotes substantial time and energy to establishing and developing the business.

Example 2. In *Whipple v. Comm.*, Whipple had made sizable cash advances to the Mission Orange Bottling Co., one of several enterprises that he owned.[7] He spent considerable effort related to these enterprises but received no type of compensation, either salary, interest, or rent. When these advances subsequently became worthless, Whipple deducted them as a business bad debt. The Supreme Court held that the loans made by the shareholder to his closely held corporation were nonbusiness bad debts even though Whipple had worked for the company. According to the Court:

> Devoting one's time and energies to the affairs of a corporation is not of itself, and without more, a trade or business of the person so engaged. Though such activities may produce income, profit or gain in the form of dividends—this return is distinctive to the process of investing—as distinguished from the trade or business of the taxpayer himself. When the only return is that of an investor, the taxpayer has not satisfied his burden of demonstrating that he is engaged in a trade or business.

---

[5] § 166(d)(1).

[6] § 166(d)(2).

[7] 63-1 USTC ¶9466, 11 AFTR2d 1454, 373 U.S. 193 (USSC, 1963).

Despite the Court's holding in *Whipple*, taxpayers have achieved limited success where they have convinced other courts that they were in the business of organizing, promoting, and financing businesses.

The other prominent area of controversy concerns a situation common to many new struggling corporations: loans made to corporations by employees who are also shareholders. Here, the issues are similar to that above. Is the taxpayer making the loan to protect an investment or to protect his or her job (i.e., the business of being an employee)? When employee-shareholders have been able to show that a loan was made to protect their jobs rather than their investment, they have been able to secure business bad debt treatment.

GENERAL REQUIREMENTS

To be deductible, the debt must not only be partially or totally worthless but must also represent a bona fide debt and have a basis.[8]

Bona Fide Debt.   A debt is considered bona fide if it arises from a true debtor-creditor relationship. For this relationship to exist, there must be a promise to repay a fixed and determinable sum, and the obligation must be enforceable under local law.

The question of whether there is valid debtor-creditor relationship usually arises when it appears that the taxpayer made the loan with little expectation of being repaid. This is typically the case where there is a close relationship between the taxpayer and the borrower. For example, loans to relatives or friends are likely to be viewed as nondeductible gifts rather than genuine debts. Such treatment is most likely where the lender makes little attempt to enforce repayment of the loan—a common occurrence when the borrower is a child or parent. In a similar fashion, advances to a closely held corporation that are not repaid may be considered nondeductible contributions to capital. On the other hand, loans made by a corporation may be something other than what they purport to be. For example, a loan to a shareholder may be treated as a disguised dividend distribution while a loan to an employee could be considered compensation.

To determine whether a bona fide debtor-creditor relationship exists requires an assessment of all of the facts and circumstances related to the debt. Besides the relationship of the parties, factors typically considered are (1) whether the debt is evidenced by a note or some other written instrument (in contrast to a mere oral promise to repay that has not been reduced to writing); (2) whether the debt is secured by collateral; (3) whether the debt bears a reasonable interest rate; and (4) whether a fixed schedule for repayment has been established.

Basis.   A taxpayer may deduct a loss from a bad debt only if he or she has a basis in the debt.[9] For this reason, cash basis taxpayers who normally do not report income until it is received are not entitled to deductions for payments they cannot collect. Their loss is represented by the unrecovered expenses incurred in providing the goods or services.

---

[8]   Reg. §§ 1.166-1(c) and (e).   [9]   Reg. §§ 1.166-1(d) and (e).

Conversely, accrual basis taxpayers who engage in credit transactions usually report income as it is earned. Accordingly, they may deduct bad debts for those amounts previously included in income. Uncollectible loans (as distinguished from accounts receivable) made by either cash or accrual basis taxpayers may be deducted, assuming the taxpayer has a basis for the loan.

> **Example 3.**   R is a tailor and uses the cash method of accounting. This year he made two suits for B for $300, which he never collected. In addition, he loaned $1,000 to a material supplier who left the country. Assuming both debts are worthless, R may deduct only the loan to the supplier for $1,000. No deduction is allowed for the uncollected $300 since R does not report the amount as income until he collects it and, therefore, has no basis in the debt. However, any expenses incurred in producing the suits (i.e., materials, etc.) are deductible.

Worthlessness.   Whether a debt is worthless ultimately depends on the facts. The Regulations indicate that a taxpayer does not have to undertake legal action to enforce payment or obtain an uncollectible judgment with respect to the debt to prove its worthlessness.[10] It is sufficient that the surrounding circumstances suggest that legal action would not result in recovery. Among the circumstances indicating a debt's worthlessness are the debtor's bankruptcy or precarious financial position, consistent failure to pay when requested, or poor health or death. As noted above, a *business* bad debt need not be totally worthless before a deduction is allowed. When events occur which suggest that the debt will not be recoverable in full, a deduction for partial worthlessness is granted.

DEDUCTION METHODS

For taxable years beginning after 1986, deductions for bad debts must be claimed using the specific charge-off method.[11] This method—often called the direct write-off method—allows a deduction only in the year when the debt actually becomes worthless. The reserve method, which allows deductions for estimated bad debts and is typically used for financial accounting purposes, was repealed for all businesses except certain financial institutions and service businesses by the Tax Reform Act of 1986.

The direct write-off method provides some flexibility in accounting for business bad debts. When the facts indicate that a specific debt is *partially* worthless, the portion considered uncollectible may be deducted, but only if such portion is actually written off the taxpayer's books for financial accounting purposes.[12] Any remaining portion of the debt that later becomes worthless can be deducted in subsequent years. Using this approach, taxpayers need not wait until the debt becomes totally worthless before any deduction is claimed. Alternatively, taxpayers can wait until the debt becomes totally worthless and claim the entire deduction at that time. Note that when the debt is totally worthless (in contrast to partially worthless), there is no requirement that the debt actually be written off the taxpayer's books.

---

[10] Reg. §§ 1.166-2(a) and (b).   [12] Reg. § 1.166-3(a).

[11] § 166(a).

Example 4.   K Company is a major supplier of lumber to homebuilders. One of its customers, which owed the company $10,000, fell on hard times in 1994 and declared bankruptcy. Because this event suggests that the debt is partially worthless, a deduction is permitted. K estimated that it would recover $7,000 of the debt, and therefore claimed a $3,000 bad debt deduction in 1994. The $3,000 amount was also charged off the taxpayer's books as required. In 1996 K Company actually received $1,000 and deducted the remainder of the loss, $6,000 ($10,000 − $3,000 previously deducted − $1,000 actually received). Alternatively, K may opt to claim no deduction for 1994 and deduct the entire $9,000 loss in 1996. Note that when the debt becomes totally worthless in either case, the taxpayer is not required to write the debt off its books for financial accounting purposes. The company should take heed, however. If the IRS later determines that the debt is partially worthless, no deduction would be allowed since the debt was not written off on the books.

Experience Method for Service Businesses.   Although the 1986 Act ostensibly eliminated the reserve method of accounting for bad debts, it provided an equivalent— but not identical—technique for service businesses. If a business uses the *accrual method* to account for income from services, the business is not required to accrue any amount that, *based on experience*, it knows will not be collected.[13] Businesses can take advantage of this exception only if they do not charge interest or a late charge on the amount billed.

As a practical matter, the actual use of this technique may be limited, since most service businesses are allowed and typically do use the cash method rather than the accrual method of accounting. Service businesses usually are exempt from the rule requiring use of the accrual method,[14] falling under the exceptions for sole proprietorships, S corporations, qualifying partnerships, personal service corporations, or taxpayers with gross receipts that generally do not exceed $5 million.

✔ CHECK YOUR KNOWLEDGE

Review Question 1.   Over the years Dr. D has done extremely well financially and has made a number of investments. Several years ago, her good friend T started a small amusement park with such attractions as a water slide and a miniature golf course. Needing some venture capital, T convinced D to lend the new business $50,000, which he would repay to D in three years with 15 percent interest. This year the note came due and T was unable to repay because his business had failed. How will D treat the bad debt?

D's loan did not arise during the ordinary course of business but rather was in the nature of an investment. Therefore, the debt is considered a nonbusiness bad debt and is deductible as a short-term capital loss (limited annually to $3,000 plus capital gains).

---

[13] § 448(d)(5).

[14] Subject to certain exceptions, § 448 requires corporations, partnerships with cor-porate partners, or tax shelters to use the accrual method of accounting.

Review Question 2.   T worked for P Corporation for 25 years. When the company began struggling this year, she worked without pay. The company finally went out of business this year, owing T six months of back pay. Does T have a business or nonbusiness bad debt?

Neither. Although most taxpayers would believe that they have a deductible loss, such is not the case. As a cash basis taxpayer, which T no doubt is, no deduction is allowed because she has no basis in her debt. Had she reported the income (i.e., had she been on the accrual basis), the IRS would be happy to allow a bad debt deduction.

Review Question 3.   At the close of 1994, Z Corporation, a lumber company, estimated that based on current year sales about $30,000 of its accounts receivable would be uncollectible. Therefore, in accordance with generally accepted accounting principles, the company adjusted its reserve account, charging bad debt expense for $22,000. May Z claim a $22,000 bad debt deduction for tax purposes?

For most businesses, the reserve method is not permitted for tax purposes. Since 1986 the law has generally required the use of the direct write-off method. Under this method, a taxpayer can claim a deduction for a bad debt only when the debt actually becomes totally or partially worthless. This requirement is relaxed for service businesses that are allowed to use a method based on their experience. Consequently, since Z is not a service business, it is not allowed to deduct $22,000 but only the amount that represents debts that are actually worthless.

CASUALTY AND THEFT LOSSES

GENERAL RULES

Unfortunately, as everyone knows, disaster may strike at any moment. Hurricanes hit, volcanoes erupt, and rivers overflow. Thieves steal, and people are mugged. The list of possible calamities is endless. Luckily, Congress has recognized that when such events occur they may seriously impair a taxpayer's ability to pay taxes. For this reason, taxpayers are generally allowed to deduct losses arising from casualty or theft. The special rules governing this deduction are the subject of this section.

   The Code generally provides that an individual's losses arising from casualty or theft are deductible regardless of the activity in which the losses are incurred. An individual's casualty and theft losses related to profit-seeking activities may be deducted under the general rules, which provide that losses incurred in a trade or business or a transaction entered into for profit are deductible.[15] In addition, § 165(c)(3) expressly allows a deduction for losses related to property used for *personal* purposes where the loss arises from fire, storm, shipwreck, theft, or other casualty.

---

[15]   §§ 162 and 212.

A deduction is allowed only for casualty losses related to property owned by the taxpayer; no deduction is allowed for damages the taxpayer may be required to pay for inflicting harm upon the person or property of another.[16] Further, the casualty must damage the property itself. A casualty that indirectly reduces the resale value of the property normally does not create a deductible loss (e.g., a mud slide near the taxpayer's residence).[17] Any expenses of cleanup, or similar expenses such as repairs to return the damaged property to its condition prior to the casualty, are usually deductible as part of the casualty loss. Incidental expenses that arise from the casualty, such as the cost of temporary housing or a rental car, are considered personal expenses and are not deductible as part of the casualty loss.

CASUALTY AND THEFT DEFINED

Casualties. The Code permits a deduction for losses arising not only from fire, storm, or shipwreck, but also from other casualties. While the terms *fire*, *storm*, and *shipwreck* are easily construed and applied, such is not the case with the phrase "other casualty." Interpretation and application of this phrase is a continuing subject of conflict. The courts and the IRS generally have agreed that to qualify as a casualty the loss must result from some *sudden, unexpected, or unusual event, caused by some external force*.[18] Losses deductible under these criteria include those resulting from earthquakes, floods, hurricanes, cave-ins, sonic booms, and similar natural causes.[19] On the other hand, losses resulting from ordinary accidents or normal everyday occurrences (e.g., breakage due to dropping) are not considered unusual and consequently are not deductible.[20] Similarly, no deduction is allowed for losses due to a gradual process, since such losses are not sudden and unexpected.[21] For this reason, losses suffered because of rust, corrosion, erosion, disease, insect infestation, or similar types of *progressive deterioration*, generally are not deductible. Unfortunately, the casualty criteria are vague, and the taxpayer may be forced to litigate to determine if his or her loss is sufficiently sudden or unusual to qualify. For example, the IRS has ruled that termite damage does not occur with the requisite swiftness to be deductible.[22] The courts, however, have found the necessary suddenness to be present in several termite cases and have allowed a deduction for the resulting losses.[23]

---

[16] *Robert M. Miller*, 34 TCM 528, T.C. Memo 1975-110.

[17] *Pulvers v. Comm.*, 48 T.C. 245, *aff'd.* in 69-1 USTC ¶9272, 23 AFTR2d 69-678, 407 F.2d 838 (CA-9, 1969).

[18] *Matheson v. Comm.*, 2 USTC ¶830, 10 AFTR 945, 54 F.2d 537 (CA-2, 1931).

[19] *Your Federal Income Tax*, IRS Publication 17 (Rev. Nov. 93), p. 190.

[20] *Diggs v. Comm.*, 60-2 USTC ¶9584, 6 AFTR2d 5095, 281 F.2d 326 (CA-2, 1960).

[21] *Supra*, Footnote 18.

[22] Rev. Rul. 63-232, 1963-2 C.B. 97.

[23] *Rosenberg v. Comm.*, 52-2 USTC ¶9377, 42 AFTR 303, 198 F.2d 46 (CA-8, 1952).

Thefts. Losses of business or personal property due to theft are deductible. The term *theft* includes, but is not limited to, larceny, embezzlement, and robbery.[24] If money or property is taken as the result of kidnapping, blackmail, threats, or extortion, it also may be a theft. Seizure or confiscation of property by a foreign government does not constitute a casualty or theft loss but may be deductible if incurred in profit-seeking activities.[25] Losing or misplacing items is not considered a theft but may qualify as a casualty if it results from some sudden, unexpected, or unusual event.[26]

> **Example 5.** H slammed a car door on his wife's hand, dislodging the diamond from her ring never to be found. The Tax Court held that the loss was deductible as an "other" casualty.[27]

LOSS COMPUTATION

The loss computation is the same whether the casualty or theft relates to property connected with profit-seeking activities or personal use.[28] As explained below, however, limitations on the amount of deductible loss may differ depending on the property's use.

The *amount* of the loss is the difference between the fair market value immediately before the casualty and the fair market value immediately after the casualty as reduced by any insurance reimbursement. Of course, when the property is completely destroyed or stolen, the loss is simply the fair market value of the property as reduced by any insurance reimbursement. Although appraisals are the preferred method of establishing fair market values, costs of repairs to restore the property to its condition immediately before the casualty may be sufficient under certain circumstances.[29]

For many years, a controversy existed concerning the deductibility of insured casualty losses for which taxpayers chose not to file a claim. The problem typically arises when taxpayers avoid filing a claim for fear that their insurance coverage may be canceled or its cost may increase. When this occurs, the Treasury is effectively acting as an insurance company, partially subsidizing the taxpayer's loss. In 1986 Congress eliminated the controversy for *nonbusiness* property by providing that no deduction is permitted for casualty losses of such property for which the taxpayer is insured, unless a timely insurance claim is filed.[30]

---

[24] Reg. § 1.165-8(d).

[25] *W.J. Powers,* 36 T.C. 1191 (1961).

[26] Rev. Rul. 72-592, 1972-2 C.B. 101.

[27] *John P. White,* 48 T.C. 430 (1967).

[28] Reg. § 1.165-7(a).

[29] Reg. § 1.165-7(a)(2)(ii).

[30] § 165(h)(4)(E).

Exhibit 10-1 *Computation of Casualty and Theft Loss Deduction*

Smaller of

        (1) Decline in value; or
        (2) Adjusted basis*

Less:

        Insurance reimbursement
        $100 floor/casualty if personal
        10% of A.G.I. if personal

Equals: Deductible casualty loss

*Adjusted basis, rather than decline in value, must be used if business or income property is completely destroyed or stolen.

The amount of the deductible loss generally is limited to the lesser of the property's adjusted basis or fair market value (decline in value if a partial casualty).[31] The lesser of these two amounts is then reduced by any insurance reimbursements. There are two exceptions to this general rule, however. First, for property used in a trade or business *or* for the production of income that is *completely* destroyed or stolen, the deductible loss is the property's adjusted basis reduced by insurance reimbursements. Second, losses to property *used for personal* purposes are deductible only to the extent they exceed a $100 floor. The $100 floor does not apply to property used in a trade or business or for the production of income. The $100 floor applies to each event, not each item. Further, if spouses file a joint return, they are subject to a single $100 floor. If spouses file separately, each one is subject to a $100 floor for each casualty.[32]

In 1982 Congress added a further limitation on the deduction for casualty or theft losses of property used for personal purposes. In addition to the $100 floor on personal losses, only total losses (after reduction by the $100 floor) in excess of 10 percent of adjusted gross income are deductible.[33] This limitation does not apply to property used in a trade or business or an income-producing activity. The computation of the casualty and theft loss deduction is summarized in Exhibit 10-1.

---

[31] Reg. § 1.165-7(b)(i).

[32] Reg. § 1.165-7(b)(4)(iii).

[33] § 165(h)(2).

Example 6. R had four casualties during the year:

Casualty	Property	Adjusted Basis	Fair Market Value Before Casualty	Fair Market Value After Casualty
1. Accident	Business car	$ 3,000	$ 9,000	$ 5,000
2. Robbery	Ring	500	800	0
	Suit	95	75	0
3. Tornado	Residence	50,000	60,000	57,000
4. Fire	Business computer	3,000	4,000	0

(handwritten: 5600 above $3,000 basis; 3100 above the After Casualty column)

R received a $600 insurance reimbursement for his loss on the residence. The deductible loss for each casualty is as follows:

1. The loss for the business car is $3,000 [lesser of the decline in value $4,000 ($9,000 − $5,000) or the adjusted basis of $3,000]. The deduction is *for* adjusted gross income unless it is related to R's business as an employee, in which case the deduction would be an itemized deduction.

2. The loss for the ring and suit is $475. The loss for the ring is $500 [lesser of decline in value of $800 ($800 − $0) or the adjusted basis of $500]. The loss for the suit is $75 [lesser of decline in value of $75 ($75 − $0) or the adjusted basis of $95]. The total loss attributable to the robbery is $575 ($500 + $75). This loss must be reduced by the $100 floor to $475 ($575 − $100). Note that the $100 floor is applied to the event, not to each item of loss. The loss, subject to the 10% overall limitation, is deductible *from* adjusted gross income.

3. The loss for the residence is $2,300 [lesser of decline in value of $3,000 ($60,000 − $57,000) or the adjusted basis of $50,000, reduced by the insurance reimbursement of $600 and the $100 floor]. The loss, subject to the 10% overall limitation, is deductible *from* adjusted gross income. Assuming R's adjusted gross income is $20,000, $775 is deductible [$2,300 + $475 − $2,000 (10% × $20,000)].

4. The loss for the computer is $3,000. Since the computer is used for business and is completely destroyed, the loss is the adjusted basis of the property regardless of its fair market value. The loss is deductible *for* adjusted gross income.

CASUALTY GAINS AND LOSSES

When the claims for some casualties are settled, the insurance reimbursement may exceed the taxpayer's adjusted basis for the property resulting in a gain. As discussed in Chapter 15, the Code provides some relief in this case, permitting the taxpayer to postpone recognition of the gain if the insurance proceeds are reinvested in similar property. Where the gain must be recognized, however, Code § 165(h) sets forth special treatment.

Under § 165(h), all gains and losses arising from a casualty unrelated to business or a transaction entered into for profit—*personal casualty gains and losses*—must first be netted. For this purpose, the personal casualty loss is computed after the $100 floor but before the 10 percent limitation. If personal casualty gains exceed personal casualty losses, each gain and each loss is treated as a gain or loss from the sale or exchange of a capital asset. The capital gain or loss would be long-term or short-term depending on the holding period of the asset. In contrast, if losses exceed gains, the net loss is deductible as an itemized deduction to the extent it exceeds 10 percent of the taxpayer's adjusted gross income.

Example 7.   T had three separate casualties involving personal use assets during the year:

			Fair Market Value	
Casualty	Property	Adjusted Basis	Before Casualty	After Casualty
1. Accident	Personal car	$12,000	$ 8,500	$ 6,000
2. Robbery	Jewelry	1,000	4,000	0
3. Hurricane	Residence	60,000	80,000	78,000

T received insurance reimbursements as follows: (1) $900 for repair of the car; (2) $3,200 for the theft of her jewelry; and (3) $1,500 for the damages to her home. Assuming T does not elect (under § 1033) to purchase replacement jewelry, her personal casualty gain exceeds her personal casualty losses by $300, computed as follows:

1.   The loss for the car is $1,500 [(lesser of $2,500 decline in value or the $12,000 adjusted basis = $2,500) − $900 insurance recovery − $100 floor].

2.   The gain for the jewelry is $2,200 ($3,200 insurance recovery − $1,000 adjusted basis).

3.   The loss from the residence is $400 [(lesser of $2,000 decline in value or the $60,000 adjusted basis = $2,000) − $1,500 insurance recovery − $100 floor].

T must report each separate gain and loss as a gain or loss from the sale or exchange of a capital asset. The classification of each gain and loss as short-term or long-term depends on the holding period of each asset.

Example 8.   Assume the same facts in *Example 7* except the loss for the personal car was not insured. In this case the loss on the car is $2,400 and the personal casualty losses exceed the gain by $600 ($2,400 + $400 − $2,200). T must treat the $600 net loss as an itemized deduction subject to the limitation of 10% of A.G.I.

YEAR DEDUCTIBLE

A casualty loss usually is deductible in the taxable year in which the loss occurs.[34] A theft loss is deductible in the *year of discovery*. If a claim for reimbursement exists and there is a reasonable prospect of recovery, the loss must be reduced by the amount the taxpayer *expects* to receive.[35] If later receipts are less than the amount originally estimated and no further reimbursement is expected, an amended return is *not* filed. Instead, the remaining loss is deductible in the year in which no further reimbursement is expected. If the casualty loss deduction was reduced by the $100 floor in the prior year, the remaining loss need not be further reduced. However, the remaining loss is subject to the 10 percent limitation of the later year.

> **Example 9.** G's diamond bracelet was stolen on December 4, 1994. Her loss was $700 before taking into account any insurance reimbursement. She expects the insurance company to reimburse her $400 for the loss. In 1994 G may deduct $200 ($700 loss − the expected reimbursement of $400 and reduced by the $100 floor) subject to the 10% limitation for 1994. If G actually receives only $300 in the following year, she may deduct an additional $100 (the difference between the expected reimbursement of $400 and the $300 received) subject to the 10% limitation for 1995. If the reimbursement was greater than that expected, the excess is included in gross income.

A special rule exists for the reporting of casualty losses sustained within an area designated by the President as a "disaster area." This rule permits the taxpayer to accelerate the tax relief provided for casualty losses by electing to deduct the disaster loss in the taxable year immediately preceding the year of the disaster loss.[36]

> **Example 10.** F, a calendar year taxpayer, suffered a loss in a "disaster area" from a flood on March 4, 1994. F may elect to deduct the loss on his 1993 return. If he has not filed the return by the casualty date, he may include the loss on the original 1993 return. If the 1993 return has been filed prior to the casualty, an amended return or refund claim is required. Alternatively, F could claim the loss on his 1994 return. In determining which year to claim the loss, F should consider the effect of the 10% limitation. For example, assume F had no other casualty losses in 1994 and his casualties in 1993 exceeded 10% of his 1993 adjusted gross income. F would derive greater tax benefits by deducting the loss in 1993 since the *entire* loss would be deductible, while the loss deduction in 1994 would be reduced by 10% of his 1994 adjusted gross income.

---

[34] Reg. § 1.165-7(a).

[35] Reg. § 1.165-1(d)(2)(i).

[36] § 165(i).

✔ **CHECK YOUR KNOWLEDGE**

Review Question 1.   While acting like a couch potato and channel surfing one rainy day, S felt a drop on the end of his nose. Then, all of a sudden, water started gushing out of the ceiling. S later determined that squirrels had eaten a hole in his roof. Can S claim a casualty loss deduction for any damage caused by the squirrels? What must S demonstrate before he can claim a casualty loss deduction?

In order to claim a deduction for an "other casualty," S must establish that the damage is sudden, unexpected, and unusual. As can be imagined, these standards are often difficult to apply. In this case, the IRS has ruled that no deduction was allowed since it is common knowledge that squirrels are destructive and because the roof holes caused by the rodents were not unexpected or unusual.[37]

Review Question 2.   In 1979 B purchased a music box as a Christmas present for his wife at a cost of $1,000. This year the box was stolen. It turned out that the music box was an antique worth more than $5,000. Because of the deductible on his homeowner's insurance policy, D received only $400 for his loss.

a.   Before considering any limitation, what is the amount of B's casualty loss deduction?

In the case of a casualty of personal use property, a taxpayer is generally allowed to deduct the lesser of the property's value or basis as reduced by any insurance reimbursement. As a result, B is allowed to deduct a loss of $600 ($1,000 − $400).

b.   After B found out that his loss in the eyes of the tax law was only $600, he went crazy. He said it was ridiculous to allow a deduction of only $600 when in fact his economic loss was really $4,600 ($5,000 − $400). Is B right or wrong?

B's belief that he has a $4,600 loss rather than a $600 loss is based on the value of the property. It is true that he has had an economic loss of $4,600, but he never had to recognize the increase in value from $1,000 to $5,000 as income for tax purposes. Therefore, the loss is measured from his basis.

c.   Answer (a) assuming the music box had been worth only $700.

In this case, the deduction would be $300 [(lesser of fair market value, $700, or basis, $1,000) − $400]. Note that B would probably believe this is unfair since he paid $1,000 for the box and was reimbursed only $400. However, the starting point for measuring the loss is the value; Congress did not want to allow a deduction for the loss in value that is not attributable to the casualty since to do so would allow the taxpayer to deduct a personal expense.

---

[37] Ltr. Rul. 8133097.

d. Even though B has a casualty loss, he will probably not receive any tax relief. Why?

Despite the loss, the deduction for *personal* casualty losses is subject to two limitations. The amount of the casualty (as measured above) must exceed the $100 floor per casualty and 10 percent of the taxpayer's adjusted gross income. After the 10 percent floor was added to the law in 1982, reported casualty loss deductions fell by 97 percent. Because of this limitation, a personal casualty loss must be almost catastrophic before a taxpayer receives any tax relief.

e. Answer (a) and (c) assuming that B was in the business of selling music boxes.

If the property is used in a trade or business, the taxpayer is entitled to a deduction equal to the basis of the property reduced by an insurance reimbursement. Consequently, in (a), where the box is worth $5,000 and has a basis of $1,000, the deduction would be $600 (adjusted basis $1,000 − insurance reimbursement $400). The same rationale provided for the solution in (b) above applies here. The deduction is limited since the taxpayer has never recognized the appreciation as income. In (c), where the box is worth $700 and has a basis of $1,000, the taxpayer is also allowed a deduction for $600 (rather than $300 as was the case when the property was used for personal purposes). Note that even though the value of the property is less than its basis, the business taxpayer is allowed to deduct the entire basis in the property. This treatment is allowed since the taxpayer would have been able to deduct the $1,000 in any event because the property is used in a trade or business. For example, the taxpayer would be able to claim a deduction when the property was sold or if the property was depreciable, through depreciation.

Review Question 3.   Checkers Pizza delivers. This year one of its cars was stolen. Does the $100 floor and 10 percent of adjusted gross income limitation apply in determining the amount of its casualty loss?

The $100 floor and 10 percent rule do not apply to casualties of property used in a trade or business or an income-producing activity. These limitations apply only to casualties of personal use property.

Review Question 4.   During 1993, the Smiths' house was destroyed by Hurricane Andrew. As a result, the Smiths moved into a motel until their home was rebuilt six months later. The cost of their motel stay was $2,000. May the couple deduct the $2,000 cost as a casualty loss?

No deduction is allowed. This is considered an incidental personal expense and is not deductible as part of the casualty loss.

NET OPERATING LOSSES

As someone once said, life is not always a bed of roses. This chapter, at least in part, is a testimonial to that. Debts do go bad, lightning may strike, and casualties can happen. Perhaps taxpayers can take some consolation in that in both of these cases, the government shares in the taxpayer's misfortune and provides some relief. Unfortunately, this section also dwells on the negative. For some taxpayers, income does not always exceed deductions. Businesses are not always profitable and catastrophic events may give rise to large expenses. In those lean or rotten years, the taxpayer may actually have a negative taxable income, usually referred to as a loss. When this happens, as might be expected, the taxpayer to his or her joy does not have to pay taxes. More importantly, the taxpayer may be able to use the loss to reduce his or her tax in a previous or subsequent year. This section examines this possibility.

In a year during which the taxpayer's deductions exceed gross income, the taxpayer is allowed to use the excess deductions to offset taxable income of prior or subsequent years.[38] Technically, the excess of deductions over income, as modified for several complex adjustments, is referred to as the taxpayer's *net operating loss* (NOL).[39] The Code generally permits the taxpayer to carry back the NOL 3 years and forward 15 years to redetermine taxable income.

Allowance of the net operating loss deduction reduces the inequity that otherwise exists due to the use of an annual reporting period and a progressive tax rate structure. For example, consider a situation involving two taxpayers, R and S, who over a two-year period have equivalent taxable incomes of $100,000 each. R earned $50,000 each year while S earned $300,000 in the first year and had a loss of $200,000 in the second year. Without the NOL provisions, S would *not* be able to offset his $200,000 loss against his $300,000 income and consequently would pay a substantially greater tax than R. Such a result clearly would be unfair since both taxpayers had identical taxable incomes over the two-year period. The NOL provision partially eliminates this inequity by allowing a loss in one year to offset income in other years.

CARRYBACK AND CARRYFORWARD YEARS

As mentioned above, an NOL resulting in the current year is generally carried back 3 years and forward 15 years.[40] The loss is first carried back to the third prior year (i.e., the earliest year first) and taxable income is recomputed for that year. If any loss remains after reducing that year's tax liability to zero, the remaining loss is carried to the second prior year and then the first prior year. If a loss still remains, the taxpayer carries it forward to the first year after the loss and so on up to the 15th year following the loss year. For example, a loss occurring in 1994 would be applied to taxable income of these years as follows: 1991, 1992, 1993, 1995, 1996, 1997, . . . , 2008, 2009.

---

[38] § 172.

[39] § 172(c).

[40] § 172(b)(1).

The taxpayer may *elect* to forego the carryback period and carry forward the loss instead.[41] The election is made simply by attaching a statement to the tax return for the year to indicate the taxpayer's intention of forgoing the carryback period. This election must be made by the due date of the return (including extensions) in which the net operating loss is reported. The election *cannot* be subsequently claimed or revoked by filing an amended return. This election normally is appropriate only where the taxpayer expects future profits. If future profits are anticipated, the taxpayer must determine whether carrying the loss back or forward will yield the greater tax benefit. This decision is often difficult since the taxpayer may be unable to predict the future with any certainty.

When the taxpayer carries the loss back to a prior year, the loss deduction is claimed on an amended return for the earlier year (Form 1040X). For this purpose, the statute-of-limitations period for returns of the earlier years normally is extended to three years after the due date (including extensions) of the return in which the loss is reported.[42] Alternatively, the loss may be claimed using Form 1045 (Form 1139 for corporations) for a so-called "quick refund." This form must be filed *after* the return of the loss year is filed and *within* one year after the *close* of the loss year. If the taxpayer fails to file Form 1045, an amended return (Form 1040X) may still be filed.

> **Example 11.** B, a calendar year taxpayer, reported a loss for 1994. He filed his 1994 return April 15, 1995. Under *normal* conditions, B must file an amended return for 1991 (the year to which the loss is carried) by April 15, 1995 (three years after April 15, 1992, the due date for the 1991 return). The Code, however, extends the period for filing an amended return for 1991 until April 15, 1998, three years after the due date of the return for the loss year. Alternatively, B may claim the loss using Form 1045 by filing the form before December 31, 1995, one year after the close of the loss year.

Where the taxpayer carries the loss forward, the loss deduction is claimed on the subsequent year's normal return (Form 1040).

If the taxpayer has losses occurring in two or more years, the loss occurring in the earliest year is used first. When the loss from the earliest year is absorbed, the losses from later years may be claimed.

NET OPERATING LOSS COMPUTATION

The term *net operating loss* (NOL) is defined as the excess of the deductions allowed over gross income, computed with certain modifications.[43] The purpose of the modifications is twofold. First, the net operating loss provisions are designed to permit a taxpayer a deduction for his or her true *economic* loss. Thus, certain artificial deductions that do not require cash outlays (such as the deductions for personal and dependent exemptions) are

---

[41] § 172(b)(3)(c).

[42] § 6511(d)(2).

[43] *Supra*, Footnote 39.

added back to negative taxable income. Second, the net operating loss provisions were enacted to provide relief only in those cases where there is a business or casualty loss. As a practical matter, a net operating loss is caused by one of the following:

- Loss from operating a sole proprietorship (e.g., a loss on Schedule C)

- Loss from rental operations in which the taxpayer actively participates subject to certain limitations

- Share of an S corporation or partnership loss

- A casualty or theft loss

Since the NOL provisions generally allow only for the carryback or carryforward of losses attributable to business or casualty, restrictions are imposed on the amount of nonbusiness expenses that may be deducted in computing the NOL. As will be seen, it is these limitations on the deduction of nonbusiness expenses and losses that make the computation of the NOL deduction so complex.

The net operating loss deduction of an individual taxpayer is computed by making the following modifications in computing taxable income.[44]

1. Any net operating loss deduction carried forward or carried back from another year is not allowed.

2. The deduction for personal and dependent exemptions is not allowed.

3. Deductions for capital losses and nonbusiness expenses are limited as explained below.

To determine the extent of any deduction for capital losses and nonbusiness expenses, gross income must be classified into *four* categories: (1) capital gains from business; (2) other income from business; (3) capital gains not from business; and (4) other income not from business. With income so classified, the following rules are applied with respect to nonbusiness expenses and capital losses in the following order: [45]

1. Nonbusiness capital losses may be deducted to the extent of any nonbusiness capital gains; thus, any excess is added back to taxable income.

2. Nonbusiness expenses may be deducted to the extent of any nonbusiness income, including any excess of nonbusiness capital gains over nonbusiness capital losses (as determined in step 1); thus, any excess is added back to taxable income.

3. Business capital losses may be deducted to the extent of any business capital gains; any excess business capital losses may be deducted to the extent of any excess of nonbusiness capital gains over nonbusiness capital losses and nonbusiness expenses (as determined in step 2).

---

[44] § 172(d)(1) through (4).   [45] § 172(d)(4).

A general formula for computing the NOL deduction is set forth in Exhibit 10-2. As may be surmised from the previous discussion and the formula, the critical first step when actually calculating the deduction is classifying income and deductions, gains and losses as either business or nonbusiness. Exhibit 10-3 identifies and classifies the most common items appearing on tax returns.

> **Example 12.**   In 1994 G quit his job and opened a car repair shop. G's filing status is married, filing jointly, and he reported the following income and deductions for the year:

Income

Business income...	$40,000
Salary from previous job..	10,000
Business capital gains—long term.............................	7,000
Business capital losses—long term............................	(2,000)
Nonbusiness capital gains—long term.........................	5,000
Nonbusiness capital losses—long term........................	(3,000)
Interest income on nonbusiness investments...................	1,000

Expenses

Business expenses...	70,000
Casualty loss on personal car.................................	5,100
Intertest on home mortgage....................................	8,000

Taxable income is computed as follows:

Net business loss ($40,000 − $70,000)........................		($30,000)
Salary..		10,000
Interest earned...		1,000
Net long-term capital gain....................................		7,000
Adjusted gross income (loss).................................		($12,000)
Less: Itemized deductions		
Casualty loss..................................	$5,000*	
Mortgage interest paid.........................	8,000	(13,000)
Less: Personal exemptions..............................		(4,900)
Taxable income (loss)..		($29,900)

* $5,100 − $100 floor. Note that the 10 percent limitation does not apply since A.G.I. is a negative number.

Following the format of Exhibit 10-2, G's net operating loss for 1994 is computed as follows:

Taxable income (loss)............................			($29,900)
Modifications			
Add back:			
Personal exemptions..........................			4,900
Excess nonbusiness expenses:			
Mortgage interest...........................		$8,000	
Nonbusiness income:			
Interest................................	$1,000		
Nonbusiness net capital			
gain ($5,000 − $3,000)..............	+ 2,000	(3,000)	5,000
Net operating loss for 1994....................			($20,000)

Computation of the real dollar loss or economic loss results in a similar deduction:

Business loss.................................	($30,000)
+ Salary...................................	10,000
+ Business capital gains...................	5,000
− Casualty loss...........................	(5,000)
Net operating loss............................	($20,000)

Note that the nonbusiness income (capital gains of $2,000 and interest income of $1,000) is not considered in this computation of economic loss since it is offset by nonbusiness expenses.

RECOMPUTING TAXABLE INCOME FOR YEAR TO WHICH NET OPERATING LOSS IS CARRIED

Once the net operating loss deduction is computed, it is carried to the appropriate year and used in the recomputation of taxable income for that year. The net operating loss deduction is a deduction *for* A.G.I. As a result, the deduction may have an effect on the amount of the deduction for certain items such as medical expenses, which are based on the taxpayer's A.G.I. All expenses based on A.G.I. except charitable contributions must be *recomputed* in determining the revised taxable income.[46] The net operating loss deduction also may have an effect on any tax credits originally claimed. For example, if a 1997 net operating loss deduction completely eliminates the taxable income of 1994, any credit originally claimed in 1994 becomes available for use in another year.

After the effect on the tax of the earliest year is computed, the amount of any loss remaining to be carried forward must be determined. In other words, a computation is required to determine how much of the net operating loss is absorbed in the year to which it is carried and how much may be carried to subsequent years. Although this calculation is somewhat similar to that explained above, additional nuances exist making the computation somewhat complex. For this reason, further reference should be made to the Regulations and Form 1045.

---

[46]   Reg. § 1.172-5(a)(3)(ii).

Exhibit 10-2 *Computation of Net Operating Loss*

Taxable loss shown on return

Add back:
Exemptions

Nonbusiness deductions
Less:
Nonbusiness ordinary income
Nonbusiness net capital gain

Nonbusiness capital losses
Less:
Nonbusiness capital gains

Business capital losses
Less:
Nonbusiness net capital gains
Less: (Nonbusiness deductions − nonbusiness income)

Equals: Net Operating Loss Deduction

Exhibit 10-3 *Calculation of Net Operating Loss Deduction:*
Classification of Business and Nonbusiness Income and Expenses

Business income

Salaries and wages
Schedule C income
Rental income
Farm income
Partnership and S corporation income
  if not passive
Gains from sale of business assets

Nonbusiness income

Interest income
Dividends
Pension income
Annuity income
Partnership and S corporation income
  if passive
Gain from sale of capital assets
  not used in business (such as stocks)

Business deductions

Schedule C expenses
Rental expenses
Farm expenses
Partnership and S corporation loss
  if not passive
Casualty or theft losses
  (business and personal)
Loss on sale of § 1244 stock
Miscellaneous itemized deductions for business
Moving expenses

Nonbusiness expenses

Standard deduction
Itemized deductions including
  medical, interest, taxes, contributions
Partnership and S corporation loss
  if passive
IRA contribution
Contribution to self-employed retirement plan
Alimony

✔ CHECK YOUR KNOWLEDGE

During 1994, C.D. opened his own computer store, specializing in sales of multimedia. He operated the business as an S corporation. Upon his first crack at computing his taxable income for the year, C.D. determined that he had a negative taxable income of $15,000 (see line 37, page 2 of Form 1040).

Review Question 1.   Assuming C.D. has a net operating loss for the year, how is it treated?

An NOL is generally carried back 3 years and forward 15 years. The 1994 loss is carried back to the third prior year (i.e., the earliest year, 1991), where taxable income is recomputed and a refund claim is filed. If any loss remains after reducing the taxable income of 1991 to zero, the loss is carried forward to the second prior year and then the first prior year. If a loss still remains, C.D. may carry it forward for up to 15 years, after which any remaining loss expires and is lost. Alternatively, C.D. may elect not to carry the loss back but to carry the loss forward for 15 years. Carrying forward the loss may make more sense if he expects to be in a tax bracket in the future that is higher than past years. In such case, the loss would produce greater benefit.

Review Question 2.   A review of C.D.'s tax return reveals that his negative taxable income of $15,000 includes several items of income and deductions. For example, his only income other than that related to his business was interest and dividends of $5,000. Indicate whether the following deductions would be allowed in computing C.D.'s net operating loss deduction and, if so, how much could be used.

a.   Personal exemption
b.   Dependency exemption
c.   Net loss from S corporation operations (sales less operating expenses)
d.   Casualty loss to personal residence from earthquake damage
e.   Interest expense on the mortgage on his personal residence of $7,000
f.   Net capital loss $8,000 ($3,000 used to offset ordinary income and $5,000 carried over)

In computing his net operating loss deduction, C.D. must make certain adjustments to negative taxable income to arrive at the taxpayer's true economic loss that the law allows to be carried over. No deduction is allowed for personal or dependency exemptions since these are artificial deductions. Therefore, the exemption deduction must be added back to negative taxable income. The net loss from his business (i.e., the S corporation) does reduce taxable income in calculating the NOL, so there is no adjustment. The casualty loss is also allowable in computing the NOL. Nonbusiness expenses such as mortgage interest and taxes are considered personal expenses and can be deducted only to the extent of nonbusiness income. Therefore, only $5,000 of the $7,000 expense is deductible, requiring an addback of $2,000. Finally, a capital loss can generally be used only to offset capital gains. Thus the $3,000 deduction attributable to the capital loss is not allowed and must be added back.

INVENTORIES

As might be expected, taxpayers who buy or produce merchandise for subsequent sale are not allowed to deduct the costs of the merchandise *at the time* the goods are produced or purchased. Instead, such costs normally must be capitalized (i.e., inventoried) and deducted when the goods are sold. The following example illustrates what might occur if taxpayers were not required to capitalize the costs of inventory.

> **Example 13.**   C Corporation began business in 1994 and purchased 10,000 gizmos at $10 each for a total of $100,000. In 1994 the corporation sold 6,000 gizmos for $120,000. In 1995 the corporation made no further purchases and sold the remaining 4,000 gizmos for $80,000. Gross profit reported with and without inventories is computed below.
>
> | | No Inventories | | Inventories | |
> | --- | --- | --- | --- | --- |
> | | *1994* | *1995* | *1994* | *1995* |
> | Sales.................................... | $120,000 | $80,000 | $120,000 | $80,000 |
> | Cost of goods sold: | | | | |
> | Beginning inventory.................. | – | – | – | $40,000 |
> | +Purchases......................... | $100,000 | – | $100,000 | – |
> | –Ending inventory.................... | – | – | (40,000) | – |
> | Costs of goods sold (4,000 @ $10)..... | $100,000 | – | $ 60,000 | $40,000 |
> | Gross profit........................... | $ 20,000 | $80,000 | $ 60,000 | $40,000 |
>
> Although the total income for the two-year period is the same under either method ($100,000), the time when it is reported differs significantly. The use of inventories produces higher income and higher taxes in the first year because only the costs of goods actually sold are deducted.

As the preceding example shows, the lack of inventories causes a mismatching of revenues and expenses and with it the possibility of widely fluctuating incomes. Without inventories, the income reported in any one year would in most cases represent a distorted picture—not a clear reflection—of how well the firm was doing. Perhaps what is more crucial, at least from the Treasury's point of view, is that taxpayers would be able to postpone the payment of taxes if inventories were not required. Note in *Example 13* that absent inventories, the taxpayer is able to defer $40,000 ($60,000 − $20,000) of income and the corresponding tax from 1994 to 1995. Congress recognized these possibilities at an early date and in 1918 took corrective action that is still intact today. Currently, Code § 471 provides the following:

> Whenever in the opinion of the Secretary the use of inventories is necessary in order clearly to determine the income of any taxpayer, inventories shall be taken by such taxpayer on such basis as the Secretary may prescribe as conforming as nearly as may be to the best accounting practice in the trade or business and as most clearly reflecting income.

With the enactment of § 471, Congress delegated its rulemaking authority concerning inventories to the IRS. The IRS has responded with a number of regulations indicating when inventories are necessary as well as what methods are acceptable for tax purposes.

The Regulations require taxpayers to maintain inventories whenever the production, purchase, or sale of merchandise is an income-producing factor.[47] As a practical matter, this means virtually all manufacturers, wholesalers, and retailers must keep track of inventories while service businesses are usually exempt. Note that inventories are required regardless of the taxpayer's method of accounting. Cash basis taxpayers must account for inventories as do accrual basis taxpayers. However, the mandatory use of the accrual method for purchases and sales does not prohibit taxpayers from using the cash method to account for other items such as advertising costs or interest income.[48]

A close reading of § 471 reveals that Congress has given the IRS two criteria to be followed in determining what inventory accounting methods are acceptable for tax purposes: (1) the method should conform as nearly as possible to the best accounting practice used in the taxpayer's trade or business; and (2) the method should clearly reflect income. Because of these requirements, the tax rules for inventory are quite similar to those used for financial accounting. Nevertheless, it is important to recognize that the IRS is the ultimate authority on determining what method represents the "best accounting practice" as well as what method most clearly reflects income. Consequently, as will be seen, taxpayers are sometimes required to adopt methods that vary from generally accepted accounting principles and cause differences between book income and taxable income.

There are three steps that must be followed in accounting for inventories and computing costs of goods sold: (1) identifying what costs (e.g., direct and indirect) are to be inventoried or capitalized; (2) evaluating the costs assigned to the ending inventory and determining whether reduction is necessary to reflect lower replacement costs (i.e., lower of cost or market); and (3) allocating the costs between ending inventory and costs of goods sold (e.g., specific identification, FIFO, LIFO). Each of these steps is discussed below.

COSTS TO BE INVENTORIED

The first step in determining costs of goods sold and ending inventory is identifying the costs that should be capitalized as part of inventory. Without guidance, taxpayers no doubt would be inclined to expense as many costs as possible. However, over the years, the IRS with help from Congress has established strict guidelines concerning what can be deducted currently (i.e., period costs) and what must be capitalized (i.e., product costs). The most recent development in this continuing debate was the enactment of the *uniform capitalization rules* (unicap) in 1986. As discussed below, the unicap provisions narrow further what the taxpayer is able to treat as a period cost.

As a general rule, the costs that must be capitalized depend on whether the taxpayer manufactures the goods (e.g., a producer of razor blades) or purchases the items for later resale (e.g., a wholesaler or a retailer such as a department store). When merchandise is bought for resale, the taxpayer must capitalize as a cost of inventory the invoice

---

[47]   Reg. § 1.471-1 and Reg. § 1.446-1(a)(4)(i).   [48]   Reg. § 1.446-1(c)(1)(iv).

price less trade discounts plus freight and other costs of acquisition. Cash discounts may be deducted from the inventory cost or reported as a separate income item. In addition, certain retailers and wholesalers are subject to the unicap rules that require capitalization of particular indirect costs as discussed below. For manufactured items, inventory cost includes costs of raw materials, direct labor, and certain indirect costs. The unicap rules apply to all manufacturers.

Many of the problems concerning inventory involve the treatment of indirect costs. Various methods have been devised to account for these costs. For example, under the *prime costing* method only the costs of direct materials and direct labor are capitalized; all indirect costs are expensed. Another method, often advocated by cost accountants, is the *variable* or *direct costing* approach. This method capitalizes only those costs varying with production and expenses all fixed costs. Despite the acceptance of these methods for managerial and internal reporting, the IRS has outlawed their use. In 1974, the IRS issued regulations requiring all manufacturers to use the *full absorption costing* method.[49] Retailers and wholesalers were not subject to the full absorption rules, and, therefore, were not required to capitalize any indirect costs.

Under the full absorption method, direct costs of material and labor must be capitalized. The treatment of indirect costs depends on which of three categories they fall into: *Category 1* includes costs that must be capitalized; *Category 2* includes costs that can be expensed; and *Category 3* includes costs whose tax treatment must conform with their financial accounting treatment. A summary of these categories and what they include appears in Exhibit 10-4.

The search for additional tax revenues brought about a substantial revision of the treatment of indirect costs in 1986 with the enactment of § 263A containing the *uniform capitalization rules*. The unicap rules apply to all manufacturers. They also apply to any retailers and wholesalers if their average annual gross receipts for the past three years exceed $10 million. Although these rules replace the full-absorption costing method, in practice many manufacturers continue to use the full-absorption method with certain modifications to meet the unicap requirements.

Section 263A requires the capitalization of direct material, direct labor costs, and, most importantly, any indirect costs that, in the words of the Regulations, "directly benefit or are incurred by reason of the performance of a production or resale activity."[50] The effect of these rules is to require taxpayers to capitalize many costs that they previously deducted. The Regulatory scheme is shown in Exhibit 10-4. In general, the Regulations categorize costs as (1) those that benefit only production and resale activities (must capitalize); (2) those that benefit only policy and management functions (do not capitalize); and (3) those that benefit both production and resale activities and policy and management functions, referred to as mixed service costs (capitalized by using any reasonable basis to allocate costs between production and policy functions).

The practical effect of the enactment of the uniform capitalization rules was to require taxpayers to adjust their accounting systems to capture the additional costs required to be capitalized. This was no small task, particularly for retailers and wholesalers that

---

[49] Reg. § 1.471-11. Absorption costing is currently used for financial statement purposes.

[50] Reg. §1.263A-1T(b)(2)(ii).

Exhibit 10-4   *Capitalizable Costs Full-Absorption vs. Uniform Capitalization*

Direct costs	Full-absorption	Unicap
Direct material	C	C
Direct labor	C	C
Indirect costs		
Repairs/maintenance (equipment and facilities)	C	C
Utilities (equipment and facilities)	C	C
Rent (equipment and facilities)	C	C
Indirect labor	C	C
Indirect material and supplies	C	C
Small tools and equipment	C	C
Quality control and inspection	C	C
Taxes other than income taxes	F	C
Depreciation and depletion for books	F	C
Depreciation and depletion: excess tax	E	C
Insurance (facilities, contents, equipment)	F	C
Current pension costs	F	C
Past service pension costs	E	C
Bidding expenses–successful bids	E	C
Engineering and design	E	C
Warehousing, purchasing, handling and general and administrative related to such functions	E	C

C: Capitalize
E: Expense currently
F: Follows financial statement treatment

* Capitalized if the produced property has a life of 20 years or more, if the property has an estimated production period of more than two years, or if the production period exceeds one year and the cost exceeds $1 million. Does not apply to property acquired for resale.

---

previously had never had to capitalize any indirect costs. As can be seen in Exhibit 10-4, the current scheme requires large retailers and wholesalers to capitalize any costs related to offsite storage (e.g., operating a warehouse), purchasing, or handling and an allocable portion of general and administrative costs. To provide all affected taxpayers with some relief, the IRS has provided several simplified techniques to account for these costs detailed in the Regulations.

ALLOCATING INVENTORIABLE COSTS

After total product costs for the year have been identified, these costs along with the cost of beginning inventory must be allocated between the goods sold during the year and ending inventory. If each item sold could be identified (e.g., a car or jewelry) or all items had the same cost, there would be little difficulty in determining the cost of items sold and those still on hand. As a practical matter, these conditions rarely exist.

Exhibit 10-4 *Continued*

Policy and Management	Full-absorption	Unicap
Marketing, selling, advertising, and distribution	E	E
Bidding expenses-unsuccessful bids	E	E
Research and experimental expenses	E	E
Losses	E	E
Depreciation on idle equipment or facilities	E	E
Income taxes	F	C
Strike costs	F	E

Interest	E	*

Mixed Service Costs		
Administrative/coordination of production or resale	F	C
Personnel department	E	C
Purchasing department	E	C
Materials handling and warehousing	E	C
Accounting and data servicing departments	E	C
Data processing	E	C
Security services	E	C
Legal department providing services to production	E	C
Overall management and policies	E	E
General business planning	E	E
Financial accounting	E	E
General financial planning	E	E
General economic analysis and forecasting	E	E
Internal audit	E	E
Shareholder and public relations	E	E
Tax department	E	E

C: Capitalize
E: Expense currently
F: Follows financial statement treatment

* Capitalized if the produced property has a life of 20 years or more, if the property has an estimated production period of more than two years, or if the production period exceeds one year and the cost exceeds $1 million. Does not apply to property acquired for resale.

Consequently, the taxpayer must make some assumptions regarding which costs should be assigned to costs of goods sold. Like financial accounting, the tax law does not require the cost flow assumption to be consistent with the physical movement of goods. There are several acceptable approaches for allocating costs: specific identification, first-in first-out (FIFO), last-in first-out (LIFO), and weighted averaged.

Example 14. K Corporation's inventory records revealed a beginning inventory of 300 units acquired at a cost of $3 per unit. This year the corporation purchased 400 units for $4 per unit, and it sold 500 units for $5,000. Gross profit using FIFO and LIFO are computed below.

	FIFO	LIFO
Sales (500 units @ $10)......................	$5,000	$5,000
Costs of goods sold:		
Beginning inventory (300 @ $3).............	$ 900	$ 900
Purchase (400 @ $4).....................	1,600	1,600
Goods available..........................	$2,500	$2,500
Ending inventory:		
FIFO (200 @ $4).........................	(800)	
LIFO (200 @ $3).........................		(600)
Costs of goods sold........................	$1,700	$1,900
Gross profit..................................	$3,300	$3,100

If K uses FIFO it is assumed that goods are used in the order that they are purchased (i.e., the first goods in are the first goods to be sold). Thus, the ending inventory consists of the most recent purchases, $800 (200 at $4 per unit). The effect of FIFO is to assign the oldest costs to costs of goods sold. In contrast, LIFO assumes that the last goods purchased are the first sold. As a result, under LIFO the most recent costs are assigned to costs of goods sold and the oldest costs to ending inventory. Thus, ending inventory under LIFO is $600 (200 at $3).

The preceding example illustrates the principal advantage of LIFO. In periods of rising prices, LIFO matches current costs against current revenue. From a financial accounting perspective, it can be reasoned that this produces a better measure of current income since both revenues and costs are stated on a comparable price basis, thereby reducing the inflationary element of earnings.[51] From a tax perspective, LIFO appears preferable because taxable income is typically lower and the corresponding tax is reduced. In effect, taxable income is not "overstated" by fictitious gains. Interestingly, LIFO became part of the tax law in 1939 for just this reason—to help businesses reduce the "paper profits" that conventional methods were yielding and that were being taxed at wartime rates of close to 80 percent.

It must be noted, however, that the advantage of LIFO is lost to the extent that sales in any one year exceed purchases (see *Example 14* above). In this case, the lower prices of goods purchased in previous periods are charged to costs of goods sold. This dipping into the past LIFO layers creates inventory profits, the specific problem that LIFO was designed to address. In a worst case scenario, a company that adopted LIFO

---

[51] Arguably, income results only to the extent that the sales price exceeds what it will cost to buy a replacement item for the merchandise sold. LIFO approximates this approach.

in 1939 might unexpectedly liquidate all of its LIFO layers, matching 1939 costs with 1992 revenues. This would no doubt lead to an unforeseen tax liability with little "real" income to pay the tax. This is a significant risk when LIFO is used. At the same time, it may represent an opportunity. Companies may be able to create income, if desirable, by liquidating LIFO layers (e.g., to absorb an expiring net operating loss).

DOLLAR VALUE LIFO

As a practical matter, applying the LIFO procedure to specific goods can be quite cumbersome and costly. In contrast to the simple one-item example above, most firms have hundreds or thousands of individual inventory items, and the number of units purchased and sold each period may amount to hundreds of thousands or more. Pricing each separate unit at the oldest costs and properly accounting for the liquidation of any LIFO layers might be a recordkeeping nightmare. Moreover, the major advantage of LIFO could be lost if old LIFO layers had to be liquidated because a specific item was discontinued or replaced. To address the problems of specific-goods LIFO, variations of LIFO have been developed. Perhaps the most widely used version of LIFO is the dollar-value method.

The dollar-value method reaches the desired result—eliminating the inflationary element of earnings attributable to inventory—in a unique way. Ending inventory is priced using the prices at the time LIFO was adopted (base-year). This value is then compared to beginning inventory to determine if there is a real increase or decrease in the pool of dollars invested in inventory. If there is no real change (i.e., ending inventory at base-year prices is the same as beginning inventory at base-year prices), the effect is to charge costs of goods sold with an amount reflecting current prices. On the other hand, if there is a real increase in inventory in terms of base-year dollars, the increase is valued at current prices and added to beginning inventory as a separate LIFO layer to determine ending inventory.

Example 15. T Corporation had an ending inventory on December 31, 1994 of 10,000 units at a cost of $20,000. During the year, T sold the original units and purchased another 10,000 units for $24,000. On December 31, 1995 ending inventory valued at current prices was $24,000. In such case, costs of goods sold would be $20,000, computed as follows.

Beginning inventory....................................	$20,000
Purchases...	24,000
Ending inventory......................................	(24,000)
Costs of goods sold..................................	$20,000

But what if, as the facts suggest, prices have increased by 20%? If so, the real amount invested in inventory has not changed ($24,000 ÷ 120% = $20,000). Consequently, valuing ending inventory at current-year prices of $24,000 (as above) effectively assigns the oldest costs of $20,000 to costs of goods sold, resulting in an inflationary profit of $4,000. Dollar-value LIFO eliminates this artificial gain—the objective of LIFO—by restating ending inventory at base-year prices. In this case, ending inventory would be restated at $20,000 ($24,000 ÷ 120%). This restatement would yield a cost of goods sold of $24,000, and would properly match current-year costs against current-year revenues.

Exhibit 10-5   *Double-Extension Dollar-Value LIFO Computation of Ending Inventory*

Step 1.   *Extension #1.* Value *ending inventory at current-year prices* (actual cost of most recent purchases, average cost, or other acceptable method).

Step 2.   *Extension #2.* Value *ending inventory at base-year prices.*

Step 3.   Compute current-year quantity increase or decrease by comparing beginning and ending inventories at base-year prices.

> Ending Inventory at base-year price (Step 2)
> −Beginning inventory at base-year price
>
> Current-year quantity increase (decrease) at base-year price

Step 4.   Calculate current-year price index.

$$\text{Index} = \frac{\text{Ending inventory at current-year price (Step 1)}}{\text{Ending inventory at base-year price (Step 2)}}$$

Step 5.   Compute the quantity increase or decrease to be added to or subtracted from beginning inventory.

    a.   For a quantity increase: convert the increase measured at base-year prices (Step 3) to current year's prices using the current-year price index (Step 4).

> Quantity increase at   Index   New
> Base-year price × (Step 4) = LIFO
> (Step 3)   Layer

    b.   For a quantity decrease: a current-year decrease consumes the layer(s) of inventory in LIFO fashion (i.e., the decrease must be subtracted from the most recently added layer). Previous layers are peeled off at the prices at which they were added.

Step 6.   Ending LIFO inventory is the beginning inventory increased by the new LIFO layer [Step 5(a)] or decreased by any liquidation of LIFO layers [Step 5(b)].

The important difference between dollar-value and specific-goods LIFO is that increases and decreases in inventory are measured in terms of dollars rather than physical units. This approach allows goods to be easily combined into pools and effectively treated as a single unit. Consequently, the likelihood of liquidating LIFO layers is reduced.

Although there are various methods of dollar-value LIFO, the most frequently used is the *double-extension method.*[52] The steps to be used in applying the double-extension method are summarized in Exhibit 10-5 and applied to the following example.

---

[52] Taxpayers may use the link-chain method or certain simplified procedures. See Code §§ 472(f) and 474 and the applicable regulations.

Example 16. In 1994 T Corporation elected to value inventories using double-extension dollar-value LIFO. Beginning inventory for 1994 consisted of the following:

Date	Pool Items	Ending Quantity	Current Cost Per Unit	Total at Current Cost
1-1-94	A	3,000	$3	$ 9,000
	B	4,000	6	24,000
Total base-year cost				$33,000

Inventory information for 1994–1996 and the computation of ending inventory using the steps in Exhibit 10-5 are shown below.

Steps 1 and 2: Double extend ending inventory.

			Ending Inventory at Current-year Prices		Ending Inventory at Base-year Prices	
Date	Pool Items	Ending Quantity	Current Cost Per Unit	Total at Current Cost	Base-year Cost Per Unit	Total at Base-year Cost
12-31-94	A	2,000	$ 4	$ 8,000	$3	$ 6,000
	B	5,000	7	35,000	6	30,000
				$43,000		$36,000
12-31-95	A	6,000	$ 5	$30,000	$3	$18,000
	B	7,000	9	63,000	6	42,000
				$93,000		$60,000
12-31-96	A	4,000	$ 6	$24,000	$3	$12,000
	B	5,000	10	50,000	6	30,000
				$74,000		$42,000

Step 3: Determine quantity increase (decrease) at base-year price.

	1994	1995	1996
Ending inventory base-year price......................	$36,000	$60,000	$42,000
Beginning inventory base-year price..................	(33,000)	(36,000)	(60,000)
Quantity increase at base-year price..................	$ 3,000	$24,000	($18,000)

Step 4: Calculate current-year price index.

$$\text{Index} = \frac{\text{Ending inventory at current-year price}}{\text{Ending inventory at base-year price}}$$

$43,000	$93,000	Decrease: use index at
$36,000	$60,000	which units were added

=	1.19	1.55	1.55

Step 5: Compute quantity increase or decrease to be added to or subtracted from beginning inventory.

	1994	1995	1996
Quantity increase at base-year price	$3,000	$24,000	($18,000)
× Index	× 1.19	× 1.55	× 1.55
= Increase or decrease to beginning inventory	$3,570	$37,200	($27,900)

Step 6: Compute ending inventory.

Base-year...	$33,000	$33,000	$33,000
1994 layer...	3,570	3,570	3,570
1995 layer...	—	37,200	9,300*
Total ending inventory................................	$36,570	$73,770	$45,870

* $37,200 − $27,900 = $9,300

THE LIFO ELECTION

Taxpayers may elect to use LIFO by filing Form 970 with the tax return for the year in which the change is made. Unlike most other changes in accounting method, prior approval by the IRS is not required. Conversely, the LIFO election cannot be revoked unless consent is obtained. As explained below, the lower of cost or market procedure may not be used with LIFO. Consequently, in the year LIFO is elected, all previous write-downs to market must be restored to income. For many years, the IRS required that all of the income due to the change had to be reported in the year of the change. In 1981, Congress expressed its disfavor with this view and enacted Code § 472(d). This provision allows the taxpayer to spread the adjustment equally over three years, the year of the change and the two following years. Nevertheless, if substantial write-downs have been made, there may be a considerable cost to elect LIFO.

Another ramification of the LIFO election concerns the *conformity requirement*. Under § 472(c), taxpayers who use LIFO for tax purposes must also use LIFO in preparing financial reports to shareholders and creditors. Failure to comply with this rule terminates the LIFO election and requires the taxpayer to change the method of accounting for inventory. As a result, taxpayers not conforming may be forced to give back any income tax savings previously obtained with LIFO.

The conformity requirement appears to have stifled the use of LIFO, presumably because during periods of rising prices it produces lower income and earnings per share than other inventory methods. This is true notwithstanding the tax savings that are available with LIFO and the relaxation of the rule over the years. The Regulations now permit the taxpayer to disclose income using an inventory method other than LIFO if the disclosure is made in the form of a footnote to the balance sheet or a parenthetical on the face of the balance sheet.[53] No comparative disclosures are allowed on the face of the income statement.

---

[53] Reg. § 1.472-2(e).

LOWER OF COST OR MARKET

In certain instances, the value of an inventory item may have dropped below the cost allocated to such items. When this occurs, financial accounting has traditionally abandoned the historical cost principle and allowed businesses to write-down their inventories to reflect the decline in value. The tax law has adopted a similar approach. Under the Regulations, taxpayers may value inventory at either (1) cost, or (2) the lower of cost or market.[54] However, the lower of cost or market approach may not be used if the LIFO method is used. Note that the lower of cost or market procedure deviates from the normal rule that losses are not deductible until they are realized.

In the phrase *the lower of cost or market,* "market" generally means replacement cost, or in the case of manufactured products, reproduction cost. When the rule is applied, the value of *each* similar item must be compared to its cost, and the lower is used in computing ending inventory.

Example 17. J's inventory records reveal the following.

Item	FIFO Cost	Market	Lower of Cost or Market
A	$ 3,100	$ 3,500	$ 3,100
B	5,100	3,000	3,000
C	6,000	7,500	6,000
	$14,200	$14,000	$12,100

If J elects to value inventories at cost, the inventory value is $14,200. Alternatively, if the lower of cost or market approach is elected, the inventory is valued at $12,100. This value is used because unsimilar items cannot be aggregated for tax purposes. For financial accounting purposes, J could combine the various items. Consequently, a difference may arise between book and taxable income.

The approach used above is that prescribed in the Regulations for normal goods. Note that these rules only allow a write-down to replacement cost. What if the firm believes that it will ultimately sell the item for less than what it would cost to replace it? Financial accountants refer to estimated sales price less costs of disposition as net realizable value. For tax purposes, a write-down below this value is allowed only for what are often referred to as "subnormal" goods.[55]

---

54 Reg. § 1.471-2(c).

55 See Reg § 1.471-2(c). Note that reduction of net realizable value by an allowance for a normal profit margin is not allowed for tax purposes.

Subnormal goods are those items in inventory that cannot be sold at normal prices because of damage (e.g., a dent in a file cabinet), imperfections (e.g., a thousand sweat-shirts with the logo improperly spelled), shop wear, changes of style, odd or broken lots, and so on. The Regulations allow the taxpayer to value these "subnormal" goods at a bona fide selling price less direct costs of disposition. However, this lower value is acceptable *only* if the goods are actually offered for sale at such price 30 days after the inventory date (e.g., cars with severe hail-damage are actually on the lot with a sales price slashed below replacement cost within 30 days of when inventory is taken).

Example 18.   In the landmark decision of *Thor Power Tool Co.*,[56] the taxpayer manufactured power tools consisting of 50 to 200 parts. Thor followed the common practice of producing additional parts at the same time it manufactured the original tool. This practice helped the company to avoid expensive retooling and special production runs as replacement parts were actually required. When accounting for these spare parts, the company initially capitalized their costs and—consistent with GAAP—subsequently wrote them down to reflect the decline in their expected sales price. The Supreme Court ultimately denied the write-down because Thor could not show that the parts (i.e., the excess inventory) were a subnormal good, and even if they had, the company had not actually offered the parts for sale at the lower price. The effect of this decision is to prohibit companies from writing down the value of slow-moving inventory.

---

[56] 79-1 USTC ¶9139, 43 AFTR2d 79-362, 439 U.S. 522 (USSC, 1979).

TAX PLANNING CONSIDERATIONS

CASUALTY AND THEFT LOSSES

Much of the controversy surrounding casualty losses results from insufficient documentation of the loss. For this reason, taxpayers should give careful attention to accumulating the evidence necessary to establish the deduction. Such evidence would include, where appropriate, pictures, eyewitnesses, police reports, and newspaper accounts. The taxpayer also should gather evidence regarding the value of the property damaged or destroyed. In situations where an item is not repaired or replaced, an appraisal may be the only method of adequately valuing the loss.

In some cases, a taxpayer may suffer a casualty loss and in seeking insurance reimbursement incur appraisal costs. Even if the casualty loss is not deductible due to the 10 percent limitation, the appraisal costs are deductible as a cost of preparing the tax return and are therefore claimed as a miscellaneous itemized deduction.

Taxpayers often measure the amount of their casualty losses by the amount paid for repairs that are necessary to bring the property back to its condition before the casualty. This method of measuring may be inappropriate, however, if the repairs do not restore the property to its same condition before the casualty. In such case, an additional loss representing the decline in value should be claimed.

The rules for determining the deductible casualty loss have important implications for the amount of insurance that a taxpayer should maintain.

> **Example 19.** T purchased a home in Boston for $70,000 15 years ago. This year, the home burned to the ground and the taxpayer received a $70,000 reimbursement from the insurance company. The cost of rebuilding the house was $200,000. Although T's economic loss was $130,000 ($200,000 − $70,000), none of the loss is deductible as a casualty loss. The casualty loss deduction is the *lesser of* the decline in value, $200,000, or the taxpayer's adjusted basis, $70,000, less the insurance reimbursement. Since the insurance reimbursement of $70,000 completely offset T's basis, there is no deductible loss.

BAD DEBTS

It is not uncommon for family members or friends to make loans to each other that are never repaid. This often occurs when a son or daughter is embarking on a business venture in which a parent is willing to invest. If the taxpayer wishes to claim a deduction if the debt is not paid, steps should be taken upon making the loan to ensure that the loan is not considered a gift. For example, the taxpayer should document the transaction in such a way that it is clear that both parties intend that repayment of the loan will occur. The best method of documenting the parties' wishes is to have a formal note drafted. Such a note would lend support to the argument that a debtor-creditor relationship existed between the parties. The note also should have a definite payment schedule, and each payment should be made on time. Collateral could be included as well. In addition, the note should call for a reasonable amount of interest. Failure to charge adequate interest could cause the imputed interest rules discussed in Chapter 5 to operate.

> **Example 20.**   In 1994 F loaned his friend K $10,000 to start a chocolate chip cookie business. The business struggled along, requiring K to ask F for another $5,000, which he gladly loaned her. The business failed after six months. If F documented the loans and sought repayment, he may claim a deduction for a nonbusiness bad debt. If he failed to do so, any deduction may be disallowed.

NET OPERATING LOSSES

When a taxpayer suffers a net operating loss, a decision must be made whether to carry the loss back or elect to carry it forward only. Due to the time value of money, a carryback is usually more advantageous since an immediate tax refund can be obtained. However, this gain must be weighed against the future benefits to be obtained by a carryforward. If the taxpayer expects to be in a higher tax bracket in the future, the present value of the higher savings may be greater than the value of an immediate refund.

PROBLEM MATERIALS

DISCUSSION QUESTIONS

10-1 *Business vs. Nonbusiness Bad Debts.*   R is employed as the chief executive officer of XYZ Corporation. Believing the company's future to be bright, he has acquired 75 percent of XYZ's stock. During the year, R loaned XYZ $10,000. Explain the tax consequences assuming XYZ is unable to repay all or a portion of the loan.

10-2 *Bad Debt Requirements.*   Under what circumstances, if any, is a cash basis taxpayer allowed to claim a deduction for a bad debt? An accrual basis taxpayer?

10-3 *Identifying Bad Debts.*   For each of the following situations, indicate whether the taxpayer would be able to claim a deduction for a bad debt.

a. Several years ago, F advanced $30,000 to his wholly owned corporation, which was experiencing financial difficulties. Last year he loaned it another $10,000. No notes were executed and no payments have been made. During the current year, the company declared bankruptcy.

b. E quit his old job as a salesman to become a sales manager for K Corporation this year. As part of his arrangement with K, he was to receive a $10,000 bonus if the company reached $1 million in sales for the year. Sales for the year were $900,000, and K Corporation did not pay E a bonus.

c. B and C each own 50 percent of ABC Incorporated. Over the years, ABC made loans to C. When C died he was penniless. He owed the company $20,000.

10-4 *Is There a Bad Debt?*   Several years ago, R's son, S, got in the restaurant business. R loaned S $10,000 to help him get the business going. No note was signed nor was any interest charged. The business was initially a huge success but as time passed, it began having financial problems. This year the son's business failed.

a. Can R claim a bad debt deduction? If so, is the debt a business or nonbusiness bad debt and how much is the deduction?

b. Same as (a) except R obtained a signed note from his son.

10-5 *Bad Debt of Related Party.*   H loaned her son $10,000 to enter the car repair business. If the son subsequently abandons the business and does not repay the loan, what are the tax consequences to H?

10-6 *Casualty Losses.*   Explain the rationale underlying the rules (lower of basis or value with certain exceptions) for computing the amount of the deduction for a casualty loss.

10-7 *Casualty Losses.* During the year, R had various losses. Explain whether each of the following would qualify as a casualty loss.

    a. Loss of stove due to electrical fire.
    b. Damage to water pipes from freezing temperatures in Southern California.
    c. Loss of tree from Dutch elm disease.
    d. Ruined carpeting from clogged sewer line.
    e. Hole in his suit from cigarette ashes he dropped; ruined shirt from pen leaking.
    f. Damage to both his and his neighbor's car while R's son drove R's car.
    g. Luggage and contents seized by a foreign government during a European vacation.

10-8 *Theft Loss Calculation.* If taxpayers could plan their taxes to account for thefts of their own personal use property (e.g., theft of their stereo and television), would they want the burglar to take all the property at once or take some property the first time and return for more later?

10-9 *Net Operating Losses in General.* Comment on each of the following:

    a. The purposes of the net operating loss deduction.
    b. The rationale underlying the complex calculation of the net operating loss deduction.
    c. How a net operating loss occurring in 1994 is utilized (i.e., the carryover process).

10-10 *Inventoriable Costs: § 263A.* HHG operates a chain of retail appliance stores. The company has grown tremendously over the last several years. It expects that its gross receipts will exceed $10 million this year. What are the implications of this growth for the company's method of accounting for inventories?

10-11 *LIFO vs. FIFO.* During the 1970s, there was a tremendous shift from the FIFO method of inventory to LIFO. Nevertheless, not every company shifted to the LIFO method. Discuss why some might shift to LIFO although others might not.

PROBLEMS

10-12 *Treatment of Bad Debts.* AAA Computer Company, an accrual basis corporation, installed a new computerized accounting system for a customer and billed him $1,500 in June, 1994. When aging its accounts receivable at year-end, the company found that the customer was experiencing financial difficulties.

    a. Assuming the company estimated that only $1,000 of the account would be collected, what is the amount of the bad debt deduction, if any, that it can claim in 1994?
    b. Would the answer to (a) change if the debt were a nonbusiness bad debt?
    c. In 1995 the company actually collected $200 and the remainder of the debt was worthless. What is the amount of the bad debt deduction, if any, that it can claim in 1995?

10-13 *Bad Debts and Accounting Methods.* Dr. D, a dentist, performed a root canal for a patient and charged him $300. The patient paid $100, then left town, never to be seen again. What is the amount of bad debt deduction, if any, that D may claim assuming that she is a cash basis taxpayer?

10-14 *Uncollectible Loan.* Several years ago, L loaned his old high-school friend B $5,000 to help him start a new business. Things did not go as well as B planned, and late in 1994 B declared bankruptcy. L expects to collect 40 cents on the dollar. In 1995 all of B's affairs were settled and L received $1,000. What are the tax consequences to L in 1994 and 1995?

10-15 *Personal Casualty.* When the waters of the Mississippi began to overflow their banks and flood the surrounding area, M was forced to leave her home and head for higher ground. On December 2, she returned to her home to find that it had been vandalized as well as damaged from the flood. After cleaning up, she determined that the following items had been stolen or damaged:

Item	Adjusted Basis	FMV Before	FMV After	Insurance Reimbursement
Fur coat	$6,000	$7,000	$0	$7,000
Computer	4,000	3,000	0	Uninsured
Couch	1,200	800	See below *700*	500
Van	7,000	5,000		

The couch had been damaged and M had it reupholstered for $700. The insurance company reimbursed her for the amounts shown on December 27. Under M's insurance policy, the company did not reimburse her for loss on the car until 45 days had passed. M expected to recover $4,000 but, after several delays, finally received a check for $2,000 on April 25, 1995. While she was waiting for reimbursement for her van, she rented a car at a total cost of $700. Although M received value for the coat, she did not replace it. In addition to the losses shown above, her real estate broker advised that even though her house had not been damaged by the flood, the value had dropped by $20,000 since it was evident that it was located in an area prone to flooding.

a. Compute M's casualty loss deduction, assuming her A.G.I. in 1994 was $18,000 and in 1995, $20,000.

b. Assume the loss occurred on January 2, 1995 and the location was officially designated a disaster area by the President. Explain when the loss could be deducted.

10-16 *Casualty Loss: Business and Investment Property.* H is a private detective. While sleuthing this year, his car was stolen. The car, which was used entirely for business, was worth $7,000 and had an adjusted basis of $12,000. H received no insurance reimbursement for his car. Also this year, his office was the victim of arson. The fire destroyed only a painting that had a basis of $1,500 and was worth $3,000. H received a reimbursement of $800 from his insurance company for the painting. H suffered yet another misfortune this year as his rental property was damaged by a flood, the first in the area in 70 years. Before the casualty, the property—which had greatly appreciated in value—was worth $90,000 and afterward only $40,000. The rental property had an adjusted basis of $30,000. He received $20,000 from the insurance company, the maximum amount for which homes in a flood plain could be insured. Compute H's casualty loss deduction assuming his A.G.I. is $30,000. Can a casualty loss create a net operating loss?

10-17 *Casualty Gains and Losses.* This year, C's jewelry, which cost $10,000, was stolen from her home. Luckily, she was insured and the insurance company reimbursed her for its current value, $19,000. In addition, while she was on vacation all of her camera equipment was stolen. The camera equipment had cost her $3,500 and was worth $3,100. She received no reimbursement since she carried a large deductible on such items. C's A.G.I. for the year was $15,000.

a. What is the effect of the casualty losses on C's taxable income?

b. Same as above except the jewelry was worth $11,000.

10-18 *Casualty and Theft Loss Computation.* In each of the following cases, compute the taxpayer's casualty loss deduction (before percentage limitations) and indicate whether it is deductible *for* or *from* adjusted gross income.

a. While G was at the theater, his house (adjusted basis $60,000, fair market value $80,000) was completely destroyed by fire. The fire also completely destroyed both his skiing equipment (cost $300, fair market value $90) and a calculator (adjusted basis $110, fair market value $80) used for business. He was reimbursed for $30,000 with respect to the house.

b. B owned a duplex which she rented. A tornado demolished the roof but did not damage the remainder of the duplex. The duplex's value before the tornado was $45,000 and after the tornado was $40,000. B's adjusted basis in the property was $30,000. The President declared the entire city a "disaster area."

c. Assume the same facts in (b) except that instead of B's duplex being partially damaged it was her personal cabin cruiser, and she received a $2,000 reimbursement from the insurance company.

d. L backed his car out of the garage and ran over his 10-speed bicycle (cost $400, fair market value $300). The bicycle is worthless.

10-19 *NOL Items.* Indicate whether the following items can *create* a net operating loss for an individual taxpayer.

a. Business capital loss

b. Nonbusiness bad debt

c. Casualty loss

d. Interest expense on mortgage secured by primary residence

e. Employee business expenses

f. Contribution to Individual Retirement Account

g. Alimony

h. Personal exemption

10-20 *Items Considered in Computing an NOL.* Indicate whether the following items are considered in computing the net operating loss deduction for an individual.

a. Salary

b. Capital gain on the sale of investment property

c. Interest income

d. Interest on a mortgage on a primary residence

10-21   *Net Operating Loss Computation.*   R, a single taxpayer, operates a bicycle shop. For the calendar year 1994 he reports the following items of income and expense:

Gross income from business..............	$150,000
Business operating expenses..............	210,000
Interest income from investments..........	7,000
Casualty loss............................	4,000
Interest expense on home mortgage........	9,000
Long-term capital gains (nonbusiness)......	3,000
Long-term capital loss (nonbusiness).......	5,000
Long-term capital gains (business)........	1,000

The casualty loss represented the uninsured theft of R's personal auto worth $4,100 ($9,000 adjusted basis).

a.   Compute R's net operating loss for 1994.

b.   Assuming R carries the loss back to 1991, when must the corrected return for 1991 be filed?

10-22   *Net Operating Loss Computation.*   V, married with two dependents, owns a hardware store. For the current year, her records reveal the following:

Gross income from sales...................	$180,000
Business operating expenses..............	230,000
Royalties from investment.................	6,000
Nonbusiness expenses.....................	9,000
Long-term capital gain (nonbusiness).......	5,000
Long-term capital gain (business)..........	3,000
Long-term capital loss (business)..........	3,500

What is V's net operating loss?

10-23   *Valuing Inventories.*   Chapters Inc., a large publishing house, prints a variety of titles, some of which are best sellers and others of which are duds. Because it is very difficult for Chapters to estimate with any accuracy which books will be successful, and because the marginal cost of printing an additional book is small, it typically prints 5,000 more copies than it expects to sell. Books that are not sold within a year of release are stored. The company's experience has shown that 95 percent of the books stored are never sold. Consequently, the company writes off any excess copies once they are delivered to storage. This practice appears permissible for financial accounting purposes. Can the same procedure be used for tax purposes?

10-24   *Applying Lower of Cost or Market.*   Fitness Galore specializes in selling physical fitness equipment. The company's inventory at the close of this year revealed the following:

Merchandise	Cost	Replacement Cost
Weight machines	$40,000	$43,000
Stationary bicycles	10,000	8,000
Stair climbers	24,000	27,000

a.   Compute the company's inventory assuming it uses the lower of FIFO cost or market.

b.   Assume the company adopts LIFO next year. Explain the tax consequences.

10-25 *Double Extension Dollar-Value LIFO.*   Unwound Sound has recently engaged an accountant to evaluate its inventory procedures and determine whether it should change from using FIFO to LIFO to account for inventories. The company's inventory records for 1993 and 1994 are shown below. Assume that the company had adopted double-extension dollar-value LIFO in 1993, and compute the ending inventory for:

a. 1993
b. 1994

Inventory Pool	1-1-93 Units	1-1-93 Cost Per Unit	12-31-93 Units	12-31-93 Cost Per Unit
Records	5,000	$2	3,000	$2
Tapes	4,000	3	6,000	4
Compact discs	2,000	6	5,000	7

Inventory Pool	12-31-94 Units	12-31-94 Cost Per Unit
Records	2,000	$3
Tapes	3,000	5
Compact discs	4,000	7

10-26 *LIFO Pooling.*   As shown in Problem 10-25 above, the inventory of Unwound Sound consists of records, tapes, and compact discs. Over the last 15 years, the components of the company's inventory have changed dramatically. Whereas once the company only carried records, now it also carries tapes and CDs. Unwound Sound expects that in the very near future it will discontinue selling records. Assuming the company uses LIFO, explain the advantages of having one single pool containing all three items rather than three different pools.

RESEARCH PROBLEMS

10-27 R has had several minor automobile accidents in the last two years. During the current year, R demolished his car (value, $7,000; adjusted basis, $8,000) when he ran into a telephone pole. He used the car solely for business. R decided not to report the accident to the insurance company and claim his reimbursement because he believes his insurance rates will be raised if he does. Will R's deduction of his unreimbursed casualty loss be allowed?

10-28 T, a cash basis taxpayer, paid a swimming pool contractor, C, the sum of $10,000 in advance for improvements that C agreed to make to T's personal residence. C performed part of the contract and then ceased activity, leaving much of the work uncompleted.

T seeks your advice concerning whether she may claim a deduction for a bad debt.

10-29   Ten years ago Mac and Beth left the stress of city life and moved to a beautiful home near Davenport overlooking the Mississippi River. Mac took a job as a dealer at a local riverboat gambling casino while Beth became a full-time mom. The couple was happily raising their four children until 1993, the year of the great flood. Their home, although several miles from the river, suffered thousands of dollars of water damage. Other homes in their small subdivision that were on somewhat lower ground had far worse damage. Mac and Beth and their neighbors were quite shocked that this could happen to them since they lived in an area where it had not flooded for over 100 years. But then some were calling this the 100-year flood. After cleaning up, several of the owners decided to move, not willing to take any more chances. Unfortunately, those people who were able to sell their homes sold them for far less than what they thought they were worth, presumably because they lived in what was now perceived as a flood-prone area. Although Mac was not planning on selling his home, he did decide it was time to refinance his mortgage, the second time in 18 months. As part of the process, he got an appraisal that revealed that the value of his home had dropped substantially from the last time it was appraised. In 1992, when he refinanced for the first time, it appeared that he had made a great investment since he had purchased the house for $150,000 and the house was appraised at a value of $225,000. However, the most recent appraisal revealed that the house was worth only $120,000. What is the amount of the couple's casualty loss deduction, if any?

LEARNING OBJECTIVES

Upon completion of this chapter you will be able to:

- Identify the personal expenses that qualify as itemized deductions

- Explain the rules regarding deductible medical expenses and compute the medical expense deduction

- Distinguish between deductible taxes and nondeductible fees or other charges

- Explain the rules regarding deductible state income taxes, including the proper treatment of such taxes by married persons filing joint or separate returns

- Distinguish between currently deductible and nondeductible interest expenses

- Explain the requirements for the deductibility of charitable contributions and compute the contribution deduction

- Identify the personal expenditures that qualify as either miscellaneous itemized deductions or other itemized deductions

- Explain the cutback rule applicable to certain itemized deductions of high-income taxpayers and compute their total deduction allowed

CHAPTER OUTLINE

Medical Expenses	11-2	Interest Expense	11-18
In General	11-2	Limitations on Deductions of Interest	
When Deductible	11-3	Expense	11-18
Deduction Limitations	11-5	Classification of Interest Expense	11-27
Special Items and Equipment	11-6	When Deductible	11-31
Special Care Facilities	11-7	Where Reported	11-32
Medical Travel and Transportation	11-8	Charitable Contributions	11-33
Medical Insurance Costs		Deduction Requirements	11-34
and Reimbursements	11-9	Limitations on Deductions	11-35
Health Insurance Costs		Contribution Carryovers	11-45
of Self-Employed Taxpayers	11-10	Miscellaneous Itemized Deductions	11-46
Personal Casualty and Theft Losses	11-11	Other Itemized Deductions	11-47
Year Deductible	11-11	Three Percent Cutback Rule	11-48
Reporting Casualty Losses	11-11	Tax Planning Considerations	11-51
Taxes	11-12	Maximizing Personal Deductions	11-51
General Requirements		Medical Expenses	11-52
for Deductibility	11-12	Charitable Contributions	11-52
Income Taxes	11-14	Miscellaneous Deductions	11-53
Property Taxes	11-15	Problem Materials	11-54
Reporting Deductions for Taxes	11-17		

Chapter 11

ITEMIZED DEDUCTIONS

Although the vast majority of deductions are those for trade or business expenses, a taxpayer's deductions are not confined to these alone. As noted in Chapter 7, since 1942 Congress has also allowed taxpayers to deduct expenses relating to profit-seeking activities—thus creating a *second* category of so-called investment or nonbusiness expenses. In addition, despite the fact that Code § 262 expressly prohibits the deduction of personal expenditures, Congress has created various exceptions. As a result, a *third* category of deductible expenses exists, which contains such personal items as medical expenses, casualty losses, interest on home mortgages, taxes on real and personal property, charitable contributions, and tax return preparation costs. The last four chapters have focused primarily on business expenses. This chapter continues the discussion of the three types of deductions by examining the specific statutory and administrative authority relating to personal itemized deductions. As defined in Chapter 3, these personal expenses are deducted by a taxpayer only if (1) they exceed the available standard deduction, or (2) the taxpayer is not eligible for the standard deduction.

Before considering these deductions in detail, it should be emphasized that a particular type of expense (e.g., interest) does not necessarily receive the same treatment in all situations. More often than not, the expense is treated differently depending on whether it is business, investment, or personal in nature. For example, the deductibility of interest expense generally depends on whether it is related to a loan that was used to make a business, investment, or personal expenditure. In contrast, real property taxes are deductible regardless of whether the property is used for business, investment, or personal purposes. The character of the expense may also affect the deduction's classification. Generally, trade or business expenses (other than the unreimbursed expenses of an employee) and expenses related to producing rents or royalties are deductions *for* A.G.I., while other expenses are *itemized deductions* which may or may not be subject to the 2 percent floor.

MEDICAL EXPENSES

IN GENERAL

Deductible medical expenses include amounts paid for the diagnosis, cure, relief, treatment, or prevention of disease of the taxpayer, his or her spouse, and dependents.[1] The status of a person as the taxpayer's spouse or dependent must exist *either* at the time the medical services are rendered *or* at the time the expenses are paid.[2] A spousal relationship does not exist if the taxpayer is legally separated from his or her spouse under a decree of separate maintenance because the two parties are not considered married.[3] For purposes of dependency status, however, *both* the gross income test and the joint return test are waived.[4]

> **Example 1.**   T pays all the medical expenses of his mother, M, during the current year. Although M had gross income in excess of the exemption amount ($2,450 in 1994) for the current year, all other dependency tests are met by T. Even though T cannot claim M as a dependent, he will be allowed to deduct all medical expenses paid on her behalf (assuming T itemizes his deductions and they exceed the percentage limitations imposed on medical deductions).

Medical expenses for children of divorced parents are deductible by the parent who pays for them, regardless of which parent is entitled to the dependency exemption. Additionally, if a taxpayer is entitled to a dependency exemption under a multiple support agreement, the taxpayer will be allowed to deduct any medical expenses which he or she actually pays on behalf of the claimed dependent.[5]

Medical expenses also include payments for treatment affecting any part or function of the body,[6] expenditures for certain medicines and drugs,[7] expenses paid for transportation primarily *for* and *essential* to the rendition of the medical care,[8] and payments made for medical care insurance for the taxpayer, his or her spouse, and dependents.[9] Again, the term *dependent* includes any person who would otherwise qualify as the taxpayer's dependent even though the gross income or separate return tests are not met, and any person claimed as a dependent under a multiple support agreement.

---

[1] See §§ 213(a) and 213(d)(1).

[2] Reg. § 1.213-1(e)(3).

[3] § 143(a).

[4] See Reg. § 1.213-1(a)(3)(i) and Chapter 4 for a discussion of the dependency tests.

[5] See § 213(d)(5) and Reg. § 1.213-1(a)(3)(i). Medical expenses taken into account under § 21 in computing a credit for the care of certain dependents are not allowed to be treated as deductible medical expenses. See § 213(e) and Reg. § 1.213-1(f) and Chapter 13 for a discussion of the tax credit allowed under § 21.

[6] § 213(d)(1)(A) and Reg. § 1.213-1(e)(1)(i).

[7] § 213(d)(2) and Reg. § 1.213-1(e)(2).

[8] § 213(d)(1)(B) and Reg. § 1.213-1(e)(1)(iv).

[9] § 213(d)(1)(C) and Reg. § 1.213-1(e)(4).

Partial lists of deductible and nondeductible medical expenses are presented in Exhibits 11-1 and 11-2. The most recent addition to the list of nondeductible medical expenses involves cosmetic surgery or other similar procedure. Cosmetic surgery is defined as any procedure which is directed at improving the patient's appearance and does not meaningfully promote the proper function of the body or prevent or treat disease. Thus, the costs of face lifts, liposuction, hair transplants, and other similar elective procedures undertaken primarily to improve the taxpayer's physical appearance are not deductible. However, deductions are allowed for procedures necessary to ameliorate a congenital deformity, a personal injury arising from an accident or trauma, or a disfiguring disease.

WHEN DEDUCTIBLE

In computing the medical expense deduction for a given tax year, the taxpayer is allowed to take into account *only* those medical expenses *actually paid* during the taxable year, regardless of when the illness or injury which occasioned the expenses occurred, and regardless of the method of accounting used by the taxpayer in computing his or her taxable income (i.e., cash or accrual).[10] Consequently, if the medical expenses are incurred but not paid during the current tax year, the deduction for

---

Exhibit 11-1 *Partial List of Deductible Medical Expenses[11]*

Fees paid for doctors, surgeons, dentists, osteopaths, opthalmologists, optometrists, chiropractors, chiropodists, podiatrists, psychiatrists, psychologists, and Christian Science practitioners

Fees paid for hospital services, therapy, nursing services (including nurse's meals while on duty), ambulance hire, and laboratory, surgical, obstetrical, diagnostic, dental, and X-ray services

Meals and lodging provided by a hospital during medical treatment, and meals and lodging provided by a center during treatment for alcoholism or drug addiction

Medical and hospital insurance premiums

Medicines and drugs, but only if prescribed by doctor (includes vitamins, iron, and pills or other birth control items)

Special foods and drinks prescribed by doctor, but only if for the treatment of an illness

Special items, including braces for teeth or limbs, false teeth, artificial limbs, eyeglasses, contact lenses, hearing aids, crutches, wheelchairs, and guide dogs for the blind or deaf

Transportation expenses for needed medical care, including air, bus, boat, railroad, and cab fares

---

[10] Reg. § 1.213-1(a)(1).

[11] See *Your Federal Income Tax*, IRS Publication 17 (Rev. 1993), pp. 166–170.

Exhibit 11-2   *Partial List of Nondeductible Expenditures[12]*

Accident insurance premiums
Bottled water
Care of a normal and healthy baby by a nurse*
Cosmetic surgery (with limited exceptions)
Diaper service
Funeral and burial expenses
Health club dues
Household help*
Illegal operation or treatment
Maternity clothes
Programs for weight loss or to stop smoking
Social activities, such as dancing lessons, for the general improvement of health, even
    though recommended by doctor
Toothpaste, toiletries, cosmetics, etc.
Trip for general improvement of health
Vitamins for general health

Note: A portion of these expenditures may qualify as expenses for the child or dependent care tax credit allowed under § 21. See Chapter 13 for further discussion of this credit.

---

such expenses will not be allowed *until* the year of payment. The IRS has ruled, however, that the use of a bank credit card to pay for medical expenses *will* qualify as payment in the year of the credit card charge regardless of when the taxpayer actually repays the bank.[13]

The *prepayment* of medical expenses does not qualify as a current deduction unless the taxpayer is required to make the payment as a condition of receiving the medical services.[14] Accordingly, the IRS has ruled that a taxpayer's nonrefundable advance payments required as a condition for admission to a retirement home or institution for future lifetime medical care are deductible as expenses in the year paid.[15]

> **Example 2.**   As a prerequisite for prenatal care and the delivery of her child, M prepays $1,750 to her doctor on November 15, 1994. Even though much of the prenatal care and the delivery of the child does not occur until 1995, M will be allowed to treat the prepayment as a medical expenditure in 1994.

---

[12]   *Supra,* Footnote 11, p. 167.

[13]   Rev. Rul. 78-39, 1978-1 C.B. 73.

[14]   See *Robert S. Basset*, 26 T.C. 619 (1956). Absent such a prohibition, a taxpayer could

maximize the tax benefits of medical deductions simply by timing the year of payment.

[15]   Rev. Rul. 75-303, 1975-2 C.B. 87.

DEDUCTION LIMITATIONS

The medical expense deduction was created by Congress with the stated social objective of providing individual taxpayers relief from a heavy tax burden during a period of medical emergency and thereby encouraging the maintenance of a high level of public health. However, the deduction was designed to provide relief for only those expenditures in excess of a normal or average amount. Currently, the medical expense deduction is allowed only to the extent medical expenditures exceed 7.5 percent of the taxpayer's adjusted gross income. This limitation ensures that only extraordinary medical costs will result in a deduction.

In addition to the percentage limitation imposed on the medical expense deduction, it is important to note that most of the everyday type of expenditures incurred by an individual for items incident to his or her general health and hygiene are excluded from the definition of qualifying medical expenses. For example, medicine and drug expenditures are deductible only if they are for insulin and *prescribed* drugs.[16] Over-the-counter medicines and drugs such as aspirin, cold remedies, skin lotions, and vitamins are not deductible. Other nondeductible expenditures are listed in Exhibit 11-2.

Example 3. F had adjusted gross income of $30,000 for 1994 and paid the following medical expenses:

Doctors	$ 500
Dentist	600
Hospital	1,300
Medical insurance premiums	800
Medicines and drugs:	
Prescription drugs	300
Nonprescription medicines	150

Assuming F is not reimbursed for any of the medical expenditures during 1994, her medical expense deduction is computed as follows:

Medical insurance premiums	$ 800
Fees paid doctors and dentist	1,100
Hospital costs	1,300
Prescription drugs only	300
Total medical expenses taken into account	$3,500
Less: 7.5% of $30,000 (A.G.I.)	− 2,250
Allowable medical deduction for 1994	$1,250

---

[16] § 213(b) and Reg. § 1.213-1(b)(2)(i).

SPECIAL ITEMS AND EQUIPMENT

The term *medical care* includes not only the diagnosis, treatment, and cure of disease, but the mitigation and prevention of disease as well. Thus, a taxpayer's expenditures for special items such as contact lenses, eyeglasses, hearing aids, artificial teeth or limbs, and ambulance hire would also qualify as medical expenditures.[17] Similarly, the cost of special equipment (e.g., wheelchairs and special controls or other equipment installed in an auto for use by a physically handicapped person) purchased *primarily* for the prevention or alleviation of a physical or mental defect or illness will be allowed as medical deductions. If the purchase of special equipment qualifies as a medical expenditure, the cost of its operation and maintenance is also a deductible medical expense.[18]

Capital expenditures generally are not deductible for Federal income tax purposes (i.e., depreciation is allowed only for property or equipment used in a taxpayer's trade or business or other income-producing activity). However, if a capital expenditure would otherwise qualify as a medical expense (i.e., it is incurred primarily for medical care), it will not be disqualified as a deduction. If the capital expenditure is for the permanent improvement or betterment of property such as the taxpayer's home, *only* the amount of the expenditure which *exceeds* the increase in value of the property improved will qualify as a medical expense.[19]

> **Example 4.**   After suffering a heart attack, T is advised by his physician to install an elevator in his residence rather than continue climbing the stairs. If the cost of installing the elevator is $6,000 and the increase in the value of his residence is determined to be only $1,000, the difference of $5,000 will be deductible by T as a medical expense in the year paid. Annual operating costs (i.e., utilities) and maintenance of the elevator also qualify as deductible medical expenses.

In two specific situations, any increase in value of the improved property is ignored (or deemed to be zero) for purposes of measuring the medical expense deduction. First, if permanent improvements are made to property *rented* by the taxpayer, the *entire* costs are deductible (subject to the 7.5% floor).[20] Likewise, the entire cost of certain home-related capital expenditures incurred by a physically handicapped individual qualifies as a medical expense. Qualifying costs include expenditures for (1) constructing

---

17 Reg. § 1.213-1(e)(1)(ii). The IRS has ruled that the costs to acquire, train, and maintain a dog that assists a blind or deaf taxpayer are deductible medical expenses (see Rev. Rul. 55-216, 1955-1 C.B. 307 and Rev. Rul. 68-295, 1968-1 C.B. 92). In the Committee Reports for the Technical and Miscellaneous Revenue Act of 1988, Congress indicated its approval of this IRS position and stated that similar costs incurred with respect to a dog *or* other service animal used to assist individuals with *other physical disabilities* would also be eligible for the medical expense deduction.

18 *Supra*, Footnote 11, p. 116.

19 Reg. § 1.213-1(e)(1)(iii).

20 Rev. Rul. 70-395, 1970-2 C.B. 65.

entrance or exit ramps to the residence; (2) widening doorways at entrances or exits to the residence; (3) widening or otherwise modifying hallways and interior doorways to accommodate wheelchairs; (4) railings, support bars, or other modifications to bathrooms to accommodate handicapped individuals; (5) lowering of or other modifications to kitchen cabinets and equipment to accommodate access by handicapped individuals; and (6) adjustment of electrical outlets and fixtures.

SPECIAL CARE FACILITIES

Expenses paid for emergency room treatment or hospital care of the taxpayer, his or her spouse, or dependents qualify for the medical deduction.[21] However, the deductibility of expenses for care in an institution other than a hospital depends upon the medical condition of the individual *and* the nature of the services he or she receives. If the *principal reason* an individual is in an institution (such as a nursing home or special school) is the availability of medical care, the *entire cost* of the medical care qualifies as a medical expenditure. This includes the cost of meals and lodging as well as any tuition expenses of special schools.[22]

> **Example 5.** T enrolled his dependent son, S, in a special school for children with hearing impairments. If the principal reason for S's attendance at the school is his medical condition *and* the institution has the resources to treat or supervise training of the hearing impaired, the entire cost of S's attendance at the school qualifies as a medical expense. This includes tuition, meals and lodging, and any other costs that are incidental to the special services furnished by the school.

If an individual's medical condition *is not* the principal reason for being in an institution, only that part of the cost of care in the institution which is attributable to medical care will qualify as a medical expense.[23]

> **Example 6.** T placed her dependent father, F, in a nursing home after F suffered a stroke and partial paralysis. Of the $6,000 total nursing home expenses, only $2,500 is attributable to the medical care and nursing attention furnished to F. If F is not in the nursing home for the principal reason of the medical and nursing care, only $2,500 will be deductible by T.

---

[21] This includes the cost of meals and lodging incurred as an in-patient of a hospital. See Reg. § 1.213-1(e)(1)(v).

[22] Reg. § 1.213-1(e)(1)(v)(a). See also *Donald R. Pfeifer*, 37 TCM 817, T.C. Memo 1978-189; *W.B. Counts*, 42 T.C. 755 (1963); Rev. Rul. 78-340, 1978-2 C.B. 124; and Rev. Rul. 58-533, 1958-2 C.B. 108.

[23] Reg. § 1.213-1(e)(1)(v)(b). This *excludes* meals and lodging and any other expenses not directly attributable to the medical care or treatment.

MEDICAL TRAVEL AND TRANSPORTATION

Expenses paid for transportation to and from the office of a doctor or dentist or to a hospital or clinic usually are deductible as medical expenses. This includes amounts paid for bus, taxi, train, and plane fares, as well as the out-of-pocket expenses for use of the taxpayer's personal vehicle (i.e., gas and oil, parking fees, and tolls). If the taxpayer uses his or her personal automobile for medical transportation and does not want to calculate actual expenses, the IRS allows a deduction of 9 cents a mile *plus* parking fees and tolls paid while traveling for medical treatment.[24]

Travel costs include *only* transportation expenses and the cost of lodging. For these expenses to qualify as a medical deduction, a trip beyond the taxpayer's locale *must* be "primarily for and essential to medical care."[25] Meal costs are deductible only if provided by a hospital or similar institution as a necessary part of medical care. Thus, meals consumed while en route between the taxpayer's home and the location of the medical care are not deductible.

If an individual receives medical treatment as an outpatient at a clinic or doctor's office, the cost of lodging while in the new locality may be deductible—but not the cost of meals. The cost of lodging will qualify as a medical expense if (1) the lodging is not lavish or extravagant under the circumstances; and (2) there is no significant element of personal pleasure, recreation, or vacation in the travel away from home. If deductible, the amount of lodging costs includible as a medical expense may not exceed *$50* for *each night* for each individual.[26] It is important to note that travel costs of a companion (including parents or a nurse) are included as medical expenses if the individual requiring medical treatment could not travel alone, or if the companion rendered medical treatment en route.[27] Thus, the lodging costs of such a person while in the new locality should also be treated as a part of any medical expenses (subject to the $50 per night limitation).

> **Example 7.** At the advice of a doctor, T travels with his three-year-old daughter, D, from Lincoln, Nebraska to Houston, Texas. D has a rare blood disease and a hospital in Houston is the nearest facility specializing in treatment of her disorder. The transportation costs and lodging for both T and his daughter while en route to and from Houston are deductible. If they stay at a nearby hotel while D receives treatment as an outpatient, the costs of lodging (but not meals) incurred in Houston—up to $100 per night—are also deductible.

---

[24] Rev. Proc. 91-67, 1991 I.R.B. 52, 11.

[25] See § 213(d)(2), Reg. § 1.213-1(e)(1)(iv), and *Comm. v. Bilder*, 62-1 USTC ¶9440, 9 AFTR2d 1355, 369 U.S. 499 (USSC, 1962).

[26] § 213(d)(2).

[27] See Rev. Rul. 75-317, 1975-2 C.B. 57.

MEDICAL INSURANCE COSTS AND REIMBURSEMENTS

Amounts paid for medical care insurance for the taxpayer, his or her spouse, and dependents qualify as medical expenses. If premiums are paid under an insurance contract which offers coverage beyond medical care (e.g., coverage for loss of life, limb, or sight, or loss of income), only the portion of the premiums paid that is attributable to medical care is deductible. To be deductible, however, the medical care portion of the premiums paid must either be separately stated in the contract itself, or included in a separate bill or statement from the insurer.[28]

Taxpayers receiving reimbursements for medical expenses in the *same year* in which the expenses were paid must reduce any medical expense deduction to a net amount. However, if the reimbursement is for medical expenses in a prior year, the income tax treatment of the reimbursement depends upon whether the taxpayer claimed a medical expense deduction for the year in which the expenses were actually paid. If no medical expense deduction was taken in the year in which the expenses were paid (e.g., taxpayer used the standard deduction or total medical expenses did not exceed the required percentage of A.G.I.), any reimbursement for such expenses will not be included in gross income. If the taxpayer claimed a deduction for the medical expenses in the prior year, however, the reimbursement must be included in gross income to the extent of the *lesser* of: (1) the previous medical expense deduction, or (2) the excess of the taxpayer's itemized deductions over his or her standard deduction. The inclusion in gross income of all or a part of the reimbursement is in accordance with the tax benefit rule.

> **Example 8.** T has adjusted gross income of $20,000 for 1994. During the year, T pays the following medical expenses:
>
> | | |
> |---|---:|
> | Hospitalization insurance premiums........... | $1,100 |
> | Doctor and dental bills....................... | 800 |
> | Eyeglasses................................... | 75 |
> | Medical transportation....................... | 25 |
>
> T's medical expense deduction is computed as follows:
>
> | | |
> |---|---:|
> | Total medical expenses................... | $2,000 |
> | Less: 7.5% of $20,000 (A.G.I.).......... | − 1,500 |
> | Medical expense deduction from 1994..... | $ 500 |
>
> T's itemized deductions (including the $500 medical expense deduction) for 1994 exceeded his standard deduction by $1,500. In 1994 T received $400 as a reimbursement from his insurance company. T must include the *entire* $400 in gross income for 1995. If T had received the $400 reimbursement in 1994, his medical expense deduction would have been limited to $100.

---

[28] Reg. § 1.213-1(e)(4). Participants in the Federal Medicare program are entitled to treat as medical care insurance premiums the amounts withheld for voluntary doctor-bill insurance.

Example 9.   Assume the same facts as in *Example 8* except that the medical expense reimbursement was $700 instead of $400. If the reimbursement was received in 1995, T would be required to include *only* $500 in gross income—the amount of the medical expenses included in his itemized deductions. If the amount by which T's itemized deductions exceeded his standard deduction was *less* than $500 for 1994, he would include in gross income for 1995 only so much of the reimbursement represented by the prior year's itemized deductions in excess of the standard deduction amount. However, if T had used the standard deduction in 1994, none of the $700 reimbursement would be included in 1995 gross income because T received no tax benefit in 1994.

The situations illustrated in *Examples 8* and *9* occur quite often because taxpayers are *not required* to reduce a current year's medical expense deduction by *anticipated* insurance reimbursements. Notice that this can result in a taxpayer receiving reimbursements early in the next tax year and not being required to pay income taxes on the reimbursement until April 15 of the following year.

HEALTH INSURANCE COSTS OF SELF-EMPLOYED TAXPAYERS

As part of the Tax Reform Act of 1986, Congress introduced a special rule allowing self-employed individuals to deduct 25 percent of the amounts paid for health insurance on behalf of a self-employed individual, his or her spouse, and dependents.[29] The deduction is allowed in determining adjusted gross income (i.e., a deduction *for* A.G.I.) rather than being treated as an itemized medical expense deduction subject to the 7.5 percent floor. The deduction may not be claimed, however, *unless* the self-employed individual provides coverage for all employees in his or her business and certain nondiscrimination requirements are satisfied.[30] Also, no deduction is allowable to the extent it *exceeds* the taxpayer's net earnings from self-employment.[31] Thus, the deduction cannot create a loss. More important, the deduction does not reduce the income base for which the taxpayer is liable for self-employment taxes.

Example 10.   K, a self-employed individual, paid $1,600 during 1993 for health insurance for himself, his wife, and their two children. K had no employees during the year. K is entitled to deduct $400 ($1,600 × 25%) in determining adjusted gross income, provided the deduction does not exceed his net earnings from self-employment, and his A.G.I. before the deduction is at least $400.

---

[29] § 162(m). This provision was scheduled to expire after June 30, 1992, but Congress has retroactively extended the deduction to July 1, 1992 through December 31, 1993.

[30] § 162(m)(2)(B).

[31] § 162(m)(2)(A).

Absent a special rule, self-employed individuals who are also employees might be tempted to opt out of an employer-provided medical insurance plan. By so doing, the 7.5 percent floor on medical expenses could be avoided and taxpayers could deduct 25 percent of what normally would be nondeductible premium payments. To prevent this course of action, the deduction is not allowed if a self-employed individual or spouse is eligible to participate in a health insurance plan of an employer.[32]

PERSONAL CASUALTY AND THEFT LOSSES

As discussed in Chapter 10, Congress has provided for a deduction of losses related to property used for *personal* purposes where the loss arises from fire, storm, shipwreck, or other casualty, or theft.[33] Like the medical expense deduction, the deduction for personal casualty and theft losses is designed to provide relief for only extraordinary losses. Thus, an individual taxpayer's deduction for personal casualty and theft losses is allowed only to the extent such losses exceed $100 per occurrence *and* the sum of all losses (after reduction by the $100 floor) for a given tax year exceeds 10 percent of the taxpayer's adjusted gross income. These deduction limitations were discussed and illustrated in Chapter 10.

YEAR DEDUCTIBLE

A personal casualty loss is generally deductible in the taxable year in which the loss occurs. Recall, however, that a theft loss is deductible only in the year of discovery. If a claim for insurance reimbursement (or any other potential recovery) exists and there is a reasonable prospect of recovery, the loss must be reduced by the amount *expected* to be received.[34] If later receipts are *less* than the amount originally estimated and no further reimbursement is expected, an amended return is not filed. Instead, the remaining loss is deductible in the year in which no further reimbursement is expected. Most important, if the casualty loss deduction claimed in the prior year was reduced by the $100 floor and exceeded the 10 percent A.G.I. limitation, the remaining loss is not further reduced. However, the remaining loss is subject to the 10 percent limitation of the later year.[35]

REPORTING CASUALTY LOSSES

Individual taxpayers are required to report and compute casualty losses on Form 4684,[36] which is to be filed with Form 1040. The casualty loss deduction, if any, is reported with other itemized deductions on Schedule A, Form 1040.

---

[32] § 162(m)(2)(C).

[33] § 165(c)(3).

[34] Reg. § 1.165-1(d)(2)(i).

[35] See *Example 9* of Chapter 10.

[36] See Appendix B for a sample of this form.

TAXES

Code § 164 is the statutory authority which permits taxpayers to deduct several types of taxes for Federal income tax purposes. If the taxes are related to an individual taxpayer's trade or business or income-producing activity, the deduction is generally allowed in arriving at adjusted gross income. However, both the IRS and the courts have taken the position that state, local, and foreign *income* taxes are deductible by an individual taxpayer *from* his or her adjusted gross income—even though it could be argued that such taxes are related to his or her trade or business. Likewise, if *property* taxes are related to personal use property (e.g., residence, car, etc.), such taxes are deductible only if the individual itemizes his or her deductions. If taxes are deductible by taxpayers other than individuals, the deductions simply reduce gross income to taxable income.[37]

The types of taxes specifically allowed as deductions under § 164 are

1. State, local, and foreign real property taxes;

2. State and local personal property taxes;

3. State, local, and foreign income, war profits, and excess profit taxes; and

4. The generation-skipping transfer tax.[38]

The generation-skipping transfer tax is imposed on income distributions from certain trusts. Discussion of this tax is beyond the scope of this text. However, each of the other three types of deductible taxes is discussed in detail below.

GENERAL REQUIREMENTS FOR DEDUCTIBILITY

A tax is deductible *only* if (1) it is imposed on the taxpayer's income or property; and (2) it is paid or incurred by the taxpayer in the taxable year for which a deduction is being claimed. Even if these two requirements are met, deductions for certain Federal, state, and local taxes are expressly denied. Exhibit 11-3 contains a list of nondeductible taxes. The most recent addition to the list of nondeductible taxes involves state and local sales taxes. Prior to 1987, if such taxes were paid or incurred in connection with a trade or business or for the production of income, taxpayers could either deduct the expenses or elect to capitalize the costs as part of the tax basis of the property purchased. Similarly, state and local sales taxes paid on purchases of personal use property (e.g., home furnishings, clothes, autos and trucks) were allowed as deductions if the taxpayer elected to itemize his or her deductions. Since 1986, however, no business *or* personal deduction is allowed for any tax paid or incurred in connection with an acquisition (i.e., a sales tax) or disposition (i.e., a transfer tax) of property. Instead, such tax *must* be treated as a part of the cost of the acquired property, or, in the case of a disposition, as a reduction in the amount realized on the disposition.[39]

---

[37] See the later section in this chapter entitled "Reporting Deductions for Taxes."

[38] § 164(a).

[39] Ibid.

Exhibit 11-3 *Nondeductible Taxes*[40]

Nondeductible Federal taxes:
Federal income taxes (including those withheld from an individual's pay)
Social security or railroad retirement taxes withheld from an individual by his or her employer (includes self-employment taxes)
Social security and other employment taxes paid on the wages of the taxpayer's employee who performed domestic or other personal services
Federal excise taxes or customs duties, *unless* they are connected with the taxpayer's business or income-producing activity
Federal estate and gift taxes

Nondeductible state and local taxes:
Motor vehicle taxes (*unless* they qualify as ad valorem taxes on personal property)
Inheritance, legacy, succession, or estate taxes
Gift taxes
Per capita or poll taxes
Cigarette, tobacco, liquor, beer, wine, etc., taxes
Sales taxes

In addition to the nondeductible taxes listed in Exhibit 11-3, deductions for *fees* (whether or not labeled as taxes) paid by taxpayers usually are denied *unless* the fees are incurred in the taxpayer's trade or business or for the production of income. Fees paid or incurred in connection with a trade or business, if ordinary and necessary, are deductible as business expenses under § 162. Similarly, fees related to the production of income generally are deductible expenses under § 212.[41]

The IRS distinguishes a "tax" from a "fee" by looking to the *purpose* of the charge.[42] If a particular charge is imposed upon the taxpayer for the purpose of *raising revenue* to be used for public or government purposes, the IRS will consider the charge to be a *tax*. However, if the charge is imposed because of either *particular acts or services* received by the taxpayer, such charge will be considered as a *fee*. Thus, fees for driver's licenses, vehicle registration and inspection, license tags for pets, hunting and fishing licenses, tolls for bridges and roads, parking meter deposits, water bills, sewer and other service charges, and postage fees are not deductible *unless* related to the taxpayer's trade or business, or income-producing activity.[43]

---

[40] See § 275, Reg. § 1.164-2 and *Your Federal Income Tax*, IRS Publication 17 (Rev. 1993), pp. 171–175.

[41] See Chapter 7 for a discussion of the requirements that must be met in order to deduct business and nonbusiness expenses of this nature.

[42] See § 275 and Reg. § 1.164-2.

[43] *Your Federal Income Tax*, IRS Publication 17 (Rev. 1992), pp. 174–175. No matter how strong an argument a taxpayer can make that his or her marriage was for business or income-producing purposes, fees for marriage licenses are considered nondeductible personal expenses.

Since most individual taxpayers use the cash receipts and disbursements method of accounting for tax purposes, the following discussion of income and property tax deductions concentrates on cash basis taxpayers and the requirement that taxes be *paid* in the year of deduction. Bear in mind throughout this discussion, however, that accrual method taxpayers are allowed a deduction for taxes in the tax year in which the obligation for payment becomes fixed and determinable (i.e., the all-events test is met).

INCOME TAXES

Most state, local, or foreign income taxes paid or accrued by a taxpayer are deductible in arriving at taxable income. For individual taxpayers, however, a deduction for state and local income taxes is allowed only if the taxpayer itemizes his or her deductions. Although the income taxes may be related solely to the individual's business income (e.g., income from a sole proprietorship or partnership), or income from rents and royalties, these taxes are considered personal in nature. Since income taxes paid to a foreign country or a U.S. possession may either be deducted as an itemized deduction or claimed as a credit against the U.S. income tax, an individual who does not itemize deductions should elect to claim foreign income taxes as credits.[44]

Cash basis taxpayers are allowed to deduct state and local income taxes *paid* during the taxable year, including those taxes imposed on interest income that is exempt from Federal income taxation. Amounts considered paid during the taxable year include

1. State and local income or foreign taxes withheld from an individual's salary by his or her employer;

2. Estimated payments made by the taxpayer under a pay-as-you-go requirement of a taxing authority; and

3. Payments made in the current year on an income tax liability of a prior year.

> **Example 11.**   During 1994 Z, a cash basis taxpayer, had $1,500 of Illinois state income taxes withheld by her employer. In 1994 she paid the remaining $450 in state income taxes due on her 1993 Illinois tax return, and also paid $300 in estimated state income tax payments during 1994. If Z itemizes her deductions for Federal income tax purposes, she is entitled to a $2,250 ($1,500 + $300 + $450) state income tax deduction for 1994.

If a cash basis taxpayer receives a refund of state, local, or foreign income taxes in the current year, the refund must be included in the current year's gross income to the extent a deduction in an earlier tax year provided a tax benefit.[45]

---

[44] For further information on this and other matters regarding the Federal income taxation of foreign source income, see *Corporate, Partnership, Estate and Gift Taxation*, 1995 Edition (Burr Ridge: Richard D. Irwin), Chapter 9.

[45] § 111.

Example 12. Assume the same facts as in *Example 11*. While preparing her 1994 Illinois state income tax return in early 1995, Z determined she had overpaid the state tax liability by $375. She received a refund of the entire overpayment on August 10, 1995. If Z claimed the total $2,250 state income taxes paid as a deduction on her 1993 Federal income tax return and her itemized deductions exceeded the standard deduction amount by at least $375, she must include the entire refund in gross income on her 1995 Federal income tax return.

Married taxpayers filing *separate* state or Federal income tax returns are subject to the following rules regarding the deduction for state income taxes:[46]

1. If separate state *and* Federal returns are filed, each spouse may deduct on his or her Federal income tax return the amount of state income tax imposed on and paid by such spouse during the tax year.

2. If separate state returns *but* a joint Federal return will be filed, the married couple may deduct on the joint Federal income tax return the sum of the state income tax imposed on both husband and wife, regardless of which spouse actually paid the tax.

3. If a joint state return *but* separate Federal returns are filed, each spouse is allowed to deduct on his or her Federal income tax return that *portion* of the total state tax imposed and paid during the year that the gross income of each spouse contributes to their total combined gross income.

PROPERTY TAXES

Personal property taxes paid to a state, local, or foreign government are deductible *only* if they are *ad valorem* taxes.[47] Ad valorem taxes are taxes imposed on the *value* of property. Quite often, state and local taxing authorities impose a combination tax and fee on personal property. In such cases, only that portion of the charge based on value of the property will qualify as a deductible tax.[48]

Example 13. State A imposes an annual vehicle registration charge of 60 cents per hundredweight. X, a resident of the state, paid $24 in 1994 for the registration of his personal automobile. Since this charge is not based on the value of the auto, X has not paid a deductible tax.

Example 14. State B imposes an annual vehicle registration charge of 1% of value plus 50 cents per hundredweight. Y, a resident of the state, owns a personal use automobile having a value of $10,000 and weighing 4,000 pounds. Of the $120 [(1% × $10,000) + (50¢ × 40 hundredweight)] total registration charge paid by Y, only $100 would be deductible as a personal property tax.

---

[46] *Your Federal Income Tax*, IRS Publication 17 (Rev. 1993), p. 172.

[47] § 164(b)(1) and Reg. § 1.164-3(c).

[48] § 164(b)(2)(E). States known to include some ad valorem tax as part of auto and boat registration fees are Arizona, California, Colorado, Indiana, Iowa, Maine, Massachusetts, Nevada, New Hampshire, Oklahoma, Washington, and Wyoming.

Real property (real estate) taxes are generally deductible only if imposed on property owned by the taxpayer and paid or accrued by the taxpayer in the year the deduction is claimed. If real property taxes are imposed on jointly held real estate, each owner may claim his or her portion of the taxes. For example, if cash basis, married taxpayers file separate Federal income tax returns and real property taxes are imposed on jointly held real estate, each spouse may claim *half* of the taxes paid.

If real estate is sold during the year, the deduction for real estate taxes *must* be *apportioned* between the buyer and seller according to the number of days in the year each held the property, regardless of which party actually paid the property taxes.[49] The taxes are apportioned to the seller up to (but not including) the date of sale, and to the buyer beginning with the date of sale.

> **Example 15.**   The real property tax year in Colorado County is April 1 to March 31. X, the owner on April 1, 1994 of real property located in Colorado County, sells the real property to Y on June 30, 1994. Y owns the real property from June 30, 1994 through March 31, 1995. The real property tax is $730 for the county's tax year April 1, 1994 to March 31, 1995. For purposes of § 164(a), $180 (90 ÷ 365 × $730 = $180 taxes for April 1, 1994 through June 29, 1994) of the real property tax is treated as imposed on X, the seller. The remaining $550 (275 ÷ 365 × $730 = $550 taxes for June 30, 1994 through March 31, 1995) of such real property tax is treated as imposed on Y, the purchaser.[50]

When both buyer and seller of real property are cash basis taxpayers and only one of the parties *actually* pays the real property taxes for the period in which both parties owned the property, *each* party to the transaction is entitled to deduct the portion of the real property taxes based on the number of days he or she held the property. As a practical matter, real property taxes are usually allocated during the closing process, and the details are provided in the closing statement for real property sales. A taxpayer need only acquire the closing statement to ascertain the proper allocation and how the sales price has been affected by the allocation.

Unless the actual real property taxes are apportioned between buyer and seller as part of the sale/purchase agreement, adjustments for the taxes must be made to determine the amount realized by the seller, as well as the buyer's cost basis of the property.[51] The treatment of the adjustments depends upon which party actually paid the real estate taxes.

---

[49]   § 164(d) and Reg. § 1.164-6(b).

[50]   Reg. § 1.164-6(b)(3), Example 1.

[51]   Reg. § 1.164-6(d); Reg. § 1.1001-1(b); and Reg. § 1.1012-1(b). A similar result should occur if buyer and seller are using different accounting methods.

Example 16. Assume that buyer and seller are both cash basis, calendar year taxpayers, and real estate taxes for the entire year are to be paid at the end of the year. Real property is sold on October 1, 1994 for $30,000, and B, the buyer, pays the real estate taxes of $365 on December 31, 1994. The real estate taxes attributable to and deductible by B are $92 (92 ÷ 365 × $365). The remaining $273 ($365 − $92) of the taxes will be apportioned to and deductible by S, the seller. As a result of this apportionment, the seller must increase the amount realized from the sale to $30,273, and the buyer will have an adjusted cost basis for the property of $30,273.

Example 17. Assume the same facts as in *Example 16*, except that the real property taxes are payable in advance for the entire year and that S, the seller, paid $365 in January 1994. The real estate taxes are apportioned in the same manner, and the buyer, B, will be entitled to deduct $92. However, B must adjust his cost basis of the property to $29,908 ($30,000 purchase price − $92 taxes paid by seller). The seller, S, is entitled to deduct $273 of the taxes and reduce his amount realized from the sale to $29,908.

Real property taxes assessed against local benefits of a kind tending to increase the value of the property assessed (e.g., special assessments for paved streets, street lights, sidewalks, drainage ditches, etc.) are not deductible.[52] Instead, the property owner simply adds the assessed amount paid to his or her cost basis of the property. However, if assessments for local benefits are made for the purpose of maintenance or repair, or for the purpose of meeting interest charges with respect to such benefits, they are deductible.[53] If an assessment is in part for the cost of an improvement and in part for maintenance, repairs or for interest charges, only *that* portion of the tax assessment relating to maintenance, repairs, or interest charges will be deductible. Unless the taxpayer can show the allocation of the amounts assessed for the different purposes, *none* of the amount paid is deductible.[54]

REPORTING DEDUCTIONS FOR TAXES

Deductible state and local taxes are reported on different forms depending on the taxpaying entity claiming the deduction. Corporations report their deductions for these taxes on Form 1120. Fiduciaries (trusts and estates) report deductible taxes on Form 1041. Partnerships and S corporations report deductible taxes on Forms 1065 and 1120S, respectively. Individuals report deductible taxes on Form 1040, but the particular schedule used depends upon whether the taxes are business expenses or personal itemized deductions.

---

[52] § 164(c)(1), Reg. § 1.164-2(g), and Reg. § 1.164-4(a).

[53] § 164(c)(1) and Reg. § 1.164-4(b)(1).

[54] Reg. § 1.164-4(b)(1).

An individual's deduction for taxes (other than income taxes) related to his or her trade or business is reported on Schedule C of Form 1040 (Schedule F for farmers and ranchers). Deductible taxes (other than income taxes) related to rents and royalties are reported on Schedule E. All other deductible taxes, including state and local income taxes on business income or income from rents or royalties, are reported by an individual taxpayer on Schedule A of Form 1040.

INTEREST EXPENSE

Interest expense is an amount paid or incurred for the use or forbearance of money.[55] Under the general rule of Code § 163(a), all interest paid or accrued on indebtedness within the taxable year is allowed as a deduction. As with most general rules in the tax law, however, there are limitations imposed on the deduction of certain interest expense as well as the complete disallowance of deductions for interest related to certain items. These restrictions are discussed below.

LIMITATIONS ON DEDUCTIONS OF INTEREST EXPENSE

Prior to 1987, interest expense for most taxpayers was totally deductible. As part of the tax reform package of 1986, however, Congress substantially limited the deduction for interest.

Over the years, Congress became concerned that by allowing a deduction for all interest expense the tax system encouraged borrowing and, conversely, discouraged savings. This problem was exacerbated by the fact that the "economic" income arising from the ownership of housing and other consumer durables is not subject to tax. For example, when a taxpayer purchases a residence, the return on the investment—the absence of having to pay rent for the item—is not subject to tax. Had the taxpayer invested in assets other than housing or other durables, the return (e.g., interest or dividends) would have been fully taxable. In those situations where the investment is financed by borrowing, allowing a deduction is equivalent to allowing a deduction for expenses related to tax-exempt income—which is expressly prohibited under Code § 265. The net result of this system is to provide an incentive to consume rather than save.

In rethinking the approach to interest in 1986, Congress believed that it would not be advisable to impute income on investments in durables and tax it. However, Congress did feel that it was appropriate and practical to address situations where consumer expenditures are financed by borrowing. Accordingly, Congress enacted rules that prohibit the deduction for personal interest (other than certain home mortgage interest). As a result, interest expense on personal auto loans, credit card purchases, and the like are no longer deductible.

---

[55] *Old Colony Railroad v. Comm.*, 3 USTC ¶880, 10 AFTR 786, 284 U.S. 552 (USSC, 1936).

In eliminating the deduction for personal interest, Congress effectively established *five* categories of interest expense, each of which is subject to its own special set of rules. The different categories of interest expense are (1) personal interest, (2) qualified residence interest, (3) trade or business interest, (4) investment interest, and (5) passive-activity interest. As explained in detail below, interest (other than qualified residence interest) is classified according to how the loan proceeds are *spent*. Consequently, taxpayers are required to determine the nature of an expenditure from loan proceeds before the amount of the interest deduction can be determined.

Personal Interest. Today, taxpayers are not allowed to deduct any *personal interest*. Personal interest is defined as all interest arising from personal expenditures *except* the following:[56]

1. Interest incurred in connection with the conduct of a trade or business (other than the performance of services as an employee);

2. Investment interest;

3. Qualified residence interest;

4. Interest taken into account in computing the income or loss from passive activities; and

5. Interest related to payment of the estate tax liability where such tax is deferred.

The effect of these rules is to severely limit the deduction for interest on consumer debt. For example, if a taxpayer borrows $2,000 from the bank and uses it to take a Caribbean cruise, none of the interest on the loan is deductible. Similarly, interest and finance charges would not be deductible on the following:

1. Automobile loans;

2. Furniture and appliance loans;

3. Credit card debt;

4. Student loans;

5. Life insurance loans;

6. Loans from qualified pension plans [including § 401(k) plans]; and

7. Delinquent tax payments and penalties.

It should be emphasized that interest incurred by an *employee* in connection with his or her trade or business is treated as consumer interest and is not deductible. In contrast, interest incurred by a self-employed person in his or her trade or business is fully deductible.

---

[56] § 163(h)(1).

Example 18.   K sells cosmetics for Fantastic Faces, Incorporated. Her job involves calling on department stores all over the state of Ohio and soliciting their orders. She uses her car entirely for business. Interest on her car loan for the year was $2,000. Since K is an employee, none of the interest is deductible.

Example 19.   R is a real estate agent working for Bungalow Brokers. All of his compensation is based on the number of homes he sells during the year. He uses his car entirely for business. Under the employment tax rules (Code § 3508), real estate agents and direct sellers are not considered employees where their remuneration is determined by sales. Since R would not be considered an employee, all of the interest on his car loan would be deductible.

Example 20.   P is a reporter for the *News-Gazette*. She purchased a portable computer for $1,000, charging it on her bank credit card. She uses the computer entirely for business. Finance charges attributable to the purchase are $25. Even though the finance charges are incurred in connection with P's business, they are not deductible since she is an employee.

Qualified Residence Interest.   The elimination of the deduction for personal interest in 1986 did not extend to interest on most home mortgages. As a general rule, interest on any debt *secured* by a taxpayer's first or second home is deductible. The interest is normally deductible whether the interest is on an original, second, or refinanced mortgage. Moreover, the interest is deductible regardless of how the taxpayer uses the money as long as the debt is *secured* by a mortgage on his or her primary or secondary residence. Unfortunately, tucked behind these seemingly simple rules are several complex restrictions.

Qualifying Indebtedness.   Technically, only "qualified residence interest" is deductible. There are two types of qualified residence interest:[57]

1. Interest on *acquisition indebtedness:* interest on debt that is incurred in acquiring, constructing, or improving a qualified residence *and* that is secured by such residence.

2. Interest on *home equity indebtedness:* interest on debt secured by a qualified residence to the extent that the debt does not exceed the property's fair market value reduced by its acquisition debt.

Note that in both cases, the crucial element in determining whether the interest qualifies is whether the debt is secured by a residence. Unsecured debt and debt secured by other property does not qualify even though the debt proceeds may be used to acquire a personal residence.

---

[57] § 163(h)(3).

Example 21.   J borrowed $50,000 from her pension plan and $10,000 from her father to buy a new home. None of the interest on the debt is deductible because neither of the debts is secured by the residence. This is true even though the borrowed amounts were used to buy a residence.

Also observe that in the case of both acquisition and home equity debt, the debt must be secured by a *qualified* residence. A qualified residence is the taxpayer's principal home and one other residence of the taxpayer.[58] This rule effectively allows taxpayers to deduct the interest on only two homes: their first home and a second of their choosing. A taxpayer with more than two homes must designate which is the second home when the return is filed. Different homes can be selected each year.

Example 22.   After winning the New York State lottery, T retired from her job and purchased a home in Tampa, Florida. She also purchased a motor home and a condominium in Vail, Colorado. All purchases were debt-financed and secured by the property. Within certain dollar limitations, T can treat the interest paid on her home in Tampa *and* the interest paid on *either* the motor home *or* the condominium as qualified residence interest.

Example 23.   Assume the same facts as above except that T converted the condominium into rental property at the advice of her tax accountant. In this case, the condominium will not qualify as T's secondary residence.[59]

In determining the deductibility of interest on a second home, special rules must be considered if the taxpayer *rents* it out. These rules are examined in conjunction with vacation homes discussed later in this chapter. If the second home is not rented out, no personal use is actually needed in order to meet the qualified residence test.

Congress also took steps to ensure that a taxpayer could not convert nondeductible interest into qualified residence interest simply by pitching a tent on the property and calling it a second home (e.g., vacant land or a car). In determining whether the debt is incurred with respect to a qualified residence, the term *residence* includes a vacation home, condominium, mobile home, boat, or recreational vehicle as long as the property contains basic living accommodations (i.e., sleeping space, toilet, and cooking facilities).

Limitations on Deductible Amount.   To prevent taxpayers from taking undue advantage of the deductibility of home mortgage interest, Congress imposed limits on the maximum amount of debt qualifying under either definition. The aggregate amount of debt that can be treated as acquisition indebtedness for any taxable year cannot exceed $1

---

[58] § 163(h)(4).

[59] This does not mean that a taxpayer's interest expense on rental property is not deductible. As discussed later, however, losses from rental property (including interest expense) may be subject to deduction limitations.

million ($500,000 in the case of a married individual filing a separate return),[60] whereas the aggregate amount of debt that will be treated as home equity indebtedness for any taxable year cannot exceed $100,000 ($50,000 if married and filing separately).[61] Collectively, the total amount of debt in any one year on which the interest paid or accrued will be treated as qualified residence interest cannot exceed $1.1 million.

> **Example 24.**   During the current year, T purchases a principal residence in Boston for $900,000 and a vacation home in Tampa for $500,000. Mortgages secured by both properties total $1.3 million. T may treat *only* the interest paid on $1 million of acquisition indebtedness as qualified residence interest. In addition, he may treat $100,000 of the loans as home equity indebtedness and, therefore, the related interest is deductible as qualified residence interest. Whether interest on the balance of the debt, $200,000, is deductible depends on how the funds are used.

> **Example 25.**   C purchased his present residence several years ago at a cost of $1.9 million. The present balance on his home mortgage is $800,000 and the property is valued at $2.5 million. This year, C borrowed $300,000 secured by a second mortgage on his home. Even though the total indebtedness does not exceed $1.1 million, C may deduct the interest on the $800,000 unpaid acquisition indebtedness and the interest on only $100,000 of the home equity mortgage. Any excess interest paid during the year will be treated as personal interest.

It is important to note that the interest paid on qualifying home equity indebtedness is allowed as a deduction *regardless* of how the taxpayer uses the loan proceeds. Thus, the obvious reason for the $100,000 limit on qualifying home equity debt is to impose a limit on the amount of an interest deduction the taxpayer may claim on loan proceeds used for personal purposes.

> **Example 26.**   K purchased her present residence 10 years ago at a cost of $70,000. The present balance on her home mortgage is $40,000 and the property is appraised at a value of $150,000. This year, K borrowed $80,000 secured by a second mortgage on her home. She used the loan proceeds to purchase new clothes and a new automobile, and to take a vacation to Hawaii. The interest on the $80,000 loan is deductible since it is qualified residence interest. The fact that K used the loan proceeds for personal purposes is irrelevant. Also note that K's original cost of $70,000 is not used to limit the amount of her $80,000 home equity loan.

---

[60] Any qualified residence indebtedness incurred before October 14, 1987—whether it is acquisition debt, home equity debt, or a combination of both—is to be treated as acquisition debt and is not subject to the $1 million limitation. If the property is later refinanced, however, the new indebtedness will be subject to this limitation. § 163(h)(3)(D).

[61] § 163(h).

Finally, any attempt to refinance acquisition indebtedness should be undertaken with caution. A qualifying residence's acquisition debt is *reduced* by principal payments and *cannot be increased* unless the loan proceeds are used for home improvements. Thus, the acquisition debt can be refinanced only to the extent that the principal amount of the refinancing does not exceed the principal amount of the acquisition debt immediately before the refinancing.[62] The interest paid on any excess refinanced debt will not be treated as acquisition indebtedness. However, any excess may be treated as home equity indebtedness. As noted above, the total qualifying indebtedness (acquisition and home equity) cannot exceed the value of the residence.

Example 27. In 1958, G purchased her California bungalow for $25,000. The house is now worth $350,000. G paid off the mortgage on the home several years ago. This year, G mortgaged her house for $120,000 and subsequently loaned the money to her grandson to enable him to buy his first home. None of the loan qualifies as acquisition debt because the balance of acquisition debt refinanced was zero. However, G may deduct interest on $100,000 of the loan, which qualifies as home equity debt.

Example 28. R purchased his present residence in 1989 for $250,000 and borrowed $210,000 on a 14% mortgage secured by the property. In 1994 R refinanced the balance of his mortgage, $190,000, by securing a new mortgage of $230,000 at 8%. Unless R used the additional loan proceeds to substantially improve the residence, only $190,000 of the new mortgage constitutes acquisition indebtedness, and the corresponding interest is therefore deductible. In addition, the $40,000 balance of the debt may be treated as home-equity debt. In such case, the interest on the entire $230,000 mortgage would be deductible as qualified residence interest.

Trade or Business Interest. While the taxpayer normally cannot deduct interest of a personal nature, interest related to a trade or business expenditure is totally deductible. Perhaps the most common example of business interest is that arising from loans used to acquire fixed assets such as buildings and equipment that are used in the business. Business interest also includes that attributable to loans used to acquire an interest in an S corporation or a partnership in which the taxpayer materially participates. Recall, however, that interest incurred in connection with performing services as an employee is not considered business interest, and thus is considered nondeductible personal interest.

As explained below, the fact that a business incurs interest expense does not necessarily mean that such interest is classified as business interest. If interest expense incurred by a business arises from an investment considered unrelated to the business, it will not be business interest (e.g., a closely held corporation purchases stock on margin).

---

[62] §163(h)(3)(B).

Investment Interest.   The fourth category of interest expense subject to limitation is investment interest. This limitation is imposed on taxpayers, other than regular corporations, who have paid or incurred interest expense to purchase or carry investments.[63] Common examples include interest on loans to purchase unimproved land and interest incurred on margin accounts used to purchase stocks and other securities. Congress imposed the investment interest limitation to eliminate what it perceived was an unfair advantage to certain wealthy investors. For example, consider the taxpayer who borrows to acquire or carry investments that produce little or no income currently but pay off handsomely when the investment is sold. This is commonly the hoped-for result with investments in such assets as growth stock or land. Without any restrictions, the taxpayer would be able to claim an immediate deduction for interest expense yet postpone any income recognition until the property was ultimately sold. Moreover, the income that the taxpayer would realize on the sale would normally be favorable capital gain. Congress apparently felt that this mismatching of income and expense was unwarranted and reacted by limiting the taxpayer's deduction for investment interest to the taxpayer's current investment income.

Before examining the investment interest limitation, the definition of investment interest should be clarified. *Investment interest* is generally any interest expense on debt used to finance property held for investment. It does not include, however, qualified residence interest or any interest related to a passive activity. As discussed in Chapter 12, interest related to a passive activity is allocated to the passive activity and is taken into account in computing the activity's income or loss. As a result, such interest is effectively limited by the passive-loss rules. Note, however, that any interest incurred by a passive activity that is related to its portfolio income (i.e., interest and dividend income) would normally be considered investment interest subject to the investment interest limitation. Because rental activities are usually treated as a passive activity, interest expense allocable to a rental activity is normally subject to the passive-loss rules.

The annual deduction for investment interest expense is limited to the taxpayer's *net investment income,* if any, for the tax year.[64] Any investment interest that exceeds the limitation and is disallowed may be carried forward until it is exhausted. Operationally, the disallowed interest is carried forward to the subsequent year, where it is combined with current year interest and is once again subject to the net investment income limitation. (Note that a sale of the financed property does not trigger the allowance of any disallowed interest.)

Net Investment Income.   Net investment income is the excess of the taxpayer's investment income over investment expenses. For this purpose, *investment income* is defined as the gross income from property held for investment (including any net gain on the disposition of such property that is to be taxed as ordinary income). Common examples of investment income include

1.   Interest.

2.   Dividends.

---

[63]   § 163(d).

[64]   § 163(d)(1).

3. Royalties.

4. Ordinary income from the recapture of depreciation or intangible drilling costs under §§ 1245, 1250, and 1254.

5. Portfolio income under the passive loss rules.

6. Income from a trade or business in which the taxpayer did not materially participate (but which is not a passive activity, e.g., a working interest in an oil or gas property).

Note that income from rental property and income from a passive activity (other than portfolio income) are not considered investment income. As noted above, any interest expense incurred in rental or passive activities is allocated to those activities and is used in computing the passive income or loss of such activity.[65] For example, mortgage interest on rental property would be deductible only to the extent of passive income.

Investment expenses are generally all those deductions (except interest) that are directly connected with the production of the investment income. Any investment expenses that are considered miscellaneous itemized deductions are considered only to the extent they exceed the 2 percent floor. For this purpose, the 2 percent floor is first absorbed by all other miscellaneous expenses.

Example 29.   G's records for 1994 revealed the following information:

Salary...	$ 40,000
Dividends and interest............................	3,500
Share of partnership income:	
Partnership ordinary income.....................	700
Portfolio income:	
Dividends....................................	50
Interest.....................................	80
Rental income from duplex........................	15,000
Rental expenses.................................	(14,000)
Adjusted gross income...........................	$ 45,330
Qualified residence interest.......................	$8,000
Real estate taxes on home........................	4,000
Property tax on land held for investment..........	1,000
Miscellaneous itemized deductions:	
Safety deposit box rental.......................	50
Financial planner..............................	1,500
Fee to maintain brokerage account.............	100
Unreimbursed employee business expenses...	725

---

[65] § 163(d)(4)(E). See Chapter 12 for a detailed discussion of the passive loss rules.

G is a limited partner in the partnership and thus treats the partnership as a passive activity. G also paid $7,700 of interest expense on the land held for investment. G's net investment income is computed as follows:

Investment income:			
Dividends and interest............................		$3,500	
Partnership income:			
Portfolio income:			
Dividends......................................		50	
Interest.......................................		80	
Total investment income............................			$3,630
Investment expenses:			
Property tax on land..............................		$1,000	
Safety deposit box rental..........................		50	
Financial planner.................................		1,500	
Fee to maintain brokerage account................		100	
Miscellaneous itemized deductions disallowed			
2% floor (2% × $45,330).....................	$ 907		
Unreimbursed employee business expenses.....	(725)		
Investment expenses classified as			
miscellaneous itemized deductions disallowed.		(182)	
Total investment expenses...........................			(2,468)
Net investment income.............................			$1,162

For 1994 G may deduct $1,162 of investment interest expense (*not* subject to the 3 percent cutback). The balance of $6,538 ($7,700 − $1,162) is carried over to the next year, 1995, and is treated as if it were paid in 1995. There is no limit on the carryover period. Note that in computing investment expenses, only investment expenses exceeding the 2% floor are allowed. In computing the disallowed portion, investment expenses are deemed to come last. Also note that rental income is not considered investment income.

Passive Activity Interest. Deductions attributable to so-called *passive activities* (e.g., those in which a taxpayer does not participate in a material fashion) are subject to special rules. Interest expense incurred by a passive activity itself (e.g., a limited partnership), or by investment in a passive activity, is treated as a deduction relating to the passive activity and is limited by the passive loss rules.[66] The passive activity loss rules are discussed in Chapter 12.

---

[66] § 163(d)(3)(B).

CLASSIFICATION OF INTEREST EXPENSE

The different rules for different types of interest expense force taxpayers to classify and allocate their interest expense among appropriate categories. The classification procedure established by the Treasury is very straightforward in principle. Under the Temporary Regulations, interest is generally classified according to how the loan proceeds are spent— that is, the character of the expenditure determines the character of interest.[67] The type of collateral that may secure the loan is irrelevant in the classification process—except in the case of the qualified residence interest which is deductible regardless of how loan proceeds are spent.[68]

> **Example 30.** This year, T pledged IBM stock held as an investment as collateral for a loan which he uses to purchase a personal car. Any interest expense on the loan is considered nondeductible personal interest since the debt proceeds were used for personal purposes. The fact that the debt is secured by investment property is irrelevant. If the loan were secured by T's primary residence, the interest could be deductible as qualified residence interest.

The classification scheme demands that the taxpayer trace how any loan proceeds were used. To simplify this task, specific rules exist for debt proceeds that are (1) deposited in the borrower's account, (2) disbursed directly by the lender to someone other than the borrower, or (3) received in cash.

Proceeds Deposited in the Borrower's Account. In most cases, taxpayers borrow money, deposit it in an account, and write checks for various expenditures. Since money is fungible (that is, one dollar cannot be distinguished from another) it would be impossible without special rules to determine how the loan proceeds were spent and therefore how the related interest should be allocated. The Temporary Regulations create such rules.[69]

The first presumption created by the Regulations concerns the treatment of interest on funds that have not been spent. To the extent borrowed funds are deposited and not spent, interest attributable to such a period is considered *investment interest* regardless of whether the account bears interest income.[70]

> **Example 31.** On November 1, K borrowed $1,000 which she intends to use to fix up her boat. She deposited the $1,000 in a separate account. No expenditures were made during the remainder of the year. In this case, K is subject to the interest allocation rules since the interest expense is considered attributable to an investment and is therefore investment interest.

> **Example 32.** Same as above except K makes several personal expenditures during the next three months. Interest must be allocated between investment interest and personal interest.

---

[67] Temp. Reg. § 1.163-8T.

[68] Temp. Reg. § 1.163-8T(c)(1). For purposes of the alternative minimum tax, however, qualified housing interest is deductible only if the debt is spent on the residence. See Chapter 13 for further discussion.

[69] Temp. Reg. § 1.163-8T(c)(4).

[70] *Ibid.*

Example 33.   R borrows $100,000 on January 1 and deposits it in a separate account where it remains until April 1 when he purchases an interest in a limited partnership for $20,000. On September 1, R purchases a new car for $30,000. Interest expense attributable to the $100,000 is allocated in the following manner:

	Debt Proceeds		
Period	Investment Interest	Passive Interest	Personal Interest
1/1-3/31	$100,000		
4/1-8/31	80,000	$20,000	
9/1-12/31	50,000	20,000	$30,000

Commingled Funds. In most situations, a taxpayer has one account in which all amounts are deposited. When this occurs, all expenditures from the account after the loan is deposited are deemed to come first from the borrowed funds.

Example 34.   On October 1, B borrowed $1,000 to purchase a snowplow attachment for the front of his truck. He plans to make some extra money this winter by plowing driveways and parking lots. B deposited the $1,000 in his only checking account. On October 20, he bought the attachment for $1,500. Prior to October 20, he wrote $700 in checks for groceries and other personal items. Of the $1,000 loan, $700 is deemed to have been spent for personal items while the remaining $300 is allocated to the snow plow. Consequently, B may deduct only the interest expense on $300.

If proceeds for more than one loan are deposited into an account, expenditures are treated as coming from the borrowed funds in the order in which they were deposited (i.e., first-in, first-out).

Example 35.   Dr. T has a personal checking account with a current balance of $3,000. On November 1, T obtained a $1,000 one-year loan (Debt A) from her bank, which it credited to her personal account. She planned to use the loan to purchase a small copier for her dental practice. After shopping, T determined she would need additional funds. Therefore, on November 30 she obtained another $1,000 loan (Debt B). On December 12, T wrote a check for $800 to pay for her husband's Christmas present, a diamond ring. On December 19, she wrote a check for $2,100 to purchase the copier. These transactions are summarized as follows:

Date	Transaction	
11/1	Borrowed (Debt A)	$1,000
11/30	Borrowed (Debt B)	1,000
12/12	Purchased ring	(800)
12/19	Purchased copier	(2,100)

For purposes of determining the deduction for the interest on the loan, $800 of Debt A is deemed to be used for personal purposes (i.e., the ring purchase) and $200 towards the copier. All of Debt B is used for the copier. Thus, interest attributable

to $800 of Debt A is nondeductible personal interest while that attributable to $200 is totally deductible. All of the interest on Debt B is deductible business interest. This may be summarized as follows:

| Expenditure | 11/1 Debt A $1,000 | | 11/30 Debt B $1,000 | | |
	Personal	Business	Personal	Business	Other
$ 800 ring	$800				
2,100 copier		$200		$1,000	$900

15-Day Rule. In lieu of allocating the debt proceeds in the above manner, an alternative method is available. A borrower can elect to treat any expenditure made within 15 days after the loan proceeds are deposited as having been made from the proceeds of that loan.

Example 36. C borrowed and deposited $5,000 in his checking account on December 1. On December 2, he wrote a check for $6,000 for his estimated income taxes. On December 10, he wrote a check for $5,000 for furniture for his business. Under the normal allocation rule, the entire $5,000 proceeds from the debt would be considered spent for personal purposes. Under the 15-day rule, however, C may treat the $5,000 as used to purchase the furniture since the proceeds were spent within 15 days of deposit.

Loan Proceeds Received Indirectly. In many transactions, a borrower incurs debt without receiving any loan proceeds directly. For example, if the taxpayer borrowed $100,000 from a bank to purchase a building, the bank typically disburses the $100,000 directly to the seller rather than to the borrower. Similarly, the borrower may purchase the building and assume the seller's $100,000 mortgage. In this and similar situations, the borrower is treated as having received the proceeds and using them to make the expenditure for the property, services, or other purpose.[71]

Loan Proceeds Received in Cash. When the borrower receives the loan proceeds in cash, the taxpayer may treat any cash expenditure made within 15 days after receiving the cash as made from the loan. If the loan proceeds are not spent within 15 days, however, the loan is deemed to have been spent for personal purposes.

Debt Repayments, Refinancings, and Reallocations. Loans that are used for several purposes present a unique problem when a portion of the loan is repaid. In this case, repayments must be applied in the following order:[72]

1. Personal expenditures.

2. Investment expenditures and passive activity expenditures (other than rental real estate in which the taxpayer actively participates).

3. Rental real estate expenditures.

4. Former passive activity expenditures.

5. Trade or business expenditures.

---

[71] Temp. Reg. § 1.163-8T(c)(3).   [72] *Ibid.*

Example 37.   R borrows $10,000, $6,000 of which is used to purchase a personal automobile and $4,000 of which is used to invest in land. On June 1 of this year she paid $7,000 on the loan. Of the $7,000 repayment, $6,000 reduces the portion of the loan allocated to personal expenditures and the remaining $1,000 reduces the portion allocated to investment.

If the taxpayer refinances an old debt, interest on the new debt is characterized in the same way as that on the old debt.

Example 38.   In 1992 S borrowed $10,000 at an annual interest rate of 14%. He used $8,000 to purchase a new boat and $2,000 to purchase a computer to use in his business. This year, he borrowed $6,000 from another bank at 10% to pay off the balance of the old loan. At the time the original loan was paid off, $4,000 of the $6,000 balance was allocated to the boat purchase and $2,000 was allocated to the computer purchase. The new debt will be allocated in the same manner as the old debt.

If the taxpayer borrows to finance a business asset, the debt must be recharacterized whenever the asset is sold or the nature of the use of the asset changes.

Example 39.   Several years ago B, a traveling salesman, borrowed $12,000 to buy a car which he used entirely for business. This year, B gave his car to his wife who uses it solely for personal use. The loan and interest thereon must be reclassified.

Computation and Allocation of Interest Expense.   The special rules governing the taxpayer's deduction for interest expense do not affect its computation. Interest is computed in the normal manner. However, allocation of the interest expense among the different categories does present certain difficulties. As a general rule, interest expense accruing on a debt for any period is allocated in the same manner as the debt. Interest which accrues on interest—that is, compound interest—is allocated in the same manner as the original interest.[73]

Example 40.   On January 1, R borrowed $100,000 at an interest rate of 10%, compounded semiannually. She deposited the loan in a separate account and on July 1 used the funds to purchase a yacht. On December 31, R paid the accrued interest of $10,250 computed as follows:

Period	Principal		Rate		Time		Interest
1/1-6/30	$100,000	×	10%	×	6/12	=	$ 5,000
7/1-12/31	105,000	×	10%	×	6/12	=	5,250
							$10,250

---

[73]   Temp. Reg. § 1.163-8T(c)(2).

Under the allocation rules, R's loan is classified as an investment loan from January 1 through June 30 and, therefore, the interest accruing for that period of $5,000 is investment interest. In addition, the interest expense which accrues on this $5,000 from July 30 through December 31 of $250 ($5,000 × 10% × $^6/_{12}$) is considered investment interest for a total of $5,250. This $250 of "compound interest" accruing from July 31 through December 31 is allocated to the investment category even though the original loan has been assigned to a new category for the same period. The remaining $5,000 of interest expense accruing from July 1 through December 31 ($100,000 × 10% × $^6/_{12}$) is personal interest.

To simplify the allocation of interest expense, the taxpayer may use a straight-line method. Using this technique, an equal amount of interest is allocated to each day of the year. For this purpose, the taxpayer may treat a year as consisting of twelve 30-day months.

> **Example 41.**   Assume the same facts as in *Example 40* above, except that R elects to allocate the interest expense on a straight-line basis, treating the year as consisting of twelve 30-day months. As a result, interest expense of $5,125 ($^{180}/_{360}$ × $10,250) would be investment interest while the remaining $5,125 of interest expense would be personal interest.

WHEN DEDUCTIBLE

The taxpayer's method of accounting generally controls the timing of an interest expense deduction. Accrual method taxpayers generally may deduct interest over the period in which the interest accrues, regardless of when the expense is actually paid. However, cash basis taxpayers must *actually* pay the interest before a deduction is allowed. Many situations arise in which the "actual payment" requirement imposed on cash basis taxpayers delays the timing of a deduction. Other situations concern measurement of the amount of interest actually paid. The most common of these situations are briefly discussed below.

Interest Paid in Advance.   If interest is paid in advance for a time period that extends beyond the end of one tax year, *both* accrual method and cash basis taxpayers generally are required to spread the interest deduction over the tax years to which it applies.[74] An important exception is made for cash basis individual taxpayers who are required to pay interest "points" in connection with indebtedness incurred to *purchase* or *improve* the taxpayer's principal residence (i.e., taxpayer's home).[75] The term *points* is often used to describe charges imposed on the borrower under such descriptions as "loan origination fees," "premium charges," and "maximum loan charges." Such charges usually are stated as a percentage (point) of the loan amount. If the payment of any of these charges is *strictly* for the use of money *and* actual payment of these charges is made out of *separate funds* belonging to the taxpayer, an interest deduction is allowed in the year of payment.[76]

---

[74] § 461(a).

[75] § 461(g).

[76] See *Roger A. Schubel*, 77 T.C. 701 (1982), and *James W. Hager*, 45 TCM 123, T.C.

Memo 1982-663. Note, however, that this interest deduction is subject to the rules regarding qualified residence interest.

Example 42. R borrowed $15,000 from State Bank to make improvements on his home. The loan is payable over a 10-year period, and the bank charged R a loan origination fee of $300 (2 points). If R pays the $300 charge from separate funds, it is currently deductible as an interest expense (assuming R itemizes his deductions). However, if the $300 charge is added to the amount of the loan, R has not currently paid interest. Instead, R will be required to treat the charge as note discount interest (see discussion below).

Note-Discount Interest. Taxpayers often sign notes calling for repayment of an amount greater than the loan proceeds actually received. This occurs when the creditor subtracts (withholds) the interest from the face amount of the loan and the taxpayer receives the balance, or when the face amount of the note simply includes add-on interest. In either case, cash basis taxpayers are not allowed a deduction until the tax year in which the interest is actually paid. Accrual method taxpayers are allowed to deduct the interest over the tax years in which it accrues.

Graduated Payment Mortgages. A creature of the high interest rate mortgage market of recent years, graduated payment mortgages provide for increasing payments in the early years of the mortgage until the payments reach some level amount. Under these plans, the payments in the early years are less than the amount of interest owed on the loan. The unpaid interest is added to the principal amount of the mortgage and future interest is computed on this revised balance. As should be expected, cash basis taxpayers may deduct *only* the interest actually paid in the current year; the increases in the principal balance of the mortgage are treated much the same as note-discount interest.

Installment Purchases. Individual taxpayers who purchase personal property or pay for educational services under a contract calling for installment payments in which carrying charges are separately stated but the interest charge cannot be determined are allowed to *impute* an interest expense. The imputed expense is allowed whether or not a payment is actually made during the tax year, and is computed at a rate of 6 percent of the *average unpaid balance* of the contract during the year.[77] The average unpaid balance is the sum of the unpaid balance outstanding on the first day of each month of the tax year, divided by 12 months.[78] Credit card and revolving charge account finance charges are generally much greater than 6 percent. Fortunately, these charges are usually stated separately at a *predetermined* interest rate (e.g., finance charge of $1\frac{1}{2}\%$ of unpaid monthly balance). Recall, however, that this type of interest expense is generally personal interest and thus nondeductible!

WHERE REPORTED

Like the deductions for taxes, the appropriate tax form or schedule on which deductible interest is reported depends upon the entity entitled to the deduction and the nature of the indebtedness to which the interest relates. A corporation's deductible interest is reported on its annual tax return Form 1120. Estates and trusts report interest deductions on Form 1041; partnerships and S corporations claim interest deductions on Forms 1065 and 1120S, respectively. Individuals claiming a deduction for interest expense must

---

[77] § 163(b)(1).   [78] *Ibid.*

report the amount on the appropriate schedule of Form 1040. If the interest is related to business indebtedness—and the business is self-employment—the individual will claim his or her deduction on Schedule C (Schedule F for farmers and ranchers). Interest on debt incurred in connection with the production of rents or royalties is reported on Schedule E. Deductible interest on indebtedness incurred for personal use must be reported as an itemized deduction on Schedule A. However, any individual who has refinanced his or her home, or is otherwise subject to the limitations imposed on qualified residence interest, should see IRS Publication 936 for instructions in computing the home mortgage interest deduction.

An individual's current deduction for investment interest expense should be calculated on Form 4952 (see Appendix B), and any disallowed deduction reported as a carryover amount. The deductible amount from Form 4952 should be transferred to and claimed as a deduction on the individual's Schedule E, Form 1040 if the interest relates to the production of royalties; otherwise, the deductible amount is reported on Schedule A. Partnerships and S corporations are not allowed to deduct investment interest expense in determining income or loss. Instead, these conduit entities are required to set out and separately report each partner's or shareholder's share of *both* investment interest expense *and* net investment income for the current year. Each partner or shareholder must claim his or her deduction subject to the previously described limitations. Recall, however, that a partner that is a regular corporation will not be subject to the investment interest expense limitation.

CHARITABLE CONTRIBUTIONS

To encourage the private sector to share in the cost of providing many needed social services, Congress allows individuals, regular corporations, estates, and trusts deductions for charitable contributions (or gifts) of money or other property to certain qualified organizations. Partnerships and S corporations are not allowed to deduct charitable contributions. Instead, these conduit entities pass the contributions through to the partners and shareholders who must claim the deduction on their own Federal income tax returns.[79]

Code § 170 contains the rules regarding deductions for charitable contributions made by individuals and regular corporations. Code § 642(c) sets forth the rules regarding the amount and timing of charitable contribution deductions claimed by estates and trusts. The rules related to the measurement, timing, and qualification of contribution deductions claimed by individuals and corporations are discussed below. A discussion of the percentage limitations imposed on current deductions by individual taxpayers is also included. The specific rules regarding limitations imposed on a corporation's annual charitable contribution deduction are discussed in Chapter 19.

---

[79] See §§ 702(a)(4) and 1366(a)(1).

DEDUCTION REQUIREMENTS

Individual taxpayers are allowed a deduction for contributions of cash or other property *only if* the gift is made to a qualifying donee organization. Additionally, individuals are required to actually pay cash or transfer property before the close of the tax year in which the deduction is claimed. An exception to the payment requirement is made in the case of contribution deductions which, due to deduction limitations, have been carried over from prior years. The deduction limitations and carryover rules are discussed later in this chapter. Finally, for any contribution of $250 or more, special substantiation requirements must be met. Basically, a deduction for any contribution of $250 or more will be denied unless the taxpayer substantiates the contribution with a written acknowledgment of the contribution by the charitable organization. For this purpose, a canceled check is not sufficient. However, separate payments (e.g., a weekly contribution to the church of $50) are not aggregated for purposes of applying the $250 threshold.

Qualifying Donees.   To be deductible, contributions of cash or other property must be made to or for the use of one of the following:[80]

1. A state, a U.S. possession, a political subdivision of a state or possession, the United States, or the District of Columbia, if the contribution is made solely for public purposes;

2. A community chest, corporation, trust, fund, or foundation that is organized or created in, or under the laws of, the United States, any state, the District of Columbia, or any possession of the United States *and* is organized and operated exclusively for religious, charitable, scientific, literary, or educational purposes or for the prevention of cruelty to children or animals;

3. A war veterans' organization;

4. A nonprofit volunteer fire company or civil defense organization;

5. A domestic fraternal society operating under the lodge system, but only if the contribution is to be used for any of the purposes stated in item 2 above; and

6. A nonprofit cemetery company if the funds are to be used solely for the perpetual care of the cemetery as a whole, and not for a particular lot or mausoleum crypt.

If the taxpayer has not been informed by the recipient organization that it is a qualifying donee, he or she may check its status in the *Cumulative List of Organizations* (IRS Publication 78). This publication contains a frequently updated listing of organizations which have applied to and received tax-exempt status from the IRS. To be a qualifying donee, however, the organization is not required to be listed in this publication.

Disallowance Possibilities.   Direct contributions to needy or worthy individuals are not deductible. In addition, contributions to qualifying organizations must not be restricted to use by a specific person; if so, deductions generally are disallowed.

---

[80]   See § 170(c) and *Your Federal Income Tax*,
IRS Publication 17 (Rev. 1993), pp. 182–183.

Example 43. F contributed cash of $10,000 to his son, S. S is a missionary for a church that is a qualified organization, and the gift proceeds were used exclusively by S to further the charitable work of the church. F is not entitled to a charitable contribution deduction since the gift was not made to a qualifying donee. Similarly, F would be denied a deduction if he made the gift to the church but restricted the use of the funds only for his missionary son.[81]

A taxpayer's contribution to a qualified organization that is motivated by the taxpayer's expectation and receipt of a significant economic benefit will not be deductible as a charitable contribution. The receipt of an unexpected and indirect economic benefit as a result of the gift should not disqualify the taxpayer's deduction, however.

Example 44. T donated two parcels of land to a nearby city for use as building sites for new public schools. The location of the building sites was such that the city had to construct two access roads through the taxpayer's remaining undeveloped land in order to make use of the gifted property. Construction of the access roads significantly enhanced the value of T's remaining acreage, and as a result, his charitable contribution deduction may be denied.[82]

Apparently because Congress does not believe that the benefit received by a taxpayer is of great significance, 80 percent of the amount paid by a taxpayer to a college or university that either directly or indirectly entitles the taxpayer to purchase tickets to the institution's athletic events is allowed as a deduction.[83] However, any amount actually paid for the tickets will not be deductible.

LIMITATIONS ON DEDUCTIONS

Unlike the requirement that an individual's medical expenses and casualty losses *exceed* some minimum percentage of adjusted gross income (referred to as the *floor* amount) *before* any deductions are allowed, deductions for charitable contributions are subject to *ceiling* limitations (i.e., not to *exceed* a percentage of A.G.I.). Generally, an individual's current deduction for charitable contributions is limited to 50 percent of the taxpayer's adjusted gross income. A 30 percent ceiling limitation is imposed on an individual's contributions of *certain appreciated property*; and a 20 percent overall limitation is imposed on an individual's contributions to *certain qualifying organizations*.

---

[81] *White v. U.S.*, 82-1 USTC ¶9232, 49 AFTR2d 82-364, 514 F. Supp. 1057 (D.Ct. Utah, 1981). For a similar result, see *Babilonia v. Comm.*, 82-2 USTC ¶9478, 50 AFTR2d 82-5442 (CA-9, 1982).

[82] See *Ottawa Silica Co. v. U.S.*, 83-1 USTC ¶9169, 51 AFTR2d 83-590, 699 F.2d 1124 (CA-Fed. Cir., 1983) where, under similar circumstances, the taxpayer's claimed contribution deduction was disallowed.

[83] See § 170(m), introduced into the Code by the Technical and Miscellaneous Revenue Act of 1988. This provision was made retroactive to tax years beginning after 1983, and set aside a longstanding position of the IRS that denied any portion of such payments as deductions.

Under the general rule, the amount of a taxpayer's charitable deduction (before any percentage limitation) is the *sum* of money *plus* the fair market value of any property other than money which is contributed to a qualifying donee. However, both the gift of property to certain organizations and the gift of certain types of property other than money may result in a deduction of an amount *less than* the property's fair market value. These exceptions to the general rule are explained below, followed by a discussion of the various percentage limitations imposed on an individual's deduction for charitable contributions.[84]

Contributions Other than Money or Property. No charitable contribution deduction is allowed for the value of time or services rendered to a charitable organization.[85] Likewise, no deduction is allowed for any "lost income" associated with the rent-free use of a taxpayer's property by a qualifying charity. However, *unreimbursed* (out-of-pocket) *expenses* incurred by the taxpayer in rendering services to a charitable institution or allowing rent-free use of property by such an organization *qualify* as charitable contributions.[86] For example, a taxpayer is allowed a deduction for the cost and upkeep of uniforms required to be worn while performing the charitable services, but only if the uniforms are not suitable for everyday use. Similarly, a taxpayer is generally allowed to deduct amounts paid for transportation to and from his or her home to the place where the charitable services are performed.[87] This includes the costs for gasoline, oil, parking, and tolls incurred by a taxpayer using his or her own vehicle in connection with the charitable services. In lieu of deducting the actual expenses for gasoline and oil, a taxpayer is allowed to use a standard mileage rate of 12 cents per mile in calculating the cost of using an automobile in charitable activities.[88] In either case, no deduction is allowed for insurance, depreciation, or the costs of general repairs and maintenance.

---

[84] Regular corporations are subject to an overall limitation of 10 percent of taxable income, determined without regard to certain deductions. See Chapter 19 for more details.

[85] Reg. § 1.170A-1(g).

[86] *Ibid.*

[87] The Tax Reform Act of 1986 added § 170(k) to the Code to disallow a deduction for travel expenses related to charitable services where there is a significant element of personal pleasure, recreation, or vacation in such travel.

[88] See § 170(j) and Rev. Proc. 91-67, 1991 I.R.B. 52, 11.

Example 45. T is the scoutmaster of a local troop of the Boy Scouts of America. During the current year, T incurred the following expenses in rendering his services to this charitable organization:

Cost and upkeep of uniforms	$ 80
Gasoline and oil expenses	200
Parking and tolls	30
Estimated value of rent-free use of den in home	1,000
Estimated value of services (500 hours @ $50 per hour)	25,000
Total	$26,310

T is entitled to a $310 charitable contribution deduction for his out-of-pocket expenses ($80 + $200 + $30) incurred in rendering the charitable services as a scoutmaster. No deduction is allowed for the estimated value of his services or the rent-free use of his home.

Example 46. Assume the same facts as in *Example 45*, except that T drove his automobile 3,000 miles in connection with the charitable services. If he did not keep records of the actual expenses for gasoline and oil, T could use the standard mileage rate of 12 cents per mile. In this case, he will be allowed to deduct $470 [(3,000 miles × 12¢ per mile for charitable use of auto = $360) + $30 for parking and tolls + $80 related to uniforms].

Fair Market Value Determination. The IRS defines fair market value as "the price at which the property would change hands between a willing buyer and a willing seller, neither being under any compulsion to buy or sell and both having reasonable knowledge of relevant facts."[89] Determination of this amount usually means the taxpayer must make an educated guess or incur the cost of an independent appraisal. Since the IRS requires that the taxpayer attach a statement to his or her return when a deduction exceeding $500 is claimed for a charitable gift of property (Form 8283, Noncash Charitable Contributions), many taxpayers seek independent appraisals to support their claimed deductions. Independent appraisals are *required*—and the donee must *attach* a summary of the appraisal to his or her return—if the claimed value of the contributed property exceeds $5,000.[90] Appraisal fees are not deductible as contributions. However, they are deductible by individuals as miscellaneous itemized deductions (subject to the 2% floor).[91]

---

[89] Reg. § 1.170-1(c)(1).

[90] § 6050L. A donee charity that sells or otherwise disposes of such property within two years of the donation *must* report the disposition (and amount received, if any) to the IRS and the donor.

[91] Under § 212(3), individuals are allowed to deduct expenses associated with the determination of their tax liability. This includes appraisal fees paid in valuing property contributions.

Ordinary Income Property. The term *ordinary income property* is used to describe any property which, if sold, would require the owner to recognize gain *other than* long-term capital gain. As such, ordinary income property includes a donor/taxpayer's property held primarily for sale to customers in his or her trade or business (i.e., inventory items), a work of art created by the donor, a manuscript prepared by the donor, letters and memorandums prepared by or for the donor, and a capital asset held by the taxpayer for not more than one year (i.e., short-term capital gain property). The term also includes property which, if sold, would result in the recognition of ordinary income under any of the depreciation recapture provisions.[92]

The charitable deduction (without regard to any percentage limitations) for the gift of ordinary income property is equal to the property's fair market value *reduced* by the amount of ordinary income that would be recognized if the property had been sold at its fair market value (this amount is often called the *ordinary income potential*).[93]

> **Example 47.** F donated 100 shares of IBM stock to his church on December 15, 1994. F had purchased the stock for $9,000 on August 7, 1994, and it was worth $12,000 on the date of the gift. Since F would have recognized a short-term capital gain if the stock had been sold on December 15, 1994 (i.e., holding period not more than one year), the stock is ordinary income property. As a result, F's charitable contribution deduction is limited to $9,000 ($12,000 fair market value − $3,000 ordinary income potential).

In most cases, the charitable deduction for ordinary income property will be limited to the taxpayer's adjusted basis in the property since its fair market value is reduced by the *unrealized appreciation* in value (fair market value − adjusted basis) which would not result in long-term capital gain if the property were sold. There are, however, four important instances when this would not be the case. First, the charitable deduction for *any property* which, if sold, would result in a *loss* (i.e., adjusted basis > fair market value) is limited to the property's fair market value. Second, any depreciable property held by the taxpayer for more than one year and used in his or her trade or business is *§ 1231 property*. The amount of gain from the sale of such property that exceeds any depreciation recapture is referred to as "§ 1231 gain." Potential § 1231 gains are treated as long-term capital gains for purposes of measuring a taxpayer's charitable contribution deduction.[94] As such, any unrealized appreciation in the value of property that is attributable to § 1231 gain will not be considered ordinary income potential for purposes of the above-described limitation.

The two remaining exceptions apply to the deduction allowed a corporation which contributes inventory items (ordinary income property) to certain qualifying charities. In one situation, the inventory must be donated to a public charity or private operating foundation *and* used by the charitable organization for the care of children, the ill, or the needy.[95] The other situation requires that the inventory item be manufactured by the

---

[92] See § 170(e)(1), Reg. §§ 1.170A-4(b)(1) and (b)(4).

[93] § 170(e)(1). For an application of this rule, see *William Glen*, 79 T.C. 208 (1982).

[94] Reg. § 1.170A-4(b)(4).

[95] § 170(e)(3).

corporate taxpayer, constitute scientific property, and be donated within two years of its construction to an educational institution for use in research.[96] In each of these situations, the corporate taxpayer is permitted to claim a contribution deduction in excess of the property's adjusted basis.

Capital Gain Property. Any property which, if sold by the donor/taxpayer, would result in the recognition of a long-term capital gain or § 1231 gain is *capital gain property*.[97] A taxpayer is generally allowed to claim the fair market value of such property as a contribution deduction. There are two important exceptions to this rule, however. *First*, if capital gain property is contributed to or for the use of a private nonoperating foundation [as defined in § 509(a)], the donor must *reduce* the contribution deduction by the *entire* amount of any long-term capital gain or § 1231 gain which would be recognized if the property were sold at its fair market value.[98] In effect, this exception treats the contribution of capital gain property to private nonoperating foundations exactly like contributions of ordinary income property, since the donor must reduce the contribution deduction to the basis of the property.

> **Example 48.** G donates stock worth $10,000 to a private nonoperating foundation on November 17, 1994. G had purchased the stock for $4,000 on August 23, 1990. G's charitable contribution deduction must be reduced to $4,000 ($10,000 fair market value − entire $6,000 appreciation).

It is important to note that this limitation *generally* does not apply to donations of capital gain property to public charities.

> **Example 49.** Assume the same facts as in *Example 48*, except that G donated the stock to her alma mater, State University (a public charity). G's charitable contribution would be $10,000 because the reduction requirement applies only to contributions to private foundations.

The *second* exception to the general rule that taxpayers are allowed to claim a deduction for the fair market value of contributed capital gain property involves contributions of tangible personalty.[99] If tangible personalty is contributed to a public charity (i.e., a university, museum, church, etc.) and the property is put to an *unrelated use* by the donee organization, the charitable contribution must be reduced by the entire amount of the property's unrealized appreciation in value (i.e., to the property's basis). For purposes of this limitation, the term *unrelated use* means that the property could not be used by

---

[96] § 170(e)(4).

[97] § 170(e)(1).

[98] § 170(e)(1)(B)(ii).

[99] As described in Chapter 9, tangible personalty is all tangible property *other than* realty (i.e., land, buildings, structural components).

the public charity in its activities for which tax-exempt status had been granted. For example, if antique furnishings are donated to a local museum that either stores, displays, or uses the items in its office in the course of carrying out its functions, the use of such property is a related use.[100] The fact that the charity later sells or exchanges the property does not alter the contribution deduction. Thus, if the taxpayer can reasonably anticipate that the tangible personalty donated to the charitable organization will be put to a related use, this limitation will not be applicable.[101]

> **Example 50.**   J contributes a painting to the local university. He had purchased the painting in 1981 for $10,000, and it was appraised at $60,000 on the date of the gift. The painting was placed in the university's library for display and study by art students. J's charitable contribution will be measured at $60,000 (the painting's fair market value) since the property was not put to an unrelated use. This is true even if the university later sells the painting.

> **Example 51.**   R donates her gun collection to the YWCA (a public charity). R had paid $8,000 for the collection 10 years ago, and the guns were appraised at $18,000 on the date of the gift. The YWCA immediately sold the collection for $18,000 to a local gun dealer. Although the property had appreciated by $10,000, R's charitable contribution must be reduced to $8,000 (the property's basis) since the property was not (and most likely could not be) put to a related use.

Fifty Percent Limitation.   An individual's deduction for contributions made to public charities may not exceed 50 percent of his or her adjusted gross income for the year.[102] This "ceiling" deduction limitation applies to contributions made to the following types of public charities:[103]

1. A church or a convention or association of churches;

2. An educational organization that normally maintains a regular faculty and curriculum;

3. An organization whose principal purposes or functions are the providing of medical or hospital care (hospitals) or medical education or medical research (medical schools);

4. An organization that receives support from the government and is organized and operated exclusively to receive, hold, invest, and administer property for the benefit of a college or university;

5. A state, a possession of the United States, or any political subdivision of any of the foregoing, or the United States or the District of Columbia;

6. An organization that normally receives a substantial part of its support from a government unit (described in item 5 above) or from the general public; and

7. Certain types of private foundations discussed below.

---

[100] Reg. § 1.170A-4(b)(3).

[101] Reg. § 1.170A-4(b)(3)(ii).

[102] § 170(b) and Reg. § 1.170A-8(b).

[103] § 170(b)(1).

Private foundations are organizations that, by definition, do not receive contributions from the general public. Examples of well-known private foundations include the Ford, Carnegie, Cullen, and Mellon Foundations. For charitable deduction purposes, private foundations are classified as either operating or nonoperating foundations. Contributions to *all* private operating foundations are subject to the 50 percent ceiling limitation.[104] The 50 percent limit also applies to contributions to certain private, nonoperating foundations if the organizations

1. Distribute the contributions they receive to public charities and private operating foundations *within* 2 ½ months following the year the contributions were received; or

2. Pool all contributions received into a common fund, and distribute *both* the income and the principal from the fund to public charities.

An individual's contributions of cash and ordinary income property to public charities, private operating foundations, and the above described nonoperating foundations which exceed the 50 percent limitation are carried forward and deducted in subsequent years. The carryover rules are discussed in a later section of this chapter. Contributions of capital gain property *and* contributions to private nonoperating foundations (other than those described above) are subject to *either* the 30 percent or 20 percent limitation. These limitations are discussed below.

Thirty Percent Limitation. There are *two* situations in which the 30 percent limitation may apply. The first situation involves the following types of contributions:

1. Contributions for the *use* of any charitable organization;

2. Contributions to veterans' organizations, fraternal societies, and not-for-profit cemetery companies; *and*

3. Contributions to most private nonoperating foundations.

The annual deduction for these contributions is limited to the *lesser of*

1. Thirty percent of adjusted gross income, *or*

2. An amount equal to 50 percent of adjusted gross income, *reduced* by contributions qualifying for the 50 percent limitation.[105]

---

[104] See § 4942(j) for the requirements for classification as a private operating foundation. For all practical purposes, an operating foundation is recognized as a public charity.

[105] See § 170(b)(1)(C).

Example 52.   R has adjusted gross income of $50,000 for the current year and contributes $5,000 cash to his church and $20,000 cash to the Veterans of Foreign Wars. R's deduction for the contribution to his church will not be limited because it does not exceed 50% of A.G.I. (i.e., $5,000 < $25,000). However, only $15,000 of the contribution to the veterans' organization will be allowed as a deduction for the current year because this donation is subject to the 30% limitation.

Contribution to church...........................	$ 5,000
Plus: Lesser of	
(1) 30% × $50,000 = $15,000	
or	
(2) 50% × $50,000 = $25,000, reduced by $5,000 gift to church = $20,000	
	15,000
Total contribution deduction......................	$20,000

Example 53.   Assume the same facts in *Example 52*, except that the contribution to the church was $20,000 and the contribution to the veterans' organization was $8,000. Again, the contribution to the church will not be limited because it does not exceed 50% of A.G.I. However, the contribution to the veterans organization will be limited to $5,000, computed as follows:

Contribution to church...........................	$20,000
Plus: Lesser of	
(1) 30% × $50,000 = $15,000	
or	
(2) 50% × $50,000 = $25,000, reduced by $20,000 gift to church = $5,000	
	5,000
Total contribution deduction......................	$25,000

Note that it is not the 30% of A.G.I. limitation that causes R's contribution to the veterans' organization to be limited. Instead, it is the fact that the overall limitation on the annual contribution deduction amount is 50% of adjusted gross income, and the contribution to the public charity is considered first.

The *second* situation in which the 30 percent limitation may apply involves contributions of captial gain property. The annual deduction allowed for contributions of capital gain property that have not been reduced by the unrealized appreciation will generally be limited to 30 percent of the taxpayer's adjusted gross income.[106] This limitation was imposed by Congress in 1969 to reduce the amount of charitable contribution deductions allowed taxpayers for gifts of substantially appreciated capital or § 1231 assets. As in the first situation discussed above, these contributions subject to the 30 percent limit are considered only after the amount of contributions allowed under the 50 percent limitation has been determined. Contributions in excess of the 30 percent limit can be carried forward and deducted in subsequent years.

> **Example 54.** K has adjusted gross income of $30,000 for the 1994 tax year. The only contribution made by K in 1994 consisted of stock worth $10,000, which she had purchased for $4,000 in 1989. The stock was given to her church. Although the contribution does not exceed 50% of her adjusted gross income, K's deduction is limited to $9,000 (30% × $30,000 A.G.I.) since the stock is capital gain property. The $1,000 excess contribution can be carried over to subsequent years.

> **Example 55.** Assume the same facts as in *Example 54*, except that K's 1994 adjusted gross income is $40,000 and she also gave $14,000 cash to her church. In this case, her deduction for the gift of the stock is limited to $6,000 (50% × $40,000 A.G.I. = $20,000 − $14,000 cash contribution) since the 50% overall limitation is applied before the 30% limitation. The remaining $4,000 ($10,000 fair market value of stock − $6,000 deduction allowed) will be carried forward to subsequent years.

When capital gain property has been contributed, the 30 percent limitation can be avoided if the taxpayer *elects* to reduce his or her claimed deduction for the capital gain property by the property's unrealized appreciation.[107] This may result in a larger deduction in the current year since the reduced amount will be subject to a higher ceiling limitation (i.e., 50% of A.G.I. rather than 30%). It is important to note that this election, if made, applies to all contributions of capital gain property made during the year.

---

[106] § 170(b)(1)(C)(i). In addition, the amount of the deduction related to unrealized appreciation is generally treated as a tax preference item for purposes of the alternative minimum tax. See Chapter 13 for more details.

[107] § 170(b)(1)(C)(iii).

Example 56.   T has adjusted gross income of $50,000 for the current year and contributes stock worth $23,000 to the American Heart Association (a public charity). T had purchased the stock for $19,000 two years earlier. Assuming this is T's only contribution for the current year, he can either claim his deduction subject to the 30% limitation and carry over any excess, or *elect* to reduce the claimed deduction by the capital gain property's unrealized appreciation and forgo any carryover. T's deduction choices are

1. $15,000 current deduction (30% × $50,000 A.G.I.) and $8,000 ($23,000 − $15,000) contribution carryover; or

2. $19,000 current deduction ($23,000 − $4,000 unrealized appreciation) and no carryover.

Obviously, the decision to reduce a current deduction by the property's unrealized appreciation *or* to claim the deduction subject to the 30 percent limit and carry over any excess amount will depend on several factors. Among the factors to be considered are

1.   The difference between the capital gain property's fair market value and its adjusted basis to the taxpayer (i.e., unrealized appreciation);

2.   The taxpayer's current marginal income tax bracket compared to his or her anticipated future marginal tax rates; and

3.   The expected remaining life of the taxpayer and his or her anticipated future contributions.

Twenty Percent Limitation.   The 50 percent ceiling limitation imposed on an individual's annual charitable contribution deduction is an "overall" limitation. The 30 percent limitation applies to most contributions of capital gain property and to contributions of cash and ordinary income property contributed to nonqualifying private nonoperating funds. However, a more severe restriction is imposed on deductions for contributions of capital gain property to such private nonoperating foundations. In addition to the required *reduction* of the contribution by any unrealized appreciation in value, the deduction allowed for contributions to *private charities* (i.e., organizations not included in the seven categories listed earlier) is limited to the *lesser of*

1.   Twenty percent of adjusted gross income; or

2.   An amount equal to 50 percent of adjusted gross income, and reduced by contributions qualifying for the 50 percent and 30 percent limitations, including any amount in excess of the 30 percent limitation.[108]

Like excess contributions to public charities, any contributions to private nonoperating foundations that exceed the 20 percent limitation are carried forward and deductible subject to the 20 percent limit, in subsequent years.[109]

---

[108]   § 170(b)(1)(B)(i).   [109]   § 170(d)(1).

Example 57.   D contributed $8,000 to his church (a public charity) and IBM stock worth $15,000 to a private nonoperating foundation in 1994. D had purchased the stock for $11,000 in 1989. His adjusted gross income for the year is $20,000. D's contribution deduction for 1994 is $10,000 [$8,000 contribution to church + $2,000 of the eligible $11,000 contribution to private foundation ($15,000 market value − $4,000 unrealized "appreciation" = $11,000)]. The deduction allowed for the contribution to the private foundation is limited to the *lesser* of

1. $4,000 (20% × $20,000 A.G.I.); or

2. $2,000 [(50% × $20,000 A.G.I. = $10,000) − $8,000 contribution qualifying for the 50% limitation].

Note that D's total contribution deduction of $10,000 does not exceed 50% of his 1994 adjusted gross income. If D had contributed $10,000 or more to his church, *none* of the $11,000 contribution to the private foundation would have been allowed. In either case, the excess contributions can be carried over to subsequent years.

CONTRIBUTION CARRYOVERS

An individual's contributions that exceed either the 20 percent limitation, the 30 percent limitation, or the 50 percent overall limitation may be carried over for five years.[110] All excess contributions due to the 20 and 30 percent limitations will *again* be subject to these limitations in the carryover years.[111] Although contribution carryovers are treated as having been made in the year to which they are carried, contributions *actually* made in the carryover year must be claimed before any carryover amounts are deducted.[112]

Example 58.   In 1994 D contributes $10,000 cash to State University (a public charity). Her adjusted gross income for 1994 is $15,000. D's contribution deduction for 1994 is limited to $7,500 (50% × $15,000 A.G.I.) and she may carry over the remaining $2,500 to 1995. If she does not make contributions in 1995 that exceed the 50% limitation, D can claim the $2,500 carryover as a deduction. If the contributions actually made in 1995 exceed 50% of D's 1995 adjusted gross income, she must carry over the 1995 excess contributions *and* the $2,500 carryover from 1994.

Example 59.   Assume the same facts as in *Example 58*, except that D's contribution was a capital gain property worth $10,000 instead of cash. Her 1994 deduction would be limited to $4,500 (30% × $15,000 A.G.I.) and she would have a $5,500 contribution carryover. Since this carryover resulted from the 30% limitation, it will be subject to the 30% limit in any carryover year. Thus if D has adjusted gross income of $10,000 and does not make contributions in 1995, she can claim a deduction of $3,000 (30% × $10,000 A.G.I.) and carry over the remaining $2,500.

---

[110]   § 170(d)(1)(A) and Reg. § 1.170A-10(a).   [112]   Reg. § 1.170A-10(c)(1).

[111]   Reg. § 1.170A-10(b)(2).

All charitable contribution carryovers are applied on a first-in, first-out basis in determining the amount of any carryovers deductible in the current year.[113] Since such carryovers will expire if not deducted within five succeeding tax years, taxpayers obviously should limit actual contributions until the carryovers are used.

MISCELLANEOUS ITEMIZED DEDUCTIONS

As discussed in Chapter 7, two major changes regarding miscellaneous itemized deductions were introduced into the tax laws in 1986. Perhaps the most significant change involves the inclusion in this category of all *unreimbursed* employee business expenses. Prior to 1987, an employee's unreimbursed travel and transportation expenses were allowed as deductions in arriving at adjusted gross income. Since 1986, *both* unreimbursed employee expenses *and* those not reimbursed under an accountable plan must be treated as miscellaneous itemized deductions.[114] Additionally, an employee's unreimbursed costs for business entertainment and meals (whether or not incurred in connection with travel) must first be reduced by a 50 percent disallowance since only 50 percent of these costs qualify for deduction.[115] It is also important to remember that interest on any indebtedness to finance an employee's business expenses is treated as *nondeductible* personal interest expense.

The second major change involves the introduction of a deduction *floor* on the total of all expenses in this category similar to the approach taken for medical and casualty loss deductions. After 1986, miscellaneous itemized deductions are deductible only to the extent they *exceed* 2 percent of A.G.I.[116] The obvious intent of this change in the law is to limit the number of taxpayers who will be able to deduct miscellaneous itemized deductions—and thereby reduce the administrative cost of policing such deductions. Exhibit 11-4 contains a partial list of items qualifying as miscellaneous itemized deductions.

> **Example 60.**   T has $40,000 of adjusted gross income in 1994. His unreimbursed employee business expenses and other miscellaneous itemized deductions include

Unreimbursed business travel expenses............	$ 90
Subscription to the Wall Street Journal...............	110
Professional dues.....................................	250
Safety deposit box rental...........................	50
Tax return preparation fee...........................	250
Total...	$750

> Since T's total miscellaneous itemized deductions of $750 do not exceed $800 (2% × $40,000 A.G.I.), he will not be able to claim any deduction for these expenses.

---

[113] Reg. § 1.170A-10(b)(2).

[114] Reg. § 1.62-2.

[115] § 274(n).

[116] § 67(a).

Exhibit 11-4 *Partial List of Miscellaneous Itemized Deductions*

Reimbursed employee expenses under
   A nonaccountable plan

Unreimbursed employee expenses for
   Travel away from home (lodging and 50% of meals)
   Transportation expenses
   Entertainment expenses (after 50% reduction)
   Home office expenses
   Outside salesperson's expenses
   Professional dues and memberships
   Subscriptions to business journals
   Uniform costs, cleaning, and maintenance expenses
   Union dues

Investment expenses for
   Investment advice
   Investment newsletter subscriptions
   Management fees charged by mutual funds
   Rentals of safety deposit boxes

Qualifying education expenses

Job seeking expenses (in the same business)

Tax determination expenses for
   Appraisal costs incurred to measure deductions for medical expenses (capital improvements), charitable contributions, and casualty losses
   Tax return preparation fees
   Tax advice, tax seminars, and books about taxes

OTHER ITEMIZED DEDUCTIONS

The final category of itemized deductions includes certain personal expenses and losses that cannot be classified in any of the other categories discussed thus far. Some of the items in this category—referred to as "Other Miscellaneous Itemized Deductions"—are discussed in other chapters.

1. Unrecovered investment in an annuity where the taxpayer's death prevents recovery of the entire investment. As discussed in Chapter 6, this deduction is allowed on the taxpayer's final tax return.

2. Impairment-related work expenses of persons with disabilities.

3. Amortizable premium on bonds purchased before October 23, 1986. Amortization of bond premium is discussed in Chapter 16.

4. Gambling losses to the extent of gambling winnings.

It is important to note that each of these items may be subject to its own unique set of limitations (e.g., gambling losses). Unlike miscellaneous itemized deductions, however, these deductions *are not* subject to the 2 percent limit.

THREE PERCENT CUTBACK RULE

As mentioned in Chapter 3, the total itemized deductions of certain high-income taxpayers are subject to another limitation. Basically, taxpayers must reduce total itemized deductions otherwise allowable (*other than* medical expenses, casualty and theft losses, investment interest, and gambling losses) by 3 percent of their A.G.I. in excess of $111,800 ($55,900 for married individuals filing separately).[117] However, this reduction cannot exceed 80 percent of the deductions. Again, this ensures that taxpayers subject to the cutback rule can deduct at least 20 percent of their so-called "3 percent" deductions. Consequently, a taxpayer's itemized deductions are never completely phased out.

Exhibit 11-5 identifies the itemized deductions that are subject to the cutback rule. Again, it is important to note that a taxpayer's medical expenses, investment interest expense, casualty and theft losses, and gambling losses are not subject to this limitation.

Exhibit 11-5 *Itemized Deductions Subject to Cutback Rule*

Taxes paid, including
State, local, and foreign income taxes
State, local, and foreign real property taxes
State and local personal property taxes
Mortgage interest on personal residences
Charitable contributions
Miscellaneous itemized deductions (in excess of 2% of A.G.I.)

---

[117] § 68. These threshold amounts were $108,450 and $54,225, respectively, for 1993, and they are adjusted annually for inflation.

Example 61.   Z is single and has adjusted gross income of $261,800 for the current year. Z has the following itemized deductions: medical expenses ($1,200 after the 7.5% limitation), real estate taxes paid ($3,000), state income taxes ($7,400), home mortgage interest ($10,300), charitable contributions ($2,500), and miscellaneous itemized deductions ($800 after the 2% limitation). The amount of itemized deductions that Z may deduct for the current year is computed as follows:

Itemized deductions subject to cutback:		
Taxes paid ($3,000 + $7,400).................................	$ 10,400	
Home mortgage interest......................................	10,300	
Charitable contributions......................................	2,500	
Miscellaneous itemized deductions............................	800	
Deductions subject to 3% cutback rule...........................		$24,000
Tentative cutback:		
Adjusted gross income..	$261,800	
Threshold amount...	(111,800)	
Excess A.G.I...	$150,000	
Times: 3%...	× 3%	
Tentative cutback...	$ 4,500	
Cutback limit:		
Itemized deductions subject to cutback........................	$ 24,000	
Times: 80%..	× 80%	
Maximum cutback..	$ 19,200	
Cutback: *Lesser* of tentative cutback		
or maximum cutback..................................		(4,500)
Amount deductible after 3% cutback..............................		$19,500
Plus: Itemized deductions not subject		
to cutback (medical expenses)...........................		1,200
Total deduction for itemized deductions...........................		$20,700

Example 62.   Assume the same facts in *Example 61* above, except that Z's adjusted gross income for the current year is $811,800.

Total itemized deductions subject to cutback......................		$24,000
Tentative cutback:		
Adjusted gross income...	$811,800	
Threshold amount...	− 111,800	
Excess A.G.I..	$700,000	
Times: 3%..	× 3%	
Tentative cutback...	$ 21,000	
Cutback limit:		
Itemized deductions subject to cutback.........................	$ 24,000	
Times: 80%...	× 80%	
Maximum cutback..	$ 19,200	
Cutback: *Lesser* of tentative cutback		
or maximum cutback...................................		−19,200
Amount deductible after 3% cutback............................		$ 4,800
Plus: Itemized deductions not subject		
to cutback (medical expenses).........................		1,200
Total deduction for itemized deductions.........................		$ 6,000

Note that in this case Z's tentative cutback ($21,000) exceeds the maximum cutback ($19,200). Thus, Z is allowed to deduct at least 20% ($24,000 × 20% = $4,800) of the itemized deductions subject to the cutback rule.

It should be obvious from the above examples that relatively few taxpayers will suffer drastic cutbacks in their itemized deductions. However, those taxpayers with adjusted gross incomes above the annual threshold amount will find that they face another complexity in computing their itemized deductions.

TAX PLANNING CONSIDERATIONS

MAXIMIZING PERSONAL DEDUCTIONS

Each year the taxpayer must choose between taking the standard deduction and itemizing actual deductions. If the standard deduction is chosen, then legitimate itemized deductions are lost. If the taxpayer chooses to itemize actual deductions, then the standard deduction is lost. One technique used to minimize the loss of personal deductions is to shift actual itemized deductions from one year to another (to the extent allowed by law) so that they are high in one year and low in the next.

Example 63. S is single and has itemized deductions that are expected to be constant in 1994 and 1995 as follows:

Mortgage interest.........................	$ 400
Dental expense (deductible portion).......	1,400
State and local taxes.....................	350
Charitable contributions..................	1,350
Total	$3,500

S cannot itemize actual deductions in 1994 or 1995 because actual deductions are less than the standard deduction for single status (assumed to be $4,000 in each year for illustration purposes). Over the two-year period, S will deduct $8,000 for personal expenses by claiming the standard deduction. However, if S were able to shift $1,000 of elective dental expenses from 1995 into 1994, and to accelerate the 1995 charitable contribution into 1994, then she would receive a greater tax benefit in the two-year period for personal expenses. Actual expenses in each year would be

	1994	1995
Mortgage interest.........................	$ 400	$ 400
Dental expense (deductible portion).......	2,400	400
State taxes...............................	350	350
Charitable contributions..................	2,700	0
Total	$5,850	$1,150

Although actual personal expenses still total $7,000 over the two-year period, S now has itemized deductions of $5,850 in 1994 and a standard deduction of $4,000 in 1995. During the 2-year period S will deduct $9,850 for personal expenses and will receive $1,850 more in deductions than if personal expenses had not been shifted.

Personal expenses should be shifted into years when adjusted gross income is lower. Not only will the 7.5 percent medical expense threshold and the 2 percent miscellaneous expense threshold be lower, but the effect of the 3 percent cutback on itemized deductions may be less. If adjusted gross income is under the prevailing threshold amount in the year that the itemized deductions are bunched, the 3 percent limitation will be avoided altogether.

MEDICAL EXPENSES

The dependency exemption under a multiple support agreement should be assigned to the taxpayer who pays the medical expenses of the dependent. The medical expenses are deductible only by the family member entitled to the dependency exemption and only if that family member actually pays on behalf of the claimed dependent. Medical expenses paid by other family members on behalf of the dependent will not be allowed as deductions.

Often expenditures incurred in the care of an ill or handicapped child may qualify for either a medical expense deduction or for the child care credit (discussed in Chapter 13). When this happens, the tax liability should be computed under each alternative to determine which is more advantageous. Usually the choice depends on the taxpayer's marginal tax rate as compared to the credit percentage rate. The choice will also depend on the 7.5 percent threshold and whether the taxpayer is itemizing or taking the standard deduction.

> **Example 64.**   In 1994 T and W spend $2,000 for care of their handicapped child. The $2,000 qualifies both as a medical expense and for the child care credit. T and W have other medical expenses that exceed the 7.5% threshold amount. T and W file a joint tax return, and their marginal tax rate is 31%. The applicable percentage for the child care credit is 20%. If T and W are able to itemize deductions, they will receive a $620 tax benefit ($2,000 × 31%) for claiming the expenditure as a medical expense, whereas they will receive only a $400 tax benefit ($2,000 × 20%) if they claim the expenditure for the child care credit. If T and W are not able to itemize deductions or if they cannot exceed the 7.5% medical expense threshold amount, then the expenditure should be claimed for the child care credit.

CHARITABLE CONTRIBUTIONS

When a taxpayer makes noncash donations of property having a fair market value lower than the adjusted tax basis, it may be more advantageous to sell the property and donate the proceeds. If the property is held for investment, the sale will yield a deductible capital loss in addition to the charitable deduction. No loss will result, however, if the property itself is donated. To recognize a loss when selling depreciated property, the property must be held for investment or business use rather than for personal use.

Example 65. T owns 100 shares of X Corporation stock that he bought for $5,000 in 1990. The stock currently has a fair market value of $2,000. If T donates the stock to a qualified charity, he will only be entitled to a $2,000 charitable deduction. If T sells the stock and donates the $2,000 proceeds to a qualified charity, he will be entitled to a $3,000 capital loss as well as a $2,000 charitable deduction.

MISCELLANEOUS DEDUCTIONS

Because certain miscellaneous itemized deductions are deductible only to the extent that they aggregately exceed 2 percent of the adjusted gross income, it is important that expenses that can be properly classified into another, nonlimited category be identified and separated. For example, if a taxpayer supplements his or her regular salary with self-employed consulting income, it may be proper to deduct some of the cost of professional publications, professional journals, and educational expenses on Schedule C rather than as a miscellaneous itemized deduction.

Some unreimbursed employee business expenses that are not presently deductible because of the 2 percent limit might be converted into deductible reimbursed employee business expenses by agreement with the employer.

Example 66. K incurs $500 of unreimbursed employee business expenses each year. Her miscellaneous itemized deductions do not exceed the 2 percent limit; she is therefore unable to deduct any of this expense. K's employer agrees, as part of next year's compensation increase, to reimburse her for $500 of employee business expenses. K will now be able to deduct the $500 of expenses against the reimbursement.

PROBLEM MATERIALS

DISCUSSION QUESTIONS

11-1 *Medical Expenses and Dependency Status.* Under what circumstances is a taxpayer entitled to deduct medical expenses attributable to other persons?

11-2 *Medical Expenses.* F and M are the divorced parents of three minor children. M, the custodial parent, has proposed to F that the current child-support payments be increased in order to pay the expected dental costs of having braces put on their oldest son's teeth. F's tax advisor has suggested that F agree to pay these costs directly to the dentist rather than increasing the support payments. From a tax perspective, why has F's advisor made this suggestion?

11-3 *Medical Expenses.* K and her two brothers currently provide more than half the support of their mother. For the past several years, they have taken turns claiming a dependency exemption deduction for their mother under a multiple support agreement. This year, K will be entitled to the exemption, and her mother needs money for cataract surgery and new eyeglasses. K's accountant has suggested that she can double up on the tax benefits by directing her share of her mother's support toward these expenses. How is this possible?

11-4 *Medical Expenses.* For the past several years, L's total itemized deductions have barely exceeded his standard deduction amount, and this pattern is not expected to change in the near future. L is currently faced with elective surgery to repair a hernia, and the procedure is not covered under his health insurance policy. Strictly from a tax perspective, and assuming that this ailment is not life-threatening, what advice would you give to L concerning the timing of the surgery?

11-5 *Prepaid Medical Expenses.* What is the requirement imposed on taxpayers who wish to deduct prepaid medical expenses? What potential abuse is prevented by this requirement?

11-6 *Medical Deductions—Percentage Limitation.* The only medical expenditures made by taxpayer T during 1994 were for prescription drugs costing $800 and new eyeglasses costing $150. If T has adjusted gross income of $10,000 for the year and itemizes his deductions, how much, if any, medical expense deduction will he be allowed?

11-7 *Medical Travel Expenses.* W resides in Gary, Indiana and suffers from chronic bronchitis. At the advice of her doctor, W spends three months each year in Flagstaff, Arizona. Under what circumstances would W be entitled to claim the costs incurred for these trips as deductible medical expenses? If deductible, which costs?

11-8 *Casualty Losses.* Taxpayer F has adjusted gross income of $20,000 during the current year and he asks you the following questions regarding the deductibility of damages to his home caused by a recent hurricane. (Hint: See Chapter 10 for discussion of limitations on casualty loss deductions.)

    a. If F does not have home insurance, how much must his loss be before any deduction is available?

    b. If F repairs the damage himself, what amount can he deduct for the value of his time?

    c. If the area in which he resides is declared a disaster area, what options are available to F as to when to claim a deduction for the casualty loss?

11-9 *Taxes versus Fees.* What is the distinction between a deductible tax and a fee? If an individual taxpayer paid appraisal fees in connection with the determination of his personal casualty loss and charitable contribution deductions, would these payments be deductible?

11-10 *Deductible Income Taxes.* Which income taxes are deductible by an individual taxpayer? Does it make any difference whether the taxes are paid directly by the taxpayer as opposed to being withheld from his or her salary and paid by an employer to the appropriate taxing authority?

11-11 *Filing Status and State Income Taxes.* If married taxpayers file separate state or Federal income tax returns, how is the Federal tax deduction for state income taxes determined?

11-12 *Personal Property Taxes.* What is an ad valorem tax? What difference does it make to a taxpayer if he or she pays a tax on nonbusiness property and the tax is based on weight or model year as opposed to value?

11-13 *Real Estate Tax Apportionment.* How are real estate taxes apportioned between the buyer and seller in the year real property is sold? What effect does the apportionment have on the seller if the buyer pays the real estate taxes for the entire year?

11-14 *Special Tax Assessments.* Under what circumstances can a property owner claim a deduction for a special tax assessment?

11-15 *Personal Interest.* What is the current limitation imposed on the deductions of personal interest? What impact do you suppose this restriction might have on debt-financed consumer purchases?

11-16 *Deductible Interest.* Your neighbor has come up with an excellent tax plan and he asks you for advice on structuring his scheme. He plans to give each of his five children a $10,000 promissory note, due in 20 years and bearing interest at 10 percent per year. The interest will be paid annually and he plans to claim a $5,000 interest expense deduction. Do you see any flaws in this plan? What advice would you give to your neighbor?

11-17 *Classifying Interest Expenses.* The local bank has just introduced a new loan program entitled "Home Equity Credit Line" under which individuals can either borrow funds or finance credit card purchases based on the equity they have in their homes. What is the tax incentive offered by this arrangement?

11-18 *Investment Interest Expense.* What is the investment interest expense limitation? Which taxpayers are not subject to this limitation? What is the purpose of the limitation?

11-19 *Types of Interest Expense.* D is a spender, not a saver. In fact, he spends money he doesn't even have. This year he borrowed over $50,000 and paid interest of close to $7,000. D was shocked when his accountant told him that only certain types of interest were deductible.

    a. Identify the different types of interest expense and explain the treatment of each.
    b. How will D classify the interest expense that he paid?

11-20 *Charitable Contribution Requirements.* What are the basic requirements imposed on an individual taxpayer's deduction for charitable contributions?

11-21 *Contributions of Ordinary Income Property.* What is ordinary income property? Does this contribution deduction limitation apply to all taxpayers? Explain.

11-22 *Contributions of Capital Gain Property.* Under what circumstances must a taxpayer reduce his or her contribution deduction by the unrealized appreciation in value of capital gain property donated to a qualifying charity? How might this limitation be avoided?

11-23 *Contribution Deduction Percentage Limitations.* What are the percentage limitations imposed on an individual taxpayer's annual charitable contribution deduction? In what order must these percentage limitations be applied to current contributions?

11-24 *Contribution Carryovers.* Which excess contributions may be carried forward by an individual taxpayer? For how many years? In determining the amount of his or her contribution deduction for the current year, how must the taxpayer treat the carryovers from prior years?

11-25 *Miscellaneous Itemized Deductions.* E's employer has offered her the option of a $50 monthly pay raise or a reimbursement plan to cover her current subscriptions to professional journals ($200) and her dues to professional organizations ($350). E files a joint return with her husband, and they expect their adjusted gross income to be $50,000 for the upcoming year. Assuming that their only miscellaneous itemized deductions are from E's subscriptions and professional dues, is this a good offer? Explain.

11-26 *Three Percent Cutback Rule.* Explain the difference between the tentative cutback and the maximum cutback amounts related to the total deduction allowed for itemized deductions. Which itemized deductions are not subject to the cutback rule?

PROBLEMS

11-27 *Medical Expense Deduction.* R, an unmarried taxpayer, has adjusted gross income of $20,000 for 1994. During the year, he paid the following amounts for medical care: $300 for prescription medicines and drugs, $600 for hospitalization insurance, and $1,100 to doctors and dentists. R filed an insurance reimbursement claim in December 1994 and received a check for $1,200 on January 24, 1995.

    a. Assuming R itemizes deductions, determine the deduction allowed for the medical expenses paid in 1994.

    b. What effect does the insurance reimbursement have on R's deduction for 1994? How should the reimbursement be treated in 1995 if R's itemized deductions for 1994 (including the medical expense deduction) were $4,500 greater than his standard deduction?

    c. How should the reimbursement be treated in 1995 if R's itemized deductions for 1994 were $400 greater than his standard deduction?

11-28 *State Income Taxes.* During 1994 K paid $500 in estimated state income taxes. An additional $400 in state income taxes was withheld from her salary by K's employer and remitted to the state. K also received a $200 refund check during 1994 for excess state income taxes paid in 1993. She had claimed a deduction for $750 of state income taxes paid in 1993. K uses the cash method of accounting and has adjusted gross income of $50,000 for the year.

    a. If K itemizes her deductions, how much may she claim as a deduction for state income taxes on her 1994 Federal tax return?

    b. If K's itemized deductions for 1993 were $1,900 greater than her standard deduction, how must the $200 refund be treated for Federal income tax purposes?

11-29 *Real Estate Tax Apportionment.*   S sells her home located in Carrolton County, Kansas, on March 1, 1994. Carrolton County assesses real property taxes at the beginning of each calendar year for the entire year, and the property tax becomes a personal liability of the owner of real property on January 1. The tax is payable on April 1, 1994. Buyer B paid $80,000 for the home on March 1, 1994 and also paid the $1,200 real estate taxes on April 1. Both S and B are cash basis, calendar year taxpayers.

    a. How much of the $1,200 in real estate taxes is deductible by S? What adjustment must S make to the amount she realized from the sale?

    b. How much of the $1,200 in taxes is deductible by B? How will he treat any of the taxes paid which are attributable to S?

11-30 *Interest Expense Limitations.*   Indicate in each of the following cases the amount of interest expense, if any, that the taxpayer is allowed to deduct.

    a. During the year, H used his bank credit card to purchase a new stereo for his teenage daughter. Finance charges for the year were $70.

    b. Over the years, G has consistently borrowed against her insurance policies because of their low rates. This year, she paid interest of $1,100 on the loans.

    c. D lives and works in Birmingham. He owns a house there as well as a summer home at Hilton Head and a condominium at Sun Valley. He paid interest expense of $6,000 on loans on each unit.

    d. B owns a home in Denver which she purchased in 1979 for $70,000. The current balance on B's mortgage loan is $60,000 and the property is worth $150,000. During the year, B obtained a second mortgage on her home, receiving $20,000 which she used to pay off her two outstanding car loans. Interest on the first mortgage was $4,000 while interest on the second mortgage was $1,000.

    e. M is a heavy trader of stocks and bonds, using his margin account frequently. This year, interest expense charged on his margin purchases was $1,200. M's investment income was $900.

    f. R is an employee of a television repair shop. He uses his own truck solely for business, making customer service calls. During the year, he paid $900 interest on a loan on his truck.

11-31 *Investment Interest Expense.*   R, a cash basis, single taxpayer, paid $17,000 of investment interest expense during 1994. R uses the calendar year for tax purposes and reports the following investment income: $1,500 interest income, and $3,500 dividends.

    a. How much of the investment interest expense is deductible by R in 1994?

    b. What must R do with any investment interest expense deduction which is disallowed for 1994?

11-32 *Investment Interest Expense Limitation.* L is an engineer. This year, she borrowed $300,000 and purchased 40 acres south of Houston. For the year, L paid interest of $30,000 on the loan. Her tax records revealed the following additional information.

Income:

Salary...	$50,000
Dividends......................................	8,000
Share of partnership income:	
Ordinary loss.................................	(3,000)
Portfolio income:	
Interest and dividends......................	1,000
Rental income..................................	8,000

Expenses:

Rental expenses................................	7,000
Qualified residence interest......................	10,000
Property tax on land............................	5,000
Investment publications.........................	400
Professional dues, licenses and subscriptions....	1,100

The items noted concerning the partnership result from L's limited partnership interest in Country Homes, a real estate development. The rental income is derived from a four-unit apartment complex that is currently filled with tenants with one-year leases. The related rental expenses include $2,000 of interest expense on the debt to acquire the apartments. Compute L's deduction for investment interest expense this year.

11-33 *Interest Expense—Note Discount.* Taxpayer T signed a note for $2,000 on August 30, 1994, agreeing to pay back the loan in 12 equal installments beginning September 30, 1994. The 12 percent interest charge ($2,000 × 12% = $240) was subtracted from the face amount of the note and T received $1,760, all of which was used to purchase furniture for his business. T uses the calendar year as his taxable year.

   a. If T is a cash basis taxpayer and he makes the four payments scheduled for 1994, what is his deduction for interest on the note in 1994? In 1995?

   b. Would your answers to (a) change if T were an accrual method taxpayer? Explain.

11-34 *Charitable Contributions.* Determine the amount of the charitable deduction (without regard to percentage limitations) allowed in each of the following situations:

   a. Rent-free use of building for three months allowed for the United Way fund drive. The building normally rents for $900 per month, and the owner paid $1,100 for utilities during this period.

   b. Gift of General Motors stock valued at $9,000 to State University. Taxpayer purchased the stock five months ago for $11,000.

   c. Donation of stamp collection valued at $4,000 to local museum for display to the general public. Taxpayer had paid $1,000 for the stamps many years ago.

   d. Gift of paintings to local hospital to be placed on the walls of a remodeled floor. The paintings were painted by the donor and were appraised at $20,000.

   e. Donation of Civil War relics to American Heart Association to be sold at its current fund-raising auction. Taxpayer paid $1,000 for the relics ten years ago and an expert appraiser valued them at $7,000 on the day of the gift.

11-35 *Contribution Deductions—Percentage Limitations.* J contributed $10,000 to the University of Miami and a long-term capital asset worth $10,000 (basis of $5,000) to a private nonoperating foundation during 1994. Assuming his adjusted gross income for the year is $24,000, answer the following:

    a. What is the amount of J's contribution deduction for 1994?

    b. How must any excess contributions be treated?

    c. If J had come to you for advice before making the gifts, what advice would you have offered?

11-36 *Contribution Deductions—Percentage Limitations.* During 1994 R donated land to her church (a public charity) to be used as a building site for a new chapel. R had purchased the land as an investment in 1983 at a cost of $10,000. The land was appraised at a fair market value of $30,000 on the date of the gift. Assuming R's adjusted gross income for 1994 is $60,000, answer the following:

    a. If R made no additional charitable contributions during 1994, what is the amount of her contribution deduction for the year?

    b. If R contributed cash of $20,000 to her church in addition to the land, what is the amount of her charitable contribution deduction for 1994?

    c. Calculate the amount of R's excess contributions from (a) and (b) and explain how these amounts are to be treated.

11-37 *Contribution Deductions—Percentage Limitations.* T, a single taxpayer, had adjusted gross income of $20,000 for 1994. During the year, T contributed cash of $1,000 and Xerox Corporation stock worth $10,000 to his church (a public charity). T inherited the stock during 1993 when it was valued at $8,000.

    a. Calculate T's total contribution deduction for 1994.

    b. How must any excess contributions be treated?

    c. If T does not anticipate being able to itemize his deductions in any future years, what might he do in 1994 to increase his current contribution deduction?

11-38 *Miscellaneous Itemized Deductions.* R, single, has the following miscellaneous itemized deductions for the current year.

Unreimbursed employee business expenses.........	$1,350
Professional dues and subscriptions.................	650
Job-seeking expenses...............................	800
Tax return preparation fee...........................	250
Safe-deposit box rental (for stocks and bonds).......	50

Assume that R itemizes his deductions for the current year.

    a. What is the amount of R's deduction for the above items if his adjusted gross income is $70,000 for the current year?

    b. What is the amount of R's deduction for these items if his adjusted gross income is $100,000 for the current year?

11-39   *Three Percent Cutback Rule.*   H and W are married and file a joint return for the current year. They have the following itemized deductions (before any percentage limitations) for the year.

Medical and dental expenses	$8,000
Real estate taxes on home	3,500
Deductible interest on home mortgage	9,000
State income taxes paid	5,500
Charitable contributions	4,000
Miscellaneous itemized deductions	2,500

Determine H and W's itemized deductions, assuming the following levels of adjusted gross income for the current year.

a. $100,000

b. $400,000

c. $800,000

11-40 *Calculating Itemized Deductions.* Robert and Jean Snyder have an adjusted gross income of $30,000 for 1993. Their expenses for 1994 are

Prescription drugs.	$ 300*
Medical insurance premiums.	900
Doctor and dental bills paid.	1,400*
Eyeglasses for Robert.	155
Hospital and clinic bills paid.	450*
Property taxes paid on home.	900
State income taxes paid:	
Remaining 1993 tax liability.	125
Withheld from wages during year.	875
State and local sales taxes paid:	
Amount paid on new automobile.	800
Amount paid on other major purchases.	280
Personal property taxes paid.	100
Interest on home mortgage**.	4,750
Interest paid on personal auto loan.	1,100
Interest paid on credit card purchases.	400
Interest paid on E.F. Hutton	
margin account***.	120
Cash contributions to church.	2,000
Fair market value of Hightech Corp. stock	
contributed to church (purchased for	
$1,000 three years ago).	5,000
Labor union dues paid by Robert.	200
Qualifying education costs paid by Jean.	300
Safe deposit box rental (for stocks and bonds).	50
Fee paid accountant for preparation of 1993	
state and Federal tax returns.	350

    *These amounts are net of insurance reimbursements received during 1994.

    **This mortgage was created at the time the home was purchased.

    ***This investment interest expense is related to the production of $1,500 of net investment income.

The Snyders drove their personal automobile 500 miles for medical and dental treatment and an additional 1,000 miles in connection with charitable services performed for their church. Assuming Robert and Jean are both under age 40 and plan to file a joint income tax return for the year, determine their total itemized deductions. If a tax form is used for the computations, complete Schedule A (Form 1040).

LEARNING OBJECTIVES

Upon completion of this chapter you will be able to:

- Discuss the basic rules governing the deduction of investment expenses

- Explain the limitations imposed on the deduction of losses incurred in an activity in which a taxpayer does not materially participate (i.e., passive losses)

- Understand the special treatment for interest expense related to a passive activity

- Discuss the restrictions imposed on deductions related to vacation homes

CHAPTER OUTLINE

Passive Activity Limitations	12-1	Recharacterized Passive Income	12-19
General Rule	12-3	Passive Activity Interest Expense	12-20
Taxpayers Subject to Limitations	12-7	Rental of Residence (Vacation Home	
Passive Activities	12-8	Rentals)	12-23
Definition of an Activity	12-9	Basic Rules	12-24
Rental Versus Nonrental Activities	12-12	Allocation of Expenses	12-26
Material Participation	12-14	Problem Materials	12-30

Chapter 12

DEDUCTIONS FOR CERTAIN INVESTMENT EXPENSES AND LOSSES

Since 1942 Congress has generally allowed taxpayers to deduct expenses and losses incurred in connection with investment activities. As explained in Chapter 7, Code § 212 currently authorizes the deduction of investment-oriented expenses. This provision specifically allows a deduction for expenses incurred for the production or collection of income or for the management, conservation, or maintenance of property held for the production of income. Deductible investment expenses typically include such items as fees paid to rent a safety deposit box to hold securities, cost of financial advice, and travel expenses incurred in managing property. Expenses incurred in operating rental property such as those for maintenance, depreciation, utilities, and insurance are also deductible under § 212. Similarly, deductions for interest expense incurred by taxpayers to finance their investments also are deductible under § 212, although certain restrictions apply (as discussed in Chapter 11). Investment expenses are normally classified as miscellaneous itemized deductions and are subject to the 2 percent limitation and the 3 percent cutback. However, expenses related to property held for the production of rents or royalties are deductible *for* A.G.I.

For many years, the general rule of § 212 adequately governed the deduction of most investment expenses. In recent times, however, Congress has enacted additional provisions to restrict investment-type deductions where it found the general rule to be insufficient. This chapter examines three areas where the Congressional ax has fallen: the deduction for losses from passive investment activities, the deduction for interest expense related to passive activities, and the deductions related to the rental of vacation homes.

PASSIVE ACTIVITY LIMITATIONS

Historically, the tax law has generally allowed taxpayers to use deductions from one activity to offset the income of another. Similarly, most credits could be used to offset tax attributable to income from any of the taxpayer's activities.

Example 1. R earns $50,000 annually working as vice president of marketing at Plentiful Products, Inc. Over the years, he has accumulated a modest portfolio of stocks which generates dividends of about $10,000 a year. In addition, he is a 10% limited partner in a partnership which owns an apartment complex consisting of 200 units. During the year, the apartment complex had operating expenses which exceeded rental income, creating a $100,000 loss. Prior to 1987, R could use his share of the loss, $10,000, to offset his other income, both salary and dividends. Assuming R's marginal tax rate was 30%, the loss produced tax savings of $3,000.

The above example illustrates the essentials of what is now a well-publicized phenomenon: under prior law, an individual could reduce his or her tax liability—even eliminate it—by investing in "tax shelters" that produced losses which could be offset against other income. The attraction of such losses for taxpayers wishing to avoid taxes was so great that the tax shelter business grew into a thriving industry.

A typical tax shelter is organized as a limited partnership. From a tax perspective, use of this form allows the losses of the activity to flow through to the individual partners to be used to reduce the investor's other taxable income. Assuming the activity carried on by the partnership is economically sound, the losses which result are artificial. They are normally attributable to a mismatching of expenses and revenues which occur in the early years of a shelter. For example, in the initial years of a traditional real estate tax shelter, expenses for interest, taxes, and accelerated depreciation normally exceed the rental income, which is often low because of the time it takes for the project to become fully occupied. Moreover, interest and accelerated depreciation are greater initially simply because of the manner in which the computations are made. As a result, in the first several years, the project "throws off" losses—many of which do not require a cash outlay due to depreciation and accrued expenses. In later years, however, these events reverse, and taxable income is produced.

Over the years, the number of stories about how taxpayers, particularly high-income taxpayers, have used tax shelters to avoid paying taxes has been legion. Perhaps one of the most revealing testimonials of the popularity of tax shelters can be found on the cover of the February, 1986 issue of *Money* magazine. The cover pictured three highly successful individuals, and indicated that each had made over a million dollars but paid no taxes. In light of this and other similar reports, it is not surprising that taxpayer confidence in the fairness of the tax system had badly eroded. Many taxpayers had come to believe that tax was paid only by the naive and the unsophisticated. This belief, in turn, was leading to noncompliance and providing incentives for expansion of the tax shelter market, often diverting investment capital from productive activities to those principally or exclusively servicing tax avoidance goals.

In order to prevent what it considered the harmful and excessive use of tax shelters, Congress took action—albeit indirect—in 1986. Perhaps fearing that they would alienate certain constituencies, Congress opted not to eliminate or limit the provisions on which shelters are built (e.g., special benefits for low-income housing and rehabilitation of old and historic buildings). Instead, Congress enacted Code § 469, which places far-reaching restrictions on how deductions, losses, and credits of a passive activity can be used to

offset the income of another activity. Although these restrictions were aimed principally at losses from a limited partnership interest, they also limit losses from rental activities, as well as losses from any trade or business in which the taxpayer does not materially participate.

GENERAL RULE

The thrust of § 469 is to divide a taxpayer's income into three types: (1) wages, salaries, and other income from activities in which the taxpayer materially participates (e.g., income from an S corporation that the taxpayer owns and operates); (2) portfolio income (e.g., interest, dividends, capital gains and losses); and (3) passive income—the sort deemed to be produced by most tax shelters and rental activities. Expenses related to passive activities can be deducted only to the extent of income from *all* such passive activities. Any excess expenses of these passive activities—the passive activity loss—may not be deducted against portfolio income or wages, salaries, or any other income from activities in which the taxpayer materially participates. Losses that cannot be used are held in suspension and carried forward to be used to offset passive income of future years.[1] Suspended losses from a passive activity can be used in full to offset portfolio or active income *only* when the taxpayer disposes of his or her entire interest in the activity. Upon disposition, any current and suspended losses (including any loss realized on the disposition) are used to offset income in the following order:[2]

1. Any gain on the disposition of the interest

2. Any *net* income from all passive activities (after taking into account any suspended losses)

3. Any other income or gain (i.e., active and portfolio income)

Observe that this special ordering rule requires the taxpayer to use up the suspended losses against gain on the disposition and any passive income before offsetting such losses against active or portfolio income. Without this rule, a taxpayer would use all of the suspended loss against active income, thus freeing up the passive gain on the disposition to absorb other passive losses.

> **Example 2.** T owned and operated her own construction company as a sole proprietorship. For the year, the company had net income of $120,000. T has a substantial portfolio that produced dividends of $15,000 and a short-term capital loss from the sale of stock of $7,000. In addition, her investment in Pleasant Properties, a limited partnership, produced a passive loss. T's share of the loss was $30,000. Her investment in Restful Recordings, another limited partnership,

---

[1] Suspended losses are carried forward to the following year, where they are treated as if they were incurred in such year. Temp. Reg. § 1.469-1T(f)(4)(B).

[2] § 469(g). To date, Regulations have not been issued on dispositions, leaving many unanswered questions. See Erickson, "Passive Activity Disposition," *The Tax Adviser* (May 1989), p. 338.

generated passive activity income. T's share of the income was $5,000. Under the capital gain and loss provisions, T may deduct $3,000 of the capital loss and carry over the remaining $4,000. The $30,000 passive loss is deductible only to the extent of passive income, which is $5,000. In effect, income and loss from the passive activities are netted, and the net loss attributable to Pleasant Properties, $25,000, is carried over to the following year.

Example 3.   Same facts as above. T held on to her investment in Pleasant Properties until this year, when she sold her entire interest, producing a gain of $40,000. Total suspended losses attributable to her investment were $70,000. Net income from Restful Recordings was $20,000 for the year. T may deduct the entire $70,000 loss: $40,000 against the gain, $20,000 against the net income from Restful Recordings, and $10,000 against any other income. Note that had there been a suspended loss from Restful Recordings, none of it would be deductible. Due to the ordering rules, the suspended loss must be used against current passive income before any active income.

As a practical matter, many taxpayers will have investments in several passive activities, some that produce income and some that produce losses. If the taxpayer has losses from more than one activity, the suspended loss for *each* activity must be determined in the event that the taxpayer subsequently disposes of one of the activities. The suspended loss of each activity is determined by allocating the total loss disallowed for the year, including any suspended losses, pro rata among the loss activities using the following formula.[3]

$$\text{Total disallowed loss for year} \times \frac{\text{Loss for this activity}}{\text{Total losses from all activities with losses}} = \frac{\text{Suspended loss}}{\text{for this activity}}$$

Note that this fraction simply represents the percentage of the total loss attributable to a particular activity. In effect, each loss activity absorbs this fraction of any passive income from other activities.

Example 4.   T owns an interest in three passive activities: A, B, and C. For 1994, activity B reports income of $2,000 while activities A and C report losses of $6,000 and $4,000, respectively. T is allowed to deduct the passive losses from A and C to the extent of the passive income from B. Thus he may deduct $2,000 of the losses. The remaining loss of $8,000 cannot be used to offset T's income from other sources (e.g., wages, dividends, or interest income) but must be suspended and carried forward to the following year. The suspended loss of $8,000 must be allocated between the loss activities pro rata. Since 60% ($6,000/$10,000) of the net loss was attributable to A, the suspended loss for

---

[3] Temp. Reg. § 1.469-1T(f)(2).

A is $4,800 (60% × $8,000). Similarly, the suspended loss for C is $3,200 [($4,000/$10,000) × $8,000]. Alternatively, the loss activities could be viewed as absorbing the passive income. Using this approach, the suspended losses would be computed somewhat differently but with the same result.

	A	C	Total
Loss for the year......................	$(6,000)	$(4,000)	$(10,000)
Loss absorbed:			
$2,000 × ($6,000/$10,000)...........	1,200	–	1,200
$2,000 × ($4,000/$10,000)...........	–	800	800
Suspended loss........................	$(4,800)	$(3,200)	$ (8,000)

These losses are carried over and treated as if they were a deduction in the following year.

Example 5.   Assume the same facts as in *Example 4*. The income and loss for 1994 of the three activities is shown below.

Activity	Current Net Income (Loss)	Carryforward from Prior Years	Total
A	$(5,200)	$(4,800)	$(10,000)
B	12,000	–	12,000
C	(1,800)	(3,200)	(5,000)
Total	$ 5,000	$(8,000)	$ (3,000)

The total passive loss disallowed in 1994 is $3,000. The $3,000 disallowed loss is allocated among the activities with total losses (taking into account both current operations and losses suspended from prior years) as follows:

Activity	Total Disallowed Loss	×	Percentage of Total Loss	=	Allocable Portion of Loss
A	$3,000	×	$10,000/($10,000 + $5,000)	=	$2,000
C	3,000	×	5,000/($10,000 + $5,000)	=	1,000

In making the allocation, the disallowed loss is allocated based on an activity's net loss *including* suspended losses (e.g., $10,000 for A) rather than the loss that actually occurred in the current year (e.g., $5,200 for A).

Example 6. J has three passive activities: R, S, and T. The suspended losses and current income and losses for each activity for 1994 are shown below. In addition, J sold activity S for a $10,000 gain in 1994. Because there has been a complete disposition of S, J is able to deduct all of the suspended losses as shown below.

	R	S	T
Suspended loss..............................	$ (9,000)	$(12,000)	$(15,000)
Current income (loss)........................	(5,000)	(6,000)	(7,000)
Total...	$(14,000)	$(18,000)	$(22,000)
Gain on disposition of S......................		10,000	
Excess loss deducted against other income...		$ (8,000)	

J must first offset the suspended and current losses of $18,000 from activity S against the $10,000 gain on the sale. The next step is to offset the $8,000 balance of losses against any net passive income for the year. In this case, the activities have no income, and thus none of the loss is absorbed by passive income. At this point, the remaining loss of $8,000 is no longer considered passive and can be used to offset any active or portfolio income that J may have.

Example 7. K has three passive activities: X, Y, and Z. The suspended losses and current income and losses for each activity for 1994 are shown below. In addition, in 1994 K sold activity Y for a $21,000 gain. K is able to deduct all of the suspended losses of Y as shown below.

	X	Y	Z
Suspended loss..............................	$ (7,000)	$(10,000)	$(18,000)
Current income (loss)........................	(8,000)	(6,000)	8,000
Total...	$(15,000)	$(16,000)	$(10,000)
Gain on disposition of Y......................	–	21,000	–
	$(15,000)	$ 5,000	$(10,000)
Loss absorbed:			
$5,000 × ($15,000/$25,000)...............	3,000		
$5,000 × ($10,000/$25,000)...............			2,000
Suspended loss..............................	$(12,000)		$ (8,000)

K must first offset Y's current and suspended losses of $16,000 against the $21,000 gain on the sale. Note that the balance of the gain ($5,000) is considered passive income that can be combined with the net losses (the sum of current income or loss and suspended losses) from the other passive activities for the year.[4]

---

[4] § 469(g)(1)(A) and Temp. Reg. § 1.469-2T(c)(2)(i)(A)(2).

Rules similar to those for passive losses apply to tax credits produced by passive activities (e.g., the low-income housing credit, rehabilitation credit, research credit, and jobs credit). Passive credits can be used *only* to offset any tax attributable to passive income. Any unused credit may be carried forward to the next taxable year to offset future taxes. In contrast to passive losses, however, credits being carried over may be *lost* when a passive activity is sold. This occurs if there is no tax attributable to passive income (including any gain on the sale of the activity) in the year of disposition.

> **Example 8.** T invested in a limited partnership that rehabilitated a historic structure. In 1995, T sold his interest, realizing a gain of $5,000. At that time, T had suspended losses of $20,000 and credits of $10,000. T is able to use $5,000 of the losses to offset the gain and the other $15,000 to offset other active or portfolio income. None of the credit can be used, however, because there is no income from the passive activity. Had T sold the property for a gain of $50,000, he would have had $30,000 of passive income. Assuming T is in the 28% tax bracket, he could have used $8,400 ($30,000 × 28%) of the credit. The remaining credit of $1,600 is lost.

TAXPAYERS SUBJECT TO LIMITATIONS

The passive loss rules apply to individuals, estates, trusts, personal service corporations, and certain closely held C corporations.[5] Partnerships and S corporations are not subject to the limitations per se. However, their activities flow through to the owners who are subject to limitation.

The passive loss rules generally do not apply to regular C corporations. Presumably, their immunity is based on the theory that individuals generally do not benefit from losses locked inside the corporate form. Congress, however, did not want taxpayers to be able to circumvent the passive loss rules merely by incorporating. Absent a special rule, a taxpayer could utilize corporate immunity to shelter income derived from personal services. Taxpayers would simply incorporate as a personal service corporation and acquire tax shelter investments at the corporate level. The losses produced by the tax shelters would offset not only the service income but also income from any investments made at the corporate level. Consequently, the passive loss rules apply to *personal service corporations*. For this purpose, a personal service corporation is one where the principal activity is the performance of personal services and such services are substantially performed by employee-owners. In addition, the employee-owners must, *in the aggregate,* own more than 10 percent of the stock of the corporation either directly or indirectly (e.g., through family members). Common examples of personal service corporations are professional corporations such as those of doctors, accountants, attorneys, engineers, actors, architects, and others where personal services are performed.

Without additional restrictions, any taxpayer—not just one who derives income from services—could incorporate his or her portfolio and offset the investment income with losses from tax shelters. To prohibit this possibility, the passive loss rules also apply in a limited fashion to all closely held C corporations (i.e., a regular C corporation where five

---

[5] § 469(a)(2).

or fewer individuals own more than 50 percent of the stock either directly or indirectly). Note that some personal service corporations that might escape the tests above may still be subject to the rules due to their status as closely held corporations. A closely held corporation may not use passive losses to offset its portfolio income. However, such corporations may offset losses from passive activities against the income of any active business carried on by the corporation.[6]

> **Example 9.**   R and his two brothers own Real Rustproofing Corporation. This year the corporation suffered a loss from operations of $10,000. In addition, it received interest income from short-term investments of working capital of $20,000. The corporation also had a passive loss from a real estate venture of $30,000. In determining taxable income, the passive activity limitation rules apply since the corporation is closely held (i.e., five or fewer individuals own more than 50 percent). As a result, none of the loss can be deducted since the loss cannot offset portfolio income of the corporation and the corporation did not have any income from operations. Had the corporation had $50,000 of operating profit, the entire loss could be deducted since passive losses can be used by a closely held corporation to offset active income—but not portfolio income.

PASSIVE ACTIVITIES

Assuming the taxpayer is subject to the passive activity rules, the most important determination is whether the activity in which the taxpayer is engaged is *passive*. The characterization of an activity as passive generally depends on the level of the taxpayer's involvement in the activity, the nature of the activity, or the form of ownership. Section 469(c) provides that the following activities are passive:

1. Any activity (other than a working interest in certain oil and gas property) that involves the conduct of a trade or business in which the taxpayer *does not materially participate*; and

2. *Any* rental activity regardless of the level of the taxpayer's participation.

Given these definitions, several questions must be addressed to determine whether a particular endeavor of the taxpayer is a passive activity.

1. What is an activity?

2. Is the activity a rental or nonrental activity?

3. What is material participation?

Unfortunately, none of these questions are easily answered. An exceedingly complex set of Regulations exists that, in large measure, creates intricate definitions designed to prohibit wily taxpayers from deducting their passive losses. The basic rules are considered below.

---

[6]   § 469(e)(2).

DEFINITION OF AN ACTIVITY

The definition of an activity serves as the foundation for the entire structure of the passive loss rules. Virtually all of the important determinations required in applying the passive loss rules are made at the activity level. Perhaps the most significant of these concerns the taxpayer's level of participation. As discussed later in this chapter, if the taxpayer participates for more than 500 hours per year in a nonrental activity, he or she is deemed to materially participate in the activity, and the activity is therefore not passive. As the following example illustrates, this test requires an unambiguous definition of an activity.

> **Example 10.** Mr. R. Rock owns and operates 10 restaurants in 10 different cities. In addition, in each of those 10 cities he owns and operates 10 movie theaters. R spends 80 hours working in each restaurant during the year for a total of 800 hours. R spends 70 hours working in each movie theater for a total of 700 hours. If *each* restaurant and each movie theater are treated as separate activities, it would appear that R would not be treated as a material participant in any one of the businesses because he devoted only a minimum amount of his time during the year, 80 or 70 hours, to each. On the other hand, if all the restaurants are aggregated and deemed a *single activity,* R's total participation in all the restaurants, 800 hours, would in fact be considered material. A similar conclusion could be reached for the movie theaters. In addition, if the restaurants are adjacent to the movie theaters (or in fact are concession stands in the theaters), it might be appropriate to treat the restaurant operation and the movie theater operation as a single activity.

The definition of an activity is not only important for the material participation test, but it is also significant should there be a disposition. As noted above, a complete disposition of an activity enables a taxpayer to deduct any suspended losses of the activity.

> **Example 11.** Same facts as in *Example 10* above. Also assume that there are suspended losses for each restaurant. If each restaurant is treated as a separate activity, a sale of one of the restaurants would enable R to deduct the suspended loss for that restaurant. In contrast, if the restaurant is not considered a separate activity, none of the loss would be recognized on the tax return for the year of sale.

Examples 10 and 11 demonstrate not only the importance of the definition of an activity but also the problems inherent in defining what constitutes an activity.

The authors of § 469 obviously anticipated the difficulty in defining an activity and therefore provided no working definition in the Code. As a result, the formidable task of defining an activity fell in the laps of those who write the Regulations. Defining an activity would not be difficult if all taxpayers were engaged in a single line of business at one location. As a practical matter, this is not always the case. Some taxpayers, such as Mr. Rock in *Example 10,* are involved in several lines of business at multiple locations. Consequently, any definition of an activity had to consider such situations. In fixing the scope of an activity, the Treasury feared that a narrow definition would allow taxpayers to generate passive income at will that could be used to offset passive losses. For example, if Mr. Rock were able to treat each restaurant as a separate activity, he could easily

manipulate his participation at each restaurant to obtain passive or active income as he deemed most beneficial. To combat this problem, the IRS initially designed a broad definition that generally required a taxpayer to aggregate various endeavors into a single activity. By establishing a broad definition that treats several undertakings as a single activity, the IRS made the material participation test easier to meet, resulting in active rather than passive income. Unfortunately, the actual definition was quite complicated, as evidenced by the Temporary Regulations, which contain 196 pages of intricate rules and examples devoted to the subject.[7] In a refreshing change of direction, however, the IRS allowed these Temporary Regulations to expire, proposing a far simpler approach all contained in only four pages![8]

Appropriate Economic Unit. Under the recently proposed regulations, taxpayers are required to treat one or more trade or business activities or one or more rental activities as a single activity if the activities constitute an *appropriate economic unit* for measuring gain or loss.[9] Whether two or more activities constitute an appropriate economic unit (AEU) is determined by taking into account all of the relevant facts and circumstances. Five factors are to be given the greatest weight in making the determination. These are as follows:

1. Similarities and differences in *types* of business;

2. The extent of common control;

3. The extent of common ownership;

4. Geographical location; and

5. Interdependencies between activities (e.g., they have the same customers or same employees, are accounted for with a single set of books, purchase or sell goods between themselves, or involve products or services that are normally provided together).

A taxpayer may use any reasonable method of applying the relevant facts and circumstances.

Example 12. C operates several businesses as a sole proprietor. These include a bakery and a movie theater at a shopping mall in Santa Fe and a bakery and a movie theater in Albuquerque. Reasonable groupings, depending on the facts and circumstances, may be as follows.

- A single activity

- `A movie theater activity and a bakery activity

- A Santa Fe activity and an Albuquerque activity

- Four separate activities

---

[7] Temp. Reg. § 1.469-4T(a)(2).

[8] Prop. Reg. § 1.469-4.

[9] Prop. Reg. § 1.469-4(c)(1).

Consistency Requirement. To ensure that taxpayers do not bounce from one grouping to another to fit their needs, the proposed regulations impose a consistency requirement. Once the activities have been grouped in a particular manner, the grouping may not be changed unless the original grouping was clearly inappropriate or there has been a material change in the facts and circumstances that makes the original grouping inappropriate.[10] For instance, in *Example 12* above, once one of the groupings is selected, the taxpayer is required to continue using the grouping unless a material change in the facts and circumstances makes it clearly inappropriate.

Although this method of defining an activity obviously lacks the mechanical precision of its predecessor, it should make compliance far easier for taxpayers. Moreover, to prevent a taxpayer from misusing the facts-and-circumstances approach, the IRS has the power to regroup activities if the taxpayer's grouping fails to reflect one or more appropriate economic units and one of the primary purposes of the taxpayer's grouping is to circumvent the passive loss rules.[11]

Activities Conducted through Conduit Entities. As a practical matter, many taxpayers will conduct activities through a partnership or an S corporation. In this case, the grouping is done at the partnership or S corporation level. Partners and S corporation shareholders then determine whether they should aggregate the entity activities with those they conduct directly or through other partnerships or S corporations.[12]

Grouping of Rental and Nonrental Activities. Rental activities and nonrental activities normally may *not* be grouped together and treated as a single activity. This rule is consistent with the basic provision that all rental activities are passive regardless of the taxpayer's participation. Therefore, it makes sense that rental and nonrental activities should not be aggregated. The practical significance of the rule is to prohibit taxpayers from sheltering active income with passive rental losses. Nevertheless, the proposed regulations do carve out an exception, allowing aggregation of rental and nonrental activities whenever either activity is insubstantial in relation to the other.[13]

> **Example 13.** PB&K, an accounting firm, operates its practice out of an office building that it owns. The firm occupies two floors of the building and leases the other three floors to third parties. This year, 90% of the firm's income is from its accounting practice and 10% is from rental of the office space. Because the rental operation is insubstantial in relation to the nonrental operation, the rental and nonrental operations are aggregated into a *single nonrental* activity. Note that in this case any net loss on the rental activity is effectively combined with the income of the accounting operation.

It should also be noted that the rental of real property and the rental of personal property cannot be grouped unless the personal property is provided in connection with the real property.[14]

---

10 Prop. Reg. § 1.469-4(g).

11 Prop. Reg. § 1.469-4(h).

12 Prop. Reg. § 1.469-4(j).

13 Prop. Reg. § 1.469-4(d).

14 Prop. Reg. § 1.469-4(e).

Example 14. T owns a small apartment building with eight units that he rents completely furnished. In addition, the building contains a small room with coin-operated laundry facilities. As a general rule, the laundry rental and apartment rental cannot be aggregated because the rental of real property cannot be grouped with the rental of personal property. In this case, however, the rental income and laundry income can be grouped since the personal property is provided in connection with the real property.

Rental and nonrental operations normally must be separated because they are subject to different rules. For example, rental activities are always passive, whereas nonrental activities are passive only if the taxpayer does not materially participate in such activities. In addition, owners of rental real estate are normally entitled to deduct up to $25,000 of rental losses annually without limitation, whereas there is no comparable rule for nonrental activities.

RENTAL VERSUS NONRENTAL ACTIVITIES

Under the general rule described above, all rental activities are deemed to be passive, regardless of whether the taxpayer materially participates. Congress adopted this view based on the belief that there is seldom any significant participation in rental activities. Therefore, it created a presumption that all rental activities would be passive. For this purpose, a rental activity is defined as any activity whereby a taxpayer receives payments that are principally for the use of property owned by the taxpayer (e.g., apartments or equipment).

Observe that this blanket rule effectively classifies many rental activities as passive even though an owner might render significant services in connection with the rental. For example, renting video tapes would be considered passive under the general rule even though the owner might perform substantial services. This approach would be unfair to those who participate yet suffer losses. Moreover, the rule creates a huge planning opportunity for those seeking passive income given that many rental businesses are profitable. Recognizing these problems, the authors of the Regulations identified six situations where what is normally a rental is to be treated as a nonrental activity.[15]

1. *1–7 Days Rental.* The activity is not a rental if the average rental period is seven days or less. Under this exception, short-term rentals of such items as cars, hotel and motel rooms, or video cassettes are not considered rental activities.

2. *8–30 Days Rental.* The activity is not a rental if the average rental period is 30 days or less and *significant services* are performed by the owner of the property. In determining whether significant services are provided, consideration is given to the type of service performed and the value of the services relative to the amount charged for the use of the property. In this regard, the Regulations indicate that telephone service and cable television are to be ignored as are those services

---

[15] Temp. Reg. § 1.469-1T(e)(3)(ii).

commonly provided in connection with long-term rentals of commercial and residential property (e.g., janitorial services, repairs, trash collection, cleaning of common areas, and security services). Unfortunately, the Regulations provide few other clues as to what constitutes significant services.

Example 15. T owns and rents a resort condominium in Florida. He provides telephone, cable, trash removal, cleaning of the common areas, and daily maid and linen service. The cost of the maid and linen services is less than 10% of the amount charged to tenants occupying the apartments. In determining whether significant services are provided, the telephone, cable, trash, and cleaning services are disregarded. Moreover, according to the Regulations, the maid and linen services would not be considered significant in this case. Because there are no significant services under the Regulations' view, the activity would be considered a rental (*assuming* the average rental use exceeds seven days) and, therefore, a passive activity.

3. *Extraordinary Services.* The activity is not a rental if extraordinary personal services are provided by the owner of the property. Services are considered extraordinary if the use of the property is merely incidental to the services performed.

Example 16. Nathan Hale Military Academy, a private college preparatory school, provides housing for its students. The school's rental of such facilities would be considered incidental to the educational services provided and thus be treated as a nonrental activity.

4. *Incidental Rentals.* The activity is not a rental activity if the rental of the property is merely incidental to the nonrental activity.

Example 17. S owns unimproved land that she is holding for future appreciation. To defray the costs of the land, she leases the land to a rancher for grazing his cattle. According to the Regulations, if the rent is less than 2% of the basis of the property (or value if less), the activity is not treated as a rental.

5. *Nonexclusive Use.* The activity is not a rental activity if the taxpayer customarily makes the property available during defined business hours for the nonexclusive use of various customers. For example, this exception would apply to a golf course that sells annual memberships but which is also open to the public on a daily basis.

6. *Property Made Available for Use in a Nonrental Activity.* The activity is not a rental activity if the taxpayer owns an interest in a partnership, S corporation, or joint venture to which the property is rented. For example, if T rents equipment to a partnership in which he is a partner, the rental is treated as a nonrental activity.

As noted above, any activity constituting a "rental" is a passive activity. Note, however, that those activities not classified as rentals (i.e., nonrental activities) may still be considered passive. Whether a *nonrental* activity is a passive activity depends on whether the taxpayer has materially participated in the activity.

MATERIAL PARTICIPATION

Material participation serves a crucial role in the application of the passive loss rules. It is the criterion that distinguishes between "passive" and "active" nonrental activities. The Code provides that an individual meets the material participation test only if he or she is involved in the operation of the activity on a regular, continuous, and substantial basis. Without further guidance, applying this nebulous criterion would essentially be left to the subjective interpretation of the taxpayer. However, the Regulations establish objective standards that look to the actual number of hours spent in the activity.

Under the regulatory scheme, a taxpayer materially participates in an activity if he or she meets one of seven tests.[16]

1. *More Than 500 Hours.* An individual materially participates if he or she spends more than 500 hours in the activity during the taxable year. Apparently the authors of the Regulations believed that this threshold (e.g., about 10 hours per week) appropriately distinguished those who truly were involved in the business from mere investors. Note that the work of a spouse is counted if it is work typically done by owners. For example, if B owned an S corporation that suffered losses (e.g., a football team), he would materially participate if he devoted more than 500 hours to the activity. However, if he spent only 300 hours and hired his wife as a receptionist who spent 250 hours, the test is not met because her work is not normally done by owners.

2. *Substantially All of the Participation.* The individual and his or her spouse materially participate if they are the sole participants or their participation constitutes substantially all of the participation of all individuals (including nonowners and nonemployees) who participate in the activity. This test, as well as the next, takes into account the fact that not all businesses require 500 hours to operate during the year. For example, if S operates a snow removal service by himself and spends only 50 hours in the activity this year because of light snow, the test is met because he was the sole participant.

3. *More Than 100 Hours and Not Less Than Anyone Else.* An individual materially participates if he or she participates for more than 100 hours and no other individual spends more time on the activity. For example, assume that S, above, occasionally hires E to help him remove snow. If S spent 160 hours and E 140, S qualifies because he spent more than 100 hours and not less than anyone else. Had S spent only 60 and E 40, S arguably would not qualify under either this or the previous test.

4. *Significant Participation in Several Activities.* An individual materially participates if his or her total participation in all *significant participation activities* (SPAs) exceeds 500 hours. A significant participation activity is defined as a trade or business in which the taxpayer participates more than 100 hours, but fails the other six tests for material participation. Thus a taxpayer must spend more than 100 hours in each activity and greater than 500 in all. The rule derives from

---

[16] Temp. Reg. § 1.469-1T(a).

the view that an individual who spends more than 500 hours in several different activities should be treated the same as those who spend an equivalent amount of time on a single activity.

Example 18.   T spends 140 hours overseeing his car wash, 160 hours supervising his quick-lube operation, and 499 hours managing his gas station. Each activity qualifies as a SPA because T spends more than 100 hours in each. More importantly, T is treated as materially participating in each because the total hours in all SPAs exceeds 500. However, if T spent 2 more hours in his gas station, then he would not be a material participant in either the car wash or quick-lube business. This occurs because the gas station would no longer be a SPA since the activity by itself satisfies the more-than-500-hours test. As a result, T's total hours in all SPAs, 300 (160 + 140), would not exceed the 500-hour benchmark. Obviously, this is a strange result.

The Regulations provide what at first glance is a curious treatment of SPAs. As expected, losses from SPAs failing to meet the 500-hour test are passive and generally not deductible. However, income from SPAs failing to meet the 500-hour test is *not* passive. Note that the IRS obtains the best of both worlds when a taxpayer is unable to combine his or her SPAs to get over the 500-hour threshold: passive loss but not passive income. This "heads I win, tails you lose" approach was designed to prevent taxpayers from creating passive income that could be used to absorb passive losses by spending small amounts of time in unrelated activities that are profitable.[17]

5. *Prior Participation.* An individual materially participates if he or she has materially participated (by tests 1 through 4) in an activity for five of the past ten years. This test prevents the taxpayer from moving in and out of material participation status. For example, D and son are partners in an appliance business that D started 30 years ago. D has essentially retired, leaving the day-to-day operations to his son. Without a special rule, D could tailor his participation year by year to obtain passive or nonpassive income as fits his needs.

6. *Prior Participation in a Personal Service Activity.* An individual materially participates in a personal service activity if he or she has materially participated in the activity for at least three years. Like the previous test, this rule eliminates the flexibility those working for personal service businesses have in tailoring their participation to obtain passive or nonpassive income as they need. For example, if a general partner in a law firm retired and converted her interest to a limited partnership interest, she would still be treated as a material participant in that law firm.

7. *Facts and Circumstances.* An individual materially participates if, based on the facts and circumstances, he or she participates in the activity on a regular, continuous, and substantial basis.

---

[17]   See Reg. § 1.469-2T(f)(2).

Rental Real Estate Exception. An extremely important exception to the passive activity rules is carved out in § 469(i) for rental real estate activities of the small investor. In many cases, the real estate held by a taxpayer is a residence that is used part-time, was formerly used, or may be used in the future. Relief was provided for this type of rental real estate because it is often held to provide financial security to individuals with moderate incomes. In such a case, these individuals share little common ground with the tax shelter investors. The relief is provided solely to individuals and certain trusts and estates. Regular C corporations are ineligible.

Under the exception, a taxpayer who *actively* participates (in contrast to materially participates) may deduct up to $25,000 of losses attributable to rental real estate annually. The $25,000 allowance is reduced by 50 percent of the excess of the taxpayer's A.G.I. over $100,000. This relationship may be expressed as follows:

$$\text{Reduction in } \$25,000 \text{ allowance} = 50\%(\text{A.G.I.} - \$100,000)$$

Consequently, high-income taxpayers (i.e., those with A.G.I. of $150,000 or more) cannot take advantage of this provision. A.G.I. for this purpose is computed without regard to contributions to individual retirement accounts, taxable social security, and any net passive losses that might be deductible. Any portion of the loss that is not deductible may be carried over and deducted subject to the same limitations in the following years.

Example 19. L moved to a new home this year. Instead of selling his old home, L decided to rent it out to supplement his income. During the first year, rents were $3,000 while expenses including maintenance, depreciation, interest, utilities, and taxes were $10,000. L's A.G.I. is $40,000. L may deduct the $7,000 loss for A.G.I. Had L's A.G.I. been $140,000, he could have deducted only $5,000 and carried over $2,000 to the following year. This computation is illustrated below.

Loss allowance..................................		$25,000
Phase out:		
A.G.I.......................................	$140,000	
Threshold..................................	(100,000)	
Excess A.G.I...............................	$ 40,000	
Rate.......................................	50%	
Phase-out.......................................		(20,000)
Maximum loss allowed..........................		$ 5,000

It should be emphasized that the taxpayer can use this exception only if the property is considered rental real estate. It cannot be used for losses from rental of personal property. More importantly, the real estate is not considered a "rental" activity where the rental period is either 1 to 7 days or between 8 and 30 days and significant services are performed.[18] For example, consider the typical investor who owns a vacation condominium. If the average rental of the condominium is 1 to 7 days, the condominium is

---

[18] For an excellent discussion of this topic and issue see Bomyea and Marucheck, "Rental of Residences," *The Tax Adviser* (September 1990), p. 543.

not considered rental property and the $25,000 exception does not apply. The result is the same if the average rental period is between 8 and 30 days and significant services are provided. Note that even though the $25,000 exception is not available in either case, all is not necessarily lost. In both situations, the condominium is treated as a nonrental activity. In such case, the taxpayer will be able to deduct all losses if there is material participation.

> **Example 20.**   M lives in Orlando, where she practices law. M owns a condominium, which she rents out on a daily basis to tourists. M runs ads in the local newspaper, makes arrangements for the rental, and cleans the unit as needed. In this case, it appears that the activity is not a rental business because of the short-term rental. As a result, the $25,000 exception for rentals does not apply. However, M still may be able to deduct a loss. Since the property by definition is not a rental activity due to the short-term rental period, it is—by default—a nonrental activity. Accordingly, the loss would be deductible if she materially participates in the activity. For example, if M spent more than 100 hours in the activity and more than anyone else or met any of the other six material participation tests, the loss would be deductible.

As noted above, the Code draws a distinction between material and active participation. The primary difference concerns the taxpayer's degree of involvement in operations. For example, a taxpayer is actively involved if he or she participates in management decisions such as approving new tenants, deciding on rental terms, approving capital or repair expenditures, or if he or she arranges for others to provide services such as repairs. In all cases, the taxpayer is not treated as actively participating in the activity if less than a 10 percent interest is owned. On the other hand, the taxpayer is not presumed to actively participate if the interest is 10 percent or more. The above standard still must be satisfied.

Real Estate Developer Exception.   Under the basic rules described above, taxpayers who are engaged in the rental real estate business (e.g., owners of warehouses, shopping centers, or office buildings) cannot deduct losses from such business activities since the law presumes that virtually all long-term rental real estate activities are passive. Note that this treatment occurs regardless of the amount of time and energy spent by the taxpayer in such activities. The level of the taxpayer's participation is irrelevant. After much debate, however, Congress finally agreed in 1993 that the passive loss rules were aimed at passive investors in real estate and not those who were in the real estate business. For this reason, it took steps to enable these individuals to deduct losses arising from these activities. This special relief is granted only if the individual can pass certain tests that effectively establish that he or she is truly in the real estate business.

An individual is *eligible* to deduct losses from rental real estate if both of the following conditions are met:[19]

1. Services representing more than 50 percent of the total personal services performed by the individual during the tax year are performed in *real property trades or businesses* in which the taxpayer materially participates during the year. For this purpose, real property trades or businesses include real property development, redevelopment, construction, acquisition, conversion, rental, operation, management, leasing, and brokerage. In the case of a closely held C corporation, this test is met if more than 50 percent of the gross receipts of such corporation are derived from real property businesses in which the corporation materially participates.

2. The individual performs more than 750 hours of services in *real property trades or businesses*.

If a joint return is filed, the special relief is available if either spouse satisfies the requirements.

Observe that satisfaction of these two tests merely opens the door for possible deduction of losses. In order to treat the losses as nonpassive, the taxpayer must still meet the material participation requirements (e.g., spend more than 500 hours in the activity). For this purpose, each activity is normally treated as a separate activity. However, the taxpayer may elect to aggregate such activities. In most cases, it would seem that those who are eligible and who elect to aggregate their real property businesses should be able to meet the material participation tests. It should also be emphasized that personal services as an *employee* in a real property business are not treated as performed in the real property business unless the individual owns at least 5 percent of the business.

> **Example 21.** G graduated from the University of Virginia law school in 1961 and has been practicing his trade ever since. Over the years, however, he has accumulated a number of properties. As a result, he is increasingly spending more time being a real estate magnate and less time being a lawyer. Currently, he owns, operates, and manages a small shopping center, a mini-warehouse, a trailer park, and several duplexes. Each of these rental activities produces a loss, primarily due to depreciation. According to G's detailed diary of how he spends his time, he worked 40 hours a week for 50 weeks during the year for a total of 2,000 hours. The majority, 1,100 hours, was devoted to his real estate ventures. The other 900 hours related to his law practice. In this case, G meets both tests that enable him to treat the rental operations as nonrental activities: (1) more than 50 percent of his personal services were performed in real property businesses, and (2) his 1,100 hours of service in these businesses exceeded the 750-hour threshold. Although the rental taint is removed, this does not necessarily mean G is allowed to deduct

---

[19]   § 469(c)(7).

the losses. He must still satisfy the material participation tests. Whether this final requirement is met depends on whether G elects to aggregate all of the activities. If so, his 1,100 hours of participation is greater than the 500 hours required and he would be entitled to deduct all of the losses.

RECHARACTERIZED PASSIVE INCOME

As is evident throughout the passive loss Regulations, the IRS was concerned that taxpayers might create passive income which could be used to absorb otherwise nondeductible passive losses. Nowhere is this more evident than in the recharacterization rules. In certain situations, income that is characterized under the general rules as passive is recharacterized under a special rule and treated as active. An example of the type of recharacterization that can occur was discussed earlier in connection with SPAs. As noted in that discussion, income from SPAs that fail to meet the 500-hour test would normally be treated as passive, but under the special recharacterization rule it is treated as active. There are several other situations when this might occur. Consequently, before it can be concluded that income is passive, the recharacterization rules must be considered. The recharacterization rules operate to convert the following types of income to nonpassive or active income (rather than passive).[20]

1. *Significant participation activities:* Income from "significant participation activities" that fail to meet the 500-hour test.

2. *Rental of nondeductible property:* Income from rental activities where less than 30 percent of the basis of the property rented is not depreciable (e.g., rental of land).

3. *Developer sales of rental property:* Rental income, including gain on the sale of rental property, if (1) gain on the sale is included in income during the taxable year; (2) rental of the property commenced less than 24 months before the date of disposition; and (3) the taxpayer performed sufficient services that enhanced the value of the rental property.

4. *Self-rented property:* Income from rental of property to an activity in which the taxpayer materially participates, other than related C corporations.

5. *Licensing of intangible property:* Royalty income from a pass-through entity that the taxpayer acquired after the entity created the intangible property.

6. *Equity-financed lending activity:* Income from the trade or business of lending money if certain conditions are satisfied.

---

[20] Temp. Reg. § 1.469-2T(f).

PASSIVE ACTIVITY INTEREST EXPENSE

One aspect related to the passive loss rules that requires special attention is the treatment of interest expense. As discussed in Chapter 11, Congress has imposed severe limitations on the deduction of interest. Interest expense incurred by a taxpayer to finance an investment in a passive activity is subject to the passive loss rules and is not considered investment interest. Similarly, interest expense incurred by an activity that is considered passive (e.g., a partnership if the taxpayer is a limited partner) is subject to the passive loss rules.[21]

> **Example 22.** Dr. P borrowed $50,000 and invested it by acquiring an interest in a limited partnership that produces movies. Interest on the loan for the year is $5,000. P can deduct the interest only to the extent of any passive income that he may have.

> **Example 23.** Assume the partnership above incurs interest expense related to loans made to acquire equipment used in its operations. The interest is treated as a normal deduction and is used in arriving at the partnership's net income or loss for the year. This year, the partnership suffered a net loss including deductions for interest expense. Dr. P is allowed to deduct his share of the loss only to the extent he has passive income from other activities.

✔ CHECK YOUR TAX KNOWLEDGE

Try the following true-false questions.

> **Review Question 1.** This year T's tax records revealed that he had income consisting of a salary of $90,000, dividends of $10,000, and a capital gain from the sale of stock of $5,000. In addition, he received a Schedule K-1 from a partnership in which he is a limited partner. According to the K-1, his share of the partnership's loss for the year was $50,000. T can deduct $15,000 of this loss (i.e., to the extent of his passive dividend and capital gain income).

> *False.* While a taxpayer is entitled to deduct passive losses to the extent of passive income, passive income does not include dividends, interest, capital gains, and the like, which are considered portfolio income.

> **Review Question 2.** A passive loss that cannot be deducted in the current year is generally suspended. The suspended loss is deductible only in the year in which the property to which the loss relates is sold, since the sale affirms the fact that the taxpayer has actually suffered an economic loss.

---

[21] § 163(d)(3)(B).

False. The above is true for the most part, but suspended passive losses are not frozen to be thawed only when the taxpayer sells his or her interest. Passive losses that cannot be deducted in a particular year are carried over to the following year and treated as if they occurred in that subsequent year. Accordingly, the suspended loss can be deducted to the extent that the taxpayer has passive income in the following year. In addition, the taxpayer is allowed to deduct the suspended losses whenever the property to which the loss relates is sold.

Review Question 3. A capital gain from the sale of stock in an S corporation in which the taxpayer does not materially participate is considered portfolio income.

False. Capital gains are normally considered portfolio income, but when such gain arises from the sale of the taxpayer's interest in a passive activity, it is treated as passive income.

Review Question 4. The passive loss rules do not apply to regular C corporations since the losses do not flow through and are not available to the individual shareholders.

False. The passive loss rules do apply to personal service corporations and closely held corporations (i.e., corporations where five or fewer individuals own more than 50 percent of the stock). Personal service corporations must play by the same rules applicable to individuals. Closely held corporations, however, are allowed to offset passive losses against income from operations other than portfolio income.

Review Question 5. Moe, Larry, and Curly pooled all of their savings to start a new restaurant, Stooges. Stooges is operated as an S corporation, and its stock is owned equally by the threesome. In its first year, the restaurant produced a loss. Depending on the circumstances, Moe may be able to deduct his share of the loss this year while Larry and Curly may not be able to deduct their shares.

True. Whether a deduction is allowed for the loss depends on whether the taxpayer materially participates in the activity. Moe may be actively involved on a daily basis, and Larry and Curly may be passive investors. In such case, only Moe would be able to deduct the loss currently.

Review Question 6. D operates a small bed and breakfast motel. Most of his customers rent rooms for one or two days. D's operation is not considered a rental activity for purposes of the passive loss rules.

True. An activity is not considered a rental for purposes of the passive loss rules if the average period of customer use is seven days or less.

Review Question 7.   T owns a duplex and rents it out. She normally signs six-month leases with her tenants. Any loss related to the rental is considered a passive loss and is not deductible regardless of T's participation.

True. This activity is considered a rental since the average period of customer use exceeds 30 days and T does not provide any extraordinary services. Losses on long-term rental real estate are normally not deductible except to the extent of passive income unless the taxpayer can qualify under one of two exceptions. First, she is permitted to deduct up to $25,000 of losses from rental real estate if she actively participates and her adjusted gross income is less than $150,000. In addition, a special exception allows individuals who spend more than 50 percent of their time in real property businesses and more than 750 hours in such businesses to treat the activities as nonrental and deduct any losses if they materially participate in such activities.

Review Question 8.   Several years ago, Q purchased an interest in a limited partnership. This year his share of the partnership's loss was $10,000. Assuming Q's adjusted gross income is $80,000, he may deduct the loss since it is less than $25,000.

False. The loss would be treated as a passive loss since Q does not materially participate in the partnership activity. The de minimis exception that enables a taxpayer to deduct up to $25,000 of passive losses annually applies only to losses from rental real estate activities in which the taxpayer actively participates.

Review Question 9.   B opened her first Planet Jupiter Cafe five years ago in Aspen. Now she has five restaurants, each located in a different resort. Since each store is located in a separate city, she must treat each store as a separate activity.

False. A taxpayer is required to treat one or more activities as a single activity if the activities constitute an appropriate economic unit (AEU). The Regulations give the taxpayer a great deal of flexibility in determining what constitutes an AEU. Thus, the taxpayer could treat each as a separate activity, combine all and treat as a single activity, or use some other grouping that may be appropriate under the Regulations.

Review Question 10.   B is a college professor who recently got involved in a mail-order smoke alarm business. This year he spent about 100 hours in the activity, taking orders and arranging to fill them. B materially participates in the business.

True. Under the general rule, a taxpayer is considered a material participant if he or she spends more than 500 hours in the activity during the year. Although B does not meet the general rule, he does meet an alternative test; that is, his participation constitutes substantially all of the participation in the activity. Therefore the activity is not a passive activity.

Review Question 11.   G owns two businesses, a convenience grocery store and a dry cleaners. For the last several years, the grocery has not done as well as G had hoped and she has lost money. This year, G did not play as much golf as usual and spent about 400 hours trying to turn the business around. She spent about 300 hours at the cleaners. Each business has a number of full-time employees. G may offset any loss attributable to the grocery store against the profits from her dry cleaners.

True. The restaurant and the dry cleaners are considered significant participation activities since G spends more than 100 hours in each. If the total participation in all SPAs exceed 500 hours, the taxpayer is deemed to materially participate in each of the activities. In this case, the total participation in all SPAs exceeds the 500-hour threshold, and G is therefore deemed to materially participate in each of the activities. Thus, she can use the loss in the grocery activity to offset the income from the cleaning business.

Review Question 12.   Same as above, except G spends 100 hours at the cleaners, 300 hours at the grocery, and the remaining time at the beach. G may offset any loss attributable to the grocery against the profits from her dry cleaners.

False. In this case, G's combined participation in the SPAs does not exceed 500 hours. This is the "heads we win, tails you lose" situation: the loss is passive, the income is nonpassive, and the two cannot be combined.

Review Question 13.   J borrowed $100,000 to purchase an interest in the Lockwood Limited Partnership, which operates several apartment complexes. This year J paid $8,000 interest on the loan to acquire his interest. In addition, J's share of the partnership's losses was $10,000. J has no passive income. The loss is a passive loss and cannot be deducted, but the interest is treated as investment interest and is deductible to the extent of J's investment income.

False. J simply treats the $8,000 of interest expense as another operating expense of the partnership, increasing the loss from $10,000 to $18,000. None of the loss, including the interest, is deductible.

RENTAL OF RESIDENCE (VACATION HOME RENTALS)

Section 280A imposes restrictions on the deduction of expenses related to rental of a residence if the taxpayer is considered as using the residence primarily for personal purposes rather than for making a profit. These restrictions are aimed at the perceived abuse existing in the area of vacation home rental. Prior to the enactment of § 280A, many felt that personal enjoyment was the predominant motive for purchasing a vacation home. Any rental of the vacation home served merely to minimize the personal expense of ownership and not to produce income.

BASIC RULES

In 1976, Congress prescribed an objective method for ascertaining the purpose of the rental activity as well as the amount of the deduction. According to this approach, the expenses incurred by the taxpayer in owning and operating the home (e.g., interest, taxes, maintenance, utilities, and depreciation) must first be allocated between personal use and rental use. The deductibility of the expenses then depends on whether the home is considered the taxpayer's *residence* or *rental property*. This latter determination is made based on the owner's personal use and the amount of rental activity.[22]

1. *Nominal Rentals:* If the residence is rented out fewer than 15 days, all rental income is excluded from gross income and no deduction is allowed for rental expenses. Otherwise allowable deductions, such as those for qualified residence interest, real estate taxes, and casualty losses may be deducted *from* A.G.I.

2. *Used as a "Residence":* If the taxpayer uses the vacation home for more than 14 days or 10 percent of the number of days the property is actually rented out, whichever is greater, the home is treated as his or her residence and deductions are restricted as explained below. A typical taxpayer caught by this rule is the owner of a vacation home who uses it for more than two weeks and rents it out to defray the cost.

    a. *Expenses allocable to the rental use:* These expenses are deductible to the extent of gross income less otherwise allowable deductions. Any deductions in excess of gross income can be carried over and deducted to the extent of any future income. These expenses are deductible *for* A.G.I. since they are related to rental use.

    b. *Expenses allocable to personal use:* Since these expenses are considered personal, they may be deducted only if they are specifically authorized by the Code. Allocable property taxes are deductible without limitation as an itemized deduction since such expenses are fully deductible regardless of the activity in which they are incurred. Interest expense *may* be deductible as an itemized deduction. Allocable interest is normally qualified residence interest since the home—*in this case*—is considered the taxpayer's residence (e.g., because it is used greater than 14 days). However, if the home is not the primary or secondary residence of the taxpayer (e.g., the taxpayer has several vacation homes), no deduction would be available. The other operating expenses are not deductible.

---

[22] §§ 280A(c)(5) and 280A(d) through (g).

3. *Used as "Rental Property":* If the taxpayer does not use the property extensively (i.e., more than the greater of 14 days or 10 percent of the number of days rented out), then the property is effectively treated as rental property.

a. *Expenses allocable to the rental use:* These expenses are deductible subject only to the restrictions on passive losses. If the property's average rental period is either (1) 1–7 days or (2) 8–30 days *and* significant services are provided, the property is *not* rental property under the passive loss rules. Thus, the treatment of any loss depends on whether the taxpayer materially participates in this "nonrental activity." If the taxpayer materially participates, any loss would not be passive and would therefore be fully deductible. (See *Example 20* earlier in this chapter.) If the property is considered a rental (e.g., perhaps under the facts-and-circumstances test or if the rental is 8–30 days and *no* significant services are provided) and the taxpayer is considered as having met the active participation standard, the taxpayer may qualify for the rental exception under the passive loss rules. This would allow the taxpayer to deduct up to $25,000 in losses annually. Any deductions would be for A.G.I.

b. *Expenses allocable to personal use:* As noted above, since these expenses are personal, they may be deducted only if they are specifically authorized by the Code. In this case, property taxes would continue to be fully deductible. On the other hand, none of the interest expense would be deductible as qualified residence interest since the vacation home is not considered a "residence" (because the taxpayer did *not* use it more than 14 days). However, the excess interest expense would be treated as investment interest and could be deducted to the extent of investment income. Other operating expenses would not be deductible.

This treatment is summarized in Exhibit 12-1.

For purposes of the owner use test, the number of days a unit is rented out does not include any day the unit is used for personal purposes. The unit is generally treated as used for personal purposes on any day where the owner or a member of his or her family uses it for any portion of the day for personal purposes or the unit is rented at less than a fair rental.[23] A day on which the taxpayer spends at least two-thirds of the time at the unit (or if less than two-thirds then at least eight hours) on repairs is not counted as a personal day. This is true even though individuals who accompany the taxpayer do not perform repairs or maintenance.[24]

---

[23] § 280A(d)(2).

[24] Prop. Reg. § 1.280A-1(e)(4) and § 280A(d)(2).

Exhibit 12-1 *Vacation Homes Summary of § 280A Rules*

Character of vacation home:	Residence	Rental property
Characterization: Personal use exceeding the greater of 1. 14 days, or 2. 10 percent of days rented out	Yes	No
Expenses allocable to rental use:	Limited to gross income by § 280A	Limited by passive loss rules Rental exception may apply
Expenses allocable to personal use: Taxes	Deductible	Deductible
Interest	Qualified residence interest	Investment interest
Other	Not deductible	Not deductible

ALLOCATION OF EXPENSES

In allocating the expenses between personal and rental use, two different methods are used. Prior to 1987, allocation of otherwise allowable deductions such as interest and taxes assumed that such expenses *accrued daily* regardless of use. Consequently, the fraction for allocating these items to the rental use was[25]

$$\text{Otherwise allowable deduction} \times \frac{\text{Number of rental days}}{365} = \text{Portion attributable to rental use}$$

In contrast, expenses such as utilities, maintenance, and depreciation were considered a *function of use*. As a result, the fraction used for allocating these items to the rental use was

$$\text{Operating expenses} \times \frac{\text{Number of rental days}}{\text{Rental + Personal days}} = \text{Portion attributable to rental use}$$

In allocating any interest and taxes, it is unclear whether the first fraction shown—which was approved by the courts prior to 1987—should still be used in light of the

---

[25] *Dorance D. Bolton*, 77 T.C. 104 (1982),
aff'd. at 82-2 USTC ¶9699, 51 AFTR2d 83-305 (CA-9, 1982).

1986 revisions.[26] The Senate Finance Committee Report indicates that the allocation of interest is to be made under rules similar to prior law. Yet, immediately thereafter the Report states that "interest" is to be allocated based on relative use (i.e., the second fraction above). The following example takes the approach under prior law.

Example 24.   A owns a condominium in a ski resort. During the year, A uses the condominium as a secondary residence for 30 days and rents it out for 90 days. The condominium is not used the remainder of the year. A's gross rental income is $3,500. Total expenses for the entire year include maintenance and utilities of $1,000, interest of $6,200, taxes of $1,100, and $2,000 depreciation on the entire cost of the unit.

A's use for 30 days is more than 14 days, the greater of 14 or 9 days (10% of the 90 days rented). For this reason, expenses attributable to the rental are deductible to the extent of gross income as reduced by otherwise allowable deductions (the interest and taxes). Deductions are computed and deducted *in the following order*:

Gross income..	$3,500
Deduct allocable portion of otherwise allowable deductions:	
Interest and taxes [$7,300 × (90 ÷ 365)]...................	− 1,800
Gross income limitation..	$1,700
Deduct allocable portion of deductions other than those otherwise allowable and depreciation: Utilities and maintenance	
[$1,000 × 90 ÷ (30 + 90)]...............................	− 750
Gross income limitation..	$ 950
Deduct allocable portion of depreciation: Depreciation [$2,000 × 90 ÷ (30 + 90)] = $1,500	
but limited to $950 balance of gross income..............	− 950
Net income...	$ 0

All of the above deductions are *for* A.G.I. The balance of interest and taxes not allocated to the rental use, $5,500 ($7,300 − $1,800), is deductible if the taxpayer itemizes deductions. Note that the interest in this case is qualified residence interest since the unit is treated as A's residence. The deduction for maintenance and utilities is not limited by gross income since all of the expenses attributable to the rental activity are deductible. The $250 ($1,000 − $750) remaining balance of maintenance and utilities would not be deductible in any case since it represents the expenses attributable to personal use. Of the remaining depreciation balance of $1,050 ($2,000 − $950), $550 ($1,500 − $950) attributable to the rental is not deductible due to the gross income limitation but may be carried over to subsequent years. The other $500 of depreciation is not deductible since it is the portion attributable to personal use. Also note that only the $950 of depreciation allowed is treated as a reduction in the basis of A's condominium.

---

[26] § 280A(e).

Example 25.   Assume the same facts as in *Example 24*, except that A used the condominium for 10 days rather than 30. Also assume that the rental is on a three-month basis to locals and no services are provided. In such case, the condominium would be treated as rental property rather than as a residence since A stayed less than 14 days. In addition, the $25,000 rental exception of the passive loss rules would apply since there is a long-term rental and no significant services are provided. A's deduction would be computed as follows:

Gross income..	$3,500
Deduct allocable portion of otherwise allowable deductions	
($7,300 × 90 ÷ 365)..	− 1,800
Deduct allocable portion of utilities and maintenance	
[$1,000 × 90 ÷ (90 + 10)]..................................	− 900
Deduct allocable portion of depreciation	
[$2,000 × 90 ÷ (90 + 10)]..................................	− 1,800
Loss..	$(1,000)

In this case, a loss is created that may offset any other income of the taxpayer under the $25,000 rental loss exception. In contrast to *Example 23* above, however, the balance of the interest expense, $5,500 ($7,300 − $1,800), would not be deductible as qualified residence interest since the property does not qualify as a residence. Nevertheless, the taxpayer may be able to deduct the amount as investment interest to the extent of any net investment income that he may have from other investments. Lacking investment income, the taxpayer would be better off by using the condominium more, in order that he could qualify it as a second residence and deduct the interest. The balance of the other expenses would not be deductible.

The vacation home rules, as discussed above, could operate to eliminate legitimate deductions for those taxpayers who convert their personal residence for rental during the year. In these cases, the owner usually uses the residence for more than 14 days and thus, deductions are limited. However, § 280A(d) provides relief for taxpayers in these situations. The provision accomplishes this goal by not counting as personal use days any days of personal use during the year immediately before (or after) the rental period begins (or ends). This rule, often referred to as the *qualified rental period exception*, applies only if the rental period is at least a year (or if less than a year, the house is sold at the end of the rental period).

Example 26.   B lived in her home from January through July. In August, she moved into a condominium and decided to convert her old home to rental property. B was able to find a tenant who leased the old home for a year. Under the normal rules of § 280A, B's deductions related to the old home would be limited to gross income since her personal use exceeded 14 days. The relief measure of § 280A(d) removes this limitation because the seven months of personal use preceding the one-year rental period are not counted as personal use days. As a result, B would treat the lease as a rental activity and could deduct expenses subject to the passive loss rules, possibly qualifying for the $25,000 exception.

✔ CHECK YOUR TAX KNOWLEDGE

Review Question 1.   During the Olympics held in Los Angeles during 1984, many Californians left town and rented their homes out for the two weeks the games were in town. It was rumored that some of the Beverly Hills mansions were rented for more than $100,000 during this time. How would these temporary landlords treat the income?

Under § 280A, if the home is rented out for less than 15 days, all of the rental income is excluded and none of the expenses allocable to the rental period are deductible. Consequently, these temporary landlords received a real windfall because they were allowed to exclude all of the income. Did you hear that, Atlanta?

Review Question 2.   T owns a condominium in Vail. This year his rental agent was able to rent it out for 100 days (most guests stayed for six days). Unfortunately, he was able to use the condo for personal purposes for only one week in January because of a skiing accident in which he broke his shoulder. Interest expense and taxes allocable to the personal use were $500. The net loss attributable to the rental during the remainder of the year was $4,000. What amount can T deduct? Is the property considered rental property subject to the passive loss rules?

Since the personal use was nominal (i.e., not more than the greater of 10% of the number of days rented or two weeks), the property is not considered a residence. Moreover, it is not considered rental property under the passive loss rules since the average rental period was less than eight days. Thus it is considered a nonrental activity with the treatment dependent on whether T materially participates in the activity. Since he does not materially participate, the loss is a passive loss and is not deductible unless he has other passive income. The interest attributable to the period of personal use is not qualified residence interest since the unit did not qualify as a residence. Instead the interest is treated as investment interest and is deductible to the extent of investment income.

Review Question 3.   W owns a condominium in St. John in the Caribbean. She rented it out for seven months (one month at a time) during the year but used it personally for the entire month of January. Can W treat the activity as a rental activity and take advantage of the $25,000 de mimimis exception that would allow her to deduct a loss from the property.

No. If a taxpayer uses a home for more than two weeks or 10 percent of the number of days the unit is rented, she treats the home as a residence. In this case, the taxpayer used the home 31 days for personal purposes, thereby exceeding the threshold and converting the property to a residence. Any interest is deductible as qualified residence interest, assuming this is a first or second home. On the other hand, rental expenses can be deducted only to the extent of rental income. The excess expenses may be carried over and deducted in subsequent years to the extent the unit generates income. The passive loss rules do not apply.

PROBLEM MATERIALS

DISCUSSION QUESTIONS

12-1 *Tax Shelters and the Solution.* In 1982, T purchased for $10,000 an interest in Neptune III, a limited partnership created by Dandy Development Company to finance and build a 25-story office building in downtown Houston. T, who was in the 50 percent tax bracket, hoped that this investment would significantly cut her taxes.

   a. Explain the features of the investment that during that period made such investments attractive and might produce the benefits desired by T.

   b. Explain what steps Congress took in 1986 to eliminate the benefits of investments in such activities as Neptune III. Comment in some detail on the approach used by Congress to accomplish its objective.

   c. What steps might you have suggested had you been advising Congress on the restriction of tax shelters?

12-2 *Effect of Code § 469.* D owns and operates several ski rental shops in Vail, Aspen, Beaver Creek, and Steamboat Springs. Over the years, the shops have had their ups and downs—profits some years, losses in others. Recently, D has spent less and less time at the shop, letting his employees do most of the work.

   a. What is the significance should the business be characterized as a passive activity?

   b. Should D worry about his business being treated as a passive activity? When is an activity considered passive?

   c. Does the fact that D's business is a rental operation have any bearing on the nature of the activity?

   d. What are the aggregation or grouping rules and why might they be important in D's case?

12-3 *Taxpayers Subject to § 469.* Dr. R has been quite successful over the years. She left St. James hospital in 1974 and started her own sports medicine practice, The Sports Institute Inc., a regular C corporation. After building this operation into a thriving practice, she branched out. In 1983, she and a good friend opened their own restaurant, The Diner, a partnership. In 1986, her college roommate persuaded R to invest and buy stock in a new venture, Compatible PCs, a corporation that manufactured personal computers. Compatible PCs was owned by R and three other individuals and operated as a regular C corporation until this year, when it converted to S status. Dr. R's other investments include a single-family house that she rents out, a limited partnership interest in an oil and gas operation, and a limited partnership interest in a business that develops land into shopping centers. Explain how R is affected by the passive loss rules.

12-4 *Definition of an Activity and Planning.* D owns several businesses, including an indoor soccer facility, a gas station adjacent to the soccer facility (he bought it with the intention of someday expanding the soccer facility), and a fast-food restaurant across the street from the soccer facility. Within the soccer facility, he has rented space to a local soccer retail store. He also rents space in the facility to another company, which operates a small bar and restaurant. In any one year, each business may be profitable or may have losses. For simplicity, assume each business is operated as a sole proprietorship.

   a. Assuming one of the businesses is profitable, would D prefer passive or active income?
   b. Assuming one of the businesses has losses, would D prefer a passive or active loss?
   c. Discuss the passive loss rules, how they might apply to D, and what planning might be considered. Identify as many questions as possible that might be asked in determining how the passive loss rules apply to D.

12-5 *Aggregation Rules.* Aggregation is mandatory for purposes of the material participation tests.

   a. Explain the general rules concerning aggregation and their purpose.
   b. Explain when this rule is beneficial and when it is detrimental for the taxpayer.

12-6 *Rental Activities and Material Participation.* T owns a 10-unit apartment complex. He not only manages the apartments but also performs all of the routine maintenance and repairs as well as keeping the books. Most of the leases that he signs with tenants are for one year. This year the complex produced a loss of $30,000. How will T treat the loss, assuming his adjusted gross income from other sources is $90,000?

12-7 *Recharacterization.* Briefly explain the purpose of the recharacterization rules and why they must not be overlooked when dealing with passive activities.

12-8 *Credits from a Passive Activity.* P is considering rehabilitating a home in a historic neighborhood. She hopes to qualify for both the rehabilitation credit as well as the low-income housing credit.

   a. Assuming she qualifies, explain how she will compute the amount of credit that she may claim.
   b. P's accountant has explained the limitations that apply to losses and has indicated to P that any losses on the rental that are denied currently will ultimately be allowed once P sells the property. Can the same be said of credits?

12-9 *Grouping Activities.* Urged by their accountants to reduce their tax liability, a group of orthopedic surgeons invested in real estate that produced passive losses. Prior to 1986, these losses did in fact serve as tax shelters. After 1986, however, the passive loss rules significantly restricted the tax benefits of the investments. Consequently, the accountants prodded the doctors to form a partnership to acquire and operate X-ray equipment. The doctors do not participate in the X-ray partnership, and, therefore, any income produced by the partnership is passive income. Most of the income from operation of the partnership is derived from services provided to the doctors themselves. Will this scheme successfully produce passive income that can be used to absorb passive losses?

12-10 *Interest Expense.* This year Dr. Z purchased a 20 percent interest in a partnership that is building an office building in downtown Dallas. To finance the acquisition, he used his line of credit at the bank and borrowed $100,000. As a result, he paid $10,000 in interest during the year.

    a. How will Dr. Z treat the interest expense?

    b. After the building was completed, the partnership secured permanent financing. This year the partnership paid mortgage interest of $700,000, of which $14,000 represented Dr. Z's allocable share. How will Dr. Z treat the interest?

PROBLEMS

12-11 *Identifying Activities.* For each of the following situations, indicate the number of activities in which the taxpayer participates.

    a. S owns and operates an ice cream store in Southwoods Mall. He is also a camera buff and owns a camera shop in the same mall.

    b. T owns a small "strip" shopping center that houses 10 businesses, including T's own video store. This year T received $40,000 in income from renting out space in the shopping center and grossed $60,000 from her video store.

    c. O owns five greeting card stores spread all around Denver.

    d. P owns 10 gas stations throughout the state of Georgia. Each station not only sells gas but also sells groceries. Seven of the stations derive 60 percent of their income from gas sales and 40 percent from food sales. Two of the stations derive 55 percent of their income from food sales and 45 percent from gas sales. One station also provides auto repair services and consequently derives one-third of its income from each operation.

    e. E owns a beer distributorship and ten liquor stores throughout Minneapolis. Sixty percent of the distributorship sales are to the liquor stores.

12-12 *Combining Activities.* T owns a 70 percent interest in each of three partnerships: a radio station (WAKO), a minor league baseball team (the Harrisville Hippos), and a video and film company (Dynamite Productions) that produces short subjects for television, including advertisements. In any particular year, one business may be profitable while another may be unprofitable. Each business is at a different location. Each business also prepares its own financial statements and has its own management, although T participates extensively in the management of all three partnerships. Any financing needed for the three partnerships is usually obtained from Second National, a local bank. The radio station broadcasts all of the Hippo games, and the production company often prepares material for local television spots on the Hippos. Occasionally, some employees in one partnership assist the other partnership in periods of peak activity or emergency. Explain how the passive loss rules apply to T in this case.

12-13 *Material Participation.* During the week, A is a mild-mannered reporter for the local paper. On the weekends, he is a partner with his brother-in-law, B, in a small van-conversion operation in Elkhart. The two typically work seven or eight hours on most Saturdays during the year. This year, the partnership suffered a loss of $10,000.

    a. How will A treat the loss?

    b. What planning might you suggest?

12-14 *Participation Defined.* Three recent Purdue graduates—C, D, and E—formed their own lawn treatment company. Each of the three participates on a part-time basis because each is otherwise employed on a full-time basis. In this, their first year of operations, C spent 40 hours, D spent 70 hours, and E contributed 80 hours. E's wife also kept the books for the partnership. Explain whether C, D, and E satisfy the material participation test.

12-15 *Material Participation.* F is an accountant with a large C.P.A. firm. She also has an interest in two partnerships: a night club and a family-owned drugstore. F maintains the accounting records for each partnership, spending 200 hours working for the night club and 400 hours for the drugstore.

    a. How will F treat any losses that the partnerships might have?
    b. How will F treat any income that the partnerships might have?

12-16 *Material Participation.* In 1975 H started his own replacement window business, Sting Construction, an S corporation. Up until 1988 H had been the sole shareholder. In 1988 he sold 90 percent of his stock to J and K, who continued the business. From time to time, H still provides advice to J and K. This year, H spent 300 hours working for the company. J and K each devoted 1,500 hours to the business. Unfortunately, the corporation suffered a loss this year because of a downturn in the economy. How will H treat the loss?

12-17 *Rental or Nonrental Activities.* Indicate whether the following are rental or nonrental activities.

    a. P owns an airplane. She has an arrangement with a flying club at a small airport to lease the plane out on a short-term basis to its students. Most of the time the plane is rented for two to three hours.
    b. Q owns a condominium in Aspen that he rents out during the year. The average stay is one week. Q has arranged to provide daily maid and linen service for the unit. In addition, his monthly condominium fee pays for maintenance of the common areas.
    c. S and his wife, T, own White Silver Sands, a posh resort on the coast of Florida. As part of its package, the resort provides everything a vacationer could want (daily maid service, free use of the golf, tennis, and pool facilities, an on-site masseuse, etc.). The average stay is two weeks.
    d. Z owns a duplex near the University of Texas that she normally rents out to students on a long-term basis. The average stay is nine months. Z provides typical landlord services such as repairs and maintenance.
    e. B owns Quiet Quarters, a retirement home for the elderly. The home's staff includes a physician and several nurses.
    f. C owns and operates Body Beautiful, a fitness club. The club has over 1,000 members, who have use of the club daily from 6 A.M. to 11 P.M.
    g. D owns a 200-acre parcel of land on the outskirts of Lubbock. The land is worth $700,000 (basis $200,000). During the year, D leased the land to a local car enthusiast who used it as a raceway. D collected rents of $5,000.

12-18 *Passive Activities.*   G is the head chef for Half-Way Airlines making a salary of $70,000 a year. In addition, his portfolio income is about $20,000 a year. Over the years, G has made numerous investments and has been a participant in many ventures. Indicate whether the passive activity rules would apply in each of the following situations.

a. A $10,000 loss from G's interest in Flimsy Flims, a limited partnership. G is a limited partner.

b. A $5,000 loss from G's interest as a shareholder in D's Bar and Grill, an S corporation. G and his wife operate the bar. Each spent 300 hours working there in the current year.

c. G and his friend, F, are equal partners in a partnership that produces and markets a Texas-style barbecue sauce. G leaves the management of the day-to-day operations to F. However, G spent 130 hours working in the business during the current year. For the year, the partnership had income of $15,000. Assume that this is G's *only* investment.

d. Same as (c) except G has an ownership interest in three other distinctly different activities (e.g., construction and consulting). He spends 130 hours in each of the four activities.

e. G is a 10 percent partner in a restaurant consulting firm. The firm operates the business on the bottom floor of a three-story building it owns. The firm leases the other two floors to a law firm and a real estate company. The consulting side of the business reported a $100,000 profit from consulting, $5,000 in interest income, and had a loss from the rental operation.

f. G is the sole owner of Try, Inc., a regular C corporation that produces G's special salad dressing. The corporation had an operating profit of $4,000. In addition, Try, Inc. had interest income of $5,000 and a $7,000 loss from its investment in a real estate limited partnership in which it was a limited partner.

12-19 *Passive Activity Limitations.*   M is a successful banker. Two years ago, M's 27-year-old son, J, asked his dad to become his partner in opening a sporting goods store. M agreed and contributed $50,000 for a 50 percent interest in the partnership. J operates the store on his own, receiving little advice from his father. Information regarding M's financial activities reveals the following for the past two years:

Year	Salary	Interest Income	Partnership Income (Loss)
1994	$100,000	$20,000	$(40,000)
1995	100,000	20,000	12,000

All parties are cash basis, calendar year taxpayers. Answer the following questions.

a. How did M's investment in the partnership affect his A.G.I. in 1994?

b. How did M's investment in the partnership affect his A.G.I. in 1995?

c. Would your answer to (b) change if the partnership had a loss in 1995 and the income shown was from M's interest as a limited partner in a real estate venture?

d. On January 1, 1996, M sold his interest in the partnership to his son for a $40,000 gain. What effect?

12-20 *Passive Activity Limitations: Rental Property.*   L, single, is the chief of surgery at a local hospital. During the year, L earned a salary of $120,000. L owns a four-unit apartment building that she rents out unfurnished. The current tenants have one-year leases, which expire at various times. This year, the property produced a loss of $30,000 due to accelerated depreciation. L is actively involved in the rental activity, making many of the decisions regarding leases, repairs, etc.

    a. How much of the loss may L deduct?

    b. Would the answer to (a) change if L materially participated?

12-21 *Rental Real Estate.*   M and H are real estate moguls. Together they have created a number of partnerships that own over 50 shopping malls as well as a few office buildings, apartments, and warehouses. Most of their lease agreements with their mall tenants are tied to the tenant's gross receipts. Unfortunately, with the downturn in the economy, several of the mall projects have produced substantial losses. How will M and H treat their share of the losses?

12-22 *Suspended Losses.*   When tax shelter activity was at its highest, G was one of its biggest proponents. Currently, she still owns an interest in several limited partnerships. She is now considering what she should do in light of the passive loss rules. To help her make this decision, she has put together her best guess as to the performance of her investments over the next two years. These are shown below.

Activity	1994	1995
X	$(7,000)	$(2,000)
Y	(3,000)	(9,000)
Z	6,000	1,000

    a. Determine the amount of suspended loss for each activity at the end of 1994 and 1995.

    b. Assume the same facts as in (a) above, except assume that in 1995 G sells the Y activity for a $4,000 gain. Explain the effect of the disposition on any suspended losses G might have, including the amount of suspended losses to be carried forward to 1996.

12-23   *Characterizing Income.*   Indicate whether the income in the following situations is passive or nonpassive.

   a.   Ten years ago, T purchased a strip of land for $300,000. Shortly thereafter, he built an office building on the land for $100,000. He currently leases the entire building to a large corporation on a ten-year lease for $90,000 annually. This year he sold the building for $700,000.

   b.   Q owns a real estate development business that she operates as an S corporation. In 1993 she purchased a vacant lot for $100,000. Q proceeded to put in roads, sewers, and other amenities at a cost of $50,000. Shortly thereafter, she contracted for the construction of a warehouse at a cost of $1 million. Upon completion of the building in September 1993, Q began leasing the space. It was completely leased by June 1994. In December 1995 she sold the property for $2 million.

   c.   T owns 100 percent of the stock of Z Corporation, an S corporation that operates a construction company. This year T purchased and leased a crane to the corporation. T received total rents of $10,000.

   d.   X operates a travel agency and an office supply store to which she devotes 300 and 100 hours, respectively. The travel agency produced a profit of $10,000 while the office supply business sustained a loss of $40,000.

12-24   *Rental versus Nonrental Activities.* Identify rental activities that would not be considered "rental activities" for purposes of the passive loss rules.

12-25   *Vacation Home Rental.*   S owns a condominium in Florida, which he and his family use occasionally. During the year, he used the condominium for 20 days and rented it for 40 days. The remainder of the year, the condominium was vacant. S compiled the following information related to the condominium for the entire year:

Rental income............................	$1,000
Expenses:	
Interest on mortgage....................	3,650
Maintenance............................	900
Depreciation............................	6,000

   a.   Compute the tax effect of the rental activity on S.
   b.   Assuming S only used the condominium personally for ten days, compute the tax effect.
   c.   Assuming S only rented the condominium for 14 days, compute the tax effect.

12-26   *Vacation Home—Personal Use Days.*   Indicate the number of personal use days in each of the following situations.

   a.   Saturday morning, March 3, S drove to Vail to replace a hot water heater in his vacation home. He arrived in Vail at 9 A.M. and skied until late afternoon when he retired to his condominium at 6 P.M. After dinner, he worked on replacing the hot water heater until midnight when he went to sleep. The following morning he awoke and went skiing until 5 P.M. when he returned home.

   b.   Same as (a) except S's wife and family accompanied him. S's family also skied but did not perform any repairs or maintenance related to the vacation home.

   c.   T owns a duplex, which he rents. On February 1 of this year, the one-year lease of the tenant living upstairs expired and she moved. Unable to rent the upstairs unit, T moved in on December 1 and remained through the end of the year.

PART **IV**

ALTERNATIVE MINIMUM TAX AND TAX CREDITS

━━━━━━━━━━━━━━━━━━ ■ CONTENTS ■ ━━━━━━━━━━━━━━

CHAPTER 13 ■ **THE ALTERNATIVE MINIMUM TAX AND TAX CREDITS**

Upon completion of this chapter you will be able to:

- Explain the tax policy reasons underlying the Alternative Minimum Tax (AMT) system

- Understand the conceptual framework of the AMT system and understand the terminology necessary to communicate AMT issues or concerns to a tax professional

- Determine the amount of AMT adjustments, preferences, and exemptions, and calculate the alternative minimum taxable income, the tentative minimum tax, and the AMT

- Complete Form 6251, Alternative Minimum Tax - Individuals

- Explain the tax policy reasons for enacting recent tax incentives in the form of tax credits rather than deductions

- Distinguish between nonrefundable tax credits subject to dollar limitations and refundable tax credits, which have no such limitations

- Understand the components of the general business credit and be able to calculate the amount of credit allowable with respect to each separate component

- Identify and calculate the nonbusiness tax credits, including the child and dependent care credit, the credit for the elderly, the earned income credit, and the minimum tax credit

- Understand and apply the tax credit carryover, carryback, and recapture rules

CHAPTER OUTLINE

Introduction	13-1	Alcohol Fuel Credit	13-38
Alternative Minimum Tax	13-2	Research and Experimental (R&E)	
Policy Objectives	13-2	Credit	13-39
Overview of AMT	13-3	Low-Income Housing Credit	13-43
AMT Rates and Exemptions	13-4	Disabled Access Credit	13-43
Adjustments and Tax Preference		Empowerment Zone Employment	
Items in General	13-6	Credit	13-44
AMT Adjustments	13-7	Other Components of the General	
AMT Adjustments Applicable to All		Business Credit	13-45
Taxpayers	13-7	General Business Credit Carryover	
AMT Adjustments Applicable Only to		Rules	13-46
Individuals	13-11	Foreign Tax Credit	13-46
Adjustment Applicable Only to		Nonbusiness Credits	13-47
Corporations	13-14	Child and Dependent Care Credit	13-48
Special Tax Shelter Loss Adjustments	13-15	Credit for the Elderly and	
Tax Preference Items	13-16	Permanently Disabled	13-53
Alternative Minimum Tax		Credit for Interest on Certain Home	
Computations	13-19	Mortgages	13-54
Minimum Tax Credit	13-23	Credit for Qualified Electric Vehicles	13-54
Income Tax Credits	13-29	Refundable Credits	13-55
Overview of Tax Credits	13-29	Tax Withheld at the Source	13-55
General Business Credit	13-31	Earned Income Credit	13-55
Investment Credit	13-32	Other Refundable Credits	13-58
Targeted Jobs Credit	13-37	Problem Materials	13-59

Chapter 13

THE ALTERNATIVE MINIMUM TAX AND TAX CREDITS

INTRODUCTION

As may be abundantly clear at this point, the U.S. tax system is replete with rules whose purpose is not simply to raise revenue but also to shape the behavior of its citizens.[1] These so-called tax incentives—or *tax preferences*—are sprinkled everywhere in the Code, and they come in every conceivable form. There are exclusions, deductions, and credits that stimulate anything and everything. For example, accelerated depreciation stimulates the acquisition of machinery and equipment, and percentage depletion boosts investment in natural resources. Research is encouraged through a quick write-off as well as a credit. There are also credits to attract investment in low-income housing and the rehabilitation of old buildings. Still other credits exhort taxpayers to use certain fuels, buy electric cars, and hire certain people. Even more tax benefits await those who invest in empowerment zones, enterprise communities, and small corporations.

Unfortunately, using the Code to solve some of the country's ills has created problems of its own. As the number of tax preferences began to grow, astute tax advisers and promoters saw an opportunity. They began to structure business and investment deals— all perfectly legal—that took advantage of the favorable treatment extended to particular investments. In fact, tax professionals did their jobs so well that it was not unusual to find wealthy individuals with large economic incomes who paid little or no income tax. Indeed, in 1966 it was determined that 154 individuals with adjusted gross incomes in excess of $200,000 were able to completely escape tax by using the various incentives. Although the revenue lost from these high-income, no-tax individuals was slight, concerns started to surface. By the late 1960s Congress recognized that an increasing number of people were losing faith in the system, believing that it was unfairly tipped in favor of the rich. Finally, amidst cries that only the poor and middle class paid taxes, the Johnson administration responded.

---

[1] See "Goals of Taxation" discussion in Chapter 1.

In 1969 legislation was enacted to guarantee that all wealthy individuals paid at least some amount of Federal income tax. The method adopted, however, was circuitous. Instead of repealing the tax preferences that created the opportunities, Congress chose to add another layer of taxation: the minimum tax. Since 1969 the minimum tax has come a long way, steadily growing in scope and importance. The first part of this chapter takes a look at these complex provisions.

The second part of this chapter is devoted to the world of credits. Over the years, Congress has established a number of credits that attempt to accomplish a variety of objectives. In addition to the business credits noted above, there are also several credits reserved for individuals. For example, there are credits to aid individuals with child care, help the elderly and disabled, and encourage individuals to get off welfare and go to work. Each of the credit provisions is discussed below.

ALTERNATIVE MINIMUM TAX

POLICY OBJECTIVES

Since its enactment in 1969, the minimum tax has gone through a virtual metamorphosis. Substantial revisions occurred in 1976, 1978, 1981, and 1982, and a complete overhaul took place in 1986. Throughout, however, the rationale behind the tax has remained virtually unchanged. The policy underlying the minimum tax was well summarized in the following excerpt from the Senate Finance Committee Report on the Tax Reform Act of 1986:

Reasons for Change

The committee believes that the minimum tax should serve one overriding objective: to ensure that no taxpayer with substantial economic income can avoid significant tax liability by using exclusions, deductions, and credits. Although these provisions may provide incentives for worthy goals, they become counterproductive when taxpayers are allowed to use them to avoid virtually all tax liability. The ability of high-income individuals and highly profitable corporations to pay little or no tax undermines respect for the entire tax system and, thus, for the incentive provisions themselves. In addition, even aside from public perceptions, the committee believes that it is inherently unfair for high-income individuals and highly profitable corporations to pay little or no tax due to their ability to utilize various tax preferences.[2]

Guided by these goals, Congress revised the AMT to ensure that the tax liability is at least a minimum percentage of a broad-based concept of income, less related expenses and certain personal or unavoidable expenditures. The intent of the legislation is to increase tax levies on certain wealthy taxpayers.

---

[2] Senate Finance Committee Report. H.R. 3838, Page 518, U.S. Government Printing Office, May 29, 1986.

Under the current AMT rules, taxpayers must make a completely separate tax calculation to determine the *tentative minimum tax*; if the tentative minimum tax is greater than the regular tax liability, the taxpayer will have to pay the higher amount. The upshot of these rules is that the separate tax calculations force taxpayers to keep a separate set of books just to compute the AMT.

OVERVIEW OF AMT

The AMT applies to all of the separate taxable entities: individuals, estates, trusts, and regular C corporations. Partnerships and S corporations are not subject to the AMT per se; but if either has items of AMT significance, such items flow through to the partners and shareholders, who must consider them in calculating their own AMT. Consequently, these flow-through entities, like any other taxpayer, cannot ignore the AMT. Nevertheless, the vast majority can rest easy since they have few tax preferences and the AMT computation contains a large exemption.

The basic formula for computing the AMT, like the basic formula for determining taxable income, is relatively uncomplicated. As can be seen from Exhibit 13-1, the calculation starts with the taxpayer's final taxable income computed in the normal fashion.[3] This amount, regular taxable income, is increased by any *tax preferences* and further modified—up or down—by certain *adjustments* (see Exhibits 13-3 and 13-4 for a list and brief explanation). The resulting amount is termed *alternative minimum taxable income* (AMTI). However, AMTI is not the amount subject to tax. AMTI is further reduced by an *exemption* to arrive at the tax base. The appropriate rate is then applied to produce

---

Exhibit 13-1   *The Alternative Minimum Tax Formula*

Start with:	Regular taxable income................................	$xxx,xxx
Plus/Minus:	AMT adjustments (see Exhibit 13-3).................	± xx,xxx
Equals:	AMT adjusted taxable income.........................	$xxx,xxx
Plus:	Sum of tax preference items (see Exhibit 13-5).......	+ xx,xxx
Equals:	Alternative minimum taxable income (AMTI)..........	$xxx,xxx
Less:	Exemption amount (adjusted for phase-out)..........	− xx,xxx
Equals:	AMT base..	$xxx,xxx
Times:	AMT rate...	× xx%
Equals:	Gross alternative minimum tax.......................	$ xx,xxx
Less:	AMT foreign tax credit...............................	− x,xxx
Equals:	Tentative minimum tax...............................	$ xx,xxx
Less:	Regular tax liability.................................	− x,xxx
Equals:	Alternative minimum tax.............................	$ xx,xxx

---

[3]   § 55(b)(2).

the gross AMT. This amount is reduced by an available AMT foreign tax credit to yield the *tentative minimum tax*. Finally, the tentative minimum tax is compared to the regular tax and the taxpayer pays the higher. Technically, the excess of the tentative minimum tax over the regular tax is the AMT, but as can be seen from the formula, the effect is to require the taxpayer to pay the higher amount.[4] It is important to observe that, in computing the AMT, tax credits (other than the AMT foreign tax credit) normally cannot be used to reduce the AMT liability.[5] This can be quite a surprise for taxpayers who have a large credit that wipes out their regular tax liability but does nothing to shield them from the AMT.

The last concern that is not revealed in the AMT formula concerns some Congressional largess. In an attempt to protect taxpayers from being taxed under both the regular tax system and the AMT system, Congress introduced what seems to make the entire computation of the AMT an exercise in futility: the minimum tax credit. As explained within, the credit provision essentially allows any alternative minimum tax paid in one year to be used (with some modifications) as a credit in the following year against the taxpayer's regular tax liability.

> **Example 1.** K is single and has taxable income of $92,500, on which she is required to pay a regular income tax of $24,197. In computing her regular taxable income, she utilized regular tax incentives that resulted in $55,000 of AMT adjustments (including her personal exemption) and $35,000 of AMT tax preference items. K's alternative minimum taxable income is $182,500 ($92,500 + $55,000 + $35,000).

As might be suspected, it is not the AMT formula that causes problems. The difficulty lies in determination of the various adjustments and preferences that must be computed to arrive at AMTI. The next several sections examine each of the items entering into the AMT calculation.

AMT RATES AND EXEMPTIONS

Tax Rates. Until 1993 the AMT was computed with two flat rates, one rate for corporations and a different rate for noncorporate taxpayers. But the increase in individual tax rates by the Revenue Reconciliation Act of 1993 (RRA) apparently necessitated a change in this approach for individuals, estates, and trusts. Consequently, these entities must use a two-tier rate system. Beginning in 1993 the rates for individuals, estates, and trusts are[6]

---

[4] § 55(a).

[5] The empowerment zone credit can offset 25% of the AMT.

[6] § 55(b). For taxable years beginning in 1991 and 1992, the minimum tax rate was 24 percent for individuals, estates, and trusts.

If the AMT base is			
Over	But not over	Tax liability is	Of the amount over
$ 0	$175,000	26%	$ 0
175,000		$45,500 + 28%	175,000

In contrast, the rate for corporate taxpayers is a flat 20 percent.

AMT Exemptions. In order to shield taxpayers with small amounts of tax preferences from the AMT, the Code provides a liberal exemption.[7] As shown in Exhibit 13-2, the exemption amount varies depending on the entity and, in the case of an individual, his or her filing status. The exemption effectively removes the vast majority of taxpayers from the AMT rolls, but its benefit to high-income taxpayers is limited. Apparently the authors of the minimum tax rules did not want high-income taxpayers to profit from the exemption. To this end, they provided for a phase-out. Specifically, the exemption amount for each taxpayer is reduced (but not below zero) by 25 cents for each $1 of AMTI exceeding a certain threshold. These thresholds are identified in Exhibit 13-2. Note that the phase-out rule completely eliminates the exemption as AMTI increases beyond a certain amount. For example, the $45,000 exemption for married taxpayers is completely eliminated when AMTI reaches $330,000[($330,000 − $150,000 = $180,000) × .25 = $45,000]. The various points at which the phase-out is complete are also shown in Exhibit 13-2.

Example 2. Assume the same facts as in *Example 1*. Because K's $182,500 AMTI exceeds the $112,500 threshold by $70,000, her exemption amount must be reduced by $17,500 ($70,000 × 0.25). Thus, the allowable exemption for the year is $16,250 ($33,750 − $17,500).

Exhibit 13-2 *Alternative Minimum Tax Exemption and Phase-out Levels*

Taxpayer	Exemption Amount	Phase-out Begins	Phase-out Complete
Married filing jointly	$45,000	$150,000	$330,000
Single individuals	33,750	112,500	247,500
Married filing separately, estates, trusts	22,500	75,000	165,000
C corporation	40,000	150,000	310,000

[7] § 55(d).

K's AMT is $19,028, computed as follows:

Regular taxable income	$ 92,500
Plus: AMT adjustments	+ 55,000
AMT adjusted taxable income	$147,500
Plus: AMT preference items	+ 35,000
AMTI	$182,500
Less: Exemption amount	− 16,250
AMTI base	$166,250
Times: AMT rate	× 26%
Gross AMT	$ 43,225
Less: AMT foreign tax credit	− 0
Tentative AMT	$ 43,225
Less: Regular tax liability	− 24,197
AMT	$ 19,028

ADJUSTMENTS AND TAX PREFERENCE ITEMS IN GENERAL

Once taxable income is determined, the search for AMTI can begin. As noted above, there are two types of modifications that must be made to regular taxable income to arrive at AMTI: adjustments and preferences. Although both of these modifications serve a similar purpose (i.e., provide a more "realistic" measure of the taxpayer's economic income), they are not identical. *Preferences* generally require only an add-back to income. For example, one tax preference item requires the taxpayer to add back the excess of accelerated depreciation actually deducted over what straight-line would have been. In contrast, *adjustments* generally call for the complete substitution of some special AMT treatment for the regular tax treatment. For instance, instead of using the regular tax rules to compute depreciation, the taxpayer must use the slower-paced methods for the AMT. Note that, when this occurs, depreciation for regular tax purposes may be more or less than AMT depreciation, resulting in either a positive or a negative adjustment. In short, AMT adjustments may increase or decrease taxable income whereas preferences only increase taxable income.

Another important distinction between adjustments and preferences concerns their effect on the taxpayer's basis in property. Adjustments, such as those for AMT depreciation, usually cause the property's basis for AMT purposes to differ from that for regular tax purposes. Consequently, when the taxpayer later disposes of the property, gain or loss for AMT purposes will normally not be the same as the gain or loss reported for regular tax purposes.[8] As might be imagined, this system effectively requires the taxpayer to maintain a separate set of records for AMT purposes. These separate records are used to

---

[8] § 56(b)(1)(F).

compute the annual adjustments as well as the adjustment when the asset is subsequently sold. Note that adjustments can generally be thought of as timing differences between regular taxable income and AMTI. In early years the adjustment normally produces an increase in AMTI. In later years, however, the trend reverses and a negative adjustment is required, actually reducing AMTI.

Although adjustments affect a property's basis, preferences do not. This approach makes accounting for preferences somewhat easier than it is for adjustments. In many cases, only a side calculation is necessary to determine the preference. The preference amount is then simply added to taxable income in the determination of AMTI. Generally, tax preference items are analogous to permanent differences between the regular tax and the minimum tax.

AMT ADJUSTMENTS

AMT adjustments can be classified into four groups. As shown in Exhibit 13-3, not all adjustments apply to all taxpayers; some apply to all taxpayers while others apply only to individuals or only to corporations.[9] In addition, there are special adjustments concerning losses from tax shelters. Although all of the adjustments are listed in Exhibit 13-3, only the more common adjustments are discussed below.

AMT ADJUSTMENTS APPLICABLE TO ALL TAXPAYERS

Depreciation. For AMT purposes, depreciation of property *placed in service after 1986* must be computed using the Alternative Depreciation System (ADS) with a slight modification for personal property discussed below.[10] As is probably apparent, this substitution of ADS for the taxpayer's normal method (e.g., MACRS) creates a difference between AMT depreciation and regular tax depreciation, and an adjustment must be made. The amount of the AMT adjustment is merely the difference between regular tax and AMT depreciation, which may be positive or negative as illustrated below.

As discussed in Chapter 9, depreciation under ADS is computed using the straight-line method, the appropriate convention, and the ADS life (the class life for personal property and 40 years for real property). While this same approach generally applies for AMT purposes, there is a modification for tangible personal property. For most personal property, ADS must be applied using a 150 percent declining-balance rate, switching to the straight-line method for the first taxable year that straight-line yields a higher deduction.[11] The 150 percent declining-balance method does not apply to assets for which the taxpayer has elected the straight-line method for regular tax purposes. An attempt to sort out this planned confusion is contained in Exhibit 13-4, where all of the allowable methods of depreciation for regular tax and AMT purposes are shown. Two observations should be made from this table. The first concerns realty: note that even

---

[9] § 56.

[10] § 56(a)(1).

[11] § 56(a)(1)(A)(ii).

Exhibit 13-3 *AMT Adjustments*

Applicable to All Taxpayers		*Brief Explanation*
§ 56(a)(1)	Depreciation	Use ADS
§ 56(a)(2)	Mining exploration and development costs	Capitalize and amortize over 10 years
§ 56(a)(3)	Income reported on the completed contract method	Use percentage completion
§ 56(a)(4)	Alternative tax net operating loss deduction	Recompute with AMT rules
§ 56(a)(5)	Pollution control facilities	Use ADS
§ 56(a)(6)	Gain from installment sales of pre-1987 inventory	No deferral
§ 56(a)(7)	Gains or losses on asset dispositions	Differing AMT basis
§ 56(a)(8)	Alcohol fuel credit	Do not include as income
Applicable Only to Individuals		
§ 56(b)(1)(A)	Itemized deductions	No taxes, miscellaneous itemized deductions (MIDs); adjust interest, medical
§ 56(b)(1)(E)	Standard deduction	Not allowed
§ 56(b)(1)(E)	Personal dependent exemptions	Not allowed
§ 56(b)(1)(D)	Income tax refunds	Do not include
§ 56(b)(2)	Circulation and research expenditures	Capitalize and amortize
§ 56(b)(3)	Incentive stock options	Include spread (FMV − option price)
Applicable Only to Corporations		
§ 56(c)	ACE (adjusted current earnings)	Add 75% (ACE − AMTI)
Specialized Tax Shelter Loss Adjustments		
§ 58(b)	Passive activity losses	Recompute with AMT rules
§ 58(a)	Farm shelter losses	Deduct in following year, if income

though the straight-line method must be used for both AMT and regular tax purposes, an adjustment is still necessary since the AMT recovery period is longer than the normal recovery period (40 years vs. 27.5 or 39 years). The second concerns personalty. Observe that the taxpayer can avoid the AMT adjustment by accepting regular tax depreciation, which uses a slower rate (150% declining-balance or straight-line) and the longer ADS life.

The scheme described above generally applies only to property placed in service after 1986. An adjustment for accelerated depreciation deductions is not required for assets placed in service before 1987, but the accelerated deductions may give rise to tax preference items, as discussed in the following section. As a rule of thumb, if the asset is depreciated under old ACRS or pre-ACRS, the accelerated depreciation will give rise to a tax preference item. However, if the asset is depreciated under the MACRS system, an adjustment may be required.

Example 3.   T placed an asset costing $100,000 in service on February 5, 1994. Assume the asset is "3-year property" and has an ADR class life of 3 years. The effect on the minimum tax is computed below assuming that the 150 percent declining-balance method was used for AMT purposes.

	1994	1995	1996	1997
Regular tax deduction (200%)...	$33,330	$44,450	$14,810	$ 7,410
AMT deduction (150%)..........	− 25,000	− 37,500	− 25,000	− 12,500
Effect of adjustment on AMTI....	$ 8,330	$ 6,950	($10,190)	($ 5,090)
	increase	increase	decrease	decrease

Note that in the first two years regular depreciation exceeds what is allowed for AMT, requiring the taxpayer to increase AMTI—a positive adjustment. In the third year, however, the trend reverses itself, and AMT depreciation is greater than what was actually deducted for regular tax purposes. Consequently, the taxpayer is allowed to decrease AMTI—a negative adjustment. Also note that the differences in regular and AMT depreciation cause the property's basis for AMT purposes to be different from the regular tax basis. Accordingly, if the property is sold, the amount of gain or loss for AMT and regular tax purposes may differ.

Recognizing the burdensome task of maintaining one set of depreciation books for each tax system, Congress took steps to coordinate the two. As shown in Exhibit 13-4, taxpayers may eliminate the AMT adjustment by electing the appropriate method

---

Exhibit 13-4   *Allowable Depreciation Methods for AMT and Regular Tax Purposes*

Type of Property	Recovery Period (years)	Allowable Methods
Realty		
Regular tax MACRS	27.5 residential, 39 nonresidential	Straight-line
Regular tax ADS	40	Straight-line
AMT ADS	40	Straight-line
Personalty		
Regular tax MACRS	MACRS life	200% declining-balance, 150% declining-balance, straight-line
Regular tax ADS	ADS life	150%, declining-balance, straight-line
AMT ADS	ADS life	150% declining-balance, straight-line

for regular tax purposes.[12] For example, the taxpayer could, for regular tax purposes, elect to use ADS with 150 percent declining balance, which would be the same as AMT depreciation. Alternatively, if the taxpayer elects to use ADS and the straight-line method for regular tax purposes, that same method must be used for the AMT. Either approach eliminates the AMT adjustment.

> **Example 4.**   Assume the same facts as in *Example 3* above, except T elects to use ADS with the 150 percent modification. In this case, the need for an AMT adjustment is eliminated, as shown below:

	1994	1995	1996	1997
Regular tax depreciation (150% ADS)	$25,000	$37,500	$25,000	$12,500
AMT depreciation (150% ADS)	− 25,000	− 37,500	− 25,000	− 12,500
AMT adjustment	$ 0	$ 0	$ 0	$ 0

Section 179 Limited Expensing.   Given the elaborate scheme to curtail accelerated depreciation deductions for AMT purposes, it is surprising that the election to expense property under § 179 does not give rise to an AMT adjustment. Currently, first-year § 179 expensing deductions are allowed for both AMT and regular tax purposes.[13]

Mining Exploration and Development Costs.   For regular tax purposes, mining exploration and development costs related to mineral property are currently expensed. For AMT purposes, however, such costs must be capitalized and amortized ratably over a 10-year period.[14]

Long-Term Contracts.   As explained in Chapter 5, for regular tax purposes, taxpayers normally must use the percentage of completion method to account for long-term contracts. However, the Code carves out two exceptions. The completed contract method may be used to account for home construction contracts and by small contractors who have gross receipts less than $10 million. AMT treatment is similar, but it is not identical. For AMT purposes, there is no exception for small contractors. Consequently, the percentage of completion method must be used for computing AMTI in all cases except in accounting for home construction contracts.[15]

Pollution Control Facilities.   While taxpayers are permitted to amortize expenditures related to pollution control facilities over 60 months for regular tax purposes, the AMT requires use of ADS.[16]

Alternative Tax Net Operating Loss (ATNOL) Deduction.   An ATNOL is allowed as a deduction for minimum tax purposes.[17] The procedure for computing the ATNOL parallels its cousin, the regular tax NOL, but the ATNOL must be determined taking into consideration all of the AMT adjustments and tax preference items. In addition, the amount of the ATNOL is *limited* to 90 percent of the AMTI determined without regard to this deduction.

---

[12] §§168(g)(7), 168(b)(2), 168(c)(2), and 56(a)(1)(A)(ii).

[13] *Supra,* footnote 2, Page 552, note 5.

[14] §§ 616 and 617.

[15] § 56(a)(3).

[16] § 169 and § 56(a)(5).

[17] § 56(a)(4).

AMT ADJUSTMENTS APPLICABLE ONLY TO INDIVIDUALS

All of the adjustments applicable only to individual taxpayers are listed in Exhibit 13-3. Each of these is discussed below.

Itemized Deductions. For the most part, itemized deductions allowed for regular tax purposes are also allowed for AMT purposes (sometimes referred to as alternative minimum tax deductions, or ATIDs). However, there are several important exceptions and modifications. These adjustments differ from those above (e.g., depreciation) in that they serve to increase the tax base instead of merely altering the timing of the item.

Two itemized deductions are totally disallowed for AMT purposes:

1. Miscellaneous itemized deductions (MIDs). For example, unreimbursed employee business expenses and tax preparation expenses are not allowed for the AMT.[18]

2. Itemized deductions related to the payment of any tax. For example, state, local, and foreign income taxes and real and personal property taxes are not allowed as deductions for AMT purposes.[19]

In computing the itemized deductions allowed for AMT purposes, the limitations for regular tax purposes normally apply (e.g., the 10% limitation on personal casualty losses or the 50% limitation for charitable contributions). However, the 3 percent cutback rule that applies to certain itemized deductions *does not* apply for AMT purposes.[20] In addition, as noted below, special rules exist for medical expenses and interest.

ATIDs generally include the following:[21]

1. Medical expenses, but *only in excess* of 10 percent of A.G.I.

2. Interest expense, but only for

    (a) Qualified housing interest

    (b) Investment interest expense to the extent of net investment income

3. Charitable contributions

4. Theft, casualty, and wagering losses

5. Estate tax deductions resulting from reporting income in respect of a decedent under § 691

6. Impairment-related work expenses[22]

7. Bond premium amortization deductions

---

[18] § 56(b)(1)(A)(i).

[19] § 56(b)(1)(A)(ii).

[20] § 56(b)(1)(F).

[21] See § 67(b) for a complete list of itemized deductions that are allowed as ATIDs. Also note that a standard deduction is not allowed for AMT purposes.

[22] § 67(d).

The above list is self-explanatory with the exception of the amount of interest that will be allowed as an ATID. Several new terms and concepts regarding the deduction for interest were developed and incorporated into the alternative minimum tax scheme. *Qualified housing interest* is interest paid or accrued on indebtedness incurred after June 30, 1982, in acquiring, constructing, or substantially rehabilitating property that is a principal residence (as defined in Code § 1034) or qualified dwelling, including a secondary residence.[23] For indebtedness incurred *before* July 1, 1982, a deduction can be taken for interest paid or accrued on a debt that, at that time, was secured by a qualified dwelling without regard for the purpose or use of the proceeds of the indebtedness. The essence of these rules is that interest on home second mortgages—home equity loans—established after 1982 will not be deductible for AMT purposes as qualified housing interest *unless* the proceeds were used to improve the principal residence.

When interest rates fall, taxpayers often refinance their homes, and a question arose about the interest paid on a loan (new loan) the proceeds of which were used to pay off the original qualified housing indebtedness (old loan). The TRA of 1986 resolved the issue by allowing an interest expense deduction for AMT purposes on the new loan used to refinance the principal residence, but only to the extent that the new loan does not exceed the outstanding balance of the old loan.[24]

Investment interest expense is allowed as an ATID, but only to the extent of qualified *adjusted* net investment income.[25] The adjustment in computing the net investment income is required for AMT purposes as a result of including a portion of the tax-exempt interest income from specified private activity bonds (SPAB) as a tax preference item that increases the AMTI (see *Example 10* for details relating to the tax-exempt income preference item). If exempt interest income from SPABs is included as a preference item for AMT purposes, the interest expense incurred with respect to it will be allowed as a deduction for AMT purposes. These adjustments for tax-exempt income and its related interest expenses are also allowed in computing the "adjusted" net investment income for AMT purposes.

Circulation and Research Expenditures.   Amounts paid or incurred that are allowable as a deduction for circulation[26] expenditures in computing the regular tax must be capitalized and amortized over a three-year period beginning with the taxable year in which the expenditures were made. The same rule applies to research and experimental

---

23   A qualified dwelling is a house, apartment, condominium, or mobile home (not used on a transient basis). Qualified dwelling for AMT is a narrow definition and differs from that of Code § 280A(f)(1), which broadly defines a dwelling unit as a house, apartment, condominium, mobile home, boat, or similar property.

24   § 56(e)(1).

25   See Chapter 11 for a discussion of the investment interest deduction limitation.

26   § 173. See footnote 46, infra, for an optional tax accounting method for circulation expenditures.

expenditures, except the amortization period is ten years.[27] However, the Revenue Reconciliation Act of 1989 repealed the AMT adjustment for research expenses of individuals who materially participate in the activity in which research expenses are incurred. The repealer is effective for taxable years beginning after December 31, 1990.[28] As with other adjustments that create a disparity between basis for regular tax and basis for AMT, separate records must be maintained to determine the allowable amortization deduction in subsequent years or the gain or loss on disposition or abandonment.

Gains from Incentive Stock Options (ISOs). For regular tax purposes, the bargain element of ISOs is *not* required to be included in income either at the time the option is granted or when the option is exercised;[29] however, an income adjustment may be required for the AMT. The income adjustment with respect to stock received from options exercised after December 31, 1987 is determined under the principles of Code § 83. Assuming the stock acquired is not subject to substantial risk of forfeiture, the adjustment to AMTI is equal to the amount by which the value of the share at the time of exercise exceeds the option price.[30] If the stock is disposed of in the option year, however, this income adjustment is not required because the income attributable to the bargain element will be reported under the regular tax system in the same year.

> **Example 5.** D receives an incentive stock option to purchase 1,000 shares of her employer's stock at $50 per share. Three years after the receipt of the option, D exercises her option when the stock is selling for $70 per share. When D exercises the option, she has an AMT adjustment of $20,000 ($70,000 − $50,000).

Since the AMT adjustment amount computed above increases the AMTI, an upward basis adjustment in the stock of an equal amount is allowed for AMT purposes. This disparity in the stock's basis for regular tax and the AMT requires the *extra set of books* to determine the amount of gain recognized upon a subsequent disposition of the stock for AMT purposes.

> **Example 6.** Assume the same facts as in *Example 5* and that D holds the stock until it further increases in value to $85,000. If D sells the stock for $85,000, she has a $35,000 gain for regular tax purposes ($85,000 − $50,000), and an AMT gain of $15,000 ($85,000 − $70,000).

Standard Deduction Not Allowed. Individuals are not permitted to take into account the standard deduction in computing the alternative minimum taxable income.[31]

Personal Exemptions. Personal exemptions authorized under § 151 are not allowed as deductions in computing the AMTI.[32]

---

[27] § 56(b)(2)(A)(ii). See footnote 46, infra, for an optional tax accounting method for research and experimental expenditures.

[28] § 56(b)(2)(D).

[29] See Chapter 18 for a discussion of ISOs and § 83.

[30] § 56(b)(3). Although no direct authority exists, arguably a § 83(b) election may be made for AMT purposes.

[31] § 56(b)(1)(E).

[32] *Ibid.*

Adjustment to Income for Tax Refunds. Generally, taxpayers who itemize deductions must report a refund of a prior year's state or local income tax as gross income in the year of receipt.[33] However, since itemized deductions for all tax expenditures are not allowed for AMT purposes, the refund or recovery in *all cases* is excluded from AMTI.

ADJUSTMENT APPLICABLE ONLY TO CORPORATIONS

The only adjustment applicable solely to corporate taxpayers is the adjustment based on a corporation's adjusted current earnings—commonly referred to as the *ACE adjustment*.[34] The ACE adjustment, like the minimum tax itself, was the Congressional response to what seemed an increasingly frequent phenomenon: corporations were reporting substantial earnings for financial accounting purposes yet paying little or no income tax. Curiously, this occurred despite the existence of the AMT. To address the problem, Congress created the ACE adjustment. This special adjustment is designed to ensure that all corporations pay some minimum tax on book income.

In theory, the ACE adjustment is relatively simple. It requires a corporation to compare book income to taxable income to determine the amount of financial accounting income, if any, that escaped tax. Part of this elusive income is then included in the corporation's AMTI. Technically, the ACE adjustment is equal to 75 percent of the difference between *adjusted current earnings* and AMTI.[35] In this calculation, adjusted current earnings essentially serve as a substitute for book income. The actual computation of adjusted current earnings is quite technical. It begins with AMTI, to which a laundry list of adjustments are made.[36] Fortunately perhaps, a discussion of the various adjustments is beyond the scope of this text. Suffice it to say that their collective purpose is to yield the corporation's economic income so its true ability to pay tax can be determined.

> **Example 7.** T corporation has AMTI of $200,000 without regard to the ACE adjustment. T's adjusted current earnings are determined to be $400,000. T's regular income tax liability is $41,750. T has an ACE adjustment of $150,000, AMTI of $350,000, a tentative AMT of $70,000, and AMT of $28,250, computed as follows:

---

[33] See § 56(b)(1)(D) and Chapter 6 for an exception based on the tax benefit rule.

[34] This adjustment *does not* apply to certain corporations, including S corporations, regulated investment companies, real estate investment trusts, or real estate mortgage investment conduits. § 56(g)(6).

[35] § 56(g)(1).

[36] § 56(g)(4).

AMTI before ACE...	$200,000
Plus: ACE adjustment [($400,000−$200,000) × 75%]..........	+ 150,000
AMTI..	$350,000
Less: Exemption amount (completely phased out)..............	− 0
AMTI base...	$350,000
Times: AMT rate..	× 20%
Gross AMT..	$ 70,000
Less: AMT foreign tax credit..................................	− 0
Tentative AMT..	$ 70,000
Less: Regular tax liability......................................	− 41,750
AMT...	$ 28,250

This portion of the alternative minimum tax system has been crafted to make certain the AMT is imposed on corporate taxpayers having an economic ability to pay.

SPECIAL TAX SHELTER LOSS ADJUSTMENTS

Certain losses that may be deductible for regular tax are *denied* for purposes of the AMT. Specifically, tax shelter farm losses and passive activity losses allowed as deductions for regular tax purposes must be recomputed under the AMT system, taking into account all of the AMT tax accounting rules.[37] Clearly, a separate set of books will be required for each activity. The amount of the AMT adjustment required by the statute is the difference between the loss allowed for the regular tax system and the loss allowed under the AMT system.

Tax Shelter Farm Losses. Noncorporate taxpayers and personal service corporations are not allowed to deduct losses from a tax shelter farm activity in computing AMTI.[38] For the AMT system, the disallowed loss will be treated as a deduction allocable to such activity in the *first* succeeding taxable year, and will be allowed to offset income from that activity in any succeeding year. Under this rule, each farm is treated as a separate activity. In the year that the taxpayer disposes of his or her entire interest in any tax shelter farm activity, the amount of previously disallowed loss related to that activity is allowed as a deduction for the year under the AMT system.

Passive Activity Losses. As discussed in Chapter 12, there are limitations on the use of losses from passive activities to offset other income of the taxpayer for regular tax purposes.[39] For AMT purposes, similar rules apply, except for AMT purposes a loss generated from a passive activity must be recomputed to reflect the AMT rules. This means that depreciation, intangible drilling and development costs, percentage depletion,

---

[37] These rules are specified in §§ 56 and 57.

[38] § 58(a).

[39] See Chapter 12 for a discussion of passive losses.

and other adjustments and preferences must be reflected in computing the loss for AMT purposes. Because of the differences in the treatment of such items, the amount of suspended losses relating to an activity may differ for minimum tax and regular tax purposes and may require that two sets of books be kept in order to track the passive loss carryover on each activity.[40]

> **Example 8.** C has $200,000 of salary income, $50,000 of gross income from passive activities, and $170,000 of deductions from passive activities for the current year. C's loss with respect to the passive activities is $120,000 for regular tax purposes. Because the recomputed expenses for AMT purposes are only $130,000, the passive activity loss is $80,000 for minimum tax purposes. For regular tax purposes, the taxpayer has taxable income of $200,000 and a suspended passive loss in the amount of $120,000 ($170,000 passive deductions − $50,000 passive income). For minimum tax purposes, the taxpayer has AMTI of $200,000 and a suspended passive loss of $80,000 ($130,000 − $50,000).

As illustrated in the example above, the recomputed passive loss using the AMT rules can be significantly different from the regular tax passive loss with respect to an activity. In fact, in some situations it is possible to have a regular tax passive loss amount *and* an AMT passive income amount on the same activity!

> **Example 9.** Assume that taxpayer C in the example above had passive activity deductions of $80,000 for regular tax purposes and $40,000 for minimum tax purposes. C would have regular taxable income of $200,000 and a suspended passive loss of $30,000 ($80,000 − $50,000) for regular tax purposes. For AMT purposes, C has alternative minimum taxable income of $210,000 [$200,000 salary + ($50,000 − $40,000)] and no suspended passive loss for minimum tax purposes.

TAX PREFERENCE ITEMS

Since tax preference items are required to be identified and computed for both corporate and noncorporate taxpayers, all the preference items are listed in Exhibit 13-5; however, only the most common items are explained below.[41]

Excess Depreciation. As noted above, there is no *adjustment* for depreciation for property placed in service before 1987. However, accelerated depreciation on pre-1987 realty does produce a tax preference. The excess of accelerated depreciation actually claimed over what straight-line would have been is a preference item.[42] Note that there is no reduction in AMTI if the straight-line depreciation required for AMT purposes

---

[40] P.L. 99-514, Tax Reform Act of 1986, Conference Committee Report, Act § 701.

[41] § 57 sets forth all of the tax preference items and the specifics of each calculation.

[42] § 57(a)(7).

Exhibit 13-5 *Alternative Minimum Tax*
Tax Preference Items

Excess depreciation on realty placed in service before 1987

Percentage depletion in excess of cost basis

Intangible drilling and development costs (in excess of 65 percent of net oil and gas income)

Reserves for losses on bad debts of financial institutions in excess of the deduction computed on the basis of actual experience*

Specified tax-exempt interest

Exclusion for gain on sale of certain small business stock

* Applies only to corporate taxpayers

exceeds regular tax depreciation, as is the case with an adjustment. Note also that the excess must be computed on an item-by-item basis. The taxpayer cannot use an aggregate approach to determine whether total accelerated depreciation exceeds total straight-line. As a practical matter, the significance of this preference is starting to wane because in most cases accelerated depreciation no longer exceeds straight-line.

Excess Depletion.   The amount of the preference item is the excess (if any) of the percentage depletion claimed for the taxable year over the adjusted basis of the property at the end of the taxable year (determined without regard to the depletion deduction for the taxable year).[43] This computation must be made for each unit of property.

Intangible Drilling and Development Costs.   In general, the amount of the tax preference is equal to the intangible drilling costs (IDC) incurred and deducted on productive oil, gas, and geothermal wells reduced by the sum of

1. The amount allowed as if the IDCs had been capitalized and amortized over a 10-year period, and

2. Sixty-five percent of the net income for the year from these properties.[44]

---

[43] § 57(a)(1), repealed for certain owners of oil and gas properties for taxable years beginning after 1992.

[44] § 57(a)(2)(E)(ii). The CNEPA of 1992 repealed this preference item for taxpayers (other than certain integrated oil and gas companies) for years beginning after December 31, 1992. However, the repeal of the excess IDCs preference "may not result in more than a 40 percent reduction (30% for taxable years beginning in 1993) in the amount of the taxpayer's AMTI computed as if the present-law excess IDC preference had not been repealed."

If the intangible drilling and development costs are capitalized and amortized in accord with special rules contained in § 59(e), they are not treated as a preference item.[45]

Private Activity Bond Interest.   This preference item pertains to interest income on specified private activity bonds (SPABs) issued after August 7, 1986.[46] The term *private activity bond* means any bond issued if 10 percent of the proceeds of the issue is used for private business use in any trade or business carried on by any person that is not a governmental unit. Where interest income on SPABs is includible in AMTI under the above rule, the regular tax rule of Code § 265 (denying deductions for expenses and interest relating to tax-exempt income) does not apply, and expenses and interest incurred to carry SPABs are deductible for minimum tax purposes.

> **Example 10.**   Taxpayer P is required to include in AMTI $10,000 of otherwise tax-exempt interest income on SPABs as a preference item. She incurred $900 of interest expense on a temporary loan in order to purchase the bonds. Code § 265 disallows a deduction of this $900 for regular tax purposes, but it is deductible for minimum tax purposes.

Charitable Contributions.   One of the time-honored planning strategies for those who make charitable contributions is to make gifts of appreciated property. By so doing, the taxpayer is normally entitled to deduct the fair market value of the property yet is not required to include the appreciation as income. As might be expected, Congress believed that this treatment was far too generous and treated the untaxed appreciation as a tax preference item. However, Congress recently had a change of heart. Believing that this rule stymied contributions to charities, it repealed the preference retroactively as part of the Revenue Reconciliation Act of 1993. As a result, the built-in gain on contributed property is no longer treated as a tax preference item for any contributions of property made after 1992. Thus, charitable contributions of tangible personal property (other than inventory or ordinary income property, or short-term capital gain property), the use of which is related to the donee's tax-exempt purpose, will give rise to a deduction equal to the fair market value of the asset for both regular tax purposes and AMT purposes. The deduction for charitable contributions of inventory or other ordinary income property and short-term capital gain property continues to be limited to the adjusted basis of the property for both regular tax and AMT systems.

Gain on the Sale of Qualified Small Business Stock.   As explained in detail in Chapter 16, the Revenue Reconciliation Act of 1993 created a special incentive to encourage taxpayers to invest in the stock of qualified small businesses (i.e., stock of a C corporation with gross assets of $50 million or less at the time the stock was issued

---

[45] Code § 59(e) was enacted to provide relief to taxpayers that are subject to the AMT, but through proper planning want to maximize the regular tax deductions and at the same time minimize the impact of the AMT. This section provides an election to capitalize "qualified expenditures" and deduct them ratably over a 10-year period (3 years in the case of circulation expenditures). Qualified expenditures include IDCs, circulation, research and experimentation, and mining exploration and development costs.

[46] § 57(a)(5)(C)(iv).

and that was held by the original owner for more than five years prior to sale). Under this special rule, a taxpayer is entitled to exclude 50 percent of the gain on the sale of the stock. However, what Congress gives with the right hand it takes away with the left. One-half of this exclusion (one-fourth of the entire gain) is treated as a tax preference item.[47]

> **Example 11.**   On October 31, 1998 J sold qualified small business stock and recognized a gain of $80,000. Only 50 percent of the gain, $40,000, is subject to regular tax, and the remaining $40,000 is excluded. For AMT purposes J has a tax preference of $20,000 (50% × $40, 000).

Note that the holding period requirement of five years means that this provision will not come into play until August 10, 1998.

ALTERNATIVE MINIMUM TAX COMPUTATIONS

Before the alternative minimum tax calculations can be made, the taxpayer's current taxable income and Federal income tax liability must first be determined. As shown in Exhibit 13-1, a taxpayer's AMT liability is the excess of the tentative AMT over the regular tax liability. To further examine this interaction, a factual situation is presented below in *Example 12* where the taxpayer's regular tax liability is determined. The same facts are then used to compute the ATIDs in *Example 13* and the taxpayer's AMT liability in *Example 14*.

---

[47]   § 57(a)(7).

Example 12.   T is a married taxpayer filing a joint return for 1994. He had the following items of income, expenses, and regular tax liability for the year.

Income:

Salary...	$88,000	
Interest...	2,000	
Dividends..	10,000	
Adjusted gross income...............................		$100,000[1]

Itemized deductions:

Medical expenses [$9,500 total − (7.5% of $100,000 A.G.I.)].............................	$ 2,000	
Real property taxes on home.......................	12,000	
Real property taxes on mountain range property..................................	8,000	
Personal property taxes............................	4,000	
Interest expense:		
Residence interest.................................	20,000[2]	
Investment interest on mountain range property ($12,000 total, but limited to)..................	4,000[3]	
Charitable contributions............................	10,000[4]	
Casualty loss [$13,000 total − (10% of A.G.I.)]...	3,000	
Miscellaneous itemized deductions [$11,000 total − (2% of A.G.I.)]...	9,000	
Total itemized deductions..........................		− 72,000
Personal exemptions (2 × $2,450)................		− 4,900
Taxable income.......................................		$ 23,100
Regular tax..		$ 3,465

[1]Although not required to be included in his taxable income, T exercised an incentive stock option for $20,000 when the fair market value of the stock was $80,000.

[2]Residence interest includes $18,000 of qualified housing interest (interest on mortgage to acquire home) and $2,000 of interest on a home equity loan to buy a boat.

[3]The mountain range property was acquired as a speculative investment and was 90% debt-financed. Recall that interest on investment indebtedness is allowed as a deduction under § 163(d) to the extent of net investment income. Net investment income = $2,000 interest + $10,000 dividends − $8,000 property taxes = $4,000. Thus the $12,000 interest expense is limited to $4,000.

[4]The charitable contribution deduction results from T's gift to his church of Ford Motor Company stock worth $10,000. T had purchased the stock two years earlier for $2,000.

Example 13. Refer to *Example 12*. T's 1994 alternative tax itemized deductions (ATIDs) and the resulting AMT adjustments are determined as follows:

	Allowed ATIDs for AMT	Allowed Itemized Deductions for Regular Tax	AMT Adjustments
Medical expenses			
(in excess of 10% of A.G.I.)................	$ 0*	$ 2,000	$ 2,000
Itemized deductions for taxes (not allowed)...	0	24,000	24,000
Qualified housing interest....................	18,000	18,000	0
Home equity loan	0	2,000	2,000
Other qualified interest			
(limited to net investment income, =			
$2,000 + $10,000 − $8,000)..............	4,000	4,000	0
Casualty losses.............................	3,000	3,000	0
Charitable contributions.....................	10,000	10,000	0
Miscellaneous itemized deductions			
(not allowed).............................	0	9,000	9,000
Totals for 1994.............................	$35,000	$72,000	$37,000

* $9,500 does not exceed 10% of $100,000, or $10,000.

Note that the computations for ATIDs are similar to those in *Example 12* for itemized deductions except (1) the reduction in medical expenses is 10% rather than 7.5%, (2) deductions for state and local taxes are not allowed, (3) the miscellaneous itemized deductions are not allowed, and (4) the interest on the home equity loan to purchase the boat is not allowed. The differences between the ATIDs allowed for AMT purposes and the itemized deductions allowed for regular tax purposes result in AMT adjustments. These adjustments are added back to T's regular taxable income to arrive at AMT adjusted taxable income and are reported on Form 6251, Computation of Alternative Minimum Tax for Individuals.

Example 14.   Refer to *Examples 12* and *13*. T's alternative minimum tax (AMT) liability for 1994 is computed as follows:

Regular taxable income...		$ 23,100
Plus:	Net adjustment for itemized deductions..................	+ 37,000[1]
	Net adjustment for exercise of ISO......................	+ 60,000[2]
	Adjustment for personal exemptions....................	+ 4,900
AMT adjusted taxable income....................................		$125,000
Plus:	Tax preference items	+ 0
Alternative minimum taxable income (AMTI)......................		$125,000
Less:	Exemption amount	
	(married filing jointly).................................	− 45,000
AMT base..		$ 80,000
Times:	AMT rate...	× 26%
Gross alternative minimum tax..................................		$ 20,800
Less:	AMT foreign tax credit................................	− 0
Tentative minimum tax..		$ 20,800
Less:	Regular tax liability...................................	− 3,465
AMT liability for 1994...		$ 17,335

[1]Regular tax itemized deductions................................	$ 72,000
ATIDs allowed for AMT..	(35,000)
Disallowed itemized deductions increase the AMTI..............	$ 37,000

[2]Stock FMV when ISO exercised................................	$ 80,000
Option price..	(20,000)
Excess is AMT adjustment that increases AMTI...	$ 60,000

Since the tentative minimum tax of $20,800 *exceeds* his $3,465 regular tax liability (computed in *Example 12*), T must pay the difference of $17,335 for 1994 because of the alternative minimum tax. Note that T must pay a total of $20,800 in taxes for 1994 ($3,465 regular income tax + $17,335 alternative minimum tax).

The previous example illustrates an unfortunate consequence of the strict application of the AMT provisions. The tax benefits of longstanding regular-tax incentive provisions such as home ownership (e.g., deductibility of interest and real property taxes) and medical expenses are either decreased or totally eliminated by the AMT. Although Congress continues to support the objectives of these incentives, their use by individuals to avoid all or most of their Federal income tax liability is not the intent of the law. Recent changes to the AMT are an attempt to minimize such perceived abuses. As illustrated

in *Example 14*, because of the limited definition of ATIDs and the decreasing Federal income tax rates, it is possible that some unsuspecting individuals (like T) will be subject to the AMT. Consequently, tax planning to avoid or minimize the AMT is becoming more important for a growing number of taxpayers. As an adjunct to planning for the impact of the AMT, it should be remembered that each taxpayer has the responsibility to maintain adequate records to support the accuracy of the amounts of tax preferences and adjustments used in the AMT computation.[48]

A completed Form 6251, based on the facts from *Examples 12*, *13*, and *14*, is contained in Exhibit 13-6. Note that the 1993 form is used because the 1994 form was not available at the publication date of this text.

With all of the potential complexity and extra reporting work required by the AMT provisions, it is noteworthy that Congress has made an attempt to make another area of the Federal tax laws more orderly—the part specifying credits against the tax liability. The remainder of this chapter is devoted to the tax incentives provided by the tax credit provisions. However, at the risk of upsetting what otherwise is an orderly presentation of the various credits, it seems only appropriate that the special minimum tax credit should be considered before we leave the AMT.

MINIMUM TAX CREDIT

One significant feature of the AMT system is that many taxpayers are required to pay the AMT long before they would have had to pay the regular income tax from certain investments. For example, taxpayers with substantial investments in depreciable personal property are *denied* the tax reduction benefits of MACRS for purposes of computing the AMT.[49] Likewise, a taxpayer who exercises an ISO must recognize income for AMT purposes to the extent the fair market value of the stock exceeds its option price, but for regular income tax purposes the taxpayer does not recognize income until the stock acquired with the ISO is sold. Without some form of relief, a taxpayer could be subject to the AMT in one year and the regular tax in a later year on the same item.

In order to limit the possibility of double taxation under the two tax systems, Congress introduced an alternative minimum tax credit. Basically, the alternative minimum tax paid in one year may be used as a credit against the taxpayer's *regular* tax liability in subsequent years. The credit may be carried forward indefinitely until used; however, the credit cannot be carried back *nor* can it be used to offset any future minimum tax liability.[50]

---

[48] Reg. § 1.57-5(a).

[49] Recall that depreciable personal property placed in service after 1986 can be depreciated using either the 150 percent declining balance or the ADS straight-line method over the asset's class life for AMT purposes.

[50] § 53(a).

Exhibit 13-6

Form **6251**	**Alternative Minimum Tax—Individuals**	OMB No. 1545-0227
	▶ See separate instructions.	**1993**
Department of the Treasury Internal Revenue Service (T)	▶ Attach to Form 1040 or Form 1040NR.	Attachment Sequence No. **32**

Name(s) shown on Form 1040   **MR. AND MRS. T**

Your social security number   **457 89 6132**

Part I   Adjustments and Preferences

1	If you itemized deductions on Schedule A (Form 1040), go to line 2. If you did not itemize deductions, enter your standard deduction from Form 1040, line 34, and skip to line 6 . .	1	
2	Medical and dental expenses. See instructions	2	2,000
3	Taxes. Enter the amount from Schedule A, line 8	3	24,000
4	Certain interest on a home mortgage not used to buy, build, or improve your home . . .	4	2,000
5	Miscellaneous itemized deductions. Enter the amount from Schedule A, line 24	5	9,000
6	Refund of taxes. Enter any tax refund from Form 1040, line 10 or 22	6	( )
7	Investment interest. Enter difference between regular tax and AMT deduction	7	
8	Post-1986 depreciation. Enter difference between regular tax and AMT depreciation . . .	8	
9	Adjusted gain or loss. Enter difference between AMT and regular tax gain or loss . . .	9	
10	Incentive stock options. Enter excess of AMT income over regular tax income	10	60,000
11	Passive activities. Enter difference between AMT and regular tax income or loss	11	
12	Beneficiaries of estates and trusts. Enter the amount from Schedule K-1 (Form 1041), line 8	12	
13	Tax-exempt interest from private activity bonds issued after 8/7/86	13	

14   Other. Enter the amount, if any, for each item and enter the total on line 14.

a	Charitable contributions .		g	Long-term contracts . .	
b	Circulation expenditures .		h	Loss limitations	
c	Depletion		i	Mining costs	
d	Depreciation (pre-1987) .		j	Pollution control facilities .	
e	Installment sales . . .		k	Research and experimental	
f	Intangible drilling costs .		l	Tax shelter farm activities.	
			m	Related adjustments . .	

	14	
15 **Total Adjustments and Preferences.** Combine lines 1 through 14 . . . . ▶	**15**	97,000

Part II   Alternative Minimum Taxable Income

16	Enter the amount from **Form 1040, line 35.** If less than zero, enter as a (loss) . . . . ▶	16	28,000
17	Net operating loss deduction, if any, from Form 1040, line 22. Enter as a positive amount .	17	
18	If Form 1040, line 32, is over $108,450 (over $54,225 if married filing separately), enter your itemized deductions limitation, if any, from line 9 of the worksheet for Schedule A, line 26	18	( )
19	Combine lines 15 through 18 . . . . ▶	19	125,000
20	Alternative tax net operating loss deduction. See instructions	20	
21	**Alternative Minimum Taxable Income.** Subtract line 20 from line 19. (If married filing separately and line 21 is more than $165,000, see instructions.) . . . . ▶	21	125,000

Part III   Exemption Amount and Alternative Minimum Tax

22   **Exemption Amount.** (If this form is for a child under age 14, see instructions.)

If your filing status is:	And line 21 is not over:	Enter on line 22:		
Single or head of household	$112,500	$33,750		
Married filing jointly or qualifying widow(er)	150,000	45,000	} . .	22 45,000
Married filing separately	75,000	22,500		

If line 21 is **over** the amount shown above for your filing status, see instructions.

23	Subtract line 22 from line 21. If zero or less, enter -0- here and on lines 26 and 28 . ▶	23	80,000
24	If line 23 is $175,000 or less ($87,500 or less if married filing separately), multiply line 23 by 26% (.26). Otherwise, see instructions	24	20,800
25	Alternative minimum tax foreign tax credit. See instructions	25	
26	Tentative minimum tax. Subtract line 25 from line 24 . . . . ▶	26	20,800
27	Enter your tax from Form 1040, line 38 (plus any amount from Form 4970 included on Form 1040, line 39), minus any foreign tax credit from Form 1040, line 43	27	3,465
28	**Alternative Minimum Tax.** (If this form is for a child under age 14, see instructions.) Subtract line 27 from line 26. If zero or less, enter -0-. Enter here and on Form 1040, line 48 . ▶	28	17,335

For Paperwork Reduction Act Notice, see separate instructions.   Cat. No. 13600G   Form **6251** (1993)

Example 15. In 1993 J paid an alternative minimum tax, and his AMT credit after making the appropriate adjustments was $20,000. In 1994 J's regular tax liability before considering the minimum tax credit is $45,000 and his *tentative minimum tax* is $40,000. Since J's regular tax exceeds his tentative minimum tax, there is no AMT for 1994. In computing his final tax liability, J is entitled to use the minimum tax credit against his regular tax liability but only to the extent that it does not create an AMT (i.e., bring his regular tax liability below his tentative minimum tax). Consequently, he may use $5,000 of the credit, reducing his regular tax liability to $40,000, as shown below. The remaining $15,000 of the credit may be carried over indefinitely.

Regular tax liability............		$45,000
Minimum tax credit:		
Limitation		
Regular tax..............	$45,000	
Tentative minimum tax....	− 40,000	
Allowable minimum tax credit		− 5,000
Total tax due.................		$40,000

Note that the minimum tax credit effectively converts the AMT from a permanent out-of-pocket tax to a prepayment of regular tax to the extent the AMT is attributable to deferral or timing preferences and adjustments rather than to exclusion items.[51]

For noncorporate taxpayers, the AMT credit for any year is the amount of the taxpayer's *adjusted net minimum tax* for all tax years after reduction for the minimum tax credit utilized for all such prior years. The adjusted net minimum tax, generally the amount of the minimum tax credit, is the difference between the AMT actually paid and the amount of AMT that would have been paid if only exclusion items were taken into account. The exclusion items are listed below:

1. Itemized deductions

2. Personal exemptions

3. Percentage depletion

4. Tax-exempt interest

5. Appreciated property charitable deductions that created a tax preference item

---

[51] § 53(d)(1)(B)(iv) authorizes corporate taxpayers to use the entire minimum tax liability as the minimum tax credit. However, this rule applies only to minimum tax credits arising in taxable years beginning after December 31, 1989.

Example 16.   J is married and files a joint return for the current year on which she reports $80,000 of taxable income and claims the standard deduction. In computing her taxable income, J excluded $56,000 of tax-exempt interest from SPABs, which creates a $56,000 AMT preference item, and she claimed a $100,000 deduction for research expenses from an activity in which she does not materially participate, which creates a $90,000 AMT adjustment for research and experimental expenditures. J's minimum tax credit to be carried forward is $29,853, as computed below.

The amount of AMT actually required to be paid is $38,798, determined as follows:

Regular taxable income..		$ 80,000
Plus: AMT adjustment for research expenses...........	+	90,000
AMT adjustment for personal exemptions.........	+	4,900
AMT adjustment for standard deduction...........	+	6,350
AMT preference item for SPAB income............	+	56,000
AMTI..		$237,250
Less: Exemption amount [after $21,813 phase-out ($237,250 − $150,000 = $87,250 × 0.25)]...	−	23,187
AMT base..		$214,063
Tentative AMT [$45,500 + 28% ($214,063 − $175,000)]....		$ 56,438
Less: Regular tax liability...............................	−	17,640
AMT liability for current year..............................		$ 38,798

The amount of AMT that would have been required to be paid if only exclusion items were taken into account is $8,945, determined as follows:

Regular taxable income.................................		$ 80,000
Plus: AMT adjustment for personal exemptions.....	+	4,900
AMT adjustment for standard deduction......	+	6,300
Tax preference item for SPAB income........	+	56,000
AMTI..		$147,250
Less: Exemption amount (no phase-out)............	−	45,000
AMT base...		$102,250
Times: AMT rate....................................	×	26%
Tentative AMT.......................................		$ 26,585
Less: Regular tax liability..........................	−	17,640
AMT using only exclusions............................		$ 8,945

The minimum tax credit is computed as follows:

AMT liability for current year...........................		$ 38,798
AMT using only exclusion items......................	−	8,945
Minimum tax credit....................................		$ 29,853

The $29,853 minimum tax credit may be carried forward and used to offset (reduce) the regular tax liability in subsequent years.

✔ CHECK YOUR TAX KNOWLEDGE

Review Question 1. After completing his tax return for the year, C has a regular tax liability of $30,000, a tentative minimum tax of $45,000, and an alternative minimum tax of $15,000. How much does C actually owe the IRS?

C owes $45,000 in taxes, consisting of a regular tax liability of $30,000 and an AMT liability of $15,000.

Review Question 2. True-False. Jack is a professional golfer, earning over $800,000 on the tour this year. He and his wife are entitled to a $45,000 exemption in computing their alternative minimum tax liability.

False. The exemption phases out once their AMTI exceeds $150,000 and is completely phased out when AMTI reaches $330,000. Based on the size of his earnings, it would appear that his AMTI exceeds $330,000 so that the exemption would provide no benefit.

Review Question 3. True-False. In determining AMTI, the taxpayer begins with taxable income and then adds back all of the loopholes. There are no negative adjustments.

False. Although the effect of the AMTI is to fill in the loopholes, adjustments may be positive or negative (e.g., when AMT depreciation exceeds regular tax depreciation). All tax preference items are positive.

Review Question 4. True-False. Steelco Corporation acquired several new copying machines for its offices this year and depreciated them under MACRS, using the 200 percent declining-balance method and a 5-year recovery period. For AMT purposes, Steelco must use the straight-line method and a 6-year life. (Hint: See Revenue Procedure 87-56 contained in Exhibit 9-2).

False. Steelco must use the ADS life of 6 years, but it is allowed to use 150 percent declining-balance in computing depreciation for personal property under ADS for AMT purposes.

Review Question 5. Fred and Ethel are married with two children. Fred is a partner in a public accounting firm. Ethel recently retired as a traveling salesperson for an athletic shoe manufacturer. After completing their return, Fred and Ethel realized that they may have to pay the alternative minimum tax. Indicate whether an adjustment is required for AMT purposes for the following items that the couple reported for regular tax purposes.

    a. Personal exemptions for Fred and Ethel

    b. Dependent exemptions for their children

    c. Social security benefits that were nontaxable, $10,000

    d. Contribution to individual retirement account, $2,000

   e.   Fred's membership dues to the Indiana C.P.A. Society reimbursed by his employer, $200

   f.   Straight-line depreciation on their newly acquired duplex, which they are currently renting out, $6,000

   g.   State income taxes, $10,000

   h.   Property taxes on their personal residence, $4,000

   i.   Tax-exempt interest from City of Indianapolis bonds used to finance its downtown mall, $2,000

   j.   State income tax refund, $500

   k.   Interest on the mortgage on their personal residence, $22,000

   l.   Interest on a second mortgage on their residence (proceeds used to add a porch), $3,600

   m.   Ethel's unreimbursed travel and entertainment expenses related to her employment, $1,000

   n.   Alimony to Fred's ex-wife, Luci, $4,000

An adjustment is required for (a) and (b) (exemptions not allowed), (f) (40- vs. 39-year life), (g) and (h) (taxes), (i) (private activity bond), (j) (no deduction for taxes), and (m) (miscellaneous itemized deduction). No adjustment is required for (c), (d), (e) (reimbursed employee business expense deductible for A.G.I.), (k) (qualified housing interest), (l) (home equity loan used for improvement to house is qualified housing interest), or (n) (no adjustment required).

Review Question 6.   For a corporation the ACE adjustment ensures that there will be a minimum tax on total financial accounting income of

   a. 20%   **b.** 15%   **c.** 26%   **d.** 75%   **e.**   None of the above

The ACE adjustment requires 75 percent of the excess of adjusted current earnings (book income) over AMTI be taxed at a 20 percent rate, ensuring a minimum tax on total accounting income of 15 percent (75% × 20%). For example, if a corporation reported $100,000 of book income but no taxable income, the ACE adjustment would be $75,000 [75% × ($100,000 − $0)]. This amount would be taxed at 20 percent, producing a tax of $15,000, which is 15 percent of book income.

Review Question 7.   GHI Construction Corporation, a calendar year taxpayer, specializes in building warehouses. Its annual gross receipts average about $5 million. The corporation began work on a building in November 1994 and finished construction in February 1995. The contract was approximately 40 percent complete as of the close of the year. For regular tax purposes, the corporation uses the completed contract method. Consequently, it reported all of the income from the contract, $100,000, in 1995.

a. What is the amount of the AMT adjustment for 1994, if any?

GHI must use the percentage of completion method for AMT purposes. Therefore, the AMT adjustment would be $40,000 (40% of $100,000).

b. Assume that the AMT attributable to the above contract was $8,000 (20% × $40,000) and that GHI paid this amount when it filed its 1994 tax return. In 1995 GHI reported the entire $100,000 profit for regular tax purposes. Is the $40,000 of profit earned in 1994 taxed twice, once under the AMT system when it is included as a $40,000 adjustment in 1994 and once under the regular tax system when it is included in the $100,000 reported in 1995?

No. The AMT paid in 1994 may be credited against the regular tax in 1995. The minimum tax credit ensures that the income is not taxed twice. Note that in this case the AMT effectively operates to accelerate the regular tax.

INCOME TAX CREDITS

One reason tax credits are popular is that a credit is viewed as providing a more equitable benefit than a comparable deduction. This is because a credit is a direct reduction of the tax liability, while a deduction merely reduces the amount of taxable income. This difference is illustrated in *Example 17*.

Example 17. Hi is in the 36% tax bracket, and Lo is in the 15% tax bracket. A credit of $100 is worth the *same* to both taxpayers since it reduces the tax liability of each by $100. On the other hand, a deduction of $100 provides a *different* benefit for each: $36 (36% × $100) for Hi and only $15 (15% × $100) for Lo.

The results from *Example 17* can be generalized for tax policy as (1) all taxpayers receive the *same dollar benefit* from credits, regardless of marginal tax rates; (2) taxpayers with higher marginal tax rates benefit more from tax deductions than do those with lower marginal rates; and (3) taxpayers receive more benefit from tax credits than from tax deductions of the same amount. In addition, the argument has been made that credits are of more benefit to those with lower incomes. This is based on the reasoning that the $100 tax saved has more relative value for those with low incomes than it has for those with high incomes. However, this line of reasoning is questionable since taxable income is just one inexact measure of a person's economic situation.

OVERVIEW OF TAX CREDITS

In recent years, the number of tax credits has been significantly increased by Congress. Most of them have been enacted into law to achieve a specified social, economic, or political goal. These goals range from encouraging taxpayers to engage in scientific research (the research credit) and the conservation of energy (energy tax credits) to providing compensatory tax reductions for those individuals who may carry greater burdens than others (credits for the elderly and for individuals with low earned incomes).

Exhibit 13-7 *Table of Tax Credits*

	Code Section	Specific Credit	Termination Date
Subpart A:	§ 21	Child and Dependent Care Credit	None
	§ 22	Credit for the Elderly	None
	§ 25	Credit for Interest on Certain Home Mortgages	None
Subpart B:	§ 27	Possession and Foreign Tax Credit	None
	§ 28	Credit for Clinical Testing of Certain Drugs	12/31/94
	§ 29	Credit for Nonconventional Fuel Production	None
	§ 30	Credit for Qualified Electric Vehicle	12/31/04
Subpart C:	§ 31	Credit for Taxes Withheld on Wages	None
	§ 32	Earned Income Credit	None
	§ 33	Credit for Taxes Withheld at Source on Nonresident Aliens and Foreign Corporations	None
	§ 34	Credit for Certain Uses of Gasoline and Special Fuels	None
Subpart D:	§ 38	General Business Credit	
		Includes	
		1. Investment Credit (§ 46)	None
		2. Targeted Jobs Credit (§ 51)	12/31/94
		3. Alcohol Fuels Credit (§ 40)	12/31/00
		4. Research Credit (§ 41)	6/30/95
		5. Low-Income Housing Credit (§ 42)	None
		6. Enhanced Oil Recovery Credit (§ 43)	None
		7. Disabled Individual Access Credit (§ 44)	None
		8. Renewable Electricity Production (§ 45)	7/1/99
		9. Empowerment Zone Employment Credit (§ 1396)	12/31/04
		10. Indian Employment Credit (§ 45A)	12/31/03
		11. Employer Social Security Credit (§ 45B)	None
Subpart G:	§ 53	Credit for Prior Year Minimum Tax Liability	

As the table in Exhibit 13-7 illustrates, the credit provisions are divided into *five* major groups or subparts. Subpart A consists of nonrefundable individual tax credits and Subpart B contains certain nonrefundable credits. All of these nonrefundable credits may be used to reduce the tax liability, but *only* to the extent of the "regular tax liability." Subpart C contains the *refundable* credits. Subpart D consists of 11 separate credits, which are combined to form the "general business credit." Finally, the minimum tax credit is contained in Subpart G.

Limitation on Nonrefundable Credits. The TRA of 1986 amended the definition of *regular tax liability* for purposes of applying the credits. This definition is significant because the nonrefundable credits may only be used to reduce the § 26 tax liability. Under revised Code § 26, a taxpayer's "regular tax liability" does not include (1) the minimum tax (§ 55); (2) the additional tax imposed on distributions from certain annuities [§ 72(m)]; (3) the additional tax imposed on income from certain retirement accounts [§ 408(f)]; (4) the accumulated earnings tax (§ 531); (5) the personal holding company tax (§ 541); (6) the tax on certain capital gains of S corporations (§ 1374); or (7) the tax on passive income of S corporations (§ 1375).[52] Thus, the nonrefundable credits cannot be used to offset penalty taxes imposed by the Code (e.g., personal holding company and accumulated earnings penalty taxes).

For taxpayers to whom two or more credits apply, the Code specifies an ascending order for the use of nonrefundable credits. Nonrefundable credits are to be used to reduce the § 26 tax liability in the following order: §§ 21, 22, 25, 27, 28, 29, 30, 38, and 53. This order is important because some of the credits may be carried forward or back and utilized in different tax years, while others "fall through the cracks" (i.e., provide no tax benefit) if they exceed the § 26 tax liability in the year they originate.

Refundable Credits. Refundable credits—listed in Exhibit 13-7 under Subpart C—are accounted for *after* the nonrefundable ones and may be applied against *any* income tax imposed by the Code—including the penalty taxes. As the name suggests, refundable credits may result in the taxpayer receiving a refund check for an amount in excess of any Federal taxes paid or withheld. In a sense, these credit provisions may result in a "negative income tax."

Due to the magnitude and relative importance of the business credits, they are examined first. A discussion of the tax credits available only to individual taxpayers follows.

GENERAL BUSINESS CREDIT

As shown in Exhibit 13-7, the general business credit actually consists of 11 separate credits that are commonly available to business. Each of these credits is separately computed under its own set of rules. The various credits are then combined to determine the current year's total business credit. The credits are combined in order to determine an overall limitation on the amount of credit that can be used.

In order to prevent taxpayers from using business credits to avoid paying all income taxes, the general business credit is limited each year by the taxpayer's *net regular tax liability*. The net regular tax liability is the § 26 tax liability reduced by the credits allowed in §§ 21 through 30.[53] In addition, taxpayers with a net regular tax liability exceeding $25,000 are subject to an additional limitation. The business credit is limited

---

[52] Other taxes imposed in special circumstances are also excluded from the regular tax liability. See § 26(b)(2) for a complete list of taxes that are excluded.

[53] § 38(c)(2).

to $25,000 *plus* 75 percent of the net regular tax liability in excess of $25,000.[54] It should also be recalled that the business credits normally are not allowed to offset the AMT. Generally, credits that are unused because of these limits can be carried back three years and then forward 15 years, applied on a first-in, first-out basis.[55]

> **Example 18.** In 1994 F has a potential general business credit of $92,000 and a net regular tax liability of $100,000. The maximum allowable business credit for 1994 is $81,250 [$25,000 + (75% × $75,000 = $56,250)]. The unused credit of $10,750 ($92,000 − $81,250) is subject to the carryover rules.

When the general business credit is limited and two or more components of the credit are applicable, special ordering rules apply to determine which credits will be utilized currently and which credits will be subject to the carryback and carryover rules. As specified in § 38(d), the order in which such credits are used is determined in the same order in which they are listed in Exhibit 13-7.

The common rules for computing the separate components of the general business credit, beginning with the investment tax credit, are detailed in the following sections.

INVESTMENT CREDIT

In 1962 Congress enacted the investment credit in hopes of stimulating the economy by encouraging taxpayers to purchase certain assets—generally tangible personal property used in a trade or business. Although application of the provision became quite difficult, the essence of the law was simple. It allowed a credit equal to a particular percentage of the cost of the property. For example, taxpayers who purchased equipment at a cost of $100,000 might be entitled to a credit equal to 10 percent of the cost, or $10,000—but only as long as they met a host of requirements.

Since its enactment, the investment credit has had a tortuous history, in the law one year and out the next. It most recently graced the pages of the Code in 1985 before it fell victim to the Tax Reform Act of 1986. In order to partially offset the significant loss of Federal tax revenues resulting from the 1986 tax rate reductions, Congress terminated the regular IC for assets placed in service after December 31, 1985.[56] However, Congress

---

54   § 38(c)(1). Married taxpayers filing separate returns are limited to $12,500 plus 75 percent of the tax liability in excess of $12,500 [§ 38(c)(4)].

55   § 39(a). Note that the credit allowed for renewable electricity production and the empowerment zone employment credit cannot be carried back to taxable years ending before January 1, 1994. The Indian employment credit and the employer social security credit cannot be carried back to a taxable year ending before August 10, 1993. See § 39(d).

56   The regular IC rules have been changed many times, resulting in several unique sets of rules applicable to different time periods in which the assets were placed in service. Because the recovery period, and thus the IC recapture period, for all assets placed in service prior to 1986 has expired, much of the complexity and detail involved in computing and recapturing the regular IC have been eliminated by the passage of time.

allowed certain portions of the old credit to continue. Under current law, the investment credit (IC) is made up of three distinct parts: (1) the credit for rehabilitation expenditures, (2) the business energy credit, and (3) the reforestation credit. Each part of the IC is computed separately under its own specific rules. The actual amount of each part of the IC is the function of two factors: the taxpayer's basis in property qualifying for the credit, and the rate of the credit. The two most frequently encountered components of the IC—the rehabilitation and energy credits—are discussed below.[57]

Rehabilitation Investment Credit. The Economic Recovery Tax Act of 1981 grafted onto the regular investment credit an additional tax credit designed to encourage the restoration of buildings constructed prior to 1936. The credit represents a unique tax incentive for the restoration of old buildings.

With an emphasis on urban renewal, the rehabilitation investment credit is limited to substantial *rehabilitation expenditures* (excluding the purchase price) of *commercial buildings* and *historic structures*.[58] *Substantial* is defined to mean qualifying expenditures that exceed the greater of (1) the property's basis, or (2) $5,000.[59] To prevent destruction of these buildings, the amended legislation requires that

1. Fifty percent or more of the existing external walls of the buildings is retained in place as external walls;

2. Seventy-five percent or more of the external walls of the building is retained in place as internal or external walls; and

3. Seventy-five percent or more of the existing internal structural framework of the building is retained in place.

If these requirements are met, the credit is available for qualified expenditures on *both* nonresidential real property and residential rental property or an addition or improvement to either type of property. However, if the rehabilitation credit is taken, the property *must* be depreciated under the straight-line method over the MACRS recovery period or the alternative depreciation system.[60]

The rate of rehabilitation credit is

Rate	Type of Structure
10%	Commercial building originally placed in service prior to 1936
20	All certified historic structures[61]

---

[57] The reforestation credit allows a 10 percent credit for qualified reforestation expenditures. See §§ 48(b) and 194 for details.

[58] § 47(a).

[59] § 47(c)(1)(C).

[60] § 47(c)(2)(B).

[61] § 47(c)(3). The designation as a certified historic structure is made by the Secretary of the Interior.

Example 19. On January 3, 1994 R purchases a commercial building that was constructed in 1920. In addition to the $300,000 of the purchase price allocated to the building, the entire core of the building is renovated at a cost of $600,000. R's rehabilitation credit is $60,000, computed as follows:

Qualified investment.......................	$600,000
Rate of credit.............................	× 10%
Current credit (before limitations)..........	$ 60,000

In some instances, rehabilitation expenditures also qualify for the energy investment credit (discussed below). When this occurs, taxpayers *must choose* between the two credits because both credits cannot be claimed for the same expenditure.[62]

Energy Investment Credit. With rising concern about conservation of energy use, Congress added the *energy credit* provisions to the Code. The objective of these credits is to encourage taxpayers to incur certain expenditures that decrease energy consumption or change the type of energy used. As originally enacted, these credit provisions applied to a broad range of alternative energy sources and were available for expenditures related not only to business property but also to residential property (e.g., insulation for one's house). In 1986, however, Congress narrowed the credit's application. Currently, the credit is available only for expenditures for solar or geothermal property that is used in a trade or business. The credit for both solar and geothermal property is 10 percent.[63]

Example 20. S is the owner of a deluxe print shop. In March 1994 S installed four solar panels to heat water to be used in a photographic development process. The panels, pumps, valves, storage tanks, control system, and installation cost a total of $80,000. S's energy tax credit is $8,000.

Qualified investment.......................	$80,000
Rate of credit.............................	× 10%
Current IC (before limitations).............	$ 8,000

Basis Reduction of Qualified Property. At one time, taxpayers were allowed to take a full 10 percent IC and any applicable energy tax credit and still recover their entire cost basis of qualifying property under ACRS. In 1986 Congress decided that this treatment was too liberal with respect to rehabilitation property and required the basis of the property to be reduced by the amount of IC taken with respect to the property.[64] A similar rule requires that the basis of energy property be reduced by *one-half* of the amount of the IC taken on such energy property.[65]

---

[62] § 48(a)(2)(B).

[63] § 48(a)(3).

[64] § 50(c)(1). Note that for determining the amount and character of gain on the disposition of the property, the downward basis adjustment is treated as a deduction allowed for depreciation. Accordingly, the amount of the basis adjustment will be subject to the § 1245 depreciation recapture rules discussed in Chapter 17.

[65] § 50(c)(3).

Example 21. Refer to the facts in *Example 19*, where R's rehabilitation credit is $60,000. R purchased the property for $300,000 and incurred $600,000 of rehabilitation expenditures. R's basis in the rehabilitated property is $840,000 ($300,000 + $600,000 − $60,000).

Example 22. Refer to the facts in *Example 20*, where S's energy tax credit is $8,000. S purchased the solar property for $80,000. S's basis in the energy property is $76,000 ($80,000 − $4,000).

The investment credit calculations discussed here provide the background for computing the recapture of IC on early dispositions required by the Code.[66] The amount of IC recapture should be an economic consideration in planning the disposition of any asset upon which the IC was claimed.

IC Recapture. When taxpayers place qualified investment property into service, they claim the full amount of IC regardless of how long they intend to use the property. However, if an asset ceases to be qualified property during a five-year period (due to a sale or other disposition, or a change in the purpose or use of the asset), taxpayers are required to recapture a portion of the "unearned" IC. The recapture percentages illustrated in Exhibit 13-8 must be used to calculate the amount of unearned credit that is recaptured as an additional tax in the year of early disposition. As a general rule, 20 percent of the credit is "earned" for each full year the property is held. For example, a qualified rehabilitation property placed in service on December 20, 1993 qualified for the rehabilitation credit in 1993 and was taken on the taxpayer's return for the year. However, none of the credit was *earned* until December 21, 1994. On that date, 20 percent of the credit allowed in 1993 was earned and thus no longer subject to recapture.

Exhibit 13-8 *ITC Recapture Percentages* [67]

If qualified property ceases to be qualified property—	The recapture percentage is:
Before one full year, after placed in service	100%
After one year, within two full years	80
After two years, within three full years	60
After three years, within four full years	40
After four years, within five full years	20

---

[66] § 50(a).   [67] § 50(a)(1)(B).

Example 23.   Assume that the commercial building (acquired on January 3, 1994) in *Example 19* was sold by R on September 1, 1995. The IC recapture is computed as follows:

Property	IC Claimed	×	Recapture Percentage	=	Amount Recaptured
Commercial bldg.	$60,000	×	80%	=	$48,000

This amount is reported on Form 4255 and is treated as an additional tax imposed on the taxpayer in the year in which an early disposition occurs. Because the building's basis was originally decreased by the entire credit claimed, its basis is increased by the amount of the recapture for purposes of computing the gain or loss to be recognized on the sale.[68]

In addition to sales and exchanges (including like-kind exchanges), dispositions generally include gifts, dividend distributions from corporations, cessation of business usage, and involuntary conversions.[69] Even though the recaptured IC is referred to as an "other tax" on Form 1040, the amount recaptured will not be treated as a tax for purposes of determining the amount of nonrefundable tax credits allowed under § 26.[70]

The recapture rules do not apply to transfers by reason of death or to assets transferred in certain corporate acquisitions.[71] The recapture rules also will not apply to transfers of property between spouses, even if the transfer is made incident to divorce.[72] Finally, property is not treated as ceasing to be qualified property when a mere change in form of conducting the trade or business occurs, so long as the property continues to be qualified property in the new business and the taxpayer retains a substantial interest in this trade or business.[73]

IC Carryovers.   The portion of the general business credit carry forward attributable to a regular IC from a tax year before June 30, 1987, *and* any regular IC allowed after 1986 on transition property must be *reduced* by 35 percent for tax years after June 30, 1987.[74] This reduction was introduced by Congress to correspond with the reduction of both individual and corporate tax rates. The amount of the credit reduction is not allowed as a credit for any other taxable year. Finally, in determining the extent to which an investment credit is used in a taxable year, the regular investment credit is deemed to be used *before* the rehabilitation credit, the energy credit, and the reforestation credit.

---

[68] § 50(c)(2). A similar rule applies to energy property, but only one-half of the amount of recapture is added to the basis of the property.

[69] Reg. § 1.47-2.

[70] § 50(a)(5)(C).

[71] § 50(a)(4).

[72] § 50(a)(5)(B).

[73] § 50(a)(4) and Reg. § 1.47-3(f).

[74] With respect to transition property, the basis of the qualifying property is required to be reduced *only* by the amount of credit that is allowable after the cutback. See § 49(d) before the amendments made by the RRA of 1990.

TARGETED JOBS CREDIT

For many years Congress has tried to spur employment by granting businesses a credit for hiring new workers. The early provisions generally granted the credit to employers that paid wages to any new employee during the year. Since 1979, however, businesses have been able to claim the credit only if they hire individuals from certain targeted groups—generally those that have had difficulty in finding jobs.[75] They are[76]

- Vocational rehabilitation referrals

- Economically disadvantaged youth (ages 18–22)

- Economically disadvantaged Vietnam-era veterans

- Social Security Supplemental Income benefits recipients

- General assistance recipients

- Youths participating in cooperative education programs (ages 16–19)

- Economically disadvantaged ex-convicts

- Eligible work incentive employees

- Qualified summer youth employees

To be eligible, each individual must obtain certification from a designated local agency, specifying that the individual meets the established criteria and therefore qualifies as a member of one of the targeted groups.

Amount of Credit.   The targeted jobs credit, as it is now known, is an elective credit equal to 40 percent of the first $6,000 of first-year wages paid to a qualified individual. Thus, the maximum credit is $2,400 for each new employee. Note that, without any restriction, the employer would be able not only to claim a credit for the wages paid to the employee but also to deduct those wages. However, employers who elect to take the credit must reduce their wage expense by the amount of the credit; this eliminates the potential windfall. Note also that, as part of the general business credit, the § 38 rules limiting the amount of the credit ($25,000 + 75% of the tax liability in excess of $25,000) are applicable, as are the 3-year carryback and 15-year carryover rules.

Special Rule for Qualified Summer Youth Employees.   Employers are allowed to claim the jobs credit for wages paid for the summer employment of teenagers that are members of economically disadvantaged families. These individuals must be 16 or 17 years of age on the hiring date and not have worked previously for the employer. To qualify for the credit, the services must be attributable to any 90-day period between May 1 and September 15. The summer youth employment credit is 40 percent of the first $3,000 of eligible wages, for a maximum credit of $1,200 per youth.[77] If a summer

---

[75] § 51(c)(4). The credit expires on December 31, 1994. Note, however, that it has been extended several times.

[76] § 51(d).

[77] § 51(d)(12)(B).

youth employee continues to work after the 90-day period, his or her wages may qualify for the general targeted jobs credit previously discussed. However, certification of this employee as a member of a second target group must be determined as of the date of the second certification rather than on the basis of the employee's original certification as a qualified summer youth employee. In addition, the $6,000 wage limit for the targeted job credit must be reduced by the qualified summer wages.

> **Example 24.**   On July 29, 1994 the owners of a farm hired 10 youths that were certified as qualified summer employees to help harvest crops. The owners paid the youths $150 a week for eight weeks (through September 22). The amount of targeted jobs credit in 1994 without regard to additional certifications is $4,200, computed in the following manner:
>
> | | |
> |---|---:|
> | Qualifying wages ($150 × 10 youths × 7 weeks)... | $10,500 |
> | Percent of credit.................................... | ×   40% |
> | Amount of credit.................................... | $ 4,200 |
>
> The wage expense deduction attributable to the youths' salaries would be $7,800, computed as follows:
>
> | | |
> |---|---:|
> | Total wages paid ($150 × 10 youths × 8 weeks)... | $12,000 |
> | Reduced by allowable credit........................ | − 4,200 |
> | Allowable wage expense........................... | $ 7,800 |

Note that the eighth week does not qualify for the credit since it occurs after the September 15th cutoff date.

ALCOHOL FUEL CREDIT

The third component of the general business credit is the alcohol fuel credit. To foster the production of gasohol, an income tax credit for alcohol and alcohol-blended fuels applies to fuel sales and uses before January 1, 2001. The alcohol fuel credit is computed and reported on Form 6478. Generally, the credit is $0.60 per gallon of alcohol used in a qualified alcohol mixture or as a straight alcohol fuel.[78] Although taxpayers are entitled to a credit, they must include an amount equal to the credit claimed in income.[79]

---

[78] § 40. A similar credit applies to small   [79] § 87.
ethanol producers.

RESEARCH AND EXPERIMENTAL (R&E) CREDIT

The fourth component of the general business credit is the research credit—commonly referred to as the R&E credit. Created in 1981 and amended several times since, the R&E credit provisions generally allow taxpayers a credit equal to 20 percent of their *incremental* expenditures that constitute either (1) qualified research expenditures or (2) basic research payments.[80] The method for identifying what qualifies as an incremental expenditure is considered in detail below, as are the types of qualifying research. First, however, the relationship of the R&E credit and the deduction for R&E must be addressed.

Impact of R&E Credit on Current Deductions. The research credit is the second part of Congress's two-prong approach for stimulating research. The first part of this plan, as might be recalled from Chapter 9, allows taxpayers either to deduct research and experimental expenditures immediately or capitalize the expenditures and amortize them over 60 months. As might be expected, taxpayers are not allowed to have their research cake and eat it too. Under § 280C(c), taxpayers must reduce their R&E deduction for the amount of R&E credit determined for the year.[81] For those taxpayers who normally expense R&E costs, this means that their deduction for R&E is simply smaller. For those taxpayers who capitalize and amortize the costs, the amount capitalized is reduced. Note that if the credit is not utilized by the taxpayer within the 15-year carryover period, a deduction equal to the amount of the expiring credit is allowed in the year following the expiration of the tax credit carryover period.[82]

Without additional rules, the cutback of the deduction for the credit could prove unduly harsh for taxpayers subject to the AMT, which generally does not allow the use of credits. For this reason taxpayers are allowed to *elect* to claim a reduced credit.[83] This election effectively enables the taxpayer to trade a credit for a deduction that could be used for AMT purposes.

Qualified Research Expenditures. The R&E credit is allowed for both in-house research and contract (outside) research. *Qualified research expenditures* are those incurred in carrying on a trade or business for in-house research expenses (e.g., wages, supplies, rental of equipment, overhead) and 65 percent of *contract research expenses* (those paid to any person other than an employee of the taxpayer for qualified research).[84] To be eligible for the credit, the expenditures must meet the same criteria that must be met for their deduction. As a general rule, these criteria extend special treatment only for research and development in the experimental or laboratory sense. This includes (1) the

---

[80] § 41(a). The credit currently extends only to amounts paid on or before December 31, 1994.

[81] For taxable years beginning before January 1, 1990, the R&E deduction was reduced by an amount equal to 50 percent of the R&E credit determined for the year.

[82] § 196. The deduction allowed is 50 percent of the expired R&E credits attributable to taxable years beginning before 1990.

[83] § 280C(c)(3).

[84] § 41(b)(4). The trade or business requirement may be met by certain start-up companies even though they are not currently in business.

development of an experimental or pilot model, plant process, formula, invention, or similar property, and (2) the improvement of such types of property already in existence.[85] In addition, the expenditures must be technological in nature *and* must relate to establishing a new or improved function, or improving the performance, reliability, or quality of a product.[86] Finally, the credit is *denied* for certain expenditure items,[87] including

1. Research undertaken outside the United States

2. Research conducted in the social sciences or humanities

3. Ordinary testing or inspection of materials or products for quality control

4. Market and consumer research

5. Research relating to style, taste, cosmetic, or seasonal design

6. Advertising and promotion expenses

7. Management studies and efficiency surveys

8. Computer software for internal use of the taxpayer

9. Research to locate and evaluate mineral deposits, including oil and gas

10. Acquisition and improvement of land and of certain depreciable or depletable property used in research (including the annual depreciation deduction)

Amount of Credit. The 20 percent credit is extended only to taxpayers who increase their research activities. As shown in the formula in Exhibit 13-9, this is accomplished by allowing a credit only for qualified research expenditures for the current year that

Exhibit 13-9 *Calculation of R&E Credit*

R&E Credit = 20% × (qualified R&E expenditures − base amount)

$$\text{Base amount} = \text{Fixed-base percentage} \times \text{Average gross receipts for four previous years}$$

$$\text{Fixed-base percentage*} = \frac{\text{Total research expenses (1984–1988)}}{\text{Total gross receipts (1984–1988)}}$$

* Subject to special rules for start-up companies and limited to a maximum of 16 percent.

---

[85] Reg. § 1.174-2(a).   [87] § 41(d)(4).

[86] § 41(d)(1)(B).

exceed the taxpayer's base amount.[88] The base amount is a fixed percentage of the taxpayer's average gross receipts for the four previous years.[89] Thus, if the taxpayer's gross receipts increase by 10 percent, the taxpayer's research activities must increase beyond 10 percent in order to secure the credit. As a result, the special incentive benefits only those taxpayers who continually increase their research.

The fixed-base percentage is computed differently for firms with a history of doing research than for firms that do not have such a history. For taxpayers reporting both qualified research expenses and gross receipts during each of at least three years from 1984 to 1988, the "fixed-base percentage" is the ratio that its total qualified research expenses for the 1984 to 1988 period bears to its total gross receipts for this period, subject to a maximum ratio of 16 percent. "Start-up companies" and those taxpayers not meeting the R&E expenditures and gross receipt requirements above are assigned a fixed-base percentage of 3 percent for the first five years in which qualified research expenditures are incurred.[90]

Example 25.   Assume R Corporation reported the following research expenditures and gross receipts:

	1986	1987	1988...	1990
Research expenditures...	$ 90,000	$100,000	$110,000...	$120,000
Gross receipts...	700,000	900,000	800,000...	700,000

	1991	1992	1993	1994
Research expenditures...	$130,000	$ 140,000	$ 150,000	$180,000
Gross receipts...	800,000	1,000,000	1,100,000	120,000

R Corporation's R&E credit is computed as follows:

(1)   Fixed-base percentage = $300,000/$2,400,000 = .125

(2)   Base amount = .125 × $3,600,000/4 = $112,500

(3)   Qualified R&E expenditures for 1994 = $180,000

(4)   R&E Credit = 20% × ($180,000 − $112,500)

         = $13,500

---

[88]   § 41 (a)(1).

[89]   § 41(c).

[90]   Special rules apply to start-up companies after the sixth taxable year in which they incur qualified research expenditures. See § 41(c)(3)(B).

Note that R's fixed-base percentage is based on the research activity and gross receipts during 1984–1988, whereas the average annual gross receipts number is based on receipts for the four previous years, 1990–1993 ($700,000 + $800,000 + $1,000,000 + $1,100,000 = $3,600,000). Also note that R must reduce its current deduction for research expenditures by $13,500, or if the deferred asset method of accounting is used, the $180,000 R&E costs must be reduced to $166,500 ($180,000 − $13,500) before being capitalized and amortized over a period of not less than 60 months.

Basic Research Expenditures.   The second category of expenditures qualifying for the research credit is the *incremental* amount of *basic research payments* made to universities and other qualified organizations. Basic research means any original investigation for the advancement of scientific knowledge not having a specific commercial objective. The term "basic research payment" means any amount paid in cash during the taxable year by a corporation to a qualified organization for basic research, but only if such payment is made pursuant to a written agreement and the basic research is to be performed by the qualified organization. Qualified organizations include educational institutions, certain scientific research organizations, and certain grant organizations.[91]

The R&E credit applies to the *excess* of corporate cash expenditures in a year over the qualified organization base period amount. The qualified organization base period amount is the *sum* of (1) the minimum basic research amount, plus (2) the maintenance-of-effort amount. The *maintenance-of-effort amount* prevents the corporation from shifting its historical charitable contribution to any qualifying educational organization over to a creditable basic research payment. It is an amount equal to the *average* nondesignated university contributions paid by the corporation during the base period, increased by the cost of living adjustment for the calendar year over the amount of nondesignated university contributions paid by the taxpayer during that year. Any portion of the basic research payments that does not exceed the qualified organization base period amount will be treated as contract research expenses for computing the incremental qualified research expenditures discussed under "qualified research expenditures" above.[92]

Credit Limitations.   As part of the general business credit, the tax liability limitation ($25,000 + 75% of the tax liability in excess of $25,000) applies, as do the 3-year carryback and 15-year carryover rules. Additional limitations are imposed in an effort to prevent the research credit from being exploited by tax shelter promoters. For individuals with ownership interests in unincorporated businesses (i.e., partners of a partnership), trust or estate beneficiaries, or S corporation shareholders, any allowable pass-through of the credit cannot exceed the *lesser of* (1) the individual's net regular tax liability limitation discussed earlier, or (2) the amount of tax attributable to the individual's taxable income resulting from the individual's interest in the entity that earned such credit.[93]

---

[91]   § 41(e)(6).

[92]   § 41(e)(1)(B).

[93]   § 41(g).

The final unique characteristic of the R&E credit is applicable to changes in business ownership. Special rules apply for computing the credit when a business changes hands, under which qualified research expenditures for periods prior to the change of ownership generally are treated as transferred with the trade or business that gave rise to those expenditures.[94]

LOW-INCOME HOUSING CREDIT

The fifth component of the general business credit is the low-income housing credit. This credit is available for low-income housing that is constructed, rehabilitated, or acquired after 1986. The credit is claimed over a 10-year period, with an annual credit of approximately 9 percent of the qualifying basis of low-income units placed in service. If Federal subsidies were used to finance the project, the credit is limited to approximately 4 percent.[95] For property place in service after 1987, the exact percentage is determined by the IRS on a monthly basis. The percentages for any month are calculated to yield, over a 10-year credit period, amounts of credit that have a present value equal to (1) 70 percent of the qualified basis of new buildings that are not Federally subsidized for the tax year, and (2) 30 percent of the qualified basis of existing buildings and new buildings that are Federally subsidized.[96]

> **Example 26.** In December 1993 H, an individual, constructed and placed in service a qualified low-income housing project. The qualified basis of the project was $1 million. The 70% present value credit for buildings placed in service in December 1993 is 8.3%.[97] Thus, the annual credit that H could claim is $83,000.

Each year, the sum of allowed low-income housing credits is subject to a nationwide cap. The cap amount is allotted among all of the states so that each state will have a cap on the amount of low-income housing credits it can authorize. A credit allocation from the appropriate state credit authority must be received by the owner of the property eligible for the low-income housing credit. The credit is available on a per-unit basis; thus, a single building may have some units that qualify for the credit and some that do not. In order to qualify, a low-income housing project must meet a host of exacting criteria throughout a 15-year compliance period.[98]

DISABLED ACCESS CREDIT

Another component of the general business credit is the disabled access credit. This credit was established in 1993 primarily as a relief measure for those businesses that are required under the Americans with Disabilities Act of 1990 to make improvements that make existing facilities accessible to the disabled. Under Code § 44, an eligible

---

[94] § 41(f)(3).

[95] § 42(b)(1).

[96] § 42(b)(2)(B). A formula for making such computations is provided in Rev. Rul. 88-6, 1988-1 C.B. 3.

[97] Rev. Rul. 93-82, 1993-39 I.R.B. 5.

[98] See §§ 42(g) and 42(l).

small business can elect to take a nonrefundable tax credit equal to 50 percent of the amount of the eligible access expenditures for any taxable year that exceed $250 but do not exceed $10,250. An eligible small business is defined as one having gross receipts for the preceding taxable year that did not exceed $1,000,000, or having no more than 30 full-time employees during the preceding taxable year. Eligible access expenditures are defined as amounts paid or incurred by an eligible small business to comply with applicable requirements of the Disabilities Act. Eligible access expenditures generally include amounts paid or incurred for the following:

1. Removing architectural, communication, physical, or transportation barriers that prevent a business from being accessible to, or usable by individuals with disabilities

2. Providing qualified interpreters or other effective methods of making aurally delivered materials available to individuals with hearing impairments

3. Providing qualified readers, taped texts, and other effective methods of making visually delivered materials available to individuals with visual impairments

4. Acquiring or modifying equipment or devices for individuals with disabilities

5. Providing other similar services, modifications, materials, or equipment

In cases where the eligible business is being conducted as a partnership or an S corporation, the dollar limitations are applied at both the entity and the owner level. Any portion of the unused general business credit attributable to the disabled access credit may not be carried back to any taxable year ending before 1990.

> **Example 27.** J, a sole proprietor, had gross receipts of $700,000 last year and incurred $5,250 of eligible access expenditures this year. J's disabled access credit for this year is $2,500 [($5,250 − $250) × 50%].

As is the case with other components of the general business credit, the depreciable basis of assets acquired subject to the credit using access expenditures must be reduced by the amount of credit claimed with respect to those expenditures. Alternatively, any current deduction attributable to the access expenditures must be reduced by the amount of credit claimed.[99]

EMPOWERMENT ZONE EMPLOYMENT CREDIT

To help rebuild distressed urban and rural areas, the RRA of 1993 created several tax incentives. The hope is that these incentives will encourage businesses to locate in these areas and hire individuals who live there. The goal is carried out in § 1396, which authorizes the Secretary of Housing and Urban Development and the Secretary of

---

[99] § 44(c)(7).

Agriculture to identify 95 enterprise communities and 9 empowerment zones where the tax benefits will be offered. The regions must meet certain criteria concerning population, size (urban areas cannot exceed 20 square miles and rural areas cannot exceed 1,000 square miles), and poverty (a minimum rate of 20 percent).

Businesses that operate within the designated areas are entitled to a variety of benefits. Perhaps the most important of these is the empowerment zone employment credit (EZEC). All employers located in an empowerment zone are entitled to a 20 percent credit for the first $15,000 of wages paid to full-time as well as part-time employees who are residents of the empowerment zone. The maximum credit per employee is $3,000 per year. If an employer is entitled to both a targeted jobs credit (TJC) and an EZEC, the first $6,000 of wages paid qualify for the higher TJC of 40 percent, and the next $9,000 qualify for the EZEC of 20 percent. Thus, the payment of $15,000 of wages could enable the employer to claim a credit as high as $4,200 ($6,000 × 40% = $2,400) + ($9,000 × 20% = $1,800). Of course, the employer's deduction for wages must be reduced by the amount of credits allowed.

Like the TJC, the EZEC is part of the general business credit and is consequently subject to the tax liability limitation as well as the carryback and carryover rule (except that an EZEC cannot be carried back to a taxable year ending before January 1, 1994). Unlike the TJC, the EZEC can offset 25 percent of the employer's AMT liability.

In addition to the EZEC, businesses within an enterprise community are entitled to increase the amount they can expense under § 179 from $17,500 to $20,000. Note that buildings do not qualify for limited expensing in any event. The increase in the § 179 amount is also allowed for the AMT, so no AMT adjustment is required.

OTHER COMPONENTS OF THE GENERAL BUSINESS CREDIT.

There are several other credits that make up the general business credit:

- *Indian Employment Credit.* Added by the RRA of 1993 to encourage the hiring of Native Americans, the Indian employment credit generally entitles employers conducting businesses located on Indian reservations to claim a credit of 20 percent for up to $20,000 of wages and insurance benefits paid to employees who are members of an Indian tribe and who work and live on the reservation.

- *Employer Social Security Credit.* This credit represents a relief measure (or perhaps a peace offering) for the restaurant industry, which presumably was detrimentally impacted by the 1993 cut in the deduction for business meals from 80 to 50 percent. Section 45B allows employers operating food and beverage establishments to claim a credit against their income tax liability for their FICA obligation (7.65%) on tips in excess of those treated as wages for purposes of satisfying the minimum wage provisions.

- *Renewable Electricity Production Credit.* Section 45, another product of the 1993 Act, provides a credit for taxpayers who produce electricity from qualified wind energy or qualified "closed-loop biomass" facilities.

- *Enhanced Oil Recovery Credit.* This is a special credit directed at owners of oil and gas properties requiring secondary or tertiary methods of production.

In addition to those credits that make up the general business credit, there are still other credits available to business. The foreign tax credit, which is available to both businesses and individuals, is discused briefly below. Two other credits, one for clinical testing of drugs (§ 28) and the other for producing fuel from a nonconventional source (§ 29), have limited applicability and are not discussed in this test.

GENERAL BUSINESS CREDIT CARRYOVER RULES

Prior to 1984, each component of the general business credit contained its own separate limitations regarding the amount of tax that could be offset by each credit. As a transitional rule, § 38 provides for pre-1984 unused credits to be combined into a single credit at the end of 1983. The resulting general business credit was allowed to be carried forward to 1984—the first year of the combined 15-year carryover period.

If the business credit carryover cannot be used within the stipulated time period, the credit expires. Without special rules, this would be a double loss for taxpayers who used the full investment tax credit percentages or other credits and who decreased the basis of property for ACRS computations. Not only have they lost the credit but they also were unable to depreciate the full cost of the assets. Because of this possibility, taxpayers are allowed to deduct the amount of the previous reductions from basis stipulated by the expired IC or other credits. This deduction may be taken in the year *following* the expiration of the tax credit carryover period.[100]

> **Example 28.**   Q originally claimed an IC of $10,000 and reduced the basis in the assets by $5,000. After the expiration of the 15-year carryforward period, an unused IC of $3,000 expires. In the first taxable year after the expiration of the credit carryover period, Q may deduct $1,500 ($\frac{1}{2}$ of $3,000). This amount equals the original decrease in basis for the expired investment credit.

FOREIGN TAX CREDIT

The new emphasis on the global economy and global investing is making the treatment of foreign income and foreign taxes a concern for far more taxpayers than ever before. As explained in Chapter 3, U.S. citizens (including U.S. corporations) and resident aliens must pay U.S. taxes on their worldwide income: income earned in the United States as well as income from foreign sources. In many cases, they pay not only U.S. taxes but also foreign taxes on the same income. To alleviate the burden of two taxes on the same income, § 27 generally allows taxpayers to claim a credit for income taxes paid or accrued to a foreign country. Alternatively, taxpayers may elect to claim a deduction for the taxes.[101] Also note that if the taxpayer elects to use the $70,000 earned income exclusion (see Chapter 3), any foreign taxes paid on such income cannot be claimed as a credit.

---

[100]   § 196.   [101]   § 164.

Although the taxpayer is normally allowed a credit for any foreign taxes paid, the amount of the credit may be limited in some cases. As a general rule, the credit for the foreign taxes cannot exceed the U.S. tax that would otherwise be paid on the same income. For example, assume a U.S. taxpayer earns $10,000 while living abroad and pays a foreign tax on such income of $3,000. If the U.S. tax on such income is only $2,000, the taxpayer's credit is limited to $2,000, and she consequently pays foreign tax and no U.S. tax. Note that, without the limitation, the United States could effectively lose $1,000 of taxes on other U.S. income that it would otherwise receive. As this example illustrates, the limitation is generally triggered when the foreign tax rate exceeds the U.S. tax rate. The actual limitation is computed using the following formula:

$$\frac{\text{Foreign source taxable income}}{\text{Worldwide taxable income*}} \times \frac{\text{U.S. tax}}{\text{before credits}} = \frac{\text{Foreign tax credit}}{\text{limitation}}$$

* U.S. source taxable income + Foreign source taxable income + Personal exemptions

Any unused foreign tax credits may be carried back two years and carried forward five years. However, the credits may be carried over only to years where the foreign tax credit limitation has not been exceeded.

Example 29.   This year Mr. and Mrs. T took their financial consultant's advice on global investing. As a result, they received $10,000 of dividends from several foreign stocks. The couple's taxable income including the dividends was $91,850, producing a tax before credits of $20,778. The maximum foreign tax credit would be $2,140, computed as follows:

$$\frac{\$10,000}{\$91,850 + \$4,900 = \$96,750} \times \$20,778 = \$2,140$$

One caveat is in order before leaving the foreign tax credit. Although the above rules normally apply, taxpayers must be careful. Not only are the rules complex, but tax treaties with a particular country may provide special rules for income earned in that country by U.S. citizens. Such treaties must be examined when dealing with foreign income.

NONBUSINESS CREDITS

In addition to the numerous business credits discussed thus far, there are several nonbusiness credits available to individual taxpayers only. These credits include (1) the child and dependent care credit, (2) the credit for the elderly, (3) the credit for interest on certain home mortgages, and (4) the earned income credit and other refundable credits. Each of these credits is discussed below.

CHILD AND DEPENDENT CARE CREDIT

The emergence of the working wife and two-earner couples during the post–World War II era produced a new tax problem. The dilemma concerned the treatment of the costs for the care of children and other dependents. The question posed was whether taxpayers who were forced to pay such costs in order to work should be entitled to deduct them as business expenses. Early court cases denied a deduction for these expenses on the grounds that they were personal in nature. In the courts' view, the expenses stemmed from a personal choice by married couples to employ others to discharge their domestic duties, a purely personal expense. Congress, however, became sensitive to the issue in the late 1960s and responded with a limited deduction in 1971. After several alterations and amendments, the deduction received a complete makeover and was converted into a credit in 1976—a far better deal for those who did not itemize. It now appears that, almost 20 years after its creation, the credit is a permanent part of the tax law, presumably justified as both a relief measure for those who have differing abilities to pay and as a stimulant that reduces the costs of entering the work force.

As the statute is now drawn, taxpayers are able to claim a credit for a portion of their child and dependent care expenses if they meet two requirements: (1) the taxpayer maintains a household for a qualifying individual and (2) the expenses—so-called *employment-related expenses*—are incurred to enable the taxpayer to be gainfully employed.[102] Each of these requirements and the computation of the credit are discussed below.

Qualifying Individual. What many believe is simply a credit for child care actually has a far broader scope. True to its name, the *child and dependent care credit* is available not only to those who have children but also to those who take care of other dependents, such as an aging parent or other relative. A taxpayer (or in the case of divorced parents, only the *custodial* parent) can claim the credit only if he or she maintains a household for one of the following individuals:[103]

- A dependent under the age of 13 (e.g., taxpayer's child)
- An incapacitated dependent
- An incapacitated spouse

Note that the year in which a dependent turns 14 is an important factor in determining the applicability of the credit. First, if the individual becomes 13 during the year, he or she normally qualifies only for the part of the year he or she was under 13. Second, once the individual reaches age 14, expenses do not qualify unless the individual is incapable of self-care.

---

[102] § 21.   [103] §§ 21(b)(1) and 21(e)(5).

Employment-Related Expenses.   Only certain expenses that enable the taxpayer to be gainfully employed or *seek* gainful employment qualify for the credit.[104] The work can be either full-time or part-time, but it must be work. Volunteer work for a nominal salary does not constitute gainful employment. For example, expenses for a baby-sitter while the taxpayer works at a church or hospital do not qualify. Note, however, that expenses incurred when one spouse works and the other attends school on a full-time basis are eligible.

Only certain types of expenses qualify as employment-related expenses. The expenses generally must be for the care of the qualifying individual (e.g., the cost of a baby-sitter). In this regard, the costs of household services qualify if the expenses are attributable at least in part to the care of a qualifying individual. Thus the IRS generally takes the position that the costs of a maid, nanny, or cook can qualify, but not those of a gardener or chauffeur. Eligible expenses normally do not include amounts paid for food, clothing, or entertainment. Similarly, the costs of transportation to a place for care do not qualify unless the qualifying individual is incapacitated. In addition, educational expenses incurred for a child in the first or higher grade level do not qualify. Observe, however, that the costs of pre-school or nursery school are eligible for the credit.

As a general rule, expenses for services both inside and outside the home qualify for the credit. However, there are several notable exceptions for the outside services:

- Care provided by a dependent care facility (e.g., a day care center) qualifies only if the facility provides care for more than six individuals.[105]

- Services outside the home for qualifying individuals other than a dependent under 13 (e.g., nursing home services for a spouse or over-13 dependent who is incapable of self-care) are eligible only if the individual spends at least eight hours a day in the employee's household.[106]

- Overnight camps do not qualify (day camps, however, can qualify).[107]

A final note on eligible expenses concerns payments made to relatives. Can the credit be claimed if the taxpayer simply pays his mother to baby-sit while he works? Payments to individuals do qualify as long as the individual is not a dependent of the taxpayer.[108] Thus payments to a child's grandparents would probably qualify since the grandparents normally are not dependents. Conversely, payments to a child's older brothers or sisters normally would not qualify since such individuals would be dependents. However, payments to the taxpayer's child can qualify if the child is not a dependent and is at least 19 years of age.

Computation of the Credit.   The credit is generally computed by multiplying the applicable percentage times employment-related expenses. A general formula for the calculation is shown in Exhibit 13-10.

---

[104] § 21(b)(2).

[105] § 21(b)(2)(C).

[106] § 21(b)(2)(B).

[107] Last sentence of § 21(b)(2)(A).

[108] § 21(e)(6).

Exhibit 13-10   *Computations of the Child and Dependent Care Credit*

Employment-related expenses
Lesser of amount paid or
1. Earned income or imputed earned income if full-time student
   or incapacitated spouse
2. $2,400 (if one qualifying individual) or $4,800 (if more than one)
× Applicable percentage (20–30%)
= Child and dependent care credit

Applicable Percentage. The applicable percentage begins at 30 percent but is reduced (but not below 20 percent) by one percentage point for each $2,000 (or fraction thereof) that the taxpayer's adjusted gross income exceeds $10,000.[109] For example, the rate for a taxpayer with an A.G.I. of $12,001 is 28 percent, one point reduction for the first $2,000 over $10,000 and another point reduction for the fractional part of the next $2,000. Based on this scheme, taxpayers with adjusted gross incomes exceeding $28,000 have a rate of 20 percent.

Limitations on Employment-Related Expenses. The Code imposes several limitations on the amount of expenses eligible for the credit. The first limitation simply sets a maximum dollar amount of expenses that may be taken into account in computing the credit. These amounts are based on the number of qualifying individuals: $2,400 for one qualifying individual and $4,800 for two or more individuals.[110] Thus, the maximum credits would be $720 (30% × $2,400) and $1,440 (30% × $4,800). As explained below, however, these amounts may be reduced.

> **Example 30.**   F is a widower and maintains a household for his two small children. He incurs $5,000 of employment-related expenses and reports A.G.I. of $27,300 for the current year. F's child care credit is determined as follows:
>
> **Step 1:**   Determine the applicable percentage:
>
> | | |
> |---|---:|
> | Adjusted gross income | $27,300 |
> | Less: Ceiling on 30% rate | (10,000) |
> | Adjusted gross income over $10,000 limit | $17,300 |
>
> Divided by $2,000 and rounded up:
> ($17,300 ÷ $2,000) = 8.65%
> Rounded up to 9%
>
> | | |
> |---|---:|
> | Maximum rate | 30% |
> | Subtracted from 30% | (9%) |
> | Allowable percentage | 21% |

---

[109]   § 21(a)(2).   [110]   § 21(c).

Step 2:   Determine the allowable employment-related
expenses:

Lesser of $5,000 paid or $4,800 limit............. $ 4,800

Step 3:   Determine the dependent care credit:

Allowable employment-related expenses...........	$ 4,800
Times: Applicable percentage.....................	× 21%
Dependent care credit............................	$ 1,008

Earned Income Limitation. In addition to the $2,400 and $4,800 limitations, employment-related expenses are limited to the individual's earned income for the year.[111] For this purpose, earned income generally includes such items as salaries, wages, and net earnings from self-employment, but not passive income such as dividends and interest.

The earned income limitation is a bit more cumbersome for married couples. If an individual is married, a joint return is required to claim the credit, and the amount of the exclusion may not exceed the lesser of the taxpayer's earned income or the earned income of the taxpayer's spouse.[112] In addition, in determining the lesser earned income for married couples, special rules apply if one spouse is either a *full-time student*[113] or an incapacitated person. The student or incapacitated spouse will be deemed to have earned income of $200 a month if there is one qualified dependent or $400 a month if there are two or more qualified dependents. This deemed income does not increase A.G.I. when determining the applicable percentage. These rules are illustrated in the following example.

Example 31. B and G are married, have one dependent child, age 9, incur employment-related expenses of $2,700, and have A.G.I. of $22,500 for the current taxable year. G is employed full-time and earns $27,000 a year. B returned to graduate school and was a full-time student for 10 months during the year. He was not employed during the year.

Step 1:   The applicable percentage is determined to be 23% [30% − ($22,500 − $10,000 = $12,500 ÷ $2,000 = 6.25%, rounded up to 7%)].

Step 2:   The allowable employment-related expenses are $2,000. This is determined by the lesser of three amounts: (1) the $2,700 spent, (2) the $2,400 limit, and (3) B's deemed earned income of $2,000 ($200 for one dependent × 10 months).

---

[111] § 21(d)(1).

[112] § 21(e)(2) and 21(d)(2).

[113] § 21(d)(2). For this purpose, a full-time student is defined exactly the same as for the dependency test (i.e., for at least five months, partial months count as full months).

Step 3:   Determine the dependent care credit:

Allowable employment-related expenses....	$2,000
Applicable percentage (30% − 7%)......... ×	23%
Dependent care credit.......................	$ 460

Relationship to Other Credits.   The child and dependent care credit is nonrefundable and is used to offset the tax liability determined under § 26. It is the *first* credit to be used in reducing an individual's tax liability, and there is no carryover or carryback available for unused credits.

Relationship to Dependent Care Assistance Programs.   Congress has addressed the problem of child and dependent care in two ways: the child care credit and the exclusion for dependent care assistance. As mentioned in Chapter 6, since 1981 employers have been allowed to establish qualified dependent care assistance plans.[114] These plans allow employers a current deduction for contributions to the plans and allow employees to exclude from gross income up to $5,000 of payments (e.g., reimbursements) received under the plan to the extent that the expenses would qualify as employment-related expenses for purposes of the child and dependent care expenses. As might be expected, the taxpayer cannot exclude the payment and at the same time use it to compute the credit. If the taxpayer elects to exclude a reimbursement for care, the limit on the amount of employment-related expenses that qualify for the credit ($2,400 or $4,800) is reduced dollar for dollar by the amount excluded.[115] Whether the taxpayer is better off using the exclusion or the credit requires careful analysis of the taxpayer's situation.

> **Example 32.**   H and W are married with two children. H works full-time as an accountant, earning $50,000 for the year. W earned $20,000 from a part-time job. The couple paid $4,000 of child care expenses, for which H was reimbursed $1,000 under his employer's qualified plan. H and W are in the 28 percent tax bracket. If the couple elects not to exclude the reimbursement, the child care credit is $800 (20% × $4,000), and they must pay taxes of $280 on the $1,000 of income, a net benefit of $520 ($800 − $280). On the other hand, if the couple elects to exclude the reimbursement, they pay no income tax on the payment, and their credit and net benefit is $760, computed as follows:

Employment-related expenses...	$4,000
Dollar limit: maximum allowable expenses for two individuals..............	$4,800
Reduction for employer-provided dependent care excluded from income...	(1,000)
Limit on expenses eligible for credit......................................	$3,800
Amount of credit (20% × lesser of $4,000 or $3,800).....................	$ 760

> Note that only the dollar limit eligible for the credit is reduced by the excluded income. The employment-related expenses total of $4,000 is still eligible for the credit.

---

[114] See § 129 and the discussion in Chapter 6.   [115] § 21(c).

CREDIT FOR THE ELDERLY AND PERMANENTLY DISABLED

A nonrefundable tax credit is available to certain taxpayers who are either 65 years of age or older or are permanently and totally disabled.[116] The credit is 15 percent of an individual's earned and investment income that does not exceed the taxpayer's appropriate § 22 amount.[117] The maximum § 22 amount is

1. $5,000 for single individuals

2. $5,000 for a joint return where only one spouse is at least 65 years old

3. $7,500 for a joint return where both spouses are 65 years or older

4. $3,750 for a married individual filing separately[118]

The maximum amount from above is then reduced by excludable pension and annuity income received during the year, including social security and railroad retirement benefits, and by one-half of the taxpayer's A.G.I. that exceeds

1. $7,500 for unmarried individuals

2. $10,000 if married filing jointly

3. $5,000 if married filing separately[119]

> **Example 33.** P is single, 65 years old, and has A.G.I. of $8,300 from interest and dividends. During the taxable year, she also received social security of $1,500. Her credit for the elderly is computed as follows:

Maximum § 22 amount..........................		$5,000
Less: Social security received...............	$1,500	
50% of A.G.I. over $7,500		
($8,300 − $7,500 = $800 ×		
50%)..................................	+ 400	(1,900)
Section 22 amount available for credit............		$3,100
Multiply by rate................................	×	15%
Amount of credit................................		$ 465

There are a number of additional special rules, and because these rules are quite complicated, individuals are allowed to file their return with a request that the IRS compute their tax liability and tax credit. However, few people are able to take advantage of the credit for the elderly since social security receipts commonly exceed the maximum § 22 amount.

---

[116] Limited rules apply to taxpayers who are under 65 years old if they are certain governmental retirees subject to the Public Retirement System and elect to have this section apply [see § 22(c)].

[117] § 22(a).

[118] § 22(b)(2).

[119] § 22(d).

The credit for the elderly or permanently disabled is limited to the § 26 tax liability reduced by the child and dependent care credit. Like the child and dependent care credit, this credit is nonrefundable and may not be carried back or forward.

CREDIT FOR INTEREST ON CERTAIN HOME MORTGAGES

In order to help provide financing for first-time home buyers, Congress has created several special programs. One of these allows state and local governments to issue mortgage credit certificates (MCCs).[120] Taxpayers who receive such certificates are allowed to claim a nonrefundable credit for a specified percentage of interest paid on mortgage loans on their principal residence. Each certificate must specify the principal amount of indebtedness that qualifies for the credit as well as the applicable percentage rate of the credit. The credit percentage may differ with each certificate but must be between 10 and 50 percent. If the credit exceeds 20 percent, the maximum credit is limited to $2,000. Of course, the amount of the taxpayer's interest deduction must be reduced by the amount of the credit claimed during the year. Any credit that cannot be used may be carried over for three years.

> **Example 34.** After saving for years, R and his wife, W, decided to buy their first house. In order to finance the purchase, R applied for and received from the state an MCC. The certificate specifies that the rate is 15% and the maximum loan amount is $70,000. The couple purchased a house for $75,000 and obtained a loan of $65,000 from a savings and loan. For the year, R and W paid interest of $5,000 on the loan. They may claim a credit of $750 ($5,000 × 15%). In addition, they may deduct interest of $4,250 ($5,000 − $750).

While the credit can provide a significant benefit, it is not available to everyone. Under the MCC program, state and local governments are limited in the volume of credits they may dispense and in the individuals to whom they may be issued. Taxpayers are eligible to receive a certificate only if they meet certain narrowly defined criteria. For example, the purchaser's income cannot generally exceed 115 percent of the area's median gross income, the price of the home cannot exceed 90 percent of the average purchase price of homes in the area, and the homes may be available only in targeted areas. Still other constraints exist that restrict the credit's use.

CREDIT FOR QUALIFIED ELECTRIC VEHICLES

One of the energy conservation provisions in the National Energy Policy Act of 1992 created an incentive for the manufacture and purchase of electric cars. Section 30 authorizes a tax credit equal to 10 percent of the cost of any qualified electric vehicle placed in service by the taxpayer after 1992 and before 2002. The maximum credit in a single year is $4,000. The credit is available to both individuals and businesses but is limited to the original owner of the vehicle.

---

[120]   § 25.

REFUNDABLE CREDITS

Refundable credits are those credits that are recoverable even though an individual has no income tax liability in the current year. They are treated as payments of taxes. Included in this category are the credit for taxes withheld at the source (§ 31), the earned income credit (§ 32), the credit for tax withheld at the source on nonresident aliens and foreign corporations (§ 33), and the gasoline and special fuels credit (§ 34).

Refundable credits may be used to offset all taxes imposed by the Code, including penalty taxes. This result is accomplished by combining all the refundable credits and accounting for them after all the nonrefundable credits have been used to offset the § 26 tax liability.

TAX WITHHELD AT THE SOURCE

The first and most important of the refundable credits is styled "Credit for Tax Withheld on Wages" and obviously includes the amount withheld by an employer as a tax on wages earned.[121] However, the credit has broader application with respect to certain taxes withheld by the payor at the source of payment, including

1. Tax on pensions and annuities withheld by the payor[122]

2. Overpaid FICA taxes (in cases where a taxpayer has two or more employers in the same year)

3. Amounts withheld as backup withholding in cases where the taxpayer fails to furnish a taxpayer identification number to the payor of interest or dividends[123]

4. Quarterly estimated tax payments

EARNED INCOME CREDIT

In 1975 Congress introduced the earned income credit to eliminate some of the disincentives that discouraged low-income taxpayers with children from working.[124] The credit was specifically designed to alleviate the increasing burden of social security taxes. In many cases, income taxes were not a concern for these low-income taxpayers since they were protected by personal and dependent exemptions as well as the standard deduction. However, they were not exempt from social security taxes. Consistent with its purpose, the credit is refundable (e.g., the taxpayer would receive the credit amount even if he or she is not required to pay income taxes since it is viewed as a refund of the social security taxes).

Since its creation, the earned income credit has been the subject of a great deal of Congressional tinkering. The most recent round of adjustments was introduced by the Clinton administration in 1993. These changes not only increased the benefits of the credit but also expanded its coverage. Beginning in 1994, the credit may apply even if the taxpayer does not have children.

---

[121] §§ 31(a) and 3401.

[122] §§ 31(a) and 3405.

[123] §§ 31(c) and 3406.

[124] § 32(a).

Exhibit 13-11   *Earned Income Credit: Credit and Phase-out Percentages*

Tax Year	Number of Qualifying Children	Credit Percentage	Earned Income Amounts	Phase-out Starts at	Phase-out Percentage
1993	1	18.50%	$7,750	$12,200	13.21%
	2	19.50	7,750	12,200	13.93
1994	0	7.65%	$4,000	$ 5,000	7.65%
	1	26.30	7,750	11,000	15.98
	2	30.00	8,425	11,000	17.68
1995	0	7.65%	$4,000*	$ 5,000*	7.65%
	1	34.00	6,000*	11,000*	15.98
	2	36.00	8,425*	11,000*	20.22

* Without adjustments for inflation.

Computation of the Credit. The starting point for determining the credit is determination of the taxpayer's earned income. As might be expected, earned income consists of wages, salaries, tips, and other employer compensation plus earnings from self-employment. It does not include pension and annuity income even if provided by an employer for past services. Nor does it include such passive income as dividends, interest, rents, capital gains, or annuities.

The initial credit is computed by multiplying the earned income of the taxpayer by a statutory percentage; however, this initial amount is phased out as the taxpayer's income increases. As can be seen from Exhibit 13-11, the maximum amounts of earned income that qualify for the credit as well as the statutory credit percentages vary depending on the number of children the taxpayer has.[125] Observe that the credit for an individual with no children is essentially designed to give the taxpayer back the FICA taxes on the first $4,000 of wages (7.65% rate × $4,000). The maximum credits for eligible individuals for 1994 are shown in Exhibit 13-12.

As noted above, the credit begins to phase out once the taxpayer's income increases. The credit is reduced if *either* the *earned income* or the *A.G.I.* of the taxpayer exceeds certain specified amounts shown in Exhibit 13-11.[126] The phase-out is computed by multiplying the applicable phase-out rate by the excess of A.G.I. or earned income (whichever is greater) over the phase-out thresholds. The credit can be computed using the following formula:

Maximum credit
    Applicable percentage × earned income (not to exceed certain maximums)
− Reduction
    Applicable percentage × [larger of Earned income or A.G.I. − Phase-out threshold]
Earned income credit

---

[125]   § 32(b)(1).   [126]   § 32(b)(2).

Exhibit 13-12	Earned Income Credit: Maximum Credits, Phase-out Completion Amounts for 1994	
Qualified Children	Maximum Credit	Phase-out Completion Amounts
0	$ 306 (7.65% × $4,000)	$ 9,000
1	2,038 (26.30% × $7,750)	23,573
2 or more	2,527 (30.00% × $8,425)	25,293

For example, the 1994 earned income credit for a taxpayer with one child is eliminated when the taxpayer's A.G.I. or earned income exceeds $23,753 [15.98% × ($23,753 − $11,000) = $2,038]. The levels at which the credit is completely phased out are shown for each type of taxpayer in Exhibit 13-12.

Example 35.   D and M are married, file a joint return for 1994, and maintain a household for their dependent son, who is three years old. D has earned income of $15,000 and M has none. The couple own investments that produce $2,475 of includible income for the year and have an A.G.I. of $17,475 ($15,000 + $2,475). The earned income credit is computed as follows:

Maximum credit (26.3% × $7,750)........................	$2,038
Less: Reduction for A.G.I. over $11,000	
($17,475 − $11,000 = $6,475 × 15.98%).......	− 1,035
Earned income credit.......................................	$1,003

To help taxpayers compute the credit, the IRS provides a work sheet and an earned income credit table to aid taxpayers in making the earned income credit calculation. The work sheet and table are included with the instructions for completing Form 1040 and Form 1040A (see Appendix B for a copy of the 1993 Table).[127]

As a refundable credit, qualified individuals may receive tax refunds equal to their earned income credit even in years when they have no tax liability.[128]

Example 36.   Y has earned income and A.G.I. of $5,600, has three exemptions (including two qualified children), and files as head of household. As a result, she has no income tax liability for the year. However, she is entitled to a tax refund equal to the earned income credit of $1,680 ($5,600 × 30%) plus any taxes (other than FICA taxes) withheld from her wages.

---

[127]   § 32(f) Note that the earned income credit table prepared annually by the IRS reflects the credit based on a mid-point of each $25 increment of an income range.

[128]   The taxpayer is required to reduce his or her earned income credit by the amount of the alternative minimum tax imposed on that individual.

Eligibility Requirements. Until 1993, the earned income credit was available only to taxpayers who had children. In a major change, the RRA of 1993 extended the earned income credit to certain individuals without children. In so doing, the Act significantly broadened the availability of the credit. The eligibility requirements for taxpayers with and without children are set forth below.

Taxpayers without Children. Taxpayers without a qualifying child are eligible to claim the credit if the taxpayer meets three conditions:[129]

1. The taxpayer must be at least 25 years old and not more than 64 years old at the end of the taxable year.

2. The taxpayer is not a dependent in the same year the credit is claimed.

3. The taxpayer has a principal residence in the United States for more than one-half of the taxable year.

Taxpayers with Children. Taxpayers are entitled to claim the credit if they have a qualifying child. The child need not be a dependent but must meet the following tests:[130]

1. *Relationship.* The individual must be a child, stepchild, foster child, or a legally adopted child of the taxpayer. A married child does not meet this test unless the taxpayer can claim the child as a dependent.

2. *Age.* The child must be either (1) less than 19 years old at the close of the calendar year, (2) less than 24 years old and a full-time student at the close of the calendar year, or (3) permanently and totally disabled any time during the year.

3. *Residency.* The child must share the same principal place of abode as the taxpayer for more than one-half of the taxable year, and that abode must be located in the United States.

Assuming all of the above requirements are met and the taxpayer properly identifies the child on the return (i.e., name, age, taxpayer identification number), the credit is allowed.

OTHER REFUNDABLE CREDITS

Three other refundable credits are allowed. Code § 33 allows as a credit the amount of tax withheld at the source for nonresident aliens and foreign corporations. Code § 34 provides an income tax credit for the amount of excise tax paid on gasoline, where the gasoline is used on a farm, for other nonhighway purposes, by local transit systems, and by operators of intercity, local, or school buses. Finally, Code § 35 provides that an overpayment of taxes resulting from filing an amended return will be treated as a refundable credit.

---

[129] § 32(c)(1)(A)(ii).

[130] § 32(c)(1)(A)(i).

PROBLEM MATERIALS

DISCUSSION QUESTIONS

13-1 *Alternative Minimum Tax.* It has been said that a taxpayer must maintain a second set of books to comply with the AMT system. Why is the extra set of books necessary?

13-2 *Alternative Minimum Tax.* The AMT requires taxpayers to keep an extra set of books for several adjustment items. What action can a taxpayer take to minimize the recordkeeping requirements with respect to depreciation deductions?

13-3 *Alternative Minimum Tax.* Assume a taxpayer has a regular tax liability of $25,000, a tentative AMT of $28,000, and an AMT of $3,000 for the current year. How much does the taxpayer actually owe the IRS?

13-4 *Alternative Minimum Tax.* A taxpayer has an AMT liability of $50,000 and a general business credit of $50,000. He is not concerned about paying the AMT because he thinks the general business credit can be used to offset the AMT. Is he correct? What if the taxpayer were a corporation?

13-5 *Alternative Minimum Tax.* Is it safe to assume that only wealthy individuals who have low taxable incomes are subject to the alternative minimum tax? Are any taxpayers whose marginal rates exceed 26 percent subject to the alternative minimum tax? Explain.

13-6 *Alternative Minimum Tax.* G will be subject to the alternative minimum tax in 1994 but not in 1995. G's property tax on her residence is due November 15, 1994. If she defers payment of the property tax until 1995, she must pay a 5 percent penalty. When should G pay the property tax? Explain.

13-7 *Alternative Minimum Tax.* Some interest expense can be taken as an itemized deduction for regular tax purposes but different rules control the interest expenses allowable as an AMT itemized deduction. Explain the differences in these rules and note which rules are more restrictive.

13-8 *Alternative Minimum Tax.* Is the § 179 (first-year expensing) deduction allowed as a deduction for the AMT system?

13-9 *Credits vs. Deductions.* Assume taxpayers have a choice of deducting $1,000 for A.G.I. or taking a $250 tax credit for the current year. Which taxpayers should choose the deduction? Why?

13-10 *Rehabilitation and Energy Credits.* A taxpayer purchases an old train station, which was placed in service in 1935, for $20,000. He plans to tear the building down and erect a new office building for $100,000. Will any of this qualify for the rehabilitation or energy investment credit? What tax advice could you give the taxpayer for his consideration in maximizing these credits?

13-11   *Rehabilitation and Energy Credit.*   When a taxpayer claims a rehabilitation credit, what impact does the credit have on the basis of the property for cost recovery purposes? What is the impact on the basis when a business energy credit is claimed? What if the disabled access credit is claimed?

13-12   *IC Recapture.*   Explain two possible consequences if a taxpayer claims an investment credit on property and then makes an early disposition of the property.

13-13   *Minimum Tax Credit.*   If a taxpayer pays an AMT in the current year, what consequences does that payment have on the AMT liability that may be owed in subsequent years? What impact does the payment of the AMT in the current year have on the regular tax liability in subsequent years?

13-14   *Dependent Care Credit.*   A husband and wife both work and employ a babysitter to watch the children during their work hours. How much of the babysitter's salary qualifies for the child and dependent care credit if

    a.   The babysitter performs cooking and cleaning services while she is watching the children.

    b.   The babysitter also performs services around the house including gardening, bartending, and chauffeuring.

13-15   *Earned Income Credit.*   A husband and wife with A.G.I. and earned income of $7,000 maintained a household for their son but were unable to claim him as a dependent because he was 20 years old and earned $3,500. Can the son or his parents qualify for the earned income credit? Explain.

13-16   *Research Credit.*   Two college students work in a garage during 1994 doing research for a new patent. They spend $15,000 on the research in 1994. In January 1995 they form an S corporation, each controlling 50 percent of the stock, and apply for the patent, which is granted in 1995. How much credit for research expenditures will the taxpayers be allowed and in what year?

13-17   *Targeted Jobs Credit.*   The purpose of the targeted jobs credit is to encourage the employment of certain groups of people with high unemployment rates. The credit has not quite achieved the desired objectives. What changes should be made to the present credit to increase its effectiveness?

PROBLEMS

13-18   *Alternative Minimum Tax—Computation.*   T is single and has taxable income of $51,900 and a regular tax liability of $11,575 for the current year. T uses the standard deduction for regular tax purposes and has $60,000 of positive adjustments for AMT purposes.

    a.   Determine T's tentative AMT and her AMT.

    b.   Determine the amount that T actually has to pay the IRS this year.

13-19   *Alternative Minimum Tax—Computation.*   V and W are married and file a joint return for the current year. They have no other dependents and they take the standard deduction. V and W's taxable income is $86,500 and their regular tax liability is $19,280. They have $60,000 of AMT preference items and $32,050 of AMT positive adjustments. Determine V and W's tentative AMT and their AMT liability.

13-20 *AMT and Qualified Small Business Stock.* T is an avid investor, always looking for that one stock that will make him rich and famous. On January 4, 1994 BC Corporation, a fast food chain, went public, and T thought this could be the one. He purchased 10,000 shares of stock for $100,000. One of the benefits from buying this initial offering was that BC's stock was eligible for treatment as qualified small business stock. After enduring the ups and downs of the market, T sold 5,000 shares of the stock for $250,000 on January 9, 1999.

    a. Determine the gain recognized on the sale of the BC stock and the amount included in T's regular taxable income.

    b. Determine the amount of tax preference or adjustment, if any, that T must take into account in computing his alternative minimum tax.

13-21 *Alternative Minimum Tax—Charitable Contribution Preference.* During the year, J contributed stock to the local university. He had purchased the stock in 1980 for $10,000, and it was appraised at $60,000 on the date of gift. The stock was sold shortly after the contribution was made, and a painting was purchased by the university with the proceeds from the sale. The university placed the painting in its Art Building for display and study by art students. J's A.G.I. in the year of contribution is $300,000.

    a. Determine J's allowable charitable contribution deduction for the regular tax system.

    b. Determine J's AMT charitable contribution preference amount with respect to the contribution of the stock.

13-22 *Alternative Minimum Tax—Computation.* B is single and reports the following items of income and deductions for the current year:

Salary...	$ 50,000
Net long-term capital gain on sale	
of investment property........................	200,000
Medical expenses...............................	17,500
Casualty loss...................................	4,500
State and local income taxes....................	10,000
Real estate taxes..............................	15,000
Charitable contributions (all cash)...............	15,000
Interest on home mortgage......................	12,000
Interest on investment loans	
(unimproved real property)....................	10,000

Taxable income 181,000

The only additional transaction during the year was the exercise of an incentive stock option of her employer's stock at an option price of $12,000 when the stock was worth $100,000. Compute B's tax liability and AMT, if any.

13-23 *Alternative Minimum Tax.* Refer to the facts in Problem 13-22 and assume B holds the stock acquired by exercising her ISO for two years and sells it for $105,000. Determine the amount of gain that must be reported for regular tax purposes and the gain that must be reflected in the AMT calculations in the year the stock was sold.

13-24 *Alternative Minimum Tax—Cost Recovery Adjustment.* In 1994 T placed a light-duty truck in service at a cost of $40,000. T uses the applicable MACRS method of depreciation for all his assets and does not elect the § 179 first-year expensing option. Identify and calculate the minimum tax adjustment that must be made for AMT purposes in 1994.

13-25 *Alternative Minimum Tax—Cost Recovery.* Refer to the facts in Problem 13-24, but assume the truck that was placed in service this year at a cost of $40,000 was a heavy-duty truck. Identify and calculate the minimum tax adjustment that must be made for AMT purposes in 1994.

13-26 *Alternative Minimum Tax—Cost Recovery Adjustment.* In January 1994 A purchases non-residential property for $200,000, excluding the cost of the land. For regular tax purposes, the 1994 depreciation on the building is $6,085 ($200,000 × $^{11.5}/_{12}$ × $^1/_{31.5}$). For AMT purposes, depreciation is $4,792 ($200,000 × $^{11.5}/_{12}$ × $^1/_{40}$). Determine the AMT adjustment for cost recovery for 1994 and 1995.

13-27 *Alternative Minimum Tax—Computation.* O is married to G and they file a joint return for 1994. O and G have A.G.I. of $70,000. One of the deductions from gross income was $50,000 of percentage depletion. Cost depletion on their gold mine was zero because the cost basis of the property was reduced to zero by prior years' depletion deductions. They do not itemize deductions. Determine O and G's tax liability for 1994.

13-28 *Alternative Minimum Tax.* T is an unmarried real estate entrepreneur. In 1990 he purchased constructed properties and leased them to tenants on long-term leases. In 1994, T has $100,000 of rental losses on his real estate activities in which he actively participates and income of $100,000 from his brokerage business. T also has a $25,000 general business credit carryover from 1993. Determine T's tax liability for 1994, assuming he does not itemize his deductions.

13-29 *Minimum Tax Credit.* Refer to the facts in Problem 13-22 and determine the minimum tax credit, if any, that is available to offset the regular tax liability in 1995.

13-30 *General Business Credit—Limited by Tax Liability.* K's tax liability before credits is $35,000. She earned a general business credit of $40,000. Determine K's tax liability after credits and any general business credit carryback or carryforward that may exist.

13-31 *Energy Credit.* In May of the current year, J invested $60,000 in a solar system to heat water for a production process.

  a. Determine the amount of business energy credit available to J.
  b. Determine the basis of the energy property that J must use for cost recovery purposes.

13-32 *Rehabilitation Credit.* During the current year, T incurred $300,000 of qualified rehabilitation expenditures with respect to 75-year-old property. Prior to these expenditures, T had a $100,000 cost basis in the depreciable building.

  a. Determine the amount of rehabilitation credit available to T.
  b. Determine the basis of the rehabilitated property that T must use for cost recovery purposes.

13-33 *Rehabilitation Credit—Computation.* During the current year, K incurred $200,000 of qualified rehabilitation expenditures with respect to property constructed in 1930. The entire block where his property is located has been designated as a Certified Historical District.

  a. Determine the amount of credit allowable to K if his structure is recognized as a historical structure.
  b. Assuming that K paid $180,000 for his building in the current year and that he would claim MACRS depreciation, calculate his adjusted basis in the building at the end of the year. Assume that the property was placed in service in July of the current year.

13-34   *IC Recapture.*   Assume D claimed a business energy credit of $30,000 for property placed in service on December 18, 1991 and that D sold this property on January 7, 1994. Determine the amount, if any, of IC recapture that D should report as an additional tax in 1994.

13-35   *IC Recapture.*   Assume L claimed rehabilitation credit of $80,000 on property placed in service on February 18, 1991 and that L exchanged this rehabilitated property for like-kind property (a § 1031 exchange) on March 17, 1994. Determine the amount of IC recapture that L should report as an additional tax in 1994, if any.

13-36   *Research and Experimentation Credit.*   M, a sole proprietor, has been in business only two years but is very successful. He has average annual gross receipts of $150,000 for this period and incurred $40,000 in qualified R&E expenses this year.

    a.   Determine M's R&E credit for the current year.
    b.   Determine the current deduction for R&E expenditures that M is entitled to, assuming he elects to deduct R&E expenditures currently.

13-37   *Disabled Access Credit—Computation.*   P Corp. had gross receipts of $500,000 last year and incurred $9,000 of eligible access expenditures to build a wheelchair ramp this year.

    a.   Determine P's disabled access credit.
    b.   Determine the basis of the wheelchair ramp that will be eligible for cost recovery deductions.

13-38   *Dependent Care Credit.*   V and J are married and file a joint return for the current year. Because they both work, they had to pay a babysitter $5,200 to watch their three children (ages 7, 8, and 9). V earned $17,000 and J earned $21,200 during the year. They do not have any other source of income nor do they claim any deductions for adjusted gross income. Determine the allowable dependent care credit for V and J.

13-39   *Dependent Care Credit.*   M and B are married, have a son three years old, and file a joint return for the current year. They incurred $500 a month for day care center expenses. During the year, B earned $23,000 but M did not work outside the home. They do not have any other source of income nor do they claim any deductions for adjusted gross income. Determine the allowable dependent care credit for the year if

    a.   M enrolled as a full-time student in a local community college on September 6 of the current year.
    b.   M was in school from January through June, and from September through December of the current year.

13-40   *Dependent Care Credit.*   C is a single parent raising a son who is eight years old. During the current year, C earned $19,500 and paid $3,000 to a sitter to watch her son after school. Determine C's dependent care credit for the current year.

13-41   *Earned Income Credit.*   R is 43, divorced, and maintains a household for his 7-year-old dependent daughter. R was laid off in 1993 and his unemployment benefits have run out. During 1994 he worked at part-time jobs earning $5,500. He has no other sources of income.

    a.   Determine R's allowable earned income credit.
    b.   Determine R's tax payment due or his refund, assuming that nothing was withheld from his wages and that he did not make any quarterly estimated tax payments.

13-42 *Earned Income Credit.* S, who is 24 and a single parent, maintains a household for her 3-year-old dependent daughter and her 10-month-old son. S earned $16,000 during this calendar year. S has no other source of income and does not itemize her deductions.

    a.   Determine S's allowable earned income credit.

    b.   Determine S's tax payment due or her refund, assuming that $200 was withheld from her wages and that she did not make any quarterly estimated tax payments.

13-43 *Integrative Credit Problem.* J, who is 32 and a single parent, maintains a household for his six-year-old dependent son. J earned $13,500 and paid $3,000 in child care payments during the calendar year. J did not have any Federal income tax withheld from his check. Determine the amount of J's refund from the IRS, if any, or the amount that J must pay the IRS, if required.

13-44 *Credit for the Elderly.* P and D are 66 years old, married, and file a joint return. The only sources of income they have are dividend income of $14,000 and social security of $2,500.

    a.   Determine the allowable credit for the elderly for the current year.

    b.   Determine the tax payable or refund due, assuming that no withholding was made on the dividends and that no quarterly estimated payments were made.

CUMULATIVE PROBLEM

13-45 R and S, married and the parents of two children ages 10 months and 6 years, file a joint return. R is a college professor of civil engineering and teaches at State University. R applied for a one-year visiting professorship with International Engineering Corporation (IEC) and was selected for the position. The visiting professor position was available from July 1 to May 31 of the following year and required R to relocate his family from Detroit to Los Angeles at a total cost of $6,500 during the last week in June. IEC reimbursed R only $5,000 for these expenses. R rented his Detroit home for the last six months of the calendar year at a net loss of $6,000 for regular tax purposes. Due to the longer life of the residential real property for AMT purposes, and therefore a smaller cost recovery deduction, the net loss for AMT purposes was only $4,000.

    S was employed by the government and was able to get a temporary transfer to Los Angeles. S earned $12,000 for the calendar year. During the calendar year, R and S paid $6,000 in child care expenses.

    R and his family incurred expenses of $2,500 a month to rent a furnished apartment (assume $1,000 a month was attributable to R and $1,000 a month was attributable to S) for the last six months of the calendar year. R and his family incurred expenses of $800 a month for food during the last six months of the year (assume 25% of the food is specifically attributable to R and that 25% is attributable to S). In addition, R incurred transportation expenses, parking fees, and laundry expenses of $2,500, and he spent $1,200 on lunches on work days during the last half of the year. S incurred transportation expenses of $500 and took her lunch to work with her. R earned $25,000 from State University for teaching half of the calendar year and $60,000 from IEC for practicing half of the year. Together, R and S had $12,000 of Federal income tax withheld from their paychecks.

During the year, R and S also incurred the following expenses:

Unreimbursed medical expenses..........................	$7,000
Charitable contribution of stock	
to State University (adjusted basis $1,000).............	5,000
State and local income taxes.............................	4,000
Real estate taxes on lake property.......................	3,000
Real estate taxes on principal residence (one-half year)...	2,000
Interest on principal residence (one-half year).............	4,800

The couple also had these additional income items:

State tax refund from previous year...............	$1,500
Interest income from private activity bonds........	7,000

R and S have a minimum tax credit carryover from last year of $5,000. Determine R and S's tax liability for the year.

RESEARCH PROBLEMS

13-46 *Rehabilitation Credit.*   Taxpayer S, a real estate developer, rehabilitated an old commercial building and was entitled to an investment credit based on the rehabilitation expenses incurred. Prior to placing the new offices into service, S is approached by P, who is interested in purchasing the building. As an inducement to get P to buy the property, S offers to transfer the IC to P. That is, S agrees not to claim the credit on his tax return with the expectation that P can claim the credit instead. Will P be allowed to take credit on her tax return in the year she places the office building into service?

13-47 *Dependent Care Credit.*   B is a single parent and his child is enrolled in a public school. The school administrators have scheduled a supervised trip to Dearborn, Michigan for one full week for the students to see Greenfield Village and the Henry Ford Museum. Total trip cost per student is $800. If B pays for his child to make the trip, will he be entitled to a child care credit for the expenditures? If so, how much of the costs will qualify?

13-48 *Alternative Minimum Tax*   This year T was the victim of his company's restructuring and downsizing. Midway through the year his employer, ABC Corporation, offered him early retirement on the condition that he would provide consulting services when needed. The offer proved so lucrative that T accepted. T ended up working for the company for the first six months of the taxable year and earned $50,000 during this period. Prior to his retirement he exercised an incentive stock option he had received several years earlier. At the time he exercised the option, the market price of the stock was $140,000 and the purchase price under the option was $50,000. After he retired, T began a new business of building toys for disabled children. He materially participated in the business and incurred a loss of $60,000, which he properly reported on Schedule C of his Form 1040 tax return. T is married and files a joint return with his wife. The couple paid $18,000 in qualified housing interest and $6,000 in real estate taxes, and made a $25,000 cash contribution to Children's Hospital during the year. Determine T's regular tax liability and AMT, if any. (Hint: Try to find authority that might support an AMT liability of zero.)

13-49 *Child Care Credit.*   K recently divorced and decided to go back to school full-time to get her Masters of Taxation at University of Denver. She has a four-year-old child who attends nursery school at a cost of $4,000 per year. As a single parent, K finds it difficult just to get by. However, she maintains her home using her alimony payments, some dividend and interest income, and her child support. She also works as a volunteer for 10 hours a week at the library and recieves $15 per week. This year she attended school for 11 months. Is K eligible for the child care credit?

PART V

PROPERTY TRANSACTIONS

CONTENTS

CHAPTER 14 ■ PROPERTY TRANSACTIONS: Basis Determination, Recognition of Gain or Loss

CHAPTER 15 ■ NONTAXABLE EXCHANGES

CHAPTER 16 ■ PROPERTY TRANSACTIONS: Capital Gains and Losses

CHAPTER 17 ■ PROPERTY TRANSACTIONS: Disposition of Trade or Business Property

Upon completion of this chapter you will be able to:

- Understand the concepts of realized and recognized gain or loss from the disposition of property
- Explain the process of determining gain or loss required to be recognized on the disposition of property, including computation of the following:
  - Amount realized from a sale, exchange, or other disposition
  - Effect of liabilities assumed or transferred
  - Adjusted basis of property involved in the transaction
- Identify the most common types of adjustments to basis of property
- Define an installment sale and identify taxpayers eligible to use the installment method of reporting gain
- Compute the amount of gain required to be recognized in the year of installment sale and the gain to be reported in any subsequent year
- Explain the limitations imposed on certain installment sales, including
  - The imputed interest rules
  - Related-party installment sales
  - Gain recognition on the disposition of installment obligations
  - Required interest payments on deferred Federal income taxes
- Identify various transactions in which loss recognition is prohibited

CHAPTER OUTLINE

Determination of Gain or Loss	14-1	Installment Sale Method	14-21
Introduction	14-1	General Rules	14-21
General Rule of Recognition	14-2	Election out of Installment Reporting	14-22
Computing Amount Realized	14-3	Gain Reported under the Installment	
Basis Determination Rules	14-6	Method	14-23
Property Acquired by Purchase	14-6	Limitations on Certain Installment	
Property Acquired by Gift	14-7	Sales	14-26
Property Acquired from a Decedent	14-9	Reporting Gain on Installment	
Property Acquired in a Nontaxable		Sales	14-30
Exchange	14-11	Disallowed Losses	14-30
Property Converted from Personal		Wash Sales	14-31
Use to Business Use	14-11	Sales between Related Parties	14-31
Property Converted from Business		Tax Planning Considerations	14-33
Use to Personal Use	14-12	Gift Versus Bequest	14-33
Adjustments to Basis	14-12	Charitable Transfers Involving	
Effect of Liabilities on Amount Realized	14-14	Property Other than Cash	14-34
Concepts Related to Realization and		Changes in the Use of Property	14-34
Recognition	14-15	Sales to Related Parties	14-34
Sale or Other Disposition	14-15	Use of Installment Sales	14-34
Allocations of Purchase Price and		Problem Materials	14-36
Basis	14-19		

Chapter **14**

PROPERTY TRANSACTIONS
Basis Determination and Recognition of Gain or Loss

Section 61(a)(3) of the Code provides that gross income includes gains derived from dealings in property. Similarly, § 165 allows a deduction, subject to limitations, for losses incurred in certain property transactions. The term *dealings in property* includes sales, exchanges, and other types of acquisitions or dispositions of property. This chapter examines the determination of the amount of gains and losses from dealings in property. Specific rules regarding gain recognition are addressed, as are the gain-deferral possibilities associated with certain installment sales. Various limitations on the deductibility of losses also are addressed.

Other topics dealing with property transactions are examined in the next three chapters. Chapter 15 deals with certain nontaxable exchanges. Chapter 16 covers the special treatment accorded gains and losses from sales or exchanges of capital assets. The unique rules governing the disposition of property used in a trade or business are examined in Chapter 17.

DETERMINATION OF GAIN OR LOSS

INTRODUCTION

Determining the gain or loss realized in a property transaction is usually a simple computation. It is the mathematical difference between the amount realized in a sale or other disposition and the adjusted basis of the property surrendered (see Exhibit 14-1). The amount realized is a measure of the consideration received in the transaction. It represents the economic value *realized* by the taxpayer.

Sale or other disposition essentially refers to any transaction in which a taxpayer realizes benefit in exchange for property. It is not necessary that there be a sale transaction or that cash be received for gain or loss to be realized by the taxpayer surrendering property other than cash.

The adjusted basis of purchased property is generally cost, plus or minus certain adjustments. Computing gain or loss realized is similar to determining gain or loss for accounting purposes, and adjusted basis is similar in concept to book value. However, the adjusted basis of a property will not always be, and frequently is not, equal to its book value for accounting purposes.

Exhibit 14-1 *Computation of Gain or Loss Realized*

Amount realized (See Exhibit 14-3)

− **Adjusted basis**

= **Gain or loss realized**

In effect, the adjusted cost, or adjusted basis, of a given property is the amount that can be recovered tax-free upon its disposition. For example, if property is sold for exactly its cost, as adjusted, there is no gain or loss realized. This concept is referred to as the *recovery of capital* or *recovery of basis* principle. If a taxpayer receives more than the adjusted basis in exchange for property, gain is realized only to the extent of that excess. The adjusted basis is recovered tax-free. The following examples illustrate this concept:

Example 1. K transferred 30 acres of land to ZX Company for $42,000 cash. K had purchased the 30 acres five years earlier for $35,000, which is his adjusted basis. As a result of this "sale or other disposition," K has a realized gain of $7,000 ($42,000 − $35,000). His $35,000 basis in the land is recovered tax-free.

Example 2. In 1992 L purchased 300 shares of W Corporation stock for $3,600 cash, including brokerage fees. When the market outlook for W Corporation's product began to weaken in 1994, L sold her shares for $3,100. The broker deducted a commission of $48 and forwarded $3,052 cash to her. L has a realized loss on this transaction of $548 ($3,052 − $3,600) in 1994.

Example 3. R transferred 200 shares of C Corporation stock worth $4,000 and $2,000 cash for an auto he will use for personal purposes. The C Corporation stock had been purchased two years earlier for $4,600. R realizes a loss of $600 [($6,000 − $2,000) − $4,600] on the "sale or other disposition" of the stock.

GENERAL RULE OF RECOGNITION

Any gain or loss realized must be recognized unless some provision of the Internal Revenue Code provides otherwise. A *recognized gain* is reported on a tax return. For example, a gain on the sale of stock generally is recognized in full in the year of sale (i.e., the gain is reported on a tax return, included in gross income, and considered in determining the tax liability for the year). In determining taxable income, the recognized gain is either offset against losses for the year or included in the computation of taxable income.[1]

---

[1] Capital gains must be offset by capital losses, and only net capital gains are included in taxable income. See the discussion of capital gains and losses in Chapter 16.

A *recognized loss* also is generally given its full tax effect in the year of realization. Depending on the type of loss, it may be either offset against gains or deducted against other forms of income in determining taxable income. Some losses, however, are not deductible[2] and others are limited.[3] For example, losses on the sale of property used for personal purposes are disallowed. Certain other losses are deferred to later tax years. Some examples of nontaxable exchanges are listed in Exhibit 14-2.

COMPUTING AMOUNT REALIZED

The amount realized from a sale or other disposition of property includes the amount of money received plus the fair market value of any other property received in a transaction. Other property includes both tangible and intangible property.

> **Example 4.** P received $20,000 and a motor home worth $80,000 in exchange for a sailing yacht that she had used for personal enjoyment. P's amount realized on the disposition of the yacht is $100,000 ($20,000 + $80,000).

The amount realized also includes any debt obligations of the buyer, and if the contract provides for inadequate interest or no interest, interest must be imputed and the sales price reduced accordingly.

> **Example 5.** Y sold his vintage Dodge automobile to C for $10,000 and a note payable from C to Y for $15,000 plus interest compounded monthly at 9%. Y's amount realized in this transaction is $25,000, the down payment plus the value of C's note.

> **Example 6.** Z sold a parcel of real estate for $100,000. Her basis in the land was $60,000. The sales contract called for $10,000 to be paid upon transfer of the property and the remaining $90,000 to be paid in full two years later.
> Since no interest was provided for in the contract, interest must be imputed on the buyer's $90,000 obligation (in this case, 9% interest, compounded semiannually, is used).[4] Accordingly, the sales price is reduced to $85,471 [$10,000 cash down payment + $75,471 (the discounted present value of the $90,000 payment in two years)]. Z will report an amount realized of $85,471 and a gain realized of $25,471 ($85,471 − $60,000 basis). When Z collects the $90,000, she must report interest income of $14,529 ($90,000 face value − $75,471 present value on date of sale).

---

[2] Losses on certain sales to related parties are disallowed under § 267, and losses on the sale of personal use property are not allowed under § 165(c).

[3] The deduction for capital losses is limited under § 1211(b).

[4] The actual rate is determined with reference to current market rates and is announced periodically by the IRS. For transactions involving $2.8 million or less, the rate cannot exceed 9 percent compounded semiannually.

Exhibit 14-2   *Partial List of Nontaxable Exchanges*

Type of Transaction	Action Required	Tax Result
Sale of Principal Residence	Reinvest in a New Principal Residence	Gain Is Deferred* See Chapter 15 and § 1034
Casualty, Theft, Condemnation (Involuntary Conversion)	Reinvest in Similar Property	Gain May Be Deferred* See Chapter 15 and § 1033
Like-Kind Exchange	Exchange Directly for Like-Kind Property	Gain or Loss Is Deferred* See Chapter 15 and § 1031
Formation of a Corporation or Subsequent Stock Issues	Transfer Property in Exchange for Stock by Controlling Shareholders	Gain or Loss Is Deferred* See § 351
Corporate Reorganizations	Examples Include Mergers, Consolidations, Divisions, Recapitalizations	Gain or Loss Is Deferred* See § 368
Partnership Formation	Transfer Property in Exchange for a Partnership Interest	Gain or Loss Is Deferred* See § 721

*When gain or loss is deferred, the deferral is only until the replacement property is sold or otherwise transferred (i.e., the deferred gain or loss is recognized along with any subsequent gain or loss when the replacement property is sold). In addition, a taxpayer who is at least 55 years of age and has owned and occupied his or her principal residence for three years may totally avoid tax on any gain on the sale of that residence up to $125,000.

The amount realized also includes the amount of any existing liabilities of the seller discharged in the transaction. Specifically, it includes any debts assumed by the buyer and any liabilities encumbering the property transferred that remain with the property in the buyer's hands.[5] Exhibit 14-3 illustrates the computation of *both* the amount realized and the gain or loss realized from the sale or other disposition of property.

---

[5] Reg. § 1.1001-2. Also, see the following discussion of the effect of liabilities in property transactions.

Exhibit 14-3   *Computation of Amount Realized and Gain or Loss Realized*

Amount realized:

	Amount of money received...................................	$xxx,xxx
Add:	Fair market value of other property received.............	+ x,xxx
	Liabilities discharged:	
	Liabilities assumed by the buyer......................	+ xx,xxx
	Liabilities encumbering the	
	property transferred................................	+ x,xxx
Less:	Selling expenses..	− xx,xxx
	Amount of money given up.............................	− x,xxx
	Liabilities incurred:	
	Liabilities assumed by the taxpayer...................	− xx,xxx
	Liabilities encumbering the property	
	received...	− x,xxx
Equals:	Amount realized..	$xxx,xxx
Less:	*Adjusted basis* in property other than	
	money given up...	− xx,xxx
Equals:	*Gain or loss realized*................................	$xxx,xxx

Example 7.   B purchased a rental house for $40,000 in 1986. She paid $8,000 down and signed a mortgage note for the balance. During the years she owned the property, B deducted depreciation totalling $16,000 and made principal payments on the note of $4,000, leaving a mortgage balance of $28,000.

During 1994 B sold the house for $62,000. The buyer paid $34,000 cash and assumed the $28,000 mortgage liability. B's amount realized is $62,000 ($34,000 cash + $28,000 relief of liability), and her adjusted basis is $24,000 ($40,000 cost reduced by $16,000 depreciation). Her gain realized is therefore $38,000 ($62,000 amount realized − $24,000 adjusted basis).

Any expenses of selling the property reduce the amount realized. Selling costs include many costs, paid by the seller, associated with offering a property for sale and transacting the sale. For example, selling costs include advertising expenses, appraisal fees, sales commissions, legal fees, transfer taxes, recording fees, and mortgage costs of the buyer paid by the seller.

BASIS DETERMINATION RULES

The adjusted basis of property may be determined in several ways, depending on how the property is acquired and whether any gain or loss is being deferred in the transaction. Various methods of acquiring property and their specific basis determination rules are discussed below.

PROPERTY ACQUIRED BY PURCHASE

Cost Basis.   In a simple purchase transaction, basis is the cost of the property acquired. Cost is the amount of money paid and the fair market value of any other property transferred in exchange for a given property.[6] The cost basis includes any payments made by the buyer with borrowed funds and any obligations (i.e., promissory notes) of the buyer given to the seller or any obligations of the seller assumed by the buyer in the exchange.[7]

Any costs of acquiring property are included in basis. For stock and securities, commissions, transfer taxes, and other acquisition costs are included. For other property, many types of acquisition costs, including commissions, legal fees related to purchase, recording fees, title insurance, appraisals, sales taxes, and transfer taxes, are added to basis.[8] Any installation and delivery costs also are part of basis.

> **Example 8.**   C purchased a new machine for his auto repair business during 1994. He paid $16,500 for the machine, $8,500 of which was made possible by a bank loan. In addition, C paid state sales taxes of $660, delivery charges of $325, and installation charges of $175. C's cost basis in the equipment is $17,660 ($16,500 purchase price + $660 sales taxes + $325 delivery charges + $175 installation charges).

Periodic operating costs such as interest and taxes are generally deducted in the year paid. However, a taxpayer may elect to *capitalize* (i.e., include in basis) certain taxes and interest related to unproductive and unimproved real property or related to real property during development or improvement rather than take a current tax deduction.[9]

> **Example 9.**   T purchased a small parcel of unimproved land near a lake known for its excellent fishing. She uses the property as a weekend retreat and plans someday to build a log cabin. T annually pays $150 for local property taxes but does not itemize deductions. T should elect to capitalize the property taxes paid each year as a part of her basis in the land.

---

[6] Reg. § 1.1012-1(a).

[7] § 1001 and *Crane v. Comm.*, 47-1 USTC ¶9217, 35 AFTR 776, 331 U.S. 1 (USSC, 1947).

[8] § 1012 and Reg. § 1.1012-1(a).

[9] § 266 and Reg. § 1.266-1(b)(1).

Identification Problems. Generally, the adjusted basis of property sold or otherwise transferred is easily traced to the acquisition of the property and certain subsequent events. However, identification of cost may be difficult if a taxpayer has multiple homogeneous assets. For example, if a taxpayer owns identical shares of stock in a corporation that were acquired in more than one transaction and sells less than his or her entire investment in that stock, it is necessary to identify which shares are sold. For tax purposes, the owner must use the *first-in, first-out* (FIFO) method of identification if it is impossible to identify which shares were sold. Specific identification of the shares sold is appropriate if the shares can be identified.[10]

Example 10. K purchased the following lots of G Corporation stock:

50 shares	Purchased 1/10/92	Cost $5,500
75 shares	Purchased 8/15/92	Cost $9,000
40 shares	Purchased 6/18/93	Cost $4,600

K sold 60 shares of her G Corporation stock in 1994 for $8,700. Unless she can specifically identify the shares sold, her basis will be determined using the FIFO method. Therefore, her basis in 50 shares sold is $5,500 and her basis in 10 shares sold is $1,200 [10 shares × $120 ($9,000 ÷ 75 shares)]. Her total gain is $2,000.

Example 11. Assuming the same facts in *Example 10*, the gain would be different if K could specifically identify the shares sold. If she directed her broker to deliver to the buyer the shares purchased on 8/15/92, referring to them by certificate number and date of purchase, her gain would be $1,500 [$8,700 sale price − $7,200 ($120 basis per share × 60)].

PROPERTY ACQUIRED BY GIFT

Generally, the basis of property received by gift is the same as the basis was to the donor.[11] This basis is *increased* by that portion of the gift tax paid by the donor, which is attributable to the appreciation in the property's value, if any, up to the date of the gift. The appreciation is measured by the difference between the fair market value of the property and the donor's adjusted basis in the property immediately before the gift.[12] The appropriate increase in basis for a given property is determined using the following formula:

$$\frac{\text{Fair market value} - \text{Donor's basis}}{\text{date of gift} \quad\quad \text{date of gift}} \times \text{Gift taxes paid}$$
$$\text{Fair market value} \atop \text{date of gift}$$

---

[10] Reg. § 1.1012-1(c).

[11] § 1015(a).

[12] § 1015(d)(6).

Gift tax returns must be filed annually. If there is more than one gift on the annual gift tax return, then the taxes paid on a *particular gift* bear the same proportion to the total gift taxes for the year as the value of that taxable gift bears to the total taxable gifts for the year.[13]

> **Example 12.** In 1994 P received a diamond necklace as a gift from her grandmother. The necklace had an adjusted basis to her grandmother of $12,000 and had a fair market value of $36,000 on the date of the gift. Gift taxes of $9,000 were paid. P's basis in the necklace is $18,000, including an adjustment for gift taxes of $6,000 ($9,000 gift taxes paid × [($36,000 − $12,000) ÷ $36,000]. If P sells the necklace for $39,000 in 1994, her gain will be $21,000 ($39,000 − $18,000).

> **Example 13.** If P, from the previous example, had sold the necklace for $15,000, she would have realized a loss of $3,000. The tax treatment of the loss depends on how she used the necklace. If she used the necklace for personal (rather than business or investment) purposes, then P would not be allowed to recognize the loss for tax purposes.

Loss Limitation Rule. Where the fair market value of the property *at the time of the gift* is less than the donor's basis, special rules must be applied to determine the basis for the donee. Perhaps the clearest expression of the rules in this case is as follows: the basis for *determining gain* is the donor's basis, while the basis for *determining loss* is the lower of either (1) the donor's basis or (2) the property's fair market value at the date of the gift.[14] Due to the way the rule for determining loss is stated, the donee will not recognize any gain or loss if the property is disposed of for any amount that *is less than* the donor's basis *but greater than* the value of the property at the date of the gift. These rules are illustrated in the following examples.

> **Example 14.** S received 200 shares of X Corporation stock as a gift from his uncle. The stock had a basis to the uncle of $32,000 and a fair market value on the date of the gift of $29,000. Gift taxes of $1,400 were paid on the transfer.
>
> During 1994 S sold all of the shares for $24,000. His loss realized on the sale is $5,000 ($24,000 sale price − $29,000 fair market value at date of gift). Note that S was not permitted to add any of the $1,400 gift taxes to his basis since such adjustments are allowed only if the fair market value is more than the donor's basis on the date of the gift (i.e., the property appreciated in the donor's hands).

---

[13] § 1015(d)(2).

[14] § 1015(a). It also should be noted that total depreciation claimed using the gain basis for computation cannot exceed the property's fair market value at date of gift. Reg. § 1.167(g)-1.

Example 15.   Assuming the same facts as in *Example 14,* if S had sold his stock for $31,000 he would not realize gain or loss on the sale. His basis for gain is $32,000 (the donor's basis) and his basis for loss is limited to $29,000 (fair market value on the date of the gift). Since the $31,000 sales price does not exceed the gain basis and is not less than his loss basis, neither gain nor loss is realized on the sale.

Example 16.   Assuming the same facts as in *Example 14,* if S's stock had been sold for $36,000, his realized gain would have been $4,000 ($36,000 sales price − $32,000 gain basis). There is no adjustment for gift taxes paid because the property did not appreciate in the donor's hands.

Application of these special rules illustrates *three* important points. First, *any gain* realized by the donee on a subsequent sale of the property is limited to the amount of gain that the donor would have realized had he or she sold it at the donee's sales price. Second, *any loss* allowed on a subsequent sale of the property is limited to the decline in the property's value that occurs while owned by the donee. Third, although the payment of a gift tax may be required as a result of the gift, the donee is not allowed to adjust the donor's basis in the property by any gift taxes paid because there is no appreciation in value of the property in the donor's hands (i.e., the fair market value of the property at the time of the gift is less than the donor's basis).

Gifts before 1977.   For gifts before 1977, the addition to the basis of property acquired by gift is the entire amount of gift taxes paid. The gift taxes, however, cannot be used to raise the basis above the fair market value of the property on the date of the gift.

Example 17.   B received a painting as a gift from her mother in 1975. The art work had a basis to her mother of $4,000 and a fair market value of $4,500. Gift taxes of $900 were paid on the gift. After further appreciation in the value of the painting, it was sold by B for $5,500 during the current year. Her realized gain is $1,000 [$5,500 sales price − $4,500 ($4,000 donor's basis + $500 of the gift taxes paid)].

Example 18.   Assuming the same facts as in *Example 17,* if the painting had a fair market value of $5,000 on the date of the gift, the entire $900 gift taxes paid would be allowed as a basis adjustment. If B sold the painting for $5,500, her realized gain would now be $600 ($5,500 sales price − $4,900 basis).

PROPERTY ACQUIRED FROM A DECEDENT

The adjusted basis of property acquired from a decedent generally is its fair market value on the date of the decedent's death.[15] This also is the value used in determining the taxable estate for estate tax purposes.[16] The fiduciary (executor or administrator) of the estate may, however, *elect* to value the estate for estate tax purposes six months after

---

[15]   § 1014(a).   [16]   § 2031(a).

the date of death.[17] This election is available only if (1) the estate is required to file a Federal estate tax return (Form 706), and (2) the alternate valuation reduces *both* the gross estate and the Federal estate tax.[18] If the fiduciary elects to use this alternate valuation date, the fair market value on the later date must also be used as the income tax basis to the heir or estate.[19]

> **Example 19.** D inherited some gold jewelry from his grandmother during 1993. The fair market value of the jewelry on the date of her death was $4,000 and its adjusted basis to the grandmother was $3,050. If D sells the jewelry in 1994 for $4,350, his realized gain will be $350 ($4,350 sale price − $4,000 basis).

> **Example 20.** If D, from the previous example, sells the jewelry for $3,000, he will have a realized loss of $1,000 ($3,000 − $4,000).

Exceptions to this basis rule are provided for *income in respect of a decedent* under § 691[20] and for certain property acquired by the decedent by gift. Income in respect of a decedent (often referred to as IRD) includes all items of income that the decedent had earned or was entitled to as of the date of death, but which were not included in the decedent's final income tax return under his or her method of accounting. For example, if a cash basis individual performed all the services required to earn a $3,000 consulting fee but had not collected the fee before his or her death, the $3,000 would be income in respect of a decedent. All IRD items are includible in the decedent's gross estate at fair market value for Federal estate tax purposes. Whoever receives the right to collect these items of income must report them in the same manner as the decedent would have been required to report them had he or she lived to collect the income. As a result, IRD items generally are fully included in the gross income of the recipient when received.[21]

If appreciated property was acquired by the decedent by gift within one year before his or her death and the property passes *back* to the donor or the donor's spouse, the recipient's adjusted basis is the decedent's adjusted basis.[22]

> **Example 21.** H transferred a parcel of lake-front real estate to his elderly grandmother when the property had an adjusted basis to H of $3,000 and a fair market value of $40,000. No gift taxes were paid on the transfer.
>
> H's grandmother died three months after the gift and left the lake-front property to H in her will. H's basis in the property is $3,000 (the rules used for gifted property apply rather than those for inherited property). If his grandmother had lived for more than a year after the gift was made, H's basis would have been determined under the general rule for property acquired from a decedent.

---

[17] § 2032(a).

[18] § 2032(c).

[19] § 1014(a)(2).

[20] § 1014(c).

[21] § 691(a)(1).

[22] § 1014(e).

Another exception is provided in the case of real property subject to special use valuation for Federal estate tax purposes. In such cases, the basis to the heir is the special value used for estate tax purposes. This special use valuation applies only to certain real property used in a trade or business and held by the heir more than 10 years.[23]

PROPERTY ACQUIRED IN A NONTAXABLE EXCHANGE

Most nontaxable exchanges provide deferral, rather than permanent nonrecognition of gain or loss. The mechanism for such deferral is typically an adjustment to the basis in some replacement property.[24] This adjustment is a reduction in basis in the case of a deferred gain and an increase in basis in the case of a deferred loss.

The specific rules for determining the basis of property acquired in nontaxable transactions, along with the requirements of each nontaxable transaction, are discussed in various parts of this text. Several such transactions are discussed in the next chapter. The following example illustrates one such transaction:

> **Example 22.** G sold his principal residence at a gain of $12,000. G met all requirements for total nonrecognition of gain under § 1034. He purchased a replacement residence for $74,000. His basis in the new residence is $62,000 ($74,000 replacement cost − $12,000 deferred gain).

PROPERTY CONVERTED FROM PERSONAL USE TO BUSINESS USE

Losses on the disposition of personal use properties are clearly not deductible. Absent some provision to the contrary, business owners could simply convert personal use assets to business use before disposing of them in order to generate business deductions for losses on their sale. Accordingly, when property is converted from personal use to trade or business use, its basis is limited for determining realized loss and for depreciation purposes. For each of those purposes, fair market value on the date of conversion is used as the property's basis if it is less than its adjusted basis.[25]

> **Example 23.** J owned a single-family home that had been her personal residence for four years. When J discontinued use of the house as her residence, she converted it to rental property. J's original basis in the property was $90,000, and the property was worth $86,000 on the date of conversion. J must determine any depreciation using the fair market value of $86,000, since it is less than her $90,000 adjusted basis. If the property is later sold, J's *gain basis* will be the original $90,000 adjusted basis reduced by the depreciation allowed after the conversion. Her *loss basis* will be the lower fair market value on the date of conversion, $86,000, reduced by the allowed depreciation. Note the similarity to the basis rules that would have applied if J had received the residence as a gift (see *Examples 14, 15,* and *16*).

---

[23] § 2032A(b).

[24] See, for example, § 1034(e), dealing with the sale of a principal residence.

[25] Reg. § 1.167(g)-1.

PROPERTY CONVERTED FROM BUSINESS USE TO PERSONAL USE

Once property is converted from business use to personal use, it is treated as personal use property. Any loss on the disposition of such property would, therefore, be disallowed; and, in the event that the property was subsequently converted back to business use, the limitations discussed above would apply.

> **Example 24.**   W has a photocopier used exclusively for business. The copier cost $4,000 and depreciation of $1,800 has been allowed, making its basis $2,200. If W converts the copier to personal and family use and later sells it for $500, no loss will be deductible. Of course, if W had immediately sold the copier at a loss rather than converting it to personal use, he would have a business loss.

ADJUSTMENTS TO BASIS

Regardless of the method used in determining a property's basis initially, certain adjustments are made to that basis. Generally, the adjustments can be broken down into three groups. Basis is *increased* by *betterments* or *improvements*[26] and *reduced* by *depreciation allowed* or *allowable*[27] and by *other capital recoveries*.[28]

Depreciation reduces basis regardless of whether it is actually deducted by the taxpayer. The *allowable depreciation* is determined using the straight-line method if no method is adopted by the taxpayer.[29]

Various types of *capital recoveries* also reduce a property's adjusted basis. The following are some of the specific items that reduce basis:

1.   Certain dividend distributions that are treated as a return of basis[30]

2.   Deductible losses with respect to property, such as casualty loss deductions[31]

3.   Credits for rehabilitation expenditures related to older commercial buildings and certified historic structures[32]

Numerous other events have an impact on a property's adjusted basis. Many of them are discussed in the remaining chapters of this text, which deal with specific types of transactions.

Exhibit 14-4 summarizes the rules for determining a property's adjusted basis.

---

[26] § 1016(a)(1).

[27] § 1016(a)(2).

[28] See following examples.

[29] § 1016(a)(2).

[30] § 1016(a)(4).

[31] See Reg. § 1.1016-6 and Rev. Rul. 74-206, 1974-1 C.B. 198.

[32] See §§ 46(a), 48(q), and 1016(a)(22).

Exhibit 14-4 *Determination of Adjusted Basis*

Method of Acquisition	Basis	Exceptions
General Rule		
Purchase	Cost	See special rules
Special Rules		
Acquired by gift	Donor's basis + gift taxes paid on appreciation	If fair market value at date of gift is less than donor's basis, use fair market value to determine loss
Acquired from a decedent	Fair market value at date of death (or alternate valuation date, if elected)	1) Income in respect of a decedent 2) Property given to the decedent by the donor/heir within one year of decedent's death 3) Property subject to special valuation under § 2032A
Converted from personal use	Adjusted basis before conversion	For determining loss and depreciation, use fair market value date of conversion if lower than original adjusted basis
Acquired in a nontaxable exchange	Fair market value less any gain not recognized or plus any loss deferred	

Note: The basis as determined under any of the above methods is subject to adjustments as provided by other provisions of the Code. Basis is increased by betterments or improvements and reduced by depreciation allowed or allowable and by other capital recoveries.

EFFECT OF LIABILITIES ON AMOUNT REALIZED

Mention has been made of the fact that the amount realized in a sale or other disposition of property includes the amount of any liabilities of the seller assumed by the buyer plus any liabilities encumbering the transferred property that remain with the property.[33] The amount realized from a transaction is reduced by any liabilities assumed by the seller plus any liabilities encumbering property received in the transaction that remain with the property. The basis of any property received includes the portion of the cost represented by the liabilities assumed by the seller or encumbering the property.[34]

Example 25.   B exchanges a vacant lot with an adjusted basis of $20,000 for a mountain cabin worth $75,000. B's vacant lot has a fair market value of $50,000 and is subject to a $15,000 mortgage. The mountain cabin B receives is subject to a mortgage of $40,000. B assumes the $40,000 mortgage on the mountain cabin and the other party to the exchange assumes the $15,000 mortgage on the vacant lot.

B's amount realized on this exchange is $50,000 ($75,000 fair market value of cabin received + $15,000 mortgage on vacant lot assumed by the other party − $40,000 mortgage on the mountain cabin assumed by B). If this exchange does not qualify for tax deferral, B has a realized and recognized gain of $30,000 ($50,000 amount realized − $20,000 adjusted basis of the vacant lot given up); and his basis in the mountain cabin is $75,000 (i.e., its fair market value).

Example 26.   D, the other party to the exchange in *Example 25,* had an adjusted basis in her mountain cabin of $65,000. D's amount realized on the exchange is $75,000 ($50,000 fair value of vacant lot received + $40,000 mortgage assumed by B − $15,000 mortgage on the vacant lot). If the exchange does not qualify for tax deferral, D has a realized and recognized gain of $10,000 ($75,000 amount realized − $65,000 adjusted basis in the mountain cabin given up); and her basis in the vacant lot is $50,000 (i.e., its fair market value).

The amount realized on a sale or exchange of property is affected by liabilities even though neither the buyer nor the seller is personally obligated for payment.[35] The rationale for such treatment is that the owner benefits from the nonrecourse liabilities as owner of the property because his or her basis in the property, or some other property, is properly increased because of the liability.[36]

---

[33]   Reg. § 1.1001-2(a)(1)

[34]   *Crane v. Comm.,* 47-1 USTC ¶9217, 35 AFTR 776, 331 U.S. 1 (USSC, 1947). Such liabilities are not included if they are contingent or not subject to valuation. Rev. Rul. 78-29, 1978-1 C.B. 62.

[35]   *Ibid.*

[36]   See *Tufts v. Comm.,* 83-1 USTC ¶9328, 51 AFTR2d 1983-1132, 461 U.S. 300 (USSC, 1983) for an excellent discussion of nonrecourse liabilities and their impact on basis.

CONCEPTS RELATED TO REALIZATION AND RECOGNITION

SALE OR OTHER DISPOSITION

Realization of gain or loss occurs upon any sale or other disposition of property. Whether such an event has occurred generally is not difficult to ascertain. A typical sale or exchange obviously constitutes a sale or other disposition, but other transactions in which the taxpayer surrenders property other than cash also may be so classified. The timing of such realization is determined according to the taxpayer's method of accounting. Under the accrual method, realization generally occurs when a transaction is closed and the seller has an unqualified right to collect the sales price.[37] Under the cash method, the taxpayer realizes gain or loss upon the receipt of cash or cash equivalents.[38] In any case, a sale is consummated and realization occurs if beneficial title or possession of the burdens and benefits of ownership are transferred to the buyer.[39]

Transactions Involving Certain Securities. Generally, a sale or other disposition occurs any time a taxpayer surrenders property in exchange for some consideration. Accordingly, if a taxpayer exchanges securities of one type for securities of another type, a taxable event has occurred.[40]

> **Example 27.** F exchanged X Corporation 12% bonds with a face value of $100,000 for Z Corporation 9% bonds with a face value of $120,000. Each group of bonds was worth $105,000 at the time of the exchange. If the X Corporation bonds that F exchanged had a basis of $100,000, he has a $5,000 gain on the exchange.

Several exceptions to this scheme do exist. In some instances, the exchange of *substantially identical* bonds of state or municipal governments has been declared a nontaxable transfer.[41] The condition of being substantially identical is usually determined in terms of rate of return and fair market value. If the bonds received do not meet this test, the exchange may be taxable.[42]

It is clearly established that converting bonds into stock under a conversion privilege contained in the bond instrument does not result in the recognition of gain.[43] Similarly, the conversion of stock into some other stock of the same corporation pursuant to a right granted under the stock certificate does not result in recognition of gain or loss.[44]

---

[37] See *Alfred Scully,* 20 TCM 1272, T.C. Memo 1961-243 (1961), and Rev. Rul. 72-381, 1972-2 C.B. 581.

[38] See, for example, *Comm. v. Union Pacific R.R. Co.,* 36-2 USTC ¶9525, 18 AFTR 636, 86 F.2d 637 (CA-2, 1936).

[39] *Ibid.*

[40] Rev. Rul. 60-25, 1960-1 C.B. 283, and Rev. Rul. 78-408, 1978-2 C.B. 203.

[41] *Motor Products Corp. v. Comm.,* 44-1 USTC ¶9308, 32 AFTR 672, 142 F.2d 449 (CA-6, 1944), and Rev. Rul. 56-435, 1956-2 C.B. 506.

[42] See *Emery v. Comm.,* 48-1 USTC ¶9165, 36 AFTR 741, 166 F.2d 27 (CA-2, 1948), and Rev. Rul. 81-169, 1981-25 I.R.B. 17. Also, see *Mutual Loan and Savings Co. v. Comm.,* 50-2 USTC ¶9420, 39 AFTR 1034, 184 F.2d 161 (CA-5, 1950) for an example of nonrecognition where the state Supreme Court held the new bonds with a lower interest rate to be a mere continuation of the original issue.

[43] Rev. Rul. 57-535, 1957-2 C.B. 513.

[44] Ltr. Rul., 2-23-45, ¶76,130 P-H Fed. 1945.

Transfer Related to Taxpayer's Debt.   When property is transferred to a creditor, the transfer may or may not be a disposition. The mere granting of a lien against property to secure a loan is not a disposition.[45] The transfer of property in satisfaction of a liability, however, is a taxable disposition.[46] Similarly, the loss of property in a foreclosure sale[47] and the voluntary transfer of mortgaged property to creditors in satisfaction of debt [48] are dispositions of property.

> **Example 28.**   M purchased a commercial property for $20,000, paying $4,000 down and signing a note secured by a mortgage for the $16,000 difference. Three years later, when M had reduced the balance on the note to $7,000, the lender accepted 300 shares of T Corporation stock in satisfaction of the obligation. The T Corporation stock had a fair market value of $7,000 and an adjusted basis to M of $5,000. Because of this disposition of stock, M has a $2,000 realized gain. Note that this result is the same as if M had sold the stock for $7,000 cash and paid the balance on the note.

> **Example 29.**   K purchased a warehouse for use in her business for $30,000, paying $5,000 down and signing a nonrecourse note (K is not personally liable) secured by a mortgage lien for the $25,000 difference. Over a three-year period, K's business suffered a decline and as a result she was able to make payments of only $3,000 on the note. During the same three-year period, K deducted depreciation of $12,000, thereby reducing her basis in the warehouse to $18,000.
>
> After the three years, K reduced the size of her business substantially and voluntarily transferred the warehouse to the lender. Upon the transfer, K's amount realized from the discharge of the remaining indebtedness is $22,000 ($25,000 original note − $3,000 payments). Since her basis in the warehouse was $18,000, K has a $4,000 realized gain on the disposition of the property.

Abandonment.   The abandonment of property used in a business or income-producing activity, whether depreciable or not, results in realization of loss to the extent of the property's adjusted basis. A loss deduction is allowed if the taxpayer takes action that demonstrates that he or she has no intention of retrieving the property for use, for sale, or other disposition in the future.[49]

> **Example 30.**   While working in a logging operation, R's truck became unoperational, and it was clear that the cost of having the truck moved to a repair site exceeded its value. R abandoned the truck with no intention of seeking its return. If R has a $2,500 adjusted basis in the truck, he is entitled to an abandonment loss deduction of $2,500.

---

[45] See *Dorothy Vickers,* 36 TCM 391, T.C. Memo 1977-90.

[46] *Carlisle Packing Co.,* 29 B.T.A. 514 (1933), and Rev. Rul. 76-111, 1976-1 C.B. 214 (1976).

[47] *O'Dell & Sons Co., Inc.,* 8 T.C. 1165 (1947).

[48] *Estate of Delman,* 73 T.C. 15 (1979).

[49] Reg. §§ 1.165-2 and 1.167(a)-8.

Demolition. No deduction is allowed for expenses related to the demolition of a building or for a loss where the adjusted basis of the building exceeds any salvage value. Both the cost of the demolition and any disallowed loss are added to the basis of the land on which the building stood.[50]

> **Example 31.** T purchased a rezoned commercial lot with a small house for $75,000. The structure was worth $2,000. In order to expedite construction of a new car wash, T simply razed the house at a cost of $1,500. No deduction is allowed for the loss of the house or the razing cost, and T's basis in the vacant lot is $76,500 ($73,000 lot + $2,000 house + $1,500 demolition costs).

Spousal Transfers. The transfer of property to one's spouse while married or as a result of dissolution of the marriage does not constitute a taxable event. This is true even if the transfer is in exchange for the release of marital rights under state law or for some other consideration. This rule applies to *any* transfer made to one's spouse during the marriage or within *one year* after the marriage is terminated. It also applies to later transfers to a former spouse if the transfers are made incident to the divorce (e.g., under a provision of the divorce decree).[51] In a consistent manner, the basis of the transferred property for the transferee (recipient) is the same as the transferor's basis.[52]

It is important to note that this nonrecognition provision applies to all transfers between spouses—including the sale of property at a fair market price. Additionally, the transferor is required to provide the transferee with records needed to determine the basis and holding period of the property.[53]

> **Example 32.** H and W were divorced this year. Under the terms of their agreement, H received marketable securities with a basis of $16,000 and a value of $10,000. W received the house with a basis of $80,000, valued at $96,000 and subject to a mortgage of $60,000. No gain or loss is recognized by either party regardless of who owned the property before the transfer. H and W have bases in their separate properties of $16,000 and $80,000, respectively.

> **Example 33.** Under an option provided in their divorce agreement, W (from the previous example) sold the house to H six months later (subject to the mortgage obligation) for $36,000. W still recognizes no gain and H's basis in the residence is $80,000.

Gift or Bequest. A transfer of property by gift or bequest generally does not constitute a sale or other disposition. Accordingly, there is no gain or loss recognized by the donor or decedent, respectively. An exception exists, however, in the case of a sale of property at a price below its fair market value. In such a *part-gift* and *part-sale,* the donor recognizes gain *only* to the extent the sales price exceeds the adjusted basis of the property transferred.[54]

---

[50] § 280B.

[51] §§ 1041(a) and (c).

[52] § 1041(b)(2).

[53] Temp. Reg. § 1.1041-1T(e).

[54] Reg. § 1.1015-4(d).

Example 34.   M sold her personal automobile to her brother for $4,000. She had a basis of $12,000 in the auto which was worth $6,000 on the date of sale. M has made a gift of $2,000 in this part-sale/part-gift transaction and she recognizes no gain or loss.

Example 35.   Assume the same facts above, except that M's basis in the auto had been reduced to $3,000 from depreciation deductions allowed in prior years. Although M has still made a $2,000 gift in this transaction, she must now recognize a $1,000 gain on the sale ($4,000 amount realized − $3,000 adjusted basis).

If the donee/buyer pays some cash and assumes debt of the donor/seller, or takes the property subject to encumbrances, the amount of the liabilities must be included by the donor/seller in the amount realized from the transaction.[55] Even if no cash changes hands, the part-gift and part-sale rules apply if there are liabilities associated with the transfer. Accordingly, if the donee assumes liabilities that exceed the donor's basis in the transferred property, the donor has taxable gain to the extent the liabilities exceed such basis.[56] Also, the donee/purchaser will take as his or her basis in the property acquired the *greater* of the basis under the gift rules or the purchase (cost) basis.

Example 36.   F gave a duplex rental unit to her grandson for his 18th birthday so he could develop property management skills. The duplex had a basis to F of $22,000 and a fair market value on the date of the gift of $40,000. The property was subject to a mortgage of $25,000, for which the grandson is now responsible. F has an amount realized on the gift transaction of $25,000 (transfer of the mortgage). Since the adjusted basis of the duplex was $22,000, F has a $3,000 taxable gain. If no gift taxes were paid, the grandson's basis in the duplex will be $25,000, the greater of the basis under the gift rules ($22,000) or the purchase (cost) basis.

Example 37.   If the property in the previous example had been subject to a mortgage of only $8,000, the general rule would have applied, and F would not have recognized gain or loss. The exception only applies when the discharged liabilities exceed the adjusted basis of the gifted property. Note also that the grandson's basis in the duplex would be $22,000, the same basis F had in the property.

---

[55]   *Reginald Fincke*, 39 B.T.A. 510 (1939).

[56]   *Levine Est. v. Comm.*, 80-2 USTC ¶9607, 46 AFTR2d, 80-5349, 634 F.2d 12 (CA-2, 1980).

Transfer of Property to Charities. The transfer of property to a charity generally is not treated as a sale or other disposition. Accordingly, no gain or loss is realized or recognized. However, an exception is provided for *bargain sales* of property to charities that result in a charitable contribution deduction to the seller. In such a case, the adjusted basis of the transferred property must be allocated between the sale portion and the contribution portion based on the fair market value of the property—and any resulting gain must be recognized.[57]

> **Example 38.** P sold land to her church for $30,000. P had an adjusted basis in the land of $25,000. The land was appraised at $50,000 at the time of the bargain sale. P is entitled to a charitable contribution deduction of $20,000 ($50,000 fair market value − $30,000 sale price). She also has taxable gain of $15,000 on the sale ($30,000 amount realized − the $15,000 pro rata share of the adjusted basis allocable to the sale portion [($30,000 sale price ÷ $50,000 fair market value) × $25,000 basis].

A charitable contribution of encumbered property is also treated as a bargain sale. The amount realized includes the amount of cash and the fair market value of any other property received plus the amount of the liabilities transferred. Accordingly, the property's adjusted basis must be allocated between the sale portion (represented by the amount realized) and the contribution portion.[58] This is true even if no cash or other property is received by the taxpayer.[59]

> **Example 39.** E made a gift of land to his alma mater. The land had a fair market value of $50,000 and was subject to a $22,000 mortgage which was assumed by the university. If the land is a long-term capital asset, E is entitled to a charitable contribution deduction of $28,000 ($50,000 fair market value reduced by the $22,000 mortgage).[60]
>
> Additionally, E's $20,000 adjusted basis in the property must be allocated between the contribution of $28,000 and the amount realized of $22,000. The basis allocated to the sale portion is $8,800 [$20,000 basis × ($22,000 amount realized ÷ $50,000 fair market value)]. The result of the bargain sale is a taxable gain to E of $13,200 ($22,000 amount realized − $8,800 allocated basis).

ALLOCATIONS OF PURCHASE PRICE AND BASIS

Properties purchased in a single transaction are often sold separately. In such a situation, the total basis must be allocated between the various items in order to determine gain or loss on the independent sales. Generally, relative fair market values at the time of

---

[57] § 1011(b); Reg. § 1.1011-2(a).

[58] See Reg. § 1.1011-2(a).

[59] *Winston Guest,* 77 T.C. 9 (1981) and Rev. Rul. 81–163, 1981-1 C.B. 433.

[60] See Chapter 11 for a discussion of charitable contributions involving long-term capital gain property.

acquisition are used to allocate the total basis among the various properties.[61] Similarly, allocation is necessary when a single sale involves properties acquired at different times in separate transactions. It may be necessary to allocate the sales price to individual assets; in such a situation, the relative fair market values on the date of sale are used for the allocation. Generally, an allocation in the sale agreement between buyer and seller will sufficiently establish the relative values unless it is shown that such assigned values were arbitrary or unreasonable.[62]

> **Example 40.**   T purchased a commercial lot in 1986 for $30,000 and built a warehouse on the site in 1989 at a cost of $60,000. During the six years he used the warehouse in his business, T deducted depreciation of $32,000. The property was sold in 1994 for $110,000. T must allocate the $110,000 sale price between the building and the land to determine the gain or loss on each. If $40,000 is allocated to the land and $70,000 is allocated to the building based on relative fair market values, T has a gain of $10,000 ($40,000 − $30,000) and $42,000 [$70,000 − ($60,000 − $32,000)], respectively, on the properties.

Sale of a Business.   When a business operated as a sole proprietorship is sold, the sale is treated as a sale of each of the individual assets of the business. Accordingly, allocations of sales price and basis must be made to the individual assets of the business.[63] The various gains and losses have separate impact, according to their character, on the taxable income of the owner.

> **Example 41.**   F has owned and operated a convenience store for 12 years. F's increased interest in her grandchildren and in fishing prompted her to sell the store and retire. The sales agreement with the buyer allocated the total sales price to the individual assets as follows:

	Value per Sales Agreement	F's Adjusted Basis
Inventory.........................	$16,000	$18,000
Furniture and fixtures..............	14,000	6,000
Leasehold and leasehold improvements...................	20,000	3,000
Goodwill..........................	0	0
Total............................	$50,000	$27,000

[61]   See, for example, *Fairfield Plaza, Inc.*, 39 T.C. 706 (1963), and Rev. Rul. 72-255, 1972-1 C.B. 221.

[62]   See *John B. Resler*, 38 TCM 153, T.C. Memo 1979-40.

[63]   See Rev. Rul. 55-79, 1955-1 C.B. 370, and *Williams v. McGowan*, 46-1 USTC ¶9120, 34 AFTR 615, 152 F.2d 570 (CA-2, 1945).

F has a $2,000 loss on the sale of inventory, and gains on the furniture and fixtures of $8,000 and on the leasehold and improvements of $17,000, each of which has its separate impact on taxable income.

The sale of an interest in a partnership or in a corporation that operates a business is generally treated as the sale of such interest, rather than of the underlying assets. Therefore, no allocation is necessary and gain or loss is recognized on the sale of the interest. For each type of entity, major exceptions to this treatment exist and are discussed in a later chapter.[64]

INSTALLMENT SALE METHOD

The general rule of Federal taxation is that all gains or losses are recognized in the year of sale or exchange. This rule could place a severe burden on taxpayers who sell their property for something other than cash, particularly deferred payment obligations. Without some relief, taxpayers would be required to pay their tax liability before obtaining the sale proceeds with which they could pay the tax. If the tax is substantial, a requirement to pay before sufficient cash collections occur might necessitate the sale of other assets the taxpayer wished to retain.

Because of the potential hardship placed on taxpayers from reporting gain without the corresponding receipt of cash, Congress enacted the installment sale method of reporting in 1926. The installment method has been significantly modified over the years, with each modification further restricting *both* the types of gains and the taxpayers eligible for its use. The eligibility requirements are discussed below.

GENERAL RULES

The installment method is used to report *gains*—not losses—from qualifying installment sales of property. An *installment sale* is defined as any sale of property whereby the seller will receive at least one payment after the close of the tax year in which the sale occurs. Unfortunately, not all gains from installment sales qualify for installment reporting.

Ineligible Sales. Currently, use of the installment method is denied for reporting gains from sales of the following:[65]

1. Property held for sale in the ordinary course of the taxpayer's trade or business (e.g., inventories)

2. Depreciable property if the depreciation recapture rules require some or all of the gain to be reported as ordinary income (see Chapter 17 for a discussion of these rules)

3. Stocks or securities that are traded on an established securities market

---

[64] See Chapter 19 for an introduction to both corporate and partnership taxation.

[65] §§ 453(b), (i), and (l). See § 453(l)(2) for certain limited exceptions.

Mandatory Reporting Requirement. Generally, gains from eligible sales *must* be reported under the installment method regardless of the taxpayer's method of accounting.[66] Thus, the installment method is considered to be *mandatory* rather than elective. However, Congress recognized the fact that for some taxpayers the installment method of reporting would not be the relief measure that it was intended to be. Consequently, taxpayers are allowed to *elect out* of the installment method simply by reporting the entire gain in the year of sale.[67]

ELECTION OUT OF INSTALLMENT REPORTING

There are various reasons why a taxpayer might wish to elect not to use the installment method of reporting gain from the sale of property. Such reasons might include the following:

1.   The taxpayer's income in the year of sale is quite low and income is expected to be higher in subsequent years.

2.   The taxpayer might have a large capital loss with which to absorb the capital gain in the year of sale.

3.   The taxpayer might have an expiring net operating loss.

4.   It might be necessary for the taxpayer to report the gain in order to utilize a tax credit carryover.

5.   The burden of complying with the installment sale rules might outweigh the advantage of the installment reporting of the gain.

If a taxpayer *elects not to use* the installment method for a given sale, the amount of gain must be computed under his or her usual method of accounting (i.e., cash or accrual) and reported in the year of sale.[68] A cash basis taxpayer must use the *fair market value* of any installment obligation received in determining the amount realized from the installment sale.[69] On the other hand, an accrual basis taxpayer must account for an installment obligation at its *face value* in computing the amount realized.[70]

---

[66]   § 453(a).

[67]   See § 453(d) and Temp. Reg. § 15a.453-1(d)(2)(ii).

[68]   *Ibid*.

[69]   § 1001(b).

[70]   Rev. Rul. 79-292, 1979-2 C.B. 287.

Example 42.   S, a cash basis taxpayer, sold land to B on December 15, 1994. S received $100,000 cash and a note from B payable in five equal annual installments of $80,000 (i.e., face value), bearing a 9% interest rate. The note has a fair market value of $300,000 and S has a $75,000 basis in the land. If S elects not to use the installment method, his gain to be reported in 1994 is computed as follows:

Amount realized:		
Cash received......................	$100,000	
FMV of installment obligations......	300,000	
	$400,000	
Less: Basis of land.................	(75,000)	
Gain to be reported in 1994...........	$325,000	

In addition to the interest income that S will recognize when the installment payments are collected, he must recognize additional income on the collection of each installment payment as follows:

Amount realized (installment payment)......	$80,000
Less: Basis in each installment	
($300,000 FMV of note ÷ 5	
installments)..........................	(60,000)
Ordinary income to be reported............	$20,000

Example 43.   Assume the same facts as in *Example 42,* except that S is an accrual basis taxpayer. His gain to be reported in the year of sale is computed as follows:

Amount realized:	
Cash received...........................	$100,000
Face value of installment obligations......	400,000
	$500,000
Less: Basis in land......................	(75,000)
Gain to be reported in 1994.................	$425,000

In this case, S will not be required to report any income other than the interest received as each of the payments are collected because his basis in each installment obligation is $100,000 (i.e., its face amount).

GAIN REPORTED UNDER THE INSTALLMENT METHOD

The following *six* factors must be taken into account by a taxpayer using the installment method of reporting gain:

1.   The gross profit on the sale

2.   The total contract price

3. The gross profit percentage

4. The payments received in the year of sale

5. The gain to be reported in the year of sale

6. The gain to be reported in the following years

Determining Gross Profit.   A taxpayer's gross profit is nothing more than the total gain that will be reported (excluding interest) from the installment sale. It is determined by subtracting the *sum* of the seller's adjusted basis and expenses of sale from the selling price:[71]

Selling price...............................	$xxx,xxx
Less: Adjusted basis in property *plus* selling expenses.................	− xx,xxx
Gross profit on sale........................	$ xx,xxx

Determining the Total Contract Price.   The total contract price is the total amount of cash (excluding interest) that the seller expects to collect from the buyer over the term of the installment sale. It is usually equal to the selling price less any liabilities of the seller that are transferred to the buyer. However, if the liabilities assumed by the buyer *exceed* the seller's adjusted basis in the property and the selling expenses, the excess must be treated as a *deemed payment* received in the year of sale. Because a deemed payment is treated as cash collected in the year of sale, it must be added to the contract price.[72]

Determining Gross Profit Percentage.   The taxpayer's gross profit percentage is the percentage of each dollar received that must be reported as gain. It is equal to the gross profit divided by the total contract price.[73]

$$\frac{\text{Gross profit}}{\text{Total contract price}} = \text{Gross profit percentage}$$

Determining Payments Received in Year of Sale.   Payments received in the year of sale include the following:[74]

1. Money received at the time of closing the sale, including any selling expenses *paid* by the buyer

2. Deemed payments (i.e., excess of seller's liabilities transferred over the property's adjusted basis plus selling expenses)

3. The fair market value of any third-party obligations received at the time of closing and the fair market value of any other property received

4. Installment payments received in the year of sale, excluding interest income

---

[71] Temp. Reg. § 15a.453-1(b)(2)(v).

[72] § 453A(a)(2) and Temp. Reg. § 15a.453-1(b)(2)(ii).

[73] § 453(c) and Temp. Reg. § 15a.453-1(b)(2)(i).

[74] Temp. Reg. § 15a.453-1(b)(3)(i).

Gain Reported in Year of Sale.   Gain reported in the year of sale is computed as follows:

$$\frac{\text{Gross profit}}{\text{Total contract price}} \times \text{Payments received} = \text{Recognized gain}$$

Gain Reported in Following Years.   Gain to be reported in the years following the year of sale equals the taxpayer's gross profit percentage multiplied by the principal payments received on the purchaser's note in that year.

Example 44.   T sold a 70-acre tract of land that she had held as an investment on March 1, 1994. The facts concerning the sale are as follows:

Sales price:		
Cash payment............................	$120,000	
Mortgage assumed by buyer.............	200,000	
Buyer's notes payable to T...............	480,000	$800,000
Less: Selling expenses.....................	$ 50,000	
T's basis in land......................	250,000	(300,000)
Gross profit on sale........................		$500,000

The contract price is $600,000 ($800,000 sales price − $200,000 debt assumed by buyer). Assuming the $120,000 payment is the only payment received in 1994, T's gain to be reported for the year is computed as follows:

$$\frac{\$500,000\ \text{(gross profit)}}{\$600,000\ \text{(contract price)}} \times \$120,000 = \$100,000 \text{ gain to be recognized}$$

As T collects the remaining $480,000 of the total contract price, she will report the remaining $400,000 gross profit from the sale (i.e., $480,000 $\times \frac{5}{6}$ gross profit percentage = $400,000).

Example 45.   Assume the same facts as in *Example 44*, except that T's basis in the land is only $100,000. In this case, the gross profit on the sale is $650,000 [$800,000 − ($50,000 + $100,000)]. T's payments received in the year of sale are computed as follows:

Cash payment...............................		$120,000
Plus: deemed payment received:		
Mortgage assumed by buyer...........	$200,000	
Less: Selling expenses.................	(50,000)	
T's basis in land.................	(100,000)	50,000
Total payments received in 1994............		$170,000

The total contract price is $650,000 ($800,000 selling price − $200,000 mortgage transferred + $50,000 excess of mortgage assumed over T's basis in property and selling expenses). T's gain to be reported in 1994 is computed as follows:

$$\frac{\$650,000 \text{ (gross profit)}}{\$650,000 \text{ (contract price)}} \times \$170,000 \text{ payments} = \$170,000$$

Note that the excess of the mortgage transferred over T's basis in the land and the selling expenses (i.e., the deemed payment) causes the gross profit percentage to become 100%. This adjustment to *both* the total contract price and the payments received in the year of sale must be made to ensure that the entire gain from the sale is ultimately reported by the seller. As a result, all payments received by T in subsequent years (excluding interest) will be reported as gain from the sale [$650,000 total gross profit − $170,000 gain reported in year of sale = $480,000 gain to be reported in subsequent years ($480,000 buyer's notes × 100%)].

LIMITATIONS ON CERTAIN INSTALLMENT SALES

As mentioned earlier, the installment sales provisions have been modified over the years to limit or stop perceived taxpayer abuse of what was intended to be simply a relief from immediate taxation of all gain from deferred payment sales. These modifications have created the following problem areas:

1. Imputed interest rules

2. Related-party rules

3. Gain recognition on dispositions of installment notes

4. Required interest payments on deferred taxes

Each of these problem areas is discussed below.

Imputed Interest Rules.   Without some limitation, a taxpayer planning a deferred payment sale of a capital asset could require the buyer to pay a higher sales price in return for a lower than prevailing market rate of interest on the deferred payments, thereby converting into capital gain what would have been ordinary (interest) income. The imputed interest rules were designed to prevent just such a scheme. Under these rules, any deferred payment sale of property with a selling price exceeding $3,000 must provide a *reasonable* interest rate.[75] Thus, in a deferred payment sale providing little or no interest, the selling price must be *restated* to equal the sum of payments received on the date of the sale and the discounted present value of the future payments. The difference between the face value of the future payments and this discounted value (i.e., the imputed interest) generally must be reported as interest income under the accrual method of accounting, regardless of the taxpayer's regular accounting method.[76]

---

[75]   See §§ 483 and 1274.

[76]   See §§ 1272(a), 1273(a), and 1274(a). Also see §§ 483 and 1274(c) for various exceptions to this requirement.

If the sales contract does not provide for interest equal to the *applicable Federal rate* (AFR), interest will be imputed at that rate.[77] The AFR is the interest rate the Federal government pays on borrowed funds, and the actual rate varies with the terms of the loan. Loans are divided into short-term (not over three years), mid-term (over three years but not over nine years), and long-term (over nine years).[78]

> **Example 46.** S, a cash basis taxpayer, sold land held as an investment on July 1, 1994 for $1 million cash and a non–interest-bearing note (face value of $4 million) due on July 1, 1996. At the time of the sale, the short-term AFR was 10% (compounded semiannually). Because the sales contract did not provide for interest of at least the AFR, the selling price must be restated and interest must be imputed at 10% (compounded semiannually).
>
> | | |
> |---|---|
> | Sale price: | |
> | Cash payment................................ | $1,000,000 |
> | Present value of $4,000,000 note due | |
> | July 1, 1996 (0.8264 × $4,000,000).... | 3,305,600 |
> | Recomputed sale price..................... | $4,305,600 |
>
> S must use this recomputed sale price in determining the total contract price, gross profit percentage, gain to be reported in the year of sale, and gain to be reported (excluding interest) when the $4 million deferred payment is received. In addition, S must report $165,280 of imputed interest income in 1994, computed as follows:
>
> | Period | Present Value | × | 10% Compounded Semiannually | = | Imputed Interest |
> |---|---|---|---|---|---|
> | 7/1/94 to 12/31/94 | $3,305,600 | × | 0.05 | = | $165,280 |
>
> S must also compute and report her imputed interest for 1995 and 1996. When the $4 million note payable is collected on July 1, 1996, S will report only the gain on the sale remaining after that portion reported in 1994.

Related-Party Sales. Generally, installment sales between related parties are subject to the same rules as other such sales *except* (1) when the related-party purchaser resells the property before payment of the original sales price;[79] and (2) when the property sold is depreciable property.[80] The primary purpose of the *resale* rule is to prevent a related-party seller from deferring his or her gain on the first sale while the related-party purchaser enjoys the use of proceeds from its resale.

---

[77] § 1274(d)(1).

[78] These three Federal rates are published monthly by the IRS.

[79] § 453(e).

[80] § 453(g).

Example 47. M plans to sell a capital asset (basis $40,000) to B, an unrelated party, for $200,000. Instead of selling the asset to B, she sells it to her son, S, for $10,000 cash and a $190,000 note due in five years and bearing a reasonable interest rate. Shortly after his purchase, S sells the asset to B for $200,000.

Without the resale rule, M would report a gain of $8,000 in the year of sale, computed as follows:

$$\frac{\$200,000 - \$40,000}{\$200,000} \times \$10,000 = \$8,000$$

M would have a deferred gain of $152,000 ($160,000 gross profit − $8,000 gain reported in year of sale). More importantly, S would have a cost basis of $200,000 in the asset and report no gain on the subsequent resale to B. The net result of the two transactions is a $152,000 deferred gain and the immediate use of the sales proceeds by a family member.

Under the resale rule, any proceeds collected by the related-party purchaser on the subsequent sale are treated as being collected by the related-party seller. Consequently, M must report her $152,000 deferred gain when S resells the property, even though she has not yet collected the $190,000 note.

For purposes of the resale rule, the term *related party* includes the spouse, children, grandchildren, and parents of the seller.[81] Any controlled corporation, partnership, trust, or estate in which the seller has an interest is also considered related under these rules.[82] It is also important to note that the resale rule does not apply when the second sale occurs (1) more than two years after the first sale, or (2) after the death of the related-party seller.[83]

The installment method is generally not allowed to be used to report a gain on the sale of depreciable property to an entity controlled by the taxpayer.[84] This rule is designed to prevent a related-party seller from deferring gain on a sale that will result in the purchaser's being able to use a higher (cost) basis to claim depreciation deductions. For this purpose, a *controlled entity* is a partnership or corporation in which the seller owns a more than 50 percent direct or indirect interest. Indirect ownership includes any interest owned by the seller's spouse and certain other family members.[85] It is important to note that this rule is based on a presumption that the related-party installment sale is motivated by tax avoidance. Thus, the related-party seller can use the installment method of reporting the sale if he or she can establish that tax avoidance *was not* the principal motive of the transaction. This makes such a sale subject to a facts and circumstances review and approval of the Internal Revenue Service.

---

[81] §§ 453(f) and 267(b).

[82] §§ 453(f) and 318(a).

[83] § 453(e)(2).

[84] *Supra*, footnote 80.

[85] §§ 1239(b) and (c).

Dispositions of Installment Obligations. After deciding to report a deferred payment sale under the installment method, rather than *electing out,* sellers ordinarily collect the payments in due course and report the remaining gain in full. However, if this process is interrupted by a sale, gift, or other transfer of some or all of the installment obligations, rules require that any unreported gain be reported at the time of the transfer. Consequently, if an installment obligation is satisfied at other than its face value or is distributed, transmitted, sold, or otherwise disposed of, the taxpayer is generally required to recognize gain or loss.

The amount of gain or loss is the difference between the obligation's basis and *either* the amount realized, if the obligation is satisfied at an amount other than its face value because it is sold or exchanged, *or* its fair market value when distributed, transmitted, or disposed of, if the transfer is not a sale or exchange.[86] The obligation's basis is its face amount less the amount of gain that would have been reported if the obligation had been satisfied in full.[87]

Taxable dispositions include most sales and exchanges. Also included are gifts, transfers to trusts, distributions by trusts and estates to beneficiaries, distributions from corporations to shareholders, net proceeds from the pledge of an installment obligation, and cancellation of the installment obligation.

The obvious purpose of the disposition rules is to prevent the seller from *either* shifting the income to another taxpayer (e.g., by gift) *or* enjoying the use of the sales proceeds prior to gain recognition (e.g., by pledging an installment obligation for borrowed funds). However, there are several exceptions to the requirement of immediate gain recognition. Transfers of installment obligations upon the death of the seller, transfers incident to divorce, transfers to or distributions from a partnership, certain transfers to controlled corporations, and certain transfers incident to corporate reorganization are among the exceptions to these rules.[88]

Required Interest Payments on Deferred Taxes. Another rule designed to reduce the benefits of installment reporting for certain taxpayers is the requirement to pay interest to the government on the deferred taxes. This rule applies if *two conditions* are met. First, the taxpayer must have outstanding installment obligations from the sale of property (other than farming property) for more than $150,000. Second, the outstanding obligations from such sales must exceed $5 million at the close of the tax year.[89] Only the deferred taxes attributable to the installment obligations in *excess* of $5 million are subject to this annual interest payment. The interest must be calculated using the tax underpayment rate in § 6621.

> **Example 48.** T has $9 million of installment obligations outstanding on December 31, 1994. These obligations arose from the sale of a vacant lot located in the downtown area of Chicago. T's gross profit percentage on the installment sale was

---

[86] § 453B(a).

[87] § 453B(b).

[88] See §§ 453B(c), (d), and (g).

[89] § 453A.

40%. Assuming the underpayment rate in § 6621 is 10% and T's 1994 marginal tax rate is 31%, the required interest payment on the deferred taxes is computed as follows:

Outstanding installment obligations............................	$9,000,000
Less: Amount not subject to rule............................	(5,000,000)
Excess installment obligations.................................	$4,000,000
Times: Gross profit percentage..............................	× 40%
Deferred gross profit..	$1,600,000
Times: T's marginal tax rate..................................	× 31%
Deferred Federal income taxes................................	$ 496,000
Times: § 6621 underpayment rate...........................	× 10%
Required interest payment....................................	$ 49,600

Because taxpayers are allowed to have up to $5 million of installment obligations outstanding without being subject to the required interest payment rule, it is apparent that only those taxpayers with one or more substantial installment sales need be concerned with this rule.

REPORTING GAIN ON INSTALLMENT SALES

Taxpayers reporting gain on the installment sale method should attach Form 6252, Computation of Installment Sale Income, to the tax return for the year of sale and each subsequent year in which a payment is collected. A sample of this form is contained in Appendix B.

DISALLOWED LOSSES

Various limitations exist regarding gain and loss recognition in certain property transactions. Several such limitations have already been discussed. Recall that any losses on the sale of personal use assets are disallowed. Similarly, losses on the sale of property acquired by gift are limited to the decline in its value subsequent to the transfer by gift. This results because the basis for determining loss is the fair market value on the date of gift, if that fair market value is less than the donor's basis (which would otherwise be the donee's basis).[90] Likewise, a loss on the disposition of property that has been converted from personal use to business use is limited to the decline in its value subsequent to the conversion. In determining any loss on such a disposition, the adjusted basis is the lesser of the taxpayer's adjusted basis or the fair market value on the date of conversion.[91]

There are several other limitations on the deductibility of losses arising from sales or other dispositions of property. As discussed in Chapter 7, losses incurred in sales between related taxpayers are not deductible. Also, certain losses incurred from the sale of stock or securities will not be allowed as a deduction.

---

[90] § 1015(a).   [91] Reg. § 1.165-9(b).

WASH SALES

A *wash sale* occurs when a taxpayer sells stock or securities at a loss and reinvests in substantially identical stock or securities within 30 days before or after the date of sale. Any loss realized on such a wash sale is not deductible.[92] In essence, a taxpayer who has a wash sale has not had a *change* in economic position—thus the transaction resulting in a loss is ignored for tax purposes. The loss is, however, taken into consideration in determining the adjusted basis in the new shares.[93]

> **Example 49.** C, a calendar year taxpayer, owns 400 shares of X Corporation stock (adjusted basis of $9,000), all of which he sells for $5,000 on December 28, 1994. On January 7, 1995 C purchases another 400 shares of X Corporation stock for $5,500. C's realized loss of $4,000 in 1994 will not be deductible because it resulted from a wash sale. Instead, his basis in the 400 shares purchased in 1995 is increased to $9,500 ($5,500 purchase price + $4,000 disallowed loss).

The *numbers* of shares purchased and sold are not always the same. When the number of shares reacquired is less than the number sold, the deduction for losses is disallowed only for the number of shares purchased.[94]

> **Example 50.** Assume the same facts as in *Example 49,* except that C purchased only 300 shares of X Corporation stock for $4,125. Because C replaced only 300 of the shares previously sold at a loss, only 75% (300 ÷ 400) of the $4,000 realized loss is disallowed. Consequently, C will report a $1,000 loss ($4,000 × 25%) in 1994 and will have a basis of $7,125 ($4,125 purchase price + $3,000 disallowed loss) in the 300 shares purchased.

When the number of shares repurchased is greater than the number of shares sold, none of the loss is deductible and the basis in a number of shares equivalent to the number of shares sold is affected by the disallowed loss.[95]

Any loss also will be disallowed if the "substantially equivalent" stock or securities are acquired by certain related parties. For example, the U.S. Supreme Court held that the wash sale provisions apply if replacement stock is acquired by a taxpayer's spouse *and* they file a joint return for the tax year of the loss.[96]

SALES BETWEEN RELATED PARTIES

The Code places numerous limitations on gain or loss recognition from transactions between certain related parties. The purpose of such restrictions is to prevent related taxpayers from entering into various property transactions solely for the tax reduction possibilities. For example, a father could sell land to his daughter at a loss, deduct the loss, and the property would still remain within the family unit. Similarly, a taxpayer

---

[92] § 1091(a).

[93] § 1091(d).

[94] Reg. § 1.1091-1(c).

[95] Reg. § 1.1091-1(d).

[96] *Helvering v. Taft,* 40-2 USTC ¶9888, 24 AFTR 1976, 311 U.S. 195 (USSC, 1940).

could sell depreciable property to her spouse and report a long-term capital gain on their joint return. For many years thereafter, she and her husband could claim ordinary deductions for depreciation on this higher basis. To control such potentially abusive situations, Congress enacted Code §§ 267 and 1239.

Section 267 disallows deductions for any losses that result from the sale or exchange of property between related parties.[97] Such losses may, however, be used by the related purchaser to offset any gain realized from a subsequent disposition of the property.[98] For purposes of § 267, related parties include the following:[99]

1. Members of an individual's family—specifically, brothers and sisters (including by half-blood), spouses, ancestors (i.e., parents and grandparents), and lineal descendants (i.e., children and grandchildren)

2. A corporation owned more than 50 percent in value by the taxpayer (directly or indirectly)

3. Two corporations owned more than 50 percent in value by the taxpayer (directly or indirectly) if either corporation is a personal holding company or a foreign personal holding company in the tax year of the transaction

4. Various partnership, S corporation, grantor, fiduciary, and trust relationships with regular corporations and individual taxpayers

> **Example 51.** M sells stock (adjusted basis of $10,000) to her daughter, D, for its fair market value of $8,000. D sells the stock two years later for $11,000. M's $2,000 loss is disallowed as a deduction. However, D's realized gain of $3,000 ($11,000 sales price − $8,000 cost basis) is reduced by the $2,000 previously disallowed loss, and she will report only $1,000 of gain.

Note the similarity between the results in *Example 51* and the situation that would result if D had received the stock as a gift from M. First, D's basis for gain would be $10,000 (M's basis) if the stock had been received as a gift; its subsequent sale for $11,000 would have resulted in the same $1,000 recognized (reported) gain. Although the disallowance of a loss deduction might discourage many related-party transactions, some taxpayers prefer to sell rather than give property to a related party in order to avoid paying state or Federal gift taxes.

Section 1239 provides that any gain realized from the sale of depreciable property between specified related parties will be taxed as ordinary income.[100] In effect, this statute precludes the possibility that any gain on the sale might be taxed as a long-term capital gain since the sale results in a higher basis in the depreciable property to a related party. Furthermore, recall that such related-party sales of depreciable property are not eligible for installment sale treatment.[101] Transactions subject to § 1239 treatment are discussed in Chapter 19.

---

[97] § 267(a)(1).

[98] § 267(d).

[99] See §§ 267(b) and (c).

[100] § 1239(a).

[101] § 453(g).

TAX PLANNING CONSIDERATIONS

GIFT VERSUS BEQUEST

In devising a plan for transferring wealth from one family member to another, several considerations related to the income tax, the transfer taxes, and the wishes of the parties involved must be evaluated. If there is a desire to transfer properties, there are relative advantages and disadvantages to lifetime transfers as opposed to testamentary transfers (transfers by will). Some of the specific factors that should be considered are as follows:

1. The income tax rate of each individual (decedent and heirs) relative to the estate and gift tax rates.

2. Whether the property is highly appreciated. If so, a testamentary transfer may be preferred since the property's basis to the heirs or the estate will be its fair market value at date of death or alternate valuation date. If the property is gifted, its basis will be the donor's basis increased by a fraction of any gift taxes paid. If the property has declined in value, only the *original* owner (donor) can benefit from any tax loss by disposing of the property to an unrelated party, due to the basis for determination of loss under § 1015(a).

3. Whether the property is expected to appreciate rapidly in the foreseeable future. If so, a current gift might be considered because the amount subject to gift taxes would be the current market value. If the property were held until death, the higher fair market value at that time would be used in calculating estate taxes. This action is, of course, speculative in nature.

4. Whether the transferee is likely to hold the property for a long period of time. If so, the basis considerations are not as important as they would be if the property were to be sold immediately upon its receipt.

5. Whether the property is income-producing property. If the property produces income, and the owner (donor) is in a high income tax bracket, a lifetime transfer could result in the profits being taxed at a lower tax rate to another family member. If the donee is in a significantly lower income tax bracket, substantial income tax savings can be accomplished.

These factors, as well as the health of the parties involved and other personal considerations, must all be considered. It is possible that the personal factors will outweigh the tax factors, or that significant amounts of taxes cannot be saved.

CHARITABLE TRANSFERS INVOLVING PROPERTY OTHER THAN CASH

Taxpayers who are considering making major charitable transfers and who have property other than cash that they would consider transferring must consider both the effects of any gain or loss if property is sold and the effects of any allowable charitable deduction. If a property has declined in value, its owner may benefit from selling the property and deducting the loss and later contributing the cash proceeds to the charity.

Planning can be even more important when the property is appreciated, since in certain instances a charitable deduction is allowed equal to the fair market value of the property. This is true when the property is long-term capital gain property that is used in the exempt function of the charity, is intangible, or is real estate (see Chapter 11). In such a case, the taxpayer will avoid paying tax on the property's unrealized appreciation and still receive full benefit from the charitable deduction.

CHANGES IN THE USE OF PROPERTY

A taxpayer who converts business property to personal use when its value is less than its adjusted basis should consider selling the asset in order to trigger a deduction for the loss. Also, a taxpayer who buys property that he or she intends to use in a business should think carefully before using the asset for personal purposes. For example, a taxpayer who purchases a new auto and drives it for personal purposes for two years before converting it to business use must use the fair value upon conversion—if less than adjusted basis—in determining both depreciation and any loss on disposition.

SALES TO RELATED PARTIES

Care must be exercised to avoid the undesirable effects of transactions between related parties. If a loss on the sale of property to a related party is disallowed, the tax benefit of a loss deduction is permanently lost unless the value of the property subsequently increases. The only way to generate a tax deduction for the loss is for the original owner to sell the property to an unrelated party. Also, characterizing gain on the sale of depreciable property as ordinary income under § 1239 should normally be avoided.

USE OF INSTALLMENT SALES

Installment sale treatment provides an excellent opportunity for deferring the tax on gain (other than depreciation recapture) when a taxpayer is willing to accept an installment obligation in exchange for property. Actually, installment reporting may provide such attractive tax deferral and tax savings possibilities that the taxpayer is induced to accept an installment obligation, even though he or she would not do so otherwise. In short, this is a tax variable which must be considered by a prudent taxpayer in planning sales of property.

A taxpayer may benefit in at least two ways from the installment method. First, benefits accrue from the deferral of the tax. The time value of money works to the taxpayer's benefit, assuming the sales contract provides for a fair rate of interest. The second benefit from installment reporting is the spreading of the gain over more than one tax year. If the gain on a sale is unusual and moves the taxpayer into a higher tax bracket, spreading the gain over several years tends to allow the overall gain to be taxed in lower tax brackets.

It is important to remember, however, that taxpayers may face several limitations on certain installment sales. First, if a reasonable interest rate is not provided in the deferred payment sale, the seller will be required to impute interest at the appropriate Federal rate. Second, a taxpayer unaware of the rules relating to related-party sales may find that he or she is required to report all the gain on such a sale long before the actual collection of cash from the installment obligations. Third, taxpayers with installment obligations must be informed of the rules requiring immediate gain recognition on certain dispositions of such obligations. These rules include treating borrowed funds as collections on the installment notes if such notes are used as collateral for a loan. Finally, taxpayers with significant amounts of installment obligations outstanding at the end of a particular tax year (i.e., in excess of $5 million) may find that the required interest payment on the deferred income taxes is greater than the interest currently being collected.

PROBLEM MATERIALS

DISCUSSION QUESTIONS

14-1 *Realization vs. Recognition.* In a few sentences, distinguish realization from recognition.

14-2 *Return-of-Capital Principle.* What is the return-of-capital principle?

14-3 *Computing Amount Realized.* Reproduce the formula for computing the amount realized in a sale or exchange.

14-4 *Impact of Liabilities.* What impact do liabilities assumed by the buyer or liabilities encumbering property transferred have on the amount realized? How are they treated if both parties to the transaction incur new liabilities?

14-5 *Cost Basis.* How does one determine cost basis for property acquired? How is this basis affected if property other than money is transferred in exchange for the new property?

14-6 *Gift Basis.* Reproduce the formula for the general rule for determining basis of property acquired by gift.

14-7 *Gift Basis Exception.* When does the general rule for determining basis of property acquired by gift (Question 14-6) not apply?

14-8 *Basis of Inherited Property.* The basis of property acquired from a decedent is generally fair market value at date of death. What are the two exceptions to this rule (do not include property subject to special-use valuation)?

14-9 *Basis Adjustments.* List the three broad categories of adjustments to basis.

14-10 *Transfers Pursuant to Divorce.* In general, do transfers of property in a divorce action result in the realization of gain or loss? Under what circumstances might gain recognition be required?

14-11 *Part-Sale/Part-Gift.* When does a bargain sale to a donee (part-gift) result in gain to the donor? Does the assumption of the donor's liabilities by the donee have any impact? Explain.

14-12 *Bargain Sales.* How is a bargain sale of property to a charitable organization treated for tax purposes?

14-13 *Allocating Sales Price.* Allocations are generally necessary when a sole proprietorship is sold as a unit. What method is normally used for such allocation? What impact does the sales agreement have if it allocates the price to the individual assets?

14-14 *Installment Sales Method—General Rules.* What is the purpose of the installment sale method of reporting gains? Is it an elective provision? How does one elect out of the installment sale method? What sales do not qualify for installment sale treatment?

14-15 *Installment Sales Method—Key Terms.* Explain how each of the following factors related to an installment sale is determined.

    a. Gross profit on deferred payment sale
    b. Total contract price
    c. Gross profit percentage
    d. Payments received in the year of sale
    e. Gain to be reported in the year of sale

14-16 *Imputed Interest Rules.* Under what circumstances must a taxpayer impute interest income from an installment sale? How is the applicable Federal rate (AFR) determined?

14-17 *Related-Party Installment Sales.* Under what circumstances will a taxpayer be faced with the related-party installment sale rules? Explain how a resale of the property by the related-party purchaser before the seller has collected the balance of the installment obligation affects the seller.

14-18 *Dispositions of Installment Obligations.* Your neighbor has $30,000 of installment obligations from a recent sale of land held for investment. He asks you for advice concerning his planned gift of these obligations to his children to be used for their future college expenses. An examination of Form 6252 attached to his most recent tax return reveals a gross profit percentage of 60% and a reasonable market rate of interest related to these installment obligations. What tax advice would you give regarding this plan?

14-19 *Wash Sale.* What is a wash sale? How is a wash sale treated for tax purposes?

14-20 *Timing of Recognition.* Under what circumstances is a realized gain actually recognized? What event generally controls the timing of gain recognition?

PROBLEMS

14-21 *Sale Involving Liabilities.* C sold a cottage in which his basis was $32,000, for cash of $12,000 and a note from the buyer worth $28,000. The buyer assumed an existing note of $30,000 secured by an interest in the property.

    a. What is C's amount realized in this sale?
    b. What is C's gain or loss realized on this sale?

14-22 *Exchange Involving Liabilities.* D exchanged a mountain cabin for a leisure yacht and $30,000 cash. The yacht was worth $25,000 and was subject to liabilities of $10,000, which were assumed by D. The cabin was subject to liabilities of $32,000, which were assumed by the other party.

    a. How much is D's amount realized?
    b. Assuming D's basis in the cabin was $42,000, what is his gain or loss realized?

14-23   *Identification of Stock Sold.* T purchased the following lots of stock in Z Corporation:

50 shares	1/12/85	Cost $1,200
100 shares	2/28/90	Cost $3,000
75 shares	10/16/91	Cost $2,500

T sold 75 shares on January 16, 1994 for $2,800. His only instruction to his broker, who actually held the shares for T, was to sell 75 shares.

   a.   How much gain or loss does T recognize on this sale?
   b.   How could this result be altered?

14-24   *Sale of Property Acquired by Gift.* J received a set of silver flatware as a gift from her grandmother in 1990, when the set was worth $5,000. The silver had a basis to the grandmother of $2,000, and gift taxes of $500 were paid.

   a.   How much gain does J recognize when she sells the set for $5,000 during the current year?
   b.   What would be your answer if the sale price were $4,200?
   c.   What would be your answer if the sale price were $1,500?

14-25   *Sale of Property Acquired by Gift.* For each of the following situations, determine the gain or loss realized by the taxpayer (donee), assuming the property was acquired by gift after 1976:

Case	Donor's Basis	Fair Market Value(*)	Gift Taxes Paid	Sales Price
A	$3,000	$4,000	$400	$4,100
B	3,000	2,500	500	3,200
C	1,200	1,400	280	1,100
D	2,000	1,600	400	1,700
E	2,400	1,800	600	1,500

* Date of gift

14-26   *Sale of Inherited Property.* D inherited two acres of commercial real estate from her grandmother, who had a basis in the property of $52,000, when it had a fair market value of $75,000. For estate tax purposes, the estate was valued as of the date of death, and estate and inheritance taxes of $8,250 were paid by the estate on this parcel of real estate.

   a.   How much gain or loss will be realized by D if she sells the property for $77,000?
   b.   What would be your answer if the sale price were $66,000?

14-27 *Basis of Inherited Property.* H inherited a parcel of real estate from his father. The property was valued for estate tax purposes at $120,000, and the father's basis was $45,000 immediately before his death. H had given the property to his father as a gift six weeks before his death. The proper portion of the gift taxes paid by H are included in his father's basis.

    a. What is H's basis in the real estate?
    b. What would be your answer if H had given the property to his father two years before his father's death?

14-28 *Basis of Converted Property.* K converted his 1991 sedan from personal use to business use as a delivery vehicle in his pizza business. The auto had an adjusted basis to K of $4,200 and a fair market value on the date of the conversion of $2,400. K properly deducted depreciation on the auto of $900 over two years before the auto was sold.

    a. How much is K's gain or loss if he sells the auto for $800?
    b. What would be your answer if the auto were sold for $3,500?

14-29 *Part-Sale/Part-Gift.* G sold a personal computer to his son for $2,000. The computer was worth $3,000, and G had a basis in the unit of $2,200. G has made a gift of $1,000 in this part-sale/part-gift.

    a. How much gain, if any, must G recognize on this sale?
    b. Would your answer differ if G's basis had been $1,700?

14-30 *Bargain Sale to Charity.* F sold a parcel of land to the city to be used as a location for a new art museum. The land had a market value of $70,000 and was sold for $40,000. F's adjusted basis in the property was $35,000. How much is F's charitable contribution deduction on this transfer? How much gain does F recognize on this sale?

14-31 *Installment Sale.* On July 1, 1994 G sold her summer cottage (basis $70,000) for $105,000. The sale contract provided for a payment of $30,000 at the time of sale and payment of the $75,000 balance in three equal installments due in July 1995, 1996, and 1997. Assuming a reasonable interest rate is charged on this deferred payment sale, compute each of the following:

    a. Gross profit on the sale
    b. Total contract price
    c. Gross profit percentage
    d. Gain to be reported (excluding interest) in 1994
    e. Gain to be reported (excluding interest) in 1995
    f. Gain to be reported in 1994 if G elects not to use the installment method

14-32 *Imputed Interest on Installment Sale.* On January 1, 1994 S sold a 100-acre tract of land for $200,000 cash and an $800,000 non–interest-bearing note due on January 1, 1997. On the date of sale, the land had a basis of $400,000. Assuming the applicable Federal rate is 10% compounded semiannually, calculate the following:

    a. Gain, excluding interest, to be reported in 1994
    b. The imputed interest to be reported by S for 1994
    c. Gain, excluding interest, to be reported in 1997

14-33 *Wash Sale.* R purchased 500 shares of Y Corporation common stock for $12,500 on August 31, 1993. She sold 200 shares of this stock for $3,000 on December 21, 1994. On January 7, 1995 R purchased an additional 100 shares of Y Corporation common stock for $1,600.

    a. What is R's realized loss for 1994?
    b. How much of the loss realized can R report in 1994?
    c. What is R's adjusted basis in the 100 shares purchased on January 7, 1995?

14-34 *Related-Party Sale.* J sold 2,000 shares of T Corporation stock, in which he had an adjusted basis of $3,000, to his brother, F, for $1,200.

    a. How much of the realized loss is recognized (reported) by J?
    b. How much gain or loss to F if he subsequently sells the stock for $1,000? for $2,000?

14-35 *Property Settlements.* H was divorced from W this year. H was required to transfer stock, which was his separate property, to W in satisfaction of his obligation for spousal support. The stock was worth $5,700 and had an adjusted basis to H of $2,900.

    a. How much gain, if any, does H recognize on the transfer?
    b. How much gain or loss does W recognize? What is her basis in the property received?

14-36 *Property Tax Allocation.* J purchased a rental property during the current year for $45,000 cash. He was required to pay all of the property taxes for the year of sale, and under the law of the state $47 is allocable to the period before J purchased the property (see Chapter 11).

    a. How much is J's property tax deduction if the total payment made during the tax year of acquisition is $700?
    b. What is J's adjusted basis in the property?

14-37 *Sales of Inherited Properties.* Each of the following involves property acquired from a decedent. None of the properties include income in respect of a decedent. Determine the gain or loss for each.

Case	Decedent's Basis	Death Taxes Paid	Fair Market Value(*)	Sales Price
A	$3,000	$600	$4,000	$6,000
B	6,000	600	4,000	5,000
C	6,000	400	4,000	3,000

* Date of decedent's death.

14-38 *Nontaxable Dividends.* M owned 300 shares of X Corporation common stock, in which her basis was $6,000 on January 1, 1994. With respect to her stock, during 1994 M collected dividends of $600 and tax-free distributions of $400. What is M's basis in the stock as of December 31, 1994?

RESEARCH PROBLEMS

14-39 *Gain Realized from Transferred Debt.* H owns a small office building and commercial complex, which he purchased for $175,000 in 1988. H invested $20,000 and signed a nonrecourse note secured by an interest in the property for the difference. The note provided for 14 percent interest, compounded annually and payable quarterly.

After six years, H decided his property was not as good an investment as he had originally thought. He found a buyer who offered him $1,000 cash for the property, subject to the existing liabilities. H eventually accepted the offer and sold the property.

During the six years he owned the property, H made timely interest payments and no payments of principal. He was allowed depreciation deductions of $37,500, using an accelerated method.

Required:

1. How much is H's gain or loss realized on this sale?
2. Would your answer differ if H's building was only worth $150,000 and instead of selling the building he had voluntarily transferred it to the obligee on the note?

Partial list of research aids:

Reg. § 1.1001-2.
Crane v. Comm., 47-1 USTC ¶9217, 35 AFTR 776, 331 U.S. 1 (USSC, 1947).
Tufts v. Comm., 83-1 USTC ¶9328, 51 AFTR2d 1983-1132, 461 U.S. 300 (USSC, 1983).
Millar v. Comm., 78-2 USTC ¶9514, 42 AFTR2d 78-4276, 577 F.2d 212, (CA-3, 1978).

14-40 *Bargain Sale to Charity.* K sold a mountain cabin for $55,000 to State University (her alma mater) for use in an annual fund-raising auction. The cabin was worth $85,000. K had purchased the cabin five years earlier as an investment for $40,000, and no depreciation has been allowed.

Required:

1. What is K's charitable contribution deduction and her gain or loss realized on this bargain sale?
2. Would your answers differ if the property were a painting instead of a mountain cabin?

Research aids:

§ 170(e)(1).
§ 1011(b).
Reg. §§ 1.170A-4(a)(2) and (c)(2).
Reg. § 1.1011-2.

LEARNING OBJECTIVES

Upon completion of this chapter you will be able to:

- Understand the rationale for deferral of gains and losses on certain property transactions

- Explain how gain or loss deferral is accomplished through adjustment to basis of the replacement property

- Apply the nonrecognition rules to the following transactions:

  - Sale of a taxpayer's principal residence

  - Involuntary conversion of property

  - Like-kind exchange of business or investment property

- Identify other common nontaxable transactions

- Recognize tax planning opportunities related to the more common types of gain-deferral transactions available to individual taxpayers

CHAPTER OUTLINE

Introduction	15-1	Treatment Mandatory	15-41
Types of Nontaxable Exchanges	15-2	Holding Period	15-41
Sale of a Personal Residence	15-3	Other Nontaxable Transactions	15-44
Section 1034	15-4	Changes in Form of Doing Business	15-44
Replacement Period	15-4	Certain Exchanges of Stock in Same	
Computation of Gain Recognized		Corporation	15-44
and Basis of New Residence	15-6	Certain Exchanges of U.S.	
Basis of Replacement Residence	15-8	Obligations	15-45
Sale of New Residence	15-10	Repossession of Real Property	15-45
Ownership by Husband and Wife	15-12	Rollover Gain from Low-Income	
Section 121 Exclusion of Gain	15-13	Housing	15-45
Involuntary Conversions	15-20	Certain Exchanges of Insurance	
Involuntary Conversion Defined	15-20	Policies	15-45
Replacement Property	15-22	Tax Planning Considerations	15-46
Replacement Period	15-24	Current Recognition versus	
Election Required	15-24	Deferral	15-46
Amount of Gain Recognized	15-25	Current Gain Resulting in Future	
Like-Kind Exchanges	15-28	Reductions	15-46
Qualified Property	15-29	Section 1034 Considerations	15-46
Like-Kind Property	15-29	Section 121 Considerations	15-47
Receipt of Property Not of a		Importance of Capital Budgeting in	
Like-Kind	15-32	Decision Making	15-47
Basis in Property Received	15-34	Problem Materials	15-48
Exchange Requirement	15-38		

Chapter **15**

NONTAXABLE EXCHANGES

INTRODUCTION

"If I could show you a perfectly legal way to pyramid your wealth to $1 million without paying tax, would you be interested?" Although this sounds like it came straight out of the con artist's guide to tax scams, its source is far more reputable.[1] More importantly, the assertion is entirely true. If a taxpayer is able to make the right investments—obviously a big if—the Internal Revenue Code is willing to lend a helping hand. The key to this wonderland without taxes can be found in the provisions concerning nontaxable exchanges, the subject of this chapter.

By now, the basic recipe for determining the tax treatment of any sale or exchange is fairly familiar. Whenever a taxpayer disposes of property, three questions must be addressed: (1) what is the gain or loss *realized,* (2) how much of this realized gain or loss is *recognized,* and (3) what is its character. This chapter focuses on the second of these questions, examining a handful of property transactions—such as the sale of a residence or a like-kind exchange—where all or at least a portion of the gain or loss realized is not recognized.

As a general rule, any gain or loss realized on a sale or other disposition of property must be recognized unless an exception is specifically provided. For the most part, this means taxpayers must include all of their realized gains and losses in determining their taxable income. However, there are a number of transactions that the Code has singled out for *nonrecognition*. These transactions appear quite different on the surface (e.g., sale of a home and condemnation of property), but they share a common thread. In each case the property sold or exchanged is replaced with new property. For example, a taxpayer might sell her old home and buy another or trade in an old business car for a new one. When this occurs, any gain or loss realized is usually not taxed—at least immediately—on the theory that the taxpayer's economic situation has not changed sufficiently to warrant taxation. Nonrecognition is deemed appropriate since the taxpayer has not liquidated her investment to cash but has continued it, albeit in another form. In substance, the taxpayer's investment has remained intact. For these situations, the law is willing to allow a taxpayer to postpone the tax until such time when the taxpayer does in fact convert the asset to cash and has the wherewithal to pay the tax.

---

[1] Robert J. Bruss, "Real Estate Exchange Provides a Way to Build Net Worth," *The Palm Beach Post*, February 19, 1989, p 57H.

It is important to observe that nonrecognition can take one of two forms: permanent exclusion or temporary deferral. The world of permanent exclusions, first introduced in Chapter 6, is relatively small. It includes such items as interest paid on state and local government bonds, insurance proceeds paid on account of death, gifts, inheritances, scholarships, child support, and a number of fringe benefits. On the other side of the ledger, losses and expenses that are personal in nature (other than casualty losses) are generally disallowed. Note that if nonrecognition is permanent, the gain or loss never affects taxable income.

> **Example 1.**   F, an elderly widow, sold her personal residence of 30 years for $92,000 (basis $21,000) and moved into a rented unit in a retirement community. F elected under Code § 121 to exclude her gain of $71,000 from gross income. Since the gain was excluded, F will never be required to pay tax on the gain from that residence.[2]

When the recognition of a gain or loss is deferred, it is normally recognized later, when the replacement property from the deferred transaction is sold in a taxable transaction. This deferral is usually achieved by building the gain or loss not recognized into the basis of the replacement property.

> **Example 2.**   D exchanged a vacant lot in San Jose that had been held for investment for unimproved farm land near Fresno. The city lot had cost $35,000 fifteen years earlier and had not been improved. Both the city lot and the rural property were worth $120,000. D recognizes no gain on the exchange and his basis in the farm land is $35,000.[3] Of course, if D later sells the farm for $130,000, his recognizable gain will be $95,000, the gain on the farm of $10,000 plus the gain deferred from the city lot of $85,000.

TYPES OF NONTAXABLE EXCHANGES

There are several types of nontaxable exchanges allowed under the Internal Revenue Code. Three are discussed in detail in this chapter. The sale of a personal residence is covered initially. This includes both the exclusion of gain for persons 55 years of age or over and the deferral of gain by persons reinvesting in another principal residence. Separate discussions of the deferral of gain on involuntary conversions and the deferral of gain or loss on like-kind exchanges follow. Then several other types of nontaxable transactions are discussed briefly.

---

[2] See discussion of § 121 following.   [3] See discussion of § 1031 following.

SALE OF A PERSONAL RESIDENCE

While a man's home may be his castle, in the United States it is also a tax shelter. The tax law contains several provisions that encourage home ownership. Two of these, the deductions for interest and property taxes, were discussed in Chapter 11. Two others considered in detail below concern the sale of a residence. The effect of these provisions, whether intended or not, is to provide what is clearly a tax bonanza. If an individual sells a residence, any gain may be deferred if the individual reinvests enough in another home. This practice—rolling over the gain from one house to another house—can be continued year after year, sale after sale. Then, once the homeowner reaches age 55, he or she can sell the home and permanently exclude up to $125,000 without having to reinvest in another home. In short, it all adds up to what are truly incredible tax benefits for homeowners.

The special treatment for the sale of a residence is not, as one might first believe, something that was established along with the enactment of the first tax law in 1913. It is a relative newcomer. Since 1951 the Internal Revenue Code has provided for the deferral of gain on the sale of an individual's *principal* residence. Gain is deferred under § 1034 when a taxpayer who sells his or her residence reinvests in another principal residence within a specified time period. In order to defer all of the gain, the amount reinvested must equal or exceed the "adjusted sales price" of the old residence.

> **Example 3.** J sold her condominium, which she used as a principal residence, for $120,000. Her basis in the residence was $82,000 and her realized gain was $38,000 ($120,000 − $82,000). Eight months after the sale, J located a suitable tract home, which she purchased for $135,000 and occupied as her principal residence. None of the $38,000 realized gain is recognized by J since she invested $135,000, which is more than the adjusted sales price of her old residence of $120,000.

As noted above, homeowners who have reached the age of 55 may take advantage of a one-time exclusion of gain on the sale of their residence. A person who qualifies may exclude up to $125,000 of the gain from the sale of his or her residence from gross income under § 121. Gain in excess of $125,000 will be either recognized or deferred by reinvesting.

> **Example 4.** T, who is 63 years of age, sold his principal residence for $224,000 on July 22, 1994. His basis in the property was $109,000 and his realized gain on the sale is $115,000 ($224,000 − $109,000). T may elect to exclude all of the $115,000 in gain from his taxable income even if he chooses not to reinvest in another personal residence.

Note that both of the above examples and § 1034 deal solely with the treatment of gains. If an individual sells a principal residence at a loss, the taxpayer receives no tax benifit since a deduction is not allowed for losses arising from sales of personal use properties. Furthermore, such losses may not be deferred under § 1034 since this provision applies only to gains.[4]

SECTION 1034

Section 1034 allows a taxpayer to postpone the recognition of gain on the sale of his or her *principal residence*. Generally, a principal residence is the one in which the taxpayer actually lives. An individual can have only *one* principal residence at a time. Therefore, a taxpayer selling two residences can only postpone gain on the *principal* residence, and a taxpayer purchasing two new residences can only treat the new *principal* residence as the replacement property.[5] Also, if an individual uses property that he or she is renting as the principal residence (e.g., a taxpayer rents an apartment and lives in it), then *no* other property that the taxpayer owns will qualify as the taxpayer's principal residence for purposes of § 1034.[6]

> **Example 5.**   Z moved out of his residence in New Jersey with no intention of returning, and offered it for rent. He immediately moved into a rented apartment in New York City. Several years later, Z sold the New Jersey residence and a year later purchased a house in Virginia that he used on weekends. Z continued to live in his New York City apartment. Neither the New Jersey residence nor the house in Virginia is Z's principal residence. Z's principal residence is the apartment in New York City. Z may not defer the gain on the sale of the New Jersey residence.

A taxpayer may still be able to use § 1034 if he or she *temporarily* rents the old residence before it is sold or rents the new residence before he or she occupies it.[7] The intent of the taxpayer is very important in such a situation. For example, if the property is rented only while the taxpayer is actively trying to sell it, then it will usually be considered the taxpayer's "principal" residence.

REPLACEMENT PERIOD

In order to qualify for the deferral, the taxpayer must acquire a replacement residence within a 48-month period: two years before or two years after the date of the sale of the old residence.[8] The taxpayer can either purchase or construct the new residence, but he or she must occupy and use the residence within this period. To the disappointment of a number of taxpayers, the time limit is strictly enforced. Closing delays, construction strikes, earthquakes, and other events over which the taxpayer has no control are disregarded in determining whether the taxpayer has made a timely investment.

---

[4] §§ 1034(a) and 165(c).

[5] Rev. Rul. 66-114, 1966-1 C.B. 181.

[6] *Stolk v. Comm.*, 64-1 USTC ¶9228, 13 AFTR2d 535, 326 F.2d 760 (CA-2, 1964),

aff'g., 40 T.C. 345 (1963), *acq.* 1964-2 C.B. 7.

[7] Reg. § 1.1034-1(c)(3)(i).

[8] § 1034(a); Reg. § 1.1034-1(a).

Example 6. M sold her principal residence and realized a gain on December 18, 1994. M can defer her gain if she reinvests in a new home by December 18, 1996. If she purchased the replacement residence *before* selling her old residence, she also qualifies for gain deferral if the replacement was not purchased before December 18, 1992. Note that merely starting construction before December 18, 1996 is not sufficient. M must occupy the residence by such date to qualify. The replacement periods are illustrated in the following diagram:

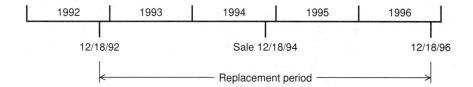

Note that with a new residence purchased or constructed before the sale of the old residence will not qualify as a replacement residence if it is sold before the sale of the old residence.[9]

Constructed Residence. The cost of a constructed residence that is *occupied* by the taxpayer within the time limits is treated the same as the cost of a purchased residence. As noted above, starting construction before the ending date is not sufficient. The taxpayer must move in and occupy the new home no later than two years after the sale of the old home. Also note that only those construction costs that are incurred within the time limits can be considered in determining the amount reinvested.[10]

Improvements to New Residence. When a replacement residence is purchased, subsequent improvements made within the reinvestment period are also considered as part of the amount reinvested. For example, if the taxpayer adds a porch or a swimming pool, these additional costs are included in the amount reinvested as long as they are no later than two years after the sale of the old home. Thus the amount reinvested includes not only the cost of the new home but also any timely improvements.

Suspension of Reinvestment Period. The rollover period is suspended in certain cases. This privilege is extended to members of the armed forces on active duty; however, the reinvestment period generally cannot extend beyond the date of the sale of the old residence by more than four years (eight years in some cases).[11] A similar suspension is provided for U.S. taxpayers while they are residents of a foreign country.[12]

---

[9] Reg. § 1.1034-1(d).

[10] § 1034(c)(2).

[11] § 1034(h). If any member of the armed forces is stationed outside the United States or required to reside in government quar-

ters, the reinvestment period is suspended an additional four years (eight years in total).

[12] § 1034(k).

basis of new resid (handwritten margin note)

Exhibit 15-1   Sale of Residence: Computation of Recognized Gain and Basis of New Residence

1. Gain realized

    | | Sales price |
    | Less: | Selling expenses |
    | | Amount realized |
    | Less: | Adjusted basis (improvements but not fixing-up expenses) |
    | | Gain (loss) realized   *3400* (handwritten) |

2. Adjusted sales price

    | | Amount realized |
    | Less: | Fixing-up expenses |
    | | Adjusted sales price |

3. Gain recognized

    | | Adjusted sales price   *94* (handwritten) |
    | Less: | Cost of replacement residence |
    | | Gain recognized (not to exceed gain realized)* |

4. Basis of replacement residence

    | | Cost of replacement residence |
    | Less: | Gain not recognized |
    | | Adjusted basis of new residence |

* If this amount is negative, the taxpayer has reinvested more than the adjusted sales price and no gain is recognized.

COMPUTATION OF GAIN RECOGNIZED AND BASIS OF NEW RESIDENCE

As illustrated in Exhibit 15-1, the calculation of the gain recognized on the sale of the house begins in the normal fashion. As usual, the computation starts with the sales price, which is then reduced by selling expenses to determine the amount realized. The sales price is usually easy to determine and presents no difficulties. Selling expenses are generally those costs paid to bring about the sale of the property. Although they are not directly deductible, they do reduce the potential gain. A few of the more common selling expenses incurred when selling a home are

Realtor's commission	Legal fees
Advertising	Title fees (abstracts, certificate, opinion)
Surveys	Transfer taxes
Buyer's points paid by the seller	Mortgage title insurance
Inspection fees (termites, radon, etc.)	Escrow fees

Gain Realized.   The amount of the gain realized is merely the difference between the amount realized and the adjusted basis. In computing the basis for the home, any improvements the owner has made should be included. Improvements include anything that adds value to the house and prolongs its useful life. Some of these are

Additions (rooms, porch, deck)	Flooring (carpeting, tile, vinyl)	Driveway, walks
Roof, siding, insulation	Fences	Curtains
Appliances, attic fan, grill	Air conditioning, furnaces	Well
Landscaping, sprinkling system	water heaters	Mailbox, house numbers
Appraisal fees	Alarm system	Septic system
Basement improvement	Basketball goal post	Sewer assessment
Shed	Solar or geothermal heating	Smoke detector

Gain Recognized.   The next concern, and no doubt the most important, is determination of the gain recognized. Most homeowners understand that they may defer the gain on the sale of their home as long as they reinvest in another one. Their confusion concerns just how much must be reinvested to avoid gain. The simple answer is that they can avoid gain as long as the cost of the new home exceeds the sales price of the old home. Although this is a good general rule, a smaller investment may suffice. Congress recognized that the gross sales price does not necessarily represent the taxpayer's wherewithal to acquire another home. Selling expenses and costs to fix up the house before selling it normally reduce the amount the taxpayer has to reinvest. For this reason, § 1034 provides that the taxpayer avoids gain recognition as long as the amount reinvested equals or exceeds the so-called *adjusted sales price,* as discussed in detail below. If the amount reinvested in the replacement residence is less than the adjusted sales price of the prior residence, the gain recognized is generally the portion of the adjusted sales price that is not reinvested.[13] For example, if a taxpayer sells her home for $200,000 (basis $120,000) and reinvests $140,000, she must recognize $60,000 of her $80,000 gain ($200,000 sales price − $140,000 reinvested = $60,000 not reinvested). (See Exhibit 15-1, part 3.)

Adjusted Sales Price.   The adjusted sales price is the amount realized on the sale of the prior residence reduced by any fixing-up expenses.[14] Note that by starting with the amount realized (see Exhibit 15-1), the taxpayer essentially begins with the sales price of the old home less any selling expenses. In effect, the taxpayer is allowed to lower the amount required for reinvestment by any expenses related to the sale.

Not to be confused with selling expenses are fixing-up expenses. Fixing-up expenses are costs incurred shortly before the closing date to assist in the sale of the home. Painting and wallpapering are common examples. Fixing-up expenses are to be distinguished from capital expenditures (e.g., an improvement such as carpeting), which are added to the home's basis, as well as from selling expenses, which reduce the amount realized. Fixing-up expenses do not affect the taxpayer's basis or gain and are not deductible elsewhere on the return. Their sole purpose is to reduce the amount that the seller must reinvest.

---

[13]   § 1034(a).   [14]   § 1034(b)(1).

Moreover, to qualify they must be for work that is performed during the 90-day period ending on the date a contract of sale is entered into and must be paid no later than 30 days after the date of sale. Costs incurred outside of this period provide no benefit.[15]

Example 7.   X entered into a contract to sell her old principal residence on June 1, 1994. The sale was final on July 1, 1994 (date of closing). X incurred the following expenses in fixing up her home for sale.

Nature of Expense	Date Work Performed	Date Paid	Amount
Painted living room	February 15, 1994	March 2, 1994	$450
Shampooed carpets	April 1, 1994	April 1, 1994	231
Wallpapered bedrooms	May 22, 1994	July 7, 1994	176
Cleaned draperies	June 15, 1994	June 16, 1994	135

All of the above items would qualify as fixing-up expenses if the work is performed and is paid for within the required time periods. In this case, the work must be performed during the 90-day period that ends on June 1, 1994 (March 3, 1994 through June 1, 1994), and must be paid within 30 days after July 1, 1994 (before July 31, 1994). Therefore, X's fixing-up expenses will be $407 (carpets shampooed and bedrooms wallpapered). The living room was painted before the 90-day period and the draperies were cleaned afterwards, so they do not qualify as fixing-up expenses.

BASIS OF REPLACEMENT RESIDENCE

The basis in the replacement residence is its cost reduced by the portion of the realized gain that is postponed by § 1034.[16] If none of the realized gain is postponed (i.e., the entire realized gain is recognized), then the basis of the replacement residence will be its cost. The cost of the new residence includes not only the purchase price and acquisition expenses, but also all capital expenditures for the construction, reconstruction, and improvement of the residence that are made during the replacement period.[17]

Example 8.   Richard Towns sold his principal residence for $96,000 on November 21, 1994. The residence had been purchased three years earlier for $73,000 and no improvements had been made. He did, however, pay $1,200 for painting and general repairs to the home on or about October 12, 1994 (which were paid for immediately), and $6,000 in realtor fees and other closing costs. Richard purchased another principal residence on December 20, 1994 for $102,000. A quick glance at the facts indicated that Richard recognized no gain on the sale of his house since

---

[15] § 1034(b)(2); Reg. § 1.1034-1(b)(6).   [17] Reg § 1.1034-1(b)(7).

[16] § 1034(e).

he reinvested more than the sales price for the old home. The actual calculations required to arrive at this result, as well as the basis for his new home, are shown below:

Sales price..	$ 96,000
Less: Selling expenses...............................	− 6,000
Amount realized..	$ 90,000
Less: Adjusted basis.................................	− 73,000
Gain (loss) realized.....................................	$ 17,000
Amount realized..	$ 90,000
Less: Fixing-up expenses............................	− 1,200
Adjusted sales price.....................................	$ 88,800
Adjusted sales price.....................................	$ 88,800
Less: Cost of replacement residence................	− 102,000
Gain recognized (if greater than zero)...................	$ None
Cost of replacement residence...........................	$102,000
Less: Gain not recognized............................	− 17,000
Adjusted basis of new residence........................	$ 85,000

Note that Richard recognizes none of the gain realized since the cost of the replacement residence exceeded the adjusted sales price. Note also that the fixing-up expenses of $1,200 are not included in determining the gain realized (i.e., they are neither selling expenses nor additions to basis). Their sole effect is to reduce the amount that has to be reinvested, or, more precisely, the adjusted sales price.

Example 9.   Assume the same facts as in *Example 8,* except that Richard reinvested only $85,000 in the new home. In this case his reinvestment is less than the adjusted sales price of $88,800, and he would recognize a gain on the sale of his home of $3,800, determined as follows:

Adjusted sales price.....................................	$88,800
Less: Cost of replacement residence................	− 85,000
Gain recognized...	$ 3,800

His basis for the new home would be $71,800, determined as follows:

Cost of replacement residence...........................	$85,000
Less: Gain not recognized ($17,000 − $3,800)......	− 13,200
Adjusted basis of new residence........................	$71,800

Example 10.   Assume the same facts as in *Example 8,* except that Richard's new residence cost only $71,000. In this case, his reinvestment is far less than the adjusted sales price, and he must consequently recognize the entire gain realized of $17,000, determined as follows:

Adjusted sales price....................................	$88,800
Less: Cost of replacement residence................	− 71,000
Gain recognized (not to exceed gain realized)...........	$17,800—but limited to $17,000

His basis for the new home would be $71,000, determined as follows:

Cost of replacement residence.........................	$71,000
Less: Gain not recognized...........................	− 0
Adjusted basis of new residence.......................	$71,000

Exhibit 15-2 is a completed Form 2119 using the information in *Example 8* above. (Note that a 1993 Form 2119 is used because the 1994 tax forms were not available on the publication date of this text.)

SALE OF NEW RESIDENCE

There is no limitation on the number of times a taxpayer can defer gain on the sale of a principal residence. As a result, gain from the sale of one's first principal residence can be deferred to the second principal residence. Subsequently, the gain from the sale of the second residence can be deferred to the third, and so on. However, there are restrictions on the period of time that the replacement residence must be held. Specifically, § 1034 generally does not apply to a replacement residence that is sold within the replacement period for the original residence.[18] Accordingly, if a taxpayer sells his or her new residence within the replacement period for the former residence and gain is deferred from the old residence, the gain on the sale of the second residence does not qualify for deferral under § 1034.[19]

Example 11.   J sold her principal residence (basis of $75,000) for $100,000 on January 15, 1994 and purchased a replacement for $105,000 on February 19, 1994. After becoming dissatisfied with the nearby schools, J sold the second residence for $112,000 on December 2, 1994 and purchased a third residence for $118,000 on January 26, 1995.

Since the third residence was purchased within the reinvestment period for the first residence, it is treated as the replacement. The $25,000 gain from the sale of the original residence is deferred, and the basis of the third residence is $93,000 ($118,000 cost − $25,000 deferred gain). Note that the $7,000 gain ($112,000 sale price − $105,000 cost) on the sale of the second residence does not qualify for deferral.

---

[18]   The holding period generally is two years. See §§ 1034(a) and 1034(c)(4).

[19]   § 1034(d)(1).

Exhibit 15-2 *Reporting Sale of Principal Residence*

Form **2119**	**Sale of Your Home**	OMB No. 1545-0072
Department of the Treasury Internal Revenue Service	▶ Attach to Form 1040 for year of sale. ▶ See separate instructions. ▶ Please print or type.	19**93** Attachment Sequence No. **20**

Your first name and initial. If a joint return, also give spouse's name and initial. RICHARD	Last name TOWNS	Your social security number 567 · 89 · 0123
Fill in Your Address Only If You Are Filing This Form by Itself and Not With Your Tax Return	Present address (no., street, and apt. no., rural route, or P.O. box no. if mail is not delivered to street address) 4321 REVERSE BLVD.	Spouse's social security number
	City, town or post office, state, and ZIP code ANNUITY, AL 33221	

Part I   General Information

1	Date your former main home was sold (month, day, year) . . . . ▶	1	11 / 21 / 94
2	Have you bought or built a new main home?		☒ Yes ☐ No
3	Is or was any part of either main home rented out or used for business? If "Yes," see instructions . .		☐ Yes ☒ No

Part II   Gain on Sale—Do not include amounts you deduct as moving expenses.

4	Selling price of home. Do not include personal property items you sold with your home . .	4	96,000
5	Expense of sale (see instructions)	5	6,000
6	Amount realized. Subtract line 5 from line 4	6	90,000
7	Adjusted basis of home sold (see instructions)	7	73,000
8	**Gain on sale.** Subtract line 7 from line 6	8	17,000

Is line 8 more than zero? — Yes ▶ If line 2 is "Yes," you **must** go to Part III or Part IV, whichever applies. If line 2 is "No," go to line 9.

— No ▶ **Stop** and attach this form to your return.

| 9 | If you haven't replaced your home, do you plan to do so within the **replacement period** (see instructions)? ☐ Yes ☐ No
• If line 9 is "Yes," stop here, attach this form to your return, and see **Additional Filing Requirements** in the instructions.
• If line 9 is "No," you **must** go to Part III or Part IV, whichever applies. |

Part III   One-Time Exclusion of Gain for People Age 55 or Older—By completing this part, you are electing to take the one-time exclusion (see instructions). If you are not electing to take the exclusion, go to Part IV now.

10	Who was age 55 or older on the date of sale? . . . . ☐ You ☐ Your spouse ☐ Both of you
11	Did the person who was age 55 or older own and use the property as his or her main home for a total of at least 3 years (except for short absences) of the 5-year period before the sale? If "No," go to Part IV now . . ☐ Yes ☐ No
12	At the time of sale, who owned the home? . . . . ☐ You ☐ Your spouse ☐ Both of you
13	Social security number of spouse at the time of sale if you had a different spouse from the one above. If you were not married at the time of sale, enter "None" . . . . ▶	13	
14	**Exclusion.** Enter the **smaller** of line 8 or $125,000 ($62,500 if married filing separate return). Then, go to line 15	14	

Part IV   Adjusted Sales Price, Taxable Gain, and Adjusted Basis of New Home

15	If line 14 is blank, enter the amount from line 8. Otherwise, subtract line 14 from line 8 . .	15	17,000
	• If line 15 is zero, stop and attach this form to your return.		
	• If line 15 is more than zero and line 2 is "Yes," go to line 16 now.		
	• If you are reporting this sale on the installment method, stop and see the instructions.		
	• All others, stop and **enter the amount from line 15 on Schedule D, col. (g), line 4 or line 12.**		
16	Fixing-up expenses (see instructions for time limits)	16	1,200
17	If line 14 is blank, enter amount from line 16. Otherwise, add lines 14 and 16	17	1,200
18	**Adjusted sales price.** Subtract line 17 from line 6	18	88,800
19a	Date you moved into new home ▶	12 / 20 / 94	b Cost of new home (see instructions)	19b	102,000
20	Subtract line 19b from line 18. If zero or less, enter -0-	20	– 0 –
21	**Taxable gain.** Enter the **smaller** of line 15 or line 20	21	– 0 –
	• If line 21 is zero, go to line 22 and attach this form to your return.		
	• If you are reporting this sale on the installment method, see the line 15 instructions and go to line 22.		
	• All others, **enter the amount from line 21 on Schedule D, col. (g), line 4 or line 12**, and go to line 22.		
22	Postponed gain. Subtract line 21 from line 15	22	17,000
23	**Adjusted basis of new home.** Subtract line 22 from line 19b	23	85,000

Sign Here Only If You Are Filing This Form by Itself and Not With Your Tax Return	Under penalties of perjury, I declare that I have examined this form, including attachments, and to the best of my knowledge and belief, it is true, correct, and complete.
	Your signature Date Spouse's signature Date
	If a joint return, both must sign.

For Paperwork Reduction Act Notice, see separate instructions.   Cat. No. 11710J   Form **2119** (1993)

An exception to the above rule is provided for taxpayers who sell their homes in connection with beginning employment (or self-employment) at a new location. Gain on the sale of a second residence purchased and sold within the reinvestment period for the original residence may be deferred, but only if the relocation to a new place of work meets both the distance and time requirements for the moving expense deduction under § 217(c).[20]

> **Example 12.** Assume the same facts as in *Example 11* except that the second residence was sold because J was promoted and transferred from Philadelphia to Atlanta. In this situation, the gain on the sale of the second residence is also deferred. J's basis in the third residence would be $86,000 ($118,000 − $32,000 total deferred gain from sale of both houses).

OWNERSHIP BY HUSBAND AND WIFE

Application of § 1034 when the house is jointly owned—as is usually the case with married couples—normally presents few problems. When a husband and wife sell a common, jointly owned principal residence, the rules operate as above so long as they reinvest in another common, jointly owned principal residence.[21] On the other hand, if the couple is considering a divorce or are divorced, the rules become a little more challenging.

Divorce. As part of a divorce agreement, the parties often agree to have the house transferred to one of the spouses as part of the property settlement. When this occurs, no gain or loss is recognized on the transfer of the property and the basis of the property carries over to the spouse receiving the property.[22] If the recipient spouse later sells the property, any gain realized on the sale is the total responsibility of the recipient spouse. In such case the selling spouse could defer any gain by reinvesting under § 1034.

In some divorce situations, the couple decides to sell the house and split the proceeds. In such case each party is then free to use the proceeds as he or she pleases. In the normal situation, the gain on a principal residence cannot be deferred by replacing it with two residences. However, the law relaxes this rule when a husband and wife divorce or agree to live apart. When this occurs, each party is assigned a portion of the gain and each must reinvest at least his or her share of the adjusted sales price of the old residence in order to defer the gain.[23]

Separate Residences and Marriage. It is not unusual to encounter two individuals who before marrying sell their separate residences and then buy a new home with their new partner. In this situation, each may defer the gain on the sale of the separate residence if an amount equal to the adjusted sales price of his or her separate residence is reinvested.[24]

---

[20] § 1034(d)(2). See Chapter 8 for a discussion of these requirements.

[21] If one spouse dies after a residence is sold but before replacement, a residence that the surviving spouse purchases and occupies may, at the election of the survivor, be treated as a replacement. § 1034(g).

[22] See discussion and examples related to § 1041 in Chapter 14.

[23] Rev. Rul. 74-250, 1974-1 C.B. 202.

[24] Rev. Rul. 75-238, 1975-1 C.B. 257.

Example 13. R and S each own their own homes. They marry each other and decide to sell their separate homes and purchase a new home together. Assuming that the amount realized equals the adjusted sales price for each sale, the results are as follows:

	R's Residence	S's Residence
Amount realized (and adjusted sales price)...	$40,000	$50,000
Less: Adjusted basis in residence.........	− 25,000	− 36,000
Realized gain.............................	$15,000	$14,000

R and S purchased a new home for $102,000, of which R and S each invested $51,000. Since each invested at least the amount of their adjusted sales price, the requirements of § 1034 are met and R and S will not recognize their realized gains. However, if R and S had invested only $80,000 ($40,000 each), then S would have to recognize $10,000 of her realized gain. This is the amount of her adjusted sales price that she did not reinvest. R reinvested his entire adjusted sales price and therefore has no recognized gain.

SECTION 121 EXCLUSION OF GAIN

A taxpayer may exclude from gross income all of his or her gain (up to a statutory limit of $125,000) from the sale of a personal residence if he or she has reached age 55 on or before the date of sale.[25] In order to qualify, the residence must have been owned and used by the taxpayer as his or her principal residence for at least three years within the five years ending with the date of its sale.[26] To meet this test, the ownership and use as a principal residence must total 36 months or 1,095 days.[27]

The § 121 exclusion is elective and applies to any gain up to $125,000 ($62,500 for a married person filing separately). If the total gain *exceeds* the limit, then $125,000 (or $62,500) of the gain may be excluded from gross income. The exclusion may be used only once by a taxpayer. Once the election has been used by either a taxpayer or the taxpayer's spouse, he or she is unable to take advantage of the provision again.[28]

Example 14. L, age 64, sold her principal residence of 10 years during 1994 for $114,000 and she does not intend to reinvest in another residence. Her adjusted basis in the property was $56,000. L may exclude her gain of $58,000 ($114,000 − $56,000) under § 121; however, if she does, she can never benefit from this provision again.

---

[25] §§ 121(a)(1) and 121(b)(1). Also see Rev. Rul. 77-382, 1977-2 C.B. 51, regarding sales on birthdays.

[26] § 121(a)(2).

[27] Reg. § 1.121-1(c).

[28] § 121(b)(2).

Example 15.   If the sales price of L's home had been $190,000, L's realized gain of $134,000 could be only partially excluded. The maximum of $125,000 could be excluded, and the remaining gain of $9,000 would be recognized in 1994.

Example 16.   After her husband died in 1989, B, age 63, sold her residence and realized a $90,000 gain. After much thought, she elected to exclude the gain, believing that she would never own a home again. But shortly thereafter B found love a second time and married H, age 64, who owned his own home. After they lived in H's home for five years, the residence was sold and no reinvestment took place. H may not elect to exclude any gain under § 121 (since B had previously benefited from a § 121 election) even though H had never benefited from the provision and the property was his separate property.

The election may, however, be made or revoked at any time before the statute of limitations expires for filing a refund claim for the year of sale. In the case of taxpayers who are married at the date of sale, both spouses must consent to the election or revocation.[29]

Example 17.   P and Q, a married couple, ages 57 and 56, sold their old home and purchased a new but smaller one in 1994. Since they only reinvested a small portion of the adjusted sales price of the former residence, they elected to exclude their remaining gain from gross income under § 121. Three years later, they decided to sell the new home and rent an apartment. Since they are still within the time allowed by the statute of limitations for filing a refund claim for the 1994 year, they may, if they wish, revoke their § 121 election for 1994 and elect § 121 for the new sale in 1997. This action would be advisable if the gain on the sale of the old residence was less than the $125,000 allowed to be excluded *and* the tax on the sale of the new home was greater than the tax from the old residence.

Incapacitated Taxpayers.   A taxpayer who purchases a residence and is soon forced to move to a rest home or similar facility may never be able to meet the time requirement for the § 121 exclusion. Fortunately, if a person in this situation lives in the residence for at least one year, he or she will be treated as having lived in that residence during any period of time that he or she has lived in a licensed facility for incapacitated individuals.[30] Thus, anyone at least 55 years of age who purchases a new home, lives in it one year, and spends two years in a rest home while still owning the home will meet all the tests for § 121.

Married Taxpayers.   If only one spouse meets the age, holding, and use requirements, husband and wife will both be treated as meeting the requirements if they own the residence jointly and file a joint return for the year of sale.[31] Also, if a taxpayer's spouse is deceased and the decedent met the holding and use requirements, the taxpayer (i.e., survivor) will be treated as meeting the holding and use requirements as long as the deceased spouse had not benefited from the § 121 election previously.[32]

---

[29] § 121(c).

[30] § 121(d)(9).

[31] § 121(d)(1).

[32] § 121(d)(2).

Example 18. R married S in 1993 and moved into S's home, which S had owned and lived in since 1985. In 1994 S died and left the home to R in her will. R, age 58, sold the home in December 1994. Because S met the three-year tests for ownership and use, and R meets the age test, R may elect to exclude gain under § 121.

Involuntary Conversions. For purposes of § 121, an involuntary conversion of a qualifying residence will be treated as the sale of that residence.[33] Thus, a person who has attained the age of 55 and meets the use and ownership tests can exclude at least a portion of any gain from the destruction, theft, or condemnation of his or her residence. Involuntary conversions are discussed in detail later in this chapter.

Interaction of §§ 121, 1033, and 1034. When a taxpayer who has made a § 121 election has a gain greater than the $125,000 that may be excluded, then he or she may be able to defer the amount of gain in excess of $125,000 by using § 1034 (sale of a residence) or § 1033 (involuntary conversions). In this situation, the amount realized for purposes of §§ 1033 and 1034 is *reduced* by the gain excluded under § 121. This reduces the amount that must be reinvested in order to defer any remaining gain.[34]

---

[33] § 121(d)(4). [34] § 121(d)(7).

Example 19.   D sold a principal residence that he had owned and occupied for 22 years for $276,000 during the current year. His selling expenses were $18,000 and he incurred no fixing-up expenses related to the sale. D was 66 years of age at the time and had purchased the residence for $86,000. Six months after the sale, D located and purchased a smaller home for $160,000.

The interaction between the § 121 exclusion and § 1034 can be seen in the following calculations.

Sales price..	$276,000
Less: Selling expenses.............................	− 18,000
Amount realized......................................	$258,000
Less: Adjusted basis...............................	− 86,000
Gain (loss) realized..................................	$172,000
Gain realized..	$172,000
Less: §121 exclusion..............................	− 125,000
Remaining gain realized..............................	$ 47,000
Amount realized......................................	$258,000
Less: §121 exclusion..............................	− 125,000
New amount realized for § 1034.......................	$133,000
New amount realized for § 1034.......................	$133,000
Less: Fixing-up expenses..........................	− 0
Adjusted sales price..................................	$133,000
Adjusted sales price..................................	$133,000
Less: Cost of replacement residence................	− 160,000
Gain recognized (if greater than zero)..................	$ None
Cost of replacement residence.........................	$160,000
Less: Gain not recognized under § 1034............	− 47,000
Adjusted basis of new residence.......................	$113,000

In this case D receives the best of all possible treatments. He has his exclusion and defers his gain too! The end result is that none of his $172,000 is gain recognized. Note that when D takes advantage of the exclusion, the computations for § 1034 simply treat D as if he had never received the amount excluded (i.e., $125,000). In this case, the effect is to reduce both the gain realized and the adjusted sales price by $125,000. Consequently, D must reinvest $125,000 less in order to exclude the entire gain.

Example 20. Assume the same facts as in *Example 19.* Had D reinvested only $110,000 (instead of $160,000), he would be required to recognize a $23,000 gain and his basis in the new residence would be $86,000, computed as follows:

Adjusted sales price...	$133,000
Less: Cost of replacement residence.........................	− 110,000
Gain recognized..	$ 23,000
Cost of replacement residence....................................	$110,000
Less: Gain not recognized under § 1034 ($47,000 − $23,000).	− 24,000
Adjusted basis of new residence................................	$ 86,000

The end result is that D reports only $23,000 of the total $172,000 gain.

✔ CHECK YOUR TAX KNOWLEDGE

Review Question 1. True-False. In order to postpone recognition of the gain on the sale of a home, the taxpayer must reinvest an amount that equals or exceeds the adjusted basis of the former residence.

False. The taxpayer must reinvest an amount equal to the adjusted sale price, generally the sales proceeds less selling and fixing-up expenses. Confusing *adjusted sales price* with *adjusted basis* could have a disastrous result.

Review Question 2. True-False. Assuming the taxpayer itemizes deductions, fixing-up expenses will reduce taxable income.

False. Fixing-up expenses serve only to reduce the amount that must be reinvested to avoid gain recognition on the sale of the home. They are not deductible in computing taxable income.

Review Question 3. True-False. Leona sold her old home for $200,000 (basis $150,000), realizing a $50,000 gain. Shortly thereafter, she acquired a new home for $225,000. The basis of her new home will be the same as the old home, $150,000, since she recognizes no gain on the sale.

False. Leona is allowed to defer the gain since she reinvested more than the adjusted sales price of her old home. To ensure the deferred gain will be recognized later, the gain not recognized, $50,000, is preserved by building it into her new basis. The basis of her new home is $175,000 (cost of $225,000 − gain not recognized of $50,000). Note that if Leona sells the new home for what she paid for it, $225,000, she will recognize the deferred gain of $50,000 ($225,000 sales price − $175,000 basis adjusted for the deferred gain).

Review Question 4.   Nathan sold his old home on January 2, 1994. He plans to build a new house. In order to defer any gain realized on the sale of the old home, when must he start construction?

The critical date is not when he starts construction but when he occupies the new house. He must occupy the newly constructed house within two years of the sale, or January 2, 1996.

Review Question 5.   Because of health problems, Mike's mom and dad, 82 and 83, decided to move from Oshkosh to Chicago to be near their son in 1994. They rented an apartment about a mile from their son's house. The couple tried to sell their 50-year-old home before they left but had little luck and were forced to rent it. After some time had passed, they were able to sell the home, realizing a $100,000 gain. What concern should the tax advisor address?

Two concerns must be considered. According to the facts, the couple converted their residence to rental property and therefore sold rental property rather than a residence. The rollover provisions of § 1034 and the exclusion under § 121 are available only if the taxpayer sells a principal residence. These benefits may be available, however, if the taxpayer can show that the rental was only temporary. Even if this problem can be sidestepped, the exclusion is available only if the taxpayer lives in the home for at least three years within the five years ending with the date of the sale.

Review Question 6. In July 1994, Tom Otto Snoop and his wife were transferred to Memphis. As a result, they sold their principal residence for $290,000. They had purchased the little bungalow in Los Angeles in 1984 for $80,000. In order to facilitate the sale, they had the entire inside of the home painted at a cost of $4,000. This expense was incurred and paid for on June 30, 1994. The couple also paid a real estate commission of $10,000. In Memphis the homes were much less expensive, and the Snoops got all the house they wanted for $270,000. They closed on the deal in September, 1994.

a. Compute the couple's gain recognized on the sale of the residence and the basis of the new residence.

Sales price..	$290,000
Less: Selling expenses..............................	− 10,000
Amount realized..	$280,000
Less: Adjusted basis................................	− 80,000
Gain (loss) realized.....................................	$200,000
Amount realized..	$280,000
Less: Fixing-up expenses...........................	− 4,000
Adjusted sales price....................................	$276,000
Adjusted sales price....................................	$276,000
Less: Cost of replacement residence................	− 270,000
Gain recognized...	$ 6,000
Cost of replacement residence.........................	$270,000
Less: Gain not recognized ($200,000 − $6,000).....	− 194,000
Adjusted basis of new residence.......................	$ 76,000

b. Assuming Tom is eligible and elects the once-in-a-lifetime exclusion, what is the minimum amount, if any, that he must reinvest in order to postpone recognition of any gain realized?

Gain realized..	$200,000
Less: § 121 exclusion..............................	− 125,000
Remaining gain realized................................	$ 75,000
Amount realized..	$280,000
Less: § 121 exclusion..............................	− 125,000
New amount realized for § 1034.......................	$155,000
New amount realized for § 1034.......................	$155,000
Less: Fixing-up expenses...........................	− 4,000
Adjusted sales price....................................	$151,000

Tom would need to reinvest the new adjusted sales price of $151,000 in order to avoid the remaining gain of $75,000.

INVOLUNTARY CONVERSIONS

Taxpayers occasionally lose their property from casualty or theft or are forced to sell their property because of some type of condemnation proceeding. When an *involuntary conversion* like this occurs, the taxpayer usually receives some type of compensation such as insurance proceeds or a condemnation award. In some cases, the compensation may actually cause the taxpayer to realize a gain from the "loss." Without any special rule, the tax resulting from this gain could produce a real hardship since the taxpayer typically uses the compensation received to acquire a replacement property. Recognizing that taxpayers may not have the wherewithal to pay the tax in this situation—which was totally beyond their control—Congress provided some relief. Special rules allow taxpayers to defer any gain realized from an involuntary conversion if they acquire qualified replacement property within a specified period of time.

> **Example 21.**   J operates a fishing boat in Miami. Unfortunately, the boat was totally destroyed when Hurricane Andrew hit the Florida coast. J's basis in the boat was $40,000 (cost of $60,000 less depreciation of $20,000). Luckily, J was insured. He filed an insurance claim and received $75,000 based on the fair market value of the boat. As a result, he realized a gain of $35,000 ($75,000 − $40,000). J may defer the gain if he reinvests at least $75,000 in similar-use property within the allowable period.

INVOLUNTARY CONVERSION DEFINED

An involuntary conversion is defined in the Code as the compulsory or involuntary conversion of property "as a result of its destruction in whole or in part, theft, seizure, or requisition or condemnation or threat or imminence thereof."[35] The terms *destruction* and *theft* have the same basic meaning as when they are used for casualty and theft losses. The IRS has ruled, however, that the destruction of property for purposes of § 1033 need not meet the *suddenness* test, which has been applied to casualty loss deductions.[36]

Seizure, Requisition, or Condemnation.   It is not as simple to determine what qualifies as a "seizure, or requisition or condemnation" as it is to identify theft or destruction. The property must be taken without the taxpayer's consent and the taxpayer must be compensated.[37]

---

[35]   § 1033(a).

[36]   Rev. Rul. 59-102, 1959-1 C.B. 200.

[37]   See, for example, *Hitke v. Comm.*, 62-1 USTC ¶9114, 8 AFTR2d 5886, 296 F.2d 639 (CA-7, 1961).

Not all types of forced dispositions will qualify. For example, the courts have found that a foreclosure sale[38] and a sale after continued insistence by a Chamber of Commerce[39] did not constitute involuntary conversions. Similarly, the IRS has ruled that the condemnation of rental properties due to structural defects or sanitary conditions does not constitute an involuntary conversion since the sale was made to avoid making property improvements necessary to meet a housing ordinance.[40] Generally, a transfer must be made to an authority that has the power to actually condemn the property, and the property must be taken for a public use.

In the case of the conversion of part of a single economic unit, § 1033 applies not only to the condemned portion, but also to the part not condemned if it is *voluntarily sold*. When a truck freight terminal was rendered virtually useless because the adjoining parking lot for the trucks was condemned, a single economic unit was found to exist and § 1033 applied to the sale of the terminal as well as the condemnation of the parking area.[41] In a similar situation when a shopping center was partially destroyed by fire and the owner chose to sell the entire shopping center rather than reconstruct the destroyed portion, the IRS ruled that no conversion existed with respect to the remaining portion since the undamaged portion could still be used and the damaged portion repaired. The fire insurance proceeds, but not the sale proceeds, qualified for deferral under § 1033.[42]

Threat or Imminence of Condemnation. The possibility of a condemnation may very well cause a taxpayer to sell property before the actual condemnation occurs. For example, a farming corporation may discover that its property is being considered as the site for a new airport and sell the property. Section 1033 extends deferral to these *voluntary* sales to someone other than the condemning authority if they are due to the *threat or imminence* of condemnation. It should be emphasized that newspaper reports, magazine articles, or rumors that property is being considered for condemnation are not sufficient.[43] Threat or imminence exists only after officials have communicated that they intend to condemn the property and the owner has good reason to believe they would.

> **Example 22.** LSA Corporation has owned a department store in downtown Indianapolis for over 50 years. The property has a value of about $2 million and a basis of only $400,000 (since the building is completely depreciated). Recently, the corporation learned that the city fathers, in an attempt to revive the downtown area, plan to build a new mall that may result in the condemnation of the building. Fearing that interest rates may rise before the city gets around to condemning the property, the corporation sold the building to another investor, who wanted to try to preserve the building as a historic structure. The corporation quickly used the

---

[38] See *Cooperative Publishing Co. v. U.S.*, 40-2 USTC ¶9823, 25 AFTR 1123, 115 F.2d 1017 (CA-9, 1940), and *Robert Recio*, 61 TCM ___, T.C. Memo. 1991-215.

[39] *Davis Co.*, 6 B.T.A. 281 (1927), *acq.* VI-2 C.B. 2.

[40] Rev. Rul. 57-314, 1957-2 C.B. 523.

[41] *Harry Masser*, 30 T.C. 741 (1958), *acq.* 1959-2 C.B. 5; Rev. Rul. 59-361, 1959-2 C.B. 183.

[42] Rev. Rul. 78-377, 1978-2 C.B. 208, distinguishing Rev. Rul. 59-361, Footnote 39.

[43] Rev. Rul. 58-557, 1958-2 C.B. 402.

sales proceeds to build another store in a nearby suburb. Unfortunately, the corporation's sale may not qualify for deferral since it has not been officially notified that the building will be condemned. The threat or imminence does not exist merely because the city is considering plans that may lead to condemnation. Nevertheless, the corporation may be able to produce facts that clearly suggest otherwise.

As noted above, the sale to a third party after the threat exists is permissible.[44] If the third party realizes gain when the property is later sold to the condemning authority, the new transaction may also qualify for involuntary conversion treatment if the proceeds are reinvested in qualified property after the condemnation of the property, even though the threat existed before the property was acquired.[45]

> **Example 23.**   T has owned and operated a successful automobile dealership for many years. This year he received legal notice from the City of New Orleans indicating that it planned to condemn his showroom and car lot for use as the site of a new convention center in approximately five years. As a result, T began searching for an acceptable new location. After finding a suitable location, T sold the old property to a person who could use it for just four or five years.
>
> T's sale and reinvestment qualifies for involuntary conversion treatment and his gain can be deferred so long as all other requirements are met. When the property is finally purchased by the city, the new owner can also qualify for involuntary conversion treatment if he or she realizes a gain and the proceeds are reinvested in qualifying property within the replacement period.

REPLACEMENT PROPERTY

To qualify for deferral of gain on an involuntary conversion, the taxpayer must reinvest in property that is *similar or related in service* or *use* to the property that is converted.[46] The IRS and taxpayers often disagree as to what qualifies as replacement property. It is clear, however, that the new property must replace the converted property, and therefore, property that was already owned by the taxpayer will not qualify.[47]

Generally, the replacement property must serve the same functional use as that served by the converted property. This *functional use* test requires that the character of service or use be the same for both properties.

> **Example 24.**   N has successfully owned and operated a bowling alley for many years. This year the bowling alley was destroyed by fire, and N replaced it with a billiard parlor. The billiard parlor is not qualified replacement property since services provided by each are not functionally equivalent. Although they both provide recreational services, the IRS believes bowling balls and billiard balls are not the same.[48]

[44] *Creative Solutions, Inc. v. U.S.*, 63-2 USTC ¶9615, 12 AFTR2d 5229, 320 F.2d 809 (CA-5, 1963); Rev. Rul. 81-180, 1981-2 C.B. 161.

[45] Rev. Rul. 81-181, 1981-2 C.B. 162.

[46] § 1033(a).

[47] § 1033(a)(1)(A)(i).

[48] Rev. Rul. 76-319, 1976-2 C.B. 242.

A different and more liberal test has been applied to rental properties involved in involuntary conversions. This test is the *taxpayer use* test, which basically requires that the replacement property be used by the taxpayer as rental property regardless of the lessee's use.

> **Example 25.** Several years ago J purchased 30 acres of land and built a large warehouse that he leased to an appliance store. This year the warehouse site was condemned, and J used the proceeds to purchase a gas station that he currently leases to an oil company. The gas station is qualified replacement property since both properties are rental properties.[49] The fact that the tenants use the properties for different purposes is irrelevant. From the owner's perspective each property is being used in the same way.

Control of Corporation. The replacement property in an involuntary conversion may be controlling stock in a corporation owning property that is "similar or related in use or service."[50] Control consists of owning at least 80 percent of all voting stock plus at least 80 percent of all other classes of stock.[51]

Condemned Real Estate. Congress provided special relief in the situation where real property is condemned by an outside authority. A more liberal interpretation of "similar or related in use" is allowed for the replacement of condemned real property if it is held by the taxpayer for use in a trade or business or for investment. The Code provides that the *like-kind* test shall be applied.[52] This is the test used for § 1031 like-kind exchanges. As explained later in this chapter, these rules allow nonrecognition whenever a taxpayer exchanges real estate for real estate regardless of the real estate's use. Thus, if the taxpayer's unimproved real estate (e.g., raw land) is condemned and replaced with improved real estate (e.g., shopping center), deferral would be granted.

Conversion of Personal Residence. Section 1033 applies to the involuntary conversion of a principal residence. However, the taxpayer may choose between § 1033 and § 1034 in the case of a condemnation, or threat or imminence of condemnation.[53] Also, if he or she qualifies, a taxpayer may elect to use § 121 instead of, or along with, § 1033 for the involuntary conversion of a personal residence.[54]

Conversion of Livestock. Section 1033 includes certain special provisions related to sales of livestock. Livestock sold because of disease[55] or solely because of drought[56] are considered involuntarily converted. Furthermore, if livestock are sold because of soil contamination or environmental contamination and it is not feasible for the owner to reinvest in other livestock, then other farm property, including real property, will qualify as replacement property.[57]

---

[49] Rev. Rul. 71-41, 1971-1 C.B. 223.

[50] § 1033(a)(2)(A).

[51] § 1033(a)(2)(E)(i).

[52] § 1033(g)(1). The similar or related in use test must be applied if the real property is destroyed or the replacement property is stock in a controlled corporation.

[53] § 1034(i).

[54] § 121(d)(4).

[55] § 1033(d).

[56] § 1033(e).

[57] § 1033(f).

REPLACEMENT PERIOD

The taxpayer is entitled to deferral only if reinvestment in the replacement property occurs within the proper time period. The replacement period usually begins on the date of disposition of the converted property; but in the case of condemnation or requisition, it begins at the earliest date of threat or imminence of the requisition or condemnation. The replacement period ends on the last day of the second taxable year after the year in which a gain is first realized,[58] but may be extended by the IRS if the taxpayer can show reasonable cause for being unable to replace within the specified time limit.[59] In the case of condemned real property used in a trade or business or held for investment, the replacement period is extended. The extension is one year, causing the replacement period to remain open until the end of the third taxable year after the first year in which gain is first realized.[60] These time periods are diagrammed below.

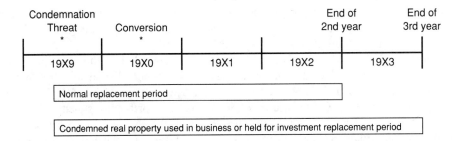

Example 26. E's rental house was condemned for public use by the county during 1994. Her basis in the residence was $32,000 and the county paid her $46,000. E is a calendar year taxpayer and her replacement period begins the day of the condemnation, or threat thereof, and ends on December 31, 1997.

Example 27. If the residence in the previous example had been used as E's personal residence, the replacement period would end on December 31, 1996. The replacement period is extended *only* for real estate held for productive use or for investment.

ELECTION REQUIRED

As a general rule, taxpayers are allowed to elect whether or not they want to defer any gain realized from an involuntary conversion. The election is made simply by not reporting any of the deferred gain on the tax return for the year in which the gain is realized. However, deferral of gain is mandatory if the property is converted directly into property that is similar or related in use.[61]

---

[58] § 1033(a)(2)(B).

[59] Reg. § 1.1033(a)-2(c)(3).

[60] § 1033(g)(4).

[61] § 1033(a).

Example 28. G owned 100 acres of land next to an airport. He had farmed the land for 25 years. All of that changed this year when the city condemned G's land to expand the airport. Pursuant to the condemnation agreement, the city transferred similar farmland to G. In this case, nonrecognition is mandatory since there was a direct conversion into similar property. Had the city paid G for the land, G would have the option to elect deferral or recognize any gain realized.

The return for that year must include detailed information relating to the involuntary conversion,[62] and if the taxpayer has not yet reinvested when the return is filed, he or she is required to notify the IRS when replacement property has been acquired or that no replacement will occur.[63] If after an election has been made under § 1033 *and* the taxpayer fails to reinvest all of the required amount within the allowable period, the tax return for the year (or years) in which gain was realized must be *amended to include the recognized gain* and the tax deficiency must be paid.[64]

AMOUNT OF GAIN RECOGNIZED

No gain is recognized by an electing taxpayer on an involuntary conversion if the amount reinvested in replacement property equals or exceeds the amount realized from the converted property (i.e., the taxpayer does not "cash out" on the transaction). If the amount reinvested is less than the amount realized, the taxpayer has "cashed out" on the transaction and *must* recognize gain to the extent of the amount *not* reinvested (see Exhibit 15-3).[65] No gain is recognized in a direct conversion.[66]

The *amount reinvested* is the *cost* of the replacement property. The property may not have been acquired by gift, inheritance, or any other method resulting in other than a cost basis.[67] The cost basis would include the amount of any debt incurred in the purchase.

The taxpayer will determine his or her basis in property acquired in an involuntary conversion by taking into consideration the deferred gain. In the case of a direct conversion, the basis of the replacement property is the same as the basis in the converted property. In conversions into money and other property, the basis in the replacement property is its cost *reduced* by the amount of gain realized but not recognized (see Exhibit 15-3).[68]

Example 29. M owned a rented industrial equipment warehouse that was adjacent to a railway. The warehouse was destroyed by fire on January 15, 1994, and M received $240,000 from her insurance carrier on March 26, 1994. Her basis in the warehouse was $130,000. M constructed a wholesale grocery warehouse on the same site since the predicted demand for such space was superior to equipment storage. The new warehouse was constructed at a cost of $280,000 and was completed May 7, 1995.

---

[62] Reg. § 1.1033(a)-2(c)(2).

[63] Reg. § 1.1033(a)-2(c)(5).

[64] Special rules extend the statute of limitations. § 1033(a)(2)(C); Reg. § 1.1033(a)-2(c)(5).

[65] § 1033(a)(2)(A).

[66] § 1033(a)(1).

[67] Reg. § 1.1033(a)-2(c)(4).

[68] § 1033(b); Reg. § 1.1033(b)-1.

Exhibit 15-3   Involuntary Conversion: Computation of Recognized Gain and Basis of Replacement Property

1. Gain realized

   Amount realized (net proceeds)

   Less: Adjusted basis

   Gain (loss) realized

2. Gain recognized

   Amount realized

   Less: Cost of replacement property

   Gain recognized (not to exceed gain realized)*

3. Basis of replacement property

   Cost of replacement property

   Less: Gain not recognized

   Adjusted basis of replacement property

* If this amount is negative, the taxpayer has reinvested more than the amount realized and no gain is recognized.

Leased (rental) property is subject to the more liberal *taxpayer use* test, rather than the *functional use* test that is applied to other properties. Therefore, the new warehouse meets the similar or related in use test since it is rental property to M.

As calculated below, M reports no gain on her 1994 return since she reinvested a sufficient amount within the reinvestment period, which ends December 31, 1996. She is required to give the IRS the details of the conversion with her 1994 return and provide a description of the replacement property when it is completed. The basis in the replacement property is $170,000 (cost of $280,000 − the gain not recognized of $110,000).

Amount realized	$240,000
Less: Adjusted basis	(130,000)
Gain (loss) realized	$110,000
Amount realized	$240,000
Less: Cost of replacement property	(280,000)
Gain recognized (not to exceed gain realized)	None
Cost of replacement property	$280,000
Less: Gain not recognized	(110,000)
Adjusted basis of replacement property	$170,000

Example 30. Assume the same facts as in *Example 29*, except that M reinvested $200,000. In this case she would be required to recognize a gain since she did not reinvest all of the insurance proceeds of $240,000. As a result, her gain would be $40,000 and her basis in the replacement property would be $130,000, as calculated below:

Amount realized.......................................	$240,000
Less: Cost of replacement property.................	− 200,000
Gain recognized (not to exceed gain realized)...........	$ 40,000
Cost of replacement property...........................	$200,000
Less: Gain not recognized ($110,000 − $40,000)....	− 70,000
Adjusted basis of replacement property................	$130,000

✔ CHECK YOUR TAX KNOWLEDGE

Over the last several years, Rock and Roller Blades Inc. opened two new roller skating rinks to capitalize on the in-line skating craze. In February 1994, however, one of the rinks was destroyed by fire. At that time, the building had a basis of $100,000. The insurance proceeds awarded to the company amounted to $160,000.

Review Question 1. If the corporation uses the insurance proceeds to build a new indoor soccer facility, will the soccer facility be considered qualified replacement property?

Probably not. In order to qualify for deferral, the replacement property must be similar to or related in service or use to the converted property. This generally means that the replacement property must provide the same functional use as the converted property. Based on the IRS ruling that a billiard parlor is not functionally equivalent to a bowling alley, it would appear that a soccer facility does not provide the same services as a roller rink.

Review Question 2. By what date must the calendar year corporation invest in qualified replacement property?

The corporation must reinvest by the close of the second taxable year following the year in which the conversion takes place, in this case December 31, 1996.

Review Question 3. Assuming the corporation immediately erects another roller rink at the cost of $190,000 and elected to defer any gain realized, the company's gain (or loss) recognized will be

a. $60,000

b. $30,000

c. $90,000

d. $0

e. $30,000 loss

f. None of the above

The answer is (d). As shown in the following computations, the corporation is allowed to defer the entire gain realized since it reinvested all of the insurance proceeds.

Amount realized..................................	$160,000
Less: Adjusted basis...........................	− 100,000
Gain (loss) realized..............................	$ 60,000

Amount realized..................................	$160,000
Less: Cost of replacement property...........	− 190,000
Gain recognized (not to exceed gain realized)....	None

Review Question 4.   Same facts as in Question 3. The basis of the replacement property is

a.	$100,000	**d.**	$0
b.	$190,000	**e.**	$160,000
c.	$170,000	**f.**	None of the above

The answer is (f). The basis is $130,000, determined as follows:

Cost of replacement property.....................	$190,000
Less: Gain not recognized.....................	− 60,000
Adjusted basis of replacement property...........	$130,000

LIKE-KIND EXCHANGES

Section 1031 of the Code provides that a taxpayer may exchange certain types of property *in kind* without the recognition of a taxable gain or loss. Specifically, no gain or loss is recognized when qualifying property is exchanged *solely* for other qualifying property that is of like-kind.

Example 31.   E traded in his 1990 automobile that was worth $4,500 and was used entirely for business purposes and also paid $15,000 cash for a new auto worth $19,500. E's basis in the old auto was $8,200, based on an original cost of $16,000 less depreciation of $7,800. E recognizes no gain or loss on the transaction since it is a qualifying like-kind exchange. His basis in the new auto is $23,200 ($8,200 basis of trade-in + $15,000 cash paid).

If property other than like-kind property—commonly called *boot*—is received in the exchange, a gain may be recognized.[69] Losses, however, are never recognized.

---

[69] § 1031(b).

QUALIFIED PROPERTY

In order to qualify for like-kind exchange treatment, a property must be held *either* for use in a trade or business *or* for investment. A qualified exchange may, however, involve the transfer of investment property for trade or business property, or vice versa.[70] No personal use properties qualify.

Unqualified Properties. Certain properties are specifically excluded from like-kind exchange treatment. For example, stocks, bonds, notes, other securities or evidences of indebtedness, and interests in partnerships do not qualify.[71] In addition, inventory items and other properties held *primarily for sale* are not eligible. Whether an item is inventory (i.e., held primarily for sale to customers in the ordinary course of a trade or business) is discussed in Chapter 16. Several courts have interpreted the phrase *held for sale* to include any property that is acquired in an exchange only to be resold shortly thereafter.[72]

> **Example 32.** K exchanged a parcel of real estate held for investment for another parcel and immediately offered the parcel received for sale. The parcel was sold on the installment basis. Since K held the new property for sale rather than for use in a trade or business or for investment, the entire gain realized on the exchange must be recognized at the time of the exchange.

LIKE-KIND PROPERTY

The concept of *like-kind* refers to the nature or character of property. An exchange of real property for real property normally will qualify, while the exchange of real property for personal property will not.[73]

Real Estate. Generally, any exchange of realty for realty will meet the like-kind test. It is immaterial whether the real property is improved or unimproved.[74] The IRS has ruled that a lease of real property with a remaining term of at least 30 years will be treated as real property for purposes of determining whether a like-kind exchange has occurred.[75] Accordingly, a realized loss from the exchange of property that had declined in value for a lease interest in that property with a life of 30 years or more resulted in a nondeductible (nonrecognized) loss.[76] Condemned real estate in an involuntary conversion is also subject to the like-kind test, as discussed previously.

[70] Reg. § 1.1031(a)-1(a).

[71] § 1031(a)(2).

[72] *Ethel Black*, 35 T.C. 90 (1960); *George M. Bernard*, 26 T.C.M. 858, T.C. Memo. 1967-176.

[73] Reg. § 1.1031(a)-1(b).

[74] Reg. § 1.1031(a)-1(b). However, an exchange of realty located within the United States for realty located outside the United States is specifically denied like-kind exchange treatment—§ 1031(h). It is im-portant to note that § 1250 may supersede § 1031 and cause the recognition of gain. Effectively, § 1250 property (generally depreciable realty) must be acquired in an amount at least as great as the § 1250 recapture potential—§ 1250(d)(4)(C). See Chapter 17 for a discussion of § 1250 recapture of depreciation.

[75] Rev. Rul. 76-301, 1976-2 C.B. 241.

[76] *Century Electric Co. v. Comm.*, 51-2 USTC ¶9482, 41 AFTR 205, 192 F.2d 155 (CA-8, 1951).

Exhibit 15-4 *General Asset Classes: Revenue Procedure 87-56*

Asset Class	Class Number
1. Office furniture, fixtures, and equipment	.11
2. Information systems (computers and peripheral equipment)	.12
3. Data handling equipment, except computers	.13
4. Airplanes and helicopters (airframes and engines), except those used in commercial or contract carrying of passengers or freight	.21
5. Automobiles, taxis	.22
6. Buses	.23
7. Light general-purpose trucks	.241
8. Heavy general-purpose trucks	.242
9. Railroad cars and locomotives	.25
10. Tractor units for use over the road	.26
11. Trailers and trailer-mounted containers	.27
12. Vessels, barges, tugs, and similar water-transportation equipment, except those used in marine construction	.28
13. Industrial steam and electric generation and/or distribution systems	.4

Tangible Depreciable Personalty. Until recently, the IRS has generally approved like-kind exchange treatment as long as personal property was exchanged for personal property. In 1991, however, the Treasury issued new Regulations that established narrow safe harbors for when personal property will be considered like-kind. These new rules provide that a like-kind exchange of personal property occurs only if the property surrendered and the property received are either within the same General Asset Class or within the same Product Class. Under this new approach, personalty must be of *like-class* in order for it to be treated as like-kind.[77]

The General Asset Classes are indentified and defined in Revenue Procedure 87-56. There are 13 classes of assets, as shown in Exhibit 15-4. If two assets fall in the same class, they are considered like-kind. For instance, a computer, printer, monitor, and modem used in a trade or business would qualify as like-kind properties since they are all part of the information systems class (General Asset Class .12). Note that these classes are quite narrow and appear to have changed what for the most part has always been considered like-kind property. For example, according to the new scheme, an automobile and a light-duty truck would not be considered like-kind since they are not in the same Class. Understand, however, that these classes serve only as safe harbors in which taxpayers have guaranteed like-kind treatment.

If a General Asset Class is not provided for a particular asset, the Product Class rules are to be used to determine if the exchanged properties are like-class. Assets are within the same product class if they have the same four-digit product code as listed in the *Standard Industrial Classification* (SIC) *Manual* published by the Department of

---

[77] Reg. § 1.1031(a)-2(b)(1).

Commerce. For example, the Regulations explain that heavy road equipment such as a grader and a scraper are like-class since neither property is within a General Asset Class and both properties have the same SIC code of 3533.

If the property does not qualify as like-class under the safe harbors created by the Regulations, it may still be treated as like-kind. As noted above, the IRS historically has allowed like-kind exchange treatment for personal property when the properties were substantially the same. For example, the IRS has ruled that the contracts of professional athletes are like-kind. Similarly, the courts have ruled that livestock used in a trade or business, but not held for sale, may qualify as like-kind. However, the Code does explain that livestock of different sexes are not like-kind.[78] While it may be obvious that a bull is not a cow, the treatment of bullion-type coins (e.g., decorative gold coins) has created a great deal of controversy. For some investors, collecting and trading gold and silver coins is a popular investment strategy. The IRS has ruled that an exchange of gold bullion held for investment for silver bullion held for the same purpose is not a like-kind exchange since gold and silver are intrinsically different minerals.[79] On the other hand, bullion-type coins of different countries constitute like-kind property.[80] Currency exchanges are not like-kind exchanges. Similarly, legal tender coins (currency) are not of like-kind with bullion-type noncurrency coins.[81]

Intangibles.   The like-class rules apply only to tangible depreciable personalty. There are no like classes for intangible personal property. Whether intangibles such as patents and copyrights are like-kind depends on the nature of the property to which the rights relate. For example, copyrights on two novels are like-kind; but a copyright on a novel and a copyright on a song are not like-kind.[82]

Multiple Property Exchanges.   In some cases an exchange may involve more than one property. When this occurs, as in an exchange of one business for another, the Regulations provide a somewhat complex set of rules. The effect of these rules is that the various assets are matched with those of the same kind or class. Note that if two businesses are exchanged, the goodwill and going concern values of similar businesses are not considered like-kind properties.[83]

---

[78] § 1031(e). Apparently, if male calves could be exchanged for female calves, a breeding herd of females could be built up more quickly and sold for capital gain treatment.

[79] Rev. Rul. 82-166, 1982-2 C.B. 190.

[80] Rev. Rul. 76-214, 1976-1 C.B. 218.

[81] Rev. Rul. 79-143, 1979-1 C.B. 264; *California Federal Life Insurance Co. v. Comm.,* 82-2 USTC ¶9464, 50 AFTR2d 82-5271,

680 F.2d 85 (CA-9, 1982), *aff'g.* 76 T.C. 107 (1981). It is interesting that the Revenue Ruling states that U.S. gold coins are currency, while the courts in these cases state that they are more like "other property" than "money."

[82] Reg. § 1.1031(a)-2(c)(3), Examples 1 and 2.

[83] Reg. § 1.1031(a)-2(c)(2).

RECEIPT OF PROPERTY NOT OF A LIKE-KIND (BOOT)

As a general rule, an exchange is nontaxable only if property is exchanged *solely* for like-kind property. But in many cases, taxpayers wanting to make an exchange do not have like-kind property of equal values. Consequently, one of the parties typically throws in cash or some other non-like-kind property—commonly called *boot*—to equalize the values exchanged. Fortunately, the receipt of boot does not totally disqualify the transaction. Instead, § 1031(b) provides that the taxpayer must recognize any gain realized to the extent of any boot received. For these purposes, *boot* includes any money received in the exchange *plus* the fair market value of any property that is either nonqualified or not like-kind. Under § 1031(c), the receipt of boot does not cause the recognition of any realized losses in such an exchange.[84]

> **Example 33.**   J transferred a vacant lot held as an investment and worth $8,000 to another party in exchange for a similar lot worth $6,000. J received $2,000 cash in addition to the new lot. J's basis in her old lot was $5,500. J's realized gain is $2,500 ($8,000 amount realized − $5,500 basis). If she holds the new lot as an investment, J still must recognize gain on this exchange in the amount of $2,000 because she received *cash boot* of $2,000.

> **Example 34.**   If J's basis in the property given up in the prior example had been $6,500, her realized gain would have been $1,500 ($8,000 amount realized − $6,500 basis). Although she received $2,000 of boot, J's recognized gain is $1,500 (recognized gain is *never* more than the realized gain).

> **Example 35.**   If J's basis in the vacant lot exchanged in the previous two examples had been $9,000, she would have a realized loss of $1,000 and a recognized loss of zero. Losses in like-kind exchanges are never recognized.

Liabilities as Boot.   In many exchanges, a taxpayer transfers property encumbered by indebtedness (e.g., land subject to a mortgage) or has liabilities assumed as part of the exchange agreement. When a taxpayer is relieved of a liability, the tax law takes the view that such relief is the economic equivalent of receiving cash and paying off the liability. In essence, the party assuming the liability is treated as having paid cash for the property. Consistent with this view, any liabilities from which the taxpayer is relieved in a like-kind exchange are treated as boot received (or boot paid in the case of the party assuming the debt).[85] Note that without these rules, taxpayers could mortgage property shortly before the exchange, receive cash, and then transfer the property along with liability without having to recognize any gain. The treatment of liability relief as boot thwarts such plans.

---

[84] If a note is received as boot, the gain may be reported using the installment sales rules. See § 453(h)(6) and (7).

[85] § 1031(d).

Example 36. Wanting to move his business out of the city, R exchanged his downtown warehouse encumbered by a mortgage of $200,000 for a new suburban building worth $700,000. R's basis in the warehouse was $600,000. As a result, R realized a gain of $300,000 ($700,000 + $200,000 − $600,000). Although R received only the building, the relief of the $200,000 liability is treated as boot received. Therefore, R must recognize a gain of $200,000.

Relief and Assumption of Liabilities. If both parties to the exchange assume a liability (e.g., the taxpayer is relieved of a liability of $100,000 but also incurs a liability of $90,000), the process becomes a bit more confusing. In this case, the taxpayer first nets the assumption and the relief. If the taxpayer has net relief (i.e., net decrease in liabilities), such amount is treated as boot received, which in turn triggers gain recognition.[86] If the taxpayer has net incurred (i.e., net increase in liabilities), such amount is treated as boot paid and no gain is recognized. Note that liabilities are the only type of boot paid or received that can be netted. Other types of boot are not netted. But what if a taxpayer receives cash and incurs liabilities? Can the taxpayer offset any cash received (and the gain that goes with it) by any liabilities incurred? And what if a taxpayer is relieved of liabilities? Can the taxpayer offset any liability relief by giving cash? The Regulations have addressed these possibilities. A taxpayer cannot offset boot received by liabilities incurred. However, liability relief can be offset by boot given (since the taxpayer could presumably pay off the debt with the boot, thereby reducing the liability relief).[87] These various situations are addressed in the next three examples.

Example 37. S exchanged a tractor worth $11,000 for a lighter duty tractor worth $9,000, both held for use in his landscaping business. The tractor given up was subject to a secured obligation of $8,000 and S incurred a liability secured by the new tractor of $6,000. S's basis in the tractor given up was $6,500, his cost of $13,500 less depreciation allowed of $7,000. S's realized gain on this exchange is $4,500, computed as follows:

Fair market value of property received......................	$ 9,000
Plus: Liabilities encumbering the property transferred.................................... +	8,000
Less: Liabilities assumed by taxpayer.................... −	6,000
Amount realized..	$11,000
Less: Adjusted basis of property given up................ −	6,500
Gain realized..	$ 4,500

S's recognized gain is $2,000 since his net liability relief ($8,000 liability relief − $6,000 liability assumed) is treated as boot.

---

[86] See Reg. §§ 1.1031(b)-1(c) and 1.1031 (d)-2. It is important to note that liabilities incurred in anticipation of a like-kind exchange will not qualify for this netting treatment. See Prop. Reg. § 1.1031 (b)-1(c).

[87] Reg. § 1.1031(d)-2, Ex. 2.

Example 38.   Use the facts in *Example 37*, but assume that instead of receiving a $9,000 tractor and incurring a $6,000 liability, S received a tractor worth $7,500 and paid $4,500 cash. S's realized gain is $4,500 computed as follows:

Fair market value of property received......................	$ 7,500
Plus: Liabilities encumbering the	
property transferred.................................+	8,000
Less: Amount of money given up.........................−	4,500
Amount realized..	$11,000
Less: Adjusted basis of property given up...............−	6,500
Gain realized..	$ 4,500

S's recognized gain is $3,500, the amount of his liability relief ($8,000) less the other boot paid ($4,500 cash).

Example 39.   If S had received a tractor worth $3,000 and incurred no liabilities and paid no cash in the transaction, his realized gain is still $4,500, computed as follows:

Fair market value of property received......................	$ 3,000
Plus: Liabilities encumbering the	
property transferred.................................. +	8,000
Amount realized..	$11,000
Less: Adjusted basis of property given up............... −	6,500
Gain realized..	$ 4,500

The amount of boot received is $8,000, the amount of his liability relief. The recognized gain is $4,500, since the gain is recognized to the extent of boot received, but never more than the gain realized.

BASIS IN PROPERTY RECEIVED

Exhibit 15-5 presents two ways of computing the basis of property received in a like-kind exchange. The first method (Method 1), prescribed by the Code, is based on the notion that the like-kind property received in the exchange is merely a continuation of the taxpayer's investment in the like-kind property given up. Thus, the basis of the property received should be the same as the property given up—a so-called *substituted* basis. This basis is *increased* by any gain recognized and by any additional consideration given or to be paid in the future, or *decreased* by the fair market value of any boot received and by any liabilities transferred.[88] The second method is derived from the basis determination

---

[88]   § 1031(d).

Exhibit 15-5   *Basis of Property Received in a Like-Kind Exchange*

Method 1:

Adjusted basis of property given up..................			$xxx,xxx
Plus:	Gain recognized.......................	$xx,xxx	
	Boot paid............................	x,xxx	
	Liabilities assumed by the taxpayer........................	xx,xxx	
	Liabilities encumbering the property received..................	xx,xxx	+ xx,xxx
			$xxx,xxx
Less:	Boot received.........................	$xx,xxx	
	Liabilities assumed by the other party (transferee)....................	xx,xxx	
	Liabilities encumbering the property transferred.................	xx,xxx	− xx,xxx
Basis of property received...........................			$xxx,xxx

Method 2:

Fair market value of like-kind property received......		$xxx,xxx
Less:	Deferred gain (realized gain − recognized gain)...................	− xx,xxx
Plus:	Realized loss (deferred)..............	+ xx,xxx
Basis of property received...........................		$xxx,xxx

method used for replacement property in involuntary conversions and sales of principal residences. Under this method, the fair market value of the like-kind property received (i.e., its cost if purchased) is *reduced* by a deferred gain or *increased* by deferred loss in determining its basis. This adjustment is made so that if the newly acquired property is later sold, any realized gain or loss that is not recognized (deferred amount) from the previous like-kind exchange will be automatically considered in the computation of the realized gain or loss. Under either method, the basis of any boot received is its fair market value.

Example 40.   J operates a charter flight business out of Ft. Lauderdale. This year he put together a deal with one of his flying buddies whereby he traded his old plane, with a basis of $40,000, for another smaller plane worth $53,000 and a hangar to park it in, worth $7,000. J's realized gain is $20,000 [($53,000 + $7,000 = $60,000) − $40,000]. Since the hanger is realty, it is treated as boot. Thus J must recognize a gain of $7,000 (lesser of the gain realized or boot received). The basis of the boot received, the hangar, is its fair market value of $7,000. J's basis in the new plane is $40,000, computed as follows:

Method 1

Adjusted basis of property given up..............	$40,000
Plus: gain recognized.........................	7,000
Less: Boot received...........................	− 7,000
Basis of property received......................	$40,000

Method 2

Fair market value of like-kind property received...	$53,000
Less: Deferred gain ($20,000 − $7,000).......	− 13,000
Basis of property received......................	$40,000

At first glance, the basis calculations may not make sense. In the substituted basis computation, the basis of the new property is initially the same as the property given up, $40,000. However, any gain recognized, in this case $7,000, must be added to ensure that upon subsequent sale of the property such gain is not taxed again. The sum of these two amounts ($40,000 + $7,000 = $47,000) represents the basis for the like-kind property and the boot received. A portion of this total is then allocated to the boot by subtracting the value of the boot, $7,000. In effect, the basis assigned to the boot is its $7,000 value, leaving the remaining $40,000 to be assigned to the like-kind property. Note how a subsequent sale of the like-kind property for its $53,000 value would cause the taxpayer to recognize the previously postponed gain of $13,000 ($53,000 − $40,000). This same result is accomplished in a much more obvious manner in the second calculation, where the deferred gain is simply subtracted from the value of the property.

The following example is a comprehensive review of the like-kind exchange rules.

Example 41.   E exchanged a rental house for T's rental condominium. E's house was worth $36,000 and her adjusted basis was $27,000. The house was not subject to any liabilities. T's condominium was worth $82,000 and was subject to a mortgage of $54,000. T also transferred $8,000 worth of Alpha Corp. stock to E in order to equalize the transaction. T's adjusted basis in his condominium and the Alpha stock were $64,000 and $5,600, respectively. The gains realized by E and T are computed as follows:

E		
Fair market value of property received		
Rental condominium (like-kind property).................		$82,000
Alpha Corp. stock (boot received).......................		+ 8,000
		$90,000
Less: Liabilities (mortgage) assumed		
by taxpayer......................................		− 54,000
Amount realized..		$36,000
Less: Adjusted basis of rent house given up..............		− 27,000
Gain realized..		$ 9,000

T		
Fair market value of rental house received.................		$36,000
Plus: Liabilities discharged (assumed by E)...............		+ 54,000
Amount realized...		$90,000
Less: Adjusted basis of properties given up:		
Rental condominium............................	$64,000	
Alpha Corp. stock (boot paid)....................	5,600	− 69,600
Gain realized..		$20,400

E's gain recognized is $8,000, the amount of boot (stock) received. The amount of boot received by T is $54,000 (the amount of liabilities discharged), which is reduced by his boot paid of $8,000 (fair market value of Alpha stock). Therefore, T's net liabilities discharged are $46,000. T's recognized gain, however, is $20,400, since recognized gain never exceeds realized gain. T's recognized gain consists of $2,400 ($8,000 fair market value − $5,600 basis) for the taxable exchange of the Alpha stock, and the remaining $18,000 is attributable to the exchange of his house.

E and T's bases in their like-kind property received are determined as follows:

	E's Condominium	T's House
Adjusted basis of like-kind property given up......................................	$27,000	$64,000
Plus: Gain recognized......................	+ 8,000	+ 20,400
Boot paid.............................	+ 0	+ 5,600
Liabilities assumed....................	+ 54,000	+ 0
Less: Boot received.........................	− 8,000	− 0
Liabilities discharged.................	− 0	− 54,000
Basis of property received....................	$81,000	$36,000

E's basis in the Alpha Corp. stock is $8,000, its fair market value.[89] E and T could have computed their bases in the like-kind property received by using the alternative method (Method 2) discussed previously.

	E	T
Fair market value of like-kind property received:		
Rental house.............................		$36,000
Rental condominium......................	$82,000	
Less: Deferred gain.........................	− 1,000	− 0
Basis of like-kind property received............	$81,000	$36,000

EXCHANGE REQUIREMENT

Generally, the determination of whether an exchange has occurred is not difficult. All that is required is a reciprocal transfer of qualifying properties. An exchange of one real estate investment for another would normally qualify. Similarly, a trade-in of a business auto along with some cash for another auto is a qualifying exchange. However, an argument can be made for collapsing seemingly independent transactions that might appear to be an exchange in substance.[90]

Example 42. B, a traveling salesperson, "sold" his business auto to a car dealership for $3,200 cash. Shortly thereafter, he purchased another auto from the same dealer for $12,000 cash. The IRS could collapse the *two* transactions (sale and purchase) between the same parties in *one* like-kind exchange. Thus, if B's basis in the old vehicle was $6,000, his loss would be disallowed, and his basis in the new auto would be $14,800 ($12,000 fair market value of new auto + $2,800 deferred loss).

---

[89] Reg. §§ 1.1031(d)-1(c) and 1.1031 (d)-1(d).

[90] Rev. Rul. 61-119, 1961-1 C.B. 395.

Three-Corner Exchanges. It is not always easy for two parties with properties of equal value, both of which are suitable to the other party, to get together. Even so, it may be possible for a taxpayer who cannot find an exchange partner to qualify for like-kind treatment through a three-corner exchange.

Several forms of multiple-party exchanges have qualified for like-kind exchange treatment. The IRS has ruled that when three property owners entered into an exchange in which each gave up and received qualifying property, like-kind exchange treatment was appropriate.[91] However, a three-corner exchange must be part of a single, integrated plan.[92]

> **Example 43.** X, Y, and Z each own rental property. They exchange the properties as follows:
>
> > X gets Y's property, Y gets Z's property, and Z gets X's property. X, Y, and Z pay or receive boot in order to equalize the difference in the values of the properties.
>
> This three-party transaction qualifies as a like-kind exchange under § 1031. Each party receiving boot must recognize gain up to the amount of the boot received.

Perhaps a more common situation involves a taxpayer who is willing to "sell" property but does not want to recognize gain. In this situation, the interested buyer purchases like-kind property identified by the "seller" and then exchanges it for the seller's property.

> **Example 44.** C owned rental property worth $70,000 (adjusted basis of $34,000), which she was willing to dispose of only if she could do so without recognizing any gain. B wanted to purchase C's property, but in order that C might defer her potential gain of $36,000, he agreed to purchase another rental property of equal value that was suitable to C. As long as she receives no boot, C would recognize no gain and her basis in the replacement property would be $34,000 ($70,000 fair market value of property received − $36,000 deferred gain). B will not qualify for § 1031 treatment since he purchased the property specifically for the exchange and thus never held it for business use or investment.[93] However, B will not have any realized gain or loss as a result of the transaction since his amount realized of $70,000 (fair market value of rental property received from C) is equal to his cost basis of the property given up.

---

[91] Rev. Rul. 57-244, 1957-1 C.B. 247; Rev. Rul. 73-476, 1973-2 C.B. 300.

[92] Rev. Rul. 75-291, 1975-2 C.B. 332; Rev. Rul. 77-297, 1977-2 C.B. 304.

[93] *Biggs v. Comm.*, 81-1 USTC ¶9114, 47 AFTR2d 81-484, 632 F.2d 1171 (CA-5, 1980).

Delayed Exchanges. The property to be accepted by the taxpayer in a like-kind exchange need not be received *simultaneously* with the transfer of his or her property. However, in order to qualify for nonrecognition treatment, the property to be acquired must be

1. Identified within 45 days after the date the taxpayer surrenders his or her property; and

2. Received within 180 days of the transfer, but no later than the due date (including extensions) of the tax return for the year of transfer.[94]

> **Example 45.**   R has agreed to purchase any real property worth $120,000 that is acceptable to S if S will immediately transfer his commercial parking lot, which is adjacent to R's store, to R. S agrees to the plan. S later identifies a duplex worth $120,000 and directs R to purchase it for him. This delayed exchange will qualify under § 1031 if the duplex is specified as the replacement property within 45 days and is transferred to S within 180 days of the transfer of the parking lot to R. Note how the taxpayer has effectively sold the property for $120,000 cash and then reinvested the cash without having to pay tax.

Delayed exchanges are frequently expedited by an escrow company that holds money that is to be used to purchase a property for the transferor. It is possible that a property would be identified within 45 days but, due to circumstances beyond the taxpayer's control, cannot be acquired. To prevent this misfortune, the taxpayer may identify one or more additional properties within the 45-day period to be acquired if the acquisition of the first property cannot be completed.[95]

Related-Party Exchanges.   Prior to 1989, related parties used a clever device to reduce gain on the sale of appreciated property. At the heart of the scheme were the substituted basis rules applied in like-kind exchanges. These rules effectively enabled the taxpayer to create a high basis for what otherwise was low-basis property that the taxpayer planned to sell.

> **Example 46.**   T owns all of the stock of D Corporation, which is planning to sell 100 acres of land for $700,000 (basis $100,000). Accordingly, D anticipates that it will recognize a gain of $600,000. To minimize the gain on the sale, however, T transfers one of his real estate investments worth $700,000 (basis $500,000) to the corporation in exchange for the land and subsequently sells the land. T's gain on the sale of the land is only $200,000 ($700,000 − $500,000) since the like-kind exchange rules enabled him to substitute the higher basis of his realty, $500,000, as the basis for the land.

---

[94] § 1031(a)(3).   [95] Reg. § 1.1031(k)-1.

To put an end to the so-called basis-swapping illustrated in *Example 46,* Congress created a special rule. If a taxpayer exchanges property with a *related party* and either taxpayer disposes of the transferred property within two years, the like-kind exchange rules do not apply to the original exchange and any deferred gain must be recognized in the year of the subsequent disposition.[96] For this purpose, the definition of a related party is the same as that used for the loss disallowance rules of §§ 267 and 707(b)(1), which generally includes the taxpayer's family (spouse, brothers, sisters, ancestors, lineal descendants) and certain entities (e.g., corporations and partnerships) in which the taxpayer owns more than a 50 percent interest.

> **Example 47.**   Assume the same facts as in *Example 46* above. Under current law T's plan would not work since T and his corporation are considered related parties and he sold the property within two years of the exchange. As a result, both T and D must recognize their deferred gains on the original exchange in the year of the sale. T recognizes a gain of $200,000 ($700,000 − $500,000) and D recognizes a gain of $600,000 ($700,000 − $100,000). T recognizes no gain on the sale itself because his basis in the land is now treated as $700,000 since the original transaction became taxable. Note that T's plan would have worked had T been patient and sold the land more than two years after the exchange.

TREATMENT MANDATORY

Like-kind exchange treatment is mandatory. Therefore, no gain or loss is recognized on any transaction that meets the like-kind exchange requirements even if the taxpayer desires otherwise. Since the provision applies to losses as well as gains, like-kind treatment may work to the disadvantage of a taxpayer, and it may be to his or her benefit to avoid exchange status.

> **Example 48.**   This year B swapped her rental property in Malibu worth $200,000 (basis $230,000) for rental property in Vail worth $175,000 and cash of $25,000. B has realized a loss of $30,000 ($200,000 − $230,000). Although she received boot of $25,000, none of the loss is recognized. In this case, B would probably be better off selling the Malibu property and purchasing the Vail property so that she could recognize her loss.

HOLDING PERIOD

The holding period of like-kind property received in a § 1031 exchange includes the holding period of the property given up on the exchange.[97] This also applies to the holding period of replacement property in an involuntary conversion. However, the holding period of any property received as boot in a § 1031 exchange *begins* on the date of its receipt. In effect, when boot received is property other than money (or liability relief), it is treated as if the taxpayer received money (equal to the property's fair market value) and used it to purchase the property. Consequently, the property's holding period starts on the day of the exchange *and* the basis of the property is its fair market value.

---

[96]   § 1031(f).   [97]   § 1223(1).

✔ CHECK YOUR TAX KNOWLEDGE

Review Question 1.   This year H retired. He decided to continue to live in Chicago but wanted to get rid of his rental property (fair market value $240,000, basis $140,000) and buy a condominium in Florida. H is now entertaining an offer to sell the property to a real estate mogul who loves the property and is hot to buy. What would you advise?

Without good advice, most taxpayers would sell the property, recognize a $100,000 gain and pay a capital gains tax of $28,000, leaving them with only $72,000 to invest. There is a much better approach. H is a perfect candidate for a delayed like-kind exchange. He could "sell" the property and have the buyer transfer the funds to an escrow agent, who would hold the money while H identifies the property in Florida he wants. He must do this within 45 days after the sale. As long as he closes on the new property within 180 days of the transfer (but no later than the due date of the return for the year of the transfer, including extensions), the like-kind exchange provisions will apply and H does not have to recognize the gain!

Review Question 2.   At the outset of this chapter, it was indicated that there is a way to pyramid one's wealth to $1 million without ever having to pay tax. How could this be done?

The first step is to make wise investments (typically real estate). After the property has appreciated, "sell" the property using the delayed like-kind exchange technique just as H did in the previous question. The effect is to invest in a higher-value property without having to pay any tax. If H can continue to invest sucessfully, he never has to pay tax along the way to $1 million. Note that H does not necessarily have to find a property of equal value, assuming the amount escrowed is reinvested in like-kind property. As long as all of the cash is used and none passes to H, he does not recognize any gain. Thus H could effectively use the property as a down payment for new property and accelerate the process.

Review Question 3.   True-False. This year D swapped her billiard parlor for a bowling alley. The transaction qualifies as a like-kind exchange.

True. Although the properties are not considered similar or related in use according to the functional use test applied to involuntary conversion rules, the two investments are considered like-kind property since they are both realty.

Review Question 4.   True-False. During the year, E exchanged her home for a rental house. The swap qualifies as a like-kind exchange.

False. The properties exchanged must be held for productive use or investment. In this case, E is not holding her home for investment, and therefore the exchange is taxable.

Review Question 5.   True-False. Under the like-kind exchange rules, a taxpayer must receive cash before any gain realized is recognized.

False. Although this may appear to be true, the taxpayer is taxed whenever boot is received. Any property other than the like-kind property received is treated as boot. For example, the boot could take the form of stock, a note, or even liability relief.

Review Question 6.   True-False. This year, F swapped her investment land for a friend's land and $10,000 of cash. As a result, F realized a $20,000 loss. F may recognize a loss of $10,000.

False. Losses are never recognized on a like-kind exchange even if the taxpayer receives boot.

Review Question 7.   True-False. G sold her rental property in Galveston for $100,000 and realized a $25,000 gain. Two months later, she used the $100,000 to purchase another rental property on Padre Island for $150,000. G does not recognize gain since she has not liquidated her investment but continued it in another rental property.

False. Although G seems to have met the spirit of the law, there must, as a general rule, be a direct exchange in order to qualify for nonrecognition under the like-kind exchange provisions. Note that G could have postponed the gain had she taken advantage of the delayed like-kind exchange rules or had she simply had the buyer of her property buy the Padre Island property and then done an exchange.

Review Question 8.   During the year, Fred traded one of his buddies a tractor used solely in his construction business for another tractor for the same use. On the date of the trade, the old tractor had an adjusted basis of $3,000. He received in exchange $500 in cash and a smaller tractor with a fair market value of $2,800. Fred should recognize a gain on the exchange of:

a.	$800	**d.**	$0
b.	$500	**e.**	None of the above
c.	$300		

The answer is (c). Fred realized a gain of $300 [($2,800 + $500 = $3,300) − $3,000]. Since he received boot of $500, he must recognize the lesser of the gain realized, $300, or the boot received, $500.

Review Question 9.   Assuming the same facts as above, the basis of the new tractor to Fred would be

a. $3,300   d. $2,300

b. $3,000   e. None of the above

c. $2,800

The answer is (c), as determined below.

Method 1

Adjusted basis of property given up..............	$3,000
Plus: Gain recognized.........................	300
Less: Boot received..........................	− 500
Basis of property received......................	$2,800

Method 2

Fair market value of like-kind property received...	$2,800
Less: Deferred gain...........................	− 0
Basis of property received......................	$2,800

OTHER NONTAXABLE TRANSACTIONS

CHANGES IN FORM OF DOING BUSINESS

Several provisions in the Internal Revenue Code are intended to allow mere changes in the form of carrying on a continuing business activity without the recognition of gain or loss. Section 721, for example, allows the transfer of property to a partnership in exchange for a partnership interest without the recognition of taxable gain or loss. Section 351 allows a similar treatment when property is transferred to a corporation solely in exchange for its stock by persons possessing control, and § 355 provides for nontaxability in certain corporate reorganizations. These specific topics are addressed in subsequent chapters.

CERTAIN EXCHANGES OF STOCK IN SAME CORPORATION

No gain or loss is recognized by the shareholder who exchanges common stock for common stock or preferred stock for preferred stock in the same corporation under § 1036. The exchange may be voting stock for nonvoting stock, and it is immaterial whether the exchange is with another shareholder or with the issuing corporation.[98] If the exchange is not solely in kind, the rules of § 1031(b) (applicable to like-kind exchanges) are applied to determine the amount of any gain recognized.[99]

---

[98] Reg. § 1.1036-1(a).   [99] Reg. § 1.1036-1(b).

CERTAIN EXCHANGES OF U.S. OBLIGATIONS

Gain may be deferred in the case of certain exchanges of U.S. obligations between the taxpayer and the U.S. Government. Section 1037 applies to exchanges of bonds of the Government issued under Chapter 31 of Title 31 (the Second Liberty Bond Act). The Treasury regulations for § 1037 discuss the application of this section.

REPOSSESSION OF REAL PROPERTY

Section 1038 provides that the seller of real property will recognize a gain on the repossession of real property only to the extent the sum of the money and other property besides the repossessed realty received exceeds the gain from the transaction previously reported. This provision applies only to repossessions to satisfy debt obligations received in exchange for the sold property (e.g., foreclosure for nonpayment of mortgage). Such purchase-money obligations must be secured by an interest in the property. If any part of these obligations has previously been deducted as a bad debt, the amount of such deductions is included in income in the year of the repossession.

ROLLOVER GAIN FROM LOW-INCOME HOUSING

The gain on the sale of "qualified housing projects" can be deferred if the property is sold to its tenants or occupants, or to a cooperative or other nonprofit organization formed solely for their benefit. To qualify, the sale must be approved by the Secretary of Housing and Urban Development.

Section 1039 provides that the owner may elect to defer the gain if another "qualified housing project" is purchased within specified time limits. The time limit may be extended by the IRS at the request of the taxpayer.

A *qualified housing project* is one subject to a mortgage insured by the Federal government under specified housing programs and, under such programs, is limited as to rates of return and occupancy charges. Properties that qualify for these guarantees provide housing for lower-income families.

CERTAIN EXCHANGES OF INSURANCE POLICIES

Section 1035 allows the deferral of gain on the exchange of a life insurance contract for another insurance policy. Additionally, it allows certain exchanges involving annuity contracts and endowment contracts.

TAX PLANNING CONSIDERATIONS

CURRENT RECOGNITION VERSUS DEFERRAL

A basic concept in tax planning, as discussed in earlier chapters, is the deferral of tax payments. Each of the provisions discussed in this chapter (as it relates to gains) is a perfect example of such a deferral. A taxpayer is usually better off by deferring any gain—unless he or she expects to be in a much higher effective tax bracket in the later year when the deferred gain would be recognized. Of course, a taxpayer is *always* better off if he or she can avoid tax altogether, as is the case under § 121. However, if a loss is deferred under § 1031, taxes are accelerated. Thus, if the adjusted basis of business or investment property being disposed of exceeds its fair market value, the nonrecognition treatment of § 1031 should be avoided.

CURRENT GAIN RESULTING IN FUTURE REDUCTIONS

In each case of deferred gain, the mechanism is a reduced basis in the replacement property. If this replacement property is depreciable property, the depreciation deductions will also be smaller. It may be advantageous to report a large gain *currently* if the tax cost is low, and reap the benefit of the larger depreciation deductions in later years.

> **Example 49.** W plans to dispose of a building that would result in capital gain if sold, and acquire similar property in a different location. W could defer gain by arranging an exchange, but his basis in the new property would be low. W also has a large capital loss carryforward that he has been deducting at the rate of $3,000 per year.
>
> If W sells the property, the gain would offset the capital loss carryforward and he would pay no tax. His basis in the new building would be its cost, resulting in larger future depreciation deductions.

SECTION 1034 CONSIDERATIONS

Qualifying for the deferral of gain on the sale of a principal residence under § 1034 involves several tax planning considerations. First, care must be exercised so that the timing requirements are met. If a taxpayer purchases a replacement residence before selling the prior residence, the later sale must occur within the two-year period.

Another use of the reinvestment period involves a situation where the taxpayer sells and reinvests an amount less than the adjusted sales price. Any improvements to the property are included in its cost if they are made prior to the expiration of the reinvestment period.

> **Example 50.** F sold her residence for $90,000, resulting in an adjusted sales price of $87,000 after selling costs and fixing-up expenses. She purchased a new residence for $65,000 three months later. Based on these facts, F must recognize gain of $22,000 ($87,000 − $65,000). However, if F adds a garage and a swimming pool to the new residence for $24,000 (or any other improvements) within two years of selling the prior residence, her amount reinvested will be $89,000 and her entire gain will be deferred.

Sale of Replacement.   A taxpayer who sells and reinvests may not defer gain from the replacement residence if it is sold before the expiration of the two-year reinvestment period from the prior residence. A taxpayer who wishes to sell the replacement and would recognize a gain should wait until that period expires.

> **Example 51.**   G purchased his first home for $56,000 and sold it for $70,000 on April 1, 1993. He purchased a replacement on July 1, 1993 for $75,000, deferring all his gain. On October 1, 1994 G received an offer to purchase his replacement residence for $92,000. Even if G reinvests on a timely basis, he will recognize the $17,000 gain ($92,000 − $75,000) if he sells before April 1, 1995. If G waits until after March 31, 1995 to sell his replacement, he can defer all of the gain by reinvesting in another replacement residence.

Business Use of Home.   If part of a home is used exclusively as an office or is otherwise dedicated to business use, the costs of that portion of the residence, including depreciation, may be deductible. However, that portion of the residence will not qualify as a principal residence and any gain on that portion of the residence cannot be deferred under § 1034. A taxpayer who anticipates selling his or her residence may wish to convert the business portion of the residence to personal use prior to the sale so that the entire residence will qualify under § 1034. In the case of an office in the home, one could begin to use the office for some nonbusiness uses (i.e., not use the office exclusively for business), resulting in disallowance of the office expenses.

SECTION 121 CONSIDERATIONS

It is often difficult to determine whether a taxpayer with a gain of less than $125,000 on the sale of a personal residence and who intends to reinvest should use his or her § 121 election. In at least two instances, the § 121 election can be very useful. *First*, it is useful when a residence is sold and the taxpayer does not anticipate ever owning another home. *Second*, it is useful when a person has a large gain and intends to invest in a significantly less expensive home. If the gain is less than $125,000, it totally escapes tax and there is no reduction in the basis of the new residence. If the gain is greater than $125,000, the amount that must be reinvested to defer all of the gain, the adjusted sales price, is reduced by the amount of gain excluded under § 121.

Age 55.   To qualify under § 121, the taxpayer must be at least 55 years of age on the date the property is sold. Accordingly, a taxpayer in his or her early fifties may wish to defer selling the residence until such time as all requirements are met. A taxpayer nearing his or her 55th birthday may wish to go ahead and offer the residence for sale, specifying that the sale cannot occur until after his or her birthday.

IMPORTANCE OF CAPITAL BUDGETING IN DECISION MAKING

In any decision of whether to defer taxes when subsequent tax years are affected, capital budgeting techniques are appropriate in making the decision. When considering possible investment opportunities, a taxpayer must *compare* current investment requirements and tax effects with the future returns from the investment and their tax effects. Some form of present-value analysis will help the taxpayer to make a sound decision. A similar analysis should be applied in deciding the appropriateness of entering into any nontaxable (tax-deferred) transaction.

PROBLEM MATERIALS

DISCUSSION QUESTIONS

15-1 *Deferral vs. Exclusion.* In what way do deferred gains differ from excluded gains?

15-2 *Adjusted Sales Price.* Write a formula for determining the adjusted sales price of a residence under § 1034 beginning with the gross sales price.

15-3 *Fixing-up Expenses.* What are "fixing-up expenses"?

15-4 *Adjusted Sales Price.* The following information was derived from B's records regarding the sale by owner of her principal residence:

Gross sales price................................	$150,000
Advertising.......................................	575
Title transfers, costs.............................	450
Food, beverages during open houses, June 1 and 8	125
Landscaping, clean-up, May 23...................	235
Repairs, July 6...................................	125

B offered the residence for sale June 1, accepted an offer to purchase June 10, and transferred title on July 10 (all in the current year). How much are B's amount realized and adjusted sales price with respect to this residence?

15-5 *Loss on Sale of Personal Assets.* Y sold his principal residence and realized a $12,000 loss. What is the proper tax treatment of this loss?

15-6 *Basis Determination.* How is the basis of a replacement residence determined under § 1034?

15-7 *Impact on Basis of Fixing-up Expenses.* How do fixing-up expenses affect the tax treatment of the sale of a principal residence under § 1034?

15-8 *Replacement Period.* T entered into a contract to sell on February 21, 1994 and sold her principal residence on April 2, 1994. What is the replacement period during which this residence must be replaced in order to defer gain from the sale?

15-9 *Required Election.* How often may the § 121 election be made? Can the taxpayer change his or her mind about a § 121 election previously made? If so, under what circumstances might you advise such action?

15-10 *Tests for Gain Exclusion.* What three tests must be met in order for a taxpayer to exclude gain on the sale of a personal residence under § 121?

15-11 *Interaction of §§ 121 and 1034.* How does an election of the § 121 exclusion affect the computation of the gain recognized and the basis of the replacement property if gain is also deferred under § 1034?

15-12 *Condemnation.* What is required in order to have "threat or imminence" of condemnation?

15-13 *Replacement Property under § 1033.* How does the concept of "similar or related in service or use" differ between an owner/user of property and an owner/lessor?

15-14 *Replacement Period.* B's beauty salon was destroyed by fire on April 21, 1994. The building was covered by current value insurance, and B realized a gain of $70,000. When must B reinvest in order to defer this gain under § 1033?

15-15 *Making the § 1033 Election.* How does a taxpayer elect to defer gain under § 1033 in involuntary conversions?

15-16 *Ineligible Property.* Property "held for sale" is not eligible for like-kind exchange treatment. Elaborate.

15-17 *Real Property under § 1031.* K proposes to exchange a downtown office building she holds as rental property for a 450-acre ranch in Virginia that she would operate as a horse ranch. Will this transaction qualify for like-kind exchange treatment?

15-18 *Personal Property under § 1031.* What constitutes personal property of "like-kind"?

15-19 *Boot.* What is the meaning of "boot" in § 1031 like-kind exchanges?

15-20 *Liabilities.* Are liabilities discharged always treated as boot received in a like-kind exchange under § 1031? Explain.

15-21 *Basis of Property Received.* How is the basis in the property received in a like-kind exchange under § 1031 determined? What is the basis in any boot received?

15-22 *§ 1031 Elective or Mandatory.* Is like-kind exchange treatment elective with the taxpayer? If not, how could such treatment be avoided if the taxpayer was so inclined?

15-23 *Holding Period.* In the current year, R received a rental house and 300 shares of IBM common stock in exchange for a vacant lot he had held as an investment since April 16, 1991. When does the holding period for the rental house begin? For the IBM stock?

PROBLEMS

15-24 *Sale of Principal Residence.* B, age 46, sold his principal residence for $96,000 on March 16, 1994. His basis in the residence was $56,000, and he paid sales commissions on the sale of $6,720. He also spent $780 on general repairs one month before entering the contract of sale. On May 7, 1995 B purchased a new residence for $90,000.

    a. What is B's "adjusted sales price" on the old residence?
    b. How much gain, if any, does B recognize on the sale of the old residence? If any gain is to be recognized, when?
    c. What is B's basis in his new residence?

15-25 *Sale of Principal Residence.* What would be your answers in Problem 15-24 if B had invested $80,000 in his new residence?

15-26 *Sale of Principal Residence.* What would be your answers to the questions in Problem 15-24 if B had reinvested $53,000?

15-27 *Sale of Principal Residence.* T realized a $66,000 gain on the sale of her personal residence. She incurred selling costs of $7,500 and allowable fixing-up expenses of $1,500 related to this sale. Assuming that T purchased a qualifying replacement residence for $187,000 and recognized a $2,000 gain, answer the following:

a. What were the sales price and adjusted basis of T's former residence?

b. What is T's basis in the replacement residence?

15-28 *Sale of Principal Residence.* M sold her principal residence for $220,000 on April 17, 1994 and reinvested in a new residence costing $190,000 on June 23, 1994. She incurred the following expenses related to the sale: sales commissions, $12,000; paint for residence, $800; general repairs, $600; new roof, $1,200; and closing costs, $500. The cost of the old residence was $124,000. The expenditures for painting and general repairs qualify as fixing-up expenses under § 1034.

a. What is M's "adjusted sales price"?

b. How much gain does M recognize on the sale of the old residence?

c. What is M's basis in her new residence?

d. How would your answers to parts b and c above change if M had reinvested $208,000?

15-29 *Sale of Principal Residence.* T sold his principal residence for $66,000 during the current year. He had an adjusted basis in the residence of $52,500 and incurred selling costs of $3,450 and qualifying fixing-up expenses of $1,300.

a. Assuming T reinvests $65,000, how much less tax does he pay because of the fixing-up expenses? What is T's basis in the replacement residence? What impact do the fixing-up expenses have on that basis?

b. How would your answers differ if, T reinvested $60,000?

15-30 *Sale of Principal Residence—Costs.* U received and accepted an offer to purchase her principal residence for $78,000 on March 12 and completed the sale on May 8 (all in the current year). Within the required reinvestment period, she purchased a replacement residence. Specify whether each of the following is properly classified as a fixing-up expense, a selling expense, an addition to the basis of the residence that was sold, or none of these.

a. New garage built during February of the current year at a cost of $12,500 because the city requires that every residence that is sold in the subdivision have a garage.

b. Real estate transfer taxes of $780 assessed by the city government.

c. Steam cleaning of carpets for $125 on April 22 and paid for upon completion.

d. Painting interior of residence completed and paid for in February.

e. Commissions of $4,680 paid to listing and selling real estate brokers.

f. Same as e, except U's sale is related to a qualifying move and U deducts $1,500 of the commission as a moving expense.

15-31 *Ownership by Husband and Wife.* J owned, as her separate property, the residence that she and her husband R lived in for many years. The residence was sold for $80,000, and J and R reinvested in a jointly owned home costing $120,000. They own equal interests in the replacement residence.

a. How much gain must J recognize on this sale under the general rules? (Assume J's basis in the former residence was $54,000.)

b. Is there any relief provision that could benefit J and R? Explain.

15-32 *Sale of Principal Residence.* During the current year, H and W ended their stormy marriage of 20 years. They had jointly owned a residence valued at $330,000 with a basis of $95,000. As part of their divorce settlement, H sold his interest in the home to W for $165,000. Assuming that there were no selling costs or fixing-up expenses, answer the following:

a. How much must H reinvest in a new principal residence in order to defer his entire gain on this sale?

b. What is W's basis in the residence?

15-33 *Sales of Principal Residences.* Provide the missing information in each of the following independent situations. Assume that each case qualifies for § 1034 treatment and that the realized gain in each case is $15,000.

Case	Sales Price	Selling Expense	Fixing-up Costs	Adjusted Sales Price	Amount Reinvested	Gain Recognized
A	$40,000	$2,400	$3,600	$_____	$34,000	$_____
B	_____	3,000	500	46,500	_____	1,000
C	40,000	2,400	_____	36,600	31,000	_____
D	70,000	_____	0	65,800	53,500	_____
E	55,000	3,300	_____	51,500	35,000	_____

15-34 *Section 121 Exclusion.* F, 65 years old, sold her principal residence of six years during the current year. The following was derived from her records.

Sales price.....................................	$225,000
Selling costs....................................	13,500
Fixing-up costs..................................	450
Adjusted basis..................................	90,000

If F uses her once-in-a-lifetime exclusion under § 121, how much gain must she recognize on her return for the current year?

15-35 *Interaction of §§ 121 and 1034.* G, age 59, sold her home during 1994 for $320,000. The property had been her principal residence for the last 15 years and had a basis to G of $172,000. She incurred selling costs of $22,000 and eligible fixing-up expenses of $5,500.

a. Assuming that G has no intention of reinvesting in a replacement residence, what is the least possible gain she may report from this sale during 1994?

b. What would be your answer if G had reinvested $180,000 in another principal residence in 1994?

15-36 *Section 121 Election Limitation.*   B and C were married in 1991. B moved into C's house, which C had owned and occupied for 10 years. The residence was sold at a large gain in 1994 when B and C decided to enjoy the peacefulness of renting. In each of the situations below, can any gain be excluded under § 121?

  a. C deferred the gain from a prior residence that he owned jointly with his deceased first spouse by reinvesting in the current residence. B has not elected § 121 before.

  b. B excluded gain on the sale of a prior residence under § 121, and B and C file jointly for 1994. C has not elected § 121 before.

  c. B excluded gain on the sale of a prior residence under § 121, and B and C file separately for 1994. C is the sole owner of the residence and has not elected § 121 before.

15-37 *Section 121 Exclusion.*   H (born May 17, 1939) and W (born November 17, 1941) are married and have lived in their jointly owned home since December 16, 1991.

  a. On what day will H and W first qualify for the exclusion of gain under § 121?

  b. Is it possible for H and W to qualify for exclusion of gain under § 1034 at an earlier date?

15-38 *When to Elect § 121.*   Z is 62 years of age and sold her principal residence during the current year for $223,000. She had an adjusted basis in the home of $167,500 and incurred fixing-up expenses of $2,300 and selling costs of $4,450. Z meets all the requirements under § 121. Analyze whether Z should use her § 121 election on this sale in each of the following circumstances.

  a. Z plans to purchase a new principal residence at a cost of $100,000.

  b. Z plans to marry Y, who has previously made a § 121 election.

  c. Z plans to move into a unit in a retirement community that she will rent, and she hopes never to own another home.

15-39 *Involuntary Conversion.*   The business office of K, a real estate broker, was destroyed by fire on August 22, 1993.

  a. By what date must K reinvest to avoid recognizing gain from the insurance proceeds received as a result of the fire?

  b. What type of property must K purchase to avoid recognition?

  c. Would your answers differ if, rather than being destroyed by fire, the office building had been condemned by the state for highway right of way?

15-40 *Involuntary Conversion.*   L owned a leased warehouse that was totally destroyed by fire on October 31, 1994. The building had a basis to L of $45,000 and his insurance paid the replacement cost of $75,000. L completed construction of a new warehouse on the same land on December 2, 1996 at a cost of $80,000.

  a. How much gain must L recognize on this conversion?

  b. What is L's basis in the replacement warehouse?

  c. Summarize L's reporting requirements.

  d. How would your answers to parts a, b, and c differ if L had invested only $65,000 in the replacement property?

15-41 *Involuntary Conversion.* Complete the following table involving certain involuntary conversions in which the taxpayer elects to defer gain. The property is converted into cash and the cash is invested in qualifying replacement property in each case. Each case is independent of the others.

Case	Amount Realized	Adjusted Basis	Amount Reinvested	Gain Recognized	Basis in Replacement
A	$3,000	$1,600	$1,200	$_____	$_____
B	3,000	1,300	1,400	$_____	$_____
C	6,000	4,000	5,500	$_____	$_____
D	7,500	3,400	7,900	$_____	$_____
E	8,400	9,000	8,700	$_____	$_____

15-42 *Involuntary Conversion Replacement Period.* For each of the following involuntary conversions, state the beginning date and the ending date of the permissible replacement period.

a. The city of Lemon Tree announced plans to condemn D's rental property on March 15, 1993 and completed condemnation proceedings on June 12, 1994 for $330,000.
b. Assume the same facts as in part a, except that the property was D's principal residence.
c. A fire destroyed G's bike shop on November 7, 1993. G received an insurance settlement on April 12, 1994.

15-43 *Involuntary Conversion-Condemned Real Estate.* The city of Orange Grove condemned T's automobile parts warehouse for use as a community park. Plans to condemn the property were announced on June 14, 1993, instituted on December 12, 1993, and completed on May 1, 1994. T's basis in the warehouse was $235,000, and the condemnation award was $366,000.

a. Describe the type of property with which T must replace this warehouse in order to qualify for involuntary conversion treatment.
b. Specify the reinvestment period during which T must reinvest in order to qualify for involuntary conversion treatment.
c. Determine the amount of gain that T must recognize and T's basis in the replacement property, which costs $387,000.

15-44 *Like-Kind Exchange.* F traded in an automobile that was used 100 percent of the time for business for a new auto for the same use. F had fully depreciated the old auto. The auto received was worth $12,000 and F paid $5,000 cash in addition to giving up her old auto.

a. How much gain must F recognize on the trade-in?
b. What is F's adjusted basis in the new auto?

15-45 *Like-Kind Exchange.* T transferred his farm land (100% business) to V in exchange for a parcel of unimproved urban real estate held by V as an investment. The farm was valued at $400,000 and was subject to a mortgage obligation of $260,000. T's basis in the farm was $340,000. The urban real estate was valued at $450,000 and was subject to a mortgage of $310,000.

a. How much gain must T recognize on this exchange?
b. What is T's basis in the urban real estate received?

15-46 *Like-Kind Exchange.* Refer to Problem 15-45. Assume that V had a basis of $360,000 in the urban real estate transferred to T.

   a. How much gain must V recognize on the exchange?
   b. What is V's basis in the farm property received?

15-47 *Like-Kind Exchange.* B exchanged undeveloped land worth $245,000 with C for developed land worth $225,000 and DEF corporation stock worth $20,000. B's adjusted basis in the land was $176,000. C's adjusted bases in the land and stock were $243,000 and $17,500, respectively.

   a. How much gain or loss must B recognize in this exchange, and what are his bases in the land and stock received?
   b. How much gain or loss must C recognize in this exchange, and what is her basis in the land received?

15-48 *Like-Kind Exchange.* F exchanged undeveloped land worth $45,000 with G for land worth $42,000 and a personal automobile worth $3,000. F's adjusted basis in the land was $36,000. G's adjusted bases in the land and automobile were $39,500 and $2,500, respectively.

   a. How much gain or loss must F recognize in this exchange, and what are his bases in the land and automobile received?
   b. How much gain or loss must G recognize in this exchange, and what is her basis in the land received?

15-49 *Like-Kind Exchange: Installment Reporting.* D entered into an agreement on December 15, 1994 under which he will immediately receive an apartment complex worth $300,000 and an installment obligation of the buyer for $200,000 with interest at 12 percent annually. D is to give up another apartment complex in which he has a basis of $320,000.

   a. What is the minimum gain that D must recognize on this exchange in 1994?
   b. How much gain must D report when he receives his first principal installment of $20,000 (plus accrued interest) in 1995?

15-50 *Like-Kind Exchanges.* Complete the following table for exchanges that qualify for like-kind exchange treatment under § 1031.

Case	Adjusted Basis of Property Given Up	FMV of Property Received	Cash Boot Received	Cash Boot Paid	Gain or Loss Recognized	Basis of Property Received
A	$3,000	$2,500	$ 0	$ 0	$_____	$_____
B	5,000	5,000	0	1,000	$_____	$_____
C	4,000	6,000	1,000	0	$_____	$_____
D	7,000	5,900	600	0	$_____	$_____
E	5,000	4,000	2,500	0	$_____	$_____
F	3,000	3,200	200	0	$_____	$_____
G	4,000	3,600	500	0	$_____	$_____

RESEARCH PROBLEMS

15-51 *Sale of Principal Residence.* R was transferred to a new location by his employer, so he attempted to sell his home for several months before moving. Concluding that he could not sell the home at a reasonable market value, R offered the property for rent and a tenant moved in the following week. The following represent the results of operations for the rental period:

Gross rental income..	$7,000
Cash rental expenses, excluding	
interest and taxes..	1,275
Interest and taxes..	6,345
Depreciation, assuming 100% rental use........................	3,225

One year later, R again offered the home for sale, this time successfully. The home was sold and R purchased a new home at an adequate price at the new work location.

a. Can R defer his gain under § 1034?

b. What amount of the rental expenses for the year may R deduct against his taxable rental income?

15-52 *Sale of Principal Residence.* S leased a duplex for $750 per month, with an option to buy it for $65,000 within two years. She moved into one part of the duplex and subleased the other to a third party. After 23 months, S announced her intention to exercise her purchase option, but the owner of the duplex refused to sell the property. S began the process of filing a lawsuit, and the owner eventually settled by paying S specific damages of $25,000. S used the proceeds as part of her down payment on a new principal residence costing $92,000, and she planned to defer her gain under § 1034. How much gain, if any, must S recognize?

15-53 *Exchange of Businesses.* T has owned and operated a taxi service (T's Taxi) for many years, but he now wishes to move to a new city. If T sells his business, he will have a substantial gain. Through a business broker, T has arranged to exchange his business for a limousine service (U's Limos) in the other city. In order to strike the deal, U insists that T sign a covenant-not-to-compete that U and T value at $25,000. The balance sheets (representing fair market values) of the two businesses are as follows:

	T's Taxi	U's Limos
Automobiles.............	$700,000	$750,000
Computers and data		
handling equipment...	60,000	30,000
Covenant-not-to-compete	25,000	
Goodwill................	65,000	60,000
Totals..................	$850,000	$840,000

In order to equalize the transaction, U will pay T $10,000 cash. T's bases are as follows: in the automobiles, $675,000; in the computers, etc., $65,000; and in the covenant and goodwill, $0. T has asked you to determine the tax effect of this proposed exchange before he completes it.

LEARNING OBJECTIVES

Upon completion of this chapter you will be able to:

- Define a capital asset and use this definition to distinguish capital assets from other types of property

- Explain the holding period rules for classifying a capital asset transaction as either short-term or long-term

- Apply the capital gain and loss netting process to a taxpayer's capital asset transactions

- Understand the differences in tax treatment of an individual's capital gains and losses

- Explain the differences in tax treatment of the capital gains and losses of a corporate taxpayer versus those of an individual taxpayer

- Identify various transactions to which capital gain or loss treatment has been extended

- Discuss the tax treatment of investments in corporate bonds and other forms of indebtedness

CHAPTER OUTLINE

General Requirements for Capital Gain	16-3	Losses on Small Business Stock:	
Capital Assets	16-3	§ 1244 Stock	16-22
Definition of a Capital Asset	16-3	Qualified Small Business Stock	16-23
Inventory	16-4	Rollover of Gain on Certain Publicly	
Disposition of a Business	16-5	Traded Securities	16-26
Sale or Exchange Requirement	16-7	Dealers in Securities	16-26
Worthless and Abandoned Property	16-7	Subdivided Real Estate	16-27
Certain Casualties and Thefts	16-8	Other Related Provisions	16-28
Other Transactions	16-10	Nonbusiness Bad Debts	16-28
Holding Period	16-10	Franchise Agreements, Trademarks,	
Stock Exchange Transactions	16-10	and Trade Names	16-28
Special Rules and Exceptions	16-11	Short Sales	16-29
Capital Gain and Loss Netting Process	16-13	Options	16-30
The Process	16-13	Corporate Bonds and Other	
The Results	16-14	Indebtedness	16-32
Treatment of Capital Gains	16-15	Original Issue Discount	16-33
Treatment of Capital Losses	16-18	Market Discount	16-36
Reporting Capital Gains and Losses	16-20	Conversion Transactions	16-37
Capital Gain Treatment Extended to		Bond Premium	16-38
Certain Transactions	16-21	Tax Planning Considerations	16-39
Patents	16-21	Timing of Capital Asset Transactions	16-39
Lease Cancellation Payments	16-22	Section 1244 Stock	16-39
Special Treatment for Certain		Problem Materials	16-41
Investments	16-22		

Chapter 16

PROPERTY TRANSACTIONS
Capital Gains and Losses

The final piece of the property transaction puzzle concerns the treatment of the taxpayer's gains and losses. In the infancy of the tax law, solving this puzzle was relatively easy. Taxpayers who sold or otherwise disposed of property needed only to determine their gain or loss realized and how much, if any, they had to recognize. The actual treatment of the gain or loss recognized—or more precisely, the rate at which it was taxed—was identical to that for other types of income. The simplicity of treating all income and loss the same was short-lived, however, lasting a mere eight years, from 1913 to 1921. Since 1921, the taxation of property transactions has been complicated by the additional need to determine not only the amount of the taxpayer's gain but also its character. Virtually all of this complication can be traced to one source: Congress's desire to provide some type of preferential treatment for capital gains.

Whether capital gains should be taxed more leniently than wages and other types of income is the subject of what seems to be a never-ending debate. When the first income tax statute was enacted, there was nothing in the definition of income to indicate that gains on dealings in property were taxable. Seizing on the omission, taxpayers relied on somewhat abstract tax theory and ingeniously argued that a gain on a sale of property (e.g., a citrus grove) was not the same as income derived from such property (e.g., sale of the fruit) and should not be taxed at all. Moreover, taxpayers who sold property and reinvested in similar property argued that they had not altered their economic position and that taxation was therefore not appropriate. While detractors cried "nonsense!" champions of favorable treatment offered additional justification, explaining that capital gain is often artificial, merely reflecting increases in the general price level. Perhaps the most defensible argument can be found in the Ways and Means Committee Report that accompanied the Revenue Act of 1921. As the following quotation shows, Congress believed that the progressive nature of the tax rates was unduly harsh on capital gains, particularly when the rate (at that time) could be as high as 77 percent.

> The sale of...capital assets is now seriously retarded by the fact that gains and profits earned over a series of years are under present law taxed as a lump sum (and the amount of surtax greatly enhanced thereby) in the year in which the profit is realized. Many of such sales...have been blocked by this feature of the present law. In order to permit such transactions to go forward without fear of a prohibitive tax, the proposed bill...adds a new section [providing a lower rate for gains from the sale or dispositions of capital assets].[1]

Although the top rate is currently much lower than it has been historically (70 percent as recently as 1980), the bunching effect is still cited as one of the major justifications for lower rates for capital gains. Proponents also reason that taxing capital gains at low rates encourages taxpayers to make riskier investments and also helps stimulate the economy by encouraging the mobility of capital. Without such rules, taxpayers, they believe, would tend to retain rather than sell their assets.

Of course, opponents of special treatment are equally vocal in their objections to the benefits extended capital gains. They reject the proposition that capital gain should not be taxed. They maintain that income is income regardless of its form. Opponents also doubt the stimulus value of preferential treatment and complain about the uneven playing field that such treatment creates. Finally, opponents offer one argument for which there is no denial. As will become all too clear in this and the following chapter, the special treatment reserved for capital gains and losses creates an inordinate amount of complexity in the tax law.

Despite the various objections, Congress has generally sided with those in favor of preferential treatment. But, as history shows, there is little agreement on exactly what that treatment should be. From 1922 to 1933, taxpayers were given the option of paying a flat 12.5 percent tax on their capital gains and the normal rate on ordinary income. From 1934 to 1937, the treatment was altered to allow an exclusion for capital gains ranging from 20 to 80 percent, depending on how long the asset was held. After some tinkering with the exclusion in 1938, Congress moved again in 1942. This time it replaced the exclusion with a deduction equal to 50 percent of the gain. The 50 percent deduction—increased in 1978 to 60 percent—made capital gains the most popular game in town for almost 45 years. In 1986, however, Congress had a complete change of heart. After lowering the top rate on ordinary income to 28 percent, it apparently believed that special treatment for capital gains was no longer needed. Accordingly, favorable capital gain treatment was repealed. This period of low rates, however, proved to be only temporary, as Congress raised the top rate to 31 percent in 1991 and 39.6 percent in 1993. The increase prompted Congress to resurrect favorable treatment for capital gains, in this case providing that the gains of an individual would be taxed at a maximum rate not to exceed 28 percent. Such treatment remains in effect today.

---

[1] House Rep. No. 350, 67th Cong. 1st Sess., pp. 10–11, as quoted in Seidman, *Legislative History of the Income Tax Laws, 1938–1961,* 813 (1938).

Although the special 28 percent rate treatment initially gave capital gains only a small advantage over ordinary income (31% vs. 28%), the 1993 rate increase to a high of 39.6 percent has once again made capital gains desirable. But, as the remainder of this chapter explains, this favorable treatment is not extended to just any gain. The taxpayer must jump through a few hoops, turn a couple of cartwheels, and clear innumerable hurdles before he or she reaches the pot of gold at the end of the capital gains rainbow.

GENERAL REQUIREMENTS FOR CAPITAL GAIN

A gain or loss is considered a capital gain or loss and receives special treatment only if each of several elements is present. The asset being transferred must be a *capital asset* and the disposition must constitute a *sale or exchange*. In addition, the exact treatment of any net gain or loss can be determined only after taking into consideration the *holding period* of the property transferred. Each of these elements is discussed below.

CAPITAL ASSETS

DEFINITION OF A CAPITAL ASSET

In order for a taxpayer to have a capital gain or loss, the Code generally requires a sale or exchange of a *capital asset*. Obviously, the definition of a capital asset is crucial. Sales involving property that qualifies as a capital asset are eligible for a reduced tax rate while sales of assets that have not been so blessed may not be as lucky.

The Internal Revenue Code takes a roundabout approach in defining a capital asset. Instead of defining what a capital asset is, the Code identifies what is not a capital asset. Under § 1221, all assets are considered capital assets unless they fall into one of five excluded classes. The following are *not* capital assets:

1. Inventory or property held primarily for sale to customers in the ordinary course of a trade or business

2. Accounts and notes receivable acquired in the ordinary course of a trade or business for services rendered or from the sale of inventory

3. Depreciable property and land used in a trade or business

4. Copyrights, literary, musical, or artistic compositions, letters or memoranda, or similar property held by the creator, or letters or memoranda held by the person for whom the property was created; in addition, such property held by a taxpayer whose basis is determined by reference to the creator's basis (e.g., acquired by gift), or held by the person for whom it was created

5. Publications of the United States Government that are received from the Government by any means other than purchase at the price at which they are offered to the public, and which are held by the taxpayer who received the publication or by a transferee whose basis is found with reference to the original recipient's basis (e.g., acquired by gift)

Before looking at some of these categories, one should appreciate the statutory scheme and the rationale behind it.

As noted above, the Code starts with the very broad premise that all property held by the taxpayer is a capital asset. Thus the sale of a home, car, jewelry, clothing, stocks, bonds, inventory, and plant, property, and equipment used in a trade or business would produce, *at least initially,* capital gain or loss since all assets are by default capital assets. However, § 1221 goes on to alter this general rule with several significant exceptions. It specifically excludes from capital asset status inventory, property held for resale, receivables related to the sales of services and inventory, and certain literary properties. As may be apparent, the purpose of these exclusions, as the Supreme Court has said, "is to differentiate between the 'profits and losses arising from the everyday operation of business' on the one hand ... and 'the realization of appreciation in value accrued over a substantial period of time' on the other."[2] In essence, the statute is drawn to deny capital gain treatment for income from regular business operations. Income that is derived from the taxpayer's routine personal efforts and services is treated as ordinary income and in effect receives the same treatment as wages, interest, and all other types of income. In contrast, capital gain, at least in the general sense, is limited to gains from the sale of investment property.

Based on the above analysis, it might seem strange that § 1221 also excludes from capital asset status a class of assets that most people would consider capital assets: the fixed assets of a business (depreciable property and land used in a business). Although it is true that these assets are not "pure" capital assets, as will be seen in Chapter 17, these assets can, if certain tests are met, sneak in the back door and receive capital gain treatment. Also observe that this rule does not exclude intangibles from capital asset treatment even though they may be amortizable. For example, goodwill is a capital asset even though it may be amortized.

One final note: it should be emphasized that the classification of an asset as a capital asset may affect more than the character of the gain or loss on its sale. For example, the amount of a charitable contribution deduction also may be affected in certain instances. Recall that the deduction for charitable contributions of appreciated capital gain property is limited.[3]

INVENTORY

The inventory exception has been the subject of much litigation and controversy. Whether property is held primarily for sale is a question of fact. The Supreme Court decided in *Malat v. Riddell*[4] that the word "primarily" should be interpreted as used in an ordinary, everyday sense, and as such, means "principally" or of "first importance." As a practical matter, such interpretations provide little guidance. In many cases, it simply boils down to whether the court views the taxpayer as a "dealer" in the particular property or merely an investor. Unfortunately, the line of demarcation is far from clear.

---

[2] *Malat v. Riddell,* 66-1 USTC ¶9317, 17 AFTR2d 604, 383 U.S. 569 (USSC, 1966).

[3] See § 170(e)(1) and Chapter 11 for a discussion of these charitable contribution limitations.

[4] *Supra,* footnote 2.

The determination of whether an item is inventory or not frequently arises in the area of sales of real property. In determining whether a taxpayer holds real estate, or a particular tract of real estate, primarily for sale, the courts seem to place the greatest emphasis on the frequency, continuity, and volume of sales.[5] Other important factors considered by the courts are subdivision and improvement,[6] solicitation and advertising,[7] purpose and manner of acquisition,[8] and reason for and method of sale.[9]

DISPOSITION OF A BUSINESS

The treatment of the sale of a business depends on the form in which the business is operated and the nature of the sale. If the business is operated as a sole proprietorship, the sale of the proprietorship business is not, as one taxpayer argued, a sale of a single integrated capital asset.[10] Rather, it is treated as a separate sale of each of the assets of the business. Accordingly, the sales price must be allocated among the various assets and gains and losses determined for each individual asset. Any gain or loss arising from the sale of inventory items and receivables would be treated separately as ordinary gains and losses. Gains and losses from the sale of depreciable property and land used in the business would be subject to special treatment discussed in Chapter 17 and may qualify for capital gain treatment. Finally, gains and losses from capital assets would of course be treated as capital gains and losses.

If the business is operated in the form of a corporation or partnership, the sale could take one of two forms: (1) a sale of the owner's interest (e.g., the owner's stock or interest in the partnership) or (2) a sale of all the assets by the entity followed by a distribution of the sales proceeds to the owner. An owner's interest—stock or an interest in a partnership—is a capital asset. Consequently, a sale of such interest normally produces capital gain or capital loss (although there are some important exceptions for sales of a partnership interest). On the other hand, a sale of assets by the entity would be treated in the same manner as the sale of a sole proprietorship, a sale of each individual asset.

[5] See, for example, *Houston Endowment, Inc. v. U.S.*, 79-2 USTC ¶9690, 44 AFTR2d 79-6074, 606 F.2d 77 (CA-5, 1979) and *Reese v. Comm.*, 80-1 USTC ¶9350, 45 AFTR2d 80-1248, 615 F.2d 226 (CA-5, 1980).

[6] See, for example, *Houston Endowment, Inc.* (Footnote 5), and *Biedenharn Realty Co., Inc. v. U.S.*, 76-1 USTC ¶9194, 37 AFTR2d 76-679, 526 F.2d 409 (CA-5, 1976).

[7] See, for example, *Houston Endowment, Inc.* (Footnote 5).

[8] See, for example, *Scheuber v. Comm.*, 67-1 USTC ¶9219, 19 AFTR2d 639, 371 F.2d 996 (CA-7, 1967), and *Biedenharn Realty Co., Inc. v. U.S.* (Footnote 6).

[9] See, for example, *Voss v. U.S.*, 64-1 USTC ¶9290, 13 AFTR2d 834, 329 F.2d 164 (CA-7, 1964).

[10] *Williams v. McGowan*, 46-1 USTC ¶9120, 34 AFTR 615, 152 F.2d 570 (CA-2, 1945); Rev. Rul. 55-79, 1955-1 C.B. 370.

✔ CHECK YOUR TAX KNOWLEDGE

Review Question 1.   Lois Price operates an office supply store, Office Discount, and owns the property listed below. Indicate whether each of the following assets is a capital asset. Respond yes or no.

a. Refrigerator in her home used solely for personal use

b. The building that houses her business

c. A picture given to her by a well-known artist

d. 100 shares of Chrysler Corporation stock held as an investment

e. Furniture in her office

f. A book of poems she has written

g. The portion of her home used as a qualifying home office

h. 1,000 boxes of 3½-inch floppy disks

i. Goodwill of the business

The following are capital assets: (a), (d), and (i). All assets are capital assets except inventory (item h), real or depreciable property used in a trade or business (items b, e, g), literary or artistic compositions held by the creator (item f), or property received by gift from the creator (item c). Note that the Code does not exclude intangible assets from capital assets status. Such assets as goodwill are treated as capital assets.

Review Question 2.   Slam-Dunk Corporation manufactures collapsible rims in Houston, Texas. Because of its tremendous growth, Mr. Slam and Ms. Dunk, the owners of the company, brought in a highly skilled executive to manage it, the famous Sam Jam. As part of the employment agreement, the company agreed to buy Sam's house if it should terminate his contract. As you might expect, Slam and Dunk did not get along with Sam and his creative management techniques. Consequently, the corporation dismissed Sam after two years and purchased his house at Sam's original cost of $300,000. Needing the cash, the corporation decided to unload the house immediately. Unfortunately, in the depressed housing market of Houston, the corporation sold the house for only $200,000. Explain the tax problems associated with the sale by the corporation. What important issue must be resolved and why?

In this situation, the corporation has realized a loss of $100,000. The critical issue is determining whether the loss is an ordinary or capital loss. The treatment, as explained below, is quite different. If the loss is ordinary, the corporation may deduct the entire loss in computing taxable income. In contrast, if the loss is a capital loss, the corporation can deduct the loss only to the extent of any capital gains that it has during the year or a three-year carryback and five-year carryforward period. The determination turns on the definition of a capital asset.

SALE OR EXCHANGE REQUIREMENT

Before capital gain or loss treatment applies, the property must be disposed of in a "sale or exchange." In most cases, determining whether a sale or exchange has occurred is not difficult. The requirement is met by most routine transactions and as a practical matter is often overlooked. Nevertheless, there are a number of situations when a sale or exchange does not actually occur but the Code steps in and creates one, thus converting what might have been ordinary income or loss to capital gain or capital loss. Several of these are considered below.

WORTHLESS AND ABANDONED PROPERTY

When misfortune strikes, leaving the taxpayer with worthless property, the taxpayer normally has a loss equal to the adjusted basis of the property. Note, however, that the loss in these situations does not technically arise from a sale or exchange, leaving the taxpayer to wonder how the loss is to be treated.

Worthless Securities. The Code has addressed this problem with respect to worthless securities (e.g., stocks and bonds). In the event that a qualifying security becomes worthless at any time during the taxable year, the resulting loss is treated as having arisen from the sale or exchange of a capital asset on the last day of the taxable year.[11] Losses from worthlessness are then treated as either short-term or long-term capital losses depending on the taxpayer's holding period.

> **Example 1.** After receiving a hot tip, N bought 200 shares of Shag Carpets Inc. for $2,000 on November 1, 1993. Just three months later, on February 1, 1994, N received a shocking notice that the company had declared bankruptcy and her investment was worthless. Because of the worthlessness, N is treated as having sold the stock for nothing on the last day of her taxable year, December 31, 1994. Because the sale is deemed to occur on December 31, 1994 (and not February 1), N is treated as if she actually held the stock for more than a year. As a result, she reports a $2,000 long-term capital loss.

The sale or exchange fiction applies only to qualifying securities. To qualify, the security must be (1) a capital asset and (2) a security as defined by the Code. Under § 165, the term *security* means stock, stock rights, and bonds, notes, or other forms of indebtedness issued by a corporation or the government. When these rules do not apply (e.g., property other than securities), the taxpayer suffers an ordinary loss. Whether a security actually becomes worthless during a given year is a question of fact, and the burden of proof is on the taxpayer to show that the security became worthless during the year in question.[12]

---

[11] § 165(g).

[12] *Young v. Comm.*, 41-2 USTC ¶9744, 28 AFTR 365, 123 F.2d 597 (CA-2, 1941). Code § 6511(d) extends the statute of limitations from three years to seven years because of the difficulty of determining the specific tax year in which stock becomes worthless.

Worthless Securities in Affiliated Corporations. The basic rule for worthless securities is modified for a corporate taxpayer's investment in securities of an affiliated corporation. If securities of an affiliated corporation become worthless, the loss is treated as an ordinary loss and the limitations that normally apply if the loss were a capital loss are avoided.[13] A corporation is considered affiliated to a parent corporation if the parent owns at least 80 percent of the voting power of all classes of stock and at least 80 percent of each class of nonvoting stock of the affiliated corporation. In addition, to be treated as an affiliated corporation for purposes of the worthless security provisions, the defunct corporation must have been truly an operating company. This test is met if the corporation has less than 10 percent of the aggregate of its gross receipts from passive sources such as rents, royalties, dividends, annuities, and gains from sales or exchanges of stock and securities. This condition prohibits ordinary loss treatment for what are really investments.

> **Example 2.**   Toy Palace Corporation is the parent corporation for over 100 subsidiary corporations that operate toy stores all over the country. Each subsidiary is 100 percent owned by Toy Palace. This year the store in Chicago, TPC Inc., declared bankruptcy. As a result, Toy Palace's investment in TPC stock of $1 million became totally worthless. Toy Palace is allowed to treat the $1 million loss as an ordinary loss since TPC was an affiliated corporation (i.e., Toy Palace owned at least 80 percent of TPC's stock and TPC was an operating corporation). Observe that without this special rule, Toy Palace would have a $1 million capital loss that it could deduct only if it had other capital gains currently or within the three-year carryback or five-year carryforward period.

Abandoned Property. While the law creates a sale or exchange for worthless securities, it takes a different approach for abandoned property. When worthless property (other than stocks and securities) is abandoned, the abandonment is not considered a sale or exchange.[14] Consequently, any loss arising from an abandonment is treated as an ordinary loss rather than a capital loss, a much more propitious result. Note, however, that the loss is deductible only if the taxpayer can demonstrate that the property has been truly abandoned and not simply taken out of service temporarily.

CERTAIN CASUALTIES AND THEFTS

Still another exception to the sale or exchange requirement involves *excess* casualty and theft gains from the involuntary conversion of *personal use assets*. As discussed in Chapter 10, § 165(h) provides that if personal casualty or theft gains *exceed* personal casualty or theft losses for any taxable year, each such gain and loss must be treated as a gain or loss from the sale or exchange of a capital asset. Each separate casualty or theft loss must be reduced by $100 before being netted with the personal casualty or theft gains.

---

[13] § 165(g)(3).

[14] Reg. §§ 1.165-2 and 1.167(a)-8.

Example 3. T had three separate casualties involving personal-use assets during the year:

			Fair Market Value	
Casualty	Property	Adjusted Basis	Before Casualty	After Casualty
1. Accident	Personal Car	$12,000	$ 8,500	$ 6,000
2. Robbery	Jewelry	1,000	4,000	0
3. Hurricane	Residence	60,000	80,000	58,000

T received insurance reimbursements as follows: (1) $900 for repair of the car; (2) $3,200 for the theft of her jewelry; and (3) $21,500 for the damages to her home. Assuming T does not elect (under § 1033) to purchase replacement jewelry, her personal casualty gain exceeds her personal casualty losses by $300, computed as follows:

1. The loss for the car is $1,500 [(lesser of $2,500 decline in value or the $12,000 adjusted basis = $2,500) − $900 insurance recovery − $100 floor].

2. The gain for the jewelry is $2,200 ($3,200 insurance recovery − $1,000 adjusted basis).

3. The loss from the residence is $400 [(lesser of $22,000 decline in value or the $60,000 adjusted basis = $22,000) − $21,500 insurance recovery − $100 floor].

T must report each separate gain and loss as a gain or loss from the sale or exchange of a capital asset. The classification of each gain and loss as short-term or long-term depends on the holding period of each asset.

It is important to note that this exception *does not* apply if the personal casualty losses exceed the gains. In such case, the *net* loss, subject to the 10 percent limitation, is deductible *from* A.G.I. Recall, however, that casualty and theft losses are among those itemized deductions that are not subject to the 3 percent cutback rule imposed on high-income taxpayers. (See Chapter 11 for a discussion of this cutback rule.)

Example 4. Assume the same facts in *Example 3* except the insurance recovery from the hurricane damage to the residence was only $11,500. In this case, the loss from the hurricane is $10,400 ($22,000 − $11,500 − $100), and the personal casualty losses exceed the gain by $9,700 ($1,500 + $10,400 − $2,200). T must treat the $9,700 net loss as an itemized deduction subject to the 10% A.G.I. limitation, but not subject to the 3% cutback rule.

OTHER TRANSACTIONS

There are still other situations where the sale or exchange requirement is an important consideration. For example, foreclosure, condemnation, and other involuntary events are treated as sales even though they may not qualify as such for state law purposes. Similarly, as discussed in greater detail later in this chapter, the collection of the face value of a corporate bond (i.e., bond redemption) at maturity is treated as a sale or exchange.

HOLDING PERIOD

As mentioned previously, in order to determine the actual treatment of capital asset transactions, it is necessary to separate the long-term capital gains and losses from those that are short-term. This is done by determining the *holding period*, or the length of time each asset has been held. In order to have a long-term capital gain or loss, the capital asset must have been held *more than* one year. The short-term holding period is one year or less.[15]

In computing the holding period, the day of acquisition is not counted but the day of sale is. The holding period is based on calendar months and fractions of calendar months, rather than on the number of days.[16] The fact that different months contain different numbers of days (i.e., 28, 30, or 31) is disregarded.

> **Example 5.**   P purchased 10 shares of EX, Inc. on March 16, 1994. Her gain or loss on the sale is short-term *if* the stock is sold on or before March 16, 1995 but long-term if sold on or after March 17, 1995.

> **Example 6.**   T purchased 100 shares of FMC Corp. stock on February 28, 1994. His gain or loss will be long-term if he sells the stock on or after March 1, 1995.

The holding period runs from the time property is acquired until the time of its disposition. Property is generally considered *acquired* or *disposed of* when title passes from one party to another. State law usually controls the passage of title and must be consulted when questions arise.

STOCK EXCHANGE TRANSACTIONS

The holding period for securities traded on a stock exchange is determined in the same manner as for other property. The trade dates, rather than the settlement dates, are used as the dates of acquisition and sale.

---

[15]   § 1222.

[16]   Rev. Rul. 66-7, 1966-1 C.B. 188.

Generally, both cash and accrual basis taxpayers must report (recognize) gains and losses on stock or security sales in the tax year of the trade, even though cash payment (settlement) may not be received until the following year. This requirement is imposed because the installment method of reporting gains is not allowed for sales of stock or securities that are traded on an established securities market.[17]

> **Example 7.** C, a cash basis calendar year taxpayer, sold 300 shares of ARA stock at a gain of $5,000 on December 29, 1994. The settlement date was January 3, 1995. C must report the gain in 1994 (the year of trade).

SPECIAL RULES AND EXCEPTIONS

Section 1223 provides several special rules for determining the holding period of certain properties. The first exception provides that the holding period of property received in an exchange *includes* the holding period of the property given up in the exchange if the basis of the property is determined by reference, in whole or in part, to the basis in that property given up.[18] It is required that the property exchanged be a capital asset or a § 1231 asset at the time of the exchange. An involuntary conversion under § 1033 is to be treated as an exchange for purposes of this special rule.

Under this provision, the holding period of a property received in a like-kind exchange under § 1031 would begin when the property given up in the exchange was originally acquired if any gain or loss was deferred in the exchange. Similarly, the holding period of a principal residence with a reduced basis because of a deferred gain from another residence under § 1034 would include the holding period of the old residence.[19]

> **Example 8.** M sold his personal residence, which he had owned for nine months, for $122,500 and does not intend to purchase a new residence. M's basis in the residence sold is $70,500, its cost of $109,000 less $38,500 of gain that was deferred from the sale of a previous residence he had owned for six years. The basis of M's residence is determined partially by referring to his basis in the previous residence (by adjusting for the deferred gain from that sale). Thus, M's holding period for the residence he has just sold is six years plus nine months, and M's gain of $52,000 ($122,500 sales price − $70,500 basis) is a long-term capital gain.

Another exception provides that if a taxpayer's basis in property is the same basis as another taxpayer had in that property, in whole or in part, the holding period will include that of the other person.[20] Therefore, the holding period of property acquired by gift generally will include the holding period of the donor. This will not be true, however, if the property is sold at a loss and the basis in the property for determining the loss is fair market value on the date of the gift.

---

[17] § 453(k)(2). See Chapter 14 for a detailed discussion of the installment sale method.

[18] § 1223(1).

[19] § 1223(7).

[20] § 1223(2).

Example 9.   G received a gold necklace from her elderly grandmother as a birthday gift on August 31, 1994. The necklace was worth $5,200 at that time and had a basis to the grandmother of $1,300. Grandmother had bought the necklace approximately 20 years earlier. Contrary to her grandmother's wishes, G sold the family heirloom for $5,000 on December 13, 1994. The $3,700 gain to G will be a long-term gain since her $1,300 basis is determined (under § 1015) by reference to her grandmother's basis, *and* her holding period includes the 20 years the necklace was held by her grandmother.

Example 10.   If G's grandmother had a basis in the necklace of $6,000, G's basis for determining loss would be $5,200, the fair market value at the date of the gift (see discussion in Chapter 14). Because G's basis is *not* determined by reference to her grandmother's basis, the grandmother's holding period is not added to G's holding period. Since G only held the necklace for three months, she will have a $200 short-term capital loss ($5,200 basis − $5,000 sales price).

A special rule is provided for property acquired from a decedent. The holding period formally begins on the date of death. However, the Code provides that, if the heir's basis in the property is its fair market value under § 1014 and the property is sold within one year after the decedent's death, the property will be treated as having been held by the heir for more than one year.[21] Therefore, the holding period of inherited property is generally long-term.

Example 11.   P sold 50 shares of Xero Corp. stock for $11,200 on July 27, 1994. The stock was inherited from P's uncle who died on May 16, 1994, and it was included in the uncle's Federal estate tax return at a fair market value of $12,000. Since P's basis in the stock ($12,000) is determined under § 1014, the $800 loss on the sale will be a long-term capital loss. This would be the case even if P's uncle had purchased the stock within days of his death. The decedent's prior holding period is irrelevant.

There are various other provisions that contain special rules for determining holding periods. The holding period of stock acquired in a transaction in which a loss was disallowed under the "wash sale" provisions (§ 1091) is added to the holding period of the replacement stock.[22] Also, when a shareholder receives stock dividends or stock rights as a result of owning stock in a corporation, the holding period of the stock or stock rights includes the holding period of the stock already owned in the corporation.[23] The holding period of any stock acquired by exercising stock rights, however, begins on the date of exercise.[24]

---

[21]   § 1223(11).

[22]   § 1223(4); Reg. § 1.1223-1(d).

[23]   § 1223(5); Reg. § 1.1223-1(e).

[24]   § 1223(6); Reg. § 1.1223-1(f).

The holding period of property acquired by exercise of an option begins on the day after the option is exercised.[25] If a taxpayer sells the property acquired by option within one year after exercising the option, then he or she will have a short-term gain or loss.

> **Example 12.**   N owned an option to purchase ten acres of land. She had owned the option more than one year when she exercised it and purchased the property. Her holding period for the property begins on the day after she exercises the option. Had she sold the option, her gain or loss would have been long-term. If she had sold the property immediately, her gain or loss would have been short-term.

The holding period of a commodity acquired in satisfaction of a commodity futures contract includes the holding period of the futures contract. However, the futures contract must have been a capital asset in the hands of the taxpayer.[26]

CAPITAL GAIN AND LOSS NETTING PROCESS

The netting process for capital gains and losses is not described as a process in the Code but is required implicitly under the definitions provided in § 1222. Gains and losses from sales or exchanges of capital assets must be combined in a particular order in determining the impact of the transactions on taxable income.

THE PROCESS

In the first step of the netting process, each taxpayer combines his or her short-term capital gains and losses and the result is either a *net* short-term capital gain (NSTCG) or a *net* short-term capital loss (NSTCL). Likewise, the taxpayer combines long-term capital gains and losses with a result of either a *net* long-term capital gain (NLTCG) or a *net* long-term capital loss (NLTCL). If the taxpayer has *both* a net short-term capital gain and a net long-term capital gain (i.e., NSTCG and NLTCG)—or a net short-term capital loss and a net long-term capital loss (i.e., NSTCL and NLTCL)—*no* further netting is allowed. However, if the taxpayer has *either* a net short-term capital gain and a net long-term capital loss (NSTCG and NLTCL), *or* a net short-term capital loss and a net long-term capital gain (NSTCL and NLTCG), these results are combined in the second stage of the netting process.

---

[25] See, for example, *Helvering v. San Joaquin Fruit & Inv. Co.*, 36-1 USTC ¶9144, 17 AFTR 470, 297 U.S. 496 (USSC, 1936), and *E.T. Weir*, 49-1 USTC ¶9190, 37 AFTR 1022, 173 F.2d 222 (CA-3, 1949).

[26] § 1223(8); Reg. § 1.1223-1(h).

THE RESULTS

The *three* possible results of the capital gain and loss netting process are defined as follows:

1. *Overall net short-term capital gain* (NSTCG)—either a net short-term capital gain with no further netting allowed, or the *excess* of a net short-term capital gain over a net long-term capital loss (i.e., NSTCG − NLTCL, if any)[27]

2. *Net capital gain* (NCG)—either a net long-term capital gain with no further netting allowed, or the *excess* of a net long-term capital gain over a net short-term capital loss (i.e., NLTCG − NSTCL, if any)[28]

3. *Net capital loss* (NCL)—either a net short-term capital loss or a net long-term capital loss with no further netting allowed (NSTCL or NLTCL), the *sum* of both net short-term and net long-term capital losses (NSTCL + NLTCL), the *excess* of a net short-term capital loss over a net long-term capital gain (NSTCL − NLTCG), or the *excess* of a net long-term capital loss over a net short-term capital gain (NLTCL − NSTCG)[29]

Note that a taxpayer could have *both* an overall net short-term capital gain (NSTCG) and a net long-term capital gain (NCG) at the end of the netting process. Unlike net losses, net short-term capital gains and net long-term capital gains are *not* combined. As discussed later in this chapter, individual taxpayers with net long-term capital gains (NCG) may receive favorable tax treatment.

The results of the netting process are illustrated below. Also, note that married persons filing a joint return net their respective capital gains and losses together, even though the asset disposed of may have been separately owned.

Example 13. The first step in the netting process is illustrated by the four independent cases below:

Case	STCG	STCL	LTCG	LTCL	Net Result	Description
A	$6,000	($2,000)			$4,000	NSTCG
B	3,000	(5,000)			(2,000)	NSTCL
C			$8,000	($1,000)	7,000	NLTCG
D			4,000	(7,000)	(3,000)	NLTCL

---

[27] Unlike the other possible results, an overall NSTCG has no special name—and as discussed below, is not eligible for any special tax treatment.

[28] § 1222(11).

[29] § 1222(10).

A taxpayer with the net results of cases A and C *or* B and D above would have no further netting of capital gains and losses. The $4,000 NSTCG from case A would be classified as an overall net short-term capital gain (NSTCG). The $7,000 NLTCG from case C would be classified as a net capital gain (NCG). The $2,000 NSTCL from case B or the $3,000 NLTCL from case D would become a net capital loss (NCL). If a taxpayer had two results, like cases B and D, the two losses would be added together and become a $5,000 net capital loss.

If a taxpayer had the results of cases A and D *or* cases B and C, however, he or she would proceed to the second step of the netting process.

Example 14.   Assume that individual K has all the capital gains and losses illustrated in cases A and D above. These results would be further combined as follows:

```
Case A: $6,000 STCG − $2,000 STCL  =  $4,000  NSTCG
Case D: $4,000 LTCG − $7,000 LTCL  =  (3,000) NLTCL

Overall NSTCG (NSTCG − NLTCL)         $1,000
```

K's $3,000 NLTCL is offset (deducted) against her $4,000 NSTCG and the result is an overall net short-term capital gain (NSTCG) of $1,000.

Example 15.   Assume that individual R has the capital gains and losses illustrated in cases B and C from *Example 13*. These results would be further combined as follows:

```
Case C: $8,000 LTCG − $1,000 LTCL  =  $7,000  NLTCG
Case B: $3,000 STCG − $5,000 STCL  =  (2,000) NSTCL

Net capital gain (NLTCG − NSTCL)      $5,000  NCG
```

R's $2,000 NSTCL is offset (deducted) against his $7,000 NLTCG and the result is a $5,000 net capital gain.

TREATMENT OF CAPITAL GAINS

The tax treatment of capital gains depends on *both* the nature of the gains and the type of taxpayer (i.e., individual, corporation, trust, or estate) involved.

Overall Net Short-term Capital Gains.   An overall net short-term capital gain is not eligible for any special tax treatment. Consequently, *all* taxpayers with this type of gain simply include it with any other ordinary taxable income in computing their tax liability.

Net Capital Gains.   The treatment of capital gains may differ depending on the entity. Regular corporations are required to treat net capital gains in the same manner as net short-term capital gains. That is, these gains are included with all other ordinary taxable income. Individuals, estates, and trusts, however, may be entitled to use a special tax computation in determining the tax on their net capital gains. The special tax computation is designed to ensure that an individual's net capital gain will (1) not be taxed at a rate greater than 28 percent, and (2) not be taxed at 28 percent when the gain falls in the 15

percent bracket.[30] Note that whenever an individual's *ordinary taxable income* exceeds the amount that would be taxed at 15 percent (e.g., $38,000 for joint returns), none of his or her net capital gain is taxed at 15 percent. In such case, the taxpayer computes the tax liability by first calculating the regular tax on ordinary taxable income and adding to that a tax of 28 percent on the net capital gain. On the other hand, if ordinary taxable income does not exceed the amount that is taxed at 15 percent, a portion of the net capital gain is taxed at the 15 percent rate, and the balance of the gain, if any, is taxed at a maximum rate of 28 percent. This special tax computation formula is presented in Exhibit 16-1.

The first step of the special tax computation formula simply seeks to determine whether the individual's ordinary taxable income is higher than the 15 percent bracket amount (e.g., $22,750 for single taxpayers and $38,000 for joint returns in 1994). If so, the entire 15 percent bracket is absorbed by ordinary taxable income, and all of the net capital gain is taxed 28 percent. To obtain this result, Step 2 computes the regular tax on ordinary taxable income (taxable income *without* the net capital gain), and Step 3 computes the tax on the net capital gain at the 28 percent rate. Normally, the taxpayer's tax will be the sum of the tax on ordinary taxable income and the 28 percent tax on the net capital gain (i.e., the *sum* of the taxes obtained in Steps 2 and 3). However, if the tax computed in the normal fashion is lower, the lower tax applies (Steps 5 and 6).

Exhibit 16-1   *Special Tax Computation for Individual Taxpayers' Net Capital Gains*

Step 1.   Determine the larger of
    a.   Ordinary taxable income (taxable income − net capital gain)
    b.   Amount of 15 percent bracket for *this* taxpayer's filing status

Step 2.   Compute the regular tax on the *greater* of (a) or (b) in Step 1 above (i.e., the regular tax on the larger of ordinary taxable income or the amount taxed at 15 percent).

Step 3.   Compute the tax on the balance of any net capital gains not taxed in Step 2 above as follows:

Taxable income (including ordinary taxable income and net capital gain)................	$xxx,xxx
Less: Greater of (a) or (b) in Step 1 above...	− xx,xxx
Balance:......................................	$xxx,xxx
Times: Maximum tax rate for net capital gains ×	28%
Equals: Tax on net capital gains.............	$ xx,xxx

Step 4.   Add the taxes computed in Steps 2 and 3 to determine the maximum tax.

Step 5.   Compute the regular tax on total taxable income.

Step 6.   Compare the taxes computed in Steps 4 and 5 and pay the smaller.

---

[30]   See § 1(h).

If the individual taxpayer's ordinary taxable income does not exceed the 15 percent bracket amount (Step 1), the 15 percent bracket amount is not entirely absorbed by ordinary taxable income. As a result, ordinary taxable income and a portion of the net capital gain are taxed at 15 percent (Step 2). The balance of the net capital gain, if any, is taxed at 28 percent. This stepwise approach to computing the tax is illustrated in *Example 16*.

Example 16. Assuming a married taxpayer filing jointly has the following amounts of ordinary taxable income and net capital gain, the tax liability for 1994 is computed as shown.

	Case 1	Case 2	Case 3
Step 1:			
a. Ordinary taxable income			
Taxable income.............................	$120,000	$120,000	$120,000
− Net capital gain..........................	− 10,000	− 40,000	− 90,000
Ordinary taxable income....................	$110,000	$ 80,000	$ 30,000
b. Amount of 15% bracket for			
taxpayer's filing status......................	$ 38,000	$ 38,000	$ 38,000
Larger of (a) or (b) above......................	$110,000	$ 80,000	$ 38,000
Step 2:			
Regular tax on larger of			
(a) ordinary income or (b) 15% bracket in *Step 1*	$ 26,405	$ 17,460	$ 5,700
Step 3:			
Total taxable income............................	$120,000	$120,000	$120,000
Less: Greater of (a) or (b)......................	− 110,000	− 80,000	− 38,000
Balance..	$ 10,000	$ 40,000	$ 82,000
Times: 28% rate...............................	× 28%	× 28%	× 28%
Tax..	$ 2,800	$ 11,200	$ 22,960
Step 4:			
Tax computed in *Step 2*........................	$ 26,405	$ 17,460	$ 5,700
Plus: Tax computed in *Step 3*..................	+ 2,800	+ 11,200	+ 22,960
Maximum tax....................................	$ 29,205	$ 28,660	$ 28,660
Step 5:			
Regular tax on total taxable income.............	$ 29,505	$ 29,505	$ 29,505
Step 6:			
1993 tax liability is lesser of			
amount from *Steps 4* or *5*......................	$ 29,205	$ 28,660	$ 28,660

In *Case 1*, the taxpayer's ordinary taxable income of $110,000 exceeds the 15% bracket amount of $38,000 for joint returns (Step 1). Consequently, the entire 15% bracket amount is absorbed by ordinary taxable income, and the net capital gain is taxed at the 28% rate. In effect, the taxpayer pulls the net capital gain out of taxable income (Step 1), computes the regular tax on $110,000 of ordinary income (Step 2 tax of $26,405), and adds to that a 28% tax on the $10,000 net capital gain (Step 3 tax of $2,800). The sum of these two taxes, $29,205 (Step 4), represents the maximum gross tax that the taxpayer will owe. The taxpayer then computes the regular tax on total taxable income of $120,000, resulting in a tax of $29,205 (Step 5). The final gross tax is $29,205 (Step 6), the lower of the regular tax of $29,505 and the maximum tax of $29,205. A similar analysis applies to *Case 2*.

In *Case 3*, the taxpayer's ordinary taxable income of $10,000 is less than the 15% bracket amount of $38,000 for joint returns (Step 1). As a result, all the $10,000 of ordinary taxable income and a portion of the $110,000 net capital gain, $28,000 ($38,000 − $10,000), a total of $38,000, is taxed at 15% (Step 2). The balance of the $110,000 net capital gain not taxed at 15%, $82,000 ($110,000 − $28,000), is taxed at 28% (Step 3). The sum of the taxes computed in Steps 2 and 3 (Step 4) is then compared to the regular tax (Step 5) to determine the final gross tax (Step 6). Note that the tax saving in *Case 2* and *Case 3* is the same ($29,505 − $28,660 = $845). This occurs because in both instances the same amount of net capital gain is removed from the 31% tax bracket ($120,000 taxable income − 28% bracket limit of $91,850 = $28,150 × 3% = $845).

TREATMENT OF CAPITAL LOSSES

There are important differences between individual and corporate taxpayers in the tax treatment of *net capital losses* [i.e., net short-term capital losses (NSTCL), net short-term capital losses in excess of net long-term capital gains (NSTCL − NLTCG), net long-term capital losses (NLTCL), and net long-term capital losses in excess of net short-term capital gains (NLTCL − NSTCG)]. Individuals are allowed a *capital loss deduction* in arriving at A.G.I. This deduction is limited to the lesser of (1) $3,000 ($1,500 in the case of a married individual filing a separate return), *or* (2) the net capital loss.[31] In either case, the capital loss deduction cannot exceed taxable income *before* the deduction.

In computing the capital loss deduction, a net short-term capital loss (NSTCL) or the excess of a net short-term capital loss over a net long-term capital gain (NSTCL − NLTCG) is taken into account *first* and offsets ordinary income up to the $3,000 limit.[32] In the absence of a net short-term capital loss *or*, if after deducting any existing net short-term capital loss the taxpayer has not reached the annual limit of the capital loss

---

[31] § 1211(b).   [32] Reg. § 1.211-1(b)(4)(i).

deduction, he or she will then be allowed to use any net long-term capital loss (or the excess of a net long-term capital loss over a net short-term capital gain) to reduce ordinary income up to the limit.[33] Any capital losses in excess of the capital loss deduction may be *carried forward* to subsequent years and offset against capital gains of the *same character* (i.e., short-term or long-term) or deducted within the same annual limitation. There is no limitation on an individual's capital loss carryover period.[34]

Example 17.   After netting all of his capital gains and losses for 1994, individual T has *both* a $2,000 NSTCL and a $5,000 NLTCL. Combining these results, T has a $7,000 net capital loss.

Assuming adequate taxable income, T will be entitled to a $3,000 capital loss deduction for 1994. In arriving at the $3,000 deduction, T must use his $2,000 NSTCL first and then use $1,000 of the NLTCL to reach the deduction limit. T must carry over to 1995 the remaining $4,000 NLTCL ($5,000 NLTCL available − $1,000 NLTCL used in the 1994 capital loss deduction). This capital loss carryover will be treated as a long-term capital loss in 1995 and must once again be put into the capital gain and loss netting process. If T has *only* the $4,000 NLTCL carryover in 1995, he will use $3,000 of the carryover amount to arrive at the $3,000 capital loss deduction for 1995 and carry over to 1996 the remaining $1,000 NLTCL.

Example 18.   After netting all of her capital gains and losses for 1994, individual R has a net capital loss consisting of only a $7,000 NSTCL. Her taxable income before the capital loss deduction is $18,000. R is entitled to a capital loss deduction of $3,000 for 1994, and she must carry over to 1995 the $4,000 unused net short-term capital loss.

If R has any short-term capital gains in 1995, she will include the $4,000 NSTCL carryover in the short-term capital gain and loss netting process. In the absence of short-term capital gains in 1995, R will then net the $4,000 NSTCL carryover against any 1995 net long-term capital gain. If any part of the carryover amount remains after this final step of the netting process, R can use it as a capital loss deduction for 1995 and carry over to 1996 any remaining NSTCL.

Example 19.   After the first step in the netting process for 1994, individual S has an $8,000 NLTCL and a $2,000 NSTCG. S must continue the netting process by offsetting the $2,000 NSTCG against the $8,000 NLTCL, with the result being a net capital loss consisting of only a $6,000 NLTCL.

Assuming adequate taxable income, S will be entitled to a $3,000 capital loss deduction for 1994 and will carry over to 1995 the remaining $3,000 NLTCL. If S has any long-term capital gains in 1995, he must *first* offset these gains with the $3,000 LTCL carryover. If any of the LTCL carryover remains, it is then used to offset any NSTCG for the year. Absent any net short-term capital gains, S can use the remaining LTCL carryover as a capital loss deduction for the year.

---

[33] For years prior to 1987, individual taxpayers were required to use $2 of NLTCL to offset $1 of ordinary income.

[34] § 1212(b).

Unlike individual taxpayers, corporations are not allowed a capital loss deduction. A corporate taxpayer's capital losses can be used *only to reduce* its capital gains.[35] Any excess losses are first *carried back* to the three preceding years and offset against any capital gains. Absent any capital gains in the three prior years, or if the loss carried back exceeds any capital gains, the excess may be *carried forward* for five years.[36]

REPORTING CAPITAL GAINS AND LOSSES

Individual taxpayers report any capital gains or losses on Schedule D of Form 1040.[37] This form is designed to facilitate the netting process, with one part used for reporting short-term gains and losses and another part used to report long-term transactions. A third part of the form is available for the second step of the netting process in the event the taxpayer has either NSTCGs and NLTCLs *or* NLTCGs and NSTCLs. The remaining parts of Schedule D provide for the special tax computation on net capital gains (following the format of *Example 16* above) and the calculation of capital loss carryovers.

Regular corporations must report capital gains and losses on Schedule D of Form 1120 in much the same manner as individual taxpayers. Partnerships and S corporations must also report capital gains and losses on a separate schedule (Schedule D of Form 1065 for partnerships and Schedule D of Form 1120S for S corporations). However, these conduit entities are limited to the *first* step of the netting process. Each owner (partner or S corporation shareholder) must include his or her share of the results from the entity with the appropriate capital transactions (i.e., short-term or long-term) being netted on the owner's Schedule D, Form 1040.

✔ CHECK YOUR TAX KNOWLEDGE

Review Question 1.   For 1994 Ms. Kulchurd earned a salary of $70,000 from her job as an art curator. In addition, she sold stock, realizing the following capital gains and losses:

LTCG	$10,000
LTCL	(17,000)
STCL	(11,000)

In 1995 she changed jobs, becoming a tax accountant and earning a salary of $300,000. In addition, she realized a long-term capital gain of $12,000.

Compute Ms. Kulchurd's adjusted gross income for 1994 and 1995 and indicate the amount, if any, that is eligible for preferential treatment as long-term capital gain.

---

[35] § 1211(a).

[36] § 1212(a). See Chapter 19 for a discussion of the unique tax treatment of a corporation's capital loss carryovers.

[37] See Appendix B for a sample of this form.

Her adjusted gross incomes for 1994 and 1995 are $67,000 and $307,000, respectively. After netting her capital gains and losses in 1994, Ms. Kulchurd has a net capital loss of $8,000, all of which is short-term. The deduction for capital losses of an individual is generally limited to $3,000. As a result, her adjusted gross income is $67,000 ($70,000 − $3,000). She is entitled to carry over the remainder of her short-term loss of $5,000. In 1995, she nets the $5,000 short-term capital loss against her $12,000 long-term capital gain to produce a net capital gain of $7,000. The $7,000 is combined with her other $300,000 of salary income to produce an adjusted gross income of $307,000. Of this amount $7,000, her net long-term capital gain, is taxed at a rate of 28 percent.

Review Question 2.   True–False. This year Mr. and Mrs. Simpson retired. The couple's only income was a long-term capital gain of $100,000 from the sale of stock. Assuming the Simpsons file a joint return, all $100,000 is taxed at a rate of 28 percent.

False. The tax computation operates to ensure that the long-term capital gain is taxed at 15 percent to the extent that ordinary income does not absorb this bracket. For 1994 the 15 percent bracket for a joint return extends to taxable income of $38,000. Therefore, $38,000 is taxed at a 15 percent rate and the remaining $62,000 is taxed at a 28 percent rate.

Review Question 3.   True–False. An individual taxpayer is generally entitled to deduct any capital loss recognized during the current year to the extent of any capital gains recognized plus $3,000. Any capital loss in excess of this amount retains its character and may be used in subsequent years until it is exhausted.

True.

CAPITAL GAIN TREATMENT EXTENDED TO CERTAIN TRANSACTIONS

The Internal Revenue Code contains several special provisions related to capital asset treatment. In some instances the concept of capital asset is expanded and in others it is limited. Some of the provisions merely clarify the tax treatment of certain transactions.

PATENTS

Section 1235 provides that certain transfers of patents shall be treated as transfers of capital assets held for more than one year. This virtually assures that a long-term capital gain will result if the patent is transferred in a taxable transaction, because the patent will have little, if any, basis since the costs of creating it are usually deducted under § 174 (research and experimental expenditures) in the tax year in which such costs are incurred. Any tranfer, other than by gift, inheritance, or devise, will qualify as long as *all substantial rights* to the patent are transferred. All substantial rights have been described as all rights that have value at the time of the transfer. For example, the

transfer must not limit the geographical coverage within the country of issuance or limit the time application to less than the remaining term of the patent.[38]

The transferor must be a *holder* as defined in § 1235(b). The term holder refers to the creator of the patented property or to an individual who purchased such property from its creator if such individual is neither the employer of the creator nor related to such creator.[39]

The sale of a patent will qualify for § 1235 treatment even if payments are made over a period that ends when the purchaser's use of the patent ceases or if payments are contingent on the productivity, use, or disposition of the patent.[40] It also is important to note that §§ 483 and 1274, which require interest to be imputed on certain sales contracts, do not apply to amounts received in exchange for patents qualifying under § 1235 that are contingent on the productivity, use, or disposition of the patent transferred.[41]

> **Example 20.**   K, a successful inventor, sold a patent (in which she had a basis of zero) to Bell Corp. The sale agreement called for K to receive a percentage of the sales of the property covered by the patent. All of K's payments received in consideration for this patent will be long-term capital gain regardless of her holding period.

LEASE CANCELLATION PAYMENTS

Section 1241 allows the treatment of payments received in cancellation of a lease or in cancellation of a distributorship agreement as having been received in a sale or exchange. Therefore, the gains or losses will be treated as capital gains or losses if the underlying assets are capital assets.[42]

SPECIAL TREATMENT FOR CERTAIN INVESTMENTS

LOSSES ON SMALL BUSINESS STOCK: § 1244 STOCK

Without special rules, the limitation on deductions for capital losses might discourage investment in new corporations. For example, if an individual invested $90,000 in stock of a new corporate venture, deductions for any loss from the investment would be limited to $3,000 annually.[43] Thus, where the stock becomes worthless it could take the investor as long as 30 years to recover the investment. This restriction on losses also is inconsistent with the treatment of losses resulting from investments by an individual in his or her sole proprietorship or in a partnership. In the case of a sole proprietorship or a partnership, losses generally may be used to offset the taxpayer's other income without limitation. For example, assume a sole proprietor sank $150,000 into a purchase of pet rocks that

---

[38] Reg. § 1.1235-2(b).

[39] For definition of "relative," see § 1235(d).

[40] § 1235(a).

[41] §§ 483(d)(4) and 1274(c)(4)(E). See Chapter 14 for a discussion of the imputed interest rules.

[42] See Chapter 17 for treatment if the asset is a § 1231 asset.

[43] A taxpayer can offset any capital losses against capital gains, if any.

he ultimately sold for only $100,000. In such case, he would have an ordinary loss of $50,000, all of which could be used to offset other ordinary income. Assume the same individual invested $150,000 in a corporation that had the same luck. If the taxpayer could at best sell the stock for $100,000, he would realize a capital loss of $50,000. Obviously the sole proprietor is in a much better position. To eliminate these problems and encourage taxpayers to invest in small corporations, Congress enacted § 1244 in 1958.

Under § 1244, losses on "Section 1244 stock" generally are treated as ordinary rather than capital losses.[44] Ordinary loss treatment normally is available *only to individuals* who are the original holders of the stock. If these individuals sell the stock at a loss or the stock becomes worthless, they may deduct up to $50,000 annually as an ordinary loss. Taxpayers who file a joint return may deduct up to $100,000 regardless of how the stock is owned (e.g., separately or jointly). When the loss in any one year exceeds the $50,000 or $100,000 limitation, the excess is considered a capital loss.

> **Example 21.**   T, married, is one of the original purchasers of RST Corporation's stock, which qualifies as § 1244 stock. She separately purchased the stock two years ago for $150,000. During the year, she sold all of the stock for $30,000, resulting in a $120,000 loss. On a joint return for the current year, she may deduct $100,000 as an ordinary loss. The portion of the loss exceeding the limitation, $20,000 ($120,000 − $100,000), is treated as a long-term capital loss.

Stock issued by a corporation (including preferred stock issued after July 18, 1984) qualifies as § 1244 stock only if the issuing corporation meets certain requirements. The most important condition is that the corporation's total capitalization (amounts received for stock issued, contributions to capital, and paid-in surplus) must not exceed $1 million at the time the stock is issued.[45] This requirement effectively limits § 1244 treatment to those individuals who originally invest the first $1 million in money and property in the corporation.

> **Example 22.**   In 1991 F provided the initial capitalization for MNO Corporation by purchasing 700 shares at a cost of $1,000 a share for a total cost of $700,000. In 1994 G purchased 500 shares at a cost of $1,000 per share or a total of $500,000. All of F's shares qualify as § 1244 stock. Only 300 of G's shares qualify for § 1244 treatment, however, since 200 of the 500 purchased were issued when the corporation's total capitalization exceeded $1 million.

QUALIFIED SMALL BUSINESS STOCK

As part of the Revenue Reconciliation Act of 1993, Congress created a new tax incentive to stimulate investment in small business. By virtue of this special rule, individuals who start their own C corporations or who are original investors in C corporations (e.g., initial public offerings) may be richly rewarded for taking the risk of investing in such enterprises. Under § 1202, noncorporate investors (i.e., individuals, partnerships, estates,

---

[44] § 1244(a).   [45] § 1244(c)(3)(A).

and trusts) are allowed to exclude 50 percent of the gain on the sale of *qualified small business* stock (QSB stock) held for more than five years.[46] The effect of this provision is to impose a maximum tax of 14 percent (50% × 28% maximum capital gain rate) on the gains from such investments, a far lower rate than the 39.6 percent that may apply to other types of income received by the taxpayer. It is important to note that because of the effective date and the five-year holding period requirement, the exclusion cannot actually be claimed until August 10, 1998.

> **Example 23.** On October 31, 1993 N purchased 1,000 shares of Boston Cod Corporation for $10,000. The stock was part of an initial public offering of the company's stock that was designed to raise $30 million to open another 200 fast fish restaurants. On December 20, 1998 N sells all of her shares for $50,000. As a result, she realizes a capital gain of $40,000, her only gain or loss during the year. Since N was one of the original investors and the stock was considered qualified small business stock at the time of its issue (assets at that time were less than $50 million), she is entitled to exclude 50 percent of her gain, or $20,000. The maximum tax on the $20,000 gain is 28 percent.

In determining net capital gain and capital losses, the taxpayer does not consider any gain excluded on the sale of QSB stock.

> **Example 24.** Same facts as above but assume that, in addition to the $40,000 gain on QSB stock, N also has other long-term capital gains of $10,000 and short-term capital losses of $5,000. N first applies the 50 percent exclusion and then nets the remainder with the other capital gains and losses. Therefore, N's net capital gain for the year is $25,000 [($40,000 − $20,000 = $20,000) + $10,000 − $5,000].

> **Example 25.** Assume N has a gain on QSB stock of $40,000 and a short-term capital loss of $23,000. N first applies the 50 percent exclusion and then nets the remaining gain with the capital loss. As a result, N has a net capital loss of $3,000 ($20,000 − $23,000).

Stock is considered QSB stock if it is issued after August 10, 1993 and meets a long list of requirements.

1. At the time the stock is issued, the corporation issuing the stock must be a *qualified small business*. A corporation is a qualified small business if

    - The corporation is a domestic C corporation
    - The corporation's gross assets do not exceed $50 million at the time the stock was issued (i.e., cash plus the fair market value of contributed property measured at the time of contribution plus the adjusted basis of other assets)

---

[46] Special rules apply for computing the exclusion on the sale of stock in a specialized small business investment company (see discussion below).

2. The seller is the original owner of the stock (i.e., the stock was acquired directly from the corporation or through an underwriter at its original issue)

3. During substantially all of the seller's holding period of the stock, the corporation was engaged in an active trade or business other than the following:

   - A business involving the performance of providing services in the fields of health, law, engineering, architecture, accounting, actuarial science, performing arts, consulting, athletics, financial services, brokerage services, or any other business where the principal asset is the reputation or skill of one or more of its employees
   - Banking, insurance, financing, leasing, or investing
   - Farming
   - Businesses involving the production or extraction of products eligible for depletion
   - Business of operating a hotel, motel, or restaurant

4. The corporation generally cannot own

   - Real property with a value that exceeds 10 percent of its total assets unless such property is used in the active conduct of a trade or business (e.g., rental real estate is not an active trade or business)
   - Portfolio stock or securities with a value that exceeds 10 percent of the corporation's total assets in excess of its liabilities

Note that the active trade or business requirement and the prohibition on real estate holdings severely limit the exclusion. These conditions effectively grant the exclusion to corporations engaged in manufacturing, retailing, or wholesaling businesses.

The new provision also imposes a restriction, albeit a liberal one, on the amount of gain eligible to be excluded on the sale of a particular corporation's stock. The maximum amount of gain that may be excluded on the sale of one corporation's stock is the *larger* of

1. $10 million, reduced by previously excluded gain on the sale of such corporation's stock; or

2. 10 times the adjusted basis of all qualified stock of the corporation that the taxpayer sold during the tax year.

This exclusion is extremely attractive, but it should be remembered that whatever Congress gives it can also take away. And that is exactly what Congress has done with QSB stock. One-half of the *excluded* gain (one-fourth of the entire gain) is a tax preference item for purposes of the alternative minimum tax. In addition, the excluded gain is generally not considered investment income for purposes of determining the investment interest limitation.

ROLLOVER OF GAIN ON CERTAIN PUBLICLY TRADED SECURITIES

Another creature of the 1993 Act encourages investment in small businesses owned by disadvantaged taxpayers. Individuals and C corporations that recognize gain on the sale of publicly traded securities are allowed to defer recognition of such gain if they reinvest the proceeds from the sale in common stock or a partnership interest in a *specialized small business investment company* (SSBIC).[47] The reinvestment must occur within 60 days of the sale. An SSBIC is generally any corporation or partnership licensed by the Small Business Administration under § 301 of the Small Business Investment Act of 1958 (as in effect on May 13, 1993). This typically includes investment companies that finance small businesses owned by disadvantaged taxpayers.

The maximum amount of gain that a taxpayer may exclude per year is generally limited to $50,000 (or, if smaller, $500,000 reduced by any previously excluded gain). These limits are increased to $250,000 and $1 million, respectively, for C corporations. Note that the special deferral privilege is not available for partnerships, S corporations, estates, or trusts.

The operation of the deferral provision is virtually identical to the rollover rules for gains on the sale of a residence and involuntary conversions. As a general rule, the taxpayer must recognize gain to the extent that the sales proceeds are not properly reinvested. Any gain deferred reduces the basis of the stock acquired.

> **Example 26.** G sold 4,000 shares of IBM stock for $200,000, recognizing a long-term capital gain of $40,000. Less than a week later, G used the entire $200,000 plus additional cash of $15,000 to purchase an interest in the P Partnership, an SSBIC. G may exclude the gain of $40,000 since she reinvested at least $200,000 in qualified property within 60 days. Her basis in the partnership interest would be $175,000 ($215,000 cost − $40,000 deferred gain).

DEALERS IN SECURITIES

The problem of determining whether a taxpayer is a dealer or investor is particularly troublesome for securities dealers. Not only do they hold stocks and bonds for sale to customers as part of their regular business operations, but they also invest in stocks and bonds for their own account. As may be apparent, the potential for abuse is great. Since long-term capital gain and ordinary loss are generally preferred, securities dealers have the natural tendency to classify the assets to provide the greatest tax benefit. On the other hand, the IRS wants to do just the opposite. To eliminate the potential controversy and prohibit taxpayers from using their hindsight, Congress enacted § 1236, which simply requires the dealer to identify that a particular security is held for investment (and is therefore a capital asset) by the end of the day on which it was acquired.[48] If the security is not properly identified on a timely basis, the dealer must characterize any gain or loss as ordinary.

---

[47] § 1202(g).   [48] § 1236(a).

SUBDIVIDED REAL ESTATE

The dealer vs. investor debate also raises its ugly head for taxpayers selling land. Is the land held for investment or primarily for resale? In an attempt to prevent disputes, Congress created a safe harbor that guarantees capital gain treatment where there is a limited amount of subdivision activity. This rule allows, as someone once said, the taxpayer to subdivide and conquer the ordinary income problem. Under § 1237, real estate is not treated as held primarily for sale if all of the following conditions are met:[49]

1. The tract of land has been held at least five years prior to the sale (except in the case of inheritance).

2. The taxpayer has made no substantial improvements to the property that increase the value of the lots sold while the property was owned.

3. The parcel sold, or any part thereof, had not previously been held by the taxpayer primarily for resale.

4. No other real property was held by the taxpayer primarily for sale during the year of the sale.

Even if the requirements are met, the taxpayer may still be required to report a portion of the gain as ordinary income. If five or fewer lots are sold from the same tract of land, the entire gain is capital gain. However, in the year that the sixth lot is sold, all lots sold in that year and later years become the target of § 1237(b). This special rule provides that 5 percent of the sales price (not gain) is ordinary income.[50] In addition, any selling expenses reduce the ordinary income portion of the gain (limited to the amount of ordinary income), rather than the amount treated as capital gain.[51]

> **Example 27.** Twenty years ago X bought 100 acres 20 miles south of Tulsa for $100,000. This year he retired and decided to sell the land. In order to sell the property, he subdivided it into 10 lots of 10 acres each. This year X sold 5 lots for $310,000 and paid a real estate commission of $10,000. As a result, he recognized a gain of $250,000 ($310,000 − $10,000 − $50,000 basis). Since he sold only 5 lots, the gain on each sale is treated as long-term capital gain. Had X sold 6 lots for the same total price, 5% of his selling price, $15,500 (5% × $310,000), would be considered ordinary income and he could reduce this amount by the selling expenses of $10,000, for net ordinary income on the sale of $5,500.

---

[49] § 1237(a).

[50] § 1237(b)(1).

[51] § 1237(b)(2).

OTHER RELATED PROVISIONS

NONBUSINESS BAD DEBTS

Bad debt losses from nonbusiness debts are deductible as short-term capital losses. Nonbusiness bad debts are deductible only in the year they become totally worthless since no deduction is allowed for partially worthless debts.[52] These rules and others related to the allowable deduction for bad debts were discussed in Chapter 10.

FRANCHISE AGREEMENTS, TRADEMARKS, AND TRADE NAMES

Section 1253 includes specific guidelines for the treatment of both the transferee and the transferor of payments with respect to franchise, trademark, and trade name agreements. The transfer of such rights is *not* treated as the sale or exchange of a capital asset by the transferor *if* he or she retains significant power, right, or continuing interest with respect to the property.[53] Capital gain and loss treatment also is denied for periodic payments that are contingent on the productivity, use, or sale of the property.[54]

"Significant power, right, or continuing interest" is defined in the Code by example. Some of the characteristics listed in the Code as indicative of such power, right, or interest retained by the transferor of the franchise are as follows:[55]

1.   The right to terminate the franchise at will;

2.   The right to disapprove any assignment;

3.   The right to prescribe quality standards;

4.   The right to require that the transferee advertise only products of the transferor;

5.   The right to require that the transferee acquire substantially all of his or her supplies or equipment from the transferor; and

6.   The right to require payments based on the productivity, use, or sale of the property.

The transferee is allowed current deductions for amounts paid or accrued that are contingent on the productivity, use, or sale of the property transferred.[56] Other payments must be at least partially deferred. They generally are amortized over the shorter of 10 years or the period covered by the transfer agreement.[57]

---

[52]   See § 166(d) and related discussion in Chapter 10.

[53]   § 1253(a).

[54]   § 1253(c).

[55]   § 1253(b)(2).

[56]   § 1253(d)(1).

[57]   § 1253(d)(2).

Example 28. M, Inc. and R enter into a franchise agreement that allows R to operate a hamburger establishment using the trade name and products of M, Inc. According to the contract, M, Inc. has retained all six rights that are listed above. R is required to pay M $50,000 upon entering the contract and 2% of all sales. The term of the contract is 25 years with provision for renewals. R must also pay for any supplies provided by M. Both the $50,000 payment and the percentage royalty payment are ordinary income to M, Inc.

R may treat the royalty payments to M, Inc. as ordinary deductions incurred in his trade or business. The initial fee of $50,000 is amortized equally over 10 years beginning with the year in which the payment is made.

SHORT SALES

Investors who believe that the price of a security will fall rather than rise may bank on their belief by using short sales. Selling short essentially means selling shares that are not actually owned. To accomplish this, the seller typically borrows shares from a broker, sells such shares, and agrees to return an equivalent number of substantially identical shares to the broker within a certain period of time. For example, an investor may sell 100 shares of borrowed stock for $100 per share, or $10,000. If the stock price falls to $80 per share, the investor can purchase 100 shares in the market for $8,000, replace the 100 borrowed shares, and have a tidy profit of $2,000. Of course, if the price goes up to $110, it costs the investor $11,000 to *cover* the short position and a loss is realized.

The tax consequences of short sales are triggered at the time the seller replaces the borrowed shares (i.e., the short position is closed or covered). No gain or loss is recognized until this time.[58] The character of the gain or loss realized depends on whether the asset involved (normally stock) is a capital asset. Determination of the holding period is more confusing. If the replacement securities have been held for a year or less before the *short sale* or are acquired after the sale, the gain or loss realized on closing the position is short-term.[59] Moreover, if the taxpayer does not use such stock to replace the borrowed shares, the holding period of such securities starts again, beginning on the date the short position was closed.[60] If the replacement property has been held for more than a year prior to the short sale, the gain or loss recognized on closing is long-term, regardless of the holding period of the actual shares used to close the short position.

Example 29. On March 15, 1993 T purchased 100 shares of SS stock for $4,000. On February 15, 1994 T sold 100 shares of SS stock short for $5,000. On June 15, 1994 T closed out his short position by delivering the March 15, 1993 shares. Because T held the replacement shares less than one year before he shorted the stock (March 15, 1993 to February 15, 1994), she reports a $1,000 short-term capital gain.

---

[58] Reg. § 1.1233-1(a)(1).

[59] § 1233(b).

[60] *Ibid.*

Example 30.   Same facts as *Example 29*, except T closed out her position by purchasing 100 new shares on June 15, 1994 for $6,500. In addition, she sold the original shares on August 15, 1994 for $7,000. T reports a capital loss of $1,500 upon covering her short position, and it is short-term since she held substantially identical stock less than a year before she shorted the stock (March 15, 1993 to February 15, 1994). In addition, T reports a *short-term* capital gain on the sale of the original stock of $3,000 ($7,000 − $4,000) even though she has held the stock for more than one year (March 15, 1993 to August 15, 1994). The holding period for the original stock begins again on the date the short sale was closed by virtue of the fact that she owned such stock less than one year before the short sale.

OPTIONS

Options of one variety or another have become commonplace in the business and investment world. They can be used in a variety of ways (e.g., an option to buy a house or buy land), but they are probably best known as a technique—sometimes a speculative one—to invest in the stock and commodities markets. The popularity of options has skyrocketed since the Chicago Board Options Exchange began organized trading in listed options in 1973. Currently, listed options on hundreds of securities can be bought and sold just like the securities themselves. One need only glance at the daily quotes in the *Wall Street Journal* or similar financial newspapers to appreciate this everyday phenomenon. This growth in the use of options requires tax advisers to have some appreciation of how they work and how they are taxed.

For some, however, options are shrouded in a cloud of mystery, an esoteric investment tool too sophisticated for the common investor. In reality, the basic operation of options is not that complicated. An option simply gives the holder the right to buy or sell a specific asset at a certain price by a specified date. A taxpayer who owns an option may either exercise the option, sell the option, or allow it to expire. The tax treatment of these actions is just as straightforward as the operation of the option itself.

Treatment of Option Buyer.   If the taxpayer exercises the option, the amount paid for the option is treated as a capital expenditure and added to the taxpayer's basis for the property. If the taxpayer sells the option or allows it to expire, the tax treatment depends on the nature of the underlying property.[61] In other words, if the taxpayer sells the option, the sale is treated as a sale of the option property. Therefore, any gain or loss recognized is a capital gain or loss only if the option property is a capital asset.

Example 31.   On May 1 J purchased for $500 an option to buy 100 shares of Wells Fargo common stock at a price of $100 per share at any time before September 15. On August 1, when Wells Fargo was trading at $130 per share, J exercised his option and bought 100 shares for $10,000. Although J is immediately better from his purchase, he has no income. The basis of his stock is $10,500 (the $500 cost of the option + the $10,000 cost of the stock) and the holding period begins on September 15.

---

[61]   § 1234(a). Note that the lapse of an option is treated as a sale or exchange [§ 1234(b)].

Example 32. On January 2 Compaq common stock was trading at what K thought was a bargain price of $65 per share. Consequently, K purchased for $700 an option to buy 100 shares of Compaq at a price of $80 on or before March 15. After the corporation reported its earnings, the stock value jumped, and by March 1 the price was bouncing between $95 and $100 per share. The value of K's option had also increased, and he sold it for $3,000. Since the option property, the stock, is a capital asset, K reports a short-term capital gain of $2,300 ($3,000 − $700).

Example 33. Same facts as *Example 32,* except Compaq's earnings were disappointing and the value of the stock as well as the value of K's option decreased. On March 15, the stock was trading at $60 per share and K decided to let the option expire. K recognizes a short-term capital loss of $700.

Options are generally billed as a way to secure a potentially large profit from a relatively small investment with a known risk. The option buyer knows in advance that the most that can be lost is the amount paid for the option. There are generally two types of options: puts and calls. A *call* is simply the shorthand term given to an option that gives the holder the right to purchase a particular security at a fixed price. All of the discussion and examples above deal with call options. For example, if an individual believes the price of IBM will rise from $50 to $70 over the next several months, she might purchase a call that enables her to buy 1,000 shares at a price far lower than the $50,000 that would be required to actually buy the stock. The ultimate tax treatment of the call depends, as explained above, on whether the taxpayer sells or exercises the option or allows it to lapse.

Treatment of Option Writer (Seller). In any option agreement, there are two parties, the party who buys the option and the person who "writes," or sells, the option. Individuals who write, or sell, call options obligate themselves to deliver a certain number of shares at a particular price in exchange for the payment of some amount referred to as the call premium. If the call is written by a person who owns the underlying stock (a "covered" call), the individual can deliver such stock if the call is exercised. If the writer does not own the stock (a "naked" call), the stock must be purchased to meet the obligation—a very risky situation. Writers of covered calls generally view the call premium as an additional source of income or as a hedge against a possible decline in the value of the stock. If the buyer exercises the call, the writer of the option adds the premium to the amount realized in determining the gain or loss realized on the stock sold. The gain or loss is long-term or short-term depending on the underlying stock. If the buyer allows the call to expire, the writer of the call treats the premium received for the option as a short-term capital gain regardless of the actual holding period. The gain is reported at the time the option expires.

Example 34.   After discussing it with her broker, W decided to write call options on her 100 shares of Colgate that she bought several years ago for $3,000. She deposited the stock with her broker and instructed him to write a call that allows an investor to purchase 100 shares of Colgate at $40 per share at a premium of $5 per share. Within a few business days, W's account was credited with $500 for writing the call. If the call is not exercised, W has a $500 short-term capital gain. If the call is exercised, W sells her stock and realizes a long-term capital gain of $1,500 ($4,000 + $500 − $3,000).

Puts.   To understand puts, one has to mentally shift gears. Puts are the exact opposites of calls. Whereas a buyer of a call buys the right to purchase stock at a fixed price, a buyer of a put buys the right to sell stock at a fixed price. As in short sales, the buyer of a put typically believes that the price of the underlying stock will drop. If the put is sold, the taxpayer reports a short-term capital gain or loss regardless of the holding period. If the put is exercised (i.e., the taxpayer does in fact sell the underlying stock), the amount realized on the sale is decreased by the premium paid for the put. If the put lapses, a loss is allowable as of the date the option expires. As a practical matter, most puts are bought with the intention of selling them.

Example 35.   After seeing reports on television that the airline industry was falling on hard times, P believed the current $47 price on Boeing stock would fall. He immediately called his broker and bought a put at a price of $200 on March 4. The put enables him to sell 100 shares of the stock at a price of $45 per share before August 24. The price did in fact fall and bottomed at $40 per share. As a result, his put, that is, his right to sell the stock at $45, became more valuable, and he sold the put for $500. P must report a short-term capital gain of $300 ($500 − $200).

CORPORATE BONDS AND OTHER INDEBTEDNESS

Investments in corporate bonds and other forms of indebtedness present several unique problems that must be considered by taxpayers who choose this form of investment. Under the general rules, mere collection of principal payments does not constitute a sale or exchange and, therefore, a capital gain or capital loss cannot result. However, the Code creates an exception for certain forms of debt. This special rule provides that any amounts received by the holder on retirement of any debt are considered as amounts received in exchange for the debt.[62] Consequently, capital gain or loss is normally recognized when the debt is redeemed or sold for more or less than the taxpayer's basis in the debt.

Example 36.   B purchased a $1,000, 10% bond issued by Z Corporation for $990. Assuming the bond is held to maturity and redeemed by the corporation, B will recognize a capital gain of $10. If B had sold the bond prior to redemption for $995, he would recognize a capital gain of $5.

---

[62]   § 1271.

A second and more difficult problem to be considered concerns the *interest element* that may be inherent in the purchase price of a corporate bond. For example, if the rate at which a bond pays interest—the stated rate—is less than the current market rate, the bond will sell for less than its face value, or at a discount. In this case, the *discount* effectively functions as a substitute for interest income. Conversely, if the stated rate exceeds the market rate, the bond will sell for more than its face value, or at a premium. Here, the *premium* essentially reduces the amount of interest income. Without special rules, the proper amount of interest income would not be captured and reported in a timely manner.

> **Example 37.** Several years ago when interest rates were 10%, T purchased a $10,000, 8% corporate bond for $8,000, or a $2,000 discount. This year the bond matured and T redeemed the bond for its par value of $10,000. Under normal accounting procedures, the redemption is treated as an exchange and the taxpayer would recognize a long-term capital gain of $2,000 ($10,000 − $8,000). In this case, the taxpayer would have converted the discount of $2,000, which from an economic view is ordinary interest income, to capital gain. Moreover, this income would be deferred until T sold the bond.

The example above illustrates the problems that the special tax rules governing bond transactions address. The provisions ensure that any premium or discount is not treated as part of the capital gain or loss realized on disposition of the bond, but rather is treated as an *adjustment* to the taxpayer's interest income received from the bond. In addition, the Code provides rules for determining how much of the premium or discount will affect interest income and *when* the additional interest income (in the case of discount) or the interest expense (in the case of premium) will be reported.

The Code provides a separate set of rules governing the treatment of premium and discount. In the case of discount, the rules differ depending on when the discount arises. One set applies when the bonds were *originally issued* at a discount (the "original issue discount" provisions) and another set applies if the discount arises when the bonds are purchased later in the open market (the "market discount" rules). The rules governing premium are the same regardless of when the premium arises.

ORIGINAL ISSUE DISCOUNT

When corporate bonds are *issued* at a price less than the stated redemption price at maturity (i.e., the bond's face value), the resulting discount is referred to as *original issued discount*, or more commonly OID. The amount of OID is easily computed as follows:

Redemption price (face value).................	$x,xxx
− Issue price....................................	− xxx
= Original issue discount........................	$x,xxx

The OID provisions generally require the holder of the bond to amortize the discount and include it in income during the period the bond is held.[63] For purposes of computing the gain or loss on disposition of the bond, the holder must increase the basis of the bond by the amount of any amortized discount. Any gain or loss on the disposition of the bond normally is capital gain. However, if at the time of issue there was an intention to call the bond before maturity, any gain on the bond is treated as ordinary income to the extent of any unamortized discount.[64]

Before examining the amortization methods, it should be emphasized that the Code furnishes a *de minimis* rule that may exempt the debt from the OID amortization requirements. OID is considered to be zero when the bond discount is less than one-fourth of one percent of the redemption price at maturity multiplied by the number of complete years to maturity.[65] This may be expressed as follows:

Redemption price at maturity..................	$x,xxx
× Percentage....................................	× 0.25%
× Number of complete years to maturity.........	× x
= De minimis amount............................	$x,xxx

In most cases, new bond issues do not create OID because the stated interest rate is set near the market rate so that the amount of discount that arises, if any, does not exceed the de minimis amount. As a result, no amortization is required.

For bonds issued after July 1, 1982, the discount is amortized into income using a technique similar to the effective interest method used in financial accounting.[66] To determine the includible OID, the OID attributable to an *accrual period* must be computed. This is done by multiplying the *adjusted issue price* at the beginning of the *accrual period* by the *yield to maturity* and reducing this amount by any interest payable on the bond during the period. The adjusted issue price is the bond's original issue price as increased for previously amortized OID. The accrual period is generally the six-month period ending on the anniversary date of the bond (date of original issue) and six months before such date. The yield to maturity must be determined using present value techniques or may be found in bond tables designed specifically for this purpose.[67]

Once the OID attributable to the entire bond period is computed, this amount is allocated ratably to each day in the bond period. The bondholder's includible OID is the sum of the daily portions of OID for each day during the taxable year that the owner held the bond.

---

[63] §§ 1271–1275.

[64] § 1271(a)(2).

[65] § 1273(a)(3).

[66] § 1272(a). For bonds issued after July 1, 1982, and before January 1, 1985, the accrual period is one year.

[67] Given the issue price, the redemption price, and the number of periods to maturity, the yield to maturity may be approximated by reference to appropriate present value tables.

Example 38.   On July 1, 1994 R purchased 100 newly issued 30-year, 8% bonds with a face value of $1,000 for $800 each or $80,000. The bonds pay interest semiannually on July 1 and December 31. The OID rules apply since the $200 discount per bond exceeds the de minimis amount of $75.

Redemption price at maturity..................	$1,000
× Percentage.....................................	× 0.25%
× Number of complete years to maturity.........	× 30
= De minimis amount...........................	$ 75

Using present value calculations, the annual yield to maturity for this bond is 10.14% (or 5.07% semiannually). The OID that R must include in income in 1994 and 1995 for all of the bonds is computed in the aggregate as follows.

	7/1–12/31 1994	1/1–6/30 1995	7/1–12/31 1995
Adjusted issue price......................	$80,000	$80,056**	$80,115
Semiannual yield.........................	× 5.07%	× 5.07%	× 5.07%
Total effective interest.....................	$ 4,056	$ 4,059	$ 4,062
Less: Interest received.................	− 4,000*	− 4,000	− 4,000
Includible OID............................	$ 56	$ 59	$ 62

* $100,000 × 4% = $4,000
** $80,000 + $56 = $80,056

R would include the amount of OID in income in addition to the interest income actually received. Note that the issuer of the bond would include in its annual deduction for interest expense the amount of OID that must be amortized.

Example 39.   Assume the same facts as above, except that R sells all of the bonds for $85,000 on July 1, 1995. Assuming there was no intention to call the bonds when issued, R will report a capital gain of $4,885 ($85,000 − $80,115).

Additional computations are required when the purchase price exceeds the original issue price as increased by OID amortized by previous holders. As a practical matter, the issuer of the bond is obligated to provide the taxpayer a Form 1099-OID, Statement of Original Issue Discount, disclosing the amount of interest income to be reported annually. For those who do not receive such a form, the IRS provides a special publication with the necessary information.

For bonds issued before July 2, 1982, the OID is generally included in the income of the holder ratably over the term of the bond (i.e., a straight-line method is used).[68]

---

[68]   § 1272(a); for bonds issued before May 28, 1969, special rules apply. See § 1272(b).

Example 40.   Assume the bond in *Example 38* was issued prior to July 2, 1982. The original issue discount included annually would be $667 ($20,000 ÷ 30).

Although the OID rules are to apply to virtually all debt instruments, there are several notable exceptions:[69]

1. U.S. Savings Bonds (which are treated as discussed in Chapter 5)

2. Tax-exempt state and local obligations (although the discount income is not included as taxable income, the taxpayer increases the basis of the instrument)

3. Debt instruments that have a fixed maturity date not exceeding one year [unless held by certain parties identified in § 1281(b), including accrual basis taxpayers]

4. Obligations issued by individuals before March 2, 1984

5. Nonbusiness loans between individuals of $10,000 or less

In 1984 the coverage of the OID rules was substantially extended to help curb abuses that occurred when a taxpayer sold property and received a note in exchange. The application of the OID rules in this area was discussed in Chapter 14 in conjunction with unstated interest.

MARKET DISCOUNT

As previously noted, without special rules, amortization of discount would not be required where the security was treated as having no OID (e.g., where the discount on the bond when originally issued was small). For example, if a bond having a $10,000 face value bearing 10 percent interest over a 30-year term was issued for $9,500, there would be no OID since the discount is less than $750 (0.25% × 30 × $10,000). In subsequent years, however, interest rates might rise, causing the bond to sell at a substantially greater discount (i.e., lower value), say $8,000 (e.g., if rates rose to 14% the bond's price might fall to $8,000). In such case, an investor could purchase the bond and ultimately report the built-in appreciation as capital gain—the $2,000 rise from the discounted price to face value at maturity—notwithstanding the fact that a portion of the increase in value actually represents interest income. Moreover, the investor could borrow amounts to purchase the investment and obtain an immediate deduction for interest on the debt, although the income from the bond was deferred until it was redeemed or sold. This highly publicized and extremely popular investment technique was foreclosed by the Deficit Reduction Act of 1984 for newly issued bonds.

---

[69]   §§ 1272(a)(2) and 1274(c)(2).

Changes made in 1993 make the rules applicable to *all* bonds purchased after April 30, 1993. Code § 1276 provides that any gain on the disposition of a bond is treated as interest income to the extent of any accrued *market discount*. Market discount, in contrast to OID, is measured at the time the purchaser acquires the bond. Hence, market discount is the excess of the stated redemption price over the basis of the bond immediately after *acquisition*.[70] Like OID, market discount is considered to be zero if it is less than one-fourth of one percent of the stated redemption price multiplied by the number of complete years to maturity after acquisition. The portion of market discount that is considered ordinary income upon disposition of the bond is computed assuming the discount accrues ratably over the number of days from the purchase of the bond to the bond's maturity date.

> **Example 41.** On January 1, 1993 T purchased a bond issued in 1992 having a face value of $10,000 for $8,000. The bond matures four years later on January 1, 1997. The market discount on the bond is $2,000, the difference between the stated redemption price of $10,000 and the taxpayer's $8,000 basis in the bond immediately after acquisition. The $2,000 is deemed to accrue on a daily basis over the 1,460 days remaining on the bond's term. Assuming T sells the bond for $9,000 on January 2, 1994, her gain is $1,000, of which $500 is ordinary interest income [$2,000 × (365 ÷ 1,460)] and the remaining $500 is long-term capital gain.

In lieu of using the daily method of computing the accrued market discount, the taxpayer may use the effective interest method similar to that used for amortizing OID. In addition, the taxpayer may elect to report accrued market discount in taxable income annually rather than at the date of disposition. If this election is made, the taxpayer increases the basis of the bond by the amount of market discount included in income.

Congress also enacted provisions limiting the taxpayer's interest deduction on loans to purchase market discount bonds. Section 1277 requires the taxpayer to defer the deduction for interest expense until that time when income from the bond is reported.

CONVERSION TRANSACTIONS

The original issue discount and market discount provisions exist in order to prevent taxpayers from converting ordinary interest income into capital gain when the interest element is in the form of a discount. In certain instances, taxpayers may still be able to avoid this treatment by structuring the transactions somewhat differently. Congress refers to these as *conversion transactions*.

---

[70] § 1277(a)(2). If the bond also has OID, the market discount is reduced by the amortized portion of OID.

Conversion transactions are certain investments on which the return is attributable to the time value of money, or for which the sales price of the investment is known at the time the investment is made. Upon the sale or disposition of such investments, any gain is treated as ordinary income, rather than capital gain, to the extent of a return on the investment calculated at 120 percent of the applicable federal rate.[71] Any gain in excess of the ordinary income or any loss realized on the investment is treated as capital gain or loss, assuming the contract is a capital asset to the taxpayer.

BOND PREMIUM

The treatment of premium depends in part on whether the interest income on the bond is taxable.[72] When the interest income is taxable, the taxpayer *may* elect to amortize and deduct the premium as interest expense and concomitantly reduce the basis in the bond. The interest expense in this case is considered investment interest and is, therefore, deductible as an itemized deduction to the extent of net investment income. If the taxpayer does not elect to amortize the premium, the unamortized premium is simply included as part of the taxpayer's basis in the bond and thus decreases the gain or increases the loss on disposition of the bond.

If the interest income on the bond is tax-exempt, the premium *must* be amortized and the bond's basis decreased. No deduction is allowed for the amortized premium since it merely represents an adjustment in the amount of nontaxable income received by the holder. In other words, no deduction for the premium is allowed since it represents interest expense related to producing tax-exempt income. Note that by requiring amortization of the premium, the taxpayer is prohibited from securing a deduction for the premium in the form of a capital loss or a reduced gain on the disposition of the bond.

> **Example 42.**   V purchased a $1,000 tax-exempt bond for $1,100. If V holds the bond to maturity, all of the premium will be amortized and his basis in the bond will be $1,000. Therefore, on redemption of the bond for $1,000, no gain or loss is recognized. However, if amortization of the premium was not required, V would report a capital loss of $100 on redemption of the bond.

The method to be used for amortizing premium depends on when the bond was issued. If the bond was issued before September 28, 1985, the premium is amortized using the straight-line method over the number of months to maturity. Premium on bonds issued on or after that date must be amortized based on the bond's yield to maturity determined when the bond was issued.

---

[71] § 1258.   [72] § 171.

```
┌─────────────────────────────────────────────────────────┐
│              TAX PLANNING CONSIDERATIONS                  │
└─────────────────────────────────────────────────────────┘
```

TIMING OF CAPITAL ASSET TRANSACTIONS

A taxpayer with investments that he or she may wish to sell should pay careful attention to the timing of those sales, particularly near the end of a year. Since the netting process takes into consideration only the sales for the year under consideration plus any capital loss carryovers, the year into which a particular transaction falls may have significant impact on the total amount of taxes paid. The taxpayer must also consider market conditions, since he or she may believe that waiting to sell a particular asset may cost more than paying any additional tax.

Strictly from a tax planning perspective, a taxpayer should consider timing the recognition of year-end capital gains and losses using the following strategy:

1. *No capital gains or losses currently*—recognize up to $3,000 STCL or LTCL to take advantage of the annual capital loss deduction.

2. *Currently have STCG*—recognize either STCL or LTCL to offset the STCG and more, if possible, to take advantage of the capital loss deduction.

3. *Currently have LTCG*—recognize either LTCL or STCL to offset the LTCG and more, if possible, to take advantage of the capital loss deduction.

4. *Currently have STCL*—if less than $3,000, recognize more STCL or LTCL to take advantage of the capital loss deduction. If more than $3,000, recognize either STCG or LTCG to offset the STCL in excess of $3,000.

5. *Currently have LTCL*—if less than $3,000, recognize more LTCL or STCL to take advantage of the capital loss deduction. If more than $3,000, recognize either STCG or LTCG to offset the LTCL in excess of $3,000.

The newly created differential between ordinary income and capital gains for non-corporate taxpayers (including flow-through entities) makes it far more important to distinguish between ordinary income and capital gain. Taxpayers should carefully plan in order to secure the benefit of this new differential, which can be as great as 11.6 percent (39.6% − 28%).

SECTION 1244 STOCK

The importance of § 1244 should not be overlooked when making an investment.

> **Example 43.**   Dr. G is extremely successful and consequently is often approached by friends, promoters, and others asking her to make an investment in one deal or another. If G loans $30,000 to a friend to start a business which ultimately fails, the loss would be governed by the worthless-security rules and thus treated as a capital loss. In such case, Dr. G's annual loss deduction is limited

to the extent of her capital gains plus $3,000. If G has no capital gains (which are not necessarily easily found), it could take her as long as ten years to deduct her loss. However, if the investment had been in the form of § 1244 stock, the entire $30,000 loss would be deductible in the year incurred.

Under § 1244, the taxpayer is allowed to deduct up to $50,000 ($100,000 in the case of a joint return) of loss *annually*. Any loss in excess of this amount is treated as a capital loss and is subject to limitation. In light of these rules, a taxpayer who anticipates a loss on § 1244 stock that exceeds the annual limitation should attempt to limit the loss recognized in any one year to $50,000 (or $100,000).

Example 44.   C, a bachelor, invested $200,000 in Risky Corporation several years ago, receiving 1,000 shares of § 1244 stock. It now appears that Risky, true to its name, will fail and that C will receive at best $100,000 for his investment. If C sells all of his shares this year, $50,000 of the loss is completely deductible as an ordinary loss under § 1244, while the remaining $50,000 of the loss would be a capital loss of which only $3,000 could be deducted (assuming he has no capital gains). C should sell half of his shares this year and half of his shares next year. By so doing, his loss for each year will be $50,000. In such case, neither loss would exceed the annual limitation, and therefore both would be deductible in full.

PROBLEM MATERIALS

DISCUSSION QUESTIONS

16-1 *Capital Asset Defined.* Define a capital asset. How would you describe the way a capital asset is defined?

16-2 *Sale of a Business.* How is the sale of an operating business treated? Discuss the sale of sole proprietorships, partnerships, and corporations in general.

16-3 *Holding Period.* What is the holding period requirement for long-term capital gains and losses? How does one determine the holding period for purchased property?

16-4 *Holding Period.* What is the rule for determining the holding period for property acquired by gift?

16-5 *Holding Period.* What is the holding period of property acquired from a decedent?

16-6 *Holding Period—Stock Exchange Transactions.* T placed an order with her stock broker to sell 100 shares of Kent Electronics, Inc. stock on December 23, 1994. Because the sale order was received after the close of the market on the 23rd, the sale was executed at 9:00 A.M. on December 30, 1994. T received a settlement check from the brokerage house on January 5, 1995. What is the date of sale and what is the last date of T's holding period?

16-7 *Holding Period—Worthless Securities.* D purchased 1,000 shares of H, Inc. for $4,450 in a speculative investment on October 25, 1993. Weeks later, on January 5, 1994, D received notice that the H, Inc. stock was worthless. What are the amount and character of D's loss in 1994?

16-8 *Capital Gain and Loss Netting Process.* Describe the three possible results of the capital gain and loss netting process. How are the gains treated for tax purposes?

16-9 *Capital Gains Tax.* D is single and has taxable income for the current year of $72,000, including a net capital gain of $7,000. Describe how D will determine the tax on his income for the year.

16-10 *Capital Loss Deduction.* How is the capital loss deduction limited for individual taxpayers?

16-11 *Capital Loss Carryover.* Capital losses in excess of the annual limit can be carried forward to the subsequent year. How long may losses be carried forward by individual taxpayers? What is the character of the loss carryover and what happens if both long-term and short-term losses are carried forward?

16-12 *Patents.* What is necessary for a patent to qualify for capital gain or loss treatment under § 1235?

16-13 *Ordinary vs. Capital Loss Treatment.* What are the tax consequences to P, a bachelor, of a $70,000 loss occurring on June 1 of the current year attributable to the following:

a. An uncollectible nonbusiness loan to XYZ Corporation
b. Worthless bonds of XYZ Corporation acquired on November 30 of the prior year
c. The sale of XYZ stock qualifying as § 1244 stock when acquired two years ago

16-14 *Section 1244 Stock.*   When is a taxpayer's stock considered § 1244 stock? Why is the designation significant?

16-15 *Fifty Percent Exclusion.*   S purchased qualified small business stock in U Corp. on October 27, 1993 for $35,000 with hopes to later qualify for the 50 percent exclusion.

    a. What two major requirements must U Corp. meet throughtout S's holding period?

    b. What is the first day on which S may sell the stock and qualify for the 50 percent exclusion?

16-16 *Rollover of Gain on Sales of Publicly Traded Securities.*   Q sold common stock in K Corp., a publicly traded corporation, for $140,000, realizing a gain of $60,000.

    a. How much must Q reinvest in a corporation or partnership that is licensed by the Small Business Administration under § 301(d) of the Small Business Investment Act of 1958 (as in effect on May 13, 1993) in order to defer all of the $60,000 gain?

    b. By what day must Q reinvest to qualify for this gain rollover (deferral)?

16-17 *Dealers in Securities.*   How does a dealer in securities guarantee that a particular "investment" will qualify for capital gain or loss treatment?

16-18 *Original Issue Discount—Deep Discount Bonds.*   Financial consulting services often advise investment in so-called *deep discount bonds* (e.g., a $1,000 par value bond maturing in 10 years with coupon rate of 6% that sells at a discounted price of $400). Explain how such an investment could provide any tax savings in light of the original issue discount rules.

16-19 *Bond Premium.*   This year, G purchased a $1,000 bond for $1,100. The bond matures in 2000 and pays interest at a rate of 10 percent. Interest is paid semiannually on February 1 and August 1. Explain the treatment of the premium on the bond if the bond was issued by:

    a. General Motors

    b. City of Sacramento

PROBLEMS

16-20 *Identifying Capital Assets.*   Which of the following items are capital assets?

    a. An automobile held for sale to customers by Midtown Motors, Inc.

    b. An automobile owned and used by Sherry Hartman to run household errands

    c. An automobile owned and used by Windowwashers, Inc.

    d. The private residence of Robert Hamilton

    e. Letters from famous U.S. President written to Jane Doe (Jane Doe has the letters.)

    f. A warehouse owned and used by Holt Packing Company

16-21 *Identifying Capital Assets.*   Which of the following properties are capital assets? Briefly explain your answers.

    a. A house built by a home-building contractor and used by her as her principal residence

    b. A house, 80 percent of which is used as a residence and 20 percent of which is used to store business inventory

    c. The same house in (b) above, used as stated for 10 years, and now used exclusively as a residence

    d. Undeveloped land held for investment by a real estate broker

    e. Stock held for investment by a stock broker

16-22 *Capital Gain Netting Process.* D sold the following capital assets during 1994:

Description	Date Acquired	Date Sold	Sales Price	Adjusted Basis
100 shares XY Corp.	1/10/74	1/12/94	$14,000	$1,000
50 shares LM Inc.	9/14/93	1/12/94	1,900	4,000
140 shares CH Corp.	11/20/93	4/10/94	3,400	3,000
Gold necklace	4/22/82	6/30/94	5,000	1,300
Personal auto	5/10/91	8/31/94	4,000	6,500

Determine each of the following amounts:

a. D's net long-term capital gain or loss
b. D's net short-term capital gain or loss
c. D's net capital gain, if any, and whether it is long- or short-term
d. D's tax liability (before prepayments and credits), assuming she is single with no dependents and her taxable income before these capital transactions is $72,000

16-23 *Capital Gain Netting Process.* Each of the following situations deals with capital gains and losses occurring during the calendar year 1994 for an individual taxpayer. For each case, determine the change in adjusted gross income and the maximum tax to be imposed on any gain.

Note:	NLTCG(L)	= Net long-term capital gain or (loss)
	NSTCG(L)	= Net short-term capital gain or (loss)

Case	NLTCG(L)	NSTCG(L)
A	$1,200	$1,200
B	1,600	(1,000)
C	(1,200)	1,800
D	4,500	(800)
E	2,400	1,800

16-24 *Capital Gain and Losses on Property Acquired by Gift.* In each of the following situations, assume that the taxpayer received the capital asset as a gift on March 19, 1994, that the donor had held the property since 1964, and that the property was sold during 1994. No gift taxes were payable on the transfer. Determine the gain or loss recognized in each case and whether it is long- or short-term.

Case	Date of Sale	Sales Price	Donor's Basis	FMV Date of Gift
A	4/19	$1,000	$ 400	$ 600
B	6/3	1,000	1,400	1,200
C	11/20	1,000	900	1,100

16-25 *Capital Gains and Losses.* K earned salaries and wages of $56,000 and interest and dividends of $3,700 for the current year. In addition, K sold the following capital assets:

100 shares of GHJ common stock, held 14 months.........	$3,400 gain
1955 Ford pickup, used five years for personal purposes...	4,500 gain
30 acres of land, held three years for investment..........	6,200 loss

    a. Compute K's net capital gain or loss.

    b. Compute K's adjusted gross income.

16-26 *Capital Gains and Losses.* L earned salaries and wages of $47,000 and interest and dividends of $6,700 for the current year. In addition, L sold the following capital assets:

10 shares LMN common stock, held ten months..............	$ 1,400 gain
1988 Dodge sedan, used four years for personal purposes....	2,600 loss
10 acres of land, held six years for investment...............	9,200 loss

    a. Compute L's net capital gain or loss.

    b. Compute L's adjusted gross income.

16-27 *Capital Gains Tax.* R is a single, calendar year taxpayer. During 1994, R recognized net capital gains of $20,000. Calculate R's tax liability (before credits and prepayments) for each of the following levels of taxable income, assuming that the net capital gains have been included in the taxable income numbers.

    a. $35,000

    b. $80,000

    c. $500,000

16-28 *Capital Gains Tax.* H and J are married, calendar year taxpayers who elect to file jointly. Their income and deductions for 1994 are summarized below.

Salaries and wages.............................	$105,000
Interest and dividend income.....................	20,000
Short-term capital loss..........................	5,000
Long-term capital gains..........................	20,000
Standard deduction..............................	6,350
Personal exemptions............................	2

Determine H and J's tax liability (before credits and prepayments).

16-29 *Effective Tax Rate on Net Capital Gains.*   T is a single, calendar year taxpayer. He provides more than one-half the support of his elderly mother, who is living in a nearby nursing home. T's income and deductions for 1994 are summarized below.

Salary...	$115,000
Interest and dividend income.....................	7,000
Itemized deductions (all subject to the 3% cut-back rule).................................	12,500
Personal and dependency exemptions............	2

   a.   Calculate T's taxable income and income tax liability (before credits and prepayments) for the year.

   b.   How would your answers to (a) above change if T also had a $20,000 long-term capital gain in 1994?

   c.   Is the additional income tax from the capital gain limited to $5,600 ($20,000 net capital gain × 28%)? If not, explain why.

16-30 *Netting Process and Capital Losses.*   T, an unmarried taxpayer, sold the following capital assets during her calendar year 1994:

Description	Date Acquired	Date Sold	Sales Price	Adjusted Basis
100 shares CZ Corp.	1/10/94	9/17/94	$14,000	$18,000
75 shares PC, Inc.	7/6/94	9/17/94	5,200	4,300
Silver coins (held as an investment)	12/2/89	11/20/94	2,000	5,000

Complete each of the following requirements based on T's taxable income of $15,000 before capital gains and losses:

   a.   T's net long-term capital gain or loss

   b.   T's net short-term capital gain or loss

   c.   T's capital loss deduction in arriving at adjusted gross income

   d.   T's capital loss carryover to 1995 (describe amount and character)

   e.   How would your answers to (c) and (d) differ if T's basis in the PC stock had been $1,000?

16-31 *Capital Loss and Carryover.*   N earned a salary of $55,000 and interest and dividends of $6,500 for the current year. N also has the following capital gains and losses for the current year:

30 shares MNO common stock, held ten months......	$ 400 gain
50 shares NOP common stock, held four years.......	3,600 loss
Long-term capital loss carryforward from prior year....	11,600 loss
10 acres of land, held six years for investment........	9,200 gain

   a.   Compute L's net capital gain.

   b.   Compute L's adjusted gross income.

16-32 *Capital Gains and Losses.* Each of the following involves capital gains and losses occurring during the calendar year 1994 for an unmarried individual taxpayer.

	Note:	NLTCG(L)	= Net long-term capital gain or (loss)
		NSTCG(L)	= Net short-term capital gain or (loss)

Case	NLTCG(L)	NSTCG(L)
A	$1,200	($4,300)
B	(5,000)	200
C	(1,200)	(2,300)
D	(7,000)	200
E	(5,000)	(200)

    a. Determine the amount deductible in arriving at adjusted gross income in each case for 1994.

    b. Which, if any, of the above case(s) generate(s) a capital loss carryover to 1995? Give the amount and character (short- or long-term).

16-33 *Capital Loss Deduction and Capital Loss Carryover.* W, an unmarried calendar year individual, had numerous capital asset transactions during the years listed. Determine the amount deductible in each year and the amount and character of any carryover.

Year	NLTCG(L)	NSTCG(L)
1993	($8,000)	$ 1,000
1994	(1,500)	(2,000)
1995	0	(4,000)
1996	2,000	(3,000)

16-34 *Capital Loss Deduction and Capital Loss Carryover.* M, an unmarried calendar year individual, had numerous capital asset transactions during the years listed. Determine the amount deductible in each year and the amount and character of any carryover.

Year	NLTCG(L)	NSTCG(L)
1993	$1,000	($5,000)
1994	(6,000)	0
1995	3,000	(3,000)
1996	(3,000)	(3,000)

16-35 *Requirements for § 1244 Stock.* During the year, X, who is single, sold stock and realized a loss. For each of the following situations, indicate whether § 1244 would apply to the taxpayer's stock loss. Unless otherwise indicated, Code § 1244 applies.

    a. The stock was that issued to X when she incorporated her business several years ago.

    b. The stock was that of General Motors Corporation and was purchased last year.

    c. X inherited the stock from her grandfather, who had started the company ten years ago.

    d. X is a corporate taxpayer.

    e. X acquired her stock interest in 1990. The other four owners had acquired their interest for $250,000 each in 1986.

    f. The loss was $60,000.

16-36 *Section 1244 Stock Computation.* S is a bachelor. During the year, he sold stock in X Corporation that qualifies as § 1244 stock at a loss of $70,000. In addition, S sold stock in Y Corporation, realizing a $4,000 long-term capital gain. Compute the effect of these transactions on S's A.G.I.

16-37 *Worthless Securities.* Several years ago, T was persuaded by his good friend W to invest in her new venture, Wobbly Corporation. T purchased 100 shares of Wobbly stock from W for $60,000. He also purchased Wobbly bonds, which had a face value of $20,000 for $18,000. This year, Wobbly declared bankruptcy and T's investment in Wobbly became worthless. What are the tax consequences to T?

16-38 *Sale of Stock.* B owned 50 percent of the stock in a small incorporated dress shop. The business was successful for several years until a new freeway diverted nearly all of the traffic away from the location. The shop was moved, but to no avail, and the stock continued to quickly decline in value. Other than small interest payments, the income of the business came exclusively from sales of women's apparel.

The total paid-in capital of the corporation was $250,000, all in the form of cash. B's basis in the stock was always $125,000. In an attempt to prevent further losses, the shop was sold to a larger competitor during 1994. B received $50,000 for all of her stock.

a. How will B report the loss on the joint return she files with her husband for 1994?

b. How would your answer to (a) differ if the stock became totally worthless rather than being sold in 1994?

16-39 *Worthless Securities.* Y purchased 30 shares of BCD Corporation common stock on March 2, 1993, for $2,475. On February 26, 1994 Y was notified by her broker that the stock was worthless.

a. What are the amount and character of Y's loss?

b. Could this loss qualify as an ordinary deduction under § 1244? Explain.

16-40 *Fifty Percent Gain Exclusion.* E purchased qualified small business stock in P, Inc. on October 27, 1993 for $75,000. The stock continued to qualify until E sold it for $400,000 on December 15, 1998.

a. How much is E's gain realized upon this sale?

b. How much of this gain may E exclude from gross income?

c. What is the maximum amount of tax that E could pay on this gain (assuming no change in tax rates)?

16-41 *Rollover of Gain on Sale of Publicly Traded Securities.* R sold common stock in L Corp., a publicly traded corporation, on March 13, 1994 for $160,000, realizing a gain of $40,000. On April 1, 1994 R reinvested $200,000 in M Partnership, a partnership licensed by the Small Business Administration under § 301(d) of the Small Business Investment Act of 1958 (as in effect on May 13, 1993).

a. How much gain must R recognize on the sale of the L Corp. stock?

b. What is R's basis in his interest in M Partnership?

16-42 *Combining the Exclusion and Rollover.*   Y sold common stock in X Corp., a publicly traded corporation, on October 1, 1993 for $200,000, realizing a gain of $35,000. On October 15, 1993 Y reinvested $250,000 in N. Inc., a corporation licensed by the Small Business Administration under § 301(d) of the Small Business Investment Act of 1958 (as in effect on May 13, 1993), the stock of which is qualified small business stock. On December 1, 1998 Y sold all of the N, Inc. stock for $625,000.

a. How much is Y's gain realized on the sale of the N, Inc. stock?
b. How much of this gain is excludable from gross income?

16-43 *Lease Cancellation Payment.*   L rents a house to T for $450 per month under a two year lease. When T is transferred, he offers L $675 to terminate the lease. If L accepts, what is the tax treatment of the transaction to L and T?

16-44 *Franchise Agreements.*   J entered into a franchise agreement with Box, Inc. under which J will operate a fast food restaurant bearing the trademark and using the products of Box. Box retained "significant power, right and continuing interest" related to the franchise agreement.

J made an initial payment under the contract of $40,000, which entitles him to the rights under the contract for 15 years with indefinite extensions at the agreement of both parties. J also is required to pay for all supplies used plus a royalty of 1.5 percent of gross sales. J's sales were $112,000 during the first year. All of the payments described, totaling $41,680, were made during the current year.

a. How will J report these payments on his cash basis tax return for the current year?
b. How would Box, Inc. treat the payments from J on its return for the current year? The corporation reports on the cash basis.

16-45 *Original Issue Discount.*   On January 1, 1994 B purchased from XYZ Corporation a newly issued, $1 million, 30-year, 4 percent bond for $300,000. The bond produces a semiannual yield to maturity of 7 percent. Interest is paid semiannually on January 1 and July 1. What is B's income with respect to the bond in 1994 and 1995?

16-46 *Market Discount.*   D purchased a $10,000, 7 percent bond, for $6,350 on January 1, 1994. The bond was issued at par on January 1, 1993 and matures January 1, 1998. On January 1, 1995 D sold the bond for $8,000. What is D's income from the sale?

16-47 *Conversion Transaction.*   J purchased a non–interest-bearing financial instrument on June 1, 1993 for $60,000. It was purchased subject to a contract that allows J to redeem the instrument for $66,000 on May 31, 1994, but it may not be redeemed early. The applicable federal rate is 5 percent throughout J's holding period. What are the amount and character of J's gain recognized in 1994?

16-48 *Comprehensive Capital Gain Problem.*   P is an unmarried full-time investor with no dependents. Her income for the year 1994 is as follows:

Taxable interest income.........................	$22,200
Excludable municipal bond interest..............	8,600
Dividends......................................	11,400
Consulting fees................................	6,400
Social security benefits.........................	8,400

Although P does not have sufficient deductions to itemize, her records reveal the following:

Investment expenses............................	$ 850
Expenses related to consulting..................	1,200

In addition to the above, P recognized the following gains and losses during the year:

Loss on sale of 100 shares of A, Inc., held three years....	$ (1,200)
Loss on sale of personal automobile.....................	(1,800)
Sales price of 100 shares of B Corp., sold short..........	8,200
(This short sale was closed the following year with shares costing $9,600.)	
Gain on sale of unimproved land held as an investment for six years..............................	45,000

Calculate P's adjusted gross income, taxable income, and gross income tax based on the above for 1994. Begin by calculating P's self-employment tax.

RESEARCH PROBLEMS

16-49 *Transfer of Patents.*   G has just completed a successful invention of a new automotive fuel conservation device. He is willing to sell his patent rights for all areas of the United States east of the Rocky Mountains.

In 1994 G entered into an agreement with a marketing firm, giving it exclusive rights to market his invention anywhere east of the Rockies. In exchange, he received a principal sum and is to receive royalties based on sales volume.

Is G entitled to capital gain treatment on this sale under § 1235? Would it make any difference if the transferee of the patent was given exclusive rights to the patent and was given the right to "sublease" the patent?

Research aids:

Kueneman v. Comm., 80-2 USTC ¶9616, 46 AFTR2d 80-5677, 628 F.2d 1196 (CA-9, 1980).

Klein Est. v. Comm., 75-1 USTC ¶9127, 35 AFTR2d 75-457, 507 F.2d 617 (CA-7, 1974).

Rouverol v. Comm., 42 T.C. 186 (1964), *non. acq.*, 1965-2 C.B. 7.

16-50 *Sale of Subdivided and Improved Real Property.*   D, a full-time physician, has owned 15 acres of unimproved suburban real estate for 10 years. The property was originally purchased for $30,000 and has been held solely for investment. D is now interested in selling the property and has several alternatives. She has come to you for advice concerning the tax treatment of these alternatives. What is the proper tax treatment of each of the following?

a. A sale of the entire acreage to an unrelated party in a single transaction for $150,000.

b. Recording the property with the county as 30 single residential lots, adding roads and improvements at a cost of $100,000, and selling the lots for $25,000 each.

c. Recording the property with the county as 30 single residential lots, and then selling them to an unrelated developer in a single transaction for $190,000.

d. Recording the property with the county as 30 single residential lots and then selling them for $190,000 in a single transaction to a partnership in which D is a 40 percent partner. The partnership then adds roads and improvements at a cost of $100,000 and sells the lots for $25,000 each.

LEARNING OBJECTIVES

Upon completion of this chapter you will be able to:

- Trace the historical development of the special tax treatment allowed for dispositions of trade or business property

- Apply the § 1231 gain and loss netting process to a taxpayer's § 1231 asset transactions

- Determine the tax treatment of § 1231 gains and losses

- Explain the purpose of the depreciation recapture rules

- Compute depreciation recapture under §§ 1245 and 1250

- Explain the additional recapture rule applicable only to corporate taxpayers

- Identify tax planning opportunities related to sales or other dispositions of trade or business property

CHAPTER OUTLINE

Introduction	17-1	Partial Recapture—§ 1250	17-18
Section 1231	17-2	Additional Recapture—Corporations	17-28
Historical Perspective	17-2	Other Recapture Provisions	17-30
Section 1231 Property	17-3	Installment Sales of Trade or	
Other § 1231 Property	17-4	Business Property	17-30
Section 1231 Netting Process	17-7	Tax Planning Considerations	17-34
Look-Back Rule	17-10	Timing of Sales and Other	
Depreciation Recapture	17-14	Dispositions	17-34
Historical Perspective	17-14	Selecting Depreciation Methods	17-35
When Applicable	17-15	Installment Sales	17-35
Types of Depreciation Recapture	17-15	Problem Materials	17-36
Full Recapture—§ 1245	17-15		

Chapter 17

PROPERTY TRANSACTIONS
Dispositions
of Trade
or Business Property

INTRODUCTION

As is no doubt clear by now, the treatment of property transactions is a complex story that seeks to answer three questions: (1) What is the gain or loss realized? (2) How much is recognized? and (3) What is its character? This chapter, the final act in the property transaction trilogy, addresses the problems in determining the character of gains or losses on the dispositions of *property used in a trade or business*.

In an uncomplicated world, it might seem logical to assume that gains or losses from property dispositions—be it stock, equipment, buildings, or whatever—would be treated just like any other type of income or deduction. But, as shown in the previous chapter, treating all items alike apparently was not part of the grand plan. Congress forever changed the process with the institution of preferential treatment for capital gains in 1921. Since that time taxpayers have been required to determine not only the gain or loss realized and recognized but also whether a disposition involved a capital asset. It is important to understand that these rules did not simply tip the scales in favor of capital gain. In the interest of fairness and equity, they also established a less than friendly environment for capital losses. The limitations on the deductibility of capital losses is clearly a major disadvantage, particularly considering that ordinary losses are fully deductible. The end result of Congress's handiwork was the creation of a system in which the preferred result is capital gain treatment for gains and ordinary treatment for losses. This chapter contains the saga of what happens when Congress attempts to provide taxpayers with the best of both worlds.

SECTION 1231

The road to tax heaven—capital gain and ordinary loss—begins at § 1231 (in tax parlance properly pronounced as "twelve thirty-one"). While § 1231 can be a completely bewildering provision, its basic operation is relatively simple. At the close of the taxable year, the taxpayer nets all gains and losses from so-called § 1231 property (e.g., land and depreciable property used in a trade or business). If there is a net gain, it is treated as a long-term capital gain. If there is a net loss, it is treated as an ordinary loss. In short, § 1231 allows taxpayers to have their cake and eat it, too. Unfortunately, this is accomplished only with a great deal of complexity, much of which makes sense only if the historical events that shaped § 1231 are considered.

HISTORICAL PERSPECTIVE.

At first glance, it seems that the productive assets of a business—its property, plant, and equipment—would be perfect candidates for capital gain treatment and would therefore be considered capital assets. Indeed, that was exactly the case initially. From 1921 to 1938, real or depreciable property used in business was in fact treated as a capital asset. At that time, the classification of such property as a capital asset seemed not only appropriate but desirable—particularly as the economy grew during the early 1920s and taxpayers were realizing gains. However, the opposite became true with the onset of the Great Depression. As the economy deteriorated, businesses that had purchased assets at inflated prices during the booming 1920s found themselves selling such properties at huge losses during the depression-plagued 1930s. To make matters worse, the tax law treated such losses as capital losses, severly limiting their deduction. But Congress apparently had a sympathetic ear for these concerns. Hoping that a change would help stimulate the economy, Congress enacted legislation that removed business properties from the list of capital assets. The legislative history to the Revenue Act of 1938 provides some insight into Congressional thinking, explaining that "corporations will not, as formerly, be deterred from disposing of partially obsolescent property, such as machinery or equipment, because of the limitations imposed . . . upon the deduction of capital losses.[1] With the 1938 changes in place, business got the ordinary loss treatment it wanted but at the same time was saddled with ordinary income treatments for its gains.

Although these rules worked well during the Depression years as businesses were reporting losses, they produced some unduly harsh results once the country moved to a wartime economy. By 1942 the build-up for World War II had the economy humming and inflation had once again set in. Businesses that earlier had sold assets for 10 cents on the dollar now found themselves realizing gains. Of course, under the 1938 changes these gains no longer benefited from preferential treatment but were taxed at extraordinarily high tax rates (88% for individuals and 40% for corporations). The shipping industry was particularly hard hit by the new treatment. Shippers not only had gains as the enemy destroyed their insured ships but also profited when they were forced to sell their property to the government for use in the war. Other businesses that had their factories and equipment condemned and requisitioned also felt the

---

[1] House Ways and Means Committee, H.R. Rep. 1860, 75th Cong., 3d Sess. (1938).

sting of higher ordinary rates. Although these companies could have deferred their gains had they replaced the property under the involuntary conversion rules of § 1033, qualified reinvestment property was in short supply, making § 1033 virtually useless. Understanding the plight of business, Congress once again came to the rescue. In 1942 Congress enacted legislation generally reinstating capital gain treatment but preserving ordinary loss treatment.

The changes in 1942 stemmed primarily from a need to provide relief for those whose property was condemned for the war effort. But in the end they went much further. For consistency, capital gain treatment was extended not only to condemnations of a business property but to other types of involuntary conversions as well. Under the new rules, casualty and theft gains from business property and capital assets also received capital gain treatment. In addition, the new legislation unexpectedly extended capital gain treatment to regular sales of property, plant, and equipment. Apparently, Congress felt that capital gain treatment was also appropriate for taxpayers who were selling out in anticipation of condemnation or simply because wartime conditions had made operations difficult. While Congress thought capital gain treatment was warranted for these gains, it also knew that other businesses had not profited from the war and were still suffering losses from their property transactions. Accordingly, it acted to preserve ordinary loss treatment. The end result of these maneuvers was the enactment of § 1231, an extremely complex provision that provides taxpayers with the best of all possible tax worlds: capital gain and ordinary loss.

The product of Congressional tinkering in 1942 still remains today. To summarize, real and depreciable property used in a trade or business is specifically denied capital asset status. But this does not necessarily mean that such property will be denied capital gain treatment. As explained at the outset, § 1231 generally extends capital gain treatment to gains and losses from these assets if the taxpayer realizes a net gain from all § 1231 transactions. On the other hand, if there is a net loss, ordinary loss treatment applies. But this summary lacks a great deal of precision. The specific rules of § 1231 are described below.

SECTION 1231 PROPERTY

The special treatment of § 1231 is generally granted only to certain transactions involving assets normally referred to as *§ 1231 property*.[2] Section 1231 property includes a variety of assets, but among them the most important is *real or depreciable property that is used in the taxpayer's trade or business* and that is held for more than one year.[3] This definition takes in most items commonly identified as a business's fixed assets, normally referred to as its property, plant, and equipment. For example, the reach of § 1231 includes depreciable personal property used in business, such as machinery, equipment, office furniture, and business automobiles. Similarly, realty used in a business, such as office buildings, warehouses, factories, and farmland, is also considered § 1231 property.

---

[2] As explained below, § 1231 also applies to involuntary conversions of pure capital assets held more than one year that are used in a trade or business or held for investment. Involuntary conversions by theft or casualty of personal assets are not included under § 1231 but are subject to a special computation.

[3] The holding period is determined in the same manner as it is for capital assets. See § 1223 discussed in Chapter 16.

The Code specifically excludes the following assets from § 1231 treatment:

1. Property held primarily for sale to customers in the ordinary course of a trade or business, or includible in inventory, if on hand at the close of the tax year;

2. A copyright; a literary, musical, or artistic composition; a letter or memorandum; or similar property held by a taxpayer whose personal efforts created such property or by certain other persons; or

3. A publication of the United States Government received from the government other than by purchase at the price at which the publication is offered to the general public.[4]

Note that the excluded assets are also excluded from the definition of a capital asset. As a result, gains or losses on the disposition of inventory, property held primarily for resale, literary compositions, and certain government publications always yield ordinary income or ordinary loss.

One of the critical conditions for § 1231 treatment requires that the property be used in a trade or business. Although this test normally presents little difficulty, from time to time it has created problems, particularly for those with rental property. As an illustration, consider the common situation of a taxpayer who sells rental property such as a house, duplex, or apartment complex. Is the property sold a capital asset or § 1231 property? Note that this is an issue only if the property is sold at a loss. If a taxpayer sells rental property at a gain, the gain would normally receive capital gain treatment regardless of whether the property is a capital asset or § 1231 property. On the other hand, if the taxpayer sells the rental property at a loss, § 1231 treatment is far more desirable. Although the Code does not provide any clear guidance on the issue, the courts have generally held that property used for rental purposes is considered as used in a trade or business and is therefore eligible for § 1231 treatment.[5]

OTHER § 1231 PROPERTY

From time to time, Congress has been convinced that particular industries deserve special tax relief. As a result, it has added a number of other properties to the § 1231 basket. Those eligible for capital gain and ordinary loss are

1. Timber, coal, and iron ore to which § 631 applies;[6]

2. Unharvested crops on land used in a trade or business and held for more than one year;[7] and

3. Certain livestock.[8]

---

4 § 1231 (b)(1).

5 See, for example, *Mary Crawford*, 16 T.C. 678 (1951) A. 1951-2 C.B. 2, and *Gilford v. Comm.*, 53-1 USTC ¶9201, 43 AFTR 221, 201 F.2d 735 (CA-2, 1953).

6 § 1231(b)(2).

7 § 1231(b)(4).

8 § 1231(b)(3).

Timber.   Under § 631, the cutting of timber by the owner of the timber, or by a person who has the right to cut the timber and has held the timber or right more than one year, is to be treated, at his or her election, as a sale or exchange of the timber that is cut during the year. The timber must be cut for sale or for use in the taxpayer's trade or business. In such case, the taxpayer would report a § 1231 gain or loss and potentially receive capital gain treatment for what otherwise might be considered the taxpayer's inventory—a very favorable result. It may appear that the timber industry has secured an unfair advantage, but timber's eligibility is arguably justified on the grounds that the value of timber normally accrues incrementally as it grows over a long period of time.

The amount of gain or loss on the "sale" of the timber is the fair market value of the timber on the first day of the taxable year minus the timber's adjusted basis for depletion. For all subsequent purposes (i.e., the sale of the cut timber), the fair market value of the timber as of the beginning of the year will be treated as the cost of the timber. The term *timber* not only includes trees used for lumber and other wood products, but also includes evergreen trees that are more than six years old when cut and are sold for ornamental purposes (e.g., Christmas trees).[9]

> **Example 1.**   B owned standing timber that he had purchased for $250,000 three years earlier. The timber was cut and sold to a lumber mill for $410,000 during 1994. The fair market value of the standing timber as of January 1, 1994 was $320,000. B has a § 1231 gain of $70,000 if he makes an election under § 631 ($320,000 fair market value of the timber on the first day of the taxable year less its $250,000 adjusted basis for depletion). The remainder of his gain on the *actual* sale of the timber, $90,000 ($410,000 selling price − $320,000 new "cost" of the timber), is ordinary income. Any expenses incurred by B in cutting the timber would be deductible as ordinary deductions.

An election under § 631 with respect to timber is binding on all timber owned by the taxpayer during the year of the election *and* in all subsequent years. The IRS may permit revocation of such election because of significant hardship. However, once the election is revoked, IRS consent must be obtained to make a new election.[10]

Section 631 also applies to the sale of timber under a contract providing a retained economic interest (i.e., a taxpayer sells the timber, but keeps the right to receive a royalty from its later sale) for the taxpayer in the timber. In such a case, the transfer is considered a sale or exchange. The gain or loss is recognized on the date the timber is cut, or when payment is received, if earlier, at the election of the taxpayer.[11]

Coal and Iron Ore.   When an owner disposes of coal or domestic iron ore under a contract that calls for a retained economic interest in the property, the disposition is treated as a sale or exchange of the coal or iron ore. The date the coal or ore is mined is considered the date of sale and since the property is § 1231 property, the gain or loss will be treated under § 1231.[12]

---

[9]   § 631(a).

[10]   *Ibid.*

[11]   § 631(b).

[12]   § 631(c).

The taxpayer may not be a co-adventurer, partner, or principal in the mining of the coal or iron ore. Furthermore, the coal or iron ore may not be sold to certain related taxpayers.[13]

Unharvested Crops.   Section 1231 also addresses the special situation where a farmer sells land with unharvested crops sitting upon the land. In this case, it seems logical that the farmer should allocate the sales price between the crops and the land to ensure ordinary income or loss for the sale of the farmer's inventory and capital gain or ordinary loss on the sale of the land. While this may be the theoretically correct result, Congress wanted to eliminate potential controversy over the allocation. Accordingly, for administrative convenience it brought the entire transaction into the § 1231 fold in 1951. Currently, whenever land used in a trade or business and unharvested crops on that land are sold at the same time to the same buyer, the gain or loss is subject to § 1231 treatment as long as the land has been held for more than a year.[14] It is worth noting that the benefits of § 1231 were not extended to farmers free of charge. At the same time, Congress eliminated the current deduction for production expenses. The law now provides that any expenses related to the production of crops cannot be deducted currently but must be capitalized as part of the basis of the crops.[15] Such treatment, in a year when land and crops are sold, reduces the farmer's capital gain on the sale rather than any other ordinary income.

> **Example 2.**   F sold 100 acres of land that she used in her farming business just days before the corn on the land was harvested. For the "package" deal, she received $600,000, including an estimated $70,000 for the unharvested crops that she figured had cost her $20,000 to produce. F had purchased the land many years ago for $200,000. In determining the character of her gain, F is not required to allocate the sales price between the crops and the land since she sold both at the same time to the same buyer, therefore qualifying for § 1231 treatment. As a result, she reports a § 1231 gain of $380,000 computed as follows:

Sales price.........................	$600,000
Adjusted basis ($200,000 + $20,000)	− 220,000
§ 1231 gain........................	$380,000

> Note that in the year of the sale F has effectively turned the $50,000 ($70,000 − $20,000) profit from the sale of her crops from ordinary income into potential capital gain.

Livestock.   As a general proposition, livestock that are used for breeding and other purposes are depreciable assets much like machinery and equipment and therefore qualify for § 1231 treatment. In many situations, however, livestock is used for these purposes for only a short period of time and then sold. If this is the farmer's or rancher's normal practice, the IRS is inclined to argue that the animals are held primarily for resale, in which case the law specifically denies § 1231 treatment. To help end this controversy, Congress specifically made all livestock (other than poultry) used for draft, breeding,

---

[13]   §§ 631(c)(1) and (2).

[14]   § 1231(b)(4).

[15]   § 268.

dairy, or sporting purposes eligible for § 1231 treatment as long as they are held for over a year.[16] In the case of cattle and horses, however, the holding period is extended to two years. Note that this treatment is extremely beneficial since the taxpayer effectively gets capital gain from animals pulled out of the breeding process and sold. Moreover, the farmer or rancher is allowed to deduct the costs of raising such animals currently against ordinary income. The extension of the holding period for cattle and horses was in part, an attempt to cut back on the benefits of this favorable treatment.

SECTION 1231 NETTING PROCESS

The treatment of § 1231 gains or losses ultimately depends on the outcome of a netting process that is far more complicated than outlined earlier.[17] As can be seen from the flow-chart in Exhibit 17-1, the taxpayer must first identify all of the gains and losses that enter into the netting process. As might be expected, these include gains and losses from what has been described above as § 1231 property. In addition, the § 1231 hotchpotch include *involuntary conversions* of certain *capital assets*. Surprisingly, gains or losses recognized from casualties, thefts, or condemnations of capital assets that are used in a trade or business or held for investment are part of the § 1231 netting process. Involuntary conversions of capital assets that are held for *personal use* are not considered under § 1231 but are subject to special rules.

After identifying all of the § 1231 transactions, the taxpayer must segregate the § 1231 gains and losses arising from casualty and theft from those attributable to sale, exchange, and condemnation. The end result is that there are two sets of § 1231 transactions:

1. **Involuntary conversions due to casualty and theft of**
   § 1231 property
   Real and depreciable property used in business held more than one year
   Timber, coal, iron ore, unharvested crops, and livestock.
   Capital assets
   Used in a trade or business or held for investment in connection with business and held more than one year

2. **Sales and exchanges of**
   § 1231 property
   Real and depreciable property used in business
   Timber, coal, iron ore, unharvested crops and livestock

   Involuntary conversion due to condemnation of
   § 1231 property
   Real and depreciable property used in business held more than one year
   Timber, coal, iron ore, unharvested crops, and livestock
   Capital assets
   Used in a trade or business or held for investment in connection with business and held more than one year

---

[16] § 1231(b)(3).   [17] § 1231(a).

Once all of the appropriate transactions have been poured into the § 1231 process, the netting process can begin. There are three steps.

1. First, all of the gains and losses in the first category of § 1231 transactions are netted. Specifically, all casualty and theft gains (after reduction for any depreciation recapture) and losses involving § 1231 assets *and* capital assets held in connection with a trade or business (including transactions entered into for profit) and held for more than one year are netted together. If the result is a net *loss*, the casualty and theft gains and losses are removed from the § 1231 netting process and treated separately. The gains are treated as ordinary income, and the losses on business use assets are deductible in arriving at adjusted gross income (i.e., deductions *for* A.G.I.). Any other casualty and theft losses are deductible *from* A.G.I. If the net result is a *gain*, it is treated as a § 1231 gain. This § 1231 gain then becomes part of the second category of other § 1231 transactions, where it will be combined with other § 1231 transactions in the next step of the netting process.

2. The second step of the process is to combine any net casualty or theft gain from the first step with the gains or losses in the second set of § 1231 transactions. In effect, the taxpayer combines any net casualty or theft gain from the first step with (1) gains (net of depreciation recapture) and losses from sales and taxable exchanges of § 1231 property, and (2) gains (net of depreciation recapture) and losses from the condemnation of § 1231 assets.

3. The third and final step in the § 1231 netting process is to characterize the gain or loss resulting from netting the transactions in the second step. If the net result is a *loss*, this net loss is treated as an ordinary deduction for adjusted gross income. It is not treated as a capital loss. If the net result is a *gain*, this gain is generally treated as a long-term capital gain and becomes part of the capital gain and loss netting process.

The § 1231 netting process is illustrated in Exhibit 17-1 and the following examples.

Example 3. During the current year, D sold a rental house for $45,000. She had purchased the house for $36,000 and had deducted depreciation of $8,400 using the straight-line method. D also sold a business car (held for more than one year) at a loss of $1,200. D's gain on the rental house is computed as follows:

Selling price.....................................		$45,000
Cost..	$36,000	
Less: Depreciation..........................	− 8,400	
Adjusted basis................................		− 27,600
Gain realized and recognized.....................		$17,400

D nets the gain and loss as follows:

Gain from sale of § 1231 asset............	$17,400
Loss from sale of § 1231 asset............	(1,200)
Net § 1231 gain for year..................	$16,200

Exhibit 17-1   *Section 1231 Netting Process*

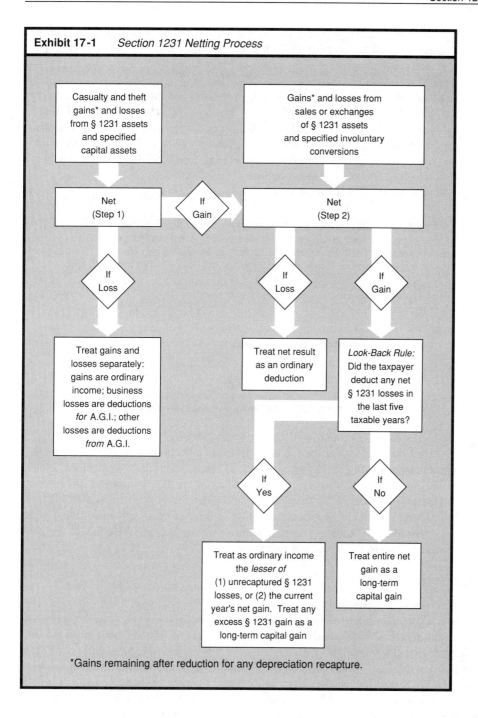

*Gains remaining after reduction for any depreciation recapture.

D's entire net § 1231 gain of $16,200 is treated as a long-term capital gain. If she had other capital gains or losses during the year, they will be subject to the capital gain and loss netting process discussed in Chapter 16.

Example 4. During 1994 R, a sole proprietor, sold a business computer for $32,000. His basis at the time of the sale was $44,000. He also sold land used in his business at a gain of $1,400 and had an uninsured theft loss of works of art used to decorate his business offices (i.e., capital assets held in connection with a trade or business). R had purchased the artwork for $1,500 four years ago and it was valued at $5,000 before the burglary.

R nets his gains and losses as follows:

Step 1:   The net loss from the casualty is $1,500 (adjusted basis). Since R has a net casualty loss, it is not treated as a § 1231 loss. Instead, the loss is treated as an ordinary loss (which is fully deductible for A.G.I. since the art works were business property).

Step 2:   Combine gains and losses from sales of § 1231 assets:

Loss from sale of business computer......... ($12,000)
Gain from sale of business land.............. 1,400

Net § 1231 loss for year.................... ($10,600)

Step 3:   A net § 1231 loss is treated as an ordinary deduction. Thus, R's $10,600 loss can be used to offset other ordinary income.

Note that the theft loss of the works of art is included in the first step of the netting process even though these items are capital assets. This loss would have offset, dollar for dollar, any casualty or theft gains (net of depreciation recapture) from § 1231 assets as well as any casualty or theft gains from other capital assets held in connection with R's business. Also note that the current year's deductible § 1231 loss may result in a change in the character of any net § 1231 gains in the next five years due to the look-back rule.

LOOK-BACK RULE

For many years, taxpayers took advantage of the § 1231 netting process. For example, assume a taxpayer in the 39.6 percent tax bracket currently owns two § 1231 assets, one with a built-in gain of $3,000 and one with a built-in loss of $2,000. If both assets are sold during the year, the loss offsets the gain and the taxpayer pays a capital gain tax of $280 $[(\$3,000 - \$2,000 = \$1,000) \times 28\%]$. If the taxpayer had sold the assets in different years, the loss would not have reduced the gain, and the tax after both transactions would have been $48 $[(\$3,000 \times 28\% = \$840) - (\$2,000 \times 39.6\% = \$792)]$. As might be imagined, taxpayers carefully planned their transactions to maximize their tax savings.

In an effort to prevent taxpayers from cleverly timing their § 1231 gains and losses to ensure that § 1231 losses reduced ordinary income and not potential capital gain, Congress enacted the so-called *look-back* rule in 1984. Under this rule a taxpayer with a net § 1231 gain in the current year must report the gain as ordinary income to the extent of any *unrecaptured net* § 1231 losses reported in the past five taxable years.[18] Unrecaptured net § 1231 losses are simply the *net* § 1231 losses that have occurred during the last five years that have not been previously recaptured (i.e., the excess of net § 1231 losses of the five preceding years over the amount of such loss that has been recaptured in the five prior years).

Example 5. Assume the same facts in *Example 4* and that R's 1994 net § 1231 loss of $10,600 is the only loss he has deducted in the past five years. In 1995 R has a $15,000 net § 1231 gain and is subject to the look-back rule. He must recapture (and report) as ordinary income $10,600 of the 1995 gain. The remaining net § 1231 gain of $4,400 ($15,000 − $10,600) is treated as a long-term capital gain. Should R have a net § 1231 gain in 1996, he will not be subject to the look-back rule since he has recaptured all prior years' net § 1231 losses.

✔ **CHECK YOUR TAX KNOWLEDGE**

Review Question 1. Indicate whether the following gains and losses are § 1231 gains or losses or capital gains and losses or neither. Make your determination prior to the § 1231 netting process and assume any holding period requirement has been met.

    a. Gain on the sale of General Motors stock held as a temporary investment by Consolidated Brands Corporation.

    b. Gain on the sale of a four-unit apartment complex owned by Lorena Smith. This was her only rental property.

    c. Loss on the sale of welding machinery used by Arco Welding in its business.

    d. Loss on theft of welding machinery used by Arco Welding in its business.

    e. Gain on sale of diamond bracelet by Nancy Jones.

    f. Income from sale of electric razors by Razor Corporation, which manufactures them.

    g. Gain on condemnation of land on which Tonya Smith's personal residence is built.

    h. Gain on condemnation of land owned by Tonya Smith's business.

    i. Loss on sale of personal automobile.

The § 1231 hotchpotch contains not only gains and losses from § 1231 property but also those from involuntary conversions by casualty, theft, or condemnation

---

[18] § 1231(c).

of capital assets that are used in a trade or business or held as an investment in connection with a trade or business.

a. The sale of the GM stock is not included in the § 1231 pot since it is a sale of a capital asset and not an involuntary conversion.

b. The rental property is generally considered property used in a trade or business and thus § 1231 property even if the owner owns only a single property.

c. The welding machinery is depreciable property used in a business and is therefore considered § 1231 property.

d. The theft of the welding machinery is also a § 1231 transaction. Note, however, that in processing the § 1231 gains and losses, the casualties must be segregated from the sales.

e. The sale of the diamond bracelet produces capital gain since it is a pure capital asset and not trade or business property.

f. The razors are inventory and are therefore neither capital assets nor § 1231 property.

g. The condemnation of the land near the residence is considered a personal casualty gain. Since the land is not held in connection with a trade or business, it does not qualify as § 1231 property.

h. The condemnation of the land held for business does enter into the § 1231 hotchpotch as a regular § 1231 gain.

i. Although the personal automobile is a capital asset, no loss is allowed from the sale.

Review Question 2. During his senior year at the University of Virginia, Bill decided that he never wanted to leave Charlottesville. After some thought, he opened his own hamburger joint, Billy's Burgers. That was 20 years ago and Bill has had great success, owning a number of businesses all over Virginia and North Carolina. Not believing in corporations, Bill and his wife, Betty, operate all of these as partnerships.

a. Information from the partnerships and his own personal records revealed the following transactions during 1994:

1. Sale of one of 50 apartment buildings that one of their partnerships owns: $50,000 gain (ignore depreciation)
2. Sale of restaurant equipment: $20,000 loss

Assuming both assets have been held for several years, how should Bill and Betty report these transactions on their 1994 return?

Answer. Under § 1231, the taxpayer generally nets gains and losses from the sale of § 1231 property. If a net gain results, the gain is treated as a long-term capital gain, whereas a net loss is treated as an ordinary loss. For this purpose, § 1231 property generally includes real or depreciable property used in a trade or

business. In this case, both the apartment complex and the restaurant equipment are § 1231 property. As a result, the couple should net the gain and loss and report a long-term capital gain of $30,000.

b. The couple's records for 1995 revealed several gains and losses:

1. Office building burned down: $20,000 loss

2. Crane for bungee jumping business stolen: $35,000 gain (assume no depreciation had been claimed)

3. Parking lot sold: $14,000 loss

4. Exxon stock sold: long-term capital loss of $10,000

5. Condemnation of Greensboro land held by the business as an investment: $15,000 gain.

Assuming each of the assets was held for several years, determine how much long-term capital gain or loss as well as the amount of ordinary income or loss that Bill and Betty will report for the year.

Answer. The § 1231 netting process requires the taxpayer to separate § 1231 casualty gains and losses from other § 1231 transactions (sometimes referred to as regular § 1231 items). The casualty loss on the office building and the casualty gain on the crane are both considered § 1231 casualties since they involve § 1231 property (i.e., real or depreciable property used in business). Note that the condemnation—even though it is an involuntary conversion—is not treated as a § 1231 casualty. The casualty items are netted to determine whether there is a net gain or loss. Here, there is a net casualty gain of $15,000 ($35,000 − $20,000). This net gain is then combined with any "regular" § 1231 items, in this case the $14,000 loss on the sale of the parking lot (real property used in a business) and the $15,000 gain on the condemnation of the land (a capital asset). After netting these items, the partnership has a net gain of $16,000. This $16,000 net § 1231 gain is treated as a long-term capital gain and is combined with $10,000 long-term capital loss on the sale of the stock. The end result is a $6,000 long-term capital gain. This process can be summarized as follows (see Exhibit 17-3):

Transaction	§ 1231 Casualties	§ 1231 Regular	Capital Gain and Losses Short-term	Capital Gain and Losses Long-term
1. Office burned	$(20,000)			
2. Crane stolen	35,000			
3. Parking lot sold		$(14,000)		
4. Exxon stock sold				$(10,000)
5. Condemnation of land		15,000		
Net casualty	$ 15,000 ⟶	15,000		
Net § 1231 gain		$ 16,000 ⟶		16,000
Net long-term capital gain				$ 6,000

c. Same as in (b), except Bill and Betty reported a net § 1231 loss of $3,000 in the previous year.

In this case, the look-back rule applies, causing $3,000 of the net § 1231 gain to be treated as ordinary income. As a result, the couple's long-term capital gain from the § 1231 netting process is $13,000 and their net long-term capital gain is only $3,000.

DEPRECIATION RECAPTURE

HISTORICAL PERSPECTIVE

For many years, taxpayers have taken advantage of the interaction of § 1231 and the depreciation rules to secure significant tax savings. Prior to 1962 there were no substantial statutory restrictions on the depreciation methods that could be adopted. Consequently, a taxpayer could quickly recover the basis of a depreciable asset by selecting a rapid depreciation method such as declining balance and using a short useful life. If the property's value did not decline as quickly as its basis was being reduced by depreciation deductions, a gain was ensured if the property was disposed of at a later date. The end result could be quite beneficial.

Example 6.   During the current year T purchased an office building for $1 million. After five years, T, using favorable depreciation rules, had claimed and deducted $600,000 of depreciation, leaving a basis of $400,000. Assume that the property did not truly depreciate in value and T was able to sell it in the sixth year for its original cost of $1 million. In such case T would report a gain of $600,000 ($1,000,000 − $400,000). Except for time value of money considerations, it appears that the $600,000 gain and the $600,000 of depreciation are simply a wash. However, the depreciation reduced ordinary income that would be taxed at ordinary rates while the gain would be a § 1231 gain and taxed at capital gain rates. As an illustration of the savings that could be achieved, assume that the law at this time provided for a top capital gain rate of 20 percent and the taxpayer's ordinary income was taxed at a 50 percent rate. In this case the deprecation would offset ordinary income and provide tax savings of $300,000, but the $600,000 gain on the sale would be treated as a capital gain and produce a tax of only $120,000. Thus, even though the taxpayer has had no economic gain or loss with respect to the property—he bought and sold the building for $1,000,000—he was able to secure a tax benefit of $180,000 ($300,000 − $120,000).

The above example clearly illustrates how taxpayers used rapid depreciation and the favorable treatment of § 1231 gains to effectively convert ordinary income into capital gain. In fact, this strategy—deferring taxes with quick depreciation write-offs at ordinary rates and giving them back later at capital gains rates—was the foundation of many tax shelter schemes.

Legislation to limit these benefits came in a number of forms, but the most important was the enactment of the so-called *depreciation recapture* rules. These rules strike right at the heart of the problem, generally treating all or some portion of any gain recognized as ordinary income, based on the amount of depreciation previously deducted. Thus, in the above example, the taxpayer's $600,000 gain, which was initially characterized as a § 1231 gain, is treated as ordinary income because of the $600,000 of depreciation previously claimed. In this way, all of the tax savings initially given away by virtue of the ordinary depreciation deductions are recaptured. Unfortunately, much like § 1231 in general, the recapture rules can become quite complex. The operations of the specific provisions are discussed below.

WHEN APPLICABLE

Before specific recapture rules are examined, there are two very important points to keep in mind. First, depreciable assets held for one year or less do not qualify for § 1231 treatment. Thus, any gain from the disposition of such assets is always reported as ordinary income. Second, the depreciation recapture rules *do not apply* if property is disposed of at a *loss*. Remember that losses from the sale or exchange of depreciable assets are treated as § 1231 losses if the long-term holding period requirement is met. In addition, casualty or theft losses of such property are included in the § 1231 netting process. Any loss from a depreciable asset held one year or less is an ordinary loss regardless of whether it was sold, exchanged, stolen, or destroyed.

TYPES OF DEPRECIATION RECAPTURE

There are essentially *three* depreciation recapture provisions in the Code. These are

1. Section 1245 Recapture—commonly called the *full recapture rule*, and applicable primarily to depreciable personalty (rather than realty)

2. Section 1250 Recapture—commonly called the *partial recapture rule*, and applicable to most depreciable realty if a method of depreciation other than straight-line was used

3. Section 291 Recapture—commonly called the *additional recapture rule*, and applicable *only* to corporate taxpayers

Each of these recapture rules is discussed below.

FULL RECAPTURE—§ 1245

The recapture concept was first introduced with the enactment of § 1245 by the Revenue Act of 1962. Section 1245 generally requires any gain recognized to be reported as ordinary income to the extent of *any* depreciation allowed on § 1245 property after 1961.

Definition of § 1245 Property.   The recapture of depreciation under § 1245 applies only to *§ 1245 property,* normally *depreciable personal property.*[19] Because the definition of personal property itself is so broad, § 1245 generally covers a wide variety of assets such as machinery, equipment, office furniture, automobiles, vans, trucks, patents, copyrights, and livestock. In practice, it is common to say that § 1245 applies to all property other than buildings and their components. This is generally true, but it may be somewhat misleading because there are exceptions. For example, nonresidential real property (e.g., warehouses and office buildings) placed in service after 1981 and before 1987 is considered § 1245 property if the taxpayer used an accelerated method of depreciation. It is also important to emphasize that § 1245 applies only if the property is depreciable or amortizable. Consequently, it pertains only to property that is used in a trade or business and property held for the production of income (i.e., investment property). In this regard, § 1245 also covers depreciable personal property that is expensed in the year of acquisition under the limited expensing provisions of § 179.[20]

Although the above definition for § 1245 property is usually sufficient, it actually embraces a number of other assets besides depreciable personalty, including the following:[21]

1. Property used as an integral part of manufacturing, production, or extraction, or in furnishing transportation, communications, electrical energy, gas, water, or sewage disposal services.

    a. However, any portion of a building or its structural components is not included.
    b. A research facility or a facility for the bulk storage of commodities related to an activity listed above is included.

2. A single-purpose agricultural or horticultural structure (e.g., greenhouses).

3. A storage structure used in connection with the distribution of petroleum or any primary product of petroleum (e.g., oil tank).

4. Any railroad grading or tunnel bore.

5. Certain other property that is subject to a special provision allowing rapid amortization (e.g., pollution control facilities and railroad rolling stock).

Operation of § 1245.   Section 1245 generally requires any gain recognized to be treated as ordinary income to the extent of *any* depreciation allowed.[22] To state the rule in another way: any gain on the disposition of § 1245 property is ordinary income to the extent of the *lesser* of the gain recognized or the § 1245 recapture potential, generally the depreciation claimed and deducted. Although both statements say the same

---

[19] § 1245(a)(3).

[20] § 1245(a)(3)(D) includes as "§ 1245 property" several other properties subject to unique expensing rules.

[21] The definition parallels that of § 38 property, which qualified for the investment tax credit. § 48(a)(1).

[22] § 1245(a).

thing, the latter helps focus attention on two points and eliminates some misconceptions. First, a taxpayer is never required to report more income than the amount of gain realized regardless of the amount of depreciation claimed and deducted (i.e., regardless of the amount of recapture potential). For example, if the taxpayer realizes a gain of $10,000 and has deducted depreciation of $15,000, the taxpayer reports only $10,000 of income, all of which would be ordinary. Note that the depreciation recapture rules do not affect the amount of gain or loss, only the character of any gain to be recognized. Second, using the term *recapture potential* helps emphasize that sometimes the amount that must be recaptured may include more than mere depreciation.

Section 1245 *recapture potential* includes *all* depreciation or amortization allowed (or allowable) with respect to a given property—regardless of the method of depreciation used. This is why § 1245 is often called the full recapture rule. Recapture potential also includes adjustments to basis related to items that are expensed (e.g., under § 179 expense election) or where tax credits have been allowed under various sections of the Code.[23]

To summarize, determining the character of gain on the disposition of § 1245 property is generally a two-step process:

1. The gain is ordinary income to the extent of the *lesser* of the gain recognized or the § 1245 recapture potential (all depreciation allowed or allowable).

2. Any recognized gain in excess of the recapture potential retains its original character, usually § 1231 gain.

Recall that there is no § 1245 depreciation recapture when a property is sold at a loss, so any loss is normally a § 1231 loss.

> **Example 7.** T owned a printing press that he used in his business. Its cost was $6,800 and T deducted depreciation in the amount of $3,200 during the three years he owned the press. T sold the press for $4,000 and his realized and recognized gain is $400 ($4,000 sales price − $3,600 adjusted basis). T's recapture potential is $3,200, the amount of depreciation taken on the property. Thus, the entire $400 gain is ordinary income under § 1245.

> **Example 8.** Assume the same facts as in *Example 7*, except that T sold his press for $7,000. In this case, T's realized and recognized gain would be $3,400 ($7,000 − $3,600). The ordinary income portion under § 1245 would be $3,200 (the amount of the recapture potential), and the remaining $200 of the gain is a § 1231 gain. Note that in order for any § 1231 gain to occur, the property must be sold for more than its original cost since all of the depreciation is treated as ordinary income.

---

[23] See § 1245(a)(2) for a listing of these adjustments and their related Code sections, including the basis adjustment related to the earned portion of any investment credit.

Example 9. Assume the same facts as in *Example 8*, except that the printing press is sold for $3,000 instead of $4,000. In this case, T has a loss from the sale of $600 ($3,000 − $3,600 adjusted basis). Because there is a loss, there is no depreciation recapture. All of T's loss is a § 1231 loss.

Exceptions and Limitations. In many ways, § 1245 operates much like the proverbial troll under the bridge. It sits ready to spring on its victim whenever the proper moment arises. Section 1245 generally applies whenever there is a transfer of property. However, § 1245 does identify certain situations where it does not apply, most of which are nontaxable events. For example, there is no recapture on a transfer by gift or bequest since both of these are nontaxable transfers.[24]

In involuntary conversions and like-kind exchanges, the depreciation recapture under § 1245 is limited to the *gain recognized*.[25] Similarly, in nontaxable business adjustments such as the formation of partnerships, transfers to controlled corporations, and certain corporate reorganizations, § 1245 recapture is limited to the gain recognized under the controlling provisions.[26] In any situation where recapture is not triggered, it is generally not lost but carried over in some fashion.

PARTIAL RECAPTURE—§ 1250

As originally enacted in 1961, the concept of recapture as set forth in § 1245 generally applied only to personalty. Gains derived from dealing in realty were not subject to recapture. In 1963, however, Congress eliminated this omission by enacting § 1250, a special recapture provision that applied to most buildings. Since that time § 1245 has generally been associated with depreciation recapture for personal property while § 1250 served that role for buildings. Although the two provisions are similar, § 1250 is far less damaging. Specifically, § 1250 calls for the recapture of only a *portion* of any *accelerated* depreciation allowed with respect to *§ 1250 property*. Note that while §§ 1250 and 1245 are essentially the same—they both convert potential capital gain into ordinary income—§ 1250 differs from § 1245 in several important ways: (1) it applies only if an accelerated method is used; (2) it does not recapture all of the depreciation deducted but only a portion—generally only the *excess of accelerated depreciation over what straight-line would have been;* and (3) it applies to a different type of property, *buildings and their components,* rather than personal property. Each of these aspects is considered below.

---

[24] §§ 1245(b)(1) and (2). Recapture of depreciation under § 1245 is required, however, to the extent § 691 applies (relating to income in respect to a decedent).

[25] § 1245(b)(4).

[26] § 1245(b)(3). See Chapter 19 for further discussion of nontaxable business adjustments.

Section 1250 Property.   Section 1250 property is generally any real property that is depreciable and is not covered by § 1245.[27] For the most part, § 1250 applies to all of the common forms of real estate such as office buildings, warehouses, apartment complexes, and low-income housing. As explained below, however, nonresidential real estate (e.g., warehouse and office buildings) placed in service after 1980 and before 1987 for which an accelerated method was used is covered by the full recapture rule of § 1245.[28]

Depreciation of Real Property.   Section 1250 applies only if an accelerated method of depreciation is used. If the straight-line depreciation method is used, § 1250 does not apply and there is no depreciation recapture for noncorporate taxpayers.[29] For this reason, a critical first step in determining the relevance of § 1250 is determining how the taxpayer has depreciated the realty.

For many years, taxpayers could choose to use either an accelerated or straight-line method to compute depreciation for realty. This was an extremely important decision, for it affected not only the amount of depreciation the taxpayer claimed but also the character of any gain on a subsequent disposition of the property. For example, a taxpayer could accelerate depreciation deductions but only at the possible expense of recapture. Alternatively, the taxpayer could accept the slower-paced straight-line method and avoid the § 1250 recapture rules. But the Tax Reform Act of 1986 ended this flexibility and at the same time simplified the law. Taxpayers who place realty in service after 1986 must use the straight-line method. As a result, § 1250 does not apply to property acquired after 1986. Unfortunately, much of the existing inventory of real property was acquired before 1987 and may therefore be subject to § 1250, depending on the method used.

Realty Placed in Service from 1981 through 1986.   For real property acquired between 1981 and the end of 1986, the taxpayer could either use the accelerated depreciation method allowed under ACRS or elect an optional straight-line method. If the taxpayer used the accelerated method of recovering cost for *nonresidential real property*, the property is classified as § 1245 property and is subject to the full recapture rule of § 1245. If the accelerated method was used for *residential realty*, the property is classified as § 1250 property and is subject to the partial recapture rule under this section.

Realty Placed in Service before 1981.   All depreciable real property acquired before 1981 is classified as § 1250 property. For such property acquired before 1981 (non-ACRS property), taxpayers were required to estimate useful lives and salvage values. Although various methods could be used, the annual deduction (during the first two-thirds of the useful life) generally could not exceed that arrived at by using the following maximum rates and methods:[30]

---

[27]   § 1250(c).

[28]   It is important to note, however, that such properties are § 1250 property if the optional straight-line method is used. § 1245(a)(5).

[29]   As explained within, corporate taxpayers are still required to recapture 20 percent of any straight-line depreciation under § 291.

[30]   § 167(j).

Maximum Allowable Deduction Type of Property	Method/Rate
New residential real estate	Declining-balance using 200% of the straight-line rate
Used residential real estate: If estimated useful life at least 20 years	Declining-balance using 125% of the straight-line rate
If estimated useful life less than 20 years	Straight-line
New nonresidential real estate	Declining-balance using 150% of the straight-line rate
Used nonresidential real estate	Straight-line

Operation of § 1250. The two critical factors in determining the amount, if any, of *§ 1250 recapture* are the gain realized *and* the amount of *excess depreciation*. Excess depreciation refers to depreciation deductions in excess of that which would be deductible using the straight-line method. For property held one year or less, all depreciation is considered excess depreciation.[31]

As a general rule, § 1250 requires recapture of the excess depreciation, that is, the excess of accelerated over straight-line. Consequently, even if the taxpayer uses an accelerated method to compute the amount of depreciation deducted on the return, the hypothetical amount of straight-line depreciation must still be computed in order to determine the excess of accelerated over straight-line when the property is sold. In determining the hypothetical amount of straight-line depreciation, the taxpayer uses the same life and salvage value, if any, that were used in computing accelerated depreciation.[32] Because of this approach, a taxpayer who uses the straight-line method would have no excess depreciation and no recapture. Because the § 1250 recapture rule applies only to any excess depreciation claimed by a taxpayer, it is sometimes referred to as the partial recapture rule.

Determining the character of any gain recognized on the disposition of § 1250 property is a two-step process:

1. The gain is ordinary income to the extent of the *lesser* of the gain recognized or the § 1250 recapture potential (generally the excess depreciation allowed).[33]

2. Any recognized gain in excess of the recapture potential is usually treated as § 1231 gain.

There is no § 1250 depreciation recapture when a property is sold at a loss, so any loss is normally a § 1231 loss.

---

[31] § 1250 (b).

[32] § 1250(b)(5).

[33] See § 1250(a) and discussion below dealing with recapture of only a portion of the excess depreciation for certain properties.

Example 10.   During 1994, L sold a small office building for $38,000. The build-
ing had cost her $22,000 in 1980, and she had deducted depreciation of $12,000 using
an accelerated method. Straight-line depreciation would have been $10,600. L's gain
recognized on the sale is $28,000 ($38,000 amount realized − $10,000 adjusted ba-
sis). Of that amount, $1,400 ($12,000 − $10,600 = $1,400 excess depreciation) is
ordinary income under § 1250 and the remainder, $26,600, is § 1231 gain.

Example 11.   M purchased a rental duplex during 1986 for $60,000. He deducted
$31,980 depreciation from 1986 through 1993 using the 19-year realty ACRS ta-
bles. Depreciation using the straight-line recovery percentages for 19-year realty
would have resulted in total depreciation of $25,260.

On January 3, 1994 M sold the property for $57,000. His gain is reported as
follows:

Sales price..		$57,000
Less: Adjusted basis		
Cost...	$ 60,000	
Depreciation...................................	(31,980)	(28,020)
Gain to be recognized...................................		$28,980
Depreciation actually claimed and deducted.............		$31,980
Straight-line depreciation (hypothetical).................		(25,260)
Excess depreciation subject to recapture...............		$ 6,720
Character of gain:		
Ordinary income (partial recapture)..................		$ 6,720
§ 1231 gain...		22,260
Total gain recognized...................................		$28,980

Although M claimed a total of $31,980 depreciation, there is only partial depre-
ciation recapture under § 1250 (i.e., the excess depreciation). M's remaining gain
of $22,260 ($28,980 − $6,720) is a § 1231 gain.

Example 12.   Assume the same facts as in *Example 11*, except that M elected
to recover his basis in the duplex using the 19-year straight-line method. In this
case, there is no § 1250 depreciation recapture potential. Consequently, M's *entire*
gain of $22,260 [$57,000 − ($60,000 − $25,260 = $34,740 basis)] is reported
as a § 1231 gain.

Example 13.   Assume the same facts as in *Example 11*, except that the property
is an office building rather than a duplex. In this case, because the property is
nonresidential real property and the accelerated method was used, the asset is
treated as § 1245 property rather than § 1250 property. Thus, M is subject to
full rather than partial depreciation recapture. The *entire* $28,980 gain must be
reported as ordinary income because it is less than the depreciation allowed (i.e.,
$28,980 < $31,980).

History of § 1250. Over the years, § 1250 has been changed frequently, with a general trend toward an expanded scope. The rules explained above apply only to depreciation allowed on nonresidential property after 1969 and residential property (other than low-income housing) after 1975. Only a *portion* of any other excess depreciation on § 1250 property is included in the recapture potential. The following percentages are applied to the gain realized in the transaction or the excess depreciation taken during the particular period, whichever is less:

1. For all excess depreciation taken after 1963 and before 1970, 100 percent less 1 percent for each full month over 20 months the property is held.[34] Any sales after 1979 would result in no recapture of pre-1970 excess depreciation since this percentage, when calculated, is zero.

2. For all excess depreciation taken after 1969 and before 1976, as follows:

   a. In the case of low-income housing, 100 percent less 1 percent for each full month the property is held over 20 months.
   b. In the case of other residential rental property (e.g., an apartment building) and property that has been rehabilitated [for purposes of § 167(k)], 100 percent less 1 percent for each full month the property is held over 100 months.[35]

   All sales from this group of real property after August 1992 will have no recapture of excess depreciation claimed before 1976. For those assets sold before September 1992, only a small percentage was recaptured.

3. For excess depreciation taken after 1975 on low-income housing and property that has been rehabilitated [for purposes of § 167(k)], 100 percent less 1 percent for each full month the property is held over 100 months.[36]

In summary, 100 percent of the excess depreciation allowed with respect to § 1250 property after 1975 is subject to recapture unless it falls into one of the above categories. The rules for the various categories are provided in § 1250(a).

Exceptions and Limitations under § 1250. Generally, the exceptions and limitations that apply under § 1245 also apply under § 1250. Thus, gifts, inheritances, and most nontaxable exchanges are allowed to occur without triggering recapture.[37] This exception is extended to any property to the extent it qualifies as a principal residence and is subject to deferral of gain under § 1034 or nonrecognition of gain under § 121.[38] In such nontaxable exchanges, the excess depreciation (that is not recaptured) taken prior to the nontaxable exchange on the property transferred carries over to the property received or purchased.[39] Similarly, in the case of gifts and certain nontaxable transfers in which the

---

[34] § 1250(a)(3).

[35] § 1250(a)(2).

[36] § 1250(a)(1).

[37] §§1250(d)(1) through (d)(4).

[38] § 1250(d)(7).

[39] Reg. §§ 1.1250-3(d)(5) and (h)(4).

property is transferred to a new owner with a carryover basis, the excess depreciation carries over to the new owner.[40] In the case of inheritances in which basis to the successor in interest is determined under § 1014, no carryover of excess depreciation occurs.[41]

Certain like-kind exchanges and involuntary conversions may result in the recognition of gain solely because of § 1250 if insufficient § 1250 property is acquired. Since not all real property is depreciable, it is possible that the replacement property would not be § 1250 property and would still qualify for nonrecognition under the appropriate rules of §§ 1033 or 1034. In such situations, gain will be recognized to the extent the amount that would be recaptured exceeds the fair market value of the § 1250 property received (property purchased in the case of an involuntary conversion).[42]

> **Example 14.** D completed a like-kind exchange in the current year in which he transferred an apartment complex (§ 1250 property) for rural farmland (not § 1250 property). The apartment had cost D $175,000 in 1980 and depreciation of $89,000 has been taken under the 200% declining-balance method. D would have deducted $62,000 under the straight-line method.
>
> The farm land was worth $200,000 at the time of the exchange. There were no improvements on the farm property. D's realized gain on the exchange is $114,000 ($200,000 amount realized − $86,000 adjusted basis in property given up). If there had been no § 1250 recapture, then D would have had no recognized gain. Because the property acquired was not § 1250 property, § 1250 supersedes (overrides) § 1031. D has a recognized gain of $27,000 [($89,000 − $62,000), the amount of excess depreciation], which is all ordinary income under § 1250.

Exhibit 17-2 provides an overview of the handling of sales and exchanges of business property. Exhibit 17-3 provides a chart that may be useful in summarizing property transactions. A comprehensive example of sales and exchanges of trade or business property is presented below.

Exhibit 17-2 *Stepwise Approach to Sales or Exchanges of Trade or Business Property—An Overview*

Step 1: Calculate any depreciation recapture on the disposition of § 1245 property and § 1250 property sold or exchanged at a taxable *gain* during the year.

Step 2: For any remaining gain (after recapture) on depreciable property held for more than one year, add to other § 1231 gains and losses and complete the § 1231 netting process.

Step 3: Complete the netting process for capital assets, taking into consideration the net § 1231 gain, if any.

---

[40] Reg. §§ 1.1250-3(a), (c), and (f).

[41] Reg. § 1.1250-3(b).

[42] § 1250(d)(4)(C). A similar rule is provided for rollovers (deferral) of gains from low-income housing under § 1039 [see § 1250(d)(8)].

Exhibit 17-3 *Summary of Property Transactions*

Recognized Gains (Losses)	Depreciation Recapture	Section 1231 Casualty and Theft	Section 1231 Other	Capital Gains/Losses Long-term Short-term		Ordinary Income (Loss)
	§ 1245 Full recapture Personalty	Casualty and theft	Sale or exchange	Sale or exchange		
		1. § 1231 property	§ 1231 property	Capital assets		
	§ 1250 Partial recapture Realty	Real or depreciable property used in business	Real or depreciable property used in business	All property except inventory, property held for resale, real and depreciable		
	§ 291 Corporations only 20% straight-line	Timber, coal, iron ore, livestock, unharvested crops	Timber, coal, iron ore, livestock, unharvested crops	property used in trade or business, literary compositions, and government		
		2. Capital assets used in trade or business or held for investment in connection with business more than a year	Condemnation 1. § 1231 property 2. Capital assets used in trade or business or held for investment in connection with business more than a year	publications		

Example 15.   Cheryl A. Reporter sold the following assets during the current year:

Description	Holding Period	Selling Price	Adjusted Basis	Recognized Gain (Loss)
Land and building (straight-line depreciation)................... Cost, $13,000 Depreciation allowed, $4,000	3 years	$14,000	$9,000	$5,000
Photocopier...................... Cost, $2,500 Depreciation allowed, $500	14 months	2,600	2,000	600
Business auto................... Cost, $4,000 Depreciation allowed, $2,080	2 years	1,800	1,920	(120)

First, any depreciation recapture must be considered. There is no recapture for the building since straight-line depreciation was used. The recapture on the photocopier is $500 (i.e., full recapture), and there is no recapture on the automobile since it is sold at a loss. Total recapture is $500.

The net § 1231 gain is $4,980, determined as follows:

Gain on sale of land and building.................	$5,000
Plus: Gain on sale of photocopier, net of depreciation recapture ($600 − $500)......	100
Less: Loss on sale of business auto.............	(120)
Net § 1231 gain................................	$4,980

This "net gain" is treated as a long-term capital gain, assuming Cheryl has not deducted § 1231 losses in any of the prior five years. The recapture of $500 is ordinary income.

A Form 4797 containing the information from *Example 15* is included in Exhibit 17-4, which follows. (Note that a 1993 form is used because the 1994 form was not available.)

Exhibit 17-4 *Completed Form 4797*

Form **4797**	**Sales of Business Property**	OMB No. 1545-0184
Department of the Treasury Internal Revenue Service (T)	(Also Involuntary Conversions and Recapture Amounts Under Sections 179 and 280F(b)(2)) ▶ Attach to your tax return. ▶ See separate instructions.	19**93** Attachment Sequence No. **27**

Name(s) shown on return: **CHERYL A. REPORTER**
Identifying number: **427-29-0121**

1 Enter here the gross proceeds from the sale or exchange of real estate reported to you for 1993 on Form(s) 1099-S (or a substitute statement) that you will be including on line 2, 11, or 22 . . . . **1**

Part I Sales or Exchanges of Property Used in a Trade or Business and Involuntary Conversions From Other Than Casualty or Theft—Property Held More Than 1 Year

(a) Description of property	(b) Date acquired (mo., day, yr.)	(c) Date sold (mo., day, yr.)	(d) Gross sales price	(e) Depreciation allowed or allowable since acquisition	(f) Cost or other basis, plus improvements and expense of sale	(g) LOSS (f) minus the sum of (d) and (e))	(h) GAIN ((d) plus (e) minus (f))
2 AUTO	3-1-92	5-2-94	1,800	2,080	4,000	120	

3 Gain, if any, from Form 4684, line 39 . . . . **3**
4 Section 1231 gain from installment sales from Form 6252, line 26 or 37 . . . . **4**
5 Section 1231 gain or (loss) from like-kind exchanges from Form 8824 . . . . **5**
6 Gain, if any, from line 34, from other than casualty or theft **6**   5,100
7 Add lines 2 through 6 in columns (g) and (h) **7**   120   5,100
8 Combine columns (g) and (h) of line 7. Enter gain or (loss) here, and on the appropriate line as follows: **8**   4,980

Partnerships—Enter the gain or (loss) on Form 1065, Schedule K, line 6. Skip lines 9, 10, 12, and 13 below.

S corporations—Report the gain or (loss) following the instructions for Form 1120S, Schedule K, lines 5 and 6. Skip lines 9, 10, 12, and 13 below, unless line 8 is a gain and the S corporation is subject to the capital gains tax.

All others—If line 8 is zero or a loss, enter the amount on line 12 below and skip lines 9 and 10. If line 8 is a gain and you did not have any prior year section 1231 losses, or they were recaptured in an earlier year, enter the gain as a long-term capital gain on Schedule D and skip lines 9, 10, and 13 below.

9 Nonrecaptured net section 1231 losses from prior years (see instructions) **9**
10 Subtract line 9 from line 8. If zero or less, enter -0-. Also enter on the appropriate line as follows (see instructions): **10**

S corporations—Enter this amount (if more than zero) on Schedule D (Form 1120S), line 13, and skip lines 12 and 13 below.

All others—If line 10 is zero, enter the amount from line 8 on line 13 below. If line 10 is more than zero, enter the amount from line 9 on line 13 below, and enter the amount from line 10 as a long-term capital gain on Schedule D.

Part II Ordinary Gains and Losses

11 Ordinary gains and losses not included on lines 12 through 18 (include property held 1 year or less):

12 Loss, if any, from line 8 . . . . **12**
13 Gain, if any, from line 8, or amount from line 9 if applicable **13**
14 Gain, if any, from line 33 . . . . **14**   500
15 Net gain or (loss) from Form 4684, lines 31 and 38a **15**
16 Ordinary gain from installment sales from Form 6252, line 25 or 36 . . . . **16**
17 Ordinary gain or (loss) from like-kind exchanges from Form 8824 . . . . **17**
18 Recapture of section 179 expense deduction for partners and S corporation shareholders from property dispositions by partnerships and S corporations (see instructions) **18**
19 Add lines 11 through 18 in columns (g) and (h) . . . . **19** (   )   500
20 Combine columns (g) and (h) of line 19. Enter gain or (loss) here, and on the appropriate line as follows: . . . **20**   500
a For all except individual returns: Enter the gain or (loss) from line 20 on the return being filed.
b For individual returns:
    (1) If the loss on line 12 includes a loss from Form 4684, line 35, column (b)(ii), enter that part of the loss here and on line 20 of Schedule A (Form 1040). Identify as from "Form 4797, line 20b(1)." See instructions . . . . **20b(1)**
    (2) Redetermine the gain or (loss) on line 20, excluding the loss, if any, on line 20b(1). Enter here and on Form 1040, line 15 . . **20b(2)**   500

For Paperwork Reduction Act Notice, see page 1 of separate instructions.   Cat. No. 13086I   Form **4797** (1993)

Exhibit 17-4 *Continued*

Form 4797 (1993)   Page **2**

Part III Gain From Disposition of Property Under Sections 1245, 1250, 1252, 1254, and 1255

	(a) Description of section 1245, 1250, 1252, 1254, or 1255 property:		(b) Date acquired (mo., day, yr.)	(c) Date sold (mo., day, yr.)
A	BUILDING AND LAND		7-14-91	11-21-94
B	PHOTOCOPIER		6-12-93	8-31-94
C				
D				

	Relate lines 21A through 21D to these columns ▶		Property A	Property B	Property C	Property D
22	Gross sales price (**Note:** *See line 1 before completing.*)	22	14,000	2,600		
23	Cost or other basis plus expense of sale	23	13,000	2,500		
24	Depreciation (or depletion) allowed or allowable	24	4,000	500		
25	Adjusted basis. Subtract line 24 from line 23	25	9,000	2,000		
26	Total gain. Subtract line 25 from line 22	26	5,000	600		
27	**If section 1245 property:**					
a	Depreciation allowed or allowable from line 24	27a		500		
b	Enter the **smaller** of line 26 or 27a	27b		500		
28	**If section 1250 property:** If straight line depreciation was used, enter -0- on line 28g, except for a corporation subject to section 291.					
a	Additional depreciation after 1975 (see instructions) . . .	28a	—0—			
b	Applicable percentage multiplied by the **smaller** of line 26 or line 28a (see instructions)	28b				
c	Subtract line 28a from line 26. If residential rental property or line 26 is not more than line 28a, skip lines 28d and 28e	28c				
d	Additional depreciation after 1969 and before 1976 . . .	28d				
e	Enter the **smaller** of line 28c or 28d	28e				
f	Section 291 amount (corporations only)	28f				
g	Add lines 28b, 28e, and 28f	28g	—0—			
29	**If section 1252 property:** Skip this section if you did not dispose of farmland or if this form is being completed for a partnership.					
a	Soil, water, and land clearing expenses	29a				
b	Line 29a multiplied by applicable percentage (see instructions)	29b				
c	Enter the **smaller** of line 26 or 29b	29c				
30	**If section 1254 property:**					
a	Intangible drilling and development costs, expenditures for development of mines and other natural deposits, and mining exploration costs (see instructions)	30a				
b	Enter the **smaller** of line 26 or 30a	30b				
31	**If section 1255 property:**					
a	Applicable percentage of payments excluded from income under section 126 (see instructions)	31a				
b	Enter the **smaller** of line 26 or 31a	31b				

Summary of Part III Gains. Complete property columns A through D, through line 31b before going to line 32.

32	Total gains for all properties. Add columns A through D, line 26	32	5,600
33	Add columns A through D, lines 27b, 28g, 29c, 30b, and 31b. Enter here and on line 14	33	500
34	Subtract line 33 from line 32. Enter the portion from casualty or theft on Form 4684, line 33. Enter the portion from casualty or theft on Form 4797, line 6	34	5,100

Part IV Recapture Amounts Under Sections 179 and 280F(b)(2) When Business Use Drops to 50% or Less
See instructions for Part IV.

			(a) Section 179	(b) Section 280F(b)(2)
35	Section 179 expense deduction or depreciation allowable in prior years	35		
36	Recomputed depreciation (see instructions)	36		
37	Recapture amount. Subtract line 36 from line 35. See instructions for where to report . . .	37		

Example 16.   Assume that Cheryl Reporter, from the previous example, had the following capital asset transactions during the same year:

Description	Holding Period	Selling Price	Adjusted Basis	Description of Gain or (Loss)
100 shares XY Corp.	4 months	$ 3,200	$4,200	($1,000) STCL
100 shares GB Corp.	3 years	3,200	4,600	(1,400) LTCL
1 acre vacant land	5 years	12,000	5,000	7,000 LTCG

Taking into consideration the net § 1231 gain of $4,980 from *Example 15*, Cheryl has a net long-term capital gain of $10,580 [$4,980 § 1231 gain + ($7,000 LTCG − $1,400 LTCL)] and a net short-term capital loss of $1,000 after the first step in the capital gain and loss netting process. After the second step, Cheryl has a $9,580 net capital gain ($10,580 NLTCG − $1,000 NSTCL). This net capital gain *cannot* be taxed at a rate greater than 28%.

ADDITIONAL RECAPTURE—CORPORATIONS

Corporations generally compute the amount of § 1245 and § 1250 ordinary income recapture on the sales of depreciable assets in the same manner as do individuals. However, Congress added Code § 291 to the tax law in 1982 with the intent of reducing the tax benefits of the accelerated cost recovery of depreciable § 1250 property available to corporate taxpayers. For sales or other taxable dispositions of § 1250 property, corporations must treat as ordinary income 20 percent of any § 1231 gain *that would have been* ordinary income if § 1245 rather than § 1250 had applied to the transaction.[43] The effect of this provision is to require the taxpayer to recapture 20 percent of any straight-line depreciation that has not been recaptured under some other provision. Technically, the amount that is treated as ordinary income under § 291 is computed in the following manner:

Amount that would be treated as ordinary income under § 1245..............................		$xx,xxx
Less:	Amount that would be treated as ordinary income under § 1250.........	(x,xxx)
Equals:	Difference between recapture amounts...	$xx,xxx
Times:	Rate specified in § 291..................	× 20%
Equals:	Amount that is treated as ordinary income......................	$xx,xxx

---

[43] § 291(a)(1).

Example 17. K Corporation sells residential rental property for $500,000 in 1994. The property was purchased for $400,000 in 1986. Assume that K claimed ACRS depreciation of $140,000 (i.e., do not attempt to verify this hypothetical amount). Straight-line depreciation would have been $105,000. K Corporation's depreciation recapture and § 1231 gain are computed as follows:

Step 1: Compute realized gain:

Sales price		$500,000
Less: Adjusted basis		
Cost	$400,000	
ACRS depreciation	(140,000)	(260,000)
Realized gain		$240,000

Step 2: Compute *excess* depreciation:

Actual depreciation	$140,000
Straight-line depreciation	(105,000)
Excess depreciation	$ 35,000

Step 3: Compute § 1250 depreciation recapture:
Lesser of realized gain of $240,000
or
Excess depreciation of $35,000

§ 1250 depreciation recapture	$ 35,000

Step 4: Compute depreciation recapture if § 1245 applied:
Lesser of realized gain of $240,000
or
Actual depreciation of $140,000
Depreciation recapture if

§ 1245 applied	$140,000

Step 5: Compute § 291 ordinary income:
Depreciation recapture if

§ 1245 applied		$140,000
§ 1250 depreciation recapture		(35,000)
Excess recapture potential		$105,000
Times: § 291 rate	×	20%
§ 291 ordinary income		$ 21,000

Step 6: Characterize recognized gain:

§ 1250 depreciation recapture	$ 35,000
Plus: § 291 ordinary income	21,000
Ordinary income	$ 56,000
Realized gain	$240,000
Less: Ordinary income	(56,000)
§ 1231 gain	$184,000

Note that without the additional recapture required under § 291, K Corporation would have reported a § 1231 gain of $205,000 ($240,000 total gain − $35,000 § 1250 recapture). If the property had been subject to § 1245 recapture, K Corporation would have only a $100,000 § 1231 gain ($240,000 − $140,000 § 1245 recapture). Section 291 requires that the corporation report 20% of this difference ($205,000 − $100,000 = $105,000 × 20%), or $21,000, as *additional* recapture. Note that this is 20% of the straight-line depreciation that is normally not recaptured on the disposition of nonresidential or residential real estate.

Example 18.   Assume the same facts as in *Example 17*, except that the property is an office building rather than residential realty *and* straight-line depreciation was elected. An individual taxpayer would report the entire gain of $205,000 [$500,000 − ($400,000 basis − $105,000 straight-line depreciation)] as a § 1231 gain. However, the corporate taxpayer must recapture $21,000 (20% × $105,000 depreciation) as ordinary income under § 291. The remaining $184,000 ($205,000 − $21,000) would be a § 1231 gain.

OTHER RECAPTURE PROVISIONS

There are several more recapture provisions than those already discussed. They include the recapture of farmland expenditures,[44] recapture of intangible drilling costs,[45] and recapture of gain from the disposition of § 126 property (relating to government cost-sharing program payments for conservation purposes).[46] Another type of recapture is investment credit recapture.[47] This is discussed in detail in Chapter 13.

INSTALLMENT SALES OF TRADE OR BUSINESS PROPERTY

As discussed in Chapter 14, gains on sales of trade or business property may be deferred using the installment sale method. However, depreciation recapture does not qualify for installment sale treatment. Thus, ordinary income from depreciation recapture must be reported in the year of sale—*regardless* of whether the seller received any payment in that year.[48] Consequently, only the § 1231 gain from such sales will qualify for installment gain deferral.

---

[44]   § 1252.

[45]   § 1254.

[46]   § 1255.

[47]   § 47.

[48]   § 453(i). See Chapter 14 for a detailed discussion of installment reporting.

Example 19. During 1994 K sold a rental house for $90,000. According to the terms of the sale, K received $10,000 down and the balance in three equal installments of $30,000 over the next three years. K had purchased the house in 1985 for $60,000 and deducted $20,000 of accelerated depreciation. Had she used the straight-line method, the straight-line depreciation would have been $15,000. K realizes a gain of $50,000 and has $5,000 of § 1250 recapture, computed as follows:

Amount realized...	$90,000
Adjusted basis ($60,000 − $20,000).........................	− 40,000
Gain realized...	$50,000
Accelerated depreciation on residential real estate before 1987	$20,000
Hypothetical straight-line depreciation.........................	− 15,000
Excess depreciation...	$ 5,000

K must report all of the depreciation recapture, $5,000, as ordinary income in the year of the sale. In addition, she must report $15,000 of the remaining gain of $45,000 as a § 1231 gain under the installment sale rules for the year of sale, computed as follows:

$$\frac{\text{Remaining gain, \$45,000}}{\text{Contract price, \$90,000}} \times \frac{\$30,000}{\text{Payment received}} = \frac{\$15,000}{\text{Gain recognized}}$$

Note that in computing the gross profit ratio, only the remaining gain is used in the numerator and not the entire $50,000 gain realized, as would normally be the case.

✔ CHECK YOUR TAX KNOWLEDGE

Review Question 1. True-False. This year T sold equipment for $6,000 (cost $15,000, depreciation $10,000), recognizing a gain of $1,000 ($6,000 − $5,000). To ensure that all of the ordinary deductions obtained from depreciation are recaptured, T must report ordinary income of $10,000 and a capital loss of $9,000, ultimately producing net income of $1,000.

False. This novel approach may seem consistent with Congressional intent, but it is incorrect. Under § 1245 any gain realized is treated as ordinary income to the extent of any depreciation allowed. As a result, the entire $1,000 is ordinary income.

Review Question 2. True-False. This year L sold a machine and recognized a small gain. Assuming L claimed straight-line depreciation, there is no depreciation recapture.

False. The machine is § 1245 property since it is depreciable personalty. Under the full recapture rule of § 1245, all depreciation is subject to recapture regardless of the method used.

Review Question 3. Several years ago Harry purchased equipment at a cost of $10,000. Over the past three years he claimed and deducted depreciation of $6,000. Assuming that Harry sold the equipment for (1) $7,000, (2) $13,000, or (3) $1,000, determine the amount of gain or loss realized and its character (i.e., ordinary income or § 1231 potential long-term capital gain).

	1	2	3
Amount realized.......................	$7,000	$13,000	$1,000
Adjusted basis ($10,000 − $6,000).....	− 4,000	− 4,000	− 4,000
Gain (loss) recognized................	$3,000	$9,000	$(3,000)

The equipment is § 1245 property since it is depreciable personalty. As a result, the full recapture rule operates and any gain recognized is ordinary income to the extent of any depreciation deducted. In the first case, the entire $3,000 is ordinary income (the lesser of the gain recognized, $3,000, or the recapture potential, $4,000). In the second situation, $4,000 is ordinary income (the lesser of the gain recognized, $9,000, or the recapture potential, $4,000) and $5,000 is § 1231 gain. In the final case, § 1245 does not apply because the property is sold at a loss. Therefore, Harry has a § 1231 loss that is potentially an ordinary loss. Its ultimate treatment depends on the outcome of the § 1231 netting process.

Review Question 4. True-False. In 1987 Sal purchased an office building to rent out. This year she sold the building, recognizing a large gain. The entire gain is a § 1231 gain since there is no recapture under either § 1245 or § 1250.

True. The office building is § 1250 property. The recapture rules of § 1250 apply only when the taxpayer uses an accelerated method, in which case the excess of accelerated depreciation over straight-line is treated as ordinary income. However, since 1986 taxpayers have been required to use the straight-line method in computing depreciation. As a result, § 1250 is inapplicable and Sal's gain retains its original § 1231 character.

Review Question 5. True-False. In 1987 Z Corporation purchased an office building to rent out. This year the corporation sold the building, recognizing a large gain. The entire gain is a § 1231 gain since there is no recapture under either § 1245 or § 1250.

False. Under § 291, corporate taxpayers are required to recapture 20 percent of any straight-line depreciation.

Review Question 6. True-False. In 1983 the Rose Partnership purchased a new office building to use as its headquarters. This year the partnership sold the building, recognizing a gain of $100,000. The partnership claimed and deducted accelerated depreciation of $40,000. Straight-line depreciation would have been $15,000. The partnership will report ordinary income of $25,000 and § 1231 gain of $75,000.

False. This would be true if the building were § 1250 property, but § 1250 does not apply. Nonresidential real estate such as this office building that was acquired from 1981 through 1986 is treated as § 1245 property and is subject to the full recapture rule if accelerated depreciation was used. In this case, the taxpayer opted for accelerated depreciation, so $40,000 is ordinary income and the remaining $60,000 is § 1231 gain.

Review Question 7. In 1983 the Daisy Partnership purchased a new apartment complex to rent out. This year the partnership sold the building, recognizing a gain of $100,000. The partnership claimed and deducted straight-line depreciation of $15,000. Accelerated depreciation would have been $40,000. The partnership will report ordinary income of $15,000 and § 1231 gain of $85,000.

False. In contrast to question 6, the property is residential real estate and is consequently treated as § 1250 property. The partial recapture rule of § 1250 applies only if the taxpayer actually uses an accelerated method. In this case the taxpayer used straight-line, so the recapture rules of § 1250 are not triggered. As a result, the entire $100,000 gain is a § 1231 gain.

TAX PLANNING CONSIDERATIONS

TIMING OF SALES AND OTHER DISPOSITIONS

Timing the sale of trade or business properties is very important and, from a tax perspective, can be critical. In the simplest case, if a taxpayer has a tax loss or is in a lower tax bracket, any contemplated sales at a gain should be considered to take advantage of the favorable tax result under § 1231. If tax rates are particularly high in the current year, loss transactions should be considered. Any net § 1231 loss is treated as an ordinary deduction for A.G.I. and avoids the $3,000 deduction limit imposed on net capital losses.

In addition, a net § 1231 gain qualifies as a long-term capital gain. For high-income taxpayers with no capital asset transactions or with a net capital gain in the current year, the net § 1231 gain qualifies for the maximum capital gains tax rate of 28 percent. The benefit can be even greater for a taxpayer with substantial capital losses for the year. Because the losses in excess of $3,000 would otherwise be suspended, any net § 1231 gain that would be offset by these losses can be currently recognized at no additional tax cost.

If a taxpayer has recognized or could recognize a § 1231 gain for the year and benefit from § 1231 treatment, additional sales of § 1231 property at a loss should be avoided. Because such losses must be netted against the gains, the favorable treatment of the gains is lost.

The look-back rule must be considered whenever a taxpayer is contemplating the timing of sales of § 1231 gain and loss assets. If no § 1231 losses have been recognized in the last five years, the gain assets should be sold in the current year to receive the favorable treatment of net § 1231 gains. The loss assets can then be sold in the next year and be treated as ordinary losses. This plan will not work, however, if the loss assets are sold first.

Finally, the timing of casualty and theft gains and losses should be considered. Obviously, a taxpayer cannot control the timing of such losses—not legally, anyway. However, the § 1033 gain deferral rules discussed in Chapter 15 may offer some tax planning opportunity. Because this deferral provision is generally elective, the taxpayer should consider existing § 1231 gains or losses before making a decision to defer gain. For example, a taxpayer with substantial capital losses may decide not to defer a capital gain or § 1231 gain under § 1033 even though the involuntarily converted asset is to be replaced. Immediate recognition of the gain will not have any negative tax consequences because it can be offset by the existing capital losses. The replacement property will have a higher (cost) basis for future depreciation. This plan is much more important to corporate taxpayers because excess capital losses can be carried forward only five years.

SELECTING DEPRECIATION METHODS

The accelerated cost recovery system provides taxpayers with several choices of depreciation methods and conventions. For example, a taxpayer with depreciable personalty may elect to use the straight-line method and either the class life or a longer alternative life. For real estate, an alternative 40-year life may be used.

Effect of Recapture.   Generally, a taxpayer should adopt the most rapid method of depreciation available because this results in a deferral of income taxes. Unless tax rates are expected to change significantly in the near future, the tax benefits produced by large depreciation deductions currently allow the taxpayer the use of the money that would otherwise have been used to pay income taxes. In addition, the availability of the like-kind exchange and involuntary conversion provisions eliminates the risk of depreciation recapture when the taxpayer plans to continue in business. It is also important to remember that, for noncorporate taxpayers, there is no depreciation recapture possibility for real estate placed in service after 1986. Because only the straight-line depreciation method can be used, there will be no excess depreciation.

Section 179.   As discussed in Chapter 9, any § 179 expense amount is treated as depreciation allowed. As a result, the comments above may also apply in deciding whether to claim the option to expense the cost of qualifying property. If more than one qualifying asset is placed in service during the year and their total cost exceeds $10,000 (or reduced limit), the taxpayer must select the assets to be expensed. Obviously, only the assets not expected to be sold should be considered for this option. Given the time value of money, however, it seems unlikely that any taxpayer should forgo the § 179 expense option—unless the additional recordkeeping is considered to outweigh the current tax benefit.

INSTALLMENT SALES

Installment sales provide an excellent tax deferral possibility. Caution must be exercised, however, if trade or business property is to be sold under a deferred-payment arrangement. Because any depreciation recapture must be reported as income in the year of sale regardless of the amount of money received, taxpayers should require a cash down payment sufficient to pay any income taxes resulting from the depreciation recapture.

PROBLEM MATERIALS

DISCUSSION QUESTIONS

17-1   *Section 1231 Assets.*   What are § 1231 assets? What is the required holding period? Does the § 1231 category of assets include § 1245 and § 1250 assets as well? Elaborate.

17-2   *Excluded Assets.*   What type of property is excluded from § 1231 treatment?

17-3   *Section 1231 Netting Process.*   Briefly describe the § 1231 netting process. Are personal use assets included in this process?

17-4   *Net § 1231 Gains.*   What is the appropriate tax treatment of net § 1231 gains? Are they offset by short-term capital losses? Can they be offset by capital loss carryovers from prior years?

17-5   *Net § 1231 Losses.*   What is the appropriate tax treatment of net § 1231 losses? Are they subject to any annual limitation? Can they be used to create or increase a net operating loss for the year?

17-6   *Certain Casualty or Theft Gains and Losses.*   Which casualty or theft gains and losses are included in the § 1231 netting process? What is the proper treatment of a net casualty or theft gain? What is the proper treatment of a net casualty or theft loss?

17-7   *Section 1231 Look-Back Rule.*   Describe how the § 1231 look-back rule operates. Why do you think Congress enacted such a rule?

17-8   *Section 1245 Property.*   What category of trade or business property is subject to § 1245? What depreciable real property has been included in this category?

17-9   *Full Depreciation Recapture – § 1245.*   What is meant by § 1245 recapture potential? Why is this rule sometimes called the full recapture rule? What is the lower limit of § 1245 recapture?

17-10   *Section 1245 Recapture Potential.*   During the current year Z sold a vacuum used in his pool-cleaning business. The vacuum had cost $3,600 three years ago, and he had expensed the entire amount under § 179.

    a.   How much is the § 1245 recapture potential with respect to this vacuum?
    b.   If the vacuum was sold for $900, what is the character of the gain?

17-11   *Asset Classification.*   When will the sale or other disposition of depreciable equipment be subject to both § 1231 and § 1245? What is the appropriate treatment of any loss from the sale of such equipment?

17-12   *Section 1245 Property.*   F gave property with § 1245 recapture potential to his daughter, D. Will F be required to recapture any of the depreciation previously claimed? How must D characterize any gain she might recognize on a subsequent disposition of the property?

17-13   *Section 1245 Recapture Potential.*   What happens to the § 1245 recapture potential when property is disposed of in a like-kind exchange?

17-14 *Section 179 Expense Treatment.* Explain the proper tax treatment of any gain recognized on the disposition of an asset that the taxpayer had earlier elected to expense under § 179. Does this mean that any amounts ever deducted under § 179 will always be subject to recapture? Explain.

17-15 *Section 1250 Property.* Is land included in the definition of § 1250 property? Is any real property depreciated under the straight-line method included in this definition?

17-16 *Section 1250 Property.* Is nonresidential real estate acquired after 1980 always § 1250 property? Explain.

17-17 *Section 1250 Property.* Why will depreciable real property placed in service after 1986 never be subject to § 1250 recapture?

17-18 *Section 1250 Recapture Potential.* Why is § 1250 sometimes called the partial recapture rule? Will the § 1250 recapture potential ever simply disappear? Explain.

17-19 *Section 1250 Recapture Potential.* This year Y sold a duplex that she had rented out for several years. The house had cost $40,000 20 years earlier and depreciation expense of $27,000 has been claimed. Straight-line depreciation would have been $24,500.

   a. How much is the § 1250 recapture potential with respect to the duplex?
   b. If the duplex was sold for $75,000, what is the character of Y's gain?

17-20 *Additional Recapture—§ 291.* Briefly describe the additional depreciation recapture rule of § 291. Which taxpayers are subject to this rule?

17-21 *Section 291 Recapture.* Can a corporation that has always elected to use the straight-line depreciation method for all real property ever be subject to additional recapture under § 291? Explain.

17-22 *Reporting § 1231 Transactions.* What tax form does a taxpayer use to report the results of § 1231 transactions? How is any depreciation recapture reported on this form?

17-23 *Planning § 1231 Transactions.* Under what circumstances should a taxpayer with an involuntary conversion gain from business property consider not electing to defer the gain under § 1033?

17-24 *Planning § 1231 Transactions.* A taxpayer plans to trade in depreciable property in order to acquire new property but is quite disappointed to find that his old equipment is worth less than its unrecovered cost basis. He is currently in the top marginal tax bracket and has no capital gains or losses or other § 1231 transactions for the year. What tax advice would you offer this taxpayer concerning the planned exchange?

17-25 *Installment Sales and Depreciation Recapture.* Briefly describe how recapture is reported when either § 1245 property or § 1250 property is disposed of in an installment sale. What tax planning should a taxpayer undertake concerning such sales?

PROBLEMS

17-26   *Characterizing Assets.*   Indicate whether the following gains and losses are § 1231 gains or losses or capital gains and losses or neither. Make your determination prior to the § 1231 netting process.

    a.   Printing press used in A's business; held for three years and sold at a loss
    b.   Goodwill sold as part of the sale of B's business
    c.   Vacant lot used five years as a parking lot in C's business; sold at a gain
    d.   House, 80 percent of which is D's home and 20 percent of which is used as a place of business; held 15 years and sold at a gain
    e.   Camera used in E's business; held for 10 months and sold at a gain
    f.   Land used by F for 10 years as a farm and sold at a loss
    g.   Personal residence sold at a loss

17-27   *Section 1231.*   During the year H sold the following assets, both of which had been held for several years:

Asset	Gain (Loss)
Vacant land held for investment	$52,000
Equipment used in his business	(12,000)

Determine how much long-term capital gain or loss as well as the amount of ordinary income or loss that H will report for the year.

17-28   *Section 1231 Netting.*   G operates the Corner Bar and Grill as a sole proprietorship. During the year he sold the following assets, all of which had been held for several years:

Asset	Gain (Loss)
IBM stock............................	$(12,000)
Land and building used in the business	34,000
Equipment used in the business.......	(3,000)

The building had been acquired in 1988. Straight-line depreciation claimed and deducted with respect to the building was $8,000. Straight-line depreciation on the equipment was $4,000. Determine how much long-term capital gain or loss as well as the amount of ordinary income or loss that G will report for the year.

17-29   *Involuntary Conversions and § 1231.*   Assume the same facts as in Problem 17-27. In addition, G's records revealed the following information:

    •   A portion of the grill's parking lot was condemned by the city when it decided to expand the adjacent street. G pocketed the cash and recognized a gain of $5,000.
    •   A pool table was destroyed as part of a barroom brawl. G realized a casualty loss of $2,000.

Determine how much long-term capital gain or loss as well as the amount of ordinary income or loss that G will report for the year.

17-30   *Section 1231 Hotchpotch.*   For 30 years Rae has operated The General Store, a hardware store in Columbus. Rae runs the business as a sole proprietorship. During the year, she recognized the following gains and losses:

1. Uninsured warehouse burned down: $10,000 loss
2. Equipment stolen: $190,000 gain (ignore depreciation)
3. Parking lot sold: $120,000 gain
4. IBM stock sold: long-term capital loss of $70,000
5. Condemnation of land: $1,000 gain

Determine how much long-term capital gain or loss as well as the amount of ordinary income or loss that Rae will report for the year.

17-31   *Section 1231 Lookback.*   J has recognized the following § 1231 gains and losses in the current year and since the inception of his business:

Year	Net § 1231 Gain (Loss)
1994	$ 50,000
1993	12,000
1992	(35,000)
1991	0
1990	65,000
1989	(13,000)

How will J treat the $50,000 gain for the current year?

17-32   *Section 1231—Timber.*   A owns timber land that she purchased in 1983. During 1994, the timber was cut and A elected § 631 treatment for the gain. Her cost assignable to the timber was $25,000 and its fair market value on January 1, 1994 was $40,000. The actual sales price of the cut timber in 1995 was $55,000.

a.   How much is A's gain or loss recognized and what is its character?
b.   Can A deduct the costs of cutting the timber?

17-33   *Section 1231—Unharvested Crops.*   This year L sold her farmland, which she had owned for 20 years. L had made minor improvements to the farm and had used straight-line depreciation to depreciate them. No personal property was sold with the farm.

   The sales price was $80,000 and L's adjusted basis was $36,000. The unharvested crops on the land represented $8,000 of the sales price, and L had spent $3,200 in producing the crop to the point of sale.

a.   How does L report the gain or loss from the sale of the farm?
b.   If L has no other sales of trade or business property or of capital assets, how much of the gain is included in her taxable income?

17-34   *Section 1245 Recapture.*   During the year D sold a drill press he had used in his wood shop business for three years. D had purchased the press for $820 and had deducted depreciation of $476. Straight-line depreciation would have been $410. Determine the amount and character of gain or loss to D under each of the following circumstances below:

a.   The press is sold for $500.
b.   The press is sold for $100.
c.   The press is sold for $900.

17-35 *Section 1245 Recapture.* This year N sold three different pieces of equipment used in her business:

Description	Holding Period	Sales Price	Cost	Depreciation Allowed
Processing machine	3 years	$1,200	$1,400	$600
Work table	4 years	1,600	1,300	500
Automatic stapler	2 years	500	900	300

What is the amount and character of N's gain or loss from these transactions?

17-36 *Section 1245 Recapture.*   Fill in the missing information for each of the three independent sales of § 1245 assets identified below. Enter a dollar amount or n/a (for not applicable) in each blank space.

	Assets		
	A	B	C
Sales price......................................	$105	$ 90	$____
Cost...	100	125	100
Depreciation allowed............................	30	____	30
Depreciation recapture..........................	____	____	20
§ 1231 gain or (loss)............................	____	(10)	____

17-37 *Basis Reductions.* Dr. T purchased a treadmill for use in his cardiology practice for $13,000 on August 14, 1992. T claimed § 179 expense of $10,000 and depreciation of $429 in 1992. The depreciation for 1993 and 1994 is scheduled to be $735 and $524, respectively. T sold the treadmill on January 13, 1994 for $3,500.

a.   What are the amount and character of T's gain on the sale?
b.   What would be your answer if the unit had been sold for $13,500?

17-38 *Section 1250 Recapture.*   Fill in the missing information for each of the three independent sales of § 1250 assets identified below. Enter a dollar amount or n/a (for not applicable) in each blank space.

	Assets		
	X	Y	Z
Sales price.......................................	100	$____	$200
Cost...	135	100	100
Depreciation allowed............................	55	____	30
Straight-line depreciation........................	____	20	____
Depreciation recapture..........................	0	10	____
§ 1231 gain or (loss)............................	____	30	120

17-39 *Real Property Acquired after 1986.*   V sold an office building in the current year that she had purchased for $60,000 in 1992. Depreciation of $4,127 was claimed before the building was sold for $75,000. What are the amount and character of V's gain on this sale?

17-40 *Section 1245, § 1250, and § 291 Recapture.*   K purchased a mini-warehouse unit on January 3, 1986 for $40,000. Using the tables under ACRS, K deducted depreciation of $19,880 for the period 1986–1994. The unit was sold on January 15, 1994 for $41,000.

    a. How much is K's gain and what is its character?

    b. If K had used the optional straight-line method and a 19-year life under ACRS, the depreciation deductions would have totaled $14,890. What would be the amount and character of K's gain using this method?

    c. What would be your answer to (b) if K were a corporation?

17-41 *Section 1250 Recapture.*   Z sold an apartment unit during 1994 for $75,000. Z purchased the property for $42,000 in 1986 and has deducted depreciation of $23,760. Straight-line depreciation using the same life and salvage value would have been $18,225. What is the amount and character of Z's gain if he receives the entire proceeds in 1994?

17-42 *Recapture and Installment Sales.*   Assume the same facts as in Problem 17-41 except that Z sold the property under an installment contract with $15,000 down and $15,000 in each of the next four years along with reasonable interest. How much gain would Z report in 1994 and 1995, and what is its character?

17-43 *Section 1231 Gain and Look-Back Rule.*   R sold land and a building used in farming at a gain of $30,000 during 1994. No other sales or dispositions of § 1231 assets were made during the year, and the § 1250 depreciation recapture for the building was $4,500.

    a. How is R's gain to be reported if he had a net § 1231 gain of $10,000 in 1991, a net § 1231 loss of $12,000 in 1992, and no § 1231 transactions in 1993?

    b. How would your answer to (a) differ if the sale of the property had resulted in a loss of $7,500?

17-44 *Section 1231 and Depreciation Recapture.*   Fill in the missing information for each of the separate sales of § 1231 assets indicated below. Enter a dollar amount or n/a (for not applicable) in each blank space.

	Land	Building	Machine	Machine
Sales price............................	$100	$____	$ 90	$____
Cost...................................	140	100	125	100
Depreciation allowed...................	0	30	____	30
Straight-line depreciation..............	0	20	____	____
Depreciation recapture.................	____	____	____	____
§ 1231 gain or (loss)..................	____	30	(10)	5

17-45 *Depreciation Recapture and the § 1231 Netting Process.* T had three § 1231 transactions during the current year.

1. Theft of electric cart used on business premises. The cart was worth $600, originally cost $800, and had an adjusted basis of $425.
2. Sale of equipment used in manufacturing. The equipment sold for $5,500, originally cost $8,000, and had an adjusted basis of $4,250.
3. Sale of land and a small building used for storage. The property was sold for $60,000, originally cost $56,000, and had an adjusted basis of $42,500. Straight-line depreciation was claimed on the building.

Determine the amount of ordinary income or loss and capital gain or loss that T must report from these transactions for the current year.

17-46 *Section 1231 Transactions.* K has the following business assets that she is interested in selling in either 1994 or 1995.

	Market Value	Basis
Manufacturing equipment.........................	$220,000	$400,000
Factory building.................................	350,000	220,000
Land used for factory............................	450,000	120,000

Straight-line depreciation was claimed on the factory. K has never sold any other § 1231 assets.

a. What are the tax results if K sells the land and building in 1994 and the equipment in 1995?
b. What are the tax results if K sells the equipment in 1994 and the land and building in 1995?
c. What are the tax results if K sells all the assets in 1994?

17-47 *Comprehensive Problem for Capital Asset and Trade or Business Property Transactions.* T owned a number of apartment units and sold several properties related to that trade or business during the current year as follows:

Description	Holding Period	Sales Price	Cost	Depreciation Allowed	Method
Apartment unit, including land (straight-line depreciation = $2,400)	3 years	$65,000	$24,000	$ 3,000	DB
Lawn tractor	5 years	1,000	3,000	2,600	SL
Spray painter	2 years	500	1,400	600	SL

During a severe winter storm, T also lost a depreciable motorscooter used in his business. The scooter, which was owned by T for two years and used exclusively in the business, had cost $2,600 and had an adjusted basis of $1,750.

In addition, T sold several capital assets during the current year as follows:

Description	Holding Period	Sales Price	Adjusted Basis
100 shares LM Corp.	16 months	$2,000	$1,000
75 shares PL, Inc.	8 months	1,600	2,900
Silver ingots	6 years	2,600	6,000

Assuming T has never deducted § 1231 losses before, calculate the following amounts based on the above information:

a. The amount of § 1245 recapture and § 1250 recapture, if any.
b. The net § 1231 gain or loss.
c. The net long-term capital gain or loss.
d. The net short-term capital gain or loss.
e. The overall impact of the above transactions on T's adjusted gross income.

17-48 *Sections 1231 and 1245 Property.* The terms *§ 1231 property* and *§ 1245 property* are often used interchangeably. However, there are times when a specific asset can be classified as (1) *both* § 1231 and § 1245 property; (2) only § 1231 property; or (3) only § 1245 property. Based on the values assigned to the letters below, indicate the appropriate classification for each of the following mathematical expressions.

Let X = asset's original cost
Y = depreciation claimed
Z = asset's adjusted basis
T = amount realized on sale

a. If $T < Z$, asset is § _____ property.
b. If $T > X$, asset is § _____ property.
c. If $X > T < Z$, asset is § _____ property.
d. If $Y > T > Z$, asset is § _____ property.

17-49 *Section 1231 and § 1250 Property.* It is possible that (1) *both* § 1231 and § 1250 apply to the sale of depreciable real property, (2) only § 1250 applies, or (3) only § 1231 applies. Based on the values assigned to the letters below, indicate which Code sections apply for each of the following mathematical expressions.

Let X = asset's original cost
Y = depreciation claimed
Z = asset's adjusted basis
T = amount realized on sale
S = amount of straight-line depreciation

a. If $Y > S$ and $T < Z$, § _____ applies.
b. If $Y > S$ and $T > X$, § _____ applies.
c. If $Y = S$, § _____ applies.
d. If $Y > S$ and $(T - Z) < (Y - S)$, § _____ applies.

17-50 *Sale of Property Converted from Personal Use — Comprehensive Problem.* L owned and used a house as her personal residence since she purchased it in 1989 for $110,000. On February 11, 1992, when it was worth $85,000, L moved out and converted the property into a rental property. She rented the house until December 15, 1994, when it was sold for $104,500.

    a. Determine L's depreciation deductions for the rental property from the time it was converted in 1992 until it was sold in 1994.

    b. What is amount and character of L's gain or loss to be recognized from the sale?

17-51 *Sale of Property Converted to Personal Use—Comprehensive Problem.* Z purchased a computer system with peripherals for $14,500 on August 12, 1991. The system was used exclusively in his business. In October 1994, when the computer was worth $8,200, Z closed the business and began using the unit for personal purposes.

    a. Determine Z's depreciation deductions for the computer system from the time it was purchased until it was converted to personal use, assuming that he elected the § 179 expensing option for other assets placed into service in 1991.

    b. Assume the computer system was sold for $5,400 on May 15, 1994 rather than being converted to personal use. What are the amount and character of Z's loss?

RESEARCH PROBLEMS

17-52 *Capital Assets versus § 1231 Assets.* R inherited a residence that had been used exclusively by her grandmother as a principal residence for 30 years. Upon receiving the property, R immediately offered the property for rent and rented to several tenants.

    After several months, R encountered an interesting potential business venture that would require a substantial capital investment. After an agonizing decision, she proceeded to sell her inherited rental unit. The unit was sold at a loss and R deducted the loss under § 1231. Since she had no § 1231 gains, the loss was deducted as an ordinary deduction.

    Is the treatment R chose the appropriate treatment for the loss? Does the character of the property to her grandmother carry over to R, resulting in disallowance of the loss or capital loss treatment?

Research aids:

    Campbell v. Comm., 5 T.C. 272 (1945).
    Crawford v. Comm., 16 T.C. 678 (1951), *acq.* 1951-2 C.B. 2.

17-53 *Business Use of Personal Residence.* J purchased a home in March 1980 for $120,000. Twenty percent of its cost was attributable to the land. From the date of purchase until March 1991, 20 percent of the house was used as a home-office, the costs of which were properly deducted annually (including depreciation). The home was used exclusively as J's residence from March 1991 until the house was sold for $325,000 on November 15, 1994.

    a. Assuming J used the declining-balance method at a 5 percent rate and a useful life of 25 years, what amount of depreciation did he claim over the 10-year period that the property was used as a home-office?

    b. Is there any depreciation recapture to be reported if gain is reported on the sale?

    c. Is there depreciation recapture to be reported if all or part of the gain is deferred under § 1034?

PART VI

EMPLOYEE COMPENSATION AND TAXATION OF BUSINESS FORMS

CONTENTS

CHAPTER 18 ■ EMPLOYEE COMPENSATION AND RETIREMENT PLANS

CHAPTER 19 ■ TAXATION OF BUSINESS FORMS AND THEIR OWNERS

Upon completion of this chapter you will be able to:

- Distinguish between taxable and nontaxable employee fringe benefits
- Determine the tax consequences of the issuance and exercise of both nonqualified and qualified stock options
- Explain the advantages and disadvantages of nonqualified deferred compensation arrangements, including
  - The deferral of both the employee's recognition of income and the employer's deduction
  - The economic risk associated with unfunded arrangements
- Specify the two basic tax benefits of qualified retirement plans
- Distinguish between a defined benefit plan and a defined contribution plan
- Calculate the limitations on annual contributions to the various types of qualified plans
- Compute the annual amount of deductible contribution to an Individual Retirement Account
- Describe the characteristics of a Simplified Employee Pension

CHAPTER OUTLINE

Introduction	18-1	Qualified Plans for Self-Employed	
Taxation of Current Compensation	18-1	Individuals	18-19
Statutory Fringe Benefits	18-2	Contribution Limitations	18-20
Deferred Compensation	18-2	Qualified Plans for Employees	18-21
Receipt of Property for Services	18-4	Cash or Deferred Arrangements	18-21
General Rule of § 83	18-4	Individual Retirement Accounts	18-23
The § 83(b) Election	18-5	Excess Contributions	18-25
Qualified Retirement Plans for		Simplified Employee Pensions	18-25
Corporations	18-5	Retirement Planning Using Nonqualified	
Tax Benefits of Qualified Plans	18-6	Deferred Compensation	18-26
Taxability of Qualified Plan Lump		Constructive Receipt	18-26
Sum Distributions	18-7	Unfunded Deferred Compensation	
A Comprehensive Example	18-9	Plans	18-27
Additional Taxes on Premature or		Funded Deferred Compensation	
Excess Distributions	18-9	Plans	18-27
Rollover Contribution	18-10	Stock Options	18-28
Plan Loans	18-10	Option Exercise	18-29
Types of Qualified Plans	18-10	Incentive Stock Options	18-29
Qualification Requirements	18-12	Holding Period Requirements	18-30
Existence of a Qualified Trust	18-13	Qualification Requirements	18-31
Anti-Discrimination Rules	18-13	Nonqualified Stock Options	18-32
Scope of Plan Participation and		Stock Appreciation Rights	18-33
Coverage	18-14	Tax Planning Considerations	18-34
Vesting Requirements and Forfeitures	18-15	Planning for Retirement Income	18-34
Funding and Contribution Limitations	18-16	Advantages of IRAs	18-34
Top Heavy Plans	18-18	Spousal IRAs	18-35
Deductibility of Contributions by		What Is an Active Participant?	18-36
Employer	18-18	Making a Nondeductible Contribution	
Determination Letters	18-19	to an IRA	18-36
		Problem Materials	18-38

Chapter **18**

EMPLOYEE COMPENSATION AND RETIREMENT PLANS

INTRODUCTION

For a large majority of individual taxpayers, compensation received for services rendered as an employee is the most significant, if not the only, source of taxable income. Because of this significance, the topic of taxation of employee compensation is of primary interest to the tax-paying public. Employee compensation consists not only of cash wage and salary payments but an incredible variety of compensation "packages" designed to accommodate the needs and desires of employer and employee alike.

The tax consequences to both the employer and employee of various types of employment compensation are examined in this chapter. Because the concept of compensation includes provisions for employee retirement income, the chapter also includes a discussion of the numerous types of retirement income plans available to both employees and self-employed taxpayers.

TAXATION OF CURRENT COMPENSATION

Under the broad authority of § 61, a taxpayer's gross income includes all compensation for services rendered including wages, salaries, fees, fringe benefits, sales commissions, customer tips, and bonuses. Compensatory payments may be made in a medium other than cash. For example, payment for services rendered may be made with property, such as marketable securities. In such cases, the fair market value of the property is the measure of the gross compensation income received.[1]

Payment for services performed by Taxpayer A for Taxpayer B could consist of services performed by Taxpayer B for Taxpayer A. For example, a lawyer might agree to draft a will for a carpenter, who in turn agrees to repair the lawyer's roof. As a result of such a *service swap*, both taxpayers must recognize gross income equal to the value of the services received.[2]

---

[1] Reg. § 1.61-2(d).   [2] *Ibid.*

STATUTORY FRINGE BENEFITS

As a general rule, any economic benefit bestowed on an employee by his or her employer that is intended to compensate the employee for services rendered represents gross income. This is true whether the benefit is in the form of a direct cash payment or an indirect noncash benefit that nonetheless improves the recipient's economic position.

Certain indirect or *fringe benefits*, however, are excludable from gross income under specific statutory authority. The following is a list of nontaxable fringe benefits and the authority for their exclusion from income. The details of these exclusions are discussed in Chapter 6.

1. Employer payment of employee group-term life insurance premiums (up to $50,000 of coverage)—§ 79

2. Employer contributions to employee accident or health plans—§ 106

3. Amounts paid to an employee under an employer's medical expense reimbursement plan—§ 105(b)

4. Employee meals or lodging furnished for the convenience of the employer—§ 119

5. Amounts received under an employer's group legal services program—§ 120

6. Amounts received under an employer's educational assistance program—§ 127

7. Amounts received under an employer's dependent care assistance program—§ 129

8. No-additional-cost services, qualified employee discounts, working condition fringes, and de minimis fringes—§ 132

The length of the above list demonstrates Congressional tolerance for the use of innovative fringe benefits to attract employees. Employers who want to design the most flexible compensation package for employees who have differing compensation needs may use a *cafeteria plan* of employee benefits. Under a cafeteria plan, an employee is allowed to choose among two or more benefits consisting of both cash and statutory nontaxable benefits.[3]

DEFERRED COMPENSATION

Deferral of compensation can be accomplished under a variety of methods that includes both "qualified" and "nonqualified" plans. A qualified plan is one that meets the requirements of Code § 401(a) and offers the employer a current deduction for money set aside for the eventual benefit of the employee. In this manner, the employees are not taxed on the amount set aside until it is distributed to them, and the income earned on the funds is exempt from tax. A nonqualified plan, on the other hand, does not possess all the specialized tax benefits, but offers a plan that is easier to administer and allows for discrimination among employees. Some of the more popular types of each of these plans are listed in Exhibit 18-1.

---

[3]   § 125.

Exhibit 18-1   *Types of Deferred Compensation Plans*

Qualified Plans

Defined Contribution Plans
Defined Benefit Plans
Money Purchase Plans
Stock Bonus Plans
Employee Stock Ownership Plans
Cash or Deferred Arrangements (401k)
Simplified Employee Plans
Individual Retirement Accounts
Incentive Stock Options

Nonqualified Plans

Restricted Stock
Deferred Payments
Rabbi Trusts
Secular Trusts
Nonqualified Stock Options

The purpose of deferred compensation plans is to allow employees to receive income at a later date when, presumably, they will have much less income. The employee's tax objective in participating in such an arrangement is to ensure that they will be taxed only when payments are received under the plan or agreement. The employer's tax objective is to offer a vehicle that will attract and compensate key personnel while obtaining a current tax deduction for any funds set aside for these employees.

Recent changes in the tax law, specifically the 1986 Tax Reform Act, reduced some of the glamour of deferred arrangements through its repeal of the capital gains differential and compression of the individual-corporate tax rate structure. However, subsequent legislation has reinstated a modest resurgence in plan activity due to the prospects of a widening capital gain differential and a probable increase in tax rates. Nevertheless, while the 1986 Act reduces the tax benefits of qualified plans, it is still possible to achieve both deferral of taxation and capital gains treatment on the eventual distribution of funds to the employee. However, most deferred compensation arrangements are not ordinarily utilized as vehicles to recharacterize the form of income.

While numerous deferred compensation arrangements focus on tax benefits, most qualified plans are flexible and have a wide range of purposes other than reducing an employee's tax liability. For example, a retirement benefit program can have a substantial psychological impact on an employee's morale because it offers an effortless program of saving for the future. In addition, a nonqualified deferred compensation arrangement can be tailored to attract and compensate new executives for benefits they may have forfeited when they left their former employer. Finally, both qualified and nonqualified deferred compensation plans can provide other benefits, such as disability guarantees, death benefits, income security, and plan loans, to safeguard and preserve the well-being of the company's most valued asset—its employees.

RECEIPT OF PROPERTY FOR SERVICES

From a corporate employer's point of view, any form of employee compensation that somehow strengthens that employee's commitment to the corporation is highly desirable. One such type of compensation is a payment made in the capital stock of the corporation itself. Such payment converts the employee into a stockholder and gives him or her an equity interest in the future prosperity of the corporation.

When stock in the corporate employer is used to compensate employees, it is typical for the employment contract to provide that the employee must continue to work for the corporation for some stated time period before he or she is given unrestricted ownership of the stock. If the employee leaves the job before the period expires, the stock received will be forfeited. In this situation, the tax consequences of the compensatory payment to both employee and employer are governed by § 83.

GENERAL RULE OF § 83

If in connection with the performance of services, property of any type is transferred to any person other than the person for whom such services are performed, § 83(a) provides that the fair market value of such property shall be included in the gross income of the person performing such services. If the recipient made any payment for the property, only the excess of the property's value over the amount of such payment is includible gross income. Such inclusion shall occur in the first taxable year in which the rights of the person having the beneficial interest in such property are *transferable* or are not subject to a *substantial risk of forfeiture*, whichever is applicable. If the property received for services is not immediately transferable by the recipient *or* is subject to risk of forfeiture, it is referred to as *restricted property*.

Regulation § 1.83-3(c)(1) explains that a substantial risk of forfeiture exists when the ownership of the transferred property is conditioned, directly or indirectly, upon the future performance (or refraining from performance) of substantial services by the recipient. The Regulation also states that the existence of a substantial risk of forfeiture can only be determined by examining the facts and circumstances of the specific situation.

Section 83(h) entitles the taxpayer for whom services were performed and who transferred property as compensation to a deduction equal to the fair market value of the property. The deduction must be taken in the taxable year in which (or with which) ends the taxable year in which the value of the property is recognized as gross income to the recipient.

> **Example 1.** Corporation M is on a fiscal year ending June 30. On November 1, 1991, the corporation gave employee E, a calendar year taxpayer, 100 shares of its own stock worth $100 per share as compensation for E's services to Corporation M. If E leaves M's employ for any reason during the three-year period beginning on November 1, 1991, he must return the shares. On November 2, 1994, E is still employed and the risk of forfeiture of the stock lapses. On this date the stock is worth $120 per share. For his taxable year 1994, E must include $12,000 in gross income; his tax basis in his shares will also be $12,000. Corporation M has a deduction of $12,000 for its fiscal year ending June 30, 1995.

The Regulations make it clear that a deduction is available to the transferor of the property only if the transfer is an expense meeting the deductibility requirements of § 162 or § 212. If the transfer constitutes a capital expenditure, it must be capitalized rather than deducted.[4]

> **Example 2.** Refer to the facts in *Example 1*. If the shares were transferred to E because E performed organizational services for Corporation M, the corporation must capitalize the $12,000 amount included in E's gross income.

THE § 83(b) ELECTION

Section 83(b) gives a taxpayer who has performed services for *restricted* property an interesting option. Within 30 days of the receipt of the property, the taxpayer may choose to include its fair market value in his or her current year's gross income. This election accelerates the recognition of gross income to the taxpayer. However, the election could be beneficial if the property were rapidly appreciating in value and consequently would have a higher fair market value on the date the risk of forfeiture or other restrictions are scheduled to lapse.

> **Example 3.** In 1992 employee Z receives property worth $10,000 as payment for services rendered. The property is subject to a substantial risk of forfeiture, but Z elects to include the $10,000 value in her 1992 gross income. In 1994, when the risk of forfeiture lapses, the property is worth $25,000. However, Z has no gross income attributable to the property in 1994. Z will have a $10,000 basis in her stock, and Z's employer has a $10,000 deduction for its taxable year that includes December 31, 1992.

The election is not without risk. If the property depreciates during the forfeiture period, the election leads to a larger gross income inclusion as well as acceleration of tax recognition. And more costly still, if the property is in fact forfeited, the taxpayer receives no deduction for the original gross income inclusion.[5] Obviously, the decision to use the § 83(b) election requires a careful analysis of both the current and expected future value of the property, current and future marginal tax rates, and the nature of the restriction involved.

QUALIFIED RETIREMENT PLANS FOR CORPORATIONS

Historically, Congress has viewed with favor the establishment of employer retirement plans as part of a total compensation package offered to employees. The existence of an employer-designed and administered plan encourages the young employee to think seriously about his or her retirement years and offers the employee a most convenient way to provide financially for such retirement.

---

[4] Reg. § 1.83-6(a)(4). [5] § 83(b)(1).

Congress provided an extremely attractive set of tax benefits available to *qualified* employer retirement plans as part of the Internal Revenue Code of 1954. Since the enactment of the 1954 Code, the scope of the benefits has been periodically expanded, and Congress has made different forms of qualified plans available to an ever-increasing number of individual taxpayers. Before examining the various types of qualified plans and the specific features of each, it will be useful to analyze the two basic tax benefits associated with qualified plans for employees—the tax-free nature of employer contributions and the tax-free growth of these contributions.

TAX BENEFITS OF QUALIFIED PLANS

When an employer makes a current contribution to a *qualified* retirement plan on behalf of an employee, §§ 402(a) and 403(a) provide that the value of the contribution is not includible gross income to the employee, even though the employee has obviously received additional compensation in the form of the contribution. In contrast, if the contribution was made by the employer to a *nonqualified* retirement plan in which the employee had a vested interest, the employee would have additional gross income equal to the value of the contribution. As a result, the net amount saved toward retirement by the employee participating in a nonqualified plan is less than the amount saved by the employee participating in a qualified plan.

The second major benefit of qualified retirement plans is that the earnings generated by employer contributions are nontaxable. Sections 401(a) and 501(a) provide that a trust created to manage and invest employer contributions to a qualified retirement plan is exempt from tax.

The effect of these two benefits on the total amount of savings available to an employee at retirement is illustrated in Exhibit 18-2. The exhibit compares two retirement plans, A and B. The plans are identical in every respect but one—A is a nonqualified personal savings plan while B is a qualified employer's trust. The exhibit is based on the following assumptions:

1. The employer will make an annual $10,000 contribution to the plan on behalf of the employee.

2. The employee has a 25 percent marginal tax rate. Therefore, the net amount saved by the employee in Plan A is only $7,500 ($10,000 − $2,500 tax on the current compensation represented by the contribution). The net amount saved in Plan B is $10,000.

3. Funds invested in both plans can earn a 12 percent before-tax return. The earnings from Plan A are taxable to the employee so that the plan's after-tax rate of return is 9 percent. Plan B is in the form of a qualified trust and therefore its earnings are tax-exempt.

The difference in the amounts available to an employee after 15 years of participation in either plan is dramatic. It is not difficult to understand why qualified retirement plans have become such an attractive fringe benefit to employees concerned with providing for their retirement years. However, before the analysis presented in Exhibit 18-2 is complete, it is necessary to examine the general rule as to the taxability of benefits paid out of a qualified plan upon an employee's retirement.

Exhibit 18-2 *Comparison of Nonqualified vs. Qualified Retirement Plans'*
Year-End Values of Employer Contributions

	Nonqualified Plan A	Qualified Plan B
Year 1.............	$ 7,500	$ 10,000
Year 2.............	15,675	21,200
Year 15.............	220,208*	372,800**

* $7,500 × 29.361 (factor for
the sum of an annuity of $1.00 at 9% for 15 years)
** $10,000 × 37.280 (factor for the sum of an annuity
of $1.00 at 12% for 15 years)

When an employee begins to withdraw funds from a nonqualified retirement savings plan, such funds represent *after-tax* dollars, and he or she will not be taxed on these funds a second time. In comparison, benefits received by an employee out of a qualified plan funded solely by employer contributions are fully taxable to the employee. Even though the income tax on such benefits may be computed using a very beneficial method (discussed below), it is important to understand that the retirement dollars available under Plan A of Exhibit 18-2 are excludable (as a return of capital), while the retirement dollars available under Plan B are fully includible in the recipient's gross income.

TAXABILITY OF QUALIFIED PLAN LUMP SUM DISTRIBUTIONS

If an employee who has made no contributions to the employer's qualified retirement plan receives a distribution from the plan, the employee has no investment in the distribution and therefore must include the entire amount in adjusted gross income.[6] When the distribution is made by a series of payments (i.e., an annuity), the taxability of the distribution is spread over a number of years.[7] If the distribution is made in a lump sum, all the retirement income is taxed in one year.[8] Given the progressive rate structure of the Federal income tax, the normal tax on a large lump sum distribution could be prohibitive.

---

[6] If the employee has made contributions to the plan, he or she will have an investment in the plan which may be recovered tax-free under the rules of § 72.

[7] § 402(a).

[8] § 402(e)(1).

To mitigate this problem, Congress provided two relief provisions that benefit the recipient of a lump sum distribution from a qualified retirement plan. First, an employee could treat the portion of a distribution attributable to the employee's participation in the retirement plan prior to 1974 as long-term capital gain.[9] The Tax Reform Act of 1986 generally repealed such capital gain treatment. However, a taxpayer who was age 50 before January 1, 1986 may elect to utilize this relief provision. In such case, the long-term capital gain portion of a distribution will be taxed at a flat 20 percent rate.[10]

A second relief provision is a special procedure for computing the amount of current tax on a lump sum distribution. Prior to the Tax Reform Act of 1986, the procedure involved a 10-year forward averaging computation; for distributions made after December 31, 1986, the averaging period has been reduced to five years.[11] A taxpayer who was age 50 before January 1, 1986 may elect to use the 10-year forward averaging computation based on 1986 income tax rates for distributions received after 1986.[12]

Under current law, the averaging computation may be elected only for lump sum distributions received on or after the taxpayer has reached $59\frac{1}{2}$ years of age, and a taxpayer may only make one such election.[13] However, a taxpayer who was age 50 before January 1, 1986 may elect to use the forward averaging computation for lump sum distributions received prior to age $59\frac{1}{2}$.[14]

The *five-year forward averaging* computation involves the following four steps:

1. Begin with the total lump sum distribution and subtract any available *minimum distribution allowance*.[15]

2. Divide the result into five equal portions.

3. Compute the tax on one portion using the rate schedule for single taxpayers.

4. Multiply the resulting tax by five.

---

[9] § 402(a)(2), repealed by the Tax Reform Act of 1986.

[10] Tax Reform Act of 1986, Act § 1122(h)(3).

[11] § 402(e).

[12] Tax Reform Act of 1986, Act § 1122(h)(5).

[13] § 402(e)(4)(B).

[14] Tax Reform Act of 1986, Act §§ 1122(h)(3) and (5).

[15] § 402(e)(1)(C) defines the minimum distribution allowance as (1) the lesser of $10,000 or half the amount of the taxable lump sum distribution, (2) reduced by 20 percent of the amount by which the distribution exceeds $20,000. Thus, for lump sum distributions of $70,000 or more there is no minimum distribution allowance.

A COMPREHENSIVE EXAMPLE

In 1994 employee E, age 64 and married, received a $90,000 lump sum distribution from a qualified retirement plan. His other taxable income for the year was $22,000. E's 1994 tax liability is computed as follows:

Tax on lump sum distribution:

Total distribution...	$90,000
Less: Minimum distribution allowance (Step 1)*.............	− 0
Amount subject to five-year averaging.........................	$90,000
$\frac{1}{5}$ of averageable amount (Step 2)...........................	$18,000
Tax on $18,000 at single rates (Step 3).......................	$ 2,700
Tax multiplied by 5 (Step 4)....................................	$13,500
Tax on $22,000 taxable income:	
At rates for married, filing jointly...............................	$ 3,300
Total tax liability ($13,500 + $3,300)...........................	$16,800

*The minimum distribution allowance is computed as follows: (1) lesser of $10,000 or $45,000 ($\frac{1}{2}$ × $90,000) = $10,000, (2) reduced by [20% × $70,000 ($90,000 − $20,000) = $14,000] = $0.

If E had simply computed his tax on $112,000 of taxable income, his total 1994 tax liability would be approximately $27,250. Note that because E was age 50 prior to January 1, 1986, he could elect to treat the amount of the distribution attributable to any pre-1974 contributions as long-term capital gain taxable at 20 percent, *and* to use the 10-year forward averaging convention based on 1986 tax rates.

ADDITIONAL TAXES ON PREMATURE OR EXCESS DISTRIBUTIONS

Congress intended for the tax-favored status of qualified plans to serve as an inducement for taxpayers to provide for a source of retirement income. Therefore, if a taxpayer makes a premature withdrawal from a qualified plan, a 10 percent penalty tax is imposed on the amount of the distribution included in the taxpayer's gross income.[16] This penalty will not be imposed if the distribution occurs after the taxpayer has reached age $59\frac{1}{2}$, or if the distribution is attributable to the death or permanent disability of the taxpayer.[17]

---

[16] § 72(t).

[17] For other exceptions to the penalty rule, see § 72(t)(2).

ROLLOVER CONTRIBUTION

There are many situations in which taxpayers receive lump sum distributions from qualified plans prior to retirement. For example, a taxpayer who quits his job with his current employer to accept a position with a new employer may have a right to a distribution from his current employer's qualified plan. Any taxpayer who receives a qualified plan distribution but does not need additional disposable income can exclude the distribution from gross income (and thus avoid both the income tax and any penalty tax on the distribution) by making a *rollover contribution* of the distributed funds. A rollover contribution must be made into another qualified employer plan, a Keogh plan, or an IRA, and it must be made within 60 days of the receipt of the distribution.[18]

Congress has also decided that taxpayers who have used qualified retirement plans to accumulate substantial amounts of wealth should bear an extra tax burden for such privilege. Consequently, § 4980A imposes a 15 percent tax on an excess distribution received by an individual during any calendar year. An excess distribution is the total amount of distributions from qualified employer retirement plans and IRAs received during the year in excess of $150,000. The amount of tax is reduced by any premature withdrawal penalty imposed on the excess distribution.[19]

PLAN LOANS

Plan participants can avoid making taxable withdrawals from qualified plans while indirectly utilizing their retirement funds by borrowing money from their qualified plans. There is a very complex limit on the amount of a plan loan. In very general terms, a plan loan to a participant is limited to the lesser of (1) one-half the participant's vested accrued benefit (but not less than $10,000) or (2) $50,000. Any amount of a loan in excess of this limit is considered a taxable distribution.[20]

> **Example 4.**   R and S are members of P Corporation's qualified plan. R has accrued vested benefits of $14,000, and S has accrued vested benefits of $80,000. R can borrow up to $10,000 even though this amount exceeds 50% of his vested benefits. If S, on the other hand, borrows $62,000 from the fund, $22,000 will be treated as a taxable distribution to her because this exceeds 50% of her benefits (which is more severe than the $50,000 ceiling violation).

TYPES OF QUALIFIED PLANS

Qualified plans fall into two basic categories, defined benefit plans and defined contribution plans. A *defined benefit plan* is one designed to systematically provide for the payment of definitely determinable benefits to retired employees for a period of years or for life. The focus of the plan is on the eventual retirement benefit to be provided.

---

[18]   § 402(a)(5).

[19]   Special rules apply to lump sum distributions and for retirement benefits accrued as of August 1, 1986.

[20]   § 72(p).

The amount of the benefit is usually based on both an employee's compensation level and years of service to the company. Defined benefit plans are commonly referred to as pension plans. The current amount of employer contributions that are required to fund future pension benefits under a given plan must be determined actuarially.[21]

Defined contribution plans provide for annual contributions to each participating employee's retirement account. Upon retirement, an employee will be entitled to the balance accumulated in his or her account. Defined contribution plans are designed to allow employees to participate in the current profitability of the business. Generally, in profitable years, an employer will make a contribution to a qualified trust and such contribution will be allocated to each employee's retirement account. However, contributions may be made to a qualified profit sharing plan without regard to current or accumulated profits of the employer corporation.[22] Although the employer may have the discretion as to the dollar amount of an annual contribution, such contributions must be recurring and substantial if the plan is to be qualified.[23]

While most defined contribution plans constitute "profit sharing plans," other types of defined contribution arrangements exist. These arrangements include *money purchase plans, stock bonus plans,* and *employee stock ownership plans.* Each of these is briefly discussed below.

Money Purchase Plans.   A money purchase plan is a defined contribution plan that is treated like a defined benefit plan. The employer's annual contribution is determined by a specific formula that involves either a percentage of compensation of covered employees or a flat dollar amount. Under a money purchase plan, unlike a defined benefit plan, a definite pension amount is not guaranteed. Rather, a participant's retirement benefit will be determined by his or her vested account balance at retirement.

Because an employee's account balance will be fashioned according to a definite formula under a money purchase plan, a certain amount of flexibility is permitted in structuring the plan's contribution formula.

> **Example 5.**   Under a company's money purchase plan formula, an employer is required to contribute to the plan 3% of an employee's compensation plus an extra 1% for each year of prior service up to a maximum of 10%. Thus, an employee with 12 years of service would receive a contribution equal to 13% [3 + (12 limited to 10)] of his covered compensation. A new employee would receive only 3%.

Note that under a money purchase plan an employer is required to make a contribution. If an employer fails to make these required contributions under the plan, however, the employer will be subject to certain excise taxes. This minimum funding standard does not apply to stock bonus or profit-sharing plans.[24]

Stock Bonus Plans.   A stock bonus plan is another type of deferred compensation arrangement in which the employer establishes a plan in order to contribute shares of the company's stock. A stock bonus plan is subject to the same requirements as a profit

[21] Reg. § 1.401-1(b)(1)(i).

[22] § 401(a)(27).

[23] Reg. § 1.401-1(b)(1)(ii).

[24] § 412(h)(1).

sharing plan; therefore, a stock bonus plan must have a predetermined formula for allocating and distributing the stock among the employees. All benefits paid from the plan must be distributed in the form of the employer company's stock. An exception is made for fractional shares distributed from the plan, which may be paid in the form of cash.[25]

Employee Stock Ownership Plans. Employee stock ownership plans (ESOPs) are defined contribution plans that qualify as a tax-exempt employee trust. The plan is established as a stock bonus plan or a combination of a stock bonus and a money purchase plan. The purpose of the trust is to invest primarily in qualified securities of the employer.[26] One of the benefits of an ESOP is that the employer can contribute the company's stock rather than cash to the plan. When this occurs, the corporation receives a tax deduction equal to the fair market value of the stock and does not recognize gain or loss on the stock contributed to the plan.[27]

> **Example 6.** P Corporation chooses to establish an ESOP plan for its employees. Under the terms of the plan, P transfers 30,000 shares of unissued stock valued at $90,000 to the trust. As a result of this transfer, P is entitled to a deduction of $90,000 without incurring a cash drain. Under § 1032, P recognizes no gain or loss on the transfer, and the shareholders are not subject to tax until they receive a subsequent distribution from the trust.

Additionally, an employer can fund an ESOP with loans to the plan to purchase the employer's securities, or it can acquire shares by a direct purchase from its shareholders. If a loan is made to the plan, the employer receives a deduction for any contributions that are made to the plan that are used to pay loan interest (a portion of which may be excluded by the lender).[28] Furthermore, the employer can deduct certain dividends paid on the securities purchased with the loan proceeds. If the employer elects to purchase the securities from its shareholders, the shareholders must recognize gain or loss upon the sale of their stock. However, a special rule exists for owners of closely held corporations that may allow the owners to elect nonrecognition treatment.

QUALIFICATION REQUIREMENTS

In order for a retirement plan to be *qualified* and therefore eligible for preferential tax treatment, it first must comply with a long list of requirements set forth in §§ 401 through 415. These requirements are extremely complex and can prove burdensome to the employer wishing to establish a qualified plan for his or her employees. The rigorous requirements are intended to ensure that a qualified retirement plan operates to benefit a company's employees in an impartial and nondiscriminatory manner.

The current requirements for plan qualification came into the law in 1974 with the enactment of the Employees Retirement Income Security Act (ERISA). Prior to ERISA, many qualified plans were designed to benefit only those employees who were officers of the company, shareholders, or highly compensated executives. Since the passage of ERISA, such discriminatory plans are no longer qualified.

---

[25] Regs. § 1.401-1(b)(1)(iii).

[26] § 4975(e)(7).

[27] § 1032.

[28] § 404(a)(9).

EXISTENCE OF A QUALIFIED TRUST

Under § 401 and the accompanying Treasury Regulations, contributions made as part of a qualified plan must be paid into a domestic (U.S.) trust, administered by a trustee for the exclusive benefit of a company's employees. The plan must be in written form and its provisions must be communicated to all employees. The plan must be established by the employer. Any type of employer—sole proprietor, partnership, trust, or corporation—may establish a plan.

ANTI-DISCRIMINATION RULES

A retirement plan will not qualify if the contributions to or benefits from the plan discriminate in favor of the *prohibited group*. The prohibited group is defined as employees who are highly compensated or who are officers or shareholders of the company. If a plan provides for contributions or benefits to be determined under an equitable and reasonable formula, the fact that the prohibited group receives a greater dollar amount of contributions or benefits than employees in the nonprohibited group will not constitute discrimination.[29] However, if the formula is based on or makes reference to an employee's current compensation, the amount of compensation that can be taken into account will be limited.[30] Prior to its amendment in 1993, the annual compensation limit was $235,840 (for 1993). Section 401(a)(17) was amended by the 1993 Tax Act to reduce the annual compensation limit to $150,000 and to modify the manner in which cost of living adjustments are made annually to the limit.

> **Example 7.** Acme Inc.'s qualified profit sharing plan provides that the employer's total annual contribution will be allocated among the various plan participants based on the relative amount of each participant's current salary. Mr. J's annual salary is $275,000 for 1993 and $280,000 for 1994. For purposes of the allocation formula, only $235,840 can be taken into account for 1993 and only $150,000 can be taken into account for 1994.

The term "highly compensated employee" means any employee who, during the year or the preceding year:[31]

1. Was at any time a 5-percent owner;

2. Received compensation from the employer in excess of $99,000 (for 1994);

3. Received compensation from the employer in excess of $66,000 (for 1994) *and* was in the top-paid group of employees for such year; or

4. Was at any time an officer and received compensation greater than 50 percent of the dollar limit for a defined benefit plan ($118,800 × 50% = $59,400 for 1994).

---

[29] §§ 401(a)(4) and (5).   [31] § 414(q).

[30] § 401(a)(17). See Exhibit 18-3.

The $66,000 and $99,000 figures are indexed annually for inflation, and the top-paid group of employees consists of the top 20 percent (based upon compensation) of all employees.

An important aspect of the statutory anti-discrimination rules for qualified plans is the fact that such plans may be integrated with public retirement benefits.[32] Thus the calculation of plan benefits may take into account the extent to which an employee is covered by social security or a state retirement program. This is often referred to as *Social Security Integration,* which allows for more benefits to be paid to more highly compensated employees.

SCOPE OF PLAN PARTICIPATION AND COVERAGE

A qualified retirement plan must provide that a substantial portion of a company's employees are eligible to participate in the plan. Specifically, any employee who has reached age 21 must be eligible to participate after completing one year of service for the employer.[33] The plan may not exclude an employee from participation on the basis of a maximum age.[34]

In addition to these *minimum* and *maximum* age and service conditions, a qualified plan must meet complex minimum coverage requirements. A qualified plan must satisfy one of the following three minimum coverage tests: the *percentage test,* the *ratio test,* or the *average benefits test.*[35]

Under the percentage test, a plan must benefit 70 percent or more of all of the employer's non–highly compensated employees. For this test, all eligible employees are considered to benefit under the plan. A plan that has no coverage requirements or highly compensated employees will automatically satisfy this test.

> **Example 8.**   P Corporation has two divisions, R and S. P Corporation adopts a plan that covers only the employees of division S. If R division has 2 highly compensated and 20 non–highly compensated employees and S division has 18 highly compensated and 80 non–highly compensated employees, P satisfies the percentage test. This is because the plan covers 80% [80% of (20 + 80)] of the non–highly paid employees.

The ratio test requires that the plan benefit a classification of employees that does not allow more than a reasonable difference between the percentage of an employer's highly compensated employees who are covered and a similarly computed percentage for non–highly compensated employees. In other words, the ratio test allows the percentage test to be proportionately reduced.

> **Example 9.**   Assume the same facts as *Example 8.* Because only 90% of the highly compensated employees are covered (18 of 20), only 90% of the percentage test must be met. Thus, the plan would meet the ratio test if as few as 63% of the non–highly compensated employees are covered (90% of 70%).

---

[32] § 401(a)(5).

[33] § 410(a)(1).

[34] § 410(a)(2).

[35] § 410(b)(1).

A plan will satisfy the average benefits test if (1) it benefits employees under a classification that the IRS finds does not discriminate and (2) the average benefit percentage for non–highly compensated employees is at least 70 percent of the average benefit percentage for highly compensated employees. The average benefit percentage, with respect to any group of employees, is the sum of all employer contributions and benefits under the plan provided to the group, expressed as a percentage of pay for all group members. An employer may compute the average benefit percentage based on either the current plan year or on a rolling average of three plan years that includes the current year. Once the employer makes this choice, it must obtain IRS consent to revoke it.[36]

The 50/40 Rule. While this rule is not a separate coverage rule, the 50/40 rule deserves attention because of the significance of the law involved. Effective for plan years beginning after 1988, a plan will lose its qualification unless on each day of the plan year, it benefits the lesser of (1) 50 employees or (2) 40 percent of all employees of the employer. The 50/40 requirement applies separately to each qualified plan, and the Regulations exempt certain plans from this rule.[37]

VESTING REQUIREMENTS AND FORFEITURES

Once an employee is participating in an employer-sponsored retirement plan, he or she may not be entitled to any benefits under the plan for a certain period of time. After the requisite period of time, the employee's benefits *vest* and become nonforfeitable regardless of his or her continued employee status.

Under a qualified plan, vesting for non–top heavy employees must occur according to one of two statutory schedules designed to guarantee that an employee obtains a right to plan benefits within a reasonable time.[38] These two schedules are often referred to as "Cliff" vesting and "Graded" vesting.

Cliff Vesting. This schedule derived its name from the tendency, before ERISA, of some employers to push off the employment "cliff" (terminate) those employees just about to become vested in the retirement plan. Effective for years beginning after 1988, plans are no longer permitted to be more restrictive than five-year cliff vesting. Under five-year cliff vesting, an employee would not be entitled to any vesting before completing five years of service. At the end of the fifth year, the employer would have to vest the employee 100 percent in his or her accrued benefit attributable to employer contributions.[39]

---

[36] § 410(b)(2)(C).

[37] § 401(a)(26) and Prop. Regs. § 1.401(a)(26)-2.

[38] § 411(a)(2).

[39] § 411(a)(2)(A).

Graded Vesting.   The second permissible non–top heavy vesting schedule is graded vesting. Effective for plan years beginning after 1988, employees must become proportionately vested over a three- to seven-year vesting period. Under seven-year graded vesting, a plan must provide at a minimum the following:

20%   vesting after three years service;
40%   vesting after four years service;
60%   vesting after five years service;
80%   vesting after six years service; and
100%   vesting after seven years service.

Under this schedule, the potential for discrimination diminishes because vesting occurs at a more gradual rate and, after three years of service, all employees are entitled to some vesting.[40]

If an employee leaves the job before some or all of the retirement benefits have vested, he or she forfeits the right to such benefits. Previous employee contributions toward these forfeited benefits are not returned to the employer, but instead transfer to remaining plan participants in a nondiscriminatory manner.[41]

FUNDING AND CONTRIBUTION LIMITATIONS

Qualified retirement plans must be *funded*. Consequently, an employer is required to make current payments into a qualified trust. For a defined benefit plan, an actuarially determined minimum current contribution is required by statute.[42] For a defined contribution plan, the annually determined contribution must be *paid* to the trustee. Because of these rules, an employer must back up its promises to the employees with actual plan contributions.

The Code limits the amount to which a qualified plan may provide tax-favored contributions or benefits on behalf of an employee. If these amounts should be exceeded, the plan will terminate.[43] In addition, § 404 establishes a limit on the amount that an employer may deduct. Sometimes the deductibility issue may have an impact on the amount that an employer may contribute on behalf of an employee.

Defined Contribution Plans.   Under a defined contribution plan, the maximum contribution that can be made to the account of an employee is limited to the lesser of the following:

1. $30,000; or

2.   25 percent of the employee's compensation.

Cost of living adjustments (indexed for inflation) are to be made to the $30,000 limitation, but they are temporarily suspended until such time that the applicable dollar limit for defined benefit plans equals $120,000. Once the $120,000 mark is reached, the two plan limits will move in tandem so as to maintain the 1:4 ratio.[44]

---

[40]   § 411(a)(2)(B).

[41]   Rev. Rul. 71-149, 1971-1 C.B. 118.

[42]   § 412.

[43]   §§ 415(a) and (b).

[44]   § 415(c)(1)(A).

Example 10.   S is a participant in Summa Inc.'s qualified profit sharing plan. If S's annual salary is $275,000, her employer can make a maximum annual contribution for her of $30,000 (the *lesser* of $30,000 or 25% of S's first $150,000 of compensation).

Example 11.   If S's current salary is $95,000, the annual contribution is limited to $23,750 (the *lesser* of $30,000 or 25% of S's compensation).

Defined Benefit Plans.   Under a defined benefit plan, the maximum annual benefit that can accrue to a participant is limited to the lesser of the following:[45]

1. $118,800 for 1994; or

2.   100 percent of the participant's average compensation for his or her three most highly compensated consecutive years of service with the employer.

Section 401(a)(17) was amended in 1993 to reduce the annual compensation limit to $150,000. Proposed regulations provide illustrations of how these new compensation limits affect *average compensation* for defined benefit plans.[46]

Example 12.   Plan X is a defined benefit plan that bases benefits on the average of an employee's three most highly compensated consecutive years of service. Employee T's annual compensation for 1991, 1992, and 1993 is $300,000 each year. Plan X cannot base Employee T's plan benefits for 1993 on compensation that exceeds $228,973 (the average of $222,220, $228,860, and $235,840, the compensation limits in effect for 1991 through 1993).

Example 13.   In January of 1994, Plan X is amended to reflect the 1993 compensation limits of $150,000. Plan X cannot acrue plan benefits for Employee T on compensation that exceeds $150,000, including compensation for years prior to 1994. Thus, if Employee T continues to make $300,000 in 1994, Plan X cannot base plan benefits for 1994 on compensation that exceeds $150,000 (the average of $150,000, $150,000, and $150,000, the compensation limits in effect for 1992 through 1994).[47]

The $118,800 is indexed annually for inflation, and adjustments to this figure are to be made if benefit payments are to begin before or after Social Security retirement age. Adjustments will be downward if payments begin before Social Security retirement age and upward if they begin after that age. The amount of the adjustment is determined actuarially based upon a straight-life annuity.[48]

---

[45]   § 415(b)(1)(A).

[46]   Prop. Regs. § 1.401(a)(17)-1(b).

[47]   Prop. Regs. § 1.401(a)(17)-1(b)(6) Example 4.

[48]   § 415(b)(2)(B).

Exhibit 18-3	Maximum Annual Inflation-Adjusted Dollar Amounts		

Plan Type	1993	1994
Defined Benefit Plan	$115,641	$118,800
Defined Contribution Plan	30,000	30,000
Annual Compensation Limit	235,840	150,000
Cash or Deferred (401k)	8,994	9,240
Highly Compensated Cap	96,368	99,000
Top-Paid Group Cap	64,245	66,000

TOP HEAVY PLANS

Section 416 contains additional requirements for qualified status of retirement plans that are deemed to be "top heavy." A *top heavy plan* is one in which more than 60 percent of the cumulative benefits provided by the plan are payable to *key employees*. Key employees include officers of the employer and highly compensated owner-employees. If a top heavy plan exists, § 416 provides an extra measure of assurance that the plan does not discriminate against non-key employees. To maintain qualified status a top heavy plan *must provide* a more rapid vesting schedule (generally 100% vesting after three years of service) and a minimum benefit to *all* employees regardless of social security or similar public retirement benefits.

DEDUCTIBILITY OF CONTRIBUTIONS BY EMPLOYER

Section 404(a) allows a deduction for employer contributions to qualified retirement plans if the contributions represent an ordinary and necessary business expense. In addition, § 404 contains complex rules that limit the dollar amount of the annual deduction. (Note that the statutory limitations on employer deductions are independent of the previously discussed limitations on the amount of contributions.) For example, the deduction for an employer's contribution to a qualified profit sharing plan is subject to a general limitation of 15 percent of total annual compensation paid to participating employees.[49] If an employer makes a contribution that exceeds this percentage limitation, the excess may be carried forward and deducted in succeeding years (subject to the percentage limitation for each succeeding year).[50]

---

[49] § 404(a)(3).   [50] *Ibid.*

DETERMINATION LETTERS

At this point, it should be obvious to the beginning tax student that the qualification rules for employer-sponsored plans are many and complex. As a result, employers are well advised to request a determination letter from the IRS before a plan is put into effect. Such determination letter is a *written approval* of the plan verifying that the plan, as described to the IRS, complies with all requirements for qualified status. If a plan treated by an employer as qualified is disqualified in an IRS audit, the employer could be liable for a considerable amount of unwithheld income and payroll taxes on employer contributions.

QUALIFIED PLANS FOR SELF-EMPLOYED INDIVIDUALS

Unincorporated taxpayers who earn money through self-employment are often precluded from retirement benefits afforded employees. To mitigate this result, Keogh (H.R. 10) plans were developed whereby contributions to such a plan are tax deductible, earnings accrue tax-free, and the self-employed individual is not taxed on any of the benefits until retirement. While Keogh plans provide substantial benefits, there are specific requirements that must be followed.

A self-employed individual who establishes an employer qualified retirement plan for his employees is not an employee eligible for participation in the plan. Self-employed individuals include sole proprietors and the partners in a business partnership. These taxpayers, however, may use the *Keogh* rules to obtain the tax benefits of a qualified plan.[51] A Keogh plan must benefit both the self-employed taxpayer and his or her employees in a nondiscriminatory manner under the wide range of rules for qualified plans previously discussed. In addition, the top heavy rules of § 416 apply to Keogh plans.[52]

To be eligible for a Keogh plan, the sole proprietor or partner must be an individual who satisfies one of the following conditions:[53]

1. Has "earned income" for the taxable year;
2. Would have had "earned income" for the year, but the trade or business being carried on had no net profits; or
3. Has been self-employed for any prior taxable year.

Generally, net earnings from self-employment will be the gross income from the trade or business less any related deductions; plus any distributive share of income or loss (if any) from a partnership. More specific definitions that are required for the tax computations are found in Exhibit 18-4.

---

[51] See § 410(c)(1). It is interesting to note that retirement plans for self-employed individuals often are referred to as Keogh *or* H.R. 10 plans. Actually, the descriptions are interchangeable since H.R. 10 designated the legislative bill introduced by Congressman Keogh and passed by Congress in 1962.

[52] § 416(i)(3).

[53] § 415(c)(1)(B).

> **Exhibit 18-4** *Special Definitions for KEOGH Plans*
>
> | | |
> |---|---|
> | *Earned Income* | Self-employment income reduced by the self-employment tax deduction *and* the amount of the allowable Keogh deduction. |
> | *Net Earnings from Self-Employment* | Earnings from self-employment without regard to the self-employment tax deduction or the allowable Keogh deduction. |
> | *Modified Net Earnings from Self-Employment* | Net earnings from self-employment reduced by the self-employment tax deduction. |
> | *Self-Employment Tax Deduction* | One-half of the self-employment taxes due for the year. |

CONTRIBUTION LIMITATIONS

Annual contributions to Keogh plans are generally subject to the same limitations that apply to employer plans. For a defined contribution plan, the annual contribution by a self-employed taxpayer is limited to the lesser of $30,000 or 25 percent of *earned income*.[54] As seen in Exhibit 18-4, the definition of earned income includes the deduction for the allowable Keogh contribution, so the computation is a circular one.[55] The computation of the allowable contribution can best be expressed in the following formula:

$$
\begin{array}{rl}
& \text{Net Earnings from Self-Employment (NE)} \\
- & \underline{\text{Self-Employment Tax Deduction}} \\[4pt]
& \text{Modified Net Earnings from Self-Employment (MNE)} \\
- & \underline{\text{Allowable Contribution (AC)}} \\[4pt]
& \text{Earned Income (EI)} \\
\times & \underline{25\%} \\[4pt]
= & \underline{\text{Allowable Contribution (AC)}}
\end{array}
$$

The results of this formula can now be restated in the form of the equation found in Exhibit 18-5. Notice that the solution to this equation demonstrates that the actual limit on a self-employed taxpayer's annual contribution to a defined contribution Keogh plan is just 20 percent of *modified net earnings*. For individuals who have self-employment income but no liability for employment taxes (e.g., they have exceeded the maximum FICA through other employment), the allowable contribution will be 20 percent of their *net earnings* from self-employment.

---

[54] §§ 415(c)(1) and (3)(B).   [55] § 401(c)(2).

Exhibit 18-5 *Circular Computation of Allowable Contribution*

$$AC = .25(EI) = .25(MNE - AC) = .25MNE - .25AC$$
or
$$1.25AC = .25MNE$$
thus
$$AC = (.25/1.25)MNE = .20MNE(20\% \text{ of } MNE)$$

Example 14. During the current year, Mr. T earned $75,924 and paid $7,848 in self-employment taxes. The maximum contribution T can make to his defined contribution plan is 25% of $72,000 [$75,924 − (½ of $7,848)] less the contribution itself. Therefore, the maximum contribution is $14,400 [25% of ($75,924 − $3,924 − $14,400)]. Note that this contribution is actually 20% of the modified net earnings of $72,000.

A different limitation applies to a Keogh plan if it is purely a discretionary profit sharing plan as opposed to the defined contribution plan discussed above. In this case, § 404(a)(3) limits the deductible contribution to only 15 percent of *modified net earnings* from self-employment. Once again, because the computation is a circular one, a calculation similar to Exhibit 18-5 would be necessary. While the computation is not illustrated, the results of such a determination indicate that the actual limit is 13.043 percent of *modified net earnings* (*net earnings* if no self-employment taxes are paid) from self-employment. For those self-employed individuals who desire to make a deductible contribution equal to the maximum of 20 percent, a defined contribution plan that combines a discretionary profit sharing plan with a money purchase plan that requires an annual contribution can be established.

QUALIFIED PLANS FOR EMPLOYEES

Since the establishment of employer-qualified plans as part of the Internal Revenue Code of 1954, Congress has expanded the scope of the law to provide similar plans for individual taxpayers who are not covered by an employer plan or who wish to supplement their employer plan.

CASH OR DEFERRED ARRANGEMENTS

Cash or deferred arrangements (CODAs), also known as salary reduction plans or 401k plans, have attained enormous popularity because these plans offer all the tax advantages of a qualified retirement plan and allow employees to make tax excludable contributions to the plan from their own funds. Contributions made on behalf of the employee can come in the form of bonuses paid to the employee, additional salary, or an agreement by the employee to reduce his or her normal salary.[56]

---

[56] Regs. § 1.401(k)-1(a).

One of the major benefits of a CODA is the flexibility it offers an employee. For example, a plan may be designed to allow an employee to defer up to 6 percent of his or her compensation. If the employee elects, he can defer 6 percent, or any smaller amount such as 1, 2, or 3 percent. This gives employees greater control of their taxable income in as much as they may choose annually how much they want in salary and how much they want to place in trust. In addition, loans from the trust are available to the plan participants.

The amount that an employee may elect to defer under a CODA many not exceed $9,240 for 1994.[57] While this figure is adjusted annually for inflation, it must be reduced by contributions to other retirement plans such as tax sheltered annuities and simplified employee plans. Any amounts in excess of this limit must be included in the individual's gross income. Furthermore, the limitations apply to the plan year and not to the calendar year of the individual. Thus, a CODA on a noncalendar year could theoretically allow an employee on a calendar year to defer up to $18,480 ($9,240 × 2) in a single year.

Employer Contributions.   One of the major benefits of a CODA to an employer is that it provides a low-cost method of financing retirement benefits to the employee. Thus, amounts that would have been paid in salaries or wages can now be directed toward the retirement plan. The offsetting administrative expenses of initiating and operating the plan should be relatively low so that they do not detract from its overall benefits. When establishing a CODA, contributions made to the trust should be treated as employer contributions as opposed to employee contributions. This is necessary to ensure the exclusion from income that is available only to contributions made by the employer.[58]

> **Example 15.**   An employee's election form to fund a CODA should not state that she elects to contribute $5,000 of her salary to a CODA. Instead, the election should request that the employer reduce her salary by $5,000 in exchange for the employer's agreement to fund a CODA by the amount of $5,000.

An employer is entitled to take a deduction for a contribution to a CODA of up to 15 percent of an employee's compensation. This 15 percent limit is reduced by the employee's active contribution. Compensation for this purpose is net compensation after considering the employee's contribution.

> **Example 16.**   E, an employee of Z Corporation, desires to make an elective contribution of $8,000 to a qualified CODA. If E's compensation for the year is $110,000, the available contribution that Z Corporation can make for the year is determined as follows:

Compensation..............	$110,000
Less: E's contribution.......	(8,000)
Net Compensation..........	$102,000
Employer limit..............	× 15%
Maximum Contribution......	$ 15,300
Less: E's contribution.......	(8,000)
Available Contribution.......	$ 7,300

---

57   § 402(g)(5).   58   § 414(h)(1).

Plan Requirements. In order to secure the benefits of a CODA, specific requirements must be satisfied. While a detailed explanation is beyond the scope of this coverage, a synopsis of these rules summarizes their features.

1. A CODA must meet the qualification requirements of a profit sharing or stock bonus plan including its participation and coverage requirements.[59]

2. A CODA must provide for an election by each eligible participant to have their employer make payments to a qualified trust or directly to them in cash.[60]

3. Amounts held under a qualified CODA are restricted as to when the funds may be distributed to the employee, and the employee's right to those benefits must be nonforfeitable.[61]

4. Under complicated rules, amounts available for tax deferral may not discriminate in favor of highly compensated employees.[62]

INDIVIDUAL RETIREMENT ACCOUNTS

Congress designed a qualified retirement plan for individuals called an Individual Retirement Account (IRA) in 1974 as part of ERISA. Currently, every taxpayer with earned income can establish an IRA with a commercial bank or savings and loan association. Even taxpayers who are participating in their employer's qualified retirement plan or who make contributions to a Keogh plan may establish an IRA. The annual contribution to an IRA is $2,000 or 100 percent of compensation, whichever is less.[63]

If a taxpayer with earned income has a spouse with minimal or no earned income, the taxpayer may establish a *spousal IRA* into which he or she may make annual contributions on behalf of the spouse. The total contribution into both IRAs is limited to $2,250 or 100 percent of compensation, with no more than $2,000 paid into either IRA.[64]

The deductibility of a taxpayer's annual IRA contribution is determined under a complex set of rules.[65]

1. For a taxpayer who is not an active participant in a qualified retirement plan, the full amount of the annual contribution is deductible.

2. For a taxpayer who is an active participant in a qualified retirement plan, but whose adjusted gross income is below an *applicable dollar amount*, the full amount of the annual contribution is deductible.

3. For a taxpayer who is an active participant in a qualified retirement plan, and whose adjusted gross income is in excess of an *applicable dollar amount*, the deductible amount of the annual contribution is reduced by a percentage. The

---

[59] § 401(k)(2) and (3).

[60] § 401(k)(2)(A).

[61] § 401(k)(2)(B) and (C).

[62] Regs. § 1.401(k)-1(a)(4)(iv).

[63] § 219(b).

[64] § 219(c).

[65] § 219(g).

percentage is calculated by dividing the excess of adjusted gross income (calculated before any deduction for an IRA contribution) over the applicable dollar amount by $10,000.

Once the excess adjusted gross income exceeds $10,000, no portion of a contribution to an IRA is deductible. However, if the excess is less than $10,000, the deductible portion of an IRA contribution shall not be reduced below $200.

The *applicable dollar amounts* are $40,000 for married taxpayers filing jointly, $25,000 for single taxpayers, and $0 for married taxpayers filing separately. On a joint return, the fact that either spouse is an active participant in a qualified plan will cause a reduction in the deductible IRA contributions of both spouses.

Example 17. In the current year, Mr. and Mrs. W had compensation income of $27,000 and $21,000, respectively. Adjusted gross income on their jointly filed tax return was $48,000. During the year, neither Mr. or Mrs. W was an active participant in a qualified retirement plan. Mr. and Mrs. W may each contribute and deduct $2,000 to an IRA.

Example 18. In the current year, Mr. and Mrs. X had compensation income of $17,000 and $8,000, respectively. Adjusted gross income on their jointly filed tax return was $25,000. During the year, Mr. X was an active participant in his employer's qualified pension plan. Mr. and Mrs. X may each contribute and deduct $2,000 to an IRA.

Example 19. In the current year, Mr. and Mrs. Y had compensation income of $20,000 and $28,000, respectively. Adjusted gross income on their jointly filed tax return was $48,000. During the year, Mr. Y was an active participant in his employer's qualified pension plan. Mr. and Mrs. Y may each contribute $2,000 to an IRA. However, the deductible amount of each contribution is *reduced* by $1,600 to $400.

$$\frac{\$8,000 \text{ (excess A.G.I. over applicable dollar amount)}}{\$10,000} \times \$2,000 = \begin{array}{c} \$1,600 \text{ (reduction in deductible} \\ \text{IRA contribution)} \end{array}$$

Example 20. In the current year, Mr. and Mrs. Z had compensation income of $20,000 and $28,000, respectively. During the year, Mr. Z was an active participant in his employer's qualified pension plan. Mr. and Mrs. Z filed separate tax returns on which adjusted gross income equaled compensation. Mr. and Mrs. Z may each contribute $2,000 to an IRA, and Mrs. Z may deduct the full amount of her contribution. However, no amount of the contribution made by Mr. Z is deductible because his excess adjusted gross income over the applicable dollar amount ($0) is more than $10,000.

Income earned in an IRA is tax-exempt, regardless of the deductibility of the contributions to the IRA.[66] When funds are withdrawn from an IRA, an amount of the withdrawal proportionate to any unrecovered non-deductible contributions in the account is not subject to tax; the balance of the withdrawal is fully includible in gross income.[67]

> **Example 21.** In the current year, taxpayer A, age 61, withdrew $9,000 from his IRA, after which the account balance was $26,000. A has made $1,500 of unrecovered nondeductible contributions to the IRA. The nontaxable portion of the withdrawal is $386, computed as follows:
>
> $$\frac{\$1,500 \text{ (nondeductible contributions)}}{\$26,000 + \$9,000 \text{ (account balance before withdrawal)}} \times \$9,000 \text{ withdrawal} = \$386$$
>
> For subsequent years, A's unrecovered nondeductible contributions are $1,114 ($1,500 − $386).

One of the more common reasons for establishing an IRA is for the purpose of *rolling over* a lump sum distribution from a qualified retirement plan. However, a taxpayer who chooses to roll over a lump sum distribution foregoes the right to use any beneficial capital gain or forward averaging rules for computing the tax on the distribution when it is withdrawn from the IRA.

EXCESS CONTRIBUTIONS

The earnings generated by contributions into an IRA are tax deferred. Therefore, taxpayers might be tempted to contribute amounts in excess of the contribution limits so that the excess contribution could yield tax-free income. Unfortunately, a 6 percent penalty tax is imposed on any excess contribution left in an IRA after the close of the taxable year.[68]

SIMPLIFIED EMPLOYEE PENSIONS

The concept of a Simplified Employee Pension (SEP) was added to the law in 1978 to provide employers with a way to avoid the fearsome complexities involved in establishing and maintaining a qualified retirement plan. By following the relatively simple rules of § 408(k), which are designed to prevent discrimination in favor of the prohibited group, an employer may establish a SEP. This qualified plan allows the employer to make contributions directly into an employee's existing IRA, thereby avoiding the necessity of a qualified trust.

The annual limit on SEP contributions is the lesser of 15 percent of employee compensation or $30,000. Employer contributions to a SEP are excludable from an employee's gross income.[69]

---

[66] § 408(c).

[67] § 408(d).

[68] § 4973.

[69] § 402(h).

RETIREMENT PLANNING USING NONQUALIFIED DEFERRED COMPENSATION

For many years employers have designed total compensation packages for valued employees that combined both a current compensation element and a *deferred* compensation element. A nonqualified deferred compensation arrangement typically is one in which the employee is compensated for current services rendered by the employer's promise to pay a certain amount at some future date. Through such an arrangement, an employee is providing for future (perhaps retirement) income. The two questions that must be answered about a deferred compensation arrangement are

1. When is the employee taxed on deferred compensation that is earned currently but will be received in a later year?

2. When is the employer entitled to a business deduction for deferred compensation that will be paid in a later year?

In order to completely answer the first question, an examination of the constructive receipt doctrine is necessary. To thoroughly answer the second, an examination of funded and unfunded plans is required.

CONSTRUCTIVE RECEIPT

The Regulations state that income (both current and deferred) is to be included in gross income for the taxable year in which it is actually or constructively received by the taxpayer.[70] Thus for a cash basis taxpayer, all items that constitute gross income (whether in the form of cash, property, or services) are to be included for the taxable year in which they are actually or constructively received. Consequently, the question to be resolved is whether deferred compensation is constructively received in the taxable year when it is authorized or in the year of actual receipt.

A mere promise to pay, not represented by notes or secured in any way, is not regarded as a receipt of income under the cash receipts and disbursements method. This should not be construed to mean that under the cash receipts and disbursements method income may be taxed only when realized in cash. Income, although not actually received, is constructively received by an individual in the taxable year during which it is credited to his account or set aside for him so that he may draw upon it at a later date.[71] Thus, under the doctrine of constructive receipt, a taxpayer may not deliberately turn his back upon income, nor may a taxpayer, by a private agreement, postpone receipt of income from one year to another.

---

[70] Regs. § 1.451-1(a).   [71] Regs. § 1.451-2(a).

Income is not constructively received if the taxpayer's control of its receipt is subject to substantial limitations or restrictions. Consequently, if a corporation credits its employees with bonus stock, but the stock is not available to those employees until some future date, the mere crediting on the books of the corporation does not constitute constructive receipt. In most cases, speculating whether an employer would have been willing to relinquish a payment earlier or determining a taxpayer's control over funds is not an easy task. As a result, in each case involving a deferral of compensation (especially nonqualified plans), the determination of whether the constructive receipt doctrine is applicable must be made on a fact-and-circumstances basis.

> **Example 22.**   T, a football player, entered into a two-year contract to play football for the California Condors. In addition to his salary, as an inducement for signing the contract, T would be paid a signing bonus of $150,000. Although T could have demanded and received his bonus at the time of signing the contract, T's attorneys suggested that the $150,000 be transferred to an escrow agent to be held for five years and then paid to T over the next five years as an annuity. If T should die, the escrow account would become part of his estate. Because T controlled the terms of payment, the $150,000 bonus must be included in T's gross income in the year in which the club unconditionally paid the amount to the escrow agent. The employer's obligation for payment terminated when the amount of the bonus was fixed at $150,000 and irrevocably set aside for T's sole benefit.[72]

UNFUNDED DEFERRED COMPENSATION PLANS

If an employer contractually promises to pay deferred compensation to an employee and does not set aside current funds in some type of trust arrangement, the employee is put in the position of an unsecured creditor of the employer. If the employee is a cash basis taxpayer and does not have any current right to payment under the deferred compensation plan, there is no constructive receipt of the compensation and thus no current taxable income to the employee. The employee will not be taxed until the year in which the deferred compensation is actually paid.[73]

From the employer's point of view, such unfunded arrangements are attractive because they do not require any current cash outflow from the business. However, neither a cash basis nor an accrual basis employer may take a deduction for deferred compensation until the deferred amount is includible in the employee's gross income.[74]

FUNDED DEFERRED COMPENSATION PLANS

Employees who agree to a nonqualified deferred compensation arrangement normally prefer that their employers secure the promise of future compensation by transferring current funds into an independent trust for the employee's benefit. While these employees desire the protection of a fund plan, they do not wish to subject those funds to current taxation. Therefore, innovative methods have been devised to allow deferral of an employee's income under a funded method by making the employee's interest in those funds forfeitable.

---

[72] Rev. Rul. 55-527, 1955-2 C.B 25.   [74] Rev. Rul. 69-650, 1969-2 C.B. 106.

[73] Rev. Rul. 69-649, 1969-2 C.B. 106.

To this end, an employer can establish one of many types of trusts. Two of the more common nonqualified arrangements are the *Rabbi trust* and the *Secular trust*. The rules of § 83, discussed earlier in the chapter, apply to these funded deferred compensation plans.[75]

Rabbi Trusts.   Rabbi trusts are so named because the first IRS ruling that approved this arrangement involved a fund established by a congregation for its rabbi. In the typical Rabbi trust arrangement, the rights of employees are forfeitable, so an employee will not recognize taxable income until he or she actually receives a distribution from the trust. If a deferred compensation arrangement provides that employees' rights in the retirement fund eventually become nonforfeitable (i.e., vested), an employee must recognize taxable income in the year his or her rights vest. In both cases, the employer will receive a deduction only in the taxable year in which the deferred compensation is includible in the gross income of the employee.[76]

> **Example 23.**   As part of a deferred compensation arrangement, employer X agrees to place $10,000 annually into a trust account for employee Y. Y's rights to the trust funds are forfeitable until he completes 10 years of service for X. In the year in which Y's risk of forfeiture lapses, the value of the trust funds is included in Y's gross income. Subsequent payments into the fund by X are fully taxable to Y.[77]

A disadvantage of the Rabbi trust is that if the employer gets into financial difficulty, the trust assets are subject to the claims of the employer's creditors. In addition, any income that is generated by the trust will be taxable to the employer.

Secular Trusts.   Designed in 1988, the secular trust is a variation of the Rabbi trust.[78] Under a Secular trust, the employee receives a vested interest in the full amount of the transfer to the trust. Because the employee has a nonforfeitable interest, the employee is taxed immediately on the transfer of funds to the trust even though he or she has not actually received the funds. In return for the transfer, the employer receives an immediate deduction. The advantage of this arrangement is that the trust assets are not subject to the claims of the employer's creditors. The disadvantage, of course, is that the funds are immediately taxable to the employee. A Secular trust differs from a Rabbi trust, because the assets of the Rabbi trust will not be protected from the creditors of the employer in the event of bankruptcy.

STOCK OPTIONS

As an alternative to the payment of compensation in the form of corporate stock, corporate employers may issue *options* to purchase stock at a specified price to employees whom the company wants to retain. As a general rule, stock options have no value on the date they are issued because the option price is equal to or greater than the market price of the stock. Consequently, the options will have value to the recipient (and become a cost to the employer) *only if* the market price of the shares increases.

---

[75]   § 402(b).

[76]   § 404(a)(5).

[77]   Reg. § 1.402(b)-1(b).

[78]   PLR8841023.

If an option has no value upon date of grant to an employee, the employee obviously has not received taxable income. However, in certain unusual cases options may have a value at date of grant. If such value can be determined with reasonable accuracy under criteria provided in Regulation § 1.83-7(b)(2), the value represents compensation income to the recipient of the option. If an option is actively traded on an established market, it is deemed to have an ascertainable value at date of grant.[79]

Example 24. Corporation C grants employee D an option to purchase 100 shares of C common stock for $10 a share at any time over the next ten years. If C stock is selling at $9 per share, D's option has no readily ascertainable value. Therefore, D has no taxable income at date of grant, and a zero tax basis in the option. If, however, D's option is actively traded on an established market and as a result can be valued at $5, D has received taxable compensation of that amount, and will have a $5 basis in the option.

OPTION EXERCISE

When the owner of a stock option that had no ascertainable value at date of grant exercises the option, the difference between the option price and the market price (bargain element) of the stock purchased represents ordinary income to the owner. If the option had an ascertainable value at date of grant, so that the recipient recognized taxable income upon receipt of the option, no additional income is recognized when the option is exercised.[80]

Example 25. In 1991 employee M received certain stock options as part of her compensation from Corporation Q. At date of grant, the options had no ascertainable value. However, in 1994 M exercised the options and purchased 1,000 shares of Q stock, market value $90 per share, for the option price of $60 per share. In 1994 M must recognize $30,000 of ordinary income ($30 per share bargain element × 1,000 shares). M's tax basis in her shares is $90,000.

From the employer's point of view, the value of a stock option can be taken as a deduction under the previously discussed rule of § 83(h). Generally, an employer will receive a deduction at date of grant if the option has a readily ascertainable value. If the option has no value at date of grant, the deduction will equal the income recognized by the owner of the option when the option is exercised.

INCENTIVE STOCK OPTIONS

In the past, Congress has experimented with a variety of *qualified stock options*—options afforded preferential tax treatment under § 421. Currently there is only a single type of qualified option, the Incentive Stock Option (ISO) of § 422A.[81]

---

[79] Reg. § 1.83-7(b)(1).

[80] Reg. § 1.83-7(a).

[81] The rules of § 422A apply to options granted on or after January 1, 1976 and outstanding on January 1, 1981.

Under § 421(a), the exercise of an ISO will not result in any income recognition to the owner. Correspondingly, the corporate employer who issued the option will never receive any deduction for the spread between option and market price at date of exercise. If and when the stock received upon exercise is sold, the employee will realize capital gain equal to the difference between the option price and selling price. The difference in tax consequences between a nonqualified stock option and an ISO is presented in the example below.

Example 26. Employee T was granted an option in 1988 to purchase *one* share of his corporate employer's stock at any time within the two succeeding calendar years. At the time the option was granted, the option price was $150 and the market price was $140. Assume that T exercised the option in 1990 when the stock had a market price of $200, and the stock acquired was sold in 1994 for $375. The tax consequences for each tax year would be as follows:

	Nonqualified Stock Option	Incentive Stock Option
1988	None	None
1990	Market price of $200 − $150 option price = $50 ordinary income and $200 basis in purchased stock ($150 cost + $50 income recognized). Employer deduction = $50	No income and $150 basis in purchased stock
1994	Sale price of $375 − $200 basis = $175 capital gain.	Sale price of $375 − $150 basis = $225 capital gain.

HOLDING PERIOD REQUIREMENTS

For the beneficial rule of § 421(a) to apply, an individual may not dispose of the stock purchased upon exercise of the ISO within two years from the date of the granting of the option and within one year from the date of exercise.[82] Additionally, the individual must be an employee of either the corporation granting the ISO or a parent, subsidiary, or successor corporation from the date of grant until the day three months before the date of exercise.[83]

If an individual violates the holding period requirement by disposing of his or her stock too quickly after purchase, § 421(b) provides that the *compensation income* (ordinary income) the individual did not recognize at date of exercise must be recognized in the year of disposition. Any gain so recognized increases the cost basis of the stock.[84] In such a situation the employer will be entitled to a corresponding deduction.

---

[82] § 422A(a)(1).

[83] § 422A(a)(2).

[84] Reg. § 1.421-5(b)(2).

Example 27.   Beta Corporation grants an ISO to employee Z on November 1, 1988. The option allows Z to purchase 500 shares of Beta stock at $3 per share. Z exercises the option on December 1, 1993, when Beta stock is selling for $7 per share. Z sells his 500 shares on March 1, 1994 for $9 per share. Because of the premature disposition (less than one year from date of exercise), Z must recognize $2,000 ordinary income [500 shares × $4 bargain price ($7 market price − $3 option price)] and a $1,000 capital gain in 1994. Additionally, Beta Corporation may claim a $2,000 deduction in 1994.

If the amount realized on a premature sale is less than the value of the stock at date of exercise, only the excess of the amount realized over the option price is recognized as ordinary income.[85]

Example 28.   Refer to the facts in *Example 27*. If Z sold his Beta stock for $6 rather than $9 a share, his ordinary income (and Beta's deduction) would be limited to $1,500 [500 shares × $3 bargain price ($6 selling price − $3 option price)].

QUALIFICATION REQUIREMENTS

An employee stock option must meet a number of statutory requirements set forth in § 422A(b) to qualify as an ISO. The primary requirements are as follows:

1. The option is granted pursuant to a plan that specifies the total number of shares that may be issued under options and the class of employees eligible to receive the options. The shareholders of the corporation must approve the plan within twelve months before or after the date the plan is adopted.

2. The options are granted within ten years of the date of adoption or the date of shareholder approval, whichever is earlier.

3. The option price is not less than the market value of the stock at date of grant.

4. The option must be exercised within ten years of date of grant.

5. The option can only be exercised by the recipient employee during his or her lifetime and can only be transferred at the employee's death.

6. The recipient of the option does not own stock possessing more than 10 percent of the total combined voting power of all classes of stock of the employer corporation or of its parent or subsidiary corporation.[86]

A major restriction on the use of ISOs is the statutory requirement that the value of stock with respect to which ISOs are *exercisable* shall not exceed $100,000 per calendar year per employee. For purposes of this requirement, the value of the stock is determined at date of grant.[87]

---

[85] § 422A(c)(2).

[86] § 422A(c)(6) waives this requirement in certain cases.

[87] § 422A(b)(7).

Example 29.   In calendar year 1993, Corporation Q granted Employee F an ISO to purchase 1,000 shares of Q stock with a current aggregate value of $200,000. In calendar year 1994, Corporation Q granted Employee F a second ISO to purchase 1,200 shares of Q stock with a current aggregate value of $300,000. If Employee F decides to exercise any of her ISOs in 1994, she may only purchase 500 shares through exercise of her 1993 option or 400 shares through exercise of her 1994 option.

NONQUALIFIED STOCK OPTIONS

A Nonqualified Stock Option (NQSO), also referred to as a nonstatutory stock option, is generally any option that does not meet the statutory requirements in the Code to be treated as an Incentive Stock Option (ISO). NQSOs are often used as implements of deferred compensation because the corporation can avail itself of a tax deduction without a cash outlay and the options themselves can be issued with more flexible terms than ISOs. The only major disadvantage of using an NQSO is the potential for income recognition to the employee. That potential is, in turn, dependent upon whether the option has a readily ascertainable fair market value.

Readily Ascertainable Fair Market Value.   If an option is actively traded on an established exchange (e.g., American Stock Exchange or Chicago Board of Options Exchange), it is deemed to have a readily ascertainable fair market value. An option that is not traded on an established exchange will not have a readily ascertainable fair market value unless it can be measured with reasonable accuracy. The Regulations support this presumption with detailed conditions for determining value.[88]

Determining value is important because, if the option has a readily ascertainable fair market value at the time of grant, the employee will be taxed immediately. Any gain or loss that accrues after the time of the grant will be recognized as capital gain or loss on the disposition of the underlying stock. When gain is recognized, the employee's basis in the stock includes any amounts paid for the stock plus the amount that was recognized as ordinary income at the time of the grant. The corporate employer takes a deduction in the same year (and for the same amount) income is recognized by the employee.[89] It is important to notice that the result of these options is conditioned on establishing a value for the option and not establishing a value for the stock of the corporation.

No Readily Ascertainable Fair Market Value.   If an option does not have a readily ascertainable fair market value, the transaction will remain "open," and the employee will not be taxed when the option is granted. Instead, the employee recognizes ordinary income when the option is exercised. The amount of income to be recognized is the spread between the value of the stock purchased and the price paid at the date of exercise. Any appreciation in the stock after the exercise date will be recognized as capital gain. The corporate employer takes a corresponding tax deduction in the same year and to the extent of ordinary income recognized by the employee.

---

[88]   Regs. § 1.83-7(b)(2).   [89]   Regs. § 1.421-6(c), (d), (e), and (f).

Example 30. On January 1, 1994 R Corporation grants S, an employee, the option to purchase 1,000 shares for $12 per share on or before August 15, 1995. At the time of the grant, R stock is valued at $20 per share. On June 3, 1995, when the value of R stock is $35, S exercises the option and acquires the stock for $12,000 (1,000 × $12). On November 1, 1995 S sells the stock for $48,000 (1,000 × $48). If the option granted has no readily ascertainable fair market value, S will recognize $23,000 ($35,000 − $12,000) of ordinary income and a $13,000 ($48,000 − $35,000) capital gain, both in 1995. R takes a deduction of $23,000 in 1995. If on the other hand, the option has a readily ascertainable value (for example $8 per share), S must recognize $8,000 of ordinary income in 1994 (the grant date) and a capital gain of $28,000 in 1995 (the sale date). R will take an $8,000 deduction in 1994.

STOCK APPRECIATION RIGHTS

Occasionally, NQSOs can create a problem for employees when they generate taxable income without providing resources to pay the tax. Unfortunately, when this occurs, some employees find it necessary to sell the stock to raise the capital, and this defeats the purpose of providing equity compensation. To ameliorate this dilemma, some employers wrap a NQSO with a Stock Appreciation Right (SAR).

An SAR is a type of right (similar to an option) that entitles the employee to a cash payment equal to the difference between the fair market value of one share of the common stock of the corporation on the date of the *exercise* of the SAR over its fair market value on the date it was *granted*. An employee need not own any stock of the corporation to receive an SAR, and SARs are granted without cost to the employee. An SAR cannot be exercised before one year after it was granted and must be exercised by the fifth year, or the SAR will be deemed exercised and cash will be paid to the employee. An SAR is not included in taxable income until the year the right is exercised. The IRS has ruled that an employee who receives an SAR will not be in constructive receipt of income in the year it was granted.[90]

---

[90] Rev. Rul. 80-300, 1980-2 C.B. 165.

TAX PLANNING CONSIDERATIONS

The area of employment compensation and retirement planning offers tremendous opportunity for creative tax planning. During a taxpayer's productive years, he or she needs to be able to analyze and appreciate the tax consequences of the various types of compensation alternatives that may be offered. The taxpayer must be aware of the tradeoff between types of compensation that will be taxed currently and fringe benefits that may not be taxable upon receipt. Sophisticated forms of compensation such as § 83 property and incentive stock options should be considered in designing a specialized compensation package.

Taxpayers should also appreciate the necessity for long-range retirement planning. An understanding of the different tax consequences of qualified and nonqualified retirement plans is essential to effective planning for post employment years. Exhibit 18-8 contains a comparison of the plans discussed in this chapter.

PLANNING FOR RETIREMENT INCOME

One of the central features of an individual's financial plan should be a provision for some source of retirement income. As the life span of the average American lengthens, the number of prospective retirement years increases. As a result, many individuals realize that some amount of current investment is necessary in order to ensure that their retirement years can be a period of financial security.

In analyzing a particular retirement plan, two basic questions must be answered:

1. Are payments into the plan deductible for Federal income tax purposes by the taxpayer?

2. To what extent are retirement benefits received from a plan includible in the recipient taxpayer's gross income?

ADVANTAGES OF IRAs

IRAs used to be among the best retirement saving plans around until Congress clipped some of their more generous features in 1986. Today they are still a useful part of many retirement portfolios; however, some limitations will apply.

Prior to 1987, IRAs were available to anyone who had not reached the age of 70½. Contributions were allowable up to the $2,000 annual limit and were fully tax deductible. Today, these rules apply to only two types of people:

- Those who are not eligible for an employer-sponsored retirement plan; or

- Those whose incomes fall below specified levels.

Exhibit 18-6 *Available IRA Deductions*

A.G.I. Before IRA Deduction	Single or Head of Household	Married, Filing Jointly, or Widower	Married, Filing Seperately
$0 – $10,000	full	full	partial
$10,000 – $25,000	full	full	NONE
$25,000 – $35,000	partial	full	NONE
$35,000 – $40,000	NONE	full	NONE
$40,000 – $50,000	NONE	partial	NONE
$50,000+	NONE	NONE	NONE

* Locate income and filing status. If the word *full* appears, a $2,000 deduction is available; if *NONE* appears, no deduction is available; and if *partial* appears, a prorated amount is deductible.

For individuals with company retirement plans, deductible IRAs are still available, provided certain tests can be satisfied. The first test of IRA deductibility is income. A taxpayer may still make a fully deductible IRA contribution as long as A.G.I does not exceed certain levels. Exhibit 18-6 provides a list of eligible individuals and the limitations on IRA deductions.

> **Example 31.**   H and W have A.G.I. of $42,000 and file a joint tax return. Their table amount indicates they are entitled to a partial deduction. To determine their deduction, subtract their A.G.I. from the limit for that particular row ($50,000 − $42,000 to get $8,000). Next, divide that amount ($8,000) by $10,000 to get a percentage ($8,000/$10,000 = 80%). This is the percentage of the IRA base, $2,000, that may be deducted. Accordingly, H and W may deduct $1,600.
>
> *Note* that the taxpayers may still *contribute* the full $2,000, but cannot deduct the extra $400.

SPOUSAL IRAs

Holding a job is not a prerequisite to opening and deducting an IRA. A nonworking spouse may start a *spousal IRA,* as long as both taxpayers file jointly and the nonworking spouse's earned income totals less than $250. When these two requirements are met, each spouse may make contributions to an IRA. Together, they may contribute as much as $2,250 in any single year. No more than $2,000 of that amount, however, may go to either account. If a spouse's earned income exceeds $250, the deduction is not lost. The spouse just opens his or her own IRA and contributes as much as 100 percent of his or her income (up to $2,000) to it.

Exhibit 18-7 *Active Participation*

Participation in any of the following plans can make a taxpayer an active participant and *not* eligible to deduct IRA contributions.

- Qualified pension, profit sharing, or stock bonus plans, including Keogh plans
- Qualified annuity plans
- Simplified employee pension plans (SEPs)
- Retirement plans for federal, state, or local government employees
- Certain union plans [so-called § 501(c)(18) plans]
- Tax-sheltered annuities for public school teachers and employees of charitable organizations.
- § 401(k) plans

WHAT IS AN ACTIVE PARTICIPANT?

As discussed earlier, an individual may not be eligible for a deductible IRA if he or she is an active participant or eligible to participate in a pension or profit sharing plan. As a general rule, the IRS considers a taxpayer an active participant in a defined plan if the plan's guidelines state that the taxpayer is covered, even if they decline to participate. As a result, just being eligible for a plan makes the taxpayer an active participant.

If an individual is not sure if he is an active participant, he can look at his W-2 form, provided by his employer. It provides a box for the taxpayer's employer to check. If this box is blank, additional research may be necessary. Exhibit 18-7 provides aid in determining whether a taxpayer is eligible to participate.

MAKING A NONDEDUCTIBLE CONTRIBUTION TO AN IRA

Even if a taxpayer is not eligible, for whatever reason, to make deductible contributions to an IRA, a nondeductible contribution is available. Whether a taxpayer should make a nondeductible IRA contribution depends on the circumstances. Some of the following pros and cons should be considered before a taxpayer makes a decision.

The most obvious pro is that even though a taxpayer may not deduct his or her annual IRA contribution, the earnings from IRA investments accumulate and compound tax-deferred. This means a faster fund build-up compared to a taxable savings account. (See Exhibit 18-2 for a similar comparison.)

The most obvious con is that once money is put into an IRA, it is locked in until the taxpayer attains the age 59 ½. Otherwise, the taxpayer is subject to pay a 10 percent penalty for early withdrawal. The penalty applies to the deductible portion of the IRA contribution and to any earnings that may have accumulated tax-deferred in the account. However, no penalty applies when nondeductible contributions are withdrawn.

Exhibit 18-8 *Comparison of Retirement Plans*

Description	Corporate Plan	Keogh [HR 10]	IRA	SEP	CODA (401(k))	Funded Rabbi	Funded Secular
Qualified	Yes	Yes	Yes	Yes	Yes	No	No
Participation	21 years old or > 1 year = 100% vested	21 years old or > 1 year = 100% vested	Limited by AGI	21 years old or 3 out of 5 years service	1 year's service	No Requirements	
Limitations	25% | $30,000 or 15% or $118,800 | 100% Avg.	20% | $30,000 or 13.043% or $118,800 | 100% Avg.	$2,000 or 100% Earned Income	$30,000 or 15% Earned Income	$8,994 (for 1993)	No limitations if paid as reasonable compensation	
Vesting	5 years Cliff or 7 years Graded	5 years Cliff or 7 years Graded	100%	100%	100% of employee's contribution	Subject to claims of creditors	100%
Premature Distributions	Rollover or 10% Penalty	Rollover or 10% Penalty	Rollover or 10% Penalty	Rollover or 10% Penalty	Rollover or 10% Penalty	Taxable only if not previously taxed	
Lump-Sum 5/10 yr Averaging Available	Yes	Yes	No, taxed as Ordinary Income	No, taxed as Ordinary Income	Yes	Not available: In some cases funds previously taxed	
Date Plan Must Be Established	By last day of plan year	By last day of plan year	Regular tax due date	Regular tax due date	By last day of plan year	By last day of plan year	
Required Date to Contribute	Extended due date	Extended due date	Regular due date	Regular due date	Extended due date	Year end	
Employee Loans From the Plan	Limited	None: Owner-Employees	None	None	Limited	Yes, but very risky	Yes

Many investment counselors suggest tax-free bonds as a reasonable alternative to making a nondeductible IRA contribution. The earnings from the bonds are tax-free and are not subject to a penalty if the taxpayer needs to withdraw any of the money. Moreover, a taxpayer is not limited to investing $2,000 ($2,250 for spousal IRAs).

Bonds, however, come with two potential drawbacks. First, a taxpayer can possibly get locked into the bonds until maturity. If interest rates rise, the value of the bonds generally declines, and a taxpayer would potentially have to sell the bonds at a loss. Second, depending on the market, the yields on bonds are sometimes low compared to the after-tax yields of other securities. So, potentially, bonds can be a very poor investment.

PROBLEM MATERIALS

DISCUSSION QUESTIONS

18-1 *Taxation of Barter Transactions.* Your friend who is a practicing dentist tells you that he filled a tooth for a friend's child "for no payment" because the friend had prepared the dentist's income tax return for the previous year. Must the dentist recognize taxable income because of this arrangement? Explain.

18-2 *Taxation of Fringe Benefits.* Define the term *fringe benefit*. As a general rule are fringe benefits taxable?

18-3 *Taxation of Fringe Benefits.* Every year, Employer E gives each employee the choice of a turkey or ham as a Christmas "gift." Is the value of this fringe benefit taxable to the employees? Would your answer be different if each employee received a Christmas bonus of $500 cash?

18-4 *Fringe Benefits—Cafeteria Plans.* What is a cafeteria plan of employee benefits?

18-5 *Reasons for Stock Options.* How does a corporation benefit from compensating valuable employees with shares of stock in the corporation rather than a cash wage or salary?

18-6 *Receipt of Restricted Property for Services.* What factors should a taxpayer consider when deciding to make an election under § 83(b) with regards to restricted property?

18-7 *ISO Plans.* An ISO (incentive stock option) allows the recipient both a deferral of income and a conversion of ordinary income into capital gain. Explain.

18-8 *Funded versus Unfunded Deferred Compensation Arrangements.* Why would an employee normally prefer a funded rather than an unfunded deferred compensation arrangement? Which would the employer normally prefer?

18-9 *Deferred Compensation and the Constructive Receipt Doctrine.* Explain the doctrine of constructive receipt as it relates to a cash basis employee who has a deferred compensation arrangement with his or her employer.

18-10 *Tax Advantages of Qualified Retirement Plans.* Discuss the tax advantages granted to qualified retirement plans.

18-11 *Defined Benefit versus Defined Contribution Plans.* Differentiate between a defined benefit retirement plan and a defined contribution retirement plan.

18-12 *Retirement Plan Qualification Requirements.* Any employee of Trion Ltd. Partnership can participate in the company's pension plan after they have been employed by Trion for 36 consecutive months. Can Trion's plan be a qualified retirement plan? Discuss.

18-13 *The Meaning of Vested Benefits.* Explain the concept of vesting as it relates to qualified retirement plans. How does it differ from the concept of participation?

18-14 *Profit Sharing Plans versus Pension Plans.* Many small, developing companies will choose to establish a qualified profit sharing plan rather than a pension plan. Why?

18-15 *Spousal IRAs.* Discuss the purpose of a spousal IRA (individual retirement account).

18-16 *Lump Sum Distribution Rollovers.* Why might an employee who receives a lump sum distribution from a qualified retirement plan choose to roll over the distribution into an IRA? What are the negative tax consequences of doing so?

PROBLEMS

18-17 *Receipt of Restricted Property for Services.* D, a calendar year taxpayer, is an employee of M Corporation, also on a calendar year for tax purposes. In 1994 M Corporation transfers 100 shares of its own common stock to D as a bonus for his outstanding work during the year. If D quits his job with M within the next three years, he must return the shares to the corporation. At date of transfer, the shares are selling on the open market at $35 per share. Three years later, when the risk of forfeiture lapses, the stock is selling at $100 per share.

  a. Assume D does not make the election under § 83(b). How much income must he recognize in 1994 because of his receipt of the stock? In 1997 when his restriction lapses?

  b. Assume D does elect under § 83(b). How much income must he recognize in 1994? In 1997?

  c. Refer to questions (a) and (b). In each case how much of a deduction may M Corporation claim and in which year should the deduction be taken?

18-18 *Tax Consequences of a Nonqualified Stock Option Plan.* In 1994 Z Corporation grants a nonqualified stock option to employee M. The option allows M to purchase 100 shares of Z Corporation stock for $20 per share at any time during the next four years. Because the current market value of Z stock is $22 per share, the option has a readily ascertainable value of $200 ($2 per share bargain element × 100 shares) at date of grant. M exercises the option in 1996 when the market value of the Z stock has increased to $28 per share.

  a. How much income does M recognize in 1994 because of the receipt of the option?
  b. How much income does M recognize in 1996 upon exercise of the option?
  c. What amount of deduction is available to Corporation Z because of the option granted to M? In what year is the deduction claimed?

18-19 *Tax Consequences of a Nonqualified Stock Option Plan.* In 1994 X Corporation grants a nonqualified stock option to E, a valued employee, as additional compensation. The option has no value at date of grant, but entitles E to purchase 1,000 shares of X stock for $20 per share at any time during the next five years. E exercises the option in 1995, when X Corporation's stock is selling on the open market at $48 per share.

  a. How much income does E recognize in 1994 because of her receipt of the option?
  b. How much income does E recognize in 1995 upon exercise of the option?
  c. What amount of deduction is available to X Corporation because of the option granted to E? In what year is the deduction claimed?

18-20 *Nonqualified Stock Option Plans.* Refer to the facts in Problems 18-18 and 18-19. In each case, what tax basis does the employee have in the purchased corporate stock?

18-21 *Incentive Stock Options (ISO) versus Nonqualified Stock Options.* Refer to the facts in Problem 18-19. If the stock option issued by X corporation had been an ISO rather than a nonqualified option, how much income would E recognize in 1995 upon option exercise?

18-22 *Incentive Stock Option Plans.* In May 1993 employee N exercised an ISO that entitled him to purchase 50 shares of Clay Corporation common stock for $120 a share. The stock was selling on the open market for $210 per share. N sold the 50 shares in 1996 for $390 per share.

    a.   How much income must N recognize in 1993 upon exercise of the option?

    b.   How much income must N recognize in 1996 upon sale of the Clay stock?

18-23 *Incentive Stock Options—Early Disposition of Stock.* Refer to the facts in Problem 18-22. What would be the tax consequences if N sold the Clay stock in August 1993 for $250 per share? For $190 per share?

18-24 *Tax Computation on Lump Sum Distributions.* T participated in his employer's qualified profit sharing plan from 1980 until his retirement at age 64 in the current year. T made no contributions to the plan. In the current year, T received a lump sum distribution of $75,000 from the plan.

    a.   How much of the distribution is taxable to T in the current year?

    b.   Assuming T is single with no dependents, does not itemize deductions, and has only $13,000 of other taxable income, use the five-year forward averaging method to compute his current-year tax liability.

18-25 *Tax Computation on Lump Sum Distributions.* In the current year, Mrs. Z, age 61, retired after a 35-year career with the same corporate employer. She received her entire $51,000 account balance from her employer's qualified profit sharing plan. In the current year, Mrs. Z and her husband will file a joint return on which they will report $21,000 of other taxable income (net of all deductions and exemptions). If Mrs. Z elects five-year averaging, compute the tax liability on the joint return.

18-26 *Qualified Pension Plan—Maximum Annual Benefits.* During his last three years as president of R Corporation, G was paid $200,000, $230,000, and $280,000 as total compensation for his services. These were the three highest compensation years of his employment. What is the maximum retirement benefit payable to G from the corporation's qualified pension plan?

18-27 *Qualified Profit Sharing Plans—Maximum Annual Contribution.* In the current year, Mr. W, a corporate vice president, earned a base salary of $350,000. His corporate employer maintains a qualified retirement plan that provides for an annual contribution equal to 10 percent of each employee's base level of compensation. Based on these facts, compute the maximum current-year contribution to Mr. W's retirement account.

18-28 *Additional Taxes on Plan Distributions.* In the current year, Mr. L, age 51 and in perfect health, resigns as President of Meta Industries, Inc. Mr. L receives a $300,000 lump sum distribution from Meta's qualified retirement plan. Before consideration of this distribution, Mr. L's taxable income for the year is over $200,000. If Mr. L decides not to "roll over" the contribution into another qualified plan or IRA, compute the net after-tax amount of the distribution that Mr. L will be able to spend.

18-29 *Maximum Annual Contributions to Keogh Plans.*   H is a self-employed businessman with several employees. He has established a profit sharing plan for himself and his employees. The annual net earned income from his business is $132,000. What is the maximum amount of a deduction available to H for his contribution to the plan for the year?

18-30 *Maximum Annual Contributions to IRAs.*   H and W file a joint tax return. W is a lawyer with current-year earned income of $65,000. H works part-time as a landscape architect and earned $22,000 in the current year.

a.   Assume that W is an active participant in the firm's qualified profit sharing plan. How much may W and H contribute to their IRAs for the current year? How much of the contribution is deductible?

b.   Assume neither H nor W is an active participant in a qualified retirement plan. How does this assumption change your answers to (a) above?

18-31 *Maximum Deductible Contributions to IRAs.*   In the current year, Ms. A, a single tax-payer, contributed $1,400 to her IRA. She also is an active participant in her employer's qualified money purchase pension plan. Ms. A's adjusted gross income (before any deduction for her IRA contribution) is $29,640. How much of the IRA contribution is deductible?

18-32 *Taxability of IRA Distributions.*   Taxpayer B, age 66, makes his first withdrawal of $8,800 from his IRA in the current year and uses the money to make a downpayment on a sailboat. At the end of the year, B's IRA balance is $36,555. During previous years, B had made nondeductible contributions to the IRA totalling $13,400. Based on these facts, what amount of the $8,800 withdrawal must B include in current-year gross income?

18-33 *Simplified Employee Pensions.*   Z is an employee of a company that has established a SEP. Z's current-year salary is $18,000.

a.   How much may Z's employer contribute to her IRA during the current year?

b.   May Z make any additional deductible contribution herself to her IRA?

RESEARCH PROBLEM

18-34 *Current versus Deferred Compensation.*   Roy Hartman is a 55-year-old executive of the Robco Oil Tool Corporation. The corporation does not have any type of qualified pension or profit sharing plan, nor does it intend to adopt one in the near future. However, in an effort to ensure the continuing services of Mr. Hartman, Robco Corporation has offered him a choice between two different compensation arrangements. One pays $40,000 additional annual salary; and the other provides for $50,000 a year deferred compensation for 10 years beginning when Roy retires at age 65. Currently, Hartman's marginal tax rate is 31 percent. Roy does not expect to be in a lower tax bracket within his last 10 years of employment or after retirement. Since he does not need the $28,800 which would remain after paying current taxes on the $40,000 additional annual salary, Mr. Hartman asks you to evaluate his alternative compensation proposals. Assuming a 10 percent pre-tax return on savings will prevail over the entire 20 year period (10 years before and 10 years after retirement), and assuming that he would save the entire $28,800 annual after-tax salary under the $40,000 additional annual compensation arrangement, which alternative would you recommend? Why?

Upon completion of this chapter you will be able to

- Understand the basic rules governing the taxation of the four business forms: sole proprietorships, partnerships, S corporations, and C corporations

- Identify the major differences between the taxation of individuals and corporations

- Compute the net taxable income or loss for the four types of business organizations

- Explain the advantages and disadvantages of each of the business forms

- Explain the basic tax consequences of forming a new business, including

  - Determination of any gain to be recognized by the owners

  - Determination of the basis of the owner's interest in the business and the business' basis in the property received

CHAPTER OUTLINE

Sole Proprietorships	19-1	C Corporations	19-19
Partnerships	19-5	Taxation of Corporate Operations in General	19-19
Taxation of Partnership Operations	19-5		
Transactions between Partnership and Partners	19-11	Differences between Corporate and Individual Taxation	19-22
S Corporations	19-13	Formation of a Business	19-30
Election of S Corporation Status	19-14	Formation of a Sole Proprietorship	19-31
Making the S Election	19-14	Formation of Partnerships	19-32
Taxation of S Corporation Operations	19-15	Formation of Corporations	19-33
Transactions between an S Corporation and Its Shareholders	19-15	Problem Materials	19-47

Chapter 19

TAXATION OF
BUSINESS FORMS
AND THEIR OWNERS

For most people, their only encounter with the income tax is the annual filing of their own personal income tax returns. It is clearly an experience that few enjoy. Having endured the filing of an individual income tax return, it would seem to most that the taxation of business must be exceedingly complex since businesses are usually involved in far more complicated transactions than individuals. While this may be the case in some instances, the truth is that the basic computation of the taxable income of a business differs little from that of an individual. In this sense, whatever one knows about individual taxation generally serves them well when trying to understand business taxation. Many are quite surprised to find that most of the general rules that apply to individuals also apply to businesses. For example, the basic tax formula used to compute taxable income is identical for each: gross income minus deductions equals taxable income. And the elements of that formula, gross income and deductions, are defined in the same manner for businesses as they are for individuals. Nevertheless, despite the similarities of individual and business taxation, there are differences. This chapter examines the tax rules that apply to the basic forms of organizations used to carry on business in the United States: sole proprietorships, partnerships, and corporations. The chapter initially focuses on the taxation of routine operations and concludes with a brief overview of the tax consequences of forming a particular type of business organization. For an in-depth discussion of these organizational forms, consult the second volume of this two-volume series, *Corporate, Partnership, Estate, and Gift Taxation*.

SOLE PROPRIETORSHIPS

More businesses are operated as sole proprietorships than any other form. This is a reflection, in part, of our entrepreneurial society. But it also is due to the fact that sole proprietorships are the simplest form of business—personally, legally, and for tax purposes.

The tax treatment of a sole proprietorship differs somewhat from the treatment used in financial accounting. For financial accounting purposes, sole proprietorships are treated as entities separate and distinct from their owners. For tax purposes, however, the sole proprietorship is not a separate taxable entity. The sole proprietorship does not file a separate tax return. Instead, the relevant information of the sole proprietorship is reported on the individual's personal income tax return along with the individual's other items of income and deduction. The proprietorship's income and deductions are not merely thrown together with all of the other items, however. They are segregated—at least somewhat. All of the *ordinary* income and deductions relating to the proprietorship's operations are captured on a separate schedule, Schedule C (or Schedule F for farming operations), which accompanies the individual's Form 1040 (see Exhibit 19-1).[1] Note that the net income of the proprietorship reported on line 31 of Schedule C is transferred to line 12 on page 1 of Form 1040 to become part of the individual's total adjusted gross income. All items subject to special tax treatment, such as capital gains and losses, charitable contributions, and dividend income are reported on the appropriate tax return schedule (e.g., Schedule D for capital gains and Schedule A for charitable contributions) as though the owner engaged in the transactions rather than the proprietorship.

Actual determination of a sole proprietorship's income simply requires the application of the basic rules applying to an individual. Like other businesses, the net income of the proprietorship is generally the gross income from operations less the costs of doing business. The major difference between the taxation of proprietorships and other forms of business lies in its lack of uniqueness. Because the sole proprietorship is not treated as a separate entity, the owner cannot enter into taxable transactions with the proprietorship as a creditor, an employee, a customer, or in any other role. For example, a sole proprietor does not receive a salary from the proprietorship. His or her "compensation" is simply the net income of the business. As a result, a sole proprietor is not subject to normal payroll taxes. Instead, a sole proprietorship's net ordinary income is subject to self-employment tax.[2] This requirement is reflected in line 31 of Schedule C, which requires the net profit of the proprietorship to be entered on Schedule SE for computing the self-employment tax.

Example 1. The records of a proprietorship owned by J show the following information for the year:

Sales	$150,000
Cost of goods sold	60,000
Operating expenses:	
Depreciation	12,000
Insurance	3,000
Office supplies	1,100
Repairs	1,800
Payroll and property taxes	3,200
Utilities and telephone	800
Employee salaries	30,000
J's compensation	25,000
Capital gain	2,000

---

[1] §§ 61(a) and 162.   [2] § 6017. See Chapter 1.

All of the amounts shown above are recorded on Schedule C (Exhibit 19-1) except for the last two. Thus, *gross income* is $90,000 ($150,000 − $60,000) and *net ordinary income* is $38,100 ($90,000 − $12,000 − $3,000 − $1,100 − $1,800 − $3,200 − $800 − $30,000). Note that line 31 of Schedule C requires the net income to be reported on Form 1040, increasing J's adjusted gross income (A.G.I.), and on Schedule SE to determine any *self-employment tax*. The amount listed above as "J's compensation" does not qualify as salary since an owner cannot be an employee of his or her own proprietorship. The $25,000 is neither deductible by the proprietorship nor includible income to J. It is simply a nontaxable withdrawal. The capital gain is reported on J's Schedule D with all her other capital gains and losses.

Example 2. Assume the same facts in *Example 1*, except that cost of goods sold is $100,000 instead of $60,000. The proprietorship now has a *net ordinary loss* of $1,900. The $1,900 loss is reported on Form 1040, reducing A.G.I., and on Schedule SE, reducing self-employment income from J's other sources (if any). The fact that the proprietorship has a net loss does not change the treatment of any other item listed in *Example 1*. If the $1,900 proprietorship loss is not offset by J's other income, she is eligible for the net operating loss (NOL) three-year carryback and/or 15-year carryforward computation (discussed in Chapter 10).[3]

The fact that a sole proprietor cannot be an employee has important implications regarding fringe benefits. Many of the fringe benefits such as medical insurance, group-term life insurance, and employer-provided meals and lodging, are not available to sole proprietors since they are not considered employees. As discussed in Chapter 6, businesses are normally allowed to deduct the costs of fringe benefits for their employees and they are nontaxable to the employees. However, when a proprietorship pays for these items, the payment is treated as if the owner made the payment directly. For example, if the proprietorship pays the medical insurance premium for the owner, it is treated as if the owner paid the premium. The expense is not reported on Schedule C but is reported as part of the taxpayer's total medical expenses. Consequently, the expense would be subject to the treatment reserved for medical expenses, which are generally not deductible unless total medical expenses exceed 7.5 percent of the taxpayer's A.G.I. Had the owner been considered an employee, the payment would have been deductible by the proprietorship and nontaxable to the owner. Without employee status, the proprietor is denied such favorable treatment. Depending on the taxpayer's situation, the loss of the special treatment for certain fringe benefits may cause him or her to opt for another form of business organization (e.g., a corporation) where employee status and, therefore, favorable fringe benefit treatment is available.

---

[3] § 172(c).

Exhibit 19-1   *Schedule C (Form 1040)*

SCHEDULE C (Form 1040) Department of the Treasury Internal Revenue Service (O)	**Profit or Loss From Business** (Sole Proprietorship) ▶ **Partnerships, joint ventures, etc., must file Form 1065.** ▶ **Attach to Form 1040 or Form 1041.** ▶ **See Instructions for Schedule C (Form 1040).**	OMB No. 1545-0074 **1993** Attachment Sequence No. **09**

Name of proprietor J	Social security number (SSN) 403 16 1792

A	Principal business or profession, including product or service (see page C-1) RETAIL APPAREL	B Enter principal business code (see page C-6) ▶ 5 6 5 1

C	Business name. If no separate business name, leave blank. J's PROPRIETORSHIP	D Employer ID number (EIN), if any 6 6 0 7 7 0 3 3 3

E Business address (including suite or room no.) ▶ 1710 NORTH SHORE ST.
   City, town or post office, state, and ZIP code   TAMPA, FL 33620

F Accounting method: **(1)** ☐ Cash   **(2)** ☒ Accrual   **(3)** ☐ Other (specify) ▶ ....

G	Method(s) used to value closing inventory:	**(1)** ☒ Cost	**(2)** ☐ Lower of cost or market	**(3)** ☐ Other (attach explanation)	**(4)** ☐ Does not apply (if checked, skip line H)	Yes	No

		Yes	No
H	Was there any change in determining quantities, costs, or valuations between opening and closing inventory? If "Yes," attach explanation		✓
I	Did you "materially participate" in the operation of this business during 1993? If "No," see page C-2 for limit on losses. . .	✓	
J	If you started or acquired this business during 1993, check here . . . . ▶ ☐		

Part I | **Income**

1	Gross receipts or sales. **Caution:** *If this income was reported to you on Form W-2 and the "Statutory employee" box on that form was checked, see page C-2 and check here* . . . . ▶ ☐	1	150,000
2	Returns and allowances	2	—
3	Subtract line 2 from line 1	3	150,000
4	Cost of goods sold (from line 40 on page 2)	4	60,000
5	**Gross profit.** Subtract line 4 from line 3	5	90,000
6	Other income, including Federal and state gasoline or fuel tax credit or refund (see page C-2) . .	6	
7	**Gross income.** Add lines 5 and 6 . . . . ▶	7	90,000

Part II | **Expenses. Caution:** *Do not enter expenses for business use of your home on lines 8–27. Instead, see line 30.*

8	Advertising	8		19	Pension and profit-sharing plans	19	
9	Bad debts from sales or services (see page C-3) . .	9		20	Rent or lease (see page C-4):		
				a	Vehicles, machinery, and equipment .	20a	
10	Car and truck expenses (see page C-3)	10		b	Other business property . .	20b	
11	Commissions and fees. . .	11		21	Repairs and maintenance . . .	21	
12	Depletion.	12		22	Supplies (not included in Part III) .	22	
13	Depreciation and section 179 expense deduction (not included in Part III) (see page C-3) . .	13	12,000	23	Taxes and licenses	23	
				24	Travel, meals, and entertainment:		
				a	Travel	24a	
14	Employee benefit programs (other than on line 19) . . .	14		b	Meals and entertainment .		
15	Insurance (other than health) .	15	3,000	c	Enter 20% of line 24b subject to limitations (see page C-4) .		
16	Interest:			d	Subtract line 24c from line 24b .	24d	
a	Mortgage (paid to banks, etc.) .	16a		25	Utilities	25	800
b	Other	16b		26	Wages (less jobs credit) . .	26	30,000
17	Legal and professional services	17		27	Other expenses (from line 46 on page 2)	27	
18	Office expense	18					

28	**Total expenses** before expenses for business use of home. Add lines 8 through 27 in columns. . ▶	28	51,900
29	Tentative profit (loss). Subtract line 28 from line 7	29	
30	Expenses for business use of your home. Attach **Form 8829**	30	
31	**Net profit or (loss).** Subtract line 30 from line 29. ● If a profit, enter on **Form 1040, line 12,** and ALSO on **Schedule SE, line 2** (statutory employees, see page C-5). Fiduciaries, enter on Form 1041, line 3. ● If a loss, you MUST go on to line 32.	31	38,100
32	If you have a loss, check the box that describes your investment in this activity (see page C-5). ● If you checked 32a, enter the loss on **Form 1040, line 12,** and ALSO on **Schedule SE, line 2** (statutory employees, see page C-5). Fiduciaries, enter on Form 1041, line 3. ● If you checked 32b, you MUST attach **Form 6198.**	32a ☐ All investment is at risk. 32b ☐ Some investment is not at risk.	

For Paperwork Reduction Act Notice, see Form 1040 instructions.   Cat. No. 11334P   Schedule C (Form 1040) 1993

PARTNERSHIPS

When two or more parties agree to go into business together, they often choose to operate as a partnership. Partnerships are quite common due in part to the fact that they are easy to form. The parties simply need to agree to do business together. Unlike the formation of a corporation, no special forms need to be filed, and there is no formal registration with the state. Perhaps surprisingly, there is no requirement that the partnership agreement be in writing. An oral agreement will suffice, although reflecting the terms of the arrangement in a written document is obviously more prudent.

There are two types of partnerships: general partnerships and limited partnerships. General partnerships are owned solely by general partners while limited partnerships have at least one general partner and one limited partner.[4] The two differ primarily in the rights and obligations of the partners. As their title suggests, limited partners are liable for partnership debts only to the extent of their contribution and have no voice in management. In contrast, general partners have unlimited liability for partnership obligations but may participate in the management and control of the partnership.

TAXATION OF PARTNERSHIP OPERATIONS

In many respects, partnerships are taxed like proprietorships. Neither are separate taxable entities. The partnership is merely a conduit through which income, deductions, credits, and other items flow to the individual partners, who report them on their own returns.[5] The amount of each item allocated to a partner is normally based on the partner's capital interest in the partnership or some other allocation method adopted by the partners.[6] Consistent with this pass-through approach, the items normally retain their character when they are allocated to the partners. For example, tax-exempt income received by the partnership flows through and is reported as tax-exempt income by the partners. To accomplish this pass-through, the partnership must file an annual information return, Form 1065 (see Exhibit 19-2). The return is simply a compilation of the items of tax consequence to the partnership and its partners. It not only reports information about the partnership's income or loss for the year but also how the income or loss must be allocated among the partners.

The various items of income, deductions, and credit that flow through to each partner are reported in one of two ways. Any item that may receive special treatment by a partner, such as capital gains, dividends, or charitable contributions, must be separately stated on Schedule K of Form 1065 (see Exhibit 19-3). In this way, the character of the item is preserved and the special treatment that the item deserves is not lost. To illustrate, consider dividends. Although dividends are treated as ordinary income by individual taxpayers, they must be separately stated since corporate taxpayers are entitled to the dividends-received deduction. Similarly, charitable contributions must be

---

4 *Uniform Partnership Act* § 6(1) and *Uniform Limited Partnership Act* § 1.

5 §§ 701 and 702(b).

6 §§ 702(a) and (c), and 704(a) and (b).

separately stated since the limitations on the deduction differ between corporations and individuals and, moreover, the limitation for each partner may differ. All other items of income and expense—those that do not receive any special treatment—are netted to arrive at the partnership's *ordinary income*. They are summarized on page 1 of Form 1065 (see line 22 on page 1 of Form 1065). Each partner's *share* of the partnership's net ordinary income and separately stated items are reported on Schedule K-1 (see Exhibit 19-4). When the partners file their own returns, they must incorporate the partnership information from Schedule K-1. For example, individual taxpayers report their share of ordinary income from the partnership on Schedule E of Form 1040 while all other items are reported on the partner's appropriate schedule as if the partner had received the income or paid the expense.[7] For instance, if the partnership reported a long-term capital gain, the individual partner would report his share of the capital gain on his own Schedule D.

Another similarity between proprietorships and partnerships concerns employment taxes. A *general* partner's share of the partnership's ordinary income (after removal of certain passive income items such as depreciation recapture income) are subject to self-employment tax.[8] In contrast, a *limited* partner's share of partnership ordinary income is not subject to self-employment tax since it represents investment income to a limited partner.

It is important to understand that the flow-through aspect of partnership taxation is just one part of a complete system that ensures that partnership income is taxed only once. While the intricacies of this system are beyond this overview, the thrust of the system is easily illustrated. Consider a typical situation in which two individuals form a partnership, each contributing $10,000 to the partnership in exchange for a 50 percent interest. Assume the partnership immediately takes the money and purchases stock for $20,000 that it subsequently sells for $22,000. In this case, the partnership has income of $2,000 ($22,000 − $20,000), and each partner reports his $1,000 share. Note that the partners report their share of partnership income even if they receive no distributions from the partnership. However, to ensure that the partnership's income is not taxed again when it is distributed, each partner must keep track of his investment, that is, the adjusted basis for his or her partnership interest. In this case, each partner has an original basis equal to the amount that he contributed to the partnership, $10,000. Upon reporting partnership income, each partner adjusts his basis in his partnership interest for his share of income, increasing it from $10,000 to $11,000. When a partner actually receives his $1,000 share of the income, the distribution is treated as tax-free to the extent of his basis. Each partner would then reduce his basis by $1,000, back to his original basis of $10,000. The end result is that the partners have reported and received income that has been subject to only *one* tax.

---

[7] Under § 704(d), the deduction for losses and separately stated expenses allocated to the partner generally cannot exceed the partner's basis in the partnership.

[8] § 1402 and Reg. § 1.707-1(c).

Exhibit 19-2 *Form 1065*

Form **1065**	U.S. Partnership Return of Income	OMB No. 1545-0099
Department of the Treasury / Internal Revenue Service	For calendar year 1993, or tax year beginning .... , 1993, and ending .... , 19 .... / ▶ See separate instructions.	**1993**

A Principal business activity RETAIL TRADE	Use the IRS label. Other- wise, please print or type.	Name of partnership H AND L PARTNERSHIP	D Employer identification number 66 : 0770333
B Principal product or service APPAREL		Number, street, and room or suite no. (If a P.O. box, see page 9 of the instructions.) 3109 STATE STREET	E Date business started 1-1-82
C Business code number 5651		City or town, state, and ZIP code STATE COLLEGE, PA 16801	F Total assets (see Specific instructions) $ 120,000

G Check applicable boxes: (1) ☐ Initial return (2) ☐ Final return (3) ☐ Change in address (4) ☐ Amended return
H Check accounting method: (1) ☐ Cash (2) ☒ Accrual (3) ☐ Other (specify) ▶ ....
I Number of Schedules K-1. Attach one for each person who was a partner at any time during the tax year ▶ ....

Caution: *Include **only** trade or business income and expenses on lines 1a through 22 below. See the instructions for more information.*

Income

1a Gross receipts or sales	1a 150,000		
b Less returns and allowances	1b – 0 –	1c	150,000
2 Cost of goods sold (Schedule A, line 8)		2	60,000
3 Gross profit. Subtract line 2 from line 1c		3	90,000
4 Ordinary income (loss) from other partnerships and fiduciaries *(attach schedule)*		4	—
5 Net farm profit (loss) *(attach Schedule F (Form 1040))*		5	—
6 Net gain (loss) from Form 4797, Part II, line 20		6	—
7 Other income (loss) (see instructions) *(attach schedule)*		7	—
8 **Total income (loss).** Combine lines 3 through 7		8	90,000

Deductions (see instructions for limitations)

9a Salaries and wages (other than to partners)	9a 30,000		
b Less employment credits	9b – 0 –	9c	30,000
10 Guaranteed payments to partners		10	25,000
11 Repairs and maintenance		11	
12 Bad debts		12	
13 Rent		13	3,200
14 Taxes and licenses. PAYROLL + PROPERTY TAXES		14	
15 Interest		15	1,800
16a Depreciation (see instructions)	16a 12,000		
b Less depreciation reported on Schedule A and elsewhere on return	16b – 0 –	16c	12,000
17 Depletion (**Do not deduct oil and gas depletion.**)		17	
18 Retirement plans, etc.		18	
19 Employee benefit programs		19	
20 Other deductions (attach schedule) OFFICE EXPENSES = $1,100; UTILITIES & TELEPHONE = $800; INSURANCE = $3,000		20	4,900
21 **Total deductions.** Add the amounts shown in the far right column for lines 9c through 20		21	76,900
22 **Ordinary income (loss)** from trade or business activities. Subtract line 21 from line 8		22	13,100

Please Sign Here

Under penalties of perjury, I declare that I have examined this return, including accompanying schedules and statements, and to the best of my knowledge and belief, it is true, correct, and complete. Declaration of preparer (other than general partner) is based on all information of which preparer has any knowledge.

▶ Signature of general partner ▶ Date

Paid Preparer's Use Only

Preparer's signature ▶	Date	Check if self-employed ▶ ☐	Preparer's social security no.
Firm's name (or yours if self-employed) and address ▶		E.I. No. ▶	
		ZIP code ▶	

For Paperwork Reduction Act Notice, see page 1 of separate instructions. Cat. No. 11390Z Form **1065** (1993)

Exhibit 19-3   *Schedule K (Form 1065)*

Form 1065 (1993)   Page **3**

Schedule K	Partners' Shares of Income, Credits, Deductions, etc.		

	(a) Distributive share items		(b) Total amount

Income (Loss)	**1** Ordinary income (loss) from trade or business activities (page 1, line 22)	**1**	13,100
	2 Net income (loss) from rental real estate activities *(attach Form 8825)*	**2**	
	3a Gross income from other rental activities 3a		
	b Expenses from other rental activities *(attach schedule)* 3b		
	c Net income (loss) from other rental activities. Subtract line 3b from line 3a	**3c**	
	4 Portfolio income (loss) (see instructions): **a** Interest income	**4a**	
	b Dividend income	**4b**	
	c Royalty income	**4c**	
	d Net short-term capital gain (loss) *(attach Schedule D (Form 1065))*	**4d**	
	e Net long-term capital gain (loss) *(attach Schedule D (Form 1065))*	**4e**	2,000
	f Other portfolio income (loss) *(attach schedule)*	**4f**	
	5 Guaranteed payments to partners	**5**	25,000
	6 Net gain (loss) under section 1231 (other than due to casualty or theft) *(attach Form 4797)*	**6**	
	7 Other income (loss) *(attach schedule)*	**7**	
Deduc-tions	**8** Charitable contributions (see instructions) *(attach schedule)*	**8**	
	9 Section 179 expense deduction *(attach Form 4562)*	**9**	
	10 Deductions related to portfolio income (see instructions) (itemize)	**10**	
	11 Other deductions *(attach schedule)*	**11**	
Invest-ment Interest	**12a** Interest expense on investment debts	**12a**	
	b (1) Investment income included on lines 4a, 4b, 4c, and 4f above	**12b(1)**	
	(2) Investment expenses included on line 10 above.	**12b(2)**	
Credits	**13a** Credit for income tax withheld	**13a**	
	b Low-income housing credit (see instructions):		
	(1) From partnerships to which section 42(j)(5) applies for property placed in service before 1990 . .	**13b(1)**	
	(2) Other than on line 13b(1) for property placed in service before 1990	**13b(2)**	
	(3) From partnerships to which section 42(j)(5) applies for property placed in service after 1989	**13b(3)**	
	(4) Other than on line 13b(3) for property placed in service after 1989	**13b(4)**	
	c Qualified rehabilitation expenditures related to rental real estate activities *(attach Form 3468)*	**13c**	
	d Credits (other than credits shown on lines 13b and 13c) related to rental real estate activities (see instructions)	**13d**	
	e Credits related to other rental activities (see instructions)	**13e**	
	14 Other credits (see instructions)	**14**	
Self-Employ-ment	**15a** Net earnings (loss) from self-employment . $ 25,000 + $ 13,100	**15a**	38,100
	b Gross farming or fishing income	**15b**	
	c Gross nonfarm income	**15c**	
Adjustments and Tax Preference Items	**16a** Depreciation adjustment on property placed in service after 1986	**16a**	
	b Adjusted gain or loss	**16b**	
	c Depletion (other than oil and gas)	**16c**	
	d (1) Gross income from oil, gas, and geothermal properties	**16d(1)**	
	(2) Deductions allocable to oil, gas, and geothermal properties	**16d(2)**	
	e Other adjustments and tax preference items *(attach schedule)*	**16e**	
Foreign Taxes	**17a** Type of income ▶ . . . . **b** Foreign country or U.S. possession ▶		
	c Total gross income from sources outside the United States *(attach schedule)*.	**17c**	
	d Total applicable deductions and losses *(attach schedule)*	**17d**	
	e Total foreign taxes (check one): ▶ ☐ Paid ☐ Accrued	**17e**	
	f Reduction in taxes available for credit *(attach schedule)*	**17f**	
	g Other foreign tax information *(attach schedule)*	**17g**	
Other	**18a** Total expenditures to which a section 59(e) election may apply	**18a**	
	b Type of expenditures ▶.		
	19 Tax-exempt interest income	**19**	
	20 Other tax-exempt income	**20**	
	21 Nondeductible expenses	**21**	
	22 Other items and amounts required to be reported separately to partners (see instructions) *(attach schedule)*		

Analysis	**23a** Income (loss). Combine lines 1 through 7 in column (b). From the result, subtract the sum of lines 8 through 12a, 17e, and 18a				**23a**		

b Analysis by type of partner:	(a) Corporate	(b) Individual		(c) Partnership	(d) Exempt organization	(e) Nominee/Other
		i. Active	ii. Passive			
(1) General partners						
(2) Limited partners						

Exhibit 19-4 *Schedule K-1 (Form 1065)*

SCHEDULE K-1 (Form 1065) Department of the Treasury Internal Revenue Service	**Partner's Share of Income, Credits, Deductions, etc.** ▶ See separate instructions. For calendar year 1993 or tax year beginning , 1993, and ending , 19	OMB No. 1545-0099 **1993**

Partner's identifying number ▶ 454-52-6467	Partnership's identifying number ▶ 66 : 0770333

Partner's name, address, and ZIP code	Partnership's name, address, and ZIP code
H. PARTNER 1615 SALEM AVENUE LANCASTER, PA 17604	H AND L PARTNERSHIP 3109 STATE STREET STATE COLLEGE, PA 16801

A This partner is a ☒ general partner ☐ limited partner ☐ limited liability company member

B What type of entity is this partner? ▶ INDIVIDUAL

C Is this partner a ☒ domestic or a ☐ foreign partner?

D Enter partner's percentage of:

	(i) Before change or termination	(ii) End of year
Profit sharing	%	50 %
Loss sharing	%	50 %
Ownership of capital	%	50 %

E IRS Center where partnership filed return: PHILADELPHIA

F Partner's share of liabilities (see instructions):

Nonrecourse	$	-0-
Qualified nonrecourse financing	$	-0-
Other	$	45,000

G Tax shelter registration number . ▶ ....

H Check here if this partnership is a publicly traded partnership as defined in section 469(k)(2) . . . . ☐

I Check applicable boxes: (1) ☐ Final K-1 (2) ☐ Amended K-1

J Analysis of partner's capital account:

(a) Capital account at beginning of year	(b) Capital contributed during year	(c) Partner's share of lines 3, 4, and 7, Form 1065, Schedule M-2	(d) Withdrawals and distributions	(e) Capital account at end of year (combine columns (a) through (d))
		1,000	( )	

	(a) Distributive share item		(b) Amount	(c) 1040 filers enter the amount in column (b) on:
Income (Loss)	1	Ordinary income (loss) from trade or business activities . . .	**1** 6,550	See Partner's Instructions for Schedule K-1 (Form 1065).
	2	Net income (loss) from rental real estate activities	**2**	
	3	Net income (loss) from other rental activities	**3**	
	4	Portfolio income (loss):		
	a	Interest	**4a**	Sch. B, Part I, line 1
	b	Dividends	**4b**	Sch. B, Part II, line 5
	c	Royalties	**4c**	Sch. E, Part I, line 4
	d	Net short-term capital gain (loss)	**4d**	Sch. D, line 5, col. (f) or (g)
	e	Net long-term capital gain (loss)	**4e** 1,000	Sch. D, line 13, col. (f) or (g)
	f	Other portfolio income (loss) (attach schedule)	**4f**	Enter on applicable line of your return.
	5	Guaranteed payments to partner	**5** 25,000	See Partner's Instructions for Schedule K-1 (Form 1065).
	6	Net gain (loss) under section 1231 (other than due to casualty or theft)	**6**	
	7	Other income (loss) (attach schedule)	**7**	Enter on applicable line of your return.
Deductions	8	Charitable contributions (see instructions) (attach schedule) . .	**8**	Sch. A, line 13 or 14
	9	Section 179 expense deduction	**9**	See Partner's Instructions for Schedule K-1 (Form 1065).
	10	Deductions related to portfolio income (attach schedule) . . .	**10**	
	11	Other deductions (attach schedule)	**11**	
Investment Interest	12a	Interest expense on investment debts	**12a**	Form 4952, line 1
	b (1)	Investment income included on lines 4a, 4b, 4c, and 4f above	**b(1)**	See Partner's Instructions for Schedule K-1 (Form 1065).
	(2)	Investment expenses included on line 10 above	**b(2)**	
Credits	13a	Credit for income tax withheld	**13a**	See Partner's Instructions for Schedule K-1 (Form 1065).
	b	Low-income housing credit:		
	(1)	From section 42(j)(5) partnerships for property placed in service before 1990	**b(1)**	
	(2)	Other than on line 13b(1) for property placed in service before 1990	**b(2)**	
	(3)	From section 42(j)(5) partnerships for property placed in service after 1989	**b(3)**	Form 8586, line 5
	(4)	Other than on line 13b(3) for property placed in service after 1989	**b(4)**	
	c	Qualified rehabilitation expenditures related to rental real estate activities (see instructions)	**13c**	
	d	Credits (other than credits shown on lines 13b and 13c) related to rental real estate activities (see instructions)	**13d**	See Partner's Instructions for Schedule K-1 (Form 1065).
	e	Credits related to other rental activities (see instructions) . . .	**13e**	
	14	Other credits (see instructions)	**14**	

For Paperwork Reduction Act Notice, see Instructions for Form 1065. Cat. No. 11394R Schedule K-1 (Form 1065) 1993

ITEM J SHOULD BE COMPLETED BEFORE THIS FORM IS FILED

Exhibit 19-4 *Continued*

Schedule K-1 (Form 1065) 1993   Page **2**

	(a) Distributive share item	(b) Amount	(c) 1040 filers enter the amount in column (b) on:
Self-em-ployment	**15a** Net earnings (loss) from self-employment **15a**	31,550	Sch. SE, Section A or B
	b Gross farming or fishing income **15b**		See Partner's Instructions for Schedule K-1 (Form 1065).
	c Gross nonfarm income **15c**		
Adjustments and Tax Preference Items	**16a** Depreciation adjustment on property placed in service after 1986 **16a**		
	b Adjusted gain or loss **16b**		See Partner's Instructions for Schedule K-1 (Form 1065) and Instructions for Form 6251.
	c Depletion (other than oil and gas) **16c**		
	d (1) Gross income from oil, gas, and geothermal properties . . **d(1)**		
	(2) Deductions allocable to oil, gas, and geothermal properties **d(2)**		
	e Other adjustments and tax preference items *(attach schedule)* **16e**		
Foreign Taxes	**17a** Type of income ▶		Form 1116, check boxes
	b Name of foreign country or U.S. possession ▶		
	c Total gross income from sources outside the United States *(attach schedule)* **17c**		Form 1116, Part I
	d Total applicable deductions and losses *(attach schedule)* . . . **17d**		
	e Total foreign taxes (check one): ▶ ☐ Paid ☐ Accrued . . . **17e**		Form 1116, Part II
	f Reduction in taxes available for credit *(attach schedule)* . . . **17f**		Form 1116, Part III
	g Other foreign tax information *(attach schedule)* **17g**		See Instructions for Form 1116.
Other	**18a** Total expenditures to which a section 59(e) election may apply **18a**		See Partner's Instructions for Schedule K-1 (Form 1065).
	b Type of expenditures ▶		
	19 Tax-exempt interest income **19**		Form 1040, line 8b
	20 Other tax-exempt income **20**		See Partner's Instructions for Schedule K-1 (Form 1065).
	21 Nondeductible expenses **21**		
	22 Recapture of low-income housing credit:		
	a From section 42(j)(5) partnerships **22a**		Form 8611, line 8
	b Other than on line 22a **22b**		
Supplemental Information	**23** Supplemental information required to be reported separately to each partner *(attach additional schedules if more space is needed)*:		

TRANSACTIONS BETWEEN PARTNERSHIP AND PARTNERS

Unlike sole proprietors, whose profit from the business is simply what's left after paying all the expenses, partners may also receive compensation for services performed for the partnership. While it may seem logical in this situation to treat the partner as an employee and the compensation as salary, the courts have taken a different approach, and the Code reflects their view. If the amount of the compensation is independent of how well the partnership fares during the year, that is, the compensation does not depend on the partnership's income, the compensation is referred to as a *guaranteed payment*.[9] In most cases, the partnership deducts the guaranteed payment to the partner just like it would a salary payment to an employee, and the partner reports the amount as income. There are several critical differences, however. Perhaps the most important of these is that a guaranteed payment, unlike a salary, is not subject to withholding. There are no income taxes withheld, no W-2 is completed, and the amount is not subject to employment taxes at the partnership or partner level. Instead, the amount of the guaranteed payment is reported on Schedule K (and deducted on page 1 in computing net income) and is treated as self-employed income subject to self-employment taxes. A guaranteed payment is treated as self-employment income whether it is received by a general or limited partner.

Partners, like proprietors, also are not considered employees for purposes of the fringe benefit rules. As noted above, employers can normally deduct the costs of providing their employees with certain benefits, yet the employee has no taxable income. For partnerships, however, the amount of the benefit is generally treated like a guaranteed payment, deductible by the partnership but taxable income to the partner. Such benefits are also subject to employment taxes. Similarly, partners are not entitled to participate with other employees in a qualified pension plan. Instead, each partner may establish his or her own Keogh plan. Although a Keogh plan provides benefits very similar to typical qualified plans, they are not identical. For example, the amount of contribution that can be made is more limited, and loans from the plan are normally prohibited.

Unlike the proprietorship, most other transactions between the partnership and its partners are treated as if each were dealing with a third party. For example, partners may lend money, rent property, or sell assets to their partnership and, with few exceptions, the partners will include interest income, rent income and gain, and perhaps loss just as if they were not dealing with their own partnership. Meanwhile, the partnership is normally allowed a deduction for the interest, rent, or depreciation expense as the case may be. Exceptions do exist, however. As discussed in Chapter 7, losses on sales between a partnership and a partner who owns more than 50 percent of the partnership are generally disallowed under § 267. The same rule applies to C and S corporations. In a similar fashion, § 267 provides that an accrual basis partnership is allowed to deduct accrued expenses payable to a related cash basis taxpayer only in the period in which the payment is included in the recipient's income. This matching rule also applies to C corporations and their more-than-50-percent shareholders as well as S corporations and any of their shareholders.

---

[9]   § 707(c).

Example 3.   The records of a partnership owned and operated equally by H and L show the following information for the year:

Sales...	$150,000
Cost of goods sold..................................	60,000
Operating expenses:	
Depreciation.......................................	12,000
Insurance..	3,000
Office supplies....................................	1,100
Repairs...	1,800
Payroll and property taxes.........................	3,200
Utilities and telephone............................	800
Employee salaries.................................	30,000
H's guaranteed payment............................	25,000
Capital gain..	2,000

Note that the above information is identical to *Example 1* except the business is a partnership with two owners. Page 1 of Form 1065 (Exhibit 19-2) is similar to Schedule C (Exhibit 19-1). The major difference is that the guaranteed payments are deductible in determining net ordinary income or loss. Thus, *gross income* is the same at $90,000 but *net ordinary income* is $13,100, which is $25,000 less than it is for the proprietorship because of the guaranteed payments. Each partner's share is $6,550 (50% × $13,100). In addition to the $13,100 net ordinary income, information relevant to the partners include guaranteed payments of $25,000, net capital gain of $2,000, and earnings from self-employment of $38,100 ($13,100 + $25,000). The total ordinary income of the partnership and each of the separately stated items is reported on Schedule K (Exhibit 19-3). The amount of each one of these items that is allocated to a partner for reporting on his or her personal return is detailed on Schedule K-1 (Exhibit 19-4). Since the Schedule K-1s are the same for H and L except for the guaranteed payments, only H's information is illustrated, showing $6,550 ordinary income, $25,000 guaranteed payments, $1,000 net capital gain, and $31,550 ($6,550 + $25,000) net earnings from self-employment. In contrast, L's Schedule K-1 has no amount for guaranteed payments and his self-employment income is only $6,550. Each partner reports the amounts from Schedule K-1 as follows: net ordinary income and guaranteed payments on page 2 of Schedule E, self-employment income on Schedule SE, and capital gain on Schedule D. Thus, the treatment of the partnership items by H and L together is the same as the treatment of the proprietorship items by J in *Example 1*.

Example 4.   Assume the same facts as in *Example 3,* except that cost of goods sold is $100,000 instead of $60,000. The partnership now has a *net ordinary loss* of $26,900. Each partner's share is $13,450 (50% × $26,900). H reports total ordinary income and self-employment income of $11,550 ($25,000 guaranteed payments − $13,450 ordinary loss) while L reports a net ordinary loss of $13,450, assuming his basis in the partnership equals or exceeds that amount. Again, the combined treatment for H and L is the same as it is for proprietor J in *Example 2*. If L's income from other sources does not exceed his loss from the partnership, he is eligible for the NOL carryback and carryforward.

Example 5. During the year, K received the following amounts from a partnership in which she has a 30% capital interest:

1. $2,750 interest on a $25,000 loan made to the partnership

2. $3,600 rental income from a storage building rented to the partnership

3. $6,000 for special tools sold to the partnership (the tools were acquired for personal use two years ago for $5,500)

Assume the partnership's net ordinary income, excluding the above items, is $40,000, and the depreciation deduction for the tools is $1,200. Thus, net income for the partnership and includible income for K, after the above three items are considered, are

	Partnership		Partner K	
Net income before..............	$40,000			
Interest on loan.................	(2,750)		$2,750	interest income
Rental of building..............	(3,600)		3,600	rental income
Tools:				
Sale.........................	0		500	capital gain
Depreciation.................	(1,200)		0	
Net income after................	$32,450	× 30% =	$9,735	partnership income

S CORPORATIONS

The final form of business organization to be considered is the corporation. A corporation, unlike a partnership, is normally viewed as an entity separate and distinct from its owners. Historically, this has been its principal advantage. The owners of the corporation, the shareholders, are insulated from the liabilities of the corporation. Shareholders are liable only to the extent of their investment in the corporation. It is this attribute, limited liability, that causes many businesses to choose the corporate form for conducting their operations.

Until 1958, all corporations were taxed in the same manner. Consistent with their treatment as separate legal entities, they were also treated as separate entities for tax purposes. Unfortunately, this treatment created the possibility for the corporation's income to be taxed *twice*: once when the corporation receives the income and again when the income is distributed as a dividend to its shareholders. Double taxation can occur because the corporation is not allowed to deduct any dividend payments to its shareholders. To the regret of many small business owners who could not easily shift the burden of double taxation to customers or employees, the risk of double taxation was the price to be paid for limited liability. Then, in 1958, bowing to pressure from small business, the Eisenhower administration proposed special rules to eliminate the trade-off between double taxation and limited liability. Congress responded to the president's wishes and enacted the new

Subchapter S of the Code, which allows certain closely held corporations to elect to be taxed like partnerships.[10]

Since the enactment of Subchapter S, there have been two types of corporations for Federal tax purposes: "S" corporations, so-called because they are governed by Subchapter S of the Internal Revenue Code, and all other corporations, referred to as regular, or "C," corporations. The latter are governed, as might be expected, by Subchapter C. For all other purposes, the law recognizes no distinction between C and S corporations— both are simply corporations, separate legal entities that provide limited liability to their shareholders. While C and S corporations are identical for nontax purposes, their tax treatment, as explained above, differs significantly. S corporations are generally taxed like partnerships and do not risk the possibility of double taxation, whereas C corporations are treated as separate taxable entities and may have their income taxed twice.

ELECTION OF S CORPORATION STATUS

The special tax treatment provided for S corporations is available only if the corporation qualifies for S treatment and all of the shareholders consent to the corporation's election to be taxed under Subchapter S. While there are several requirements that a corporation must satisfy in order to qualify for the election, the most important concerns its shareholders.[11] The corporation can have no more than 35 *eligible* shareholders. For this purpose, only individuals, estates, and certain trusts are eligible to own the stock. Corporations and partnerships cannot own the stock of an S corporation. Nonresident aliens (individuals who are not U.S. citizens and who do not live in the U.S.) are also barred from owning stock in an S corporation. The S election is terminated if any of these conditions are violated or a majority of the shareholders revoke the election. When either of these events occurs, the S election terminates, and the corporation becomes a C corporation and normally cannot reelect S status for five years.

MAKING THE S ELECTION

The S election is made by filing Form 2553, to which all shareholders must consent. For the election to be effective for the current year, the election must be filed within two months and 15 days after the corporation's taxable year begins. If the S election is not made within this period, the election is effective for the corporation's following taxable year. It should be noted, particularly for newly formed corporations, that a failure to obtain S status for the corporation's first taxable year means that it will be treated as a C corporation until the S election becomes effective. While the consequences of this are beyond the scope of this overview, suffice it to say that numerous problems can arise when a C corporation converts to S status. These difficulties are ignored in the discussion below, but the reader should be forewarned that these converted corporations may be subject to special rules.

---

[10]   §§ 1361 and 1362. Some states do not recognize S corporations and treat them as C corporations for state tax purposes.

[11]   §§ 1361(b) and (c).

TAXATION OF S CORPORATION OPERATIONS

Like a partnership, an S corporation is normally treated as a conduit. Consequently, the method of reporting the amount of S corporation income that flows through to the shareholders is virtually identical to that for a partnership.[12] The various nonseparately stated items that make up the S corporation's ordinary income are summarized on page 1 of Form 1120S (see Exhibit 19-5). The separately stated items are reported on Schedule K (see Exhibit 19-6). Each shareholder's *share* of the S corporation's ordinary income and separately stated items are reported on Schedule K-1 (see Exhibit 19-7). Like partners, when S corporation shareholders file their own returns, they must incorporate the information on Schedule K-1. As a result, *Examples 3* and *4*, which illustrate how a partnership's income is summarized and passed through to its partners, are equally applicable to S corporations and their shareholders (other than the treatment of the owner's compensation discussed below). Exhibits 19-5, 19-6, and 19-7 contain a completed Form 1120S, including Schedules K and K-1, using the facts of *Example 3*. Note the similarity in the forms and the reporting.

TRANSACTIONS BETWEEN AN S CORPORATION AND ITS SHAREHOLDERS

Although the taxation of routine operations of an S corporation and that of a partnership are virtually identical, there are differences. The most important of these concerns the treatment of the owners' compensation, including employment taxes. In the discussion of partnerships, it was observed that partners are not considered "employees" of the partnership. As a result, they were not eligible for many nontaxable fringe benefits. In addition, any compensation paid to them was generally treated as a guaranteed payment that was not reported on a Form W-2 but on Schedule K-1 and was subject to self-employment tax. In contrast, shareholders of an S corporation may be "employees" of the S corporation. Consequently, salaries paid to S shareholders in their capacity as employees are subject to withholding, including normal social security and Medicare taxes, and, therefore, the salary does not qualify as self-employment income. Also in contrast to partnerships, the shareholder's share of the S corporation's ordinary income is not considered self-employment income. Thus, the S corporation's Schedules K and K-1 do not contain a line for self-employment income. Despite these differences, the treatment of the fringe benefits of S shareholders closely resembles that for partners. For purposes of fringe benefits, any shareholder owning more than 2 percent of the stock is treated in the same manner as a partner. Consequently, the benefits are treated as compensation that is included on the shareholder-employee's W-2 and that the S corporation can deduct. Such benefits are not subject to employment taxes, however. The net effect for those who own more than a 2 percent share is that they are denied many nontaxable fringe benefits.

Most other transactions between the S corporation and its shareholders are treated as if they each were dealing with a third party, again like a partnership. For instance, losses on sales between an S corporation and a shareholder who owns more than 50 percent of the stock are generally disallowed.

---

[12] §§ 1363 and 1366.

Exhibit 19-5 *Form 1120S, p.1*

Form **1120S**	**U.S. Income Tax Return for an S Corporation**	OMB No. 1545-0130
Department of the Treasury Internal Revenue Service	▶ Do not file this form unless the corporation has timely filed Form 2553 to elect to be an S corporation. ▶ See separate instructions.	19**93**

For calendar year 1993, or tax year beginning .... , 1993, and ending .... , 19 ......

A Date of election as an S corporation **1-1-82**	Use IRS label. Other- wise, please print or type.	Name **H AND L CORPORATION**	**C** Employer identification number **66 : 0770333**
B Business code no. (see Specific Instructions) **5651**		Number, street, and room or suite no. (If a P.O. box, see page 9 of the instructions.) **3109 STATE ST.**	**D** Date incorporated **1-1-82**
		City or town, state, and ZIP code **STATE COLLEGE, PA 16801**	**E** Total assets (see Specific Instructions) $ **120,000**

F Check applicable boxes: (1) ☐ Initial return   (2) ☐ Final return   (3) ☐ Change in address   (4) ☐ Amended return
G Check this box if this S corporation is subject to the consolidated audit procedures of sections 6241 through 6245 (see instructions before checking this box) . ▶ ☐
H Enter number of shareholders in the corporation at end of the tax year . . . . ▶ **2**

Caution: Include **only** trade or business income and expenses on lines 1a through 21. See the instructions for more information.

Income

1a Gross receipts or sales **150,000** **b** Less returns and allowances **—0—** **c** Bal ▶	**1c**	**150,000**	
2 Cost of goods sold (Schedule A, line 8)	**2**	**60,000**	
3 Gross profit. Subtract line 2 from line 1c	**3**	**90,000**	
4 Net gain (loss) from Form 4797, Part II, line 20 *(attach Form 4797)*	**4**		
5 Other income (loss) (see instructions) *(attach schedule)* . . .	**5**		
6 **Total income (loss).** Combine lines 3 through 5 . . . . ▶	**6**	**90,000**	

Deductions (See instructions for limitations.)

7 Compensation of officers	**7**	**25,000**	
8a Salaries and wages **30,000** **b** Less employment credits **—0—** **c** Bal ▶	**8c**	**30,000**	
9 Repairs and maintenance.	**9**	**1,800**	
10 Bad debts	**10**		
11 Rents	**11**		
12 Taxes and licenses. PAYROLL & PROPERTY TAXES	**12**	**3,200**	
13 Interest	**13**		
14a Depreciation (see instructions) **14a** **12,000**			
b Depreciation claimed on Schedule A and elsewhere on return . . **14b** **—0—**			
c Subtract line 14b from line 14a	**14c**	**12,000**	
15 Depletion **(Do not deduct oil and gas depletion.)**	**15**		
16 Advertising	**16**		
17 Pension, profit-sharing, etc., plans	**17**		
18 Employee benefit programs . INSURANCE = $3,000	**18**		
19 Other deductions (see instructions) *(attach schedule)* OFFICE = $1,100 UTILITIES = $800	**19**	**4,900**	
20 **Total deductions.** Add lines 7 through 19 . . . EXPENSES TELEPHONE ▶	**20**	**76,900**	
21 Ordinary income (loss) from trade or business activities. Subtract line 20 from line 6	**21**	**13,100**	

Tax and Payments

22 **Tax: a** Excess net passive income tax *(attach schedule)*. . . .	**22a**		
b Tax from Schedule D (Form 1120S)	**22b**		
c Add lines 22a and 22b (see instructions for additional taxes) . .	**22c**		
23 **Payments: a** 1993 estimated tax payments	**23a**		
b Tax deposited with Form 7004	**23b**		
c Credit for Federal tax paid on fuels *(attach Form 4136)* . . .	**23c**		
d Add lines 23a through 23c	**23d**		
24 Estimated tax penalty (see instructions). Check if Form 2220 is attached. . . . . ▶ ☐	**24**		
25 **Tax due.** If the total of lines 22c and 24 is larger than line 23d, enter amount owed. See instructions for depositary method of payment . . . . ▶	**25**		
26 **Overpayment.** If line 23d is larger than the total of lines 22c and 24, enter amount overpaid ▶	**26**		
27 Enter amount of line 26 you want: **Credited to 1994 estimated tax** ▶	Refunded ▶	**27**	

Please Sign Here

Under penalties of perjury, I declare that I have examined this return, including accompanying schedules and statements, and to the best of my knowledge and belief, it is true, correct, and complete. Declaration of preparer (other than taxpayer) is based on all information of which preparer has any knowledge.

▶		
Signature of officer	Date	Title

Paid Preparer's Use Only

Preparer's signature ▶		Date	Check if self- employed ▶ ☐	Preparer's social security number
Firm's name (or yours if self-employed) and address ▶			E.I. No. ▶	
			ZIP code ▶	

For Paperwork Reduction Act Notice, see page 1 of separate instructions.   Cat. No. 11510H   Form **1120S** (1993)

Exhibit 19-6 *Schedule K (Form 1120S)*

Form 1120S (1993)   Page 3

Schedule K	Shareholders' Shares of Income, Credits, Deductions, etc.		
	(a) Pro rata share items		**(b) Total amount**

Income (Loss)	1 Ordinary income (loss) from trade or business activities (page 1, line 21)	1	13,100	
	2 Net income (loss) from rental real estate activities *(attach Form 8825)*	2		
	3a Gross income from other rental activities	3a		
	b Expenses from other rental activities *(attach schedule)*. .	3b		
	c Net income (loss) from other rental activities. Subtract line 3b from line 3a	3c		
	4 Portfolio income (loss):			
	a Interest income	4a		
	b Dividend income.	4b		
	c Royalty income	4c		
	d Net short-term capital gain (loss) *(attach Schedule D (Form 1120S))*	4d	2,000	
	e Net long-term capital gain (loss) *(attach Schedule D (Form 1120S))*.	4e		
	f Other portfolio income (loss) *(attach schedule)*	4f		
	5 Net gain (loss) under section 1231 (other than due to casualty or theft) *(attach Form 4797)*	5		
	6 Other income (loss) *(attach schedule)*	6		
Deductions	7 Charitable contributions (see instructions) *(attach schedule)*	7		
	8 Section 179 expense deduction *(attach Form 4562)*.	8		
	9 Deductions related to portfolio income (loss) (see instructions) (itemize)	9		
	10 Other deductions *(attach schedule)*	10		
Investment Interest	11a Interest expense on investment debts	11a		
	b (1) Investment income included on lines 4a, 4b, 4c, and 4f above	11b(1)		
	(2) Investment expenses included on line 9 above	11b(2)		
Credits	12a Credit for alcohol used as a fuel *(attach Form 6478)*	12a		
	b Low-income housing credit (see instructions):			
	(1) From partnerships to which section 42(j)(5) applies for property placed in service before 1990	12b(1)		
	(2) Other than on line 12b(1) for property placed in service before 1990.	12b(2)		
	(3) From partnerships to which section 42(j)(5) applies for property placed in service after 1989	12b(3)		
	(4) Other than on line 12b(3) for property placed in service after 1989	12b(4)		
	c Qualified rehabilitation expenditures related to rental real estate activities *(attach Form 3468)* .	12c		
	d Credits (other than credits shown on lines 12b and 12c) related to rental real estate activities (see instructions).	12d		
	e Credits related to other rental activities (see instructions)	12e		
	13 Other credits (see instructions)	13		
Adjustments and Tax Preference Items	14a Depreciation adjustment on property placed in service after 1986	14a		
	b Adjusted gain or loss	14b		
	c Depletion (other than oil and gas)	14c		
	d (1) Gross income from oil, gas, or geothermal properties	14d(1)		
	(2) Deductions allocable to oil, gas, or geothermal properties	14d(2)		
	e Other adjustments and tax preference items *(attach schedule)*	14e		
Foreign Taxes	15a Type of income ▶			
	b Name of foreign country or U.S. possession ▶			
	c Total gross income from sources outside the United States *(attach schedule)*	15c		
	d Total applicable deductions and losses *(attach schedule)*	15d		
	e Total foreign taxes (check one): ▶ ☐ Paid ☐ Accrued	15e		
	f Reduction in taxes available for credit *(attach schedule)*	15f		
	g Other foreign tax information *(attach schedule)*	15g		
Other	16a Total expenditures to which a section 59(e) election may apply	16a		
	b Type of expenditures ▶			
	17 Tax-exempt interest income	17		
	18 Other tax-exempt income	18		
	19 Nondeductible expenses	19		
	20 Total property distributions (including cash) other than dividends reported on line 22 below	20		
	21 Other items and amounts required to be reported separately to shareholders (see instructions) *(attach schedule)*			
	22 Total dividend distributions paid from accumulated earnings and profits	22		
	23 **Income (loss).** (Required only if Schedule M-1 must be completed.) Combine lines 1 through 6 in column (b). From the result, subtract the sum of lines 7 through 11a, 15e, and 16a	23		

Exhibit 19-7 *Schedule K-1 (Form 1120S)*

SCHEDULE K-1 (Form 1120S)	Shareholder's Share of Income, Credits, Deductions, etc.	OMB No. 1545-0130
Department of the Treasury Internal Revenue Service	▶ See separate instructions. For calendar year 1993 or tax year beginning , 1993, and ending , 19	1993

Shareholder's identifying number ▶	Corporation's identifying number ▶
Shareholder's name, address, and ZIP code H. SHAREHOLDER 1615 SALEM AVENUE LANCASTER, PA 17604	Corporation's name, address, and ZIP code H AND L CORPORATION 3109 STATE STREET STATE COLLEGE, PA 16801

A Shareholder's percentage of stock ownership for tax year (see Instructions for Schedule K-1) . . . . ▶ **50** %
B Internal Revenue Service Center where corporation filed its return ▶ . . . . PHILADELPHIA . . . .
C Tax shelter registration number (see Instructions for Schedule K-1) . . . . ▶ . . . .
D Check applicable boxes: **(1)** ☐ Final K-1   **(2)** ☐ Amended K-1

		(a) Pro rata share items		(b) Amount	(c) Form 1040 filers enter the amount in column (b) on:
Income (Loss)	1	Ordinary income (loss) from trade or business activities . . .	1	6,550	See Shareholder's Instructions for Schedule K-1 (Form 1120S).
	2	Net income (loss) from rental real estate activities	2		
	3	Net income (loss) from other rental activities	3		
	4	Portfolio income (loss):			
	a	Interest	4a		Sch. B, Part I, line 1
	b	Dividends	4b		Sch. B, Part II, line 5
	c	Royalties	4c		Sch. E, Part I, line 4
	d	Net short-term capital gain (loss)	4d		Sch. D, line 5, col. (f) or (g)
	e	Net long-term capital gain (loss)	4e	1,000	Sch. D, line 13, col. (f) or (g)
	f	Other portfolio income (loss) *(attach schedule)*	4f		(Enter on applicable line of your return.)
	5	Net gain (loss) under section 1231 (other than due to casualty or theft)	5		See Shareholder's Instructions for Schedule K-1 (Form 1120S)
	6	Other income (loss) *(attach schedule)*	6		(Enter on applicable line of your return.)
Deductions	7	Charitable contributions (see instructions) *(attach schedule)* . .	7		Sch. A, line 13 or 14
	8	Section 179 expense deduction	8		See Shareholder's Instructions for Schedule K-1 (Form 1120S).
	9	Deductions related to portfolio income (loss) *(attach schedule)* .	9		
	10	Other deductions *(attach schedule)*	10		
Investment Interest	11a	Interest expense on investment debts	11a		Form 4952, line 1
	b	(1) Investment income included on lines 4a, 4b, 4c, and 4f above	b(1)		See Shareholder's Instructions for Schedule K-1 (Form 1120S)
		(2) Investment expenses included on line 9 above	b(2)		
Credits	12a	Credit for alcohol used as fuel	12a		Form 6478, line 10
	b	Low-income housing credit:			
		(1) From section 42(j)(5) partnerships for property placed in service before 1990.	b(1)		
		(2) Other than on line 12b(1) for property placed in service before 1990	b(2)		Form 8586, line 5
		(3) From section 42(j)(5) partnerships for property placed in service after 1989	b(3)		
		(4) Other than on line 12b(3) for property placed in service after 1989	b(4)		
	c	Qualified rehabilitation expenditures related to rental real estate activities (see instructions)	12c		
	d	Credits (other than credits shown on lines 12b and 12c) related to rental real estate activities (see instructions)	12d		See Shareholder's Instructions for Schedule K-1 (Form 1120S).
	e	Credits related to other rental activities (see instructions) . . .	12e		
	13	Other credits (see instructions)	13		
Adjustments and Tax Preference Items	14a	Depreciation adjustment on property placed in service after 1986	14a		See Shareholder's Instructions for Schedule K-1 (Form 1120S) and Instructions for Form 6251
	b	Adjusted gain or loss	14b		
	c	Depletion (other than oil and gas)	14c		
	d	(1) Gross income from oil, gas, or geothermal properties . .	d(1)		
		(2) Deductions allocable to oil, gas, or geothermal properties	d(2)		
	e	Other adjustments and tax preference items *(attach schedule)* .	14e		

For Paperwork Reduction Act Notice, see page 1 of Instructions for Form 1120S.   Cat. No. 11520D   **Schedule K-1 (Form 1120S) 1993**

C CORPORATIONS

Of the four business forms discussed in this chapter, only the C corporation is a separate taxable entity. And, as the only separate taxable entity, it is the only form of business for which the income may be taxed twice. The possibility of double taxation became a virtual certainty for owners of closely held businesses after 1986, and, consequently, most businesses that were eligible to elect the S corporate form usually did. There are many corporations, however, for which the S corporation election was not an alternative, and these corporations continue to operate as C corporations. As a practical matter, although the number of S corporations may be greater than the number of C corporations, the vast majority of business conducted in the United States is conducted by C corporations (e.g., publicly traded corporations).

TAXATION OF CORPORATE OPERATIONS IN GENERAL

The overall taxation of a corporation closely resembles that for an individual. Nevertheless, differences do exist. This section looks at the basic rules for computing the corporation's tax liability, identifying the similarities and differences between corporate and individual taxation.

Tax Formula.   The basic formula for computing the corporation's taxable income, although similar to that for an individual, is really far simpler. A quick comparison of the two formulas (given in Chapter 3 in Exhibits 3-1 and 3-2 and on the inside back cover of this text) reveals that taxable income for both entities is computed in the same manner—total income less exclusions and deductions. Note, however, that the corporate formula is not confused with such items as adjusted gross income, itemized deductions, and exemptions. These latter items, as discussed below, are all unique to individual taxation.

Accounting Periods and Methods.   Before determining the taxable income of any entity, the entity must select a reporting period and the accounting methods used to allocate items between periods. Corporations, like individuals, can use the calendar year or a fiscal year. In this regard, corporations have far greater flexibility than partnerships and S corporations, which are generally restricted to using the calendar year for reporting purposes (unless they are willing to prepay the tax on the deferred income).

With respect to accounting methods, individuals, partnerships, and S corporations have somewhat greater flexibility than C corporations. As discussed in Chapter 5, individuals, partnerships, and S corporations may use the cash or accrual method. In contrast, corporations generally are required to use the accrual method. However, there are several broad exceptions. Personal service corporations and corporations whose average annual gross receipts do not exceed $5 million are allowed to use the cash method. It is important to emphasize, however, that both individuals and corporations must use the accrual method in determining sales and costs of goods sold if they maintain an inventory of items to sell to customers.

Income.   The all-inclusive definition of income contained in Code § 61 applies to all taxpayers. Section 61 simply states that "gross income means all income from whatever source derived. . . ." It makes no distinction between individuals or corporations. Consequently, the determination of a corporation's or an individual's income is based on the same definition. Just as important, all of the concepts underlying that definition are equally applicable to both individuals and corporations.

Exclusions. Both individuals and corporations are entitled to exclude certain types of income. For example, both entities are entitled to exclude interest on municipal bonds. Similarly, both are normally allowed to exclude life insurance proceeds, although such proceeds are received in a different context. Corporations often receive proceeds on the death of an insured officer or shareholder, and individuals receive amounts upon the death of a family member. Most of the other exclusions, such as those for scholarships and child support, are obviously personal in nature and, therefore, unique to individuals. The exclusion rules for gifts and inheritances do apply to both individuals and corporations; but as a practical matter, corporations rarely receive gifts or inheritances. However, corporations may receive contributions to their capital from both shareholders and nonshareholders (e.g., a city gives a corporation land on which to build a plant), in which case they are allowed to exclude such contributions. Many of the exclusions for individuals are those for employee benefits, such as social security, meals and lodging, group-term life insurance, health insurance, disability insurance, educational assistance, child and dependent care, tuition reduction, qualified employee discounts, and working condition fringe benefits. Once again, these exclusions are unique to individuals and not a concern when determining a corporation's income.

Deductions in General. Section 162 provides the general rule governing deductions, allowing taxpayers to deduct all the ordinary and necessary expenses incurred in carrying on a trade or business. Like its counterpart in the income area, this provision applies to both individuals and corporations. Both are allowed to deduct business expenses. The critical feature of corporate taxation is that all activities of a corporation are considered business. Therefore, corporations normally do not have the often exasperating problem that individuals do in determining whether an expense is a business or personal expense. Because all of a corporation's expenses are business related, the complexity in the individual tax formula attributable to personal expenses cannot be found in the corporate tax formula. Corporations have no adjusted gross income, and, therefore, there is no need to classify deductions as *for* adjusted gross income or as itemized deductions. All expenditures are either deductible or not deductible. Similarly, corporations are not entitled to such personal deductions as the standard deduction or the deduction for personal and dependency exemptions.

The treatment of salaries and fringe benefits to owners deserves special mention, given the differing treatment of these items in the partnership and S corporation area. Salaries and fringe benefits of *shareholders* who are *employees* of their C corporations are normally treated the same as salaries and fringe benefits paid to any other employee. Salaries are deductible corporate expenses, subject to withholding and regular employment taxes (not self-employment taxes). This is the same treatment that applies to salaries paid to shareholders of an S corporation. Fringe benefits are deductible by the corporation and nontaxable to the shareholder-employees. This treatment of fringe benefits allows shareholders in a C corporation to obtain their advantages while more-than-2-percent shareholders in S corporations and partners cannot.

There are several deductions that corporations have that individuals do not have. In addition, there are often differences in the manner in which certain deductions are computed. The most important of these are considered below.

Exhibit 19-8 *If Taxable Income Is*

Over	But Not Over	Tax Liability	Of the Amount Over
$ 0	$ 50,000	15%	$ 0
50,000	75,000	$ 7,500+25%	50,000
75,000	100,000	13,750+34%	75,000
100,000	335,000	22,250+39%	100,000
335,000	10,000,000	113,900+34%	335,000
10,000,000	15,000,000	3,400,000+35%	10,000,000
15,000,000	18,333,333	5,150,000+38%	15,000,000
18,333,333		6,416,666+35%	18,333,333

There is a 5 percent surcharge for taxable income in excess of $100,000, up to a maximum surtax of $11,750. Similarly, there is a 3 percent surcharge for taxable income in excess of $15 million up to a maximum surtax of $100,000.

Credits. Many of the tax credits available to individuals are also available to corporations. For example, corporations may claim the credits for rehabilitation of buildings, building and improving low-income housing, investment in solar and geothermal property, hiring certain targeted persons, research and experimentation, providing access for the disabled, and the use of alcohol as fuel. Certain credits that are personal in nature are obviously not available to corporations. These include the child and dependent care credit, credit for the elderly and permanently disabled, and the earned income credit.

Tax Rates. Corporations have their own unique tax rate schedule. The tax rates for corporations can be found in Exhibit 19-8. The rates for individuals and corporations can be easily compared by turning to the inside front cover of this text. As can be seen in the corporate tax rate schedule, the tax rates for corporations are progressive, increasing from a low of 15 percent on the first $50,000 of income to a high of 35 percent on incomes over $10 million. In an effort to restrict the tax benefit of the lower graduated rates to small corporate businesses with taxable income of $100,000 or less, a 5 percent surtax is imposed on corporate taxable income in excess of $100,000, up to a maximum surtax of $11,750—the net "savings" of having the first $100,000 of corporate income taxed at the lower rates rather than 34 percent. The effect is to create a 39-percent bracket for incomes from $100,000 to $335,000. In a similar fashion, the tax rate increases by 3 percentage points from 35 to 38 percent when income exceeds $15 million. The 3 percent surtax from $15 million to $18,333,333 million wipes out the 1 percent benefit derived from the lower 34 percent bracket on the first $10 million of taxable income [$100,000 surtax (3% × $3,333,333) eliminates $100,000 benefit ((35% − 34% = 1%) × $10,000,000)].

Reporting. A corporation reports all of its relevant tax information on Form 1120. The return is due on the 15th day of the third month after the close of its taxable year. An automatic extension of six months is available.

Example 6.   The records of a C corporation owned equally by D and E show the following information for the year:

Sales...	$150,000
Cost of goods sold....................................	60,000
Operating expenses:	
Depreciation.......................................	12,000
Insurance..	3,000
Office supplies.....................................	1,100
Repairs..	1,800
Payroll and property taxes..........................	3,200
Utilities and telephone.............................	800
Employee salaries..................................	30,000
H's guaranteed payment............................	25,000
Capital gain..	2,000

The above information is the same as it is with the proprietorship (*Example 1*), the partnership (*Example 3*), and the S corporation (Exhibit 19-5). Page 1 of Form 1120 (Exhibit 19-9) is similar to Forms 1065 (Exhibit 19-2) and 1120S (Exhibit 19-5). There are two differences. First, the computation is for *taxable income*, not net ordinary income. As a result, *gross income* is $92,000 ($150,000 − $60,000 + $2,000) which is $2,000 greater than it is for the partnership and S corporation because of the net capital gain. *Taxable income* of $15,100 also is $2,000 greater than the net ordinary income for the partnership and S corporation. The second difference is that the C corporation has a *tax liability* of $2,265 ($15,100 × 15%), which is calculated on Schedule J (Exhibit 19-10) of Form 1120. D has includible salary income of $25,000 but the corporate activities have no effect on E's tax return.

DIFFERENCES BETWEEN CORPORATE AND INDIVIDUAL TAXATION

As may be apparent from the discussion above, the *basic* rules to determine a corporation's taxable income are essentially the same as those applied to determine the taxable income of individuals, sole proprietors, partnerships, and S corporations. The organization form simply does not affect the tax treatment of most transactions that occur during the ordinary course of business. For example, the computations related to sales, costs of goods sold, and numerous operating expenses such as those for salaries and wages paid to nonowner employees, repairs and maintenance, utilities, insurance, rent, supplies, travel, entertainment, interest, repairs, bad debts, and advertising are all the same regardless of the form of business. However, despite all of these similarities, there are differences. The most significant of these are covered below. Note that while the following discussion is couched in terms of the differences between corporate and individual taxation, it effectively includes a comparison of corporate taxation to the taxation of partnerships and S corporations as well since they are merely conduits.

Dividend Income.   Dividend income received by an individual receives no special treatment and is simply included along with other items in the taxpayer's gross income. As explained earlier, this treatment results in double taxation since the income is also taxed at the corporate level and is not deductible by the corporation when distributed to the shareholders. Note that if the shareholder is a corporation, *triple* taxation or more could

Exhibit 19-9 *Form 1120*

Form **1120**	U.S. Corporation Income Tax Return	OMB No. 1545-0123

Department of the Treasury / Internal Revenue Service

For calendar year 1993 or tax year beginning .... , 1993, ending .... , 19 ...
► **Instructions are separate. See page 1 for Paperwork Reduction Act Notice.**

19 93

A Check if a:
1 Consolidated return (attach Form 851) ☐
2 Personal holding co. (attach Sch. PH) ☐
3 Personal service corp. (as defined in Temporary Regs. sec. 1.441-4T— see instructions) ☐

Use IRS label. Otherwise, please print or type.

Name **H AND L CORPORATION**

Number, street, and room or suite no. (If a P.O. box, see page 7 of instructions.) **3109 STATE ST.**

City or town, state, and ZIP code **STATE COLLEGE, PA 16801**

B Employer identification number **66 : 0770333**

C Date incorporated **1-1-82**

D Total assets (see Specific Instructions) $ **120,000**

E Check applicable boxes: (1) Initial return ☐ (2) Final return ☐ (3) Change of address ☐

1a	Gross receipts or sales **150,000**	b Less returns and allowances **—0—** c Bal ►	1c **150,000**
2	Cost of goods sold (Schedule A, line 8)		2 **60,000**
3	Gross profit. Subtract line 2 from line 1c		3 **90,000**
4	Dividends (Schedule C, line 19)		4 **—**
5	Interest		5 **—**
6	Gross rents		6 **—**
7	Gross royalties		7 **—**
8	Capital gain net income (attach Schedule D (Form 1120))		8 **2,000**
9	Net gain or (loss) from Form 4797, Part II, line 20 (attach Form 4797)		9 **—**
10	Other income (see instructions—attach schedule)		10 **—**
11	**Total income.** Add lines 3 through 10 ►		11 **92,000**

(Income)

12	Compensation of officers (Schedule E, line 4)		12 **25,000**
13a	Salaries and wages _____ b Less employment credits _____ c Bal ►		13c **30,000**
14	Repairs and maintenance		14 **1,800**
15	Bad debts		15 **—**
16	Rents		16 **—**
17	Taxes and licenses **PAYROLL & PROPERTY TAXES**		17 **3,200**
18	Interest		18 **—**
19	Charitable contributions (see instructions for 10% limitation)		19 **—**
20	Depreciation (attach Form 4562) . . . 20 **12,000**		
21	Less depreciation claimed on Schedule A and elsewhere on return . . . 21a **—0—**		21b **12,000**
22	Depletion		22 **—**
23	Advertising		23 **—**
24	Pension, profit-sharing, etc., plans		24 **—**
25	Employee benefit programs **INSURANCE = $3,000**		25 **—**
26	Other deductions (attach schedule) **OFFICE EXPENSES=$1,100 ; UTILITIES+TELEPHONE = $800**		26 **4,900**
27	**Total deductions.** Add lines 12 through 26 ►		27 **76,900**
28	Taxable income before net operating loss deduction and special deductions. Subtract line 27 from line 11		28 **15,100**
29	**Less:** a Net operating loss deduction (see instructions) 29a		
	b Special deductions (Schedule C, line 20) 29b		29c **—**

(Deductions (See instructions for limitations on deductions.))

30	**Taxable income.** Subtract line 29c from line 28		30 **15,100**
31	**Total tax** (Schedule J, line 10)		31 **2,265**
32	Payments: a 1992 overpayment credited to 1993 32a		
b	1993 estimated tax payments . . 32b		
c	Less 1993 refund applied for on Form 4466 32c ( ) d Bal ► 32d		
e	Tax deposited with Form 7004 . . . . 32e		
f	Credit from regulated investment companies (attach Form 2439) . . 32f		
g	Credit for Federal tax on fuels (attach Form 4136). See instructions . . . 32g		32h **—**
33	Estimated tax penalty (see instructions). Check if Form 2220 is attached . . . . ► ☐		33 **—**
34	**Tax due.** If line 32h is smaller than the total of lines 31 and 33, enter amount owed		34 **2,265**
35	**Overpayment.** If line 32h is larger than the total of lines 31 and 33, enter amount overpaid		35 **—**
36	Enter amount of line 35 you want: **Credited to 1994 estimated tax** ► Refunded ►		36 **—**

(Tax and Payments)

Please Sign Here

Under penalties of perjury, I declare that I have examined this return, including accompanying schedules and statements, and to the best of my knowledge and belief, it is true, correct, and complete. Declaration of preparer (other than taxpayer) is based on all information of which preparer has any knowledge.

► Signature of officer _____ Date ____ ► Title ____

Paid Preparer's Use Only

Preparer's signature _____ Date ____ Check if self-employed ☐ Preparer's social security number ____

Firm's name (or yours if self-employed) and address _____ E.I. No. ► ZIP code ►

Cat. No. 11450Q

Exhibit 19-10 *Schedule J (Form 1120)*

Form 1120 (1993)   Page 3

Schedule J   Tax Computation (See instructions.)

1   Check if the corporation is a member of a controlled group (see sections 1561 and 1563) . . . . ▶ ☐

2a   If the box on line 1 is checked, enter the corporation's share of the $50,000, $25,000, and $9,925,000 taxable
     income brackets (in that order):

    (1) $ _____   (2) $ _____   (3) $ _____

b   Enter the corporation's share of:

    (1) additional 5% tax (not more than $11,750) $ _____

    (2) additional 3% tax (not more than $100,000) $ _____

3   Income tax. Check this box if the corporation is a qualified personal service corporation as defined in section
     448(d)(2) (see instructions on page 15) . . . . ▶ ☐ | **3** | 2,265

4a Foreign tax credit (attach Form 1118)	**4a**
b Possessions tax credit (attach Form 5735)	**4b**
c Orphan drug credit (attach Form 6765)	**4c**
d Check: ☐ Nonconventional source fuel credit ☐ QEV credit (attach Form 8834)	**4d**

e   General business credit. Enter here and check which forms are attached:

    ☐ Form 3800 ☐ Form 3468 ☐ Form 5884 ☐ Form 6478 ☐ Form 6765

    ☐ Form 8586 ☐ Form 8830 ☐ Form 8826 ☐ Form 8835 . . . . | **4e**

f   Credit for prior year minimum tax (attach Form 8827) . . . . | **4f**

5 **Total credits.** Add lines 4a through 4f	**5**	
6 Subtract line 5 from line 3	**6**	2,265
7 Personal holding company tax (attach Schedule PH (Form 1120))	**7**	
8 Recapture taxes. Check if from: ☐ Form 4255 ☐ Form 8611	**8**	
9a Alternative minimum tax (attach Form 4626)	**9a**	
b Environmental tax (attach Form 4626)	**9b**	
10 **Total tax.** Add lines 6 through 9b. Enter here and on line 31, page 1	**10**	2,265

Schedule K   Other Information (See pages 17 and 18 of instructions.)

	Yes	No
1 Check method of accounting: a ☐ Cash		
b ☒ Accrual c ☐ Other (specify) ▶		

2   Refer to page 19 of the instructions and state the principal:

a   Business activity code no. ▶ .....5651.....

b   Business activity ▶ ....RETAIL TRADE.......

c   Product or service ▶ ....APPAREL...........

	Yes	No
3 Did the corporation at the end of the tax year own, directly or indirectly, 50% or more of the voting stock of a domestic corporation? (For rules of attribution, see section 267(c).)		✓

    If "Yes," attach a schedule showing: (a) name and identifying number, (b) percentage owned, and (c) taxable income or (loss) before NOL and special deductions of such corporation for the tax year ending with or within your tax year.

	Yes	No
4 Is the corporation a subsidiary in an affiliated group or a parent-subsidiary controlled group?		✓

    If "Yes," enter employer identification number and name of the parent corporation ▶ ....

	Yes	No
5 Did any individual, partnership, corporation, estate or trust at the end of the tax year own, directly or indirectly, 50% or more of the corporation's voting stock? (For rules of attribution, see section 267(c).)	✓	

    If "Yes," attach a schedule showing name and identifying number. (Do not include any information already entered in **4** above.) Enter percentage owned ▶ .....50%....

	Yes	No
6 During this tax year, did the corporation pay dividends (other than stock dividends and distributions in exchange for stock) in excess of the corporation's current and accumulated earnings and profits? (See secs. 301 and 316.)		✓

    If "Yes," file Form 5452. If this is a consolidated return, answer here for the parent corporation and on **Form 851,** Affiliations Schedule, for each subsidiary.

	Yes	No
7 Was the corporation a U.S. shareholder of any controlled foreign corporation? (See sections 951 and 957.) . . .		✓

    If "Yes," attach Form 5471 for each such corporation. Enter number of Forms 5471 attached ▶ ....

	Yes	No
8 At any time during the 1993 calendar year, did the corporation have an interest in or a signature or other authority over a financial account in a foreign country (such as a bank account, securities account, or other financial account)? .		✓

    If "Yes," the corporation may have to file Form TD F 90-22.1. If "Yes," enter name of foreign country ▶ ....

	Yes	No
9 Was the corporation the grantor of, or transferor to, a foreign trust that existed during the current tax year, whether or not the corporation has any beneficial interest in it? If "Yes," the corporation may have to file Forms 926, 3520, or 3520-A		✓

	Yes	No
10 Did one foreign person at any time during the tax year own, directly or indirectly, at least 25% of: **(a)** the total voting power of all classes of stock of the corporation entitled to vote, or **(b)** the total value of all classes of stock of the corporation? If "Yes,"		✓

a   Enter percentage owned ▶ ....

b   Enter owner's country ▶ ....

c   The corporation may have to file Form 5472. Enter number of Forms 5472 attached ▶ ....

11   Check this box if the corporation issued publicly offered debt instruments with original issue discount . . ▶ ☐

    If so, the corporation may have to file Form 8281.

12   Enter the amount of tax-exempt interest received or accrued during the tax year ▶ $ ....

13   If there were 35 or fewer shareholders at the end of the tax year, enter the number ▶ 2 ....

14   If the corporation has an NOL for the tax year and is electing to forego the carryback period, check here ▶ ☐

15   Enter the available NOL carryover from prior tax years (Do not reduce it by any deduction on line 29a.) ▶ $

result. To prevent this, Congress provided corporations with a deduction for dividends received.

The amount of the deduction for dividends received normally is 70 percent of the amount of the dividend.[13] However, this may be increased to 80 or 100 percent depending on the corporate shareholder's ownership in the dividend-paying corporation as summarized below:

Relationship to Dividend-Paying Corporation	Dividends-Received Deduction
Owns 20% or less..	70%
Owns more than 20%, but less than 80%.....................	80%
Is an affiliated group member (80% of stock is owned by other members of the group)......	100%

The 70 and 80 percent dividends-received deductions may be limited to 70 and 80 percent of taxable income, respectively. For this purpose, taxable income is computed before the dividends-received deduction, net operating loss (NOL) carryovers and carrybacks, and capital loss carrybacks. By ignoring the carrybacks, the dividends-received deduction is not affected when a corporation subsequently incurs a capital loss or an NOL and carries either back.

The taxable income limitation does not always apply. The taxable income limitation is ignored if the dividends-received deduction when subtracted from taxable income either creates an NOL or adds to an existing NOL.

Example 7.   This year, three corporations—R, S, and T—each received $40,000 of dividends from less than 20 percent owned corporations. Consequently, the tentative dividends-received deduction of each corporation is $28,000 (70% × $40,000). However, to determine the amount of the dividends-received deduction actually allowed, each corporation must compute its taxable income limitation and determine if it is applicable. The computation of the taxable income limitation is shown below.

	R	S	T
Dividends received...................................	$40,000	$40,000	$40,000
Sales..	60,000	20,000	10,000
Costs of goods sold and other operating expenses....	−30,000	−30,000	−30,000
Taxable income before the dividends-received deduction...	$70,000	$30,000	$20,000
Taxable income before the dividends-received deduction...	$70,000	$30,000	$20,000
	× 70%	× 70%	× 70%
Taxable income limitation.............................	$49,000	$21,000	$14,000

---

[13]   §§ 243 through 246.

R may claim a dividends-received deduction of $28,000 since it is less than its taxable income limitation of $49,000. In S's situation, however, the dividends-received deduction is limited to $21,000 *unless* the tentative dividends-received deduction of $28,000 *adds to or creates a net operating loss*. In this case, subtracting the tentative dividends-received deduction of $28,000 from $30,000 does not add to or create a loss, so S's dividends-received deduction is limited to $21,000. T's situation presents the third possibility. Similar to S's, T's dividends-received deduction is limited to $14,000 *unless* the tentative dividends-received deduction of $28,000 *adds to or creates a net operating loss*. In this case, subtracting the tentative dividends-received deduction of $28,000 from $20,000 creates an NOL of $8,000. Consequently, T is allowed to deduct the normal dividends-received deduction of $28,000.

Capital Gains and Losses. The world of capital gains and capital losses is virtually identical for corporations and individuals. The definition of a capital asset, the determination of the holding period, and the capital gain and loss netting process are the same for all.[14] However, the treatment of these items may differ. If a corporation or an individual has a net short-term capital gain (i.e., capital gain net income), there is no special treatment. They both treat net short-term capital gain as ordinary income. While the treatment of net short-term capital gains is the same, the treatment of net long-term capital gains differs. If an individual has a net long-term capital gain (i.e., a net capital gain), a special tax calculation ensures that the gain is taxed at the lesser of the individual's marginal rate or 28 percent. In contrast, a corporation receives no favorable treatment for long-term capital gains. Corporations simply include both net long-term capital gains and net short-term capital gains along with other ordinary income and compute the tax liability using the current rates. Thus, a corporation's capital gains could be taxed at a rate as high as 39 percent (34% plus a 5% surcharge).

The treatment of a net capital loss of a corporation differs significantly from that for an individual. As a general rule, individuals are allowed to offset capital losses against capital gains and up to $3,000 of ordinary income annually.[15] If both a net short-term capital loss and a net long-term capital loss exist, an individual taxpayer first offsets the net short-term capital loss against ordinary income. Any short-term or long-term capital loss not absorbed is carried *forward* until it is exhausted.[16] Capital losses retain their character as either short-term or long-term when they are carried forward.

Capital losses of a corporation offset *only* capital gains.[17] A corporation is never permitted to reduce ordinary income by a capital loss. As a result, corporations cannot deduct their excess capital losses for the year. Instead, a corporation must carry the excess capital losses *back* for three years and *forward* for five years, to use them to offset capital gains in those years. The losses are first carried back three years. All of the losses, whether short-term or long-term, are carried back as short-term capital losses. They are treated as if they occurred in the prior year and reduce the amount of capital

---

[14] §§ 1222(5), (6), (7), and (8).

[15] § 1211(b)(1) and Reg. §§ 1.1211-1(b)(2) and (6).

[16] § 1212(b).

[17] §§ 1211(a) and 1212(a).

gains reported in the earliest year. Any amount not used to offset gain in the third previous year can offset gain in the second previous year and then the first previous year. If the sum of the capital gains reported in the three previous years is less than the capital loss, the excess is carried forward. Losses carried forward may be used to offset capital gains recognized in the succeeding five tax years. Losses unused at the end of the five-year carryforward period expire.

Example 8. B Corporation has income, gains, and losses as follows:

	1991	1992	1993	1994
Ordinary income......................	$100,000	$100,000	$100,000	$100,000
Net capital gain or (loss)..............	4,000	3,000	2,000	(10,000)
Total income.........................	$ 104,000	$ 103,000	$ 102,000	$ 90,000

B reported taxable income in years 1991, 1992, and 1993 of $104,000, $103,000, and $102,000, respectively, since net capital gains are added into taxable income. In 1993 B must report $100,000 taxable income because capital losses are non-deductible. However, B Corporation is entitled to carry the net capital loss back to years 1991, 1992, and 1993 and file a claim for refund for the taxes paid on the capital gains for each year. Because the 1994 capital loss carryback ($10,000) exceeds the sum of the capital gains in the prior three years ($9,000), B has a $1,000 capital loss carryforward. This loss carryforward can be used to offset the first $1,000 of capital gains recognized in years 1995 through 1999.

Corporations treat all capital loss carrybacks and carryovers as short-term losses. At present, this has no effect on the tax due and it is often immaterial whether the carryover is considered long-term or short-term. However, if Congress ever reinstates special treatment for long-term capital gains, keeping short-term and long-term carryovers separate will once again have meaning.

Sales of Depreciable Property and Recapture. Corporations, like individuals, must recapture depreciation on the sales of most depreciable property under the normal recapture provisions of § 1245 and § 1250. Unlike the other entities, however, C corporations (and in certain cases S corporations) are subject to the special recapture rules of § 291. These rules, explained in detail in Chapter 17, require the corporation to recapture 20 percent of any straight-line depreciation that normally is not recaptured on the sale of depreciable realty.

Example 9. Business T sells a shopping center for $800,000; $200,000 allocated to land and $600,000 to buildings. The basis for the land is $125,000 and for the building is $120,000 ($450,000 cost − $330,000 accumulated depreciation, based on the straight-line method). T's § 1231 gain on the land is $75,000 ($200,000 −

$125,000), regardless of whether T is an S or C corporation, a proprietorship, or a partnership. T's gain on the buildings is $480,000 ($600,000 − $120,000). Since only straight-line depreciation was used, all gain on the buildings is § 1231 gain for a proprietorship or a partnership. However, if T is a C corporation (or an S corporation that was a C corporation at any time during the three prior years), $66,000 of the $480,000 gain is ordinary income, computed as follows:

Amount that would have been recaptured under § 1245 (lesser of accumulated depreciation or gain)...................	$330,000
Less § 1250 gain..	− 0
	$330,000
Multiplied by the statutory rate.....................................	× 20%
§ 291(a)(1) ordinary income......................................	$ 66,000

The C or S corporation has ordinary income of $66,000 and § 1231 gain of $489,000 [$75,000 + ($480,000 − $66,000)].

Charitable Contributions.   A corporation's charitable contribution deduction, although similar to that for individuals, differs in several important respects. The first difference concerns timing of the deduction. Normally, charitable contributions can be deducted only in the year in which payment is actually made. However, accrual basis corporations are permitted to deduct the contribution prior to the year of payment—in effect, accrue the deduction—if all of the following requirements are met.

- The corporation is an accrual basis taxpayer.

- The charitable contribution is authorized during the year by the board of directors.

- The contribution is paid to the charity by the 15th day of the third month following the close of the tax year (March 15 for calendar year corporations).

The second difference between corporate and individual contribution deduction rules concerns the limitation on the amount of the annual deduction. An individual's charitable contributions are generally limited to 50 percent of adjusted gross income, although the limitation can be 30 or 20 percent in certain cases. In contrast, the corporation's deduction is limited to 10 percent of taxable income before the contribution deduction, the dividends-received deduction, and NOL carrybacks.[18] Any amount in excess of this limitation may be carried forward and deducted in any of the five succeeding years. In any year in which there are both *current* contributions and carryforwards, the current contributions are deducted first. If any portion of the 10 percent limitation is still available, the carryforwards are used on a first-in, first-out basis.[19] At the end of the five-year period, any carryover not deducted expires.

---

[18]   §170(b)(2).   [19]   §170(d)(2).

Example 10. W Inc. has the following information for its 1994, 1995, and 1996 tax years:

	1994	1995	1996
Taxable income before charitable deductions............................	$50,000	$57,000	$65,000
Charitable contributions....................	6,200	6,000	5,100

Assume W did not have dividend income in any of the three years. Taxable income and carryforwards are computed as follows:

	1994	1995	1996
Taxable income before charitable deductions............................	$50,000	$57,000	$65,000
Less charitable contributions:			
Current year............................	5,000	5,700	5,100
Carryforward from 1994.................			1,200
Carryforward from 1995.................			200
Taxable income...........................	$45,000	$51,300	$58,500
Charitable contributions:			
Carryforward from 1994.................	$ 1,200	$ 1,200	$ 0
Carryforward from 1995.................		300	100
Carryforward from 1996.................			0

Net Operating Losses. Section 172 allows corporations, like individuals, to deduct net operating losses occurring in other years. Fortunately, the NOL for a corporation is much simpler to compute. The difficulty in computing the NOL of an individual stems from trying to isolate the individual's true business loss. Consider an individual's tax return that after all is said and done reveals a negative number on the line for taxable income. This negative number on an individual's return is not simply attributable to the fact that business expenses exceeded business revenues. The number also reflects many nonbusiness items as well as artificial deductions (e.g., mortgage interest, medical expenses, and exemptions). Consequently, a series of complex adjustments are required to determine the loss attributable solely to business activities. For example, no deduction is allowed for personal exemptions, nonbusiness expenses can be deducted only to the extent of nonbusiness income, and special rules exist for capital gains and losses. The calculation of a corporation's NOL is far easier since a corporation's negative taxable income is also its business loss. The only modification in computing the NOL of a corporation concerns NOLs from other years.[20] Any NOL from another year is omitted from the computation of the current year's NOL. Note also that the dividends-received deduction, although artificial in nature, is not limited if, as explained above, it either creates an NOL or adds to an existing NOL.[21]

---

[20] § 172(d)(1).

[21] § 172(d)(5).

The carryover period for a corporate NOL is the same as that for individuals. The corporation normally carries the NOL back three years and forward 15 years.[22] A corporation may elect not to carry the loss back. If this election is made, the loss would be carried forward for 15 years.[23] This election is irrevocable.

Example 11.   A corporation's records show the following:

	1991	1992	1993	1994
Net operating income (loss)........	$11,000	$25,000	$17,000	($45,000)

Assume the corporation has never had dividend income and its only NOL occurred in 1994. The $45,000 NOL is carried back to offset the entire ordinary income in 1991 ($11,000) and 1992 ($25,000). The remaining $9,000 ($45,000 − $11,000 − $25,000) of NOL is deducted in 1993, leaving $8,000 ($17,000 − $9,000) ordinary income in 1993. Tax refunds are obtained for three years based on decreases in taxable income due to the 1994 NOL. Thus, all of the tax paid in 1991 and 1992 and a portion of the tax paid in 1993 are refunded. An election may be made, however, to carry the 1994 NOL forward instead of back. This may be advisable if the corporate marginal tax rates in 1995 (or later years if applicable) are expected to exceed those in the past three years. Of course, the present value of receiving a current refund for a carryback compared with paying a reduced tax in the future for the carryforward election *must* be included in the decision.

FORMATION OF A BUSINESS

The formation of a business normally requires the transfer of assets from the owner to the business in exchange for an interest in the business. For example, when two individuals decide to incorporate, they typically transfer property to the corporation in exchange for stock. If the individuals were to form a partnership, they would exchange property for an interest in the partnership. Without special rules, these exchanges would be taxable events and, consequently, could deter the owners from using the corporate or partnership form where otherwise it is perfectly appropriate. However, Congress recognized this problem early on and created special rules. These rules generally provide that any gain or loss realized on the transfer of property to a corporation or partnership in exchange for an interest in the entity is not recognized. The treatment is very similar to that for like-kind exchanges (discussed in Chapter 15). This section provides a brief overview of the specific tax consequences of forming a sole proprietorship, a partnership, or a corporation.

---

[22] § 172(b)(1).

[23] § 172(b)(3)(C). This is the same carryover available to individuals (see Chapter 10).

FORMATION OF A SOLE PROPRIETORSHIP

When an individual starts a business and decides to operate it as a sole proprietorship, the transfer of assets from the owner to the business is not a taxable event. In the eyes of the tax law, there is nothing to tax. No exchange has occurred since the owner still legally owns the assets and the sole proprietorship is not considered a separate taxable entity. Consequently, there are no tax consequences. The primary tax consideration is the property's basis for depreciation, any depreciation recapture potential, and the holding period. In those situations when the individual uses assets from another business activity in the new operation, the assets retain all of these tax attributes (basis, potential recapture, and holding period). This is not necessarily the case if personal assets are converted to business use. In this situation, the property's basis is the *lesser* of its value or basis. This rule ensures that the owner is not allowed a deduction for any decline in value that occurred while the property was held for personal use.

Example 12. T operates a proprietorship. During the year, T transfers the following assets from personal to business use:

Asset	Cost	Market Value
Automobile	$10,100	$ 5,200
Land	8,200	15,300

This is a nontaxable transfer. The assets are recorded on the proprietorship's books at the lower of (1) T's basis, which is the cost of the assets, or (2) market value on the transfer date. Thus, the automobile is recorded at $5,200 and the land at $8,200.

Example 13. V operates a proprietorship. After using the following equipment for two years of its five-year MACRS life, V transfers it from business to personal use (numbers are rounded for convenience):

Asset	Cost	Accumulated Depreciation	Basis	Market Value
Equipment	$10,000	$5,200	$4,800	$6,300

This is a nontaxable transfer. The market value of $6,300 is not considered when assets are transferred from the proprietorship to the owner. V records the equipment at its $4,800 basis and the potential § 1245 recapture of $5,200 transfers to him. If V sells the equipment, the first $5,200 of gain is § 1245 ordinary gain (see Chapter 17). This same treatment generally applies if the equipment is transferred to another business in a tax-free exchange.

FORMATION OF PARTNERSHIPS

A partnership is formed by contributions of cash, property, or services in exchange for an interest in the partnership. While most exchanges are taxable events, as suggested above, special rules provide that the transfer of *property* to a partnership in exchange for an interest in the partnership is nontaxable for both the partner and the partnership.[24] Any gain or loss realized is normally not recognized. This rule only applies to contributions of property. If the partner receives an interest in exchange for past services or services to be performed in the future, the receipt of the interest is treated as compensation and the partner normally reports income equal to the value of the interest. In this instance, additional special rules apply to the partnership and the remaining partners.

Although the partner and the partnership do not recognize any of the gain or loss realized on the exchange, such gain or loss does not escape tax. The gain or loss is preserved in the basis assigned to the partnership's basis in the assets received and the partner's basis in the partnership interest. The partner's initial basis in the partnership is generally the sum of the amount of cash contributed plus the adjusted basis of any property contributed.[25] The partnership's basis for the property received is generally the same as it was in the hands of the contributing partner.[26] In other words, the partner's basis for the property normally carries over to the partnership and becomes the partnership's basis for the property. As noted above, however, if the contributed property was formerly used for personal purposes, the lesser of the property's basis or fair market value is used in computing the partner's basis for the interest received as well as the partnership's basis for the property.

> **Example 14.** This year T contributed the following assets to the ST partnership in exchange for a 50 percent interest worth $26,000.

Assets	Cost	Accumulated Depreciation	Basis	FMV
Property used in proprietorship:				
Equipment..............................	$10,000	$5,200	$ 4,800	$ 6,000
Converted personal assets:				
Automobile.............................	10,000		10,000	5,000
Land....................................	8,000		8,000	15,000
Total.....................................			$22,800	$26,000

> Although T has realized a gain on the exchange of $3,200 ($26,000 − $4,800 − $10,000 − $8,000), the gain is not recognized. T's basis in his partnership interest is $17,800 ($4,800 + $5,000 + $8,000). The partnership's bases for the assets received are $4,800 for the equipment, $5,000 for the automobile, and $8,000 for the land. Note that when the property contributed is being converted from

---

[24] § 721.

[25] § 722.

[26] § 723.

personal use, the lower of the property's value or basis is used in computing both the partner's basis for his interest and the partnership's bases for the assets. The result is identical to that found in *Examples 12* and *13* for a sole proprietor.

It is important to note that for financial accounting purposes, the treatment of the partner and partnership is quite different than it is for tax purposes. For financial accounting, the assets are recorded at their fair market value and the contributing partner's capital account reflects the total fair market value of the property contributed. For example, in *Example 14* above, the partnership's financial accounting records would show the assets at a total value of $26,000 rather than their tax basis of $17,800. Similarly, the partner's capital account would reflect the value of his interest, $26,000, rather than his tax basis of $17,800. This obviously creates some interesting and difficult problems that must be considered when accounting for partnership transactions.

FORMATION OF CORPORATIONS

Like the formation of a partnership, the transfer of assets to a corporation in exchange for stock is normally a nontaxable transaction. Section 351 provides nonrecognition of any gain or loss realized on the exchange if the following requirements are met.

- The transferors of property, as a group, must control the corporation immediately after the exchange. Control is generally defined as ownership of at least 80 percent of the stock outstanding.

- The transferors must receive solely stock on the exchange. If the shareholders receive any other property—so-called boot—the shareholder must recognize any realized gain to the extent of the boot received. Losses are not recognized. Special rules apply when the transferor contributes liabilities to a corporation.

If these conditions are met, the transferors of property do not recognize any gain or loss realized. Note, however, that shareholders who contribute services in exchange for stock are not covered by § 351 and must recognize gain equal to the value of services. Service shareholders are treated as if they were paid cash for their services and then used such cash to purchase an interest in the corporation.

Any gain or loss not recognized is merely postponed and, as with a partnership, is preserved in the basis of the assets to the corporation and the basis of the stock to the shareholders. As a general rule, the basis of the shareholder's stock is the same as the basis of the property transferred increased by any gain recognized on the exchange and reduced by the value of the boot received.[27] This basis is generally referred to as a substituted basis and may be expressed as follows:

> Transferor's adjusted basis for the property transferred
> + Gain recognized
> − Boot received
>
> = Adjusted basis in stock received

---

[27]   § 358.

The corporation's basis for the assets received is the same as it was in the hands of the transferor increased by any gain recognized by the transferor.[28] The corporation's basis in the property received is referred to as a *carryover basis* and may be expressed as follows:

Transferor's adjusted basis for the property transferred
+ Gain recognized by the shareholder
= Corporation's adjusted basis for property received

Example 15.   This year R and S formed T Corporation. R transferred land worth $70,000 (basis $20,000) for 70 shares of stock worth $70,000. S transferred cash of $40,000 for 40 shares of stock. R has realized a gain of $50,000 computed as

Amount realized:	
Fair market value of stock received......................	$70,000
Adjusted basis of property transferred.....................	(20,000)
Gain realized...	$50,000

Although R has realized a gain of $50,000, none of it is recognized since the transaction meets the conditions of § 351. In this case, the transferors of property, R and S, together own 100 percent of the stock immediately after the exchange, thus satisfying the 80 percent control test. R's basis in her stock is a substituted basis of $20,000, whereas S's basis is $40,000. The corporation would have a carryover basis in the land contributed by R of $20,000. The basis calculations are shown below.

	R	S
Transferor's adjusted basis for the property transferred.........	$20,000	$40,000
+ Gain recognized...	0	0
− Boot received..	0	0
Shareholder's adjusted basis in stock received	$20,000	$40,000
Transferor's adjusted basis for the property transferred.........	$20,000	$40,000
+ Gain recognized by the shareholder...........................	0	0
Corporation's adjusted basis for property received	$20,000	$40,000

Note that if R were to sell her stock immediately for its value of $70,000, she would recognize the gain deferred on the exchange of $50,000 ($70,000 − $20,000).

---

[28]   § 362.

Example 16. Same facts as in *Example 15*, except R receives 65 shares of stock worth $65,000 and cash of $5,000. In this case, the requirements of § 351 are still satisfied but because R received boot of $5,000 she must recognize $5,000 of her $50,000 realized gain. The basis calculations for R and the corporation are shown below.

	Transferor's adjusted basis for the property transferred......	$20,000
+	Gain recognized...	5,000
−	Boot received...	(5,000)
	Shareholder's adjusted basis in stock received	$20,000

	Transferor's adjusted basis for the property transferred......	$20,000
+	Gain recognized by the shareholder.......................	5,000
	Corporation's adjusted basis for property received	$25,000

Formation of an S Corporation. While the taxation of ordinary operations of an S corporation mirrors that for a partnership, other transactions in which an S corporation engages are often governed by the rules applying to C corporations, sometimes modified to reflect the fact that an S corporation is a conduit. This is true for the tax consequences of forming an S corporation where the rules for C corporations and S corporations are identical. For this reason, the rules governing formation of an S corporation are identical to that discussed above for C corporations.

Finally, a comprehensive summary of the differences in computing the income tax liability of each of the four business operating forms is presented in *Example 17* below, and Exhibit 19-11 contains a comparison of some of the key features of the four business forms.

Example 17. T Company, organized January 1, 1993, has the following information for 1994, its second calendar year:

Gross profit		
Sales..		$470,000
Cost of goods sold................................		300,000
Operating expenses		
Salary (or compensation) to T, the owner............		24,000
Salaries to others (2 nonowners)...................		48,000
Payroll taxes for T................................		[1]
Payroll taxes for others...........................		4,000[1]
Employee benefits:		
Life insurance for T.............................		700[2]
Life insurance for others........................		1,400[2]
Utilities and telephone............................		2,500
Office expenses...................................		1,100
Insurance..		3,100
Interest to T ($300 not paid until 2/1/95)............		3,600
Property taxes....................................		3,000
Repairs...		12,000
Depreciation......................................		15,000
Charitable contributions...........................		7,000

Other items

Dividend income (from 25% owned corporation).....	2,000
Capital gain (CG)....................................	2,200
Capital loss (CL).....................................	1,200
Rehabilitation investment credit......................	2,000
Cash distributed to owner T..........................	12,000
Land distributed to owner T (basis).................	7,000[3]

1. Each employee was paid $2,000 per month. FICA is 7.65% × $24,000 = $1,836 and unemployment taxes are 6.2% × $7,000 = $434 for each employee and $2,270 for both taxes. This is rounded to $4,000 to simplify the illustration. If the company is a corporation, payroll taxes for T are $2,000 (rounded). If the company is a proprietorship or partnership, there are no payroll taxes for T. Instead, T is subject to self-employment taxes on his personal tax return.

2. Life insurance is group-term life insurance of $50,000 for T and each of the other two employees. The $700 paid by T Company for the life insurance for its owner/employee has not been included as part of T's salary or other compensation.

3. Market value of the land distributed is $10,000. It was purchased for the $7,000 on May 2, 1993.

If the business is a proprietorship, T is the owner. For the sake of comparison, assume T is allocated all of the partnership items and is the sole shareholder of the S or C corporation. The Ts (Mr. and Mrs. T) file a joint return, have two exemptions, and have $8,000 of personal itemized deductions of interest, taxes, and charitable contributions. They have no other includible income or deductible expenses for the year. On December 31, 1993 T's basis was $100,000.

A. The taxable business income for each of the four organizational forms is computed on the following page.

	Proprietorship	Partnership	S Corporation	C Corporation
Income				
Sales........................	$470,000	$470,000	$470,000	$470,000
Cost of goods sold...........	(300,000)	(300,000)	(300,000)	(300,000)
Gross profit................	$170,000	$170,000	$170,000	$170,000
Dividend income..............	0	0	0	2,000
Net capital gain..............	0	0	0	4,000 [1]
Total income................	$170,000	$170,000	$170,000	$176,000

	Proprietorship	Partnership	S Corporation	C Corporation
Deductions				
Salary (or compensation) to T....	0	24,700 (2)	24,700 (2)	24,000
Salaries to others.................	48,000	48,000	48,000	48,000
Payroll taxes for T................	0	0	2,000 (3)	2,000
Payroll taxes for others...........	4,000	4,000	4,000	4,000
Life insurance for T...............	0	0	0	700 (2)
Life insurance for others..........	1,400	1,400	1,400	1,400
Utilities and telephone............	2,500	2,500	2,500	2,500
Office supplies....................	1,100	1,100	1,100	1,100
Insurance.........................	3,100	3,100	3,100	3,100
Interest to T......................	0	3,300 (4)	3,300 (4)	3,300 (4)
Property taxes....................	3,000	3,000	3,000	3,000
Repairs...........................	12,000	12,000	12,000	12,000
Depreciation......................	15,000	15,000	15,000	15,000
Charitable contributions...........	0	0	0	5,590 (5)
Dividend deduction...............	0	0	0	1,600
Total deductions................	$ 90,100	$118,100	$120,100	$127,290
Taxable income.................	$ 79,900	$ 51,900	$ 49,900	$ 48,710
Tax liability.......................				$ 7,306 (6)
Rehabilitation credit..............				(2,000)
Tax due........................				$ 5,306

1. The C corporation must recognize the $3,000 ($10,000 − $7,000) § 1231 gain on the land distributed, which is treated as capital gain. Thus, $3,000 + $2,200 − $1,200 = $4,000 net capital gain.

2. As a partnership or an S corporation, T Company can deduct the $700 cost of life insurance provided to T. However, the amount is treated as an additional salary (or guaranteed payment) to be included as income to T. As a C corporation, T Company can deduct the $700 as an additional cost of providing employee benefits, and T can exclude the cost from gross income.

3. Even though the $700 cost of owner/employee benefits provided by T Company is included as salary to T, the amount is not subject to payroll taxes.

4. Accrued expenses to a cash-basis related party are not deductible until paid. The $300 is deductible in 1995.

5. Charitable contributions may not exceed 10% of taxable income computed before the dividends-received deduction, charitable contribution deduction, and net operating and capital loss carrybacks ($48,710 + $5,590 + $1,600 = $55,900 × 10% = $5,590). The $1,410 ($7,000 − $5,590) is carried forward.

6. 15% × $48,710 = $7,306.

B. The Ts' Federal income tax for each of the organizational forms is computed below.

	Proprietorship	Partnership	S Corporation	C Corporation
Net business income.............	$79,900	$51,900	$49,900	$ 0
Business dividend income.......	2,000	2,000	2,000	0
Net capital gain..................	1,000[1]	1,000[1]	4,000[1]	0
Salary income....................	0	24,700	24,700	24,000
Interest income..................	0	3,300	3,300	3,300
Cash distribution................	0	0	0	12,000
Land distribution................	0	0	0	10,000
Self-employment tax[4]..........	(4,827)	(4,783)	0	0
Adjusted gross income......	$78,073	$78,117	$83,900	$49,300
Itemized deductions from the business:				
Charitable contributions.......	7,000	7,000	7,000	0
Other itemized deductions[2].....	8,000	8,000	8,000	8,000
Exemptions......................	4,900	4,900	4,900	4,900
Deductions from A.G.I.........	19,900	19,900	19,900	12,900
Taxable income...............	$58,173	$58,217	$64,000	$36,400
Federal income tax[3]............	$11,348	$11,361	$12,980	$ 5,460
Self-employment tax[4]..........	9,654	9,566	0	0
Rehabilitation credit.............	(2,000)	(2,000)	(2,000)	0
Tax due......................	$19,002	$18,927	$10,980	$ 5,460

1. Net capital gains for the proprietor and the partner total $2,200 capital gain − $1,200 capital loss = $1,000. The S corporation must recognize the $3,000 ($10,000 − $7,000) gain on the land distributed. This $3,000 capital gain also flows out to T. Thus, the S shareholder's net capital gains total $1,000 + $3,000 = $4,000.

2. Itemized deductions exceed the standard deduction.

3. 1994 tax rates used: (15% × $38,000 = $5,700) + (28% × remaining taxable income). The surtax is not assessed since taxable income is below the surtax requirement.

4. The self-employment (SE) tax is composed of a social security tax (12.4% rate) and a Medicare tax (2.9% rate). Only 92.35 percent of an individual's self-employment income is subject to either tax. Also, the social security tax is imposed on a base limited to $60,600 for 1994. Thus the maximum social security tax for 1994 is $7,514.40 ($60,600 × 12.4%).

T's self-employment tax is

Proprietorship: $7,514.40 + ($79,900 × .9235 × 2.9% = $2,139.84) = $9,654.24, rounded to $9,654

Partnership: $7,514.40 + ($51,900 + $24,700 = $76,600 × .9235 × 2.9% = $2,051.46) = $9,565.86, rounded to $9,566

T may deduct 50% of the self-employment tax for A.G.I.

Proprietorship: $9,654 × 50% = $4,827

Partnership: $9,566 × 50% = $4,783

C.   The combined taxes on income, self-employment, and owner salary for T and each of the organizational forms is computed below.

	Proprietorship	Partnership	S Corporation	C Corporation
Employee taxes on T's salary.....	$ 0	$ 0	$ 2,000	$ 2,000
FICA taxes paid by T..............	0	0	2,000	2,000
Corporate Federal income tax............................	0	0	0	5,306
T's Federal income and self-employment tax.............	19,002	18,927	10,980	5,460
Total tax.......................	$19,002	$18,927	$14,980	$14,766

No conclusion should be drawn from this comparison and applied to other situations. For example, the self-employment tax is a substantial cost in the illustration. An owner who has salary income from another source would avoid part of the self-employment tax. Different cash and property distributions also would affect the total taxes. In addition, a proprietor and partner would have a $7,000 basis in the land whereas the S and C shareholders would have a $10,000 basis in the land.

D.   T's basis in the business or stock for the organizational forms is computed below.

	Partnership	S Corporation	C Corporation
Basis 12/31/93............	$100,000	$100,000	$100,000
Net business income.....	51,900	49,900	0
Dividend income.........	2,000	2,000	0
Net capital gain..........	1,000	4,000	0
Life insurance...........	0[1]	0[1]	0
Charitable contributions...	(7,000)	(7,000)	0
Cash distributed.........	(12,000)	(12,000)	0
Property distributed.......	(7,000)	(10,000)	0
Basis 12/31/94............	$128,900	$126,900	$100,000

The proprietor has a basis in each asset and liability, not in the business itself.

1.   This amount is includible compensation and has no effect on basis.

Exhibit 19-11   *Comparative Analysis of Business Forms*

Basic Concepts	*Items for Comparison*	*Proprietorship/ Proprietor*	*Partnership/ Partner*	*S Corporation/ Shareholder*	*C Corporation/ Shareholder*
	1. What are the restrictions on the number of owners or who may be an owner?	1. One owner who must be an individual	1. None, except there must be at least two owners	1. No more than 35 shareholders (and some states set a minimum number) who must be individuals, estates, or certain trusts	1. None, except some states set minimum number of shareholders
	2. Are owners liable for business debts that they have not personally guaranteed?	2. Yes	2. Yes, for general partners but no for limited partners	2. No	2. No
	3. What are the appropriate tax forms and schedules and who files them?	3. Schedules C, SE, and all supporting schedules and forms are filed with proprietor's Form 1040	3. Form 1065 and Schedules K-1 are prepared at the partnership level; partners report their shares on Schedules E, SE, and other supporting schedules and file them with their Form 1040s	3. Same as partnership except Form 1120S and its Schedules K-1 are prepared at the S corporation level	3. Form 1120 and all supporting schedules are filed for the C corporation; shareholders report dividend income on Schedule B and file it with their Form 1040s

Exhibit 19-11 *Continued*

Basic Concepts Continued:	Items for Comparison	Proprietorship/ Proprietor	Partnership/ Partner	S Corporation/ Shareholder	C Corporation/ Shareholder
	4. Who is the taxpayer?	4. Proprietor	4. Partners (but the partnership may be subject to tax if a year-end different from the partners is used)	4. Shareholders (but the S corporation may be subject to a special tax on certain built-in gains and excess passive investment income or if a year-end different from the share-holders is used)	4. C corporation and shareholders are taxed on dividend income when corporate earnings are distributed
	5. Do owners have self-employment income from the business?	5. Yes, the net income from Schedule C	5. Yes, each *general* partner's share of net ordinary income less passive income from Form 1065 plus his or her guaranteed payments; but for *limited* partners, only their guaranteed payments from services provided to the partnership	5. No	5. No
	6. Must the business' taxable year be the same as the majority owners?	6. Yes	6. Generally, but a different year may be used if the partnership pays a tax on the deferred income	6. Same as partnership	6. No, any generally accepted accounting period may be used

Exhibit 19-11 *Continued*

Asset Transfers between Owners and Their Business	Items for Comparison	Proprietorship/ Proprietor	Partnership/ Partner	S Corporation/ Shareholder	C Corporation/ Shareholder
	1. Are contributions of assets for an ownership interest taxable transactions?	1. No, tax-free exchange, all tax attributes transfer to the business except the lower of basis or market value must be used for nonbusiness assets transferred; the term "ownership interest" is not applicable	1. No, same as proprietorship except ownership (capital) interest is applicable	1. No, same as partnership *if* parties to the exchange own more than 80 percent of the corporation after the contribution, but otherwise, a taxable exchange with no carryover of tax attributes	1. Same as S corporation
	2. May an owner enter into taxable transactions (sales, loans, lease arrangements, etc.) with the business?	2. No	2. Yes, when acting in a nonpartner capacity, but subject to related party restrictions	2. Yes, subject to related party restrictions	2. Same as S corporation
	3. May an accrual basis business deduct accrued expenses to cash basis owners?	3. No, not applicable	3. No, deductible only when paid (except see 4 below)	3. Same as partnership	3. Same as partnership and S corporation

Exhibit 19-11 *Continued*

Asset Transfers between Owners and Their Business Continued:	Items for Comparison	Proprietorship/ Proprietor	Partnership/ Partner	S Corporation/ Shareholder	C Corporation/ Shareholder
	4. Are accrued expenses of the business includible income to cash basis owners? If yes, when?	4. No, not applicable	4. Yes, when received, except guaranteed salary and interest on capital are includible when accrued to a partner whose capital interest exceeds 5 percent	4. Yes, when received	4. Yes, when received
	5. Can owners be employees of the business and be paid salaries subject to employment taxes and withholding?	5. No.	5. No, unless partner's capital interest does not exceed 5 percent	5. Yes	5. Yes
	6. Are fringe benefits for owner/ employees deductible expenses?	6. No	6. Yes, but partner must include in gross income.	6. Yes, but a more-than-2-percent shareholder must include in gross income	6. Yes
	7. May the business use the cash method?	7. Yes	7. Yes, unless it qualifies as a tax shelter or has a C corporation as a partner	7. Yes, unless it qualifies as a tax shelter	7. No, unless gross receipts do not exceed $5 million or it qualifies under "type of business" exception

Exhibit 19-11   *Continued*

Income, Deductions, and Credits	*Items for Comparison*	*Proprietorship/ Proprietor*	*Partnership/ Partner*	*S Corporation/ Shareholder*	*C Corporation/ Shareholder*
	1. Is the business a conduit with the original character of the items flowing through to its owners as of the last day of the business' taxable year?	1. Yes	1. Yes	1. Yes	1. No, the business is an entity and the flow through concept is not applicable
	2. How are capital gains and losses treated?	2. As though received by the proprietor	2. Flow through to each partner	2. Same as partnership	2. Net capital gain includible in corporate taxable income and taxed at regular rates; net capital losses are subject to the carryover rules (back 3 years and forward 5 years) and deductible against capital gains
	3. How is dividend income treated?	3. Includible income as though received by the proprietor	3. Flow through to each partner as dividend income	3. Same as partnership	3. Includible income with a 70 percent dividend deduction (80% if at least 20% of the distributing corporation's stock is owned; 100% if from an affiliated corporation)

Exhibit 19-11 *Continued*

Income, Deductions, and Credits Continued:	*Items for Comparison*	*Proprietorship/ Proprietor*	*Partnership/ Partner*	*S Corporation/ Shareholder*	*C Corporation/ Shareholder*
	4. How are charitable contributions treated?	4. An itemized deduction as though contributed by the proprietor	4. Flow through to each partner as an itemized deduction	4. Same as partnership	4. Deductions may not exceed 10 percent of taxable income before certain deductions
	5. Who pays state and local income taxes on the business net income and how are they treated?	5. Proprietor; an itemized deduction as though paid by the proprietor	5. Each partner; an itemized deduction	5. Same as partnership, except some state and local income taxes are assessed on the S corporation and are a deductible expense	5. Deductible expense
	6. How are tax credits treated?	6. As though the credit was earned	6. Qualifying credits flow through to each partner subject to any limitations applicable at the partner level	6. Same as partnership	6. Computed at the corporate level and reduces corporate tax liability
	7. How is net ordinary income treated?	7. Includible with proprietor's A.G.I.	7. Flows through to each partner	7. Same as partnership	7. Included in corporate taxable income
	8. How is net ordinary loss treated?	8. Includible as a reduction of proprietor's A.G.I.	8. Flows through to each partner up to that partner's basis in the partnership; any excess is carried forward	8. Same as partnership	8. Subject to carryover rules (back 3 years and forward 15 years or forward 15 years only) and deductible against net ordinary income

Exhibit 19-11 *Continued*

Income, Deductions, and Credits Continued:	*Items for Comparison*	*Proprietorship/ Proprietor*	*Partnership/ Partner*	*S Corporation/ Shareholder*	*C Corporation/ Shareholder*
	9. Is § 291(a)(1) applicable?	9. No	9. No	9. Yes, if C corporation for any of 3 prior tax years	9. Yes
	10. How are items allocated among the owners?	10. Not applicable	10. According to profit and loss ratio or may be specially allocated	10. According to stock ownership ratio	10. Not applicable

PROBLEM MATERIALS

DISCUSSION QUESTIONS

19-1 *Basic Comparison.* List the tax advantages of each of the following:

    a. Proprietorship
    b. Partnership
    c. S corporation
    d. C corporation

19-2 *Transactions between Owners and the Business.* An owner leases a building to his business at the market value of $500 per month. Is this a deductible expense for any of the organizational forms? Is this includible gross income to the owner?

19-3 *Assets Exchanged for a Capital Interest.* When must an owner recognize gain on appreciated assets exchanged solely for an ownership interest?

19-4 *Losses on Sale.* May an owner sell equipment ($4,000 basis and $3,200 market value) to her business and recognize the loss?

19-5 *Compensation Paid to Owner.* Which organizational forms treat compensation paid to owners in the following manner?

    a. The compensation is a deductible business expense.
    b. The compensation is subject to FICA withholding.

19-6 *Business Deductions.* How are the following items treated by each of the four organizational forms?

    a. Property insurance expense
    b. Life insurance premiums (that qualify as employee benefits) paid for employees who are owners
    c. Life insurance premiums (that qualify as employee benefits) paid for employees who are *not* owners
    d. Net capital loss
    e. Charitable contributions of $5,000 when taxable income before this deduction is $40,000

19-7 *Operating Expense.* Taxpayers with substantial income from investments are establishing a new retail business. They expect the business to have net losses for the first three to four years and continually increasing net income after that. They plan to withdraw very little cash from the business other than compensation for their services.

    a. Which organizational form should they choose now? Why?
    b. Will this form be appropriate if the business begins to have net income? Why? What should they do then?

19-8 *Limited Partnerships.* When are limited partnerships preferable to general partnerships? Why?

19-9   *Partnership vs. S Corporation.*   List the tax advantages of each of the following:

   a.   A partnership when compared with an S corporation.
   b.   An S corporation when compared with a partnership.

19-10   *Schedule K-1.*   Why must each partner and each S corporate shareholder be provided with a Schedule K-1 or the information that would appear on it?

19-11   *Business Income.*   How are the following items treated by each of the four organizational forms?

   a.   Dividend income of $5,000
   b.   Net capital gain of $2,000
   c.   Tax-exempt interest income of $1,100

19-12   *Accrued Expenses.*   At the end of its taxable year, the accrual basis business accrues $800 interest expense owed to a cash basis owner on a long-term note. In which year is the $800 deductible by the business and includible by the owner for each of the four organizational forms if the interest is paid one month after the business year?

PROBLEMS

19-13   *Dividends-Received Deduction.*   K Corporation has the following items of revenue and expense for the current year:

Sales revenue, net of returns....................................	$100,000
Cost of sales..	30,000
Operating expenses...	40,000
Dividends (from less than 20% owned corporation)...............	20,000

   a.   What is K Corporation's dividends-received deduction for the current year?
   b.   Assuming that K Corporation's operating expenses were $72,000 instead of $40,000, compute its dividends-received deduction for the current year.

19-14   *Dividends-Received Deduction.*   During 1994, R Corporation (a cash method, calendar year taxpayer) has the following income and expenses:

Revenues from operations.......................................	$170,000
Operating expenses...	178,000
Dividends (from less than 20% owned corporation)...............	40,000

   a.   What is R Corporation's 1994 dividends-received deduction?
   b.   Assuming R Corporation's 1994 tax year has not yet closed, compute the effect on its dividends-received deduction if R accelerated $5,000 of operating expenses to 1994 that were planned for 1995.

19-15 *Contributions.* L transfers the following assets in exchange for an ownership interest in a business that has been owned and operated for several years by three of his friends.

Asset	Cost	Accumulated Depreciation	Basis	Market Value
Land	$12,000	$ 0	$12,000	$18,000
Building	80,000	18,000	62,000	95,000
Van	15,000	0	15,000	10,000

The land and building were rented to an unrelated person in the past and the van was used as a nonbusiness family vehicle. All of the accumulated depreciation is recapturable. Determine (1) L's recognized gain or loss, (2) L's basis in the business, (3) the business' basis in each asset, and (4) any potential depreciation recapture that is transferred to the business. Assume L receives the following ownership interest:

a. 20 percent of a partnership;

b. 30 percent of an S corporation;

c. 85 percent of an S corporation; or

d. 40 percent of a C corporation.

19-16 *Net Income.* A calendar year business has the following information for the current taxable year:

Sales..	$180,000
Cost of goods sold...............................	70,000
Dividend income...................................	5,000
Net capital loss...................................	(4,000)
Compensation to Z................................	12,000
Other operating expenses.........................	40,000

Assume Z is single and her only other income is $30,000 salary from an unrelated employer.

a. Assume the business is a proprietorship. Calculate its net ordinary income and Z's adjusted gross income.

b. Assume the business is a partnership. Calculate its net ordinary income and Z's adjusted gross income if Z is a 20 percent owner and no special allocations are made.

c. Assume the business is an S corporation. Calculate its net ordinary income and Z's adjusted gross income if Z is a 20 percent owner.

d. Assume the business is a C corporation. Calculate its *taxable income* and Z's adjusted gross income if Z is a 25 percent owner.

19-17 *Owner/Employee Benefits.* A business pays medical insurance premiums of $3,200 during the year for its 60 percent owner, J. Net income before this expense is considered is $36,000. FICA taxes are 7.65 percent. Calculate the business' net income for the year and all tax effects on J, after the premium payments are considered if the business is each of the following:

a. A proprietorship

b. A partnership

c. An S corporation

d. A C corporation

19-18   *Net Losses.*   A calendar year business has the following information for the current taxable year:

Sales	$180,000
Cost of goods sold	130,000
Net capital gain	6,000
Compensation to Z	18,000
Charitable contributions	1,000
Other operating expenses	65,000

Assume Z is single and her only other income is $30,000 salary from an unrelated employer.

a.   Assume the business is a proprietorship. Calculate its net ordinary loss and Z's adjusted gross income.

b.   Assume the business is a partnership. Calculate its net ordinary loss and Z's adjusted gross income if Z is a 20 percent owner and no special allocations are made.

c.   Assume the business is an S corporation. Calculate its net ordinary loss and Z's adjusted gross income if Z is a 20 percent owner.

d.   Assume the business is a C corporation. Calculate its *taxable loss* and Z's adjusted gross income if Z is a 20 percent owner.

19-19   *Self-employment Income.*   G Enterprises has the following information:

Net ordinary income *before* the items below are considered	$40,000
Compensation to Y	12,000
Dividend income	2,000
Net capital gain	5,000

Y performs services for business and receives $1,000 per month whether the business has net income or net losses. Determine Y's self-employment income for each of the following assumptions.

a.   G is a proprietorship and Y is its proprietor.

b.   G is a general partnership and Y is a 40 percent partner.

c.   G is a limited partnership and Y is a 40 percent limited partner.

d.   G is an S corporation and Y is a 40 percent shareholder.

e.   G is a C corporation and Y is a 40 percent shareholder.

19-20   *Transactions.*   V purchased land as an investment in 1979 for $25,000. She sells the land to a business for its $100,000 market value. The business will develop, subdivide, and sell the land in one-acre plots. Determine the amount and character of the gain (ordinary or capital) in each of the following situations:

a.   The business is a partnership and V is a 40 percent owner.

b.   The business is a partnership and V is a 90 percent owner.

c.   The business is an S corporation and V is a 90 percent owner.

d.   The business is a C corporation and V is a 90 percent owner.

19-21 *Gains and Losses.* E, Inc. has operated as a regular C corporation for many years. The corporation is owned equally by P and J. In 1985 the corporation purchased a small apartment building for a total of $150,000. Appraisals indicated that the building was worth $100,000 and the land was worth $50,000. The corporation used the ACRS method to compute depreciation totaling $75,000 in the first nine years. Straight-line depreciation would have been $60,000. In 1993, the corporation sold the apartment building for $500,000. An appraisal indicated that the land was worth $150,000.

a. How much gain does the corporation recognize and what is its character?

b. How would your answer to (a) change if the business had been a partnership instead of a corporation?

19-22 *Charitable Contributions.* XYZ, Inc. is a regular C corporation and has no dividends-received deduction or other loss carrybacks. The corporation reported the following items:

	1993	1994
Net income (before contributions)	$100,000	$200,000
Charitable contributions	22,000	15,000

How much net income will the corporation report in 1993 and 1994 and what are the consequences of any carryovers that may exist?

19-23 *Owner/Employee Relationships.* X and Y are doctors who have been operating as a partnership but are considering incorporating. They want to pay themselves salaries of $150,000 each. In addition, since they will now be employees, they wish to establish a group life insurance plan to pay their yearly (1) life insurance premiums of $15,000 each and (2) medical insurance premiums of $4,000 each. The other employees are covered under a life insurance plan. A typical year for the doctors is as follows:

Revenue	$700,000
Operating expense	190,000
Owner compensation	300,000
Life insurance premiums	30,000

a. Calculate the business' ordinary net income if the partnership is incorporated and S status is elected. An employer's share of FICA taxes is 6.2 percent of the first $60,600 *and* 1.45 percent of each person's salary, and unemployment taxes are 6.2 percent of the first $7,000 of each person's salary. The employee must also pay the same FICA tax as the employer.

b. Ignoring limited liability considerations, should the partners incorporate and elect S status? A self-employed person must pay 12.4 percent of the first $60,600 and 2.9 percent of self-employment income. However, one-half of the self-employment tax is a deductible business expense. Assume X and Y have no other includible income, have total itemized deductions and exemptions of $20,000 each, and file as single taxpayers.

19-24 *Comprehensive Comparison.* A service business has the following information for the current calendar year:

Revenues from services	$200,000
Operating expenses:	
Depreciation	22,000
Insurance	1,400
Office supplies	1,800
Repairs	2,300
Salary (or compensation) to owner/employee W	25,000
Payroll taxes for W	(1)
Salary to nonowner employees	50,000
Payroll taxes for nonowner employees	4,600
Group-term life insurance premiums:	
For W	750
For nonowner employees	1,320
Utilities and telephone	7,900
Charitable contributions	1,100
Rent expense	4,800 (2)
Other items:	
Capital gain	2,000
Capital loss	5,000 (3)
Dividend income (from 10% owned corporation)	6,000
Rehabilitation credit	3,000

(1) Payroll taxes for W are $2,300 ($25,000 $\times$ 7.65% = $1,912.50 FICA + $434 FUTA = $2,346.50, rounded to $2,300 for simplicity) if the business is an S or C corporation.

(2) The rent expense is for a building rented from W. $400 of the rent expense was accrued at the end of the year but not paid until January of the next year.

(3) There have been no capital gains in prior years.

W is a 90 percent owner. W has no other includible income, files a married joint return, has four exemptions, and has other itemized deductions of $8,500 (including no medical expenses and no miscellaneous deductions).

a. Calculate the net business income for the partnership and the S corporation, and the taxable income and tax liability for the C corporation.

b. Calculate W's Federal income tax liability and self-employment tax liability for each of the three organizational forms.

RESEARCH PROBLEMS

19-25 *Family Business.* B operates a proprietorship that manufactures and sells utility tables. Net ordinary income has been increasing approximately 20 percent each year. Last year, net ordinary income was $60,000 on net assets of $225,000. B needs $75,000 to expand the business. Although B's daughter is only 11 years old, she plans to join her father in the business at some point in the future. B is considering forming either a partnership or corporation with his daughter. His ownership interest would be 75 percent and hers would be 25 percent. If the daughter's interest is held in trust until she reaches age 18, can B serve as the trustee without disqualifying the joint-ownership arrangement?

19-26 *Incorporating a Proprietorship or Partnership.*   E and F have operated competing businesses for several years. Recently, they agreed to combine their assets and form a corporation. They plan to transfer appreciated property to the newly organized corporation in exchange for stock and notes. The assets have a market value of $320,000 and a basis to the owners of $175,000. After the exchange, each of them will own stock valued at $100,000 and long-term notes with a face value of $60,000 and an annual interest rate of 10 percent. The term of the notes has not been established yet but E and F are considering making a third of them ($20,000 to E and $20,000 to F) payable at the end of three years, a third payable at the end of five years, and the remainder payable at the end of 10 years. Based on their present plans, will the transfer of appreciated property to the corporation for stock and notes qualify as a nontaxable exchange?

Some suggested research materials:

§ 351 and accompanying Regulations
Pinellas Ice & Cold Storage Co. v. Comm., 3 USTC ¶1023, 11 AFTR 1112, 287 U.S. 462 (1933).
Camp Wolters Enterprises, Inc., 22 T.C. 737 (1955) *aff'd.* in 56-1 USTC ¶9314, 49 AFTR 283, 230 F.2d 555 (CA-5, 1956).
Robert W. Adams, 58 T.C. 4 (1972).

APPENDICES

CONTENTS

APPENDIX A ▪ TAX RATE SCHEDULES AND TABLES

APPENDIX B ▪ TAX FORMS

APPENDIX C ▪ MODIFIED ACRS AND ORIGINAL ACRS TABLES

APPENDIX D ▪ TABLE OF CASES CITED

APPENDIX E ▪ TABLE OF CODE SECTIONS CITED

APPENDIX F ▪ TABLE OF REGULATIONS CITED

APPENDIX G ▪ TABLE OF REVENUE PROCEDURES AND REVENUE RULINGS CITED

APPENDIX H ▪ GLOSSARY OF TAX TERMS

APPENDIX I ▪ TWO INDIVIDUAL COMPREHENSIVE TAX RETURN PROBLEMS FOR 1993

Appendix **A**

TAX RATE SCHEDULES AND TABLES

		Page Nos.
A-1	1993 Income Tax Rate Schedules..................................	**A-2**
A-2	1993 Income Tax Tables...	**A-3**
A-3	Unified Transfer Tax Rate Schedule...............................	**A-15**
A-4	Estate and Gift Tax Valuation Tables..............................	**A-16**

A-1　1993 Income Tax Rate Schedules

1993
Tax Rate
Schedules

Caution: *Use **only** if your taxable income (Form 1040, line 37) is $100,000 or more. If less, use the **Tax Table**. Even though you cannot use the tax rate schedules below if your taxable income is less than $100,000, all levels of taxable income are shown so taxpayers can see the tax rate that applies to each level.*

Schedule X—Use if your filing status is **Single**

If the amount on Form 1040, line 37, is: Over—	But not over—	Enter on Form 1040, line 38		of the amount over—
$0	$22,100	....	15%	$0
22,100	53,500	$3,315.00 +	28%	22,100
53,500	115,000	12,107.00 +	31%	53,500
115,000	250,000	31,172.00 +	36%	115,000
250,000	....	79,772.00 +	39.6%	250,000

Schedule Y-1—Use if your filing status is **Married filing jointly** or **Qualifying widow(er)**

If the amount on Form 1040, line 37, is: Over—	But not over—	Enter on Form 1040, line 38		of the amount over—
$0	$36,900	....	15%	$0
36,900	89,150	$5,535.00 +	28%	36,900
89,150	140,000	20,165.00 +	31%	89,150
140,000	250,000	35,928.50 +	36%	140,000
250,000	....	75,528.50 +	39.6%	250,000

Schedule Y-2—Use if your filing status is **Married filing separately**

If the amount on Form 1040, line 37, is: Over—	But not over—	Enter on Form 1040, line 38		of the amount over—
$0	$18,450	....	15%	$0
18,450	44,575	$2,767.50 +	28%	18,450
44,575	70,000	10,082.50 +	31%	44,575
70,000	125,000	17,964.25 +	36%	70,000
125,000	....	37,764.25 +	39.6%	125,000

Schedule Z—Use if your filing status is **Head of household**

If the amount on Form 1040, line 37, is: Over—	But not over—	Enter on Form 1040, line 38		of the amount over—
$0	$29,600	....	15%	$0
29,600	76,400	$4,440.00 +	28%	29,600
76,400	127,500	17,544.00 +	31%	76,400
127,500	250,000	33,385.00 +	36%	127,500
250,000	....	77,485.00 +	39.6%	250,000

A-2 1993 Income Tax Tables

Section 7.
1993 Tax Table

Use if your taxable income is less than $100,000.
If $100,000 or more, use the Tax Rate Schedules.

Example. Mr. and Mrs. Brown are filing a joint return. Their taxable income on line 37 of Form 1040 is $25,300. First, they find the $25,300–25,350 income line. Next, they find the column for married filing jointly and read down the column. The amount shown where the income line and filing status column meet is $3,799. This is the tax amount they must enter on line 38 of their Form 1040.

Sample Table

At least	But less than	Single	Married filing jointly	Married sepa-rately	Head of a house-hold
			Your tax is—		
25,200	25,250	4,190	3,784	4,665	3,784
25,250	25,300	4,204	3,791	4,679	3,791
25,300	25,350	4,218	(3,799)	4,693	3,799
25,350	25,400	4,232	3,806	4,707	3,806

If line 37 (taxable income) is—		And you are—				If line 37 (taxable income) is—		And you are—				If line 37 (taxable income) is—		And you are—			
At least	But less than	Single	Married filing jointly *	Married sepa-rately	Head of a house-hold	At least	But less than	Single	Married filing jointly *	Married sepa-rately	Head of a house-hold	At least	But less than	Single	Married filing jointly *	Married sepa-rately	Head of a house-hold
			Your tax is—						**Your tax is—**						**Your tax is—**		
0	5	0	0	0	0	1,300	1,325	197	197	197	197	2,700	2,725	407	407	407	407
5	15	2	2	2	2	1,325	1,350	201	201	201	201	2,725	2,750	411	411	411	411
						1,350	1,375	204	204	204	204	2,750	2,775	414	414	414	414
15	25	3	3	3	3	1,375	1,400	208	208	208	208	2,775	2,800	418	418	418	418
25	50	6	6	6	6	1,400	1,425	212	212	212	212	2,800	2,825	422	422	422	422
50	75	9	9	9	9	1,425	1,450	216	216	216	216	2,825	2,850	426	426	426	426
75	100	13	13	13	13	1,450	1,475	219	219	219	219	2,850	2,875	429	429	429	429
						1,475	1,500	223	223	223	223	2,875	2,900	433	433	433	433
100	125	17	17	17	17	1,500	1,525	227	227	227	227	2,900	2,925	437	437	437	437
125	150	21	21	21	21	1,525	1,550	231	231	231	231	2,925	2,950	441	441	441	441
150	175	24	24	24	24	1,550	1,575	234	234	234	234	2,950	2,975	444	444	444	444
175	200	28	28	28	28	1,575	1,600	238	238	238	238	2,975	3,000	448	448	448	448
200	225	32	32	32	32	1,600	1,625	242	242	242	242						
225	250	36	36	36	36	1,625	1,650	246	246	246	246	**3,000**					
250	275	39	39	39	39	1,650	1,675	249	249	249	249						
275	300	43	43	43	43	1,675	1,700	253	253	253	253	3,000	3,050	454	454	454	454
300	325	47	47	47	47	1,700	1,725	257	257	257	257	3,050	3,100	461	461	461	461
325	350	51	51	51	51	1,725	1,750	261	261	261	261	3,100	3,150	469	469	469	469
350	375	54	54	54	54	1,750	1,775	264	264	264	264	3,150	3,200	476	476	476	476
375	400	58	58	58	58	1,775	1,800	268	268	268	268	3,200	3,250	484	484	484	484
400	425	62	62	62	62	1,800	1,825	272	272	272	272	3,250	3,300	491	491	491	491
425	450	66	66	66	66	1,825	1,850	276	276	276	276	3,300	3,350	499	499	499	499
450	475	69	69	69	69	1,850	1,875	279	279	279	279	3,350	3,400	506	506	506	506
475	500	73	73	73	73	1,875	1,900	283	283	283	283	3,400	3,450	514	514	514	514
500	525	77	77	77	77	1,900	1,925	287	287	287	287	3,450	3,500	521	521	521	521
525	550	81	81	81	81	1,925	1,950	291	291	291	291	3,500	3,550	529	529	529	529
550	575	84	84	84	84	1,950	1,975	294	294	294	294	3,550	3,600	536	536	536	536
575	600	88	88	88	88	1,975	2,000	298	298	298	298	3,600	3,650	544	544	544	544
600	625	92	92	92	92							3,650	3,700	551	551	551	551
625	650	96	96	96	96	**2,000**						3,700	3,750	559	559	559	559
650	675	99	99	99	99							3,750	3,800	566	566	566	566
675	700	103	103	103	103	2,000	2,025	302	302	302	302	3,800	3,850	574	574	574	574
700	725	107	107	107	107	2,025	2,050	306	306	306	306	3,850	3,900	581	581	581	581
725	750	111	111	111	111	2,050	2,075	309	309	309	309	3,900	3,950	589	589	589	589
750	775	114	114	114	114	2,075	2,100	313	313	313	313	3,950	4,000	596	596	596	596
775	800	118	118	118	118	2,100	2,125	317	317	317	317						
800	825	122	122	122	122	2,125	2,150	321	321	321	321	**4,000**					
825	850	126	126	126	126	2,150	2,175	324	324	324	324						
850	875	129	129	129	129	2,175	2,200	328	328	328	328	4,000	4,050	604	604	604	604
875	900	133	133	133	133	2,200	2,225	332	332	332	332	4,050	4,100	611	611	611	611
900	925	137	137	137	137	2,225	2,250	336	336	336	336	4,100	4,150	619	619	619	619
925	950	141	141	141	141	2,250	2,275	339	339	339	339	4,150	4,200	626	626	626	626
950	975	144	144	144	144	2,275	2,300	343	343	343	343	4,200	4,250	634	634	634	634
975	1,000	148	148	148	148	2,300	2,325	347	347	347	347	4,250	4,300	641	641	641	641
						2,325	2,350	351	351	351	351	4,300	4,350	649	649	649	649
1,000						2,350	2,375	354	354	354	354	4,350	4,400	656	656	656	656
						2,375	2,400	358	358	358	358	4,400	4,450	664	664	664	664
1,000	1,025	152	152	152	152	2,400	2,425	362	362	362	362	4,450	4,500	671	671	671	671
1,025	1,050	156	156	156	156	2,425	2,450	366	366	366	366	4,500	4,550	679	679	679	679
1,050	1,075	159	159	159	159	2,450	2,475	369	369	369	369	4,550	4,600	686	686	686	686
1,075	1,100	163	163	163	163	2,475	2,500	373	373	373	373	4,600	4,650	694	694	694	694
1,100	1,125	167	167	167	167	2,500	2,525	377	377	377	377	4,650	4,700	701	701	701	701
1,125	1,150	171	171	171	171	2,525	2,550	381	381	381	381	4,700	4,750	709	709	709	709
1,150	1,175	174	174	174	174	2,550	2,575	384	384	384	384	4,750	4,800	716	716	716	716
1,175	1,200	178	178	178	178	2,575	2,600	388	388	388	388	4,800	4,850	724	724	724	724
1,200	1,225	182	182	182	182	2,600	2,625	392	392	392	392	4,850	4,900	731	731	731	731
1,225	1,250	186	186	186	186	2,625	2,650	396	396	396	396	4,900	4,950	739	739	739	739
1,250	1,275	189	189	189	189	2,650	2,675	399	399	399	399	4,950	5,000	746	746	746	746
1,275	1,300	193	193	193	193	2,675	2,700	403	403	403	403						

Continued on next page

* This column must also be used by a qualifying widow(er).

1993 Tax Table—Continued

Columns for each panel: **If line 37 (taxable income) is— At least / But less than** and **And you are— Single / Married filing jointly* / Married filing separately / Head of a household** — Your tax is—

5,000

At least	But less than	Single	Married filing jointly*	Married filing separately	Head of a household
5,000	5,050	754	754	754	754
5,050	5,100	761	761	761	761
5,100	5,150	769	769	769	769
5,150	5,200	776	776	776	776
5,200	5,250	784	784	784	784
5,250	5,300	791	791	791	791
5,300	5,350	799	799	799	799
5,350	5,400	806	806	806	806
5,400	5,450	814	814	814	814
5,450	5,500	821	821	821	821
5,500	5,550	829	829	829	829
5,550	5,600	836	836	836	836
5,600	5,650	844	844	844	844
5,650	5,700	851	851	851	851
5,700	5,750	859	859	859	859
5,750	5,800	866	866	866	866
5,800	5,850	874	874	874	874
5,850	5,900	881	881	881	881
5,900	5,950	889	889	889	889
5,950	6,000	896	896	896	896

8,000

At least	But less than	Single	Married filing jointly*	Married filing separately	Head of a household
8,000	8,050	1,204	1,204	1,204	1,204
8,050	8,100	1,211	1,211	1,211	1,211
8,100	8,150	1,219	1,219	1,219	1,219
8,150	8,200	1,226	1,226	1,226	1,226
8,200	8,250	1,234	1,234	1,234	1,234
8,250	8,300	1,241	1,241	1,241	1,241
8,300	8,350	1,249	1,249	1,249	1,249
8,350	8,400	1,256	1,256	1,256	1,256
8,400	8,450	1,264	1,264	1,264	1,264
8,450	8,500	1,271	1,271	1,271	1,271
8,500	8,550	1,279	1,279	1,279	1,279
8,550	8,600	1,286	1,286	1,286	1,286
8,600	8,650	1,294	1,294	1,294	1,294
8,650	8,700	1,301	1,301	1,301	1,301
8,700	8,750	1,309	1,309	1,309	1,309
8,750	8,800	1,316	1,316	1,316	1,316
8,800	8,850	1,324	1,324	1,324	1,324
8,850	8,900	1,331	1,331	1,331	1,331
8,900	8,950	1,339	1,339	1,339	1,339
8,950	9,000	1,346	1,346	1,346	1,346

11,000

At least	But less than	Single	Married filing jointly*	Married filing separately	Head of a household
11,000	11,050	1,654	1,654	1,654	1,654
11,050	11,100	1,661	1,661	1,661	1,661
11,100	11,150	1,669	1,669	1,669	1,669
11,150	11,200	1,676	1,676	1,676	1,676
11,200	11,250	1,684	1,684	1,684	1,684
11,250	11,300	1,691	1,691	1,691	1,691
11,300	11,350	1,699	1,699	1,699	1,699
11,350	11,400	1,706	1,706	1,706	1,706
11,400	11,450	1,714	1,714	1,714	1,714
11,450	11,500	1,721	1,721	1,721	1,721
11,500	11,550	1,729	1,729	1,729	1,729
11,550	11,600	1,736	1,736	1,736	1,736
11,600	11,650	1,744	1,744	1,744	1,744
11,650	11,700	1,751	1,751	1,751	1,751
11,700	11,750	1,759	1,759	1,759	1,759
11,750	11,800	1,766	1,766	1,766	1,766
11,800	11,850	1,774	1,774	1,774	1,774
11,850	11,900	1,781	1,781	1,781	1,781
11,900	11,950	1,789	1,789	1,789	1,789
11,950	12,000	1,796	1,796	1,796	1,796

6,000

At least	But less than	Single	Married filing jointly*	Married filing separately	Head of a household
6,000	6,050	904	904	904	904
6,050	6,100	911	911	911	911
6,100	6,150	919	919	919	919
6,150	6,200	926	926	926	926
6,200	6,250	934	934	934	934
6,250	6,300	941	941	941	941
6,300	6,350	949	949	949	949
6,350	6,400	956	956	956	956
6,400	6,450	964	964	964	964
6,450	6,500	971	971	971	971
6,500	6,550	979	979	979	979
6,550	6,600	986	986	986	986
6,600	6,650	994	994	994	994
6,650	6,700	1,001	1,001	1,001	1,001
6,700	6,750	1,009	1,009	1,009	1,009
6,750	6,800	1,016	1,016	1,016	1,016
6,800	6,850	1,024	1,024	1,024	1,024
6,850	6,900	1,031	1,031	1,031	1,031
6,900	6,950	1,039	1,039	1,039	1,039
6,950	7,000	1,046	1,046	1,046	1,046

9,000

At least	But less than	Single	Married filing jointly*	Married filing separately	Head of a household
9,000	9,050	1,354	1,354	1,354	1,354
9,050	9,100	1,361	1,361	1,361	1,361
9,100	9,150	1,369	1,369	1,369	1,369
9,150	9,200	1,376	1,376	1,376	1,376
9,200	9,250	1,384	1,384	1,384	1,384
9,250	9,300	1,391	1,391	1,391	1,391
9,300	9,350	1,399	1,399	1,399	1,399
9,350	9,400	1,406	1,406	1,406	1,406
9,400	9,450	1,414	1,414	1,414	1,414
9,450	9,500	1,421	1,421	1,421	1,421
9,500	9,550	1,429	1,429	1,429	1,429
9,550	9,600	1,436	1,436	1,436	1,436
9,600	9,650	1,444	1,444	1,444	1,444
9,650	9,700	1,451	1,451	1,451	1,451
9,700	9,750	1,459	1,459	1,459	1,459
9,750	9,800	1,466	1,466	1,466	1,466
9,800	9,850	1,474	1,474	1,474	1,474
9,850	9,900	1,481	1,481	1,481	1,481
9,900	9,950	1,489	1,489	1,489	1,489
9,950	10,000	1,496	1,496	1,496	1,496

12,000

At least	But less than	Single	Married filing jointly*	Married filing separately	Head of a household
12,000	12,050	1,804	1,804	1,804	1,804
12,050	12,100	1,811	1,811	1,811	1,811
12,100	12,150	1,819	1,819	1,819	1,819
12,150	12,200	1,826	1,826	1,826	1,826
12,200	12,250	1,834	1,834	1,834	1,834
12,250	12,300	1,841	1,841	1,841	1,841
12,300	12,350	1,849	1,849	1,849	1,849
12,350	12,400	1,856	1,856	1,856	1,856
12,400	12,450	1,864	1,864	1,864	1,864
12,450	12,500	1,871	1,871	1,871	1,871
12,500	12,550	1,879	1,879	1,879	1,879
12,550	12,600	1,886	1,886	1,886	1,886
12,600	12,650	1,894	1,894	1,894	1,894
12,650	12,700	1,901	1,901	1,901	1,901
12,700	12,750	1,909	1,909	1,909	1,909
12,750	12,800	1,916	1,916	1,916	1,916
12,800	12,850	1,924	1,924	1,924	1,924
12,850	12,900	1,931	1,931	1,931	1,931
12,900	12,950	1,939	1,939	1,939	1,939
12,950	13,000	1,946	1,946	1,946	1,946

7,000

At least	But less than	Single	Married filing jointly*	Married filing separately	Head of a household
7,000	7,050	1,054	1,054	1,054	1,054
7,050	7,100	1,061	1,061	1,061	1,061
7,100	7,150	1,069	1,069	1,069	1,069
7,150	7,200	1,076	1,076	1,076	1,076
7,200	7,250	1,084	1,084	1,084	1,084
7,250	7,300	1,091	1,091	1,091	1,091
7,300	7,350	1,099	1,099	1,099	1,099
7,350	7,400	1,106	1,106	1,106	1,106
7,400	7,450	1,114	1,114	1,114	1,114
7,450	7,500	1,121	1,121	1,121	1,121
7,500	7,550	1,129	1,129	1,129	1,129
7,550	7,600	1,136	1,136	1,136	1,136
7,600	7,650	1,144	1,144	1,144	1,144
7,650	7,700	1,151	1,151	1,151	1,151
7,700	7,750	1,159	1,159	1,159	1,159
7,750	7,800	1,166	1,166	1,166	1,166
7,800	7,850	1,174	1,174	1,174	1,174
7,850	7,900	1,181	1,181	1,181	1,181
7,900	7,950	1,189	1,189	1,189	1,189
7,950	8,000	1,196	1,196	1,196	1,196

10,000

At least	But less than	Single	Married filing jointly*	Married filing separately	Head of a household
10,000	10,050	1,504	1,504	1,504	1,504
10,050	10,100	1,511	1,511	1,511	1,511
10,100	10,150	1,519	1,519	1,519	1,519
10,150	10,200	1,526	1,526	1,526	1,526
10,200	10,250	1,534	1,534	1,534	1,534
10,250	10,300	1,541	1,541	1,541	1,541
10,300	10,350	1,549	1,549	1,549	1,549
10,350	10,400	1,556	1,556	1,556	1,556
10,400	10,450	1,564	1,564	1,564	1,564
10,450	10,500	1,571	1,571	1,571	1,571
10,500	10,550	1,579	1,579	1,579	1,579
10,550	10,600	1,586	1,586	1,586	1,586
10,600	10,650	1,594	1,594	1,594	1,594
10,650	10,700	1,601	1,601	1,601	1,601
10,700	10,750	1,609	1,609	1,609	1,609
10,750	10,800	1,616	1,616	1,616	1,616
10,800	10,850	1,624	1,624	1,624	1,624
10,850	10,900	1,631	1,631	1,631	1,631
10,900	10,950	1,639	1,639	1,639	1,639
10,950	11,000	1,646	1,646	1,646	1,646

13,000

At least	But less than	Single	Married filing jointly*	Married filing separately	Head of a household
13,000	13,050	1,954	1,954	1,954	1,954
13,050	13,100	1,961	1,961	1,961	1,961
13,100	13,150	1,969	1,969	1,969	1,969
13,150	13,200	1,976	1,976	1,976	1,976
13,200	13,250	1,984	1,984	1,984	1,984
13,250	13,300	1,991	1,991	1,991	1,991
13,300	13,350	1,999	1,999	1,999	1,999
13,350	13,400	2,006	2,006	2,006	2,006
13,400	13,450	2,014	2,014	2,014	2,014
13,450	13,500	2,021	2,021	2,021	2,021
13,500	13,550	2,029	2,029	2,029	2,029
13,550	13,600	2,036	2,036	2,036	2,036
13,600	13,650	2,044	2,044	2,044	2,044
13,650	13,700	2,051	2,051	2,051	2,051
13,700	13,750	2,059	2,059	2,059	2,059
13,750	13,800	2,066	2,066	2,066	2,066
13,800	13,850	2,074	2,074	2,074	2,074
13,850	13,900	2,081	2,081	2,081	2,081
13,900	13,950	2,089	2,089	2,089	2,089
13,950	14,000	2,096	2,096	2,096	2,096

* This column must also be used by a qualifying widow(er).

Continued on next page

1993 Tax Table—*Continued*

If line 37 (taxable income) is—		And you are—			
At least	But less than	Single	Married filing jointly *	Married filing sepa-rately	Head of a house-hold
		Your tax is—			
14,000					
14,000	14,050	2,104	2,104	2,104	2,104
14,050	14,100	2,111	2,111	2,111	2,111
14,100	14,150	2,119	2,119	2,119	2,119
14,150	14,200	2,126	2,126	2,126	2,126
14,200	14,250	2,134	2,134	2,134	2,134
14,250	14,300	2,141	2,141	2,141	2,141
14,300	14,350	2,149	2,149	2,149	2,149
14,350	14,400	2,156	2,156	2,156	2,156
14,400	14,450	2,164	2,164	2,164	2,164
14,450	14,500	2,171	2,171	2,171	2,171
14,500	14,550	2,179	2,179	2,179	2,179
14,550	14,600	2,186	2,186	2,186	2,186
14,600	14,650	2,194	2,194	2,194	2,194
14,650	14,700	2,201	2,201	2,201	2,201
14,700	14,750	2,209	2,209	2,209	2,209
14,750	14,800	2,216	2,216	2,216	2,216
14,800	14,850	2,224	2,224	2,224	2,224
14,850	14,900	2,231	2,231	2,231	2,231
14,900	14,950	2,239	2,239	2,239	2,239
14,950	15,000	2,246	2,246	2,246	2,246
15,000					
15,000	15,050	2,254	2,254	2,254	2,254
15,050	15,100	2,261	2,261	2,261	2,261
15,100	15,150	2,269	2,269	2,269	2,269
15,150	15,200	2,276	2,276	2,276	2,276
15,200	15,250	2,284	2,284	2,284	2,284
15,250	15,300	2,291	2,291	2,291	2,291
15,300	15,350	2,299	2,299	2,299	2,299
15,350	15,400	2,306	2,306	2,306	2,306
15,400	15,450	2,314	2,314	2,314	2,314
15,450	15,500	2,321	2,321	2,321	2,321
15,500	15,550	2,329	2,329	2,329	2,329
15,550	15,600	2,336	2,336	2,336	2,336
15,600	15,650	2,344	2,344	2,344	2,344
15,650	15,700	2,351	2,351	2,351	2,351
15,700	15,750	2,359	2,359	2,359	2,359
15,750	15,800	2,366	2,366	2,366	2,366
15,800	15,850	2,374	2,374	2,374	2,374
15,850	15,900	2,381	2,381	2,381	2,381
15,900	15,950	2,389	2,389	2,389	2,389
15,950	16,000	2,396	2,396	2,396	2,396
16,000					
16,000	16,050	2,404	2,404	2,404	2,404
16,050	16,100	2,411	2,411	2,411	2,411
16,100	16,150	2,419	2,419	2,419	2,419
16,150	16,200	2,426	2,426	2,426	2,426
16,200	16,250	2,434	2,434	2,434	2,434
16,250	16,300	2,441	2,441	2,441	2,441
16,300	16,350	2,449	2,449	2,449	2,449
16,350	16,400	2,456	2,456	2,456	2,456
16,400	16,450	2,464	2,464	2,464	2,464
16,450	16,500	2,471	2,471	2,471	2,471
16,500	16,550	2,479	2,479	2,479	2,479
16,550	16,600	2,486	2,486	2,486	2,486
16,600	16,650	2,494	2,494	2,494	2,494
16,650	16,700	2,501	2,501	2,501	2,501
16,700	16,750	2,509	2,509	2,509	2,509
16,750	16,800	2,516	2,516	2,516	2,516
16,800	16,850	2,524	2,524	2,524	2,524
16,850	16,900	2,531	2,531	2,531	2,531
16,900	16,950	2,539	2,539	2,539	2,539
16,950	17,000	2,546	2,546	2,546	2,546

If line 37 (taxable income) is—		And you are—			
At least	But less than	Single	Married filing jointly *	Married filing sepa-rately	Head of a house-hold
		Your tax is—			
17,000					
17,000	17,050	2,554	2,554	2,554	2,554
17,050	17,100	2,561	2,561	2,561	2,561
17,100	17,150	2,569	2,569	2,569	2,569
17,150	17,200	2,576	2,576	2,576	2,576
17,200	17,250	2,584	2,584	2,584	2,584
17,250	17,300	2,591	2,591	2,591	2,591
17,300	17,350	2,599	2,599	2,599	2,599
17,350	17,400	2,606	2,606	2,606	2,606
17,400	17,450	2,614	2,614	2,614	2,614
17,450	17,500	2,621	2,621	2,621	2,621
17,500	17,550	2,629	2,629	2,629	2,629
17,550	17,600	2,636	2,636	2,636	2,636
17,600	17,650	2,644	2,644	2,644	2,644
17,650	17,700	2,651	2,651	2,651	2,651
17,700	17,750	2,659	2,659	2,659	2,659
17,750	17,800	2,666	2,666	2,666	2,666
17,800	17,850	2,674	2,674	2,674	2,674
17,850	17,900	2,681	2,681	2,681	2,681
17,900	17,950	2,689	2,689	2,689	2,689
17,950	18,000	2,696	2,696	2,696	2,696
18,000					
18,000	18,050	2,704	2,704	2,704	2,704
18,050	18,100	2,711	2,711	2,711	2,711
18,100	18,150	2,719	2,719	2,719	2,719
18,150	18,200	2,726	2,726	2,726	2,726
18,200	18,250	2,734	2,734	2,734	2,734
18,250	18,300	2,741	2,741	2,741	2,741
18,300	18,350	2,749	2,749	2,749	2,749
18,350	18,400	2,756	2,756	2,756	2,756
18,400	18,450	2,764	2,764	2,764	2,764
18,450	18,500	2,771	2,771	2,775	2,771
18,500	18,550	2,779	2,779	2,789	2,779
18,550	18,600	2,786	2,786	2,803	2,786
18,600	18,650	2,794	2,794	2,817	2,794
18,650	18,700	2,801	2,801	2,831	2,801
18,700	18,750	2,809	2,809	2,845	2,809
18,750	18,800	2,816	2,816	2,859	2,816
18,800	18,850	2,824	2,824	2,873	2,824
18,850	18,900	2,831	2,831	2,887	2,831
18,900	18,950	2,839	2,839	2,901	2,839
18,950	19,000	2,846	2,846	2,915	2,846
19,000					
19,000	19,050	2,854	2,854	2,929	2,854
19,050	19,100	2,861	2,861	2,943	2,861
19,100	19,150	2,869	2,869	2,957	2,869
19,150	19,200	2,876	2,876	2,971	2,876
19,200	19,250	2,884	2,884	2,985	2,884
19,250	19,300	2,891	2,891	2,999	2,891
19,300	19,350	2,899	2,899	3,013	2,899
19,350	19,400	2,906	2,906	3,027	2,906
19,400	19,450	2,914	2,914	3,041	2,914
19,450	19,500	2,921	2,921	3,055	2,921
19,500	19,550	2,929	2,929	3,069	2,929
19,550	19,600	2,936	2,936	3,083	2,936
19,600	19,650	2,944	2,944	3,097	2,944
19,650	19,700	2,951	2,951	3,111	2,951
19,700	19,750	2,959	2,959	3,125	2,959
19,750	19,800	2,966	2,966	3,139	2,966
19,800	19,850	2,974	2,974	3,153	2,974
19,850	19,900	2,981	2,981	3,167	2,981
19,900	19,950	2,989	2,989	3,181	2,989
19,950	20,000	2,996	2,996	3,195	2,996

If line 37 (taxable income) is—		And you are—			
At least	But less than	Single	Married filing jointly *	Married filing sepa-rately	Head of a house-hold
		Your tax is—			
20,000					
20,000	20,050	3,004	3,004	3,209	3,004
20,050	20,100	3,011	3,011	3,223	3,011
20,100	20,150	3,019	3,019	3,237	3,019
20,150	20,200	3,026	3,026	3,251	3,026
20,200	20,250	3,034	3,034	3,265	3,034
20,250	20,300	3,041	3,041	3,279	3,041
20,300	20,350	3,049	3,049	3,293	3,049
20,350	20,400	3,056	3,056	3,307	3,056
20,400	20,450	3,064	3,064	3,321	3,064
20,450	20,500	3,071	3,071	3,335	3,071
20,500	20,550	3,079	3,079	3,349	3,079
20,550	20,600	3,086	3,086	3,363	3,086
20,600	20,650	3,094	3,094	3,377	3,094
20,650	20,700	3,101	3,101	3,391	3,101
20,700	20,750	3,109	3,109	3,405	3,109
20,750	20,800	3,116	3,116	3,419	3,116
20,800	20,850	3,124	3,124	3,433	3,124
20,850	20,900	3,131	3,131	3,447	3,131
20,900	20,950	3,139	3,139	3,461	3,139
20,950	21,000	3,146	3,146	3,475	3,146
21,000					
21,000	21,050	3,154	3,154	3,489	3,154
21,050	21,100	3,161	3,161	3,503	3,161
21,100	21,150	3,169	3,169	3,517	3,169
21,150	21,200	3,176	3,176	3,531	3,176
21,200	21,250	3,184	3,184	3,545	3,184
21,250	21,300	3,191	3,191	3,559	3,191
21,300	21,350	3,199	3,199	3,573	3,199
21,350	21,400	3,206	3,206	3,587	3,206
21,400	21,450	3,214	3,214	3,601	3,214
21,450	21,500	3,221	3,221	3,615	3,221
21,500	21,550	3,229	3,229	3,629	3,229
21,550	21,600	3,236	3,236	3,643	3,236
21,600	21,650	3,244	3,244	3,657	3,244
21,650	21,700	3,251	3,251	3,671	3,251
21,700	21,750	3,259	3,259	3,685	3,259
21,750	21,800	3,266	3,266	3,699	3,266
21,800	21,850	3,274	3,274	3,713	3,274
21,850	21,900	3,281	3,281	3,727	3,281
21,900	21,950	3,289	3,289	3,741	3,289
21,950	22,000	3,296	3,296	3,755	3,296
22,000					
22,000	22,050	3,304	3,304	3,769	3,304
22,050	22,100	3,311	3,311	3,783	3,311
22,100	22,150	3,322	3,319	3,797	3,319
22,150	22,200	3,336	3,326	3,811	3,326
22,200	22,250	3,350	3,334	3,825	3,334
22,250	22,300	3,364	3,341	3,839	3,341
22,300	22,350	3,378	3,349	3,853	3,349
22,350	22,400	3,392	3,356	3,867	3,356
22,400	22,450	3,406	3,364	3,881	3,364
22,450	22,500	3,420	3,371	3,895	3,371
22,500	22,550	3,434	3,379	3,909	3,379
22,550	22,600	3,448	3,386	3,923	3,386
22,600	22,650	3,462	3,394	3,937	3,394
22,650	22,700	3,476	3,401	3,951	3,401
22,700	22,750	3,490	3,409	3,965	3,409
22,750	22,800	3,504	3,416	3,979	3,416
22,800	22,850	3,518	3,424	3,993	3,424
22,850	22,900	3,532	3,431	4,007	3,431
22,900	22,950	3,546	3,439	4,021	3,439
22,950	23,000	3,560	3,446	4,035	3,446

* This column must also be used by a qualifying widow(er).

Continued on next page

1993 Tax Table—Continued

Columns for each section: At least | But less than | Single | Married filing jointly * | Married filing separately | Head of a household — Your tax is—

23,000

At least	But less than	Single	Married filing jointly*	Married filing separately	Head of a household
23,000	23,050	3,574	3,454	4,049	3,454
23,050	23,100	3,588	3,461	4,063	3,461
23,100	23,150	3,602	3,469	4,077	3,469
23,150	23,200	3,616	3,476	4,091	3,476
23,200	23,250	3,630	3,484	4,105	3,484
23,250	23,300	3,644	3,491	4,119	3,491
23,300	23,350	3,658	3,499	4,133	3,499
23,350	23,400	3,672	3,506	4,147	3,506
23,400	23,450	3,686	3,514	4,161	3,514
23,450	23,500	3,700	3,521	4,175	3,521
23,500	23,550	3,714	3,529	4,189	3,529
23,550	23,600	3,728	3,536	4,203	3,536
23,600	23,650	3,742	3,544	4,217	3,544
23,650	23,700	3,756	3,551	4,231	3,551
23,700	23,750	3,770	3,559	4,245	3,559
23,750	23,800	3,784	3,566	4,259	3,566
23,800	23,850	3,798	3,574	4,273	3,574
23,850	23,900	3,812	3,581	4,287	3,581
23,900	23,950	3,826	3,589	4,301	3,589
23,950	24,000	3,840	3,596	4,315	3,596

24,000

At least	But less than	Single	Married filing jointly*	Married filing separately	Head of a household
24,000	24,050	3,854	3,604	4,329	3,604
24,050	24,100	3,868	3,611	4,343	3,611
24,100	24,150	3,882	3,619	4,357	3,619
24,150	24,200	3,896	3,626	4,371	3,626
24,200	24,250	3,910	3,634	4,385	3,634
24,250	24,300	3,924	3,641	4,399	3,641
24,300	24,350	3,938	3,649	4,413	3,649
24,350	24,400	3,952	3,656	4,427	3,656
24,400	24,450	3,966	3,664	4,441	3,664
24,450	24,500	3,980	3,671	4,455	3,671
24,500	24,550	3,994	3,679	4,469	3,679
24,550	24,600	4,008	3,686	4,483	3,686
24,600	24,650	4,022	3,694	4,497	3,694
24,650	24,700	4,036	3,701	4,511	3,701
24,700	24,750	4,050	3,709	4,525	3,709
24,750	24,800	4,064	3,716	4,539	3,716
24,800	24,850	4,078	3,724	4,553	3,724
24,850	24,900	4,092	3,731	4,567	3,731
24,900	24,950	4,106	3,739	4,581	3,739
24,950	25,000	4,120	3,746	4,595	3,746

25,000

At least	But less than	Single	Married filing jointly*	Married filing separately	Head of a household
25,000	25,050	4,134	3,754	4,609	3,754
25,050	25,100	4,148	3,761	4,623	3,761
25,100	25,150	4,162	3,769	4,637	3,769
25,150	25,200	4,176	3,776	4,651	3,776
25,200	25,250	4,190	3,784	4,665	3,784
25,250	25,300	4,204	3,791	4,679	3,791
25,300	25,350	4,218	3,799	4,693	3,799
25,350	25,400	4,232	3,806	4,707	3,806
25,400	25,450	4,246	3,814	4,721	3,814
25,450	25,500	4,260	3,821	4,735	3,821
25,500	25,550	4,274	3,829	4,749	3,829
25,550	25,600	4,288	3,836	4,763	3,836
25,600	25,650	4,302	3,844	4,777	3,844
25,650	25,700	4,316	3,851	4,791	3,851
25,700	25,750	4,330	3,859	4,805	3,859
25,750	25,800	4,344	3,866	4,819	3,866
25,800	25,850	4,358	3,874	4,833	3,874
25,850	25,900	4,372	3,881	4,847	3,881
25,900	25,950	4,386	3,889	4,861	3,889
25,950	26,000	4,400	3,896	4,875	3,896

26,000

At least	But less than	Single	Married filing jointly*	Married filing separately	Head of a household
26,000	26,050	4,414	3,904	4,889	3,904
26,050	26,100	4,428	3,911	4,903	3,911
26,100	26,150	4,442	3,919	4,917	3,919
26,150	26,200	4,456	3,926	4,931	3,926
26,200	26,250	4,470	3,934	4,945	3,934
26,250	26,300	4,484	3,941	4,959	3,941
26,300	26,350	4,498	3,949	4,973	3,949
26,350	26,400	4,512	3,956	4,987	3,956
26,400	26,450	4,526	3,964	5,001	3,964
26,450	26,500	4,540	3,971	5,015	3,971
26,500	26,550	4,554	3,979	5,029	3,979
26,550	26,600	4,568	3,986	5,043	3,986
26,600	26,650	4,582	3,994	5,057	3,994
26,650	26,700	4,596	4,001	5,071	4,001
26,700	26,750	4,610	4,009	5,085	4,009
26,750	26,800	4,624	4,016	5,099	4,016
26,800	26,850	4,638	4,024	5,113	4,024
26,850	26,900	4,652	4,031	5,127	4,031
26,900	26,950	4,666	4,039	5,141	4,039
26,950	27,000	4,680	4,046	5,155	4,046

27,000

At least	But less than	Single	Married filing jointly*	Married filing separately	Head of a household
27,000	27,050	4,694	4,054	5,169	4,054
27,050	27,100	4,708	4,061	5,183	4,061
27,100	27,150	4,722	4,069	5,197	4,069
27,150	27,200	4,736	4,076	5,211	4,076
27,200	27,250	4,750	4,084	5,225	4,084
27,250	27,300	4,764	4,091	5,239	4,091
27,300	27,350	4,778	4,099	5,253	4,099
27,350	27,400	4,792	4,106	5,267	4,106
27,400	27,450	4,806	4,114	5,281	4,114
27,450	27,500	4,820	4,121	5,295	4,121
27,500	27,550	4,834	4,129	5,309	4,129
27,550	27,600	4,848	4,136	5,323	4,136
27,600	27,650	4,862	4,144	5,337	4,144
27,650	27,700	4,876	4,151	5,351	4,151
27,700	27,750	4,890	4,159	5,365	4,159
27,750	27,800	4,904	4,166	5,379	4,166
27,800	27,850	4,918	4,174	5,393	4,174
27,850	27,900	4,932	4,181	5,407	4,181
27,900	27,950	4,946	4,189	5,421	4,189
27,950	28,000	4,960	4,196	5,435	4,196

28,000

At least	But less than	Single	Married filing jointly*	Married filing separately	Head of a household
28,000	28,050	4,974	4,204	5,449	4,204
28,050	28,100	4,988	4,211	5,463	4,211
28,100	28,150	5,002	4,219	5,477	4,219
28,150	28,200	5,016	4,226	5,491	4,226
28,200	28,250	5,030	4,234	5,505	4,234
28,250	28,300	5,044	4,241	5,519	4,241
28,300	28,350	5,058	4,249	5,533	4,249
28,350	28,400	5,072	4,256	5,547	4,256
28,400	28,450	5,086	4,264	5,561	4,264
28,450	28,500	5,100	4,271	5,575	4,271
28,500	28,550	5,114	4,279	5,589	4,279
28,550	28,600	5,128	4,286	5,603	4,286
28,600	28,650	5,142	4,294	5,617	4,294
28,650	28,700	5,156	4,301	5,631	4,301
28,700	28,750	5,170	4,309	5,645	4,309
28,750	28,800	5,184	4,316	5,659	4,316
28,800	28,850	5,198	4,324	5,673	4,324
28,850	28,900	5,212	4,331	5,687	4,331
28,900	28,950	5,226	4,339	5,701	4,339
28,950	29,000	5,240	4,346	5,715	4,346

29,000

At least	But less than	Single	Married filing jointly*	Married filing separately	Head of a household
29,000	29,050	5,254	4,354	5,729	4,354
29,050	29,100	5,268	4,361	5,743	4,361
29,100	29,150	5,282	4,369	5,757	4,369
29,150	29,200	5,296	4,376	5,771	4,376
29,200	29,250	5,310	4,384	5,785	4,384
29,250	29,300	5,324	4,391	5,799	4,391
29,300	29,350	5,338	4,399	5,813	4,399
29,350	29,400	5,352	4,406	5,827	4,406
29,400	29,450	5,366	4,414	5,841	4,414
29,450	29,500	5,380	4,421	5,855	4,421
29,500	29,550	5,394	4,429	5,869	4,429
29,550	29,600	5,408	4,436	5,883	4,436
29,600	29,650	5,422	4,444	5,897	4,447
29,650	29,700	5,436	4,451	5,911	4,461
29,700	29,750	5,450	4,459	5,925	4,475
29,750	29,800	5,464	4,466	5,939	4,489
29,800	29,850	5,478	4,474	5,953	4,503
29,850	29,900	5,492	4,481	5,967	4,517
29,900	29,950	5,506	4,489	5,981	4,531
29,950	30,000	5,520	4,496	5,995	4,545

30,000

At least	But less than	Single	Married filing jointly*	Married filing separately	Head of a household
30,000	30,050	5,534	4,504	6,009	4,559
30,050	30,100	5,548	4,511	6,023	4,573
30,100	30,150	5,562	4,519	6,037	4,587
30,150	30,200	5,576	4,526	6,051	4,601
30,200	30,250	5,590	4,534	6,065	4,615
30,250	30,300	5,604	4,541	6,079	4,629
30,300	30,350	5,618	4,549	6,093	4,643
30,350	30,400	5,632	4,556	6,107	4,657
30,400	30,450	5,646	4,564	6,121	4,671
30,450	30,500	5,660	4,571	6,135	4,685
30,500	30,550	5,674	4,579	6,149	4,699
30,550	30,600	5,688	4,586	6,163	4,713
30,600	30,650	5,702	4,594	6,177	4,727
30,650	30,700	5,716	4,601	6,191	4,741
30,700	30,750	5,730	4,609	6,205	4,755
30,750	30,800	5,744	4,616	6,219	4,769
30,800	30,850	5,758	4,624	6,233	4,783
30,850	30,900	5,772	4,631	6,247	4,797
30,900	30,950	5,786	4,639	6,261	4,811
30,950	31,000	5,800	4,646	6,275	4,825

31,000

At least	But less than	Single	Married filing jointly*	Married filing separately	Head of a household
31,000	31,050	5,814	4,654	6,289	4,839
31,050	31,100	5,828	4,661	6,303	4,853
31,100	31,150	5,842	4,669	6,317	4,867
31,150	31,200	5,856	4,676	6,331	4,881
31,200	31,250	5,870	4,684	6,345	4,895
31,250	31,300	5,884	4,691	6,359	4,909
31,300	31,350	5,898	4,699	6,373	4,923
31,350	31,400	5,912	4,706	6,387	4,937
31,400	31,450	5,926	4,714	6,401	4,951
31,450	31,500	5,940	4,721	6,415	4,965
31,500	31,550	5,954	4,729	6,429	4,979
31,550	31,600	5,968	4,736	6,443	4,993
31,600	31,650	5,982	4,744	6,457	5,007
31,650	31,700	5,996	4,751	6,471	5,021
31,700	31,750	6,010	4,759	6,485	5,035
31,750	31,800	6,024	4,766	6,499	5,049
31,800	31,850	6,038	4,774	6,513	5,063
31,850	31,900	6,052	4,781	6,527	5,077
31,900	31,950	6,066	4,789	6,541	5,091
31,950	32,000	6,080	4,796	6,555	5,105

* This column must also be used by a qualifying widow(er).

Continued on next page

1993 Tax Table—*Continued*

If line 37 (taxable income) is—		And you are—				If line 37 (taxable income) is—		And you are—				If line 37 (taxable income) is—		And you are—			
At least	But less than	Single	Married filing jointly *	Married filing sepa-rately	Head of a house-hold	At least	But less than	Single	Married filing jointly *	Married filing sepa-rately	Head of a house-hold	At least	But less than	Single	Married filing jointly *	Married filing sepa-rately	Head of a house-hold
		Your tax is—						Your tax is—						Your tax is—			
32,000						**35,000**						**38,000**					
32,000	**32,050**	6,094	4,804	6,569	5,119	**35,000**	**35,050**	6,934	5,254	7,409	5,959	**38,000**	**38,050**	7,774	5,850	8,249	6,799
32,050	**32,100**	6,108	4,811	6,583	5,133	**35,050**	**35,100**	6,948	5,261	7,423	5,973	**38,050**	**38,100**	7,788	5,864	8,263	6,813
32,100	**32,150**	6,122	4,819	6,597	5,147	**35,100**	**35,150**	6,962	5,269	7,437	5,987	**38,100**	**38,150**	7,802	5,878	8,277	6,827
32,150	**32,200**	6,136	4,826	6,611	5,161	**35,150**	**35,200**	6,976	5,276	7,451	6,001	**38,150**	**38,200**	7,816	5,892	8,291	6,841
32,200	**32,250**	6,150	4,834	6,625	5,175	**35,200**	**35,250**	6,990	5,284	7,465	6,015	**38,200**	**38,250**	7,830	5,906	8,305	6,855
32,250	**32,300**	6,164	4,841	6,639	5,189	**35,250**	**35,300**	7,004	5,291	7,479	6,029	**38,250**	**38,300**	7,844	5,920	8,319	6,869
32,300	**32,350**	6,178	4,849	6,653	5,203	**35,300**	**35,350**	7,018	5,299	7,493	6,043	**38,300**	**38,350**	7,858	5,934	8,333	6,883
32,350	**32,400**	6,192	4,856	6,667	5,217	**35,350**	**35,400**	7,032	5,306	7,507	6,057	**38,350**	**38,400**	7,872	5,948	8,347	6,897
32,400	**32,450**	6,206	4,864	6,681	5,231	**35,400**	**35,450**	7,046	5,314	7,521	6,071	**38,400**	**38,450**	7,886	5,962	8,361	6,911
32,450	**32,500**	6,220	4,871	6,695	5,245	**35,450**	**35,500**	7,060	5,321	7,535	6,085	**38,450**	**38,500**	7,900	5,976	8,375	6,925
32,500	**32,550**	6,234	4,879	6,709	5,259	**35,500**	**35,550**	7,074	5,329	7,549	6,099	**38,500**	**38,550**	7,914	5,990	8,389	6,939
32,550	**32,600**	6,248	4,886	6,723	5,273	**35,550**	**35,600**	7,088	5,336	7,563	6,113	**38,550**	**38,600**	7,928	6,004	8,403	6,953
32,600	**32,650**	6,262	4,894	6,737	5,287	**35,600**	**35,650**	7,102	5,344	7,577	6,127	**38,600**	**38,650**	7,942	6,018	8,417	6,967
32,650	**32,700**	6,276	4,901	6,751	5,301	**35,650**	**35,700**	7,116	5,351	7,591	6,141	**38,650**	**38,700**	7,956	6,032	8,431	6,981
32,700	**32,750**	6,290	4,909	6,765	5,315	**35,700**	**35,750**	7,130	5,359	7,605	6,155	**38,700**	**38,750**	7,970	6,046	8,445	6,995
32,750	**32,800**	6,304	4,916	6,779	5,329	**35,750**	**35,800**	7,144	5,366	7,619	6,169	**38,750**	**38,800**	7,984	6,060	8,459	7,009
32,800	**32,850**	6,318	4,924	6,793	5,343	**35,800**	**35,850**	7,158	5,374	7,633	6,183	**38,800**	**38,850**	7,998	6,074	8,473	7,023
32,850	**32,900**	6,332	4,931	6,807	5,357	**35,850**	**35,900**	7,172	5,381	7,647	6,197	**38,850**	**38,900**	8,012	6,088	8,487	7,037
32,900	**32,950**	6,346	4,939	6,821	5,371	**35,900**	**35,950**	7,186	5,389	7,661	6,211	**38,900**	**38,950**	8,026	6,102	8,501	7,051
32,950	**33,000**	6,360	4,946	6,835	5,385	**35,950**	**36,000**	7,200	5,396	7,675	6,225	**38,950**	**39,000**	8,040	6,116	8,515	7,065
33,000						**36,000**						**39,000**					
33,000	**33,050**	6,374	4,954	6,849	5,399	**36,000**	**36,050**	7,214	5,404	7,689	6,239	**39,000**	**39,050**	8,054	6,130	8,529	7,079
33,050	**33,100**	6,388	4,961	6,863	5,413	**36,050**	**36,100**	7,228	5,411	7,703	6,253	**39,050**	**39,100**	8,068	6,144	8,543	7,093
33,100	**33,150**	6,402	4,969	6,877	5,427	**36,100**	**36,150**	7,242	5,419	7,717	6,267	**39,100**	**39,150**	8,082	6,158	8,557	7,107
33,150	**33,200**	6,416	4,976	6,891	5,441	**36,150**	**36,200**	7,256	5,426	7,731	6,281	**39,150**	**39,200**	8,096	6,172	8,571	7,121
33,200	**33,250**	6,430	4,984	6,905	5,455	**36,200**	**36,250**	7,270	5,434	7,745	6,295	**39,200**	**39,250**	8,110	6,186	8,585	7,135
33,250	**33,300**	6,444	4,991	6,919	5,469	**36,250**	**36,300**	7,284	5,441	7,759	6,309	**39,250**	**39,300**	8,124	6,200	8,599	7,149
33,300	**33,350**	6,458	4,999	6,933	5,483	**36,300**	**36,350**	7,298	5,449	7,773	6,323	**39,300**	**39,350**	8,138	6,214	8,613	7,163
33,350	**33,400**	6,472	5,006	6,947	5,497	**36,350**	**36,400**	7,312	5,456	7,787	6,337	**39,350**	**39,400**	8,152	6,228	8,627	7,177
33,400	**33,450**	6,486	5,014	6,961	5,511	**36,400**	**36,450**	7,326	5,464	7,801	6,351	**39,400**	**39,450**	8,166	6,242	8,641	7,191
33,450	**33,500**	6,500	5,021	6,975	5,525	**36,450**	**36,500**	7,340	5,471	7,815	6,365	**39,450**	**39,500**	8,180	6,256	8,655	7,205
33,500	**33,550**	6,514	5,029	6,989	5,539	**36,500**	**36,550**	7,354	5,479	7,829	6,379	**39,500**	**39,550**	8,194	6,270	8,669	7,219
33,550	**33,600**	6,528	5,036	7,003	5,553	**36,550**	**36,600**	7,368	5,486	7,843	6,393	**39,550**	**39,600**	8,208	6,284	8,683	7,233
33,600	**33,650**	6,542	5,044	7,017	5,567	**36,600**	**36,650**	7,382	5,494	7,857	6,407	**39,600**	**39,650**	8,222	6,298	8,697	7,247
33,650	**33,700**	6,556	5,051	7,031	5,581	**36,650**	**36,700**	7,396	5,501	7,871	6,421	**39,650**	**39,700**	8,236	6,312	8,711	7,261
33,700	**33,750**	6,570	5,059	7,045	5,595	**36,700**	**36,750**	7,410	5,509	7,885	6,435	**39,700**	**39,750**	8,250	6,326	8,725	7,275
33,750	**33,800**	6,584	5,066	7,059	5,609	**36,750**	**36,800**	7,424	5,516	7,899	6,449	**39,750**	**39,800**	8,264	6,340	8,739	7,289
33,800	**33,850**	6,598	5,074	7,073	5,623	**36,800**	**36,850**	7,438	5,524	7,913	6,463	**39,800**	**39,850**	8,278	6,354	8,753	7,303
33,850	**33,900**	6,612	5,081	7,087	5,637	**36,850**	**36,900**	7,452	5,531	7,927	6,477	**39,850**	**39,900**	8,292	6,368	8,767	7,317
33,900	**33,950**	6,626	5,089	7,101	5,651	**36,900**	**36,950**	7,466	5,542	7,941	6,491	**39,900**	**39,950**	8,306	6,382	8,781	7,331
33,950	**34,000**	6,640	5,096	7,115	5,665	**36,950**	**37,000**	7,480	5,556	7,955	6,505	**39,950**	**40,000**	8,320	6,396	8,795	7,345
34,000						**37,000**						**40,000**					
34,000	**34,050**	6,654	5,104	7,129	5,679	**37,000**	**37,050**	7,494	5,570	7,969	6,519	**40,000**	**40,050**	8,334	6,410	8,809	7,359
34,050	**34,100**	6,668	5,111	7,143	5,693	**37,050**	**37,100**	7,508	5,584	7,983	6,533	**40,050**	**40,100**	8,348	6,424	8,823	7,373
34,100	**34,150**	6,682	5,119	7,157	5,707	**37,100**	**37,150**	7,522	5,598	7,997	6,547	**40,100**	**40,150**	8,362	6,438	8,837	7,387
34,150	**34,200**	6,696	5,126	7,171	5,721	**37,150**	**37,200**	7,536	5,612	8,011	6,561	**40,150**	**40,200**	8,376	6,452	8,851	7,401
34,200	**34,250**	6,710	5,134	7,185	5,735	**37,200**	**37,250**	7,550	5,626	8,025	6,575	**40,200**	**40,250**	8,390	6,466	8,865	7,415
34,250	**34,300**	6,724	5,141	7,199	5,749	**37,250**	**37,300**	7,564	5,640	8,039	6,589	**40,250**	**40,300**	8,404	6,480	8,879	7,429
34,300	**34,350**	6,738	5,149	7,213	5,763	**37,300**	**37,350**	7,578	5,654	8,053	6,603	**40,300**	**40,350**	8,418	6,494	8,893	7,443
34,350	**34,400**	6,752	5,156	7,227	5,777	**37,350**	**37,400**	7,592	5,668	8,067	6,617	**40,350**	**40,400**	8,432	6,508	8,907	7,457
34,400	**34,450**	6,766	5,164	7,241	5,791	**37,400**	**37,450**	7,606	5,682	8,081	6,631	**40,400**	**40,450**	8,446	6,522	8,921	7,471
34,450	**34,500**	6,780	5,171	7,255	5,805	**37,450**	**37,500**	7,620	5,696	8,095	6,645	**40,450**	**40,500**	8,460	6,536	8,935	7,485
34,500	**34,550**	6,794	5,179	7,269	5,819	**37,500**	**37,550**	7,634	5,710	8,109	6,659	**40,500**	**40,550**	8,474	6,550	8,949	7,499
34,550	**34,600**	6,808	5,186	7,283	5,833	**37,550**	**37,600**	7,648	5,724	8,123	6,673	**40,550**	**40,600**	8,488	6,564	8,963	7,513
34,600	**34,650**	6,822	5,194	7,297	5,847	**37,600**	**37,650**	7,662	5,738	8,137	6,687	**40,600**	**40,650**	8,502	6,578	8,977	7,527
34,650	**34,700**	6,836	5,201	7,311	5,861	**37,650**	**37,700**	7,676	5,752	8,151	6,701	**40,650**	**40,700**	8,516	6,592	8,991	7,541
34,700	**34,750**	6,850	5,209	7,325	5,875	**37,700**	**37,750**	7,690	5,766	8,165	6,715	**40,700**	**40,750**	8,530	6,606	9,005	7,555
34,750	**34,800**	6,864	5,216	7,339	5,889	**37,750**	**37,800**	7,704	5,780	8,179	6,729	**40,750**	**40,800**	8,544	6,620	9,019	7,569
34,800	**34,850**	6,878	5,224	7,353	5,903	**37,800**	**37,850**	7,718	5,794	8,193	6,743	**40,800**	**40,850**	8,558	6,634	9,033	7,583
34,850	**34,900**	6,892	5,231	7,367	5,917	**37,850**	**37,900**	7,732	5,808	8,207	6,757	**40,850**	**40,900**	8,572	6,648	9,047	7,597
34,900	**34,950**	6,906	5,239	7,381	5,931	**37,900**	**37,950**	7,746	5,822	8,221	6,771	**40,900**	**40,950**	8,586	6,662	9,061	7,611
34,950	**35,000**	6,920	5,246	7,395	5,945	**37,950**	**38,000**	7,760	5,836	8,235	6,785	**40,950**	**41,000**	8,600	6,676	9,075	7,625

* This column must also be used by a qualifying widow(er).

Continued on next page

1993 Tax Table—Continued

If line 37 (taxable income) is— At least	But less than	Single	Married filing jointly *	Married filing separately	Head of a household	If line 37 (taxable income) is— At least	But less than	Single	Married filing jointly *	Married filing separately	Head of a household	If line 37 (taxable income) is— At least	But less than	Single	Married filing jointly *	Married filing separately	Head of a household
41,000						**44,000**						**47,000**					
41,000	41,050	8,614	6,690	9,089	7,639	44,000	44,050	9,454	7,530	9,929	8,479	47,000	47,050	10,294	8,370	10,842	9,319
41,050	41,100	8,628	6,704	9,103	7,653	44,050	44,100	9,468	7,544	9,943	8,493	47,050	47,100	10,308	8,384	10,858	9,333
41,100	41,150	8,642	6,718	9,117	7,667	44,100	44,150	9,482	7,558	9,957	8,507	47,100	47,150	10,322	8,398	10,873	9,347
41,150	41,200	8,656	6,732	9,131	7,681	44,150	44,200	9,496	7,572	9,971	8,521	47,150	47,200	10,336	8,412	10,889	9,361
41,200	41,250	8,670	6,746	9,145	7,695	44,200	44,250	9,510	7,586	9,985	8,535	47,200	47,250	10,350	8,426	10,904	9,375
41,250	41,300	8,684	6,760	9,159	7,709	44,250	44,300	9,524	7,600	9,999	8,549	47,250	47,300	10,364	8,440	10,920	9,389
41,300	41,350	8,698	6,774	9,173	7,723	44,300	44,350	9,538	7,614	10,013	8,563	47,300	47,350	10,378	8,454	10,935	9,403
41,350	41,400	8,712	6,788	9,187	7,737	44,350	44,400	9,552	7,628	10,027	8,577	47,350	47,400	10,392	8,468	10,951	9,417
41,400	41,450	8,726	6,802	9,201	7,751	44,400	44,450	9,566	7,642	10,041	8,591	47,400	47,450	10,406	8,482	10,966	9,431
41,450	41,500	8,740	6,816	9,215	7,765	44,450	44,500	9,580	7,656	10,055	8,605	47,450	47,500	10,420	8,496	10,982	9,445
41,500	41,550	8,754	6,830	9,229	7,779	44,500	44,550	9,594	7,670	10,069	8,619	47,500	47,550	10,434	8,510	10,997	9,459
41,550	41,600	8,768	6,844	9,243	7,793	44,550	44,600	9,608	7,684	10,083	8,633	47,550	47,600	10,448	8,524	11,013	9,473
41,600	41,650	8,782	6,858	9,257	7,807	44,600	44,650	9,622	7,698	10,098	8,647	47,600	47,650	10,462	8,538	11,028	9,487
41,650	41,700	8,796	6,872	9,271	7,821	44,650	44,700	9,636	7,712	10,114	8,661	47,650	47,700	10,476	8,552	11,044	9,501
41,700	41,750	8,810	6,886	9,285	7,835	44,700	44,750	9,650	7,726	10,129	8,675	47,700	47,750	10,490	8,566	11,059	9,515
41,750	41,800	8,824	6,900	9,299	7,849	44,750	44,800	9,664	7,740	10,145	8,689	47,750	47,800	10,504	8,580	11,075	9,529
41,800	41,850	8,838	6,914	9,313	7,863	44,800	44,850	9,678	7,754	10,160	8,703	47,800	47,850	10,518	8,594	11,090	9,543
41,850	41,900	8,852	6,928	9,327	7,877	44,850	44,900	9,692	7,768	10,176	8,717	47,850	47,900	10,532	8,608	11,106	9,557
41,900	41,950	8,866	6,942	9,341	7,891	44,900	44,950	9,706	7,782	10,191	8,731	47,900	47,950	10,546	8,622	11,121	9,571
41,950	42,000	8,880	6,956	9,355	7,905	44,950	45,000	9,720	7,796	10,207	8,745	47,950	48,000	10,560	8,636	11,137	9,585
42,000						**45,000**						**48,000**					
42,000	42,050	8,894	6,970	9,369	7,919	45,000	45,050	9,734	7,810	10,222	8,759	48,000	48,050	10,574	8,650	11,152	9,599
42,050	42,100	8,908	6,984	9,383	7,933	45,050	45,100	9,748	7,824	10,238	8,773	48,050	48,100	10,588	8,664	11,168	9,613
42,100	42,150	8,922	6,998	9,397	7,947	45,100	45,150	9,762	7,838	10,253	8,787	48,100	48,150	10,602	8,678	11,183	9,627
42,150	42,200	8,936	7,012	9,411	7,961	45,150	45,200	9,776	7,852	10,269	8,801	48,150	48,200	10,616	8,692	11,199	9,641
42,200	42,250	8,950	7,026	9,425	7,975	45,200	45,250	9,790	7,866	10,284	8,815	48,200	48,250	10,630	8,706	11,214	9,655
42,250	42,300	8,964	7,040	9,439	7,989	45,250	45,300	9,804	7,880	10,300	8,829	48,250	48,300	10,644	8,720	11,230	9,669
42,300	42,350	8,978	7,054	9,453	8,003	45,300	45,350	9,818	7,894	10,315	8,843	48,300	48,350	10,658	8,734	11,245	9,683
42,350	42,400	8,992	7,068	9,467	8,017	45,350	45,400	9,832	7,908	10,331	8,857	48,350	48,400	10,672	8,748	11,261	9,697
42,400	42,450	9,006	7,082	9,481	8,031	45,400	45,450	9,846	7,922	10,346	8,871	48,400	48,450	10,686	8,762	11,276	9,711
42,450	42,500	9,020	7,096	9,495	8,045	45,450	45,500	9,860	7,936	10,362	8,885	48,450	48,500	10,700	8,776	11,292	9,725
42,500	42,550	9,034	7,110	9,509	8,059	45,500	45,550	9,874	7,950	10,377	8,899	48,500	48,550	10,714	8,790	11,307	9,739
42,550	42,600	9,048	7,124	9,523	8,073	45,550	45,600	9,888	7,964	10,393	8,913	48,550	48,600	10,728	8,804	11,323	9,753
42,600	42,650	9,062	7,138	9,537	8,087	45,600	45,650	9,902	7,978	10,408	8,927	48,600	48,650	10,742	8,818	11,338	9,767
42,650	42,700	9,076	7,152	9,551	8,101	45,650	45,700	9,916	7,992	10,424	8,941	48,650	48,700	10,756	8,832	11,354	9,781
42,700	42,750	9,090	7,166	9,565	8,115	45,700	45,750	9,930	8,006	10,439	8,955	48,700	48,750	10,770	8,846	11,369	9,795
42,750	42,800	9,104	7,180	9,579	8,129	45,750	45,800	9,944	8,020	10,455	8,969	48,750	48,800	10,784	8,860	11,385	9,809
42,800	42,850	9,118	7,194	9,593	8,143	45,800	45,850	9,958	8,034	10,470	8,983	48,800	48,850	10,798	8,874	11,400	9,823
42,850	42,900	9,132	7,208	9,607	8,157	45,850	45,900	9,972	8,048	10,486	8,997	48,850	48,900	10,812	8,888	11,416	9,837
42,900	42,950	9,146	7,222	9,621	8,171	45,900	45,950	9,986	8,062	10,501	9,011	48,900	48,950	10,826	8,902	11,431	9,851
42,950	43,000	9,160	7,236	9,635	8,185	45,950	46,000	10,000	8,076	10,517	9,025	48,950	49,000	10,840	8,916	11,447	9,865
43,000						**46,000**						**49,000**					
43,000	43,050	9,174	7,250	9,649	8,199	46,000	46,050	10,014	8,090	10,532	9,039	49,000	49,050	10,854	8,930	11,462	9,879
43,050	43,100	9,188	7,264	9,663	8,213	46,050	46,100	10,028	8,104	10,548	9,053	49,050	49,100	10,868	8,944	11,478	9,893
43,100	43,150	9,202	7,278	9,677	8,227	46,100	46,150	10,042	8,118	10,563	9,067	49,100	49,150	10,882	8,958	11,493	9,907
43,150	43,200	9,216	7,292	9,691	8,241	46,150	46,200	10,056	8,132	10,579	9,081	49,150	49,200	10,896	8,972	11,509	9,921
43,200	43,250	9,230	7,306	9,705	8,255	46,200	46,250	10,070	8,146	10,594	9,095	49,200	49,250	10,910	8,986	11,524	9,935
43,250	43,300	9,244	7,320	9,719	8,269	46,250	46,300	10,084	8,160	10,610	9,109	49,250	49,300	10,924	9,000	11,540	9,949
43,300	43,350	9,258	7,334	9,733	8,283	46,300	46,350	10,098	8,174	10,625	9,123	49,300	49,350	10,938	9,014	11,555	9,963
43,350	43,400	9,272	7,348	9,747	8,297	46,350	46,400	10,112	8,188	10,641	9,137	49,350	49,400	10,952	9,028	11,571	9,977
43,400	43,450	9,286	7,362	9,761	8,311	46,400	46,450	10,126	8,202	10,656	9,151	49,400	49,450	10,966	9,042	11,586	9,991
43,450	43,500	9,300	7,376	9,775	8,325	46,450	46,500	10,140	8,216	10,672	9,165	49,450	49,500	10,980	9,056	11,602	10,005
43,500	43,550	9,314	7,390	9,789	8,339	46,500	46,550	10,154	8,230	10,687	9,179	49,500	49,550	10,994	9,070	11,617	10,019
43,550	43,600	9,328	7,404	9,803	8,353	46,550	46,600	10,168	8,244	10,703	9,193	49,550	49,600	11,008	9,084	11,633	10,033
43,600	43,650	9,342	7,418	9,817	8,367	46,600	46,650	10,182	8,258	10,718	9,207	49,600	49,650	11,022	9,098	11,648	10,047
43,650	43,700	9,356	7,432	9,831	8,381	46,650	46,700	10,196	8,272	10,734	9,221	49,650	49,700	11,036	9,112	11,664	10,061
43,700	43,750	9,370	7,446	9,845	8,395	46,700	46,750	10,210	8,286	10,749	9,235	49,700	49,750	11,050	9,126	11,679	10,075
43,750	43,800	9,384	7,460	9,859	8,409	46,750	46,800	10,224	8,300	10,765	9,249	49,750	49,800	11,064	9,140	11,695	10,089
43,800	43,850	9,398	7,474	9,873	8,423	46,800	46,850	10,238	8,314	10,780	9,263	49,800	49,850	11,078	9,154	11,710	10,103
43,850	43,900	9,412	7,488	9,887	8,437	46,850	46,900	10,252	8,328	10,796	9,277	49,850	49,900	11,092	9,168	11,726	10,117
43,900	43,950	9,426	7,502	9,901	8,451	46,900	46,950	10,266	8,342	10,811	9,291	49,900	49,950	11,106	9,182	11,741	10,131
43,950	44,000	9,440	7,516	9,915	8,465	46,950	47,000	10,280	8,356	10,827	9,305	49,950	50,000	11,120	9,196	11,757	10,145

* This column must also be used by a qualifying widow(er).

Continued on next page

1993 Tax Table—Continued

If line 37 (taxable income) is— At least	But less than	Single	Married filing jointly	Married filing separately	Head of a household
50,000					
50,000	50,050	11,134	9,210	11,772	10,159
50,050	50,100	11,148	9,224	11,788	10,173
50,100	50,150	11,162	9,238	11,803	10,187
50,150	50,200	11,176	9,252	11,819	10,201
50,200	50,250	11,190	9,266	11,834	10,215
50,250	50,300	11,204	9,280	11,850	10,229
50,300	50,350	11,218	9,294	11,865	10,243
50,350	50,400	11,232	9,308	11,881	10,257
50,400	50,450	11,246	9,322	11,896	10,271
50,450	50,500	11,260	9,336	11,912	10,285
50,500	50,550	11,274	9,350	11,927	10,299
50,550	50,600	11,288	9,364	11,943	10,313
50,600	50,650	11,302	9,378	11,958	10,327
50,650	50,700	11,316	9,392	11,974	10,341
50,700	50,750	11,330	9,406	11,989	10,355
50,750	50,800	11,344	9,420	12,005	10,369
50,800	50,850	11,358	9,434	12,020	10,383
50,850	50,900	11,372	9,448	12,036	10,397
50,900	50,950	11,386	9,462	12,051	10,411
50,950	51,000	11,400	9,476	12,067	10,425
51,000					
51,000	51,050	11,414	9,490	12,082	10,439
51,050	51,100	11,428	9,504	12,098	10,453
51,100	51,150	11,442	9,518	12,113	10,467
51,150	51,200	11,456	9,532	12,129	10,481
51,200	51,250	11,470	9,546	12,144	10,495
51,250	51,300	11,484	9,560	12,160	10,509
51,300	51,350	11,498	9,574	12,175	10,523
51,350	51,400	11,512	9,588	12,191	10,537
51,400	51,450	11,526	9,602	12,206	10,551
51,450	51,500	11,540	9,616	12,222	10,565
51,500	51,550	11,554	9,630	12,237	10,579
51,550	51,600	11,568	9,644	12,253	10,593
51,600	51,650	11,582	9,658	12,268	10,607
51,650	51,700	11,596	9,672	12,284	10,621
51,700	51,750	11,610	9,686	12,299	10,635
51,750	51,800	11,624	9,700	12,315	10,649
51,800	51,850	11,638	9,714	12,330	10,663
51,850	51,900	11,652	9,728	12,346	10,677
51,900	51,950	11,666	9,742	12,361	10,691
51,950	52,000	11,680	9,756	12,377	10,705
52,000					
52,000	52,050	11,694	9,770	12,392	10,719
52,050	52,100	11,708	9,784	12,408	10,733
52,100	52,150	11,722	9,798	12,423	10,747
52,150	52,200	11,736	9,812	12,439	10,761
52,200	52,250	11,750	9,826	12,454	10,775
52,250	52,300	11,764	9,840	12,470	10,789
52,300	52,350	11,778	9,854	12,485	10,803
52,350	52,400	11,792	9,868	12,501	10,817
52,400	52,450	11,806	9,882	12,516	10,831
52,450	52,500	11,820	9,896	12,532	10,845
52,500	52,550	11,834	9,910	12,547	10,859
52,550	52,600	11,848	9,924	12,563	10,873
52,600	52,650	11,862	9,938	12,578	10,887
52,650	52,700	11,876	9,952	12,594	10,901
52,700	52,750	11,890	9,966	12,609	10,915
52,750	52,800	11,904	9,980	12,625	10,929
52,800	52,850	11,918	9,994	12,640	10,943
52,850	52,900	11,932	10,008	12,656	10,957
52,900	52,950	11,946	10,022	12,671	10,971
52,950	53,000	11,960	10,036	12,687	10,985

If line 37 (taxable income) is— At least	But less than	Single	Married filing jointly	Married filing separately	Head of a household
53,000					
53,000	53,050	11,974	10,050	12,702	10,999
53,050	53,100	11,988	10,064	12,718	11,013
53,100	53,150	12,002	10,078	12,733	11,027
53,150	53,200	12,016	10,092	12,749	11,041
53,200	53,250	12,030	10,106	12,764	11,055
53,250	53,300	12,044	10,120	12,780	11,069
53,300	53,350	12,058	10,134	12,795	11,083
53,350	53,400	12,072	10,148	12,811	11,097
53,400	53,450	12,086	10,162	12,826	11,111
53,450	53,500	12,100	10,176	12,842	11,125
53,500	53,550	12,115	10,190	12,857	11,139
53,550	53,600	12,130	10,204	12,873	11,153
53,600	53,650	12,146	10,218	12,888	11,167
53,650	53,700	12,161	10,232	12,904	11,181
53,700	53,750	12,177	10,246	12,919	11,195
53,750	53,800	12,192	10,260	12,935	11,209
53,800	53,850	12,208	10,274	12,950	11,223
53,850	53,900	12,223	10,288	12,966	11,237
53,900	53,950	12,239	10,302	12,981	11,251
53,950	54,000	12,254	10,316	12,997	11,265
54,000					
54,000	54,050	12,270	10,330	13,012	11,279
54,050	54,100	12,285	10,344	13,028	11,293
54,100	54,150	12,301	10,358	13,043	11,307
54,150	54,200	12,316	10,372	13,059	11,321
54,200	54,250	12,332	10,386	13,074	11,335
54,250	54,300	12,347	10,400	13,090	11,349
54,300	54,350	12,363	10,414	13,105	11,363
54,350	54,400	12,378	10,428	13,121	11,377
54,400	54,450	12,394	10,442	13,136	11,391
54,450	54,500	12,409	10,456	13,152	11,405
54,500	54,550	12,425	10,470	13,167	11,419
54,550	54,600	12,440	10,484	13,183	11,433
54,600	54,650	12,456	10,498	13,198	11,447
54,650	54,700	12,471	10,512	13,214	11,461
54,700	54,750	12,487	10,526	13,229	11,475
54,750	54,800	12,502	10,540	13,245	11,489
54,800	54,850	12,518	10,554	13,260	11,503
54,850	54,900	12,533	10,568	13,276	11,517
54,900	54,950	12,549	10,582	13,291	11,531
54,950	55,000	12,564	10,596	13,307	11,545
55,000					
55,000	55,050	12,580	10,610	13,322	11,559
55,050	55,100	12,595	10,624	13,338	11,573
55,100	55,150	12,611	10,638	13,353	11,587
55,150	55,200	12,626	10,652	13,369	11,601
55,200	55,250	12,642	10,666	13,384	11,615
55,250	55,300	12,657	10,680	13,400	11,629
55,300	55,350	12,673	10,694	13,415	11,643
55,350	55,400	12,688	10,708	13,431	11,657
55,400	55,450	12,704	10,722	13,446	11,671
55,450	55,500	12,719	10,736	13,462	11,685
55,500	55,550	12,735	10,750	13,477	11,699
55,550	55,600	12,750	10,764	13,493	11,713
55,600	55,650	12,766	10,778	13,508	11,727
55,650	55,700	12,781	10,792	13,524	11,741
55,700	55,750	12,797	10,806	13,539	11,755
55,750	55,800	12,812	10,820	13,555	11,769
55,800	55,850	12,828	10,834	13,570	11,783
55,850	55,900	12,843	10,848	13,586	11,797
55,900	55,950	12,859	10,862	13,601	11,811
55,950	56,000	12,874	10,876	13,617	11,825

If line 37 (taxable income) is— At least	But less than	Single	Married filing jointly	Married filing separately	Head of a household
56,000					
56,000	56,050	12,890	10,890	13,632	11,839
56,050	56,100	12,905	10,904	13,648	11,853
56,100	56,150	12,921	10,918	13,663	11,867
56,150	56,200	12,936	10,932	13,679	11,881
56,200	56,250	12,952	10,946	13,694	11,895
56,250	56,300	12,967	10,960	13,710	11,909
56,300	56,350	12,983	10,974	13,725	11,923
56,350	56,400	12,998	10,988	13,741	11,937
56,400	56,450	13,014	11,002	13,756	11,951
56,450	56,500	13,029	11,016	13,772	11,965
56,500	56,550	13,045	11,030	13,787	11,979
56,550	56,600	13,060	11,044	13,803	11,993
56,600	56,650	13,076	11,058	13,818	12,007
56,650	56,700	13,091	11,072	13,834	12,021
56,700	56,750	13,107	11,086	13,849	12,035
56,750	56,800	13,122	11,100	13,865	12,049
56,800	56,850	13,138	11,114	13,880	12,063
56,850	56,900	13,153	11,128	13,896	12,077
56,900	56,950	13,169	11,142	13,911	12,091
56,950	57,000	13,184	11,156	13,927	12,105
57,000					
57,000	57,050	13,200	11,170	13,942	12,119
57,050	57,100	13,215	11,184	13,958	12,133
57,100	57,150	13,231	11,198	13,973	12,147
57,150	57,200	13,246	11,212	13,989	12,161
57,200	57,250	13,262	11,226	14,004	12,175
57,250	57,300	13,277	11,240	14,020	12,189
57,300	57,350	13,293	11,254	14,035	12,203
57,350	57,400	13,308	11,268	14,051	12,217
57,400	57,450	13,324	11,282	14,066	12,231
57,450	57,500	13,339	11,296	14,082	12,245
57,500	57,550	13,355	11,310	14,097	12,259
57,550	57,600	13,370	11,324	14,113	12,273
57,600	57,650	13,386	11,338	14,128	12,287
57,650	57,700	13,401	11,352	14,144	12,301
57,700	57,750	13,417	11,366	14,159	12,315
57,750	57,800	13,432	11,380	14,175	12,329
57,800	57,850	13,448	11,394	14,190	12,343
57,850	57,900	13,463	11,408	14,206	12,357
57,900	57,950	13,479	11,422	14,221	12,371
57,950	58,000	13,494	11,436	14,237	12,385
58,000					
58,000	58,050	13,510	11,450	14,252	12,399
58,050	58,100	13,525	11,464	14,268	12,413
58,100	58,150	13,541	11,478	14,283	12,427
58,150	58,200	13,556	11,492	14,299	12,441
58,200	58,250	13,572	11,506	14,314	12,455
58,250	58,300	13,587	11,520	14,330	12,469
58,300	58,350	13,603	11,534	14,345	12,483
58,350	58,400	13,618	11,548	14,361	12,497
58,400	58,450	13,634	11,562	14,376	12,511
58,450	58,500	13,649	11,576	14,392	12,525
58,500	58,550	13,665	11,590	14,407	12,539
58,550	58,600	13,680	11,604	14,423	12,553
58,600	58,650	13,696	11,618	14,438	12,567
58,650	58,700	13,711	11,632	14,454	12,581
58,700	58,750	13,727	11,646	14,469	12,595
58,750	58,800	13,742	11,660	14,485	12,609
58,800	58,850	13,758	11,674	14,500	12,623
58,850	58,900	13,773	11,688	14,516	12,637
58,900	58,950	13,789	11,702	14,531	12,651
58,950	59,000	13,804	11,716	14,547	12,665

* This column must also be used by a qualifying widow(er).

Continued on next page

1993 Tax Table—Continued

59,000

At least	But less than	Single	Married filing jointly *	Married filing separately	Head of a household
59,000	59,050	13,820	11,730	14,562	12,679
59,050	59,100	13,835	11,744	14,578	12,693
59,100	59,150	13,851	11,758	14,593	12,707
59,150	59,200	13,866	11,772	14,609	12,721
59,200	59,250	13,882	11,786	14,624	12,735
59,250	59,300	13,897	11,800	14,640	12,749
59,300	59,350	13,913	11,814	14,655	12,763
59,350	59,400	13,928	11,828	14,671	12,777
59,400	59,450	13,944	11,842	14,686	12,791
59,450	59,500	13,959	11,856	14,702	12,805
59,500	59,550	13,975	11,870	14,717	12,819
59,550	59,600	13,990	11,884	14,733	12,833
59,600	59,650	14,006	11,898	14,748	12,847
59,650	59,700	14,021	11,912	14,764	12,861
59,700	59,750	14,037	11,926	14,779	12,875
59,750	59,800	14,052	11,940	14,795	12,889
59,800	59,850	14,068	11,954	14,810	12,903
59,850	59,900	14,083	11,968	14,826	12,917
59,900	59,950	14,099	11,982	14,841	12,931
59,950	60,000	14,114	11,996	14,857	12,945

60,000

At least	But less than	Single	Married filing jointly *	Married filing separately	Head of a household
60,000	60,050	14,130	12,010	14,872	12,959
60,050	60,100	14,145	12,024	14,888	12,973
60,100	60,150	14,161	12,038	14,903	12,987
60,150	60,200	14,176	12,052	14,919	13,001
60,200	60,250	14,192	12,066	14,934	13,015
60,250	60,300	14,207	12,080	14,950	13,029
60,300	60,350	14,223	12,094	14,965	13,043
60,350	60,400	14,238	12,108	14,981	13,057
60,400	60,450	14,254	12,122	14,996	13,071
60,450	60,500	14,269	12,136	15,012	13,085
60,500	60,550	14,285	12,150	15,027	13,099
60,550	60,600	14,300	12,164	15,043	13,113
60,600	60,650	14,316	12,178	15,058	13,127
60,650	60,700	14,331	12,192	15,074	13,141
60,700	60,750	14,347	12,206	15,089	13,155
60,750	60,800	14,362	12,220	15,105	13,169
60,800	60,850	14,378	12,234	15,120	13,183
60,850	60,900	14,393	12,248	15,136	13,197
60,900	60,950	14,409	12,262	15,151	13,211
60,950	61,000	14,424	12,276	15,167	13,225

61,000

At least	But less than	Single	Married filing jointly *	Married filing separately	Head of a household
61,000	61,050	14,440	12,290	15,182	13,239
61,050	61,100	14,455	12,304	15,198	13,253
61,100	61,150	14,471	12,318	15,213	13,267
61,150	61,200	14,486	12,332	15,229	13,281
61,200	61,250	14,502	12,346	15,244	13,295
61,250	61,300	14,517	12,360	15,260	13,309
61,300	61,350	14,533	12,374	15,275	13,323
61,350	61,400	14,548	12,388	15,291	13,337
61,400	61,450	14,564	12,402	15,306	13,351
61,450	61,500	14,579	12,416	15,322	13,365
61,500	61,550	14,595	12,430	15,337	13,379
61,550	61,600	14,610	12,444	15,353	13,393
61,600	61,650	14,626	12,458	15,368	13,407
61,650	61,700	14,641	12,472	15,384	13,421
61,700	61,750	14,657	12,486	15,399	13,435
61,750	61,800	14,672	12,500	15,415	13,449
61,800	61,850	14,688	12,514	15,430	13,463
61,850	61,900	14,703	12,528	15,446	13,477
61,900	61,950	14,719	12,542	15,461	13,491
61,950	62,000	14,734	12,556	15,477	13,505

62,000

At least	But less than	Single	Married filing jointly *	Married filing separately	Head of a household
62,000	62,050	14,750	12,570	15,492	13,519
62,050	62,100	14,765	12,584	15,508	13,533
62,100	62,150	14,781	12,598	15,523	13,547
62,150	62,200	14,796	12,612	15,539	13,561
62,200	62,250	14,812	12,626	15,554	13,575
62,250	62,300	14,827	12,640	15,570	13,589
62,300	62,350	14,843	12,654	15,585	13,603
62,350	62,400	14,858	12,668	15,601	13,617
62,400	62,450	14,874	12,682	15,616	13,631
62,450	62,500	14,889	12,696	15,632	13,645
62,500	62,550	14,905	12,710	15,647	13,659
62,550	62,600	14,920	12,724	15,663	13,673
62,600	62,650	14,936	12,738	15,678	13,687
62,650	62,700	14,951	12,752	15,694	13,701
62,700	62,750	14,967	12,766	15,709	13,715
62,750	62,800	14,982	12,780	15,725	13,729
62,800	62,850	14,998	12,794	15,740	13,743
62,850	62,900	15,013	12,808	15,756	13,757
62,900	62,950	15,029	12,822	15,771	13,771
62,950	63,000	15,044	12,836	15,787	13,785

63,000

At least	But less than	Single	Married filing jointly *	Married filing separately	Head of a household
63,000	63,050	15,060	12,850	15,802	13,799
63,050	63,100	15,075	12,864	15,818	13,813
63,100	63,150	15,091	12,878	15,833	13,827
63,150	63,200	15,106	12,892	15,849	13,841
63,200	63,250	15,122	12,906	15,864	13,855
63,250	63,300	15,137	12,920	15,880	13,869
63,300	63,350	15,153	12,934	15,895	13,883
63,350	63,400	15,168	12,948	15,911	13,897
63,400	63,450	15,184	12,962	15,926	13,911
63,450	63,500	15,199	12,976	15,942	13,925
63,500	63,550	15,215	12,990	15,957	13,939
63,550	63,600	15,230	13,004	15,973	13,953
63,600	63,650	15,246	13,018	15,988	13,967
63,650	63,700	15,261	13,032	16,004	13,981
63,700	63,750	15,277	13,046	16,019	13,995
63,750	63,800	15,292	13,060	16,035	14,009
63,800	63,850	15,308	13,074	16,050	14,023
63,850	63,900	15,323	13,088	16,066	14,037
63,900	63,950	15,339	13,102	16,081	14,051
63,950	64,000	15,354	13,116	16,097	14,065

64,000

At least	But less than	Single	Married filing jointly *	Married filing separately	Head of a household
64,000	64,050	15,370	13,130	16,112	14,079
64,050	64,100	15,385	13,144	16,128	14,093
64,100	64,150	15,401	13,158	16,143	14,107
64,150	64,200	15,416	13,172	16,159	14,121
64,200	64,250	15,432	13,186	16,174	14,135
64,250	64,300	15,447	13,200	16,190	14,149
64,300	64,350	15,463	13,214	16,205	14,163
64,350	64,400	15,478	13,228	16,221	14,177
64,400	64,450	15,494	13,242	16,236	14,191
64,450	64,500	15,509	13,256	16,252	14,205
64,500	64,550	15,525	13,270	16,267	14,219
64,550	64,600	15,540	13,284	16,283	14,233
64,600	64,650	15,556	13,298	16,298	14,247
64,650	64,700	15,571	13,312	16,314	14,261
64,700	64,750	15,587	13,326	16,329	14,275
64,750	64,800	15,602	13,340	16,345	14,289
64,800	64,850	15,618	13,354	16,360	14,303
64,850	64,900	15,633	13,368	16,376	14,317
64,900	64,950	15,649	13,382	16,391	14,331
64,950	65,000	15,664	13,396	16,407	14,345

65,000

At least	But less than	Single	Married filing jointly *	Married filing separately	Head of a household
65,000	65,050	15,680	13,410	16,422	14,359
65,050	65,100	15,695	13,424	16,438	14,373
65,100	65,150	15,711	13,438	16,453	14,387
65,150	65,200	15,726	13,452	16,469	14,401
65,200	65,250	15,742	13,466	16,484	14,415
65,250	65,300	15,757	13,480	16,500	14,429
65,300	65,350	15,773	13,494	16,515	14,443
65,350	65,400	15,788	13,508	16,531	14,457
65,400	65,450	15,804	13,522	16,546	14,471
65,450	65,500	15,819	13,536	16,562	14,485
65,500	65,550	15,835	13,550	16,577	14,499
65,550	65,600	15,850	13,564	16,593	14,513
65,600	65,650	15,866	13,578	16,608	14,527
65,650	65,700	15,881	13,592	16,624	14,541
65,700	65,750	15,897	13,606	16,639	14,555
65,750	65,800	15,912	13,620	16,655	14,569
65,800	65,850	15,928	13,634	16,670	14,583
65,850	65,900	15,943	13,648	16,686	14,597
65,900	65,950	15,959	13,662	16,701	14,611
65,950	66,000	15,974	13,676	16,717	14,625

66,000

At least	But less than	Single	Married filing jointly *	Married filing separately	Head of a household
66,000	66,050	15,990	13,690	16,732	14,639
66,050	66,100	16,005	13,704	16,748	14,653
66,100	66,150	16,021	13,718	16,763	14,667
66,150	66,200	16,036	13,732	16,779	14,681
66,200	66,250	16,052	13,746	16,794	14,695
66,250	66,300	16,067	13,760	16,810	14,709
66,300	66,350	16,083	13,774	16,825	14,723
66,350	66,400	16,098	13,788	16,841	14,737
66,400	66,450	16,114	13,802	16,856	14,751
66,450	66,500	16,129	13,816	16,872	14,765
66,500	66,550	16,145	13,830	16,887	14,779
66,550	66,600	16,160	13,844	16,903	14,793
66,600	66,650	16,176	13,858	16,918	14,807
66,650	66,700	16,191	13,872	16,934	14,821
66,700	66,750	16,207	13,886	16,949	14,835
66,750	66,800	16,222	13,900	16,965	14,849
66,800	66,850	16,238	13,914	16,980	14,863
66,850	66,900	16,253	13,928	16,996	14,877
66,900	66,950	16,269	13,942	17,011	14,891
66,950	67,000	16,284	13,956	17,027	14,905

67,000

At least	But less than	Single	Married filing jointly *	Married filing separately	Head of a household
67,000	67,050	16,300	13,970	17,042	14,919
67,050	67,100	16,315	13,984	17,058	14,933
67,100	67,150	16,331	13,998	17,073	14,947
67,150	67,200	16,346	14,012	17,089	14,961
67,200	67,250	16,362	14,026	17,104	14,975
67,250	67,300	16,377	14,040	17,120	14,989
67,300	67,350	16,393	14,054	17,135	15,003
67,350	67,400	16,408	14,068	17,151	15,017
67,400	67,450	16,424	14,082	17,166	15,031
67,450	67,500	16,439	14,096	17,182	15,045
67,500	67,550	16,455	14,110	17,197	15,059
67,550	67,600	16,470	14,124	17,213	15,073
67,600	67,650	16,486	14,138	17,228	15,087
67,650	67,700	16,501	14,152	17,244	15,101
67,700	67,750	16,517	14,166	17,259	15,115
67,750	67,800	16,532	14,180	17,275	15,129
67,800	67,850	16,548	14,194	17,290	15,143
67,850	67,900	16,563	14,208	17,306	15,157
67,900	67,950	16,579	14,222	17,321	15,171
67,950	68,000	16,594	14,236	17,337	15,185

* This column must also be used by a qualifying widow(er).

Continued on next page

1993 Tax Table—Continued

68,000 / 71,000 / 74,000

At least	But less than	Single	Married filing jointly *	Married filing separately	Head of a household	At least	But less than	Single	Married filing jointly *	Married filing separately	Head of a household	At least	But less than	Single	Married filing jointly *	Married filing separately	Head of a household
68,000	68,050	16,610	14,250	17,352	15,199	71,000	71,050	17,540	15,090	18,333	16,039	74,000	74,050	18,470	15,930	19,413	16,879
68,050	68,100	16,625	14,264	17,368	15,213	71,050	71,100	17,555	15,104	18,351	16,053	74,050	74,100	18,485	15,944	19,431	16,893
68,100	68,150	16,641	14,278	17,383	15,227	71,100	71,150	17,571	15,118	18,369	16,067	74,100	74,150	18,501	15,958	19,449	16,907
68,150	68,200	16,656	14,292	17,399	15,241	71,150	71,200	17,586	15,132	18,387	16,081	74,150	74,200	18,516	15,972	19,467	16,921
68,200	68,250	16,672	14,306	17,414	15,255	71,200	71,250	17,602	15,146	18,405	16,095	74,200	74,250	18,532	15,986	19,485	16,935
68,250	68,300	16,687	14,320	17,430	15,269	71,250	71,300	17,617	15,160	18,423	16,109	74,250	74,300	18,547	16,000	19,503	16,949
68,300	68,350	16,703	14,334	17,445	15,283	71,300	71,350	17,633	15,174	18,441	16,123	74,300	74,350	18,563	16,014	19,521	16,963
68,350	68,400	16,718	14,348	17,461	15,297	71,350	71,400	17,648	15,188	18,459	16,137	74,350	74,400	18,578	16,028	19,539	16,977
68,400	68,450	16,734	14,362	17,476	15,311	71,400	71,450	17,664	15,202	18,477	16,151	74,400	74,450	18,594	16,042	19,557	16,991
68,450	68,500	16,749	14,376	17,492	15,325	71,450	71,500	17,679	15,216	18,495	16,165	74,450	74,500	18,609	16,056	19,575	17,005
68,500	68,550	16,765	14,390	17,507	15,339	71,500	71,550	17,695	15,230	18,513	16,179	74,500	74,550	18,625	16,070	19,593	17,019
68,550	68,600	16,780	14,404	17,523	15,353	71,550	71,600	17,710	15,244	18,531	16,193	74,550	74,600	18,640	16,084	19,611	17,033
68,600	68,650	16,796	14,418	17,538	15,367	71,600	71,650	17,726	15,258	18,549	16,207	74,600	74,650	18,656	16,098	19,629	17,047
68,650	68,700	16,811	14,432	17,554	15,381	71,650	71,700	17,741	15,272	18,567	16,221	74,650	74,700	18,671	16,112	19,647	17,061
68,700	68,750	16,827	14,446	17,569	15,395	71,700	71,750	17,757	15,286	18,585	16,235	74,700	74,750	18,687	16,126	19,665	17,075
68,750	68,800	16,842	14,460	17,585	15,409	71,750	71,800	17,772	15,300	18,603	16,249	74,750	74,800	18,702	16,140	19,683	17,089
68,800	68,850	16,858	14,474	17,600	15,423	71,800	71,850	17,788	15,314	18,621	16,263	74,800	74,850	18,718	16,154	19,701	17,103
68,850	68,900	16,873	14,488	17,616	15,437	71,850	71,900	17,803	15,328	18,639	16,277	74,850	74,900	18,733	16,168	19,719	17,117
68,900	68,950	16,889	14,502	17,631	15,451	71,900	71,950	17,819	15,342	18,657	16,291	74,900	74,950	18,749	16,182	19,737	17,131
68,950	69,000	16,904	14,516	17,647	15,465	71,950	72,000	17,834	15,356	18,675	16,305	74,950	75,000	18,764	16,196	19,755	17,145

69,000 / 72,000 / 75,000

At least	But less than	Single	Married filing jointly *	Married filing separately	Head of a household	At least	But less than	Single	Married filing jointly *	Married filing separately	Head of a household	At least	But less than	Single	Married filing jointly *	Married filing separately	Head of a household
69,000	69,050	16,920	14,530	17,662	15,479	72,000	72,050	17,850	15,370	18,693	16,319	75,000	75,050	18,780	16,210	19,773	17,159
69,050	69,100	16,935	14,544	17,678	15,493	72,050	72,100	17,865	15,384	18,711	16,333	75,050	75,100	18,795	16,224	19,791	17,173
69,100	69,150	16,951	14,558	17,693	15,507	72,100	72,150	17,881	15,398	18,729	16,347	75,100	75,150	18,811	16,238	19,809	17,187
69,150	69,200	16,966	14,572	17,709	15,521	72,150	72,200	17,896	15,412	18,747	16,361	75,150	75,200	18,826	16,252	19,827	17,201
69,200	69,250	16,982	14,586	17,724	15,535	72,200	72,250	17,912	15,426	18,765	16,375	75,200	75,250	18,842	16,266	19,845	17,215
69,250	69,300	16,997	14,600	17,740	15,549	72,250	72,300	17,927	15,440	18,783	16,389	75,250	75,300	18,857	16,280	19,863	17,229
69,300	69,350	17,013	14,614	17,755	15,563	72,300	72,350	17,943	15,454	18,801	16,403	75,300	75,350	18,873	16,294	19,881	17,243
69,350	69,400	17,028	14,628	17,771	15,577	72,350	72,400	17,958	15,468	18,819	16,417	75,350	75,400	18,888	16,308	19,899	17,257
69,400	69,450	17,044	14,642	17,786	15,591	72,400	72,450	17,974	15,482	18,837	16,431	75,400	75,450	18,904	16,322	19,917	17,271
69,450	69,500	17,059	14,656	17,802	15,605	72,450	72,500	17,989	15,496	18,855	16,445	75,450	75,500	18,919	16,336	19,935	17,285
69,500	69,550	17,075	14,670	17,817	15,619	72,500	72,550	18,005	15,510	18,873	16,459	75,500	75,550	18,935	16,350	19,953	17,299
69,550	69,600	17,090	14,684	17,833	15,633	72,550	72,600	18,020	15,524	18,891	16,473	75,550	75,600	18,950	16,364	19,971	17,313
69,600	69,650	17,106	14,698	17,848	15,647	72,600	72,650	18,036	15,538	18,909	16,487	75,600	75,650	18,966	16,378	19,989	17,327
69,650	69,700	17,121	14,712	17,864	15,661	72,650	72,700	18,051	15,552	18,927	16,501	75,650	75,700	18,981	16,392	20,007	17,341
69,700	69,750	17,137	14,726	17,879	15,675	72,700	72,750	18,067	15,566	18,945	16,515	75,700	75,750	18,997	16,406	20,025	17,355
69,750	69,800	17,152	14,740	17,895	15,689	72,750	72,800	18,082	15,580	18,963	16,529	75,750	75,800	19,012	16,420	20,043	17,369
69,800	69,850	17,168	14,754	17,910	15,703	72,800	72,850	18,098	15,594	18,981	16,543	75,800	75,850	19,028	16,434	20,061	17,383
69,850	69,900	17,183	14,768	17,926	15,717	72,850	72,900	18,113	15,608	18,999	16,557	75,850	75,900	19,043	16,448	20,079	17,397
69,900	69,950	17,199	14,782	17,941	15,731	72,900	72,950	18,129	15,622	19,017	16,571	75,900	75,950	19,059	16,462	20,097	17,411
69,950	70,000	17,214	14,796	17,957	15,745	72,950	73,000	18,144	15,636	19,035	16,585	75,950	76,000	19,074	16,476	20,115	17,425

70,000 / 73,000 / 76,000

At least	But less than	Single	Married filing jointly *	Married filing separately	Head of a household	At least	But less than	Single	Married filing jointly *	Married filing separately	Head of a household	At least	But less than	Single	Married filing jointly *	Married filing separately	Head of a household
70,000	70,050	17,230	14,810	17,973	15,759	73,000	73,050	18,160	15,650	19,053	16,599	76,000	76,050	19,090	16,490	20,133	17,439
70,050	70,100	17,245	14,824	17,991	15,773	73,050	73,100	18,175	15,664	19,071	16,613	76,050	76,100	19,105	16,504	20,151	17,453
70,100	70,150	17,261	14,838	18,009	15,787	73,100	73,150	18,191	15,678	19,089	16,627	76,100	76,150	19,121	16,518	20,169	17,467
70,150	70,200	17,276	14,852	18,027	15,801	73,150	73,200	18,206	15,692	19,107	16,641	76,150	76,200	19,136	16,532	20,187	17,481
70,200	70,250	17,292	14,866	18,045	15,815	73,200	73,250	18,222	15,706	19,125	16,655	76,200	76,250	19,152	16,546	20,205	17,495
70,250	70,300	17,307	14,880	18,063	15,829	73,250	73,300	18,237	15,720	19,143	16,669	76,250	76,300	19,167	16,560	20,223	17,509
70,300	70,350	17,323	14,894	18,081	15,843	73,300	73,350	18,253	15,734	19,161	16,683	76,300	76,350	19,183	16,574	20,241	17,523
70,350	70,400	17,338	14,908	18,099	15,857	73,350	73,400	18,268	15,748	19,179	16,697	76,350	76,400	19,198	16,588	20,259	17,537
70,400	70,450	17,354	14,922	18,117	15,871	73,400	73,450	18,284	15,762	19,197	16,711	76,400	76,450	19,214	16,602	20,277	17,552
70,450	70,500	17,369	14,936	18,135	15,885	73,450	73,500	18,299	15,776	19,215	16,725	76,450	76,500	19,229	16,616	20,295	17,567
70,500	70,550	17,385	14,950	18,153	15,899	73,500	73,550	18,315	15,790	19,233	16,739	76,500	76,550	19,245	16,630	20,313	17,583
70,550	70,600	17,400	14,964	18,171	15,913	73,550	73,600	18,330	15,804	19,251	16,753	76,550	76,600	19,260	16,644	20,331	17,598
70,600	70,650	17,416	14,978	18,189	15,927	73,600	73,650	18,346	15,818	19,269	16,767	76,600	76,650	19,276	16,658	20,349	17,614
70,650	70,700	17,431	14,992	18,207	15,941	73,650	73,700	18,361	15,832	19,287	16,781	76,650	76,700	19,291	16,672	20,367	17,629
70,700	70,750	17,447	15,006	18,225	15,955	73,700	73,750	18,377	15,846	19,305	16,795	76,700	76,750	19,307	16,686	20,385	17,645
70,750	70,800	17,462	15,020	18,243	15,969	73,750	73,800	18,392	15,860	19,323	16,809	76,750	76,800	19,322	16,700	20,403	17,660
70,800	70,850	17,478	15,034	18,261	15,983	73,800	73,850	18,408	15,874	19,341	16,823	76,800	76,850	19,338	16,714	20,421	17,676
70,850	70,900	17,493	15,048	18,279	15,997	73,850	73,900	18,423	15,888	19,359	16,837	76,850	76,900	19,353	16,728	20,439	17,691
70,900	70,950	17,509	15,062	18,297	16,011	73,900	73,950	18,439	15,902	19,377	16,851	76,900	76,950	19,369	16,742	20,457	17,707
70,950	71,000	17,524	15,076	18,315	16,025	73,950	74,000	18,454	15,916	19,395	16,865	76,950	77,000	19,384	16,756	20,475	17,722

* This column must also be used by a qualifying widow(er).

Continued on next page

1993 Tax Table—Continued

If line 37 (taxable income) is— At least	But less than	Single	Married filing jointly *	Married filing separately	Head of a household	If line 37 (taxable income) is— At least	But less than	Single	Married filing jointly *	Married filing separately	Head of a household	If line 37 (taxable income) is— At least	But less than	Single	Married filing jointly *	Married filing separately	Head of a household
77,000						**80,000**						**83,000**					
77,000	77,050	19,400	16,770	20,493	17,738	80,000	80,050	20,330	17,610	21,573	18,668	83,000	83,050	21,260	18,450	22,653	19,598
77,050	77,100	19,415	16,784	20,511	17,753	80,050	80,100	20,345	17,624	21,591	18,683	83,050	83,100	21,275	18,464	22,671	19,613
77,100	77,150	19,431	16,798	20,529	17,769	80,100	80,150	20,361	17,638	21,609	18,699	83,100	83,150	21,291	18,478	22,689	19,629
77,150	77,200	19,446	16,812	20,547	17,784	80,150	80,200	20,376	17,652	21,627	18,714	83,150	83,200	21,306	18,492	22,707	19,644
77,200	77,250	19,462	16,826	20,565	17,800	80,200	80,250	20,392	17,666	21,645	18,730	83,200	83,250	21,322	18,506	22,725	19,660
77,250	77,300	19,477	16,840	20,583	17,815	80,250	80,300	20,407	17,680	21,663	18,745	83,250	83,300	21,337	18,520	22,743	19,675
77,300	77,350	19,493	16,854	20,601	17,831	80,300	80,350	20,423	17,694	21,681	18,761	83,300	83,350	21,353	18,534	22,761	19,691
77,350	77,400	19,508	16,868	20,619	17,846	80,350	80,400	20,438	17,708	21,699	18,776	83,350	83,400	21,368	18,548	22,779	19,706
77,400	77,450	19,524	16,882	20,637	17,862	80,400	80,450	20,454	17,722	21,717	18,792	83,400	83,450	21,384	18,562	22,797	19,722
77,450	77,500	19,539	16,896	20,655	17,877	80,450	80,500	20,469	17,736	21,735	18,807	83,450	83,500	21,399	18,576	22,815	19,737
77,500	77,550	19,555	16,910	20,673	17,893	80,500	80,550	20,485	17,750	21,753	18,823	83,500	83,550	21,415	18,590	22,833	19,753
77,550	77,600	19,570	16,924	20,691	17,908	80,550	80,600	20,500	17,764	21,771	18,838	83,550	83,600	21,430	18,604	22,851	19,768
77,600	77,650	19,586	16,938	20,709	17,924	80,600	80,650	20,516	17,778	21,789	18,854	83,600	83,650	21,446	18,618	22,869	19,784
77,650	77,700	19,601	16,952	20,727	17,939	80,650	80,700	20,531	17,792	21,807	18,869	83,650	83,700	21,461	18,632	22,887	19,799
77,700	77,750	19,617	16,966	20,745	17,955	80,700	80,750	20,547	17,806	21,825	18,885	83,700	83,750	21,477	18,646	22,905	19,815
77,750	77,800	19,632	16,980	20,763	17,970	80,750	80,800	20,562	17,820	21,843	18,900	83,750	83,800	21,492	18,660	22,923	19,830
77,800	77,850	19,648	16,994	20,781	17,986	80,800	80,850	20,578	17,834	21,861	18,916	83,800	83,850	21,508	18,674	22,941	19,846
77,850	77,900	19,663	17,008	20,799	18,001	80,850	80,900	20,593	17,848	21,879	18,931	83,850	83,900	21,523	18,688	22,959	19,861
77,900	77,950	19,679	17,022	20,817	18,017	80,900	80,950	20,609	17,862	21,897	18,947	83,900	83,950	21,539	18,702	22,977	19,877
77,950	78,000	19,694	17,036	20,835	18,032	80,950	81,000	20,624	17,876	21,915	18,962	83,950	84,000	21,554	18,716	22,995	19,892
78,000						**81,000**						**84,000**					
78,000	78,050	19,710	17,050	20,853	18,048	81,000	81,050	20,640	17,890	21,933	18,978	84,000	84,050	21,570	18,730	23,013	19,908
78,050	78,100	19,725	17,064	20,871	18,063	81,050	81,100	20,655	17,904	21,951	18,993	84,050	84,100	21,585	18,744	23,031	19,923
78,100	78,150	19,741	17,078	20,889	18,079	81,100	81,150	20,671	17,918	21,969	19,009	84,100	84,150	21,601	18,758	23,049	19,939
78,150	78,200	19,756	17,092	20,907	18,094	81,150	81,200	20,686	17,932	21,987	19,024	84,150	84,200	21,616	18,772	23,067	19,954
78,200	78,250	19,772	17,106	20,925	18,110	81,200	81,250	20,702	17,946	22,005	19,040	84,200	84,250	21,632	18,786	23,085	19,970
78,250	78,300	19,787	17,120	20,943	18,125	81,250	81,300	20,717	17,960	22,023	19,055	84,250	84,300	21,647	18,800	23,103	19,985
78,300	78,350	19,803	17,134	20,961	18,141	81,300	81,350	20,733	17,974	22,041	19,071	84,300	84,350	21,663	18,814	23,121	20,001
78,350	78,400	19,818	17,148	20,979	18,156	81,350	81,400	20,748	17,988	22,059	19,086	84,350	84,400	21,678	18,828	23,139	20,016
78,400	78,450	19,834	17,162	20,997	18,172	81,400	81,450	20,764	18,002	22,077	19,102	84,400	84,450	21,694	18,842	23,157	20,032
78,450	78,500	19,849	17,176	21,015	18,187	81,450	81,500	20,779	18,016	22,095	19,117	84,450	84,500	21,709	18,856	23,175	20,047
78,500	78,550	19,865	17,190	21,033	18,203	81,500	81,550	20,795	18,030	22,113	19,133	84,500	84,550	21,725	18,870	23,193	20,063
78,550	78,600	19,880	17,204	21,051	18,218	81,550	81,600	20,810	18,044	22,131	19,148	84,550	84,600	21,740	18,884	23,211	20,078
78,600	78,650	19,896	17,218	21,069	18,234	81,600	81,650	20,826	18,058	22,149	19,164	84,600	84,650	21,756	18,898	23,229	20,094
78,650	78,700	19,911	17,232	21,087	18,249	81,650	81,700	20,841	18,072	22,167	19,179	84,650	84,700	21,771	18,912	23,247	20,109
78,700	78,750	19,927	17,246	21,105	18,265	81,700	81,750	20,857	18,086	22,185	19,195	84,700	84,750	21,787	18,926	23,265	20,125
78,750	78,800	19,942	17,260	21,123	18,280	81,750	81,800	20,872	18,100	22,203	19,210	84,750	84,800	21,802	18,940	23,283	20,140
78,800	78,850	19,958	17,274	21,141	18,296	81,800	81,850	20,888	18,114	22,221	19,226	84,800	84,850	21,818	18,954	23,301	20,156
78,850	78,900	19,973	17,288	21,159	18,311	81,850	81,900	20,903	18,128	22,239	19,241	84,850	84,900	21,833	18,968	23,319	20,171
78,900	78,950	19,989	17,302	21,177	18,327	81,900	81,950	20,919	18,142	22,257	19,257	84,900	84,950	21,849	18,982	23,337	20,187
78,950	79,000	20,004	17,316	21,195	18,342	81,950	82,000	20,934	18,156	22,275	19,272	84,950	85,000	21,864	18,996	23,355	20,202
79,000						**82,000**						**85,000**					
79,000	79,050	20,020	17,330	21,213	18,358	82,000	82,050	20,950	18,170	22,293	19,288	85,000	85,050	21,880	19,010	23,373	20,218
79,050	79,100	20,035	17,344	21,231	18,373	82,050	82,100	20,965	18,184	22,311	19,303	85,050	85,100	21,895	19,024	23,391	20,233
79,100	79,150	20,051	17,358	21,249	18,389	82,100	82,150	20,981	18,198	22,329	19,319	85,100	85,150	21,911	19,038	23,409	20,249
79,150	79,200	20,066	17,372	21,267	18,404	82,150	82,200	20,996	18,212	22,347	19,334	85,150	85,200	21,926	19,052	23,427	20,264
79,200	79,250	20,082	17,386	21,285	18,420	82,200	82,250	21,012	18,226	22,365	19,350	85,200	85,250	21,942	19,066	23,445	20,280
79,250	79,300	20,097	17,400	21,303	18,435	82,250	82,300	21,027	18,240	22,383	19,365	85,250	85,300	21,957	19,080	23,463	20,295
79,300	79,350	20,113	17,414	21,321	18,451	82,300	82,350	21,043	18,254	22,401	19,381	85,300	85,350	21,973	19,094	23,481	20,311
79,350	79,400	20,128	17,428	21,339	18,466	82,350	82,400	21,058	18,268	22,419	19,396	85,350	85,400	21,988	19,108	23,499	20,326
79,400	79,450	20,144	17,442	21,357	18,482	82,400	82,450	21,074	18,282	22,437	19,412	85,400	85,450	22,004	19,122	23,517	20,342
79,450	79,500	20,159	17,456	21,375	18,497	82,450	82,500	21,089	18,296	22,455	19,427	85,450	85,500	22,019	19,136	23,535	20,357
79,500	79,550	20,175	17,470	21,393	18,513	82,500	82,550	21,105	18,310	22,473	19,443	85,500	85,550	22,035	19,150	23,553	20,373
79,550	79,600	20,190	17,484	21,411	18,528	82,550	82,600	21,120	18,324	22,491	19,458	85,550	85,600	22,050	19,164	23,571	20,388
79,600	79,650	20,206	17,498	21,429	18,544	82,600	82,650	21,136	18,338	22,509	19,474	85,600	85,650	22,066	19,178	23,589	20,404
79,650	79,700	20,221	17,512	21,447	18,559	82,650	82,700	21,151	18,352	22,527	19,489	85,650	85,700	22,081	19,192	23,607	20,419
79,700	79,750	20,237	17,526	21,465	18,575	82,700	82,750	21,167	18,366	22,545	19,505	85,700	85,750	22,097	19,206	23,625	20,435
79,750	79,800	20,252	17,540	21,483	18,590	82,750	82,800	21,182	18,380	22,563	19,520	85,750	85,800	22,112	19,220	23,643	20,450
79,800	79,850	20,268	17,554	21,501	18,606	82,800	82,850	21,198	18,394	22,581	19,536	85,800	85,850	22,128	19,234	23,661	20,466
79,850	79,900	20,283	17,568	21,519	18,621	82,850	82,900	21,213	18,408	22,599	19,551	85,850	85,900	22,143	19,248	23,679	20,481
79,900	79,950	20,299	17,582	21,537	18,637	82,900	82,950	21,229	18,422	22,617	19,567	85,900	85,950	22,159	19,262	23,697	20,497
79,950	80,000	20,314	17,596	21,555	18,652	82,950	83,000	21,244	18,436	22,635	19,582	85,950	86,000	22,174	19,276	23,715	20,512

* This column must also be used by a qualifying widow(er).

Continued on next page

1993 Tax Table—Continued

If line 37 (taxable income) is—		And you are—			
At least	But less than	Single	Married filing jointly *	Married filing separately	Head of a household
		Your tax is—			

86,000

At least	But less than	Single	Married filing jointly	Married filing separately	Head of a household
86,000	86,050	22,190	19,290	23,733	20,528
86,050	86,100	22,205	19,304	23,751	20,543
86,100	86,150	22,221	19,318	23,769	20,559
86,150	86,200	22,236	19,332	23,787	20,574
86,200	86,250	22,252	19,346	23,805	20,590
86,250	86,300	22,267	19,360	23,823	20,605
86,300	86,350	22,283	19,374	23,841	20,621
86,350	86,400	22,298	19,388	23,859	20,636
86,400	86,450	22,314	19,402	23,877	20,652
86,450	86,500	22,329	19,416	23,895	20,667
86,500	86,550	22,345	19,430	23,913	20,683
86,550	86,600	22,360	19,444	23,931	20,698
86,600	86,650	22,376	19,458	23,949	20,714
86,650	86,700	22,391	19,472	23,967	20,729
86,700	86,750	22,407	19,486	23,985	20,745
86,750	86,800	22,422	19,500	24,003	20,760
86,800	86,850	22,438	19,514	24,021	20,776
86,850	86,900	22,453	19,528	24,039	20,791
86,900	86,950	22,469	19,542	24,057	20,807
86,950	87,000	22,484	19,556	24,075	20,822

87,000

At least	But less than	Single	Married filing jointly	Married filing separately	Head of a household
87,000	87,050	22,500	19,570	24,093	20,838
87,050	87,100	22,515	19,584	24,111	20,853
87,100	87,150	22,531	19,598	24,129	20,869
87,150	87,200	22,546	19,612	24,147	20,884
87,200	87,250	22,562	19,626	24,165	20,900
87,250	87,300	22,577	19,640	24,183	20,915
87,300	87,350	22,593	19,654	24,201	20,931
87,350	87,400	22,608	19,668	24,219	20,946
87,400	87,450	22,624	19,682	24,237	20,962
87,450	87,500	22,639	19,696	24,255	20,977
87,500	87,550	22,655	19,710	24,273	20,993
87,550	87,600	22,670	19,724	24,291	21,008
87,600	87,650	22,686	19,738	24,309	21,024
87,650	87,700	22,701	19,752	24,327	21,039
87,700	87,750	22,717	19,766	24,345	21,055
87,750	87,800	22,732	19,780	24,363	21,070
87,800	87,850	22,748	19,794	24,381	21,086
87,850	87,900	22,763	19,808	24,399	21,101
87,900	87,950	22,779	19,822	24,417	21,117
87,950	88,000	22,794	19,836	24,435	21,132

88,000

At least	But less than	Single	Married filing jointly	Married filing separately	Head of a household
88,000	88,050	22,810	19,850	24,453	21,148
88,050	88,100	22,825	19,864	24,471	21,163
88,100	88,150	22,841	19,878	24,489	21,179
88,150	88,200	22,856	19,892	24,507	21,194
88,200	88,250	22,872	19,906	24,525	21,210
88,250	88,300	22,887	19,920	24,543	21,225
88,300	88,350	22,903	19,934	24,561	21,241
88,350	88,400	22,918	19,948	24,579	21,256
88,400	88,450	22,934	19,962	24,597	21,272
88,450	88,500	22,949	19,976	24,615	21,287
88,500	88,550	22,965	19,990	24,633	21,303
88,550	88,600	22,980	20,004	24,651	21,318
88,600	88,650	22,996	20,018	24,669	21,334
88,650	88,700	23,011	20,032	24,687	21,349
88,700	88,750	23,027	20,046	24,705	21,365
88,750	88,800	23,042	20,060	24,723	21,380
88,800	88,850	23,058	20,074	24,741	21,396
88,850	88,900	23,073	20,088	24,759	21,411
88,900	88,950	23,089	20,102	24,777	21,427
88,950	89,000	23,104	20,116	24,795	21,442

89,000

At least	But less than	Single	Married filing jointly	Married filing separately	Head of a household
89,000	89,050	23,120	20,130	24,813	21,458
89,050	89,100	23,135	20,144	24,831	21,473
89,100	89,150	23,151	20,158	24,849	21,489
89,150	89,200	23,166	20,173	24,867	21,504
89,200	89,250	23,182	20,188	24,885	21,520
89,250	89,300	23,197	20,204	24,903	21,535
89,300	89,350	23,213	20,219	24,921	21,551
89,350	89,400	23,228	20,235	24,939	21,566
89,400	89,450	23,244	20,250	24,957	21,582
89,450	89,500	23,259	20,266	24,975	21,597
89,500	89,550	23,275	20,281	24,993	21,613
89,550	89,600	23,290	20,297	25,011	21,628
89,600	89,650	23,306	20,312	25,029	21,644
89,650	89,700	23,321	20,328	25,047	21,659
89,700	89,750	23,337	20,343	25,065	21,675
89,750	89,800	23,352	20,359	25,083	21,690
89,800	89,850	23,368	20,374	25,101	21,706
89,850	89,900	23,383	20,390	25,119	21,721
89,900	89,950	23,399	20,405	25,137	21,737
89,950	90,000	23,414	20,421	25,155	21,752

90,000

At least	But less than	Single	Married filing jointly	Married filing separately	Head of a household
90,000	90,050	23,430	20,436	25,173	21,768
90,050	90,100	23,445	20,452	25,191	21,783
90,100	90,150	23,461	20,467	25,209	21,799
90,150	90,200	23,476	20,483	25,227	21,814
90,200	90,250	23,492	20,498	25,245	21,830
90,250	90,300	23,507	20,514	25,263	21,845
90,300	90,350	23,523	20,529	25,281	21,861
90,350	90,400	23,538	20,545	25,299	21,876
90,400	90,450	23,554	20,560	25,317	21,892
90,450	90,500	23,569	20,576	25,335	21,907
90,500	90,550	23,585	20,591	25,353	21,923
90,550	90,600	23,600	20,607	25,371	21,938
90,600	90,650	23,616	20,622	25,389	21,954
90,650	90,700	23,631	20,638	25,407	21,969
90,700	90,750	23,647	20,653	25,425	21,985
90,750	90,800	23,662	20,669	25,443	22,000
90,800	90,850	23,678	20,684	25,461	22,016
90,850	90,900	23,693	20,700	25,479	22,031
90,900	90,950	23,709	20,715	25,497	22,047
90,950	91,000	23,724	20,731	25,515	22,062

91,000

At least	But less than	Single	Married filing jointly	Married filing separately	Head of a household
91,000	91,050	23,740	20,746	25,533	22,078
91,050	91,100	23,755	20,762	25,551	22,093
91,100	91,150	23,771	20,777	25,569	22,109
91,150	91,200	23,786	20,793	25,587	22,124
91,200	91,250	23,802	20,808	25,605	22,140
91,250	91,300	23,817	20,824	25,623	22,155
91,300	91,350	23,833	20,839	25,641	22,171
91,350	91,400	23,848	20,855	25,659	22,186
91,400	91,450	23,864	20,870	25,677	22,202
91,450	91,500	23,879	20,886	25,695	22,217
91,500	91,550	23,895	20,901	25,713	22,233
91,550	91,600	23,910	20,917	25,731	22,248
91,600	91,650	23,926	20,932	25,749	22,264
91,650	91,700	23,941	20,948	25,767	22,279
91,700	91,750	23,957	20,963	25,785	22,295
91,750	91,800	23,972	20,979	25,803	22,310
91,800	91,850	23,988	20,994	25,821	22,326
91,850	91,900	24,003	21,010	25,839	22,341
91,900	91,950	24,019	21,025	25,857	22,357
91,950	92,000	24,034	21,041	25,875	22,372

92,000

At least	But less than	Single	Married filing jointly	Married filing separately	Head of a household
92,000	92,050	24,050	21,056	25,893	22,388
92,050	92,100	24,065	21,072	25,911	22,403
92,100	92,150	24,081	21,087	25,929	22,419
92,150	92,200	24,096	21,103	25,947	22,434
92,200	92,250	24,112	21,118	25,965	22,450
92,250	92,300	24,127	21,134	25,983	22,465
92,300	92,350	24,143	21,149	26,001	22,481
92,350	92,400	24,158	21,165	26,019	22,496
92,400	92,450	24,174	21,180	26,037	22,512
92,450	92,500	24,189	21,196	26,055	22,527
92,500	92,550	24,205	21,211	26,073	22,543
92,550	92,600	24,220	21,227	26,091	22,558
92,600	92,650	24,236	21,242	26,109	22,574
92,650	92,700	24,251	21,258	26,127	22,589
92,700	92,750	24,267	21,273	26,145	22,605
92,750	92,800	24,282	21,289	26,163	22,620
92,800	92,850	24,298	21,304	26,181	22,636
92,850	92,900	24,313	21,320	26,199	22,651
92,900	92,950	24,329	21,335	26,217	22,667
92,950	93,000	24,344	21,351	26,235	22,682

93,000

At least	But less than	Single	Married filing jointly	Married filing separately	Head of a household
93,000	93,050	24,360	21,366	26,253	22,698
93,050	93,100	24,375	21,382	26,271	22,713
93,100	93,150	24,391	21,397	26,289	22,729
93,150	93,200	24,406	21,413	26,307	22,744
93,200	93,250	24,422	21,428	26,325	22,760
93,250	93,300	24,437	21,444	26,343	22,775
93,300	93,350	24,453	21,459	26,361	22,791
93,350	93,400	24,468	21,475	26,379	22,806
93,400	93,450	24,484	21,490	26,397	22,822
93,450	93,500	24,499	21,506	26,415	22,837
93,500	93,550	24,515	21,521	26,433	22,853
93,550	93,600	24,530	21,537	26,451	22,868
93,600	93,650	24,546	21,552	26,469	22,884
93,650	93,700	24,561	21,568	26,487	22,899
93,700	93,750	24,577	21,583	26,505	22,915
93,750	93,800	24,592	21,599	26,523	22,930
93,800	93,850	24,608	21,614	26,541	22,946
93,850	93,900	24,623	21,630	26,559	22,961
93,900	93,950	24,639	21,645	26,577	22,977
93,950	94,000	24,654	21,661	26,595	22,992

94,000

At least	But less than	Single	Married filing jointly	Married filing separately	Head of a household
94,000	94,050	24,670	21,676	26,613	23,008
94,050	94,100	24,685	21,692	26,631	23,023
94,100	94,150	24,701	21,707	26,649	23,039
94,150	94,200	24,716	21,723	26,667	23,054
94,200	94,250	24,732	21,738	26,685	23,070
94,250	94,300	24,747	21,754	26,703	23,085
94,300	94,350	24,763	21,769	26,721	23,101
94,350	94,400	24,778	21,785	26,739	23,116
94,400	94,450	24,794	21,800	26,757	23,132
94,450	94,500	24,809	21,816	26,775	23,147
94,500	94,550	24,825	21,831	26,793	23,163
94,550	94,600	24,840	21,847	26,811	23,178
94,600	94,650	24,856	21,862	26,829	23,194
94,650	94,700	24,871	21,878	26,847	23,209
94,700	94,750	24,887	21,893	26,865	23,225
94,750	94,800	24,902	21,909	26,883	23,240
94,800	94,850	24,918	21,924	26,901	23,256
94,850	94,900	24,933	21,940	26,919	23,271
94,900	94,950	24,949	21,955	26,937	23,287
94,950	95,000	24,964	21,971	26,955	23,302

* This column must also be used by a qualifying widow(er).

Continued on next page

1993 Tax Table—*Continued*

If line 37 (taxable income) is—		And you are—				If line 37 (taxable income) is—		And you are—			
At least	But less than	Single	Married filing jointly *	Married filing sepa-rately	Head of a house-hold	At least	But less than	Single	Married filing jointly *	Married filing sepa-rately	Head of a house-hold
		Your tax is—						Your tax is—			

95,000 / 98,000

At least	But less than	Single	Married filing jointly	Married filing separately	Head of household	At least	But less than	Single	Married filing jointly	Married filing separately	Head of household
95,000	95,050	24,980	21,986	26,973	23,318	98,000	98,050	25,910	22,916	28,053	24,248
95,050	95,100	24,995	22,002	26,991	23,333	98,050	98,100	25,925	22,932	28,071	24,263
95,100	95,150	25,011	22,017	27,009	23,349	98,100	98,150	25,941	22,947	28,089	24,279
95,150	95,200	25,026	22,033	27,027	23,364	98,150	98,200	25,956	22,963	28,107	24,294
95,200	95,250	25,042	22,048	27,045	23,380	98,200	98,250	25,972	22,978	28,125	24,310
95,250	95,300	25,057	22,064	27,063	23,395	98,250	98,300	25,987	22,994	28,143	24,325
95,300	95,350	25,073	22,079	27,081	23,411	98,300	98,350	26,003	23,009	28,161	24,341
95,350	95,400	25,088	22,095	27,099	23,426	98,350	98,400	26,018	23,025	28,179	24,356
95,400	95,450	25,104	22,110	27,117	23,442	98,400	98,450	26,034	23,040	28,197	24,372
95,450	95,500	25,119	22,126	27,135	23,457	98,450	98,500	26,049	23,056	28,215	24,387
95,500	95,550	25,135	22,141	27,153	23,473	98,500	98,550	26,065	23,071	28,233	24,403
95,550	95,600	25,150	22,157	27,171	23,488	98,550	98,600	26,080	23,087	28,251	24,418
95,600	95,650	25,166	22,172	27,189	23,504	98,600	98,650	26,096	23,102	28,269	24,434
95,650	95,700	25,181	22,188	27,207	23,519	98,650	98,700	26,111	23,118	28,287	24,449
95,700	95,750	25,197	22,203	27,225	23,535	98,700	98,750	26,127	23,133	28,305	24,465
95,750	95,800	25,212	22,219	27,242	23,550	98,750	98,800	26,142	23,149	28,323	24,480
95,800	95,850	25,228	22,234	27,261	23,566	98,800	98,850	26,158	23,164	28,341	24,496
95,850	95,900	25,243	22,250	27,279	23,581	98,850	98,900	26,173	23,180	28,359	24,511
95,900	95,950	25,259	22,265	27,297	23,597	98,900	98,950	26,189	23,195	28,377	24,527
95,950	96,000	25,274	22,281	27,315	23,612	98,950	99,000	26,204	23,211	28,395	24,542

96,000 / 99,000

At least	But less than	Single	Married filing jointly	Married filing separately	Head of household	At least	But less than	Single	Married filing jointly	Married filing separately	Head of household
96,000	96,050	25,290	22,296	27,333	23,628	99,000	99,050	26,220	23,226	28,413	24,558
96,050	96,100	25,305	22,312	27,351	23,643	99,050	99,100	26,235	23,242	28,431	24,573
96,100	96,150	25,321	22,327	27,369	23,659	99,100	99,150	26,251	23,257	28,449	24,589
96,150	96,200	25,336	22,343	27,387	23,674	99,150	99,200	26,266	23,273	28,467	24,604
96,200	96,250	25,352	22,358	27,405	23,690	99,200	99,250	26,282	23,288	28,485	24,620
96,250	96,300	25,367	22,374	27,423	23,705	99,250	99,300	26,297	23,304	28,503	24,635
96,300	96,350	25,383	22,389	27,441	23,721	99,300	99,350	26,313	23,319	28,521	24,651
96,350	96,400	25,398	22,405	27,459	23,736	99,350	99,400	26,328	23,335	28,539	24,666
96,400	96,450	25,414	22,420	27,477	23,752	99,400	99,450	26,344	23,350	28,557	24,682
96,450	96,500	25,429	22,436	27,495	23,767	99,450	99,500	26,359	23,366	28,575	24,697
96,500	96,550	25,445	22,451	27,513	23,783	99,500	99,550	26,375	23,381	28,593	24,713
96,550	96,600	25,460	22,467	27,531	23,798	99,550	99,600	26,390	23,397	28,611	24,728
96,600	96,650	25,476	22,482	27,549	23,814	99,600	99,650	26,406	23,412	28,629	24,744
96,650	96,700	25,491	22,498	27,567	23,829	99,650	99,700	26,421	23,428	28,647	24,759
96,700	96,750	25,507	22,513	27,585	23,845	99,700	99,750	26,437	23,443	28,665	24,775
96,750	96,800	25,522	22,529	27,603	23,860	99,750	99,800	26,452	23,459	28,683	24,790
96,800	96,850	25,538	22,544	27,621	23,876	99,800	99,850	26,468	23,474	28,701	24,806
96,850	96,900	25,553	22,560	27,639	23,891	99,850	99,900	26,483	23,490	28,719	24,821
96,900	96,950	25,569	22,575	27,657	23,907	99,900	99,950	26,499	23,505	28,737	24,837
96,950	97,000	25,584	22,591	27,675	23,922	99,950	100,000	26,514	23,521	28,755	24,852

97,000

At least	But less than	Single	Married filing jointly	Married filing separately	Head of household
97,000	97,050	25,600	22,606	27,693	23,938
97,050	97,100	25,615	22,622	27,711	23,953
97,100	97,150	25,631	22,637	27,729	23,969
97,150	97,200	25,646	22,653	27,747	23,984
97,200	97,250	25,662	22,668	27,765	24,000
97,250	97,300	25,677	22,684	27,783	24,015
97,300	97,350	25,693	22,699	27,801	24,031
97,350	97,400	25,708	22,715	27,819	24,046
97,400	97,450	25,724	22,730	27,837	24,062
97,450	97,500	25,739	22,746	27,855	24,077
97,500	97,550	25,755	22,761	27,873	24,093
97,550	97,600	25,770	22,777	27,891	24,108
97,600	97,650	25,786	22,792	27,909	24,124
97,650	97,700	25,801	22,808	27,927	24,139
97,700	97,750	25,817	22,823	27,945	24,155
97,750	97,800	25,832	22,839	27,963	24,170
97,800	97,850	25,848	22,854	27,981	24,186
97,850	97,900	25,863	22,870	27,999	24,201
97,900	97,950	25,879	22,885	28,017	24,217
97,950	98,000	25,894	22,901	28,035	24,232

$100,000 or over — use Tax Rate Schedules

* This column must also be used by a qualifying widow(er).

A-3 Unified Transfer Tax Rate Schedule

Unified Transfer Tax Rate Schedule

If the amount with respect to which the tentative tax to be computed is:	The tentative tax is:
Not over $10,000..............................	18 percent of such amount
Over $10,000 but not over $20,000............	$1,800 plus 20 percent of the excess of such amount over $10,000
Over $20,000 but not over $40,000............	$3,800 plus 22 percent of the excess of such amount over $20,000
Over $40,000 but not over $60,000............	$8,200 plus 24 percent of the excess of such amount over $40,000
Over $60,000 but not over $80,000............	$13,000 plus 26 percent of the excess of such amount over $60,000
Over $80,000 but not over $100,000...........	$18,200 plus 28 percent of the excess of such amount over $80,000
Over $100,000 but not over $150,000..........	$23,800 plus 30 percent of the excess of such amount over $100,000
Over $150,000 but not over $250,000..........	$38,800 plus 32 percent of the excess of such amount over $150,000
Over $250,000 but not over $500,000..........	$70,800 plus 34 percent of the excess of such amount over $250,000
Over $500,000 but not over $750,000..........	$155,800 plus 37 percent of the excess of such amount over $500,000
Over $750,000 but not over $1,000,000........	$248,300 plus 39 percent of the excess of such amount over $750,000
Over $1,000,000 but not over $1,250,000......	$345,800 plus 41 percent of the excess of such amount over $1,000,000
Over $1,250,000 but not over $1,500,000......	$448,300 plus 43 percent of the excess of such amount over $1,250,000
Over $1,500,000 but not over $2,000,000......	$555,800 plus 45 percent of the excess of such amount over $1,500,000
Over $2,000,000 but not over $2,500,000......	$780,800 plus 49 percent of the excess of such amount over $2,000,000
Over $2,500,000 but not over $3,000,000......	$1,290,800 plus 53 percent of the excess of such amount over $2,500,000
Over $3,000,000..............................	$1,290,800 plus 55 percent of the excess of such amount over $3,000,000

A-4   Estate and Gift Tax Valuation Tables

Table A

Single Life Remainder Factors
Various Interest Rates
(See Notes to Table A)

Age	9.8%	10.0%	10.2%	Age	9.8%	10.0%	10.2%
0	.01954	.01922	.01891	25	.02902	.02784	.02673
1	.00834	.00801	.00770	26	.03052	.02928	.02811
2	.00819	.00784	.00751	27	.03219	.03088	.02965
3	.00832	.00795	.00760	28	.03403	.03264	.03134
4	.00862	.00822	.00786	29	.03604	.03458	.03322
5	.00904	.00862	.00824	30	.03825	.03671	.03527
6	.00954	.00910	.00869	31	.04067	.03905	.03753
7	.01013	.00966	.00923	32	.04329	.04160	.04000
8	.01081	.01031	.00986	33	.04616	.04438	.04269
9	.01159	.01107	.01059	34	.04926	.04738	.04561
10	.01249	.01194	.01142	35	.05260	.05063	.04877
11	.01351	.01293	.01239	36	.05617	.05411	.05215
12	.01463	.01402	.01345	37	.05999	.05783	.05578
13	.01582	.01517	.01457	38	.06407	.06180	.05965
14	.01698	.01630	.01567	39	.06841	.06604	.06379
15	.01810	.01738	.01672	40	.07303	.07055	.06820
16	.01917	.01842	.01772	41	.07794	.07535	.07288
17	.02018	.01940	.01866	42	.08312	.08041	.07784
18	.02118	.02035	.01958	43	.08858	.08576	.08308
19	.02218	.02131	.02050	44	.09434	.09141	.08861
20	.02320	.02229	.02143	45	.10042	.09736	.09445
21	.02424	.02328	.02238	46	.10680	.10363	.10060
22	.02532	.02430	.02336	47	.11352	.11022	.10707
23	.02644	.02538	.02438	48	.12055	.11713	.11386
24	.02767	.02655	.02550	49	.12787	.12433	.12094

(Continued)

Table A *(Continued)*

Age	9.8%	10.0%	10.2%	Age	9.8%	10.0%	10.2%
50	.13548	.13182	.12831	80	.53248	.52705	.52171
51	.14342	.13963	.13600	81	.55035	.54499	.53974
52	.15172	.14780	.14405	82	.56796	.56270	.55753
53	.16038	.15635	.15247	83	.58523	.58007	.57500
54	.16940	.16524	.16124	84	.60218	.59713	.59216
55	.17878	.17450	.17039	85	.61886	.61392	.60906
56	.18854	.18414	.17991	86	.63511	.63030	.62555
57	.19870	.19419	.18984	87	.65071	.64602	.64139
58	.20927	.20464	.20018	88	.66574	.66117	.65666
59	.22024	.21551	.21093	89	.68045	.67601	.67163
60	.23158	.22674	.22206	90	.69502	.69071	.68646
61	.24325	.23831	.23353	91	.70921	.70504	.70093
62	.25524	.25020	.24532	92	.72267	.71864	.71466
63	.26754	.26240	.25742	93	.73524	.73135	.72750
64	.28016	.27493	.26987	94	.74680	.74303	.73931
65	.29317	.28787	.28271	95	.75727	.75362	.75001
66	.30663	.30124	.29601	96	.76657	.76303	.75953
67	.32053	.31508	.30978	97	.77504	.77160	.76819
68	.33488	.32937	.32401	98	.78267	.77931	.77599
69	.34961	.34405	.33863	99	.78971	.78644	.78319
70	.36468	.35907	.35361	100	.79624	.79304	.78987
71	.38000	.37436	.36886	101	.80245	.79932	.79622
72	.39558	.38991	.38439	102	.80892	.80586	.80283
73	.41143	.40575	.40021	103	.81577	.81279	.80983
74	.42763	.42195	.41639	104	.82338	.82048	.81760
75	.44424	.43856	.43301	105	.83282	.83003	.82726
76	.46129	.45563	.45009	106	.84659	.84397	.84137
77	.47873	.47311	.46761	107	.86676	.86443	.86211
78	.49652	.49094	.48548	108	.90020	.89840	.89660
79	.51488	.50897	.50356	109	.95537	.95455	.95372

Notes to Table A:

1. These single life remainder factors are excerpts from Notice 89-60, 1989-22 I.R.B. (May 30, 1989). The IRS released tables for various interest rates beginning at 8.2 percent and incrementing by 0.2 percent up to 12.0 percent. Only three different rates are illustrated here.

2. These single life remainder factors can be used to determine the appropriate income factor for valuation of an income interest by using the following formula:

$$\text{Income factor} = 1.000000 - \text{Remainder factor}$$

Table B

Term Certain Remainder Factors
Various Interest Rates

Number of Years	9.8%	10.0%	10.2%	Number of Years	9.8%	10.0%	10.2%
1	.910747	.909091	.907441	31	.055122	.052099	.049246
2	.829460	.826446	.823449	32	.050202	.047362	.044688
3	.755428	.751315	.747232	33	.045722	.043057	.040552
4	.688003	.683013	.678069	34	.041641	.039143	.036798
5	.626597	.620921	.615307	35	.037924	.035584	.033392
6	.570671	.564474	.558355	36	.034539	.032349	.030301
7	.519737	.513158	.506674	37	.031457	.029408	.027497
8	.473349	.466507	.459777	38	.028649	.026735	.024952
9	.431101	.424098	.417221	39	.026092	.024304	.022642
10	.392624	.385543	.378603	40	.023763	.022095	.020546
11	.357581	.350494	.343560	41	.021642	.020086	.018645
12	.325666	.318631	.311760	42	.019711	.018260	.016919
13	.296599	.289664	.282904	43	.017951	.016600	.015353
14	.270127	.263331	.256719	44	.016349	.015091	.013932
15	.246017	.239392	.232957	45	.014890	.013719	.012642
16	.224059	.217629	.211395	46	.013561	.012472	.011472
17	.204061	.197845	.191828	47	.012351	.011338	.010410
18	.185848	.179859	.174073	48	.011248	.010307	.009447
19	.169260	.163508	.157961	49	.010244	.009370	.008572
20	.154153	.148644	.143340	50	.009330	.008519	.007779
21	.140395	.135131	.130073	51	.008497	.007744	.007059
22	.127864	.122846	.118033	52	.007739	.007040	.006406
23	.116452	.111678	.107108	53	.007048	.006400	.005813
24	.106058	.101562	.097195	54	.006419	.005818	.005275
25	.096592	.092296	.088198	55	.005846	.005289	.004786
26	.087971	.083905	.080035	56	.005324	.004809	.004343
27	.080119	.076278	.072627	57	.004849	.004371	.003941
28	.072968	.069343	.065905	58	.004416	.003974	.003577
29	.066456	.063039	.059804	59	.004022	.003613	.003246
30	.060524	.057309	.054269	60	.003663	.003284	.002945

Note: Like Table A, this table contains excerpts from Notice 89-60, but only 3 different interest rates are illustrated. The Table B from Notice 89-60 contains factors for 8.2 percent through 12.0 percent.

Appendix B

TAX FORMS

		Page Nos.
B-1	Form 1040A U.S. Individual Income Tax Return	**B-3**
B-2	Form 1040EZ Income Tax Return for Single Filers With No Dependents	**B-6**
B-3	Form 1040 U.S. Individual Income Tax Return and Schedules	**B-8**
	Schedules A&B Itemized Deductions and Interest and Dividend Income	**B-10**
	Schedule C Profit or Loss From Business	**B-12**
	Schedule D Capital Gains and Losses and Reconciliation of Forms 1099-B	**B-14**
	Schedule E Supplemental Income and Loss	**B-16**
	Schedule F Farm Income and Expenses	**B-18**
	Schedule R Credit for the Elderly or the Disabled	**B-20**
	Schedule SE Self-Employment Tax	**B-22**
	Schedule EIC Earned Income Credit	**B-24**
B-4	Amended Tax Return Forms	
	Form 1040X Amended U.S. Individual Income Tax Return	**B-26**
	Form 1120X Amended U.S. Corporation Income Tax Return	**B-32**
B-5	Application for Extension of Time to File Income Tax Returns	
	Form 4868 Application for Automatic Extension of Time to File U.S. Individual Income Tax Return	**B-34**
	Form 2688 Application for Additional Extension of Time to File U.S. Individual Income Tax Return	**B-35**
B-6	Underpayment of Estimated Tax	
	Form 2210 Underpayment of Estimated Tax by Individuals and Fiduciaries	**B-37**
	Form 2220 Underpayment of Estimated Tax by Corporations	**B-39**
B-7	Forms for Computation of Minimum Tax	
	Form 4626 Alternative Minimum Tax—Corporations	**B-45**
	Form 6251 Alternative Minimum Tax—Individuals	**B-50**

B-8 Forms for Tax Credits
  Form 2441 Child and Dependent Care Expenses.............. **B-55**
  Form 3468 Investment Credit................................. **B-60**
  Form 3800 General Business Credit.......................... **B-64**

B-9 Other Tax Forms
  Form 2106 Employee Business Expenses..................... **B-66**
  Form 2119 Sale of Your Home............................... **B-72**
  Form 2120 Multiple Support Declaration..................... **B-75**
  Form 3903 Moving Expenses................................ **B-76**
  Form 4562 Depreciation and Amortization................... **B-79**
  Form 4684 Casualties and Thefts............................ **B-81**
  Form 4797 Sales of Business Property....................... **B-87**
  Form 4952 Investment Interest Expense Deduction............ **B-89**
  Form 4970 Tax on Accumulation Distribution of Trusts......... **B-91**
  Form 6252 Installment Sale Income.......................... **B-93**
  Form 8283 Noncash Charitable Contributions................. **B-96**
  Form 8582 Passive Activity Loss Limitations.................. **B-98**
  Form 8615 Tax for Children Under Age 14 Who
    Have Investment Income of More Than $12100............... **B-101**
  Form 8814 Parent's Election to Report
    Child's Interest and Dividends............................ **B-103**
  Form 8829 Expenses for Business
    Use of Your Home....................................... **B-105**

B-1 Form 1040A   U.S. Individual Income Tax Return

Form **1040A**
Department of the Treasury—Internal Revenue Service
U.S. Individual Income Tax Return (T)   **1993**   IRS Use Only—Do not write or staple in this space.

OMB No. 1545-0085

Label
(See page 15.)

Use the IRS label.
Otherwise, please print or type.

L A B E L   H E R E

Your first name and initial   Last name

If a joint return, spouse's first name and initial   Last name

Home address (number and street). If you have a P.O. box, see page 16.   Apt. no.

City, town or post office, state, and ZIP code. If you have a foreign address, see page 16.

Your social security number

Spouse's social security number

For Privacy Act and Paperwork Reduction Act Notice, see page 4.

Presidential Election Campaign Fund (See page 16.)
Do you want $3 to go to this fund?
If a joint return, does your spouse want $3 to go to this fund?

Yes No

Note: Checking "Yes" will not change your tax or reduce your refund.

Check the box for your filing status
(See page 16.)

Check only one box.

1 ☐ Single
2 ☐ Married filing joint return (even if only one had income)
3 ☐ Married filing separate return. Enter spouse's social security number above and full name here. ▶
4 ☐ Head of household (with qualifying person). (See page 17.) If the qualifying person is a child but not your dependent, enter this child's name here. ▶
5 ☐ Qualifying widow(er) with dependent child (year spouse died ▶ 19___). (See page 18.)

Figure your exemptions
(See page 19.)

If more than seven dependents, see page 22.

6a ☐ **Yourself.** If your parent (or someone else) can claim you as a dependent on his or her tax return, **do not** check box 6a. But be sure to check the box on line 18b on page 2.

b ☐ **Spouse**

c **Dependents:**

(1) Name (first, initial, and last name)	(2) Check if under age 1	(3) If age 1 or older, dependent's social security number	(4) Dependent's relationship to you	(5) No. of months lived in your home in 1993

d If your child didn't live with you but is claimed as your dependent under a pre-1985 agreement, check here . . . . ▶ ☐
e Total number of exemptions claimed.

No. of boxes checked on 6a and 6b ___

No. of your children on 6c who:
• lived with you
• didn't live with you due to divorce or separation (see page 22)

Dependents on 6c not entered above

Add numbers entered on lines above

Figure your total income

Attach Copy B of your Forms W-2 and 1099-R here.

If you didn't get a W-2, see page 24.

If you are attaching a check or money order, put it on top of any Forms W-2 or 1099-R.

7 Wages, salaries, tips, etc. This should be shown in box 1 of your W-2 form(s). Attach Form(s) W-2. | 7

8a **Taxable** interest income (see page 25). If over $400, also complete and attach Schedule 1, Part I. | 8a
b **Tax-exempt** interest. DO NOT include on line 8a. 8b

9 Dividends. If over $400, also complete and attach Schedule 1, Part II. | 9

10a Total IRA distributions. 10a | 10b Taxable amount (see page 26). | 10b

11a Total pensions and annuities. 11a | 11b Taxable amount (see page 26). | 11b

12 Unemployment compensation (see page 30). | 12

13a Social security benefits. 13a | 13b Taxable amount (see page 30). | 13b

14 Add lines 7 through 13b (far right column). This is your **total income.** ▶ 14

Figure your adjusted gross income

15a Your IRA deduction (see page 32). 15a
b Spouse's IRA deduction (see page 32). 15b
c Add lines 15a and 15b. These are your **total adjustments.** 15c

16 Subtract line 15c from line 14. This is your **adjusted gross income.** If less than $23,050 and a child lived with you, see page 63 to find out if you can claim the "Earned income credit" on line 28c. ▶ 16

Cat. No. 11327A   **1993 Form 1040A page 1**

■ 1993 Form 1040A page 2

Name(s) shown on page 1	Your social security number

Figure your standard deduction, exemption amount, and taxable income

17 Enter the amount from line 16.   17

18a Check if: ☐ **You** were 65 or older ☐ Blind   ☐ **Spouse** was 65 or older ☐ Blind } **Enter number of boxes checked ▶** 18a

b If your parent (or someone else) can claim you as a dependent, check here . . . . ▶ 18b ☐

c If you are married filing separately and your spouse files Form 1040 and itemizes deductions, see page 36 and check here ▶ 18c ☐

19 Enter the **standard deduction** shown below for your filing status. **But if you checked any box on line 18a or b,** go to page 36 to find your standard deduction. **If you checked box 18c,** enter -0-.

- Single—$3,700   ● Head of household—$5,450
- Married filing jointly or Qualifying widow(er)—$6,200
- Married filing separately—$3,100   19

20 Subtract line 19 from line 17. If line 19 is more than line 17, enter -0-.   20

21 Multiply $2,350 by the total number of exemptions claimed on line 6e.   21

22 Subtract line 21 from line 20. If line 21 is more than line 20, enter -0-. This is your **taxable income.** ▶ 22

Figure your tax, credits, and payments

If you want the IRS to figure your tax, see the instructions for line 22 on page 37.

23 Find the tax on the amount on line 22. Check if from: ☐ Tax Table (pages 50–55) or ☐ Form 8615 (see page 38).   23

24a Credit for child and dependent care expenses. Complete and attach Schedule 2.   24a

b Credit for the elderly or the disabled. Complete and attach Schedule 3.   24b

c Add lines 24a and 24b. These are your **total credits.**   24c

25 Subtract line 24c from line 23. If line 24c is more than line 23, enter -0-.   25

26 Advance earned income credit payments from Form W-2.   26

27 Add lines 25 and 26. This is your **total tax.** ▶ 27

28a Total Federal income tax withheld. If any tax is from Form(s) 1099, check here. ▶ ☐   28a

b 1993 estimated tax payments and amount applied from 1992 return.   28b

c **Earned income credit.** Complete and attach Schedule EIC.   28c

d Add lines 28a, 28b, and 28c. These are your **total payments.** ▶ 28d

Figure your refund or amount you owe

29 If line 28d is more than line 27, subtract line 27 from line 28d. This is the amount you **overpaid.**   29

30 Amount of line 29 you want **refunded to you.**   30

31 Amount of line 29 you want **applied to your 1994 estimated tax.**   31

32 If line 27 is more than line 28d, subtract line 28d from line 27. This is the **amount you owe.** For details on how to pay, including what to write on your payment, see page 42.   32

33 Estimated tax penalty (see page 43). Also, include on line 32.   33

Sign your return

Keep a copy of this return for your records.

Under penalties of perjury, I declare that I have examined this return and accompanying schedules and statements, and to the best of my knowledge and belief, they are true, correct, and accurately list all amounts and sources of income I received during the tax year. Declaration of preparer (other than the taxpayer) is based on all information of which the preparer has any knowledge.

Your signature	Date	Your occupation
Spouse's signature. If joint return, BOTH must sign.	Date	Spouse's occupation

Paid preparer's use only

Preparer's signature ▶	Date	Check if self-employed ☐	Preparer's social security no.
Firm's name (or yours if self-employed) and address ▶		E.I. No.	
		ZIP code	

1993 Form 1040A page 2

Schedule 1
(Form 1040A)

Department of the Treasury—Internal Revenue Service

**Interest and Dividend Income
for Form 1040A Filers** (T)

1993

OMB No. 1545-0085

Name(s) shown on Form 1040A | Your social security number

Part I

Interest income

(See pages 25 and 56.)

Note: *If you received a Form 1099–INT, Form 1099–OID, or substitute statement from a brokerage firm, enter the firm's name and the total interest shown on that form.*

1   List name of payer. If any interest is from a seller-financed mortgage and the buyer used the property as a personal residence, see page 56 and list this interest first. Also, show that buyer's social security number and address.

Amount

| | 1 | |

2   Add the amounts on line 1.   **2**

3   Excludable interest on series EE U.S. savings bonds issued after 1989 from Form 8815, line 14. You MUST attach Form 8815 to Form 1040A.   **3**

4   Subtract line 3 from line 2. Enter the result here and on Form 1040A, line 8a.   **4**

Part II

Dividend income

(See pages 25 and 57.)

Note: *If you received a Form 1099–DIV or substitute statement from a brokerage firm, enter the firm's name and the total dividends shown on that form.*

5   List name of payer

Amount

| | 5 | |

6   Add the amounts on line 5. Enter the total here and on Form 1040A, line 9.   **6**

For Paperwork Reduction Act Notice, see Form 1040A instructions.   Cat. No. 12075R   **1993 Schedule 1 (Form 1040A) page 1**

B-2   Form 1040EZ   Income Tax Return for Single Filers With No Dependents

Department of the Treasury—Internal Revenue Service

Form 1040EZ

Income Tax Return for Single and Joint Filers With No Dependents (T) **1993**

OMB No. 1545-0675

Use the IRS label (See page 10.) Otherwise, please print.

L A B E L
H E R E

Print your name (first, initial, last)

If a joint return, print spouse's name (first, initial, last)

Home address (number and street). If you have a P.O. box, see page 11.   Apt. no.

City, town or post office, state and ZIP code. If you have a foreign address, see page 11.

Your social security number

Spouse's social security number

See instructions on back and in Form 1040EZ booklet.

Presidential Election Campaign (See page 11.)

Note: *Checking "Yes" will not change your tax or reduce your refund.*

Do you want $3 to go to this fund? ▶

If a joint return, does your spouse want $3 to go to this fund? ▶

Yes   No

Filing status

1   ☐ Single   ☐ Married filing joint return (even if only one had income)

Dollars   Cents

Report your income

Attach Copy B of Form(s) W-2 here. Attach any tax payment on top of Form(s) W-2.

Note: *You must check Yes or No.*

2   Total wages, salaries, and tips. This should be shown in box 1 of your W-2 form(s). Attach your W-2 form(s).   2

3   Taxable interest income of $400 or less. If the total is over $400, you cannot use Form 1040EZ.   3

4   Add lines 2 and 3. This is your **adjusted gross income.**   4

5   Can your parents (or someone else) claim you on their return?
☐ **Yes.** Do worksheet on back; enter amount from line G here.   ☐ **No.** If **single,** enter 6,050.00. If **married,** enter 10,900.00. For an explanation of these amounts, see back of form.   5

6   Subtract line 5 from line 4. If line 5 is larger than line 4, enter 0. This is your **taxable income.**   6

Figure your tax

7   Enter your Federal income tax withheld from box 2 of your W-2 form(s).   7

8   **Tax.** Look at line 6 above. Use the amount on **line 6** to find your tax in the tax table on pages 24–28 of the booklet. Then, enter the tax from the table on this line.   8

Refund or amount you owe

9   If line 7 is larger than line 8, subtract line 8 from line 7. This is your **refund.**   9

10   If line 8 is larger than line 7, subtract line 7 from line 8. This is the **amount you owe.** For details on how to pay, including what to write on your payment, see page 16.   10

Sign your return

Keep a copy of this form for your records.

I have read this return. Under penalties of perjury, I declare that to the best of my knowledge and belief, the return is true, correct, and accurately lists all amounts and sources of income I received during the tax year.

Your signature

Spouse's signature if joint return

Date   Your occupation

Date   Spouse's occupation

For IRS Use Only — Please do not write in boxes below.

For Privacy Act and Paperwork Reduction Act Notice, see page 4.   Cat. No. 11329W   Form 1040EZ (1993)

1993   **Instructions for Form 1040EZ**

Use this form if
- Your filing status is single or married filing jointly.
- You do not claim any dependents.
- You (and your spouse if married) were under 65 on January 1, 1994, and not blind at the end of 1993.
- Your taxable income (line 6) is less than $50,000.
- You had **only** wages, salaries, tips, and taxable scholarship or fellowship grants, and your taxable interest income was $400 or less. **But** if you earned tips, including allocated tips, that are not included in box 5 and box 7 of your W-2, you may not be able to use Form 1040EZ. See page 13.
- You did not receive any advance earned income credit payments.

  Caution: If married and either you or your spouse had total wages of over $57,600, you may not be able to use this form. See page 6.

  If you are not sure about your filing status, see page 12. If you have questions about dependents, call Tele-Tax (see page 22) and listen to topic 354. If you **can't use this form,** call Tele-Tax (see page 22) and listen to topic 352.

Filling in your return

Because this form is read by a machine, please print your numbers inside the boxes like this:

9 8 7 6 5 4 3 2 1 0   Do not type your numbers. Do not use dollar signs.

Most people can fill in the form by following the instructions on the front. But you will have to use the booklet if you received a scholarship or fellowship grant or tax-exempt interest income, such as on municipal bonds. Also, use the booklet if you received a Form 1099-INT showing income tax withheld (backup withholding).

Remember, you must report all wages, salaries, and tips even if you don't get a W-2 form from your employer. You must also report all your taxable interest income, including interest from banks, savings and loans, credit unions, etc., even if you don't get a Form 1099-INT.

If you paid someone to prepare your return, see page 17.

Worksheet for dependents who checked "Yes" on line 5

Use this worksheet to figure the amount to enter on line 5 if someone can claim you (or your spouse if married) as a dependent, even if that person chooses not to do so. To find out if someone can claim you as a dependent, call Tele-Tax (see page 22) and listen to topic 354.

A. Enter the amount from line 2 on the front.	A. _____
B. Minimum standard deduction.	B. _____ 600.00
C. Enter the LARGER of line A or line B here.	C. _____
D. Maximum standard deduction. If single, enter 3,700.00; if married, enter 6,200.00.	D. _____
E. Enter the SMALLER of line C or line D here. This is your standard deduction.	E. _____
F. Exemption amount.	
• If single, enter 0.	
• If married and both you and your spouse can be claimed as dependents, enter 0.	
• If married and only one of you can be claimed as a dependent, enter 2,350.00.	F. _____
G. Add lines E and F. Enter the total here and on line 5 on the front.	G. _____

If you checked "No" on line 5 because no one can claim you (or your spouse if married) as a dependent, enter on line 5 the amount shown below that applies to you.

- Single, enter 6,050.00. This is the total of your standard deduction (3,700.00) and personal exemption (2,350.00).
- Married, enter 10,900.00. This is the total of your standard deduction (6,200.00), exemption for yourself (2,350.00), and exemption for your spouse (2,350.00).

Avoid mistakes

Please see page 17 of the Form 1040EZ booklet for a list of common mistakes to avoid that will help you make sure your form is filled in correctly.

Mailing your return

Mail your return by **April 15, 1994**. Use the envelope that came with your booklet. If you don't have that envelope, see page 29 for the address to use.

B-3 Form 1040 U.S. Individual Income Tax Return and Schedules

Form **1040**
Department of the Treasury—Internal Revenue Service

U.S. Individual Income Tax Return (T) **1993**

For the year Jan. 1–Dec. 31, 1993, or other tax year beginning _____, 1993, ending _____, 19 ___

IRS Use Only—Do not write or staple in this space.

OMB No. 1545-0074

Label
(See instructions on page 12.)

Use the IRS label. Otherwise, please print or type.

LABEL HERE

Your first name and initial | Last name

If a joint return, spouse's first name and initial | Last name

Home address (number and street). If you have a P.O. box, see page 12. | Apt. no.

City, town or post office, state, and ZIP code. If you have a foreign address, see page 12.

Your social security number

Spouse's social security number

For Privacy Act and Paperwork Reduction Act Notice, see page 4.

Presidential Election Campaign
(See page 12.)

Do you want $3 to go to this fund? . . . .
If a joint return, does your spouse want $3 to go to this fund? . . . . . .

Yes | No | Note: Checking "Yes" will not change your tax or reduce your refund.

Filing Status
(See page 12.)

Check only one box.

1 ☐ Single
2 ☐ Married filing joint return (even if only one had income)
3 ☐ Married filing separate return. Enter spouse's social security no. above and full name here. ▶ _____
4 ☐ Head of household (with qualifying person). (See page 13.) If the qualifying person is a child but not your dependent, enter this child's name here. ▶ _____
5 ☐ Qualifying widow(er) with dependent child (year spouse died ▶ 19___). (See page 13.)

Exemptions
(See page 13.)

If more than six dependents, see page 14.

6a ☐ **Yourself.** If your parent (or someone else) can claim you as a dependent on his or her tax return, **do not** check box 6a. But be sure to check the box on line 33b on page 2
b ☐ **Spouse** . . . .
c **Dependents:**

(1) Name (first, initial, and last name)	(2) Check if under age 1	(3) If age 1 or older, dependent's social security number	(4) Dependent's relationship to you	(5) No. of months lived in your home in 1993

No. of boxes checked on 6a and 6b ___

No. of your children on 6c who:
• lived with you ___
• didn't live with you due to divorce or separation (see page 15) ___

Dependents on 6c not entered above ___

d If your child didn't live with you but is claimed as your dependent under a pre-1985 agreement, check here ▶ ☐
e Total number of exemptions claimed

Add numbers entered on lines above ▶ ☐

Income

Attach Copy B of your Forms W-2, W-2G, and 1099-R here.

If you did not get a W-2, see page 10.

If you are attaching a check or money order, put it on top of any Forms W-2, W-2G, or 1099-R.

7 Wages, salaries, tips, etc. Attach Form(s) W-2 . . . . | 7 |
8a **Taxable** interest income (see page 16). Attach Schedule B if over $400 . . . . | 8a |
b Tax-exempt interest (see page 17). DON'T include on line 8a | 8b |
9 Dividend income. Attach Schedule B if over $400 . . . . | 9 |
10 Taxable refunds, credits, or offsets of state and local income taxes (see page 17) . . | 10 |
11 Alimony received . . . . | 11 |
12 Business income or (loss). Attach Schedule C or C-EZ . . . . | 12 |
13 Capital gain or (loss). Attach Schedule D . . . . | 13 |
14 Capital gain distributions not reported on line 13 (see page 17) . . . . . | 14 |
15 Other gains or (losses). Attach Form 4797 . . . . | 15 |
16a Total IRA distributions . | 16a | b Taxable amount (see page 18) | 16b |
17a Total pensions and annuities | 17a | b Taxable amount (see page 18) | 17b |
18 Rental real estate, royalties, partnerships, S corporations, trusts, etc. Attach Schedule E | 18 |
19 Farm income or (loss). Attach Schedule F . . . . | 19 |
20 Unemployment compensation (see page 19) . . . . | 20 |
21a Social security benefits | 21a | b Taxable amount (see page 19) | 21b |
22 Other income. List type and amount—see page 20 .... | 22 |
23 Add the amounts in the far right column for lines 7 through 22. This is your **total income** ▶ | 23 |

Adjustments to Income
(See page 20.)

24a Your IRA deduction (see page 20) . . . . . . | 24a |
b Spouse's IRA deduction (see page 20) . . . . . . | 24b |
25 One-half of self-employment tax (see page 21) . . . . | 25 |
26 Self-employed health insurance deduction (see page 22) | 26 |
27 Keogh retirement plan and self-employed SEP deduction | 27 |
28 Penalty on early withdrawal of savings . . . . . | 28 |
29 Alimony paid. Recipient's SSN ▶ | 29 |
30 Add lines 24a through 29. These are your **total adjustments** . . . . ▶ | 30 |

Adjusted Gross Income

31 Subtract line 30 from line 23. This is your **adjusted gross income.** If this amount is less than $23,050 and a child lived with you, see page EIC-1 to find out if you can claim the "Earned Income Credit" on line 56 . . . . ▶ | 31 |

Cat. No. 11320B

Form **1040** (1993)

Form 1040 (1993)   Page 2

Tax Computation

(See page 23.)

32	Amount from line 31 (adjusted gross income)	32
33a	Check if: ☐ **You** were 65 or older, ☐ Blind; ☐ **Spouse** was 65 or older, ☐ Blind.	
	Add the number of boxes checked above and enter the total here . . . ▶ **33a**	
b	If your parent (or someone else) can claim you as a dependent, check here . ▶ **33b** ☐	
c	If you are married filing separately and your spouse itemizes deductions or you are a dual-status alien, see page 24 and check here . . . . . ▶ **33c** ☐	
34	Enter the larger of your: { **Itemized deductions** from Schedule A, line 26, **OR** **Standard deduction** shown below for your filing status. **But if you checked any box on line 33a or b,** go to page 24 to find your standard deduction. If you checked **box 33c,** your standard deduction is zero. ● Single—$3,700 ● Head of household—$5,450 ● Married filing jointly or Qualifying widow(er)—$6,200 ● Married filing separately—$3,100 }	34
35	Subtract line 34 from line 32	35
36	If line 32 is $81,350 or less, multiply $2,350 by the total number of exemptions claimed on line 6e. If line 32 is over $81,350, see the worksheet on page 25 for the amount to enter .	36
37	**Taxable income.** Subtract line 36 from line 35. If line 36 is more than line 35, enter -0- .	37
38	Tax. Check if from **a** ☐ Tax Table, **b** ☐ Tax Rate Schedules, **c** ☐ Schedule D Tax Work-sheet, or **d** ☐ Form 8615 (see page 25). Amount from Form(s) 8814 ▶ **e**	38
39	Additional taxes (see page 25). Check if from **a** ☐ Form 4970 **b** ☐ Form 4972 . . .	39
40	Add lines 38 and 39 . . . . ▶	40

If you want the IRS to figure your tax, see page 24.

Credits

(See page 25.)

41	Credit for child and dependent care expenses. Attach Form 2441	41	
42	Credit for the elderly or the disabled. Attach Schedule R . .	42	
43	Foreign tax credit. Attach Form 1116	43	
44	Other credits (see page 26). Check if from **a** ☐ Form 3800 **b** ☐ Form 8396 **c** ☐ Form 8801 **d** ☐ Form (specify)_____	44	
45	Add lines 41 through 44	45	
46	Subtract line 45 from line 40. If line 45 is more than line 40, enter -0- . . . . . ▶	46	

Other Taxes

47	Self-employment tax. Attach Schedule SE. Also, see line 25	47
48	Alternative minimum tax. Attach Form 6251	48
49	Recapture taxes (see page 26). Check if from **a** ☐ Form 4255 **b** ☐ Form 8611 **c** ☐ Form 8828	49
50	Social security and Medicare tax on tip income not reported to employer. Attach Form 4137 .	50
51	Tax on qualified retirement plans, including IRAs. If required, attach Form 5329	51
52	Advance earned income credit payments from Form W-2	52
53	Add lines 46 through 52. This is your **total tax** . . . . ▶	53

Payments

Attach Forms W-2, W-2G, and 1099-R on the front.

54	Federal income tax withheld. If any is from Form(s) 1099, check ▶ ☐	54	
55	1993 estimated tax payments and amount applied from 1992 return .	55	
56	**Earned income credit.** Attach Schedule EIC	56	
57	Amount paid with Form 4868 (extension request)	57	
58a	Excess social security, Medicare, and RRTA tax withheld (see page 28) .	58a	
b	Deferral of additional 1993 taxes. Attach Form 8841	58b	
59	Other payments (see page 28). Check if from **a** ☐ Form 2439 **b** ☐ Form 4136	59	
60	Add lines 54 through 59. These are your **total payments** . . . . ▶	60	

Refund or Amount You Owe

61	If line 60 is more than line 53, subtract line 53 from line 60. This is the amount you **OVERPAID.** ▶	61	
62	Amount of line 61 you want **REFUNDED TO YOU.** . . . . ▶	62	
63	Amount of line 61 you want **APPLIED TO YOUR 1994 ESTIMATED TAX** ▶	63	
64	If line 53 is more than line 60, subtract line 60 from line 53. This is the **AMOUNT YOU OWE.** For details on how to pay, including what to write on your payment, see page 29 . . .	64	
65	Estimated tax penalty (see page 29). Also include on line 64	65	

Sign Here

Keep a copy of this return for your records.

Under penalties of perjury, I declare that I have examined this return and accompanying schedules and statements, and to the best of my knowledge and belief, they are true, correct, and complete. Declaration of preparer (other than taxpayer) is based on all information of which preparer has any knowledge.

Your signature ▶	Date	Your occupation
Spouse's signature. If a joint return, BOTH must sign.	Date	Spouse's occupation

Paid Preparer's Use Only

Preparer's signature ▶	Date	Check if self-employed ☐	Preparer's social security no.
Firm's name (or yours if self-employed) and address ▶		E.I. No.	
		ZIP code	

SCHEDULES A&B
(Form 1040)

Department of the Treasury
Internal Revenue Service (T)

Schedule A—Itemized Deductions

(Schedule B is on back)

▶ Attach to Form 1040. ▶ See Instructions for Schedules A and B (Form 1040).

OMB No. 1545-0074

1993

Attachment
Sequence No. **07**

Name(s) shown on Form 1040

Your social security number

Medical and Dental Expenses		**Caution:** *Do not include expenses reimbursed or paid by others.*	
	1	Medical and dental expenses (see page A-1)	1
	2	Enter amount from Form 1040, line 32. ⌊ **2** ⌋	
	3	Multiply line 2 above by 7.5% (.075)	3
	4	Subtract line 3 from line 1. If zero or less, enter -0- . . . . ▶	4
Taxes You Paid (See page A-1.)	5	State and local income taxes	5
	6	Real estate taxes (see page A-2)	6
	7	Other taxes. List—include personal property taxes ▶	7
	8	Add lines 5 through 7 . . . . ▶	8
Interest You Paid (See page A-2.)	9a	Home mortgage interest and points reported to you on Form 1098	9a
	b	Home mortgage interest not reported to you on Form 1098. If paid to the person from whom you bought the home, see page A-3 and show that person's name, identifying no., and address ▶	
Note: Personal interest is not deductible.			9b
	10	Points not reported to you on Form 1098. See page A-3 for special rules	10
	11	Investment interest. If required, attach Form 4952. (See page A-3.)	11
	12	Add lines 9a through 11 . . . . ▶	12
Gifts to Charity (See page A-3.)		**Caution:** *If you made a charitable contribution and received a benefit in return, see page A-3.*	
	13	Contributions by cash or check	13
	14	Other than by cash or check. If over $500, you **MUST** attach Form 8283	14
	15	Carryover from prior year	15
	16	Add lines 13 through 15 . . . . ▶	16
Casualty and Theft Losses	17	Casualty or theft loss(es). Attach Form 4684. (See page A-4.) . . . . . . ▶	17
Moving Expenses	18	Moving expenses. Attach Form 3903 or 3903-F. (See page A-4.) . . . . . ▶	18
Job Expenses and Most Other Miscellaneous Deductions (See page A-5 for expenses to deduct here.)	19	Unreimbursed employee expenses—job travel, union dues, job education, etc. If required, you **MUST** attach Form 2106. (See page A-4.) ▶	19
	20	Other expenses—investment, tax preparation, safe deposit box, etc. List type and amount ▶	20
	21	Add lines 19 and 20	21
	22	Enter amount from Form 1040, line 32. ⌊ **22** ⌋	
	23	Multiply line 22 above by 2% (.02)	23
	24	Subtract line 23 from line 21. If zero or less, enter -0- . . . . ▶	24
Other Miscellaneous Deductions	25	Other—from list on page A-5. List type and amount ▶	25
Total Itemized Deductions	26	Is the amount on Form 1040, line 32, more than $108,450 (more than $54,225 if married filing separately)? • **NO.** Your deduction is not limited. Add lines 4, 8, 12, 16, 17, 18, 24, and 25 and enter the total here. Also enter on Form 1040, line 34, the **larger** of this amount or your standard deduction. • **YES.** Your deduction may be limited. See page A-5 for the amount to enter.	▶ 26

For Paperwork Reduction Act Notice, see Form 1040 instructions.   Cat. No. 11330X   Schedule A (Form 1040) 1993

Schedules A&B (Form 1040) 1993

Name(s) shown on Form 1040. Do not enter name and social security number if shown on other side.

OMB No. 1545-0074   Page **2**

Your social security number

Schedule B—Interest and Dividend Income

Attachment Sequence No. **08**

Part I
Interest Income

(See pages 16 and B-1.)

Note: If you received a Form 1099-INT, Form 1099-OID, or substitute statement from a brokerage firm, list the firm's name as the payer and enter the total interest shown on that form.

Note: *If you had over $400 in taxable interest income, you must also complete Part III.*

Interest Income	Amount
1 List name of payer. If any interest is from a seller-financed mortgage and the buyer used the property as a personal residence, see page B-1 and list this interest first. Also show that buyer's social security number and address ►	

1

2 Add the amounts on line 1	**2**	
3 Excludable interest on series EE U.S. savings bonds issued after 1989 from Form 8815, line 14. You MUST attach Form 8815 to Form 1040	**3**	
4 Subtract line 3 from line 2. Enter the result here and on Form 1040, line 8a ►	**4**	

Part II
Dividend Income

(See pages 17 and B-1.)

Note: If you received a Form 1099-DIV or substitute statement from a brokerage firm, list the firm's name as the payer and enter the total dividends shown on that form.

Note: *If you had over $400 in gross dividends and/or other distributions on stock, you must also complete Part III.*

Dividend Income	Amount
5 List name of payer. Include gross dividends and/or other distributions on stock here. Any capital gain distributions and nontaxable distributions will be deducted on lines 7 and 8 ►	

5

6 Add the amounts on line 5	**6**	
7 Capital gain distributions. Enter here and on Schedule D* .	**7**	
8 Nontaxable distributions. (See the inst. for Form 1040, line 9.)	**8**	
9 Add lines 7 and 8	**9**	
10 Subtract line 9 from line 6. Enter the result here and on Form 1040, line 9 . ►	**10**	

If you received capital gain distributions but do not need Schedule D to report any other gains or losses, see the instructions for Form 1040, lines 13 and 14.

Part III
Foreign Accounts and Trusts

(See page B-2.)

If you had over $400 of interest or dividends OR had a foreign account or were a grantor of, or a transferor to, a foreign trust, you must complete this part.

	Yes	No
11a At any time during 1993, did you have an interest in or a signature or other authority over a financial account in a foreign country, such as a bank account, securities account, or other financial account? See page B-2 for exceptions and filing requirements for Form TD F 90-22.1		
b If "Yes," enter the name of the foreign country ►		
12 Were you the grantor of, or transferor to, a foreign trust that existed during 1993, whether or not you have any beneficial interest in it? If "Yes," you may have to file Form 3520, 3520-A, or 926 .		

For Paperwork Reduction Act Notice, see Form 1040 instructions.

Schedule B (Form 1040) 1993

SCHEDULE C
(Form 1040)

Department of the Treasury
Internal Revenue Service   (O)

Profit or Loss From Business
(Sole Proprietorship)

▶ Partnerships, joint ventures, etc., must file Form 1065.

▶ **Attach to Form 1040 or Form 1041.**   ▶ **See Instructions for Schedule C (Form 1040).**

OMB No. 1545-0074

1993

Attachment
Sequence No. **09**

Name of proprietor

Social security number (SSN)

A   Principal business or profession, including product or service (see page C-1)

B Enter principal business code
(see page C-6) ▶

C   Business name. If no separate business name, leave blank.

D Employer ID number (EIN), if any

E   Business address (including suite or room no.) ▶ ....
City, town or post office, state, and ZIP code

F   Accounting method: **(1)** ☐ Cash   **(2)** ☐ Accrual   **(3)** ☐ Other (specify) ▶ ....

G   Method(s) used to
value closing inventory: **(1)** ☐ Cost   **(2)** ☐ Lower of cost or market   **(3)** ☐ Other (attach explanation)   **(4)** ☐ Does not apply (if checked, skip line H) | Yes | No |

H   Was there any change in determining quantities, costs, or valuations between opening and closing inventory? If "Yes," attach explanation . . . .

I   Did you "materially participate" in the operation of this business during 1993? If "No," see page C-2 for limit on losses. . .

J   If you started or acquired this business during 1993, check here . . . . ▶ ☐

Part I   Income

1	Gross receipts or sales. **Caution:** *If this income was reported to you on Form W-2 and the "Statutory employee" box on that form was checked, see page C-2 and check here* . . . . ▶ ☐	**1**
2	Returns and allowances	**2**
3	Subtract line 2 from line 1	**3**
4	Cost of goods sold (from line 40 on page 2)	**4**
5	**Gross profit.** Subtract line 4 from line 3	**5**
6	Other income, including Federal and state gasoline or fuel tax credit or refund (see page C-2) . . .	**6**
7	**Gross income.** Add lines 5 and 6 . . . . ▶	**7**

Part II   Expenses. Caution: *Do not enter expenses for business use of your home on lines 8–27. Instead, see line 30.*

8	Advertising	**8**	**19**	Pension and profit-sharing plans	**19**
9	Bad debts from sales or services (see page C-3) . .	**9**	**20**	Rent or lease (see page C-4):	
10	Car and truck expenses (see page C-3)	**10**	**a**	Vehicles, machinery, and equipment .	**20a**
11	Commissions and fees. . .	**11**	**b**	Other business property . .	**20b**
12	Depletion.	**12**	**21**	Repairs and maintenance . .	**21**
13	Depreciation and section 179 expense deduction (not included in Part III) (see page C-3) . .	**13**	**22**	Supplies (not included in Part III) .	**22**
			23	Taxes and licenses	**23**
14	Employee benefit programs (other than on line 19) . . .	**14**	**24**	Travel, meals, and entertainment:	
			a	Travel	**24a**
15	Insurance (other than health) .	**15**	**b**	Meals and entertainment .	
16	Interest:		**c**	Enter 20% of line 24b subject to limitations (see page C-4)	
a	Mortgage (paid to banks, etc.) .	**16a**			
b	Other	**16b**	**d**	Subtract line 24c from line 24b .	**24d**
17	Legal and professional services	**17**	**25**	Utilities	**25**
			26	Wages (less jobs credit) . .	**26**
18	Office expense	**18**	**27**	Other expenses (from line 46 on page 2)	**27**

28	**Total expenses** before expenses for business use of home. Add lines 8 through 27 in columns. . ▶	**28**
29	Tentative profit (loss). Subtract line 28 from line 7	**29**
30	Expenses for business use of your home. Attach **Form 8829**	**30**
31	**Net profit or (loss).** Subtract line 30 from line 29.	
	• If a profit, enter on **Form 1040, line 12,** and ALSO on **Schedule SE, line 2** (statutory employees, see page C-5). Fiduciaries, enter on Form 1041, line 3.	**31**
	• If a loss, you MUST go on to line 32.	
32	If you have a loss, check the box that describes your investment in this activity (see page C-5).	
	• If you checked 32a, enter the loss on **Form 1040, line 12,** and ALSO on **Schedule SE, line 2** (statutory employees, see page C-5). Fiduciaries, enter on Form 1041, line 3.	**32a** ☐ All investment is at risk.
	• If you checked 32b, you MUST attach **Form 6198.**	**32b** ☐ Some investment is not at risk.

For Paperwork Reduction Act Notice, see Form 1040 instructions.   Cat. No. 11334P   **Schedule C (Form 1040) 1993**

Part III **Cost of Goods Sold** (see page C-5)

33	Inventory at beginning of year. If different from last year's closing inventory, attach explanation . .	33
34	Purchases less cost of items withdrawn for personal use	34
35	Cost of labor. Do not include salary paid to yourself	35
36	Materials and supplies	36
37	Other costs	37
38	Add lines 33 through 37	38
39	Inventory at end of year	39
40	**Cost of goods sold.** Subtract line 39 from line 38. Enter the result here and on page 1, line 4 . .	40

Part IV **Information on Your Vehicle.** Complete this part **ONLY** if you are claiming car or truck expenses on line 10 and are not required to file Form 4562 for this business.

41 When did you place your vehicle in service for business purposes? (month, day, year) ▶ ..../........./..... .

42 Of the total number of miles you drove your vehicle during 1993, enter the number of miles you used your vehicle for:

a Business .... **b** Commuting .... **c** Other ....

43 Do you (or your spouse) have another vehicle available for personal use? . . . . ☐ Yes ☐ No

44 Was your vehicle available for use during off-duty hours? . . . . ☐ Yes ☐ No

45a Do you have evidence to support your deduction? . . . . ☐ Yes ☐ No
  b If "Yes," is the evidence written? . . . . ☐ Yes ☐ No

Part V **Other Expenses.** List below business expenses not included on lines 8–26 or line 30.

....		
....		
....		
....		
....		
....		
....		
....		
....		

46	**Total other expenses.** Enter here and on page 1, line 27	46

SCHEDULE D
(Form 1040)

Department of the Treasury
Internal Revenue Service   (T)

Name(s) shown on Form 1040

Capital Gains and Losses

▶ Attach to Form 1040.   ▶ See Instructions for Schedule D (Form 1040).

▶ Use lines 20 and 22 for more space to list transactions for lines 1 and 9.

OMB No. 1545-0074

1993

Attachment
Sequence No. **12**

Your social security number

Part I **Short-Term Capital Gains and Losses—Assets Held One Year or Less**

(a) Description of property (Example: 100 sh. XYZ Co.)	(b) Date acquired (Mo., day, yr.)	(c) Date sold (Mo., day, yr.)	(d) Sales price (see page D-3)	(e) Cost or other basis (see page D-3)	(f) LOSS If (e) is more than (d), subtract (d) from (e)	(g) GAIN If (d) is more than (e), subtract (e) from (d)
1						

2 Enter your short-term totals, if any, from line 21 . . . . | **2** |

3 Total short-term sales price amounts. Add column (d) of lines 1 and 2 . . . | **3** |

4 Short-term gain from Forms 2119 and 6252, and short-term gain or (loss) from Forms 4684, 6781, and 8824 . . . . **4**

5 Net short-term gain or (loss) from partnerships, S corporations, and fiduciaries from Schedule(s) K-1 . . . . **5**

6 Short-term capital loss carryover from 1992 Schedule D, line 38 . . . . **6**

7 Add lines 1, 2, and 4 through 6, in columns (f) and (g) . . . . **7** ( )

8 Net short-term capital gain or (loss). Combine columns (f) and (g) of line 7 . . . . **8**

Part II **Long-Term Capital Gains and Losses—Assets Held More Than One Year**

(a)	(b)	(c)	(d)	(e)	(f)	(g)
9						

10 Enter your long-term totals, if any, from line 23 . . . . | **10** |

11 Total long-term sales price amounts. Add column (d) of lines 9 and 10 . . . | **11** |

12 Gain from Form 4797; long-term gain from Forms 2119, 2439, and 6252; and long-term gain or (loss) from Forms 4684, 6781, and 8824 . . . . **12**

13 Net long-term gain or (loss) from partnerships, S corporations, and fiduciaries from Schedule(s) K-1 . . . . **13**

14 Capital gain distributions **14**

15 Long-term capital loss carryover from 1992 Schedule D, line 45 . . . . **15**

16 Add lines 9, 10, and 12 through 15, in columns (f) and (g) . . . . . . **16** ( )

17 Net long-term capital gain or (loss). Combine columns (f) and (g) of line 16 . . . . . . **17**

Part III **Summary of Parts I and II**

18 Combine lines 8 and 17. If a loss, go to line 19. If a gain, enter the gain on Form 1040, line 13.
Note: *If both lines 17 and 18 are gains, see the Schedule D Tax Worksheet on page D-4* . . | **18** |

19 If line 18 is a (loss), enter here and as a (loss) on Form 1040, line 13, the **smaller** of these losses:

a The (loss) on line 18; **or**

b ($3,000) or, if married filing separately, ($1,500) . . . . **19** ( )

Note: *See the Capital Loss Carryover Worksheet on page D-4 if the loss on line 18 exceeds the loss on line 19 or if Form 1040, line 35, is a loss.*

For Paperwork Reduction Act Notice, see Form 1040 instructions.   Cat. No. 11338H   **Schedule D (Form 1040) 1993**

Schedule D (Form 1040) 1993   Attachment Sequence No. **12**   Page **2**

Name(s) shown on Form 1040. Do not enter name and social security number if shown on other side. | **Your social security number**

Part IV   Short-Term Capital Gains and Losses—Assets Held One Year or Less *(Continuation of Part I)*

(a) Description of property (Example: 100 sh. XYZ Co.)	(b) Date acquired (Mo., day, yr.)	(c) Date sold (Mo., day, yr.)	(d) Sales price (see page D-3)	(e) Cost or other basis (see page D-3)	(f) LOSS If (e) is more than (d), subtract (d) from (e)	(g) GAIN If (d) is more than (e), subtract (e) from (d)
20						

21 Short-term totals. Add columns (d), (f), and (g) of line 20. Enter here and on line 2 . | **21** | | | | | |

Part V   Long-Term Capital Gains and Losses—Assets Held More Than One Year *(Continuation of Part II)*

22						

23 Long-term totals. Add columns (d), (f), and (g) of line 22. Enter here and on line 10 . | **23** | | | | | |

SCHEDULE E
(Form 1040)

Department of the Treasury
Internal Revenue Service (T)

Supplemental Income and Loss

(From rental real estate, royalties, partnerships,
S corporations, estates, trusts, REMICs, etc.)
▶ Attach to Form 1040 or Form 1041.   ▶ See Instructions for Schedule E (Form 1040).

OMB No. 1545-0074

1993

Attachment
Sequence No. **13**

Name(s) shown on return

Your social security number

Part I   **Income or Loss From Rental Real Estate and Royalties**   Note: *Report income and expenses from your business of renting personal property on Schedule C or C-EZ (see page E-1). Report farm rental income or loss from Form 4835 on page 2, line 39.*

1 Show the kind and location of each **rental real estate property:**

A ....

B ....

C ....

2 For each rental real estate property listed on line 1, did you or your family use it for personal purposes for more than the greater of 14 days or 10% of the total days rented at fair rental value during the tax year? (See page E-1.)

	Yes	No
A		
B		
C		

		Properties			Totals
Income:		A	B	C	(Add columns A, B, and C.)
3 Rents received	**3**				**3**
4 Royalties received	**4**				**4**
Expenses:					
5 Advertising	**5**				
6 Auto and travel (see page E-2) .	**6**				
7 Cleaning and maintenance . . .	**7**				
8 Commissions	**8**				
9 Insurance	**9**				
10 Legal and other professional fees	**10**				
11 Management fees	**11**				
12 Mortgage interest paid to banks, etc. (see page E-2)	**12**				**12**
13 Other interest	**13**				
14 Repairs	**14**				
15 Supplies	**15**				
16 Taxes	**16**				
17 Utilities	**17**				
18 Other (list) ▶	**18**				
19 Add lines 5 through 18	**19**				**19**
20 Depreciation expense or depletion (see page E-2)	**20**				**20**
21 Total expenses. Add lines 19 and 20	**21**				
22 Income or (loss) from rental real estate or royalty properties. Subtract line 21 from line 3 (rents) or line 4 (royalties). If the result is a (loss), see page E-2 to find out if you must file **Form 6198** . .	**22**				
23 Deductible rental real estate loss. **Caution:** *Your rental real estate loss on line 22 may be limited. See page E-3 to find out if you must file* **Form 8582**	**23** (	)(	)(	)	

24 **Income.** Add positive amounts shown on line 22. **Do not** include any losses **24**

25 **Losses.** Add royalty losses from line 22 and rental real estate losses from line 23. Enter the total losses here . . . .   **25** (   )

26 Total rental real estate and royalty income or (loss). Combine lines 24 and 25. Enter the result here. If Parts II, III, IV, and line 39 on page 2 do not apply to you, also enter this amount on Form 1040, line 18. Otherwise, include this amount in the total on line 40 on page 2 . . . .   **26**

For Paperwork Reduction Act Notice, see Form 1040 instructions.   Cat. No. 11344L   Schedule E (Form 1040) 1993

Schedule E (Form 1040) 1993   Attachment Sequence No. **13**   Page **2**

Name(s) shown on return. Do not enter name and social security number if shown on other side. | Your social security number

Note: *If you report amounts from farming or fishing on Schedule E, you must enter your gross income from those activities on line 41 below.*

Part II — Income or Loss From Partnerships and S Corporations

If you report a loss from an at-risk activity, you MUST check either column **(e)** or **(f)** of line 27 to describe your investment in the activity. See page E-4. If you check column **(f)**, you must attach **Form 6198.**

27	(a) Name	(b) Enter P for partnership; S for S corporation	(c) Check if foreign partnership	(d) Employer identification number	Investment At Risk? (e) All is at risk	(f) Some is not at risk
A						
B						
C						
D						
E						

	Passive Income and Loss		Nonpassive Income and Loss		
	(g) Passive loss allowed (attach **Form 8582** if required)	(h) Passive income from **Schedule K-1**	(i) Nonpassive loss from **Schedule K-1**	(j) Section 179 expense deduction from **Form 4562**	(k) Nonpassive income from **Schedule K-1**
A					
B					
C					
D					
E					
28a Totals					
b Totals					

29   Add columns (h) and (k) of line 28a . . . . | **29** |
30   Add columns (g), (i), and (j) of line 28b . . . . | **30** (   )
31   Total partnership and S corporation income or (loss). Combine lines 29 and 30. Enter the result here and include in the total on line 40 below . . . . | **31**

Part III — Income or Loss From Estates and Trusts

32	(a) Name	(b) Employer identification number
A		
B		
C		

	Passive Income and Loss		Nonpassive Income and Loss	
	(c) Passive deduction or loss allowed (attach **Form 8582** if required)	(d) Passive income from **Schedule K-1**	(e) Deduction or loss from **Schedule K-1**	(f) Other income from **Schedule K-1**
A				
B				
C				
33a Totals				
b Totals				

34   Add columns (d) and (f) of line 33a . . . . | **34** |
35   Add columns (c) and (e) of line 33b . . . . | **35** (   )
36   Total estate and trust income or (loss). Combine lines 34 and 35. Enter the result here and include in the total on line 40 below . . . . | **36**

Part IV — Income or Loss From Real Estate Mortgage Investment Conduits (REMICs)—Residual Holder

37	(a) Name	(b) Employer identification number	(c) Excess inclusion from Schedules Q, line 2c (see page E-4)	(d) Taxable income (net loss) from **Schedules Q**, line 1b	(e) Income from **Schedules Q**, line 3b

38   Combine columns (d) and (e) only. Enter the result here and include in the total on line 40 below | **38**

Part V — Summary

39   Net farm rental income or (loss) from **Form 4835.** Also, complete line 41 below . . . . . | **39**
40   TOTAL income or (loss). Combine lines 26, 31, 36, 38, and 39. Enter the result here and on Form 1040, line 18 . . . . ▶ | **40**
41   **Reconciliation of Farming and Fishing Income:** Enter your **gross** farming and fishing income reported in Parts II and III and on line 39 (see page E-4) . . . . | **41**

SCHEDULE F
(Form 1040)

Department of the Treasury
Internal Revenue Service   (T)

Profit or Loss From Farming

▶ **Attach to Form 1040, Form 1041, or Form 1065.**

▶ **See Instructions for Schedule F (Form 1040).**

OMB No. 1545-0074

19**93**

Attachment
Sequence No. **14**

Name of proprietor

Social security number (SSN)

A Principal product. Describe in one or two words your principal crop or activity for the current tax year.

B Enter principal agricultural activity code (from page 2) ▶

D Employer ID number (EIN), if any

C Accounting method: (1) ☐ Cash   (2) ☐ Accrual

E Did you "materially participate" in the operation of this business during 1993? If "No," see page F-2 for limit on losses.   ☐ Yes ☐ No

Part I **Farm Income—Cash Method. Complete Parts I and II** (Accrual method taxpayers complete Parts II and III, and line 11 of Part I.)
Do not include sales of livestock held for draft, breeding, sport, or dairy purposes; report these sales on Form 4797.

1	Sales of livestock and other items you bought for resale	1		
2	Cost or other basis of livestock and other items reported on line 1 . . .	2		
3	Subtract line 2 from line 1		3	
4	Sales of livestock, produce, grains, and other products you raised		4	
5a	Total cooperative distributions (Form(s) 1099-PATR)	5a	5b Taxable amount	5b
6a	Agricultural program payments (see page F-2)	6a	6b Taxable amount	6b
7	Commodity Credit Corporation (CCC) loans (see page F-2):			
a	CCC loans reported under election		7a	
b	CCC loans forfeited or repaid with certificates	7b	7c Taxable amount	7c
8	Crop insurance proceeds and certain disaster payments (see page F-2):			
a	Amount received in 1993	8a	8b Taxable amount	8b
c	If election to defer to 1994 is attached, check here ▶ ☐	8d Amount deferred from 1992 . .	8d	
9	Custom hire (machine work) income		9	
10	Other income, including Federal and state gasoline or fuel tax credit or refund (see page F-3)		10	
11	**Gross income.** Add amounts in the right column for lines 3 through 10. If accrual method taxpayer, enter the amount from page 2, line 51. . . . . ▶		11	

Part II **Farm Expenses—Cash and Accrual Method. Do not** include personal or living expenses such as taxes, insurance, repairs, etc., on your home.

12	Car and truck expenses (see page F-3—also attach **Form 4562**) .	12	25	Pension and profit-sharing plans	25
13	Chemicals	13	26	Rent or lease (see page F-4):	
14	Conservation expenses. Attach **Form 8645**.	14	a	Vehicles, machinery, and equipment	26a
15	Custom hire (machine work).	15	b	Other (land, animals, etc.) .	26b
16	Depreciation and section 179 expense deduction not claimed elsewhere (see page F-4) . .	16	27	Repairs and maintenance . .	27
			28	Seeds and plants purchased .	28
			29	Storage and warehousing . .	29
17	Employee benefit programs other than on line 25	17	30	Supplies purchased	30
18	Feed purchased	18	31	Taxes	31
19	Fertilizers and lime	19	32	Utilities	32
20	Freight and trucking . . .	20	33	Veterinary, breeding, and medicine .	33
21	Gasoline, fuel, and oil . . .	21	34	Other expenses (specify):	
22	Insurance (other than health) .	22	a	....	34a
23	Interest:		b	....	34b
a	Mortgage (paid to banks, etc.) .	23a	c	....	34c
b	Other	23b	d	....	34d
24	Labor hired (less jobs credit) .	24	e	....	34e
			f		34f

35	**Total expenses.** Add lines 12 through 34f . . . . ▶	35	
36	**Net farm profit or (loss).** Subtract line 35 from line 11. If a profit, enter on **Form 1040, line 19,** and ALSO on **Schedule SE, line 1.** If a loss, you MUST go on to line 37 (fiduciaries and partnerships, see page F-5) . . .	36	
37	If you have a loss, you MUST check the box that describes your investment in this activity (see page F-5). If you checked 37a, enter the loss on **Form 1040, line 19,** and ALSO on **Schedule SE, line 1.** If you checked 37b, you MUST attach **Form 6198.**	37a ☐ All investment is at risk. 37b ☐ Some investment is not at risk.	

For Paperwork Reduction Act Notice, see Form 1040 instructions.   Cat. No. 11346H   Schedule F (Form 1040) 1993

Schedule F (Form 1040) 1993   Page **2**

Part III **Farm Income—Accrual Method** (see page F-5)

Do not include sales of livestock held for draft, breeding, sport, or dairy purposes; report these sales on Form 4797 and do not include this livestock on line 46 below.

38	Sales of livestock, produce, grains, and other products during the year.	**38**	
39a	Total cooperative distributions (Form(s) 1099-PATR) **39a** | **39b** Taxable amount	**39b**	
40a	Agricultural program payments **40a** | **40b** Taxable amount	**40b**	
41	Commodity Credit Corporation (CCC) loans:		
a	CCC loans reported under election	**41a**	
b	CCC loans forfeited or repaid with certificates **41b** | **41c** Taxable amount	**41c**	
42	Crop insurance proceeds	**42**	
43	Custom hire (machine work) income	**43**	
44	Other income, including Federal and state gasoline or fuel tax credit or refund	**44**	
45	Add amounts in the right column for lines 38 through 44	**45**	
46	Inventory of livestock, produce, grains, and other products at beginning of the year.	**46**	
47	Cost of livestock, produce, grains, and other products purchased during the year.	**47**	
48	Add lines 46 and 47	**48**	
49	Inventory of livestock, produce, grains, and other products at end of year	**49**	
50	Cost of livestock, produce, grains, and other products sold. Subtract line 49 from line 48*	**50**	
51	**Gross income.** Subtract line 50 from line 45. Enter the result here and on page 1, line 11 ▶	**51**	

*If you use the unit-livestock-price method or the farm-price method of valuing inventory and the amount on line 49 is larger than the amount on line 48, subtract line 48 from line 49. Enter the result on line 50. Add lines 45 and 50. Enter the total on line 51.

Part IV **Principal Agricultural Activity Codes**

Caution: File *Schedule C (Form 1040), Profit or Loss From Business,* or *Schedule C-EZ (Form 1040), Net Profit From Business,* instead of Schedule F if:

• *Your principal source of income is from providing agricultural services such as soil preparation, veterinary, farm labor, horticultural, or management for a fee or on a contract basis,* or

• *You are engaged in the business of breeding, raising, and caring for dogs, cats, or other pet animals.*

Select one of the following codes and write the 3-digit number on page 1, line B:

120 **Field crop,** including grains and nongrains such as cotton, peanuts, feed corn, wheat, tobacco, Irish potatoes, etc.

160 **Vegetables and melons,** garden-type vegetables and melons, such as sweet corn, tomatoes, squash, etc.

170 **Fruit and tree nuts,** including grapes, berries, olives, etc.

180 **Ornamental floriculture and nursery products**

185 **Food crops grown under cover,** including hydroponic crops

211 **Beefcattle feedlots**

212 **Beefcattle,** except feedlots

215 **Hogs, sheep, and goats**

240 **Dairy**

250 **Poultry and eggs,** including chickens, ducks, pigeons, quail, etc.

260 **General livestock,** not specializing in any one livestock category

270 **Animal specialty,** including bees, fur-bearing animals, horses, snakes, etc.

280 **Animal aquaculture,** including fish, shellfish, mollusks, frogs, etc., produced within confined space

290 **Forest products,** including forest nurseries and seed gathering, extraction of pine gum, and gathering of forest products

300 **Agricultural production,** not specified

Schedule R
(Form 1040)

Department of the Treasury
Internal Revenue Service (T)

Credit for the Elderly or the Disabled

▶ **Attach to Form 1040.**   ▶ **See separate instructions for Schedule R.**

OMB No. 1545-0074

19**93**

Attachment
Sequence No. **16**

Name(s) shown on Form 1040

Your social security number

You may be able to use Schedule R to reduce your tax if by the end of 1993:

● You were age 65 or older, **OR** ● You were under age 65, you retired on **permanent and total** disability, and you received
   taxable disability income.

But you must also meet other tests. See the separate instructions for Schedule R.
Note: *In most cases, the IRS can figure the credit for you. See page 25 of the Form 1040 instructions.*

Part I   **Check the Box for Your Filing Status and Age**

If your filing status is:	And by the end of 1993:	Check only one box:
Single, Head of household, or Qualifying widow(er) with dependent child	1 You were 65 or older 1	☐
	2 You were under 65 and you retired on permanent and total disability . . . 2	☐
Married filing a joint return	3 Both spouses were 65 or older 3	☐
	4 Both spouses were under 65, but only one spouse retired on permanent and total disability 4	☐
	5 Both spouses were under 65, and both retired on permanent and total disability 5	☐
	6 One spouse was 65 or older, and the other spouse was under 65 and retired on permanent and total disability 6	☐
	7 One spouse was 65 or older, and the other spouse was under 65 and **NOT** retired on permanent and total disability 7	☐
Married filing a separate return	8 You were 65 or older and you lived apart from your spouse for all of 1993 . . 8	☐
	9 You were under 65, you retired on permanent and total disability, and you lived apart from your spouse for all of 1993 9	☐

If you checked box 1, 3, 7, or 8, skip Part II and complete Part III on the back. All others, complete Parts II and III.

Part II   **Statement of Permanent and Total Disability** (Complete **only** if you checked box 2, 4, 5, 6, or 9 above.)

IF: 1 You filed a physician's statement for this disability for 1983 or an earlier year, or you filed a statement for tax years
   after 1983 and your physician signed line B on the statement, **AND**

2 Due to your continued disabled condition, you were unable to engage in any substantial gainful activity in 1993,
   check this box   . . . . ▶ ☐

● If you checked this box, you do not have to file another statement for 1993.
● If you **did not** check this box, have your physician complete the following statement.

Physician's Statement (See instructions at bottom of page 2.)

I certify that _____
                              Name of disabled person

was permanently and totally disabled on January 1, 1976, or January 1, 1977, **OR** was permanently and totally disabled on the
date he or she retired. If retired after December 31, 1976, enter the date retired. ▶ _____
Physician: Sign your name on **either** line A or B below.

A The disability has lasted or can be expected to
   last continuously for at least a year . . . . . _____
                                                       Physician's signature   Date

B There is no reasonable probability that the
   disabled condition will ever improve . . . . . _____
                                                       Physician's signature   Date

Physician's name   Physician's address

For Paperwork Reduction Act Notice, see Form 1040 instructions.   Cat. No. 11359K   **Schedule R (Form 1040) 1993**

Part III   Figure Your Credit

10   **If you checked (in Part I):**   **Enter:**

Box 1, 2, 4, or 7 . . . . $5,000 ⎤

Box 3, 5, or 6 . . . . $7,500 ⎬ **10**

Box 8 or 9 . . . . $3,750 ⎦

   Caution: *If you checked box 2, 4, 5, 6, or 9 in Part I, you* **MUST** *complete line 11 below. All others, skip line 11 and enter the amount from line 10 on line 12.*

11   **If you checked:**

   ● Box 6 in Part I, add $5,000 to the taxable disability income of the spouse who was under age 65. Enter the total.   ⎤

   ● Box 2, 4, or 9 in Part I, enter your taxable disability income.   ⎬ **11**

   ● Box 5 in Part I, add your taxable disability income to your spouse's taxable disability income. Enter the total.   ⎦

   TIP: *For more details on what to include on line 11, see the instructions.*

12   ● If you completed line 11, look at lines 10 and 11. Enter the **smaller** of the two amounts.   ⎬ **12**

   ● All others, enter the amount from line 10.

13   Enter the following pensions, annuities, or disability income that you (and your spouse if filing a joint return) received in 1993:

   a Nontaxable part of social security benefits, and   ⎤

      Nontaxable part of railroad retirement benefits treated as   ⎬ . . . **13a**

      social security. See instructions.   ⎦

   b Nontaxable veterans' pensions, and   ⎤

      Any other pension, annuity, or disability benefit that is   ⎬ . . . **13b**

      excluded from income under any other provision of law.   ⎦

      See instructions.

   c Add lines 13a and 13b. (Even though these income items are not taxable, they **must** be included here to figure your credit.) If you did not receive any of the types of nontaxable income listed on line 13a or 13b, enter -0- on line 13c **13c**

14   Enter the amount from Form 1040, line 32   **14**

15   **If you checked (in Part I):**   **Enter:**

   Box 1 or 2 . . . . $7,500 ⎤

   Box 3, 4, 5, 6, or 7 . . . . $10,000 ⎬ **15**

   Box 8 or 9 . . . . $5,000 ⎦

16   Subtract line 15 from line 14. If line 15 is more than line 14, enter -0- **16**

17   Divide line 16 above by 2 . . . . **17**

18   Add lines 13c and 17 . . . . **18**

19   Subtract line 18 from line 12. If line 18 is more than line 12, stop here; you **cannot** take the credit. Otherwise, go to line 21 . . . . **19**

20   Decimal amount used to figure the credit . . . . **20**   × .15

21   Multiply line 19 above by the decimal amount (.15) on line 20. Enter the result here and on Form 1040, line 42. **Caution:** *If you file Schedule C, C-EZ, D, E, or F (Form 1040), your credit may be limited. See the instructions for line 21 for the amount of credit you can claim* **21**

Instructions for Physician's Statement

Taxpayer

If you retired after December 31, 1976, enter the date you retired in the space provided in Part II.

Physician

A person is permanently and totally disabled if **both** of the following apply:

   1. He or she cannot engage in any substantial gainful activity because of a physical or mental condition, and

2. A physician determines that the disability has lasted or can be expected to last continuously for at least a year or can lead to death.

SCHEDULE SE
(Form 1040)

Department of the Treasury
Internal Revenue Service (T)

Self-Employment Tax

▶ See Instructions for Schedule SE (Form 1040).

▶ **Attach to Form 1040.**

OMB No. 1545-0074

1993

Attachment
Sequence No. **17**

Name of person with **self-employment** income (as shown on Form 1040)	Social security number of person with **self-employment** income ▶

Who Must File Schedule SE

You must file Schedule SE if:

- Your wages (and tips) subject to social security AND Medicare tax (or railroad retirement tax) were less than $135,000; **AND**
- Your net earnings from self-employment from other than church employee income (line 4 of Short Schedule SE or line 4c of Long Schedule SE) were $400 or more; **OR**
- You had church employee income of $108.28 or more. Income from services you performed as a minister or a member of a religious order **is not** church employee income. See page SE-1.

Note: *Even if you have a loss or a small amount of income from self-employment, it may be to your benefit to file Schedule SE and use either "optional method" in Part II of Long Schedule SE. See page SE-3.*

Exception. If your only self-employment income was from earnings as a minister, member of a religious order, or Christian Science practitioner, **AND** you filed Form 4361 and received IRS approval not to be taxed on those earnings, **DO NOT** file Schedule SE. Instead, write "Exempt–Form 4361" on Form 1040, line 47.

May I Use Short Schedule SE or MUST I Use Long Schedule SE?

Did you receive wages or tips in 1993?

No → Are you a minister, member of a religious order, or Christian Science practitioner who received IRS approval **not** to be taxed on earnings from these sources, **but** you owe self-employment tax on other earnings? — Yes →

No ↓

Are you using one of the optional methods to figure your net earnings (see page SE-3)? — Yes →

No ↓

Did you receive church employee income reported on Form W-2 of $108.28 or more? — Yes →

No ↓

YOU MAY USE SHORT SCHEDULE SE BELOW

Yes → Was the total of your wages and tips subject to social security or railroad retirement tax **plus** your net earnings from self-employment more than $57,600? — Yes →

No ↓

Was the total of your wages and tips subject to Medicare tax **plus** your net earnings from self-employment more than $135,000? — Yes →

No ↓

No ← Did you receive tips subject to social security or Medicare tax that you **did not** report to your employer? — Yes →

YOU MUST USE LONG SCHEDULE SE ON THE BACK

Section A—Short Schedule SE. Caution: *Read above to see if you can use Short Schedule SE.*

1	Net farm profit or (loss) from Schedule F, line 36, and farm partnerships, Schedule K-1 (Form 1065), line 15a	**1**	
2	Net profit or (loss) from Schedule C, line 31; Schedule C-EZ, line 3; and Schedule K-1 (Form 1065), line 15a (other than farming). Ministers and members of religious orders see page SE-1 for amounts to report on this line. See page SE-2 for other income to report	**2**	
3	Combine lines 1 and 2	**3**	
4	**Net earnings from self-employment.** Multiply line 3 by 92.35% (.9235). If less than $400, **do not** file this schedule; you do not owe self-employment tax . . . . ▶	**4**	
5	**Self-employment tax.** If the amount on line 4 is:		
	• $57,600 or less, multiply line 4 by 15.3% (.153) and enter the result.		
	• More than $57,600 but less than $135,000, multiply the amount in excess of $57,600 by 2.9% (.029). Then, add $8,812.80 to the result and enter the total.		
	• $135,000 or more, enter $11,057.40.		
	Also enter on **Form 1040, line 47. (Important:** You are allowed a deduction for **one-half** of this amount. Multiply line 5 by 50% (.5) and enter the result on **Form 1040, line 25.)**	**5**	

For Paperwork Reduction Act Notice, see Form 1040 instructions.   Cat. No. 11358Z   **Schedule SE (Form 1040) 1993**

Schedule SE (Form 1040) 1993 | Attachment Sequence No. **17** | Page **2**

Name of person with **self-employment** income (as shown on Form 1040) | Social security number of person with **self-employment** income ▶

Section B—Long Schedule SE

Part I Self-Employment Tax

Note: *If your only income subject to self-employment tax is church employee income, skip lines 1 through 4b. Enter -0- on line 4c and go to line 5a. Income from services you performed as a minister or a member of a religious order **is not** church employee income. See page SE-1.*

A If you are a minister, member of a religious order, or Christian Science practitioner **AND** you filed Form 4361, but you had $400 or more of **other** net earnings from self-employment, check here and continue with Part I . . . . . ▶ ☐

1 Net farm profit or (loss) from Schedule F, line 36, and farm partnerships, Schedule K-1 (Form 1065), line 15a. **Note:** *Skip this line if you use the farm optional method. See page SE-3* | **1**

2 Net profit or (loss) from Schedule C, line 31; Schedule C-EZ, line 3; and Schedule K-1 (Form 1065), line 15a (other than farming). Ministers and members of religious orders see page SE-1 for amounts to report on this line. See page SE-2 for other income to report. **Note:** *Skip this line if you use the nonfarm optional method. See page SE-3* . . . . | **2**

3 Combine lines 1 and 2 . . . . | **3**

4a If line 3 is more than zero, multiply line 3 by 92.35% (.9235). Otherwise, enter amount from line 3 | **4a**

b If you elected one or both of the optional methods, enter the total of lines 17 and 19 here . . | **4b**

c Combine lines 4a and 4b. If less than $400, **do not** file this schedule; you do not owe self-employment tax. **Exception.** If less than $400 and you had church employee income, enter -0- and continue . ▶ | **4c**

5a Enter your church employee income from Form W-2. **Caution:** *See page SE-1 for definition of church employee income* . . . . . | **5a** |

b Multiply line 5a by 92.35% (.9235). If less than $100, enter -0- . . . . | **5b**

6 **Net earnings from self-employment.** Add lines 4c and 5b . . . . | **6**

7 Maximum amount of combined wages and self-employment earnings subject to social security tax or the 6.2% portion of the 7.65% railroad retirement (tier 1) tax for 1993 . . . . . . | **7** | 57,600 | 00

8a Total social security wages and tips (from Form(s) W-2) and railroad retirement (tier 1) compensation . . . . | **8a** |

b Unreported tips subject to social security tax (from Form 4137, line 9) | **8b** |

c Add lines 8a and 8b . . . . | **8c**

9 Subtract line 8c from line 7. If zero or less, enter -0- here and on line 10 and go to line 12a ▶ | **9**

10 Multiply the **smaller** of line 6 or line 9 by 12.4% (.124) . . . . | **10**

11 Maximum amount of combined wages and self-employment earnings subject to Medicare tax or the 1.45% portion of the 7.65% railroad retirement (tier 1) tax for 1993 . . . . | **11** | 135,000 | 00

12a Total Medicare wages and tips (from Form(s) W-2) and railroad retirement (tier 1) compensation . . . . | **12a** |

b Unreported tips subject to Medicare tax (from Form 4137, line 14) . | **12b** |

c Add lines 12a and 12b . . . . | **12c**

13 Subtract line 12c from line 11. If zero or less, enter -0- here and on line 14 and go to line 15 . | **13**

14 Multiply the **smaller** of line 6 or line 13 by 2.9% (.029) . . . . | **14**

15 **Self-employment tax.** Add lines 10 and 14. Enter here and on **Form 1040, line 47.** (**Important:** You are allowed a deduction for **one-half** of this amount. Multiply line 15 by 50% (.5) and enter the result on **Form 1040, line 25.**) . . . . | **15**

Part II Optional Methods To Figure Net Earnings (See page SE-3.)

Farm Optional Method. You may use this method only if **(a)** Your gross farm income[1] was not more than $2,400 **or (b)** Your gross farm income[1] was more than $2,400 and your net farm profits[2] were less than $1,733.

16 Maximum income for optional methods . . . . | **16** | 1,600 | 00

17 Enter the **smaller** of: two-thirds (⅔) of gross farm income[1] (not less than zero) **or** $1,600. Also, include this amount on line 4b above . . . . | **17**

Nonfarm Optional Method. You may use this method **only** if **(a)** Your net nonfarm profits[3] were less than $1,733 and also less than 72.189% of your gross nonfarm income,[4] **and (b)** You had net earnings from self-employment of at least $400 in 2 of the prior 3 years. **Caution:** *You may use this method no more than five times.*

18 Subtract line 17 from line 16 . . . . | **18**

19 Enter the **smaller** of: two-thirds (⅔) of gross nonfarm income[4] (not less than zero) **or** the amount on line 18. Also, include this amount on line 4b above . . . . | **19**

[1]From Schedule F, line 11, and Schedule K-1 (Form 1065), line 15b.   [3]From Schedule C, line 31; Schedule C-EZ, line 3; and Schedule K-1 (Form 1065), line 15a.
[2]From Schedule F, line 36, and Schedule K-1 (Form 1065), line 15a.   [4]From Schedule C, line 7; Schedule C-EZ, line 1; and Schedule K-1 (Form 1065), line 15c.

SCHEDULE EIC
(Form 1040A or 1040)

Department of the Treasury   (O)
Internal Revenue Service

Earned Income Credit

▶ Attach to Form 1040A or 1040.

▶ See Instructions for Schedule EIC.

OMB No. 1545-0074

1993

Attachment
Sequence No. **43**

Name(s) shown on return

Your social security number

Want the IRS to figure the credit for you? Just fill in this page. We'll do the rest.

General Information

To take
this credit

- You **must** have worked and earned **less** than $23,050, **and**
- Your adjusted gross income (Form 1040A, line 16, or Form 1040, line 31) **must** be **less** than $23,050, **and**
- Your filing status can be any status **except** married filing a separate return, **and**
- You **must** have at least one qualifying child (see boxes below), **and**
- You **cannot** be a qualifying child yourself.

A **qualifying child** is a child who:

is your:

son
daughter
adopted child
grandchild
stepchild
or
foster child

A N D

was (at the end of 1993):

under age 19
or
under age 24 and a full-time student
or
any age and permanently and totally disabled

A N D

who:

lived with you
in the U.S.
for
more than half of 1993*
(or all of 1993 if a foster child*)

*If the child didn't live with you for the required time (for example, was born in 1993), see the **Exception** on page 64 (1040A) or page EIC-2 (1040).

| **Do you have at least one qualifying child?** | **No** ▶ | You **cannot** take the credit. Enter "NO" next to line 28c of Form 1040A (or line 56 of Form 1040). |
| | **Yes** ▶ | Go to line 1. But if the child was married or is also a qualifying child of another person (other than your spouse if filing a joint return), first see page 64 (1040A) or page EIC-2 (1040). |

Information About Your Qualifying Child or Children

If more than two qualifying children, see page 65 (1040A) or page EIC-2 (1040). **1(a)** Child's name (first, initial, and last name)	**(b)** Child's year of birth	For a child born **before 1975,** check if child was—		**(e)** If child was born **before 1993,** enter the child's social security number	**(f)** Child's relationship to you (for example, son, grandchild, etc.)	**(g)** Number of months child lived with you in the U.S. in 1993
		(c) a student under age 24 at end of 1993	**(d)** disabled (see booklet)			
	19					
	19					

Caution: *If a child you listed above was born in 1993* **and** *you chose to claim the credit or exclusion for child care expenses for this child on* **Schedule 2** *(Form 1040A) or* **Form 2441** *(Form 1040), check here* . . . . ▶ ☐

| **Do you want the IRS to figure the credit for you?** | **Yes** ▶ | Fill in lines 2 and 3; **and** enter the amount from Form 1040A, line 16, or Form 1040, line 31, here. ▶ $ |
| | **No** ▶ | Go to page 2 on the back now. |

Other Information

| **2** | Enter any **nontaxable earned income** (see page 65 (1040A) or page EIC-2 (1040)) such as military housing and subsistence or contributions to a 401(k) plan. Also, list type and amount here. ▶ .... | **2** | |
| **3** | Enter the total amount you paid in 1993 for health insurance that covered at least one qualifying child. See instructions . . . . | **3** | |

| **If you want the IRS to figure the credit for you:** | **S T O P** ▶ | **Attach this schedule to your return.**
• If filing Form 1040A, print "EIC" on the line next to line 28c.
• If filing Form 1040, print "EIC" on the dotted line next to line 56. |

For Paperwork Reduction Act Notice, see Form 1040A or 1040 instructions.   Cat. No. 13339M   **Schedule EIC (Form 1040A or 1040) 1993**

Schedule EIC (Form 1040A or 1040) 1993   Page **2**

Figure Your Basic Credit

4 Enter the amount from line 7 of Form 1040A or Form 1040. If you received a taxable scholarship or fellowship grant, see instructions **4**

5 Enter any **nontaxable earned income** (see page 65 (1040A) or page EIC-2 (1040)) such as military housing and subsistence or contributions to a 401(k) plan. Also, list type and amount here. ▶ **5**

6 **Form 1040 Filers Only:** If you were self-employed **or** used Sch. C or C-EZ as a statutory employee, enter the amount from the worksheet on page EIC-3 . . . . **6**

7 **Earned income.** Add lines 4, 5, and 6. If $23,050 or more, you **cannot** take the credit. Enter "NO" next to line 28c of Form 1040A (or line 56 of Form 1040) . . . . ▶ **7**

8 Use **line 7** above to find your credit in **TABLE A** on pages **69 and 70** (1040A) or pages **EIC-4 and 5** (1040). Enter here . . . . . . | **8** |

9 **Adjusted gross income.** Enter the amount from Form 1040A, line 16, or Form 1040, line 31 ▶ **9**

10 **Is line 9 $12,200 or more?**

 YES. Use **line 9** to find your credit in **TABLE A** on pages **69 and 70** (1040A) or pages **EIC-4 and 5** (1040). Enter here . . . . . | **10** |
 NO. Go to line 11.

11 **Basic credit:**
 ● If you answered "YES" to line 10, enter the **smaller** of line 8 or line 10. ⎫ . . . .
 ● If you answered "NO" to line 10, enter the amount from line 8. ⎭   **11**

 Next: To take the health insurance credit, fill in lines 12–16. To take the extra credit for a child born in 1993, fill in lines 17–19. Otherwise, go to line 20 now.

Figure Your Health Insurance Credit

12 Use **line 7** above to find your credit in **TABLE B** on page **71** (1040A) or page **EIC-6** (1040). Enter here . . . . | **12** |

13 **Is line 9 above $12,200 or more?**

 YES. Use **line 9** to find your credit in **TABLE B** on page **71** (1040A) or page **EIC-6** (1040). Enter here. . . . . | **13** |
 NO. Go to line 14.

14 ● If you answered "YES" to line 13, enter the **smaller** of line 12 ⎫
 or line 13.   ⎬ | **14** |
 ● If you answered "NO" to line 13, enter the amount from line 12. ⎭

15 Enter the total amount you paid in 1993 for health insurance that covered at least one qualifying child. See instructions . . . . . | **15** |

16 **Health insurance credit.** Enter the **smaller** of line 14 or line 15 . . . . **16**

Figure Your Extra Credit for Child Born in 1993

 Take this credit **only** if you did not take the credit or exclusion for child care expenses on **Schedule 2** or **Form 2441** for the same child.

 TIP: You can take **both** the basic credit and the **extra credit** for your child born in 1993.

17 Use **line 7** above to find your credit in **TABLE C** on page **72** (1040A) or page **EIC-7** (1040). Enter here . . . . | **17** |

18 **Is line 9 above $12,200 or more?**

 YES. Use **line 9** to find your credit in **TABLE C** on page **72** (1040A) or page **EIC-7** (1040). Enter here . . . . | **18** |
 NO. Go to line 19.

19 **Extra credit for child born in 1993:**
 ● If you answered "YES" to line 18, enter the **smaller** of line 17 or line 18. ⎫ . . . . . .
 ● If you answered "NO" to line 18, enter the amount from line 17. ⎭   **19**

Figure Your Total Earned Income Credit

20 Add lines 11, 16, and 19. Enter the total here and on Form 1040A, line 28c (or on Form 1040, line 56). This is your **total earned income credit** . . . . ▶ **20**

 TIP: Do you want the earned income credit added to your take-home pay in 1994? To see if you qualify, get **Form W-5** from your employer or by calling the IRS at 1-800-829-3676.

B-4   Amended Tax Return Forms

Form **1040X**
(Rev. October 1993)

Department of the Treasury—Internal Revenue Service

Amended U.S. Individual Income Tax Return

▶ See separate instructions.

OMB No. 1545-0091
Expires 10-31-96

This return is for calendar year ▶ 19 , OR fiscal year ended ▶ , 19 .

Please print or type

Your first name and initial	Last name	Your social security number
If a joint return, spouse's first name and initial	Last name	Spouse's social security number
Home address (number and street). If you have a P.O. box, see instructions.	Apt. no.	Telephone number (optional) ( )
City, town or post office, state, and ZIP code. If you have a foreign address, see instructions.		For Paperwork Reduction Act Notice, see page 1 of separate instructions.

Enter name and address as shown on original return. If same as above, write "Same." If changing from separate to joint return, enter names and addresses from original returns.

A Service center where original return was filed

B Has original return been changed or audited by the IRS? ☐ Yes ☐ No
If "No," have you been notified that it will be? . . . . ☐ Yes ☐ No
If "Yes," identify the IRS office ▶

C Are you amending your return to include any item (loss, credit, deduction, other tax benefit, or income) relating to a tax shelter required to be registered? . . . . ☐ Yes ☐ No
If "Yes," you must attach **Form 8271,** Investor Reporting of Tax Shelter Registration Number.

D Filing status claimed. **Note:** *You cannot change from joint to separate returns after the due date has passed.*
On original return ▶ ☐ Single ☐ Married filing joint return ☐ Married filing separate return ☐ Head of household ☐ Qualifying widow(er)
On this return ▶ ☐ Single ☐ Married filing joint return ☐ Married filing separate return ☐ Head of household ☐ Qualifying widow(er)

	Income and Deductions (see instructions) Caution: *Be sure to complete Part II on page 2.*		**A.** As originally reported or as previously adjusted (see instructions)	**B.** Net change— Increase or (Decrease)—explain on page 2	**C.** Correct amount
Tax Liability	1 Total income	1			
	2 Total adjustments (such as IRA deduction, alimony paid, etc.)	2			
	3 Adjusted gross income. Subtract line 2 from line 1 . . .	3			
	4 Itemized deductions or standard deduction	4			
	5 Subtract line 4 from line 3	5			
	6 Exemptions. If changing, fill in Parts I and II on page 2 . .	6			
	7 Taxable income. Subtract line 6 from line 5	7			
	8 Tax (see instructions). Method used in col. C	8			
	9 Credits (see instructions)	9			
	10 Subtract line 9 from line 8. Enter the result but not less than zero .	10			
	11 Other taxes (such as self-employment tax, alternative minimum tax, etc.)	11			
	12 Total tax. Add lines 10 and 11	12			
Payments	13 Federal income tax withheld and excess social security, Medicare, and RRTA taxes withheld. If changing, see instructions	13			
	14 Estimated tax payments	14			
	15 Earned income credit	15			
	16 Credits for Federal tax paid on fuels, regulated investment company, etc.	16			
	17 Amount paid with Form 4868, Form 2688, or Form 2350 (application for extension of time to file) .	17			
	18 Amount paid with original return plus additional tax paid after it was filed	18			
	19 Total payments. Add lines 13 through 18 in column C	19			

Refund or Amount You Owe

20 Overpayment, if any, as shown on original return or as previously adjusted by the IRS . . .	20		
21 Subtract line 20 from line 19 (see instructions)	21		
22 **AMOUNT YOU OWE.** If line 12, column C, is more than line 21, enter the difference and see instructions	22		
23 **REFUND** to be received. If line 12, column C, is less than line 21, enter the difference . . .	23		

Sign Here
Keep a copy of this return for your records.

Under penalties of perjury, I declare that I have filed an original return and that I have examined this amended return, including accompanying schedules and statements, and to the best of my knowledge and belief, this amended return is true, correct, and complete. Declaration of preparer (other than taxpayer) is based on all information of which the preparer has any knowledge.

▶ Your signature   Date   ▶ Spouse's signature. If a joint return, BOTH must sign.   Date

Paid Preparer's Use Only

Preparer's signature	Date	Check if self-employed ☐	Preparer's social security no.
Firm's name (or yours if self-employed) and address ▶		E.I. No.	
		ZIP code	

Cat. No. 11360L   Form **1040X** (Rev. 10-93)

Form 1040X (Rev. 10-93)   Page **2**

Part I   Exemptions. See Form 1040 or Form 1040A instructions.

If you are not changing your exemptions, do not complete this part.
If claiming more exemptions, complete lines 24–30 and, if applicable, line 31.
If claiming fewer exemptions, complete lines 24–29.

		A. Number originally reported	B. Net change	C. Correct number
24	Yourself and spouse	24		
	Caution: *If your parents (or someone else) can claim you as a dependent (even if they chose not to), you cannot claim an exemption for yourself.*			
25	Your dependent children who lived with you	25		
26	Your dependent children who did not live with you due to divorce or separation	26		
27	Other dependents	27		
28	Total number of exemptions. Add lines 24 through 27	28		

29 Multiply the number of exemptions claimed on line 28 by the amount listed below for the tax year you are amending. Enter the result here and on line 6.

Tax Year	Exemption Amount	But see the instructions if the amount on line 3 is over:
1993	$2,350	$81,350
1992	2,300	78,950
1991	2,150	75,000
1990	2,050	Not applicable for tax year 1990.

29

30   Dependents (children and other) not claimed on original return:

(a) Dependent's name (first, initial, and last name)	(b) Check if under age 1 (under age 2 if a 1990 return)	(c) If age 1 or older (age 2 or older if a 1990 return), enter dependent's social security number	(d) Dependent's relationship to you	(e) No. of months lived in your home

No. of your children on line 30 who lived with you . . ▶ ☐

No. of your children on line 30 who **didn't** live with you due to divorce or separation (see instructions) ▶ ☐

No. of dependents on line 30 not entered above . ▶ ☐

31   If your child listed on line 30 didn't live with you but is claimed as your dependent under a pre-1985 agreement, check here ▶ ☐

Part II   Explanation of Changes to Income, Deductions, and Credits

Enter the line number from page 1 for each item you are changing and give the reason for each change. **Attach all supporting forms and schedules for items changed. If you don't, your Form 1040X may be returned. Be sure to include your name and social security number on any attachments.**

If the change pertains to a net operating loss carryback or a general business credit carryback, attach the schedule or form that shows the year in which the loss or credit occurred. See instructions. Also, check here . . . . ▶ ☐

Part III   Presidential Election Campaign Fund. Checking below will not increase your tax or reduce your refund.

If you did not previously want to have $3 (or $1 if a 1992 return) go to the fund but now want to, check here . . . . ▶ ☐ $3 for 1993   ☐ $1 for 1992

If a joint return and your spouse did not previously want to have $3 (or $1 if a 1992 return) go to the fund but now wants to, check here . . . . ▶ ☐ $3 for 1993   ☐ $1 for 1992

Department of the Treasury
Internal Revenue Service

Instructions for Form 1040X
(Revised October 1993)
Amended U.S. Individual Income Tax Return
Section references are to the Internal Revenue Code.

Paperwork Reduction Act Notice

We ask for the information on this form to carry out the Internal Revenue laws of the United States. You are required to give us the information. We need it to ensure that you are complying with these laws and to allow us to figure and collect the right amount of tax.

The time needed to complete and file this form will vary depending on individual circumstances. The estimated average time is: **Recordkeeping,** 1 hr., 12 min.; **Learning about the law or the form,** 20 min.; **Preparing the form,** 1 hr., 11 min.; and **Copying, assembling, and sending the form to the IRS,** 35 min.

If you have comments concerning the accuracy of these time estimates or suggestions for making this form more simple, we would be happy to hear from you. You can write to both the **Internal Revenue Service,** Attention: Reports Clearance Officer, PC:FP, Washington, DC 20224; and the **Office of Management and Budget,** Paperwork Reduction Project (1545-0091), Washington, DC 20503. **DO NOT** send this form to either of these offices. Instead, see **Where To File** on page 2.

General Instructions

Purpose of Form

Use Form 1040X to correct **Form 1040, Form 1040A, Form 1040EZ, Form 1040NR,** or **Form 1040PC.** If you used TeleFile to file your original return, you can call 1-800-829-1040 for details on how to complete Form 1040X. You may also use Form 1040X to make certain elections after the prescribed deadline. For details, see Rev. Proc. 92-85, 1992-2 C.B. 490.

File a separate Form 1040X for each year you are amending. If you are changing your Federal return, you may also have to change your state return. Please note that it often takes 2 to 3 months to process Form 1040X.

Filing Form 1045

You may use **Form 1045,** Application for Tentative Refund, instead of Form 1040X if:

● You are applying for a refund resulting from a net operating loss or general business credit carryback, AND

● Less than 1 year has elapsed since the end of the year in which the loss or credit arose.

For more details, see the separate instructions for Form 1045.

When To File

File Form 1040X only after you have filed your original return. Generally, Form 1040X must be filed within 3 years after the date the original return was filed, or within 2 years after the date the tax was paid, whichever is later. A return filed early is considered filed on the date it was due.

A Form 1040X based on a bad debt or worthless security must generally be filed within 7 years after the due date of the return for the tax year in which the debt or security became worthless. For more details, see section 6511.

A Form 1040X based on a net operating loss carryback or a general business credit carryback generally must be filed within 3 years after the due date of the return for the tax year of the net operating loss or unused credit.

Carryback Claims

You must attach copies of the following to Form 1040X if it is used as a carryback claim.

● Pages 1 and 2 of Form 1040 and Schedules A and D, if applicable, for the year in which the loss or credit originated. At the top of these forms, write "Attachment to Form 1040X—Copy Only—Do Not Process."

● Any Schedules K-1 you received from any partnership, S corporation, estate, or trust for the year of the loss or credit that contribute to the loss or credit carryback.

● Any form or schedule from which the carryback results such as Form 3800 or Schedule C or F.

● The forms or schedules for items refigured in the carryback year such as Form 6251, Form 3468, or Schedule A.

All information described above **must be attached to your Form 1040X, if applicable, or your Form 1040X will be returned for the attachments.**

Note: *If you filed a joint or separate return for some, but not all, of the years involved in figuring the loss or credit carryback, you may have to allocate your income, deductions, and credits. For details, get the publication that explains the type of carryback you are claiming. For example, get Pub. 536, Net Operating Losses, if you are claiming a net operating loss carryback, or Pub. 514, Foreign Tax Credit for Individuals, for a foreign tax credit carryback.*

Net Operating Loss

Attach a computation of your net operating loss using **Schedule A (Form 1045)** and, if applicable, your net operating loss carryover using **Schedule B (Form 1045).**

A refund based on a net operating loss should not include the refund of any self-employment tax reported on line 11 of Form 1040X. For more details, see Pub. 536.

Other Claims

Injured Spouse Claim.—Do not use Form 1040X to file an injured spouse claim. Instead, file only **Form 8379,** Injured Spouse Claim and Allocation.

Resident and Nonresident Aliens.— Use Form 1040X to amend **Form 1040NR,** U.S. Nonresident Alien Income Tax Return. Also, use Form 1040X if you filed Form 1040NR and you should have filed a Form 1040, 1040A, or 1040EZ, or vice versa. For details on resident and nonresident alien filing requirements, get **Pub. 519,** U.S. Tax Guide for Aliens.

To amend Form 1040NR or to file the correct return, you must do the following:

1. On Form 1040X, fill in your name, address, and identifying or social security number. Also, complete lines A and B, and Part II on page 2. Include in Part II an explanation for the changes or corrections made.

2. Attach the corrected return (Form 1040, Form 1040NR, etc.) to Form

Cat. No. 11362H

1040X. Write "Amended" across the top of the corrected return.

3. If Form 1040X includes a Form 1040NR, file it with the Internal Revenue Service, Philadelphia, PA 19255, U.S.A. Otherwise, file Form 1040X with the service center for the place where you live. For the address, see **Where To File** below.

Where To File

Mail your return to the **Internal Revenue Service Center** for the place where you live. No street address is needed.

If you live in:	Use this address:
Florida, Georgia, South Carolina	Atlanta, GA 39901
New Jersey, New York (New York City and counties of Nassau, Rockland, Suffolk, and Westchester)	Holtsville, NY 00501
New York (all other counties), Connecticut, Maine, Massachusetts, New Hampshire, Rhode Island, Vermont	Andover, MA 05501
Illinois, Iowa, Minnesota, Missouri, Wisconsin	Kansas City, MO 64999
Delaware, District of Columbia, Maryland, Pennsylvania, Virginia	Philadelphia, PA 19255
Indiana, Kentucky, Michigan, Ohio, West Virginia	Cincinnati, OH 45999
Kansas, New Mexico, Oklahoma, Texas	Austin, TX 73301
Alabama, Arkansas, Louisiana, Mississippi, North Carolina, Tennessee	Memphis, TN 37501
Alaska, Arizona, California (counties of Alpine, Amador, Butte, Calaveras, Colusa, Contra Costa, Del Norte, El Dorado, Glenn, Humboldt, Lake, Lassen, Marin, Mendocino, Modoc, Napa, Nevada, Placer, Plumas, Sacramento, Shasta, Sierra, Siskiyou, Solano, Sonoma, Sutter, Tehama, Trinity, Yolo, and Yuba), Colorado, Idaho, Montana, Nebraska, Nevada, North Dakota, Oregon, South Dakota, Utah, Washington, Wyoming	Ogden, UT 84201
California (all other counties), Hawaii	Fresno, CA 93888
American Samoa	Philadelphia, PA 19255
Guam: Permanent residents	Department of Revenue and Taxation Government of Guam 378 Chalan San Antonio Tamuning, GU 96911
Guam: Nonpermanent residents Puerto Rico (or if excluding income under section 933) Virgin Islands: Nonpermanent residents	Philadelphia, PA 19255
Virgin Islands: Permanent residents	V.I. Bureau of Internal Revenue Lockhart Gardens No. 1-A Charlotte Amalie St. Thomas, VI 00802
Foreign country: U.S. citizens and those filing Form 2555, Form 2555-EZ, or Form 4563	Philadelphia, PA 19255
All A.P.O. and F.P.O. addresses	Philadelphia, PA 19255

Information on Income, Deductions, etc.

If you have questions, such as what income is taxable or what expenses are deductible, the instructions for the return you are amending may help you. Be sure to use the Tax Table or Tax Rate Schedules for the right year to figure the corrected tax. The related schedules and forms may also help you. To get prior year forms, schedules, and instructions, call 1-800-TAX-FORM (1-800-829-3676).

Death of Taxpayer

If you are filing a Form 1040X for a deceased taxpayer, write **"DECEASED,"** the taxpayer's name, and the date of death across the top of Form 1040X.

If you are filing Form 1040X as a surviving spouse filing a joint return with the deceased, write "Filing as surviving spouse" in the area where you sign the return. If someone else is the personal representative, he or she must also sign.

Claiming a Refund for a Deceased Taxpayer.—If you are a surviving spouse filing a joint return with the deceased, file only Form 1040X to claim the refund. If you are a court-appointed personal representative or any other person claiming a deceased taxpayer's refund, file Form 1040X and attach **Form 1310,** Statement of Person Claiming a Refund Due a Deceased Taxpayer, and any other information required by its instructions.

For more details, get **Pub. 559,** Survivors, Executors, and Administrators.

Paid Preparers

Generally, anyone you pay to prepare your return must sign it. A preparer who is required to sign your return must sign it by hand in the space provided (signature stamps or labels cannot be used) and give you a copy of the return for your records. Someone who prepares your return for you but does not charge you should not sign your return.

Specific Instructions

Above your name, enter the calendar year or fiscal year of the return you are amending.

Name, Address, and Social Security Number

If amending a joint return, list your names and social security numbers in the same order as shown on the original return. If changing from a separate to a joint return and your spouse did not file an original return, enter your name and social security number first.

P.O. Box.—If your post office does not deliver mail to your home and you have a P.O. box, enter the box number instead of your home address.

Foreign Address.—If your address is outside the United States or its possessions or territories, enter the information on the line for "City, town or post office, state, and ZIP code" in the following order: city, province or state, postal code, and the name of the country. **Do not** abbreviate the country name.

Line D—Filing Status

If you and your spouse are changing from separate returns to a joint return, enter in column A the amounts from your return as originally filed or as previously adjusted (either by you or the IRS). Next, combine the amounts from your spouse's return as originally filed or as previously adjusted with any other changes you or your spouse are making to determine the amounts to enter in column B. If your spouse did not file an original return, include your spouse's income, deductions, credits, other taxes, etc., in determining the amounts to enter in column B. Then, read the instructions for column C on this page to figure the amounts to enter in that column. Both of you must sign Form 1040X. If there is any tax due, it must be paid in full.

Columns A–C

In **column A,** enter the amounts from your return as originally filed or as you later amended it. If your return was changed or audited by the IRS, enter the adjusted amounts.

In **column B,** enter the net increase or net decrease for each line you are changing. Show all decreases in parentheses. Explain each change in Part II on page 2 of the form and attach any related schedule or form. For example, if you are amending your return to itemize deductions, attach **Schedule A (Form 1040).** If you need more space, show the required information on an attached statement.

For **column C,** add the increase in column B to the amount in column A, or subtract the column B decrease from column A. For any item you do not

Page 2

change, enter the amount from column A in column C.

Example. Anna Arbor had originally reported $11,000 as her total income on her 1992 Form 1040EZ. She received an additional Form W-2 for $500 after she filed her tax return. Ms. Arbor would complete line 1 of Form 1040X as follows:

	Col. A	Col. B	Col. C
Line 1	$11,000	$500	$11,500

Ms. Arbor would also report any additional income tax withheld on line 13 in column B.

Lines 1–31

If you are changing only credits or other taxes, skip lines 1–7 and start with line 8. If changing only payments, skip lines 1–11 and start with line 12.

If you are only providing additional information and there are no changes to the amounts you originally reported, skip lines 1–31 and complete Part II and, if applicable, Part III.

Line 1

Enter income from all sources, such as wages, taxable interest, dividends, and net profit from business. On Form 1040, use line 23.

On Form 1040A, use line 14.

On Form 1040EZ for 1990–1992, use line 3. For 1993, use line 4.

If you are correcting wages or other employee compensation, attach the first copy or Copy B of all additional or corrected Forms W-2 you got after you filed your original return.

Line 2

Enter all adjustments to income, such as an IRA deduction or alimony paid. On Form 1040, use lines 24a–29. Be sure to include any write-in adjustment. For more details, see your Form 1040 instructions.

On Form 1040A, use lines 15a and 15b.

If you are changing the amount of your IRA deduction, write in Part II of Form 1040X "IRA deduction" and the amount of the increase or decrease. If you are changing a deductible IRA contribution to a nondeductible IRA contribution, also complete and attach **Form 8606,** Nondeductible IRAs.

Line 3

Changes you make to your adjusted gross income (AGI) can cause other amounts to increase or decrease. For example, increasing your AGI may decrease your miscellaneous itemized deductions or your credit for child and dependent care expenses. It may also increase the allowable deduction for charitable contributions or the amount of social security benefits that is taxable.

Also, changes to your AGI may change your **total** itemized deductions or your deduction for exemptions. You should refigure these items whenever you change your AGI.

Effect on Exemption Deduction.—Use the **Deduction for Exemptions Worksheet** in the Form 1040 instructions for the year you are amending to figure the amount to enter on Form 1040X, line 6, and if applicable, line 29, if any of the following apply:

● You are amending your 1993 return **and** your AGI in column A or C is over $162,700 ($108,450 if single; $135,600 if head of household; $81,350 if married filing separately).

● You are amending your 1992 return **and** your AGI in column A or C is over $157,900 ($105,250 if single; $131,550 if head of household; $78,950 if married filing separately).

● You are amending your 1991 return **and** your AGI in column A or C is over $150,000 ($100,000 if single; $125,000 if head of household; $75,000 if married filing separately).

Line 4

Itemized Deductions.—If you itemize deductions on **Schedule A (Form 1040),** enter on line 4 your total itemized deductions. On Schedule A for 1990, use line 27. For 1991–1993, use line 26.

Standard Deduction.—If you **do not** itemize, enter on line 4 your standard deduction. On Form 1040, use line 34.

On Form 1040A, use line 19.

On Form 1040EZ for 1990-1992, if you checked the **"Yes"** box on line 4 of that form, enter the amount from line 4 of Form 1040EZ on line 4 of Form 1040X. If you checked the **"No"** box, enter on line 4 of Form 1040X the amount listed below for the tax year you are amending.

Tax Year	Amount
1992	$3,600
1991	3,400
1990	3,250

On Form 1040EZ for 1993, if you checked the **"Yes"** box on line 5 of that form, enter on line 4 of Form 1040X the amount from line E of the worksheet on the back of Form 1040EZ. If you checked the **"No"** box, enter $3,700 ($6,200 if married filing jointly) on line 4 of Form 1040X.

Line 6

If you are changing the number of exemptions claimed, complete the applicable lines in Part I of the form to figure the amounts to enter on line 6. Otherwise, enter in columns A and C of line 6 the amount you claimed for exemptions on your original return. On Form 1040, use line 36. But if changes to your AGI affect your deduction for exemptions (see the line 3 instructions),

enter the net change in column B of line 6 and the correct amount in column C.

On Form 1040A, use line 21.

On Form 1040EZ for 1990–1992, if you checked the **"Yes"** box on line 4 of that form, enter zero on line 6 of Form 1040X. If you checked the **"No"** box, enter the amount listed below for the tax year you are amending.

Tax Year	Amount
1992	$2,300
1991	2,150
1990	2,050

On Form 1040EZ for 1993, if you checked the **"Yes"** box on line 5 of that form, enter on line 6 of Form 1040X the amount from line F of the worksheet on the back of Form 1040EZ. If you checked the **"No"** box, enter $2,350 ($4,700 if married filing jointly) on line 6 of Form 1040X.

Line 8

Enter your income tax before subtracting any credits. Show on this line the method you use in column C to figure your tax. For example, if you use the Tax Rate Schedules, write "TRS." If you use **Schedule D (Form 1040)** or, for 1993, the Schedule D Tax Worksheet, write "Sch. D."

Figure the tax on the taxable income you reported on line 7, column C. Attach the appropriate schedule or forms. Include on line 8 any additional taxes from **Form 4970,** Tax on Accumulation Distribution of Trusts, or **Form 4972,** Tax on Lump-Sum Distributions.

Line 9

Enter your total credits, such as the credit for the elderly or the disabled, credit for child and dependent care expenses, or credit for prior year minimum tax. On Form 1040 for 1990, use lines 41–45. For 1991–1993, use lines 41–44. Be sure to include any write-in credit.

On Form 1040A, use lines 24a and 24b.

Line 11

Include other taxes, such as alternative minimum tax, self-employment tax, tax on early distributions from qualified retirement plans, or advance earned income credit payments. Also, include any recapture of investment credit, low-income housing credit, or Federal mortgage subsidy. On Form 1040 for 1990, use lines 48–53. For 1991–1993, use lines 47–52. Be sure to include any write-in tax.

On Form 1040A, use line 26.

Lines 13–17

Enter on the applicable lines your payments and credits. On Form 1040 for 1990, use lines 55–61. For 1991–1993, use lines 54–59. If you are amending

Page 3

your 1993 Form 1040 and you filed **Form 8841,** Deferral of Additional 1993 Taxes, see the instructions for line 14.

On Form 1040A, use lines 28a–28c. Be sure to include any write-in payment.

On Form 1040EZ for 1990–1992, use line 6. For 1993, use line 7.

Line 13.—If you change these amounts, attach to the front of Form 1040X the first copy or Copy B of all additional or corrected Forms W-2 or Forms 1099-R that you got after you filed your original return. Enter in column B any additional Federal income tax withheld shown on Forms W-2 or 1099.

Line 14.—Enter the estimated tax payments you claimed on your original return. If you filed **Form 1040-C,** U.S. Departing Alien Income Tax Return, include the amount you paid as the balance due with the return.

If you are amending your 1993 Form 1040, include any deferral of additional 1993 taxes from line 58b of that form on line 14 of Form 1040X. Write "Form 8841" in the space to the left of line 14. The amount reported on your original return as deferred additional 1993 taxes cannot be changed even if your taxable income has increased or decreased.

Line 18

Enter the amount you paid from the "Amount You Owe" line on your **original** return. Also, include any additional tax that may have resulted if your original return was changed or examined. **Do not** include payments of interest or penalties.

Line 20

Enter the overpayment from your original return. On Form 1040 for 1990, use line 63. For 1991–1993, use line 61. On Form 1040A, use line 29. On Form 1040EZ for 1990–1992, use line 8. For 1993, use line 9. The overpayment amount must be considered in preparing Form 1040X since any refund you have not yet received from your original return will be refunded separately from any additional refund claimed on your Form 1040X.

If your original return was changed or audited by the IRS and as a result there was an additional overpayment of tax, also include that amount on line 20. **Do not** include any interest you received on any refund.

Lines 21 and 22

If line 21 is a negative amount, treat it as a positive amount and add it to the amount on line 12, column C. Enter the

result on line 22. This is the amount you owe.

Attach your check or money order payable to the Internal Revenue Service for the full amount. Write your name, address, social security number, and daytime phone number on your payment. Also, write the year and type of return you are amending. For example, "1992 Form 1040." We will figure the interest due and send you a bill.

If you cannot pay the full amount shown on line 22, you may ask to make monthly installment payments. Get **Form 9465,** Installment Agreement Request, for more information. But if you and your spouse are changing from separate returns to joint returns, you cannot request an installment agreement.

Line 23

If you are entitled to a larger refund than you claimed on your original return, show only the additional amount due you. This will be refunded separately from the amount claimed on your original return (see the instructions for line 20). We will figure the interest and include it in your refund.

Lines 24–28

In column A, enter the number of exemptions claimed on your original return. In column B, enter any changes to exemptions claimed on your original return. Enter in column C the corrected number of exemptions you are claiming.

Line 29

You may have to use the **Deduction for Exemptions Worksheet** in the Form 1040 instructions to figure the amount to enter on line 29 if the amount in column A or C of line 3 is—

● Over $81,350 if amending your 1993 return,

● Over $78,950 if amending your 1992 return, or

● Over $75,000 if amending your 1991 return.

For details, see **Effect on Exemption Deduction** on page 3. If you don't have to use the worksheet, multiply the applicable dollar amount on line 29 by the number of exemptions on line 28.

Line 30

If you are amending your return to claim an exemption for a dependent, you may have to enter the dependent's social security number (SSN) in column (c) of line 30. For 1990, you must enter the SSN of any dependent who was age 2

or older on December 31, 1990. For tax years after 1990, you must enter the SSN of any dependent who was age 1 or older on December 31 of the year you are amending. If you do not enter the number or if the number is wrong, you may have to pay a $50 penalty. If your dependent does not have an SSN, see your 1993 Form 1040 or Form 1040A instructions for line 6c.

If you are claiming more than five additional dependents, show the information requested in columns (a) through (e) on an attached statement. When entering the total number of dependents in the boxes to the right of line 30, be sure to include these dependents.

If you are claiming a child who didn't live with you under the special rules for children of divorced or separated parents, you **must** do one of the following:

● **Check the box on line 31** if your divorce decree or written separation agreement was in effect before 1985 and it states that you can claim the child as your dependent.

● Attach **Form 8332,** Release of Claim to Exemption for Child of Divorced or Separated Parents, or similar statement. If your divorce decree or separation agreement went into effect after 1984 and it unconditionally states that you can claim the child as your dependent, you may attach a copy of the following pages from the decree or agreement instead of Form 8332:

1. Cover page (write the other parent's social security number on this page), and

2. The page that unconditionally states you can claim the child as your dependent, and

3. Signature page showing the date of the agreement.

For more details, see your 1993 Form 1040 or Form 1040A instructions for line 6c.

Part III—Presidential Election Campaign Fund

You may use Form 1040X to have $3 (or $1 if amending a 1992 return) go to the Presidential Election Campaign Fund if you (or your spouse on a joint return) did not do so on your original return. This must be done within 20½ months after the original due date for filing the return. For calendar year 1993, this period ends on December 31, 1995. For calendar year 1992, this period ends on December 31, 1994. A **"Yes"** designation cannot be changed.

Page 4

Form **1120X**
(Rev. May 1991)
Department of the Treasury
Internal Revenue Service

**Amended U.S. Corporation
Income Tax Return**

OMB No. 1545-0132
Expires 4-30-94

For tax year ending in
▶ ....
(Enter month and year)

Please Type or Print	Name	Employer identification number
	Number, street, and room or suite no. (If a P.O. box, see instructions.)	
	City or town, state, and ZIP code	Telephone number (optional) ( )

Enter name and address used on original return (If same as above, write "Same.")

Internal Revenue Service Center
where original return was filed ▶

Fill in Applicable Items and Use Part II To Explain Any Changes

Part I Income and Deductions	**(a)** As originally reported or as adjusted (see Specific Instructions)	**(b)** Net change (increase or decrease— explain in Part II)	**(c)** Correct amount
1 Total income (Form 1120 or 1120-A, line 11)			
2 Total deductions (total of lines 27 and 29c, Form 1120, or lines 23 and 25c, Form 1120-A)			
3 Taxable income. Subtract line 2 from line 1			
4 Tax (Form 1120, line 31, or Form 1120-A, line 27) . . .			

Payments and Credits

5a Estimated tax payments. Include overpayment in prior year allowed as a credit			
b Amount of refund applied for on Form 4466			
c Subtract line 5b from line 5a			
6 Tax deposited with Form 7004 (see instructions) . . .			
7 Credit from regulated investment companies			
8 Credit for Federal tax on fuels			
9 Other payment or refundable credit (specify) ▶			
10 Tax deposited or paid with (or after) the filing of the original return			
11 Add lines 5c through 10, column (c)			
12 Overpayment, if any, as shown on original return or as later adjusted			
13 Subtract line 12 from line 11			

Tax Due or Refund

14 **Tax due.** Subtract line 13 from line 4, column (c). Make check payable to "Internal Revenue Service" (see instructions) . . . . ▶			
15 **Refund.** Subtract line 4, column (c), from line 13 . . . . ▶			

Please Sign Here

Under penalties of perjury, I declare that I have filed an original return and that I have examined this amended return, including accompanying schedules and statements, and to the best of my knowledge and belief, this amended return is true, correct, and complete. Declaration of preparer (other than taxpayer) is based on all information of which preparer has any knowledge.

▶ _____   ▶ _____   ▶ _____
Signature of officer   Date   Title

Paid Preparer's Use Only

Preparer's signature		Date	Check if self-employed ▶ ☐	Preparer's social security no.
Firm's name (or yours if self-employed) and address			E.I. No. ▶	
			ZIP code ▶	

For Paperwork Reduction Act Notice, see instructions on back.   Cat. No. 11530Z   Form **1120X** (Rev. 5-91)

Form 1120X (Rev. 5-91)   Page **2**

| **Part II** | **Explanation of Changes to Income, Deductions, Credits, etc.** Enter the line number from page 1 for the items you are changing, and give the reason for each change. Show any computation in detail. Attach additional sheets if necessary. |

If the change is due to a net operating loss carryback, a capital loss carryback, or a general business credit carryback (see **Carryback Claims,** below), check here . . . . ▶ ☐

General Instructions

(Section references are to the Internal Revenue Code.)

Paperwork Reduction Act Notice

We ask for the information on this form to carry out the Internal Revenue laws of the United States. You are required to give us this information. We need it to ensure that you are complying with these laws and to allow us to figure and collect the right amount of tax.

The time needed to complete and file this form will vary depending on individual circumstances. The estimated average time is:

Recordkeeping	11 hr., 14 min.
Learning about the law or the form	40 min.
Preparing the form	1 hr., 49 min.
Copying, assembling, and sending the form to IRS	16 min.

If you have comments concerning the accuracy of these time estimates or suggestions for making this form more simple, we would be happy to hear from you. You can write to both the **Internal Revenue Service,** Washington, DC 20224, Attention: IRS Reports Clearance Officer, T:FP; and the **Office of Management and Budget,** Paperwork Reduction Project (1545-0037), Washington, DC 20503. DO NOT send the tax form to either of these offices. Instead, see **Where To File** below.

Purpose of Form.—Use Form 1120X to correct **Form 1120,** U.S. Corporation Income Tax Return, or **Form 1120-A,** U.S. Corporation Short-Form Income Tax Return, as you originally filed it or as it was later adjusted by an amended return, a claim for refund, or an examination. Please note that it often takes 3 to 4 months to process Form 1120X.

Do not use Form 1120X to apply for a tentative refund or a quick refund of estimated tax. Use the following forms instead:

● **Form 4466,** Corporation Application for Quick Refund of Overpayment of Estimated Tax. For a quick refund of estimated tax, file Form 4466 within 2½ months after the end of the tax year and before the corporation files its tax return.

● **Form 1139,** Corporation Application for Tentative Refund. For a tentative refund due to the carryback of a net operating loss, a net capital loss, unused credits, or overpaid tax resulting from a claim-of-right adjustment under section 1341(b)(1), file Form 1139. You may use Form 1139 only if one year or less has passed since the tax year in which the carryback or adjustment occurred. For additional information on net operating losses and a worksheet to help figure the corporation's net operating loss deduction in a carryback year, see **Pub. 536,** Net Operating Losses.

When To File.—File Form 1120X only after the corporation has filed its original return. Generally, Form 1120X must be filed within 3 years after the date the original return was due or 3 years after the date the corporation filed it, whichever is later. A Form 1120X based on a net operating loss carryback, a capital loss carryback, or a general business credit carryback, generally must be filed within 3 years after the due date of the return for the tax year of the net operating loss, capital loss, or unused credit. Other claims for refund must be filed within 3 years after the date the original return was due, 3 years after the date the corporation filed it, or 2 years after the date the tax was paid, whichever is later.

What To Attach.—If the change you are making involves an item of income, deduction, or credit, that the corporation income tax return (or its instructions) requires the corporation to support with a schedule, statement, or form, attach the appropriate schedule, statement, or form to Form 1120X.

Tax Shelters. If you are amending your return to include any item (loss, credit, deduction, other tax benefit, or income) relating to a tax shelter required to be registered, you must attach **Form 8271,** Investor Reporting of Tax Shelter Registration Number.

Carryback Claims. If Form 1120X is used as a carryback claim, attach copies of Form 1120 (pages 1 and 3) or Form 1120-A (pages 1 and 2), for both the year the loss or credit originated and for the carryback year. Also attach any other forms, schedules, or statements that are necessary to support the claim. At the top of these attachments, write "Copy Only—Do Not Process."

Information on Income, Deductions, Tax Computation, etc.—See the instructions for Forms 1120 and 1120-A for the year you are amending for information about the taxability of certain types of income, the allowability of certain expenses as deductions from income, computation of tax, etc.

Note: *Deductions for such items as charitable contributions and the dividends-received deduction may have to be refigured because of changes made to other items of income or expense.*

Where To File.—Mail this form to the Internal Revenue Service Center where the corporation filed its original return.

Specific Instructions

Tax Year.—In the space above the employer identification number, enter the ending month and year of the calendar or fiscal year for the tax return you are amending.

P.O. Box.—If the post office does not deliver mail to the street address and the corporation has a P.O. box, show the P.O. box number instead of the street address.

Column (a)

Enter the amounts from your return as originally filed or as you later amended it. If

your return was changed or audited by IRS, enter the amounts as adjusted.

Column (b)

Enter the net increase or net decrease for each line you are changing. Use parentheses around all amounts that are decreases. Explain the increase or decrease in Part II.

Column (c)

Lines 1 and 2.—Add the increase in column (b) to the amount in column (a) or subtract the column (b) decrease from column (a). Enter the result in column (c). For any item not changed, enter the amount from column (a) in column (c).

Line 4.—Figure the new amount of tax using the taxable income on line 3, column (c). Use Schedule J, Form 1120, or Part I, Form 1120-A, of the original return to make the necessary tax computation.

Line 6.—Enter the amount of tax deposited with **Form 7004,** Application for Automatic Extension of Time To File Corporation Income Tax Return.

Line 12—Overpayment.—Enter the amount from the "Overpayment" line of the original return, even if the corporation chose to credit all or part of this amount to the next year's estimated tax. This amount must be considered in preparing Form 1120X since any refund due from the original return will be refunded separately (or credited to estimated tax) from any additional refund claimed on Form 1120X

Line 14—Tax due.—Make the check payable to "Internal Revenue Service" for the amount shown on line 14 and attach it to this form. Do not use the depositary method of payment.

Line 15—Refund.—If the corporation is entitled to a refund larger than the amount claimed on the original return, line 15 will show only the additional amount of refund. This additional amount will be refunded separately from the amount claimed on the original return.

Signature.—The return must be signed and dated by the president, vice president, treasurer, assistant treasurer, chief accounting officer, or any other corporate officer (such as tax officer) authorized to sign. A receiver, trustee, or assignee must sign and date any return required to be filed on behalf of a corporation.

If a corporate officer filled in Form 1120X, the Paid Preparer's space should remain blank. If someone prepares Form 1120X and does not charge the corporation, that person should not sign the return. Certain others who prepare Form 1120X should not sign. See the instructions for Forms 1120 and 1120-A for more information.

Note: *IRS will figure any interest due and will either include it in the refund or bill the corporation for the interest.*

B-5   Application for Extension of Time to File Income Tax Returns

Form **4868**	**Application for Automatic Extension of Time To File U.S. Individual Income Tax Return**	OMB No. 1545-0188

Department of the Treasury
Internal Revenue Service

▶ This is not an extension of time to pay your tax.
▶ See separate instructions.

19 93

Please Type or Print

| Your first name and initial | Last name | Your social security number |
| If a joint return, spouse's first name and initial | Last name | Spouse's social security number |

Home address (number, street, and apt. no. or rural route). If you have a P.O. box, see the instructions.

City, town or post office, state, and ZIP code

I request an automatic 4-month extension of time to August 15, 1994, to file Form 1040EZ, Form 1040A, or Form 1040 for the calendar year 1993 or to _____, 19 ____, for the fiscal tax year ending _____, 19 ____.

Part I   Individual Income Tax—You must complete this part.

1   **Total tax liability for 1993.** This is the amount you expect to enter on Form 1040EZ, line 8; Form 1040A, line 27; or Form 1040, line 53. If you expect this amount to be zero, enter -0-. . | **1** |

   Caution: You **MUST** enter an amount on line 1 or your extension will be denied. You can estimate this amount, but be as exact as you can with the information you have. If we later find that your estimate was not reasonable, the extension will be null and void.

2   **Total payments for 1993.** This is the amount you expect to enter on Form 1040EZ, line 7; Form 1040A, line 28d; or Form 1040, line 60 . . . . | **2** |

3   **BALANCE DUE.** Subtract line 2 from line 1. If line 2 is more than line 1, enter -0-. For details on how to pay, including what to write on your payment, see the instructions . . . . . ▶ | **3** |

Part II   Gift or Generation-Skipping Transfer (GST) Tax—Complete this part if you expect to owe either tax.

Caution: Do not include income tax on lines 5a and 5b. See the instructions.

4   If you or your spouse plan to file a gift tax return (Form 709 or 709-A) for 1993, generally due by April 15, 1994, see the instructions and check here . . . } Yourself ▶ ☐   Spouse ▶ ☐

5a Enter the amount of gift or GST tax **you** are paying with this form . . . . | **5a** |

b   Enter the amount of gift or GST tax **your spouse** is paying with this form . . . . . . | **5b** |

Signature and Verification

Under penalties of perjury, I declare that I have examined this form, including accompanying schedules and statements, and to the best of my knowledge and belief, it is true, correct, and complete; and, if prepared by someone other than the taxpayer, that I am authorized to prepare this form.

▶ _____   _____   ▶ _____   _____
Your signature   Date   Spouse's signature, if filing jointly   Date

▶ _____
Preparer's signature (other than taxpayer)   Date

If you want correspondence regarding this extension to be sent to you at an address other than that shown above or to an agent acting for you, please enter the name of the agent and/or the address where it should be sent.

Please Type or Print

Name

Number and street (include suite, room, or apt. no.) or P.O. box number if mail is not delivered to street address

City, town or post office, state, and ZIP code

For Paperwork Reduction Act Notice, see separate instructions.   Cat. No. 13141W   Form **4868** (1993)

Form **2688**

Department of the Treasury
Internal Revenue Service

**Application for Additional Extension of Time To File
U.S. Individual Income Tax Return**

▶ See instructions on back.
▶ You MUST complete all items that apply to you.

OMB No. 1545-0066

1993

Attachment
Sequence No. **59**

**Please type
or print.**

**File the
original and
one copy by
the due date
for filing
your return.**

Your first name and initial	Last name	Your social security number
If a joint return, spouse's first name and initial	Last name	Spouse's social security number

Home address (number, street, and apt. no. or rural route). If you have a P.O. box, see the instructions.

City, town or post office, state, and ZIP code

1   I request an extension of time until .... , 19........ , to file Form 1040EZ, Form 1040A, or Form 1040 for the
calendar year 1993, or other tax year ending .... , 19........ .

2   Have you filed Form 4868 to request an extension of time to file for this tax year? . . . . ☐ **Yes**   ☐ **No**
If you checked "No," we will grant your extension only for undue hardship. Fully explain the hardship on line 3.

3   Explain why you need an extension ▶ ....
....
....
....
....

If you expect to owe gift or generation-skipping transfer (GST) tax, complete line 4.

4   If you or your spouse plan to file a gift tax return (Form 709 or 709-A) for 1993, generally due   } Yourself . . ▶ ☐
by April 15, 1994, see the instructions and check here . . . .   } Spouse . . ▶ ☐

Signature and Verification

Under penalties of perjury, I declare that I have examined this form, including accompanying schedules and statements, and to
the best of my knowledge and belief, it is true, correct, and complete; and, if prepared by someone other than the taxpayer, that
I am authorized to prepare this form.

Signature of taxpayer ▶ _____ Date ▶ _____

Signature of spouse ▶ _____ Date ▶ _____
          (If filing jointly, BOTH must sign even if only one had income)

Signature of preparer
other than taxpayer ▶ _____ Date ▶ _____

File original and one copy. The IRS will show below whether or not your application is approved and will return the copy.

Notice to Applicant—To Be Completed by the IRS

☐   We **HAVE** approved your application. Please attach this form to your return.

☐   We **HAVE NOT** approved your application. Please attach this form to your return. However, because of your reasons stated
above, we have granted a 10-day grace period from the date shown below or due date of your return, whichever is later.
This grace period is considered to be a valid extension of time for elections otherwise required to be made on returns filed
on time.

☐   We **HAVE NOT** approved your application. After considering your reasons stated above, we cannot grant your request for
an extension of time to file. We are not granting the 10-day grace period.

☐   We cannot consider your application because it was filed after the due date of your return.

☐   We **HAVE NOT** approved your application. The maximum extension of time allowed by law is 6 months.

☐   Other ....

_____ Director

_____ By _____
        Date

Please type or print

Name	
Number and street (include suite, room, or apt. no.) or P.O. box number if mail is not delivered to street address	If you want the copy of this form returned to you at an address other than that shown above or to an agent acting for you, enter the name of the agent and/or the address where the copy should be sent.
City, town or post office, state, and ZIP code	

For Paperwork Reduction Act Notice, see back of form.   Cat. No. 11958F   Form **2688** (1993)

General Instructions

Paperwork Reduction Act Notice.—We ask for the information on this form to carry out the Internal Revenue laws of the United States. You are required to give us the information. We need it to ensure that you are complying with these laws and to allow us to figure and collect the right amount of tax.

The time needed to complete and file this form will vary depending on individual circumstances. The estimated average time is: **Learning about the law or the form,** 7 min.; **Preparing the form,** 10 min.; and **Copying, assembling, and sending the form to the IRS,** 20 min.

If you have comments concerning the accuracy of these time estimates or suggestions for making this form more simple, we would be happy to hear from you. You can write to both the **Internal Revenue Service,** Attention: Reports Clearance Officer, PC:FP, Washington, DC 20224; and the **Office of Management and Budget,** Paperwork Reduction Project (1545-0066), Washington, DC 20503. **DO NOT** send this form to either of these offices. Instead, see **Where To File** later.

Purpose of Form

Caution: *If the new tax rates for high-income taxpayers apply to you, you may be able to defer part of your 1993 tax liability. But to do so, you **must** pay by the regular due date of your return, at least 90% of your 1993 tax liability, minus the tax you would be eligible to defer. For details, get* **Form 8841,** *Deferral of Additional 1993 Taxes.*

Use Form 2688 to ask for more time to file **Form 1040EZ, Form 1040A,** or **Form 1040.** Generally, use it only if you already asked for more time on **Form 4868** (the "automatic" extension form) and that time was not enough. We will make an exception to this rule only for undue hardship.

To get the extra time you **MUST:**

● Complete and file Form 2688 on time, **AND**

● Have a good reason why the first 4 months were not enough. Explain the reason on line 3.

Generally, we will not give you more time to file just for the convenience of your tax return preparer. But if the reasons for being late are beyond his or her control or, despite a good effort, you cannot get professional help in time to file, we will usually give you the extra time.

You cannot have the IRS figure your tax if you file after the regular due date of your return. An extension of time to file a 1993 calendar year income tax return also extends the time to file a gift tax return for 1993.

Caution: *If we give you more time to file and later find that the statements made on this form are false or misleading, the extension is null and void. You will owe the late filing penalty explained on this page.*

If You Live Abroad.—U.S. citizens or resident aliens living abroad may qualify for special tax treatment if they meet the required residence or presence tests. If you do not expect to meet either of those tests by the due date of your return,

request an extension to a date after you expect to qualify. Ask for it on **Form 2350,** Application for Extension of Time To File U.S. Income Tax Return. Get **Pub. 54,** Tax Guide for U.S. Citizens and Resident Aliens Abroad.

Total Time Allowed

We cannot extend the due date of your return for more than 6 months. This includes the 4 extra months allowed by Form 4868. There may be an exception if you live abroad. See previous discussion.

When To File

If you filed Form 4868, file Form 2688 by the extended due date of your return. For most people, this is August 15, 1994. If you didn't file Form 4868 first because of undue hardship, file Form 2688 by the due date of your return, April 15, 1994, for a calendar year return. Be sure to fully explain why you are filing Form 2688 first. Also, file Form 2688 early so that if your request is not approved you can still file your return on time.

Out of the Country.—You may have been allowed 2 extra months to file if you were a U.S. citizen or resident out of the country on the due date of your return. "Out of the country" means either (1) you live outside the United States and Puerto Rico **and** your main place of work is outside the United States and Puerto Rico, **or** (2) you are in military or naval service outside the United States and Puerto Rico.

Where To File

Mail Form 2688 AND a copy to the Internal Revenue Service Center where you send your return.

Filing Your Tax Return

You may file Form 1040EZ, 1040A, or Form 1040 any time before your extension of time is up. But remember, Form 2688 does not extend the time to pay taxes. If you do not pay the amount due by the regular due date, you will owe interest. You may also be charged penalties.

Interest.—You will owe interest on any tax not paid by the regular due date of your return. The interest runs until you pay the tax. Even if you had a good reason for not paying on time, you will still owe interest.

Late Payment Penalty.—The penalty is usually ½ of 1% of any tax (other than estimated tax) not paid by the regular due date. It is charged for each month or part of a month the tax is unpaid. The maximum penalty is 25%. You might not owe this penalty if you have a good reason for not paying on time. Attach a statement to your return, not Form 2688, explaining the reason.

Late Filing Penalty.—A penalty is usually charged if your return is filed after the due date (including extensions). It is usually 5% of the tax not paid by the regular due date for each month or part of a month your return is late. Generally, the maximum penalty is 25%. If your return is more than 60 days late, the minimum penalty is $100 or the balance of tax due on your return, whichever is smaller. You might not owe the penalty if you have a good reason for filing late. Attach a full explanation to your return, not Form 2688, if you file late.

How To Claim Credit for Payment Made With This Form.—Include any payment you sent with Form 2688 on the appropriate line of your tax return. If you file Form 1040EZ, the instructions for line 7 will tell you how to report the payment. If you file Form 1040A, see the instructions for line 28d. If you file Form 1040, enter the payment on line 57.

If you and your spouse each filed a separate Form 2688 but later file a joint return for 1993, enter the total paid with both Forms 2688 on the appropriate line of your joint return.

If you and your spouse jointly filed Form 2688 but later file separate returns for 1993, you may enter the total amount paid with Form 2688 on either of your separate returns. Or you and your spouse may divide the payment in any agreed amounts. Be sure each separate return has the social security numbers of both spouses.

Specific Instructions

Name, Address, and Social Security Number (SSN).—Enter your name, address, and SSN. If you plan to file a joint return, also enter your spouse's name and SSN. If the post office does not bring mail to your street address and you have a P.O. box, enter the box number instead.

Note: *If you changed your mailing address after you filed your last return, you should use* **Form 8822,** *Change of Address, to notify the IRS of the change. A new address shown on Form 2688 will not update your record. You can get Form 8822 by calling 1-800-829-3676.*

Line 3.—Clearly describe the reasons that will delay your return. We cannot accept incomplete reasons, such as "illness" or "practitioner too busy," without adequate explanations. If it is clear that you have no important reason but only want more time, we will deny your request. The 10-day grace period will also be denied.

If because of undue hardship you are filing Form 2688 without filing Form 4868 first, clearly explain why on line 3. Attach any information you have that helps explain the hardship.

Line 4.—If you or your spouse plan to file Form 709 or 709-A for 1993, check whichever box applies. But if your spouse files a separate Form 2688, do not check the box for your spouse.

Your Signature.—This form must be signed. If you plan to file a joint return, both of you should sign. If there is a good reason why one of you cannot, the other spouse may sign for both. Attach a statement explaining why the other spouse cannot sign.

Others Who Can Sign for You.—Anyone with a power of attorney can sign. But the following can sign for you without a power of attorney:

● Attorneys, CPAs, and enrolled agents.

● A person in close personal or business relationship to you who is signing because you cannot. There must be a good reason why you cannot sign, such as illness or absence. Attach an explanation to this form.

B-6 Underpayment of Estimated Tax

Form **2210**

Department of the Treasury
Internal Revenue Service

**Underpayment of
Estimated Tax by Individuals and Fiduciaries**
▶ See separate instructions.
▶ Attach to Form 1040, Form 1040A, Form 1040NR, or Form 1041.

OMB No. 1545-0140

19**93**

Attachment
Sequence No. **06**

Name(s) shown on tax return   Identifying number

Note: In most cases, you **do not** need to file Form 2210. The IRS will figure any penalty you owe and send you a bill. File Form
2210 **only** if one or more boxes in Part I apply to you. If you do not need to file Form 2210, you still may use it to figure your penalty.
Enter the amount from line 20 or line 32 on the penalty line of your return, but do not attach Form 2210.

| **Part I** | Reasons For Filing—If 1a, b, c, or d below applies to you, you may be able to lower or eliminate your penalty. But you MUST check the boxes that apply and file Form 2210 with your tax return. If 1e or f below applies to you, check that box and file Form 2210 with your tax return. |

1   Check whichever boxes apply (if none apply, see the **Note** above):

a ☐ You request a **waiver.** In certain circumstances, the IRS will waive all or part of the penalty. See the instructions for **Waiver
       of Penalty.**

b ☐ You use the **annualized income installment method.** If your income varied during the year, this method may reduce the
       amount of one or more required installments. See the **Instructions for Schedule B.**

c ☐ You had Federal income tax withheld from wages and you treat it as paid for estimated tax purposes when it was **actually**
       withheld instead of in equal amounts on the payment due dates. See the instructions for line 22.

d ☐ **(1)** You made estimated tax payments for 1990, 1991, or 1992 (or were charged an estimated tax penalty for any of those years), **AND**
       (2) Your adjusted gross income (AGI) is more than $75,000 (more than $37,500 if married filing separately), **AND**
       (3) Your 1993 **modified** AGI exceeds your 1992 AGI by more than $40,000 (more than $20,000 if married filing separately), **AND**
       (4) Your 2nd, 3rd, or 4th required installment (column (b), (c), or (d) of line 21) is based on **either** your 1992 tax **or** 90%
               of your 1993 **modified** tax.
       See the **Instructions for Schedule A** for more information.

e ☐ Conditions (1), (2), and (4) (but not condition (3)) in box 1d apply to you, and your 1993 AGI exceeds your 1992 AGI by
       more than $40,000 (more than $20,000 if married filing separately). If you check this box, you must also attach a computation
       of your 1993 modified AGI.

f ☐ One or more of your required installments (line 21) are based on your 1992 tax and you filed or are filing a joint return for
       either 1992 or 1993 but not for both years.

| **Part II** | All Filers Must Complete This Part |

2	Enter your 1993 tax after credits (see instructions)	2	
3	Other taxes (see instructions)	3	
4	Add lines 2 and 3	4	
5	Earned income credit	5		
6	Credit for Federal tax paid on fuels	6		
7	Add lines 5 and 6	7	
8	Current year tax. Subtract line 7 from line 4	8	
9	Multiply line 8 by 90% (.90)	9		
10	Withholding taxes. **Do not** include any estimated tax payments on this line (see instructions) .	10	
11	Subtract line 10 from line 8. If less than $500, stop here; **do not** complete or file this form. You do not owe the penalty	11	
12	Tax shown on your prior year (1992) return. **(Caution:** See instructions.**)**	12	
13	Enter the **smaller** of line 9 or line 12 (see instructions)	13	

| **Part III** | Short Method **(Caution:** Read the instructions to see if you can use the short method. If you checked box **1b, c,** or **d** in Part I, skip this part and go to Part IV.**)** |

14	Enter the amount, if any, from line 10 above	14		
15	Enter the total amount, if any, of estimated tax payments you made	15		
16	Add lines 14 and 15	16	
17	**Total underpayment for year.** Subtract line 16 from line 13. If zero or less, stop here; you do not owe the penalty. Do not file Form 2210 unless you checked box 1e or f above	17	
18	Multiply line 17 by .04655	18	
19	● If the amount on line 17 was paid **on or after** 4/15/94, enter -0-.		
	● If the amount on line 17 was paid **before** 4/15/94, make the following computation to find the amount to enter on line 19. Amount on × Number of days paid × .00019 . . . . . . line 17 before 4/15/94	19	
20	**PENALTY.** Subtract line 19 from line 18. Enter the result here and on Form 1040, line 65; Form 1040A, line 33; Form 1040NR, line 66; or Form 1041, line 26 . . . . ▶	20	

For Paperwork Reduction Act Notice, see page 1 of separate instructions.   Cat. No. 11744P   Form **2210** (1993)

Form 2210 (1993)   Page **2**

Part IV   **Regular Method** (See the instructions if you are filing Form 1040NR.)

		Payment Due Dates			
Section A—Figure Your Underpayment		(a) 4/15/93	(b) 6/15/93	(c) 9/15/93	(d) 1/15/94
21	**Required installments.** If box 1b applies, enter the amounts from Schedule B, line 26. If you must use Schedule A to figure your penalty (and box 1b does not apply), enter the amounts from Schedule A, line 5, 8, or 19, whichever applies. All others, enter ¼ of line 13, Form 2210, in each column **21**				
22	Estimated tax paid and tax withheld (see instructions). For column (a) only, also enter the amount from line 22 on line 26. If line 22 is equal to or more than line 21 for all payment periods, stop here; you do not owe the penalty. Do not file Form 2210 unless you checked a box in Part I **22**				
	Complete lines 23 through 29 of one column before going to the next column.				
23	Enter amount, if any, from line 29 of previous column **23**				
24	Add lines 22 and 23 . . . . **24**				
25	Add amounts on lines 27 and 28 of the previous column **25**				
26	Subtract line 25 from line 24. If zero or less, enter -0-. For column (a) only, enter the amount from line 22 . **26**				
27	If the amount on line 26 is zero, subtract line 24 from line 25. Otherwise, enter -0- **27**				
28	**Underpayment.** If line 21 is equal to or more than line 26, subtract line 26 from line 21. Then go to line 23 of next column. Otherwise, go to line 29 . . ▶ **28**				
29	Overpayment. If line 26 is more than line 21, subtract line 21 from line 26. Then go to line 23 of next column **29**				

Section B—Figure the Penalty (Complete lines 30 and 31 of one column before going to the next column.)

		4/15/93	6/15/93	9/15/93	1/15/94
30	Number of days FROM the date shown above line 30 TO the date the amount on line 28 was paid **or** 4/15/94, whichever is earlier **30**	Days:	Days:	Days:	Days:
31	$\dfrac{\text{Underpayment}}{\text{on line 28}} \times \dfrac{\text{Number of days on line 30}}{365} \times .07$ ▶ **31**	$	$	$	$
32	**PENALTY.** Add the amounts in each column of line 31. Enter the total here and on Form 1040, line 65; Form 1040A, line 33; Form 1040NR, line 66; or Form 1041, line 26 . . . . ▶ **32**	$			

Form **2220**

Department of the Treasury
Internal Revenue Service

Underpayment of Estimated Tax by Corporations

▶ See separate instructions.
▶ Attach to the corporation's tax return.

OMB No. 1545-0142

19**93**

Name

Employer identification number

Note: *In most cases, the IRS will figure the penalty and the corporation will not have to complete this form. See the instructions for more information.*

Part I Figuring the Underpayment

1	Total tax (see instructions)	1
2a	Personal holding company tax included on line 1 (Schedule PH (Form 1120), line 26).	2a
b	Interest due under the look-back method of section 460(b)(2) for completed long-term contracts included on line 1	2b
c	Credit for Federal tax paid on fuels (see instructions)	2c
d	**Total.** Add lines 2a through 2c	2d
3	Subtract line 2d from line 1. If the result is less than $500, **do not** complete or file this form. The corporation does not owe the penalty	3
4a	Multiply line 3 by 97%	4a
b	Tax shown on the corporation's 1992 income tax return. *(CAUTION: See instructions before completing this line.)*	4b
c	Enter the **smaller** of line 4a or line 4b. If the corporation is required to skip line 4b, enter the amount from line 4a on line 4c	4c

		(a)	(b)	(c)	(d)
5	**Installment due dates.** Enter in columns (a) through (d) the 15th day of the 4th, 6th, 9th, and 12th months of the corporation's tax year . . . . ▶				
6	**Required installments.** Enter 25% of line 4c in columns (a) through (d) unless **a** or **b** below applies to the corporation.				
a	**Annualized income installment method and/or the adjusted seasonal installment method:** If the corporation uses one or both of these methods, complete the worksheet in the instructions and enter on line 6 the amounts from line 45 of the worksheet. Also check this box ▶ ☐ and attach a copy of the worksheet.				
b	**"Large corporations:"** Check this box ▶ ☐ and see the instructions for the amount to enter in each column of line 6				
7	Estimated tax paid or credited for each period (see instructions). For column (a) only, enter the amount from line 7 on line 11				
	Complete lines 8 through 14 of one column before going to the next column.				
8	Enter amount, if any, from line 14 of the preceding column				
9	Add lines 7 and 8				
10	Add amounts on lines 12 and 13 of the preceding column.				
11	Subtract line 10 from line 9. If zero or less, enter -0-. For column (a) only, enter the amount from line 7				
12	If the amount on line 11 is zero, subtract line 9 from line 10. Otherwise, enter -0-				
13	**Underpayment.** If line 11 is less than or equal to line 6, subtract line 11 from line 6. Then go to line 8 of the next column. Otherwise, go to line 14 (see instructions) . . .				
14	**Overpayment.** If line 6 is less than line 11, subtract line 6 from line 11. Then go to line 8 of the next column				

Complete Part II on the back of this form to figure the penalty. *If there are no entries on line 13, no penalty is owed.*

For Paperwork Reduction Act Notice, see page 1 of instructions.

Cat. No. 11746L

Form **2220** (1993)

Form 2220 (1993)   Page **2**

Part II   Figuring the Penalty

		(a)	(b)	(c)	(d)
15	Enter the date of payment or the 15th day of the 3rd month after the close of the tax year, whichever is earlier (see instructions). *(Form 990-PF and Form 990-T filers:* Use 5th month instead of 3rd month.) **15**				
16	Number of days from due date of installment on line 5 to the date shown on line 15 . . . . **16**				
17	Number of days on line 16 after 4/15/93 and before 4/1/94 . **17**				
18	Number of days on line 16 after 3/31/94 and before 7/1/94 . **18**				
19	Number of days on line 16 after 6/30/94 and before 10/1/94. **19**				
20	Number of days on line 16 after 9/30/94 and before 1/1/95 . **20**				
21	Number of days on line 16 after 12/31/94 and before 2/16/95 **21**				
22	Underpayment on line 13 $\times \dfrac{\text{Number of days on line 17}}{365} \times$ 7% . . **22**	\$	\$	\$	\$
23	Underpayment on line 13 $\times \dfrac{\text{Number of days on line 18}}{365} \times$ *% . . **23**	\$	\$	\$	\$
24	Underpayment on line 13 $\times \dfrac{\text{Number of days on line 19}}{365} \times$ *% . . **24**	\$	\$	\$	\$
25	Underpayment on line 13 $\times \dfrac{\text{Number of days on line 20}}{365} \times$ *% . . **25**	\$	\$	\$	\$
26	Underpayment on line 13 $\times \dfrac{\text{Number of days on line 21}}{365} \times$ *% . . **26**	\$	\$	\$	\$
27	Add lines 22 through 26 . . . . **27**	\$	\$	\$	\$
28	**PENALTY.** Add columns (a) through (d), line 27. Enter here and on line 33, Form 1120; line 29, Form 1120-A; or comparable line for other income tax returns **28**			\$	

1993    Department of the Treasury
Internal Revenue Service

Instructions for Form 2220

Underpayment of Estimated Tax by Corporations

Section references are to the Internal Revenue Code.

Paperwork Reduction Act Notice

We ask for the information on this form to carry out the Internal Revenue laws of the United States. You are required to give us the information. We need it to ensure that you are complying with these laws and to allow us to figure and collect the right amount of tax.

The time needed to complete and file this form will vary depending on individual circumstances. The estimated average time is:

Form	Recordkeeping	Learning about the law or the form	Preparing and sending the form to the IRS
2220	24 hr., 9 min.	35 min.	1 hr., 1 min.
Worksheet, Pt. I	11 hr., 43 min.	12 min.	24 min.
Worksheet, Pt. II	24 hr., 23 min.	- - -	24 min.
Worksheet, Pt. III	5 hr., 16 min.	- - -	5 min.

If you have comments concerning the accuracy of these time estimates or suggestions for making this form more simple, we would be happy to hear from you. You can write to both the IRS and the Office of Management and Budget at the addresses listed in the instructions for the tax return with which this form is filed.

A Change To Note

The Revenue Reconciliation Act of 1993 (Act) made changes in the tax law that may affect the corporation's tax liability. The IRS will waive all or part of the estimated tax penalty to the extent the underpayment is attributable to changes made by the new law. See the instructions for line 13 under **Waiver of Penalty** on page 2.

Purpose of Form

Corporations (including S corporations), tax-exempt organizations subject to the unrelated business income tax, and private foundations use Form 2220 to determine if they are subject to the penalty for underpayment of estimated tax and, if so, the amount of the penalty.

Who Must Pay the Underpayment Penalty

If the corporation did not pay enough estimated tax by any of the due dates, it may be charged a penalty. This is true even if the corporation is due a refund when its return is filed. The penalty is figured separately for each installment due date. Therefore, the corporation may owe a penalty for an earlier installment due date, even if it paid enough tax later to make up the underpayment.

Generally, a corporation is subject to the penalty if its tax liability is $500 or more and it did not timely pay the smaller of 97% of its tax liability for 1993, or 100% of its tax liability for 1992 (if it filed a 1992 return that showed a liability for at least some amount of tax and the return covered a full 12 months). However, a large corporation (see the instructions for line 6(b)) may base only its first required installment on 100% of the prior year's tax liability. A corporation may be able to reduce or eliminate the penalty by using

the annualized income installment method or the adjusted seasonal installment method.

IRS May Be Able To Figure the Penalty

Generally, the corporation does not have to file this form because the IRS will figure the amount of any penalty and bill the corporation. However, even if the corporation does not owe a penalty, complete and attach this form if:

1. The annualized income installment method and/or the adjusted seasonal installment method is used (see the instructions for line 6(a)),

2. The corporation is a large corporation computing its first required installment based on the prior year's tax, or

3. The corporation is claiming a waiver of the penalty as discussed in the instructions for line 13 under **Waiver of Penalty.**

How To Use This Form

Complete Part I of Form 2220 to determine the underpayment for any of the four installment due dates. If there is an underpayment on line 13 (column (a), (b), (c), or (d)), go to Part II to figure the penalty. Attach Form 2220 to the income tax return and check the box on line 33, page 1 of Form 1120; line 29 of Form 1120-A; or the comparable line of any other income tax return the corporation is required to file (e.g., Form 990-C, 1120-L, 1120S, etc.).

Part I. Figuring the Underpayment

Complete lines 1 through 14 of Part I.

Line 1.—Enter the tax from line 31, Form 1120; line 27, Form 1120-A; or the comparable line for other income tax returns (except as noted below).

Filers of Forms 990-PF, 990-T, 1120-L, 1120-PC, 1120-REIT, 1120-RIC, and 1120S.—See the instructions for the appropriate tax return for the definition of tax for estimated tax purposes.

Line 2c.—Enter the amount from line 32g, Form 1120; line 28g, Form 1120-A; or the comparable line for other income tax returns.

Line 4b. All filers other than S corporations.—Figure the corporation's 1992 tax in the same manner as the amount on line 3 of this form was determined, using the taxes and credits from its 1992 tax return.

Skip line 4b and enter the amount from line 4a on line 4c if either of the following apply:

1. The corporation did not file a tax return for 1992 that showed a liability for at least some amount of tax; or

2. The corporation had a 1992 tax year of less than 12 months.

S corporations.—Enter on line 4b the sum of: (a) 97% of the sum of the investment credit recapture tax and the built-in gains tax (or the tax on certain capital gains) shown on the return for the 1993 tax year, and (b) 100% of any excess net passive income tax shown on the S corporation's return for the 1992 tax year. If the 1992 tax year was less than 12 months, do not complete line 4b. Instead, enter the amount from line 4a on line 4c.

Line 6a. Annualized Income Installment Method and/or Adjusted Seasonal Installment Method.—If the corporation's income varied during the year because, for example, it operated its business on a seasonal basis, it may be able to lower or eliminate the amount of one or more required installments by using the annualized income installment method or the adjusted seasonal installment method. For example, a ski shop, which receives most of its income during the winter months, may benefit from using one or both of these methods in figuring its required installments. The annualized income installment or adjusted seasonal installment may be less than the required installment under the regular method for one or more due dates. This will reduce or eliminate the penalty for those due dates.

To use one or both of these methods to figure one or more required installments, use the worksheet on pages 3 and 4 of these instructions. If the worksheet is used for any payment due date, it must be used for **all** payment due dates. To arrive at the amount of each required installment, the worksheet automatically selects the smallest of: (a) the annualized income installment, (b) the adjusted seasonal installment (if applicable), or (c) the regular installment under section 6655(d) (increased by any reduction recapture under section 6655(e)(1)(B)).

If the corporation is using only the annualized income installment method, it must complete Parts I and III of the worksheet. If it is using only the adjusted seasonal installment method, it must complete Parts II and III of the worksheet. If the corporation is using both methods, it must complete the entire worksheet. Enter in each column on line 6 of Form 2220 the amount from the corresponding column of line 45 of the worksheet. Also attach a copy of the worksheet to Form 2220 and check the box on line 6a.

Line 6b. Large corporations.—A large corporation is a corporation (other than an S corporation) that had, or its predecessor had, taxable income of $1 million or more for any of the 3 tax years immediately preceding the current tax year. For this purpose, taxable income is modified to exclude net operating loss or capital loss carrybacks or carryovers. Members of a controlled group, as defined in section 1563, must divide the $1 million amount among themselves in accordance with rules similar to those in section 1561.

If the annualized income installment method or the adjusted seasonal installment method is not used, follow the instructions below to figure the amount to enter on line 6. Also check the box on line 6b. (If the corporation is using the annualized income installment method and/or the adjusted seasonal installment method, these instructions apply to line 41 of the worksheet.)

If line 4a is smaller than line 4b.—Enter 25% of line 4a in columns (a) through (d) of line 6.

If line 4b is smaller than line 4a.—Enter 25% of line 4b in column (a) of line 6. In column (b), determine the amount to enter as follows:

1. Subtract line 4b from line 4a,

2. Add the result to the amount on line 4a, and

3. Multiply the total in 2 above by 25% and enter the result in column (b).

In columns (c) and (d), enter 25% of line 4a.

Line 7.—In column (a), enter the estimated tax payments deposited by the 15th day of the 4th month of the corporation's tax year; in column (b), enter payments made after the 15th day of the 4th month through the 15th day of the 6th month of the tax year; in column (c), enter payments made after the 15th day of the 6th month through the 15th day of the 9th month of the tax year; and, in column (d), enter payments made after the 15th day of the 9th month through the 15th day of the 12th month of the tax year.

Include in the estimated tax payments any overpayment of tax from the corporation's 1992 return that was credited to the corporation's 1993 estimated tax.

Line 13.—If any of the columns in line 13 shows an underpayment, complete Part II to figure the penalty.

Waiver of Penalty.—If the corporation has an underpayment of tax for any installment due date before March 15, 1994, no penalty will be imposed on any underpayment of estimated tax attributable to changes made by the Act for any period before March 16, 1994. Accordingly, if a corporation has an underpayment on line 13 that is due only to

changes made by the Act, the penalty for that underpayment will be waived for the period from the installment due date to March 15, 1994.

To claim the waiver, affected corporations should write the word "WAIVER" in the bottom margin of page 1. Compute the penalty by refiguring Form 2220 through line 27 on the basis of the law in effect before the changes were made. Subtract the total of columns (a) through (d) of line 27 on the refigured Form 2220 from the total of those columns on Form 2220 based on the changes made by the Act. On the dotted line to the left of line 28, write "Amount waived" and the amount. Subtract the waiver amount from the total of columns (a) through (d), line 27, to arrive at the amount to enter on line 28. Attach a statement showing the computation of the amount of the penalty to be waived (with references to the changes in the law that justify the waiver).

Part II. Figuring the Penalty

Complete lines 15 through 28 to determine the amount of the penalty. The penalty is figured for the period of underpayment determined under section 6655 using the underpayment rate determined under section 6621(a)(2). For underpayments paid after March 31, 1994, see the instructions below for lines 23 through 26.

Line 15.—A payment of estimated tax is applied against underpayments of required installments in the order that installments are required to be paid, regardless of which installment the payment pertains to.

For example, a corporation has an underpayment for the April 15 installment of $1,000. The June 15 installment requires a payment of $2,500. On June 10, the corporation deposits $2,500 to cover the June 15 installment. However, $1,000 of this payment is considered to be for the April 15 installment. The penalty for the April 15 installment is figured to June 10 (56 days). The payment to be applied to the June 15 installment will then be $1,500.

If the corporation has made more than one payment for a required installment, attach a separate computation for each payment.

Lines 23 through 26.—For underpayments paid after March 31, 1994, use the penalty rate for each calendar quarter that the IRS will determine during the first month in the preceding quarter. These rates are published quarterly in the Internal Revenue Bulletin. You can also call toll-free 1-800-829-1040 to get rate information.

Instructions for Worksheet

Part I—Annualized Income Installment Method

Line 4. Filers of Forms 990-PF and 990-T.—The period to be used to figure taxable income for each column is as follows: **column (a)**, first 2 months; **column (b)**, first 4 months; **column (c)**, first 7 months; and **column (d)**, first 10 months.

Line 5. Filers of Forms 990-PF and 990-T.—The annualization amount to be used in each column is as follows: **column (a)**, 6; **column (b)**, 3; **column (c)**, 1.71429; and **column (d)**, 1.2.

Line 9.—Enter the taxes the corporation owed because of events that occurred during

the months shown in the column headings used to figure annualized taxable income. Include the same taxes used to figure line 1 of Form 2220, but do not include the personal holding company tax or interest due under the look-back method of section 460(b)(2) for completed long-term contracts.

Figure the alternative minimum tax and environmental tax on **Form 4626**, Alternative Minimum Tax–Corporations. Figure alternative minimum taxable income and modified alternative minimum taxable income based on the corporation's income and deductions during the months shown in the column headings used to figure annualized taxable income. Multiply the alternative minimum taxable income and modified alternative minimum taxable income by the annualization amounts used to figure annualized taxable income (on line 2 or line 5) before subtracting the exemption amounts (see sections 55(d) and 59A(a)(2)).

Line 11.—Enter the credits allowed due to events that occurred during the months shown in the column headings used to figure annualized taxable income.

Line 15.—Before completing line 15 in columns (b) through (d), complete line 16; Part II (if applicable); and lines 40 through 45, in each of the preceding columns. For example, complete line 16, lines 17 through 39 (if using the adjusted seasonal installment method), and lines 40 through 45, in column (a) before completing line 15 in column (b).

Part II—Adjusted Seasonal Installment Method

Do not complete this part unless the corporation's base period percentage for any 6 consecutive months of the tax year equals or exceeds 70%. The base period percentage for any period of 6 consecutive months is the average of the 3 percentages figured by dividing the taxable income for the corresponding 6 consecutive month period in each of the 3 preceding tax years by the taxable income for each of their respective tax years.

Example. An amusement park that has a calendar year as its tax year receives the largest part of its taxable income during the 6-month period from May through October. To compute its base period percentage for the period May through October 1993, it must figure its taxable income for the period May through October in each of the years: 1990, 1991, and 1992. The taxable income for each May-through-October period is then divided by the total taxable income for the tax year in which the period is included, resulting in the following quotients: .69 for May through October 1990, .74 for May through October 1991, and .67 for May through October 1992. Since the average of .69, .74, and .67 is equal to .70, the base period percentage for May through October 1993 is 70%. Therefore, the amusement park qualifies for the adjusted seasonal installment method.

Line 33.—Enter the taxes the corporation owed because of events that occurred during the months shown in the column headings above line 17. Include the same taxes used to figure line 1 of Form 2220, but do not include the personal holding company tax or interest due under the look-back method of section 460(b)(2) for completed long-term contracts.

Figure the alternative minimum tax and environmental tax on Form 4626. Figure alternative minimum taxable income and modified alternative minimum taxable income based on the corporation's income and deductions during the months shown in the column headings above line 17. Divide the alternative minimum taxable income and modified alternative minimum taxable income by the amounts shown on line 24 before subtracting the exemption amounts (see sections 55(d) and 59A(a)(2)). For columns (a) through (c) only, multiply the alternative minimum tax and environmental tax determined by the amounts shown on line 31.

Line 35.—Enter the credits allowed due to events that occurred during the months shown in the column headings above line 17.

Line 38.—Before completing line 38 in columns (b) through (d), complete lines 39 through 45 in each of the preceding columns. For example, complete lines 39 through 45 in column (a) before completing line 38 in column (b).

Worksheet to Figure Required Installments Using the Annualized Income Installment Method and/or the Adjusted Seasonal Installment Method Under Section 6655(e)

Form 1120S filers: *For lines 1, 4, 17, 18, and 19, below, "taxable income" refers to excess net passive income or the amount on which tax is imposed under section 1374(a) (or the corresponding provisions of prior law), whichever applies.*

Part I	Annualized Income Installment Method		(a)	(b)	(c)	(d)
				Period		
				First 3 months	First 6 months	First 9 months
1	Enter taxable income for each period.	1				
2	Annualization amounts.	2		4	2	1.33333
3	Multiply line 1 by line 2.	3				
	Form 990-PF and Form 990-T filers: *Do not use the periods shown directly above line 4 or the annualization amounts shown on line 5 when figuring lines 4 and 6. Instead, see the instructions for Worksheet lines 4 and 5.*			**Period**		
			First 3 months	First 5 months	First 8 months	First 11 months
4	Enter taxable income for each period.	4				
5	Annualization amounts.	5	4	2.4	1.5	1.09091
6	Multiply line 4 by line 5.	6				
7	Annualized taxable income. In column (a), enter the amount from line 6, column (a). In columns (b), (c), and (d), enter the **smaller** of the amounts in each column on line 3 or line 6.	7				
8	Figure the tax on the amount in each column on line 7 using the instructions for Form 1120, Schedule J, line 3 (or the comparable line of the tax return).	8				
9	Enter other taxes for each payment period (see instructions).	9				
10	Total tax. Add lines 8 and 9.	10				
11	For each period, enter the same type of credits as allowed on Form 2220, lines 1 and 2c (see instructions).	11				
12	Total tax after credits. Subtract line 11 from line 10. If zero or less, enter -0-.	12				
13	Applicable percentage.	13	24.25%	48.5%	72.75%	97%
14	Multiply line 12 by line 13.	14				
15	Add the amounts in all preceding columns of line 45 (see instructions).	15				
16	Subtract line 15 from line 14. If zero or less, enter -0-.	16				

Part II	Adjusted Seasonal Installment Method (Caution: *Use this method only if the base period percentage for any 6 consecutive months is at least 70%. See the instructions for more information.*)		(a)	(b)	(c)	(d)
				Period		
			First 3 months	First 5 months	First 8 months	First 11 months
17	Enter taxable income for the following periods:					
a	Tax year beginning in 1990	17a				
b	Tax year beginning in 1991	17b				
c	Tax year beginning in 1992	17c				
18	Enter taxable income for each period for the tax year beginning in 1993.	18				

Page 3

		(a)	(b)	(c)	(d)
				Period	
		First 4 months	First 6 months	First 9 months	Entire year
19	Enter taxable income for the following periods:				
a	Tax year beginning in 1990 **19a**				
b	Tax year beginning in 1991 **19b**				
c	Tax year beginning in 1992 **19c**				
20	Divide the amount in each column on line 17a by the amount in column (d) on line 19a. **20**				
21	Divide the amount in each column on line 17b by the amount in column (d) on line 19b. **21**				
22	Divide the amount in each column on line 17c by the amount in column (d) on line 19c. **22**				
23	Add lines 20 through 22. **23**				
24	Divide line 23 by 3. **24**				
25	Divide line 18 by line 24. **25**				
26	Figure the tax on the amount on line 25 using the instructions for Form 1120, Schedule J, line 3 (or the comparable line of the return). **26**				
27	Divide the amount in columns (a) through (c) on line 19a by the amount in column (d) on line 19a. **27**				
28	Divide the amount in columns (a) through (c) on line 19b by the amount in column (d) on line 19b. **28**				
29	Divide the amount in columns (a) through (c) on line 19c by the amount in column (d) on line 19c. **29**				
30	Add lines 27 through 29. **30**				
31	Divide line 30 by 3. **31**				
32	Multiply the amount in columns (a) through (c) of line 26 by the amount in the corresponding column of line 31. In column (d), enter the amount from line 26, column (d). **32**				
33	Enter other taxes for each payment period (see instructions). **33**				
34	Total tax. Add lines 32 and 33. **34**				
35	For each period, enter the same type of credits as allowed on Form 2220, lines 1 and 2c (see instructions). **35**				
36	Total tax after credits. Subtract line 35 from line 34. If zero or less, enter -0-. **36**				
37	Multiply line 36 by 97%. **37**				
38	Add the amounts in all preceding columns of line 45 (see instructions). **38**				
39	Subtract line 38 from line 37. If zero or less, enter -0-. **39**				

Part III   Required Installments

		1st installment	2nd installment	3rd installment	4th installment
40	If only one of the above parts is completed, enter the amounts in each column from line 16 or line 39. If both parts are completed, enter the smaller of the amounts in each column from line 16 or line 39. **40**				
41	Divide line 4c, Form 2220, by 4 and enter the result in each column. **(Note:** *"Large corporations" see the instructions for line 6(b) on page 2 for the amount to enter.)* **41**				
42	Enter the amount from line 44 of the preceding column. **42**				
43	Add lines 41 and 42. **43**				
44	If line 43 is more than line 40, subtract line 40 from line 43. Otherwise, enter -0-. **44**				
45	**Required installments.** Enter the smaller of line 40 or line 43 here and on Form 2220, line 6. **45**				

B-7 Forms for Computation of Minimum Tax

Form **4626**	**Alternative Minimum Tax—Corporations** (including environmental tax) ▶ See separate instructions. ▶ Attach to the corporation's tax return.	OMB No. 1545-0175

Department of the Treasury
Internal Revenue Service

19**93**

Name | Employer identification number

1 Taxable income or (loss) before net operating loss deduction. (**Important:** See instructions if the corporation is subject to the environmental tax.) **1**

2 Adjustments:

a Depreciation of tangible property placed in service after 1986 . . . . . . | **2a**

b Amortization of certified pollution control facilities placed in service after 1986 . | **2b**

c Amortization of mining exploration and development costs paid or incurred after 1986 . | **2c**

d Amortization of circulation expenditures paid or incurred after 1986 (personal holding companies only) . . . . | **2d**

e Basis adjustments in determining gain or loss from sale or exchange of property . | **2e**

f Long-term contracts entered into after February 28, 1986. . . . . | **2f**

g Installment sales of certain property . . . . | **2g**

h Merchant marine capital construction funds . . . . | **2h**

i Section 833(b) deduction (Blue Cross, Blue Shield, and similar type organizations only) . | **2i**

j Tax shelter farm activities (personal service corporations only) . . . . . . | **2j**

k Passive activities (closely held corporations and personal service corporations only) | **2k**

l Certain loss limitations . . . . | **2l**

m Other adjustments . . . . | **2m**

n Combine lines 2a through 2m **2n**

3 Tax preference items:

a Depletion . . . . | **3a**

b Tax-exempt interest from private activity bonds issued after August 7, 1986 . | **3b**

c Charitable contributions . . . . | **3c**

d Intangible drilling costs . . . . | **3d**

e Reserves for losses on bad debts of financial institutions . . . . | **3e**

f Accelerated depreciation of real property placed in service before 1987 . . . | **3f**

g Accelerated depreciation of leased personal property placed in service before 1987 (personal holding companies only). . . . . | **3g**

h Add lines 3a through 3g **3h**

4 Preadjustment alternative minimum taxable income (AMTI). Combine lines 1, 2n, and 3h **4**

5 Adjusted current earnings (ACE) adjustment:

a Enter the corporation's ACE from line 10 of the worksheet on page 8 of the instructions | **5a**

b Subtract line 4 from line 5a. If line 4 exceeds line 5a, enter the difference as a negative number (see instructions for examples) . . . . | **5b**

c Multiply line 5b by 75% and enter the result as a positive number . . . . . | **5c**

d Enter the excess, if any, of the corporation's total increases in AMTI from prior year ACE adjustments over its total reductions in AMTI from prior year ACE adjustments (see instructions). **Note:** You **must** enter an amount on line 5d (even if line 5b is positive) . . . . | **5d**

e ACE adjustment:

• If you entered a positive number or zero on line 5b, enter the amount from line 5c on line 5e as a positive amount.

• If you entered a negative number on line 5b, enter the smaller of line 5c or line 5d on line 5e as a negative amount. | **5e**

6 Combine lines 4 and 5e. If zero or less, stop here (the corporation is not subject to the alternative minimum tax). **6**

7 Alternative tax net operating loss deduction (see instructions) **7**

8 Alternative minimum taxable income. Subtract line 7 from line 6. . . . . **8**

For Paperwork Reduction Act Notice, see separate instructions.   Cat. No. 12955I   Form **4626** (1993)

1993

**Department of the Treasury
Internal Revenue Service**

Instructions for Form 4626
Alternative Minimum Tax—Corporations
Section references are to the Internal Revenue Code unless otherwise noted.

Paperwork Reduction Act Notice

We ask for the information on this form to carry out the Internal Revenue laws of the United States. You are required to give us the information. We need it to ensure that you are complying with these laws and to allow us to figure and collect the right amount of tax.

The time needed to complete and file this form will vary depending on individual circumstances. The estimated average time is:

Recordkeeping . . . . 18 hr., 39 min.

Learning about the law or the form . . . . 14 hr.

Preparing and sending the form to the IRS . . . 14 hr., 56 min.

If you have comments concerning the accuracy of these time estimates or suggestions for making this form more simple, we would be happy to hear from you. You can write to both the IRS and the Office of Management and Budget at the addresses listed in the instructions for the tax return with which this form is filed.

General Instructions

Changes To Note

The Energy Policy Act of 1992 made the following changes that affect the alternative minimum tax for tax years beginning after 1992:

● The preference for depletion no longer applies to independent producers or royalty owners claiming percentage depletion for oil and gas wells under section 613A(c).

● The preference for intangible drilling costs generally no longer applies to corporations that are independent producers (i.e., not integrated oil companies as defined in section 291(b)(4)). However, the benefit of this exclusion may be limited. See page 4.

● The adjusted current earnings (ACE) adjustment for depletion no longer applies to independent producers or royalty owners claiming percentage depletion for oil and gas wells under section 613A(c).

● The ACE adjustment for intangible drilling costs for oil or gas wells no longer applies to corporations that are independent producers (i.e., not integrated oil companies as defined in section 291(b)(4)).

● The adjustment based on energy preferences has been repealed.

The Revenue Reconciliation Act of 1993 made the following additional changes:

● The preference for contributions of appreciated property was repealed for contributions of tangible personal property made after June 30, 1992, and for all other contributions made after 1992. In addition, no adjustment related to the earnings and profits effects of any contribution is included in ACE.

● The ACE depreciation adjustment does not apply to property placed in service after 1993.

Who Must File

File Form 4626 if the corporation's taxable income or (loss) before the net operating loss **(NOL)** deduction when combined with its adjustments and tax preference items (including the ACE adjustment) totals more than the smaller of: **(a)** $40,000 or **(b)** its allowable exemption amount.

Short Period Return

If this is a short period return, use the formula in section 443(d) to determine the corporation's alternative minimum taxable income **(AMTI)** and alternative minimum tax **(AMT)**.

Apportionment of Differently Treated Items in Case of Certain Entities

If you are preparing Form 4626 for a regulated investment company, a real estate investment trust, or a common trust fund, see section 59(d).

Credit for Prior Year Minimum Tax

See **Form 8827**, Credit for Prior Year Minimum Tax—Corporations, for details concerning the computation of the credit.

Specific Instructions

Line 1. Taxable income or (loss) before net operating loss deduction.—Enter the corporation's taxable income or (loss) before the NOL deduction. For example, if you file Form 1120, subtract line 29b from line 28 of that form.

Important: *If the corporation is subject to the environmental tax, you will generally need to figure that tax on line 17 before completing line 1 (see instructions for line 17).*

Line 2a. Depreciation of tangible property placed in service after 1986.—The following rules apply to tangible property placed in service after 1986 (or after July 31, 1986, if you made the transitional election under section 203(a)(1)(B) of the Tax Reform Act of 1986):

Caution: *Do not include depreciation adjustments attributable to passive activities or tax shelter farm activities on line 2a. Instead, include them on line 2j or 2k.*

The depreciation expense allowable for regular tax purposes under section 167 with respect to any tangible property placed in service after 1986 must be recomputed for AMT purposes under the alternative depreciation system **(ADS)** described in section 168(g) as follows:

1. For any real property described in section 1250(c) (generally nonresidential real and residential rental), use the straight line method over 40 years with the same mid-month convention used for regular tax purposes;

2. For any tangible property (other than the real property described in **1** above) for which depreciation for regular tax purposes is determined using the straight line method, recompute the depreciation expense using the straight line method over the property's class life with the same convention used for regular tax purposes;

3. For all tangible property other than property described in **1** or **2** above, use the 150% declining balance method, switching to the straight line method the first tax year it gives a larger deduction, over the property's class life. Use the same convention used for regular tax purposes.

In applying the above rules:

1. The class life you use for AMT purposes is not necessarily the same as the recovery period used for regular tax purposes. The class lives you use for AMT purposes are listed in Rev. Proc. 87-56, 1987-2 C.B. 674, or in **Pub. 534**, Depreciation. Use 12 years for any tangible personal property that does not have an assigned class life;

2. See Rev. Proc. 87-57, 1987-2 C.B. 687, for optional tables (14 through 18) that you can use to figure depreciation for AMT purposes. (These optional tables also appear in Pub. 534.);

3. Do not make an adjustment for: **(a)** property for which the corporation made a section 168(g)(7) election (to use the ADS of section 168(g)) for regular tax purposes, **(b)** property expensed under section 179 for regular tax purposes, or **(c)** property described in sections 168(f)(1) through (4); and

4. You must consider the transitional rules (described in section 56(a)(1)(C)) and the normalization rules (described in section 56(a)(1)(D)).

Subtract the recomputed AMT expense from the depreciation expense claimed for regular tax purposes and enter the result on line 2a. If the recomputed AMT expense is more than the depreciation expense claimed for regular tax purposes, enter the difference as a negative amount.

Note: *Depreciation that is capitalized to inventory under the uniform capitalization rules must be refigured using the rules described above.*

Line 2b. Amortization of certified pollution control facilities placed in service after 1986.—The amortization deduction claimed

for regular tax purposes is not allowed for AMT purposes.

For AMT purposes, use the ADS described in section 168(g) (i.e., use the straight line method over the facility's class life). The facility's class life is listed in Rev. Proc. 87-56 or in Pub. 534.

Note: *Section 168(g) applies to 100% of the asset's amortizable basis. Do not reduce the corporation's AMT basis by the 20% section 291 adjustment that applied for regular tax purposes.*

Subtract the recomputed AMT expense from the expense claimed for regular tax purposes and enter the result on line 2b. If the recomputed AMT expense is more than the expense claimed for regular tax purposes, enter the difference as a negative amount.

Line 2c. Amortization of mining exploration and development costs paid or incurred after 1986.—*If, for regular tax purposes, the corporation elected the optional 10-year writeoff under section 59(e) for all assets in this category, skip this line (no adjustment is necessary).*

The deduction claimed for regular tax purposes under sections 616(a) and 617(a) is not allowed for AMT purposes. Instead, capitalize those costs and amortize them ratably over a 10-year period beginning with the tax year in which the corporation made them.

Note: *The 10-year amortization applies to 100% of the mining development and exploration costs paid or incurred during the tax year. Do not reduce the corporation's AMT basis by the 30% section 291 adjustment that applied for regular tax purposes.*

Subtract the recomputed AMT expense from the expense claimed for regular tax purposes and enter the result on line 2c. If the recomputed AMT expense is more than the expense claimed for regular tax purposes, enter the difference as a negative amount. See section 56(a)(2)(B) if the corporation had a loss from any mine or other natural deposit (other than an oil, gas, or geothermal well).

Line 2d. Amortization of circulation expenditures paid or incurred after 1986 (personal holding companies only).—*If, for regular tax purposes, the corporation elected the optional 3-year writeoff under section 59(e) for all of these expenditures, skip this line (no adjustment is necessary).*

The deduction claimed for regular tax purposes (under section 173) for these expenditures incurred after 1986 is not allowed for AMT purposes. For AMT purposes, capitalize these expenditures and amortize them ratably over a 3-year period beginning with the tax year in which the corporation made them.

Subtract the recomputed AMT expense from the expense claimed for regular tax purposes and enter the result on line 2d. If the recomputed AMT expense is more than the expense claimed for regular tax purposes, enter the difference as a negative amount. See section 56(b)(2)(B) if the corporation had a loss from circulation expenditures deducted under section 173.

Line 2e. Basis adjustments in determining gain or loss from sale or exchange of property.—If, during the tax year, the corporation disposed of property for which

you are making (or have previously made) any of the adjustments described in lines 2a through 2d above, recompute the property's adjusted basis for AMT purposes. Then recompute the gain or loss on the disposition.

The property's adjusted basis for AMT purposes is its cost minus all applicable depreciation or amortization deductions allowed for AMT purposes during the current tax year and previous tax years. Then, subtract this recomputed basis from the sales price to arrive at the gain or loss for AMT purposes.

Note: *The corporation may also have gains or losses from lines 2j, 2k, and 2l that must be taken into consideration on line 2e. For example, if for regular tax purposes the corporation reports a loss from the disposition of an asset used in a passive activity, include the loss in the computations for line 2k to determine whether any passive activity loss is limited for AMT purposes. Then, include the portion of the AMT passive activity loss allowed that pertains to the disposition of the asset on line 2e in determining the corporation's AMT basis adjustment. It may be helpful to refigure Form 8810 and related worksheets and Schedule D (Form 1120), Form 4684 (Section B), or Form 4797 for AMT purposes.*

Enter the difference between the gain or loss for regular tax purposes and the recomputed gain or loss for AMT purposes. Enter the difference as a negative amount if:

● The gain recomputed for AMT purposes is less than the gain computed for regular tax purposes, OR

● The loss recomputed for AMT purposes is more than the loss computed for regular tax purposes, OR

● The corporation recomputed a loss for AMT purposes and computed a gain for regular tax purposes.

Line 2f. Long-term contracts entered into after February 28, 1986.—For AMT purposes, use the percentage-of-completion method rules described in section 460(b) to determine the taxable income from any "long-term contract" (defined in section 460(f)) entered into after February 28, 1986. However, this rule does not apply to: **(1)** any "home construction contract" (as defined in section 460(e)(6)) entered into after June 20, 1988, for which the corporation meets the "small" home construction contract requirements of section 460(e)(1)(B) or **(2) any** home construction contract entered into in a tax year beginning after September 30, 1990, regardless of whether the corporation meets the "small" home construction contract requirements of section 460(e)(1)(B).

Note: *In the case of a contract described in section 460(e)(1), determine the percentage of the contract completed using the simplified procedures for allocating costs outlined in section 460(b)(4).*

Subtract the income reported for regular tax purposes from the income recomputed for AMT purposes and enter the difference on line 2f. If the recomputed AMT income is less than the income reported for regular tax purposes, enter the difference as a negative amount.

Line 2g. Installment sales of certain property.—For either of the following kinds of dispositions in which the corporation used the installment method for regular tax purposes,

refigure its income for AMT purposes without regard to the installment method:

1. Any disposition after March 1, 1986, of property used or produced in the corporation's farming business that it held primarily for sale to customers.

2. Any nondealer disposition of property that occurred after August 16, 1986, but before the first day of the corporation's tax year that began in 1987, if an obligation that arose from the disposition was an installment obligation to which the proportionate disallowance rule applied.

Enter on line 2g the difference between the income recomputed for AMT purposes and the income reported for regular tax purposes. If the income recomputed for regular tax purposes is more than the income recomputed for AMT purposes, enter the difference as a negative amount.

Line 2h. Merchant marine capital construction funds.—Amounts deposited in these funds (established under section 607 of the Merchant Marine Act of 1936) after 1986 are not deductible for AMT purposes. Earnings on these funds are not excludable from gross income for AMT purposes. If the corporation deducted these amounts or excluded them from income for regular tax purposes, add them back on line 2h. See section 56(c)(2) for more information.

Line 2i. Section 833(b) deduction (Blue Cross, Blue Shield, and similar type organizations only).—This deduction is not allowed for AMT purposes. If the corporation took this deduction for regular tax purposes, add it back on line 2i.

Line 2j. Tax shelter farm activities (personal service corporations only).—Complete line 2j only if the corporation has a gain or loss from a tax shelter farm activity (as defined in section 58(a)(2)) that is **not** a passive activity. If the tax shelter farm activity **is** a passive activity, you must include the gain or loss in the computations for line 2k below.

Recompute all gains and losses reported for regular tax purposes from tax shelter farm activities by taking into account the corporation's AMT adjustments and tax preference items.

Important: *To avoid duplication, do not include any AMT adjustment or tax preference item taken into account on line 2j in the amounts to be entered on any other line of this form.*

Determine the corporation's tax shelter farm activity gain or loss for AMT purposes using the same rules used for regular tax purposes with the following modification: No recomputed loss is allowed, except to the extent the personal service corporation is insolvent (see section 58(c)(1)). Do not use a recomputed loss in the current tax year to offset gains from other tax shelter farm activities. Instead, suspend any recomputed loss and carry it forward indefinitely until: **(1)** the corporation has a gain in a subsequent tax year from that same tax shelter farm activity, OR **(2)** it disposes of the activity.

Note: *The amount of any tax shelter farm activity loss that is not deductible (and is therefore carried forward) for AMT purposes is likely to differ from the amount (if any) that is suspended and carried forward for regular tax*

Page 2

purposes. Keep adequate records for both AMT purposes and regular tax purposes.

Enter on line 2j the difference between the gain or loss recomputed for AMT purposes and the gain or loss reported for regular tax purposes. Enter the difference as a negative amount if the corporation:

• Reported a loss for AMT purposes and a gain for regular tax purposes, OR

• Recomputed a loss for AMT purposes that exceeds the loss reported for regular tax purposes, OR

• Reported a gain for regular tax purposes that exceeds the gain recomputed for AMT purposes.

Line 2k. Passive activities (closely held corporations and personal service corporations only).—Recompute all passive activity gains and losses reported for regular tax purposes by taking into account the corporation's AMT adjustments, tax preference items, and AMT prior year unallowed losses.

Important: *To avoid duplication, do not include any AMT adjustment or tax preference item taken into account on line 2k in the amounts to be entered on any other line of this form.*

Determine the corporation's passive activity gain or loss for AMT purposes using the same rules used for regular tax purposes. If the corporation is insolvent, see section 58(c)(1).

Disallowed losses of a personal service corporation are suspended until the corporation has income from that (or any other) passive activity or until the passive activity is disposed of (i.e., its passive losses cannot offset "net active income" (defined in section 469(e)(2)(B)) or "portfolio income"). Disallowed losses of a closely held corporation that is not a personal service corporation are treated the same except that, in addition, they may be used to offset "net active income."

Note: *The amount of any passive activity loss that is not deductible (and is therefore suspended and carried forward) for AMT purposes is likely to differ from the amount (if any) that is carried forward for regular tax purposes. Keep adequate records for both AMT purposes and regular tax purposes.*

Enter on line 2k the difference between the gain or loss recomputed for AMT purposes and the gain or loss reported for regular tax purposes. Enter the difference as a negative amount if the corporation:

• Reported a loss for AMT purposes and a gain for regular tax purposes, OR

• Recomputed a loss for AMT purposes that exceeds the loss reported for regular tax purposes, OR

• Reported a gain for regular tax purposes that exceeds the gain recomputed for AMT purposes.

Tax shelter farm activities that are passive activities.—Recompute all gains and losses reported for regular tax purposes by taking into account the corporation's AMT adjustments, tax preference items, and AMT prior year unallowed losses.

Important: *To avoid duplication, do not include any AMT adjustment or tax preference item taken into account here in the amounts to be entered on any other line of this form.*

Take into account these recomputed gains and losses when figuring the corporation's passive activity gain or loss for AMT purposes described above. Use the same rules outlined above, with the following additional modification: Recomputed gains from tax shelter farm activities that are passive activities may be used to offset recomputed losses from other passive activities. However, recomputed losses from tax shelter farm activities that are passive activities may not be used to offset recomputed gains from other passive activities. (Recomputed losses from tax shelter farm activities that are passive activities are disallowed and must be suspended and carried forward as explained in the instructions for line 2j.)

Line 2l. Certain loss limitations.—Recompute gains and losses reported for regular tax purposes from at-risk activities and partnerships by taking into account the corporation's AMT adjustments and tax preference items. If the corporation has recomputed losses that must (in accordance with section 59(h)) be limited for AMT purposes by section 465 or by section 704(d) OR if, for regular tax purposes, the corporation reported losses from at-risk activities or partnerships that were limited by those sections, compute the difference between the loss limited for AMT purposes and the loss limited for regular tax purposes for each applicable at-risk activity or partnership. For this purpose, "loss limited" means the amount of loss that is not allowable for the year due to the limitation of section 465 or 704(d).

Enter on line 2l the excess of the loss limited for AMT purposes over the loss limited for regular tax purposes. If the loss limited for regular tax purposes is more than the loss limited for AMT purposes, enter the difference as a negative amount.

Line 2m. Other adjustments.—Include on this line:

1. Income eligible for the possessions tax credit—The corporation's AMTI must not include any income (from the sources described in section 936(a)(1)) that is eligible for the possessions tax credit of section 936. If you included this type of income in the corporation's taxable income for regular tax purposes, enter the amount on line 2m as a negative amount.

2. Income with respect to the alcohol fuel credit—The corporation's AMTI must not include any amount with respect to the alcohol fuel credit that was included in the corporation's gross income under section 87. If this type of income was included in the corporation's income for regular tax purposes, enter the amount on line 2m as a negative amount.

3. Income as the beneficiary of an estate or trust—If the corporation is the beneficiary of an estate or trust, enter the minimum taxable income adjustment from Schedule K-1 (Form 1041), line 8.

4. Related adjustments—AMT adjustments and tax preference items may affect deductions that are based on an income limit. Refigure these deductions using the income limit as modified for AMT purposes. Include on line 2m an adjustment for the total difference between the regular tax and AMT amounts for all such deductions and include it on line 2m. If the AMT deduction is more

than the regular tax deduction, enter the difference as a negative amount.

Note: *Do not make an adjustment on line 2m for an item you refigured on another line of this form (e.g., line 3a or 3c).*

Example. The corporation has taxable income derived from the active conduct of a trade or business of $9,000 (before the net operating loss deduction, special deductions, and the section 179 expense deduction). During the year, the corporation purchased a business asset for $10,000 for which it elects to take the section 179 expense deduction. The corporation also has an AMT depreciation adjustment of $700 for other depreciable assets. The corporation's section 179 expense deduction is limited to $9,000, its taxable income derived from the active conduct of a trade or business (before the net operating loss deduction, special deductions, and the section 179 expense deduction). The $1,000 excess is a section 179 expense deduction carryforward for regular tax purposes. But, for AMT purposes, the section 179 taxable income limit is $9,700, so it is allowed a section 179 expense deduction of $9,700 for AMT purposes. The corporation has a section 179 expense deduction carryforward of $300 for AMT purposes. Therefore, it includes a $700 negative adjustment on line 2m because its section 179 expense deduction for AMT purposes is $700 greater than its allowable regular tax deduction. In the following year, when the corporation uses the $1,000 regular tax carryforward, it will have a $700 positive adjustment for AMT purposes because its AMT carryforward is only $300.

Line 3a. Depletion.—The corporation's depletion deduction must be refigured for AMT purposes. To do so, use only income and deductions allowed for AMT purposes when refiguring the limit based on taxable income from the property under section 613(a) and the limit based on taxable income, with certain adjustments, under section 613A(d)(1). Also, the depletion deduction for mines, wells, and other natural deposits under section 611 is limited to the property's adjusted basis at the end of the year, as refigured for AMT purposes, unless the corporation is an independent producer or royalty owner claiming percentage depletion for oil and gas wells under section 613A(c). Figure this limit separately for each property. When refiguring the property's adjusted basis, take into account any AMT adjustments the corporation made this year or in previous years that affect basis (other than the current year's depletion). Do not include in the property's adjusted basis any unrecovered costs of depreciable tangible property used to exploit the deposits (e.g., machinery, tools, pipes, etc.).

Enter on line 3a the difference between the regular tax and the AMT deduction. If the AMT deduction is more than the regular tax deduction, enter the difference as a negative amount.

Note: *For iron ore and coal (including lignite), apply the section 291 adjustment before figuring this tax preference item.*

Line 3b. Tax-exempt interest from private activity bonds issued after August 7, 1986.—Enter interest earned on specified private activity bonds reduced by any deduction that would have been allowable if the interest were includible in gross income

for regular tax purposes. Generally, a "specified private activity bond" is any private activity bond (as defined in section 141) issued after August 7, 1986. See section 57(a)(5) for exceptions and for more information.

Line 3c. Charitable contributions.—The corporation's charitable contributions deduction must be refigured for AMT purposes. To do so, use only income and deductions allowed for AMT purposes when refiguring the limit based on taxable income under section 170(b)(2). Also, any AMT carryover of charitable contributions is limited to the cost or other basis (instead of fair market value) for any contribution of capital gain or section 1231 property for which the preference for charitable contributions of appreciated property applied. The preference for charitable contributions of appreciated property does not apply to any contribution made after 1992 or to any contribution of tangible personal property made in a tax year beginning after 1990. It also does not apply to contributions of property for which you elected under section 170(b)(1)(C)(iii) to figure the deduction using the property's adjusted basis rather than its fair market value.

Enter on line 3c the difference between the regular tax purposes and the AMT deduction. If the AMT deduction is more than the regular tax deduction, enter the difference as a negative amount.

Line 3d. Intangible drilling costs.—*If, for regular tax purposes, the corporation elected the optional 60-month writeoff under section 59(e) for all assets in this category, skip this line (no adjustment is necessary).*

Intangible drilling costs (**IDCs**) from oil, gas, and geothermal properties are a tax preference item to the extent that excess IDCs exceed 65% of the net income from the properties. The tax preference item is computed separately for geothermal deposits, and for oil and gas properties that is not geothermal deposits.

"Excess IDCs" are the excess of: **(1)** the amount of IDCs the corporation paid or incurred with respect to oil, gas, or geothermal properties that it elected to expense for regular tax purposes under section 263(c) (not including any section 263(c) deduction for nonproductive wells) reduced by the section 291 adjustment for integrated oil companies; over **(2)** the amount that would have been allowed if the corporation had amortized that amount over a 120-month period starting with the month the well was placed in production.

Note: *If the corporation prefers not to use the 120-month period, it can elect to use any method that is permissible in determining cost depletion.*

"Net income" is the gross income the corporation received or accrued from all oil, gas, and geothermal wells minus the deductions allocable to these properties (reduced by the excess IDCs). When refiguring net income, use only income and deductions allowed for AMT purposes.

Exception. The preference for IDCs does not apply to corporations that are independent producers (i.e., not integrated oil companies as defined in section 291(b)(4)). However, this benefit may be limited. First, figure the IDC preference as if this exception did not apply. Then, for purposes of this exception,

complete a second Form 4626 through line 6, including the IDC preference. On line 7, enter the corporation's regular tax net operating loss deduction (e.g., if the corporation files Form 1120, this would be line 29a of Form 1120). Subtract the amount on line 7 from line 6, and enter the result on line 8 (if zero or less, enter zero). If the amount of the IDC preference exceeds 30% of the amount figured for line 8, enter the excess on line 3d (the benefit of this exception is limited). If the amount of the IDC preference is equal to or less than 30% of the amount figured for line 8, do not enter an amount on line 3d (the benefit of this exception is not limited).

Line 3e. Reserves for losses on bad debts of financial institutions.—Enter the excess of: **(1)** the deduction allowable for a reasonable addition to a reserve for bad debts of a financial institution to which section 593 applies (reduced by the section 291 adjustment), over **(2)** the amount that would have been allowable had the financial institution maintained its bad debt reserve for all tax years on the basis of actual experience.

Line 3f. Accelerated depreciation of real property placed in service before 1987.—Enter the excess of the depreciation claimed for the property for regular tax purposes over the depreciation allowable for AMT purposes as refigured using the straight line method. Figure this amount separately for each property and include only positive adjustments on line 3f. For 15-, 18-, or 19-year real property, use the straight line method over 15, 18, or 19 years, respectively. For low-income housing property, use the straight line method over 15 years.

Line 3g. Accelerated depreciation of leased personal property placed in service before 1987 (personal holding companies only).—For leased personal property, other than recovery property, enter the excess of the depreciation claimed for the property for regular tax purposes over the depreciation allowable for AMT purposes as refigured using the straight line method. Figure this amount separately for each property and include only positive adjustments on line 3g.

For leased recovery property, other than 15-, 18-, or 19-year real property, or low-income housing, enter the amount by which the corporation's depreciation deduction for regular tax purposes is more than the deduction allowable for AMT purposes using the straight line method over the following recovery period:

5-year property . . . . 8 years
10-year property . . . . . . 15 years
15-year public utility property . . 22 years

Adjusted Current Earnings (ACE) Adjustment

Lines 5a through 5e

If you are preparing Form 4626 for a regulated investment company or a real estate investment trust, skip lines 5a through 5e (they do not apply).

Line 5b.—*If you are preparing Form 4626 for an affiliated group that has filed a consolidated tax return for the current tax year under the rules of section 1501, you must figure line 5b on a consolidated basis.*

The following examples illustrate the manner in which line 4 is subtracted from line 5a to arrive at the amount to enter on line 5b:

Example 1: Corporation A has line 5a ACE of $25,000. If Corporation A has line 4 pre-adjustment AMTI in the amounts shown below, its line 4 pre-adjustment AMTI and line 5a ACE would be combined as shown below to determine the amount to enter on line 5b:

Line 5a ACE	$25,000	$25,000	$25,000
Line 4 pre-adjustment AMTI	10,000	30,000	(50,000)
Amount to enter on line 5b	$15,000	($5,000)	$75,000

Example 2: Corporation B has line 5a ACE of negative $25,000. If Corporation B has line 4 pre-adjustment AMTI in the amounts shown below, its line 4 pre-adjustment AMTI and line 5a ACE would be combined as shown below to determine the amount to enter on line 5b:

Line 5a ACE	($25,000)	($25,000)	($25,000)
Line 4 pre-adjustment AMTI	(10,000)	(30,000)	50,000
Amount to enter on line 5b	($15,000)	$5,000	($75,000)

Line 5d.—Section 56(g)(2)(B) provides that a potential negative ACE adjustment (i.e., a negative amount on line 5b multiplied by 75%) is allowed as a negative ACE adjustment on line 5e only to the extent that the corporation's total increases in AMTI from prior year ACE adjustments exceed its total reductions in AMTI from prior year ACE adjustments (line 5d). The purpose of line 5d is to provide a "running balance" of this limitation amount. As such, you must keep adequate records (e.g., a copy of Form 4626 completed at least through line 6) from year to year (even in years in which the corporation does not owe any AMT).

Regulations section 1.56(g)-1(a)(2)(ii) provides that any potential negative ACE adjustment that is not allowed as a negative ACE adjustment in a tax year because of the line 5d limitation may not be used to reduce a positive ACE adjustment in any other tax year.

Combine lines 5d and 5e of the 1992 Form 4626 and enter the result here on line 5d of the 1993 Form 4626. Do not enter a negative amount on line 5d for the reason given in the preceding paragraph.

Example 3: Corporation C, a calendar-year corporation, has ACE and pre-adjustment AMTI in the following amounts for 1990 through 1993:

Year	ACE	Pre-adjustment AMTI
1990	$700,000	$800,000
1991	900,000	600,000
1992	400,000	500,000
1993	(100,000)	300,000

Corporation C subtracts its pre-adjustment AMTI from its ACE in each of the years and then multiplies the result by 75% to arrive at the following potential ACE adjustments for 1990 through 1993:

Page 4

Form **6251**	**Alternative Minimum Tax—Individuals**	OMB No. 1545-0227

Department of the Treasury
Internal Revenue Service (T)

► See separate instructions.

► **Attach to Form 1040 or Form 1040NR.**

19**93**

Attachment
Sequence No. **32**

Name(s) shown on Form 1040

Your social security number

Part I   Adjustments and Preferences

1 If you itemized deductions on Schedule A (Form 1040), go to line 2. If you did not itemize deductions, enter your standard deduction from Form 1040, line 34, and skip to line 6 . .	**1**
2 Medical and dental expenses. See instructions	**2**
3 Taxes. Enter the amount from Schedule A, line 8 . .	**3**
4 Certain interest on a home mortgage not used to buy, build, or improve your home	**4**
5 Miscellaneous itemized deductions. Enter the amount from Schedule A, line 24	**5**
6 Refund of taxes. Enter any tax refund from Form 1040, line 10 or 22	**6** ( )
7 Investment interest. Enter difference between regular tax and AMT deduction . . .	**7**
8 Post-1986 depreciation. Enter difference between regular tax and AMT depreciation . . .	**8**
9 Adjusted gain or loss. Enter difference between AMT and regular tax gain or loss	**9**
10 Incentive stock options. Enter excess of AMT income over regular tax income	**10**
11 Passive activities. Enter difference between AMT and regular tax income or loss	**11**
12 Beneficiaries of estates and trusts. Enter the amount from Schedule K-1 (Form 1041), line 8	**12**
13 Tax-exempt interest from private activity bonds issued after 8/7/86	**13**

14 Other. Enter the amount, if any, for each item and enter the total on line 14.

a Charitable contributions .	**g** Long-term contracts . .	
b Circulation expenditures .	**h** Loss limitations	
c Depletion	**i** Mining costs	
d Depreciation (pre-1987) .	**j** Pollution control facilities .	
e Installment sales . . .	**k** Research and experimental	
f Intangible drilling costs .	**l** Tax shelter farm activities .	
	m Related adjustments . .	**14**

15 Total Adjustments and Preferences. Combine lines 1 through 14 . . . . ►	**15**

Part II   Alternative Minimum Taxable Income

16 Enter the amount from **Form 1040, line 35.** If less than zero, enter as a (loss) . . . . ►	**16**
17 Net operating loss deduction, if any, from Form 1040, line 22. Enter as a positive amount .	**17**
18 If Form 1040, line 32, is over $108,450 (over $54,225 if married filing separately), enter your itemized deductions limitation, if any, from line 9 of the worksheet for Schedule A, line 26	**18** ( )
19 Combine lines 15 through 18 . . . . ►	**19**
20 Alternative tax net operating loss deduction. See instructions	**20**
21 Alternative Minimum Taxable Income. Subtract line 20 from line 19. (If married filing separately and line 21 is more than $165,000, see instructions.) . . . . ►	**21**

Part III   Exemption Amount and Alternative Minimum Tax

22 Exemption Amount. (If this form is for a child under age 14, see instructions.)

If your filing status is:	And line 21 is not over:	Enter on line 22:	
Single or head of household	$112,500	$33,750	
Married filing jointly or qualifying widow(er)	150,000	45,000	**22**
Married filing separately	75,000	22,500	

If line 21 is **over** the amount shown above for your filing status, see instructions.

23 Subtract line 22 from line 21. If zero or less, enter -0- here and on lines 26 and 28 . . ►	**23**
24 If line 23 is $175,000 or less ($87,500 or less if married filing separately), multiply line 23 by 26% (.26). Otherwise, see instructions	**24**
25 Alternative minimum tax foreign tax credit. See instructions	**25**
26 Tentative minimum tax. Subtract line 25 from line 24 . . . . ►	**26**
27 Enter your tax from Form 1040, line 38 (plus any amount from Form 4970 included on Form 1040, line 39), minus any foreign tax credit from Form 1040, line 43	**27**
28 Alternative Minimum Tax. (If this form is for a child under age 14, see instructions.) Subtract line 27 from line 26. If zero or less, enter -0-. Enter here and on Form 1040, line 48 . . ►	**28**

For Paperwork Reduction Act Notice, see separate instructions.   Cat. No. 13600G   Form **6251** (1993)

93

 **Department of the Treasury**
Internal Revenue Service

Instructions for Form 6251

Alternative Minimum Tax—Individuals

Section references are to the Internal Revenue Code.

Paperwork Reduction Act Notice

We ask for the information on this form to carry out the Internal Revenue laws of the United States. You are required to give us the information. We need it to ensure that you are complying with these laws and to allow us to figure and collect the right amount of tax.

The time needed to complete and file this form will vary depending on individual circumstances. The estimated average time is:

Recordkeeping . . . 2 hr., 17 min.

Learning about the law or the form . . . 1 hr., 16 min.

Preparing the form . . 2 hr., 2 min.

Copying, assembling, and sending the form to the IRS . . . . 20 min.

If you have comments concerning the accuracy of these time estimates or suggestions for making this form more simple, we would be happy to hear from you. You can write to both the IRS and the Office of Management and Budget at the addresses listed in the instructions of the tax return with which this form is filed.

General Instructions

Purpose of Form

The tax laws give special treatment to some types of income and allow special deductions for some types of expenses. These laws enable some taxpayers with substantial economic income to significantly reduce their regular tax. The purpose of the alternative minimum tax (AMT) is to ensure that these taxpayers pay a minimum amount of tax on their economic income. Use Form 6251 to figure the amount, if any, of your AMT.

Changes To Note

Form 6251 Revised

The format of Form 6251 has been revised for 1993. We grouped many of the less common adjustments and preferences together and clarified the explanations for many of the lines. Also, we added a chart to figure the exemption amount on line 22. Most people will be able to quickly enter their

exemption amount after reading the chart.

If you are filing this form for a child under age 14, we have made several changes that will affect you. We expanded the exemption worksheet used to figure the child's exemption amount. We also added a worksheet to figure the child's limit on AMT. This limit was previously figured on Form 8803, which is now obsolete.

Filing Requirements

The filing requirements for Form 6251 have been changed. Most taxpayers who complete Form 6251 and aren't liable for the AMT won't have to attach the form. See **Who Must File** below.

Rates and Exemption Amounts

The AMT tax rate and exemption amounts have increased. See lines 22 and 24 and their instructions.

Appreciated Contributions

The preference for contributions of appreciated property has been repealed for all contributions made after 1992. See the instructions for line 14a on page 4 for more details.

Depletion

The preference for depletion does not apply to 15% depletion for oil and gas wells by independent producers and royalty owners. See page 4.

Intangible Drilling Costs

The preference for intangible drilling costs generally does not apply to taxpayers who are independent producers. However, the benefit of this exclusion may be limited. See page 4.

Who Must File

Complete Form 6251 to see if the AMT applies to you. Attach it to your return **only** if:

● You are liable for the AMT,

● You have certain credits (such as the credit for child and dependent care expenses, etc.) that are limited by the amount shown on line 24 (or in some cases, line 26) (the forms used to figure these credits have details on the limits), or

● The total of lines 7 through 14 is negative and you would be liable for the

AMT without taking those lines into account. This will help show us why you are not liable for the AMT.

Children Under Age 14

Form 6251 must be filed for a child under age 14 if the child's AMT is limited by using the worksheet for line 28 or if line 22 is more than $1,000 plus the child's earned income. A "child under age 14" is any child who was under age 14 on January 1, 1994, at least one of whose parents was alive at the end of 1993.

Additional Information

For more details, get **Pub. 909,** Alternative Minimum Tax for Individuals.

Recordkeeping

For the AMT, certain items of income, deductions, etc., receive different tax treatment than for the regular tax. Therefore, you need to recompute items for the AMT that you figured for the regular tax. In some cases, you may wish to do this by completing the applicable tax form a second time. If you do complete another form, **do not** attach it to your tax return (except for **Form 1116,** Foreign Tax Credit—see the instructions for line 25 on page 7), but keep it for your records.

For the regular tax, some deductions and credits may result in carrybacks or carryforwards to other tax years. Examples are investment interest expense, a net operating loss, a capital loss, and the foreign tax credit. Because you may have to refigure these items for the AMT, the carryback or carryforward amount may be different for the AMT than for the regular tax. Therefore, you should keep records of these different amounts. An AMT carryforward amount will be important in completing Form 6251 the next year.

Partners, Shareholders, etc.

If you are a member of a partnership or a shareholder in an S corporation, your Schedule K-1 will give you information on any adjustments or preferences from the partnership or S corporation that you have to take into account for Form 6251.

Nonresident Aliens

If you are a nonresident alien and you disposed of U.S. real property interests at a gain, see the instructions for line 45 of **Form 1040NR,** U.S. Nonresident Alien Income Tax Return. You may have to enter a different figure on line 23 of Form 6251 if the amount figured on the worksheet in the instructions for line 45 of Form 1040NR is more than the tentative amount you figured on line 23 of Form 6251.

Cat. No. 64277P

Credit For Prior Year Minimum Tax

Get **Form 8801,** Credit For Prior Year Minimum Tax—Individuals and Fiduciaries, if you paid AMT for 1992, or if you had a minimum tax credit carryforward on line 26 of your 1992 Form 8801. If you pay AMT for 1993, you may be able to take a credit on your 1994 Form 8801.

Earned Income Credit

If you have an earned income credit, you must reduce it by any AMT.

Optional Write-Off for Certain Adjustments and Preferences

If you elect to deduct certain adjustments and preferences ratably over a period of time for the regular tax, they are not treated as adjustments or preferences for the AMT. These items are: circulation expenditures (section 173), research and experimental expenditures (section 174(a)), intangible drilling and developmental costs (section 263(c)), development expenditures (section 616(a)), and mining exploration expenditures (section 617(a)). You may elect to deduct circulation expenditures over 3 years, intangible drilling and development costs over 60 months, and the other items over 10 years.

You make the election in the year of the expenditure. You can revoke it only with IRS consent. If you made the election for one of the above items, do not make an adjustment for that item on Form 6251. See section 59(e) for more details.

Specific Instructions

Part I—Adjustments and Preferences

Caution: *To avoid duplication, any adjustment or preference for line 5, 11, 14h, or 14l should not be taken into account in figuring the amount to enter for any other adjustment or preference (except when completing the worksheet on page 6.)*

Line 2—Medical and Dental Expenses

If you do not have an entry on line 1 of Schedule A (Form 1040), skip Form 6251, line 2, and go to Form 6251, line 3. Otherwise, if **none** of the adjustments and preferences on lines 6, 7 (from investment interest on Schedule E (Form 1040)), 8 through 13, 14b through 14l, 17, and 20 apply to you, enter on Form 6251, line 2, the smaller of Schedule A, line 4, or 2.5% of Form 1040, line 32. If **any** of these adjustments and preferences apply to you, complete the **Medical and Dental Expenses Page 2**

Worksheet on this page. Before you start the worksheet, complete Form 6251, lines 6, 7 (if you deducted investment interest on Schedule E), 8 through 13, 14b through 14m, 17, and 20.

Line 3—Taxes

Enter the amount from Schedule A, line 8, but do not include any generation-skipping transfer taxes on income distributions.

Line 4—Certain Home Mortgage Interest

Include on this line home mortgage interest from line 9a, 9b, or 10 of Schedule A (Form 1040) that is for a mortgage whose proceeds were **not** used to buy, build, or substantially improve your main home or a qualified dwelling that is your second home. See section 163(h)(4).

Exception. If the mortgage was taken out before July 1, 1982, do not include interest on the mortgage if it was secured by property that was your main home or a qualified dwelling used by you or a member of your family at the time the mortgage was taken out. See section 56(e)(3).

A qualified dwelling is any house, apartment, condominium, or mobile home not used on a transient basis.

Line 6—Refund of Taxes

Include any refund from line 10 of Form 1040 that is attributable to state or local income taxes deducted in a tax year after 1986.

Also include any refunds received in 1993 and included in income on Form 1040, line 22, that are attributable to state or local personal property taxes, foreign income taxes, or state, local, or foreign real property taxes, deducted in a tax year after 1986. If you include such amounts, you **must** write a description and the amount on the dotted line to the left of the entry space for line 6. For example, if you include a refund of real property taxes, write "real property" and the amount to the left of the entry space.

Line 7—Investment Interest

If you completed **Form 4952,** Investment Interest Expense Deduction, figure your AMT investment interest expense on another Form 4952 as follows:

Step 1. Complete line 1 of Form 4952. Follow the Form 4952 instructions for line 1, but add to line 1 any interest expense on line 4 of Form 6251 that was paid or accrued on indebtedness attributable to property held for investment within the meaning of section 163(d)(5). An example is interest on a home equity loan whose proceeds were invested in preferred stock. It is deductible as home mortgage interest expense for the regular tax, but not for the AMT. Add to this amount any interest expense that would have been deductible if interest earned on private activity bonds issued after August 7, 1986, had been includible in gross income.

Step 2. Enter your **AMT** disallowed investment interest expense from 1992 on line 2. Complete line 3.

Step 3. When completing Part II, recompute your gross income from property held for investment, any net gain from the disposition of property held for investment, and any investment expenses, taking into account all adjustments and preferences. Include any interest income and investment expenses from private activity bonds issued after August 7, 1986. Complete Part III.

Enter on Form 6251, line 7, the difference between line 8 of your AMT Form 4952 and line 8 of your regular tax Form 4952. If your AMT investment interest expense is more than the regular tax amount, enter the difference as a negative amount.

Note: *If you took the standard deduction instead of itemizing your deductions and you had investment interest expense, do not enter an amount on Form 6251, line 7, unless you reported investment interest expense on Schedule E. If you did, follow the steps above for completing Form 4952. Allocate the investment interest expense allowed on line 8 of Form 4952 in the same way you did for the regular tax. Enter on Form 6251, line 7, the difference between the amount allowed on Schedule E for the regular tax and the amount allowed on Schedule E for the AMT.*

Medical and Dental Expenses Worksheet—Line 2 (keep for your records)

1. Enter the amount from Schedule A, line 1	**1.**	_____
2. Complete the ATAGI worksheet on page 6 for purposes of this line, and enter the ATAGI from line 7 . . . . **2.** _____		
3. Multiply line 2 above by 10% (.10). If zero or less, enter -0-	**3.**	_____
4. Enter the amount from Schedule A, line 4	**4.**	_____
5. Subtract line 3 from line 1. If zero or less, enter -0- . . .	**5.**	_____
6. Subtract line 5 from line 4. Enter the result on Form 6251, line 2	**6.**	_____

Line 8—Post-1986 Depreciation

Caution: *Do not include on this line any depreciation adjustment from:*
(a) incurring employee business expenses deducted on Schedule A; (b) a passive activity; (c) an activity for which you are not at risk, or from a partnership or an S corporation if the basis limitations under section 704(d) or 1366(d) apply; or (d) a tax shelter farm activity. Instead, take these depreciation adjustments into account when figuring the amount to enter on line 5, 11, 14h, or 14l.

For the AMT, depreciation must be recomputed using the alternative depreciation system of section 168(g) for tangible property placed in service after 1986 (or after July 31, 1986, if an election was made under the transitional provision of section 203(a)(1) of the Tax Reform Act of 1986) as follows:

1. For any section 1250(c) real property (generally nonresidential real and residential rental), use the straight line method over 40 years.

2. For any tangible property not described in **1** above that is depreciated using the straight line method for the regular tax, recompute your depreciation using the straight line method over the property's class life (explained below).

3. For all other tangible property, use the 150% declining balance method over the property's class life, switching to the straight line method in the first tax year it yields a larger deduction.

In applying the above rules:

1. Use the same convention you used for the regular tax;

2. The class life to be used for the AMT is not necessarily the same as the recovery period used for the regular tax. The class lives you need to use for the AMT can be found in Rev. Proc. 87-56, 1987-2 C.B. 674, or in **Pub. 534,** Depreciation. Use 12 years for any tangible personal property that does not have an assigned class life;

3. See Rev. Proc. 87-57, 1987-2 C.B. 687, for optional tables (14 through 18) that can be used in figuring AMT depreciation. (These optional tables are also included in Pub. 534.) Rev. Proc. 89-15, 1989-1 C.B. 816, has special rules for applying Rev. Proc. 87-57 for short years and for property disposed of before the end of the recovery period;

4. Do not make an adjustment for motion picture films, videotapes, sound recordings, or property depreciated under the unit-of-production method or any other method not expressed in a term of years; and

5. Do not recompute depreciation for any part of the cost of any property for which you made the election under section 179 to treat the cost of the property as an expense deduction. The

section 179 expense deduction is allowed for the AMT.

Enter on line 8 the difference between the regular tax and the AMT depreciation. If the AMT depreciation is more than the regular tax depreciation, enter the difference as a negative amount.

If depreciation is capitalized to inventory under the uniform capitalization rules, refigure the inventory using the rules above.

Note: *Pub. 534 has examples of how to figure depreciation for the AMT.*

Line 9—Adjusted Gain or Loss

Use this line to report any AMT adjustment resulting from the recomputation of a gain or loss from the sale or exchange of property during the year, or from the recomputation of a casualty gain or loss to business or income-producing property.

Make an entry on this line only if you reported gain or loss on **Form 4797,** Sales of Business Property, **Schedule D** (Form 1040), or Section B of **Form 4684,** Casualties and Thefts. Recompute your gain or loss for those forms. When figuring your adjusted basis, take into account any AMT adjustments you made this year or in previous years that affect basis.

Enter on line 9 the difference between the gain or loss reported for the regular tax and that figured for the AMT. If **(a)** the AMT gain is less than the regular tax gain, **(b)** the AMT loss is more than the regular tax loss, **or (c)** you have an AMT loss and a regular tax gain, enter the difference as a negative amount.

Line 10—Incentive Stock Options

For the regular tax, no income is recognized when an incentive stock option (ISO), as defined in section 422(b), is granted or exercised. However, this rule does not apply for the AMT. Instead, you must generally include on line 10 the excess, if any, of:

1. The fair market value of the option (determined without regard to any lapse restriction) at the first time your rights in the option become transferable or when these rights are no longer subject to a substantial risk of forfeiture, over

2. The amount you paid for the option.

Increase your AMT basis of any stock acquired through the exercise of an ISO by the amount of the adjustment. If you acquired stock by exercising an ISO and you disposed of that stock in the same year, the tax treatment under the regular tax and the AMT is the same (no adjustment is required). See section 83 for more details.

Note: *Your AMT basis in stock acquired through an ISO is likely to differ from your regular tax basis. Therefore, keep adequate records for both the AMT and regular tax so that you can compute*

your adjusted gain or loss in the year you sell the stock. See the instructions for line 9.

Line 11—Passive Activities

Your passive activity gains and losses must be refigured for the AMT by taking into account all adjustments, preferences, and any AMT prior year unallowed losses that apply to that activity. You may wish to fill out a second **Form 8582,** Passive Activity Loss Limitations, and the other forms or schedules on which your passive activities are reported, to determine your passive activity loss allowed for AMT purposes, but do not file the second set of forms and schedules.

If the special allowance for rental real estate with active participation applies to you, you must use ATAGI (see the worksheet on page 6) instead of AGI as the starting point for figuring modified AGI on Form 8582, line 6.

Example. Assume you are a partner in a partnership and the Schedule K-1 (Form 1065) you received shows the following:

- A passive activity loss of ($4,125),
- A depreciation adjustment of $500 on post-1986 property, and
- A preference of $225 for tax-exempt interest from private activity bonds issued after August 7, 1986.

Because the depreciation adjustment and the tax-exempt interest preference are items that are not allowed for the AMT, you must first reduce the passive activity loss by those amounts. The result is a passive activity loss for the AMT of ($3,400). You would then enter this amount on Worksheet 2 of the AMT Form 8582 and refigure the allowable passive activity loss for the AMT.

Note: *The amount of any AMT passive activity loss that is not deductible and is carried forward is likely to differ from the regular tax amount, if any. Therefore, keep adequate records for both the AMT and regular tax.*

Enter on line 11 the difference between the amount that would be reported for the activity on Schedule C, C-EZ, E, F, or **Form 4835,** Farm Rental Income and Expenses, for the AMT and the amount that was reported for the activity on that form or schedule for the regular tax. If **(a)** the AMT loss is more than the regular tax loss, **(b)** the AMT gain is less than the regular tax gain, **or (c)** you have an AMT loss and a regular tax gain, enter the adjustment as a negative amount.

Enter any adjustment for amounts reported on Schedule D, Form 4684, or Form 4797 for the activity on line 9 instead of line 11. See the instructions for line 9.

Publicly traded partnership (PTP).—If you had losses from a PTP, you will have to refigure the loss using any AMT

Page 3

adjustments and preferences and any AMT prior year unallowed loss.

Tax shelter passive farm activities.— Refigure any gain or loss from a tax shelter passive farm activity taking into account all AMT adjustments and preferences and any AMT prior year unallowed losses. If the amount is a gain, it can be included on the AMT Form 8582, but if it is a loss, the adjustment for the tax shelter passive farm activity is the loss you reported for the regular tax. The AMT loss to carry forward is the refigured AMT loss.

Insolvency.— If at the end of the tax year your liabilities exceed the fair market value of your assets, increase your passive activity loss allowed by that excess (but not by more than your total loss). See section 58(c)(1).

Line 13—Tax-Exempt Interest From Private Activity Bonds

Enter on line 13 interest you earned on "specified private activity bonds" reduced (but not below zero) by any deduction that would have been allowable if the interest were includible in gross income for the regular tax. Generally, the term "specified private activity bonds" means any private activity bond (as defined in section 141) issued after August 7, 1986. See section 57(a)(5) for exceptions and more details.

Exempt-interest dividends paid by a regulated investment company are treated as interest on a specified private activity bond to the extent the company received interest on the bond.

If you are filing **Form 8814,** Parents' Election To Report Child's Interest and Dividends, any tax-exempt interest from line 1b of that form that is a preference must be included on Form 6251, line 13.

Line 14—Other Adjustments and Preferences

Enter the amounts of any other adjustments or preferences that apply to you on lines 14a through 14m. Enter the total on line 14.

Line 14a—Charitable contributions.— If your charitable contribution deduction is subject to the 50%, 30%, or 20% limitation for the AMT or the regular tax **or** you have an AMT or regular tax carryforward of charitable contributions, you must refigure your deduction for the AMT. First refigure your charitable contribution deduction using your AMT carryover instead of your regular tax carryover (see **Note** below). Then, refigure the 50%, 30%, and 20% limitations using alternative tax adjusted gross income (ATAGI) instead of adjusted gross income (AGI) from Form 1040, line 32. Use the worksheet on page 6 to figure ATAGI. See **Pub. 526,** Charitable Contributions, for details on the charitable contribution deduction

limits, but be sure to use ATAGI instead of AGI when figuring the limits.

Enter on line 14a the difference between the regular tax and AMT deduction. If the AMT deduction is larger than the regular tax deduction, enter the difference as a negative amount.

Note: *Your AMT carryforward of contributions must be figured (a) using ATAGI instead of AGI for the charitable contribution limitations and (b) using the cost or other basis (instead of fair market value) for any contribution of capital gain or section 1231 property for which the preference for charitable contributions of appreciated property applies. The preference for charitable contributions of appreciated property does not apply for any contribution made after 1992 or any contribution of tangible personal property made after 1990. It also does not apply to contributions of property for which you elected under section 170(b)(1)(C)(iii) to figure the deduction using the property's adjusted basis rather than its fair market value.*

Line 14b—Circulation expenditures.— For the regular tax, section 173 allows circulation expenditures to be deducted in full in the tax year they were paid or incurred. However, for the AMT these expenditures must be capitalized and amortized over 3 years beginning with the year they were paid or incurred. Refigure these circulation expenditures for the AMT. Enter on line 14b the difference between the regular tax expense and the AMT expense. If the current year deduction for the AMT is more than that figured for the regular tax, enter the difference as a negative amount.

If you had a loss on property for which a deduction for circulation expenditures was allowed for the regular tax, see section 56(b)(2)(B).

Note: *Do not make this adjustment if you elected to take the optional 3-year write-off period for circulation expenditures under section 59(e) for the regular tax.*

Line 14c—Depletion.— Your depletion deduction must be refigured for the AMT. To do so, you must use only income and deductions allowed for the AMT when refiguring the limit based on taxable income from the property under section 613(a) and the limit based on taxable income, with certain adjustments, under section 613A(d)(1). Also, your depletion deduction for mines, wells, and other natural deposits under section 611 is limited to the property's adjusted basis at the end of the year, as refigured for the AMT, unless you are an independent producer or royalty owner claiming percentage depletion for oil and gas wells under section 613A(c). Figure this limit separately for each property. When refiguring the property's adjusted basis, take into account any AMT adjustments

you made this year or in previous years that affect basis (other than the current year's depletion).

Enter on line 14c the difference between the regular tax and AMT deduction. If the AMT deduction is more than the regular tax deduction, enter the difference as a negative amount.

Line 14d—Depreciation (pre-1987).— For the AMT, you must use the straight line method to figure depreciation on real property for which accelerated depreciation was determined using the pre-1987 rules. Figure the excess of the regular tax depreciation over the AMT depreciation separately for each property and include on line 14d only positive amounts. For 19-year real property, use the straight line method over 19 years. For low-income housing property, use the straight line method over 15 years. (This preference will generally only apply to property that was placed in service after 1987, but is depreciated using the pre-1987 rules due to transitional provisions of the Tax Reform Act of 1986.)

You must also use the straight line method to figure depreciation for the AMT on leased personal property placed in service before 1987. Figure the excess of the regular tax depreciation over the AMT depreciation separately for each property and include on line 14d only positive amounts. For leased recovery property, other than 15-, 18-, or 19-year real property, or low-income housing, enter the amount by which your depreciation deduction figured for the regular tax exceeds the deduction allowable using the straight line method with a half-year convention, no salvage value, and a recovery period of 15 years for 10-year property (22 years for 15-year public utility property).

Line 14e—Installment sales.— For either of the following kinds of dispositions in which you used the installment method for the regular tax, you must refigure your income for the AMT without regard to the installment method:

1. Any disposition after March 1, 1986, of property used or produced in your farming business that you held primarily for sale to customers.

2. Any nondealer disposition of property that occurred after August 16, 1986, but before January 1, 1987, if an obligation that arose from the disposition was an installment obligation to which the proportionate disallowance rule applied.

Enter on line 14e the difference between the AMT income and the regular tax income. If the AMT income is less than the regular tax income, enter the difference as a negative amount.

Line 14f—Intangible drilling costs (IDCs).— IDCs from oil, gas, and geothermal wells are a preference to the

Page 4

B-8   Forms for Tax Credits

Form **2441**	**Child and Dependent Care Expenses**	OMB No. 1545-0068

Department of the Treasury
Internal Revenue Service (T)

▶ Attach to Form 1040.

▶ See separate instructions.

1993

Attachment
Sequence No. **21**

Name(s) shown on Form 1040

Your social security number

You need to understand the following terms to complete this form: **Dependent Care Benefits, Earned Income, Qualified Expenses,** and **Qualifying Person(s).** See **Important Terms** on page 1 of the Form 2441 instructions. Also, if you had a child born in 1993 and line 32 of Form 1040 is less than $23,050, see **A Change To Note** on page 2 of the instructions.

Part I   Persons or Organizations Who Provided the Care—You **must** complete this part.
(If you need more space, use the bottom of page 2.)

1	**(a)** Care provider's name	**(b)** Address (number, street, apt. no., city, state, and ZIP code)	**(c)** Identifying number (SSN or EIN)	**(d)** Amount paid (see instructions)

2 Add the amounts in column (d) of line 1 . . . .   **2**

3 Enter the number of **qualifying persons** cared for in 1993 . . . . ▶ ☐

Did you receive **dependent care benefits?**

— NO ——▶ Complete only Part II below.

— YES ——▶ Complete Part III on the back now.

Part II   Credit for Child and Dependent Care Expenses

4 Enter the amount of **qualified expenses** you incurred and paid in 1993. DO NOT enter more than $2,400 for one qualifying person or $4,800 for two or more persons. If you completed Part III, enter the amount from line 25 . . . .   **4**

5 Enter YOUR **earned income** **5**

6 If married filing a joint return, enter YOUR SPOUSE'S earned income (if student or disabled, see instructions); **all others,** enter the amount from line 5 . . . .   **6**

7 Enter the **smallest** of line 4, 5, or 6 . . . .   **7**

8 Enter the amount from Form 1040, line 32 . . . .   **8**

9 Enter on line 9 the decimal amount shown below that applies to the amount on line 8

If line 8 is—		Decimal amount is	If line 8 is—		Decimal amount is
Over	But not over		Over	But not over	
$0	10,000	.30	$20,000	22,000	.24
10,000	12,000	.29	22,000	24,000	.23
12,000	14,000	.28	24,000	26,000	.22
14,000	16,000	.27	26,000	28,000	.21
16,000	18,000	.26	28,000	No limit	.20
18,000	20,000	.25			

9   × .

10 Multiply **line 7** by the decimal amount on line 9. Enter the result. Then, see the instructions for the amount of credit to enter on Form 1040, line 41 . . . .   **10**

Caution: If you paid $50 or more in a calendar quarter to a person who worked in your home, you must file an employment tax return. Get **Form 942** for details.

For Paperwork Reduction Act Notice, see separate instructions.   Cat. No. 11862M   Form **2441** (1993)

Form 2441 (1993)   Page **2**

Part III **Dependent Care Benefits**—Complete this part **only** if you received these benefits.

11   Enter the total amount of **dependent care benefits** you received for 1993. This amount should
     be shown in box 10 of your W-2 form(s). DO NOT include amounts that were reported to you
     as wages in box 1 of Form(s) W-2 . . . .   **11**

12   Enter the amount forfeited, if any. See the instructions **12**

13   Subtract line 12 from line 11 . . . .   **13**

14   Enter the total amount of **qualified expenses** incurred in 1993
     for the care of the qualifying person(s) **14**

15   Enter the **smaller** of line 13 or 14 . . . .   **15**

16   Enter YOUR **earned income** **16**

17   If married filing a joint return, enter YOUR SPOUSE'S earned
     income (if student or disabled, see the line 6 instructions); if
     married filing a separate return, see the instructions for the
     amount to enter; **all others,** enter the amount from line 16 . .   **17**

18   Enter the **smallest** of line 15, 16, or 17. . . . .   **18**

19   **Excluded benefits.** Enter here the **smaller** of the following:

     • The amount from line 18, or
     • $5,000 ($2,500 if married filing a separate return
        and you were required to enter your spouse's   } **19**
        earned income on line 17).

20   **Taxable benefits.** Subtract line 19 from line 13. Also, include this amount on Form 1040,
     line 7. On the dotted line next to line 7, write "DCB" **20**

                    To claim the child and dependent care credit, complete
                    lines 21–25 below, and lines 4–10 on the front of this form.

21   Enter the amount of qualified expenses you incurred and paid in 1993. DO NOT include on
     this line any excluded benefits shown on line 19 . . . .   **21**

22   Enter $2,400 ($4,800 if two or more qualifying persons) . . .   **22**

23   Enter the amount from line 19 . . . .   **23**

24   Subtract line 23 from line 22. If zero or less, **STOP**. You cannot take the credit. **Exception.** If
     you paid 1992 expenses in 1993, see the line 10 instructions **24**

25   Enter the **smaller** of line 21 or 24 here **and** on line 4 on the front of this form **25**

19**93**

 Department of the Treasury
Internal Revenue Service

Instructions for Form 2441

Child and Dependent Care Expenses

Paperwork Reduction Act Notice. We ask for the information on this form to carry out the Internal Revenue laws of the United States. You are required to give us the information. We need it to ensure that you are complying with these laws and to allow us to figure and collect the right amount of tax.

The time needed to complete and file this form will vary depending on individual circumstances. The estimated average time is: **Recordkeeping,** 40 min.; **Learning about the law or the form,** 24 min.; **Preparing the form,** 59 min.; and **Copying, assembling, and sending the form to the IRS,** 28 min.

If you have comments concerning the accuracy of these time estimates or suggestions for making this form more simple, we would be happy to hear from you. You can write to both the IRS and the Office of Management and Budget at the addresses listed on page 4 of the Instructions for Form 1040.

Purpose of Form

If you paid someone to care for your child or other qualifying person so you (and your spouse if filing a joint return) could work or look for work in 1993, you may be able to take the credit for child and dependent care expenses. But you must have had earned income to take the credit. If you can take the credit, fill in Parts I and II of Form 2441 and attach it to your return. Part II is used to figure the amount of your credit.

If you received **any dependent care benefits** for 1993, you **MUST** fill in Parts I and III of Form 2441 and attach it to your return. Part III is used to figure the amount, if any, of the benefits you may exclude from your income on Form 1040, line 7. You must complete Part III before you can figure the credit, if any, in Part II.

Important Terms

Dependent Care Benefits

These include amounts your employer paid directly to either you or your care provider for the care of your qualifying person(s) while you worked. These benefits also include the fair market value of care in a day-care facility provided or sponsored by your employer. Your salary may have been reduced to pay for these benefits. If you received dependent care benefits, they should be shown in box 10 of your 1993 W-2 form(s).

Earned Income

Generally, this is your wages, salaries, tips, and other employee compensation. This is usually the amount shown on Form 1040, line 7. But earned income does not include a scholarship or fellowship grant if you did not get a W-2 form for it. For purposes of Part III of Form 2441, earned income does not include any dependent care benefits shown on line 11 of Form 2441.

If you were a statutory employee and are filing **Schedule C** or **C-EZ** to report income and expenses as a statutory employee, earned income also includes the amount from line 1 of that Schedule C or C-EZ.

If you were self-employed, earned income also includes the amount shown on **Schedule SE,** line 3, minus any deduction you claim on Form 1040, line 25. If you use either optional method to figure self-employment tax, subtract any deduction you claim on Form 1040, line 25, from the total of the amounts on Schedule SE, Section B, lines 3 and 4b, to figure earned income.

Note: *You must reduce your earned income by any loss from self-employment.*

If you are **filing a joint return,** disregard community property laws. If your spouse died in 1993 and had no earned income, get **Pub. 503,** Child and Dependent Care Expenses. If your spouse was a student or disabled in 1993, see the line 6 instructions.

Qualified Expenses

These include amounts paid for household services and care of the qualifying person while you worked or looked for work. Child support payments are **not** qualified expenses.

Household Services. These are services needed to care for the qualifying person as well as to run the home. They include, for example, the services of a cook, maid, babysitter, housekeeper, or cleaning person if the services were partly for the care of the qualifying person. Do not include services of a chauffeur or gardener.

You may also include your share of the employment taxes paid on wages for qualifying child and dependent care services.

Care of the Qualifying Person. Care includes the cost of services for the qualifying person's well-being and protection. It does not include the cost of clothing or entertainment.

You may include the cost of care provided outside your home for your dependent under age 13 or any other

qualifying person who regularly spends at least 8 hours a day in your home. If the care was provided by a dependent care center, the center must meet all applicable state and local regulations. A dependent care center is a place that provides care for more than six persons (other than persons who live there) and receives a fee, payment, or grant for providing services for any of those persons, even if the center is not run for profit.

Do not include amounts paid for food or schooling. But if these items are included as part of the total care and they are incident to and cannot be separated from the total cost, you may include the total cost. Also, **do not** include the cost of schooling for a child in the first grade or above or the expenses for sending your child to an overnight camp.

Medical Expenses. Some disabled spouse and dependent care expenses may qualify as medical expenses if you itemize deductions on **Schedule A.** Get Pub. 503 and **Pub. 502,** Medical and Dental Expenses, for details.

Qualifying Person(s)

A qualifying person is:

● Any child **under age 13** whom you can claim as a dependent (but see **Exception for Children of Divorced or Separated Parents** below). If the child turned 13 during the year, the child is a qualifying person for the part of the year he or she was under age 13.

● Your disabled spouse who is not able to care for himself or herself.

● Any disabled person not able to care for himself or herself whom you can claim as a dependent (or could claim as a dependent except that the person had gross income of $2,350 or more). But if this person is your child, see **Exception for Children of Divorced or Separated Parents** below.

To find out who is a dependent, see the instructions for Form 1040, line 6c.

Caution: *To be a qualifying person, the person must have shared the same home with you in 1993.*

Exception for Children of Divorced or Separated Parents. If you were divorced, legally separated, or lived apart from your spouse during the last 6 months of 1993, you may be able to take the credit or the exclusion even if your child is not your dependent. If your child is not your dependent, he or she is a qualifying person only if **all five** of the following apply:

1. You had custody of the child for a longer time in 1993 than the other parent. Get **Pub. 501,** Exemptions, Standard

Cat. No. 10842K

Deduction, and Filing Information, for the definition of custody.

2. One or both of the parents provided over half of the child's support in 1993.

3. One or both of the parents had custody of the child for more than half of 1993.

4. The child was under age 13 or was disabled and could not care for himself or herself.

5. The other parent claims the child as a dependent because—

• As the custodial parent, you signed **Form 8332** or a similar statement agreeing not to claim the child's exemption for 1993, or

• Your divorce decree or written agreement went into effect before 1985 and it states that the other parent can claim the child as a dependent, and the other parent gave at least $600 for the child's support in 1993. But this rule does not apply if your decree or agreement was changed after 1984 to say that the other parent cannot claim the child as a dependent.

If you can take the credit or the exclusion because of this exception, enter your child's name on the dotted line next to line 3. The other parent cannot treat this child as a qualifying person even though the other parent claims this child as a dependent.

A Change To Note

If you have a child who was born in 1993 and the amount on Form 1040, line 32, is less than $23,050, you may be able to take the extra credit for a child born in 1993 on **Schedule EIC**, Earned Income Credit. To find out if you can take the extra credit, see Schedule EIC and its instructions. But if you take the extra credit, you **cannot** take the credit for child care expenses or the exclusion of dependent care benefits on Form 2441 for the same child.

If you qualify for both the child care credit **and** the extra credit for a child born in 1993, **you should figure the amount of tax you overpaid (or the amount of tax you owe) both ways to see which way is better for you.** You should also do this if you received dependent care benefits and qualify for the extra credit on Schedule EIC. But see the **Exception** on this page.

To see which way is better, first get Schedule EIC and fill in lines 1(a)–1(g) and all the lines on page 2 that apply to you. Be sure to figure the extra credit for a child born in 1993. Then, follow the steps below.

Step 1. Figure the child care credit or exclusion on Form 2441. **Include** the qualified expenses for your child born in 1993. Fill in Form 1040 through line 55. On line 56, enter the total of the amounts from lines 11 and 16 of Schedule EIC. Fill in the rest of Form 1040 through line 61 (or line 64).

Step 2. Again, figure the child care credit or exclusion on Form 2441. But this time, **don't include** the qualified expenses for your child born in 1993. Fill in Form 1040 through line 55. On line 56, enter the

Page 2

amount from line 20 of Schedule EIC. Fill in the rest of Form 1040 through line 61 (or line 64).

Step 3. Compare the amount on line 61 (or line 64) of Form 1040 figured using Step 1 to the amount figured using Step 2. File your return using the one that benefits you more. If you choose to use Step 1 and the amount on line 4 of Form 2441 includes expenses for more than one person, write in the amount of qualified expenses for your child born in 1993 on the dotted line to the left of your line 4 entry. If you are completing Part III, write this amount on the dotted line to the left of your line 14 entry.

Exception. If you didn't receive any dependent care benefits and the amount on line 40 of your Form 1040 is zero, you should take the extra credit for a child born in 1993. Don't file Form 2441.

Additional Information

For more details, see **Pub. 503.**

Who May Take the Credit or Exclude Dependent Care Benefits?

You may take the credit or the exclusion if **all six** of the following apply:

1. Your filing status is Single, Head of household, Qualifying widow(er) with dependent child, or Married filing jointly. But see **Special Rule for Married Persons Filing Separate Returns** below.

2. The care was provided so you (and your spouse if you were married) could work or look for work. However, if you did not find a job and have no earned income for the year, you cannot take the credit or the exclusion. But if your spouse was a student or disabled, see the line 6 instructions.

3. You (and your spouse if you were married) paid over half the cost of keeping up your home. The cost includes rent, mortgage interest, real estate taxes, utilities, home repairs, and food eaten at home.

4. You and the qualifying person(s) lived in the same home.

5. The person who provided the care was not your spouse or a person whom you can claim as a dependent. If your child provided the care, he or she must have been age 19 or older by the end of 1993.

6. You report the required information about the care provider on line 1.

Special Rule for Married Persons Filing Separate Returns. If your filing status is married filing separately and **all** of the following apply, you are considered unmarried for purposes of figuring the credit and the exclusion on Form 2441.

• You lived apart from your spouse during the last 6 months of 1993, and

• The qualifying person lived in your home more than half of 1993, and

• You provided over half the cost of keeping up your home.

If you meet **all** the requirements to be treated as unmarried and meet items **2** through **6** listed earlier, you may take the credit or the exclusion. If you do not meet all the requirements to be treated as unmarried, you **cannot** take the credit. However, you may take the exclusion if you meet items **2** through **6**.

Other Forms You May Have To File

If you paid someone who worked in your home cash wages of $50 or more in any calendar quarter in 1993, you usually must file **Form 942,** Employer's Quarterly Tax Return for Household Employees.

Also, if you paid someone who worked in your home cash wages of $1,000 or more in any calendar quarter in 1992 or 1993, you must file a 1993 **Form 940** or **Form 940-EZ,** Employer's Annual Federal Unemployment (FUTA) Tax Return, by January 31, 1994.

Get **Pub. 926,** Employment Taxes for Household Employers, for more details.

Line Instructions

Line 1

Complete columns **(a)** through **(d)** for each person or organization that provided the care. You can use **Form W-10,** Dependent Care Provider's Identification and Certification, or any other source listed in its instructions, to get the information from the care provider. If you do not give correct or complete information, your credit (and exclusion, if applicable) may be disallowed unless you can show you used due diligence in attempting to provide the required information.

Due Diligence. You can show due diligence by keeping in your records a Form W-10 properly completed by the care provider or one of the other sources of information listed in the instructions for Form W-10. If the provider does not comply with your request for one of these items, complete the entries you can on line 1 of Form 2441, such as the provider's name and address. Write "See Page 2" in the columns for which you do not have the information. On the bottom of page 2, explain that you requested the information from the care provider, but the provider did not comply with your request.

Columns (a) and (b). Enter the care provider's name and address. If you were covered by your employer's dependent care plan and your employer furnished the care (either at your workplace or by hiring a care provider), enter your employer's name in column **(a)**, write "See W-2" in column **(b)**, and leave columns **(c)** and **(d)** blank. But if your employer paid a third party (not hired by your employer) on your behalf to provide the care, you must give information on the third party in columns **(a)** through **(d)**.

Column (c). If the care provider is an individual, enter his or her social security number (SSN). Otherwise, enter the provider's employer identification number

(EIN). If the provider is a tax-exempt organization, write "Tax-Exempt" in column (c).

Column (d). Enter the total amount you **actually paid** in 1993 to the care provider. Also, include amounts your employer paid to a third party on your behalf. It does not matter when the expenses were incurred. Do not reduce this amount by any reimbursement you received.

Line 4

Do not include the following expenses on line 4:

● Qualified expenses you incurred in 1993 but did not pay until 1994. You may be able to use these expenses to increase your 1994 credit.

● Qualified expenses you incurred in 1992 but did not pay until 1993. Instead, see **Prior Year's Expenses** below.

Line 6

Spouse Who Was a Student or Disabled. Your spouse was a **student** if he or she was enrolled as a full-time student at a school during any 5 months of 1993. Your spouse was **disabled** if he or she was not capable of self-care. Figure your spouse's earned income on a monthly basis.

For each month or part of a month your spouse was a student or was disabled, he or she is considered to have worked and earned income. His or her earned income for each month is considered to be at least $200 ($400 if more than one qualifying person was cared for in 1993). If your spouse also worked during that month, use the higher of $200 (or $400) or his or her actual earned income for that month. If, in the same month, both you and your spouse were either students or disabled, this rule applies to only one of you for that month.

For any month that your spouse was not disabled or a student, use your spouse's actual earned income if he or she worked during the month.

Line 10

If you had qualified expenses for 1992 that you didn't pay until 1993, see **Prior Year's Expenses** below. Otherwise, see **Credit Limit** on this page.

Prior Year's Expenses. If you had qualified expenses for 1992 that you didn't pay until 1993, you may be able to increase the amount of credit you can take in 1993. For details, see **Amount of Credit** in Pub. 503. If you can take a credit for your 1992 expenses, write "PYE" and the amount of the credit on the dotted line next to line 10. Add the credit to the amount on line 10 and replace the amount on line 10 with that total. Also, attach a statement showing how you figured the credit. See **Credit Limit** next.

Credit Limit. The amount of your credit may be limited. Some people need to complete **Form 6251,** Alternative Minimum Tax—Individuals, because the amount from line 24 of that form is used to figure the limit. Use the worksheet on this page to see if you need to complete Form 6251 and to figure the amount of credit you may claim.

Line 12

If you had a flexible spending account, any amount included on line 11 that you did not receive because you did not incur the expense is considered forfeited. Enter the forfeited amount on line 12. **Do not** include amounts you expect to receive at a future date.

Example. Under your employer's dependent care plan, you elected to have your employer set aside $5,000 to cover your 1993 dependent care expenses. The $5,000 is shown in box 10 of your W-2 form. In 1993, you incurred and were reimbursed for $4,950 of qualified expenses. You would enter $5,000 on line 11 and $50, the amount forfeited, on line 12.

Line 14

Enter the total of all qualified expenses incurred in 1993 for the care of your qualifying person(s). It does not matter when the expenses were paid.

Example. You received $2,000 in cash under your employer's dependent care plan for 1993. The $2,000 is shown in box 10 of your W-2 form. Only $900 of qualified expenses were incurred in 1993 for the care of your 5-year-old dependent child. You would enter $2,000 on line 11 and $900 on line 14.

Line 17

If your filing status is married filing separately, see **Special Rule for Married Persons Filing Separate Returns** earlier. If you are considered unmarried under that rule, enter your earned income (from line 16) on line 17. On line 19, enter the smaller of the amount from line 18 or $5,000. If you are **not** considered unmarried under that rule, enter your spouse's earned income on line 17. If your spouse was a student or disabled in 1993, see the line 6 instructions. On line 19, enter the smaller of the amount from line 18 or $2,500.

Credit Limit Worksheet—Line 10 (keep for your records)

1. Enter the amount from Form 2441, line 10 . . . . . . 1. _____

2. Enter the amount from Form 1040, line 23, plus any net operating loss deduction and tax-exempt interest from private activity bonds issued after August 7,1986 . . . . . . 2. _____

   Next: If line 2 is more than $150,000 ($112,500 if single or head of household; $75,000 if married filing separately) **OR** you file Schedule C, C-EZ, D, E, or F, complete Form 6251 through line 24. Then, complete only lines 5 and 8–10 below. Otherwise, go to line 3.

3. Enter $45,000 ($33,750 if single or head of household; $22,500 if married filing separately) . . . . 3. _____

4. Subtract line 3 from line 2. If zero or less, **stop here;** enter on Form 1040, line 41, the amount from line 1 above. Otherwise, go to line 5 . . . . 4. _____

5. Enter the amount from Form 1040, line 40 . . . . . . 5. _____

6. Multiply line 4 by 26% (.26) . . . . 6. _____

7. Subtract line 6 from line 5 (if zero or less, enter -0-) . . . 7. _____

   Next: If line 7 is equal to or more than line 1, **stop here;** enter the amount from line 1 above on Form 1040, line 41. Otherwise, complete Form 6251 through line 24 and lines 8–10 below.

8. Enter the amount from Form 6251, line 24 . . . . . . 8. _____

9. Subtract line 8 from line 5 (if zero or less, enter -0-) . . . 9. _____

10. Enter the **smaller** of line 1 or line 9 here and on Form 1040, line 41. If line 9 is the smaller amount, write "AMT" in the left margin next to line 41 and replace the amount on Form 2441, line 10, with that amount . . . . 10. _____

Page 3

Form **3468**

Department of the Treasury
Internal Revenue Service

Investment Credit

► Attach to your return.

► See separate instructions.

OMB No. 1545-0155

19**93**

Attachment
Sequence No. **52**

Name(s) as shown on return

Identifying number

Part I   Current Year Investment Credit

Note: *Generally, you cannot claim the regular investment credit for property placed in service after December 31, 1985 (see instructions).*

1   Rehabilitation credit. Enter the amount of qualified rehabilitation expenditures and multiply by the percentage shown:

a   Pre-1936 buildings . . . . _____ × 10% (.10) | **1a** |

b   Certified historic structures (attach NPS certificate) . . _____ × 20% (.20) | **1b** |

Enter NPS number assigned or the flow-through entity's identifying number (see instructions). . . . . . . _____

Transition property:

c   30-year-old buildings . . . . _____ × 10% (.10) | **1c** |

d   40-year-old buildings . . . . _____ × 13% (.13) | **1d** |

e   Certified historic structures (attach NPS certificate) . . _____ × 25% (.25) | **1e** |

Enter NPS number assigned or the flow-through entity's identifying number (see instructions). . . . . . . _____

2a   Energy credit. Enter the basis of energy property placed in service during the tax year (see instructions) . . . . . _____ × 10% (.10) | **2a** |

b   Transition property. Attach computation (see instructions) . . . . | **2b** |

3   Reforestation credit. Enter the amortizable basis of qualified timber property acquired during the tax year (see instructions for limitations) . . . . _____ × 10% (.10) | **3** |

4   Regular investment credit for transition property. Enter qualified investment (see instructions) . . . . _____ × 6.5% (.065) | **4** |

5   Credit from cooperatives. Enter the unused regular investment credit for transition property and the unused energy credit from cooperatives . . . . | **5** |

6   **Total current year investment credit.** Add lines 1a through 5 . . . . | **6** |

Part II   Tax Liability Limitation (See **Who Must File Form 3800** to see if you complete Part II or file Form 3800.)

7a   Individuals. Enter amount from Form 1040, line 40 . . . .

b   Corporations. Enter amount from Form 1120, Schedule J, line 3 (or Form 1120-A, Part I, line 1) } . . | **7** |

c   Other filers. Enter regular tax before credits from your return . . . . }

8   Credits that reduce regular tax before the investment credit:

a   Credit for child and dependent care expenses (Form 2441, line 10) . | **8a** |

b   Credit for the elderly or the disabled (Schedule R (Form 1040), line 21) | **8b** |

c   Mortgage interest credit (Form 8396, line 11) . . . . | **8c** |

d   Foreign tax credit (Form 1116, line 32, or Form 1118, Sch. B, line 12) | **8d** |

e   Possessions tax credit (Form 5735, line 14) . . . . | **8e** |

f   Orphan drug credit (Form 6765, line 10) . . . . | **8f** |

g   Credit for fuel from a nonconventional source . . . . | **8g** |

h   Qualified electric vehicle credit (Form 8834, line 17) . . . . . . | **8h** |

i   Add lines 8a through 8h . . . . | **8i** |

9   Net regular tax. Subtract line 8i from line 7 . . . . | **9** |

10   Tentative minimum tax (see instructions):

a   Individuals. Enter amount from Form 6251, line 26 . . . . }

b   Corporations. Enter amount from Form 4626, line 14 . . . . } | **10** |

c   Estates and trusts. Enter amount from Form 1041, Schedule H, line 37 . . . }

11   Net income tax:

a   Individuals. Add line 9 above and line 28 of Form 6251 . . . . }

b   Corporations. Add line 9 above and line 16 of Form 4626 . . . . } | **11** |

c   Estates and trusts. Add line 9 above and line 39 of Form 1041, Schedule H . }

12   If line 9 is more than $25,000, enter 25% (.25) of the excess (see instructions) . . . . . | **12** |

13   Subtract line 10 or line 12, whichever is greater, from line 11. If less than zero, enter -0-. . . . | **13** |

14   **Investment credit allowed for current year.** Enter the **smaller** of line 6 or line 13. This is your **General Business Credit** for 1993. Enter here and on Form 1040, line 44; Form 1120, Schedule J, line 4e; Form 1120-A, Part I, line 2a; or on the appropriate line of other income tax returns . | **14** |

For Paperwork Reduction Act Notice, see separate instructions.   Cat. No. 12276E   Form **3468** (1993)

Department of the Treasury
Internal Revenue Service

Instructions for Form 3468

Investment Credit

Section references are to the Internal Revenue Code unless otherwise noted.

Paperwork Reduction Act Notice.—We ask for the information on this form to carry out the Internal Revenue laws of the United States. You are required to give us the information. We need it to ensure that you are complying with these laws and to allow us to figure and collect the right amount of tax.

The time needed to complete and file this form will vary depending on individual circumstances. The estimated average time is:

Recordkeeping . . . 12 hr., 40 min.

Learning about the law or the form . . . 3 hr., 28 min.

Preparing and sending the form to the IRS . . . 3 hr., 50 min.

If you have comments concerning the accuracy of these time estimates or suggestions for making this form more simple, we would be happy to hear from you. You can write to both the IRS and the Office of Management and Budget at the addresses listed in the instructions of the tax return with which this form is filed.

Items To Note

The "regular percentage" investment credit expired for property placed in service after December 31, 1990. But see the **Exception** below. Generally, the 1993 investment credit consists of:

1. The rehabilitation credit (see the instructions for line 1),

2. The energy credit, which is now permanent (see the instructions for lines 2a and 2b), and

3. The reforestation credit (see the instructions for line 3).

Exception. Because of transitional and certain computation rules, you may be able to claim a current year investment credit for the following section 38 property (as defined in section 48(a) as in effect on November 4, 1990, before amendment by the Revenue Reconciliation Act of 1990):

1. Regular percentage for transition property (as defined in section 49(e) as in effect on November 4, 1990).

2. Regular percentage for progress expenditure property that is transition property when placed in service (see section 46(d) as in effect on November 4, 1990).

3. Energy percentage for certain long-term energy projects (as defined in section 46(b)(2)(C) as in effect on November 4, 1990).

Recapture of credit.—You may have to refigure the credit and recapture all or a portion of it if:

• You dispose of the property before the end of the property class life or life years,

• You change the use of the property,

• The business use of the property decreases so that it no longer qualifies (in whole or in part) as investment credit property,

• You reduce your proportionate interest in a partnership or other "pass-through" entity that allocated the cost or basis of property to you for which you claimed a credit, or

• You return leased property (on which you claimed a credit) to the lessor before the end of the recapture period or useful life.

For more information, see **Form 4255,** Recapture of Investment Credit.

General Instructions

Purpose of Form

Use Form 3468 to claim a rehabilitation, energy, or reforestation credit. Also, use Form 3468 to claim a regular investment credit for certain transition property.

If you are a partner in a partnership, beneficiary of an estate or trust, shareholder in an S corporation, or lessee, use Form 3468 to figure the credit based on your share of the investment that was allocated to you by the partnership, estate, trust, S corporation, or lessor.

Who Must File Form 3800

The general business credit consists of the investment credit (Form 3468), jobs credit (Form 5884), credit for alcohol used as fuel (Form 6478), credit for increasing research activities (Form 6765), low-income housing credit (Form 8586), enhanced oil recovery credit (Form 8830), disabled access credit (Form 8826), and renewable electricity production credit (Form 8835). The Revenue Reconciliation Act of 1993 added the following new credits to the general business credit: empowerment

zone employment credit (Form 8844), Indian employment credit (Form 8845), credit for employer social security taxes paid on certain employee cash tips (Form 8846), and credit for contributions to certain community development corporations (Form 8847). Generally, the new credits are allowed for expenditures incurred after December 31, 1993. See the new credit forms and **Form 3800,** General Business Credit, for other details.

If you have (1) more than one of these credits for 1993, (2) a carryback or a carryforward of any of these credits, or (3) an investment credit from a passive activity, you must also file Form 3800, which is used instead of Part II of Form 3468 to figure the tax liability limitation.

C corporations that are required to file **Form 4626,** Alternative Minimum Tax—Corporations, may also use Schedule A of Form 3800 to determine if they are entitled to an additional general business credit for any regular investment credit carryforward to 1993 for property placed in service before January 1, 1991, under section 38(c)(2) before amendment by the Revenue Reconciliation Act of 1990.

Investment Credit Property

You may claim an investment credit for property placed in service only if it qualifies as one of the properties listed under **Items To Note.** Enter only the business part if property is for both business and personal use.

Exceptions. You cannot claim an investment credit for property that is:

1. Used mainly outside the United States,

2. Used by governmental units and foreign persons and entities,

3. Used by a tax-exempt organization (other than a section 521 farmers' cooperative) unless the property is used mainly in an unrelated trade or business, or

4. Used for lodging or for furnishing the lodging (see section 50(b)(2) for exceptions).

Election for certain leased property.—If you lease property to someone else, you may elect to treat all or part of your investment in new property as if it were made by the person who is leasing it from you. Lessors and lessees should see section 48(d), as in effect on November 4, 1990, and related

Cat. No. 12277P

regulations for rules on making this election. For limitations, see sections 46(e)(3) and 48(d), as in effect on November 4, 1990.

At-Risk Limitation for Individuals and Closely Held Corporations

The cost or basis of property for investment credit purposes may be limited if you borrowed against the property and are protected against loss, or if you borrowed money from a person who is related or who has other than a creditor interest in the business activity. The cost or basis must be reduced by the amount of this "nonqualified nonrecourse financing" related to the property as of the close of the tax year in which it is placed in service. If, at the close of a tax year following the year property was placed in service, the nonqualified nonrecourse financing for any property has increased or decreased, then the credit base for the property changes accordingly. The changes may result in an increased credit or a recapture of the credit in the year of the change. See sections 49 and 465 for details.

Specific Instructions

Partnerships, S Corporations, Estates, and Trusts

To figure the cost or basis of property to pass through to the individual partners, shareholders, or beneficiaries, complete only the following lines:

● The qualified rehabilitation expenditures shown on lines 1a through 1e,

● The basis of energy property placed in service shown on line 2a and the basis and credit rate of any transitional energy property shown on the attachment to line 2b,

● The amortizable basis of qualified timber property shown on line 3, and

● The qualified investment for transitional regular investment credit property shown on line 4.

Attach the completed form to the partnership, S corporation, estate, or trust income tax return to show the total cost or basis (or unused credit from a cooperative) that is passed through.

Special Limitations for Lines 1a Through 1e, 4, and 12

The qualified rehabilitation expenditures on lines 1a through 1e, the qualified investment on line 4, and the tax liability on line 12 are limited as follows:

● For mutual savings institutions, the line 1, 4, and 12 amounts are limited to

50% of the amounts otherwise determined.

● For regulated investment companies and real estate investment trusts, the line 1, 4, and 12 amounts are limited to a percentage of the amounts otherwise determined. Figure this percentage by dividing taxable income for the year by taxable income computed without regard to the corporation's deduction for dividends paid.

See Regulations section 1.46-4 for other details.

Part I—Current Year Investment Credit

Lines 1a–1e—Rehabilitation credit.— You are allowed a credit for certain capital costs incurred for additions or improvements to qualified existing buildings and for rehabilitation of certified historic structures. The expenditures must be added to the basis of the building, depreciated by the straight-line method, and incurred in connection with the rehabilitation of a qualified rehabilitated building.

Decrease the depreciable basis by the amount of the credit.

For filers placing property in service in 1993, the qualified rehabilitation expenditures must be for:

1. Nonresidential real property,

2. Residential rental property (certified historic structures only—see Regulations section 1.48-1(h)), or

3. Real property that has a class life of more than 12½ years.

Your building must also meet the following requirements:

1. The building must be substantially rehabilitated.

2. The building must have been placed in service before the beginning of rehabilitation. This requirement is met if the building was placed in service by any person at any time before the rehabilitation begins.

3. At least 75% of the external walls must be retained with 50% or more kept in place as external walls. Also, at least 75% of the existing internal structural framework of the building must be retained in place. This does not apply to certified historic structures.

A building is considered to be "substantially rehabilitated" if your rehabilitation expenses during a 24-month period that you select and that ends with or within your tax year are more than the greater of:

1. $5,000, or

2. Your adjusted basis in the building and its structural components.

Figure your adjusted basis on the first day of the 24-month period or the first day of your holding period, whichever is later.

If you are rehabilitating the building in phases under a written architectural plan and specifications that were completed before the rehabilitation began, substitute "60-month period" for "24-month period."

Enter in the applicable entry space next to lines 1a and 1b the qualified rehabilitation expenditures for rehabilitation property. This is property that is not covered by the transition rules. To qualify for the credit, the building must have been originally placed in service before 1936 or must be a certified historic structure. See section 47(c) for details.

Enter in the applicable entry space next to lines 1c, 1d, and 1e the qualified rehabilitation expenditures for transition rehabilitation property and certain projects. See section 251(d) of the Tax Reform Act of 1986 for details.

If you are claiming a credit for a certified historic structure on line 1b or 1e, you must attach a copy of your request for final National Park Service (NPS) certification (NPS Form 10-168c). Enter the building number assigned by the NPS in the space provided. If the qualified rehabilitation expenditures are from a partnership, S corporation, estate, or trust, enter the identifying number of the flow-through entity in the space provided.

Line 2a—Energy credit.—Enter the basis of energy property placed in service during the tax year. Energy property is equipment that uses solar energy to generate electricity, to heat or cool (or provide hot water for use in) a structure, or to provide solar process heat. Energy property is also equipment used to produce or use energy derived from a geothermal deposit (within the meaning of section 613(e)(2)). For electricity produced by geothermal power, include equipment up to, but not including, the electrical transmission stage.

To qualify, the property must be constructed, reconstructed, or erected by the taxpayer. If acquired by the taxpayer, the original use of such property must commence with the taxpayer. The property must be subject to depreciation (or amortization in lieu of depreciation). The property must meet the performance and quality standards, if any, that have been prescribed by regulations and are in effect at the time the property is acquired.

Energy property does not include any property that is public utility property as defined by section 46(f)(5) as in effect on November 4, 1990.

If energy property is financed in whole or in part by subsidized energy financing or by tax-exempt private activity bonds, the amount that you can claim as basis is a fraction that is 1 reduced by the fraction, the numerator of which is that

portion of the basis allocable to such financing or proceeds, and the denominator of which is the basis of the property. For example, if the basis of the property is $100,000 and the portion allocable to such financing or proceeds is $20,000, the fraction of the basis that you may claim the credit on is 4/5 (i.e., 1 minus $20,000/$100,000).

Subsidized energy financing means financing provided under a Federal, state, or local program, a principal purpose of which is to provide subsidized financing for projects designed to conserve or produce energy.

You must reduce the basis by 50% of the energy credit determined.

Line 2b—Transition energy property.— If you have energy property that is transition property defined in section 49(e) as in effect on November 4, 1990, attach a statement showing your computation of the allowable credit.

Reduce any credit by 35% as required by section 49(c) as in effect on November 4, 1990.

Line 3—Reforestation credit.—Enter the portion of the amortizable basis of any qualified timber property that was acquired during the tax year and is taken into account under section 194. Only direct costs for planting and seeding can be amortized. These include costs for site preparation, seed, seedlings, labor, tools, and depreciation on equipment such as tractors, trucks, and tree planters used in planting or seeding. Depreciation is a direct cost only for the period of time the equipment is used in these activities.

You cannot claim more than $10,000 (or $5,000 in the case of a married person filing a separate return) of amortizable basis acquired during the tax year. For more information, see Regulations sections 1.194-2 and 1.48-1(p).

You must reduce the amortizable basis by 50% of the reforestation credit determined.

Line 4—Regular investment credit for transition property.—Enter the qualified investment of any property that qualified for "regular" investment credit as transition property (as defined in section 49(e) as in effect on November 4, 1990). You must reduce the regular 10% credit for transition property by 35%, thus making the credit for this type of property 6.5%.

You must reduce the basis in the property by the amount of the credit.

Line 5—Credit from cooperatives.— Section 1381(a) cooperative organizations may claim the investment credit. If the cooperative cannot use any of the credit because of the tax liability limitation, the unused credit must be allocated to the patrons of the cooperative. The recapture provisions of section 50 apply as if the cooperative had kept the credit and not allocated it. Patrons should enter their unused regular investment credit and their unused energy credit from cooperatives.

Part II—Tax Liability Limitation

If item (1), (2), or (3) listed in **Who Must File Form 3800** on page 1 applies, do not complete Part II. Instead complete Form 3800.

Line 8g—Credit for fuel from a nonconventional source.—Corporations enter the nonconventional source fuel credit from Form 1120, Schedule J, line 4d. For individuals, the credit is included in the total for line 45 of Form 1040 (report only the portion of line 45 that is the nonconventional source fuel credit). Other filers, enter the credit from the appropriate line of your return.

Line 10—Tentative minimum tax.— Enter the tentative minimum tax (TMT) that was figured on the appropriate alternative minimum tax (AMT) form or schedule. Although you may not owe AMT, you must still compute the TMT to figure your credit.

Line 12.—If a husband and wife file separate returns, each must use $12,500 instead of $25,000. But if one of them has no investment credit (or no carryforwards or carrybacks to the current year), then the other may use the entire $25,000.

A member of a controlled group must enter only its apportioned share of the $25,000.

A mutual savings institution, a regulated investment company, or a real estate investment trust should see **Special Limitations for Lines 1a Through 1e, 4, and 12** on page 2.

For estates and trusts, the $25,000 limitation is reduced by the same proportionate share of income that was allocated to the beneficiaries.

Note: *If you cannot use all of the credit because of the tax liability limitation (line 6 is greater than line 13), carry the excess back 3 years and then forward 15 years. See the separate Instructions for Form 3800 for details.*

Form 3800

Department of the Treasury
Internal Revenue Service

General Business Credit

▶ Attach to your tax return.

▶ See separate instructions.

OMB No. 1545–0895

19**93**

Attachment
Sequence No. **22**

Name(s) as shown on return

Identifying number

Part I   Tentative Credit

1a	Current year investment credit (Form 3468, Part I)	1a
b	Current year jobs credit (Form 5884, Part I)	1b
c	Current year credit for alcohol used as fuel (Form 6478)	1c
d	Current year credit for increasing research activities (Form 6765, Part III)	1d
e	Current year low-income housing credit (Form 8586, Part I)	1e
f	Current year enhanced oil recovery credit (Form 8830, Part I)	1f
g	Current year disabled access credit (Form 8826, Part I)	1g
h	Current year renewable electricity production credit (Form 8835, Part I)	1h
i	Other current year credit(s). Check if from ☐ Form 8845 ☐ Form 8846 ☐ Form 8847	1i
j	**Current year general business credit.** Add lines 1a through 1i	1j
2	Passive activity credits included on lines 1a through 1i (see instructions).	2
3	Subtract line 2 from line 1j	3
4	Passive activity credits allowed for 1993 (see instructions)	4
5	Carryforward of general business, WIN, or ESOP credit to 1993 (see instructions for the schedule to attach)	5
6	Carryback of general business credit to 1993 (see instructions)	6
7	**Tentative general business credit.** Add lines 3 through 6	7

Part II   General Business Credit Limitation Based on Amount of Tax

8a	Individuals. Enter amount from Form 1040, line 40		
b	Corporations. Enter amount from Form 1120, Schedule J, line 3 (or Form 1120-A, Part I, line 1)	8	
c	Other filers. Enter regular tax before credits from your return		
9	Credits that reduce regular tax before the general business credit—		
a	Credit for child and dependent care expenses (Form 2441, line 10)	9a	
b	Credit for the elderly or the disabled (Schedule R (Form 1040), line 21)	9b	
c	Mortgage interest credit (Form 8396, line 11)	9c	
d	Foreign tax credit (Form 1116, line 32, or Form 1118, Sch. B, line 12)	9d	
e	Possessions tax credit (Form 5735, line 14)	9e	
f	Orphan drug credit (Form 6765, line 10)	9f	
g	Credit for fuel from a nonconventional source	9g	
h	Qualified electric vehicle credit (Form 8834, line 17)	9h	
i	Add lines 9a through 9h	9i	
10	Net regular tax. Subtract line 9i from line 8	10	
11	Tentative minimum tax (see instructions):		
a	Individuals. Enter amount from Form 6251, line 26		
b	Corporations. Enter amount from Form 4626, line 14	11	
c	Estates and trusts. Enter amount from Form 1041, Schedule H, line 37		
12	Net income tax:		
a	Individuals. Add line 10 above and line 28 of Form 6251		
b	Corporations. Add line 10 above and line 16 of Form 4626	12	
c	Estates and trusts. Add line 10 above and line 39 of Form 1041, Schedule H		
13	If line 10 is more than $25,000, enter 25% (.25) of the excess (see instructions)	13	
14	Subtract line 11 or line 13, whichever is greater, from line 12. If less than zero, enter -0- . .	14	
15	**General business credit allowed for current year.** Enter the **smaller** of line 7 or line 14. Also enter this amount on Form 1040, line 44; Form 1120, Schedule J, line 4e; Form 1120-A, Part I, line 2a; or on the appropriate line of your return. (Individuals, estates, and trusts, see instructions if the credit for increasing research activities is claimed. C corporations, see instructions for Schedule A if any regular investment credit carryforward is claimed. See the instructions if the corporation has undergone a post-1986 "ownership change.")	15	

For Paperwork Reduction Act Notice, see page 2 of this form.   Cat. No. 12392F   Form **3800** (1993)

Form 3800 (1993)   Page **2**

Schedule A— **Additional General Business Credit Allowed By Section 38(c)(2) (Before Repeal by the Revenue Reconciliation Act of 1990)—Only Applicable to C Corporations**

16 Enter the portion of the credit shown on line 5, page 1, that is attributable to the regular investment credit under section 46 (before amendment by the Revenue Reconciliation Act of 1990) . . .   **16**

17 Tentative minimum tax (from line 11, page 1) **17**

18 Multiply line 17 by 25% (.25) **18**

19 Enter the amount from line 14, page 1. . . . .   **19**

20 Enter the portion of the credit shown on line 7, page 1, that is NOT attributable to the regular investment credit under section 46 (before amendment by the Revenue Reconciliation Act of 1990). **20**

21 Subtract line 20 from line 19 (if less than zero, enter -0-) **21**

22 Subtract line 21 from line 16 (if less than zero, enter -0-) **22**

23 For purposes of this line only, recompute the amount on line 12, Form 4626, by using zero on line 7, Form 4626, and enter the result here .   **23**

24 Multiply line 23 by 10% (.10) **24**

25 Net income tax (from line 12, page 1) **25**

26 General business credit (from line 15, page 1) **26**

27 Subtract line 26 from line 25 . . . .   **27**

28 Subtract line 24 from line 27 . . . .   **28**

29 Enter the smallest of line 18, line 22, or line 28 . . . .   **29**

30 Subtract line 29 from line 17 . . . .   **30**

31 Enter the greater of line 30 or line 13, page 1 . . . .   **31**

32 Subtract line 31 from line 25 . . . .   **32**

33 Enter the smaller of line 32 or line 10, page 1. Enter this amount also on line 15, page 1, instead of the amount previously computed on that line. Write "Sec. 38(c)(2)" in the margin next to your entry on line 15, page 1 . . . .   **33**

34 If line 32 is greater than line 33, enter the excess here (see instructions) **34**

Paperwork Reduction Act Notice

We ask for the information on this form to carry out the Internal Revenue laws of the United States. You are required to give us the information. We need it to ensure that you are complying with these laws and to allow us to figure and collect the right amount of tax.

The time needed to complete and file this form will vary depending on individual circumstances. The estimated average time is:

Recordkeeping . . . .11 hr., 29 min.
Learning about the law or the form . . . . 1 hr., 17 min.
Preparing and sending the form to the IRS . . 1 hr., 32 min.

If you have comments concerning the accuracy of these time estimates or suggestions for making this form more simple, we would be happy to hear from you. You can write to both the IRS and the Office of Management and Budget at the addresses listed in the instructions for the tax return with which this form is filed.

B-9   Other Tax Forms

Form **2106**	**Employee Business Expenses**	OMB No. 1545-0139
Department of the Treasury Internal Revenue Service (T)	▶ See separate instructions. ▶ **Attach to Form 1040.**	19**93** Attachment Sequence No. **54**

Your name	Social security number	Occupation in which expenses were incurred

Part I   Employee Business Expenses and Reimbursements

STEP 1 Enter Your Expenses		**Column A** Other Than Meals and Entertainment	**Column B** Meals and Entertainment
1	Vehicle expense from line 22 or line 29	1	
2	Parking fees, tolls, and transportation, including train, bus, etc., that **did not** involve overnight travel	2	
3	Travel expense while away from home overnight, including lodging, airplane, car rental, etc. **Do not** include meals and entertainment	3	
4	Business expenses not included on lines 1 through 3. **Do not** include meals and entertainment	4	
5	Meals and entertainment expenses (see instructions)	5	
6	**Total expenses.** In Column A, add lines 1 through 4 and enter the result. In Column B, enter the amount from line 5	6	

Note: *If you were not reimbursed for any expenses in Step 1, skip line 7 and enter the amount from line 6 on line 8.*

STEP 2   Enter Amounts Your Employer Gave You for Expenses Listed in STEP 1

7	Enter amounts your employer gave you that were **not** reported to you in box 1 of Form W-2. Include any amount reported under code "L" in box 13 of your Form W-2 (see instructions) . . .	7	

STEP 3   Figure Expenses To Deduct on Schedule A (Form 1040)

8	Subtract line 7 from line 6	8	
	Note: *If **both columns** of line 8 are zero, **stop here.** If Column A is less than zero, report the amount as income on Form 1040, line 7, and enter -0- on line 10, Column A.*		
9	Enter 20% (.20) of line 8, Column B	9	
10	In Column A, enter the amount from line 8. In Column B, subtract line 9 from line 8	10	
11	Add the amounts on line 10 of both columns and enter the total here. **Also, enter the total on Schedule A (Form 1040), line 19.** (Qualified performing artists and individuals with disabilities, see the instructions for special rules on where to enter the total.) . . . . ▶	11	

For Paperwork Reduction Act Notice, see instructions.   Cat. No. 11700N   Form **2106** (1993)

Form 2106 (1993)   Page **2**

Part II	**Vehicle Expenses** (See instructions to find out which sections to complete.)		**(a)** Vehicle 1	**(b)** Vehicle 2

Section A.—General Information

			(a) Vehicle 1	(b) Vehicle 2
12	Enter the date vehicle was placed in service	12	/ /	/ /
13	Total miles vehicle was driven during 1993	13	miles	miles
14	Business miles included on line 13	14	miles	miles
15	Percent of business use. Divide line 14 by line 13	15	%	%
16	Average daily round trip commuting distance	16	miles	miles
17	Commuting miles included on line 13	17	miles	miles
18	Other personal miles. Add lines 14 and 17 and subtract the total from line 13	18	miles	miles

19 Do you (or your spouse) have another vehicle available for personal purposes? . . . . □ Yes □ No

20 If your employer provided you with a vehicle, is personal use during off duty hours permitted? □ Yes □ No □ Not applicable

21a Do you have evidence to support your deduction? . . . . □ Yes □ No

21b If "Yes," is the evidence written? . . . . □ Yes □ No

Section B.—Standard Mileage Rate (Use this section only if you own the vehicle.)

22	Multiply line 14 by 28¢ (.28). Enter the result here and on line 1. (Rural mail carriers, see instructions.)	22	

Section C.—Actual Expenses

			(a) Vehicle 1		(b) Vehicle 2	
23	Gasoline, oil, repairs, vehicle insurance, etc.	23				
24a	Vehicle rentals	24a				
b	Inclusion amount (see instructions)	24b				
c	Subtract line 24b from line 24a	24c				
25	Value of employer-provided vehicle (applies only if 100% of annual lease value was included on Form W-2—see instructions)	25				
26	Add lines 23, 24c, and 25 . .	26				
27	Multiply line 26 by the percentage on line 15 . . .	27				
28	Depreciation. Enter amount from line 38 below	28				
29	Add lines 27 and 28. Enter total here and on line 1.	29				

Section D.—Depreciation of Vehicles (Use this section only if you own the vehicle.)

			(a) Vehicle 1		(b) Vehicle 2	
30	Enter cost or other basis (see instructions)	30				
31	Enter amount of section 179 deduction (see instructions) .	31				
32	Multiply line 30 by line 15 (see instructions if you elected the section 179 deduction) . . .	32				
33	Enter depreciation method and percentage (see instructions) .	33				
34	Multiply line 32 by the percentage on line 33 (see instructions) . .	34				
35	Add lines 31 and 34	35				
36	Enter the limitation amount from the table in the line 36 instructions	36				
37	Multiply line 36 by the percentage on line 15 . . .	37				
38	Enter the **smaller** of line 35 or line 37. Also, enter this amount on line 28 above	38				

1993 Department of the Treasury Internal Revenue Service

Instructions for Form 2106

Employee Business Expenses

Section references are to the Internal Revenue Code.

Paperwork Reduction Act Notice

We ask for the information on this form to carry out the Internal Revenue laws of the United States. You are required to give us the information. We need it to ensure that you are complying with these laws and to allow us to figure and collect the right amount of tax.

The time needed to complete and file this form will vary depending on individual circumstances. The estimated average time is:

Recordkeeping . . . . 1 hr., 38 min.

Learning about the law or the form . . . . 18 min.

Preparing the form . . . 1 hr., 14 min.

Copying, assembling, and sending the form to the IRS . . 42 min.

If you have comments concerning the accuracy of these time estimates or suggestions for making this form more simple, we would be happy to hear from you. You can write to both the IRS and the Office of Management and Budget at the addresses listed on **page 4** of the Instructions for Form 1040.

General Instructions

Purpose of Form

Use Form 2106 if you are an employee deducting expenses attributable to your job. See the chart at the bottom of this page to find out if you must file this form.

A Change To Note

For amounts paid or incurred after 1992, you cannot deduct any expenses for travel away from your tax home if the period of temporary employment is more than 1 year.

Additional Information

If you need more information about employee business expenses, you will find the following publications helpful:

Pub. 463, Travel, Entertainment, and Gift Expenses

Pub. 529, Miscellaneous Deductions

Pub. 534, Depreciation

Pub. 587, Business Use of Your Home

Pub. 907, Information for Persons With Disabilities

Pub. 917, Business Use of a Car

Pub. 946, How To Begin Depreciating Your Property

Specific Instructions

Part I—Employee Business Expenses and Reimbursements

Fill in ALL of Part I if you were reimbursed for employee business expenses. If you were not reimbursed for your expenses, fill in only Steps 1 and 3 of Part I.

Step 1—Enter Your Expenses

Line 1—Enter your vehicle expenses from Part II, line 22 or line 29.

Line 2—Enter parking fees, etc., that did not involve overnight travel. Do not include transportation expenses for commuting to and from work. See the line 16 instructions for the definition of **commuting**.

Line 3—Enter expenses for lodging and transportation connected with overnight travel away from your **tax home**. Do not include expenses for meals and entertainment. For details, including limitations, see Pub. 463.

Generally, your **tax home** is your main place of business or post of duty regardless of where you maintain your family home. If you do not have a regular or main place of business because of the nature of your work, then your tax home is the place where you

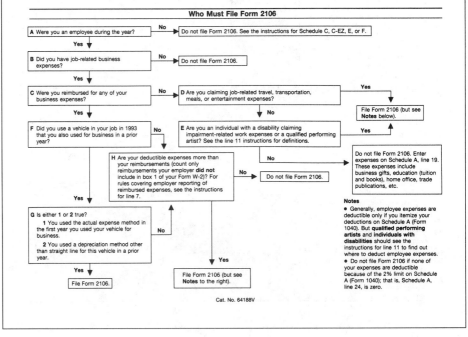

Who Must File Form 2106

A Were you an employee during the year? — No → Do not file Form 2106. See the instructions for Schedule C, C-EZ, E, or F.

Yes ↓

B Did you have job-related business expenses? — No → Do not file Form 2106.

Yes ↓

C Were you reimbursed for any of your business expenses? — No → D Are you claiming job-related travel, transportation, meals, or entertainment expenses? — Yes → File Form 2106 (but see **Notes** below).

C — Yes ↓

D — No ↓

F Did you use a vehicle in your job in 1993 that you also used for business in a prior year? — No → E Are you an individual with a disability claiming impairment-related work expenses or a qualified performing artist? See the line 11 instructions for definitions. — Yes → Do not file Form 2106. Enter expenses on Schedule A, line 19. These expenses include business gifts, education (tuition and books), home office, trade publications, etc.

F — Yes ↓

H Are your deductible expenses more than your reimbursements (count only reimbursements your employer **did not** include in box 1 of your Form W-2)? For rules covering employer reporting of reimbursed expenses, see the instructions for line 7. — No → Do not file Form 2106.

H — Yes ↓ File Form 2106 (but see **Notes** to the right).

G Is either 1 or 2 true?
1 You used the actual expense method in the first year you used your vehicle for business.
2 You used a depreciation method other than straight line for this vehicle in a prior year.

G — No → (to H)

G — Yes ↓ File Form 2106.

Notes
- Generally, employee expenses are deductible only if you itemize your deductions on Schedule A (Form 1040). But **qualified performing artists** and **individuals with disabilities** should see the instructions for line 11 to find out where to deduct employee expenses.
- Do not file Form 2106 if none of your expenses are deductible because of the 2% limit on Schedule A (Form 1040); that is, Schedule A, line 24, is zero.

Cat. No. 64188V

regularly live. If you do not fit either of these categories, you are considered an itinerant and your tax home is wherever you work. As an itinerant, you are not away from home and cannot claim a travel expense deduction. For more details on tax home, see Pub. 463.

Line 4—Enter other job-related expenses not listed on any other line on this form. Include expenses for business gifts, education (tuition and books), home office, trade publications, etc. For details, including limitations, see Pub. 463 and Pub. 529. If you are deducting home office expenses, see Pub. 587 for special instructions on how to report your expenses. If you are deducting depreciation or claiming a section 179 deduction on a cellular telephone or other similar telecommunications equipment, a home computer, etc., get **Form 4562,** Depreciation and Amortization, to figure the depreciation and section 179 deduction. Enter the depreciation and section 179 deduction on line 4.

Do not include expenses for meals and entertainment, taxes, or interest. Deductible taxes are entered on lines 5 through 8 of Schedule A.

Line 5—Enter your allowable meals and entertainment expense. Include meals while away from your tax home overnight and other business meals and entertainment. Instead of actual cost, you may be able to claim the "standard meal allowance" for your daily meals and incidental expenses while away from your tax home overnight. Under this method, you deduct a specified amount, depending on where you travel, instead of keeping records of your actual meal expenses. However, you must still keep records to prove the time, place, and business purpose of your travel. See Pub. 463 to figure your deduction using the standard meal allowance.

Step 2—Enter Amounts Your Employer Gave You for Expenses Listed in Step 1

Line 7—Enter the amounts your employer (or third party) gave you for expenses shown in Step 1 that were NOT reported to you in box 1 of your Form W-2. This includes any amount reported under code "L" in box 13 of Form W-2. Amounts reported under code "L" are certain reimbursements you received for business expenses that were not included as wages on Form W-2 because the expenses were treated as meeting specific IRS substantiation requirements.

Generally, when your employer pays for your expenses, the payments should not be included in box 1 of your Form W-2 if, within a reasonable period of time, you (a) accounted to your employer for the expenses, AND (b) were required to return, and did return, any payments not spent (or considered not spent) for business expenses. If these payments were included in box 1, ask your employer for a corrected Form W-2.

Accounting to your employer means that you gave your employer documentary evidence and an account book, diary, or similar statement to verify the amount, time, place, and business purpose of each expense. You are also treated as having accounted for your expenses if either of the following applies:

• Your employer gave you a fixed travel allowance that is similar in form to the per

Page 2

diem allowance specified by the Federal Government and you verified the time, place, and business purpose of each expense. See Pub. 463 for more details.

• Your employer reimbursed you for vehicle expenses at the standard mileage rate or according to a flat rate or stated schedule, and you verified the date of each trip, mileage, and business purpose of the vehicle use. See Pub. 917 for more details.

Allocating Your Reimbursement. If your employer paid you a single amount that covers both meals and entertainment, as well as other business expenses, you must allocate the reimbursement so that you know how much to enter in Column A and Column B of line 7. Use the following worksheet to figure this allocation.

Worksheet
1. Enter the total amount of reimbursements your employer gave you that **were not** reported to you in box 1 of Form W-2 . . . . . . _____
2. Enter the total amount of your expenses for the periods covered by this reimbursement . . . . . . _____
3. Of the amount on line 2, enter your total expense for meals and entertainment . . . . _____
4. Divide line 3 by line 2. Enter the result as a decimal (to at least two places) _____
5. Multiply line 1 by line 4. Enter the result here and in Column B, line 7 . . _____
6. Subtract line 5 from line 1. Enter this result here and in Column A, line 7 . _____

Step 3—Figure Expenses To Deduct on Schedule A (Form 1040)

Line 11—Special Rules. If you are a qualified performing artist (defined below), include your performing-arts-related expenses in the total on Form 1040, line 30. Write "QPA" and the amount in the space to the left of line 30. Your performing-arts-related business expenses are deductible whether or not you itemize deductions on Schedule A. The expenses are not subject to the 2% limit that applies to most other employee business expenses.

A **qualified performing artist** is an individual who (1) performed services in the performing arts as an employee for at least two employers during the tax year, (2) received from at least two of those employers wages of $200 or more per employer, (3) had allowable business expenses attributable to the performing arts of more than 10% of gross income from the performing arts, and (4) had adjusted gross income of $16,000 or less before deducting expenses as a performing artist. To be treated as a qualified performing artist, a married individual must also file a joint return, unless the individual and his or her spouse lived apart for all of 1993. On a joint return, requirements (1), (2), and (3) must be figured separately for each spouse. However, requirement (4) applies to the combined adjusted gross income of both spouses.

If you are an **individual with a disability** and are claiming impairment-related work expenses (defined below), enter the part of the line 11 amount attributable to those expenses on Schedule A, line 25, instead of on Schedule A, line 19. Your impairment-related work expenses are not subject to the

2% limit that applies to most other employee business expenses.

Impairment-related work expenses are the allowable expenses of an individual with physical or mental disabilities for attendant care at his or her place of employment. They also include other expenses in connection with the place of employment that enable the employee to work.

See Pub. 907 for more details.

Part II—Vehicle Expenses

There are two methods for computing vehicle expenses—the Standard Mileage Rate and the Actual Expense Method. In some cases, you must use the Actual Expense Method instead of the Standard Mileage Rate. Use the following two flowcharts to see which method you should use. Rural mail carriers should see the line 22 instructions instead of using the flowcharts for special rules that apply to them.

If you have the option of using either the Standard Mileage Rate or Actual Expense Method, you should calculate your expenses using each method, and use the method most advantageous to you.

For Vehicles Placed in Service After 1980

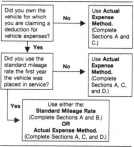

For Vehicles Placed in Service Before 1981

Section A.—General Information

All individuals claiming vehicle expenses must complete Section A.

If you used two vehicles for business during the year, use a separate column for each vehicle in Sections A, C, and D. If you

used more than two, attach a computation using the format in Sections A, C, and D.

Line 12—Date placed in service is generally the date you first start using your vehicle. However, if you first start using your vehicle for personal use and later convert it to business use, the vehicle is treated as placed in service on the date you started using it for business.

Line 13—Enter the total miles you drove each vehicle during the year for all purposes. However, if you converted your vehicle during the year from personal to business use (or from business to personal use), enter the total miles only for the months during which you drove the vehicle for business purposes.

Line 14—Do not include commuting miles on this line; commuting miles are not considered business miles. See the line 16 instructions for the definition of **commuting**.

Line 15—Divide line 14 by line 13 to figure your business use percentage. However, if you converted your vehicle during the year from personal to business use (or from business to personal use), multiply this percentage by the number of months during which you drove the vehicle for business purposes and divide the result by 12.

Line 16—Enter your average daily round trip commuting distance. If you went to more than one regular place of business, figure the average.

Commuting is travel between your home and any location at which you work or perform services on a regular basis even if you do not go to the same location each day. However, travel between your home and a location at which you perform services on an irregular or short-term basis (generally a matter of days or weeks) is not commuting.

Line 17—If you do not know the total actual miles you used your vehicle for commuting during the year, figure the amount to enter on line 17 by multiplying the number of days during the year that you used each vehicle to drive to and from your regular place of business by the average daily round trip commuting distance in miles. However, if you converted your vehicle during the year from personal to business use (or from business to personal use), enter the miles you used your vehicle for commuting only for the same period of time you drove your vehicle for business purposes.

Section B.—Standard Mileage Rate

If you do not own the vehicle, skip Section B and go to Section C.

You may use the standard mileage rate instead of actual expenses to figure the deductible costs of operating a passenger car, including a van, pickup, or panel truck. If you want to use the standard mileage rate for a car placed in service after 1980, you must do so in the first year you place your car in service. In later years, you may deduct actual expenses but you may not use a depreciation method other than straight line. If you do not use the standard mileage rate in the first year, you may not use it for that car for any subsequent year.

You may also deduct state and local personal property taxes. Include state and local personal property taxes on Schedule A, line 7.

Line 22—If you are a rural mail carrier (defined below) and you use the standard mileage rate to figure your vehicle expense, multiply the number of miles on line 14 by 42 cents (.42) instead of 28 cents.

You may use the higher mileage rate if you (1) were an employee of the U.S. Postal Service in 1993, (2) used your own vehicle to collect and deliver mail on a rural route, and (3) did not claim depreciation for the vehicle for any tax year beginning after 1987.

If you are also claiming the standard mileage rate for mileage driven in another business activity, you must figure the deduction for that mileage on a separate Form 2106.

See Pub. 917 for more details.

Section C.—Actual Expenses

Line 23—Enter your total annual expenses for gasoline, oil, repairs, insurance, tires, license plates, or similar items. Do not include state and local personal property taxes or interest expense you paid. Include state and local personal property taxes on Schedule A, line 7.

Line 24a—If you rented or leased a vehicle during the year instead of using one you own, enter the cost of renting. Also, include on this line any temporary vehicle rentals not included on line 3, such as when your car was being repaired.

Line 24b—If you leased a vehicle for a term of 30 days or more after June 18, 1984, you may have to reduce your deduction for vehicle lease payments by an amount called the **inclusion amount.** You may have to enter the inclusion amount on line 24b if—

The lease term began:	And the vehicle's fair market value on the first day of the lease exceeded:
During 1993	$14,300
During 1992	$13,700
During 1991	$13,400
After 1986 but before 1991 . .	$12,800

If the lease term began after June 18, 1984, but before January 1, 1987, see Pub. 917 to find out if you have an inclusion amount.

See Pub. 917 to figure the inclusion amount. Enter the inclusion amount on line 24b. If you have no inclusion amount, leave line 24b blank.

Line 25—If during 1993 your employer provided a vehicle for your business use and included 100% of its annual lease value in box 1 of your Form W-2, enter this amount on line 25. If less than 100% of the annual lease value was included in box 1 of your Form W-2, skip line 25.

Section D.—Depreciation of Vehicles

Depreciation is an amount you can deduct to recover the cost or other basis of your vehicle over a certain number of years. In some

cases, you may elect to expense, under section 179, part of the cost of your vehicle in the year of purchase. For more details, see Pub. 917.

Line 30—Enter the vehicle's actual cost or other basis (unadjusted for prior years' depreciation). If you traded in your vehicle, your basis is the adjusted basis of the old vehicle (figured as if 100% of the vehicle's use had been for business purposes) plus any additional amount you pay for your new vehicle. Reduce your basis by any diesel fuel tax credit, qualified electric vehicle credit, or deduction for clean-fuel vehicles you claimed. For any vehicle purchased after 1986, add to your basis any sales tax paid on the vehicle.

If you converted the vehicle from personal use to business use, your basis for depreciation is the smaller of the vehicle's adjusted basis or its fair market value on the date of conversion.

Line 31—If 1993 is the first year your vehicle was placed in service and the percentage on line 15 is more than 50%, you may elect to deduct as an expense a portion of the cost (subject to a yearly limit). To calculate this section 179 deduction, multiply the part of the cost of the vehicle that you choose to expense by the percentage on line 15. The total of your depreciation and section 179 deduction cannot be more than $2,860 multiplied by the percentage on line 15. Your section 179 deduction for the year cannot be more than the income from your job and any other active trade or business on your Form 1040.

Caution: *If you are claiming a section 179 deduction on other property, or you placed more than $200,000 of section 179 property in service during the year, use Form 4562 to figure your section 179 deduction. Enter the amount of the section 179 deduction allocable to your vehicle (from Form 4562, line 12) on Form 2106, line 31.*

Note: *For section 179 purposes, the cost of the new vehicle does not include the adjusted basis of the vehicle you traded in.*

Example:

Cost including taxes	$15,000
Adjusted basis of trade-in . .	− $ 2,000
Section 179 basis	= $13,000
Limit on depreciation and section 179 deduction	$ 2,860

Smaller of:

Section 179 basis, or Limit on depreciation and section 179 deduction	$ 2,860
Percentage on line 15	x 75%
Section 179 deduction	= $ 2,145

Line 32—To figure the basis for depreciation, multiply line 30 by the percentage on line 15. From that result, subtract the full amount of any section 179 deduction (and half of any investment credit taken before 1986 unless you took the reduced credit).

Line 33—If you used the standard mileage rate in the first year the vehicle was placed in service and now elect to use the actual expense method, you **MUST** use the straight line method of depreciation for the vehicle's estimated useful life. Otherwise, use the chart below to find the depreciation method and percentage to enter on line 33. (For example, if you placed a car in service on December 1, 1993, and you use the method and percentage in column (a), enter "200 DB 5%" on line 33.) To use the chart, first find the date you placed the vehicle in service (line 12). Then, select the depreciation method and percentage from column (a), (b), (c), or (d). For vehicles placed in service before 1993, use the same method you used on last year's return unless a decline in your business use requires a change to the straight line method. For vehicles placed in service during 1993, select the depreciation method and percentage after reading the explanation for each column below.

Column (a)—You may use column (a) only if the business use percentage on line 15 is more than 50%. The method in this column, the 200% declining balance method, will give you the largest deduction in the year your vehicle is placed in service. This column is also used for vehicles placed in service before 1987 and depreciated under ACRS (accelerated cost recovery system).

Column (b)—You may use column (b) only if the business use percentage on line 15 is more than 50%. The method in this column, the 150% declining balance method, will give you a smaller depreciation deduction than in column (a) for the first 3 years. However, you will not have a "depreciation adjustment" on this item for alternative minimum tax purposes. This may result in a smaller tax liability if you must file **Form 6251,** Alternative Minimum Tax—Individuals.

Column (c)—You must use column (c), or column (d) if applicable, if the business use percentage on line 15 is 50% or less. The method in this column is the straight line method over 5 years. It is optional if the business use percentage on line 15 is more than 50%.

Note: If your vehicle was used more than 50% for business in the year it was placed in service and used 50% or less in a later year, part of the depreciation and section 179 deduction previously claimed may have to be added back to your income in the later year. Figure the amount to be included in income on **Form 4797,** Sales of Business Property.

Column (d)—You must use column (d) if you placed your vehicle in service before 1987 and you elected the straight line method over a recovery period of 12 years.

Caution: If you placed other business property in service during the year you placed your vehicle in service (for any year after 1986), you may not be able to use the chart shown below. See Pub. 534 for the proper depreciation rate to use.

Depreciation Method and Percentage Chart

Date Placed in Service	(a)	(b)	(c)	(d)
Oct. 1—Dec. 31, 1993	200 DB 5%	150 DB 3.75%	SL 2.5%	
Jan. 1—Sept. 30, 1993	200 DB 20%	150 DB 15%	SL 10%	
Oct. 1—Dec. 31, 1992	200 DB 38%	150 DB 28.88%	SL 20%	
Jan. 1—Sept. 30, 1992	200 DB 32%	150 DB 25.5%	SL 20%	
Oct. 1—Dec. 31, 1991	200 DB 22.8%	150 DB 20.21%	SL 20%	
Jan. 1—Sept. 30, 1991	200 DB 19.2%	150 DB 17.85%	SL 20%	
Oct. 1—Dec. 31, 1990	200 DB 13.68%	150 DB 16.4%	SL 20%	
Jan. 1—Sept. 30, 1990	200 DB 11.52%	150 DB 16.66%	SL 20%	
Oct. 1—Dec. 31, 1989	200 DB 10.94%	150 DB 16.41%	SL 20%	
Jan. 1—Sept. 30, 1989	200 DB 11.52%	150 DB 16.66%	SL 20%	
Oct. 1—Dec. 31, 1988	200 DB 9.58%	150 DB 14.35%	SL 17.5%	
Jan. 1—Sept. 30, 1988	200 DB 5.76%	150 DB 8.33%	SL 10%	
Jan. 1—Dec. 31, 1987	MACRS*	MACRS*	SL*	
June 19, 1984—Dec. 31, 1986	ACRS*		SL*	SL 8.333%
Jan. 1, 1982—June 18, 1984				SL 8.333%
Jan. 1—Dec. 31, 1981				Sl. 4.167%

*Enter your unrecovered basis, if any, on line 34. See Pub. 917 for more information.

Line 34—If during the year you sold or exchanged your vehicle that was placed in service: **(a)** Before 1987, enter -0- on line 34 for that vehicle; **(b)** After 1986, multiply the result for line 34 by 50% and enter on line 34. However, do not multiply by 50% if you originally placed the vehicle in service during the last 3 months of a year after 1986. Instead, multiply the result for line 34 by the percentage shown below for the month you disposed of the vehicle:

Month	Percentage
Jan., Feb., March	12.5%
April, May, June	37.5%
July, Aug., Sept.	62.5%
Oct., Nov., Dec.	87.5%

Line 36—Using the chart below, find the date you placed your vehicle in service. Then, enter on line 36 the corresponding amount from the **Limitation** column. If your vehicle was placed in service before June 19, 1984, skip lines 36 and 37 and enter on line 38 the amount from line 35.

Date Vehicle Was Placed in Service	Limitation
Jan. 1—Dec. 31, 1993	$2,860
Jan. 1—Dec. 31, 1992	$4,400
Jan. 1—Dec. 31, 1991	$2,550
Jan. 1, 1987—Dec. 31, 1990	$1,475
Apr. 3, 1985—Dec. 31, 1986	$4,800
Jan. 1—Apr. 2, 1985	$6,200
June 19—Dec. 31, 1984	$6,000

Form **2119**

Department of the Treasury
Internal Revenue Service

Sale of Your Home

▶ Attach to Form 1040 for year of sale.

▶ **See separate instructions.**   ▶ **Please print or type.**

OMB No. 1545-0072

1993

Attachment
Sequence No. **20**

Your first name and initial. If a joint return, also give spouse's name and initial.	Last name	Your social security number

Fill in Your Address Only If You Are Filing This Form by Itself and Not With Your Tax Return	Present address (no., street, and apt. no., rural route, or P.O. box no. if mail is not delivered to street address)	Spouse's social security number
	City, town or post office, state, and ZIP code	

Part I   General Information

1	Date your former main home was sold (month, day, year) . . . . ▶	1	/ /
2	Have you bought or built a new main home?		☐ Yes ☐ No
3	Is or was any part of either main home rented out or used for business? If "Yes," see instructions . .		☐ Yes ☐ No

Part II   Gain on Sale—Do not include amounts you deduct as moving expenses.

4	Selling price of home. Do not include personal property items you sold with your home . .	4	
5	Expense of sale (see instructions)	5	
6	Amount realized. Subtract line 5 from line 4	6	
7	Adjusted basis of home sold (see instructions)	7	
8	**Gain on sale.** Subtract line 7 from line 6	8	

Is line 8 more than zero?

Yes ▶ If line 2 is "Yes," you **must** go to Part III or Part IV, whichever applies. If line 2 is "No," go to line 9.

No ▶ **Stop** and attach this form to your return.

9	If you haven't replaced your home, do you plan to do so within the **replacement period** (see instructions)? ☐ Yes ☐ No

● If line 9 is "Yes," stop here, attach this form to your return, and see **Additional Filing Requirements** in the instructions.

● If line 9 is "No," you **must** go to Part III or Part IV, whichever applies.

Part III   One-Time Exclusion of Gain for People Age 55 or Older—By completing this part, you are electing to take the one-time exclusion (see instructions). If you are not electing to take the exclusion, go to Part IV now.

10	Who was age 55 or older on the date of sale? . . . . ☐ You ☐ Your spouse ☐ Both of you
11	Did the person who was age 55 or older own and use the property as his or her main home for a total of at least 3 years (except for short absences) of the 5-year period before the sale? If "No," go to Part IV now . . ☐ Yes ☐ No
12	At the time of sale, who owned the home? . . . . ☐ You ☐ Your spouse ☐ Both of you

13	Social security number of spouse at the time of sale if you had a different spouse from the one above. If you were not married at the time of sale, enter "None" . . . . ▶	13	
14	**Exclusion.** Enter the **smaller** of line 8 or $125,000 ($62,500 if married filing separate return). Then, go to line 15	14	

Part IV   Adjusted Sales Price, Taxable Gain, and Adjusted Basis of New Home

15	If line 14 is blank, enter the amount from line 8. Otherwise, subtract line 14 from line 8 . .	15	

● If line 15 is zero, stop and attach this form to your return.

● If line 15 is more than zero and line 2 is "Yes," go to line 16 now.

● If you are reporting this sale on the installment method, stop and see the instructions.

● All others, stop and **enter the amount from line 15 on Schedule D, col. (g), line 4 or 12.**

16	Fixing-up expenses (see instructions for time limits)	16	
17	If line 14 is blank, enter amount from line 16. Otherwise, add lines 14 and 16	17	
18	**Adjusted sales price.** Subtract line 17 from line 6	18	
19a	Date you moved into new home ▶ [/ /] **b** Cost of new home (see instructions)	19b	
20	Subtract line 19b from line 18. If zero or less, enter -0-	20	
21	**Taxable gain.** Enter the **smaller** of line 15 or line 20	21	

● If line 21 is zero, go to line 22 and attach this form to your return.

● If you are reporting this sale on the installment method, see the line 15 instructions and go to line 22.

● All others, **enter the amount from line 21 on Schedule D, col. (g), line 4 or line 12,** and go to line 22.

22	Postponed gain. Subtract line 21 from line 15	22	
23	**Adjusted basis of new home.** Subtract line 22 from line 19b	23	

Sign Here Only If You Are Filing This Form by Itself and Not With Your Tax Return

Under penalties of perjury, I declare that I have examined this form, including attachments, and to the best of my knowledge and belief, it is true, correct, and complete.

Your signature	Date	Spouse's signature	Date

▶ If a joint return, both must sign.

For Paperwork Reduction Act Notice, see separate instructions.   Cat. No. 11710J   Form **2119** (1993)

1993

 Department of the Treasury
Internal Revenue Service

Instructions for Form 2119

Sale of Your Home

General Instructions

Paperwork Reduction Act Notice

We ask for the information on this form to carry out the Internal Revenue laws of the United States. You are required to give us the information. We need it to ensure that you are complying with these laws and to allow us to figure and collect the right amount of tax.

The time needed to complete and file this form will vary depending on individual circumstances. The estimated average time is:

Recordkeeping . . . . . 46 min.

**Learning about the law
or the form** . . . . 17 min.

Preparing the form . . 1 hr., 26 min.

**Copying, assembling, and
sending the form to the IRS** . 20 min.

If you have comments concerning the accuracy of these time estimates or suggestions for making this form more simple, we would be happy to hear from you. You can write to both the **Internal Revenue Service,** Attention: Reports Clearance Officer, T:FP, Washington, DC 20224; and the **Office of Management and Budget,** Paperwork Reduction Project (1545-0072), Washington, DC 20503. **DO NOT** send this form to either of these offices. Instead, see **When and Where To File** on page 2.

Purpose of Form

Use Form 2119 to report the sale of your main home. If you replaced your main home within the replacement period, also use Form 2119 to postpone paying tax on all or part of the gain. Form 2119 is also used by people who were age 55 or older on the date of sale to elect a one-time exclusion of gain on the sale.

Caution: *If the home you sold was financed (in whole or in part) from a qualified mortgage credit certificate or the proceeds of a tax-exempt qualified mortgage bond, you may owe additional tax. Get* **Form 8828,** *Recapture of Federal Mortgage Subsidy, for details.*

Who Must File

You must file Form 1040 with Form 2119 for the year in which you sell your main home, even if the sale resulted in a loss,

you are electing the one-time exclusion for people age 55 or older, or you are postponing all or part of the gain. There may be other filing requirements as well. See **When and Where To File** on page 2.

Loss on the Sale of Your Home.—You cannot deduct a loss on the sale of your home. However, you must file Form 2119 to report the sale. Complete lines 1 through 8 of Form 2119 and attach it to your return for the year of sale. If you replace your home, the loss has no effect on the basis of your new home.

Additional Information

You may find **Pub. 523,** Selling Your Home, helpful. It has examples of how to complete Form 2119.

Definitions

Adjusted Basis.—This is your basis in the property increased or decreased by certain amounts. For details on how to figure the adjusted basis of the home you sold, see the instructions for line 7 on page 3.

Basis.—If you bought your home, your basis is the purchase price of the home. If you acquired your home other than by purchase, such as by gift, inheritance, or trade, or you built your home, see Pub. 523. For a complete discussion of basis, get **Pub. 551,** Basis of Assets.

Date of Sale.—See the instructions for line 1 on page 3.

Main Home.—Your main home is the one you live in most of the time. It can be a house, houseboat, housetrailer, cooperative apartment, condominium, etc.

Replacement Period.—This is the time period during which you must replace your old main home to postpone any of the gain from its sale. It starts 2 years before and ends 2 years after the date of sale. But this period may be longer if you are on active duty in the U.S. Armed Forces for more than 90 days or if you live and work outside the United States. For details, see Pub. 523.

Special Situations

More Than One Owner.—If you owned the old home jointly with a person other than your spouse, you may postpone gain or elect the one-time exclusion only on your ownership interest in the home. For more details, see Pub. 523.

Surviving Spouse.—If your spouse died before the old home was sold and you

owned the home jointly with your deceased spouse, you must make a special computation to figure the adjusted basis of the home you sold. For details, see **Inheritance** under **Basis** in Pub. 523.

Divorced or Separated Taxpayers.—If your home was sold in connection with a divorce or separation, see Pub. 523. Also, get **Pub. 504,** Divorced or Separated Individuals.

Condemned Property.—If your old home was condemned for public use, you can choose either to postpone gain under the rules for a condemnation or to treat the transaction as a sale of your home. See Pub. 523. Also, get **Pub. 544,** Sales and Other Dispositions of Assets.

Partial Rental or Business Use of Home.—If part of your old home was rented out or used for business, you may have to report that part of the sale on **Form 4797,** Sales of Business Property. See the instructions for line 3 on page 3.

Installment Sale.—If you provided financing for the buyer of your home, you may be able to choose to report the gain on the sale using the installment method. For details, get **Pub. 537,** Installment Sales. If you qualify and choose to do so, complete Form 2119 first and then complete **Form 6252,** Installment Sale Income. Also, see the instructions for line 15 on page 4. **Do not** report the gain from Form 2119 on Schedule D (Form 1040).

Note: *Be sure to report on Form 1040, line 8a, any interest you received on the note or other financial instrument. If the buyer used the property as a personal residence, be sure you report that buyer's name, social security number, and address on Schedule B (Form 1040).*

Casualty Damage.—If your home was damaged by fire, storm, or other casualty, get **Form 4684,** Casualties and Thefts, and its separate instructions. Also, get **Pub. 547,** Nonbusiness Disasters, Casualties, and Thefts.

Which Parts To Complete

Parts I and II.—All filers must complete Parts I and II.

Part III.—Complete this part only if you qualify for the **One-Time Exclusion for People Age 55 or Older** (see page 2) and you want to make the election for this sale.

Part IV.—Complete line 15 even if you did not take the exclusion in Part III. Complete lines 16 through 23 only if line 15 is more than zero and you answered "Yes" on line 2.

Cat. No. 18038W

When and Where To File

File Form 2119 with your tax return for the year of sale. If the amount on line 8 of Form 2119 is zero or less, you have no additional filing requirements, even if you replace your home.

Additional Filing Requirements.—If you have not replaced your home but plan to do so within the replacement period (defined on page 1), you will also have to complete a second Form 2119.

• You must file the second Form 2119 by itself if **all three** of the following apply:

1. You planned to replace your home within the replacement period.

2. You later replaced your home within the replacement period.

3. Your taxable gain (line 21 on the second Form 2119) is zero.

If your taxable gain is zero, no tax is due. But you must still file the second form to show that you replaced your home within the replacement period. Enter your name and address, and sign and date the second form. If a joint return was filed for the year of sale, both you and your spouse must sign the second Form 2119. Send the form to the place where you would file your next tax return based on the address where you now live.

• You must file **Form 1040X,** Amended U.S. Individual Income Tax Return, for the year of sale with the second Form 2119 attached if **any** of the following apply:

1. You planned to replace your home when you filed your tax return, you later replaced your home within the replacement period, **and** you had a taxable gain on line 21 of the second Form 2119.

2. You planned to replace your home when you filed your tax return but **did not** do so within the replacement period.

3. You **did not** plan to replace your home when you filed your tax return and included the gain in income, but later you did replace your home within the replacement period.

Report the correct amount of gain from Form 2119 on Schedule D (Form 1040) and attach both forms to Form 1040X. Interest will be charged on any additional tax due. If you are due a refund, interest will be included with the refund.

Recordkeeping

Keep a copy of Form 2119 (and any documents used to complete it) with your tax return for the year of sale until the statute of limitations runs out for that return. Usually, this is 3 years from the date the return was due or filed, or 2 years from the date the tax was paid, whichever is later. But if you postpone tax on any gain, keep a copy of the Form 2119 (and any documents used to complete it) with your records for the basis of your new home.

One-Time Exclusion for People Age 55 or Older

Generally, you can elect to exclude from your income up to $125,000 ($62,500 if married filing a separate return) of the gain from one sale of any main home you choose. But for sales after July 26, 1978, the exclusion is available only once. To make the election for this sale, complete Part III. You can make the election if **all three** of the following apply:

1. You or your spouse were age 55 or older on the date of sale.

2. Neither you nor your spouse have ever excluded gain on the sale of a home after July 26, 1978.

3. The person who was age 55 or older owned and lived in the home for periods adding up to at least 3 years within the 5-year period ending on the date of sale. But see **Exception for Disabled Individuals** below.

The gain excluded is never taxed. But if the gain is more than the amount excluded, also complete Part IV to figure whether the excess gain is included in your income or postponed. If the gain is less than $125,000 ($62,500 if married filing a separate return), the difference **cannot** be excluded on a future sale of another main home. Generally, you can make or revoke the election within 3 years from the due date of your return (including extensions) for the year of sale. To do so, file Form 1040X with Form 2119 attached. For more details, see Pub. 523.

Exception for Disabled Individuals.—If you meet this exception, you are treated as having lived in the home sold during any time that you lived in a facility such as a nursing home. The facility must be licensed by a state or political subdivision to care for people with your condition. You meet this exception if, during the 5-year period ending on the date of sale—

• You became physically or mentally unable to care for yourself, and

• You owned and lived in your home as your main home for a total of at least 1 year.

Married Taxpayers.—If you and your spouse owned the property jointly and file a joint return, only one of you must meet the age, ownership, and use tests to be able to make the election. If you did not own the property jointly, the spouse who owned the property must meet these tests.

If you were married at the time of sale, both you and your spouse must agree to exclude the gain. If you do not file a joint return with that spouse, your spouse must agree to exclude the gain by signing a statement saying, "I agree to the Part III election." The statement and signature may be made on a separate sheet or in the bottom margin of Form 2119.

If you sell a home while you are married and one spouse already made the election prior to the marriage, neither of you can exclude gain on the sale.

The election to exclude gain does not apply separately to you and your spouse. If you elect to exclude gain during marriage and later divorce, neither of you can make the election again.

Postponing Gain

If you buy or build another main home and move into it within the replacement period (defined on page 1), you must postpone all or part of the gain in most cases. The amount of gain postponed is shown on line 22.

If one spouse dies after the old home is sold and before the new home is bought, the gain from the sale of the old home is postponed if the above requirements are met, the spouses were married on the date of death, and the surviving spouse uses the new home as his or her main home. This rule applies whether the title of the old home is in one spouse's name or is held jointly. For more details, see Pub. 523.

If you bought more than one main home during the replacement period, only the last one you bought qualifies as your new main home for postponing gain. If you sold more than one main home during the replacement period, any sale after the first one does not qualify for postponing gain. But these rules do not apply if you sold your home because of a job change that qualifies for a moving expense deduction. If this is the case, file a Form 2119 for each sale, for the year of the sale, and attach an explanation for each sale (except the first) to Form 2119. For more details on moving expenses, get **Pub. 521,** Moving Expenses.

Applying Separate Gain to Basis of New Home.—If you are married and you or your spouse owned the old home separately but own the new home jointly, you and your spouse may elect to divide the gain and the adjusted basis. If you owned the old home jointly but you now own new homes separately, you may elect to divide the gain to be postponed. In either situation, you both must:

1. Use the old and new homes as your main homes, and

2. Sign a statement that says, "We agree to reduce the basis of the new home(s) by the gain from selling the old home." This statement can be made in the bottom margin of Form 2119 or on an attached sheet.

If you both do not meet these two requirements, you must report the gain in the regular way without allocation. For more details and examples, see **Allocation between you and your spouse** under **New Home** in Pub. 523.

Form **2120**
(Rev. January 1994)

Department of the Treasury
Internal Revenue Service

Multiple Support Declaration

▶ **Attach to Form 1040 or Form 1040A of Person
Claiming the Dependent.**

OMB No. 1545-0071
Expires 1-31-97

Attachment
Sequence No. **50**

Name of person claiming the dependent

Social security number

During the calendar year 19 ...., I paid over 10% of the support of

....
Name of person

I could have claimed this person as a dependent except that I did not pay over 50% of his or her support. I understand that this person named above is being claimed as a dependent on the income tax return of

....
Name

....
Address

I agree not to claim this person as a dependent on my Federal income tax return for any tax year that began in this calendar year.

....
Your signature

Your social security number

....
Date

Address (number, street, apt. no.)

....
City, state, and ZIP code

Instructions

Paperwork Reduction Act Notice

We ask for the information on this form to carry out the Internal Revenue laws of the United States. You are required to give us the information. We need it to ensure that you are complying with these laws and to allow us to figure and collect the right amount of tax.

The time needed to complete and file this form will vary depending on individual circumstances. The estimated average time is: **Recordkeeping**, 7 minutes; **Learning about the law or the form**, 2 minutes; **Preparing the form**, 7 minutes; and **Copying, assembling, and sending the form to the IRS**, 10 minutes.

If you have comments concerning the accuracy of these time estimates or suggestions for making this form more simple, we would be happy to hear from you. You can write to both the IRS and the Office of Management and Budget at the addresses listed in the instructions of the tax return with which this form is filed.

Purpose of Form

When two or more individuals together pay over 50% of another person's support, Form 2120 or a similar statement is used to allow one of them to claim the person as a dependent for tax purposes.

The similar statement must contain the same information that is required by this form.

Who Can Claim the Dependent

To claim someone as a dependent, you must pay over 50% of that person's living expenses (support).

If no one meets this support test, but two or more of you together provide over 50% of a person's support, then one of you can claim that person as a dependent.

To claim the dependent, you must meet **all three** of the following requirements:

1. You paid over 10% of the support, and

2. All others who paid over 10% agree not to claim the person as a dependent, and

3. The other four dependency tests are met. See **Dependents** in the Form 1040 or Form 1040A instructions.

All contributors who provided over 10% support must choose which one of them will claim the dependent. If you will be claiming the dependent, see **How To File** below.

If you are a 10% contributor but **will not** be claiming the dependent, complete and sign a Form 2120 or similar statement. Give it to the person claiming the dependent.

How To File

If you are claiming the dependent, you must attach to your tax return a Form 2120 or similar statement that is completed and signed by each of the 10% contributors who are not claiming the dependent for the tax year. Be sure your name and social security number are at the top of each Form 2120 or similar statement.

Additional Information

See **Pub. 501,** Exemptions, Standard Deduction, and Filing Information, for more information.

Cat. No. 11712F

Form **2120** (Rev. 1-94)

Form **3903**

Department of the Treasury
Internal Revenue Service

Moving Expenses

▶ Attach to Form 1040.

▶ See separate instructions.

OMB No. 1545-0062

19**93**

Attachment
Sequence No. **62**

Name(s) shown on Form 1040

Your social security number

Caution: *If you are a member of the armed forces, see the instructions before completing this form.*

1	Enter the number of miles from your **old home** to your **new workplace**	1	
2	Enter the number of miles from your **old home** to your **old workplace**	2	
3	Subtract line 2 from line 1. Enter the result but not less than zero . . . . ▶	3	

If line 3 is 35 or more miles, complete the rest of this form. Also, see **Time Test** in the instructions. If line 3 is less than 35 miles, you may not deduct your moving expenses.

Part I   Moving Expenses

Note: *Any payments your employer made for any part of your move (including the value of any services furnished in kind) should be included on your W-2 form. Report that amount on **Form 1040, line 7**. See **Reimbursements** in the instructions.*

Section A—Transportation of Household Goods

4   Transportation and storage for household goods and personal effects   4

Section B—Expenses of Moving From Old To New Home

5   Travel and lodging **not** including meals   5

6   Total meals   6

7   Multiply line 6 by 80% (.80)   7

8   Add lines 5 and 7   8

Section C—Pre-move Househunting Expenses and Temporary Quarters
         (for any 30 days in a row after getting your job)

9   Pre-move travel and lodging **not** including meals   9

10   Temporary quarters expenses **not** including meals   10

11   Total meal expenses for both pre-move househunting and temporary quarters   11

12   Multiply line 11 by 80% (.80)   12

13   Add lines 9, 10, and 12   13

Section D—Qualified Real Estate Expenses

14   Expenses of (check one)   a ☐ selling or exchanging your old home, or   }   14
                         b ☐ if renting, settling an unexpired lease.   }

15   Expenses of (check one)   a ☐ buying your new home, or   }   15
                         b ☐ if renting, getting a new lease.   }

Part II   Dollar Limits and Moving Expense Deduction

Note: *If you and your spouse moved to separate homes, see the instructions.*

16   Enter the **smaller** of:
     ● The amount on line 13, or
     ● $1,500 ($750 if married filing a separate return and at the end of   } . .   16
       1993 you lived with your spouse who also started work in 1993).   }

17   Add lines 14, 15, and 16   17

18   Enter the **smaller** of:
     ● The amount on line 17, or
     ● $3,000 ($1,500 if married filing a separate return and at the end   }   18
       of 1993 you lived with your spouse who also started work in 1993).   }

19   Add lines 4, 8, and 18. Enter the total here and on Schedule A, line 18. This is your **moving expense deduction** . . . . ▶   19

For Paperwork Reduction Act Notice, see separate instructions.   Cat. No. 12490K   Form **3903** (1993)

19**93**

 Department of the Treasury
Internal Revenue Service

Instructions for Form 3903

Moving Expenses

Paperwork Reduction Act Notice

We ask for the information on this form to carry out the Internal Revenue laws of the United States. You are required to give us the information. We need it to ensure that you are complying with these laws and to allow us to figure and collect the right amount of tax.

The time needed to complete and file this form will vary depending on individual circumstances. The estimated average time is: **Recordkeeping,** 1 hr., 5 min.; **Learning about the law or the form,** 7 min.; **Preparing the form,** 31 min.; and **Copying, assembling, and sending the form to the IRS,** 20 min.

If you have comments concerning the accuracy of these time estimates or suggestions for making this form more simple, we would be happy to hear from you. You can write to both the IRS and the Office of Management and Budget at the addresses listed in the Instructions for Form 1040.

General Instructions

Purpose of Form

Use Form 3903 to figure your moving expense deduction if you moved to a new principal place of work (workplace) within the United States or its possessions. If you qualify to deduct expenses for more than one move, use a separate Form 3903 for each move.

Note: Use **Form 3903-F,** Foreign Moving Expenses, instead of this form if you are a U.S. citizen or resident alien who moved to a new principal workplace outside the United States or its possessions.

Additional Information

For more details, get **Pub. 521,** Moving Expenses.

Who May Deduct Moving Expenses

If you moved to a different home because of a change in job location, you may be able to deduct your moving expenses. You may be able to take the deduction whether you are self-employed or an employee. But you must meet certain tests explained next.

Distance Test.—Your new principal workplace must be at least 35 miles farther from your old home than your old workplace was. For example, if your old workplace was 3 miles from your old

home, your new workplace must be at least 38 miles from that home. If you did not have an old workplace, your new workplace must be at least 35 miles from your old home. The distance between the two points is the shortest of the more commonly traveled routes between them.

Time Test.—If you are an employee, you must work full time in the general area of your new workplace for at least 39 weeks during the 12 months right after you move. If you are self-employed, you must work full time in the general area of your new workplace for at least 39 weeks during the first 12 months and a total of at least 78 weeks during the 24 months right after you move.

You may deduct your moving expenses for 1993 even if you have not met the time test before your 1993 return is due. You may do this if you expect to meet the 39-week test by the end of 1994 or the 78-week test by the end of 1995. If you deduct your moving expenses on your 1993 return but do not meet the time test, you will have to either:

● Amend your 1993 tax return by filing **Form 1040X,** Amended U.S. Individual Income Tax Return, or

● Report the amount of your 1993 moving expense deduction that reduced your 1993 income tax as income in the year you cannot meet the test. For more details, see **Time Test** in Pub. 521.

If you do not deduct your moving expenses on your 1993 return and you later meet the time test, you may take the deduction by filing an amended return for 1993. To do this, use Form 1040X.

Exceptions to the Time Test.—The time test does not have to be met in case of death. You do not have to meet the time test if any of the following apply:

● Your job ends because of disability.

● You are transferred for your employer's benefit.

● You are laid off or discharged for a reason other than willful misconduct.

● You meet the requirements (explained later) for retirees or survivors living outside the United States.

Members of the Armed Forces

If you are in the armed forces, you do not have to meet the **distance and time tests** if the move is due to a permanent change of station. A permanent change of station includes a move in connection with and within 1 year of retirement or other termination of active duty.

Note: If the total reimbursements and allowances you received from the government in connection with the move are more than your actual moving expenses, include the excess in income on Form 1040, line 7. **Do not** complete Form 3903.

How To Complete Form 3903.—If your total reimbursements and allowances are less than your actual moving expenses, first complete Part I of Form 3903 using your actual expenses. **Do not** reduce your expenses by any reimbursements or allowances you received from the government in connection with the move. Also, do not include any expenses for moving services that were provided by the government. If you and your spouse and dependents are moved to or from different locations, treat the moves as a single move.

Next, complete lines 16 through 18 of Form 3903. Then, read the instructions for line 19 on the next page to figure your moving expense deduction.

Qualified Retirees or Survivors Living Outside the United States

If you are a retiree or survivor who moved to a home in the United States or its possessions and you meet the requirements below, you are treated as if you moved to a new workplace located in the United States. You are subject to the distance test and other limitations explained on Form 3903. Use this form instead of Form 3903-F to figure your moving expense deduction.

Retirees.—You may deduct moving expenses for a move to a new home in the United States when you actually retire if both your old principal workplace and your old home were outside the United States.

Survivors.—You may deduct moving expenses for a move to a home in the United States if you are the spouse or dependent of a person whose principal workplace at the time of death was outside the United States. In addition, the expenses must be for a move (1) that begins within 6 months after the decedent's death, and (2) from a former home outside the United States that you lived in with the decedent at the time of death.

Deductible Moving Expenses

You may deduct most of the reasonable expenses you incur in moving your family and dependent household members. These include the following:

● Costs to move to the new location (Part I, Sections A and B).

● Pre-move househunting expenses and temporary quarters once you arrive in the new location (Section C).

● Certain qualified real estate expenses (Section D).

You **may not** deduct expenses of a loss on the sale of your home, mortgage penalties, refitting draperies and carpets,

Cat. No. 64324D

or canceling club memberships. Do not deduct expenses for employees such as a servant, governess, or nurse.

Reimbursements

You must include in gross income as compensation for services any reimbursement of, or payment for, moving expenses. If your employer paid for any part of your move, you must report that amount as income on **Form 1040, line 7.** Your employer should include the amount paid in your total income on Form W-2. However, if you are not sure that the reimbursements have been included on your Form W-2, check with your employer. Your employer must give you a statement showing a detailed breakdown of reimbursements or payments for moving expenses. Your employer may use **Form 4782,** Employee Moving Expense Information, or his or her own form.

You may choose to deduct moving expenses in the year you are reimbursed by your employer, even though you paid for the moving expenses in a different year. However, special rules apply. See **How To Report** in Pub. 521.

Meal Expenses

Only 80% of your meal expenses are deductible. This limit is figured on lines 7 and 12.

No Double Benefits

You may not take double benefits. For example, you may not use the moving expenses on line 14 that are part of your moving expense deduction to lower the amount of gain on the sale of your old home. In addition, you may not use the moving expenses on line 15 that are part of your moving expense deduction to add to the basis of your new home. Use **Form 2119,** Sale of Your Home, to figure the gain, if any, you must report on the sale of your old home and the adjusted basis of the new one.

Specific Instructions

Part I—Moving Expenses

Line 4.—Enter the actual cost to pack, crate, and move your household goods and personal effects. You may also include the cost to store and insure household goods and personal effects within any period of 30 days in a row after the items were moved from your old home and before they were delivered to your new home.

Lines 5 and 6.—Enter the costs of travel from your old home to your new home.

These include transportation, meals, and lodging on the way. Include costs for the day you arrive. Report the cost of transportation and lodging on line 5. Report your meal expenses separately on line 6. Although not all the members of your household have to travel together or at the same time, you may only include expenses for one trip per person.

If you use your own car(s), you may figure the expenses by using either:

- Actual out-of-pocket expenses for gas and oil, or
- Mileage at the rate of 9 cents a mile.

You may add parking fees and tolls to the amount claimed under either method. Keep records to verify your expenses.

Lines 9 through 11.—Enter the costs of travel to look for a new home before you move and temporary quarters expenses after you move. Report pre-move househunting travel and lodging on line 9, temporary quarters expenses on line 10, and the combined cost of meals on line 11.

Pre-move househunting expenses are deductible only if you:

- Took the trip after you got the job, **and**
- Returned to your old home after looking for a new one, **and**
- Traveled to the new work area primarily to look for a new home.

There is no limit on the number of househunting trips you may take and you do not have to be successful in finding a home to qualify for this deduction. If you used your own car, figure transportation costs as explained in the instructions for lines 5 and 6. If you are self-employed, you may deduct househunting costs only if you had already made substantial arrangements to begin work in the new location. See Pub. 521 for factors used to determine if substantial arrangements were made.

You may deduct the cost of meals and lodging while occupying temporary quarters in the area of your new workplace. Include the costs for any period of 30 days in a row after you get the job, but before you move into permanent quarters. If you are self-employed, you may count these expenses only if you had already made substantial arrangements to begin work in the new location.

Lines 14 and 15.—Enter your qualified real estate expenses. Also, check the appropriate box, **a** or **b.** You may include most of the costs to sell or buy a home or to settle or get a lease. Examples of expenses you **may** include are:

- Sales commissions.

- Advertising costs.
- Attorney's fees.
- Title and escrow fees.
- State transfer taxes.
- Costs to settle an unexpired lease such as attorney's fees, real estate commissions, or amounts paid to the lessor.
- Fees or commissions to get a lease, sublease, or an assignment of a lease.

Examples of expenses you **may not** include are:

- Costs to improve your home to help it sell.
- Charges for payment or prepayment of interest.
- Payments or prepayments of rent (including security deposits) to get a new lease.

Part II—Dollar Limits and Moving Expense Deductions

Lines 16 and 18.—The dollar limits on these lines apply to the total expenses **per move** even though you may claim expenses related to the same move in more than 1 year. For more details, see **How To Report** in Pub. 521.

If both you and your spouse began work at new workplaces and shared the same new home at the end of 1993, you must treat this as one move rather than two. If you file separate returns, each of you is limited to a total of $750 on line 16, and to a total of $1,500 on line 18.

If both you and your spouse began work at new workplaces but each of you moved to separate new homes, this is treated as two separate moves. If you file a joint return, line 16 is limited to a total of $3,000, and line 18 is limited to a total of $6,000. If you file separate returns, each of you is limited to a total of $1,500 on line 16, and a total of $3,000 on line 18.

Note: *If you checked box **a** on line 14, any amount on line 14 that you cannot deduct because of the dollar limits should be used on Form 2119 to decrease the gain on the sale of your old home. If you checked box **a** on line 15, use any amount on line 15 that you cannot deduct because of the dollar limit to increase the basis of your new home.*

Line 19.—If you are a member of the armed forces, add the amounts on lines 4, 8, and 18. From that total, subtract the total reimbursements and allowances you received from the government in connection with the move. If the result is more than zero, enter the result on line 19 and on Schedule A, line 18.

Form **4562**

Department of the Treasury
Internal Revenue Service (T)

Depreciation and Amortization
(Including Information on Listed Property)

▶ See separate instructions. ▶ Attach this form to your return.

OMB No. 1545-0172

1993

Attachment
Sequence No. **67**

Name(s) shown on return

Identifying number

Business or activity to which this form relates

Part I **Election To Expense Certain Tangible Property (Section 179)** (**Note:** *If you have any "Listed Property," complete Part V before you complete Part I.*)

1	Maximum dollar limitation (If an enterprise zone business, see instructions.)	**1**	$17,500
2	Total cost of section 179 property placed in service during the tax year (see instructions) . .	**2**	
3	Threshold cost of section 179 property before reduction in limitation	**3**	$200,000
4	Reduction in limitation. Subtract line 3 from line 2, but do not enter less than -0-	**4**	
5	Dollar limitation for tax year. Subtract line 4 from line 1, but do not enter less than -0-. (If married filing separately, see instructions.)	**5**	

	(a) Description of property	(b) Cost	(c) Elected cost
6			

7	Listed property. Enter amount from line 26.	**7**	
8	Total elected cost of section 179 property. Add amounts in column (c), lines 6 and 7 . . .	**8**	
9	Tentative deduction. Enter the smaller of line 5 or line 8	**9**	
10	Carryover of disallowed deduction from 1992 (see instructions).	**10**	
11	Taxable income limitation. Enter the smaller of taxable income or line 5 (see instructions) . .	**11**	
12	Section 179 expense deduction. Add lines 9 and 10, but do not enter more than line 11 . .	**12**	
13	Carryover of disallowed deduction to 1994. Add lines 9 and 10, less line 12 ▶	**13**		

Note: *Do not use Part II or Part III below for listed property (automobiles, certain other vehicles, cellular telephones, certain computers, or property used for entertainment, recreation, or amusement). Instead, use Part V for listed property.*

Part II **MACRS Depreciation For Assets Placed in Service ONLY During Your 1993 Tax Year (Do Not Include Listed Property)**

(a) Classification of property	(b) Month and year placed in service	(c) Basis for depreciation (business/investment use only—see instructions)	(d) Recovery period	(e) Convention	(f) Method	(g) Depreciation deduction
14 General Depreciation System (GDS) (see instructions):						
a 3-year property						
b 5-year property						
c 7-year property						
d 10-year property						
e 15-year property						
f 20-year property						
g Residential rental property			27.5 yrs.	MM	S/L	
			27.5 yrs.	MM	S/L	
h Nonresidential real property				MM	S/L	
				MM	S/L	
15 Alternative Depreciation System (ADS) (see instructions):						
a Class life					S/L	
b 12-year			12 yrs.		S/L	
c 40-year			40 yrs.	MM	S/L	

Part III **Other Depreciation (Do Not Include Listed Property)**

16	GDS and ADS deductions for assets placed in service in tax years beginning before 1993 (see instructions)	**16**	
17	Property subject to section 168(f)(1) election (see instructions)	**17**	
18	ACRS and other depreciation (see instructions)	**18**	

Part IV **Summary**

19	Listed property. Enter amount from line 25.	**19**	
20	**Total.** Add deductions on line 12, lines 14 and 15 in column (g), and lines 16 through 19. Enter here and on the appropriate lines of your return. (Partnerships and S corporations—see instructions)	**20**	
21	For assets shown above and placed in service during the current year, enter the portion of the basis attributable to section 263A costs (see instructions)	**21**		

For Paperwork Reduction Act Notice, see page 1 of the separate instructions. Cat. No. 12906N Form **4562** (1993)

Form 4562 (1993)　　　　　　　　　　　　　　　　　　　　　　　　　Page **2**

Part V　Listed Property—Automobiles, Certain Other Vehicles, Cellular Telephones, Certain Computers, and Property Used for Entertainment, Recreation, or Amusement

*For any vehicle for which you are using the standard mileage rate or deducting lease expense, complete **only** 22a, 22b, columns (a) through (c) of Section A, all of Section B, and Section C if applicable.*

Section A—Depreciation and Other Information (Caution: *See instructions for limitations for automobiles.*)

22a Do you have evidence to support the business/investment use claimed? ☐ **Yes** ☐ **No** **22b** If "Yes," is the evidence written? ☐ **Yes** ☐ **No**

(a) Type of property (list vehicles first)	(b) Date placed in service	(c) Business/investment use percentage	(d) Cost or other basis	(e) Basis for depreciation (business/investment use only)	(f) Recovery period	(g) Method/ Convention	(h) Depreciation deduction	(i) Elected section 179 cost
23 Property used more than 50% in a qualified business use (see instructions):								
		%						
		%						
		%						
24 Property used 50% or less in a qualified business use (see instructions):								
		%				S/L –		
		%				S/L –		
		%				S/L –		

25 Add amounts in column (h). Enter the total here and on line 19, page 1 . . . . . . **25**

26 Add amounts in column (i). Enter the total here and on line 7, page 1 . . . . **26**

Section B—Information Regarding Use of Vehicles—*If you deduct expenses for vehicles:*

• *Always complete this section for vehicles used by a sole proprietor, partner, or other "more than 5% owner," or related person.*
• *If you provided vehicles to your employees, first answer the questions in Section C to see if you meet an exception to completing this section for those vehicles.*

	(a) Vehicle 1		(b) Vehicle 2		(c) Vehicle 3		(d) Vehicle 4		(e) Vehicle 5		(f) Vehicle 6	
27 Total business/investment miles driven during the year (DO NOT include commuting miles)												
28 Total commuting miles driven during the year												
29 Total other personal (noncommuting) miles driven												
30 Total miles driven during the year. Add lines 27 through 29												
	Yes	No	Yes	No	Yes	No	Yes	No	Yes	No	Yes	No
31 Was the vehicle available for personal use during off-duty hours?												
32 Was the vehicle used primarily by a more than 5% owner or related person?												
33 Is another vehicle available for personal use?												

Section C—Questions for Employers Who Provide Vehicles for Use by Their Employees

Answer these questions to determine if you meet an exception to completing Section B. **Note:** *Section B must always be completed for vehicles used by sole proprietors, partners, or other more than 5% owners or related persons.*

	Yes	No
34 Do you maintain a written policy statement that prohibits all personal use of vehicles, including commuting, by your employees?		
35 Do you maintain a written policy statement that prohibits personal use of vehicles, except commuting, by your employees? (See instructions for vehicles used by corporate officers, directors, or 1% or more owners.)		
36 Do you treat all use of vehicles by employees as personal use?		
37 Do you provide more than five vehicles to your employees and retain the information received from your employees concerning the use of the vehicles?		
38 Do you meet the requirements concerning qualified automobile demonstration use (see instructions)? . .		

Note: *If your answer to 34, 35, 36, 37, or 38 is "Yes," you need not complete Section B for the covered vehicles.*

Part VI　Amortization

(a) Description of costs	(b) Date amortization begins	(c) Amortizable amount	(d) Code section	(e) Amortization period or percentage	(f) Amortization for this year
39 Amortization of costs that begins during your 1993 tax year:					

40 Amortization of costs that began before 1993 . . . . **40**

41 **Total.** Enter here and on "Other Deductions" or "Other Expenses" line of your return . . . **41**

Form **4684**

Department of the Treasury
Internal Revenue Service

Casualties and Thefts

▶ See separate instructions.
▶ Attach to your tax return.
▶ Use a separate Form 4684 for each different casualty or theft.

OMB No. 1545-0177

19**93**

Attachment
Sequence No. **26**

Name(s) shown on tax return

Identifying number

SECTION A—Personal Use Property (Use this section to report casualties and thefts of property **not** used in a trade or business or for income-producing purposes.)

1   Description of properties (show type, location, and date acquired for each):

Property **A** ....
Property **B** ....
Property **C** ....
Property **D** ....

		Properties (Use a separate column for each property lost or damaged from one casualty or theft.)			
		A	**B**	**C**	**D**
2 Cost or other basis of each property	2				
3 Insurance or other reimbursement (whether or not you filed a claim). See instructions . . . . . **Note:** If line 2 is **more than** line 3, skip line 4.	3				
4 Gain from casualty or theft. If line 3 is **more than** line 2, enter the difference here and skip lines 5 through 9 for that column. See instructions if line 3 includes insurance or other reimbursement you did not claim, or you received payment for your loss in a later tax year	4				
5 Fair market value **before** casualty or theft . . .	5				
6 Fair market value **after** casualty or theft	6				
7 Subtract line 6 from line 5	7				
8 Enter the **smaller** of line 2 or line 7	8				
9 Subtract line 3 from line 8. If zero or less, enter -0-	9				

10   Casualty or theft loss. Add the amounts on line 9. Enter the total **10**

11   Enter the amount from line 10 or $100, whichever is **smaller** **11**

12   Subtract line 11 from line 10 . . . . **12**
     Caution: Use only one Form 4684 for lines 13 through 18.
13   Add the amounts on line 12 of all Forms 4684 . . . . **13**

14   Combine the amounts from line 4 of all Forms 4684 . . . . **14**
15   • If line 14 is **more than** line 13, enter the difference here and on Schedule D. Do not complete the rest of this section (see instructions).
     • If line 14 is **less than** line 13, enter -0- here and continue with the form. **15**
     • If line 14 is **equal to** line 13, enter -0- here. Do not complete the rest of this section.

16   If line 14 is **less than** line 13, enter the difference **16**

17   Enter 10% of your adjusted gross income (Form 1040, line 32). Estates and trusts, see instructions **17**

18   Subtract line 17 from line 16. If zero or less, enter -0-. Also enter result on Schedule A (Form 1040), line 17. Estates and trusts, enter on the "Other deductions" line of your tax return **18**

For Paperwork Reduction Act Notice, see page 1 of separate instructions.   Cat. No. 12997O   Form **4684** (1993)

Form 4684 (1993)   Attachment Sequence No. **26**   Page **2**

Name(s) shown on tax return. Do not enter name and identifying number if shown on other side. | Identifying number

SECTION B—Business and Income-Producing Property (Use this section to report casualties and thefts of property used in a trade or business or for income-producing purposes.)

Part I **Casualty or Theft Gain or Loss** (Use a separate Part I for each casualty or theft.)

19 Description of properties (show type, location, and date acquired for each):

Property **A** ....

Property **B** ....

Property **C** ....

Property **D** ....

	Properties (Use a separate column for each property lost or damaged from one casualty or theft.)			
	A	**B**	**C**	**D**
20 Cost or adjusted basis of each property **20**				
21 Insurance or other reimbursement (whether or not you filed a claim). See the instructions for line 3 . **Note:** *If line 20 is* **more than** *line 21, skip line 22.* **21**				
22 Gain from casualty or theft. If line 21 is **more than** line 20, enter the difference here and on line 29 or line 34, column (c), except as provided in the instructions for line 33. Also, skip lines 23 through 27 for that column. See the instructions for line 4 if line 21 includes insurance or other reimbursement you did not claim, or you received payment for your loss in a later tax year **22**				
23 Fair market value **before** casualty or theft . . . **23**				
24 Fair market value **after** casualty or theft **24**				
25 Subtract line 24 from line 23 . . . . . . **25**				
26 Enter the **smaller** of line 20 or line 25 . . . . **26**				
Note: *If the property was totally destroyed by casualty or lost from theft, enter on line 26 the amount from line 20.*				
27 Subtract line 21 from line 26. If zero or less, enter -0- **27**				

28 Casualty or theft loss. Add the amounts on line 27. Enter the total here and on line 29 or line 34 (see instructions). | **28** |

Part II **Summary of Gains and Losses** (from separate Parts I)

(a) Identify casualty or theft	(b) Losses from casualties or thefts		(c) Gains from casualties or thefts includible in income
	(i) Trade, business, rental or royalty property	(ii) Income-producing property	

Casualty or Theft of Property Held One Year or Less

29	( )	( )	
	( )	( )	
30 Totals. Add the amounts on line 29 . . . . **30**	( )	( )	

31 Combine line 30, columns (b)(i) and (c). Enter the net gain or (loss) here and on Form 4797, line 15. If Form 4797 is not otherwise required, see instructions . . . . | **31** |

32 Enter the amount from line 30, column (b)(ii) here and on Schedule A (Form 1040), line 20. Partnerships, S corporations, estates and trusts, see instructions . . . . | **32** |

Casualty or Theft of Property Held More Than One Year

33 Casualty or theft gains from Form 4797, line 34 . . . . | **33** |

| **34** | | ( ) | ( ) | |
| | | ( ) | ( ) | |

35 Total losses. Add amounts on line 34, columns (b)(i) and (b)(ii) . . . **35** ( ) | ( ) |

36 Total gains. Add lines 33 and 34, column (c) . . . . | **36** |

37 Add amounts on line 35, columns (b)(i) and (b)(ii) . . . . | **37** |

38 If the loss on line 37 is **more than** the gain on line 36:

a Combine line 35, column (b)(i) and line 36, and enter the net gain or (loss) here. Partnerships and S corporations see the note below. All others enter this amount on Form 4797, line 15. If Form 4797 is not otherwise required, see instructions . . . . | **38a** |

b Enter the amount from line 35, column (b)(ii) here. Partnerships and S corporations see the note below. Individuals enter this amount on Schedule A (Form 1040), line 20. Estates and trusts, enter on the "Other deductions" line of your tax return | **38b** |

39 If the loss on line 37 is **equal to** or **less than** the gain on line 36, combine these lines and enter here. Partnerships, see the note below. All others, enter this amount on Form 4797, line 3 . . . . | **39** |

Note: *Partnerships, enter the amount from line 38a, 38b, or line 39 on Form 1065, Schedule K, line 7. S corporations, enter the amount from line 38a or 38b on Form 1120S, Schedule K, line 6.*

19**93**

 Department of the Treasury
Internal Revenue Service

Instructions for Form 4684

Casualties and Thefts

Paperwork Reduction Act Notice

We ask for the information on this form to carry out the Internal Revenue laws of the United States. You are required to give us the information. We need it to ensure that you are complying with these laws and to allow us to figure and collect the right amount of tax.

The time needed to complete and file this form will vary depending on individual circumstances. The estimated average time is:

Recordkeeping. . . . . 1 hr., 12 min.

**Learning about the
law or the form** . . . . . 10 min.

Preparing the form . . . . 58 min.

**Copying, assembling, and
sending the form to the IRS** . 35 min.

If you have comments concerning the accuracy of these time estimates or suggestions for making this form more simple, we would be happy to hear from you. You can write to both the IRS and the Office of Management and Budget at the addresses listed in the instructions for the tax return with which this form is filed.

General Instructions

Changes To Note

If your main home was located in an area declared after August 31, 1991, by the President of the United States to warrant Federal assistance as the result of a disaster, and that home or any of its contents were damaged or destroyed due to the disaster, the following new rules apply for tax years ending after August 31, 1991:

● No gain is recognized from receiving any insurance proceeds for unscheduled personal property that was part of the contents of the home.

● Any other insurance proceeds you receive for the home or its contents is treated as received for a single item of property, and any replacement property you purchase that is similar or related in service or use to the home or its contents is treated as similar or related in service or use to that single item of property. Therefore, you can choose to recognize gain only to the extent the insurance proceeds treated as received

for that single item of property exceed the cost of the replacement property.

● If you choose to postpone any gain from the receipt of insurance or other reimbursement for your main home or any of its contents, the period in which you must purchase replacement property is extended until 4 years after the end of the first tax year in which any part of the gain is realized.

● Renters receiving insurance proceeds for damaged or destroyed property in a rented home also qualify for relief under these rules if their rented home is their main home.

Example. Your main home and its contents were completely destroyed in 1993 by a flood in a Presidentially-declared disaster area. You received insurance proceeds of $200,000 for the home, $25,000 for unscheduled personal property in your home, $5,000 for jewelry, and $10,000 for a stamp collection. The jewelry and stamp collection were kept in your home and were scheduled property on your insurance policy. No gain is recognized on the $25,000 you received for the unscheduled personal property. If you reinvest the remaining proceeds of $215,000 in property similar or related in service or use to your home, jewelry, or stamp collection, you can elect to postpone any gain on that home, jewelry, or stamp collection. If you want to reinvest all of the remaining proceeds in a new main home, you can still qualify to postpone all of your gain even if you do not purchase any jewelry or stamps. If you reinvest less than $215,000, any gain is recognized only to the extent $215,000 exceeds the amount you reinvest in property similar or related in service or use to your home, jewelry, or stamp collection. To postpone gain, you must purchase the replacement property before 1998. Your basis in the replacement property equals its cost decreased by the amount of any postponed gain.

If you reported a gain in a prior year ending after August 31, 1991, that is not taxable under the new rules, or you want to change your mind about reporting or postponing a prior year gain, file an amended return for that year.

Purpose of Form

Use Form 4684 to report gains and losses from casualties and thefts. Attach Form 4684 to your tax return.

Deductible Losses

You may deduct losses from fire, storm, shipwreck, or other casualty, or theft (for example, larceny, embezzlement, and robbery).

If your property is covered by insurance, you must file a timely insurance claim for reimbursement of your loss. Otherwise, you cannot deduct the loss as a casualty or theft loss. However, the part of the loss that is not covered by insurance is still deductible.

Related expenses.—The related expenses you have due to a casualty or theft, such as expenses for the treatment of personal injuries or for the rental of a car, are not deductible as casualty or theft losses.

Costs for protection against future casualties are not deductible but should be capitalized as permanent improvements. An example would be the cost of a levee to stop flooding.

Gain on Reimbursement

If the amount you receive in insurance or other reimbursement is more than the cost or other basis of the property, you have a gain. If you have a gain, you may have to pay tax on it, or you may be able to postpone reporting the gain.

Do not report the gain on damaged, destroyed, or stolen property if you receive property that is similar or related to it in service or use. Your basis for the new property is the same as your basis for the old property.

Generally, you must report the gain if you receive unlike property or money as reimbursement. But you can choose to postpone all or part of the gain if, within 2 years of the end of the first tax year in which any part of the gain is realized, you purchase:

1. Property similar or related in service or use to the damaged, destroyed, or stolen property, or

2. A controlling interest (at least 80%) in a corporation owning such property.

To postpone all of the gain, the cost of the replacement property must be equal to or more than the reimbursement you received for your property. If the cost of the replacement property is less than the

Cat. No. 12998Z

reimbursement received, you must report the gain to the extent the reimbursement exceeds the cost of the replacement property.

For details on how to postpone the gain, get **Pub. 334,** Tax Guide for Small Business.

Which Sections To Complete

Use **Section A** to figure casualty or theft gains and losses for property that is not used in a trade or business or for income-producing purposes.

Use **Section B** to figure casualty or theft gains and losses for property that is used in a trade or business or for income-producing purposes.

If property is used partly in a trade or business and partly for personal purposes, such as a personal home with a rental unit, figure the personal part in Section A and the business part in Section B.

Additional Information

You may want to get the following publications for more information:

Pub. 225, Farmer's Tax Guide.

Pub. 525, Taxable and Nontaxable Income.

Pub. 529, Miscellaneous Deductions.

Pub. 534, Depreciation.

Pub. 547, Nonbusiness Disasters, Casualties, and Thefts.

Pub. 550, Investment Income and Expenses.

Pub. 551, Basis of Assets.

Pub. 584, Nonbusiness Disaster, Casualty, and Theft Loss Workbook.

When To Deduct a Loss

Deduct the part of your casualty or theft loss that is not reimbursable. Deduct it in the tax year the casualty occurred or the theft was discovered. However, a disaster loss and a loss from deposits in insolvent or bankrupt financial institutions may be treated differently. See **Disaster Losses** and **Special Treatment for Losses on Deposits in Insolvent or Bankrupt Financial Institutions** below.

If you are not sure whether part of your casualty or theft loss will be reimbursed, do not deduct that part until the tax year when you are reasonably certain that it will not be reimbursed.

If you are reimbursed for a loss you deducted in an earlier year, include the reimbursement in your income in the year you received it, but only to the extent the deduction reduced your tax in an earlier year.

See Pub. 547 for special rules on when to deduct losses from casualties and thefts to leased property.

Disaster Losses

A disaster loss is a loss that occurred in an area determined by the President of

Page 2

the United States to warrant Federal disaster assistance.

If your home was located in a disaster area and your state or local government ordered you to tear it down or move it because it was no longer safe to use as a home, the loss in value because it is no longer safe is treated as a disaster loss. The order for you to tear down or move the home must have been issued within 120 days after the area was officially declared a disaster area.

Use the value of your home before you moved it or tore it down as its fair market value after the casualty for purposes of figuring the disaster loss.

You may elect to deduct a disaster loss in the prior tax year as long as the loss would otherwise be allowed as a deduction in the year it occurred.

This election must be made by filing your return or amended return for the prior year, and claiming your disaster loss on it, by the later of the following two dates:

1. The due date for filing your original return (without extensions) for the tax year in which the disaster actually occurred.

2. The due date for filing your original return (including extensions) for the tax year immediately before the tax year in which the disaster actually occurred.

You may revoke your election within 90 days after making it by returning to the Internal Revenue Service any refund or credit you received from the election. If you revoke your election before receiving a refund, you must repay the refund within 30 days after receiving it.

On the return on which you claim the disaster loss, specify the date(s) of the disaster and the city, town, county, and state in which the damaged or destroyed property was located.

Note: To determine the amount to deduct for a disaster loss, you must take into account as reimbursements any benefits you received from Federal or state programs to restore your property.

Special Treatment for Losses on Deposits in Insolvent or Bankrupt Financial Institutions

If you are an individual who incurred a loss from a deposit in a bank, credit union, or other financial institution because it became insolvent or bankrupt, and you can reasonably estimate your loss, you can choose to deduct the loss as:

● A casualty loss to personal use property on Form 4684, or

● An ordinary loss (miscellaneous itemized deduction) on Schedule A (Form 1040), line 20. The maximum amount you can claim is $20,000 ($10,000 if you are married filing separately). Your deduction is reduced

by any expected state insurance proceeds and is subject to the 2% limit.

If you choose, you can wait until the year of final determination of the actual loss and treat that amount as a nonbusiness bad debt. A nonbusiness bad debt is deducted on Schedule D (Form 1040) as a short-term capital loss.

If you are a 1% or more owner, an officer of the financial institution, or related to any such owner or officer, you cannot deduct the loss as a casualty loss or as an ordinary loss. See Pub. 550 for the definition of "related."

You cannot choose the ordinary loss deduction if any part of the deposits related to the loss is federally insured.

If you decide to deduct the loss as a casualty loss or as an ordinary loss and you have more than one account in the same financial institution, you must include all your accounts. Once you make the choice, you cannot change it without permission from the IRS.

To choose to deduct the loss as a casualty loss, complete Form 4684 as follows: On line 1, show the name of the financial institution and write "Insolvent Financial Institution." Skip lines 2 through 9. Enter the amount of the loss on line 10, and complete the rest of Section A.

If, in a later year, you recover an amount you deducted as a loss, you may have to include in your income the amount recovered for that year. For details, see **Recoveries** in Pub. 525.

Specific Instructions

Section A—Personal Use Property

Use a separate column for lines 1 through 9 to show each item lost or damaged from a single casualty or theft. If more than four items were lost or damaged, use additional sheets following the format of lines 1 through 9.

Use a separate Form 4684 through line 12 for each casualty or theft involving property not used in a trade or business or for income-producing purposes.

Do not include any loss previously deducted on an estate tax return.

If you are liable for casualty or theft losses to property you **lease** from someone else, see Pub. 547.

Line 2.—Cost or other basis usually means original cost plus improvements. Subtract any postponed gain from the sale of a previous main home. Special rules apply to property received as a gift or inheritance.

Line 3.—Enter on this line the amount of insurance or other reimbursement you received or expect to receive for each property. Include your insurance coverage whether or not you are filing a

claim for reimbursement. For example, your car worth $2,000 is totally destroyed in a collision. You are insured with a $500 deductible, but decide not to report it to your insurance company because you are afraid the insurance company will cancel your policy. In this case, enter $1,500 on this line.

If you expect to be reimbursed but have not yet received payment, you must still enter the expected reimbursement from the loss. If, in a later tax year, you determine with reasonable certainty that you will not be reimbursed for all or part of the loss, you can deduct for that year the amount of the loss that is not reimbursed.

Types of reimbursements.—Insurance is the most common way to be reimbursed for a casualty or theft loss, but if:

● Part of a Federal disaster loan under the Disaster Relief Act is forgiven, the part you do not have to pay back is considered a reimbursement.

● The person who leases your property must make repairs or must repay you for any part of a loss, the repayment and the cost of the repairs are considered reimbursements.

● A court awards you damages for a casualty or theft loss, the amount you are able to collect, minus lawyers' fees and other necessary expenses, is a reimbursement.

● You accept repairs, restoration, or cleanup services provided by relief agencies, it is considered a reimbursement.

● A bonding company pays you for a theft loss, the payment is also considered a reimbursement.

Lump-sum reimbursement.—If you have a casualty or theft loss of several assets at the same time and you receive a lump-sum reimbursement, you must divide the amount you receive among the assets according to the fair market value of each asset at the time of the loss.

Grants, gifts, and other payments.—Grants and other payments you receive to help you after a casualty are considered reimbursements only if they are specifically designated to repair or replace your property. Such payments, if so designated, will reduce your casualty loss deduction. If there are no conditions on how you have to use the money you receive, it is not a reimbursement.

Use and occupancy insurance.—If insurance reimburses you for your loss of business income, it does not reduce your casualty or theft loss. The reimbursement is income, however, and is taxed in the same manner as your business income.

Line 4.—If you are entitled to an insurance payment or other reimbursement for any part of a casualty or theft loss but you choose not to file a claim for the loss, you cannot realize a gain from that payment or reimbursement. Therefore, figure the gain on line 4 by subtracting your cost or other basis in the property (line 2) **only** from the amount of reimbursement you actually received. Enter the result on line 4, but do not enter less than zero.

If you filed a claim for reimbursement but did not receive it until after the year of the casualty or theft, see Pub. 547 for information on how to report the reimbursement.

Lines 5 and 6.—Fair market value is the price at which the property would change hands between a willing buyer and a willing seller, each having a knowledge of the relevant facts. The difference between the fair market value immediately before the casualty or theft and the fair market value immediately after represents the decrease in fair market value because of the casualty or theft.

The fair market value of property after a theft is zero if the property is not recovered.

Fair market value is generally determined by competent appraisal. The appraiser's knowledge of sales of comparable property about the same time as the casualty or theft, knowledge of your property before and after the occurrence, and the methods of determining fair market value are important elements in proving your loss.

The appraised value of property immediately after the casualty must be adjusted (increased) for the effects of any general market decline that may occur at the same time as the casualty or theft. For example, the value of all nearby property may become depressed because it is in an area where such occurrences are commonplace. This general decline in market value is not part of the property's decrease in fair market value as a result of the casualty or theft.

Replacement cost or the cost of repairs is not necessarily fair market value. However, you may be able to use the cost of repairs to the damaged property as evidence of loss in value if:

● The repairs are necessary to restore the property to the condition it was in immediately before the casualty;

● The amount spent for repairs is not excessive;

● The repairs only correct the damage caused by the casualty; and

● The value of the property after the repairs is not, as a result of the repairs, more than the value of the property immediately before the casualty.

To figure a casualty loss to real estate not used in a trade, business, or for income-producing purposes, measure the decrease in value of the property as a whole. All improvements, such as buildings, trees, and shrubs, are considered together as one item. Figure the loss separately for other items. For example, figure the loss separately for each piece of furniture.

Line 15.—If there is a net gain on this line, combine your short-term gains with your short-term losses, and enter the net short-term gain or loss on Schedule D (Form 1040), line 4. Fiduciaries enter this amount on Schedule D (Form 1041), line 1, and write "Form 4684, Section A." Combine your long-term gains with your long-term losses and enter the net long-term gain or loss on Schedule D (Form 1040), line 12. Fiduciaries enter this amount on Schedule D (Form 1041), line 7, and write "Form 4684, Section A."

The holding period for long-term gains and losses is more than 1 year. For short-term gains and losses it is 1 year or less. To figure the holding period, begin counting on the day after you received the property and include the day the casualty or theft occurred.

Line 17.—Estates and trusts figure adjusted gross income in the same way as individuals, except that the costs of administration are allowed in figuring adjusted gross income.

Section B—Business and Income-Producing Property

Use a separate column of Part I, lines 19 through 27, to show each item lost or damaged from a single casualty or theft. If more than four items were lost or damaged, use additional sheets following the format of Part I, lines 19 through 27.

Use a separate Section B, Part I, of Form 4684 for each casualty or theft involving property used in a trade or business or for income-producing purposes. Use one Section B, Part II, to combine all Sections B, Part I.

For details on the treatment of casualties or thefts to business or income-producing property, including rules on the loss of inventory through casualty or theft, see Pub. 334.

Note: *A gain or loss from a casualty or theft of property used in a passive activity is not taken into account in determining the loss from a passive activity unless losses similar in cause and severity recur regularly in the activity. See* **Form 8582,** *Passive Activity Loss Limitations, and its instructions for details.*

Line 20.—Cost or adjusted basis usually means original cost plus improvements, minus depreciation allowed or allowable (including any section 179 expense deduction), amortization, depletion, etc. Special rules apply to property received as a gift or inheritance. See Pub. 551 for details.

Line 21.—See the instructions for line 3.
Line 22.—See the instructions for line 4.

Page 3

Lines 23 and 24.—See the instructions for lines 5 and 6 for details on determining fair market value.

Loss on each item figured separately.—Unlike a casualty loss to personal use real estate, in which all improvements are considered one item, a casualty loss to business or income-producing property must be figured separately for each item. For example, if casualty damage occurs to both a building and to trees on the same piece of real estate, measure the loss separately for the building and for the trees.

Line 26.—If you have business or income-producing property that is completely lost (becomes totally worthless) because of a casualty or theft, figure your loss without taking into account any decrease in fair market value.

Line 28.—If the amount on line 28 includes losses on property held 1 year or less, and on property held for more than 1 year, you must allocate the amount between lines 29 and 34 according to how long you held each property. Enter on line 29 all gains and losses to property held 1 year or less. Enter on line 34 all gains and losses to property held more than 1 year, except as provided in the instructions for line 33 below.

Part II, Column (a).—Use a separate line for each casualty or theft.

Part II, Column (b)(i).—Enter the part of line 28 from trade, business, rental, or royalty property (other than property you used in performing services as an employee). Enter in column (b)(ii) the part of line 28 from property you used in performing services as an employee.

Part II, Column (b)(ii).—Enter the part of line 28 from income-producing property and from property you used in performing services as an employee. Income-producing property is property held for investment, such as stocks, notes, bonds, gold, silver, vacant lots, and works of art.

Line 31.—If **Form 4797**, Sales of Business Property, is not otherwise required, enter the amount from this line on page 1 of your tax return, on the line identified as from Form 4797. Write "Form 4684."

Line 32.—Estates and trusts, enter on the "Other deductions" line of your tax return. Partnerships, enter on Form 1065, Schedule K, line 11. S corporations, enter on Form 1120S, Schedule K, line 10. Write "Form 4684."

Line 33.—If you had a casualty or theft gain from certain trade, business, or income-producing property held more than 1 year, you may have to recapture part or all of the gain as ordinary income. See the instructions for Form 4797, Part III, for more information on the types of property subject to recapture. If recapture applies, complete Form 4797, Part III, and this line, instead of Form 4684, line 34.

Line 38a.—Taxpayers, other than partnerships and S corporations, if Form 4797 is not otherwise required, enter the amount from this line on page 1 of your tax return, on the line identified as from Form 4797. Write "Form 4684."

Form 4797

Department of the Treasury
Internal Revenue Service   (T)

Sales of Business Property

(Also Involuntary Conversions and Recapture Amounts
Under Sections 179 and 280F(b)(2))

▶ Attach to your tax return.   ▶ See separate instructions.

OMB No. 1545-0184

1993

Attachment
Sequence No. **27**

Name(s) shown on return | Identifying number

1   Enter here the gross proceeds from the sale or exchange of real estate reported to you for 1993 on Form(s) 1099-S (or a substitute statement) that you will be including on line 2, 11, or 22 . . . .   **1**

Part I   Sales or Exchanges of Property Used in a Trade or Business and Involuntary Conversions From Other Than Casualty or Theft—Property Held More Than 1 Year

(a) Description of property	(b) Date acquired (mo., day, yr.)	(c) Date sold (mo., day, yr.)	(d) Gross sales price	(e) Depreciation allowed or allowable since acquisition	(f) Cost or other basis, plus improvements and expense of sale	(g) LOSS ((f) minus the sum of (d) and (e))	(h) GAIN ((d) plus (e) minus (f))
2							

3   Gain, if any, from Form 4684, line 39 . . . .   **3**
4   Section 1231 gain from installment sales from Form 6252, line 26 or 37 . . . .   **4**
5   Section 1231 gain or (loss) from like-kind exchanges from Form 8824 . . . .   **5**
6   Gain, if any, from line 34, from other than casualty or theft **6**
7   Add lines 2 through 6 in columns (g) and (h) . . . .   **7** ( )
8   Combine columns (g) and (h) of line 7. Enter gain or (loss) here, and on the appropriate line as follows: **8**

    Partnerships—Enter the gain or (loss) on Form 1065, Schedule K, line 6. Skip lines 9, 10, 12, and 13 below.

    S corporations—Report the gain or (loss) following the instructions for Form 1120S, Schedule K, lines 5 and 6. Skip lines 9, 10, 12, and 13 below, unless line 8 is a gain and the S corporation is subject to the capital gains tax.

    All others—If line 8 is zero or a loss, enter the amount on line 12 below and skip lines 9 and 10. If line 8 is a gain and you did not have any prior year section 1231 losses, or they were recaptured in an earlier year, enter the gain as a long-term capital gain on Schedule D and skip lines 9, 10, and 13 below.

9   Nonrecaptured net section 1231 losses from prior years (see instructions) **9**
10   Subtract line 9 from line 8. If zero or less, enter -0-. Also enter on the appropriate line as follows (see instructions):   **10**

    S corporations—Enter this amount (if more than zero) on Schedule D (Form 1120S), line 13, and skip lines 12 and 13 below.

    All others—If line 10 is zero, enter the amount from line 8 on line 13 below. If line 10 is more than zero, enter the amount from line 9 on line 13 below, and enter the amount from line 10 as a long-term capital gain on Schedule D.

Part II   Ordinary Gains and Losses

11   Ordinary gains and losses not included on lines 12 through 18 (include property held 1 year or less):

12   Loss, if any, from line 8 . . . .   **12**
13   Gain, if any, from line 8, or amount from line 9 if applicable **13**
14   Gain, if any, from line 33 . . . .   **14**
15   Net gain or (loss) from Form 4684, lines 31 and 38a **15**
16   Ordinary gain from installment sales from Form 6252, line 25 or 36 . . . .   **16**
17   Ordinary gain or (loss) from like-kind exchanges from Form 8824 . . . .   **17**
18   Recapture of section 179 expense deduction for partners and S corporation shareholders from property dispositions by partnerships and S corporations (see instructions) **18**
19   Add lines 11 through 18 in columns (g) and (h) . . . .   **19** ( )
20   Combine columns (g) and (h) of line 19. Enter gain or (loss) here, and on the appropriate line as follows: . . .   **20**
a   For all except individual returns: Enter the gain or (loss) from line 20 on the return being filed.
b   For individual returns:
   (1)   If the loss on line 12 includes a loss from Form 4684, line 35, column (b)(ii), enter that part of the loss here and on line 20 of Schedule A (Form 1040). Identify as from "Form 4797, line 20b(1)." See instructions . . .   **20b(1)**
   (2)   Redetermine the gain or (loss) on line 20, excluding the loss, if any, on line 20b(1). Enter here and on Form 1040, line 15 .   **20b(2)**

For Paperwork Reduction Act Notice, see page 1 of separate instructions.   Cat. No. 13086I   Form **4797** (1993)

Form 4797 (1993)   Page **2**

Part III Gain From Disposition of Property Under Sections 1245, 1250, 1252, 1254, and 1255

21	**(a)** Description of section 1245, 1250, 1252, 1254, or 1255 property:	**(b)** Date acquired (mo., day, yr.)	**(c)** Date sold (mo., day, yr.)
A			
B			
C			
D			

	Relate lines 21A through 21D to these columns ▶		Property A	Property B	Property C	Property D
22	Gross sales price (**Note:** *See line 1 before completing.*)	22				
23	Cost or other basis plus expense of sale	23				
24	Depreciation (or depletion) allowed or allowable	24				
25	Adjusted basis. Subtract line 24 from line 23	25				
26	Total gain. Subtract line 25 from line 22	26				
27	**If section 1245 property:**					
a	Depreciation allowed or allowable from line 24	27a				
b	Enter the **smaller** of line 26 or 27a	27b				
28	**If section 1250 property:** If straight line depreciation was used, enter -0- on line 28g, except for a corporation subject to section 291.					
a	Additional depreciation after 1975 (see instructions)	28a				
b	Applicable percentage multiplied by the **smaller** of line 26 or line 28a (see instructions)	28b				
c	Subtract line 28a from line 26. If residential rental property or line 26 is not more than line 28a, skip lines 28d and 28e	28c				
d	Additional depreciation after 1969 and before 1976	28d				
e	Enter the **smaller** of line 28c or 28d	28e				
f	Section 291 amount (corporations only)	28f				
g	Add lines 28b, 28e, and 28f	28g				
29	**If section 1252 property:** Skip this section if you did not dispose of farmland or if this form is being completed for a partnership.					
a	Soil, water, and land clearing expenses	29a				
b	Line 29a multiplied by applicable percentage (see instructions)	29b				
c	Enter the **smaller** of line 26 or 29b	29c				
30	**If section 1254 property:**					
a	Intangible drilling and development costs, expenditures for development of mines and other natural deposits, and mining exploration costs (see instructions)	30a				
b	Enter the **smaller** of line 26 or 30a	30b				
31	**If section 1255 property:**					
a	Applicable percentage of payments excluded from income under section 126 (see instructions)	31a				
b	Enter the **smaller** of line 26 or 31a	31b				

Summary of Part III Gains. Complete property columns A through D, through line 31b before going to line 32.

32	Total gains for all properties. Add columns A through D, line 26	32	
33	Add columns A through D, lines 27b, 28g, 29c, 30b, and 31b. Enter here and on line 14	33	
34	Subtract line 33 from line 32. Enter the portion from casualty or theft on Form 4684, line 33. Enter the portion from other than casualty or theft on Form 4797, line 6	34	

Part IV Recapture Amounts Under Sections 179 and 280F(b)(2) When Business Use Drops to 50% or Less
See instructions for Part IV.

			(a) Section 179	(b) Section 280F(b)(2)
35	Section 179 expense deduction or depreciation allowable in prior years	35		
36	Recomputed depreciation (see instructions)	36		
37	Recapture amount. Subtract line 36 from line 35. See instructions for where to report	37		

Form **4952**

Department of the Treasury
Internal Revenue Service

Investment Interest Expense Deduction

▶ Attach to your tax return.

OMB No. 1545-0191

1993

Attachment
Sequence No. **12A**

Name(s) shown on return

Identifying number

Part I   Total Investment Interest Expense

1	Investment interest expense paid or accrued in 1993. See instructions	1
2	Disallowed investment interest expense from 1992 Form 4952, line 5	2
3	**Total investment interest expense.** Add lines 1 and 2	3

Part II   Net Investment Income

4a	Gross income from property held for investment (excluding any net gain from the disposition of property held for investment)	4a
b	Net gain from the disposition of property held for investment . . . 4b	
c	Net capital gain from the disposition of property held for investment 4c	
d	Subtract line 4c from line 4b. If zero or less, enter -0-	4d
e	Enter all or part of the amount on line 4c that you elect to include in investment income. Do not enter more than the amount on line 4b. See instructions . . . . ▶	4e
f	Investment income. Add lines 4a, 4d, and 4e. See instructions	4f
5	Investment expenses. See instructions	5
6	**Net investment income.** Subtract line 5 from line 4f. If zero or less, enter -0-	6

Part III   Investment Interest Expense Deduction

7	Disallowed investment interest expense to be carried forward to 1994. Subtract line 6 from line 3. If zero or less, enter -0-	7
8	**Investment interest expense deduction.** Enter the smaller of line 3 or 6. See instructions . .	8

Paperwork Reduction Act Notice

We ask for the information on this form to carry out the Internal Revenue laws of the United States. We are required to give us the information. We need it to ensure that you are complying with these laws and to allow us to figure and collect the right amount of tax.

The time needed to complete and file this form will vary depending on individual circumstances. The estimated average time is:

Recordkeeping . . . . . . 13 min.
**Learning about the
law or the form** . . . . . . 15 min.
Preparing the form . . . . . 21 min.
**Copying, assembling, and
sending the form to the IRS** . . 10 min.

If you have comments concerning the accuracy of these time estimates or suggestions for making this form more simple, we would be happy to hear from you. You can write to both the IRS and the Office of Management and Budget at the addresses listed in the instructions for the tax return with which this form is filed.

General Instructions

Section references are to the Internal Revenue Code unless otherwise noted.

A Change To Note

Beginning in 1993, for purposes of computing your investment interest deduction, net capital gain from the disposition of property held for investment is excluded from investment income. However, you may elect to include in your investment income all or

part of the net capital gain from the disposition of property held for investment if you also reduce the amount of net capital gain eligible for the 28% maximum capital gains rate by the same amount. See the instructions for line 4e on page 2.

Purpose of Form

Interest expense paid by an individual, estate, or a trust on a loan that is allocable to property held for investment may not be fully deductible in the current year. Form 4952 is used to figure the amount of investment interest expense deductible for the current year and the amount, if any, to carry forward to future years.

For more details, get **Pub. 550**, Investment Income and Expenses.

Cat. No. 13177Y

Form **4952** (1993)

Form 4952 (1993)   Page **2**

Who Must File

If you are an individual, estate, or a trust, and you claim a deduction for investment interest expense, you must complete and attach Form 4952 to your tax return, unless **all** of the following apply:

● Your only investment income was from interest or dividends,

● You have no other deductible expenses connected with the production of interest or dividends,

● Your investment interest expense is not more than your investment income, and

● You have no carryovers of investment interest expense from 1992.

Allocation of Interest Expense Under Temporary Regulations Section 1.163-8T

If you paid or accrued interest on a loan and you used the proceeds of the loan for more than one purpose, you may have to allocate the interest paid. This is necessary because of the different rules that apply to investment interest, personal interest, trade or business interest, home mortgage interest, and passive activity interest. See Pub. 550.

Specific Instructions

Part I—Total Investment Interest Expense

Line 1

Enter the investment interest paid or accrued during the tax year, regardless of when the indebtedness was incurred. Investment interest is interest paid or accrued on a loan (or part of a loan) that is allocable to property held for investment (as defined below).

Be sure to include investment interest expense reported to you on Schedule K-1 from a partnership or an S corporation. Include amortization of bond premium on taxable bonds purchased after October 22, 1986, but before January 1, 1988, unless you elected to offset amortizable bond premium against the interest payments on the bond. A taxable bond is a bond on which the interest is includible in gross income.

Investment interest expense does not include the following:

● Home mortgage interest.

● Interest expense that is properly allocable to a passive activity. A passive activity is any business activity in which you **do not** materially participate and any rental activity regardless of participation. See the separate instructions for **Form 8582,** Passive Activity Loss Limitations, for the material participation tests and the definition of "rental activity."

● Any interest expense that is capitalized, such as construction interest subject to section 263A.

● Interest expense related to tax-exempt interest income under section 265.

Property held for investment.—Property held for investment includes property that produces income (unless derived in the ordinary course of a trade or business) from interest, dividends, annuities, or royalties; and gains from the disposition of property that produces those types of income or is held for investment. However, it does not include an interest in a passive activity.

Property held for investment also includes an interest in an activity of conducting a trade or business in which you did not materially participate and that is not a passive activity. For example, a working interest in an oil or gas property that is not a passive activity is property held for investment if you did not materially participate in the activity.

Part II—Net Investment Income

Line 4a

Gross income from property held for investment to be entered on line 4a includes income (unless derived in the ordinary course of a trade or business) from:

● Interest,

● Dividends (except Alaska Permanent Fund dividends),

● Annuities, and

● Royalties.

If you are filing **Form 8814,** Parents' Election To Report Child's Interest and Dividends, part or all of your child's income may be included on line 4a. See Form 8814 for details.

Also, include on line 4a net income from the following passive activities:

● Rental of substantially nondepreciable property,

● Equity-financed lending activities, and

● Acquisition of certain interests in a pass-through entity licensing intangible property.

See Regulations section 1.469-2(f)(10) for details.

Net passive income from a passive activity of a publicly traded partnership (as defined in section 469(k)(2)) is also included in investment income. See Notice 88-75, 1988-2 C.B. 386, for details.

Include investment income reported to you on Schedule K-1 from a partnership or an S corporation. Also include net investment income from an estate or a trust.

Do not include on line 4a any net gain from the disposition of property held for investment. Instead, enter this amount on line 4b.

Line 4b

Net gain from the disposition of property held for investment is the excess, if any, of total gains over total losses from the disposition of property held for investment. When figuring this amount, be sure to include capital gain distributions from mutual funds.

Line 4c

Net capital gain from the disposition of property held for investment is the excess, if any, of net long-term capital gain over net short-term capital loss from the disposition of property held for investment. When figuring this amount, be sure to include capital gain distributions from mutual funds.

Line 4e

Enter all or part of the amount on line 4c, but not more than the amount on line 4b, that you choose to include in investment income. If you make an entry on line 4e and you are using the **Schedule D Tax Worksheet** on page D-4 of the Form 1040 instructions (or Part VI of Schedule D (Form 1041)), you must also reduce the amount of net capital gain eligible for the 28% maximum capital gains

rate by the amount on this line. Therefore, you should consider the effect on your tax using the maximum capital gains rate before making an entry on this line.

Line 5

Investment expenses are your allowed deductions, other than interest expense, directly connected with the production of investment income. For example, depreciation or depletion allowed on assets that produce investment income is an investment expense.

Be sure to include investment expenses reported to you on Schedule K-1 from a partnership or an S corporation.

Investment expenses do not include any deductions taken into account in determining your income or loss from a passive activity.

If you have investment expenses that are included as a miscellaneous itemized deduction on Schedule A (Form 1040), line 20, you may not have to use all of the amount for purposes of Form 4952, line 5. The 2% adjusted gross income limitation on Schedule A may reduce the amount.

To figure the amount to use, compare the amount of the investment expenses included on Schedule A, line 20, with the total miscellaneous expenses on Schedule A, line 24. The smaller of the investment expenses included on line 20 or the total of line 24 is the amount to use to figure the investment expenses from Schedule A for line 5.

Example. Assume Schedule A, line 20, includes investment expenses of $3,000, and line 24 is $1,300 after the 2% adjusted gross income limitation. Investment expenses from Schedule A of $1,300 are used to figure the amount of investment expenses for line 5. If investment expenses of $800 were included on line 20 and line 24 was $1,300, investment expenses from Schedule A of $800 would be used.

Part III—Investment Interest Expense Deduction

Line 8

This is the amount you may deduct as investment interest expense.

Individuals.—Enter the amount from line 8 on Schedule A (Form 1040), line 11, even if all or part of it is attributable to a partnership or an S corporation. However, if any portion of this amount is attributable to royalties, enter that part of the interest expense on Schedule E (Form 1040).

Estates and trusts.—Enter the amount from line 8 on Form 1041, line 10.

Form 6198.—If any portion of the deductible investment interest expense is attributable to an activity for which you are not at risk, you must also use **Form 6198,** At-Risk Limitations, to figure your deductible investment interest expense. Enter the portion attributable to the at-risk activity on Form 6198, line 4. Reduce Form 4952, line 8, by the amount entered on Form 6198. See Form 6198 and its instructions for more details, especially the instructions for line 4 of that form.

Alternative minimum tax.—Deductible interest expense is an adjustment for alternative minimum tax purposes. Get **Form 6251,** Alternative Minimum Tax—Individuals, or Form 1041, Schedule H, for estates and trusts.

Form **4970**	**Tax on Accumulation Distribution of Trusts**	OMB No. 1545-0192
Department of the Treasury Internal Revenue Service	▶ Attach to beneficiary's tax return. ▶ See instructions on back.	19**93** Attachment Sequence No. **73**

A Name(s) as shown on return	**B** Social security number

C Name and address of trust	**D** Employer identification number

E Type of trust: ☐ Domestic ☐ Foreign	**F** Beneficiary's date of birth	**G** Enter number of trusts from which you received accumulation distributions in this tax year . . . . ▶

Part I   Average Income and Determination of Computation Years

1	Amount of current distribution that is considered distributed in earlier tax years. (From Schedule J (Form 1041), line 37, column (a))	1
2	Distributions of income accumulated before you were born or reached age 21	2
3	Subtract line 2 from line 1	3
4	Taxes imposed on the trust on amounts from line 3. (From Schedule J (Form 1041), line 37, column (b)).	4
5	Total (add lines 3 and 4)	5
6	Tax-exempt interest included on line 5. (From Schedule J (Form 1041), line 37, column (c)) . . .	6
7	Taxable part of line 5 (subtract line 6 from line 5)	7
8	Number of trust's earlier tax years in which amounts on line 7 are considered distributed . . .	8
9	Average annual amount considered distributed (divide line 3 by line 8) . .	9	
10	Multiply line 9 by .25	10	
11	Number of earlier tax years to be taken into account (see instructions)	11
12	Average amount for recomputing tax (divide line 7 by line 11). Enter here and in each column on line 15	12

13	Enter your taxable income before this distribution for the 5 immediately preceding tax years	(a) 1992	(b) 1991	(c) 1990	(d) 1989	(e) 1988

Part II   Tax Attributable to the Accumulation Distribution

			(a) 19......	(b) 19......	(c) 19......
14	Enter the amounts from line 13, eliminating the highest and lowest taxable income years	14			
15	Enter amount from line 12 in each column	15			
16	Recomputed taxable income (add lines 14 and 15)	16			
17	Income tax on amounts on line 16	17			
18	Income tax before credits on line 14 income	18			
19	Additional tax before credits (subtract line 18 from line 17) . .	19			
20	Tax credit adjustment	20			
21	Subtract line 20 from line 19	21			
22	Alternative minimum tax adjustments	22			
23	Combine lines 21 and 22	23			

24	Add columns (a), (b), and (c), line 23	24
25	Divide the line 24 amount by 3	25
26	Multiply the amount on line 25 by the number of years on line 11	26
27	Enter the amount from line 4	27
28	Partial tax (subtract line 27 from line 26) (If line 27 is more than line 26, enter -0-.)	28
29	Interest charge on accumulation distribution from foreign trusts	29
30	Tax attributable to the accumulation distribution (add lines 28 and 29)	30

For Paperwork Reduction Act Notice, see back of form.   Cat. No. 13180V   Form **4970** (1993)

General Instructions

Section references are to the Internal Revenue Code unless otherwise noted.

Paperwork Reduction Act Notice

We ask for the information on this form to carry out the Internal Revenue laws of the United States. You are required to give us the information. We need it to ensure that you are complying with these laws and to allow us to figure and collect the right amount of tax.

The time needed to complete and file this form will vary depending on individual circumstances. The estimated average time is:

Recordkeeping	1 hr., 12 min.
Learning about the law or the form	16 min.
Preparing the form	1 hr., 30 min.
Copying, assembling, and sending the form to the IRS	20 min.

If you have comments concerning the accuracy of these time estimates or suggestions for making this form more simple, we would be happy to hear from you. You can write to both the IRS and the Office of Management and Budget at the addresses listed in the instructions of the tax return with which this form is filed.

Purpose of Form

If you are the beneficiary of a trust that accumulated its income, instead of distributing it currently, use Form 4970 to figure the partial tax under section 667. The fiduciary notifies the beneficiary of an "accumulation distribution" by completing Part IV of Schedule J (Form 1041).

Thus, if you received a distribution for this tax year from a trust that accumulated its income, instead of distributing it each year (and the trust paid taxes on that income), you must complete Form 4970 to compute any additional tax liability. The trustee must give you a completed Part IV of Schedule J (Form 1041) so you can complete this form.

If you received accumulation distributions from more than one trust during the current tax year, prepare a separate Form 4970 for each trust from which you received an accumulation distribution. You can arrange the distributions in any order you want them considered to have been made.

Definitions

Undistributed Net Income (UNI).—Undistributed net income is the distributable net income (DNI) of the trust for any tax year less: **(1)** the amount of income required to be distributed currently and any other amounts properly paid or credited or required to be distributed to beneficiaries in the tax year; and **(2)** the taxes imposed on the trust attributable to such DNI.

Accumulation Distribution.—An accumulation distribution is the excess of amounts properly paid, credited, or required to be distributed (other than income required to be distributed currently) over the DNI of the trust reduced by income required to be distributed currently.

Generally, except for tax-exempt interest, the distribution loses its character upon distribution to the beneficiary. See section 667(d) for special rules for foreign trusts.

Specific Instructions

Line 1.—For a nonresident alien or foreign corporation, include only the part of the accumulation distribution that is attributable to U.S. sources or is effectively connected with a trade or business carried on in the United States.

Line 2.—Enter any amount from line 1 that represents UNI of a domestic trust accumulated before you were born or reached age 21. However, if the multiple trust rule applies, see the instructions for line 4.

Line 4—Multiple Trust Rule.—If you received accumulation distributions from two or more other trusts that were considered to have been made in any of the earlier tax years in which the current accumulation distribution is considered to have been made, do not include on line 4 the taxes attributable to the current accumulation distribution considered to have been distributed in the same earlier tax year(s).

For this special rule, only count as trusts those trusts for which the sum of this accumulation distribution and any earlier accumulation distributions from the trust, which are considered under section 666(a) to have been distributed in the same earlier tax year, is $1,000 or more.

Foreign Trust.—If the trust is a foreign trust, see section 665(d)(2).

Line 8.—You can determine the number of years in which the UNI is deemed to have been distributed by counting the "throwback years" for which there are entries on lines 32 through 36 of Part IV of Schedule J (Form 1041). These throwback rules apply even if you would not have been entitled to receive a distribution in the earlier tax year if the distribution had actually been made then. **Note:** *There can be more than 5 "throwback years."*

Line 11.—From the number of years entered on line 8, subtract any year in which the distribution from column (a), Part IV of Schedule J (Form 1041) is less than the amount on line 10 of Form 4970. If the distribution for each throwback year is more than line 10, then enter the same number on line 11 as you entered on line 8.

Line 13.—Enter your taxable incomes for years 1988–1992, even if less than 5 years of the trust had accumulated income after you became 21. Use the taxable income as reported, amended by you, or as changed by the IRS. Include in the taxable income amounts considered distributed in that year as a result of prior accumulation distributions, whether from the same or another trust, and whether made in an earlier year or the current year.

If your taxable income as adjusted is less than zero, enter zero.

Line 17.—Figure the income tax (not including any alternative minimum tax) on the income on line 16 using the tax rates in effect for your particular earlier tax year shown in each of the three columns. You may use the Tax Rate Schedules, etc., as applicable. You can get the Tax Rate Schedules and earlier year forms from many IRS offices.

Line 18.—Enter your income tax (not including any alternative minimum tax) as originally reported, corrected, or amended,

before reduction for any credits for your particular earlier year shown in each of the three columns.

Line 20.—Nonrefundable credits that are limited to tax liability, such as the general business credit, may be changed because of an accumulation distribution. If the total allowable credits for any of the 3 computation years increases, enter the increase on line 20. However, do not treat as an increase the part of the credit that was allowable as a carryback or carryforward credit in the current or any preceding year other than the computation year.

To refigure these credits, you must consider changes to the tax before credits for each of the 3 computation years due to previous accumulation distributions.

If the accumulation distribution is from a domestic trust that paid foreign income taxes, the limitation on the foreign tax credit under section 904 is applied separately to the accumulation distribution. If the distribution is from a foreign trust, see sections 667(d) and 904(f)(4) for special rules.

Attach the proper form for any credit you refigure. The amount determined for items on this line is limited to tax law provisions in effect for those years involved.

Line 22.—Use and attach a separate **Form 4626, Form 6251, Form 8656,** or **Schedule H, Form 1041** to recompute the alternative minimum tax for each earlier year and show any change in those taxes in the bottom margin of the forms. Enter the adjustments on this line.

Line 28.—If estate taxes or generation-skipping transfer taxes apply to the accumulation distribution, reduce the partial tax proportionately for those taxes. See section 667(b)(6) for the computation.

Line 29.—For an accumulation distribution from a foreign trust, an interest charge must be added to the partial tax. This interest charge is not deductible under any Code section and is figured as follows:

1. Figure 6% of line 28.

2. Total the number of years from the year(s) of allocation to the year of distribution (including the year of allocation, but not the year of distribution).

3. Divide the number in step **2** by the total years of allocation (line 8).

4. Multiply the answer in step **1** by the decimal in step **3**.

5. Subtract line 28 from line 1. This is the maximum interest.

6. Enter on line 29 the amount from step **4** or step **5**, whichever is less.

If this form is not being used for distributions from a foreign trust, enter zero on line 29. However, if the distributions are from a domestic trust that used to be a foreign trust, see Rev. Rul. 91-6, 1991-1 C.B. 89.

Line 30—Individuals.—Enter the amount from this line on 39, Form 1040.

Trusts and Decedent's Estates.—Include the amount on line 1b, Schedule G, Form 1041.

Other Filers.—Add the result to the total tax liability before credits on your income tax return for the year of the accumulation distribution. Attach this form to that return.

Form **6252**

Department of the Treasury
Internal Revenue Service

Installment Sale Income

▶ See separate instructions.   ▶ Attach to your tax return.
▶ Use a separate form for each sale or other disposition of
property on the installment method.

OMB No. 1545-0228

1993

Attachment
Sequence No. **79**

Name(s) shown on return

Identifying number

1	Description of property ▶		
2a	Date acquired (month, day, and year) ▶ ____ / ____ / ____	**b** Date sold (month, day, and year) ▶ ____ / ____ / ____	
3	Was the property sold to a related party after May 14, 1980? See instructions	☐ Yes	☐ No
4	If the answer to question 3 is "Yes," was the property a marketable security? If "Yes," complete Part III. If "No," complete Part III for the year of sale and for 2 years after the year of sale.	☐ Yes	☐ No

Part I   **Gross Profit and Contract Price.** Complete this part for the year of sale only.

5	Selling price including mortgages and other debts. Do not include interest whether stated or unstated	**5**	
6	Mortgages and other debts the buyer assumed or took the property subject to, but not new mortgages the buyer got from a bank or other source .	**6**	
7	Subtract line 6 from line 5	**7**	
8	Cost or other basis of property sold	**8**	
9	Depreciation allowed or allowable	**9**	
10	Adjusted basis. Subtract line 9 from line 8	**10**	
11	Commissions and other expenses of sale.	**11**	
12	Income recapture from Form 4797, Part III. See instructions . .	**12**	
13	Add lines 10, 11, and 12		**13**	
14	Subtract line 13 from line 5. If zero or less, **stop here.** Do not complete the rest of this form .	**14**	
15	If the property described on line 1 above was your main home, enter the total of lines 14 and 22 from Form 2119. Otherwise, enter -0-	**15**	
16	**Gross profit.** Subtract line 15 from line 14	**16**	
17	Subtract line 13 from line 6. If zero or less, enter -0-	**17**	
18	**Contract price.** Add line 7 and line 17	**18**	

Part II   **Installment Sale Income.** Complete this part for the year of sale and any year you receive a payment or have certain debts you must treat as a payment on installment obligations.

19	Gross profit percentage. Divide line 16 by line 18. For years after the year of sale, see instructions	**19**	
20	**For year of sale only**—Enter amount from line 17 above; otherwise, enter -0-	**20**	
21	Payments received during year. See instructions. Do not include interest whether stated or unstated	**21**	
22	Add lines 20 and 21	**22**	
23	Payments received in prior years. See instructions. Do not include interest whether stated or unstated	**23**	
24	**Installment sale income.** Multiply line 22 by line 19	**24**	
25	Part of line 24 that is ordinary income under recapture rules. See instructions	**25**	
26	Subtract line 25 from line 24. Enter here and on Schedule D or Form 4797. See instructions .	**26**	

Part III   **Related Party Installment Sale Income.** Do not complete if you received the final payment this tax year.

27	Name, address, and taxpayer identifying number of related party ....

28 Did the related party, during this tax year, resell or dispose of the property ("second disposition")? . . . ☐ Yes   ☐ No

29 **If the answer to question 28 is "Yes,"** complete lines 30 through 37 below unless one of the following conditions is met. Check only the box that applies.

  a ☐ The second disposition was more than 2 years after the first disposition (other than dispositions of marketable securities). If this box is checked, enter the date of disposition (month, day, year) ▶ ____ / ____ / ____

  b ☐ The first disposition was a sale or exchange of stock to the issuing corporation.

  c ☐ The second disposition was an involuntary conversion where the threat of conversion occurred after the first disposition.

  d ☐ The second disposition occurred after the death of the original seller or buyer.

  e ☐ It can be established to the satisfaction of the Internal Revenue Service that tax avoidance was not a principal purpose for either of the dispositions. If this box is checked, attach an explanation. See instructions.

30	Selling price of property sold by related party	**30**	
31	Enter contract price from line 18 for year of first sale	**31**	
32	Enter the **smaller** of line 30 or line 31	**32**	
33	Total payments received by the end of your 1993 tax year. Add lines 22 and 23	**33**	
34	Subtract line 33 from line 32. If zero or less, enter -0-	**34**	
35	Multiply line 34 by the gross profit percentage on line 19 for year of first sale	**35**	
36	Part of line 35 that is ordinary income under recapture rules. See instructions	**36**	
37	Subtract line 36 from line 35. Enter here and on Schedule D or Form 4797. See instructions .	**37**	

For Paperwork Reduction Act Notice, see separate instructions.   Cat. No. 13601R   Form **6252** (1993)

1993  Department of the Treasury
Internal Revenue Service

Instructions for Form 6252

Installment Sale Income

(Section references are to the Internal Revenue Code unless otherwise noted.)

Paperwork Reduction Act Notice

We ask for the information on this form to carry out the Internal Revenue laws of the United States. You are required to give us the information. We need it to ensure that you are complying with these laws and to allow us to figure and collect the right amount of tax.

The time needed to complete and file this form will vary depending on individual circumstances. The estimated average time is:

Recordkeeping	1 hr., 25 min.
Learning about the law or the form	39 min.
Preparing the form	56 min.
Copying, assembling, and sending the form to the IRS	20 min.

If you have comments concerning the accuracy of these time estimates or suggestions for making this form more simple, we would be happy to hear from you. You can write to both the IRS and the Office of Management and Budget at the addresses listed in the instructions for the tax return with which this form is filed.

General Instructions

Purpose of Form

Use Form 6252 to report income from casual sales of real or personal property (other than inventory) if you will receive any payments in a tax year after the year of sale.

Do not use Form 6252 to report sales after 1986 of stock or securities traded on an established securities market. Treat all payments from these sales as received in the year you sold the stock.

Do not use Form 6252 if you elect not to report the sale on the installment method. To elect, report the full amount of the gain on a timely filed return (including extensions), using **Form 4797,** Sales of Business Property, or the **Schedule D** for your return, whichever applies.

Note: *Generally, once you file Form 6252, you cannot later elect out of the installment method. Get* **Pub. 537,** *Installment Sales, for details.*

Which Parts To Complete

For the Year of Sale.—Complete lines 1 through 26.

For Years After the Year of Sale.—Complete lines 1 through 4, and Part II, for

any year you receive a payment from an installment sale.

Related Party Sales.—If you sold marketable securities to a related party (defined below), complete Form 6252 for each year of the installment agreement even if you did not receive a payment. For any year after the year of sale, complete lines 1 through 4, and Part III. If you received a payment, also complete Part II.

If you sold property other than marketable securities to a related party, complete Form 6252 for the year of sale and for 2 years after the year of sale even if you did not receive a payment. If during this 2-year period you did not receive an actual or deemed payment, complete lines 1 through 4, and Part III. After this 2-year period, see **For Years After the Year of Sale,** above.

Special Rules

Interest.—If any part of an installment payment you received is for interest, be sure to report that interest on the appropriate form or schedule. Do not report interest received, carrying charges received, or unstated interest on Form 6252. See Pub. 537 for details on unstated interest.

Installment Sales to Related Party.—A special rule applies to a first disposition (sale or exchange) of property under the installment method to a related party who then makes a second disposition (sale, exchange, gift, or cancellation of installment note) before making all payments on the first disposition. For this purpose, a **related party** includes your spouse, child, grandchild, parent, brother, sister, or a related corporation, S corporation, partnership, estate, or trust. See section 453(f)(1) for more details.

Under this rule, you treat part or all of the amount the related party realized (or the fair market value if the disposed property is not sold or exchanged) from the second disposition as if you received it from the first disposition at the time of the second disposition. Figure the gain, if any, on lines 30 through 37. This rule does not apply if any of the exceptions listed on line 29 are met.

Sale of Depreciable Property to Related Person.—Generally, if you sell depreciable property to a related person (as defined in section 453(g)(3)), you may not report the sale using the installment method. For this purpose, depreciable property is any property that can be depreciated by the person or entity to whom you transfer it.

However, you may use the installment method if you can show to the satisfaction of the IRS that avoidance of Federal income taxes was not one of the principal purposes of the sale (e.g., no significant tax deferral benefits will result from the sale).

If the installment method does not apply, report the sale on Schedule D or Form 4797, whichever applies. Treat all payments you will receive as if they were received in the year of sale. Use fair market value for any payment that is contingent as to amount. If the fair market value cannot be readily determined, basis is recovered ratably.

Pledge Rule.—If an installment obligation from a nondealer disposition of real property used in a trade or business or held for the production of rental income with a sales price over $150,000 is pledged as security on debt after December 17, 1987, treat the net proceeds of the secured debt as a payment on the installment obligation. This rule applies to the disposition of any property under the installment method after 1988 with a sales price over $150,000, except for farm property and personal use property disposed of by an individual. The amount treated as a payment cannot exceed the excess of the total contract price over any payments received under the contract before the secured debt was obtained.

The pledge rule does not apply to pledges made after December 17, 1987, if the debt is incurred to refinance the principal amount of a debt that was outstanding on December 17, 1987, AND was secured by nondealer real property installment obligations on that date and at all times after that date until the refinancing occurred. However, this exception does not apply to the extent that the principal amount of the debt resulting from the refinancing exceeds the principal amount of the refinanced debt immediately before the refinancing. Also, the pledge rule does not affect refinancing due to the calling of a debt by the creditor as long as the debt is then refinanced by a person other than this creditor or someone related to the creditor.

Interest on Deferred Tax.—Generally, interest must be paid on the deferred tax related to any obligation that arises during a tax year from the disposition of property under the installment method if:

● The property had a sales price over $150,000 AND

● The aggregate balance of all nondealer installment obligations arising during, and

Cat. No. 64262Q

outstanding at the close of, the tax year is more than $5 million.

Interest must be paid in subsequent years if installment obligations, which originally required interest to be paid, are still outstanding at the close of a tax year.

These rules **do not** apply to dispositions of:

- Farm property,
- Personal use property by an individual,
- Real property in tax years beginning before 1988, or
- Personal property before 1989.

How to report the interest. The interest is not figured on Form 6252. See section 453A to figure the interest. Enter the interest as an additional tax on your tax return. Include it in the amount to be entered on the total tax line after credits and other taxes. For individuals, this is line 53 of the 1993 Form 1040. For corporations, it is line 10 of Schedule J (Form 1120). Write "Section 453A(c) interest" to the left of the amount.

Corporations may deduct the interest in the year it is paid or accrued. For individuals and other taxpayers, this interest is not deductible.

Additional Information

See Pub. 537 for additional information, including details about reductions in selling price, the single sale of several assets, like-kind exchanges, dispositions of installment obligations, and repossessions.

Specific Instructions

Part I—Gross Profit and Contract Price

Line 5.—Enter the total of any money, face amount of the installment obligation, and the fair market value of other property that you received or will receive in exchange for the property sold. Include on line 5 any existing mortgage or other debt the buyer assumed or took the property subject to.

If there is no stated maximum selling price, such as in a contingent sale, attach a schedule showing the computation of gain. Enter the taxable part on line 24 and also on line 35 if Part III applies. See Temporary Regulations section 15A.453.

Line 6.— Enter only mortgages or other debts the buyer assumed from the seller or took the property subject to. Do not include new mortgages the buyer gets from a bank, the seller, or other sources.

Line 8.—Enter the original cost and other expenses you incurred in buying the property. Add the cost of improvements, etc., and subtract any qualified electric vehicle credit, diesel-powered highway vehicle credit, enhanced oil recovery credit, disabled access credit, or casualty losses previously allowed. For more details, get **Pub. 551**, Basis of Assets.

Line 9.—Enter all depreciation or amortization you deducted or should have

deducted from the date of purchase until the date of sale. Add any section 179 expense deduction; the downward basis adjustment under section 50(c) (or the corresponding provision of prior law); the deduction for qualified clean-fuel vehicle property or refueling property; and deductions claimed under section 190, 193, or 1253(d)(2) or (3) (as in effect before the enactment of P.L. 103-66). Subtract any investment tax credit recapture amount if the basis of the property was reduced under section 50(c) (or the corresponding provision of prior law); any section 179 or 280F recapture amount included in gross income in a prior tax year; and any qualified clean-fuel vehicle property or refueling property deduction you were required to recapture because the property ceased to be eligible for the deduction. Do not include on this line any section 179 expense deduction for a partnership or an S corporation that passed through the deduction to its partners or shareholders.

Line 11.—Enter sales commissions, advertising expenses, attorney and legal fees, etc., in selling the property.

Line 12.—Any ordinary income recapture under section 1245 or 1250 (including sections 179 and 291) is fully taxable in the year of sale even if no payments were received. To figure the recapture, complete Form 4797, Part III. The ordinary income recapture is the amount on line 33 of Form 4797. Enter it on line 12 of Form 6252 and also on line 14 of Form 4797. Do not enter any gain for this property on line 34 of Form 4797. If you used Form 4797 only to figure the recapture on line 12 of Form 6252, enter "N/A" on line 34 of Form 4797.

Part II—Installment Sale Income

Line 19.—Enter the gross profit percentage determined for the year of sale even if you did not file Form 6252 for that year.

Line 21.—Enter all money and the fair market value of any property you received in 1993. Include as payments any amount withheld to pay off a mortgage or other debt, such as broker and legal fees. Do not include the buyer's note, any mortgage, or other liability assumed by the buyer. If you did not receive any payments in 1993, enter zero.

If in prior years an amount was entered on the equivalent of line 32 of the 1993 form, do not include it on this line. Instead, enter it on line 23.

See **Pledge Rule** on page 1 for details about proceeds of debt secured by installment obligations that must be treated as payments on installment obligations.

Line 23.—Enter all money and the fair market value of property you received before 1993 from the sale. Include allocable installment income and any other deemed payments from prior years.

Line 25.—Enter here and on Form 4797, line 16, any ordinary income recapture on section 1252, 1254, or 1255 property. This includes recapture for the year of sale or

any remaining recapture from a prior year sale. Do not enter ordinary income from a section 179 expense deduction. If this is the year of sale, complete Form 4797, Part III. The amount from line 29c, 30b, or 31b of Form 4797 is the ordinary income recapture. Do not enter any gain for this property on line 33 or 34 of Form 4797. If you used Form 4797 only to figure the recapture on line 25 or 36, enter "N/A" on lines 33 and 34 of Form 4797.

Also report on this line any ordinary income recapture remaining from prior years on section 1245 or 1250 property sold before June 7, 1984.

Do not enter on line 25 more than the amount shown on line 24. The excess **must** be reported in future years on Form 6252 up to the taxable part of the installment sale until all of the recapture has been reported.

Line 26.—For trade or business property, enter this amount on Form 4797, line 4, if the property was held more than 1 year. If the property was held 1 year or less, or if you have an ordinary gain from a noncapital asset (even if the holding period is more than 1 year), enter this amount on Form 4797, line 11, and write "From Form 6252."

For capital assets, enter this amount on Schedule D as a short-term or long-term gain. Use the lines identified as from Form 6252.

Part III—Related Party Installment Sale Income

Line 29.—If one of the exceptions apply, check the appropriate box. Skip lines 30 through 37. If you checked box 29e, attach an explanation. Generally, the nontax avoidance exception will apply to the second disposition if:

- The disposition was involuntary (e.g., a creditor of the related person foreclosed on the property, or the related person declared bankruptcy), or

- The disposition was an installment sale under which the terms of payment were substantially equal to or longer than those for the first sale. However, the resale terms must not permit significant deferral of recognition of gain from the first sale (e.g., amounts from the resale are being collected sooner).

Line 30.—If the related party sold all or part of the property from the original sale in 1993, enter the selling price of the part resold. If part was sold in an earlier year and part was sold this year, enter the cumulative amount of the selling price.

Line 36.—See the instructions for line 25, above. **Do not** enter on line 36 more than the amount shown on line 35. The excess **must** be reported in future years on Form 6252 up to the taxable part of the installment sale until all of the recapture has been reported.

Line 37.—See the instructions for line 26, above.

Page 2

Form **8283**
(Rev. November 1992)

Department of the Treasury
Internal Revenue Service

Noncash Charitable Contributions

▶ **Attach to your tax return if the total deduction claimed
for all property contributed exceeds $500.**

▶ **See separate instructions.**

OMB No. 1545-0908
Expires 11-30-95

Attachment
Sequence No. **55**

Name(s) shown on your income tax return

Identifying number

Note: *Figure the amount of your contribution deduction before completing this form. See your tax return instructions.*

Section A—Include in this section **only** items (or groups of similar items) for which you claimed a deduction of $5,000 or less per item or group, and certain publicly traded securities (see instructions).

Part I   **Information on Donated Property**—If you need more space, attach a statement.

1	**(a)** Name and address of the donee organization	**(b)** Description of donated property
A		
B		
C		
D		
E		

Note: *If the amount you claimed as a deduction for an item is $500 or less, you do not have to complete columns (d), (e), and (f).*

	(c) Date of the contribution	**(d)** Date acquired by donor (mo., yr.)	**(e)** How acquired by donor	**(f)** Donor's cost or adjusted basis	**(g)** Fair market value	**(h)** Method used to determine the fair market value
A						
B						
C						
D						
E						

Part II   **Other Information**—If you gave less than an entire interest in property listed in Part I, complete lines 2a–2e. If restrictions were attached to a contribution listed in Part I, complete lines 3a–3c.

2   If less than the entire interest in the property is contributed during the year, complete the following:

a   Enter letter from Part I that identifies the property _____. If Part II applies to more than one property, attach a separate statement.

b   Total amount claimed as a deduction for the property listed in Part I: **(1)** For this tax year _____
(2) For any prior tax years _____

c   Name and address of each organization to which any such contribution was made in a prior year (complete only if different than the donee organization above).

Name of charitable organization (donee)

Address (number, street, and room or suite no.)

City or town, state, and ZIP code

d   For tangible property, enter the place where the property is located or kept _____
e   Name of any person, other than the donee organization, having actual possession of the property _____

3   If conditions were attached to any contribution listed in Part I, answer the following questions and attach the required statement (see instructions):

		Yes	No
a	Is there a restriction, either temporary or permanent, on the donee's right to use or dispose of the donated property?		
b	Did you give to anyone (other than the donee organization or another organization participating with the donee organization in cooperative fundraising) the right to the income from the donated property or to the possession of the property, including the right to vote donated securities, to acquire the property by purchase or otherwise, or to designate the person having such income, possession, or right to acquire?		
c	Is there a restriction limiting the donated property for a particular use?		

For Paperwork Reduction Act Notice, see separate instructions.   Cat. No. 62299J   Form **8283** (Rev. 11-92)

Form 8283 (Rev. 11-92)   Page **2**

Name(s) shown on your income tax return	Identifying number

Section B—Appraisal Summary—Include in this section only items (or groups of similar items) for which you claimed a deduction of more than $5,000 per item or group. Report contributions of certain publicly traded securities only in Section A.

If you donated art, you may have to attach the complete appraisal. See the **Note** in Part I below.

Part I   **Information on Donated Property**—To be completed by the taxpayer and/or appraiser.

4 Check type of property:

☐ Art* (contribution of $20,000 or more)   ☐ Real Estate   ☐ Gems/Jewelry   ☐ Stamp Collections

☐ Art* (contribution of less than $20,000)   ☐ Coin Collections   ☐ Books   ☐ Other

*Art includes paintings, sculptures, watercolors, prints, drawings, ceramics, antique furniture, decorative arts, textiles, carpets, silver, rare manuscripts, historical memorabilia, and other similar objects.

Note: *If your total art contribution deduction was $20,000 or more, you must attach a complete copy of the signed appraisal. See instructions.*

5	(a) Description of donated property (if you need more space, attach a separate statement)	(b) If tangible property was donated, give a brief summary of the overall physical condition at the time of the gift	(c) Appraised fair market value
A			
B			
C			
D			

	(d) Date acquired by donor (mo., yr.)	(e) How acquired by donor	(f) Donor's cost or adjusted basis	(g) For bargain sales, enter amount received	See instructions	
					(h) Amount claimed as a deduction	(i) Average trading price of securities
A						
B						
C						
D						

Part II   **Taxpayer (Donor) Statement**—List each item included in Part I above that is separately identified in the appraisal as having a value of $500 or less. See instructions.

I declare that the following item(s) included in Part I above has to the best of my knowledge and belief an appraised value of not more than $500 (per item). Enter identifying letter from Part I and describe the specific item: _____

Signature of taxpayer (donor) ▶   Date ▶

Part III   **Certification of Appraiser**

I declare that I am not the donor, the donee, a party to the transaction in which the donor acquired the property, employed by, married to, or related to any of the foregoing persons, or an appraiser regularly used by any of the foregoing persons and who does not perform a majority of appraisals during the taxable year for other persons.

Also, I declare that I hold myself out to the public as an appraiser or perform appraisals on a regular basis; and that because of my qualifications as described in the appraisal, I am qualified to make appraisals of the type of property being valued. I certify that the appraisal fees were not based upon a percentage of the appraised property value. Furthermore, I understand that a false or fraudulent overstatement of the property value as described in the qualified appraisal or this appraisal summary may subject me to the civil penalty under section 6701(a) (aiding and abetting the understatement of tax liability). I affirm that I have not been barred from presenting evidence or testimony by the Director of Practice.

Sign Here   Signature ▶   Title ▶   Date of appraisal ▶

Business address (including room or suite no.)	Identifying number
City or town, state, and ZIP code	

Part IV   **Donee Acknowledgment**—To be completed by the charitable organization.

This charitable organization acknowledges that it is a qualified organization under section 170(c) and that it received the donated property as described in Section B, Part I, above on _____

                                          (Date)

Furthermore, this organization affirms that in the event it sells, exchanges, or otherwise disposes of the property (or any portion thereof) within 2 years after the date of receipt, it will file an information return (**Form 8282**, Donee Information Return) with the IRS and furnish the donor a copy of that return. This acknowledgment does not represent concurrence in the claimed fair market value.

Name of charitable organization (donee)	Employer identification number	
Address (number, street, and room or suite no.)	City or town, state, and ZIP code	
Authorized signature	Title	Date

Form **8582**	Passive Activity Loss Limitations	OMB No. 1545-1008
	► See separate instructions.	**1993**
Department of the Treasury Internal Revenue Service	► Attach to Form 1040 or Form 1041.	Attachment Sequence No. **88**
Name(s) shown on return		Identifying number

Part I   **1993 Passive Activity Loss**
Caution: *See the instructions for Worksheets 1 and 2 on page 7 before completing Part I.*

Rental Real Estate Activities With Active Participation (For the definition of active participation see **Active Participation in a Rental Real Estate Activity** on page 3 of the instructions.)

1a Activities with net income (from Worksheet 1, column (a)) . . . | **1a**

  b Activities with net loss (from Worksheet 1, column (b)) . . . . | **1b** (   )

  c Prior year unallowed losses (from Worksheet 1, column (c)) . . | **1c** (   )

  d Combine lines 1a, 1b, and 1c . . . . | **1d**

All Other Passive Activities

2a Activities with net income (from Worksheet 2, column (a)) . . . | **2a**

  b Activities with net loss (from Worksheet 2, column (b)) . . . . | **2b** (   )

  c Prior year unallowed losses (from Worksheet 2, column (c)) . . | **2c** (   )

  d Combine lines 2a, 2b, and 2c . . . . | **2d**

3 Combine lines 1d and 2d. If the result is net income or zero, see the instructions for line 3. If this line and line 1d are losses, go to line 4. Otherwise, enter -0- on line 9 and go to line 10 . | **3**

Part II   **Special Allowance for Rental Real Estate With Active Participation**
Note: *Enter all numbers in Part II as positive amounts. (See instructions on page 7 for examples.)*

4 Enter the **smaller** of the loss on line 1d or the loss on line 3 . . . . | **4**

5 Enter $150,000. If married filing separately, see the instructions . | **5**

6 Enter modified adjusted gross income, but not less than zero (see instructions) . . . . | **6**

Note: *If line 6 is equal to or greater than line 5, skip lines 7 and 8, enter -0- on line 9, and then go to line 10. Otherwise, go to line 7.*

7 Subtract line 6 from line 5 . . . . | **7**

8 Multiply line 7 by 50% (.5). **Do not** enter more than $25,000. If married filing separately, see instructions . . . . | **8**

9 Enter the **smaller** of line 4 or line 8 . . . . | **9**

Part III   **Total Losses Allowed**

10 Add the income, if any, on lines 1a and 2a and enter the total . . . . | **10**

11 **Total losses allowed from all passive activities for 1993.** Add lines 9 and 10. See the instructions to find out how to report the losses on your tax return . . . . | **11**

For Paperwork Reduction Act Notice, see separate instructions.   Cat. No. 63704F   Form **8582** (1993)

Form 8582 (1993)   Page **2**

Caution: *The worksheets are not required to be filed with your tax return and may be detached before filing Form 8582. Keep a copy of the worksheets for your records.*

Worksheet 1—For Form 8582, Lines 1a, 1b, and 1c (See instructions on page 7.)

Name of activity	Current year		Prior year	Overall gain or loss	
	(a) Net income (line 1a)	(b) Net loss (line 1b)	(c) Unallowed loss (line 1c)	(d) Gain	(e) Loss
Total. Enter on Form 8582, lines 1a, 1b, and 1c. . . . . ▶					

Worksheet 2—For Form 8582, Lines 2a, 2b, and 2c (See instructions on page 7.)

Name of activity	Current year		Prior year	Overall gain or loss	
	(a) Net income (line 2a)	(b) Net loss (line 2b)	(c) Unallowed loss (line 2c)	(d) Gain	(e) Loss
Total. Enter on Form 8582, lines 2a, 2b, and 2c. . . . . ▶					

Worksheet 3—Use this worksheet if an amount is shown on Form 8582, line 9 (See instructions on page 8.)

Name of activity	Form or schedule to be reported on	(a) Loss (See instructions.)	(b) Ratio (See instructions.)	(c) Special allowance (See instructions.)	(d) Subtract column (c) from column (a) (See instructions.)
Total . . . . ▶			1.00		

Worksheet 4—Allocation of Unallowed Losses (See instructions on page 8.)

Name of activity	Form or schedule to be reported on	(a) Loss (See instructions.)	(b) Ratio (See instructions.)	(c) Unallowed loss (See instructions.)
Total . . . . ▶			1.00	

Worksheet 5—Allowed Losses (See instructions on page 8.)

Name of activity	Form or schedule to be reported on	(a) Loss (See instructions.)	(b) Unallowed loss (See instructions.)	(c) Allowed loss (See instructions.)
Total . . . . ▶				

Worksheet 6—Activities With Losses Reported on Two or More Different Forms or Schedules (See instructions on page 8.)

Name of Activity:	(a) (See instr.)	(b) (See instr.)	(c) Ratio (See instr.)	(d) Unallowed loss (See instr.)	(e) Allowed loss (See instr.)
Form or Schedule To Be Reported on:					
1a Net loss plus prior year unallowed loss from form or schedule . ▶					
b Net income from form or schedule . . . . . . ▶					
c Subtract line 1b from line 1a. If zero or less, enter -0- . . . . . . ▶					
Form or Schedule To Be Reported on:					
1a Net loss plus prior year unallowed loss from form or schedule . ▶					
b Net income from form or schedule . . . . . . ▶					
c Subtract line 1b from line 1a. If zero or less, enter -0- . . . . . . ▶					
Form or Schedule To Be Reported on:					
1a Net loss plus prior year unallowed loss from form or schedule . ▶					
b Net income from form or schedule . . . . . . ▶					
c Subtract line 1b from line 1a. If zero or less, enter -0- . . . . . . ▶					
Total . . . . ▶			1.00		

Form **8615**	**Tax for Children Under Age 14**	OMB No. 1545-0998
	Who Have Investment Income of More Than $1,200	**19**93
Department of the Treasury Internal Revenue Service	▶ See instructions below and on back. ▶ Attach ONLY to the child's Form 1040, Form 1040A, or Form 1040NR.	Attachment Sequence No. **33**

Child's name shown on return | Child's social security number

A Parent's name (first, initial, and last). **Caution:** See instructions on back before completing. | **B** Parent's social security number

C Parent's filing status (check one):
☐ Single   ☐ Married filing jointly   ☐ Married filing separately   ☐ Head of household   ☐ Qualifying widow(er)

Step 1 Figure child's net investment income

1 Enter child's investment income, such as taxable interest and dividend income. See instructions. If this amount is $1,200 or less, **stop here;** do not file this form . . . . | **1**

2 If the child DID NOT itemize deductions on Schedule A (Form 1040 or Form 1040NR), enter $1,200. If the child ITEMIZED deductions, see instructions . . . . | **2**

3 Subtract line 2 from line 1. If the result is zero or less, **stop here;** do not complete the rest of this form but ATTACH it to the child's return . . . . | **3**

4 Enter child's **taxable** income from Form 1040, line 37; Form 1040A, line 22; or Form 1040NR, line 36 | **4**

5 Enter the **smaller** of line 3 or line 4 here . . . . ▶ | **5**

Step 2 Figure tentative tax based on the tax rate of the parent listed on line A

6 Enter parent's **taxable** income from Form 1040, line 37; Form 1040A, line 22; Form 1040EZ, line 6; or Form 1040NR, line 36. If the parent transferred property to a trust, see instructions . . | **6**

7 Enter the total net investment income, if any, from Forms 8615, line 5, of ALL OTHER children of the parent identified above. **Do not** include the amount from line 5 above . . . . . . | **7**

8 Add lines 5, 6, and 7 . . . . | **8**

9 Tax on line 8 based on the **parent's** filing status. See instructions. If from Schedule D Tax Worksheet, enter amount from line 4 of that worksheet here ▶ | **9**

10 Enter parent's tax from Form 1040, line 38; Form 1040A, line 23; Form 1040EZ, line 8; or Form 1040NR, line 37. If from Schedule D Tax Worksheet, enter amount from line 4 of that worksheet here ▶ | **10**

11 Subtract line 10 from line 9. If line 7 is blank, enter on line 13 the amount from line 11; skip lines 12a and 12b . . . . | **11**

12a Add lines 5 and 7 . . . . **12a** |
b Divide line 5 by line 12a. Enter the result as a decimal (rounded to two places) . . . . . . | **12b** | × .

13 Multiply line 11 by line 12b . . . . ▶ | **13**

Step 3 Figure child's tax—If lines 4 and 5 above are the same, go to line 16 now.

14 Subtract line 5 from line 4 . . . . **14** |

15 Tax on line 14 based on the **child's** filing status. See instructions. If from Schedule D Tax Worksheet, enter amount from line 4 of that worksheet here ▶ | **15**

16 Add lines 13 and 15 . . . . | **16**

17 Tax on line 4 based on the **child's** filing status. See instructions. If from Schedule D Tax Worksheet, check here . . . . ▶ ☐ | **17**

18 Enter the **larger** of line 16 or line 17 here and on Form 1040, line 38; Form 1040A, line 23; or Form 1040NR, line 37. Be sure to check the box for "Form 8615" even if line 17 is more than line 16 . ▶ | **18**

General Instructions

A Change To Note.—If line 8 of Form 8615 is over $70,000 (over $140,000 if the parent's filing status is married filing jointly or qualifying widow(er)), the election to defer additional 1993 taxes may apply to the child. Get **Form 8841,** Deferral of Additional 1993 Taxes, for details. If the election is made, Form 1040A **cannot** be filed for the child.

Purpose of Form.—For children under age 14, investment income over $1,200 is taxed at the parent's rate if the parent's rate is higher than the child's rate. If the child's investment income is more than $1,200, use this form to figure the child's tax.

Investment Income.—As used on this form, "investment income" includes all taxable income other than earned income as defined on page 2. It includes income such as taxable interest, dividends, capital gains, rents, royalties, etc. It also includes pension and annuity income and income (other than earned income) received as the beneficiary of a trust.

Who Must File.—Generally, Form 8615 must be filed for any child who was under age 14 on January 1, 1994, had more than $1,200 of investment income, and is required to file a tax return. If neither parent was alive on December 31, 1993, do not use Form 8615.

Instead, figure the child's tax in the normal manner.

Note: The parent may be able to elect to report the child's interest and dividends on his or her return. If the parent makes this election, the child will not have to file a return or Form 8615. For more details, see the instructions for Form 1040 or Form 1040A, or get **Form 8814,** Parents' Election To Report Child's Interest and Dividends.

Additional Information.—For more details, get **Pub. 929,** Tax Rules for Children and Dependents.

Incomplete Information for Parent.—If the parent's taxable income or filing status or the net investment income of

For Paperwork Reduction Act Notice, see back of form.   Cat. No. 64113U   Form **8615** (1993)

the parent's other children is not known by the due date of the child's return, reasonable estimates may be used. Write "Estimated" on the appropriate line(s) of Form 8615. For more details, see Pub. 929.

Amended Return.—If after the child's return is filed, the parent's taxable income is changed or the net investment income of any of the parent's other children is changed, the child's tax must be refigured using the adjusted amounts. If the child's tax is changed as a result of the adjustment(s), file **Form 1040X,** Amended U.S. Individual Income Tax Return, to correct the child's tax.

Alternative Minimum Tax.—A child whose tax is figured on Form 8615 may owe the alternative minimum tax. For details, get **Form 6251,** Alternative Minimum Tax—Individuals, and its instructions.

Line Instructions

Section references are to the Internal Revenue Code.

Lines A and B.—If the child's parents were married to each other and filed a joint return, enter the name and social security number (SSN) of the parent who is listed first on the joint return. For example, if the father's name is listed first on the return and his SSN is entered in the block labeled "Your social security number," enter his name on line A and his SSN on line B.

If the parents were married but filed separate returns, enter the name and SSN of the parent who had the **higher** taxable income. If you do not know which parent had the higher taxable income, see Pub. 929.

If the parents were unmarried, treated as unmarried for Federal income tax purposes, or separated either by a divorce or separate maintenance decree, enter the name and SSN of the parent who had custody of the child for most of the year (the custodial parent).

Exception. If the custodial parent remarried and filed a joint return with his or her new spouse, enter the name and SSN of the person listed first on the joint return, even if that person is not the child's parent. If the custodial parent and his or her new spouse filed separate returns, enter the name and SSN of the person with the **higher** taxable income, even if that person is not the child's parent.

Note: *If the parents were unmarried but lived together during the year with the child, enter the name and SSN of the parent who had the **higher** taxable income.*

Line 1.—If the child had no earned income (defined later), enter the child's adjusted gross income from Form 1040, line 32; Form 1040A, line 17; or Form 1040NR, line 32.

If the child had earned income, use the following worksheet to figure the amount to enter on line 1. But if the child files **Form 2555,** Foreign Earned Income, or **Form 2555-EZ,** Foreign Earned Income Exclusion, has a net loss from self-employment, or claims a net operating loss deduction, **do not** use the worksheet below. Instead, use the worksheet in Pub. 929 to figure the amount to enter on line 1.

Worksheet (keep a copy for your records)

1. Enter the amount from the child's Form 1040, line 23; Form 1040A, line 14; or Form 1040NR, line 24, whichever applies . . . _____
2. Enter the child's **earned income** (defined below) plus any deduction the child claims on Form 1040, line 28, or Form 1040NR, line 28, whichever applies _____
3. Subtract line 2 from line 1. Enter the result here and on Form 8615, line 1 . . _____

Earned income includes wages, tips, and other payments received for personal services performed. Generally, earned income is the total of the amounts reported on Form 1040, lines 7, 12, and 19; Form 1040A, line 7; or Form 1040NR, lines 8, 13, and 20.

Line 2.—If the child itemized deductions, enter on line 2 the **greater** of:

- $600 plus the portion of the amount on Schedule A (Form 1040), line 26, or Schedule A (Form 1040NR), line 17, that is directly connected with the production of the investment income on Form 8615, line 1; **OR**
- $1,200.

Line 6.—If the parent's taxable income is less than zero, enter zero on line 6. If the parent filed a joint return, enter the taxable income shown on that return even if the parent's spouse is not the child's parent. If the parent transferred property to a trust which sold or exchanged the property during the year at a gain, include any gain that was taxed to the trust under section 644 in the amount entered on line 6. Enter "Section 644" and the amount to the right of the line 6 entry. Also, see the instructions for line 10.

Line 9.—Figure the tax using the Tax Table, Tax Rate Schedules, or the Schedule D Tax Worksheet, whichever applies. If any net capital gain is included on lines 5, 6, and/or 7, the tax on the amount on line 8 may be less if the Schedule D Tax Worksheet can be used to figure the tax. See Pub. 929 for details on how to figure the net capital gain included on line 8 and how to complete the worksheet. The Schedule D Tax Worksheet should be used to figure the tax if:

the parent's filing status is:	AND	the amount on Form 8615, line 8, is over:
• Single		$53,500
• Married filing jointly or Qualifying widow(er)		$89,150
• Married filing separately		$44,575
• Head of household		$76,400

If the Schedule D Tax Worksheet is used to figure the tax, enter on Form 8615, line 9, the amount from line 13 of that worksheet. Also, enter the amount from line 4 of that worksheet in the space next to line 9 of Form 8615.

Line 10.—If the parent filed a joint return, enter the tax shown on that return even if the parent's spouse is not the child's parent. If the parent filed Form 8814, enter "Form 8814" and the total tax from line 8 of Form(s) 8814 in the space next to line 10 of Form 8615.

If line 6 includes any gain taxed to a trust under section 644, add the tax imposed under section 644(a)(2)(A) to the tax shown on the parent's return. Enter the total on line 10 instead of the tax from the parent's return. Also, enter "Section 644" next to line 10.

Line 15.—Figure the tax using the Tax Table, Tax Rate Schedule X, or the Schedule D Tax Worksheet, whichever applies. If line 14 is more than $53,500 and includes any net capital gain, the tax may be less if the Schedule D Tax Worksheet is used to figure the tax. See Pub. 929 for details on how to figure the net capital gain included on line 14 and how to complete the worksheet.

Line 17.—Figure the tax as if these rules did not apply. For example, if the child files Schedule D and can use the Schedule D Tax Worksheet to figure his or her tax, complete that worksheet.

Paperwork Reduction Act Notice.—We ask for the information on this form to carry out the Internal Revenue laws of the United States. You are required to give us the information. We need it to ensure that you are complying with these laws and to allow us to figure and collect the right amount of tax.

The time needed to complete and file this form will vary depending on individual circumstances. The estimated average time is: **Recordkeeping,** 13 min.; **Learning about the law or the form,** 12 min.; **Preparing the form,** 45 min.; and **Copying, assembling, and sending the form to the IRS,** 17 min.

If you have comments concerning the accuracy of these time estimates or suggestions for making this form more simple, we would be happy to hear from you. You can write to both the IRS and the Office of Management and Budget at the addresses listed in the instructions of the tax return with which this form is filed.

Form **8814**

Department of the Treasury
Internal Revenue Service

Parents' Election To Report
Child's Interest and Dividends
▶ See instructions below and on back.
▶ Attach to parents' Form 1040 or Form 1040NR.

OMB No. 1545-1128

1993

Attachment
Sequence No. **40**

Name(s) shown on your return

Your social security number

A Child's name (first, initial, and last)

B Child's social security number

C If more than one Form 8814 is attached, check here . . . . ▶

Step 1 **Figure amount of child's interest and dividend income to report on your return**

1a Enter your child's **taxable** interest income. If this amount is different from the amounts shown on the child's Forms 1099-INT and 1099-OID, see the instructions . . . . | **1a** |

b Enter your child's **tax-exempt** interest income. **DO NOT** include this amount on line 1a . . . . | **1b** |

2a Enter your child's gross dividends, including any Alaska Permanent Fund dividends. If none, enter -0- on line 2c and go to line 3. If your child received any capital gain distributions or dividends as a nominee, see the instructions . . . . | **2a** |

b Enter your child's nontaxable distributions that are included on line 2a. These should be shown in box 1d of Form 1099-DIV . . . . | **2b** |

c Subtract line 2b from line 2a . . . . | **2c** |

3 Add lines 1a and 2c. If the total is $1,000 or less, skip lines 4 and 5 and go to line 6. If the total is $5,000 or more, **do not** file this form. Your child **must** file his or her own return to report the income . . . . | **3** |

4 Base amount . . . . | **4** | 1,000 | 00

5 Subtract line 4 from line 3. If you checked the box on line C above or if line 2a includes any capital gain distributions, see the instructions. Also, include this amount in the total on Form 1040, line 22, or Form 1040NR, line 22. In the space next to line 22, enter "Form 8814" and show the amount. Go to line 6 below . . . . ▶ | **5** |

Step 2 **Figure your tax on the first $1,000 of child's interest and dividend income**

6 Amount not taxed . . . . | **6** | 500 | 00

7 Subtract line 6 from line 3. If the result is zero or less, enter -0- . . . . | **7** |

8 **Tax.** Is the amount on line 7 less than $500?
  • **NO.** Enter $75 here and see the **Note** below.
  • **YES.** Multiply line 7 by 15% (.15). Enter the result here and see the **Note** below. | **8** |

Note: *If you checked the box on line C above, see the instructions. Otherwise, include the amount from line 8 in the tax you enter on Form 1040, line 38, or Form 1040NR, line 37. Also, enter the amount from line 8 in the space provided next to line 38 on Form 1040, or next to line 37 on Form 1040NR.*

General Instructions

Purpose of Form.—Use this form if you elect to report your child's income on your return. If you do, your child will not have to file a return. You can make this election if your child meets **all** of the following conditions:

• Was under age 14 on January 1, 1994.

• Is required to file a 1993 return.

• Had income only from interest and dividends, including Alaska Permanent Fund dividends.

• Had gross income for 1993 that was less than $5,000.

• Had no estimated tax payments for 1993.

• Did not have any overpayment of tax shown on his or her 1992 return applied to the 1993 return.

• Had no Federal income tax withheld from his or her income (backup withholding).

You must also qualify as explained on page 2 of these instructions.

Step 1 of the form is used to figure the amount of your child's income to report on your return. **Step 2** is used to figure an additional tax that must be added to your tax.

How To Make the Election.—To make the election, complete and attach Form 8814 to your tax return and file your return by the due date (including extensions). A separate Form 8814 must be filed for **each** child whose income you choose to report.

Caution: *The Federal income tax on your child's income may be less if you file a tax return for the child instead of making this election. This is because you cannot take certain deductions that your child would be entitled to on his or her own return. For details, see **Deductions You May Not Take** on page 2.*

For Paperwork Reduction Act Notice, see back of form.

Cat. No. 10750J

Form **8814** (1993)

Parents Who Qualify To Make the Election.—You qualify to make this election if you file Form 1040 or Form 1040NR and any of the following apply:

• You are filing a joint return for 1993 with the child's other parent.

• You and the child's other parent were married to each other but file separate returns for 1993 AND you had the **higher** taxable income. If you do not know if you had the higher taxable income, get **Pub. 929**, Tax Rules for Children and Dependents.

• You were unmarried, treated as unmarried for Federal income tax purposes, or separated from the child's other parent by a divorce or separate maintenance decree. You must have had custody of your child for most of the year (you were the custodial parent). If you were the custodial parent and you remarried, you may make the election on a joint return with your new spouse. But if you and your new spouse do not file a joint return, you qualify to make the election only if you had **higher** taxable income than your new spouse.

Note: *If you and the child's other parent were not married but lived together during the year with the child, you qualify to make the election only if you are the parent with the **higher** taxable income.*

Deductions You May Not Take.—If you elect to report your child's income on your return, you may not take any of the following deductions that your child would be entitled to on his or her own return.

• Standard deduction of $600 ($1,500 for a blind child).

• Penalty on early withdrawal of child's savings.

• Itemized deductions such as child's investment expenses or charitable contributions.

If any of the above apply to your child, first figure the tax on your child's income as if he or she is filing a return. Next, figure the tax as if you are electing to report your child's income on **your** return. Then, compare the methods to determine which results in the lower tax.

Alternative Minimum Tax.—If your child received any tax-exempt interest (or exempt-interest dividends paid by a regulated investment company) from certain private activity bonds, you must take this into account in determining if you owe the alternative minimum tax. Get **Form 6251**, Alternative Minimum Tax—Individuals, and its instructions for details.

Investment Interest Expense.—Your child's income (excluding Alaska Permanent Fund dividends and capital gain distributions) that you report on your return is considered to be **your** investment income for purposes of figuring your investment interest expense deduction. If your child received Alaska Permanent Fund dividends or capital gain distributions, get **Pub. 550**, Investment Income and Expenses, to figure the amount you may treat as your investment income.

Foreign Accounts and Trusts.—If your child had a foreign financial account or was the grantor of, or transferor to, a foreign trust, complete Part III of **Schedule B** (Form 1040) for the child. If you answered "Yes" to either of the questions, you must file this Schedule B with **your** return. Also, complete line 11b if applicable. Write "Form 8814" next to line 11a or line 12, whichever applies.

Change of Address.—If your child filed a return for a year before 1993 and the address shown on the last return filed is not your child's current address, be sure to notify the IRS, in writing, of the new address. To do this, you may use **Form 8822**, Change of Address, or you may write to the Internal Revenue Service Center where your child's last return was filed, or to the Chief, Taxpayer Service Division, in your local IRS district office.

Additional Information.—For more details, see Pub. 929.

Line Instructions

Name and Social Security Number.—Enter your name as shown on your return. If filing a joint return, include your spouse's name but enter the social security number of the person whose name is shown first on the return.

Line 1a.—Enter **ALL** taxable interest income received by your child in 1993. If your child received a **Form 1099-INT** for tax-exempt interest, such as from municipal bonds, write the amount and "Tax-exempt interest" on the dotted line next to line 1a. Be sure to include this interest on line 1b but **do not** include it in the total for line 1a.

If your child received, as a **nominee**, interest that actually belongs to another person, write the amount and "ND" (for nominee distribution) on the dotted line next to line 1a. **Do not** include interest received as a nominee in the total for line 1a.

If your child had accrued interest that was paid to the seller of a bond, amortizable bond premium (ABP) allowed as a reduction to interest income, or if any original issue discount (OID) included on line 1a is less than the amount shown on your child's **Form 1099-OID**, follow the instructions above for nominee interest to see how to report the nontaxable amounts. But on the dotted line next to line 1a, write the nontaxable amount and "Accrued interest," "ABP adjustment," or "OID adjustment," whichever applies. **Do not** include any nontaxable amounts in the total for line 1a.

Line 1b.—If your child received any tax-exempt interest income, such as interest on certain state and municipal bonds, enter the total tax-exempt interest on line 1b. Also, include any exempt-interest dividends your child received as a shareholder in a mutual fund or other regulated investment company. **Do not** include this interest on lines 1a or 3.

Note: *If line 1b includes tax-exempt interest or exempt-interest dividends paid by a regulated investment company from private activity bonds, see **Alternative Minimum Tax** on this page.*

Line 2a.—Enter gross dividends received by your child in 1993, including capital gain distributions and nontaxable distributions. Gross dividends should be shown in box 1a of **Form 1099-DIV.** Also, include dividends your child received through a partnership, an S corporation, or an estate or trust.

If line 2a includes any **capital gain distributions** see the line 5 instructions below. These should be shown in box 1c of Form 1099-DIV.

If your child received, as a **nominee**, dividends that actually belong to another person, write the amount and "ND" on the dotted line next to line 2a. **Do not** include amounts received as a nominee in the total for line 2a.

Line 5.—If you checked the box on line C, add the amounts from line 5 of **all** your Forms 8814. Include the total on line 22 of Form 1040 or Form 1040NR, whichever applies. Be sure to write "Form 8814" and show the total of the line 5 amounts in the space next to line 22.

If line 2a includes any **capital gain distributions** and you are filing **Schedule D** (Form 1040), part or all of your child's capital gain distributions should be reported on your Schedule D instead of on Form 8814, line 5. Before you enter an amount on line 5, see Pub. 929 for details on how to figure the amount to report on your Schedule D.

Line 8.—If you checked the box on line C, add the amounts from line 8 of **all** your Forms 8814. Include the total on Form 1040, line 38, or Form 1040NR, line 37. Be sure to enter the total of the line 8 amounts in the space provided next to line 38 on Form 1040 or next to line 37 on Form 1040NR.

Paperwork Reduction Act Notice.—We ask for the information on this form to carry out the Internal Revenue laws of the United States. You are required to give us the information. We need it to ensure that you are complying with these laws and to allow us to figure and collect the right amount of tax.

The time needed to complete and file this form will vary depending on individual circumstances. The estimated average time is: **Recordkeeping**, 20 min.; **Learning about the law or the form**, 8 min.; **Preparing the form**, 16 min.; and **Copying, assembling, and sending the form to the IRS**, 35 min.

If you have comments concerning the accuracy of these time estimates or suggestions for making this form more simple, we would be happy to hear from you. You can write to both the IRS and the Office of Management and Budget at the addresses listed in the instructions of the tax return with which this form is filed.

Form **8829**

Department of the Treasury
Internal Revenue Service (O)

Expenses for Business Use of Your Home

▶ File only with Schedule C (Form 1040). Use a separate Form 8829 for each home you used for business during the year.

▶ See separate instructions.

OMB No. 1545-1266

1993

Attachment
Sequence No. **66**

Name(s) of proprietor(s)

Your social security number

Part I	**Part of Your Home Used for Business**		
1	Area used regularly and exclusively for business, regularly for day care, or for inventory storage. See instructions	1	
2	Total area of home	2	
3	Divide line 1 by line 2. Enter the result as a percentage	3	%

• For day-care facilities not used exclusively for business, also complete lines 4–6.
• All others, skip lines 4–6 and enter the amount from line 3 on line 7.

4	Multiply days used for day care during year by hours used per day	4		hr.
5	Total hours available for use during the year (365 days × 24 hours). See instructions	5	8,760	hr.
6	Divide line 4 by line 5. Enter the result as a decimal amount	6	.	
7	Business percentage. For day-care facilities not used exclusively for business, multiply line 6 by line 3 (enter the result as a percentage). All others, enter the amount from line 3 ▶	7		%

Part II	**Figure Your Allowable Deduction**			
8	Enter the amount from Schedule C, line 29, **plus** any net gain or (loss) derived from the business use of your home and shown on Schedule D or Form 4797. If more than one place of business, see instructions		8	

See instructions for columns (a) and (b) before completing lines 9–20.

			(a) Direct expenses	(b) Indirect expenses	
9	Casualty losses. See instructions	9			
10	Deductible mortgage interest. See instructions	10			
11	Real estate taxes. See instructions	11			
12	Add lines 9, 10, and 11	12			
13	Multiply line 12, column (b) by line 7			13	
14	Add line 12, column (a) and line 13				14
15	Subtract line 14 from line 8. If zero or less, enter -0-				15
16	Excess mortgage interest. See instructions	16			
17	Insurance	17			
18	Repairs and maintenance	18			
19	Utilities	19			
20	Other expenses. See instructions	20			
21	Add lines 16 through 20	21			
22	Multiply line 21, column (b) by line 7		22		
23	Carryover of operating expenses from 1992 Form 8829, line 41		23		
24	Add line 21 in column (a), line 22, and line 23				24
25	Allowable operating expenses. Enter the **smaller** of line 15 or line 24				25
26	Limit on excess casualty losses and depreciation. Subtract line 25 from line 15				26
27	Excess casualty losses. See instructions		27		
28	Depreciation of your home from Part III below		28		
29	Carryover of excess casualty losses and depreciation from 1992 Form 8829, line 42		29		
30	Add lines 27 through 29				30
31	Allowable excess casualty losses and depreciation. Enter the **smaller** of line 26 or line 30				31
32	Add lines 14, 25, and 31				32
33	Casualty loss portion, if any, from lines 14 and 31. Carry amount to **Form 4684**, Section B				33
34	Allowable expenses for business use of your home. Subtract line 33 from line 32. Enter here and on Schedule C, line 30. If your home was used for more than one business, see instructions ▶				34

Part III	**Depreciation of Your Home**		
35	Enter the **smaller** of your home's adjusted basis or its fair market value. See instructions	35	
36	Value of land included on line 35	36	
37	Basis of building. Subtract line 36 from line 35	37	
38	Business basis of building. Multiply line 37 by line 7	38	
39	Depreciation percentage. See instructions	39	%
40	Depreciation allowable. Multiply line 38 by line 39. Enter here and on line 28 above. See instructions	40	

Part IV	**Carryover of Unallowed Expenses to 1994**		
41	Operating expenses. Subtract line 25 from line 24. If less than zero, enter -0-	41	
42	Excess casualty losses and depreciation. Subtract line 31 from line 30. If less than zero, enter -0-	42	

19**93**

 Department of the Treasury
Internal Revenue Service

Instructions for Form 8829
Expenses for Business Use of Your Home

Paperwork Reduction Act Notice

We ask for the information on this form to carry out the Internal Revenue laws of the United States. You are required to give us the information. We need it to ensure that you are complying with these laws and to allow us to figure and collect the right amount of tax.

The time needed to complete and file this form will vary depending on individual circumstances. The estimated average time is: **Recordkeeping,** 52 min.; **Learning about the law or the form,** 7 min.; **Preparing the form,** 1 hr., 13 min.; and **Copying, assembling, and sending the form to the IRS,** 20 min.

If you have comments concerning the accuracy of these time estimates or suggestions for making this form more simple, we would be happy to hear from you. You can write to both the IRS and the Office of Management and Budget at the addresses listed in the instructions for Form 1040.

General Instructions

Purpose of Form

Use Form 8829 to figure the allowable expenses for business use of your home on **Schedule C** (Form 1040) and any carryover to 1994 of amounts not deductible in 1993.

If all of the expenses for business use of your home are properly allocable to inventory costs, do not complete Form 8829. These expenses are figured in Part III of Schedule C and not on Form 8829.

You must meet specific requirements to deduct expenses for the business use of your home. Even if you meet these requirements, your deductible expenses are limited. For details, get **Pub. 587,** Business Use of Your Home.

Note: If you file **Schedule F** (Form 1040) or you are an employee or a partner, **do not** use this form. Instead, use the worksheet in Pub. 587.

Who May Deduct Expenses for Business Use of a Home

Generally, you may deduct business expenses that apply to a part of your home **only** if that part is exclusively used on a regular basis:

1. As your principal place of business for any of your trades or businesses; or

2. As a place of business used by your patients, clients, or customers to meet or

deal with you in the normal course of your trade or business; or

3. In connection with your trade or business if it is a separate structure that is not attached to your home.

In determining whether a business location in your home qualifies as your principal place of business, you must consider the following two factors:

1. The relative importance of the activities performed at each business location; and

2. The amount of time spent at each location.

A comparison of the relative importance of the activities performed at each business location depends on the characteristics of each business. If the nature of your business requires that you meet or confer with clients or patients, or that you deliver goods or services to a customer, the place where that contact occurs must be given a greater weight in determining where the most important activities are performed. Performance of necessary or essential activities at the business location in your home (such as planning for services or the delivery of goods, or the accounting or billing for those activities or goods) is not controlling.

In addition to comparing the relative importance of the activities performed at each business location, you should also compare the amount of time spent on business at each location. The time consideration is particularly significant when a comparison of the importance of the activities performed at each business location does not clearly identify the location of your principal place of business. This may happen when you perform income-producing activities at both your home and some other location.

Exception for storage of inventory.— You may also deduct expenses that apply to space within your home if it is the **only** fixed location of your trade or business. The space must be used on a regular basis to store inventory from your trade or business of selling products at retail or wholesale.

Exception for day-care facilities.—If you use space in your home on a regular basis in the trade or business of providing day care, you may be able to deduct the business expenses even though you use the same space for nonbusiness purposes. To qualify for this exception, you must have applied for (and not have been rejected), been granted (and still have in effect), or be exempt from having a license, certification, registration, or approval as a day-care center or as a

family or group day-care home under state law.

Specific Instructions

Part I

Lines 1 and 2.—To determine the area on lines 1 and 2, you may use square feet or any other reasonable method if it accurately figures your business percentage on line 7.

Do not include on line 1 the area of your home you used to figure any expenses allocable to inventory costs. The business percentage of these expenses should have been taken into account in Part III of Schedule C.

Special computation for certain day-care facilities.—If the part of your home used as a day-care facility included areas used exclusively for business as well as other areas used only partly for business, you **cannot** figure your business percentage using Part I. Instead, follow these three steps:

1. Figure the business percentage of the part of your home used exclusively for business by dividing the area used exclusively for business by the total area of the home.

2. Figure the business percentage of the part of your home used only partly for business by following the same method used in Part I of the form, but enter on line 1 of your computation only the area of the home used partly for business.

3. Add the business percentages you figured in the first two steps and enter the result on line 7. Attach your computation and write "See attached computation" directly above the percentage you entered on line 7.

Line 4.—Enter the total number of hours the facility was used for day care during the year.

Example. Your home is used Monday through Friday for 12 hours per day for 250 days during the year. It is also used on 50 Saturdays for 8 hours per day. Enter 3,400 hours on line 4 (3,000 hours for weekdays plus 400 hours for Saturdays).

Line 5.—If you started or stopped using your home for day care in 1993, you must prorate the number of hours based on the number of days the home was available for day care. Cross out the preprinted entry on line 5. Multiply 24 hours by the number of days available and enter the result.

Part II

Line 8.—If all of the gross income from your trade or business is from the business

use of your home, enter on line 8 the amount from Schedule C, line 29, **plus** any net gain or (loss) derived from the business use of your home and shown on Schedule D or Form 4797. If you file more than one Form 8829, include only the income earned and the deductions attributable to that income during the period you owned the home for which Part I was completed.

If part of the income is from a place of business other than your home, you must first determine the part of your gross income (Schedule C, line 7, and gains from Schedule D and Form 4797) from the business use of your home. In making this determination, consider the amount of time you spend at each location as well as other facts. After determining the part of your gross income from the business use of your home, subtract from that amount the **total expenses** shown on Schedule C, line 28, plus any losses from your business shown on Schedule D or Form 4797. Enter the result on line 8 of Form 8829.

Columns (a) and (b).—Enter as direct or indirect expenses only expenses for the business use of your home (i.e., expenses allowable only because your home is used for business). Other expenses not allocable to the business use of your home such as salaries, supplies, and business telephone expenses, are deductible elsewhere on Schedule C and should not be entered on Form 8829.

Direct expenses benefit only the business part of your home. They include painting or repairs made to the specific area or room used for business. Enter 100% of your direct expenses on the appropriate expense line in column (a).

Indirect expenses are for keeping up and running your entire home. They benefit both the business and personal parts of your home. Generally, enter 100% of your indirect expenses on the appropriate expense line in column (b).

Exception. If the business percentage of an indirect expense is different from the percentage on line 7, enter only the business part of the expense on the appropriate line in column (a), and leave that line in column (b) blank. For example, your electric bill is $800 for lighting, cooking, laundry, and television. If you reasonably estimate $300 of your electric bill is for lighting and you use 10% of your home for business, enter $30 on line 19 in column (a). **Do not** make an entry on line 19 in column (b) for any part of your electric bill.

Lines 9, 10, and 11.—Enter only the amounts that would be deductible whether or not you used your home for business (i.e., amounts allowable as itemized deductions on **Schedule A (Form 1040)**).

Treat **casualty losses** as personal expenses for this step. Figure the amount

to enter on line 9 by completing Form 4684, Section A. When figuring line 17, enter 10% of your adjusted gross income excluding the gross income from business use of your home and the deductions attributable to that income. Include on line 9 of Form 8829 the amount from Form 4684, line 18. See line 27 to deduct part of the casualty losses not allowed because of the limits on Form 4684.

Do not file or use that Form 4684 to figure the amount of casualty losses to deduct on Schedule A. Instead, complete a separate Form 4684 to deduct the personal portion of your casualty losses.

On line 10, include only **mortgage interest** that would be deductible on Schedule A and that qualifies as a direct or indirect expense. **Do not** include interest on a mortgage loan that did not benefit your home (e.g., a home equity loan used to pay off credit card bills, to buy a car, or to pay tuition costs).

If you itemized your deductions, be sure to claim **only** the personal portion of your deductible mortgage interest and real estate taxes on Schedule A. For example, if your business percentage on line 7 is 30%, you can claim 70% of your deductible mortgage interest and real estate taxes on Schedule A.

Line 16.—If the amount of home mortgage interest you deduct on Schedule A is limited, enter the part of the excess mortgage interest that qualifies as a direct or indirect expense. Do not include mortgage interest on a loan that did not benefit your home (explained above).

Line 20.—If you rent rather than own your home, include the rent you paid on line 20, column (b).

Line 27.—Multiply your casualty losses in excess of the amount on line 9 by the business percentage of those losses and enter the result.

Line 34.—If your home was used in more than one business, allocate the amount shown on line 34 to each business using any method that is reasonable under the circumstances. For each business, enter on Schedule C, line 30, only the amount allocated to that business.

Part III

Lines 35 through 37.—Enter on line 35 the cost or other basis of your home, or if less, the fair market value of your home on the date you first used the home for business. **Do not** adjust this amount for depreciation claimed or changes in fair market value after the year you first used your home for business. Allocate this amount between land and building values on lines 36 and 37.

Show on an attached schedule the cost or other basis of additions and

improvements placed in service after you began to use your home for business. Do not include any amounts on lines 35 through 38 for these expenditures. Instead, see the instructions for line 40.

Line 39.—If you first used your home for business in 1993, enter the percentage for the month you first used it for business.

Jan.	3.042%	May 1–12	1.984%	*Sept.	0.749%
Feb.	2.778%	*May 13–31	1.605%	*Oct.	0.535%
March	2.513%	*June	1.391%	*Nov.	0.321%
April	2.249%	*July	1.177%	*Dec.	0.107%
		*Aug.	0.963%		

*If you started construction before May 13, 1993, on a home used for business, or you had a binding written contract to buy or build it before that date, a larger percentage applies. Get **Pub. 534**, Depreciation, for the percentage to enter on line 39.

If you first used your home for business before 1993 and after 1986, enter 3.175%. If the business use began before 1987 or you stopped using your home for business before the end of the year, see Pub. 534 for the percentage to enter.

Line 40.—If no additions and improvements were placed in service after you began using your home for business, multiply line 38 by the percentage on line 39. Enter the result on lines 40 and 28.

If additions and improvements were placed in service during 1993 (but after you began using your home for business), figure the amount of depreciation allowed on these expenditures by multiplying the business part of their cost or other basis by the percentage shown in the line 39 instructions for the month placed in service. If additions and improvements were placed in service before 1993 and after 1986 (but after you began using your home for business), figure the depreciation by multiplying the business part of their cost or other basis by 3.175%. If additions and improvements were placed in service before 1987 (but after you began using your home for business) or you stopped using your home for business before the end of the year, see Pub. 534 to figure the depreciation.

Attach a schedule showing your computation and include the amount you figured in the total for line 40. Write "see attached" below the entry space.

Complete and attach **Form 4562,** Depreciation and Amortization, **only** if:

1. You first used your home for business in 1993, or

2. You are depreciating additions and improvements placed in service in 1993.

If you first used your home for business in 1993, enter on Form 4562, in column (c) of line 14h, the amount from line 38 of Form 8829. Then enter on Form 4562, in column (g) of line 14h, the amount from line 40 of Form 8829 (but **do not** include it on Schedule C, line 13).

Page 2

Appendix C

MODIFIED ACRS AND ORIGINAL ACRS TABLES

MODIFIED ACRS TABLES

Accelerated Depreciation Percentages
Using the Half-Year Convention
for 3-, 5-, 7-, 10-, 15-, and 20-Year Property **C-3**

Depreciation Percentages
Residential Rental Property
Placed in Service after December 31, 1986.............................. **C-4**

Depreciation Percentages
Nonresidential Real Property
Placed in Service after December 31, 1986.............................. **C-6**

Accelerated Depreciation Percentages
Using the Mid-Quarter Convention
for 3-, 5-, 7-, 10-, 15-, and 20-Year Property **C-8**

Alternative Depreciation System
Recovery Periods.. **C-10**

ACRS and ADS Straight-Line Depreciation Percentages
Using the Half-Year Convention
for Property with Certain Recovery Periods **C-11**

ADS Straight-Line Depreciation Percentages
Real Property
Using the Mid-Month Convention **C-12**

ORIGINAL ACRS TABLES

Accelerated Recovery Percentages
for 3-, 5-, 10-, and 15-Year Public Utility Property **C-13**

Accelerated Recovery Percentages
for 15-Year Realty **C-14**

Accelerated Recovery Percentages
for Low-Income Housing **C-15**

Accelerated Recovery Percentages
for 18-Year Realty **C-16**

Accelerated Cost Recovery Percentages
for 19-Year Realty **C-17**

Straight-Line Recovery Percentages
for 3-, 5-, 10-, and 15-Year Public Utility Property **C-18**

Straight-Line Recovery Percentages
for 18-Year Realty **C-19**

Straight-Line Recovery Percentages
for 19-Year Realty **C-20**

Modified ACRS Accelerated Depreciation Percentages
Using the Half-Year Convention
for 3-, 5-, 7-, 10-, 15-, and 20-Year Property
Placed in Service after December 31, 1986

Recovery Year	Property Class					
	3-Year	5-Year	7-Year	10-Year	15-Year	20-Year
1	33.33	20.00	14.29	10.00	5.00	3.750
2	44.45	32.00	24.49	18.00	9.50	7.219
3	14.81	19.20	17.49	14.40	8.55	6.677
4	7.41	11.52	12.49	11.52	7.70	6.177
5		11.52	8.93	9.22	6.93	5.713
6		5.76	8.92	7.37	6.23	5.285
7			8.93	6.55	5.90	4.888
8			4.46	6.55	5.90	4.522
9				6.56	5.91	4.462
10				6.55	5.90	4.461
11				3.28	5.91	4.462
12					5.90	4.461
13					5.91	4.462
14					5.90	4.461
15					5.91	4.462
16					2.95	4.461
17						4.462
18						4.461
19						4.462
20						4.461
21						2.231

Source: Rev. Proc. 87-57, Table 1.

Modified ACRS Depreciation Rates
for Residential Rental Property
Placed in Service after December 31, 1986

Recovery Year	Month Placed in Service					
	1	2	3	4	5	6
1	3.485	3.182	2.879	2.576	2.273	1.970
2	3.636	3.636	3.636	3.636	3.636	3.636
3	3.636	3.636	3.636	3.636	3.636	3.636
4	3.636	3.636	3.636	3.636	3.636	3.636
5	3.636	3.636	3.636	3.636	3.636	3.636
6	3.636	3.636	3.636	3.636	3.636	3.636
7	3.636	3.636	3.636	3.636	3.636	3.636
8	3.636	3.636	3.636	3.636	3.636	3.636
9	3.636	3.636	3.636	3.636	3.636	3.636
10	3.637	3.637	3.637	3.637	3.637	3.637
11	3.636	3.636	3.636	3.636	3.636	3.636
12	3.637	3.637	3.637	3.637	3.637	3.637
13	3.636	3.636	3.636	3.636	3.636	3.636
14	3.637	3.637	3.637	3.637	3.637	3.637
15	3.636	3.636	3.636	3.636	3.636	3.636
16	3.637	3.637	3.637	3.637	3.637	3.637
17	3.636	3.636	3.636	3.636	3.636	3.636
18	3.637	3.637	3.637	3.637	3.637	3.637
19	3.636	3.636	3.636	3.636	3.636	3.636
20	3.637	3.637	3.637	3.637	3.637	3.636
21	3.636	3.636	3.636	3.636	3.636	3.636
22	3.637	3.637	3.637	3.637	3.637	3.637
23	3.636	3.636	3.636	3.636	3.636	3.636
24	3.637	3.637	3.637	3.637	3.637	3.637
25	3.636	3.636	3.636	3.636	3.636	3.636
26	3.637	3.637	3.637	3.637	3.637	3.637
27	3.636	3.636	3.636	3.636	3.636	3.636
28	1.970	2.273	2.576	2.879	3.182	3.485
29	0.000	0.000	0.000	0.000	0.000	0.000

Recovery Year	Month Placed in Service					
	7	8	9	10	11	12
1	1.667	1.364	1.061	0.758	0.455	0.152
2	3.636	3.636	3.636	3.636	3.636	3.636
3	3.636	3.636	3.636	3.636	3.636	3.636
4	3.636	3.636	3.636	3.636	3.636	3.636
5	3.636	3.636	3.636	3.636	3.636	3.636
6	3.636	3.636	3.636	3.636	3.636	3.636
7	3.636	3.636	3.636	3.636	3.636	3.636
8	3.636	3.636	3.636	3.636	3.636	3.636
9	3.636	3.636	3.636	3.636	3.636	3.636
10	3.636	3.636	3.636	3.636	3.636	3.636
11	3.637	3.637	3.637	3.637	3.637	3.637
12	3.636	3.636	3.636	3.636	3.636	3.636
13	3.637	3.637	3.637	3.637	3.637	3.637
14	3.636	3.636	3.636	3.636	3.636	3.636
15	3.637	3.637	3.637	3.637	3.637	3.637
16	3.636	3.636	3.636	3.636	3.636	3.636
17	3.637	3.637	3.637	3.637	3.637	3.637
18	3.636	3.636	3.636	3.636	3.636	3.636
19	3.637	3.637	3.637	3.637	3.637	3.637
20	3.636	3.636	3.636	3.636	3.636	3.636
21	3.637	3.637	3.637	3.637	3.637	3.637
22	3.636	3.636	3.636	3.636	3.636	3.636
23	3.637	3.637	3.637	3.637	3.637	3.637
24	3.636	3.636	3.636	3.636	3.636	3.636
25	3.637	3.637	3.637	3.637	3.637	3.637
26	3.636	3.636	3.636	3.636	3.636	3.636
27	3.637	3.637	3.637	3.637	3.637	3.637
28	3.636	3.636	3.636	3.636	3.636	3.636
29	0.152	0.455	0.758	1.061	1.364	1.667

Source: Rev. Proc. 87-57, Table 7.

Modified ACRS Depreciation Percentages
for Nonresidential Real Property
Placed in Service after December 31, 1986

Recovery Year	Month Placed in Service					
	1	2	3	4	5	6
1	3.042	2.778	2.513	2.249	1.984	1.720
2	3.175	3.175	3.175	3.175	3.175	3.175
3	3.175	3.175	3.175	3.175	3.175	3.175
4	3.175	3.175	3.175	3.175	3.175	3.175
5	3.175	3.175	3.175	3.175	3.175	3.175
6	3.175	3.175	3.175	3.175	3.175	3.175
7	3.175	3.175	3.175	3.175	3.175	3.175
8	3.175	3.174	3.175	3.174	3.175	3.174
9	3.174	3.175	3.174	3.175	3.174	3.175
10	3.175	3.174	3.175	3.174	3.175	3.174
11	3.174	3.175	3.174	3.175	3.174	3.175
12	3.175	3.174	3.175	3.174	3.175	3.174
13	3.174	3.175	3.174	3.175	3.174	3.175
14	3.175	3.174	3.175	3.174	3.175	3.174
15	3.174	3.175	3.174	3.175	3.174	3.175
16	3.175	3.174	3.175	3.174	3.175	3.174
17	3.174	3.175	3.174	3.175	3.174	3.175
18	3.175	3.174	3.175	3.174	3.175	3.174
19	3.174	3.175	3.174	3.175	3.174	3.175
20	3.175	3.174	3.175	3.174	3.175	3.174
21	3.174	3.175	3.174	3.175	3.174	3.175
22	3.175	3.174	3.175	3.174	3.175	3.174
23	3.174	3.175	3.174	3.175	3.174	3.175
24	3.175	3.174	3.175	3.174	3.175	3.174
25	3.174	3.175	3.174	3.175	3.174	3.175
26	3.175	3.174	3.175	3.174	3.175	3.174
27	3.174	3.175	3.174	3.175	3.174	3.175
28	3.175	3.174	3.175	3.174	3.175	3.174
29	3.174	3.175	3.174	3.175	3.174	3.175
30	3.175	3.174	3.175	3.174	3.175	3.174
31	3.174	3.175	3.174	3.175	3.174	3.175
32	1.720	1.984	2.249	2.513	2.778	3.042
33	0.000	0.000	0.000	0.000	0.000	0.000

| | Month Placed in Service | | | | | |
Recovery Year	7	8	9	10	11	12
1	1.455	1.190	0.926	0.661	0.397	0.132
2	3.175	3.175	3.175	3.175	3.175	3.175
3	3.175	3.175	3.175	3.175	3.175	3.175
4	3.175	3.175	3.175	3.175	3.175	3.175
5	3.175	3.175	3.175	3.175	3.175	3.175
6	3.175	3.175	3.175	3.175	3.175	3.175
7	3.175	3.175	3.175	3.175	3.175	3.175
8	3.175	3.175	3.175	3.175	3.175	3.175
9	3.174	3.175	3.175	3.175	3.174	3.175
10	3.175	3.174	3.175	3.174	3.175	3.174
11	3.174	3.175	3.174	3.175	3.174	3.175
12	3.175	3.174	3.175	3.174	3.175	3.174
13	3.174	3.175	3.174	3.175	3.174	3.175
14	3.175	3.174	3.175	3.174	3.175	3.174
15	3.174	3.175	3.174	3.175	3.174	3.175
16	3.175	3.174	3.175	3.174	3.175	3.174
17	3.174	3.175	3.174	3.175	3.174	3.175
18	3.175	3.174	3.175	3.174	3.175	3.174
19	3.174	3.175	3.174	3.175	3.174	3.175
20	3.175	3.174	3.175	3.174	3.175	3.174
21	3.174	3.175	3.174	3.175	3.174	3.175
22	3.175	3.174	3.175	3.174	3.175	3.174
23	3.174	3.175	3.174	3.175	3.174	3.175
24	3.175	3.174	3.175	3.174	3.175	3.174
25	3.174	3.175	3.174	3.175	3.174	3.175
26	3.175	3.174	3.175	3.174	3.175	3.174
27	3.174	3.175	3.174	3.175	3.174	3.175
28	3.175	3.174	3.175	3.174	3.175	3.174
29	3.174	3.175	3.174	3.175	3.174	3.175
30	3.175	3.174	3.175	3.174	3.175	3.174
31	3.174	3.175	3.174	3.175	3.174	3.175
32	3.175	3.174	3.175	3.174	3.175	3.174
33	0.132	0.397	0.661	0.926	1.190	1.455

Source: Rev. Proc. 87-57, Table 7.

Modified ACRS Accelerated Depreciation Percentages
Using the Mid-Quarter Convention
for 3-, 5-, 7-, 10-, 15-, and 20-Year Property
Placed in Service after December 31, 1986

3-Year Property:

Recovery Year	Quarter Placed in Service			
	1	2	3	4
1	58.33	41.67	25.00	8.33
2	27.78	38.89	50.00	61.11
3	12.35	14.14	16.67	20.37
4	1.54	5.30	8.33	10.19

5-Year Property:

1	35.00	25.00	15.00	5.00
2	26.00	30.00	34.00	38.00
3	15.60	18.00	20.40	22.80
4	11.01	11.37	12.24	13.68
5	11.01	11.37	11.30	10.94
6	1.38	4.26	7.06	9.58

7-Year Property:

1	25.00	17.85	10.71	3.57
2	21.43	23.47	25.51	27.55
3	15.31	16.76	18.22	19.68
4	10.93	11.37	13.02	14.06
5	8.75	8.87	9.30	10.04
6	8.74	8.87	8.85	8.73
7	8.75	8.87	8.86	8.73
8	1.09	3.33	5.53	7.64

10-Year Property:

1	17.50	12.50	7.50	2.50
2	16.50	17.50	18.50	19.50
3	13.20	14.00	14.80	15.60
4	10.56	11.20	11.84	12.48
5	8.45	8.96	9.47	9.98
6	6.76	7.17	7.58	7.99
7	6.55	6.55	6.55	6.55
8	6.55	6.55	6.55	6.55
9	6.56	6.56	6.56	6.56
10	0.82	6.55	6.55	6.55
11		2.46	4.10	5.74

Recovery Year	Quarter Placed in Service			
	1	2	3	4

15-Year Property:

	1	2	3	4
1	8.75	6.25	3.75	1.25
2	9.13	9.38	9.63	9.88
3	8.21	8.44	8.66	8.89
4	7.39	7.59	7.80	8.00
5	6.65	6.83	7.02	7.20
6	5.99	6.15	6.31	6.48
7	5.90	5.91	5.90	5.90
8	5.91	5.90	5.90	5.90
9	5.90	5.91	5.91	5.90
10	5.91	5.90	5.90	5.91
11	5.90	5.91	5.91	5.90
12	5.91	5.90	5.90	5.91
13	5.90	5.91	5.91	5.90
14	5.91	5.90	5.90	5.91
15	5.90	5.91	5.91	5.90
16	.74	2.21	3.69	5.17

20-Year Property:

	1	2	3	4
1	6.563	4.688	2.813	0.938
2	7.000	7.148	7.289	7.430
3	6.482	6.612	6.742	6.872
4	5.996	6.116	6.237	6.357
5	5.546	5.658	5.769	5.880
6	5.130	5.233	5.336	5.439
7	4.746	4.841	4.936	5.031
8	4.459	4.478	4.566	4.654
9	4.459	4.463	4.460	4.458
10	4.459	4.463	4.460	4.458
11	4.459	4.463	4.460	4.458
12	4.460	4.463	4.460	4.458
13	4.459	4.463	4.461	4.458
14	4.460	4.463	4.460	4.458
15	4.459	4.462	4.461	4.458
16	4.460	4.463	4.460	4.458
17	4.459	4.462	4.461	4.458
18	4.460	4.463	4.460	4.459
19	4.459	4.462	4.461	4.458
20	4.460	4.463	4.460	4.459
21	.557	1.673	2.788	3.901

Source: Rev. Proc. 87-57.

Alternative Depreciation System
Recovery Periods

General Rule: Recovery period is the property's class life unless:

1. There is no class life (see below), or
2. A special class life has been designated (see below).

Type of Property	*Recovery Period*
Personal property with no class life	12 years
Nonresidential real property with no class life	40 years
Residential rental property with no class life............	40 years
Cars, light general purpose trucks, certain technological equipment, and semiconductor manufacturing equipment............................	5 years
Computer-based telephone central office switching equipment..	9.5 years
Railroad track...	10 years
Single purpose agricultural or horticultural structures ...	15 years
Municipal waste water treatment plants, telephone distribution plants.....................................	24 years
Low-income housing financed by tax-exempt bonds....	27.5 years
Municipal sewers	50 years

Modified ACRS and ADS Straight-Line Depreciation Percentages
Using the Half-Year Convention
for 3-, 5-, 7-, 10-, 15-, and 20-Year Property
Placed in Service after December 31, 1986

Recovery Year	Property Class					
	3-Year	5-Year	7-Year	10-Year	15-Year	20-Year
1	16.67	10.00	7.14	5.00	3.33	2.50
2	33.33	20.00	14.29	10.00	6.67	5.00
3	33.33	20.00	14.29	10.00	6.67	5.00
4	16.67	20.00	14.28	10.00	6.67	5.00
5		20.00	14.29	10.00	6.67	5.00
6		10.00	14.28	10.00	6.67	5.00
7			14.29	10.00	6.67	5.00
8			7.14	10.00	6.66	5.00
9				10.00	6.67	5.00
10				10.00	6.66	5.00
11				5.00	6.67	5.00
12					6.66	5.00
13					6.67	5.00
14					6.66	5.00
15					6.67	5.00
16					3.33	5.00
17						5.00
18						5.00
19						5.00
20						5.00
21						2.50

Source: Rev. Proc. 87-57.

ADS Straight-Line Depreciation Percentages
Real Property
Using the Mid-Month Convention
for Property Placed in Service after December 31, 1986

| Month Placed | Recovery Year | | |
In Service	1	2-40	41
1	2.396	2.500	0.104
2	2.188	2.500	0.312
3	1.979	2.500	0.521
4	1.771	2.500	0.729
5	1.563	2.500	0.937
6	1.354	2.500	1.146
7	1.146	2.500	1.354
8	0.938	2.500	1.562
9	0.729	2.500	1.771
10	0.521	2.500	1.979
11	0.313	2.500	2.187
12	0.104	2.500	2.396

Source: Rev. Proc. 87-57, Table 13.

Original ACRS
Accelerated Recovery Percentages
for 3-, 5-, 10-, and 15-Year Public Utility Property

Personalty Placed in Service after 1980 and before 1987

Recovery Year	Property Class			
	3-Year	5-Year	10-Year	15-Year Public Utility
1	25%	15%	8%	5%
2	38	22	14	10
3	37	21	12	9
4		21	10	8
5		21	10	7
6			10	7
7			9	6
8			9	6
9			9	6
10			9	6
11				6
12				6
13				6
14				6
15				6

Original ACRS
Accelerated Recovery Percentages
for 15-Year Realty

Placed in Service after 1980 and before March 16, 1984

Recovery Year	Month Placed in Service											
	1	2	3	4	5	6	7	8	9	10	11	12
1	12	11	10	9	8	7	6	5	4	3	2	1
2	10	10	11	11	11	11	11	11	11	11	11	12
3	9	9	9	9	10	10	10	10	10	10	10	10
4	8	8	8	8	8	8	9	9	9	9	9	9
5	7	7	7	7	7	7	8	8	8	8	8	8
6	6	6	6	6	7	7	7	7	7	7	7	7
7	6	6	6	6	6	6	6	6	6	6	6	6
8	6	6	6	6	6	6	5	6	6	6	6	6
9	6	6	6	6	5	6	5	5	5	6	6	6
10	5	6	6	6	5	5	5	5	5	5	6	5
11	5	5	5	5	5	5	5	5	5	5	5	5
12	5	5	5	5	5	5	5	5	5	5	5	5
13	5	5	5	5	5	5	5	5	5	5	5	5
14	5	5	5	5	5	5	5	5	5	5	5	5
15	5	5	5	5	5	5	5	5	5	5	5	5
16			1	1	2	2	3	3	4	4	4	5

Original ACRS
Accelerated Recovery Percentages
for Low-Income Housing

Placed in Service after 1980 and before March 16, 1984

Recovery Year	Month Placed in Service											
	1	2	3	4	5	6	7	8	9	10	11	12
1	13	12	11	10	9	8	7	6	4	3	2	1
2	12	12	12	12	12	12	12	13	13	13	13	13
3	10	10	10	10	11	11	11	11	11	11	11	11
4	9	9	9	9	9	9	9	9	10	10	10	10
5	8	8	8	8	8	8	8	8	8	8	8	9
6	7	7	7	7	7	7	7	7	7	7	7	7
7	6	6	6	6	6	6	6	6	6	6	6	6
8	5	5	5	5	5	5	5	5	5	5	6	6
9	5	5	5	5	5	5	5	5	5	5	5	5
10	5	5	5	5	5	5	5	5	5	5	5	5
11	4	5	5	5	5	5	5	5	5	5	5	5
12	4	4	4	5	4	5	5	5	5	5	5	5
13	4	4	4	4	4	4	5	4	5	5	5	5
14	4	4	4	4	4	4	4	4	4	5	4	4
15	4	4	4	4	4	4	4	4	4	4	4	4
16			1	1	2	2	2	3	3	3	4	4

Original ACRS
Accelerated Recovery Percentages
for 18-Year Realty

Realty Placed in Service after March 15, 1984 and before May 9, 1985

Recovery Year	Month Placed in Service											
	1	2	3	4	5	6	7	8	9	10	11	12

The applicable percentage is:

Recovery Year	1	2	3	4	5	6	7	8	9	10	11	12
1	9	9	8	7	6	5	4	4	3	2	1	0.4
2	9	9	9	9	9	9	9	9	9	10	10	10.0
3	8	8	8	8	8	8	8	8	9	9	9	9.0
4	7	7	7	7	7	8	8	8	8	8	8	8.0
5	7	7	7	7	7	7	7	7	7	7	7	7.0
6	6	6	6	6	6	6	6	6	6	6	6	6.0
7	5	5	5	5	6	6	6	6	6	6	6	6.0
8	5	5	5	5	5	5	5	5	5	5	5	5.0
9	5	5	5	5	5	5	5	5	5	5	5	5.0
10	5	5	5	5	5	5	5	5	5	5	5	5.0
11	5	5	5	5	5	5	5	5	5	5	5	5.0
12	5	5	5	5	5	5	5	5	5	5	5	5.0
13	4	4	4	5	4	4	5	4	4	4	5	5.0
14	4	4	4	4	4	4	4	4	4	4	4	4.0
15	4	4	4	4	4	4	4	4	4	4	4	4.0
16	4	4	4	4	4	4	4	4	4	4	4	4.0
17	4	4	4	4	4	4	4	4	4	4	4	4.0
18	4	3	4	4	4	4	4	4	4	4	4	4.0
19		1	1	1	2	2	2	3	3	3	3	3.6

Original ACRS
Accelerated Cost Recovery Percentages
for 19-Year Realty

Realty Placed in Service after May 8, 1985 and before 1987

Recovery Year	Month Placed in Service											
	1	*2*	*3*	*4*	*5*	*6*	*7*	*8*	*9*	*10*	*11*	*12*
	The applicable percentage is:											
1	8.8	8.1	7.3	6.5	5.8	5.0	4.2	3.5	2.7	1.9	1.1	0.4
2	8.4	8.5	8.5	8.6	8.7	8.8	8.8	8.9	9.0	9.0	9.1	9.2
3	7.6	7.7	7.7	7.8	7.9	7.9	8.0	8.1	8.1	8.2	8.3	8.3
4	6.9	7.0	7.0	7.1	7.1	7.2	7.3	7.3	7.4	7.4	7.5	7.6
5	6.3	6.3	6.4	6.4	6.5	6.5	6.6	6.6	6.7	6.8	6.8	6.9
6	5.7	5.7	5.8	5.9	5.9	5.9	6.0	6.0	6.1	6.1	6.2	6.2
7	5.2	5.2	5.3	5.3	5.3	5.4	5.4	5.5	5.5	5.6	5.6	5.6
8	4.7	4.7	4.8	4.8	4.8	4.9	4.9	5.0	5.0	5.1	5.1	5.1
9	4.2	4.3	4.3	4.4	4.4	4.5	4.5	4.5	4.5	4.6	4.6	4.7
10	4.2	4.2	4.2	4.2	4.2	4.2	4.2	4.2	4.2	4.2	4.2	4.2
11	4.2	4.2	4.2	4.2	4.2	4.2	4.2	4.2	4.2	4.2	4.2	4.2
12	4.2	4.2	4.2	4.2	4.2	4.2	4.2	4.2	4.2	4.2	4.2	4.2
13	4.2	4.2	4.2	4.2	4.2	4.2	4.2	4.2	4.2	4.2	4.2	4.2
14	4.2	4.2	4.2	4.2	4.2	4.2	4.2	4.2	4.2	4.2	4.2	4.2
15	4.2	4.2	4.2	4.2	4.2	4.2	4.2	4.2	4.2	4.2	4.2	4.2
16	4.2	4.2	4.2	4.2	4.2	4.2	4.2	4.2	4.2	4.2	4.2	4.2
17	4.2	4.2	4.2	4.2	4.2	4.2	4.2	4.2	4.2	4.2	4.2	4.2
18	4.2	4.2	4.2	4.2	4.2	4.2	4.2	4.2	4.2	4.2	4.2	4.2
19	4.2	4.2	4.2	4.2	4.2	4.2	4.2	4.2	4.2	4.2	4.2	4.2
20	0.2	0.5	0.9	1.2	1.6	1.9	2.3	2.6	3.0	3.3	3.7	4.0

Original ACRS Straight-Line Recovery Percentages
for 3-, 5-, 10-, and 15-Year Public Utility Property

Personalty Placed in Service before 1987

Recovery Year	Optional Recovery Period in Years							
	3	5	10	12	15	25	35	45
The applicable percentage is:								
1	17	10	5	4	3	2	1	1.1
2	33	20	10	9	7	4	3	2.3
3	33	20	10	9	7	4	3	2.3
4	17	20	10	9	7	4	3	2.3
5		20	10	9	7	4	3	2.3
6		10	10	8	7	4	3	2.3
7			10	8	7	4	3	2.3
8			10	8	7	4	3	2.3
9			10	8	7	4	3	2.3
10			10	8	7	4	3	2.3
11			5	8	7	4	3	2.3
12				8	6	4	3	2.2
13				4	6	4	3	2.2
14					6	4	3	2.2
15					6	4	3	2.2
16					3	4	3	2.2
17						4	3	2.2
18						4	3	2.2
19						4	3	2.2
20						4	3	2.2
21						4	3	2.2
22						4	3	2.2
23						4	3	2.2
24						4	3	2.2
25						4	3	2.2
26						2	3	2.2
27							3	2.2
28							3	2.2
29							3	2.2
30							3	2.2
31							3	2.2
32							2	2.2
33							2	2.2
34							2	2.2
35							2	2.2
36							1	2.2
37								2.2
38								2.2
39								2.2
40								2.2
41								2.2
42								2.2
43								2.2
44								2.2
45								2.2
46								1.1

Original ACRS
Straight-Line Recovery Percentages
for 18-Year Realty

Realty Placed in Service after March 15, 1984 and before May 9, 1985

Recovery Year	Month Placed in Service					
	1-2	3-4	5-7	8-9	10-11	12
	The applicable percentage is:					
1	5	4	3	2	1	0.2
2	6	6	6	6	6	6.0
3	6	6	6	6	6	6.0
4	6	6	6	6	6	6.0
5	6	6	6	6	6	6.0
6	6	6	6	6	6	6.0
7	6	6	6	6	6	6.0
8	6	6	6	6	6	6.0
9	6	6	6	6	6	6.0
10	6	6	6	6	6	6.0
11	5	5	5	5	5	5.8
12	5	5	5	5	5	5.0
13	5	5	5	5	5	5.0
14	5	5	5	5	5	5.0
15	5	5	5	5	5	5.0
16	5	5	5	5	5	5.0
17	5	5	5	5	5	5.0
18	5	5	5	5	5	5.0
19	1	2	3	4	5	5.0

Original ACRS
Straight-Line Recovery Percentages
for 19-Year Realty

Realty Placed in Service after May 8, 1985 and before 1987

Recovery Year	Month Placed in Service											
	1	2	3	4	5	6	7	8	9	10	11	12

The applicable percentage is:

	1	2	3	4	5	6	7	8	9	10	11	12
1	5.0	4.6	4.2	3.7	3.3	2.9	2.4	2.0	1.5	1.1	.7	.2
2	5.3	5.3	5.3	5.3	5.3	5.3	5.3	5.3	5.3	5.3	5.3	5.3
3	5.3	5.3	5.3	5.3	5.3	5.3	5.3	5.3	5.3	5.3	5.3	5.3
4	5.3	5.3	5.3	5.3	5.3	5.3	5.3	5.3	5.3	5.3	5.3	5.3
5	5.3	5.3	5.3	5.3	5.3	5.3	5.3	5.3	5.3	5.3	5.3	5.3
6	5.3	5.3	5.3	5.3	5.3	5.3	5.3	5.3	5.3	5.3	5.3	5.3
7	5.3	5.3	5.3	5.3	5.3	5.3	5.3	5.3	5.3	5.3	5.3	5.3
8	5.3	5.3	5.3	5.3	5.3	5.3	5.3	5.3	5.3	5.3	5.3	5.3
9	5.3	5.3	5.3	5.3	5.3	5.3	5.3	5.3	5.3	5.3	5.3	5.3
10	5.3	5.3	5.3	5.3	5.3	5.3	5.3	5.3	5.3	5.3	5.3	5.3
11	5.3	5.3	5.3	5.3	5.3	5.3	5.3	5.3	5.3	5.3	5.3	5.3
12	5.3	5.3	5.3	5.3	5.3	5.3	5.3	5.3	5.3	5.3	5.3	5.3
13	5.3	5.3	5.3	5.3	5.3	5.3	5.3	5.3	5.3	5.3	5.3	5.3
14	5.2	5.2	5.2	5.2	5.2	5.2	5.2	5.2	5.2	5.2	5.2	5.2
15	5.2	5.2	5.2	5.2	5.2	5.2	5.2	5.2	5.2	5.2	5.2	5.2
16	5.2	5.2	5.2	5.2	5.2	5.2	5.2	5.2	5.2	5.2	5.2	5.2
17	5.2	5.2	5.2	5.2	5.2	5.2	5.2	5.2	5.2	5.2	5.2	5.2
18	5.2	5.2	5.2	5.2	5.2	5.2	5.2	5.2	5.2	5.2	5.2	5.2
19	5.2	5.2	5.2	5.2	5.2	5.2	5.2	5.2	5.2	5.2	5.2	5.2
20	.2	.6	1.0	1.5	1.9	2.3	2.8	3.2	3.7	4.1	4.5	5.0

Appendix **D**

TABLE OF CASES CITED

— A —

Abrams, Arnold A., 6-37
Adams, Joe J., 8-23
Alex, James, 7-33
Allen, Louis, 7-28
Allen, Richard A., 5-47
American Viscose Corp. v. Comm., 6-7
Anderson, Charles N., 2-44, 2-46, 6-26
Anderson, Clayton & Co. v. U.S., 2-25
Arizona Governing Committee v. Norris, 6-11
Atlanta Biltmore Hotel Corp., et al. v. Comm., 6-25
Avery, S.L., 5-22

— B —

Babilonia v. Comm., 11-35
Baie, Rudolph, 8-12
Basset, Robert S., 11-4
Bedell v. Comm., 5-21
Bell Electric Co., 7-13
Benedict, Douglas G., 6-33
Bernard, George, 15-29
Biedenharn Realty Co., Inc. v. U.S., 16-5
Biggs v. Comm., 15-39
Bilder, Comm. v., 11-8
Black, Ethel, 15-29
Blair, Frank S. III, 8-2
Bonaire Development Co., 7-11
Borbonus, W.E., 6-37
Bowers, F.C., v. Comm., 7-26
Brushaber v. Union Pacific Railroad Co., 1-4
Burke et al. v. U.S., 6-46
Butler, U.S. v., 1-1

— C —

California Federal Life Ins. Co. v. Comm., 15-31
Carlisle Packing Co. v. Comm., 14-16
Carmichael, Lemuel A., 6-34
Century Electric Co. v. Comm., 15-29
Cesarini v. Comm., 6-45
Chauls, Robert, 8-12
Christiansen, 6-34
Clinton Hotel Realty Corp. v. Comm., 5-32
Cohan v. Comm., 7-40
Cohen, Max, 7-33
Colorado Springs National Bank v. U.S., 7-29
Coombs, Lee E., 8-27
Cooperative Publishing Co. v. U.S., 15-21
Correll, U.S. v., 8-26
Counts, W.B., 11-7
Crane v. Comm., 14-6, 14-14
Crawford, Mary, 17-4
Creative Solutions, Inc. v. U.S., 15-22
Crescent Wharf & Warehouse Co. v. Comm., 7-13
Curphey, Edwin R., 7-4

— D —

Dancer, Harold, 7-6
Davis Co., 15-21
Delman Est. v. Comm., 14-16
Deputy v. DuPont, 7-7
Dickman v. Comm., 5-42
Diggs v. Comm., 10-8
Doggett v. Burnett, 7-4
Dole, et.al., Comm. v., 6-26
Dowell, Cam F., Jr. v. U.S., 8-43
Downey, Burns P., 6-47
Doyle v. Mitchell Bros., 5-10

Drucker v. Comm., 8-12
Duberstein, Comm. v., 5-8, 6-15
Dunn and McCarthy, Inc. v. Comm., 7-7
Durkee v. Comm., 6-42

— E —

Eisner v. Macomber, 5-5, 5-6
Emery v. Comm., 14-15

— F —

Fairfield Plaza, Inc. v. Comm., 14-20
Farmers' and Merchants Bank of Cattletsburg,
        Ky. v. Comm., 6-42
Fausner v. Comm., 8-19
Fincke v. Comm., 14-18
Flint v. Stone Tracy Co., 1-4
Frank, Morton, 7-29
Franklin Life Insurance v. U.S., 5-32
Freedman, Julian D. v. Comm., 7-6

— G —

Garner, Raymond, 8-23
Gilford v. Comm., 17-4
Gilmore, U.S. v., 7-6
Glen, William, 11-38
Glenshaw Glass Co., 5-6, 6-42
Goedel, 7-7
Golsen, Jack E., 2-34
Gordon, A.Z., 6-37
Grayson, J.F., 8-19
Green, John W., 8-13
Gregory v. Helvering, 6-49
Grier v. U.S., 7-4
Guest v. Comm., 14-19

— H —

Hager, James W., 11-31
Harding, R.L., 6-40
Harold, Paul v. Comm., 7-13
Hawaiian Trust Co., Ltd. v. U.S., 7-42
Hawkins, C.A., 5-11
Heininger, Comm. v., 7-8
Higgins v. Comm., 7-5
Holland v. U.S., 5-5
Hornung, Paul V., 5-28
Hoover Motor Express Co., Inc. v. U.S.,
        7-31
Horst, Helvering v., 5-41
Hort v. Comm., 6-42

Houston Endowment, Inc. v. U.S.,
        16-5
Hughes Properties, Inc., 7-12
Hundley Jr., Cecil Randolph, 5-47
Huntsman, James R., 7-12

— J —

Jacob v. Comm., 6-26
James v. U.S., 5-31
James, George H. v. U.S., 8-27
Johnston, A.V., 5-23
Jones v. U.S., 5-13
Jones, Joseph M., 7-28

— K —

Kahler, C. F., 5-22
Kowalski v. Comm., 6-26

— L —

Landfield Finance Co. v. Comm., 6-21
Lester, Comm. v., 6-37
Levin, Samuel B. v. U.S., 7-5
Levine Est. v. Comm., 14-18
Lewis, U.S. v., 5-31
Lincoln Electric Co., Comm. v., 7-8
Lindeman, J.B., 6-25, 6-26
Los Angeles Dept. of Water & Power v.
        Manhart, 6-11
Lucas v. Earl, 5-40
Lucas v. North Texas Lumber Co.,
        5-25
Lutter v. Comm., 4-5

— M —

Malat v. Riddell, 16-4
Maleszewski, Chester J. v. U.S., 6-47
Markarian v. Comm., 4-4
Masser, Harry, 15-21
Matheson v. Comm., 10-8
Mazzei, R., 7-32
McCoy, Lawrence W., 6-38
McDonald, L., 5-11
McDonough, B.P. v. Comm., 7-36
McEuen, H.B. v. Comm., 5-22
Miller, Robert M., 10-8
Moller, Joseph v. U.S., 7-5
Motor Products Corp. v. Comm., 14-15
Mutual Loan and Savings Co. v. Comm.,
        14-15

— N —

National Life Insurance Co., 6-5
New Colonial Ice Co. v. Helvering, 7-1
Nodiak v. Comm., 7-26
North American Oil Consolidated v. Burnet,
   5-29

— O —

O'Dell & Sons Co., Inc. v. Comm., 14-16
Old Colony Railroad v. Comm., 11-18
Ottawa Silica Co. v. U.S., 11-35

— P —

Papineau, George A., 6-25
Patterson, George D. v. Thomas, 5-13
Pfeifer, Donald R., 11-7
Phillips, Michael v. Comm., 5-31
Phoenix Coal Co. v. Comm., 5-11
Pistillo v. Comm., 6-46
Pollock v. Farmers' Loan & Trust Co., 1-4
Pool, H.A., 8-19
Powers, W.J., 10-9
Pulvers v. Comm., 10-8

— R —

Raytheon Production Corp. v. Comm., 5-12
Recio, Robert, 15-21
Reese v. Comm., 16-5
Resler v. Comm., 14-20
Roemer, Jr. v. Comm., 6-47
Rosenberg v. Comm., 10-8
Rosenspan v. U.S., 8-26
Rothensies v. Electric Storage Battery Co.,
   4-40

— S —

San Joaquin Fruit & Inv. Co., Helvering v.,
   16-13
Sanders v. Comm., 8-18
Scheuber v. Comm., 16-5
Schubel, Roger A., 7-43, 11-31
Scott, W.M., 5-32
Scully v. Comm., 14-15
Seed, Harris W., 7-30
Shilling, H.N., Jr., 7-26
Skidmore v. Swift and Co., 2-26
Sklar, Margaret R., 6-37
Smith, Ronald T., 8-2

Soliman, Nader E., 8-12, 8-13, 8-16
South Dade Farms, Inc. v. Comm.,
   5-32
Southern Pacific Co. v. Lowe, 5-10
Sparrow v. Comm., 6-46
Springer v. U.S., 1-3, 1-4
St. Louis Refrigerating & Cold Storage
       Co. v. Comm., 6-21
State Fish Corp., 6-42
Stolk v. Comm., 15-4
Sullivan v. Comm., 7-33

— T —

Taft, Helvering v., 14-31
Tar Products Corp. v. Comm.,
   5-26
Tauferner v. Comm., 8-18
Tellier, Comm. v., 7-26
Thomson v. Comm., 6-42, 6-46
Thor Power Tool Co., 5-20, 10-34
Threlkeld, James E. v. Comm.,
   6-47
Tufts v. Comm., 14-14
Turner, Reginald, 6-38
Turney, U.S. v., 5-31

— U —

Union Pacific Railroad Co., Comm. v.,
   14-15
U.S. Jr. Chamber of Commerce,
   2-46
U.S. Trust Co. of N.Y. v. Anderson,
   6-7

— V —

Van Raden, Kenneth, 7-11
Vickers v. Comm., 14-16
Voss v. U.S., 16-5

— W —

Warwick, Pierre C., 8-30
Watson, T., 5-22
Weightman, George, 8-11
Weir, E.T., 16-13
Weissman v. Comm., 8-12
Welch v. Helvering, 7-7
Wexler, Jan J., 2-46
Whipple v. Comm., 10-3, 10-4
White v. U.S., 11-35

White, John P., 10-9
Wilcox, Comm. v., 5-1
Wilhelm, et.al., Comm. v., 6-25
Wilkins, Fraser, 8-30
Williams v. McGowan, 14-20, 16-5
Willcuts v. Bunn, 6-5, 6-7
Wilson v. Comm., 6-25
Wolfson, A.W., 5-21

— Y —

York v. Comm., 7-29
Young v. Comm., 16-7

— Z —

Zaninovich, Martin J., 7-10

Appendix E

TABLE OF CODE SECTIONS CITED

I.R.C. Sec. | **Page**

1 .... 3-2, 3-11, 4-23
1(c).............................. 4-20
1(e) 3-6
1(f) 4-2, 4-44
1(g)(4)......................... 4-44
1(h) 16-16
1(i) 4-25, 5-41
1(i)(4) 4-27
1(i)(7) 4-30
2(a) 4-16
2(b)(1)........................... 4-16
2(b)(3)........................... 4-17
2(c).............................. 4-18
3 4-21
11 .... 3-4, 13-30
21 .... 6-26, 11-2,
11-4, 13-31, 13-48
21(a)(2) 13-50
21(b)(1) 13-48
21(b)(2) 13-49
21(b)(2)(A) 13-49
21(b)(2)(B) 13-49
21(b)(2)(C) 13-49
21(c) 13-50, 13-52
21(d)(1) 13-51
21(d)(2) 13-51
21(e)(2) 13-51
21(e)(5) 13-48
21(e)(6) 13-49
22 .... 13-30, 13-31, 13-53

I.R.C. Sec. | **Page**

22(a) 13-53
22(b)(2) 13-53
22(c) 13-53
22(d) 13-53
25 .... 13-30, 13-31, 13-54
26 .... 13-31, 13-36,
13-52, 13-54, 13-55
26(b)(2) 13-31
27 .... 13-30, 13-31, 13-46
28 .... 13-30, 13-31, 13-46
29 .... 13-30, 13-31, 13-46
30 .... 13-30, 13-31, 13-54
31 .... 13-30, 13-55
31(a) 13-55
31(c) 13-55
32 .... 13-30, 13-55
32(a) 13-55
32(b)(1) 13-56
32(b)(2) 13-56
32(c)(1)(A)(i) 13-58
32(c)(1)(A)(ii) 13-58
32(f).........................13-57
33 .... 13-30, 13-55, 13-58
34 .... 13-30, 13-55, 13-58
35 13-58
38 .... 13-30, 13-31,
13-37, 13-46, 17-16
38(c)(1).......................13-32
38(c)(2).......................13-31
38(c)(4).......................13-32

I.R.C.

Sec.	Page
38(d)	13-32
39(a)	13-32
40	13-30, 13-38
41	9-44, 13-30
41(a)	13-39
41(a)(1)	13-41
41(b)(4)	13-39
41(c)	13-41
41(c)(3)(B)	13-41
41(d)(1)(B)	13-40
41(d)(4)	13-40
41(e)(1)(B)	13-42
41(e)(6)	13-42
41(f)(3)	13-43
41(g)	13-42
42	13-30
42(b)(1)	13-43
42(b)(2)(B)	13-43
42(g)	13-43
42(l)	13-43
43	13-30
44	13-30, 13-44
44(c)(7)	13-44
45	13-30, 13-45
45A	13-30
45B	13-30, 13-45
46	13-30
46(a)	14-12
47	17-30
47(a)	13-33
47(c)(1)(C)	13-33
47(c)(2)(B)	13-33
47(c)(3)	13-33
48(a)(1)	17-16
48(a)(2)(B)	13-34
48(a)(3)	13-34
48(b)	13-33
48(q)	14-12
49(d)	13-36
50(a)	13-35
50(a)(1)(B)	13-35
50(a)(4)	13-36
50(a)(5)(B)	13-36
50(a)(5)(C)	13-36

I.R.C.

Sec.	Page
50(c)(1)	13-34
50(c)(3)	13-34
51	13-30
51(c)(4)	13-37
51(d)	13-37
51(d)(12)(B)	13-37
53	13-31
53(a)	13-23
53(d)(1)(B)(iv)	13-25
55	13-31
55(a)	13-4
55(b)	13-4
55(b)(2)	13-3
55(d)	13-5
56	13-7, 13-15
56(a)(1)	13-7, 13-8
56(a)(1)(A)(ii)	13-7, 13-10
56(a)(2)	13-8
56(a)(3)	13-8, 13-10
56(a)(4)	13-8, 13-10
56(a)(5)	13-8, 13-10
56(a)(6)	13-8
56(a)(7)	13-8
56(a)(8)	13-8
56(b)(1)(A)	13-8
56(b)(1)(A)(i)	13-11
56(b)(1)(D)	13-8, 13-14
56(b)(1)(E)	13-8, 13-13
56(b)(1)(F)	13-6, 13-11
56(b)(2)	13-8
56(b)(2)(A)(ii)	13-13
56(b)(2)(D)	13-13
56(b)(3)	13-8, 13-13
56(c)	13-8
56(e)(1)	13-12
56(g)(1)	13-14
56(g)(4)	13-14
56(g)(6)	13-14
57	13-15, 13-16
57(a)(1)	13-17
57(a)(2)(E)(ii)	13-17
57(a)(5)(C)(iv)	13-18
57(a)(7)	13-16, 13-19
58	13-30

I.R.C.

Sec.	Page
58(a)	13-8, 13-15
58(b)	13-8
59(e)	13-18
60(c)(2)	13-36
61	2-44, 5-2, 5-3, 5-4, 5-8, 5-14, 18-1, 19-19
61(a)	3-11, 6-1, 19-2
61(a)(1)	6-14, 6-27
61(a)(3)	14-1
61(a)(5)	6-2
61(a)(6)	6-2
61(a)(12)	6-43
62	3-15, 3-16, 7-16, 7-17
63	3-11, 3-17, 7-1
63(c)	3-18
63(c)(6)(A)	3-21
63(c)(6)(B)	3-21
63(c)(6)(C)	3-21
67(a)	11-46
67(b)	13-11
67(d)	13-11
68	11-48
71	6-35
71(a)	6-33
71(a)(1)	6-32
71(b)	6-33
71(c)(2)	6-37
71(d)	6-36
71(f)	6-35
72	5-12, 6-13, 18-7
72(b)(1)	6-10
72(b)(2)	6-11
72(b)(3)	6-11
72(c)(3)	6-11
72(m)	13-31
72(p)	18-10
72(q)(2)	6-10
72(t)	18-9
72(t)(2)	18-9
74(b)	6-38
74(c)	6-16
79	18-2

I.R.C.

Sec.	Page
79(a)(1)	6-20
83	13-13, 18-4 to 18-5, 18-28, 18-34
83(a)	18-4
83(b)	13-13, 18-5
83(b)(1)	18-5
83(h)	18-4, 18-29
85(a)	6-19
86	6-17
87	13-38
101	5-12
101(a)(1)	6-21
101(a)(2)	6-22
101(a)(2)(B)	6-22
101(b)	6-24
101(b)(3)	6-24
102	5-6, 6-32
102(a)	6-32
102(b)	5-9
103	3-4, 5-6
103(a)	6-5
103(b)	6-6
103(c)	6-5
104	5-11
104(a)	5-11, 6-47
104(a)(1)	6-40
104(a)(2)	6-46, 6-47
104(a)(3)	6-23
105(a)	6-23
105(b)	6-22, 6-23, 18-2
105(c)	6-23
105(h)	6-23
106	6-22, 18-2
108	6-44
108(a)	6-43
108(a)(3)	6-43
108(b)	6-43
108(b)(5)	6-43
108(d)(3)	6-43
108(e)(1)	6-43
109	6-44
111	11-14
111(a)	6-22, 6-46
117	6-39

I.R.C.

Sec.	Page
117(c)	6-31
117(d)	6-31, 6-39
118	6-45
119	2-44, 5-13, 9-29, 18-2
119(a)(2)	6-25
120	18-2
121	15-2, 15-3, 15-13, 15-14, 15-15, 15-16, 15-18, 15-19, 15-23, 15-46, 15-47, 17-22
121(a)(1)	15-13
121(a)(2)	15-13
121(b)(1)	15-13
121(b)(2)	15-13
121(c)	15-14
121(d)(1)	15-14
121(d)(2)	15-14
121(d)(4)	15-15, 15-23
121(d)(7)	15-15
121(d)(9)	15-14
123	6-46
125	18-2
126	6-40, 17-30
127	6-27, 18-2
129	13-52, 18-2
129(a)(1)	6-26
132	6-28, 6-29, 18-2
132(a)(1)	6-27
132(b)	6-28, 6-29
132(c)	6-28, 6-29
132(d)	6-27, 6-28
132(e)	6-28, 6-30
132(g)(1)	6-29
132(h)	6-29
132(h)(4)	6-29
132(h)(5)(B)	6-30
132(h)(6)	6-28
135	6-7
143(a)	11-2
151	13-13
151(a)	4-1
151(b)	4-1, 4-2
151(c)(1)(A)	4-7

I.R.C.

Sec.	Page
151(c)(1)(B)	4-8
151(c)(2)	4-10
151(d)	3-20, 4-11
151(d)(1)	3-21
151(d)(2)	3-21, 4-2
151(d)(3)	3-20, 4-2, 4-44
151(e)(4)	6-39
152	3-21, 4-9
152(a)	4-3, 4-8
152(a)(6)	4-9
152(a)(7)	4-9
152(a)(9)	4-17
152(b)(3)	4-11
152(b)(5)	4-9
152(c)	4-6, 4-17
152(e)(1)	4-7
152(e)(2)	4-7
152(e)(3)	4-7
152(e)(4)	4-7
152(e)(5)	4-7
161	7-1
162	3-4, 3-14, 6-27, 7-2 to 7-7, 7-9, 7-15, 7-26, 7-35, 8-1, 8-18, 8-26, 8-34, 8-41, 8-44, 10-7, 11-13, 18-5, 19-2, 19-20
162(a)	7-2, 7-3, 7-8, 8-22, 8-27
162(a)(2)	8-17
162(c)	7-32
162(e)	7-33, 7-35
162(e)(2)	7-34
162(f)	7-32
162(g)	7-32
162(m)	11-10
162(m)(2)(A)	11-10
162(m)(2)(B)	11-10
162(m)(2)(C)	11-11
163	7-2
163(a)	11-18
163(b)(1)	11-32
163(d)	11-24
163(d)(1)	11-24
163(d)(3)(B)	11-26, 12-20

I.R.C.

Sec.	Page
163(d)(4)(E)	11-25
163(h)	11-22
163(h)(1)	11-19
163(h)(3)	11-20
163(h)(3)(B)	11-23
163(h)(3)(D)	11-22
163(h)(4)	11-21
164	7-2, 7-24, 7-28, 11-12, 13-46
164(a)	3-3, 11-12, 11-16
164(b)(1)	11-15
164(b)(2)(E)	11-15
164(c)(1)	11-17
164(d)	11-16
164(f)	1-21
165	7-2, 7-6, 7-15, 14-1, 16-7
165(c)	14-3, 15-4
165(c)(3)	10-7, 11-11
165(g)	16-7
165(g)(3)	16-8
165(h)	10-11, 10-12, 16-8
165(h)(2)	10-10
165(h)(4)(E)	10-9
165(i)	10-13
166	7-6, 10-1
166(a)	10-5
166(d)	16-28
166(d)(1)	10-3
166(d)(1)(B)	10-2
166(d)(2)	10-2, 10-3
167	6-27, 7-27
167(a)	9-2
167(g)	9-3
167(j)	17-19
167(k)	9-36, 17-22
168	7-27, 9-4, 9-19
168(a)	9-5
168(b)(2)	13-10
168(b)(3)(C)	9-18
168(c)(2)	13-10
168(c)	9-7
168(d)	9-7
168(d)(2)	9-13

I.R.C.

Sec.	Page
168(d)(3)	9-15, 9-16
168(d)(4)	9-7
168(d)(4)(B)	9-13
168(e)	9-6
168(e)(2)	9-7
168(e)(4)	9-33
168(f)	9-5
168(g)	9-19
168(g)(1)	9-20
168(g)(1)(C)	9-34
168(g)(7)	9-20, 13-10
168(i)(4)	9-20
168(i)(8)	9-36
169	7-27, 9-36, 13-10
170	3-14, 9-42, 11-33
170(a)(2)(B)	2-24
170(b)	11-40
170(b)(1)	11-40
170(b)(1)(B)(i)	11-44
170(b)(1)(C)	11-41
170(b)(1)(C)(i)	11-43
170(b)(1)(C)(iii)	11-43
170(b)(2)	19-28
170(c)	11-34
170(d)(1)	11-44
170(d)(1)(A)	11-45
170(d)(2)	19-28
170(e)(1)	11-38, 11-39, 16-4
170(e)(1)(B)(ii)	11-39
170(e)(3)	11-38
170(e)(4)	11-39
170(j)	11-36
170(k)	11-36
170(m)	11-35
171	16-38
172	5-18, 10-16, 19-29
172(b)(1)	10-16, 19-30
172(b)(3)(C)	10-17, 19-30
172(c)	10-16, 19-3
172(d)(1)	10-18, 19-29
172(d)(4)	10-18
172(d)(5)	19-29
173	13-12
174	7-29, 9-40, 16-21

I.R.C.

Sec.	Page
174(a)	9-41
174(a)(2)	9-41
174(b)	9-41
174(b)(2)	9-41
174(c)	9-41
175	7-29, 9-43
178	7-27, 9-36
178(a)	9-36
179	7-6, 9-6, 9-15, 9-22 to 9-24, 9-25, 9-26, 13-10, 13-45, 17-16, 17-17, 17-35
179(d)(1)	9-23
179(d)(2)	9-23
179(d)(10)	9-24
180	7-29, 9-43
183	7-23, 7-24
183(b)	7-24
183(d)	7-24
183(d)(4)	7-24
184	7-27, 9-36
186	6-42
188	7-27, 9-36
194	13-33
195	7-30
195(a)	7-29
195(c)(1)	7-30
196	13-39, 13-46
197	9-35, 9-36
212	3-14, 7-2 to 7-7, 7-9, 7-26, 7-35, 8-18, 10-7, 11-13, 12-1, 18-5
212(1)	8-26
212(2)	8-26
212(3)	11-37
213	3-14, 6-22
213(a)	11-2
213(a)(1)	7-39
213(b)	11-5
213(d)(1)	11-2
213(d)(1)(A)	11-2
213(d)(1)(B)	11-2
213(d)(1)(C)	11-2
213(d)(2)	11-2, 11-8
213(d)(5)	11-2

I.R.C.

Sec.	Page
213(e)	11-2
215	6-36
215(a)	6-32
217	8-5, 8-6
217(b)(1)(A)	8-7
217(b)(1)(B)	8-7, 8-8
217(c)	15-12
217(c)(1)	8-6
217(c)(2)	8-6
217(d)	8-7
219(b)	18-23
219(c)	18-23
219(g)	18-23
243–246	6-2, 19-23
262	7-26, 11-1
263	7-10, 7-28
263(a)	7-28
263A	10-25
264	7-36
265	7-3, 7-35, 11-18, 13-18
265(1)	7-35
265(2)	7-35
266	14-6
267	7-36, 7-37, 7-38, 7-39 9-23, 14-3, 14-32, 15-41, 19-11
267(a)(1)	14-32
267(a)(2)	7-38, 7-39
267(b)	7-37, 14-28, 14-32
267(c)	7-37, 14-32
267(c)(5)	7-37
267(d)	7-38, 14-32
268	17-6
274	8-33, 8-34, 8-35, 8-38, 8-44
274(a)	8-37
274(a)(1)	8-34
274(a)(1)(B)	8-38
274(a)(3)	8-38
274(b)	6-15, 6-24, 8-37, 8-41
274(c)	8-30
274(d)	8-34, 8-42, 8-43, 9-32

I.R.C.

Sec.	Page
274(e)	8-40, 8-46
274(e)(1)–(9)	8-38
274(e)(3)	8-40
274(e)(5)	8-38
274(h)(1)	8-31
274(h)(2)	8-32
274(h)(3)	8-31
274(h)(6)	8-31
274(h)(7)	8-29
274(j)	6-16, 8-42
274(k)(1)(B)	8-37
274(l)(1)	8-41
274(l)(2)	8-38
274(m)	8-29
274(m)(1)	8-31
274(m)(2)	8-3
274(n)	8-39, 11-46
274(n)(1)	8-41
274(n)(2)	8-40
274(n)(2)(B)	8-40
274(n)(2)(C)	8-41
275	11-13
276	7-34
280	2-22
280A	2-22, 7-6, 8-10, 8-11, 8-17, 12-23, 12-26, 12-28, 12-29
280A(c)	8-11
280A(c)(1)	8-11
280A(c)(2)	8-15
280A(c)(4)	8-15
280A(c)(5)	8-14, 12-24
280A(c)(6)	8-15
280A(d)	12-28
280A(d)(2)	12-25
280A(d)–(g)	12-24
280A(e)	12-27
280A(f)(1)	13-12
280B	2-22, 7-28, 14-17
280C	2-22
280C(c)	9-42, 13-39
280C(c)(3)	13-39
280E	7-33

I.R.C.

Sec.	Page
280F	9-24, 9-25, 9-26, 9-29, 9-30
280F(b)	9-26
280F(b)(1)	9-27
280F(b)(2)	9-27
280F(c)	9-26
280F(d)(3)	9-29
280F(d)(4)	9-27
280F(d)(5)	9-24
280F(d)(5)(B)	9-24
280F(d)(6)	9-27
291	17-15, 17-19, 17-24, 17-28, 19-27
291(a)(1)	17-29, 17-30, 17-32, 19-28
301	5-12
301(b)	6-2
301(c)(2)	6-3
301(c)(3)	6-3
305(a)	6-3, 6-4
305(b)(1)	6-4
305(b)(2)	6-4
305(b)(5)	6-4
306	6-4
307(a)	6-3
316	5-12
316(a)	6-3
316(b)(1)	6-3
318(a)	14-28
351	14-4, 15-44, 19-34, 19-35, 19-53
355	15-44
358	19-33
362	19-34
368	14-4
401	18-13
401–415	18-12
401(a)	6-12, 18-2, 18-6
401(a)(4)	18-13
401(a)(5)	18-13, 18-14
401(a)(17)	18-13, 18-17
401(a)(27)	18-11
401(a)(26)	18-15
401(c)(2)	18-20

I.R.C. Sec.	Page
401(k)	11-19, 18-3, 18-18, 18-36
401(k)(2)	18-23
401(k)(2)(A)	18-23
401(k)(2)(B)	18-23
401(k)(2)(C)	18-23
401(k)(3)	18-23
402(a)	18-6, 18-7
402(a)(2)	18-8
402(a)(5)	18-10
402(b)	18-28
402(e)	18-8
402(e)(1)	18-7
402(e)(1)(C)	18-8
402(e)(4)(B)	18-8
402(g)(5)	18-22
402(h)	18-25
403(a)	18-6
403(b)	6-12
404	18-16, 18-18
404(a)	18-18
404(a)(3)	18-18, 18-21
404(a)(5)	18-28
404(a)(9)	18-12
408(c)	18-25
408(d)	18-25
408(f)	13-31
408(k)	18-25
410(a)(1)	18-14
410(a)(2)	18-14
410(b)(1)	18-14
410(b)(2)(c)	18-15
410(c)(1)	18-19
411(a)(2)	18-15
411(a)(2)(A)	18-15
411(a)(2)(B)	18-16
412	18-16
412(h)(1)	18-11
414(h)(1)	18-22
414(q)	18-13
415(a)	18-16
415(b)	18-16
415(b)(1)(A)	18-17
415(b)(2)(B)	18-17

I.R.C. Sec.	Page
415(c)(1)	18-20
415(c)(1)(A)	18-16
415(c)(1)(B)	18-19
415(c)(3)(B)	18-20
416	18-18
416(i)(3)	18-19
421	18-29
421(a)	18-30
421(b)	18-30
422A	18-29
422A(a)(1)	18-30
422A(a)(2)	18-30
422A(b)	18-31
422A(b)(7)	18-31
422A(c)(2)	18-31
422A(c)(6)	18-31
441(a)	5-16
441(b)	5-16
441(i)	5-17
442	5-16
443	5-16
444	5-17
446(b)	5-19
446(c)	5-19
446(f)	5-26
447	9-44
448	10-6
448(a)	5-24
448(b)	5-24
448(d)(5)	10-6
453(a)	14-22
453(b)	14-21
453(c)	14-24
453(d)	14-22
453(e)	14-27
453(e)(2)	14-28
453(f)	14-28
453(g)	14-27, 14-32
453(h)(6)	15-32
453(h)(7)	15-32
453(i)	14-21, 17-30
453(k)(2)	16-11
453(l)	14-21
453(l)(2)	14-21

I.R.C.

Sec.	Page
453A	14-29
453A(a)(2)	14-24
453B(a)	14-29
453B(b)	14-29
453B(c)	14-29
453B(d)	14-29
453B(g)	14-29
454(a)	5-37
454(b)	5-38
454(c)	5-38
455	5-35
456	5-35
460	5-33
460(a)	5-34
460(b)(2)	5-35
460(b)(5)	5-34
460(e)	5-34
461(a)	7-9, 11-31
461(g)	7-12, 11-31
461(h)	7-12
461(h)(3)	7-14
464	9-44
464(f)	9-44
469	7-23, 12-2, 12-3, 12-9, 12-30
469(a)(2)	12-7
469(c)	12-18
469(c)(7)	12-18
469(e)(2)	12-8
469(g)	12-3
469(g)(1)(A)	12-6
469(i)	12-16
471	10-23, 10-24
472(c)	10-32
472(d)	10-32
472(f)	10-30
474	10-30
481	5-26
481(a)	5-26
481(c)	5-27
482(b)	5-27
483	14-26, 16-22
483(d)(4)	16-22
501(a)	3-4, 18-6

I.R.C.

Sec.	Page
501(b)	3-4
501(c)(18)	18-36
509(a)	11-39
531	13-31
541	13-31
611	7-27, 9-37
613	9-38
613(a)	9-37
613A(c)	9-37
616	13-10
617	13-10
631	17-4, 17-5
631(a)	17-5
631(b)	17-5
631(c)	17-5
631(c)(1)	17-6
631(c)(2)	17-6
639(c)(4)	4-44
641(a)	3-6
641(b)	3-6
642(c)	11-33
651	3-6
661	3-6
662	3-6
663(a)(1)	6-32
691	13-11, 14-10, 17-18
691(a)(1)	14-10
701	3-6, 19-5
702(a)	3-6, 19-5
702(a)(4)	11-33
702(b)	6-2, 19-5
702(c)	6-2, 19-5
703(b)	3-7
704(a)	19-5
704(b)	19-5
704(d)	19-6
706(b)	5-17
707(a)	3-7
707(b)	7-37
707(b)(1)	15-41
707(c)	19-11
721	6-45, 14-4, 15-44, 19-32

I.R.C.

Sec.	Page
722	19-32
723	19-32
731(a)	3-7
741	3-7
852(b)(3)(D)	6-2
871	3-3
882(a)	3-4
901	3-3
911(a)	3-4
1001	14-6
1001(a)	5-10
1001(b)	3-28, 14-22
1011(b)	14-19
1011-1116	3-28
1012	14-6
1014	16-12, 17-23
1014(a)	14-9
1014(a)(2)	14-10
1014(c)	14-10
1014(e)	14-10
1015	16-12
1015(a)	14-7, 14-8, 14-30, 14-33
1015(d)(2)	14-8
1015(d)(6)	14-7
1016(a)(1)	14-12
1016(a)(2)	14-12
1016(a)(4)	14-12
1016(a)(22)	14-12
1031	14-4, 15-2, 15-23, 15-28, 15-29, 15-32, 15-40, 15-39, 15-41, 15-46, 16-11, 17-23
1031(a)(2)	15-29
1031(a)(3)	15-40
1031(b)	15-28, 15-44
1031(c)	15-32
1031(d)	15-32, 15-34
1031(e)	15-31
1031(f)	15-41
1031(h)	15-29
1032	18-12
1033	14-4, 15-15, 15-20, 15-21, 15-23, 15-25, 16-9, 16-11, 17-2, 17-3, 17-23, 17-34
1033(a)	15-20, 15-22, 15-24
1033(a)(1)	15-25
1033(a)(1)(A)(i)	15-22
1033(a)(2)(A)	15-23, 15-25
1033(a)(2)(B)	15-24
1033(a)(2)(C)	15-25
1033(a)(2)(E)(i)	15-23
1033(b)	15-25
1033(d)	15-23
1033(e)	15-23
1033(f)	15-23
1033(g)(1)	15-23
1033(g)(4)	15-24
1034	13-12, 14-4, 15-3, 15-4, 15-7, 15-8, 15-10, 15-12, 15-13, 15-15, 15-16, 15-18, 15-19, 15-46, 15-47, 16-11, 17-22, 17-23
1034(a)	15-4, 15-7, 15-10
1034(b)(1)	15-7
1034(b)(2)	15-8
1034(c)(2)	15-5
1034(c)(4)	15-10
1034(d)(1)	15-10
1034(d)(2)	15-12
1034(e)	14-11, 15-8
1034(g)	15-12
1034(h)	15-5
1034(i)	15-23
1034(k)	15-5
1036	15-44
1037	5-38, 15-45
1038	15-45
1039	15-45, 17-23
1041	15-12
1041(a)	14-17
1041(b)(2)	6-36, 14-17
1041(c)	14-17
1060	6-41
1091	16-12
1091(a)	14-31
1091(d)	14-31
1202	16-23

I.R.C.

Sec.	Page
1202(g)	16-26
1211(a)	3-34, 16-20
1211(b)	3-33, 14-3, 16-18
1211(b)(1)	19-25
1212(a)	3-34, 16-20, 19-25
1212(b)	16-19, 19-25
1221	3-13, 7-6, 16-3, 16-4
1222	16-10, 16-13
1222(1)	3-31
1222(3)	3-31
1222(4)	3-31
1222(5)	19-25
1222(6)	19-25
1222(7)	19-25
1222(8)	19-25
1222(10)	16-14
1222(11)	16-14
1223	3-31, 16-11, 17-3
1223(1)	15-41, 16-11
1223(2)	16-11
1223(4)	16-12
1223(5)	6-4, 16-12
1223(6)	16-12
1223(7)	16-11
1223(8)	16-13
1223(11)	16-12
1231	3-34, 3-35, 3-43, 11-38, 11-39, 11-43, 16-11, 16-22, 17-2 to 17-33, 17-34, 19-27, 19-28, 19-37
1231(a)(1)	17-7
1231(b)(1)	17-4
1231(b)(2)	17-4
1231(b)(3)	17-4, 17-7
1231(b)(4)	17-4, 17-6
1231(c)	17-11
1233(b)	16-29
1234(a)	16-30
1235	16-21, 16-22
1235(a)	16-22
1235(b)	16-22
1235(d)	16-22
1236	16-26
1236(a)	16-26

I.R.C.

Sec.	Page
1237	16-27
1237(a)	16-27
1237(b)	16-27
1237(b)(1)	16-27
1237(b)(2)	16-27
1239	14-32, 14-34
1239(a)	14-32
1239(b)	14-28
1239(c)	14-28
1241	6-42, 16-22
1244	10-21, 16-22, 16-23, 16-39, 16-40
1244(a)	16-23
1244(c)(3)(A)	16-23
1245	3-34, 11-25, 13-34, 17-15 to 17-18, 17-19, 17-21, 17-22, 17-24, 17-28, 17-29, 17-30, 17-31, 17-32, 17-33, 19-27, 19-28, 19-31
1245(a)	17-16
1245(a)(2)	17-17
1245(a)(3)	17-16
1245(a)(3)(D)	17-16
1245(a)(5)	17-19
1245(b)(1)	17-18
1245(b)(2)	17-18
1245(b)(3)	17-18
1245(b)(4)	17-18
1250	3-34, 11-25, 15-29, 17-15, 17-18 to 17-30, 19-27, 19-28
1250(a)	17-20, 17-22
1250(a)(1)	17-22
1250(a)(2)	17-22
1250(a)(3)	17-22
1250(b)	17-20
1250(b)(5)	17-20
1250(c)	17-19
1250(d)(1)	17-22
1250(d)(2)	17-22
1250(d)(3)	17-22
1250(d)(4)	17-22
1250(d)(4)(C)	15-29, 17-23
1250(d)(7)	17-22

I.R.C.

Sec.	Page
1250(d)(8)	17-23
1252	17-30
1253	16-28
1253(a)	16-28
1253(b)(2)	16-28
1253(c)	16-28
1253(d)(1)	16-28
1253(d)(2)	16-28
1254	11-25, 17-30
1255	17-30
1258	16-38
1271	16-32
1271(a)(2)	16-34
1271-1275	16-34
1272(a)	14-26, 16-34, 16-35
1272(a)(2)	16-36
1272(b)	16-35
1273(a)	14-26
1273(a)(3)	16-34
1274	14-26, 16-22
1274(a)	14-26
1274(c)	14-26
1274(c)(2)	16-36
1274(c)(4)(E)	16-22
1274(d)(1)	14-27
1276	16-37
1277	16-37
1277(a)(2)	16-37
1281(a)	5-38
1281(b)	16-36
1341	5-31
1361	19-13
1361-1379	3-8
1361(b)	19-14
1361(c)	19-14
1362	19-13
1363	19-14
1366	19-14
1366(a)(1)	11-33
1374	13-31
1375	13-31
1378	5-17
1382(b)	6-3
1385(b)	6-3

I.R.C.

Sec.	Page
1396	13-30, 13-44
1402	19-6
1402(a)(12)	1-21
1502	2-25
2011	1-17
2031(a)	14-9
2032A	14-13
2032A(b)	14-11
2032(a)	14-10
2032(c)	14-10
3306(a)(1)	1-24
3401	13-55
3405	13-55
3406	13-55
3508	11-20
4942(j)	11-41
4973	18-25
4975(e)(7)	18-12
4980A	18-10
6012(a)(1)	4-31
6012(a)(1)(C)(i)	4-31
6013(a)	4-15
6013(a)(2)	4-15
6013(e)	4-15
6013(g)	4-15
6017	19-2
6050L	11-37
6072(a)	4-35
6501(e)	4-41
6511(a)	4-37
6511(d)	16-7
6511(d)(2)	10-17
6551(f)	4-36
6591	2-28
6601(a)	4-36
6621	14-29, 14-30
6651(a)(1)	4-36
6651(a)(2)	4-36
6653(a)(1)	4-37
6653(b)	4-37
6654(a)	4-38
6654(d)	4-38, 4-39
6654(d)(1)(c)	4-34
6662	2-6, 2-10

I.R.C.

Sec.	Page
6662(c)	2-6
6662(d)	2-8
6662(e)	2-9
6663	2-10
6694(a)	2-14, 2-15, 2-19
6694(b)	2-16
7206	2-16

I.R.C.

Sec.	Page
7207	2-16
7216	2-16
7701(b)	3-2
7703(a)(1)	4-15
7703(b)	4-18
7805(a)	2-25
7872	2-24, 5-43, 5-45

Appendix **F**

TABLE OF REGULATIONS CITED

Regulations

Reg. §	Page	Reg. §	Page
1.2-2(d)	4-18	1.102-1(a)	6-32
1.47-2	13-36	1.104-1(d)	6-23
1.47-3(f)	13-36	1.109-1	6-44
1.57-5(a)	13-23	1.117-3(a)	6-39
1.61-1(a)	5-9	1.117-3(b)	6-39
1.61-2(a)	6-14	1.117-4(c)	6-39
1.61-2(d)	18-1	1.119-1(a)(2)	6-25
1.61-2(d)(1)	6-27	1.119-1(a)(3)	6-25
1.61-3	4-7	1.119-1(b)	6-25
1.61-3(a)	5-11	1.119-1(c)(2)	6-25
1.61-4(a)(4)	6-40	1.121-1(c)	15-13
1.61-7(a)	6-3	1.132-1(e)(1)	6-30
1.61-8	6-2	1.132-1(e)(2)	6-30
1.62-1(f)	8-54	1.132-1(e)(5)	6-30
1.62-1(g)	8-7	1.132-5	6-27
1.62-2	11-46	1.132-5(n)	5-15
1.71-1	6-33	1.151-1(c)(2)	3-20
1.71-1(b)(4)	6-34	1.151-3(a)	4-8
1.71-1(e)	6-36, 6-37	1.151-3(b)	4-8
1.72-9	6-11	1.152-1(a)(2)(i)	4-4
1.74-1(a)(2)	6-38	1.152-1(a)(2)(ii)	4-5
1.79-0	6-20	1.152-1(c)	4-4
1.79-1(a)(4)	6-20	1.152-2(d)	4-9
1.79-3	6-20, 6-21	1.162-1(a)	7-6
1.83-3(c)(1)	18-4	1.162-2(a)	8-26
1.83-6(a)(4)	18-5	1.162-2(b)(1)	8-28
1.83-7(a)	18-29	1.162-2(c)	8-29
1.83-7(b)(1)	18-29	1.162-4	7-28
1.83-7(b)(2)	18-29, 18-32	1.162-5(a)	8-2

Reg. §	Page
1.162-5(b)(2)	8-2
1.162-5(b)(3)	8-2, 8-3
1.162-5(b)(3)(ii)	8-3
1.162-7(b)(1)	7-8
1.162-8	7-8
1.162-12	9-43
1.162-20(a)(2)	7-34
1.162-20(b)	7-34
1.162-21(b)	7-32
1.164-2	11-13
1.164-2(g)	11-17
1.164-3(c)	11-15
1.164-4(a)	11-17
1.164-4(b)(1)	11-17
1.164-6(b)	11-16
1.164-6(b)(3)	11-16
1.164-6(d)	11-16
1.165-1(d)(2)(i)	10-13, 11-11
1.165-2	14-16, 16-8
1.165-7(a)	10-9, 10-13
1.165-7(a)(2)(ii)	10-9
1.165-7(b)(i)	10-10
1.165-7(b)(4)(iii)	10-10
1.165-8(d)	10-9
1.165-9(b)	14-30
1.166-1(c)	10-4
1.166-1(d)	10-4
1.166-1(e)	10-4
1.166-2(a)	10-5
1.166-2(b)	10-5
1.166-3(a)	10-5
1.166-5(a)(2)	10-2
1.167(a)-2	9-2
1.167(a)-3	9-2
1.167(a)-8	14-16, 16-8
1.167(a)-10	9-3
1.167(g)-1	9-3, 14-8, 14-11
1.170A-1(g)	11-36
1.170A-4(b)(1)	11-38
1.170A-4(b)(3)	11-40
1.170A-4(b)(3)(ii)	11-40
1.170A-4(b)(4)	11-38
1.170A-8(b)	11-40
1.170A-10(a)	11-45
1.170A-10(b)(2)	11-45, 11-46

Reg. §	Page
1.170A-10(c)(1)	11-45
1.170-1(c)(1)	11-37
1.172-5(a)(3)(ii)	10-20
1.102-1(a)	6-32
1.174-2(a)	9-40, 13-40
1.183-2(a)	7-23
1.183-2(b)	7-23
1.186-1	6-42
1.211-1(b)(4)(i)	16-18
1.212-1(b)	7-7
1.212-1(d)	7-6
1.212-1(k)	7-28
1.213-1(a)(1)	11-3
1.213-1(a)(3)(i)	11-2
1.213-1(b)(2)(i)	11-5
1.213-1(e)(1)(i)	11-2
1.213-1(e)(1)(ii)	11-6
1.213-1(e)(1)(iii)	11-6
1.213-1(e)(1)(iv)	11-2, 11-8
1.213-1(e)(1)(v)	11-7
1.213-1(e)(1)(v)(a)	11-7
1.213-1(e)(1)(v)(b)	11-7
1.213-1(e)(2)	11-2
1.213-1(e)(3)	11-2
1.213-1(e)(4)	11-2, 11-9
1.213-1(f)	11-2
1.217-2(b)(3)	8-7
1.263(a)-1(b)	7-28
1.263(a)-2	7-28
1.266-1(b)(1)	14-6
1.274-2(b)(1)(iii)	8-41
1.274-2(c)(3)	8-35
1.274-2(c)(7)	8-35
1.274-2(d)	8-36
1.274-2(d)(4)	8-36, 8-37
1.274-2(d)(5)	8-36
1.274-2(e)(2)	8-38
1.274-4	8-30
1.274-5(c)(3)	8-43
1.280A-1(e)(4)	12-25
1.401-1(b)(1)(i)	18-11
1.401-1(b)(1)(ii)	18-11
1.401-1(b)(1)(iii)	18-12
1.401(k)-1(a)	18-21
1.401(k)-1(a)(4)(iv)	18-23

Reg. §	Page
1.402(b)-1(b)	18-28
1.421-5(b)(2)	18-30
1.421-6(c)	18-32
1.421-6(d)	18-32
1.421-6(e)	18-32
1.421-6(f)	18-32
1.441-1(d)	5-16
1.441-1(e)	5-16
1.441-2	5-16
1.446-1(a)(1)	7-9, 7-10
1.446-1(a)(2)	5-20
1.446-1(a)(3)	5-9, 5-21
1.446-1(a)(4)(i)	10-24
1.446-1(c)(1)(i)	5-21
1.446-1(c)(1)(ii)	5-19, 5-25, 5-30
1.446-1(c)(1)(iv)	10-24
1.446-1(c)(2)	7-10
1.451-1(a)	5-25, 18-26
1.451-2(a)	5-21, 18-26
1.451-2(b)	5-22, 5-26
1.451-3	5-33
1.451-4(c)(1)	5-33
1.451-5(b)	5-33
1.454-1(a)	5-38
1.471-1	10-24
1.471-2(c)	10-33
1.471-11	10-25
1.472-2(e)	10-32
1.611-1(a)	9-37
1.611-1(b)	9-37
1.611-2(a)	9-37
1.707-1(c)	19-6
1.852-4(a)	6-2
1.852-4(b)	6-2
1.871-2(b)	3-3
1.1001-1(b)	11-16
1.1001-2	14-4
1.1001-2(a)(1)	14-14
1.1011-2(a)	14-19
1.1012-1(a)	14-6
1.1012-1(b)	11-16
1.1012-1(c)	14-7
1.1015-4(d)	14-17
1.1016-6	14-12
1.1031(a)-1(a)	15-29

Reg. §	Page
1.1031(a)-1(b)	15-29
1.1031(a)-2(a)	15-31
1.1031(a)-2(b)(1)	15-30
1.1031(b)-1(c)	15-33
1.1031(d)-1(c)	15-38
1.1031(d)-1(d)	15-38
1.1031(d)-2	15-33
1.1031(k)-1	15-40
1.1033(a)-2(c)(2)	15-25
1.1033(a)-2(c)(3)	15-24
1.1033(a)-2(c)(4)	15-25
1.1033(a)-2(c)(5)	15-25
1.1033(a)-2(c)(8)	6-42
1.1033(b)-1	15-25
1.1034-1(a)	15-4
1.1034-1(b)(6)	15-8
1.1034-1(b)(7)	15-8
1.1034-1(c)(3)(i)	15-4
1.1034-1(d)	15-5
1.1036-1(a)	15-44
1.1036-1(b)	15-44
1.1091-1(c)	14-31
1.1091-1(d)	14-31
1.1211-1(b)(2)	19-25
1.1211-1(b)(6)	19-25
1.1223-1(d)	16-12
1.1223-1(e)	16-12
1.1223-1(f)	16-12
1.1223-1(h)	16-13
1.1235-2(b)	16-22
1.1250-3(a)	17-23
1.1250-3(b)	17-23
1.1250-3(c)	17-23
1.1250-3(d)(5)	17-22
1.1250-3(f)	17-23
1.1250-3(h)(4)	17-22
1.6001-1(a)	7-40
1.6041-2	6-27
1.6041-3(i)	7-20
1.6081-4(a)	4-35
1.6694-2(b)	2-14
1.6662-3(b)(3)	2-8
1.6694-2(c)(2)	2-8
1.6662-4(d)	2-8
1.6692-4(d)(3)(iii)	2-9

Reg. §	Page
1.6694-2(c)(3)	2-9
31.3401(c)-1(a)	7-22
1.401(a)(17)-1(b)	18-17

Proposed Regulations

Reg. §	Page
1.401(a)(17)-1(b)(6)	18-7
1.401(a)(26)-2	18-15
1.469-4	12-10
1.469-4(c)(1)	12-10
1.469-4(d)	12-11
1.469-4(e)	12-11
1.469-4(g)	12-11
1.469-4(h)	12-11
1.469-4(j)	12-11
1.7872-4(d)(2)	5-43

Temporary Regulations

Reg. §	Page
1.61-2T(d)(2)(iii)	9-31
1.62-2T	8-47
1.62-2T(e)(2)	8-51
1.71-1T	6-33, 6-37
1.71-1T(b)	6-33, 6-34
1.163-8T	11-27
1.163-8T(c)(1)	11-27

Reg. §	Page
1.163-8T(c)(2)	11-30
1.163-8T(c)(3)	11-29
1.163-8T(c)(4)	11-27
1.263A-1T(b)(2)(ii)	10-25
1.274-5T(a)(4)	8-42
1.274-5T(b)(6)	9-32
1.274-5T(g)	8-51
1.280F-6T(a)(2)	9-29
1.280F-6T(d)(2)	9-27
1.280F-6T(d)(4)(iv)	9-30
1.448-1T(f)(2)(iv)	5-24
1.469-1T(a)	12-14
1.469-1T(e)(3)(ii)	12-12
1.469-1T(f)(2)	12-14
1.469-1T(f)(4)(B)	12-3
1.469-2T(c)(2)(i)(A)(2)	12-6
1.469-2T(f)	12-19
1.469-2T(f)(2)	12-15
1.469-4T(a)(2)	12-10
1.1041-1T(e)	14-17
15a.453-1(b)(2)(i)	14-24
15a.453-1(b)(2)(ii)	14-24
15a.453-1(b)(2)(v)	14-24
15a.453-1(b)(3)(i)	14-24
15a.453-1(d)(2)(ii)	14-22
16A.126-1	6-40

Appendix G

TABLE OF REVENUE PROCEDURES AND REVENUE RULINGS CITED

Revenue Procedures

Rev. Proc.	Page
71-21	5-32
72-18	7-35
74-8	7-35
77-10	9-4
82-22	2-28
87-56	9-6, 15-30
87-57	9-11, 9-12, 9-14, 9-15, 9-17, 9-18, 9-19, 9-21
88-22	9-6
91-67	8-24, 9-31, 11-8, 11-36
92-12	7-43
92-20	5-27
93-51	9-31

Revenue Rulings

Rev. Rul.	Page
190(1953)	8-21
53-61	6-45
53-80	6-25
54-567	4-10
55-57	8-29
55-79	14-20, 16-5
55-109	8-23
55-216	11-6
55-264	6-42
55-527	18-27
55-555	6-45
56-435	14-15
57-244	15-39
57-314	15-21
57-398	6-45
57-535	14-15
58-52	6-37
58-533	11-7
58-557	15-21
59-58	6-15
59-80	6-39
59-102	15-20
59-307	6-25
59-361	15-21
60-25	14-15
60-31	5-23
60-32	6-40
61-119	15-38
63-136	6-40
63-144	8-37
63-232	10-8
66-7	16-10
66-114	15-4
66-262	7-35
68-20	6-39
68-38	6-40
68-295	11-6
68-579	6-26

Rev. Rul.	Page	Rev. Rul.	Page
69-292	8-3	76-301	15-29
69-649	18-27	76-319	15-22
69-650	18-27	76-373	6-40
70-217	6-16	77-16	7-31
70-218	6-34	77-254	7-30
70-254	6-21	77-297	15-39
70-341	6-40	77-323	6-40
70-395	11-6	77-382	15-13
70-413	7-11	78-39	7-10, 11-4
70-474	7-15	78-80	6-40
71-41	15-23	78-111	7-34
71-149	18-16	78-112	7-34
71-411	6-26	78-180	6-40
71-416	6-37	78-340	11-7
71-425	6-40	78-377	15-21
71-468	4-5	78-408	14-15
72-255	14-20	79-143	15-31
72-340	6-40	79-229	7-11
72-341	6-46	79-292	14-22
72-381	14-15	80-55	7-35
72-545	7-27	80-300	18-33
72-592	10-9	80-335	7-10
73-99	7-10	81-163	14-19
73-476	15-39	81-169	14-15
73-529	8-27	81-180	15-22
74-74	6-40	81-181	15-22
74-77	5-11, 6-47	82-166	15-31
74-153	6-40	85-143	6-47
74-206	14-12	87-22	7-12
74-250	15-12	87-41	7-22
74-291	8-26	87-56	13-27
74-407	7-34	88-6	13-43
74-413	6-40	90-23	8-21
75-14	7-24	93-82	13-43
75-120	7-31		
75-230	6-47		
75-238	15-12		
75-291	15-39		
75-303	11-4		
75-317	11-8		
75-380	8-19		
76-71	6-39		
76-111	14-16		
76-144	6-40		
76-214	15-31		

Private Letter Rulings

Private Letter Ruling	Page
2-23-45	14-15
8122017	6-27
8133097	10-14
8527082	7-42
8615024	9-29
8634040	6-33
8841023	18-28

Appendix H

GLOSSARY OF
TAX TERMS

—A—

A. (*see* Acquiescence).

Accelerated Cost Recovery System (ACRS).   An alternate form of depreciation enacted by the Economic Recovery Tax Act of 1981 and significantly modified by the Tax Reform Act of 1986. The modified cost recovery system applies to assets placed into service after 1986 and is referred to as MACRS. Under both systems, the cost of a qualifying asset is recovered over a set period of time. Salvage value is ignored. § 168.

Accelerated Depreciation.   Various depreciation methods that produce larger depreciation deductions in the earlier years of an asset's life than straight-line depreciation. Examples: double-declining balance method (200% declining balance) and sum-of-the-years'-digits method. § 167 (*see* Depreciation).

Accounting Method.   A method by which an entity's income and expenses are determined. The primary accounting methods used are the accrual method and the cash method. Other accounting methods include the installment method; the percentage-of-completion method (for construction); and various methods for valuing inventories, such as FIFO and LIFO. §§ 446 and 447 (*see also specific accounting methods*).

Accounting Period.   A period of time used by a taxpayer in determining his or her income, expenses, and tax liability. An accounting period is generally a year for tax purposes, either a calendar year, a fiscal year, or a 52–53 week year. §§ 441 and 443.

Accrual Method of Accounting.   The method of accounting that reflects the income earned and the expenses incurred during a given tax period. However, unearned income of an accrual basis taxpayer must generally be included in an entity's income in the year in which it is received, even if it is not actually earned by the entity until a later tax period. § 446.

Acquiescence.   The public endorsement of a regular Tax Court decision by the Commissioner of the Internal Revenue Service. When the Commissioner acquiesces to a regular Tax Court decision, the IRS generally will not dispute the result in cases involving substantially similar facts (*see* Nonacquiescence).

Ad Valorem Tax. A tax based on the value of property.

Adjusted Basis. The basis (i.e., cost or other basis) of property plus capital improvements minus depreciation allowed or allowable. See § 1016 for other adjustments to basis. § 1016 (*see* Basis).

Adjusted Gross Income. A term used with reference to individual taxpayers. Adjusted gross income consists of an individual's gross income less certain deductions and business expenses. § 62.

AFTR (American Federal Tax Reports). These volumes contain the Federal tax decisions issued by the U.S. District Courts, U.S. Claims Court, U.S. Circuit Courts of Appeal, and the U.S. Supreme Court (*see* AFTR2d).

AFTR2d (American Federal Tax Reports, Second Series). The second series of the American Federal Tax Reports. These volumes contain the Federal tax decisions issued by the U.S. District Courts, U.S. Claims Court, U.S. Circuit Courts of Appeal, and the U.S. Supreme Court (*see* AFTR).

Alternate Valuation Date. The property contained in a decedent's gross estate must be valued at either the decedent's date of death or the alternate valuation date. The alternate valuation date is six months after the decedent's date of death, or, if the property is disposed of prior to that date, the particular property disposed of is valued as of the date of its disposition. § 2032.

Alternative Minimum Tax. A tax imposed on taxpayers only if it exceeds the "regular" tax of the taxpayer. Regular taxable income is adjusted by certain timing differences, then increased by tax preferences to arrive at alternative minimum taxable income.

Amortization. The systematic write-off (deduction) of the cost or other basis of an intangible asset over its estimated useful life. The concept is similar to depreciation (used for tangible assets) and depletion (used for natural resources) (*see* Goodwill; Intangible Asset).

Amount Realized. Any money received, plus the fair market value of any other property or services received, plus any liabilities discharged on the sale or other disposition of property. The determination of the amount realized is the first step in determining realized gain or loss. § 1001(b).

Annual Exclusion. The amount each year that a donor may exclude from Federal gift tax for each donee. Currently, the annual exclusion is $10,000 per donee per year. The annual exclusion does not generally apply to gifts of future interests. § 2503(b).

Annuity. A fixed amount of money payable to a person at specific intervals for either a specific period of time or for life.

Appellate Court. A court to which other court decisions are appealed. The appellate courts for Federal tax purposes include the Courts of Appeals and the Supreme Court.

Arm's-Length Transaction.   A transaction entered into by unrelated parties, all acting in their own best interests. It is presumed that in an arm's length transaction the prices used are the fair market values of the properties or services being transferred in the transaction.

Assessment of Tax.   The imposition of an additional tax liability by the Internal Revenue Service (i.e., as the result of an audit).

Assignment of Income.   A situation in which a taxpayer assigns income or income-producing property to another person or entity in an attempt to avoid paying taxes on that income. An assignment of income or income-producing property is generally not recognized for tax purposes, and the income is taxable to the assignor.

Attribution.   (*see* Constructive Ownership).

Audit.   The examination of a taxpayer's return or other taxable transactions by the Internal Revenue Service in order to determine the correct tax liability. Types of audits include correspondence audits, office audits, and field audits (*see also* Correspondence Audit; Field Audit; Office Audit).

—B—

Bad Debt.   An uncollectible debt. A bad debt may be classified either as a business bad debt or a nonbusiness bad debt. A business bad debt is one that has arisen in the course of the taxpayer's business (with a business purpose). Nonbusiness bad debts are treated as short-term capital losses rather than as ordinary losses. § 166.

Bargain Sale, Rental, or Purchase.   A sale, rental, or purchase of property for less than its fair market value. The difference between the sale, rental, or purchase price and the property's fair market value may have its own tax consequences, such as consideration as a constructive dividend or a gift.

Bartering.   The exchange of goods and services without using money.

Basis.   The starting point in determining the gain or loss from the sale or other disposition of an asset, or the depreciation (or depletion or amortization) on an asset. For example, if an asset is purchased for cash, the basis of that asset is the cash paid. §§ 1012, 1014, 1015, 334, 358, 362.

Beneficiary.   Someone who will benefit from an act of another, such as the beneficiary of a life insurance contract, the beneficiary of a trust (i.e., income beneficiary), or the beneficiary of an estate.

Bequest.   A testamentary transfer (by will) of personal property (personalty).

Board of Tax Appeals (B.T.A.).   The predecessor of the United States Tax Court, in existence from 1924 to 1942.

Bona Fide.   Real; in good faith.

Boot.   Cash or property that is not included in the definition of a particular type of non-taxable exchange [see §§ 351(b) and 1031(b)]. In these nontaxable exchanges, a taxpayer who receives boot must recognize gain to the extent of the boot received or the realized gain, whichever is less.

Burden of Proof.   The weight of evidence in a legal case or in a tax proceeding. Generally, the burden of proof is on the taxpayer in a tax case. However, the burden of proof is on the government in fraud cases. § 7454.

Business Purpose.   An actual business reason for following a course of action. Tax avoidance alone is not considered to be a business purpose. In areas such as corporate formation and corporate reorganizations, business purpose is especially important.

—C—

Capital Asset.   All property held by a taxpayer (e.g., house, car, clothing) except for certain assets that are specifically excluded from the definition of a capital asset, such as inventory and depreciable and real property used in a trade or business.

Capital Contribution.   Cash, services, or property contributed by a partner to a partnership or by a shareholder to a corporation. Capital contributions are not income to the recipient partnership or corporation. §§ 721 and 118.

Capital Expenditure.   Any amount paid for new buildings or for permanent improvements; any expenditures that add to the value or prolong the life of property or adapt the property to a new or different use. Capital expenditures should be added to the basis of the property improved. § 263.

Capital Gain.   A gain from the sale or other disposition of a capital asset. § 1222.

Capital Loss.   A loss from the sale or other disposition of a capital asset. § 1222.

Cash Method of Accounting.   The method of accounting that reflects the income received (or constructively received) and the expenses paid during a given period. However, prepaid expenses of a cash basis taxpayer that benefit more than one year may be required to be deducted only in the periods benefited (e.g., a premium for a three-year insurance policy may have to be spread over three years).

CCH.   (*see* Commerce Clearing House).

C Corporation.   A so-called regular corporation that is a separate tax-paying entity and is subject to the tax rules contained in Subchapter C of the Internal Revenue Code (as opposed to an S corporation, which is subject to the tax rules of Subchapter S of the Code).

Certiorari. A Writ of Certiorari is the form used to appeal a lower court (U.S. Court of Appeals) decision to the Supreme Court. The Supreme Court then decides, by reviewing the Writ of Certiorari, whether it will accept the appeal or not. The Supreme Court generally does not accept the appeal unless a constitutional issue is involved or the lower courts are in conflict. If the Supreme Court refuses to accept the appeal, then the certiorari is denied (cert. den.).

Claim of Right Doctrine. If a taxpayer has an unrestricted claim to income, the income is included in that taxpayer's income when it is received or constructively received, even if there is a possibility that all or part of the income may have to be returned to another party.

Closely Held Corporation. A corporation whose voting stock is owned by one or a few shareholders and is operated by this person or closely knit group.

Commerce Clearing House. A publisher of tax materials, including a multivolume tax service, volumes that contain the Federal courts' decisions on tax matters (USTC) and the Tax Court regular (T.C.) and memorandum (TCM) decisions.

Community Property. Property that is owned together by husband and wife, where each has an undivided one-half interest in the property due to their marital status. The nine community property states are Arizona, California, Idaho, Louisiana, Nevada, New Mexico, Texas, Washington, and Wisconsin.

Condemnation. The taking of private property for a public use by a public authority, an exercise of the power of eminent domain. The public authority compensates the owner of the property taken in a condemnation (*see also* Involuntary Conversion).

Conduit Principle. The provisions in the tax law that allow specific tax characteristics to be passed through certain entities to the owners of the entity without losing their identity. For example, the short-term capital gains of a partnership would be passed through to the partners and retain their character as short-term capital gains on the tax returns of the partners. This principle applies in varying degrees to partnerships, S corporations, estates, and trusts.

Constructive Dividends. The constructive receipt of a dividend. Even though a taxable benefit was not designated as a dividend by the distributing corporation, a shareholder may be designated by the IRS as having received a dividend if the benefit has the appearance of a dividend. For example, if a shareholder uses corporate property for personal purposes rent-free, he or she will have a constructive dividend equal to the fair rental value of the corporate property.

Constructive Ownership. In certain situations the tax law attributes the ownership of stock to persons "related" to the person or entity that actually owns the stock. The related party is said to constructively own the stock of that person. For example, under § 267(c) a father is considered to constructively own all stock actually owned by his son. §§ 267, 318, and 544(a).

Constructive Receipt.   When income is available to a taxpayer, even though it is not actually received by the taxpayer, the amount is considered to be constructively received by the taxpayer and should be included in income (e.g., accrued interest on a savings account). However, if there are restrictions on the availability of the income, it is generally not considered to be constructively received until the restrictions are removed (e.g., interest on a 6-month certificate of deposit is not constructively received until the end of the 6-month period if early withdrawal would result in loss of interest or principal).

Contributions to the Capital of a Corporation.   (*see* Capital Contributions).

Corpus.   The principal of a trust, as opposed to the income of the trust. Also called the *res* of the trust.

Correspondence Audit.   An IRS audit conducted through the mail. Generally, verification or substantiation for specified items is requested by the IRS, and the taxpayer mails the requested information to the IRS (*see* Field Audit; Office Audit).

Cost Depletion.   (*see* Depletion).

Court of Appeals.   The U.S. Federal court system has 13 circuit Courts of Appeals, which consider cases appealed from the U.S. Claims Court, the U.S. Tax Court, and the U.S. District Courts. A writ of certiorari is used to appeal a case from a Court of Appeals to the U.S. Supreme Court (*see* Appellate Court).

Creditor.   A person or entity to whom money is owed. The person or entity who owes the money is called the debtor.

---D---

Death Tax.   A tax imposed on property upon the death of the owner, such as an estate tax or inheritance tax.

Debtor.   A person or entity who owes money to another. The person or entity to whom the money is owed is called the creditor.

Decedent.   A deceased person.

Deficiency.   An additional tax liability owed to the IRS by a taxpayer. A deficiency is generally proposed by the IRS through the use of a Revenue Agent's Report.

Deficit.   A negative balance in retained earnings or in earnings and profits.

Dependent.   A person who derives his or her primary support from another. In order for a taxpayer to claim a dependency exemption for a person, there are five tests that must be met: support test, gross income test, citizenship or residency test, relationship or member of household test, and joint return test. § 152.

Depletion. As natural resources are extracted and sold, the cost or other basis of the resource is recovered by the use of depletion. Depletion may be either cost or percentage (statutory) depletion. Cost depletion has to do with the recovery of the cost of natural resources based on the units of the resource sold. Percentage depletion uses percentages given in the Internal Revenue Code multiplied by the gross income from the interest, subject to limitations. §§ 613 and 613A.

Depreciation. The systematic write-off of the basis of a tangible asset over the asset's estimated useful life. Depreciation is intended to reflect the wear, tear, and obsolescence of the asset (*see* Amortization; Depletion).

Depreciation Recapture. The situation in which all or part of the realized gain from the sale or other disposition of depreciable business property could be treated as ordinary income. See text for discussion of §§ 291, 1245, and 1250.

Determination Letter. A written statement regarding the tax consequences of a transaction issued by an IRS District Director in response to a written inquiry by a taxpayer that applies to a particular set of facts. Determination letters are frequently used to state whether a pension or profit-sharing plan is qualified or not, to determine the tax-exempt status of nonprofit organizations, and to clarify employee status.

Discriminant Function System (DIF). The computerized system used by the Internal Revenue Service in identifying and selecting returns for examination. This system uses secret mathematical formulae to select those returns that have a probability of tax errors.

Dissent. A disagreement with the majority opinion. The term is generally used to mean the explicit disagreement of one or more judges in a court with the majority decision on a particular case.

District Court. A trial court in which Federal tax matters can be litigated; the only trial court in which a jury trial can be obtained.

Dividend. A payment by a corporation to its shareholders authorized by the corporation's board of directors to be distributed pro rata among the outstanding shares. However, a constructive dividend does not need to be authorized by the shareholders (*see also* Constructive Dividend).

Donee. The person or entity to whom a gift is made.

Donor. The person or entity who makes a gift.

Double Taxation. A situation in which income is taxed twice. For example, a regular corporation pays tax on its taxable income, and when this income is distributed to the corporation's shareholders, the shareholders are taxed on the dividend income.

—E—

Earned Income.   Income from personal services. § 911(d)(2).

Earnings and Profits (E&P).   The measure of a corporation's ability to pay dividends to its shareholders. Distributions made by a corporation to its shareholders are dividends to the extent of the corporation's earnings and profits. §§ 312 and 316.

Eminent Domain.   (*see* Condemnation).

Employee.   A person in the service of another, where the employer has the power to specify how the work is to be performed (*see* Independent Contractor).

Employee Achievement Award.   An award of tangible personalty that is made for length of service achievement or safety achievement. § 274(j).

Encumbrance.   A liability.

Entity.   For tax purposes, an organization that is considered to have a separate existence, such as a partnership, corporation, estate, or trust.

Escrow.   Cash or other property that is held by a third party as security for an obligation.

Estate.   All of the property owned by a decedent at the time of his or her death.

Estate Tax.   A tax imposed on the transfer of a decedent's taxable estate. The estate, not the heirs, is liable for the estate tax. §§ 2001–2209 (*see* Inheritance Tax).

Estoppel.   A bar or impediment preventing a party from asserting a fact or a claim in court that is inconsistent with a position he or she had previously taken.

Excise Tax.   A tax imposed on the sale, manufacture, or use of a commodity or on the conduct of an occupation or activity; considered to include every Internal Revenue Tax except the income tax.

Executor.   A person appointed in a will to carry out the provisions in the will and to administer the estate of the decedent. (Feminine of *executor* is *executrix.*)

Exempt Organization.   An organization (such as a charitable organization) that is exempt from Federal income taxes. §§ 501–528.

Exemption.   A deduction allowed in computing taxable income. Personal exemptions are available for the taxpayer and his or her spouse. Dependency exemptions are available for the taxpayer's dependents. §§ 151–154 (*see* Dependent).

—F—

F.2d (Federal Reporter, Second Series).   Volumes in which the decisions of the U.S. Claims Court and the U.S. Courts of Appeals are published.

F. Supp. (Federal Supplement).   Volumes in which the decisions of the U.S. District Courts are published.

Fair Market Value.   The amount that a willing buyer would pay a willing seller in an arm's-length transaction.

Fed. (Federal Reporter).   Volumes in which the decisions of the U.S. Claims Court and the U.S. Courts of Appeals are published.

FICA (Federal Insurance Contributions Act).   The law dealing with social security taxes and benefits. §§ 3101–3126.

Fiduciary.   A person or institution who holds and manages property for another, such as a guardian, trustee, executor, or administrator. § 7701(a)(6).

Field Audit.   An audit conducted by the IRS at the taxpayer's place of business or at the place of business of the taxpayer's representative. Field audits are generally conducted by Revenue Agents (*see* Correspondence Audit; Office Audit).

FIFO (First-in, First-out).   A method of determining the cost of an inventory. The first inventory units acquired are considered to be the first sold. Therefore, the cost of the inventory would consist of the most recently acquired inventory.

Filing Status.   The filing status of an individual taxpayer determines the tax rates that are applicable to that taxpayer. The filing statuses include Single, Head of Household, Married Filing Jointly, Married Filing Separately, and Surviving Spouse (Qualifying Widow or Widower).

Fiscal Year.   A period of 12 consecutive months, other than a calendar year, used as the accounting period of a business. § 7701(a)(24).

Foreign Corporation.   A corporation that is not organized under U.S. laws, other than a domestic corporation. § 7701(a)(5).

Fraud.   A willful intent to evade tax. For tax purposes, fraud is divided into civil fraud and criminal fraud. The IRS has the burden of proof of proving fraud. Civil fraud has a penalty of 75 percent of the underpayment [§ 6653(b)]. Criminal fraud requires a greater degree of willful intent to evade tax (§§ 7201–7207).

Freedom of Information Act.   The means by which the public may obtain information held by Federal agencies.

Fringe Benefits.   Benefits received by an employee in addition to his or her salary or wages, such as insurance and recreational facilities.

FUTA (Federal Unemployment Tax Act).   A tax imposed on the employer on the wages of the employees. A credit is generally given for amounts contributed to state unemployment tax funds. §§ 3301–3311.

Future Interest.   An interest, the possession or enjoyment of which will come into being at some point in the future. The annual exclusion for gifts applies only to gifts of present interests, as opposed to future interests.

—G—

General Partner.   A partner who is jointly and severally liable for the debts of the partnership. A general partner has no limited liability (see Limited Partner).

Gift.   A transfer of property or money given for less than adequate consideration in money or money's worth.

Gift-Splitting.   A tax provision that allows a married person who makes a gift of his or her property to elect, with the consent of his or her spouse, to treat the gift as being made one-half by each the taxpayer and his or her spouse. The effect of gift-splitting is to take advantage of the annual gift tax exclusions for both the taxpayer and his or her spouse. § 2513.

Goodwill.   An intangible that has an indefinite useful life, arising from the difference between the purchase price and the value of the assets of an acquired business. Goodwill is amortizable over a 15-year period. § 197.

Grantor.   The person who creates a trust.

Gross Estate.   The value of all property, real or personal, tangible or intangible, owned by a decedent at the time of his or her death. §§ 2031–2046.

Gross Income.   Income that is subject to Federal income tax. All income from whatever source derived, unless it is specifically excluded from income (e.g., interest on state and local bonds). § 61.

Guaranteed Payment.   A payment made by a partnership to a partner for services or the use of capital, without regard to the income of the partnership. The payment generally is deductible by the partnership and taxable to the partner. § 707(c).

—H—

Half-Year Convention.   When a taxpayer is using MACRS, personalty placed in service at any time during the year is treated as placed in service in the middle of the year, and personalty disposed of or retired at any time during the year is treated as disposed of in the middle of the year. However, if more than 40 percent of all personalty placed in service during the year is placed in service during the last three months of the year, the mid-quarter convention applies. § 168(d)(4)(A).

Heir.   One who inherits property from a decedent.

Hobby.   An activity not engaged in for profit. § 183.

Holding Period.   The period of time that property is held. Holding period is used to determine whether a gain or loss is short-term or long-term. §§ 1222 and 1223.

H.R. 10 Plans.   (*see* Keogh Plans).

—I—

Income Beneficiary.   The person or entity entitled to receive the income from property. Generally used in reference to trusts.

Income in Respect of a Decedent (IRD).   Income that had been earned by a decedent at the time of his or her death, but is not included on the final tax return because of the decedent's method of accounting. Income in respect of a decedent is included in the decedent's gross estate and also on the tax return of the person who receives the income. § 691.

Independent Contractor.   One who contracts to do a job according to his or her own methods and skills. The employer has control over the independent contractor only as to the final result of his or her work (*see* Employee).

Indirect Method.   A method used by the IRS in order to determine whether a taxpayer's income is correctly reported when adequate records do not exist. Indirect methods include the Source and Applications of Funds Method and the Net Worth Method.

Information Return.   A return that must be filed with the Internal Revenue Service even though no tax is imposed, such as a partnership return (Form 1065), Form W-2, and Form 1099.

Inheritance Tax.   A tax imposed on the privilege of receiving property of a decedent. The tax is imposed on the heir.

Installment Method.   A method of accounting under which a taxpayer spreads the recognition of his or her gain ratably over time as the payments are received. §§ 453, 453A, and 453B.

Intangible Asset.   A nonphysical asset, such as goodwill, copyrights, franchises, or trademarks.

Inter Vivos Transfer.   A property transfer during the life of the owner.

Internal Revenue Service.   Part of the Treasury Department, it is responsible for administering and enforcing the Federal tax laws.

Intestate.   No will existing at the time of death.

Investment Tax Credit.   A credit against tax that was allowed for investing in depreciable tangible personalty before 1986. The credit was equal to 10 percent of the qualified investment. §§ 38 and 46–48.

Investment Credit Recapture.   When property on which an investment credit has been taken is disposed of prior to the full time period required under the law to earn the credit, then the amount of unearned credit must be added back to the taxpayer's tax liability—this is called recapture of the investment credit. § 47.

Involuntary Conversion.   The complete or partial destruction, theft, seizure, requisition, or condemnation of property. § 1033.

Itemized Deductions.   Certain expenditures of a personal nature that are specifically allowed to be deductible from an individual taxpayer's adjusted gross income. Itemized deductions (e.g., medical expenses, charitable contributions, interest, taxes, and miscellaneous itemized deductions) are deductible if they exceed the taxpayer's standard deduction.

—J—

Jeopardy Assessment.   If the IRS has reason to believe that the collection or assessment of a tax would be jeopardized by delay, the IRS may assess and collect the tax immediately. §§ 6861–6864.

Joint and Several Liability.   The creditor has the ability to sue one or more of the parties who have a liability, or all of the liable persons together. General partners are jointly and severally liable for the debts of the partnership. Also, if a husband and wife file a joint return, they are jointly and severally liable to the IRS for the taxes due.

Joint Tenancy.   Property held by two or more owners, where each has an undivided interest in the property. Joint tenancy includes the right of survivorship, which means that upon the death of an owner, his or her share passes to the surviving owner(s).

Joint Venture.   A joining together of two or more persons in order to undertake a specific business project. A joint venture is not a continuing relationship like a partnership, but may be treated as a partnership for Federal income tax purposes. § 761(a).

—K—

Keogh Plans.   A retirement plan available for self-employed taxpayers. § 401.

Kiddie Tax.   Unearned income of a child under age 14 is taxed at the child's parents' marginal tax rate. § 1(i).

—L—

Leaseback. A transaction in which a taxpayer sells property and then leases back the property.

Lessee. A person or entity who rents or leases property from another.

Lessor. A person or entity who rents or leases property to another.

Life Insurance. A form of insurance that will pay the beneficiary of the policy a fixed amount upon the death of the insured person.

LIFO (Last-in, First-out). A method of determining the cost of an inventory. The last inventory units acquired are considered to be the first sold. Therefore, the cost of the inventory would consist of the earliest acquired inventory.

Like-Kind Exchange. The exchange of property held for productive use in a trade or business or for investment (but not inventory, stock, bonds, or notes) for property that is also held for productive use or for investment (i.e., realty for realty; personalty for personalty). No gain or loss is generally recognized by either party unless boot (other than qualifying property) is involved in the transaction. § 1031.

Limited Liability. The situation in which the liability of an owner of an organization for the organization's debts is limited to the owner's investment in the organization. Examples of taxpayers with limited liability are corporate shareholders and the limited partners in a limited partnership.

Limited Partner. A partner whose liability for partnership debts is limited to his or her investment in the partnership. A limited partner may take no active part in the management of the partnership according to the Uniform Limited Partnership Act (*see* General Partner).

Lump Sum Distribution. Payment at one time of an entire amount due, or the entire proceeds of a pension or profit-sharing plan, rather than installment payments.

—M—

Majority. Of legal age (*see* Minor).

Marital Deduction. Upon the transfer of property from one spouse to another, either by gift or at death, the Internal Revenue Code allows a transfer tax deduction for the amount transferred.

Market Value. (*see* Fair Market Value).

Material Participation. Occurs when a taxpayer is involved in the operations of an activity on a regular, continuous, and substantial basis. § 469(h).

Mid-Month Convention.   When a taxpayer is using ACRS or MACRS, realty placed in service at any time during a month is treated as placed in service in the middle of the month, and realty disposed of or retired at any time during a month is treated as disposed of in the middle of the month. § 168(d)(4)(B).

Mid-Quarter Convention.   Used for all personalty placed in service during the year if more than 40 percent of all personalty placed in service during the year is placed in service during the last three months of the year. § 168(d)(4)(C).

Minimum Tax.   (*see* Alternative Minimum Tax).

Minor.   A person who has not yet reached the age of legal majority. In most states, a minor is a person under 18 years of age.

Mortgagee.   The person or entity that holds the mortgage; the lender; the creditor.

Mortgagor.   The person or entity that is mortgaging the property; the debtor.

—N—

NA.   (*see* Nonacquiescence).

Negligence Penalty.   A penalty imposed by the IRS on taxpayers who are negligent or intentionally disregard the rules or regulations (but are not fraudulent), in the determination of their tax liability. § 6662.

Net Operating Loss (NOL).   The amount by which deductions exceed a taxpayer's gross income. § 172.

Net Worth Method.   An indirect method of determining a taxpayer's income used by the IRS when adequate records do not exist. The net worth of the taxpayer is determined for the end of each year in question, and adjustments are made to the increase in net worth from year to year for nontaxable sources of income and nondeductible expenditures. This method is often used when a possibility of fraud exists.

Ninety-day Letter.   (*see* Statutory Notice of Deficiency).

Nonacquiescence.   The public announcement that the Commissioner of the Internal Revenue Service disagrees with a regular Tax Court decision. When the Commissioner nonacquiesces to a regular Tax Court decision, the IRS generally will litigate cases involving similar facts (*see* Acquiescence).

Nonresident Alien.   A person who is not a resident or citizen of the United States.

—O—

Office Audit. An audit conducted by the Internal Revenue Service on IRS premises. The person conducting the audit is generally referred to as an Office Auditor (*see* Correspondence Audit; Field Audit).

Office Auditor. An IRS employee who conducts primarily office audits, as opposed to a Revenue Agent, who conducts primarily field audits (*see also* Revenue Agent).

—P—

Partner. (*see* General Partner; Limited Partner).

Partnership. A syndicate, group, pool, joint venture, or other unincorporated organization, through or by means of which any business, financial operation, or venture is carried on, and which is not a trust, estate, or corporation. §§ 761(a) and 7701(a)(2).

Passive Activity. Any activity that involves the conduct of any trade or business in which the taxpayer does not materially participate. Losses from passive activities generally are deductible only to the extent of passive activity income. § 469.

Pecuniary Bequest. Monetary bequest (*see* Bequest).

Percentage Depletion. (*see* Depletion).

Percentage of Completion Method of Accounting. A method of accounting that may be used on certain long-term contracts in which the income is reported as the contract reaches various stages of completion.

Personal Property. All property that is not realty; personalty. This term is also often used to mean personal use property (*see* Personal Use Property; Personalty).

Personal Use Property. Any property used for personal, rather than business, purposes. Distinguished from "personal property."

Personalty. All property that is not realty (e.g., automobiles, trucks, machinery, and equipment).

Portfolio Income. Interest and dividends. Portfolio income, annuities, and royalties are not considered to be income from a passive activity for purposes of the passive activity loss limitations. § 469(e).

Present Interest.   An interest in which the donee has the present right to use, possess, or enjoy the donated property. The annual exclusion is available for gifts of present interests, but not for gifts of future interests (*see* Future Interest).

Private Letter Ruling.   A written statement from the IRS to a taxpayer in response to a request by the taxpayer for the tax consequences of a specific set of facts. The taxpayer who receives the Private Letter Ruling is the only taxpayer that may rely on that specific ruling in case of litigation.

Probate.   The court-directed administration of a decedent's estate.

Prop. Reg. (Proposed Regulation).   Treasury (IRS) Regulations are generally issued first in a proposed form in order to obtain input from various sources before the regulations are changed (if necessary) and issued in final form.

Pro Rata.   Proportionately.

—Q—

Qualified Pension or Profit-Sharing Plan.   A pension or profit-sharing plan sponsored by an employer that meets the requirements set forth by Congress in § 401. §§ 401–404.

Qualified Residence Interest.   Interest on indebtedness that is secured by the principal residence or one other residence of a taxpayer. §§ 162(h)(3) and (5)(A).

—R—

RAR.   (*see* Revenue Agent's Report).

Real Property.   (*see* Realty).

Realized Gain or Loss.   The difference between the amount realized from the sale or other disposition of an asset and the adjusted basis of the asset. § 1001.

Realty.   Real estate; land, including any objects attached thereto that are not readily movable (e.g., buildings, sidewalks, trees, and fences).

Recapture.   The recovery of the tax benefit from a previously taken deduction or credit. The recapture of a deduction results in its inclusion in income, and the recapture of a credit results in its inclusion in tax (*see* Depreciation Recapture; Investment Credit Recapture).

Recognized Gain or Loss.   The amount of the realized gain or loss that is subject to income tax. § 1001.

Reg.   (*see* Regulations).

Regulations (Treasury Department Regulations). Interpretations of the Internal Revenue Code by the Internal Revenue Service.

Related Party. A person or entity that is related to another under the various code provisions for constructive ownership. §§ 267, 318, and 544(a).

Remand. The sending back of a case by an appellate court to a lower court for further action by the lower court. The abbreviation for "remanding" is "rem'g."

Research Institute of America (RIA). A publisher of tax materials, including a multi-volume tax service and volumes that contain the Federal courts' decisions on tax matters (AFTR, AFTR2d).

Resident Alien. A person who is not a citizen of the United States, and who is a resident of the United States or meets the substantial presence test. § 7701(b).

Revenue Agent. An employee of the Internal Revenue Service who performs primarily field audits.

Revenue Agent's Report (RAR). The report issued by a Revenue Agent in which adjustments to a taxpayer's tax liability are proposed. (IRS Form 4549; Form 1902 is used for office audits.)

Revenue Officer. An employee of the Internal Revenue Service whose primary duty is the collection of Tax. (As opposed to a Revenue Agent, who audits returns.)

Revenue Procedure. A procedure published by the Internal Revenue Service outlining various processes and methods of handling various matters of tax practice and administration. Revenue Procedures are published first in the Internal Revenue Bulletin and then compiled annually in the Cumulative Bulletin.

Revenue Ruling. A published interpretation by the Internal Revenue Service of the tax law as applied to specific situations. Revenue Rulings are published first in the Internal Revenue Bulletin and then compiled annually in the Cumulative Bulletin.

Reversed (Rev'd). The reverse of a lower court's decision by a higher court.

Reversing (Rev'g). The reversing of a lower court's decision by a higher court.

Rev. Proc. (*see* Revenue Procedure).

Rev. Rul. (*see* Revenue Ruling).

Right of Survivorship. (*see* Joint Tenancy).

Royalty. Compensation for the use of property, such as natural resources or copyrighted material.

—S—

S Corporation. A corporation that qualifies as a small business corporation and elects to have §§ 1361–1379 apply. Once a Subchapter S election is made, the corporation is treated similarly to a partnership for tax purposes. An S corporation uses Form 1120S to report its income and expenses. (*see* C Corporation).

Section 38 Property. Property subject to the investment tax credit (*see* Investment Tax Credit).

Section 1231 Property. Depreciable property and real estate used in a trade or business held for more than one year. Section 1231 property may also include timber, coal, domestic iron ore, livestock, and unharvested crops.

Section 1244 Stock. Stock of a small business corporation issued pursuant to § 1244. A loss on § 1244 stock is treated as an ordinary loss (rather than a capital loss) within limitations. § 1244.

Section 1245 Property. Property that is subject to depreciation recapture under § 1245.

Section 1250 Property. Property that is subject to depreciation recapture under § 1250.

Securities. Evidences of debt or of property, such as stock, bonds, and notes.

Separate Property. Property that belongs separately to only one spouse (as contrasted with community property in a community property state). In a community property state, a spouse's separate property generally includes property acquired by the spouse prior to marriage, or property acquired after marriage by gift or inheritance.

Severance Tax. At the time they are severed or removed from the earth, a tax on minerals or timber.

Sham Transaction. A transaction with no substance or bona fide business purpose that may be ignored for tax purposes.

Simple Trust. A trust that is required to distribute all of its income currently and does not pay, set aside, or use any funds for charitable purposes. § 651(a).

Small Business Corporation. There are two separate definitions of a small business corporation, one relating to S corporations and one relating to § 1244. If small business corporation status is met under § 1361(b), a corporation may elect Subchapter S. If small business corporation status is met under § 1244(c)(3), losses on § 1244 stock may be deducted as ordinary (rather than capital) losses, within limitations.

Specific Bequest. A bequest made by a testator in his or her will giving an heir a particular piece of property or money.

Standard Deduction. A deduction that is available to most individual taxpayers. The standard deduction or total itemized deductions, whichever is larger, is subtracted in computing taxable income. §§ 63(c) and (f).

Statute of Limitations. Law provisions that limit the period of time in which action may be taken after an event occurs. The limitations on the IRS for assessments and collections are included in §§ 6501–6504, and the limitations on taxpayers for credits or refunds are included in §§ 6511–6515.

Statutory Depletion. (*see* Depletion).

Stock Option. A right to purchase a specified amount of stock for a specified price at a given time or times.

Subchapter S. Sections 1361–1379 of the Internal Revenue Code (*see also* S Corporation).

Substance vs. Form. The essence of a transaction as opposed to the structure or form that the transaction takes. For example, a transaction may formally meet the requirements for a specific type of tax treatment, but if what the transaction is actually accomplishing is different from the form of the transaction, the form may be ignored.

—T—

Tangible Property. Property that may be touched (e.g., machinery, automobile, desk) as opposed to intangibles, that may not be touched (e.g., goodwill, copyrights, patents).

Tax Avoidance. Using the tax laws to avoid paying taxes or to reduce one's tax liability (*see* Tax Evasion).

Tax Benefit Rule. The doctrine by which the amount of income that a taxpayer must include in income when the taxpayer has recovered an amount previously deducted is limited to the amount of the previous deduction that produced a tax benefit.

Tax Court (United States Tax Court). One of the three trial courts that hears cases dealing with Federal tax matters. A taxpayer need not pay his or her tax deficiency in advance if he or she decides to litigate the case in Tax Court (as opposed to the District Court or Claims Court).

Tax Credits. An amount that is deducted directly from a taxpayer's tax liability, as opposed to a deduction, which reduces taxable income.

Tax Evasion. The illegal evasion of the tax laws. § 7201 (*see* Tax Avoidance).

Tax Preference Items. Those items specifically designated in § 57 that may be subject to a special tax (*see also* Alternative Minimum Tax).

Tax Shelter. A device or scheme used by taxpayers either to reduce taxes, or defer the payment of taxes.

T.C. (Tax Court: United States Tax Court). This abbreviation is also used to cite the Tax Court's Regular Decisions (*see* Tax Court; T.C. Memo).

T.C. Memo.   The term used to cite the Tax Court's Memorandum Decisions (*see* Tax Court; T.C.).

Tenancy by the Entirety.   A form of ownership between a husband and wife wherein each has an undivided interest in the property, with the right of survivorship.

Tenancy in Common.   A form of joint ownership wherein each owner has an undivided interest in the property, with no right of survivorship.

Testator.   A person who makes or has made a will; one who dies and has left a will.

Treasury Regulations.   (*see* Regulations).

Trial Court.   The first court to consider a case, as opposed to an appellate court.

Trust.   A right in property that is held by one person or entity for the benefit of another. §§ 641–683.

—U—

Unearned Income.   Income that is not earned or is not yet earned. The term is used to refer to both prepaid (not yet earned) income and to passive (not earned) income.

Unearned Income of a Minor Child.   (*see* Kiddie tax).

Unified Transfer Tax.   The Federal tax that applies to both estates and gifts after 1976.

Unified Transfer Tax Credit.   A credit against the unified transfer tax that allows a taxpayer to make a certain amount of gifts and/or have a certain size estate without incurring any Federal estate or gift tax.

Uniform Gift to Minors Act.   An Act that provides a way to transfer property to minors. A custodian manages the property on behalf of the minor, and the custodianship terminates when the minor achieves majority.

USSC (U.S. Supreme Court).   This abbreviation is used to cite U.S. Supreme Court cases.

U.S. Tax Court.   (*see* Tax Court).

USTC (U.S. Tax Cases).   Published by Commerce Clearing House. These volumes contain all the Federal tax-related decisions of the U.S. District Courts, the U.S. Claims Court, the U.S. Courts of Appeals, and the U.S. Supreme Court.

—V—

Valuation.   (*see* Fair Market Value).

Vested.   Fixed or settled; having the right to absolute ownership, even if ownership will not come into being until some time in the future.

Appendix I

TWO INDIVIDUAL COMPREHENSIVE TAX RETURN PROBLEMS FOR 1993

1. David R. and Susan L. Holman

   a. David and Susan Holman are married and file a joint return. David is 38 years of age and Susan is 36. David is a self-employed certified real estate appraiser (C.R.E.), and Susan is employed by Wells Fargo Bank as a trust officer. They have two children: Richard Lawrence, age 7, and Karen Ann, age 4. The Holmans currently live at 5901 W. 75th Street, Los Angeles, California 90034, in a home they purchased and occupied on September 6, 1993.

   Until August 12, 1993 the Holman family lived at 3085 Windmill Lane in Dallas, Texas, where David was employed by Vestpar Company, a real estate appraisal company and Susan was a bank officer for First National Bank. They sold their home in Dallas and moved to Los Angeles so that Susan could assume her new job as a trust officer and David could become self-employed.

   b. David and Susan sold their home in Dallas for $95,000 and incurred the following expenses:

Sales commission	$5,700
Attorney's fee	300
Title insurance	450
Document preparation fee	60
Recording fee	10
Pest inspection fee	80
Prepayment penalty for early retirement of home mortgage (3 points)	1,500

The Holmans had purchased the Dallas home on March 4, 1984 and never held it for rent or used it for business purposes. The home originally cost $62,500, and they had paid $1,200 for a cedar fence and $300 for landscaping. Within seven weeks of receiving a contract of sale on their house, the Holmans paid $800 for interior and exterior painting and $200 for steam-cleaning of the carpets. The sale was closed on August 1, 1993 and the Holmans were required to move out of the home by August 15, 1993.

c.   In moving from Dallas to Los Angeles, the Holmans incurred the following expenses, none of which were reimbursed:

Cost of moving household goods.......................	$6,250
Meals...	100
Lodging...	250
House-hunting expenses (including	
$150 for meals).....................................	1,000
Temporary living expenses (20 days;	
including meals costing $400)........................	1,700

Not included in any of the above expenses are the costs for driving two automobiles from Dallas to Los Angeles. David and Susan each drove a car, taking turns driving with the children. Although neither one of them kept receipts, Susan noted that her auto mileage was 1,500 miles. In addition, David noted that the number of miles from their old home to their old workplace was 24 miles, and the number of miles from their old home to their new workplace is 1,514 miles.

d.   The Holmans purchased their new home for $230,000 by making a $30,000 down payment and financing the remaining balance with a 30-year, 7% conventional mortgage loan from California Federal Savings and Loan. They were required to prepay 2 points ($4,000) in return for the favorable mortgage terms. New furniture and drapes cost an additional $7,500.

e.   The Holmans received the following Forms W-2, reporting their salaries for 1993:

1) David R. Holman, Social Security No. 452-64-5837:

Gross salary..	$45,000
Federal income taxes withheld.........................	6,750
F.I.C.A. taxes withheld:	
Social security......................................	2,790
Medicare..	653

2) Susan L. Holman, Social Security No. 467-32-5452:

	First Nat'l Bank	Wells Fargo Bank	Total
Gross salary............................	$17,500	$24,000	$41,500
Federal income taxes withheld........................	1,100	3,150	4,250
F.I.C.A. taxes withheld:			
Social security........................	1,085	1,488	2,573
Medicare............................	254	348	602
California income taxes withheld........................	—	700	700

f. On October 1, 1993 David rented office space at 5510 Wacker Drive, Los Angeles, California 90025. The terms of the one-year lease agreement called for a monthly rent of $800, with the first and last month's rent paid in advance.

David decided to operate his business in the name of "David R. Holman, Certified Real Estate Appraiser," and he elected to use the cash method of accounting for his revenues and expenses. The following items relate to his business for 1993:

Gross receipts...	$35,000
Expenses:	
Advertising..	250
Bank service charges................................	50
Dues and publications................................	450
Insurance..	600*
Interest..	275
Professional services................................	525
Office rent..	3,200**
Office supplies..	700
Meals and entertainment.............................	500
Miscellaneous expenses..............................	75

*Three months of coverage
**Includes prepayment of rent for September, 1994

David drove his personal automobile, a 1992 Buick LeSabre, 5,000 miles for business purposes from October 1 through December 31. Rather than keeping receipts, he elected to use the automatic mileage method (29 cents per mile) for determining his auto expenses. David's total auto mileage for the year was 20,000 miles.

On October 3, 1993 David purchased the following furniture and equipment for use in his business:

Office furniture..	$11,000
Copying machine......................................	3,800
Computers..	6,500
Laser printers..	2,500
Phone answering machine.............................	200

David elects to expense the maximum amount allowed under the optional expensing rules of § 179. He also elects to compute the maximum depreciation allowance using the appropriate MACRS percentages.

g. The Holmans received interest income during 1993 from the following:

U.S. Treasury bills......................................	$1,475
First National Bank, Dallas.............................	625
Wells Fargo Bank.......................................	400
Tarrant County municipal bonds........................	800

h. David and Susan received the following dividends during 1993:

Ford Motor Company....................................	$ 300
Eastman Kodak Company...............................	575
IBM Corporation..	125
General Motors stock dividend (20 new shares of stock valued at $60 per share, received March 9, 1993).......................................	1,200

i. The Holmans have never maintained foreign bank accounts or created foreign trusts.

j. The Holmans report the following stock transactions for 1993:

1) Sold 100 shares of IBM stock for $120 per share on August 1, 1993. David had inherited 500 shares of IBM stock from his uncle on July 18, 1990, and the stock was valued at $170 per share on the date of his uncle's death (the value used for estate tax purposes).

2) Sold 400 shares of General Motors stock for $78 per share on September 20, 1993. Susan had received 1,000 shares of General Motors stock as a wedding present from her grandfather on June 3, 1985. Her grandfather had purchased the stock for $35 per share on May 7, 1970, and the stock was valued at $50 per share on the date of the gift. Susan's grandfather paid gift taxes of $10,000 as a result of the gift.

3) Sold 300 shares of Eastman Kodak stock for $40 per share on December 28, 1993, but did not receive the sales proceeds until January 3, 1994. The Holmans had paid $25 per share for the stock on October 21, 1991.

k. Susan has summarized the following cash expenditures for 1993 from canceled checks, mortgage company statements, and other documents:

Prescription medicines and drugs......................	$ 982
Medical insurance premiums...........................	2,830
Doctors' and hospital bills (net of reimbursements)......	1,535
Contact lenses for David..............................	218
Real estate taxes paid on	
Dallas residence.....................................	1,400
Los Angeles residence...............................	2,600
Sales taxes paid on new auto..........................	1,485
Ad valorem taxes paid on both autos...................	350
Interest paid for	
Dallas home mortgage...............................	3,250*
Los Angeles home mortgage.........................	7,200**
Credit card interest..................................	480
Personal car loan....................................	620
Cash contributions to	
United Methodist Church.............................	3,000
American Heart Fund................................	200
United Way Campaign...............................	300
George Bush Campaign Fund.........................	250
Susan's unreimbursed employee expenses..............	470***
David's unreimbursed employee expenses..............	360***
Tax return preparation fee.............................	375

*Does not include the mortgage prepayment penalty identified in item (b) above.

**Does not include the interest points charged for the new mortgage identified in item (d) above.

***Does not include any costs for meals or entertainment.

Susan also noted that she and David had driven their personal automobiles 500 miles to receive medical treatment for themselves and their children. She also has a receipt for 100 shares of General Motors stock that she gave to her alma mater, Southern Methodist University, on November 12, 1993. The stock was valued at $70 per share on the date of the gift and was from the block of General Motors stock Susan had received as a wedding present from her grandfather [see item (j)(2) above for details].

l. The Holmans paid the following child care expenses during 1993:

1) Kindergarten Day Care School......................... $2,800
    1177 Valley View
    Dallas, Texas 75210
    EIN: 74-0186254

2) Happy Trails Day Center............................... 2,200
    3692 Airport Blvd.
    Los Angeles, California 90034
    EIN: 78-0593676

m.   Social security numbers for the Holman children are provided below:

Richard L. Holman, Social Security No. 582-60-4732
Karen A. Holman, Social Security No. 582-60-5840

n.   David and Susan made estimated Federal income tax payments of $1,250 each quarter, on 4/15/93, 6/15/93, 9/15/93, and 1/15/94.

o.   The Holmans have always directed that $6 go to the Presidential Election Campaign by checking the "yes" boxes on their Form 1040.

Required:

Complete the Holmans' Federal income tax return for 1993. If they have a refund due, they would prefer having it credited against their 1994 taxes.

2. Richard M. and Anna K. Wilson

   a. Richard and Anna Wilson are married and file a joint return. Richard is 47 years of age and Anna is 46. Richard is employed by Telstar Corporation as its controller and Anna is self-employed as a travel agent. They have three children: Michael, age 20; Lisa, age 17; and Laura, age 14. Michael is a full-time student at Rutgers University. Lisa and Laura both live at home and attend school full-time. The Wilsons currently live at 3721 Chestnut Ridge Road, Montvale, New Jersey 07645, in a home they have owned since July 1979.

   Richard and Anna provided over half of the support of Anna's mother, who currently lives in a nursing home in Mahwah, New Jersey. They also provided over half of the support of their son, Michael, who earned $2,750 during the summer as an accounting student intern for a national accounting firm.

   b. Richard received a Form W-2 from his employer reporting the following information for 1993:

   Richard M. Wilson, Social Security No. 294-38-6249:

Gross wages and taxable benefits..................	$63,000
Federal income taxes withheld...................	12,400
F.I.C.A. taxes withheld:	
Social security...................................	3,571
Medicare.......................................	914
State income taxes withheld....................	1,850

   The taxable benefits reported on his W-2 Form include $2,700 ($0.29 per mile) for Richard's personal use of the company car provided by his employer.

   c. Anna operates her business under the name "Wilson's Travel Agency," located at 7200 Treeline Drive, Montvale, NJ 07645. Anna has one full-time employee, and her Federal employer identification number is 74-2638596.

Anna uses the cash method of accounting for her business, and her records for 1993 show the following:

Fees and commissions....................................	$114,000
Expenses:	
Advertising..	1,425
Bank service charges....................................	75
Dues and subscriptions.................................	560
Insurance...	1,100
Interest on furniture loan...............................	960
Professional services....................................	700
Office rent..	6,000
Office supplies..	470
Meals and entertainment................................	1,000
Payroll taxes..	2,170
Utilities and telephone...................................	3,480
Wages paid to full-time employee.......................	22,800
Miscellaneous expenses.................................	20

Automobile expenses and amounts paid to her children are not included in the above expenses. Anna paid her daughters Lisa and Laura $750 and $450, respectively, for working part-time during the summer. Since she did not withhold or pay any Federal income or employment taxes on these amounts, Anna is not certain that she is allowed a deduction. She does feel that the amounts paid to her children were reasonable, however.

Anna purchased a new 1992 Oldsmobile on November 20 of last year, and her tax accountant used the actual cost method in determining the deductible business expenses for her 1992 Federal tax return. Because the deductible amount seemed so small, she is not certain whether she should claim actual expenses (including depreciation), or simply use the automatic mileage method. She has the following records relating to the business auto:

Original cost (including sales tax	
and auto title)..	$18,000
Depreciation claimed in 1992.............................	900
Gas, oil, and repairs in 1993.............................	1,790
Parking and tolls paid in 1993............................	410
Insurance for 1993.......................................	650
Interest on car loan for 1993.............................	750

Anna drove the auto 20,000 miles for business purposes and 5,000 miles for personal purposes during the year. The above expenses for 1993 have not been reduced to reflect her personal use of the vehicle.

On January 7, 1993 Anna purchased the following items for use in her business:

Office furniture..	$2,900
Copying machine..	1,700
Zenith portable computer...............................	1,500
Printer..	600
Fax machine..	1,300

Anna wishes to claim the maximum amount of depreciation deductions or other cost recovery allowed on the office furniture and equipment.

d. Richard attended an accounting convention in Washington, D.C. for three days in October. He incurred the following unreimbursed expenses related to the trip:

Air fare (round-trip).....................................	$270
Registration fee for meeting.............................	425
Hotel cost..	375
Meals..	130
Taxis...	20
Airport parking...	18
Road tolls..	2

e. Richard and Anna received Forms 1099-INT reporting interest income earned during 1993 from the following:

Citibank of Mahwah.....................................	$845
Montvale National Bank.................................	900
Telstar Employees' Credit Union........................	755

f. The Wilsons received the following dividends during 1993:

Telstar Corporation.....................................	$300
Exxon Corporation.....................................	200

g. The Wilsons have never had a foreign bank account or created a foreign trust.

h. The Wilsons had the following property transactions for 1993:

1) Anna sold 300 shares of Exxon Corporation stock on September 9, 1993 in order to pay for Michael's fall semester of college. She received a check in the amount of $14,950 from Shearson Lehman on September 16, 1993. The stock was from a block of 1,000 shares that Richard and Anna had purchased for $35 per share on February 1, 1970.

2) They gave each of the children 100 shares of Exxon stock on December 30, 1993, when the stock was valued at $62.50 per share. The stock was from the same block of stock purchased for $35 per share in February, 1970. No gift taxes were paid on these gifts.

3) They gave 100 shares of Exxon stock to Richard's alma mater, Rider College, on December 29, 1993. The average trading price of Exxon stock on that day was $61.25. This stock was also from the original block of 1,000 shares the Wilsons had purchased for $35 per share in 1970. Rider College is located in Lawrenceville, New Jersey.

4) On May 17, 1993, Richard and Anna were notified by the bankruptcy judge handling the affairs of Bubbling Crude Oil Company in Houston, Texas that the company's shareholders would not receive anything for their stock ownership because all of the assets were used to satisfy claims of creditors. Richard had purchased 2,000 shares of the stock for $6 per share on April 1, 1984. Unfortunately, the stock did not meet the requirements of § 1244.

i. Richard and Anna own a rental condominium located at 7777 Boardwalk in Atlantic City, New Jersey. The unit was purchased on July 29, 1992 for $25,000 cash and a $125,000 mortgage. The following items relate to the rental unit for 1993:

Gross rents	$15,400
Expenses:	
Management fee	2,310
Cleaning and maintenance	1,200
Insurance	840
Property taxes	2,750
Interest paid on mortgage	13,675
Utilities	150

Although the unfurnished unit was vacant for 11 weeks during the year, the Wilsons never used the property for personal purposes. When the property is rented, the tenant is required to pay for all utilities, and the Wilsons are charged a management fee equal to 15 percent of the rents collected.

j. The Wilsons have prepared the following summary of their other expenditures for 1993:

Prescription medicines and drugs......................	$ 425
Medical insurance premiums...........................	1,595
Doctors' and hospital bills (net of reimbursements)	805*
Dentist...	2,750**
Real estate taxes paid on home.......................	1,625
State income taxes paid during 1993...................	2,100***
Interest paid for	
Original home mortgage.............................	2,690
Home equity loan...................................	6,410****
Credit card interest................................	275
Personal car loan..................................	725
Cash contributions to First Presbyterian Church.........	1,200
Fee for preparation of 1992 tax return..................	450

   *Does not include $1,485 of doctor bills paid by Richard and Anna for medical treatment provided to Anna's mother at the nursing home. Also not included is $115 that Anna paid for a new pair of eyeglasses for her mother.

   **$2,350 of this amount represents a prepayment for Laura's braces. The dentist required the prepayment before he would begin the two-year dental program involved.

   ***Does not include amounts withheld from Richard's wages.

   ****Represents interest paid on a $75,000 home equity loan made by the Wilsons in 1992.

k. Anna made an $11,500 deductible contribution to her Keogh plan on December 15, 1993.

l. Richard paid the following unreimbursed employee business expenses:

Professional dues...	$450
Professional journals......................................	385
Office gifts to subordinates (none over $25)................	115

m. The Wilsons received a state income tax refund of $130 in 1993. They had $18,750 of itemized deductions for 1992, and their 1992 taxable income was $52,825.

n. Richard and Anna made timely estimated Federal income tax payments of $2,250 each quarter on 4/15/93, 6/15/93, 9/15/93, and 1/15/94.

o. Social security numbers for Anna, the children, and Anna's mother are pro-
    vided below:

	Number
Anna K. Wilson	296-48-2385
Michael D. Wilson	256-83-4421
Lisa M. Wilson	257-64-7573
Laura D. Wilson	258-34-2894
Ruth Knapp	451-38-3790

p. The Wilsons have always checked the "no" boxes on their Form 1040 re-
    garding the Presidential Election Campaign fund contribution.

Required:

Complete the Wilsons' Federal income tax return for 1993. If they have a refund due,
they would prefer having it credited against their 1994 taxes.

INDEX

— A —

Abandoned spouse, 4-18 to 4-20, 5-46
Abandonment losses, 14-16
Accelerated Cost Recovery System (ACRS) (*see also* Modified Accelerated Cost Recovery System), 1-28
Accelerated depreciation (*see* Depreciation and amortization)
Accident and health benefits (*see also* Employee fringe benefits), 6-22 to 6-23, 6-23 to 6-24, 6-40, 6-51 to 6-52, 18-2
Accounting methods, 5-7, 5-16 to 5-28
  accrual basis (*see* Accrual method of accounting)
  bad debts (*see* Bad debts)
  cash basis (*see* Cash method of accounting)
  cash receipts and disbursements method (*see* Cash method of accounting)
  changes in method, 5-19, 5-26 to 5-28
  choice of method, 5-19
  claim of right doctrine, 5-29 to 5-31
  completed contract method, 5-19, 5-33 to 5-34
  constructive receipt, 5-21 to 5-23, 5-41
  deferral of advance payments (*see* Advance payments)
  installment method (*see* Installment method of accounting)
  inventories (*see* Inventories)
  long-term contracts, 5-19, 5-33 to 5-35
  percentage of completion method, 5-33 to 5-34
  permissible methods, 5-19
  personal service corporations, 19-19
  prepaid expenses, 7-9 to 7-12
  prepaid income, 5-31 to 5-35
  prepaid insurance, 7-11
  prepaid interest, 5-32, 7-12, 11-31 to 11-32
  prepaid rent, 7-11
Accounting periods, 5-16 to 5-18
  annual accounting period, 5-17 to 5-18
  calendar year, 5-16, 5-17, 19-19
  choice of accounting period, 5-16, 19-19
  corporations, 19-19
  fiscal year, 5-16 to 5-17, 19-19
  partnerships, 19-19
  S corporation, 19-19
  taxable year, 5-16 to 5-18

Accrual method of accounting, 5-19, 5-25 to 5-26, 5-31 to 5-35, 7-12 to 7-15, 10-5, 10-6, 11-14, 19-19
  advance payments (*see* Advance payments)
  all events test (*see* All events test)
  claim of right doctrine, 5-29 to 5-31
  inventoriable goods, 10-24
  prepaid income, 5-31 to 5-35
Accumulated adjustments account (AAA) (*see* S corporations)
Accumulated earnings and profits (*see* Earnings and profits)
Accumulated taxable income (*see* Accumulated earnings tax)
Accumulation of earnings (*see* Accumulated earnings tax)
Accuracy-related penalties, 2-6 to 2-10
Acquiescence, 2-37
Acquisition costs, 7-28
Acquisition indebtedness, 11-20
ACRS (*see* Accelerated Cost Recovery System)
Activity, definition of, 12-9 to 12-10
  activities conducted through conduit entities, 12-11
  appropriate economic unit, 12-10
  consistency requirement, 12-11
  grouping of rental and nonrental activities, 12-11 to 12-12
Activity not engaged in for profit (*see* Hobby losses)
Additions to tax (*see* Interest assessments; Penalties)
Adjusted basis (*see also* Basis), 3-28 to 3-29, 5-10, 14-2, 14-6 to 14-13
Adjusted gross income, 3-15, 3-16 to 3-17, 18-7
  defined, 3-15
Adjusted ordinary gross income (AOGI) (*see* Personal holding company)
Adjusted sale price (*see* Sale of principal residence)
Adjustments, 3-24
ADR (Asset depreciation range) (*see* Depreciation and amortization)
ADS (Alternative Depreciation System) (*see* Depreciation and amortization)
Ad valorem tax, 11-15
Advance payments, 5-33
  deferral, 5-32 to 5-34
  prepaid income, 5-31 to 5-35

Advertising, 7-28

AFTR (American Federal Tax Reports), 2-38

Alcohol fuel credit, 13-30, 13-38

Aliens (*see also* Nonresident aliens; Resident aliens), 3-2, 3-21

Alimony, 6-32 to 6-38, 6-53, 7-18

All events test, 5-25, 7-12 to 7-15, 11-14

All-inclusive concept, 7-1

Allocation of partnership income (*see* Partnerships)

Allowance for bad debts (*see* Bad debts)

Alternate valuation (*see* Estate tax)

Alternative Depreciation System (ADS), 9-5, 9-6, 9-19 to 9-21, 13-7

Alternative minimum tax, 3-23, 13-1 to 13-26

American Federal Tax Reports (AFTR), 2-38

Americans with Disabilities Act, 9-24

Amortization (*see also* Depreciation and amortization), 7-30 to 7-31

Amount realized, 3-28 to 3-30, 5-10, 14-1, 14-3 to 14-5, 14-14, 15-34, 15-35

Annual exclusion (*see* Gift tax)

Annuities, 5-12, 6-9 to 6-14, 6-49, 7-18, 13-53, 18-7

Anti-churning rules, 9-33 to 9-34

Anti-discrimination rules, 18-13 to 18-14

Appellate Courts (*see also* Court of Appeals), 2-32 to 2-35

Appreciated inventory (*see* Appreciated property)

Appreciated property, 14-10
  charitable contributions, 11-36, 11-41

Artists, expenses of, 7-21

Assessments for local benefits, 11-17

Assessments of tax
  deficiency assessment, 4-41
  statute of limitations (*see* Statute of limitations)

Asset depreciation range (ADR) (*see* Depreciation and amortization)

Assets (*see* Property)

Assignment of income, 5-40, 6-31
  compensation, 5-40
  income-producing property, 5-41

Assumption of liabilities—(§ 357) (*see* Liabilities assumed)

Attribution of stock ownership (*see* Constructive ownership)

Audit of returns assessments (*see* Assessments of tax)

Automobile expenses (*see* Transportation expenses)

Avoidance (*see* Tax avoidance)

Awards (*see* Prizes and awards)

— B —

Backup withholding, 13-55

Bad debts, 10-1 to 10-6, 16-28
  allowable methods, 10-5 to 10-6
  bona-fide debt, 10-4
  business vs. nonbusiness, 10-2 to 10-4, 16-28
  charge-off method, 10-5
  loans between related parties (*see* Related party transactions)
  reserve method, 10-5, 10-6 to 10-7
  specific charge-off method, 10-5
  tax benefit rule, 6-42
  tax planning, 10-36
  worthlessness, 10-5

Bankruptcy, 6-43 to 6-44

Bankruptcy Court, 2-31

Bargain sale, rental, or purchase, 14-19
  bargain sale to charity, 14-19

Base period research expense (*see* Research and experimental expenditures)

Basis, 9-3, 14-6 to 14-13, 19-8, 19-33
  adjusted basis defined, 3-28 to 3-29, 9-3, 14-6 to 14-13
  adjustments to basis, 3-28 to 3-30, 14-12
  allocation of basis, 14-19 to 14-21
  bad debt, 10-4 to 10-5
  capital additions, 3-28 to 3-29, 14-12
  capital recoveries, 14-12
  conversion to business or income-producing use, 14-12
  corporation's basis in contributed property, 19-34
  cost basis, 3-28 to 3-30, 14-6
  decedent, property acquired from a, 14-9 to 14-11
  depreciation, 9-3, 9-13, 14-12
  determination of (chart), 14-13
  gift, property acquired by, 14-7 to 14-9
  gift tax, effect on basis, 14-7 to 14-9
  identification problems, 14-7
  income in respect of a decedent, 14-9 to 14-11
  installment obligations (*see* Installment obligations)
  inventories (*see* Inventories)
  involuntary conversion (*see* Involuntary conversion)
  liabilities in excess of, 14-14
  like-kind exchanges, 15-34 to 15-38
  nontaxable transactions (*see also specific items*), 15-1 to 15-47

Basis (*cont.*)
options (*see* Options)
    partnership changes in liabilities (*see*
        Partnerships)
    partnership interest (*see* Partnerships)
    personal residence (*see* Sale of principal
        residence)
    stock dividends, 6-3 to 6-4
    wash sales (*see* Wash sales)
Below-market loans, 5-42 to 5-45
Beneficiaries
    death benefits, 6-24
    insurance, 6-21
Benefits (*see* Accident and health benefits;
        Employee fringe benefits; Qualified
        pension and profit sharing plans)
    death benefits (*see* Death benefits)
Bequests of property, 6-32, 14-17 to 14-18
    tax planning, 14-33 to 14-35
Blindness, additional standard deduction, 1-29,
        3-20, 4-31
Board of Tax Appeals (BTA), 2-35
Bonds
    government bonds issued at a discount (*see*
        Series E and EE savings bonds)
    government obligations, state and local, 6-5
        to 6-7, 6-50, 14-15
    interest (*see* Interest income)
Books and records (*see* Accounting methods)
Boot
    corporate formation, 19-33
    like-kind exchanges, 15-32 to 15-34
Bracket creep, 4-41 to 4-42
Bribes and illegal payments, 7-32 to 7-33
Burden of proof, 7-24
Business, defined, 7-6
Business assets (*see* Section 1231 property)
Business bad debts (*see* Bad debts)
Business energy tax credit, 13-29, 13-34
Business expenses and losses, 3-14, 7-2
        to 7-15
    bad debts (*see* Bad debts)
    educational expenses (*see* Educational
        expenses)
    employee (*see* Employee)
    health insurance, 11-10 to 11-11
    losses, 7-16
    ordinary and necessary, 7-3, 7-7 to 7-8
    reasonable, 7-3, 7-8 to 7-9
    rules for deductibility, 7-2 to 7-16
    violation of public policy (*see* Public policy
        restriction)
Business form, change in, 3-38, 15-44
Business gifts, 6-15 to 6-16, 6-24, 8-34, 8-41
        to 8-42

Business interest, 11-23
Business interruption insurance proceeds,
        6-41 to 6-42
Business meals (*see* Entertainment expenses;
        Meals and lodging)
Business, sale of a, 14-20 to 14-21

— C —

Calculation of tax liability, 4-1, 4-21 to 4-30
Calendar year (*see* Accounting periods)
Cancellation of debt (*see* Discharge of
        indebtedness)
Capital additions (*see* Basis)
Capital assets (*see also* Capital gains and
        losses), 3-31, 19-26 to 19-27
    business assets (*see* Section 1231 property)
    capital gains and losses (*see* Capital gains
        and losses)
    defined, 3-31
    franchises, 16-28 to 16-29
    holding period (*see* Holding period)
    inventories, 16-4 to 16-5
    lease cancellation payments, 6-41, 6-42
    options, 16-30 to 16-32
    partnership, sale of interest in, 14-21
    patents, 16-21 to 16-22
    personal use property, 3-31
    property excluded, 3-31
    residence (*see* Sale of principal residence)
    sale or exchange (*see* Capital gains and
        losses)
worthless securities (*see* Worthless securities)
Capital budgeting, 15-47
Capital contributions (*see* Corporations;
        Partnerships)
Capital expenditures, 7-28, 18-5
    acquisition costs, 7-28
    advertising, 7-28
    basis adjustments (*see* Basis)
    defined, 7-27
    election to capitalize or deduct, 7-29
    improvements (*see* Capital additions)
    medical care purposes (*see* Medical and
        dental expenses)
    repairs and maintenance vs., 7-28
    research and experimental expenses (*see*
        Research and experimental expenses)
Capital gain deduction, 3-31 to 3-34, 16-13
        to 16-20
Capital gain or loss holding period (*see*
        Holding period)
Capital gain property (*see* Capital assets;
        Capital gains and losses; Charitable
        contributions)

Capital gains and losses, 3-31 to 3-34, 16-1
        to 16-40, 18-30, 19-5
    basis (*see* Basis)
    beneficiaries (*see* Beneficiaries)
    bonds, corporate, 16-32 to 16-38
    capital assets (*see* Capital assets)
    capital gain deduction (*see* Capital gain
        deduction)
    capital loss carryover, 3-34, 16-19 to 16-20,
        19-25
    capital loss deduction, 3-31 to 3-34, 16-18
        to 16-20, 19-26 to 19-27
    computation of, 3-31 to 3-34, 16-10, 16-13
        to 16-16
    corporate bonds, 16-32 to 16-38
    corporations, 3-34, 19-5
    dealers in securities, 16-26
    franchises, 16-28 to 16-29
    holding period, 3-31, 16-10 to 16-13
    installment sales (*see* Installment method of
        accounting)
    involuntary conversions (*see* Involuntary
        conversions)
    lease cancellation payments (*see* Leases,
        cancellation payments)
    long- or short-term, 3-31 to 3-33, 16-10
        to 16-13
    long-term capital gains, 3-31 to 3-33, 6-2,
        6-3, 16-13 to 16-20, 18-9, 18-30
      capital gain deduction, 16-13 to 16-20
    long-term capital losses, 3-31 to 3-33, 16-13
        to 16-20
    lump-sum distributions from qualified plans,
        18-7 to 18-8
    net capital gains and losses, 3-31 to 3-33,
        16-13 to 16-20
    netting process, 3-31 to 3-32, 16-13 to
        16-20
    nonbusiness bad debts (*see also* Bad
        debts), 10-2 to 10-4
    nontaxable transactions, 15-1 to 15-47
    options, 16-30 to 16-32
    patents, 16-21 to 16-22
    related party transactions (*see* Related party
        transactions)
    reporting procedures, 16-20
    sale or exchange, 16-7 to 16-10
    Section 1231 (*see* Section 1231 property)
    short-term capital gain or loss, 3-31 to 3-33,
        10-2, 16-13 to 16-20
    tax planning, 15-46 to 15-47, 16-39 to 16-40
    worthless securities, 10-2, 16-7 to 16-8,
        16-22
Capital losses (*see* Capital gains and losses)
Capital recoveries (*see also* Return of capital),
        9-1 to 9-47, 14-12

Capital stock (*see* Securities)
Car pools, 6-45
Carryovers
    basis, 19-34
    capital losses, 3-34, 16-18 to 16-20
    charitable contributions, 11-41, 11-44, 11-45
        to 11-46
    net operating loss, 10-16 to 10-17, 19-25
Cash basis (*see* Cash method of accounting)
Cash dividends (*see* Dividend distributions)
Cash equivalent doctrine, 5-21
Cash method of accounting, 5-19, 5-21 to
        5-25, 5-35 to 5-36, 7-9 to 7-11,
        10-4, 11-14
    claim of right doctrine, 5-29 to 5-31
    constructive receipt, 5-21 to 5-23, 5-41
    income, when to report, 5-30 to 5-31
    inventoriable goods, 10-24
    prepaid expenses, 7-11 to 7-12
    prepaid income, 5-31 to 5-35
    restrictions on use of, 7-10 to 7-11
    savings bonds (*see* Savings bonds)
    time of payment, 7-10
Cash or deferred arrangements (CODAs),
        18-21 to 18-23
Casualty and theft gains, 16-8 to 16-9, 17-8
Casualty and theft losses, 3-30, 7-16, 7-18,
        10-7 to 10-13, 11-1, 11-11, 16-8 to 16-9
    amount of loss, 10-9 to 10-11
    appraisals, 10-9
    business property, 10-10
    defined, 10-8 to 10-9
    disaster area losses, 10-13
    limitations on deductibility, 10-9 to 10-11,
        11-11
    reimbursements, 10-9 to 10-11
    tax planning, 10-35
    theft losses, 10-9, 11-11
    when to deduct, 10-13, 11-11
Category A method, 5-27
Category B method, 5-27, 5-28
Change in accounting method (*see* Accounting
        methods)
Change in accounting period (*see* Accounting
        periods)
Change in form of doing business, 15-44
Charge cards (*see* Interest expense)
Charitable contributions, 1-28, 7-16, 11-1,
        11-33 to 11-46, 16-4, 19-5
    appraisal fees, 11-37, 11-47
    appreciated property, 11-35
    bargain sales, 14-19
    capital gain property, 11-39 to 11-45
    carryovers, 11-41, 11-44, 11-45 to 11-46
    ceiling limitations, 11-33, 11-35 to 11-45,
        19-28 to 19-29

Charitable contributions (*cont.*)
  corporations, 11-33, 11-38 to 11-39, 19-28 to 19-29
  deduction, 11-34 to 11-35, 19-5
  estates, 1-12 to 1-13
  excess contributions, 11-45
  fair market value, 11-37
  limitations, 11-33, 11-35 to 11-45, 19-5 to 19-6
  ordinary income property, 11-38 to 11-39
  partnerships, 11-33
  percentage limitations, 11-33, 11-35 to 11-45
    corporations, 11-33
    individuals, 11-35 to 11-45
  private foundations, 11-38, 11-44
  property contributions, 11-38 to 11-45
  public charities, 11-34 to 11-35, 11-39 to 11-41
    qualified organizations, 11-34
  S corporations, 11-33
  tax planning, 11-52 to 11-53
  unrelated use, 11-39
  valuation problems, 11-37
Child and dependent care credit, 4-30, 6-26, 11-4, 13-48 to 13-52, 18-2
  amount of credit, 13-48 to 13-52
  dependents qualifying, 13-48
  earned income limitation, 13-51 to 13-52
  employment related expenses, 13-49
Child support payments, 6-36 to 6-38
Children
  care (*see* Child and dependent care credit)
  exemption for, 3-21, 4-3 to 4-12
  medical expenses of, 7-39, 11-2 to 11-11
  unearned income of, 4-25 to 4-30, 5-41
Citations, 2-24, 2-26 to 2-27, 2-28, 2-29, 2-35 to 2-40
Citizenship or residency requirement (*see also* Dependency exemptions), 4-3, 4-11
CLADR (Class Life Asset Depreciation Range) (*see* Depreciation and amortization)
Claim of right doctrine, 5-29 to 5-31
Claims Court, 2-31, 2-37, 2-38
Cliff vesting, 18-15
Club dues, 8-38
Coal and iron ore, 17-5 to 17-6
Cohan Rule, 7-40, 8-42
Collection of tax, 4-40 to 4-41
  employee tax withholding (*see* Withholding tax)
  employment taxes (*see* Employment taxes)
  estimated tax payments (*see* Estimated tax)
  interest (*see* Interest assessments)
  penalties (*see* Penalties)
  statute of limitations (*see* Statute of limitations)

Commissioner of the Internal Revenue Service, 2-39
Commodity futures, 16-13
Community property, 4-14, 5-46 to 5-47
  community income, 4-14, 5-46 to 5-47
  community property states, 4-14, 5-46
  defined, 4-14, 5-46
  separate property, 5-46
  tax returns, 4-14
Commuting expense, 8-17 to 8-25
Comparison of business forms, 6-52 to 6-53
Compensation, 7-2, 7-3, 7-8
  deferred compensation, 5-23, 5-41, 18-2 to 18-3
  independent contractors, 7-19 to 7-22
  injury or sickness (*see* Employee fringe benefits)
Compensation for personal services
  assignment of income (*see* Assignment of income)
  educational expenses (*see* Educational expenses)
  fringe benefits (*see* Employee fringe benefits)
  receipt of property, 18-4 to 18-5
  shareholder-employees, 7-8
  when to report (*see* Accounting methods)
Compete, agreement not to, 6-41
Completed contract method of accounting, 5-19, 5-33 to 5-34
Comprehensive Energy Policy Act of 1992, 1-5
Computation of tax (*see* Tax computation)
Computers, 9-28, 9-29
Condemnation (*see* Involuntary conversions)
Conduit principle, 3-1, 3-6
  partnerships, 3-6
  S corporations, 19-35
Conservation programs, 6-40, 9-43
Construction contracts (*see* Long-term contracts)
Constructive ownership (*see* Related party transactions), 7-36 to 7-39
Constructive receipt, 5-21 to 5-23, 5-49, 18-26 to 18-27
Consumer Price Index, 1-27
Contributions, charitable (*see* Charitable contributions)
Contributions to the capital of a corporation (*see* Controlled corporations; Corporations)
Contributions to partnerships (*see* Partnerships)
Controlled corporations (*see also* Corporations), 19-18
  accounting periods and methods, 19-19
  analysis of, 19-40 to 19-46
  deductions, 19-20

Controlled corporations (*cont.*)
  reporting, 19-21 to 19-22
  sales of depreciable property and recapture, 19-27 to 19-28
Conventions and seminars (*see* Travel and entertainment)
Conversions (*see* Involuntary conversions)
Conversion transactions, 16-37 to 16-38
Corporations, 3-4 to 3-5, 6-41, 19-13 to 19-14, 19-40 to 19-46
  accounting periods and methods, 19-19
  alternative minimum tax (*see* Minimum tax)
  capital contributions, 6-41, 6-45, 19-20
  by shareholders, 6-45
  capital losses, limitation, 3-34, 16-20, 19-26 to 19-27
  charitable contributions (*see also* Charitable contributions), 11-33, 11-38 to 11-39, 19-28 to 19-29
  controlled (*see* Controlled corporations)
  credits, 19-21
  deductions, 19-20
  differences between corporate and individual taxation, 19-22 to 19-30
  dividend distributions (*see* Dividend distributions)
  dividend income, 19-23 to 19-26
  dividends received deduction, 19-25, 19-29
  double taxation, 19-22
  estimated tax payments (*see* Estimated tax)
  exclusions, 19-20
  filing requirements, 4-35
  formation of corporation, 19-33 to 19-35
  fringe benefits, 19-20
  income, 19-19
  net operating loss (NOL), 19-25, 19-29 to 19-30
  recapture, 17-28 to 17-30, 19-27 to 19-28
  reporting, 19-21 to 19-22
  sale of depreciable property, 19-27 to 19-28
  stock (*see* Securities)
  subchapter S corporations (*see* S corporations)
  tax-exempt, 3-4
  tax formula, 3-11 to 3-25, 19-19
  tax rates, 3-21 to 3-22, 19-21
  transfers to controlled corporations (*see* Controlled corporations)
Cosmetic surgery, 11-3
Cost depletion, 9-1, 9-37 to 9-39
Court of Appeals, 2-32 to 2-34, 2-37, 2-38
Court of Appeals for the Federal Circuit, 2-32 to 2-34
Court of Claims, 2-31, 2-32, 2-34, 2-37, 2-38
Court system, Federal, 2-29 to 2-40
Covenants not to compete, 6-41, 9-34 to 9-35, 9-46

Credit cards (*see also* Interest expense), 7-10
Credits (*see* Estate tax credits; Tax credits)
Crops, unharvested, 17-6
Cruise ships, 8-32
Cumulative bulletin (C.B.), 2-22, 2-27, 2-28, 2-37

— D —

Damages, 5-11 to 5-12, 6-42, 6-46 to 6-48
  breach of contract, 5-11, 6-46, 6-47
  compensatory, 5-11, 6-42
  libel or slander, 5-11, 6-46, 6-47
  loss of profits, 5-11, 6-42
  patent infringement, 5-12, 6-42
  personal injuries, 5-11, 6-46, 6-47
  punitive, 5-6, 5-11, 6-42
Daycare, home used for, 8-15
Dealers in securities, 16-26
Death benefits, 6-14, 6-24, 6-50
Death tax (Federal) (*see* Estate tax)
Debts (*see* Bad debts; Discharge of indebtedness)
Decedent (*see also* Estate tax)
  basis of property acquired from a, 14-9 to 14-11, 16-12
  income in respect of a, 14-9 to 14-11
Deductions and losses, 1-7, 3-11 to 3-16
  accounting methods (*see* Accounting methods)
  adjusted gross income for (*see also* Employee expenses), 3-15, 7-5, 7-16 to 7-18, 8-47, 11-12
  adjusted gross income from (*see also* Itemized deductions), 3-15 to 3-20, 7-5, 7-16 to 7-18, 11-1
  bad debts (*see* Bad debts)
  business expenses (*see* Business expenses and losses)
  capital losses (*see* Capital gains and losses)
  casualty and theft losses (*see* Casualty and theft losses)
  charitable contributions (*see* Charitable contributions)
  depreciation (*see* Depreciation and amortization)
  general rules for deductibility, 7-2 to 7-15
  illegal business, 7-32 to 7-33
  itemized (*see* Itemized deductions)
  net operating losses (*see* Net operating loss)
  office in the home (*see* Office in the home)
  ordinary and necessary expenses, 7-3, 7-7 to 7-8
  standard (*see* Itemized deductions)
  when to deduct (*see* Accounting methods)

Deferral of advance payments (*see* Advance payments)
Deferred compensation, 5-23, 5-49, 18-2 to 18-3, 18-27 to 18-28
Deficiency assessments, 4-41
Demolition, 14-17
Dental expenses (*see* Medical and dental expenses)
Dependency exemptions (*see also* Personal and dependency exemptions), 3-21, 4-3 to 4-12, 4-25 to 4-30, 6-2, 8-29
Dependent familial relative, 4-16
Depletion, 9-1, 9-37 to 9-39
Depreciation and amortization, 9-2 to 9-37
  accelerated methods, 8-25, 9-46
  ACRS (Accelerated Cost Recovery System) (*see* Accelerated Cost Recovery System)
  Alternative Depreciation System (ADS), 9-5, 9-6, 9-19 to 9-21
  Alternative minimum tax, 13-7 to 13-10
  amortization, 5-39, 9-1, 9-34 to 9-36
  automobiles, 9-24 to 9-34
  basis (*see* Basis)
  component depreciation, 9-36, 9-46
  computers, 9-27, 9-28, 9-29
  cost-segregation, 9-46
  declining-balance method, 17-14
  defined, 9-1 to 9-2
  historical perspective, 9-3 to 9-4
  qualifying property, 9-1, 9-2, 9-5 to 9-6
  real property, 9-1, 9-7, 9-8, 9-9, 9-15
  recapture (*see* Recapture, depreciation)
  recordkeeping requirements, 9-32 to 9-33
  salvage value, 9-19
  straight-line, 9-18 to 9-21, 9-28
  tax planning, 9-45 to 9-47
Devise, 6-32
Disability and sick pay, 6-19, 6-23 to 6-24
Disabled access credit, 13-30, 13-43 to 13-44
Disabled dependent care credit (*see* Child and dependent care credit)
Disallowance of expenses and losses, 14-30 to 14-32
  capital expenditures, 7-28
  hobby losses (*see* Hobby losses)
  personal expenditures, 3-14, 7-26 to 7-27
  public policy restriction, 7-31 to 7-33
  related party transactions (*see* Related party transactions)
  to produce tax-exempt income, 7-4, 7-35 to 7-36, 7-42
  unrealized losses, 7-16
  wash sales, 14-31
Discharge of indebtedness, 6-41, 6-43 to 6-44
Discovery of cash or other assets, 6-45

District Court, 2-31, 2-32, 2-34, 2-37, 2-38
Dividend distributions, 6-2 to 6-4
  cash dividends, 6-2
  property dividends, 6-2
  stock dividends, 6-2, 6-3 to 6-4
Dividend income, 6-2 to 6-4, 7-8, 19-5
Dividends-received deduction, 19-5, 19-25, 19-29
Divorce legal expenses, 7-27
Divorce settlements (*see also* Alimony; Child support payments), 4-6 to 4-7, 14-17, 15-12
Documentation requirements, 7-40, 8-43, 9-32 to 9-33
Dollar-value inventory method, 10-29 to 10-32
Donations (*see* Charitable contributions)
Double-extension method, 10-30
Double taxation, 3-3 to 3-5, 19-13, 19-22
Due dates for filing returns (*see* Filing requirements)
Dues, 7-15, 7-19

— E —

E and EE bonds (*see* Series E and EE savings bonds)
Earned income credit, 4-31, 13-29, 13-55 to 13-58
Earnings and profits, 6-2, 6-3, 6-50
  accumulated earnings and profits, 6-2, 6-3
  current earnings and profits, 6-2, 6-3
Economic performance, 7-12 to 7-15
Economic Recovery Tax Act of 1981 (ERTA), 1-28
Educational expenses, 6-14, 6-27, 6-31, 8-1 to 8-5
  educational savings bonds, 6-7 to 6-9
  requirements for deductibility, 8-2 to 8-3
  travel, 8-3, 8-4
  where to deduct, 8-4
Elderly tax credit, 3-20, 13-29, 13-53 to 13-54
Electric vehicles, 13-54
Electricity production credit, renewable, 13-45
Embezzlement proceeds, 5-1, 5-31
Employee, 7-15
  achievement awards, 6-16, 8-42
  annuities, 6-9 to 6-14, 18-7
  benefits (*see* Employee fringe benefits)
  compensation and retirement plans, 18-1 to 18-37
  death benefits, 6-14, 6-24, 6-50
  discounts, 6-14, 6-28, 6-29 to 6-30, 6-51
  expenses, 3-40, 7-15, 7-16 to 7-22
    dues, 7-15, 7-19
    educational expenses (*see* Educational expenses)

Employee expenses (cont.)
    employment-seeking expenses, 7-19, 7-31
  entertainment expenses, 7-19, 8-33 to 8-42
  moving expenses, 6-14, 8-5 to 8-10
  office in the home (*see* Office in the home)
  reimbursed expenses, 6-14 to 6-15, 7-17 to
    7-19, 7-20 to 7-21, 8-47
  residential phone service, 8-16
  transportation expenses, 6-14, 7-19, 8-17 to
    8-25, 9-30 to 9-33
    travel expenses, 6-14, 7-19, 8-26 to 8-32,
      8-42 to 8-43
    unreimbursed expenses, 8-25
    work clothes and uniforms, 7-15
  gifts to, 6-14, 6-15
  retirement plans, 18-1 to 18-37
Employee awards, 6-15 to 6-16, 8-42
Employee fringe benefits, 5-13 to 5-14, 6-26
    to 6-31, 18-2, 19-3, 19-11
  accident and health benefits, 6-22 to 6-23,
    6-40, 6-51, 18-2
  annuities, 6-9 to 6-14, 6-49, 18-7
  athletic facilities, 6-28, 6-30
  cafeteria plans, 18-2
  child care, 6-26, 18-2
  company automobile, 6-27, 6-28, 6-29, 9-30
    to 9-33
  corporation, 19-20
  de minimus, 6-14, 6-15 to 6-16, 6-28, 6-30
  death benefits (*see* Death benefits)
  disability payments, 6-19, 6-23 to 6-24, 6-52
  discounts, 6-14, 6-28, 6-29 to 6-30, 6-51
  educational assistance payments, 6-14,
    6-27, 6-31
  group-term life insurance, 6-14, 6-20 to
    6-22, 6-51, 18-2
  insurance, 6-20 to 6-22
  meals and lodging, 5-13, 6-14, 6-25 to 6-26,
    6-51, 18-2
  medical reimbursement plans, 6-22 to 6-23, 18-2
  no-additional-cost services, 6-28, 6-29, 18-2
  qualified pension and profit sharing plans
    (*see* Qualified pension and profit
    sharing plans)
  stock option plans (ESOPS), 18-12
  tax planning, 6-49 to 6-53, 18-34 to 18-37
  tuition reduction, 6-14, 6-27, 6-31
  working condition fringe, 6-28
Employees Retirement Income Security Act
    (ERISA), 18-12
Employer awards, 6-15 to 6-16, 8-42
Employer deductions, 18-29
Employer social security credit, 13-45
Employment related expenses (*see* Child
    and dependent care credit; Employee,
    expenses)

Employment taxes, 1-19 to 1-24, 11-13
  FICA, 1-19 to 1-23
  FUTA, 1-19, 1-23 to 1-24
  self-employment tax, 1-19 to 1-23, 7-18
  state unemployment taxes, 1-19, 6-19
Empowerment zone employment credit, 13-44
    to 13-45
Energy tax credits, 13-29, 13-34
  business, 13-29, 13-34
Entertainment expenses, 7-19, 8-33 to 8-42
  associated with, 8-36
  business gifts, 6-14, 6-15 to 6-16, 8-34,
    8-41 to 8-42
  business meals, 8-37
  country club, 8-34, 8-38
  directly related, 8-35 to 8-36
  documentation required, 7-40, 8-42 to 8-43
  eighty percent limitation, 8-39 to 8-44
  entertainment facilities, 8-38
  reimbursed, 6-14 to 6-15, 8-40
  tax planning, 8-55 to 8-56
Equity, 1-30 to 1-31
ERTA (Economic Recovery Tax Act of 1981),
    1-28
Estate tax, 1-2, 1-5, 1-12 to 1-13, 11-13,
    14-9 to 14-11
  alternate valuation date, 14-10
  computation, 1-12 to 1-13
  credits, 1-13
    charitable deduction, 1-13
    expenses indebtedness and taxes, 1-13
    gift taxes, 1-13
    marital deduction, 1-13
    state estate taxes, 1-16 to 1-17
  Federal, 1-12 to 1-13, 4-35
  filing requirements, 4-35
  formula, 1-12
  gross estate (*see* Gross estate)
  marital deduction, 1-13
  special use valuation, 14-11
  state, 1-16, 1-17
  taxable estate, 1-13
  unified transfer tax (rates), 1-12
  valuation of estate, 14-9 to 14-11
Estates—income taxation (*see also*
    Beneficiaries; Income in respect of a
    decedent; Trusts), 3-5 to 3-6
  basis of property, 14-9 to 14-11
  distributions, 3-6
  filing requirements, 4-35
  holding period, 16-12
  received from decedent, 14-9 to 14-11
Estimated tax, 3-22, 4-30, 4-37 to 4-40, 13-55
  corporations, 4-38
  failure to pay, 4-38, 4-39
  individuals, 4-37 to 4-40

Estimated tax (*cont.*)
  penalties for failure to pay, 4-38, 4-39
  underpayment penalty, 4-38 to 4-40
Ethics, 2-4 to 2-19
Evasion of tax, 1-32
Excess itemized deductions (*see* Itemized
    deductions)
Exchanges of property (*see also* Capital
    gains and losses; Like-kind exchanges;
    Property transactions; Recapture) stock
    in same corporation, 15-44, 17-22 to
    17-23
Excise taxes, 1-2, 1-24 to 1-25, 11-13
Exclusion, annual (Federal gift tax) (*see*
    Gift tax)
Exclusions from gross income, 1-7, 3-11, 3-11
    to 3-14
  accident and health benefits, 6-22 to 6-23,
    6-23 to 6-24, 6-40, 6-51 to 6-52, 18-2
  disability and sick pay, 6-19, 6-23 to 6-24
  discharge of indebtedness, 6-41, 6-43 to 6-44
  employee death benefits (*see* Death
    benefits)
  employee fringe benefits (*see* Employee
    fringe benefits)
  expenses related to, 7-4, 7-35 to 7-36, 7-42
  fellowships (*see* Scholarships and
    fellowships)
  gifts and bequests (*see* Bequests of
    property; Gifts)
  group-term life insurance, 6-14, 6-20 to 6-22,
    6-51, 18-2
  inheritances (*see* Inheritances)
  interest on state and local government
    obligations, 6-5 to 6-7, 6-50
  life insurance proceeds, 6-20 to 6-22
  meals and lodging (*see* Meals and lodging)
  medical reimbursements, 6-22 to 6-23, 18-2
  scholarships (*see* Scholarships and
    fellowships)
  social security benefits (*see* Social security)
  tax benefit rule (*see* Tax benefit rule)
  tax-exempt interest, 6-5 to 6-9, 6-50
  unemployment compensation, 6-19
  worker's compensation, 6-40
Executor, 6-45
Exempt organizations, 3-4
Exemptions (*see also* Personal and
    dependency exemptions), 3-21, 4-1
    to 4-12, 6-2
  dependency, 3-21, 4-1, 4-3 to 4-12, 4-31, 4-32
  personal, 3-21, 4-2, 4-32
Expenses
  business (*see* Business expenses
    and losses)
  capital expenditures vs., 7-28

child care (*see* Child and dependent care
    credit)
Cohan rule, 7-40, 8-42
deduction of (*see* Deductions and losses)
employee (*see* Employee, expenses)
for the benefit of another, 7-39
illegal business expenses, 7-32 to 7-33
obligations of another taxpayer, payment
    of, 7-39
ordinary and necessary, 7-3, 7-7 to 7-8
prepaid, 7-11 to 7-12
related to the production or collection of
    income, 7-3, 7-4 to 7-7, 9-22
related to tax-exempt income, 7-3, 7-35
    to 7-36, 9-21, 9-34
Extension of time
  to file tax return, 4-35 to 4-36
  to pay taxes, 4-35 to 4-36

— F —

Failure to pay penalty, 4-36 to 4-37
Fair market value (FMV), 3-28, 19-33
  charitable contributions, 11-37
  defined, 11-37
  estate tax, 14-10
Family (*see* Related party transactions)
Farming, 5-24, 6-40, 9-2, 9-42 to 9-44,
    17-30
  expenses, 9-2, 9-42 to 9-44
  subsidies, 6-40
Federal estate tax (*see* Estate tax)
Federal Insurance Contributions Act (FICA),
    1-19 to 1-23
Federal Supplement, 2-38
Federal Unemployment Tax Act (FUTA), 1-19,
    1-23 to 1-24
Fellowships (*see* Scholarships and
    fellowships)
Fertilizer, 9-43
FICA taxes (*see also* Employment taxes),
    1-19 to 1-23
Fiduciary, 3-5 to 3-6
  defined, 3-5
FIFO method (first-in first-out) (*see also*
    Inventories), 10-27, 10-28, 14-7
Filing requirements, 4-31 to 4-42
  corporations, 4-35
  estates, 4-35
  estimated tax (*see* Estimated tax)
  extensions of time to file, 4-35 to 4-36
  gift tax (Federal), 4-35
  individuals, 4-2, 4-35 to 4-37
  partnerships, 4-35
  trusts, 4-35

Filing status, 4-1, 4-13 to 4-20
  head of household, 4-14 to 4-15, 4-16 to
    4-18, 4-32
  married filing jointly, 4-14, 4-15 to 4-16,
    4-19, 4-32
  married filing separately, 4-16, 4-19, 4-32
  single, 4-15, 4-19, 4-20, 4-32
  surviving spouse, 4-16, 4-18, 4-19, 4-32
Fines (*see also* Penalties), 7-32
First-in first-out (FIFO) (*see also* Inventories),
  10-27, 10-28, 14-7
Fiscal year (*see* Accounting periods)
FMV (fair market value) (*see* Fair market
  value)
Foreign conventions (*see* Travel expenses)
Foreign Corrupt Practices Act, 7-32
Foreign source income, 3-3
Foreign tax credit, 3-3, 6-43, 13-46 to 13-47
Foreign tax treaties, 2-24, 3-4
Foreign travel (*see* Travel expenses)
Forward averaging, 18-8
Franchise tax, 1-25, 16-28 to 16-29
Fraud, 2-10 to 2-12, 4-41
Fringe benefits (*see* Employee fringe benefits)
Full absorption costing of inventories (*see*
  Inventories, full absorption)
Funeral expenses, 1-13
FUTA (Federal Unemployment Tax Act), 1-19,
  1-23 to 1-24

— G —

Gains and losses (*see also* Capital gains and
  losses)
  character of, 3-31 to 3-34
  computation of, 3-31 to 3-34, 14-2
  property transactions, 3-27 to 3-35, 14-1
    to 14-35, 17-1 to 17-35
  realized, 3-28 to 3-30, 5-10, 14-3 to 14-5
  recognized, 3-30, 14-2 to 14-3
Gambling, 7-18
General business credit, 13-31 to 13-32,
  13-46
General partners, 19-5, 19-8, 19-11
General sales tax, 1-26
Generation-skipping tax, 11-12
Gift splitting, 1-16
Gift tax—Federal (*see also* Gifts), 1-5, 1-14
  to 1-16, 11-13
  annual exclusion, 1-14
  charitable contributions (*see* Charitable
    contributions)
  computation, 1-14 to 1-15
  filing requirements, 4-35
  gift splitting, 1-16
  marital deduction, 1-15

  political contributions (*see* Political
    contributions)
  rates of tax, 1-14 to 1-15
  unified transfer tax, 1-15
  unified transfer tax credit, 1-15
Gift tax—State, 1-17, 1-19
Gifts (*see also* Gift tax—Federal), 6-32,
  14-17 to 14-18, 17-22 to 17-23
  basis of, 14-7 to 14-9
  business, 6-14, 6-15 to 6-16, 8-34, 8-41 to
    8-42
  charitable (*see* Charitable contributions)
  exclusion from gross income, 6-32
  holding period, 16-11
  liabilities in excess of basis, 14-18
  part-gift part-sale, 14-17 to 14-18
  tax planning, 14-33 to 14-35
Goodwill, 6-41, 7-27 to 7-28, 9-34 to 9-35,
  9-46 to 9-47
Government bonds issued at a discount (*see*
  Series E and EE savings bonds)
Government obligations, state and local, 6-5
  to 6-7, 6-50, 11-13, 14-15
Government transfer payments, 6-38, 6-40
Graded vesting, 18-15 to 18-16
Gross estate (*see also* Estate tax), 1-13
Gross income (*see also specific items*), 3-11,
  3-11 to 3-14, 5-1 to 5-51, 6-1 to 6-53
  accounting methods (*see* Accounting
    methods)
  accounting periods (*see* Accounting periods)
  adjusted gross income, 3-16 to 3-17
  alimony and separate maintenance
    payments, 6-32 to 6-38, 6-53, 7-18
  annuities, 5-12, 6-9 to 6-14, 6-49, 7-18,
    13-53, 18-7
  assignment of income, 5-40 to 5-42, 6-31
  awards, 6-38
  business, 6-41 to 6-45
  claim of right doctrine, 5-29 to 5-31
  community property, 4-14, 5-46 to 5-47
  constructive receipt, 5-21 to 5-23, 5-41
  corporations, 6-41, 19-19
  damages (*see* Damages)
  deductions from (*see* Deductions and
    losses)
  defined, 5-2 to 5-7, 6-1
  dependency exemption requirement, 4-2
    to 4-3, 4-7 to 4-8, 6-2
  discharge of indebtedness (*see* Discharge
    of indebtedness)
  dividend income (*see* Dividend income)
  employee fringe benefits (*see* Employee
    fringe benefits)
  exclusions (*see* Exclusions from gross
    income)

Gross income (*cont.*)
fees, 6-45
filing requirements, 4-31
form of benefit, 5-9 to 5-10
form of receipt, 5-9 to 5-10
gains (*see* Capital gains and losses; Gains
    and losses)
group-term life insurance, 6-14, 6-20 to 6-22,
    6-51, 18-2
hobby (*see also* Hobby losses), 6-41, 7-4,
    7-23 to 7-25
illegal income, 5-31, 6-41
inclusions (*see specific items*)
indirect economic benefits, 5-9 to 5-10, 5-13 to
    5-14
installment sales (*see* Installment method
    of accounting)
original issue discount, 5-39
return of capital, 5-10, 6-2, 6-3, 6-10, 6-50
    savings bonds (*see* Savings bonds)
    social security benefits (*see* Social security)
    sole proprietorship, 19-2
    taxable income (*see* Taxable income)
    tax planning, 5-49 to 5-51
    unemployment compensation, 6-19
Gross income test (*see also* Dependency
    exemptions), 4-3, 4-7 to 4-8, 6-2
Group-term life insurance, 6-14, 6-20 to 6-22,
    6-51, 18-2
Guaranteed payment, 19-11, 19-12

— H —

Head of household, 4-14 to 4-15, 4-16 to 4-18,
    4-32
Health and accident insurance plans, 6-22
    to 6-23, 6-40, 6-51, 11-10 to 11-11,
    18-2
Heirs (*see* Beneficiaries)
Hobby losses, 7-4, 7-23 to 7-25, 7-43
    burden of proof, 7-24
    defined, 7-23
    tax planning, 7-43
Holding period, 3-31, 16-10 to 16-13
    capital assets (*see* Capital assets)
    carryover basis, 16-11
    commodity futures, 16-13
    computation of, 16-10
    gift, property acquired by, 16-11
    incentive stock options, 18-30 to 18-33
    inheritance, property acquired by, 16-12
    involuntary conversions, 16-11
    like-kind exchanges, 16-11
    "long-term" defined, 3-31, 16-10
    nontaxable transactions, 16-10 to 16-13
    sale of a residence, 16-11

Section 1231 assets, 17-3
    "short-term" defined, 3-31, 16-10
    stock dividends, 16-12
    stock exchange transactions, 16-10 to 16-11
    stock rights, 16-12
    wash sales, 16-12
Home equity indebtedness, 11-20, 11-21
Home office (*see* Office in the home)
H.R. (Keogh) Plans (*see* Keogh Plans)

— I —

Illegal expenses, deductibility of, 7-32 to 7-33
Illegal income, 5-31, 6-41
Immediate expensing election, 9-22 to 9-24, 9-28
Imputed interest, 11-18
Inaccurate return penalty, 2-9 to 2-10
Incapacitated taxpayers, 15-14
Incentive stock options, 13-13, 18-29 to 18-33
Income (*see also* Gross income;
    Taxable income), 1-6, 3-11, 5-1 to 5-7
Income-producing property, 5-41
Income in respect of a decedent, 3-13, 14-9
    to 14-11
Income shifting, 5-41 to 5-42, 5-50
Income splitting, 5-49 to 5-51
Income tax (Federal), 1-3 to 1-5, 1-5 to
    1-6, 1-9 to 1-11
    avoidance (*see* Tax avoidance)
    penalties (*see* Penalties)
    rates, 1-7 to 1-8, 3-21 to 3-22
        corporate, 3-21
        individuals, 3-21 to 3-22, 4-15, 4-21 to 4-23
    statute of limitations (*see* Statute of
        limitations)
    withholding tax (*see* Withholding tax)
Income tax (state and local), 7-17, 11-12,
    11-14 to 11-15
Incorporation (*see* Controlled corporations)
Indebtedness, discharge of (*see* Discharge of
    indebtedness)
Independent contractors, 7-19 to 7-22
Indexation, 1-27, 4-41 to 4-42
Indian employment credit, 13-45
Individual retirement accounts (IRAs), 5-41,
    7-18, 18-10, 18-23 to 18-25, 18-34
    to 18-36
    contributions to, 7-18, 18-25, 18-36 to 18-37
    distributions, taxation of, 18-25
    spousal, 18-35
Individual taxpayers (*see also specific items*),
    3-2 to 3-4
Industrial development bonds, 6-6
Information returns, 4-35 to 4-37
Inheritances, 6-32, 17-22 to 17-23
Inheritance taxes, 1-16 to 1-19, 11-13

Innocent spouse provision, 4-15
Installment sale method of accounting,
        5-41, 14-21 to 14-30, 17-30 to 17-31
    disposition of installment notes, 14-29
    electing out, 14-22 to 14-23
    gain computation, 14-23 to 14-26
    imputed interest, 14-26 to 14-27
    interest payments on deferred taxes,
        14-29 to 14-30
    limitations on, 14-26 to 14-30
    related party sales, 14-27 to 14-28
    tax planning, 14-34, 14-35
Insurance policies, exchange of, 15-45
Insurance premiums, 6-20 to 6-22
    group-term life insurance, 6-14, 6-20
        to 6-22, 6-51, 18-2
    health and accident insurance, 6-19, 6-22
        to 6-23, 6-40, 6-51, 18-2
    life insurance, 5-12, 6-20 to 6-22, 6-34,
        6-49, 6-50
    medical expense, 6-22 to 6-23
Insurance proceeds, 6-20 to 6-22
    health and accident insurance, 6-19, 6-22
        to 6-23
    interruption of business, 6-41
    life insurance, 6-20 to 6-22
    medical expense reimbursements, 6-22
        to 6-23
Intangible assets (see Depreciation and
    amortization; specific items)
Intangible drilling costs, recapture, 17-30
Interest assessments (by IRS) rate of, 4-36
    to 4-37
Interest exclusion, 6-4
Interest expense, 11-18
    business, 11-23
    classification of, 11-27 to 11-31
        commingled funds, 11-28 to 11-29
        debt repayments, refinancings, and
            reallocations, 11-29 to 11-30
        loan proceeds received in cash, 11-29
        loan proceeds received indirectly, 11-29
        proceeds deposited in borrower's account,
            11-27 to 11-28
    computation and allocation of, 11-30 to 11-31
    credit cards, 7-10
    graduated payment mortgages, 11-32
    imputed interest, 11-18
    installment purchases, 11-32
    investment, 11-24 to 11-26
    itemized deduction, 1-28 to 1-29, 7-18
    limitation on deductibility, 11-18 to 11-26
    mortgage, 11-32, 13-54
    note discount interest, 11-32
    passive activity, 12-20
    personal, 11-19 to 11-20

    points, 7-12
    prepaid, 5-31 to 5-35, 7-12
    qualified residence, 11-20 to 11-23
    related party transactions (see Related
        party transactions)
    tax-exempt securities related to, 7-35 to
        7-36, 7-42
    tax planning, 7-43
    trade, 11-23
    when deductible, 11-31 to 11-32
    where reported, 11-32 to 11-33
Interest-free loans, 5-42 to 5-45
Interest income, 5-35 to 5-39, 5-42 to 5-45,
        6-4 to 6-9
    exempt, 6-4 to 6-9
    original issue discount (see Original issue
        discount)
    Series E and EE bonds (see Series E
        and EE savings bonds)
    tax-exempt securities, 6-4 to 6-9
Internal Revenue Bulletins (IRB), 2-22, 2-27,
        2-28, 2-37
Internal Revenue Code, 2-20, 2-45
Internal Revenue Service (IRS)
    compliance functions, 4-39
Inventories, 10-23 to 10-34, 16-4 to 16-5
    charitable contributions, 11-38 to 11-39
    first-in, first-out (FIFO), 10-27, 10-28, 14-7
    full absorption, 10-25
    indirect costs, 10-24, 10-25
    last-in, first-out (LIFO), 10-24, 10-27 to 10-33
    lower of cost or market, 10-33 to 10-34
    specific goods, 10-30
Investigation of new business, 7-29 to 7-31
Investment credit, 9-23, 13-32 to 13-36, 17-30
    amount, 13-32
    carrybacks and carryovers, 13-36 to 13-37
    computation, 13-32
    recapture, 13-35 to 13-36
    Section 179 immediate expensing election,
        effect on, 9-22 to 9-24, 9-28
Investment expenses, 11-24 to 11-26, 12-1
        to 12-20
    passive activity limitations, 12-1 to 12-19
Investment income, 11-24 to 11-26, 19-8
Investment interest, 11-24 to 11-26
Involuntary conversions, 14-4, 15-2, 15-20
        to 15-27, 16-8, 16-11
    capital gains, 15-25
    defined, 15-20 to 15-22
    election, 15-24 to 15-25
    gain or loss, 15-25 to 15-27
        computation, 15-25 to 15-27
        nonrecognition, 15-25 to 15-27
    personal residence, 15-15
    replacement period, 15-24

Involuntary Conversions (*cont.*)
  replacement property, 15-22 to 15-23
  reporting requirements, 15-25
IRA (*see* Individual retirement accounts)
IRD (*see* Income in respect of a decedent)
Iron ore, 17-5 to 17-6
IRS (*see* Internal Revenue Service)
Itemized deductions (*see also* Deductions and
        losses; *specific items*), 3-15 to 3-16,
        3-17 to 3-20, 7-18 to 7-19, 8-4
  casualty and theft losses (*see* Casualty and
      theft losses)
  charitable contributions (*see* Charitable
      contributions)
  classification of expenses, 7-5, 7-16 to 7-22
  educational expenses (*see* Educational
      expenses)
  employee business expenses, 7-17
  entertainment expenses (*see* Entertainment
      expenses)
  interest (*see* Interest expense)
  medical expenses (*see* Medical and dental
      expenses)
  miscellaneous itemized, 3-18, 7-15, 7-18 to
      7-19, 7-31, 8-4, 11-46 to 11-47
  standard deduction, 1-29, 3-17 to 3-20,
      3-39, 4-25, 7-41
  taxes (*see* Taxes)
  three-percent deductions, 3-20, 11-48 to 11-50

— J —

Jobs credit (*see* Targeted jobs tax credit)
Job-seeking expenses, 7-19
Joint ownership (*see* Community property
      forms)
Joint return test (*see also* Dependency
      exemptions), 4-3, 4-10
Joint tenancies (*see* Community property)
Judicial process, 2-29 to 2-40
Judicial sources of tax law, 2-29 to 2-40, 2-45
      to 2-46

— K —

Keogh Plans, 5-41, 7-18, 18-10, 18-19
      to 18-21, 19-11
Kickbacks, 7-32 to 7-33
Kiddie tax, 4-25, 5-41, 5-50 to 5-51

— L —

Land (*see* Realty)
Land clearing, 9-43
Last-in, first-out (LIFO) (*see also* Inventories),
      10-24, 10-27 to 10-33

Leasehold improvements, 6-41, 6-44, 9-36
Leases, 6-41, 6-44
  cancellation payments, 6-41, 6-42, 16-22
  improvements by lessee, 6-44
Legal expenses, 7-26 to 7-27
  divorce, 7-27
  nonbusiness expenses, 7-26 to 7-27
  tax related, 7-26 to 7-27
Legislative grace, 7-1
Legislative process, 2-21 to 2-22
Liabilities assumed
  amount realized, effect on, 14-5, 14-14
  in excess of basis, 14-18
Life insurance premiums, 6-20 to 6-22, 6-34,
      6-49, 6-50, 7-36
  group-term, 6-14, 6-20 to 6-22, 6-51, 18-2
Life insurance proceeds, 6-20 to 6-22, 6-49
      to 6-50
  keyman, 6-22
LIFO (last-in, first-out) (*see also* Inventories),
      10-24, 10-27 to 10-33
Like-kind exchanges, 15-2, 15-23, 15-28
      to 15-42, 16-11
  amount realized, 15-33, 15-35
  basis of property received, 15-34 to 15-38
  boot, effect of, 15-32 to 15-34
  defined, 15-29
  exchange requirement, 15-38 to 15-41
  holding period, 15-41
  liabilities, effect of, 15-32 to 15-33
  like-kind property, 15-29 to 15-31
  mandatory treatment, 15-41
  qualified property, 15-29
  three-corner exchanges, 15-39
Limitation period (*see* Statute of limitations)
Limited liability, 19-5, 19-13
Limited liability company (LLC), 3-8, 3-38
Limited partner, 19-5, 19-8, 19-11
Listed property, 9-26 to 9-33
Livestock, 9-44 to 9-43, 15-23, 15-31, 17-6 to
      17-7
Living expenses, 6-46, 7-26 to 7-27
Loans between related parties (*see* Related
      party transactions)
Lobbying expenditures, 7-33 to 7-34
Lodging (*see* Meals and lodging)
Long-term capital gains and losses (*see*
      Capital gains and losses)
Long-term contracts, 5-19, 5-33 to 5-35
Look back rule, 17-9, 17-10 to 17-11
Losses (*see* Capital gains and losses;
      Casualty and theft losses; Deductions
      and losses; Gains and losses; Net
      operating losses; *specific items*)
Losses between related parties (*see* Related
      party transactions)

Low-income housing, 13-30, 13-43, 15-45
Lump sum distributions, 18-7 to 18-9, 18-25

— M —

Marginal tax rate, 5-41
Marital deduction (*see* Estate tax; Gift tax),
    1-13
Marital property settlement (*see* Community
    property; Divorce settlements)
Marital status, 4-14
Market value (*see* Fair market value)
Meals and lodging, 5-13, 6-14, 6-25 to 6-26,
    6-51, 18-2
Medical and dental expenses, 7-16, 7-18,
    7-39, 11-2 to 11-11
    accident and health insurance premiums,
        6-23 to 6-24, 11-4, 11-9 to 11-11
    capital expenditures, 11-6 to 11-7
    child care expenses, 11-4
    dependents', 7-39, 11-2
    insurance premiums, 6-22 to 6-23, 11-4,
        11-9 to 11-11
    limitations, 11-5
    medicine and drugs, 11-2, 11-3, 11-5
    nursing homes, 11-7
    reimbursement of, 6-22 to 6-23, 11-9 to 11-10
    tax benefit rule, 11-9 to 11-10
    tax planning, 11-52
    transportation expenses, 11-3, 11-8
    when deductible, 11-3 to 11-4
Medical reimbursement plans, 6-22 to 6-23,
    18-2
Medicare benefits, 6-40
Medicine and drugs (*see* Medical and dental
    expenses)
Memorandum decisions (Tax Court) 2-37
Method of accounting (*see* Accounting
    methods)
Military personnel, 6-31
Minimum tax
    alternative minimum tax, 9-20, 13-1 to 13-26,
    computation, 13-1 to 13-26
    individuals, 13-1 to 13-26
Minor children, unearned income of, 4-25
    to 4-30, 5-41, 5-50 to 5-51
Miscellaneous itemized deductions, 3-18, 7-15,
    7-18 to 7-19, 7-31, 8-4, 11-46 to 11-47
Modified Accelerated Cost Recovery System
    (MACRS), 8-25, 9-4 to 9-34
    computation, 9-7 to 9-18
    depreciation recapture, 9-24, 9-32, 17-14
        to 17-31
    election to expense accounts, 9-22 to 9-24,
        9-28
    eligible property, 9-5 to 9-6, 9-23

half-year convention, 9-7 to 9-13, 9-18,
    9-19
mass asset accounts, 9-21
mid-month convention, 9-7, 9-13 to 9-15
mid-quarter convention, 9-7, 9-15 to 9-18
personalty, 9-8 to 9-9, 9-15 to 9-16
qualifying property, 9-5 to 9-6
realty, 9-9
recapture (*see* MACRS, depreciation
    recapture)
recovery periods, 9-4, 9-5, 9-6, 9-7, 9-10,
    9-20
recovery property, 9-5 to 9-6, 9-8, 9-9, 9-20
salvage value, 9-19
straight-line, 9-18 to 9-21, 9-28
tax planning, 9-45 to 9-47
Money purchase plans, 18-11
Mortgage Credit Certificates, 13-54
Moving expenses, 6-14, 7-18, 8-5 to 8-10
    direct expenses, 8-7 to 8-9
    distance requirement, 8-5 to 8-6
    indirect expenses, 8-7 to 8-9
    tax planning, 8-55
    time test, 8-6 to 8-7
Multiple support agreement (*see also*
    Dependency exemptions), 4-6, 4-18,
    11-2

— N —

Natural resources, 9-37 to 9-39
Negative income tax (*see* Earned income
    credit)
Negligence penalty, 2-6 to 2-8
Net capital gains and losses (*see* Capital
    gains and losses)
Net earnings from self-employment (*see*
    Self-employment tax)
Net operating loss (NOL), 5-18, 6-43, 10-16
    to 10-21, 13-10, 19-25
    carrybacks and carryovers, 10-16 to 10-17,
        19-25
    computation of, 10-17 to 10-20
    corporations, 19-25, 19-29 to 19-30
    deduction, 10-18, 19-25
    individuals, 10-18 to 10-20
    modifications, 10-18 to 10-20
    tax planning, 10-36
Net unearned income, 4-26 to 4-27
Net worth method, 5-3 to 5-5
NOL (*see* Net operating loss)
Nonacquiescence (Non Acq. or NA), 2-37
Nonbusiness bad debts (*see* Bad debts)
Nonprofit organizations, 3-4
Nonqualified Stock Option (NQSO), 18-32
    to 18-33

Nonresident aliens, 3-3, 3-21, 19-14
Nontaxable transactions, 14-11, 15-1 to 15-47,
       16-10 to 16-13
Note discount interest, 11-32

— O —

Obligations of another, 7-39
Office in the home, 7-19, 8-10 to 8-16,
       8-56, 15-47
   allocation of expenses, 8-13 to 8-15
   amount of deduction, 8-13 to 8-15
   daycare and storage use, 8-15
   deductible expenses, 8-13 to 8-15
   depreciation on home, 8-13 to 8-14
   employee of, 8-11
   limitation on deduction, 8-10
   requirements for deductibility, 8-11 to
       8-13
   tax planning, 8-56
Oil recovery credit, enhanced, 13-45
Options (see also Stock options), 16-30 to 16-32
Ordinary and necessary expenses (see
       Deductions and losses)
Ordinary dividends, 6-2
Original issue discount, 5-39
Outside salesperson, 7-19
   expenses of, 7-19

— P —

Partnerships, 3-6 to 3-7, 6-2, 6-41, 16-5,
       19-5, 19-40 to 19-46
   accounting periods, 5-16
   basis adjustment, 19-32
   basis in, 19-32
   basis of property, 19-32
   conduit concept, 3-6
   contributions, 6-45, 11-33
   entity concept, 3-7
   estimated taxes (see Estimated tax)
   filing requirements, 4-35
   formation of, 19-30 to 19-33
   general partnership, 19-5, 19-8, 19-11
   guaranteed payments, 19-11, 19-12
   limited partnership, 19-5, 19-8, 19-11
   net income, 19-12
   sale of interest in, 14-21, 19-11
   self-employment income, 19-8, 19-11, 19-12
   tax planning, 19-5 to 19-10
   transactions between partner and
       partnership, 3-6 to 3-7, 19-8 to 19-13
Passive activity interest, 12-20
Passive activity limitations, 12-1 to 12-19
Passive loss rules, 12-7

Patents, 16-21 to 16-22
Payment of tax
   estimated taxes (see Estimated tax)
   withholding (see Withholding tax)
Penalties
   accuracy-related, 2-6 to 2-10
   deductibility of, 7-32
   failure to pay tax, 4-36 to 4-37
   taxpayer, 2-5 to 2-6
   tax preparer, 2-12 to 2-17
Pension plans (see Qualified pension and
       profit-sharing plans)
Percentage depletion, 9-37 to 9-39
Percentage of completion method, 5-33 to
       5-34
Perquisites (see Employee fringe benefits)
Personal and dependency exemptions, 1-27,
       3-21, 4-1 to 4-12, 6-2
   age 65 or over, 1-29, 3-20
   blindness, 1-29, 3-20
   citizenship or residency test, 4-3, 4-11
   dependency exemption tests, 4-1, 4-3
       to 4-12, 4-32
   gross income test, 4-3, 4-7 to 4-8
   joint return test, 4-3, 4-10
   phase-out, 4-11 to 4-12
   relationship or member of household test,
       4-3, 4-8 to 4-10
   support test, 4-3, 4-3 to 4-5
Personal expenditures, 3-14, 7-26 to 7-27
   medical expenses, 11-2 to 11-11
   personal casualty and theft losses, 11-11
   taxes, 11-12 to 11-18
Personal holding company dividends paid
       deduction, 6-53
Personal interest, 11-19 to 11-20
Personal liability (see Partnerships)
Personal residence (see Involuntary
       conversions; Sale of principal
       residence—§ 121; Sale of principal
       residence—§ 1034)
Personal service corporation, 12-7, 19-19
Points, 7-12, 7-42 to 7-43
Political contributions, 7-33 to 7-35
Preference items, 3-24
Prepaid expenses, 7-11 to 7-12
Prepaid income, 5-31 to 5-35
Prepaid insurance, 7-11
Prepaid interest, 5-32, 7-12
Prepaid rent, 7-11
Preparation of returns (see Returns)
Prepayment of tax (see Estimated tax)
Prime costing method, 10-25
Principal residence (see Sale of a principal
       residence—§ 121; Sale of a principal
       residence—§ 1034)

Private letter rulings, 2-25, 2-28 to 2-29, 2-46
Prizes and awards, 6-38, 8-42
Progressive tax structure, 1-7
Property, 3-1, 3-27 to 3-35, 11-12, 11-15 to 11-17, 14-1 to 14-35, 15-1 to 15-47
  ad valorem, 11-15
  adjusted basis, 3-28 to 3-30, 5-10, 14-1, 14-2, 14-6 to 14-13
  basis (see Basis)
  capital assets (see Capital assets)
  capital gains and losses (see Capital gains and losses)
  charitable contributions (see Charitable contributions)
  community property (see Community property)
  condemned (see Involuntary conversions)
  conversion (see Involuntary conversions)
  depreciation (see Depreciation and amortization)
  depreciation recapture (see Recapture, depreciation)
  gains and losses, 15-1 to 15-47
  intangible, 9-1
  investment tax credit (see Investment tax credit)
  LIFO (see LIFO)
  personalty, 1-26, 9-2
  personal use, 9-2
  realty, 1-26, 9-2
  recapture, 3-34
  Section 1231 definition, 3-35
  settlements, 6-36, 14-17
  tangible, 9-1 to 9-2, 9-5
Property taxes, 11-12, 11-15 to 11-17
  ad valorem, 11-15
  deductibility of, 11-15 to 11-17
  personalty, 1-26, 11-12, 11-15
  real estate taxes apportionment of, 11-16 to 11-17
  realty, 1-26, 11-12, 11-16 to 11-17
Property transactions (see also Involuntary conversions; Like-kind exchanges), 3-1, 3-27 to 3-35, 14-1 to 14-35, 15-1 to 15-47
  gains and losses (see also Gains and losses)
  nonrecognition of gains and losses (see specific provisions), 15-1 to 15-47
Property transfers to creditors, 14-16
Proportional tax rate, 1-7
Proprietorship, 16-5, 19-40 to 19-46
Public assistance payments, 6-40
Public policy restriction, 7-31 to 7-33

— Q —

Qualified investment (see Investment credit)
Qualified pension and profit-sharing plans, 6-12, 18-5 to 18-12, 19-11
  annuities (see Annuities)
  contributions to, 18-6 to 18-7, 18-18
  defined benefit plan, 18-17
  defined contribution plan, 18-16
  determination letters, 18-18
  lump-sum distribution, 18-7 to 18-8
  nonqualified vs., 18-6 to 18-7
  plan loans, 18-10
  premature distributions, 18-9
  qualification requirements, 18-12 to 18-19
  rollover contribution, 18-10
  scope of plan participation and coverage, 18-14 to 18-15
  self-employed individuals, 18-19 to 18-21
  tax benefits, 18-6 to 18-7
  tax planning, 18-34 to 18-37
  types of, 18-10 to 18-12
Qualified personal service corporations, 5-24
Qualified residence interest, 11-20 to 11-23
Qualified retirement plans (see Qualified pension and profit-sharing plans)
Qualified small business stock, 16-23 to 16-25
Qualified trust, 18-13

— R —

Rabbi trusts, 18-28
Railroad Retirement Tax Act benefits (RRTA), 11-13
Ranching expenses, 9-42 to 9-44
Rates of tax (see Tax rates)
Real estate, rental, 12-16 to 12-17
  vs. nonrental, 12-12 to 12-13
Real estate developer, 12-17 to 12-19
Real property (see Realty)
Realized amount (see Amount realized)
Realized gain or loss, 3-28 to 3-30, 5-10 to 5-11, 14-3 to 14-5
  adjusted basis, 3-28 to 3-30, 5-10, 14-1, 14-2, 14-6 to 14-13
  amount realized, 3-28 to 3-30, 5-10, 14-1, 14-3 to 14-5, 14-14, 15-34, 15-35
  like-kind exchanges, 16-11
  recognition of, 3-30, 14-2 to 14-3
  sale of a residence, 16-11
Realty, subdivided, 16-27
Reasonableness requirement, 7-8 to 7-9
  compensation, 7-8
Recapture, 3-34, 17-14 to 17-31, 19-27 to 19-28
  ACRS, 17-19

Recapture (*cont.*)
  corporations, 17-28 to 17-30, 19-27 to
      19-28
  depreciation, 3-34, 9-24, 9-32, 17-14 to 17-31,
      19-27 to 19-28
  exceptions to, 17-18, 17-22 to 17-23
  farm recapture, 17-30
  intangible drilling costs, 17-30
  investment credit (*see* Investment credit,
      recapture)
  nontaxable transactions, 17-18, 17-22 to
      17-23
  Section 291, 17-28 to 17-30
  Section 1245, 17-15 to 17-18
  Section 1250, 17-18 to 17-28
Receivables, 16-3 to 16-4, 16-5
Recognition of gain or loss, 3-30, 14-3
Recordkeeping requirements, 7-40, 8-42
      to 8-43, 9-32 to 9-33
  in general, 8-42 to 8-43
  travel, entertainment, and gift expenses,
      7-40, 8-42 to 8-43
Recoveries
  bad debts (*see* Bad debts)
  capital (*see* Return of capital)
Refunds of tax (*see* Tax refunds)
Regular decisions (Tax Court), 2-35 to 2-37
Regulations, 2-25 to 2-27
Reimbursed expenses, 6-14, 7-17, 8-25
  deductibility of, 7-17
  educational, 6-14
  employees, 6-14 to 6-15, 7-18, 8-46 to 8-54
  medical expenses, 11-9 to 11-10
  mileage allowances, 8-51 to 8-53
  per diem allowances, 8-51 to 8-53
  recordkeeping requirements, 7-40, 8-42
      to 8-43
  where to deduct, 7-18, 8-47
Reinvested dividends, 6-4
Related party transactions, 7-36 to 7-39, 9-23,
      15-40 to 15-41
  accrued expenses payable to related party,
      7-38 to 7-39
  constructive ownership, 7-37
  defined, 7-37
  interest expense, 7-38 to 7-39
  losses, 7-38, 14-31
  related taxpayers, 7-36 to 7-39, 14-31
      to 14-32
  sale of depreciable property, 14-31 to 14-32
  tax planning, 14-34
  unpaid expenses, 7-38 to 7-39
Relationship or member of household test
      (*see also* Dependency exemptions),
      4-3, 4-8 to 4-10
Rental real estate, 12-16 to 12-17

  vs. nonrental, 12-12 to 12-13
Repairs vs. capital expenditures, 7-28
Repossessions, 15-45
Research (*see* Tax research)
Research and experimental expenditures
  credit, 1-28, 9-42, 13-30, 13-39 to 13-43
  elections, 7-29, 9-41 to 9-42
  expenditures, 9-39 to 9-42
  qualified expenditures, 9-40, 13-39 to 13-42
Reserve for bad debts (*see* Bad debts)
Residence (*see also* Sale of principal
      residence—§ 121; Sale of principal
      residence—§ 1034)
  rental of, 12-23 to 12-28
Resident aliens, 3-2
Retirement plans, 18-1 to 18-37
Return of capital, 5-11, 6-3, 6-10, 6-50, 14-2
Returns, of a dependent, 4-11
Revenue Act of 1987, 1-5
Revenue Procedure (Rev. Proc.), 2-27
Revenue Reconciliation Act (RRA) of 1990,
      1-5, 13-45
Revenue Reconciliation Act (RRA) of 1993,
      16-23
Revenue Ruling (Rev. Rul.), 2-27, 2-46
Revenue sources, 1-5
Rollovers, 18-10, 18-25
Royalties, 5-32
Rulings (*see also* Revenue Ruling), 2-46

— S —

S corporations, 3-4, 3-8, 6-1, 19-13 to 19-15,
      19-40 to 19-46
  accounting periods, 5-16
  conduit concept, 19-15, 19-35
  election, 19-14
  eligibility for election
    corporations, 19-14
    number of shareholders, 19-14
  formation of, 19-35
  related persons (*see* Related party transactions)
  shareholders
    corporate distributions, 19-15
    number of shareholders, 19-14
    taxation of shareholders, 19-15
    transactions with, 19-15
  taxation of, 19-14 to 19-18
Sale of principal residence (§ 121), 15-2,
      15-13 to 15-17
  computations, 15-13 to 15-17
  exclusion of gain if taxpayer 55 or older,
      15-13, 15-47
  incapacitated taxpayers, 15-14
  interaction with other provisions, 15-15
      to 15-17, 15-24

Sale of principal residence (*cont.*)
  married taxpayers, 15-14 to 15-15
  once-in-a-lifetime exclusion, 15-13 to 15-14
  revocation of election, 15-14
  tax planning, 15-47
Sale of principal residence (§ 1034), 15-3 to
    15-17, 15-46 to 15-47
  adjusted sales price, 15-3, 15-7 to 15-8
  basis of new residence, 15-6 to 15-8,
    15-15
  capital improvement, 15-5
  holding period, 16-11
  postponed gain, 15-8
  principal residence defined, 15-4
  replacement period, 15-4 to 15-5
  sale of new residence, 15-10 to 15-12
Salesperson, outside (*see* Outside
    salesperson)
Sales tax (*see* General sales tax)
Salvage value (*see* Accelerated Cost
    Recovery System; Depreciation and
    amortization)
Savings bonds, 5-37 to 5-38, 5-41, 6-7 to 6-9
Scholarships and fellowships, 6-39
Section 280F, 9-24 to 9-33
Section 1231 property (real and depreciable
    business property), 3-35, 17-3 to 17-11,
    17-34
  casualty and theft losses, 10-11 to 10-12,
    17-8
  computations, 17-7 to 17-11
  gains and losses, 3-35
  holding period requirement, 17-3
  netting process, 17-7 to 17-11
  tax planning, 17-34
Section 1244 stock, 16-23
Section 1245 property (*see also* Recapture),
    17-15 to 17-18
  depreciation recapture, 17-15 to 17-18
  included property, 17-16
Section 1250 property (*see also* Recapture),
    17-18 to 17-28
  applicable percentages, 17-22
  depreciation recapture, 17-18 to 17-20
  included property, 17-19
Secular trusts, 18-28
Securities (*see also* Worthless securities),
    16-7 to 16-8
  capital gains and losses (*see* Capital gains
    and losses)
  dealers in, 16-26
  holding period (*see* Holding period)
Self-employed business expenses (*see*
    Business expenses and losses)
Self employed vs. employee status, 6-52
    to 6-53, 7-22 to 7-23

Self-employment income, 4-31, 19-8, 19-11,
    19-12
Self-employment tax, 1-19, 1-21, 3-23, 7-18
SEP (*see* Simplified employee pensions)
Separate maintenance payments (*see also*
    Alimony), 6-32 to 6-38, 6-53
Series E and EE savings bonds, 5-37 to 5-38,
    5-41, 6-7
Series HH savings bonds, 5-38
Short Sales, 16-29 to 16-30
Short-term capital gains and losses (*see*
    Capital gains and losses)
Sick pay (*see* Disability and sick pay)
Simplified employee pensions, 18-25
Single filing status, 4-15, 4-19, 4-20, 4-32
Sixteenth Amendment, 2-20, 6-1
Small business corporations
  Section 1244 stock, 16-23
Small Claims Division (*see also* Tax Court), 2-31
Social objectives of taxation, 1-28 to 1-29
Social security, 1-19 to 1-23, 6-16 to 6-19,
    11-13, 18-14
  benefits, 4-5
  credit for the elderly, effect on, 13-29, 13-53
    to 13-54
  employer's deduction, 1-20
  self-employment tax, 1-21 to 1-23
  tax rates, 1-19 to 1-23
Soil and water conservation, 9-43
Sole proprietorship, 3-3, 14-20, 16-5, 19-1
    to 19-4, 19-31, 19-40 to 19-46
Special tax computations (*see* Tax
    computation)
Specific charge-off method (*see* Bad debts)
Standard deduction, 1-29, 3-15 to 3-21, 3-39,
    4-25, 7-41
Standard mileage deduction, 9-31
Start-up expenditures, 7-29 to 7-31
State and local government obligations, 6-5
    to 6-7, 6-50, 14-15
State and local taxes (*see* Taxes)
Statute of limitations, 4-40 to 4-41
  fraud, 4-41
  no return filed, 4-41
  omission of 25% gross income, 4-41
Stock (*see* Securities)
Stock bonus plans, 18-11 to 18-12
Stock dividends, 6-2, 6-3 to 6-4, 16-12
  basis, 6-3
  holding period, 16-12
  tax treatment of, 6-3
Stock options, 16-30 to 16-32, 18-28 to 18-33,
    18-34
Stock rights, 16-12
Straight-line depreciation (*see* Depreciation
    and amortization)

Subchapter S corporations (*see* S corporations)
Subdivided real estate, 16-27
Substantiation requirements of travel and entertainment expenses, 7-40, 8-42 to 8-43, 9-32 to 9-33
Sum-of-the-years'-digits depreciation (*see* Depreciation and amortization)
Support (*see* Child support payments; Personal and dependency exemptions)
Surviving spouse, 4-16, 4-18, 4-19, 4-32

— T —

Targeted jobs tax credit, 1-29, 13-30, 13-37 to 13-38
Tax avoidance, 1-32
Tax benefit rule, 6-42, 11-14
    bad debts (*see* Bad debts)
    exclusion from gross income, 6-20, 6-45, 11-14
    medical expenses, 11-9 to 11-10
    state and local income taxes, 6-50, 11-14
Tax, characteristics of good, 1-29 to 1-31
Tax collection (*see* Collection of tax)
Tax compliance, 2-1 to 2-2
Tax computation, 4-1, 4-21 to 4-30
    minimum tax on tax preferences, 13-1 to 13-26
    tax schedules, 4-23 to 4-25
    tax tables, 4-21 to 4-23
Tax Court, 2-30 to 2-31, 2-32, 2-35 to 2-37
Tax Court Memorandum Decisions (TCM), 2-37
Tax credits, 1-9, 1-13, 3-22, 13-29 to 13-54
    alcohol fuels credit, 13-30, 13-38
    child and dependent care credit, 4-30, 6-26, 11-4, 13-48 to 13-52
    deductions vs., 13-29
    earned income credit, 4-31, 13-29, 13-55 to 13-58
    elderly, credit for the, 3-20, 13-29, 13-53 to 13-54
    energy credits, 13-29, 13-34
    general business credit, 13-31 to 13-32, 13-46
    investment credit (*see* Investment tax credit)
    mortgage credit certificates, 13-54
    nonbusiness credits, 13-47 to 13-54
    refundable credits, 13-31, 13-55 to 13-58
    research and experimental expenditures, 1-28, 13-30, 13-39 to 13-43
    table of, 13-30
    targeted jobs credit, 1-29, 13-30, 13-37 to 13-38
Tax evasion, 1-32

Tax-exempt income (*see* Exclusions from gross income)
Tax-exempt organizations, 3-4, 9-34
Tax formula, 3-1, 3-11 to 3-25
    components (*see also specific items*), 3-11 to 3-25
    illustration of, 1-10, 1-11, 3-12
Tax goals, 1-26 to 1-31, 5-20, 13-29
    economic objectives, 1-27 to 1-28, 13-29
    social objectives, 1-28 to 1-29, 13-29
Tax home, 8-21, 8-26 to 8-27
Tax litigation, 2-2
Tax periodicals, 2-42
Tax planning, 1-31 to 1-33, 2-2
    annuity, 6-49
    bequests, 14-33
    capital budgeting, 15-47
    capital gains and losses, 15-46 to 15-47, 17-34
    charitable contributions, 11-52 to 11-53
    deductions and losses, 7-41 to 7-43
    depreciation and amortization, 9-45 to 9-47
    divorce, 6-53
    employee compensation and retirement plans, 18-34 to 18-37
    employee fringe benefits, 6-50 to 6-52, 18-34
    entertainment expense, 8-55 to 8-56
    form of business, 3-38
    gifts, 14-33
    gross income, 5-49 to 5-51
    hobby losses, 7-43
    home office deduction, 8-56
    income deferral, 5-49 to 5-51
    installment sales, 14-34 to 14-35
    interest expense, 7-41
    investments, 6-49 to 6-50
    itemized deductions vs. standard deductions, 3-39
    medical expenses, 11-52
    moving expenses, 8-55
    personal deductions, 11-51 to 11-52
    planning chart, 1-33
    recapture, 17-35
    related taxpayers, 14-34
    residence, sale of, 15-47
    Section 1231 assets, 17-34
    self-employed vs. employee, 6-52 to 6-53
    stock options, 18-34
    tax-exempt income expenses, 7-42
    travel expenses, 8-55 to 8-56
Tax preference items, 13-6 to 13-7, 13-16 to 13-19
    alternative minimum tax, 13-1 to 13-26
    minimum tax, 13-16 to 13-19

Tax preparation, 7-19
  penalties related to, 2-12 to 2-17
Tax rates, 1-7 to 1-9, 3-21 to 3-22, 19-21
  corporations, 19-21
  individuals, 1-7 to 1-9, 3-21 to 3-22, 4-15,
    4-18, 4-19
Tax rate schedules, 3-21 to 3-22, 4-23 to 4-25
Tax Reform Act of 1986 (TRA), 6-31, 10-5,
    10-6, 11-10, 11-36, 18-8
Tax refunds, 6-46
Tax research, 2-1 to 2-47
Tax services, 2-41
Tax shelters, 5-25, 12-2, 12-7, 13-15 to 13-16
Tax tables, 4-21 to 4-23
Tax treaties, 2-24, 3-4
Taxable dividends (see Dividend income)
Taxable entities, 3-1 to 3-8
Taxable estate (see Estate tax)
Taxable income, 3-21 to 3-22
Taxation
  equity of, 1-30 to 1-31
  history of, 1-2 to 1-5
  as a professional career, 2-3 to 2-4
Taxes, deductibility of, 11-12 to 11-18
  ad valorem tax, 11-15
  assessments, special, 11-17
  employment taxes (see also Employment
    taxes), 11-13
  estate taxes, 11-13
  excise taxes, 11-13
  gift tax, 11-13
  income taxes, 11-14 to 11-15
  inheritance taxes, 11-13
  nondeductible taxes, 11-13
  personal property taxes, 11-12, 11-15
  real property taxes, 11-12, 11-16 to 11-17
  social security taxes, 11-13
  state and local, 7-17, 11-12, 11-14
  when deductible, 11-14
  windfall profits tax, 11-12
Teachers (see Educational expenses)
Technical advice, 2-29
Technical and Miscellaneous Revenue Act
    of 1988, 11-6, 11-35, 11-36
Telephone service, residential, 8-16
Tenancy in common (see Community property)
Termite damage, 10-8
Theft losses (see Casualty and theft losses)
Three percent cutback rule, 3-20
Timber, 17-5
Trade interest, 11-23
Trade or business, defined, 7-6, 8-13
Trade or business expenses (see Business
    expenses and losses)
Trademarks, 16-28 to 16-29

Transfer payment (see Government transfer
    payments)
Transportation expenses, 7-19, 8-17 to 8-25,
    11-3, 11-8
  automobile expenses, 8-23 to 8-25, 9-24
    to 9-33
  commuting, 8-17 to 8-25
  reimbursements, 6-14 to 6-15
  where to deduct, 8-18
Travel expenses, 7-3, 7-19, 8-17, 8-25 to 8-32,
    8-42 to 8-43
  away from home requirement, 8-26
    to 8-27
  combined business and pleasure, 8-28
    to 8-29, 8-55 to 8-56
  cruise ships, 8-32
  defined, 8-26
  education, 8-3, 8-4
  foreign conventions, 8-31 to 8-32
  foreign travel, 8-30 to 8-31
  luxury water travel, 8-31
  meals and lodging, 8-17, 8-26
  reimbursed expenses, 6-14 to 6-15
  spouse and dependents, 8-29 to 8-30
  substantiation requirements, 7-40, 8-42
    to 8-43
  tax planning, 8-55 to 8-56
Treasury Bills, 5-38, 5-41
Treasury Department Regulations, 2-25 to
    2-27, 2-45
Trusts (see also Beneficiaries), 3-5 to 3-6
  distributions, 3-6
  fiduciary, 3-5
  filing requirements, 4-35

— U —

Understatement penalty, 2-8 to 2-9
Unearned income of dependent child, 4-25
    to 4-30, 5-41, 5-50 to 5-51
  prepaid income, 5-31 to 5-35
Unemployment benefits, 6-19
Unemployment compensation, 6-19
Unemployment Compensation Amendments
    Act of 1992, 1-5
Unemployment tax, Federal, 1-19, 6-19
Unharvested crops, 17-6
Unified transfer tax (see also Estate tax; Gift
    tax), 1-12, 1-13 to 1-15
Unified transfer tax credit (see Estate tax; Gift
    tax), 1-13 to 1-15
Uniform capitalization rules, 10-24 to 10-26
Unitary tax, 1-11
Unrealized losses, disallowed, 7-16
Unreasonable compensation, 7-9

U. S. Board of Tax Appeals Report (BTA),
    2-35
U. S. Supreme Court Reports (USSC), 2-39
U. S. Tax Cases (USTC), 2-39
U. S. Tax Court (*see* Tax Court)
U. S. Tax Court Reports (T.C.), 2-36
Use tax, 1-26

— V —

Vacation home rentals, 12-23 to 12-28
Valuation misstatement penalty, 2-9
Value added tax (VAT), 1-9
Vesting, 18-15 to 18-16

— W —

Wash sales, 14-31, 16-12
Welfare payments, 6-40
Wherewithal to pay concept, 1-30
Withholding tax, 1-10, 1-20, 3-22, 4-30,
    13-55
Worker's compensation, 6-40
Working capital requirements (*see*
    Accumulated earnings tax)
Worthless securities, 16-7 to 16-8, 16-22
Writ of Certiorari, 2-35

— Y —

Year taxable (*see* Accounting periods)